THE HISTORY OF THE JEWISH PEOPLE
IN THE AGE OF JESUS CHRIST

40.67

THE HISTORY
OF THE JEWISH PEOPLE
IN THE AGE OF JESUS CHRIST
(175 B.C.–A.D. 135)

BY

EMIL SCHÜRER

A NEW ENGLISH VERSION
REVISED AND EDITED BY

GEZA VERMES   FERGUS MILLAR
MARTIN GOODMAN

Literary Editor
PAMELA VERMES

Organizing Editor
MATTHEW BLACK

VOLUME III, PART I

EDINBURGH T. & T. CLARK LTD 59 GEORGE STREET

1986

13070

Revised English Edition

Copyright © 1986 T. & T. CLARK LTD.

SET IN MONOTYPE BASKERVILLE 10 ON 11 POINT
BY BRADLEY COMPUTING, LOWER SOUDLEY, GLOS.
ON A MONOTYPE LASERCOMP PHOTOTYPESETTER
AT OXFORD UNIVERSITY COMPUTING SERVICE

PRINTED BY PAGE BROS (NORWICH) LIMITED

BOUND BY HUNTER & FOULIS LIMITED, EDINBURGH

FOR

T. & T. CLARK LTD EDINBURGH

FIRST EDITION AND REPRINTS 1885–1924
REVISED EDITION 1986

British Library Cataloguing in Publication Data

Schürer, Emil
    The history of the Jewish people in the age of Jesus Christ.
    —New English version
    Vol. 3 Pt. 1
    1. Jews—History—175 B.C.–135 A.D.
    I. Title   II. Vermes, Geza   III. Millar, Fergus
    IV. Goodman, Martin   V. Geschichte des jüdischen
    Volkes im Zeitalter Jesu Christi. English
    933   DS122

    ISBN 0–567–02244–7

Preface

Launched in 1964 by Professor Matthew Black, the revised English edition of Emil Schürer's *Geschichte des jüdischen Volkes im Zeitalter Jesu Christi* has, with the present volume, reached its completion after twenty-one years of concerted effort.

The basic principles underlying the revision are set out in the Preface to volume I, where it is also made plain that the intention of the editors (or rather co-authors) is to offer students of today a rejuvenated and enlarged compendium to serve as a basis for historical research. In pursuing this task, they have felt free throughout to introduce new evidence, and to replace those views and interpretations of Schürer which appear untenable in the light of contemporary knowledge.

Modernization reaches a climax in volume III. Diaspora Judaism (§31), for which Fergus Millar has taken primary responsibility, has required extensive revision and supplementation in the wake of the considerable archaeological and epigraphic discoveries of the last seventy-five years. In the Jewish literature sections (§§32–33) substantial reorganization has been necessary because the old distinction between Palestinian and Hellenistic Judaism, with its mechanical corollary that all Hebrew and Aramaic compositions originated in the Holy Land, and every Jewish book written in Greek derived from the Hellenistic diaspora (if not from Alexandria itself), is no longer acceptable. A fresh classification has therefore been introduced. §32 deals with writings of Semitic origin; §33A with works composed in Greek; and §33B with Jewish books the primitive language of which can no longer be ascertained. Geza Vermes has revised §32, Martin Goodman §33A, and both of them jointly, §33B.

The Semitic section has been enriched to a large extent thanks to the Qumran finds. Scrolls material judged to be free from sectarian features has been inserted into the existing divisions of §32. An additional lengthy chapter (§32.VIII) accommodates the literary creations of the Qumran (Essene) community.

The editors are particularly grateful to Mrs Jenny Morris (Wycombe Abbey School) for reworking the whole of §34; to Dr Philip Alexander (Manchester University) for contributing an appendix on 3 Enoch

v

(§32.V.2), and an instructive and comprehensive essay on Jewish incantations and magic (§32.VII); and to Dr Sebastian Brock (Oxford University) for discussing the Odes of Solomon (§33B. Appendix 1) and for the generous loan of his unpublished supplements to A.-M. Denis, *Introduction aux pseudépigraphes grecs d'Ancien Testament*.

As usual, Pamela Vermes has checked the entire typescript, comparing it to the surviving German original, and generally emending it wherever necessary.

Bibliographical coverage extends normally to 1983, although occasionally a few later studies are also used. The editors regret that they have been unable to avail themselves to two important books, bearing the date 1984, *Die aramäischen Texte vom Toten Meer* by Klaus Beyer, and *The Apocryphal Old Testament*, edited by H. F. D. Sparks.

At an advanced stage, it became clear that volume III would be too large to be conveniently handled. It has therefore been divided into III.1, containing §§31, 32 and 33A, and III.2, with §§33B and 34, as well as the index to the entire work, compiled by Dr Léonie Archer (Oxford Centre for Postgraduate Hebrew Studies). III.2 is also due to appear in the course of 1986. Continuous page-numbering has been retained throughout.

The publication of this final volume of *The History of the Jewish People in the Age of Jesus Christ* is to take place a century after the first English translation of Schürer saw the light of day under the imprint of the same publishing house of T. & T. Clark. The editors and publishers hope that by bringing to completion this revised and reshaped version of one of the outstanding text-books of the late nineteenth century, they will have secured its useful survival into the twenty-first.

1 October 1985

Contents

Volume III, Part 1

Translators/Revisers*

The Rev. C. H. CAVE, Exeter University (§31).
Professor G. J. KUIPER, Johnson C. Smith University (§33).
Professor A. R. C. LEANEY, Nottingham University (§31).
Professor R. McL. WILSON, St. Andrews University (§34).

* The figures in parentheses indicate the sections for which the Translators/Revisers
supplied the Editors with a first draft.

Abbreviations

AAAScHung	Acta Antiqua Academiae Scientiarum Hungaricae
AAB	Abhandlungen der Deutschen (Preussischen) Akademie der Wissenschaften zu Berlin
AAM	Abhandlungen der Bayerischen Akademie der Wissenschaften, München
AArchAcSc Hung	Acta Archaeologica Academiae Scientiarum Hungaricae
AfO	Archiv für Orientforschung
AIPhOS	Annuaire de l'Institut de Philologie et d'Histoire Orientales et Slaves
AJA	American Journal of Archaeology
AJAH	American Journal of Ancient History
AJPh	American Journal of Philology
AJS Review	Association for Jewish Studies Review
AJSL	American Journal of Semitic Languages and Literatures
AJTh	American Journal of Theology
ALGHJ	*Arbeiten zur Literatur und Geschichte des hellenistischen Judentums*
ALUOS	Annual of Leeds University Oriental Society
ANET	J. B. Pritchard (ed.), *Ancient Near Eastern Texts Relating to the Old Testament* (1969)
AnglThR	Anglican Theological Review
ANRW	H. Temporini (ed.), *Aufstieg und Niedergang der römischen Welt*
AP	A. Cowley, *Aramaic Papyri of the Fifth Century B.C.* (1923)
APAT	E. Kautzsch (ed.), *Die Apokryphen und Pseudepigraphen des Alten Testaments* (1900)
APO	E. Sachau, *Aramäische Papyrus und Ostraka aus einer Militär-Kolonie zu Elephantine* (1911)
APOT	R. H. Charles, *Apocrypha and Pseudepigrapha of the Old Testament* I–II (1912–13)
ARW	Archiv für Religionswissenschaft
AS	Anatolian Studies

ASTI	Annual of the Swedish Theological Institute
Ath. Mitt.	Mitteilungen des Deutschen Archäologischen Instituts, Athenische Abteilung
AWH	Akademie der Wissenschaften, Heidelberg
BA	Biblical Archaeologist
BAAJ	J. J. Collins, *Between Athens and Jerusalem* (1983)
BAC	Bulletino di Archeologia Cristiana
BAR	*British Archaeological Reports*
BASOR	Bulletin of the American Schools of Oriental Research
BASP	Bulletin of the American Society of Papyrologists
BAW	Bayerische Akademie der Wissenschaften
BBB	Bonner Biblische Beiträge
BCH	Bulletin de Correspondance Hellénique
BE	Bulletin Épigraphique, in REG
BGU	*Aegyptische Urkunden aus den Koeniglichen (Staatlichen) Museen zu Berlin, Griechische Urkunden*
Bibl	Biblica
BIFAO	Bulletin de l'Institut français d'archéologie orientale
BIOSCS	Bulletin of the International Organization for Septuagint and Cognate Studies
BJPES	Bulletin of the Jewish Palestine Exploration Society
BJRL	Bulletin of the John Rylands Library
BL	British Library
BMC	*Catalogue of the Greek Coins in the British Museum*
BO	Bibliotheca Orientalis
BP	E. G. Kraeling, *The Brooklyn Museum Aramaic Papyri* (1953)
BSAA	Bulletin de la Société d'Archéologie d'Alexandrie
BSOAS	Bulletin of the School of Oriental and African Studies
Bull. arch.	Bulletin Archéologique du Comité des Travaux Historiques et Scientifiques
BWA(N)T	Beiträge zur Wissenschaft vom Alten (und Neuen) Testament
Byz. Z	Byzantinische Zeitschrift
BZ	Biblische Zeitschrift
BZAW	Beihefte zur Zeitschrift für die Alttestamentliche Wissenschaft
BZNW	Beihefte zur Zeitschrift für die Neutestamentliche Wissenschaft
CBQ	Catholic Biblical Quarterly
CCAGr	Catalogus Codicum Astrologorum Graecorum
CCAR	Central Conference of the American Rabbis
CCL	Corpus Christianorum, series Latina
CE	Chronique d'Égypte

CERP	A. H. M. Jones, *Cities of the Eastern Roman Provinces* (^{2}1971)
CG	P. E. Kahle, *The Cairo Geniza* (^{2}1959)
CIG	*Corpus Inscriptionum Graecarum*
CIH	*Corpus Inscriptionum Hebraicarum*
CIHJ	A. Scheiber, *Corpus Inscriptionum Hungariae Judaicarum* (1960)
CIJ	J. B. Frey, *Corpus Inscriptionum Iudaicarum* I–II (1939, 1951)
CIL	*Corpus Inscriptionum Latinarum*
CIRB	I. Struve, *Corpus Inscriptionum Regni Bosporani* (1965)
CIS	*Corpus Inscriptionum Semiticarum*
CJZC	G. Luederitz, *Corpus jüdischer Zeugnisse aus der Cyrenaika* (1983)
CNRS	Centre National de la Recherche Scientifique
CPh	Classical Philology
CPJ	V. Tcherikover, A. Fuks, M. Stern, *Corpus Papyrorum Judaicarum* I–III (1957–64)
CPR	C. Wessely *et al.*, *Corpus Papyrorum Raineri*
CQ	Classical Quarterly
CRAI	Comptes-rendus de l'Académie des Inscriptions et Belles-lettres
CSCO	*Corpus Scriptorum Christianorum Orientalium*
CSEL	*Corpus Scriptorum Ecclesiasticorum Latinorum*
CSHB	*Corpus Scriptorum Historiae Byzantinae*
C–W	L. Cohn, P. Wendland and S. Reiter, *Philonis opera quae supersunt*
DAC(L)	*Dictionnaire d'Archéologie Chrétienne et de Liturgie*
DB	*Dictionnaire de la Bible*
DBS	*Dictionnaire de la Bible, Supplément*
DCB	*Dictionary of Christian Biography*
DF	B. Lifshitz, *Donateurs et fondateurs dans les synagogues juives* (1967)
DJD	*Discoveries in the Judaean Desert*
DOP	Dumbarton Oaks Papers
DSS	G. Vermes, *The Dead Sea Scrolls: Qumran in Perspective* (1977, 1982)
DSSE	G. Vermes, *The Dead Sea Scrolls in English* (1962, ^{2}1975)
DThC	*Dictionnaire de la Théologie Catholique*
DWA	Denkschriften der Wiener Akademie
EB	Estudios Biblicos
EE	A. Dupont-Sommer, *Les écrits esséniens découverts près de la Mer Morte* (1959, ^{3}1964)
EHR	Etudes sur l'Histoire des Religions

EJ	*Encyclopaedia Judaica*
ESJL	B. Z. Wacholder, *Eupolemus: A Study of Judaeo-Greek Literature* (1974)
EThL	Ephemerides Theologicae Lovanienses
EvTh	Evangelische Theologie
FGrH	F. Jacoby, *Die Fragmente der griechischen Historiker*
FHG	I. Müller, *Fragmenta Historicorum Graecorum*
FHJA	C. R. Holladay, *Fragments from Hellenistic Jewish Authors*, I: *Historians* (1983)
FIRA	S. Riccobono, *Fontes Iuris Romani Anteiustiniani*
FJB	Frankfurter Judaistische Beiträge
FPG	A.-M. Denis, *Fragmenta Pseudepigraphorum quae supersunt Graeca* (1970)
FRLANT	*Forschungen zur Religion und Literatur des Alten und Neuen Testaments*
GAQ	J. A. Fitzmyer, *The Genesis Apocryphon of Qumran Cave I: A Commentary* (1966, ²1971)
GCS	*Die Griechischen Christlichen Schriftsteller der ersten drei Jahrhunderte*
GJV	E. Schürer, *Geschichte des jüdischen Volkes im Zeitalter Jesu Christi*
GLAJJ	M. Stern, *Greek and Latin Authors on Jews and Judaism* I–III (1974–84)
GRBS	Greek, Roman and Byzantine Studies
HDB	*Hastings' Dictionary of the Bible*
Hell.	L. Robert, *Hellenica* I–XIII (1940–65)
HERE	*Hastings' Encyclopaedia of Religion and Ethics*
HJ	Historisches Jahrbuch
HSCPh	Harvard Studies in Classical Philology
HThR	Harvard Theological Review
HUCA	Hebrew Union College Annual
HZ	Historische Zeitschrift
IBM	C. T. Newton *et al.*, *The Collection of Ancient Greek Inscriptions in the British Museum*
ICC	*International Critical Commentary*
ID	*Inscriptions de Délos*
IDB	*The Interpreter's Dictionary of the Bible*
IDBS	*The Interpreter's Dictionary of the Bible, Supplementary Volume*
IEJ	Israel Exploration Journal
IG	*Inscriptiones Graecae*
IG Bulg	*Inscriptiones Graecae in Bulgaria Repertae*
IGLS	*Inscriptions grecques et latines de la Syrie*
IGR	R. Cagnat *et al.*, *Inscriptiones Graecae ad Res Romanas Pertinentes*

IGUR	*Inscriptiones Graecae Urbis Romae*
IK	*Inschriften griechischer Städte aus Kleinasien*
ILAlg	*Inscriptions latines de l'Algérie*
ILChV	*Inscriptiones Latinae Christianae Veteres*
ILS	*Inscriptiones Latinae Selectae*
Ins. Cret.	*Inscriptiones Creticae*
IOSCS	International Organization for Septuagint and Cognate Studies
IOSPE	I. Latyschev, *Inscriptiones Antiquae Orae Septentrionalis Ponti Euxini Graecae et Latinae*
IOTG	H. B. Swete and R. Ottley, *Introduction to the Old Testament in Greek* (1920)
IPGAT	A.-M. Denis, *Introduction aux pseudépigraphes grecs d'Ancien Testament* (1970)
Ist. Mitt.	Mitteilungen des Deutschen Archäologischen Instituts, Istanbuler Abteilung
JAC	Jahrbuch für Antike und Christentum
JAOS	Journal of the American Oriental Society
JBL	Journal of Biblical Literature
JBR	Journal of Bible and Religion
JDAI	Jahrbuch des Deutschen Archäologischen Instituts
JE	*The Jewish Encyclopedia*
JEA	Journal of Egyptian Archaeology
JHS	Journal of Hellenic Studies
JIH	A. Scheiber (ed.), *Jewish Inscriptions in Hungary* (1983)
JJP	Journal of Juristic Papyrology
JJS	Journal of Jewish Studies
JLBBM	G. W. E. Nickelsburg, *Jewish Literature between the Bible and the Mishnah* (1981)
JNES	Journal of Near Eastern Studies
JÖAI	Jahrbuch des Österreichischen Archäologischen Instituts
JPFC	S. Safrai and M. Stern (eds.), *The Jewish People in the First Century* I–II (1974–76)
JPOS	Journal of the Palestine Oriental Society
JPTh	Jahrbücher für Protestantische Theologie
JQR	Jewish Quarterly Review
JRAS	Journal of the Royal Asiatic Society
JRS	Journal of Roman Studies
JS	Journal des Savants
JSHRZ	*Jüdische Schriften aus hellenistischer und römischer Zeit*
JSJ	Journal for the Study of Judaism
JSS(t)	Journal of Semitic Studies
JThSt	Journal of Theological Studies

JWSTP	M. E. Stone (ed.), *Jewish Writings of the Second Temple Period* (1984)
JZWL	Jüdische Zeitschrift für Wissenschaft und Leben
KAI	H. Donner and W. Röllig, *Kanaanäische und Aramäische Inschriften* I–II (³1971–6)
LASBF	Liber Annuus Studii Biblici Franciscani
LThK	Lexikon für Theologie und Kirche
MAMA	*Monumenta Asiae Minoris Antiqua*
MDAI	Mitteilungen des Deutschen Archäologischen Instituts
MEFR	Mélanges de l'École française de Rome
MGH	*Monumenta Germaniae Historica*
MGWJ	Monatsschrift für Geschichte und Wissenschaft des Judentums
MPAT	J. A. Fitzmyer and D. J. Harrington, *A Manual of Palestinian Aramaic Texts* (1978)
MQ	L. Moraldi, *I manoscritti di Qumrān* (1971)
MRR	T. R. S. Broughton, *Magistrates of the Roman Republic* I–II
MT	Masoretic Text
MUSJ	Mélanges de l'Université St. Joseph
NA(W)G	Nachrichten der Akademie der Wissenschaften in Göttingen
NC	Numismatic Chronicle
NedThT	Nederlands Theologische Tijdschrift
NESE	Neue Ephemeris für die Semitische Epigraphik
NGGW	Nachrichten von der (Kgl.) Gesellschaft der Wissenschaften zu Göttingen
Not. d. Sc.	Notizie degli Scavi
NRTh	Nouvelle Revue Théologique
NT	Novum Testamentum
NTS(t)	New Testament Studies
NTT	Norsk Teologisk Tidsskrift
ÖAW	Österreichische Akademie der Wissenschaften
OGIS	W. Dittenberger, *Orientis Graeci Inscriptiones Selectae* I–II
OLZ	Orientalische Literaturzeitung
OTP	J. H. Charlesworth, *Old Testament Pseudepigrapha* I (1983)
PA	P. M. Fraser, *Ptolemaic Alexandria* I–III (1972)
PAAJR	Proceedings of the American Academy for Jewish Research
PBJS	G. Vermes, *Post-Biblical Jewish Studies*
PBSR	Papers of the British School at Rome
PCPhS	Proceedings of the Cambridge Philological Society
PEFQSt	Palestine Exploration Fund, Quarterly Statement
PEQ	Palestine Exploration Quarterly
PG	J.-P. Migne, *Patrum Graecorum Cursus Completus*

PGM	K. Preisendanz, *Papyri Graecae Magicae*
P. Hib.	B. P. Grenfell and A. S. Hunt, *The Hibeh Papyri* I (1906)
PIR	*Prosopographia Imperii Romani*
PL	J.-P. Migne, *Patrum Latinorum Cursus Completus*
PMRS	J. H. Charlesworth, *The Pseudepigrapha and Modern Research with a Supplement* (1981)
PRE	*Realencyclopädie für Protestantische Theologie und Kirche*
PSBA	Proceedings of the Society of Biblical Archaeology
PVTG	*Pseudepigrapha Veteris Testamenti Graeca*
QAL	Quaderni di Archeologia della Libia
Q-E	J. Maier and K. Schubert, *Die Qumran-Essener* (1973)
RA	Revue Archéologique
RAC	*Reallexikon für Antike und Christentum*
RB	Revue Biblique
RBibIt	Rivista Biblica Italiana
RBT	*Realencyclopädie für Bibel und Talmud*
RE	Pauly-Wissowa, *Realencyclopädie der classischen Altertumswissenschaft*
REA	Revue des Études Anciennes
REG	Revue des Études Grecques
REJ	Revue des Études Juives
REtSl	Revue des Études Slaves
RGG	*Religion in Geschichte und Gegenwart*
RhM	Rheinisches Museum
RHP(h)R	Revue d'Histoire et de Philosophie Religieuses
RHR	Revue de l'Histoire des Religions
RIU	L. Barkóczi and A. Mócsy, *Die römischen Inschriften Ungarns*
Riv. fil.	Rivista di filologia e d'istruzione pubblica
RN	Revue Numismatique
RPh	Revue de Philologie
RQ	Revue de Qumrân
RQCA	Römische Quartalschrift für Christliche Altertumskunde
RS(c)R	Recherches de Science Religieuse
RSem	Revue sémitique
RSPhTh	Revue des sciences philosophiques et théologiques
RS(t)O(r)	Rivista degli Studi Orientali
RThLouv	Revue Théologique de Louvain
RThPhil	Revue de Théologie et de Philosophie
SAB	Sitzungsberichte der Deutschen Akademie der Wissenschaften zu Berlin
SAM	Sitzungsberichte der Bayerischen Akademie der Wissenschaften

SAW	Sitzungsberichte der Österreichischen Akademie der Wissenschaften
SB	F. Preisigke, *Sammelbuch griechischer Urkunden aus Ägypten*
SBFLA	Studii Biblici Franciscani Liber Annuus
SBL	Society of Biblical Literature
SC	*Sources Chrétiennes*
SCI	Scripta Classica Israelica
SCO	Studi Classici e Orientali
SEG	Supplementum Epigraphicum Graecum
SEHHW	M. Rostovtzeff, *Social and Economic History of the Hellenistic World*
SIG	W. Dittenberger, *Sylloge Inscriptionum Graecarum*³
SMS	S. Jellicoe, *The Septuagint and Modern Study* (1968)
SNTS(MS)	Studiorum Novi Testamenti Societas (Monograph Series)
SP	Studia Patristica
ST	*Studi e Testi*
STJ	G. Vermes, *Scripture and Tradition in Judaism* (1961, ²1973)
Str.-B.	H. L. Strack and P. Billerbeck, *Kommentar zum Neuen Testament aus Talmud und Midrasch* (1924–28)
StTh	Studia Theologica
SVT	Supplements to Vetus Testamentum
TAM	*Tituli Asiae Minoris*
TAPhA	Transactions of the American Philological Association
TDNT	*Theological Dictionary of the New Testament*
Theol. Bl.	Theologische Blätter
ThLZ	Theologische Literaturzeitung
ThQ	Theologische Quartalschrift
ThR	Theologische Revue
ThStKr	Theologische Studien und Kritiken
ThStud	Theological Studies
ThWNT	*Theologisches Wörterbuch zum Neuen Testament*
ThZ	Theologische Zeitschrift
TLS	Times Literary Supplement
TQ	J. Carmignac, *Les textes de Qumrân* I–II (1961–63)
TQHD	E. Lohse, *Die Texte von Qumran hebräisch und deutsch* (1964, ²1971)
TS	Y. Yadin, *The Temple Scroll* I–II (1983)
TTM	J. Maier, *Die Texte vom Toten Meer* I–II (1960)
TU	*Texte und Untersuchungen*
VC	Vigiliae Christianae
VDI	Vestnik Drevne Istorii
VT	Vetus Testamentum
VTS	Vetus Testamentum, Supplement

WUNT	Wissenschaftliche Untersuchungen zum Neuen Testament
WZKM	Wiener Zeitschrift zur Kunde des Morgenlandes
YCS	Yale Classical Studies
ZAW	Zeitschrift für die Alttestamentliche Wissenschaft
ZDPV	Zeitschrift des Deutschen Palästina-Vereins
ZKTh	Zeitschrift für Katholische Theologie
ZNW	Zeitschrift für die Neutestamentliche Wissenschaft
ZPE	Zeitschrift für Papyrologie und Epigraphik
ZRGG	Zeitschrift für Religions- und Geistesgeschichte
ZSS	Zeitschrift der Savigny-Stiftung: Romanistische Abteilung
ZTK	Zeitschrift für Theologie und Kirche
ZWTh	Zeitschrift für Wissenschaftliche Theologie

§ 31. JUDAISM IN THE DIASPORA: GENTILES AND JUDAISM

Bibliography

Ewald, H., *Geschichte des Volkes Israel* IV (³1864), pp. 305 ff., V (³1867), pp. 108 ff., VI (³1868), pp. 396 ff.

Neubauer, A., *La Géographie du Talmud* (1868), pp. 289–419.

Hamburger, J., *Real-Encyclopädie für Bibel und Talmud* II (1883), s.v. 'Zehn Stämme', 'Zerstreuung', 'Alexandria', 'Antiochia', 'Rom', etc., and Supplementband III (1892) pp. 9–24, 'Ausbreitung des Judentums'.

Mommsen, T., *Römische Geschichte* V (1885), pp. 489–99.

Grätz, H., *Geschichte der Juden* IV (⁴1888), pp. 24–49.

Pressel, W., *Die Zerstreuung des Volkes Israel* (1889).

Renan, E., *Histoire du peuple d'Israël* V (1893), pp. 221–47.

Friedländer, M., *Das Judenthum in der vorchristlichen griechischen Welt* (1897).

Guthe, H., 'Dispersion', EB I, cols. 1106–17.

Reinach, T., 'Judaei', in *Dictionnaire des antiquités grecques et romaines*, ed. Daremberg and Saglio, III (1900), cols. 619–32; translated into English, 'Diaspora', JE IV (1903) cols. 559–74.

Ramsay, W. M., 'The Jews in the Graeco-Asiatic Cities', *Exp.* (1902), pp. 19–33, 92–109.

Schürer, E., 'Diaspora', HDB extra volume (1904), cols. 91–109.

de Ricci, S., 'Palaeography', in JE II (1905), cols. 471–5: 'Greek and Latin Inscriptions' (with complete geographical list of Inscriptions).

Lévi, I., 'Le prosélytisme juif', REJ 50 (1905), pp. 1–9; 51 (1906), pp. 1–31; 33 (1907), pp. 56–61.

Harnack, A., *Die Mission und Ausbreitung des Christentums* I-II (1902; ⁴1924), especially I, pp. 5–23.

Bludau, A., *Juden und Judenverfolgung im alten Alexandria* (1906).

Wendland, P., *Die hellenistisch-römische Kultur* (*Handbuch zum N.T.* I.2) (1907), pp. 106–20; (²⁻³1912; ⁴1972, with bibliog. supp. by H. Dörrie), pp. 192–211.

Oehlers, J., 'Epigraphische Beiträge zur Geschichte des Judentums', MGWJ 53 (1909), pp. 292–302.

Juster, J., *Les Juifs dans l'Empire Romain* I-II (1914).

Bell, H. I., *Jews and Christians in Egypt* (1924).

Bell, H.I., *Juden und Griechen im römischen Alexandreia* (1926).

Sukenik, E. L., *Ancient Synagogues in Palestine and Greece* (1934).

Frey, J. B., *Corpus Inscriptionum Judaicarum* I (1938; ²1975, rev. B. Lifschitz); II (1952).

Bamberger, B. J., *Proselytism in the Talmudic Period* (1939; ²1968).

Braude, W. G., *Jewish Proselytizing in the First Five Centuries of the Common Era. The Age of the Tannaim and Amoraim* (1940).

Simon, M., *Verus Israel: étude sur les relations entre Chrétiens et Juifs dans l'Empire romain (135-425)* (1948; ²1964).

Feldman, L. H., '"Jewish Sympathisers" in Classical Literature and Inscriptions', TAPhA 81 (1950), pp. 200–8.

Tcherikover, V. A., and Fuks, A., *Corpus Papyrorum Judaicarum* I-III (1957–64).

Scheiber, A., *Corpus Inscriptionum Hungariae Iudaicarum* (1960); rev. Eng. ed., *Jewish Inscriptions in Hungary* (1983).

Leon, H. J., *The Jews of Ancient Rome* (1960).

Lerle, E., *Proselytenwerbung und Urchristentum* (1960).

Tcherikover, V. A., *Hellenistic Civilization and the Jews*, translated from the Hebrew by S. Applebaum (1961), pp. 269–377.

Kuhn, K. G., Stegemann, H., 'Proselyten', RE Suppl. IX (1962), cols. 1248–83.

Neusner, J., *A History of the Jews in Babylonia* I (1965; ²1969), pp. 1–67.

Lifshitz, B., *Donateurs et fondateurs dans les synagogues juives. Répertoire des dédicaces grecques relatives à la construction et la réfection des synagogues (Cahiers de la Revue Biblique* VII, 1967).

Hirschberg, H. Z. (J. W.), *A History of the Jews in North Africa* I (1974), pp. 21–86.

Stern, M., *Greek and Latin Authors on Jews and Judaism* I (1974); II (1980); III (1984).

Stern, M., 'The Jewish Diaspora', JPFC I (1974), pp. 117–83.

Applebaum, S., 'The Legal Status of the Jewish Communities in the Diaspora', *ibid.* 420–63.

Applebaum, S., 'The Organisation of the Jewish Communities in the Diaspora', *ibid.* 464–503.

Gutmann, J. (ed.), *The Synagogue: Studies in Origins, Archaeology and Architecture* (1975).

Bowers, W. P., 'Jewish Communities in Spain in the Time of Paul the Apostle', JThSt 26 (1975), pp. 395–402.

Smallwood, E. M., *The Jews under Roman Rule, from Pompey to Diocletian* (1976), ch. 6, 9–10, 14, 19.

Kasher, A., *The Jews in Hellenistic and Roman Egypt* (1978) (Hebrew).

Applebaum, S., *Jews and Greeks in Ancient Cyrene* (1979).

Kraabel, A. T., 'The Diaspora Synagogue: Archaeological and Epigraphic Evidence since Sukenik', ANRW II.19 (1979), pp. 477–510.

Rabello, A. M., 'The Legal Condition of the Jews in the Roman Empire', ANRW II.13 (1980), pp. 662–762.

Gutmann, J. (ed.), *Ancient Synagogues: The State of Research* (1981).

Le Bohec, Y., 'Inscriptions juives et judaïsantes de l'Afrique romaine', Antiquités Africaines 17 (1981), pp. 165–207.

Conzelmann, H., *Heiden-Juden-Christen. Auseinandersetzung in der Literatur der hellenistisch-römischen Zeit* (1981).

Mélèze-Modrzejewski, J., 'Splendeurs grecques et misères romaines: les Juifs d'Égypte dans l'Antiquité', J. Hassoun (ed.), *Les Juifs du Nil* (1981), pp. 15–48.

Pucci, M., *La rivolta ebraica al tempo di Traiano* (1981).

Paul, P., *Le monde juif à l'heure de Jésus* (1981).

Saulnier, C., 'Lois romaines sur les Juifs selon Flavius Josèphe', RB 88 (1981), pp. 161–98.

Kraabel, A. T., 'The Disappearance of the "God-fearers"', Numen 28 (1981), pp. 113–26.

Kraabel, A. T., 'The Roman Diaspora: Six Questionable Assumptions', *Essays in Honour of Y. Yadin*, ed. Vermes, G., and Neusner, J. = JJS 33 (1982), pp. 445–64.

Brooten, B., *Women Leaders in the Ancient Synagogue* (Brown Judaic Studies XXXVI, 1982).

Oppenheimer, A. (with Isaac, B., and Lecker, M.), *Babylonia Judaica in the Talmudic Period (Beihefte zum Tübinger Atlas des Vorderen Orients*, Reihe B, Geisteswissenschaften, XLVII, 1983).

Collins, J. J., *Between Athens and Jerusalem: Jewish Identity in the Hellenistic Diaspora* (1983).

Solin, H., 'Juden und Syren im westlichen Teil der römischen Welt. Eine ethnisch-demographische Studie mit besonderer Berücksichtigung der sprachlichen Zustände', ANRW II.29.2 (1983), pp. 587–789, 1222–49.

Hanfmann, G. M. A., *Sardis from Prehistoric to Roman Times* (1983), ch. 9, 'The Synagogue and the Jewish Community' (by A. R. Seager and A. T. Kraabel).

Hengel, M., 'Messianische Hoffnung und politischer "Radikalismus" in der "jüdisch-hellenistischen Diaspora". Zur Frage der Voraussetzungen des jüdischen Aufstandes unter Trajan 115–117 n. Chr.', Hellholm, D. (ed.), *Apocalypticism in the Mediterranean World and the Near East* (1983), pp. 655–86.
Luederitz, G., *Corpus jüdischer Zeugnisse aus der Cyrenaika. Mit einem Anhang von J. M. Reynolds* (Beih. Tübinger Atlas Vord. Or., Reihe B, LIII, 1983).
Gager, J. G., *The Origins of Anti-Semitism: Attitudes towards Judaism in Pagan and Christian Antiquity* (1983).
Davies, W. D., and Finkelstein, L. (eds.), *The Cambridge History of Judaism* I. *Introduction; The Persian Period* (1984), ch. 13B, 'The Babylonian Captivity' (by E. J. Bickerman); 13D, 'The Jews in Egypt' (by B. Porten).
Rajak, T., 'Was there a Roman Charter for the Jews?', JRS 74 (1984), pp. 107–23.

I. Diaspora : Geographical Survey

The history of Judaism in the time of Jesus Christ is not limited to the narrow confines of the Holy Land. Jewish communities of greater or lesser extent and significance had settled in almost every part of the then civilized world, and remaining on the one hand in lasting relation with the motherland and, on the other, in active contact with the non-Jewish world, they were of great importance to the internal development of Judaism as well as to its influence on the rest of the civilized nations. The causes of this dispersion were various. In the earlier period, the Assyrian and Babylonian conquerors had forcibly deported large masses of the people to their eastern provinces. The same happened later, though to a far smaller degree, as for example when Pompey carried off hundreds of Jews to Rome as prisoners of war. But of greater significance in the Hellenistic-Roman age was the voluntary migration of Jewish settlers into the areas bordering on Palestine, and indeed into all the major cities of the civilized world. These movements must have been specially numerous at the beginning of the Hellenistic era. The sucessors of Alexander the Great and their descendants were frequently in need of considerable numbers of settlers for the foundation of their new cities, and immigrants to these places were often granted citizenship or privileges without further ado. Attracted by such conditions, Jews in particular appear to have been persuaded to emigrate on a generous scale. Difficult circumstances in their own land, in particular its exposed position—for Palestine served as a theatre of war for every imbroglio between Syria and Egypt—may have contributed to this. Many Jews therefore made their way to neighbouring Syria and Egypt, where, notably in the capitals, Antioch and Alexandria, but also in other newly-founded Hellenistic cities, specific rights seem to have been granted to them. They also moved in large numbers into Asia Minor, particularly to the cities of the Ionian coast, and to many of the more important places in the Greek-speaking parts of the Mediterranean and the Black Sea.

Notwithstanding the reasons adduced for it, the extent of this Jewish Diaspora continues to puzzle when one considers how small the Jewish community in the motherland was, even as late as the beginning of the Maccabaean period. It scarcely reached beyond the borders of 'Judaea' proper (see vol. II, pp. 1–13). Can this small population have provided such multitudes of settlers as are found, at least as early as the first century B.C., throughout the world? Or was it greatly increased by converts to Judaism in the last centuries B.C.?

Already in the first century B.C. (as it seems), the Sibyl was able to declare of the Jewish people that every land and every sea was filled with them.[1] In the previous century (139–138 B.C.), the Roman Senate issued a circular letter to the kings of Egypt, Syria, Pergamum, Cappadocia and Parthia, and to many of the areas, cities and islands of the Mediterranean, in support of the Jews (1 Mac. 15:23–4).[2] We must therefore assume that they were already present in greater or smaller numbers in all these regions and cities. As regards the time of Sulla (c. 85 B.C.), Strabo says that the Jewish people at that time 'had already made their way into every city, and scarcely any place in the world can be found which has not received members of this race and not been conquered by them'.[3] Josephus[4] and Philo[5] express themselves similarly from time to time. But the extent of the Jewish dispersion is described best in the letter of King Agrippa I to Caligula reported by Philo. 'Jerusalem', it states, 'is the capital city, not only of Judaea, but of most countries, because of the colonies which it has sent out at suitable opportunities into the neighbouring lands of *Egypt, Phoenicia, Syria, Coele-Cyria,* and into the more distant *Pamphylia* and *Cilicia,* into most parts of Asia as far as *Bithynia* and the remotest corner of *Pontus*;

---

1. *Or. Sib.* iii 271: πᾶσα δὲ γαῖα σέθεν πλήρης καὶ πᾶσα θάλασσα. For a detailed discussion of the date of this work, see V. Nikiprowetzky, *La troisième Sibylle* (1970), pp. 195-217.

2. For problems about the authenticity of the letter of the Roman consul 'Lucius' (1 Mac. 15:16–21), see vol. I, pp. 194-7. Besides the kings of *Egypt, Syria, Pergamum, Cappadocia* and *Parthia*, 1 Mac. 15:22–3 mentions also *Sampsame* (?), *Sparta, Sicyon* (in the Peloponnese), the islands of *Delos* and *Samos*, the city of *Gortyn* in Crete, the district of *Caria* with the cities of *Myndus, Halicarnassus* and *Cnidus*, the islands of *Cos* and *Rhodes*, and the district of *Lycia* with the city of *Phaselis*, the district of *Pamphylia* with the city of *Side*, the Phoenician city of *Aradus*, and finally *Cyprus* and *Cyrene*. The individual districts, cities and islands mentioned together with the five kingdoms, were more or less independent, and were listed separately for that reason (see vol. I, pp. 194–5). For a highly speculative identification of 'Sampsame' with Amisus (later Samsun), see Abel *ad loc.*

3. Strabo *ap.* Jos. *Ant.* xiv 7, 2 (115) = FGrH 91 F 7 = GLAJJ I, no. 105.

4. Jos. *B.J.* ii 16, 4 (398); vii 3, 3 (43).

5. Philo, *In Flaccum* 7 (45–6).

likewise into *Europe, Thessaly, Boeotia, Macedonia, Aetolia, Attica, Argus, Corinth,* and into most of the finest parts of the *Peloponnese.* And not only is the mainland full of Jewish colonies, but also the most important islands : *Euboea, Cyprus* and *Crete.* And I say nothing of the lands beyond the *Euphrates.* For except for a very small part, the whole of *Babylonia,* and those satrapies which encircle the fertile land, have Jewish inhabitants.'[6] Acts also mentions Jews and proselytes from *Parthia, Media, Elam* and *Mesopotamia,* from *Cappadocia, Pontus* and *Asia, Phrygia* and *Pamphylia, Egypt* and *Cyrenaica,* from *Rome, Crete* and *Arabia* (Acts 2 : 9–11).[7]

In *Mesopotamia, Media* and *Babylonia* lived the descendants of members of the kingdom of the ten tribes, and of the kingdom of Judah, once deported there by the Assyrians and the Babylonians.[8] It was agreed in Antiquity that the 'ten tribes' had never returned from exile,[9] and it was still disputed at the time of Akiba whether they would ever do so.[10] Even the return of the tribes of Judah and Benjamin cannot be regarded as having been total. The deportations, particularly those by the Assyrians from the kingdom of the ten tribes, took place at a time when the religion of Israel was still much more fluid, less consolidated and less differentiated from paganism than it became later. It is therefore open to doubt how far the great expansion of normative Judaism in the later period is to be related to the ancient deportations. Some sort of connection is nevertheless probable. Relations with the homeland will have never been wholly severed. The ancient tribal confederation formed the point of departure for the later propagation of Judaism. This at least applies to Babylonia, where the descendants of the tribes of Judah and Benjamin lived. Documents from Babylonia in the Persian period, at any rate from the fifth century, now provide substantial evidence of the Jewish community still settled there, and illustrate both their exposure to foreign influences and their continued

---

6. Philo, *Legatio* 36 (281–2).

7. The words Ἰουδαῖοί τε καὶ προσήλυτοι, Acts 2 : 10, are probably only in apposition to Ῥωμαῖοι (see further Haenchen's commentary *ad loc.*). But even if only proselytes or sympathisers are meant, their existence implies the presence of Jews in the countries listed.

8. On the Assyrian deportations see A. Malamat s.v. 'Exile, Assyrian', EJ VI (1971), cols. 1034–6, and B. Oded, *Mass Deportations and Deportees in the Neo-Assyrian Empire* (1979).

9. Jos. *Ant.* xi 5, 2 (133) ; 4 Ezra 13 :39–47 ; Origen, *Epist. ad Africanum* 14 ; Commodian, *Carmen apologet.* 936–40/943–6 (9 ? tribes are still *trans Persida flumine clausi*).

10. mSanh. x 3 *fin*; 'The ten tribes shall not return, for it is written of them (Dt. 29 :28) : "He shall cast them into another land, as at this day." As this day passes and does not return, so shall they pass and not return.' So R. Akiba. But R. Eliezer says: 'As the day becomes dark and again light, so for the ten tribes for whom it became dark, it shall also one day become again light.' Cf. on this above, vol. II, pp. 530–1.

attachment to the God of Israel.[11] Moreover, further dispersals are reported by late sources to have taken place during the Persian period. According to Eusebius and later chroniclers, Artaxerxes Ochus, during one of his Egyptian campaigns, perhaps that of 345–343 B.C., took Jewish prisoners and settled them in Hyrcania by the Caspian Sea, and perhaps also in Babylonia.[12] Faustus of Byzantium also alleges that Tigranes, during his domination of Syria (83–69 B.C., see vol. I, pp.134–6), transported a large number of Jews to Armenia (iv 55, French translation in FHG V, p.275). Voluntary emigration, moreover, will no doubt have served to increase the scale of Jewish settlement

---

11. For Jews in Babylonia under the Persians, see e.g., S. Daiches, *The Jews in Babylonia at the Time of Ezra and Nehemiah* (1910); E. Klamroth, *Die jüdischen Exulanten in Babylonien* (1912); E. Ebeling, *Aus dem Leben der jüdischen Exulanten in Babylon* (1914); D. Sidersky, 'L'onomastique hébraïque des tablettes de Nippur', REJ 78 (1929), pp. 177–99; B. Meissner, 'Die Achämeniden-Könige und das Judentum', AAB, Ph.-hist. Kl. (1938), pp. 6–26; G. Cardascia, *Les archives de Muraŝû* (1951); B. Porten, s.v. 'Exile, Babylonian', EJ VI (1971), cols. 1036–41; M. D. Coogan, 'Life in the Diaspora: Jews at Nippur in the Fifth Century B.C.', BA 37 (1974), pp. 6–12; *idem, West Semitic Personal Names in the Muraŝû Documents* (1976); R. Zadok, *The Jews in Babylonia in the Chaldaean and Achaemenian Periods in the Light of the Babylonian Sources* (1976; [2]1979); *On West Semites in Babylonia during the Chaldaean and Achaemenian Periods: An Onomastic Study* (1977); E. J. Bickerman, 'The Babylonian Captivity', in W. D. Davies and L. Finkelstein (eds.), *The Cambridge History of Judaism* I (1984), pp. 342–58.

12. Euseb. *Chron.*, ed. A. Schoene, II, p. 112 *ad ann. Abr.* 1657 (according to the Armenian text): 'Ochus partem aliquam de Romanis Judaeisque cepit et habitare fecit in Hyrcania juxta mare Cazbium'. Cf. Jerome, ed. R. Helm (1956), p. 121; Syncellus, ed. Dindorf, I, p. 486; Orosius iii 7. Those who follow Eusebius merely copy this. In the Armenian translation, the text is distorted through the addition of 'de Romanis'; Syncellus adds τοὺς δὲ ἐν Βαβυλῶνι. This may receive some support from Hecataeus of Abdera, quoted by Jos. *C. Ap.* i 194 (GLAJJ I, no. 12), who states that 'many myriads' of Jews had been deported to Babylonia by the Persians. For a possible historical context and for archaeological evidence of destruction which might be associated with such deportations, see D. Barag, 'The Effects of the Tennes Rebellion on Palestine', BASOR 183 (1966), pp. 6–12. The events narrated in Josephus, *Ant.* xi 7, 1 (297–301) may have occurred, not in the time of Artaxerxes III Ochus, but earlier, under Artaxerxes II Mnemon (404–358 B.C.), since the personalities named there—the high priest Yohanan and the governor Bagoas— can reasonably be identified with those who, according to an Aramaic papyrus originally published by Sachau, were in office under Darius II (424–4 B.C.). See E. Sachau, *Drei aramäische Papyrusurkunden* (1907), pp. 16 ff. = A. Cowley, *Aramaic Papyri*, nos. 30–1 = P. Grelot, *Documents araméens*, no. 102. Τοῦ ἄλλου Ἀρταξέρξου in the text of Josephus would thus be confirmed. But for a different sequence, based on the Samaria papyri, see F. M. Cross, 'A Reconstruction of the Judean Restoration', JBL 94 (1975), pp. 3–18.

Cf. on Artaxerxes and the Jews in general, W. Judeich, *Kleinasiatische Studien, Untersuchungen zur griechisch-persischen Geschichte des IV. Jahrhunderts v. Chr.* (1892), pp. 170–6, and in RE II, cols. 1318 ff. s.v. 'Artaxerxes'; G. Hölscher, *Palästina in der persischen und hellenistischen Zeit* (1903), pp. 46–50; J. Bright, *History of Israel* ([3]1980), pp. 410–14.

The confused notice in Solinus concerning the conquest of Jericho is usually related to the war of Artaxerxes Ochus, Solin. 35 4: 'Iudaeae caput fuit Hierosolyma, sed excisa est. Successit Hierichus: et haec desivit, Artaxerxis bello subacta.'

beyond the Euphrates. As a result, the Jewish population there during the Roman period is reported as numbering tens of thousands.[13] Because they lived near the eastern frontier of the Roman Empire— until the second century A.D., as subjects of the Parthians, and later (those settled in N. Mesopotamia) as inhabitants of the Roman province of Mesopotamia, which was disputed first by Parthia and then by Sassanid Persia[14]—their attitude was of strategic concern to the Roman Empire. For instance, the legate of Syria, P. Petronius, regarded it as hazardous in A.D. 40 to provoke them to enmity vis-à-vis Rome.[15] During the revolt of A.D. 66–73-4 the rebels in Palestine attempted to arouse such hostility among their co-religionists beyond the Euphrates.[16] It was a source of danger for Trajan, in his advance

---

13. Jos. *Ant.* xi 5, 2 (133): Αἱ δὲ δέκα φυλαὶ πέραν εἰσὶν Εὐφράτου ἔως δεῦρο, μυριάδες ἄπειροι καὶ ἀριθμῷ γνωσθῆναι μὴ δυνάμεναι. Cf. *Ant.* xv 2, 2 (14) and 3, 1 (39). On the history of Babylonian Jewry in the Parthian period, cf. especially also *Ant.* xviii 9 (310–73): in the reign of Tiberius, in the region of Nehardea on the Euphrates, two brothers named Asinaus and Anilaus founded a Jewish robber-state which, owing to the weakness of the Parthian king, held firm for several decades, namely for fifteen years during the lifetime of Asinaus (*Ant.* xviii 9, 4 (330)), and after his death, for a further long period under Anilaus. For comments see also A. von Gutschmid, *Kl. Schr.* iii, pp. 53–5. Note also xvii 2, 1–2 (23–8); *C. Ap.* i 7 (33).

In the Mishnah, account is taken from time to time of the Babylonian and Median Jews. See mShek. 3:4 (half-shekel tax from Babylon and Media); mHal. 4:11 (first fruits not accepted from Babylon); mYom. 6:4 (Babylonians plucked the hair of the scapegoat on the Day of Atonement); mMen. 11:7 (Babylonian priests); mB.M. 7:9 (Yaddua the Babylonian); mShab. 6:6 (Median Jewesses); mB.K. 9:5 = mB.M. 4:7 (on the obligation to restore stolen goods even to Media); mShab. 2:1, mNaz. 5:4, mB.B. 5:2 (Nahum the Median). That Jews lived in Media is attested also by the book of Tobit (Tob. 1:14, 3:7 etc.).

On the subject in general, see S. Funk, *Die Juden in Babylonien* (1908); S. Krauss, s.v. 'Babylonia', JE II (1902), pp. 403–15; J. Engel, *Die Juden in Babylonien unter den persischen Königen während des zweiten Tempels bis nach dem barkochbäischen Kriege*, (Diss. Bern, 1907); J. Juster, *Les Juifs dans l'empire romain* I (1914), pp. 199–203; G. F. Moore, *Judaism in the first centuries of the Christian Era* I (1927), pp. 102–6; J. Newman, *The Agricultural Life of the Jews in Babylonia* (1932); J. Neusner, *A History of the Jews in Babylonia* I: *The Parthian Period* (1965; [2]1969); II: *The Early Sasanian Period* (1966); III: *From Shapur I to Shapur II* (1968); IV: *The Age of Shapur II* (1969); V: *The Later Sasanian Times* (1970). Note also the important discussion by G. Widengren, 'The Status of the Jews in the Sassanian Empire', Iranica Antiqua 1 (1961), pp. 117–62. See now the major work of reference by A. Oppenheimer, *Babylonia Judaica in the Talmudic Period* (1983).

14. For relations between Rome and Parthia, see W. C. Debevoise, *A Political History of Parthia* (1938); M. G. A. Bertinelli, 'I Romani oltre l'Euphrate nel II sec. d. c.', ANRW IX.1 (1976), pp. 3–45; *Cambridge History of Iran* III.1 (1983), pp. 21–99; R. N. Frye, *The History of Ancient Iran* (1984), pp. 233–44.

15. Philo, *Legatio* 31 (216–17). For all these issues, see J. Neusner, 'The Jews East of the Euphrates and the Roman Empire I. 1st–3rd Centuries A.D.', ANRW IX.1 (1976), pp. 46–69.

16. Jos. *B.J.* vi 6, 2 (343). Titus reproaches the Jews: καὶ πρεσβεῖαι μὲν ὑμῶν πρὸς τοὺς ὑπὲρ Εὐφράτην ἐπὶ νεωτερισμῷ. Jews from beyond the Euphrates fought also among the

against the Parthians, that he was threatened in the rear by an uprising of Mesopotamian Jews (see vol. I, p. 532).

Josephus names the fortified towns of *Nehardea* and *Nisibis* as the principal settlements of Jews in *Babylonia*. Nehardea (נהרדעא) is clearly attested both in Josephus and in Talmudic sources as a major Jewish centre in Babylonia proper, and as a strong-point of the semi-independent Jewish 'state' which, according to Josephus' narrative flourished between about A.D. 20 and 35.[17] By 'Nisibis' it would seem natural to understand the well-known city of that name in Northern Mesopotamia since it is situated in the centre of the districts to which the ten tribes were deported by the Assyrians, whereas Nehardea lies further south, in Babylonia proper, where the tribes of Judah and Benjamin were settled by the Babylonians.[18] However, in the context of Josephus' narrative, 'Nisibis' seems also to be a town in Babylonia near Nehardea and not far from the major cities of Seleucia and Ctesiphon.[19] If this view is correct, we are left on the one hand with the evidence of the Assyrian deportations to this area, and on the other with a fair amount of Talmudic evidence for a Jewish presence there from at least the second century A.D. onwards.[20] There may therefore

rebels in Palestine (Dio lxvi 4, 3; Jos. *B.J.* ii 19, 2 (520), vi 6, 4 (356) mentions relatives of Monobazus and Izates in particular. Neusner, *op. cit.*, pp. 58–64.

17. Jos. *Ant.* xviii 9, 1 (310–13) and 9 (379). See the full account by Oppenheimer, *Babylonia Judaica*, pp. 276–93.

18. On *Nisibis* see RE XVII, cols. 714–57; C. Ritter, *Erdkunde* XI, pp. 413 ff.; Oppenheimer, *Babylonia Judaica*, pp. 311–25. For the geographical context see L. Dillemann, *Haute Mésopotamie orientale et pays adjacents* (1962). Nisibis lay on the Mygdonius, a tributary of the Chaboras, itself a tributary of the Euphrates. It served as the centre of the localities named in 2 Kings 17:6, 18:11, to which the members of the kingdom of the ten tribes were deported by the Assyrians. Nehardea, by contrast, lay much further south, in Babylonia proper.

19. For this point, see J. Wellhausen, *Israelitische und jüdische Geschichte* (⁴1901), 206n., and W. Bousset, *Die Religion des Judentums* (³1926), p. 62. The existence of a separate place called 'Nisibis', and situated in Babylonia proper, is assumed by Oppenheimer, *Babylonia Judaica*, pp. 319 and 325. According to Jos. *Ant.* xviii 9, 1 (311), *Nehardea* was not easily accessible because it was completely encircled by the Euphrates and its canals. 'Nisibis' was also situated on the same stretch surrounded by the Euphrates (ἔστιν δὲ καὶ Νίσιβις πόλις κατὰ τὸν αὐτὸν τοῦ ποταμοῦ περίρρουν). Both cities, according to the account in xviii 9, 8–9 (371–2) were not far from *Seleucia* and *Ctesiphon*. bKidd. 70b reports that *Nehardea* (נהרדעא) lay on the King's Canal (נהר מלכא) connecting the Euphrates with the Tigris. It is mentioned also in the Mishnah (mYeb. 16:7) and was a centre of rabbinical learning (Hamburger, RBT II, pp. 852 f.; C. Ritter, *Erdkunde* X, pp. 146 f.).

20. The 'Nisibis' referred to by Josephus (*loc. cit.*) may perhaps be identical with the נציבין in rabbinical literature, but the reference in bKidd. 72a is clearly to the major northern city, and Oppenheimer, *Babylonia Judaica*, pp. 311–25, is probably correct to take all the rabbinic allusions as referring to 'the' Nisibis.

For the places of residence of Jews in Babylonia in general, cf. especially A. Neubauer, *La géographie du Talmud* (1868), pp. 343–68; A. Berliner, *Beiträge zur Geographie und Ethnographie Babyloniens im Talmud und Midrasch* (1884), and S. Funk in *Monumenta Judaica*,

have been continuity of settlement, but it can not be proved.

Documentary evidence, or dated and localisable literary references, for Jewish settlement in Northern Mesopotamia, which we might use to furnish evidence on the question of whether Josephus' Nisibis could have been 'the' Nisibis, is not extensive. Of the towns of Northern Mesopotamia, three grave inscriptions in Hebrew lettering are reported from *Edessa*: one of them has a parallel Greek text identifying the persons buried there as Jews, and is thought to be of the early third century A.D.[21] By the fourth century at least, there was a Jewish community, with a synagogue, at *Nicephorium* (*Callinicum*) on the Euphrates (Ambrose, *Ep.* 40–1).

In *Babylonia*, the individual places attested, apart from *Nehardea* (above) are *Seleuceia*, *Ant.* xviii 9, 8 (372–7) and *Ctesiphon*, xviii 9, 5 (377–8). For these places see Oppenheimer, *Babylonia Judaica*, pp. 200–16 (Seleuceia) and 191–200 (Ctesiphon).

As regards the area south of Babylonia, a story in Josephus reveals a Jewish merchant named Ananias operating in *Spasinou Charax*, in the region known as Characene or Mesene at the head of the Persian Gulf, *Ant.* xx 2, 3 (34); and in the third or fourth century, a Jewish lady named Sara from *Mesene* was buried at Beth Shearim (CIJ II, no. 1124; M. Schwabe, B. Lifshitz, *Beth Shearim* II, no. 101). For the background see S. A. Nodelman, 'A Preliminary History of Characene', *Berytus* 13 (1960), pp. 83–121, especially pp. 100 and 112. The questions of the purity of the Jews of Mesene is discussed in bKid 71b. See the excellent account in Oppenheimer, *Babylonia Judaica*, pp. 235–49.

The conversion of Queen Helena of *Adiabene* near the Tigris, and her son Izates, in the middle of the first century, was also effected by a Jew there, *Ant.* xx 2, 3 (35); another, named Eleazar, later arrived from

---

Altera pars: Monumenta Talmudica I (1906), pp. 20–4 (a full collection of the source material concerning the cities and localities of Babylonia from rabbinical literature). Juster, *op. cit.* I, pp. 199–202; G. F. Moore, *Judaism* I, pp. 102–4. Note however that J. Neusner, *op. cit.*, p. 47, n. 2, does not accept the hypothesis of a second 'Nisibis' in Babylonia, and prefers the view that Josephus' geographical indications are vague. See now above all Oppenheimer, *Babylonia Judaica* (1983), passim.

The ninth-century account by Eldad ha-Dani is legendary: for critical editions see A. Epstein, *Eldad ha-Dani, seine Berichte über die Stämme und deren Ritus in verschiedenen Versionen nach Handschriften und alten Drücken* (1891); H. Müller, 'Die Recensionen und Versionen des Eldad had-Dani u.s.w. veröffentlicht und kritisch untersucht', DWA ph.-h.Kl. 41 (1892), pp. 1–80; Epstein, REJ 25 (1892), p. 43. H. L. Strack and P. Billerbeck, *Kommentar zum Neuen Testament aus Talmud und Midrasch* II (1924), pp. 606–8, 683 ff., IV (1928), pp. 903–6; G. F. Moore, *Judaism* II, p. 368 ff. See EJ VI (1972), cols. 576–8 s.v. 'Eldad ha-Dani'.

21. Published by G. H. Pognon, *Inscriptions sémitiques de la Syrie, de la Mésopotamie et de la region de Mossoul* (1907), pp. 78 ff., nos. 40, 41, 43 (bilingual); note also J. B. Segal, *Edessa the Blessed City* (1970), pp. 41 ff. (speculative).

Galilee. For the full evidence on the conversion, and Jewish presence in this region see Oppenheimer, *Babylonica Judaica*, pp. 14–17.

Acts 2, if taken literally, implies the presence of Jews further east of the Tigris, in *Parthia, Media* and *Elam* (Elymais Susiana). It may be relevant that II Kings 17:6 records Assyrian deportation of Jews to Media, and that the book of Tobit (see pp. 222–32 below) vividly reflects Jewish settlement there, while bKid 71b indicates suspicion of the purity of Jews from Media, as from Mesene. See further Widengren, *op. cit.* pp. 118 f.

According to Armenian sources, Tigranes (see above, p. 6) also deported Jews to Armenia, while the Persians deported significant numbers from Armenia in the later fourth century A.D. For a discussion see J. Neusner, 'The Jews in Pagan Armenia', JAOS 84 (1964), pp. 230–40, accepting as a fact that there will have been Jewish settlement there at any rate by the fourth century.

For one place on the Euphrates itself, namely *Dura-Europos*, we now have substantial evidence of a Jewish community and its synagogue.[22] A Macedonian settlement of the early Hellenistic period, the town passed under Parthian rule in the late second century B.C., and under Roman rule in the second century A.D. It was destroyed by the Persians in about A.D. 256. Excavations conducted in the 1920s and 1930s have revealed, amid much else of the greatest interest, the synagogue created by two successive re-modellings of a private house. The first version was constructed in the late second and early third century A.D., and the second, notable for its magnificent narrative frescoes depicting Old Testament scenes and others, was completed in A.D. 244–5. The central room contained a niche in the west wall (towards Jerusalem), presumably for the Torah scrolls, and was surrounded by benches.

The excavations have revealed no archaeological or documentary evidence for the community prior to the period of the construction of the two phases of the synagogue. From that time, however, there is some written evidence: (a) an inscription in Palmyrene characters reveals a Jewish painter Thomas Benaia (תאנ]מ[א בניה) at work, along with non-Jews, on a Palmyrene house in Dura (CIJ II, no.825); (b) three fragments of a Hebrew parchment, thought to be of the third century A.D. and containing a benediction after meals, were found in the vicinity of the synagogue (*Excavations at Dura-Europos, Final Report*

22. Only the essential bibliography on the Synagogue and the Jewish community can be given here: C. H. Kraeling, *Excavations at Dura-Europos, Final Report* VIII.1: *The Synagogue* (1956; augmented 2nd ed., 1979); E. R. Goodenough, *Jewish Symbols in the Greco-Roman Period* IX–XI: *Symbolism in the Dura Synagogue* (1964); EJ VI (1971), cols. 275–98 s.v. 'Dura Europos'; J. Gutmann (ed.), *The Dura-Europos Synagogue: A Re-Evaluation* (1972).

V.1. *The Parchments and Papyri* (1959), no.11; a fragmentary Aramaic papyrus, probably of A.D. 200, is also likely to have emanated from the Jewish community, see J. T. Milik, 'Parchemin judéo-araméen de Doura-Europos, an 200 ap. J.-C.', Syria 45 (1968), pp. 97–104; (c) four Aramaic graffiti from the first synagogue, recording (perhaps) the painter (CIJ II, 826a; *Final Report* VIII.1. p.274, no.20), and probably the donors (826b–c; nos. 21–2) of the painted panels of that stage, as well as the single name אבל (827); (d) important Greek and Aramaic graffiti relating to the construction of the final version of the synagogue:
1. An Aramaic graffito giving the date 556 of the Seleucid era (see vol. I, p. 126) and the second year of Philip (A.D. 244–9), so 244–5, in the presbyterate (בקשישותה) of Samuel *cohen*, son of Ydyw, *archon* (ארכון) (CIJ II, no. 828a; definitive text in *Final Report* VIII.1., p. 267, no. 1b) 2. The same date, and the presbyter Samuel, along with the officials of the community, appear in the painted Aramaic inscription on two ceiling tiles, constituting the formal record of the completion of the synagogue.

(Tile A)

ה

הדין ביתאתני	1
בשנה חמש מאה חמאין	2
ושית דאינין שנת תרתן לפלפוס	3
[[יוליס]] קסר בקשישותה דשמואל	4
כהנה בר ידעי ארכן. ודקמו	5
על עיבידה הדין אברם גיזב־	6
רה ושמואל [בר] סְפרה ו.....	7
גיורה. ברוח [מיתרעיה שוין למיבנין	8
בשנת שית וחמשין אילין ושדרו ל..	9
....ר............ורהטו....	10
......ב........תה ועמלו ב...	11
...........ברכתה מן שביה	12
וכל בני.......עמלו ולאין...	13
שלמה [להון ולנ]שׁיהון ובניהון כלהון.	14
וכשים	15

(Tile B)

וב

וכשים כלהון דעמלו [כך אחיהון]...	2
כלהון דבכספה..............	3
ובחמידת נפ[ן]שהון]	4

אגרהון כלמה.......... עלמה [ההבא]   5
דאתי ה..........   6
קימה להון..........שם....   7
בכל שבת......פרסין [ידיהון]   8
בה.   9

(Tile A) This house was built in the year 556, this corresponding to the second year of Philip Julius Caesar; in the eldership of the priest Samuel son of Yeda'ya, the Archon. Now those who stood in charge of this work were: Abram the Treasurer, and Samuel son of Sapharah, and ..... the proselyte. With a willing spirit they [began to build] in this fifty-sixth year; and they sent .... and they made haste .... and they labored in .... a blessing from the elders and from all the children of .... they labored and toiled .... Peace to them, and to their wives and children all.

(Tile B) And like all those who labored [were their brethren ....], all of them, who with their money .... and in the eager desire of their souls .... Their reward, all whatever .... that the world which is to come .... assured to them .... on every sabbath .... spreading out [their hands] in it (in prayer)   (CIJ II, 828b; text and translation from *Final Report* VIII.1., p. 263 no. 1a).

3. Samuel is named also in a briefer Greek text: Σαμουὴλ Εἰδδέου πρεσβύτερος τῶν Ἰουδέων ἔκτισεν (CIJ II, no. 829; best text in *Final Report* VIII.1., p. 277, no. 23, whence Lifshitz, DF, no.58). 'Founded' (ἔκτισεν) must here, as Welles and Lifshitz comment, mean 'made' or built, for a second 'founder' appears on another very similar inscription (4): Σαμουὴλ Βαρσαφάρα μνησθῇ ἔκ[τ]ισεν ταῦτα οὕτως (CIJ II, no. 831; best text in *Final Report* VIII., p. 277, no. 24, whence Lifshitz, DF, no. 59).   5. Four other persons who 'aided' (the construction, evidently) are also named: Ἄβραμ καὶ Ἀροάχου καὶ Σίλας κὲ Σαλμάνη ἐβοήθησαν (CIJ II, no. 830; *Final Report*, p. 278, no. 25, whence Lifshitz, DF, no. 60.   7. Two Greek graffiti from the synagogue record single names, Ὄρβαζ and Ἰαω (CIJ II, nos. 832–3).   7. On the narrative frescoes representing O.T. scenes, a series of painted inscriptions in Aramaic and Greek identify some of the characters and occasionally describe their actions (CIJ II, nos. 834–42; *Final Report* VIII.1, pp. 269–74).   8. A graffito in Aramaic perhaps records one 'Uzzi who made the Torah shrine (אנא עזי עבדת בית ארונא), *Final Report* VIII.1, p. 269 no. 2. For a quite different reading see le Comte Mesnil de Buisson, 'L'inscription de la niche centrale de la synagogue de Dura-Europos', Syria 40

(1963), pp. 303–14: 'MRTYN' who [made] the work of the Byt 'aron
...' Note also an Aramaic graffito from a detached block in the
synagogue **שׁאמוּאל בר חנני אני** (CIJ II, no. 843; *Final Report* VIII.1, p.
273, no. 16); a brick stamp of Eulalis, with what may be a lulab (844)
and an Aramaic epitaph (?) found some 100m north of the synagogue
(845). There are also a number of painted or scratched middle-Iranian
inscriptions made by visitors to the synagogue (*Final Report* VIII.1, pp.
263–317). It should be noted that the synagogue both could and did
draw on the artistic resources of its environment to create a form of
narrative art, ignoring the long-established rules about representation
(cf. vol. I, p. 556, n. 192). For what can be known or surmised
concerning the history and nature of the community and its relations to
a wider background see *Final Report* VIII.1, pp. 322–39.

Syria is described by Josephus as the region with the largest
percentage of Jewish inhabitants. Again, the capital, *Antioch*, was
especially prominent in this respect.[23] The historian states that Jews
were settled there and given ἡ πολιτεία (see pp. 126–7 below) by the
founder, Seleucus I (312–271 B.C.), see *Ant.* xii 3, 1 (119); *C. Ap.* ii 4
(39). He also claims, *B.J.* vii 3, 3 (44), that the successors of Antiochus
Epiphanes (175–164 B.C.) restored to the *synagoge* at Antioch brass
offerings taken from the Temple; given the ambiguity of the term, it
remains uncertain whether the allusion is to the community or its
building, but the latter is quite probable. Josephus' narrative of events
in A.D. 67 and 70, *B.J.* vii 3, 3–4 (43–62), reveals that there was a
significant level of proselytism (see pp. 160–4 below) and that the
community possessed a chief official with the title *archon*. A pagan
petition to Titus in A.D. 70 failed to obtain the removal of Jewish
privileges, allegedly recorded on bronze tablets, vii 5, 2 (100–11). In the
second half of the fourth century, whence comes the next substantial
evidence on the community, more than one synagogue stood in the city
and there were officials with the titles *archon* and *prostates* (see Kraeling,
op. cit.). But in other towns of Syria also, the Jews could sometimes be
counted by thousands, as for example in *Damascus*, where, so Josephus

---

23. *B.J.* vii 3, 3 (43): τὸ γὰρ Ἰουδαίων γένος πολὺ μὲν κατὰ πᾶσαν τὴν οἰκουμένην
παρέσπαρται τοῖς ἐπιχωρίοις, πλεῖστον δὲ τῇ Συρίᾳ κατὰ τὴν γειτνίασιν ἀναμεμιγμένον,
ἐξαιρέτως δ' ἐπὶ τῆς Ἀντιοχείας ἦν πολὺ διὰ τὸ τῆς πόλεως μέγεθος. Cf. also A. Neubauer,
La géographie du Talmud, pp. 311 ff.; J. Hamburger, RE s.v. 'Antiochien'; S. Krauss, REJ
45 (1902), pp. 27–49; C. H. Kraeling, 'The Jewish Community at Antioch', JBL 51
(1932), pp. 130–60 (the fullest account); G. Haddad, *Aspects of Social Life in Antioch*
(1949); V. Tcherikover, *Hellenistic Civilization and the Jews* (1962), p. 289. See G. Downey,
A History of Antioch in Syria from Seleucus to the Arab Conquest (1961); W. A. Meeks, R. L.
Wilken, *Jews and Christians in Antioch in the First Four Centuries of the Common Era* (1978); R.
L. Wilken, *John Chrysostom and the Jews* (1983).

reports, 10,500 (in another passage 18,000) Jews were massacred at the time of the war.[24] This is related in the context of the violent inter-communal disturbances which took place in A.D. 66, on the outbreak of the great revolt (*B.J.* ii 18, 1–5 (457–80), see vol. I, p. 487). Most of them occurred in the Greek cities closest to the main Jewish area (discussed in vol. II, pp. 85–183), such as Damascus itself, where we could naturally expect Jewish settlement. But while Josephus informs us that 'the whole of Syria' was filled with disaster, and that every city had both Jews and 'Judaisers' (ii 18, 2 (462–3) : ἰουδαΐζοντας), of the cities not discussed above, he mentions by name only *Tyre*, ii 18, 5 (428), where Jews were executed or imprisoned, and *Sidon, Apamea* and *Antioch*, where the Jewish residents were spared, ii 18, 5 (479).

As is the case in regard to other parts of the Greek world (see below), significant, if scattered and incomplete, documentary evidence now exists for Jewish communities in the cities of Syria in the Graeco-Roman period; as elsewhere, much of it comes from the late-Roman period. For example, the Greek epitaphs from the Jewish necropolis at Beth She'arim, dating to the third and early fourth centuries, published by M. Schwabe and B. Lifshitz, *Beth She'arim II : The Greek Inscriptions* (1967), record Jews from the following places in Syria : *Palmyra* (nos. 92, 100); *Byblos* (136–7); *Tyre* (147, 149) *Phaene* (178), and *Antioch* (141, a *gerousiarches*); also an *archisynagogos* from *Sidon*, B. Lifshitz, *ZDPV* 72 (1966), p. 57); *Beirut* (148, and especially 164, also recording an *archisynagogos*).

From *Apamea* in Syria we have a group of nineteen mosaic inscriptions from the floor of a synagogue, dating to the late fourth century. One is specifically dated to the year 703 of the Seleucid era, A.D. 391. See CIJ II, nos. 803–18, and three extra inscriptions (with improved texts and extended commentaries) in IGLS IV (1955), nos. 1319–37, whence Lifshitz, DF, nos. 38–56. Note especially IGLS, no. 1319, showing that in A.D. 391 the synagogue had three *archisynagogi*, a *gerousiarchos* and at least four *presbyteri* at the moment when the mosaic was constructed by Ilasios, ἀρχισυνάγωγος Ἀντιοχέων, who was related by marriage to the community of Apamea (IGLS, no. 1320). He was also a descendant of the *gerousiarchos* from Antioch buried at Beth She'arim (above). Note also IGLS, no. 1321, dated by Neemiah, *hazzan* and 'deacon' (ἐπὶ Νεμία ἀζζανα καὶ τοῦ διάκονος).

As regards *Palmyra*, large claims have often been made, on the basis of nomenclature, for a Jewish presence. See most recently L.D. Merino, 'Influencias judia y cristiana en los signos e inscripciones palmirenas', *LASBF* 21 (1971), pp. 76–148. But taking only the certain evidence,

---

24. 10,500 : *B.J.* ii 20, 2 (561) ; 18,000 : *B.J.* vii 8, 7 (368).

three Hebrew inscriptions survive, from what may be the door of a
synagogue, containing Old Testament texts (CIJ II, nos. 821–3). The
only text that indubitably reflects a Jewish family is a bilingual
Palmyrene-Greek inscription of A.D. 212, which two brothers, Zeno-
bios-Zebeidah and Samuel, put up on their family tomb in honour of
their father Levi son of Jacob son of Samuel (CIJ II, no.820). An
Aramaic graffito from the temple of Bel *may* be read צדיק כהנא בר
אלעזר and *may* therefore be Jewish (CIJ II, no.824). Better evidence is
provided by a number of third-century epitaphs in Palmyrene from
Beth She'arim, clearly suggesting that the persons referred to were Jews
from Palmyra, buried there like others (see above) from outside
Palestine. See B. Mazar, *Beth She'arim* I: *Catacombs 1–4* (1973), p. 198,
no. 12; 199, nos. 17–18; 202, no. 83; 203, no. 86; 206, no. 126; 207,
nos. 130, 132, 133. Cf. also Oppenheimer, *Babylonia Judaica*, pp. 432–5.

A number of Jewish, or possibly Jewish, inscriptions originate from
the area on the borders of Palestine where, as mentioned above, a
Jewish presence is to be expected (e.g., CIJ II, nos. 848–69); for nos.
866–7 see C. H. Kraeling (ed.), *Gerasa* (1938), p. 473, nos. 283, 287. The
more substantial of these inscriptions are re-edited in Lifshitz, DF, nos.
61–3).

For the *Phoenician coast*, the evidence is very slight: a few Jewish
names from *Tyre* (CIJ II, nos. 879–80; see also J.-P. Rey-Coquais,
Inscriptions de la nécropole (1977), nos. 164; 167: priests, presumably
Jewish; 168: Samaritans); a bronze plaque from *Ornithopolis* with
συναγογῆς (sic) Ὀρνιθοκόμης (878); two certainly Jewish inscriptions
from *Beirut* (873–4); and a few fragments from *Byblos* (869–72). A
heavily damaged late Greek inscription from *Sepphoris* (CIJ II, no. 991)
seems to mention *archisynagogi* from *Tyre* and *Sidon*. It is not yet possible
to say whether the limited epigraphic record of Jewish settlement in
Syria, compared for instance to Asia Minor, reflects a historical fact, a
less well-established tradition of inscribing on stone, or the relatively
limited progress of archaeology and epigraphy in that area.

As far as the expansion of Judaism in the *Arabian Peninsula* is
concerned, it is no longer possible to determine when this first took
place.[25] Evidence however exists of Jewish settlement and influence

25. For Jewish presence and influence in Arabia before the Hegira, a complex topic
which cannot be pursued here, see e.g. R. Leszynski, *Die Juden in Arabien zur Zeit
Mohammeds* (1910); H. Lammens, *L'Arabie occidentale avant l'Hégire* (1928); D. S.
Margoliouth, *The Relations between Arabs and Israelites prior to the Rise of Islam* (1924); C. C.
Torrey, *The Jewish Foundations of Islam* (1933); H. Z. Hirschberg, *Yisra'l bArav* (1946);
J. A. Montgomery, *Arabia and the Bible* ([2]1969). It is not easy to accept as evidence
for Jewish settlement in North Arabia in the sixth century B.C. the documents discussed
by C. J. Gadd, 'The Harran Inscriptions of Nabonidus', AS 9 (1958), pp. 35-92.

there from, at the latest, the fourth century A.D. onwards. The most significant item of documentary evidence is probably the epitaph from Beth She'arim (hence third-fourth century A.D.) which is to be read Μαναὴ πατήρ, πρεσ(βύτερος) Ὁμηριτῶν (CIJ II, nos. 1137 + 8 = *Beth She'arim* II, no. 11, to be read as one, see B. Lifshitz, RB 67 (1960), p. 61). The deceased Menahem was therefore an elder of the 'Himyarites', the Jews from Himyar, i.e., the Yemen. From the Yemen itself there have now been published a Sabean-Hebrew bilingual inscription probably of the late fourth century, and a list of priestly courses in Hebrew, perhaps of the fifth century; see NESE 2 (1974), pp. 111 ff.; 117 ff.; 166 ff. Thus it is not impossible that when, under Constantius, efforts were made to spread Christianity in Himyar, the mission met with Jewish opposition, as Philostorgius reports.[26] An Ethiopic hagiographic narrative set in the fifth century also presupposes Jewish opponents.[27] In the beginning of the sixth century, the king of Himyar, Yūsuf Musuf As'ar, was a convert to Judaism. He was overthrown by the Christian king of Abyssinia *c.* A.D. 525 because he persecuted Christians.[28]

Jewish women from Arabia are also mentioned in the Mishnah.[29] The reference might be to 'Himyarites', or to people from the N-E of the Arabian peninsula or even from within the Roman province of 'Arabia', the former kingdom of *Nabataea*, absorbed in A.D. 106. Documents discovered in the Nahal Hever in 1961, but never fully published, reveal a Jewish family settled and owning property at Mahoza near Zoar, from the later first century A.D. to shortly before the revolt of A.D. 132.[30]

It is accepted however by I. Ben-Zvi, 'The Origins of the Settlement of Jewish Tribes in Arabia', *Eretz Israel* 6 (1960), pp. 130–48 (Hebrew), which is speculative.

26. Philostorgius iii 4 (ed. J. Bidez, F. Winkelmann, 1972). Philostorgius says here that of the population there οὐκ ὀλίγον πλῆθος Ἰουδαίων ἀνεπέφυρται.

27. Trans. H. Winckler, 'Zur Geschichte des Judentums in Jemen', *Altorientalische Forschungen*, Erste Reihe IV (1896), pp. 329–36. See J. Ryckmans, 'Le christianisme en Arabie du Sud préislamique', *L'Oriente cristiano* (Acc. naz. Lincei, Quad. 62, 1964), pp. 413–54.

28. Cf. T. Nöldeke, *Geschichte der Perser und Araber zur Zeit der Sasaniden, aus der arabischen Chronik des Tabari übersetzt* (1879), pp. 174 ff., 185, 187 ff.; for subsequent work and surveys of new evidence see e.g. J. Ryckmans, *La persécution des chrétiens himyarites au sixième siècle* (1956); I. Shahid, *The Martyrs of Najran: New Documents* (1971); 'Byzantium in South Arabia', *DOP* 33 (1979), pp. 23–94.

29. According to mShab. 6:6, Arabian Jewesses are permitted to wear their veils also on the Sabbath.

30. See the report in *IEJ* 12 (1962), pp. 235–48, of the archive of Babatha, which remains unpublished. For publication of a few of these documents, see H. J. Polotsky, 'Three Greek Documents from the Family Archive of Babatha', *Eretz Israel* 8 (1967), pp. 46–51 (Hebrew). The three documents are republished as SB, no. 10288; two are also

From the southernmost part of the Nabataean kingdom, the ancient Egra or Hegra (Mada' in Salih) there is an extensive grave-inscription from the facade of a tomb, written in Nabataean but explicitly identifying the family as Jewish. It is dated to the third year of Mlkw king of Nabataea (Malichus II, A.D. 40–70), hence A.D. 42 (CIS II.1, no. 219 = CIS II, no. 1422). For further reports of Jewish and possibly Jewish inscriptions from this area see F. Altheim and R. Stiehl, *Die Araber in der Alten Welt* V.1 (1968), pp. 305–9.

Concerning *Asia Minor*, Philo says, as of Syria, that Jews inhabited every town in great throngs.[31] As early as the mid-fourth century B.C. Aristotle, during his stay in Asia Minor (348–345 B.C.), had encountered an educated Jew who had come there and who 'was Greek not only in language but in spirit'; this is reported by Clearchus, a pupil of Aristotle, in his *On Sleep*, which gives further details.[32] Antiochus the Great (223–187 B.C.) is said to have settled two thousand Jewish families from Mesopotamia and Babylonia in Phrygia and Lydia.[33]

---

republished, with an English translation, by N. Lewis, Illinois Classical Studies 3 (1978), pp. 100–14. See Y. Yadin, 'The Nabataean Kingdom, Provincia Arabia, Petra and Engeddi in the Documents from Nahal Hever', Ex Oriente Lux 6 (1959–61), pp. 227–41, and G. W. Bowersock, *Roman Arabia* (1983), esp. pp. 75–9.

31. Philo, *Legatio* 33 (245): Ἰουδαῖοι καθ' ἑκάστην πόλιν εἰσὶ παμπληθεῖς Ἀσίας τε καὶ Συρίας.

32. The report of Clearchus is preserved by Josephus, *C. Ap.* i 22 (176–82) = FHG II, p. 323 (Clearchus F 69) = GLAJJ I, no. 15. Josephus is the source of the story in Eus. *Praep. Ev.* ix 5. There is also a brief mention in Clem. Alex. *Strom.* i 15, 70. Cf. A. von Gutschmid, *Neue Beiträge zur Geschichte des alten Orients* (1876) p. 77 = *Kl. Schr.* IV (1893), pp. 578 ff.; on the authenticity of Clearchus' information see E. Silberschlag, 'The Earliest Record of Jews in Asia Minor', JBL 52 (1933), pp. 66–77; H. Lewy, 'Aristotle and the Jewish Sage according to Clearchus of Soli', HThR 31 (1938), pp. 205–35; D. M. Lewis, 'The First Greek Jew', JSS 2 (1957), pp. 264–6; V. Tcherikover, *Hellenistic Civilisation and the Jews* (1961), pp. 278 ff.; and Stern, GLAJJ ad loc.

33. *Ant.* xii 3, 4 (147–53). The authenticity of the letter of Antiochus, giving instructions for this settlement, has often been disputed, see e.g., H. Willrich, *Juden und Griechen* (1895), pp. 41 ff., cf. A. Büchler, *Die Tobiaden und die Oniaden* (1899), pp. 144 ff.; for further literature R. Marcus, Loeb Josephus VII, App. D; note A. Schalit, 'The Letter of Antiochus III to Zeuxis', JQR 50 (1959–60), pp. 289–318, and most recently J. D. Gauger, *Beiträge zur jüdischen Apologetik: Untersuchungen zur Authentizität von Urkunden bei Flavius Josephus und im I. Makkebäerbuch* (1977). But there are no conclusive formal or historical arguments against authenticity. An interesting parallel is the settlement in Lydia, as early as the Persian period, of colonists from Hyrcania. 'The Hyrcanian Plain' in the triangle between Thyatira, Magnesia and Sardis, as well as a community of Hyrcanians situated there, owe their names to them. For the plain: Strabo xii 4, 13 (629); Livy xxxvii 38, 1; Stephanus, Byz. s.v. For the city: Tac. *Ann.* ii 47, 3 ('Macedones Hyrcani'); Pliny, *Nat. Hist.* v 120 (as Tacitus). For inscriptions see Robert, op. cit. below. For coins: B. V. Head, *Historia Numorum* ([2]1911), p. 652; BMC Lydia, pp. lxiv–vi; 122–6. On the site: W. M. Ramsay, *Historical Geography of Asia Minor* (1890), p. 124. On its importance as a Macedonian military colony: A. Schulten, *Hermes* 32 (1897), p. 533.

From the first century B.C., substantial testimony exists of a considerable Jewish diaspora in Asia Minor. Most of the material derives from Josephus, *Ant.* xiv 10 (185–267) and xvi 6 (160–178). Next to it in importance is the passage from Cicero's *pro Flacco* 28 (see the text below, p. 118). This information is supported by a notable and growing muster of inscriptions, many however of later date. On the basis of this evidence, it is possible to establish the existence of Jews and Jewish communities in the following districts and cities of Asia Minor in the Graeco-Roman period (the list begins in the north-west corner of Asia Minor and moves round approximately anti-clockwise to Bithynia).[34]

In *Adramyttium*, Jewish funds were confiscated in the time of Cicero (62–61 B.C.) by the *legatus* of Flaccus (*pro Flacco* 28/68).

For *Pergamum*, the earliest definite evidence is the same passage of Cicero (*pro Flacco* 28/68). Cicero says that 'not much' was taken from there. Josephus, *Ant.* xiv 10, 22 (247–55), refers to a public decree through which the Pergamenes assured the Jews and their high priest Hyrcanus of Pergamene friendship. Allusion is made in the decree to the existence of friendly relations between Jews and Pergamenes since the time of Abraham (ὡς καὶ ἐν τοῖς κατὰ Ἄβραμον καιροῖς, ὃς ἦν πάντων Ἑβραίων πατήρ, οἱ πρόγονοι ἡμῶν ἦσαν αὐτοῖς φίλοι, καθὼς καὶ ἐν τοῖς δημοσίοις εὑρίσκομεν γράμμασιν). That something of this sort was believed in the Hellenistic-Roman period under the influence of Judaism is not impossible. It therefore provides no conclusive reason to doubt the authenticity of this decree; on the contrary it might be taken as proof of the influence of Judaism in that region. The text of the decree as Josephus gives it contains the terms of part of a Roman *senatus consultum*. If in fact this belonged to it originally, the Pergamene decree will have been issued already in the time of the high priest Hyrcanus I. But the *senatus consultum* was probably inserted into the Pergamene decree by mistake, and should be dissociated from it completely; (see vol. I, p. 197, and note now T. Rajak, GRBS 22 (1981), pp. 65–81). The name of the *prytanis*, Kratippos, by which the Pergamene decree is dated, appears also as that of an eponymous official in a fragmentary inscribed list of ephebes from Pergamum (MDAI (Athens) 27 (1902),

Note especially L. Robert, *Hell.* VI (1948), pp. 16–26, for a full review of the evidence.

34. For surveys see e.g., J. Weiss, s.v. 'Kleinasien' in Herzog-Hauck, *Real-Enc.* III ([10]1901), cols. 535–63; W. M. Ramsay, 'The Jews in the Graeco-Asiatic Cities', *Exp.* (Jan. 1902), pp. 19–33; (Feb. 1902) pp. 92–109; Juster, *op. cit.* I, pp. 188–94; F. Blanchetière, 'Juifs et non-Juifs. Essai sur la Diaspora en Asie Mineure', RHPhR 54 (1974), pp. 367–82, and A. J. Marshall, 'Flaccus and the Jews of Asia (Cicero, *Pro Flacco* 28, 67–69)', Phoenix 29 (1975), pp. 139–54; A. Ovadiah, 'Ancient Synagogues in Asia-Minor', *Proc. X. Int. Cong. Class. Arch.*, *1973* (1978), pp. 857–66. A full study of Judaism in Asia Minor is expected from A. T. Kraabel.

p. 126) and also in a festal calendar from there (*Ins. v. Pergamon*, no. 247); see JOAI 8 (1905), p. 238. For an altar from Pergamum with the judaising inscription Θεός Κύριος, ὁ ὤν εἰς ἀεί see BE 1958, no. 413, and Lifshitz, DF, no. 12.

In *Lydia* generally, as noted above, Jewish colonists were settled by Antiochus the Great, *Ant.* xii 34 (147–153).

In *Phocaea*, or *Kyme*, on the Ionian coast the following Jewish inscription was found. It is interesting from several points of view (reported by Th. Reinach REJ 12 (1886), pp. 236–43 and BCH 10 (1886), pp. 327–35 = IGR IV, no. 1327 = CIJ II, no. 738 = DF, no. 13 = IK Kyme, no. 45): Τάτιον Στράτωνος τοῦ Ἐνπέδωνος τὸν οἶκον καὶ τὸν περίβολον τοῦ ὑπαίθρου κατασκευάσασα ἐκ τῶ[ν ἰδ]ίων ἐχαρίσατο τ[οῖς Ἰο]υδαίοις. Ἡ συναγωγὴ ἐ[τείμη]σεν τῶν Ἰουδαίων Τάτιον Σ[τράτ]ωνος τοῦ Ἐνπέδωνος χρυσῷ στεφάνῳ καὶ προεδρίᾳ. On the personal names in -ιον (masculine and feminine pet-forms) see A. Zimmerman, *Philologus* 64 (1905), pp. 499–505, and L. Robert, *Hellenica* VI (1948), p. 90.

From *Thyatira* the retailer of purple originated, named Lydia (Acts 16:14), a σεβομένη τὸν θεόν. Since she is met only in Philippi, it is not known whether she had already been converted to the Jewish faith in her homeland. A Σαμβαθεῖον is mentioned on an inscription from Thyatira, dating from between the mid-second and earlier third century; IGR IV, no. 1281; CIJ II, no. 752. The notion that such a building might be a sanctuary of the Chaldaean Sybil Sambethe mentioned in the Sibylline Oracles has been adequately refuted by S. Krauss, *Synagogale Altertümer*, pp. 25 ff. See also V. Tcherikover, 'The Sambathions', Scripta Hierosolymitana 1 (1954), pp. 78–98, on pp. 83–4, and the further discussion in CPJ III, pp. 43–87, 'The Sambathions'. It is much more probable that σαμβαθεῖον is simply the equivalent of σαββατεῖον, meaning 'Sabbath House' (cf. Josephus, *Ant.* xvi, 6, 2 (164) and vol. II, p. 440). The community to which this 'Sabbath House' belonged cannot, however, have been a fully orthodox Jewish one for, according to the inscription, a burial place was situated in its vicinity.

In *Magnesia ad Sipylum* the following inscription has been found (REJ 10 (1885), p. 76; CIJ II, no. 753; IK Magnesia, no. 27): Στράτων Τυράννου Ἰουδαῖος ζῶν τὸ μνημεῖον κατεσκέασε (sic) ἑαυτῷ καὶ γυναικὶ καὶ τέκνοις.

Smyrna was certainly inhabited by a Jewish community, one reported as having shown hostility to Christians (cf. e.g., R. Knopf, *Das Nachapostol. Zeitalter* (1905), pp. 142–4; C.J. Cadoux, *Ancient Smyrna* (1938), ch. 11–12). 1). As early as the book of Revelation mention is made of the abuse that Christians in Smyrna had to endure at the

hands of the Jews (Rev. 2:9). 2). The Jews there play a prominent part
in the martyr-act of Polycarp, paras. 17–18; see J. B. Lightfoot, *Apostolic
Fathers* II, pt. 3, pp. 363–401; K. Lake, *Apostolic Fathers* (Loeb ed.) II,
pp. 312–45; Knopf-Krüger-Ruhbach, *Ausgewählte Martyrerakten*, no.
1; H. A. Musurillo, *Acts of the Christian Martyrs*, no. 1. Cf. also the
legendary *Vita Polycarpi auctore Pionio*, ed. L. Duchesne (1881), dating
from about the fourth century A.D.; see Th. Reinach, REJ 11 (1885),
pp. 235–8); other literature about this *Vita* in O. Bardenhewer, *Gesch.
der altkirchl. Literatur* II, p. 616; B. Altaner, *Patrology*, p. 112. 3).
Similarly in the *Martyrium Pionii*, relating to the Decian persecution,
A.D. 250, the Jews in Smyrna appear as enemies of the Christians; see
Knopf, *op. cit.*, pp. 96–143 f. Text in O. von Gebhardt, *Ausgewählte
Martyrerakten* (1902), pp. 96–114; Knopf-Krüger-Ruhbach, no. 10;
Musurillo, no. 10; other literature on this *Martyrium* in Bardenhewer,
op. cit., II, pp. 631 f.; Altaner, *op. cit.*, p. 112. An important study of this
text was expected from L. Robert.

An inscription from the time of Hadrian, giving a list of donors of
gifts to the city, mentions also οἱ ποτὲ Ἰουδαῖοι (CIG, no. 3148 = IGR IV,
no. 1431 = CIJ II, no. 742, line 29; cf. also 740 = DF, nos. 14–15).

Apart from a brief Jewish inscription, a building-inscription put up
by Irenopoios son of Jacob, and ending שלום, CIG, no. 9897 = CIJ II, no.
739, the most informative inscription from Smyrna is IGR IV, no. 1452
= CIJ II, no. 741 = IK Smyrna I, no. 295: Ῥουφεῖνα Ἰουδαία
ἀρχισυνάγωγος κατεσκεύασεν τὸ ἐνσόριον τοῖς ἀπελευθέροις καὶ θρέμασιν.
μηδενὸς ἄλ⟨λ⟩ου ἐξουσίαν ἔχοντος θάψαι τινά. εἰ δέ τι τολμήσει, δώσει
τῷ ἱερωτάτῳ ταμείῳ (δηνάρια) αφ´ καὶ τῷ ἔθνει τῶν Ἰουδαίων (δηνάρια)
α´. ταύτης τῆς ἐπιγραφῆς τὸ ἀντίγραφον ἀπόκειται εἰς τὸ ἀρχεῖον. The
inscription dates at the earliest to the third century A.D. Note also IK
Smyrna I, no. 296, a γραμματεὺς τοῦ ἐν Σμύρνῃ λαοῦ (for the Jewish
connotations of λαός see L. Robert, *Hellenica* XI-XII (1960), pp. 260–2),
and no. 297, a gravestone of Judas, erected by his mother Anna.

In *Sardis* a Jewish community *may* have been in existence as early as
the sixth century B.C. Obadiah v. 20, writing in the late sixth or fifth
century, refers to '(the) captivity of Jerusalem which is in Sepharad'
(בספרד) in the course of a prophecy of destruction. No indication of
the localisation of the place is given. However, in 1916 a Lydian-
Aramaic bilingual inscription from Sardis was published, belonging to
the Persian period, from either the fifth or the fourth century; see
Donner and Röllig, KAI, no. 260, with text, translation and commentary. It is dated 'on the fifth of Marheshvan, year 10 of King Artaxerxes
in the fortress Sepharad (בספרד בירתא)'. The two place-names are
identical. But although there is late evidence for Persian settlement of
Jews in Hyrcania (p. 6 above), there is none for such settlement in

the Sardis area, i.e., Lydia, until the Seleucid period (p. 17). In any case, the identity of the two names is hardly an adequate basis. In short, though Sardis *may* have been the 'Sepharad' to which Obadiah alludes, Jewish settlement in this area is not attested until a later period. The existence of a Jewish community there in the first century B.C. is recorded by various passages in Josephus. In a letter of L. Antonius to the authorities in Sardis (50–49 B.C.), it is said that the Jews in the city have their own court. Hence even Jews who are Roman citizens are authorized to bring their disputes before the Jewish court instead of before that set up for Roman citizens, *Ant.* xiv 10, 17 (235). Through a decree of the city of Sardis, of uncertain date, the Jews there are assured of the unhindered practice of their religion, *Ant.* xiv 10, 24 (259–61). In a letter of the proconsul, C. Norbanus Flaccus, to the authorities in Sardis in the time of Augustus, the city authorities are requested not to prevent the Jews from consigning money for sacred purposes to Jerusalem, *Ant.* xvi 6, 6 (171).

There is now extensive inscriptional and archaeological evidence for the Jewish community of Sardis and their synagogue in the Imperial period. The older evidence consists of two fragmentary inscriptions, one mentioning a woman described as Ἑβρέα (CIJ II, no. 750) and the other listing among the fountains of the city that of the synagogue, συναγωγῆ[ς κρήνη] (no. 751). By far the most important recent evidence for Jewish communities in Asia Minor is however provided by the synagogue itself, discovered in 1962, and excavated and restored since.[35] It is thought that the building, clearly identified as Jewish by decorative elements and inscriptions, had originally been constructed as part of a large bath and gymnasium complex begun in the first century A.D., with work continuing well into the second, and had come into use as a synagogue by the second half of the third century. It was then further remodelled in the fourth century, and may have remained in service until the early seventh. Including a number of small fragments, more than eighty inscriptions have been found there. The only group to be fully published so far includes two mosaic inscriptions of persons described as θεοσεβής (Robert, *Sardes*, nos. 4–5 = DF, nos. 17–18); a plaque recording someone's contribution to the building ἐκ τῶν δωρεῶν

35. The bibliography of the Sardis synagogue, including many annual or semi-popular reports, is already extensive. The essential items are: L. Robert, *Nouvelles Inscriptions de Sardes* I (1964), pp. 37–58, 'Inscriptions de la Synagogue'; A. R. Seager, 'The Building History of the Sardis Synagogue', AJA 76 (1972), pp. 425–35; G. M. A. Hanfmann, *Sardis from Prehistoric to Roman Times* (1983), ch. 9, 'The Synagogue and the Jewish Community' (by A. R. Seager and A. T. Kraabel); A. R. Seager et al., *The Synagogue and its Setting* (*Archaeological Exploration of Sardis, Report V*), forthcoming. For a brief account, Kraabel, 'The Diaspora Synagogue', pp. 483–8.

τοῦ παντοκράτορος Θ⟨εο⟩ῦ (no. 7 = DF, no. 20); and three pottery fragments with the names Sabbatios, Theoktistos and Jacob (nos. 20–2). See DF, nos. 21–7. The remainder, on which a brief report has been made (BASOR 187 (1967), pp. 27–32), include a notice of the presentation of a menorah (*heptamyxion*); a plaque which probably comes from the Torah shrine (*nomophylakion*); and the fourth-century inscription of a man described as *hiereus* and *sophodidaskalos*. A number of fragmentary Hebrew inscriptions have also been found and await publication.

That Jews lived in *Philadelphia*, south-east of Sardis, is apparent from the letter in the book of Revelation to the Christian communities there (Rev. 3:9). It is confirmed by an inscription from Deliler nearby, CIJ II, no. 754 = DF, no. 28: [τ]ῇ ἁγιοτ[άτῃ σ]υναγωγῇ τῶν Ἑβραίων Εὐστάθιος ὁ θεοσεβὴς ὑπὲρ μνίας (sic) τοῦ ἀδελφοῦ Ἑρμοφίλου τὸν μασκαύλην...

In *Hypaepa*, south of Sardis, the following inscription has been found: Ἰουδα[ί]ων νεωτέρων. It dates from about the end of the second, or the beginning of the third, century A.D., Th. Reinach, REJ 10 (1885), pp. 74 ff. = CIJ II, no. 755.

It is perhaps a sign of Jewish influence in *Colophon* that the Oracle of Apollo Clarius once issued a reply there concerning the god Ἰάω (see the oracle in Macrobius, *Sat.* i 18, 19–21 = Stern, GLAJJ II, no. 445); on its authenticity see G. Baudissin, *Studien zur semitischen Religionsgeschichte* I (1876), pp. 213–18; C. Buresch, *Klaros* (1889), pp. 48–55); Ch. Picard, *Éphèse et Claros* (1922), pp. 705, 715.

The *archisynagogos* attested at nearby *Teos* (CIJ II, no. 744) was probably a Jewish official. The name was correctly re-read by L. Robert, *Hell.* I (1940), pp. 27–8, as *T.* Ῥουτ(ίλιος) Ἰωσῆς: hence a Roman citizen, perhaps of the third century A.D. See Lifshitz, DF, no. 16.

References to the Jews in *Ephesus* are numerous. Josephus claims that they were granted local citizenship as early as the time of the Diadochi, probably through Antiochus II Theos (261–246 B.C.), Josephus, *Ant.* xii 3, 2 (125); C. *Ap.* ii 4; cf. p. 129. When the consul, L. Cornelius Lentulus Crus, acting in the interest of the Pompeian party in Asia Minor, summoned Roman citizens to military service in 49 B.C., the Jews in Ephesus with Roman citizenship were exempted, *Ant.* xiv 10, 13 (228–30); 16 (234); 19 (239–40). This privilege was renewed in 43 B.C. by Dolabella, and they were at the same time assured of the freedom to practise their religion in general, *Ant.* xiv 10, 11–12 (223–27). The same guarantee was given by M. Iunius Brutus in 42 B.C., *Ant.* xiv 10, 25 (262–4), where the corrupt name is probably to be read in this way. Under Augustus, the authorities in Ephesus were often sharply reminded that the Jews were not to be prevented from despatching sacred money to Jerusalem; see the letters of C. Norbanus Flaccus in Philo, *Legatio* 40 (315); of Agrippa, Josephus *Ant.* xvi 6, 4 (167–8); of Iullus Antonius, *Ant.* xvi 6, 7 (172–3). The latter was consul in 10 B.C. and proconsul of Asia a few years later.

The synagogue in Ephesus is mentioned in Acts 18:19, 26; 19:8. A fragmentary inscription of uncertain date from the city seems to refer to the officials of the synagogue: τῶν ἀρχι⟨σ⟩υναγώγ⟨ω⟩ν καὶ τῶν πρεσβ(υτέρων), JÖAI 52 (1978–80), p. 50, no. 94 (BE 1981, no. 428) = IK Ephesos, no. 1251. From the second to third century A.D. come the following two epitaphs found in Ephesus: 1) Published in the form, τὸ μνημεῖόν ἐστι Μὰρ Μουσσίου Ἰαίρεος. ζῇ. κήδονται οἱ Ἰουδαῖοι (IBM III.2, Ephesos (1890), no. 676 = CIJ II, no. 746). Μάρ has been supposed equivalent to *mar*, title of a respected rabbi, and Μούσσιος to Moses. But it is more likely that what we have is the abbreviated name of a Roman citizen, Μ(ᾶρκος) Α⟨ὐ⟩ρ(ήλιος) Μούσσιος. The word ἰαίρεως is probably not a proper name but the genitive ἱερέως, 'priest'. So L. Robert, *Hell.* XI-XII (1960), pp. 381–4, followed in IK Ephesos, no. 1676. 2) [τὸ μνημεῖόν ἐστι] Ἰο[υλίου ? ...] ἀρχιάτρου [καὶ τῆς γυναικ]ὸς αὐτοῦ Ἰουλίας [....]ης καὶ τέκνων αὐτῶν. [ζῶ]σιν. [ταύτης τῆ]ς σοροῦ κήδον[ται οἱ ἐν Ἐφέσ]ῳ Ἰουδέοι (IBM III.2, no. 677 = CIJ II, 745 = IK Ephesos, no. 1677). The title 'chief doctor' may imply that the man was among the doctors recognized by a city in the province of Asia; they enjoyed immunity from all obligations. According to a letter of Antoninus Pius (*Dig.* xxvii 1, 6, 2), immunities could be granted for five in the small towns, seven in *conventus* centres and ten in *metropoleis*. For these city chief physicians in general, see J. Marquardt, *Das Privatleben der Römer* II (1882), pp. 749 ff.; RE II, cols. 464–6; W. Liebenam, *Städteverwaltung in röm. Kaiserreiche* (1900), pp. 100–4; J. Keil, 'Arzteinschriften aus Ephesos', JÖAI 8 (1905), pp. 128–38; P. Wolters, JÖAI 9 (1906), pp. 295–7). There was a Jewish ἀρχίατρος also in Venosa (CIJ I², no. 600). For a full discussion of the meaning of the term, concluding that, in the context of an Asia Minor city after Antoninus Pius' letter, it most probably does refer to one of the doctors granted immunity, see V. Nutton, 'Archiatri and the Medical Profession in Antiquity', PBSR 45 (1977), pp. 191–226. Cf. also the discussion of *archiatri* in G. H. R. Horsley, *New Documents Illustrating Early Christianity* II (1982), no. 2.

For the later period note also the inscribed letter of bishop Hypatios mentioning the φιλαργυρία Ἰουδαϊκή, H. Grégoire, *Rec. Ins. Gr. Asie Min.* I, no. 108; *Ephesos* IV: *die Marienkirche* (1932), no. 35 = IK Ephesos, no. 4135. This is of course not evidence for Jewish settlement in the city. For the fragmentary evidence available from this period see C. Foss, *Ephesus after Antiquity* (1979), p. 45.

It was necessary for a Roman proconsul, probably in the time of Caesar, to compel the authorities in *Tralles* to allow Jews to practise their religion, as appears from a chance allusion in the letter of the Laodiceans in *Ant.* xiv 10, 20 (242). The inscription of a grand lady from Tralles, Capitolina, ἡ ἀξιόλογ(ος?) καὶ ⟨θ⟩εοσεβ(ής), may refer to her Jewish beliefs (see also the formula ὑπὲρ εὐχῆς, ll. 6–7), as argued by L. Robert, *Études Anatoliennes* (1937), pp. 409–12), followed by Lifshitz, DF, no. 30.

In the neighbourhood of *Nysa*, in the Maeander valley, the following inscription has been found: Μένανδρος 'Απολλων⟨ί⟩δου ἐποίησεν οἰκο⟨δ⟩ομήσας τὸν τόπον ἀπὸ τῆς ἐπιγραφῆς τῆς πρὸς ἀνατ[ολ]ὴν τῷ λαῷ καὶ τῇ συνόδῳ τ[ῶν περὶ] Δωσίθεον Θεογένου (Ath. Mitt. 22 (1897), p. 484, no. 2). The editor notes: 'The expression λαός might suggest that the σύνοδος was a Jewish community'. This is very probable, see L. Robert, *Hell.* XI-XII (1960), p. 261 (from which the text given here is taken); DF, no. 31. With regard to λαός, compare the inscriptions from Hierapolis in Phrygia, Mantinea, and Larissa collected on p. 89. Personal names with θεός were specially popular among Jews. Nysa lies between Tralles and Laodicea.

That Jews were living in *Caria*, particularly in the towns of *Myndus*, *Halicarnassus* and *Cnidus*, as early as the second century B.C. may be deduced from 1 Mac. 15:23 (see above, p. 4). Good evidence exists for Hyllarima, Priene (?), Miletus, Iasus, Halicarnassus and Myndus.

At *Hyllarima* in the interior, an inscription of the late-Roman period records a dedication by Αὐρ. Εὐσάνθιος (sic) πρε⟨σ⟩βύτερος and Αὐρ. Εὐτυνχ⟨αν⟩οῦσα which mentions (l. 5) τῇ ἁγιωτάτῃ συναγωγῇ (BCH 58 (1934), p. 379, no. 44 and pp. 516–17); note L. Robert, *Hell.* III, p. 105, n. 5, recording from autopsy that the inscription is *in situ* in the ruins of what may well be the synagogue. Cf. DF, no. 32.

At *Priene*, no literary or epigraphic evidence exists for a Jewish community, but a house originally built in the Hellenistic period and reconstructed under the Empire has clearly Jewish decorative motifs (menorah, lulab, ethrog, shofar) and can reasonably be regarded as a synagogue. See Kraabel, 'Diaspora Synagogue', pp. 489–91.

The authorities in *Miletus* were specifically instructed by a letter of the proconsul of Asia not to hinder the Jews in the practice of their religious customs, *Ant.* xiv 10, 21 (244–6). The letter probably dates to the time of Caesar; in our text of Josephus, the proconsul's name is corrupt (see below, p. 116, n. 37).

In the theatre of Miletus belonging to the Roman period, the following has been found, besides many other inscriptions on seats: τόπος Εἰουδέων τῶν καὶ Θεοσεβίον (published by A. Deissman, *Licht vom Osten* (1908; ⁴1923), pp. 391–2 f.; ET, *Light from the Ancient East* (1910), pp. 446 f. = CIJ II, no. 748). This inscription has given rise to very extensive discussion. See most recently H. Hommel, 'Juden und Christen im kaiserzeitlichen Milet. Überlegungen zur Theaterinschrift', Ist. Mitt. 25 (1975), pp. 167–95. See pp. 167–8 below.

Miletus also has a small oblong building which the excavators hypothetically identified as a synagogue of the late Roman period. See *Milet* I.6 (1922), pp. 80–2 and 17 (plan), and Kraabel, 'Diaspora Synagogue', pp. 488–9.

In *Iasus* on the coast between Miletus and Halicarnassus, a list of contributors to the festival of the Dionysia includes a certain Nicetas, a Jerusalemite, who is qualified furthermore as a *metoikos* (a foreigner living in Iasus). He donated one hundred drachmas (Le Bas et Waddington, *Inscriptions*, III, no. 294 = CIJ II, no. 749). The inscription dates from some time in the middle of the second century B.C. (see the discussion in Le Bas et Waddington III.2, p. 87, on nos. 252 ff.). Jewish support of a pagan festival recalls parallel events in Jerusalem before the beginning of the Maccabaean uprising. It is however not certain that Nicetas was a Jew. Two other inscriptions (L. Robert, *Hell.* I, pp. 28–9; III, pp. 100–1) each mention the name Judas.

A decree of the city of *Halicarnassus* guarantees the Jews of the city free exercise of their religion, *Ant.* xiv 10, 23 (256–8). This decree was also passed under Roman influence, perhaps in the time of Caesar.

In *Myndus*, west of Halicarnassus and on the same peninsula, a woman appears on an inscription from the beginning of the Byzantine period as *archisynagogos* (REJ 42 (1901), 1–4 = CIJ II, no. 756 = DF, no. 29).

From the newly excavated city of *Aphrodisias* in inland Caria, there is a new inscription of major importance which is to be published by J. M. Reynolds, O. Masson and R. Tannenbaum as a Supplementary Volume of the Proceedings of the Cambridge Philological Society.

The text is inscribed on two faces of a marble block which may possibly have functioned as a door-jamb. The lettering on face *b.* (see below) suggests a date in the late second or early third century. That on face *a.* is different, and cannot be assigned to a specific century within the Imperial or late-Roman period. It remains unclear whether or not the two inscribed faces contain a single text.

Face *a.* contains the names and functions of persons who contributed for the foundation of something (presumably a building?) described in l. 1 by the transliterated Latin word *patella*, meaning dish. Its function is described as being 'for the relief of sorrow (*apenthesia*) among the people'. These and other problems arising from the heading cannot be discussed here. The Jewish character of the inscription is unmistakeable from the names which follow, including a female patroness (*prostates*) named Iael, with her son Iosoua, an *arch(on)* ; Samouel, a *presbeutes* and priest; Beniamin, a *psalmo(logos?)* ; three persons described as *proselutos* (variously abbreviated), with the names Samouel, Ioses, and Eioseph son of Eusebios; and two persons described as *theoseb(es)*.

The concluding lines of this face are lost, as is perhaps one line at the top of face *b*. Two further lines here are completely or almost completely lost. It is therefore unclear whether the list of names which follows (in a different epigraphic hand, see above) had a separate heading, or continues the list of contributors.

What is clear is, once again, that this is a list of the male members of a Jewish community. Amid the Greek, and transliterated Latin names, there are a substantial number of Hebrew names: Iakob (3 times), Manases, Ioudas (7), Ioseph (3), Rouben, Samouel, Symeon, Zacharias; the name Eusabbathios also occurs four times.

After this list there is a one-line break and then a sub-heading: 'and such as are *theosebis*' (*sic*). The new list begins with nine persons each described as 'town-councillor' (*bouleutes*); here and in the rest of it, again recording only males, there are no Hebrew names, although the name Eusabbathios occurs once. The new inscription thus provides the conclusive evidence for the reality of a defined category of gentile 'God-fearers' attached to a Jewish community (see pp. 166–8 below).

Note also that the editors will publish, along with other minor Jewish, or possibly Jewish, inscriptions, some late-Roman graffiti from the Odeon at Aphrodisias: one reads 'place of (the) Hebreoi', and another 'place of (the) blue Hebreoi, the elders' (*paleoi*). The reference is to the circus- and theatre-faction of the 'blues'.

In *Sala*, on the borders of Lydia and Phrygia, eponymous magistrates (Melito and Andronicus) whose father was named 'Salamon' appear on coins from the time of Trajan, Antoninus Pius and Marcus Aurelius. a) In the time of Trajan: ἐπὶ Μελίτωνος Σαλ(αμῶνος) ἀρχιερέως Σαλήνων, RN 4ᵉ sér. 2 (1898), pp. 535–6, nos. 6436, 6441, 6446. BMC Lydia, p. 227. b) Under Antoninus Pius: ἐπὶ Ἀνδρονείκου Σαλαμῶνος Σαλήνων, BMC Lydia, p. 232; F. Imhoof-Blumer, *Kleinasiatische Münzen* (1901), p. 183. The name Σαλαμῶνος is written in full on both examples and thereby makes possible the restoration of the name on the coins of Melito. c) In the time of Marcus Aurelius: ἐπὶ Ἀνδρο(νείκου) Σαλαμῶνος Σαλήνων, RN 4ᵉ ser. 2 (1898), p. 556, no. 6453.

The city officials whose names appear on these coins were presumably not practising Jews. Melito was even a pagan high priest. The name 'Salamon' has suggested nevertheless that they were of Jewish origin. Cf. W. M. Ramsay, *Exp.* (Feb. 1902) p. 102. But it is however more likely that the name is Lydian, see L. Zgusta, *Kleinasiatische Personennamen* (1964), p. 451.

In *Phrygia*, a considerable number of Jews were settled by Antiochus the Great, *Ant.* xii 3, 4 (147–53) ; see above, p. 17. Their main centres of population seem to have been Laodicea and Apamea. For Jews in Phrygia in general, see Ramsay, *The Cities and Bishoprics of Phrygia* I.2 (1897), pp. 667–76.

In *Laodicea*, rather more than twenty pounds of gold destined for the Temple were confiscated on the orders of Flaccus (62–61 B.C.) (Cicero, *pro Flacco* 28-68 : 'Laodiceae viginti pondo paullo amplius per hunc L. Peducaeum iudicem nostrum').

In a letter to the proconsul, C. Rabirius, perhaps in the time of Caesar (both name and title are uncertain, see below p. 116), the authorities of Laodicea assure him that, in obedience to Roman orders, they will not hinder the Jews in the free practice of their religion, *Ant.* xiv 10, 20 (241–3).

In *Hierapolis* a number of Jewish epitaphs have been found.

1) ἡ σορὸς... Αὐρηλίας Γλυκωνήδος Ἀμμιανοῦ καὶ τ[οῦ] ἀνδρὸς αὐτῆς Μ(άρκου) Αὐρ(ηλίου) Ἀλεξάνδρου Θεοφίλου ἐπίκλ[ην Ἀσ?]αφ [λα]οῦ Ἰουδαίων.. ἑτέρῳ δὲ οὐδενὶ ἐξέσται κηδεῦσαι ἐν αὐτῇ τινα. εἰ δὲ μὴ, ἀποτείσει τῷ λαῷ τῶν Ἰουδαί[ω]ν προστε⟨ί⟩μου ὀν[όμ]ατι δηνάρια χείλια. ταύτης τῆς ἐπιγραφῆς ἀπλοῦν ἀ[ν]τίγραφον ἀπετέθη εἰς τὰ ἀρχία (*Altertümer von Hierapolis*, by Humann, Cichorius, Judeich, Winter; JDAI, 4. Ergänzungsheft (1898), ins. no. 69 = CIJ II, no. 776.

2) ἡ σορὸς.. Αὐρ(ηλίας) Αὐγούστας Ζωτεικοῦ ... εἰ δὲ ἔτι ἕτερος κηδεύσει, δώσει τῇ κατοικίᾳ τῶν ἐν Ἱεραπόλει κατοικούντων Ἰουδαίων προστείμου (δηνάρια) [...] καὶ τῷ ἐκζητήσαντι (δηνάρια δισχίλια). ἀντίγραφον ἀπετέθη ἐν τῷ ἀρχίῳ τῶν Ἰουδαίων (*Altertümer von Hierapolis*, ins. no. 212 = IGR IV, no. 834 = CIJ II, no. 775. The Jewish archive mentioned here is probably the one meant also in the previous inscription.

3) Especially remarkable is the epitaph of a certain Publius Aelius Glykon, in which it is stated that the dead man has bequeathed a sum to the guild of purple-dyers (τῇ σεμνοτάτῃ προεδρίᾳ τῶν πορφυροβάφων) so that, out of the interest, his grave could be decorated yearly with a wreath ἐν τῇ ἑορτῇ τῶν ἀζύμων. Further, he left to another guild (τῷ συνεδρίῳ τῶν καιροδαπιστῶν) a sum for the decoration of his grave ἐν τῇ ἑορτῇ πεντηκο[στῆς]. According to this, the dead man at least was a Jew, since τὰ ἄζυμα can only refer to Passover, not to the Christian festival of Easter. But the members of the guilds must also have been influenced by Judaism. The inscription was published by A. Wagener, Rev. de l'Instruction publique en Belgique XVIᵉ année 11 (1869), pp. 1 ff. See Philologus 32 (1873), p. 380; Ramsay, *The Cities and Bishoprics of Phrygia* I 2, p. 545; and Judeich, *Altertümer von Hierapolis*, no. 342 = CIJ II, no. 777. For discussion see Ramsay, *Exp.* (Feb. 1902), 98–100. On the

custom of decorating graves yearly with flowers, see also Judeich, *op. cit.*, 129 ff. (on no. 195) and the inscriptions nos. 133, 153, 195, 209, 234, 278, 293, 310, 336. It occurs also in the west: CIL V, nos. 2315, 4017; XI, no. 132. J.P. Waltzing, *Étude historique sur les corporations professionnelles chez les Romains* IV (1900), p. 542. Note also the epitaph of Αὐρηλίου Ἀννίου Εἰνόνιος (?) Ἰουδέ[ου?] (CIJ II, no. 778. Nos. 779 and 780 may perhaps be Jewish), and the more recently published epitaph from a tomb with Jewish symbols: ἡ σορὸς καὶ ὁ βωμὸς καθ' οὗ ἐπεικεέται Μάρ(κου) Αὐρ(ηλίου) Φιλουμένου Στρηνείωνος Ἰουδαίου, as well as a sarcophagus with menorah and the word Ἰουδέων (BE 1971, no. 645).

In *Apamea*, Jewish money amounting to about one hundred pounds of gold was confiscated on the orders of Flaccus (62–61 B.C.). (Cicero, *pro Flacco* 28-68: 'Apameae manifesto comprehensum ante pedes praetoris in foro expensum esse auri pondo centum paullo minus per Sex. Caesium, equitem Romanum, castissimum hominem atque integerrimum'.)

An inscription in Apamea runs as follows: Αὐρ. Ῥοῦφος Ἰουλιανοῦ Βʹ ἐποί[ησα τὸ ἡρῷον ἐμαυτῷ κὲ [τῇ συμβίῳ μ]ου Αὐρ. Τατιανῇ· ἰς ὃ ἕτερος οὐ τεθῇ. εἰ δέ' τις ἐπιτηδεύσει, τὸν νόμον οἶδεν τῶν Εἰουδέων (Ramsay, *The Cities and Bishoprics of Phrygia* II.2, p. 538 = CIJ II, no. 774). Note also the parallel inscription from Apamea (CIJ II, no. 773 dating to A.D. 253-4), on the construction of a ἡρῷον and using the formula ἔσται αὐτῷ πρὸς, τ[ὸν] θεόν. On heroon = tomb or burial-place, see below, p. 33, the remarks on the inscription from Tlos.

It is also possible that the localisation and adoption of the Noah saga in Apamea is to be ascribed to Jewish influence. Definite evidence for this localization admittedly derives only from the Christian period. Iulius Africanus notes that some believe Ararat to be in the neighbourhood of Celaenae in Phrygia (quoted by Georgius Syncellus, *Chron.* ed. Dindorf I, pp. 38–42; also in Routh, *Reliquiae Sacrae* II, p. 243). It is located in the same place, i.e. near the sources of the Marsyas, by the author of *Or. Sib.* i 261 ff. According to Strabo xii 8, 15 (577 ff.), Celaenae lay near the sources of the Marsyas and the Meander. The inhabitants were forced by Antiochus Soter to leave the town, and to settle further downstream at the junction of the Marsyas and Meander, where Antiochus founded the city of Apamea in honour of his mother, Apama. Apamea thus took the place of Celaenae (Strabo, *loc. cit.*; Livy xxxviii 13, 5; Pliny, *Nat. Hist.* v 29-106. On the location and history of the town, see especially the thorough treatment by G. Hirschfeld, AAB (1875), pp. 1–26; also D.G. Hogarth, JHS 9 (1888), pp. 343–9; G. Weber, *Dinair, Célènes, Apamée Cibotos, avec un plan et deux cartes* (1892); Hirschfeld in RE I, cols. 2664 ff.; Ramsay, *The Cities and Bishoprics of*

Phrygia I.2 (1897), pp. 396–483; H. Leclercq in DAC I.2 (1907), cols. 2500–23; RE XX (1941), col. 815 (bibliography); D. Magie, *Roman Rule in Asia Minor* (1950), pp. 983–4; Jones, CERP², pp. 69–71. We now have coins from Apamea dating from the first half of the third century A.D., from the time of Septimius Severus, Macrinus, Severus Alexander and Philip the Arab, depicting Noah and his wife stepping out of the Ark. The name *ΝΩΕ* is added in explanation. The coins, already known to earlier numismatists, P. Eckhel, *Doctr. Num.* III, pp. 132 ff., were described and published in greatest detail in F.W. Madden, NC (1866), pp. 173–219 and pl. 6; new examples in the Waddington collection, RN (1898), pp. 397 ff., nos. 5723, 5730, 5731; BMC *Phrygia*, p. 101; full bibliography in Leclercq, DAC *loc. cit.*; B.V. Head, *Hist. Num.* (²1911), pp. 665–7; note also E. R. Goodenough, *Jewish Symbols* II (1953), pp. 119–20. Since the coins were struck by the pagan authorities of Apamea, they testify to the acceptance of the legend in these districts also. But it is improbable that this first came about through Christian influence; Judaism obtained a foothold there long before Christianity. The adoption of the Noah saga may be in some way connected to the previous adoption of the nickname *Κιβωτός,* by which Apamea was known as early as Strabo, xii 8, 13 (576): *Ἀπάμεια ἡ Κιβωτὸς λεγομένη.* Cf. Pliny, *Nat. Hist.* v 29-106: 'Apameam ante appellatam Celaenas dein Ciboton'; Ptolem. V 2, 25: *Ἀπάμεια Κιβωτός. Κιβωτός* is the term usually employed in the LXX for Noah's Ark. It is therefore possible that Apamea received its nickname directly in consequence of adopting the Noah saga (so S. von Gutschmid, RhM (1864), p. 400; *Kl. Schr.* II, p. 392; E. Babelon, RHR 23 (1891), p. 176). It must however be admitted that *kibotos* occurs elsewhere as a place-name. According to Strabo xvii 1, 10 (p. 795), the inner, artificially-excavated harbour of Alexandria was called *kibotos* and Anna Comnena, *Alexias* xi 1; xiv 5; xv 1, mentions a *Kibotos* on the coast of Bithynia, in the eastern corner of the Propontis (see Ramsay, *Historical Geography of Asia Minor* (1890), p. 186). It should further be noted that on the coins of Apamea, *Κιβωτοί* appears also in the plural as an adjective (F. Imhoof-Blumer, *Kleinasiatische Münzen* I (1901), p. 211: coins from the time of Hadrian with the inscription *Ἀπαμέων Μαρσύας Κιβωτοί,* the plural being quite clearly legible in some examples). Five chests are depicted in the field, at the top. Presumably, therefore, the town's nickname had some other origin and only subsequently provided the reason for the localization of the Noah saga (Ramsay expressed doubts in *The Cities and Bishoprics of Phrygia* I.2, pp. 669–72). On the other hand, there appear to be no grounds whatever for supposing that a pagan flood legend originally existed in Apamea, and that it was later combined with the Jewish story (as for example

J.G. Droysen, *Gesch. des Hellenismus*, III.2 (²1877), p. 271 ; Reinach, *Les monnaies juives* (1887), pp. 71 ff. ; H. Usener, *Die Sintfluthsagen* (1899), pp. 48–50). Against this, see especially Babelon, 'La tradition phrygienne du déluge', RHR 23 (1891), pp. 174–83) ; Juster, *Les Juifs dans l'empire romain* I (1914), p. 191, n. 19. It should therefore be made clear at the end of this discussion that the background and context of the appearance of Noah and the Ark on these coins remains wholly unintelligible

Besides the legend of Noah, literary evidence also relates the Enoch legend to Phrygia. In *Steph. Byz.* s.v. Ἰκόνιον (= FGrH 800 F 3), it is stated that at the time of a certain Annacus, who lived to be over three hundred years old, the Phrygians were informed by the Oracle that after his death all would be destroyed as happened after the flood of Deucalion . Thence there derived the saying τὸ ἐπὶ Ἀννακοῦ κλαύσειν. The appeal to the proverbial saying indicates that the note originates from the same source as the closely similar saying in Zenobius, *Prov.* vi 10 (*Paroemiographi graeci*, edd. E. L. von Leutsch and F. W. Schneidewin I.1, p. 164) and the Suda s.v. Νάννακος. Zenobius, whose work is simply an extract from older collections of sayings, lived at the time of Hadrian. He, and after him the Suda, has Nannacus instead of Annacus, call him 'King of the Phrygians', and quote as authority 'Hermogenes in the *Phrygia*'. Whether this Hermogenes is identical with the author of the same name known from other sources, is impossible to say (see FHG III, p. 523: texts in FGrH 795). He may be the person referred to by Josephus among writers who also mention Jews, *C. Ap.* i 23 (216). In any case, because of their substantial agreement with the biblical story, there is no doubt concerning the Jewish origin of the legends, despite the strong attestation of the form 'Nannacus' (H. Usener, *Die Sintfluthsagen*, p. 50). Probably, the proverbial saying spoke of κλαύσειν ἐπὶ Ναννάκου, and under Jewish influence this was subsequently explained on the basis of the Enoch legend. Here also, therefore, there is no reason to assume the existence of an original related Phrygian saga (as for example in P. C. Buttman, *Mythologus* I, pp. 176 ff., and Ramsay, *Exp.* (Sept. 1905), pp. 199 ff.) On a Jewish origin see Babelon, RHR 23 (1891), p. 180. For a rightly sceptical view of these connections see Stern, GLAJJ I, no. lxxiv (Hermogenes).

In the territory of *Acmonia* in Phrygia an inscription has been found honouring several synagogue officials who restored 'the synagogue built by Iulia Severa' (first reported from a copy made by Ramsay in RA 12 (1888), p. 225 ; a fresh and better copy by Ramsay in REA 3 (1901), p. 272 ; following this RA 41 (1902), p. 357 = IGR IV no. 655 = MAMA VI, no. 264 (the best text), followed in DF, no. 33) ; cf. also CIJ II, no. 766 (on whose deficiencies see L. Robert, BE 1954, no. 24) :

τὸν κατασκευασθὲ[ν]τα ο[ἶ]κον ὑπὸ Ἰουλίας Σεουήρας Π. Τυρρώνιος Κλάδος ὁ διὰ βίου ἀρχισυνάγωγος καὶ Λούκιος Λουκίου ἀρχισυνάγωγος καὶ Ποπίλιος Ζωτικὸς ἄρχων ἐπεσκεύασαν ἔκ τε τῶν ἰδίων καὶ τῶν συνκαταθεμένων καὶ ἔγραψαν τοὺς τοίχους καὶ τὴν ὀροφὴν καὶ ἐποίησαν τὴν τῶν θυρίδων ἀσφάλειαν καὶ τὸν [λυ]πὸν πάντα κόσμον, οὕστινας κα[ὶ] ἡ συναγωγὴ ἐτείμησαν ὅπλῳ ἐπιχρύσῳ διά τε τὴν ἐνάρετον αὐτῶν δ[ι]άθ[ε]σιν καὶ τὴν πρὸς τὴν συναγωγὴν εὔνοιάν τε καὶ σ[που]δήν. The Iulia Severa named here as builder is known from inscriptions and coins from Acmonia as a lady of high rank (CIG no. 3858, or better, Ramsay, *Cities and Bishoprics* I.2, p. 637; another inscription *ibid.* p. 647, no. 550; full evidence in PIR² I 701. Along with her husband, Servenius Capito, she was several times 'high priestess' (on coins: ἐπὶ ἀρχ. τὸ γ´ Σερουηνίου Καπίτωνος καὶ Ἰουλίας Σεουήρας, BMC Phrygia, pp. 6, 10, similarly pp. 9, 10, 11; cf. p. xxii; other examples in the survey by Waddington, RN (1898), p. 384, nos. 5488, 5490, 5494. Older material on these coins in T. E. Mionnet, *Description de médailles* IV, pp. 198 ff. Suppl. vii, p. 484. The view that ἀρχ. = ἀρχιερέων (and not ἀρχόντων) is recommended in view of the inscription in Ramsay, p. 647, no. 550: Ἰουλίᾳ Σεουήρᾳ ἀρχιερείᾳ καὶ ἀγωνοθέτιδι. Cf. also PIR¹ S 404; Ramsay, *The Cities and Bishoprics*, I.2, pp. 637–40, 673 ff. The coins in question all date to the time of Nero. The Jewish community in Acmonia therefore had friends in the highest social circles at that time. Iulia Severa cannot, of course, have been Jewish: she was a 'high priestess', i.e., of the Imperial cult. But she built the synagogue for the Jews as their patroness. Our inscription belongs to a later age; the people it honours had *restored* the synagogue she had once built.

Substantial further evidence now exists of Jewish settlement in Acmonia. See most recently L. Robert, JS 1975, pp. 158–60, and A.R.R. Sheppard, 'Jews, Christians and Heretics in Acmonia and Eumeneia', AS 29 (1979), pp. 169–80. Note CIJ II, no. 764, the epitaph of a man described as Ἰουδαῖος; no. 769 (from Yenice near Acmonia) a grave-curse with the formula (derived from Zech. 5:2–4 LXX) [ἔσ]ται αὐτῷ πρὸς τὸν θεὸν τὸν ὕψιστον, καὶ τὸ ἀράς δρέπανον εἰς τὸ ὖκον (*sic*) αὐτου [ἐσελθοῖτο]; for grave-curses showing (at least) Jewish influence see also MAMA VI, nos. 277; 287; 316 (CIJ II, no. 768); 325; 335–335a (= CIJ II, no. 760, wrongly attributed to Blaundos). On these inscriptions note the explicit reference to Deuteronomy—ὅσαι ἀραὶ ἐν τῷ Δευτερονομίῳ εἰσὶ γεγραμμέναι *et sim.* etc. The second of them shows that the donor of the monument, dated to A.D. 248-9, had filled a number of local magistracies. For this feature compare also an inscription of A.D. 233, copied at Uşak but almost certainly from Acmonia (see L. Robert, *Hell.* X, pp. 249–53). For another sepulchral inscription (B. Laum, *Stiftungen* II, no. 174) of the third century, almost certainly emanating from a Jewish milieu in Acmonia, see L. Robert, *Hell.* XI-XII, pp. 409–13. MAMA VI, no. 334 is a bilingual inscription in Greek (fragmentary) and Hebrew, of uncertain date. For menorahs, see CIJ II, no. 771, MAMA VI, no. 347.

For two further dedications to *Theos Hypsistos* from *Yenice Köy* and *Corum* (Jorumlar) near Acmonia, see T. Drew-Bear, 'Local Cults in Graeco-Roman Phrygia', GRBS 17 (1976), pp. 247–68, nos. 1–2, reproduced in SEG XXVI, nos. 1355–6, and by G. H. R. Horsley, *New Documents Illustrating Early Christianity* (1981), no. 5, with a valuable discussion. For the question of the Jewish or pagan character of the worship of the 'Highest God', see pp. 38, 67–8, 70–2, 169 below.

For traces of Judaism or Jewish influence at *Eumeneia*, see L. Robert, *Hell.* XI-XII, pp. 414–39, and Sheppard, *op. cit.*, with CIJ II, no. 761 (grave-curses). The inscriptions of the area also show a clear and extensive Christian presence, see E. Gibson, *The 'Christians for Christians' Inscriptions of Phrygia* (1978).

From *Synnada*, further east, a fragmentary inscription (MAMA IV, no. 90 = CIJ II, no. 759) has [ἀ]ρχισυν[άγωγος?].

Antioch in Pisidia, where a Jewish synagogue stood at the time of the apostle Paul (Acts 13:14), also belonged originally to Phrygia. A Jewish woman, Deborah, from a city called 'Antioch', is named on an epitaph in Apollonia: ['A]ντιόχισσα πάτρης γονέων πολυτείμων οὔνομα Δεββωρά BCH 17 (1893), p. 257; CIJ II, no. 772, not using the revised text in MAMA IV, no. 202, see L. Robert, *Noms indigènes* (1963), pp. 401–6. She evidently had parents who had won many honours in their native land. The date is the end of the second or the third century A.D. The tone of the epitaph nevertheless strongly suggests that she had come from an Antioch more distant than this one, perhaps the Carian Antioch on the river Meander; so MAMA VII, p. x, n. 1, followed by B. M. Levick, *Roman Colonies in Southern Asia Minor* (1967), p. 128.

From *Sidibunda* (modern Zivint) in Pisidia comes a dedication θεῷ ὑψίστῳ καὶ Ἀγείᾳ Καταφυγῇ (AS 10 (1960), p. 70, no. 122) which can reasonably be argued to reflect Judaism or Jewish influence (so L. Robert in BE 1961, no. 750; 1965, no. 412).

In *Lycia*, particularly in the town of *Phaselis*, Jews are assumed to have lived, according to 1 Mac. 15:23, already in the second century B.C. (cf. p. 4 above).

In *Limyra* in Lycia there is an epitaph with the words Εἰούδα εἱρόν (Petersen and Luschan, *Reisen in Lykien, Milyas und Kibyratis* (1889), p. 66 = CIJ II, no. 758).

In *Tlos* in Lycia, a remarkably interesting inscription has been found (publ. by Hula in *Eranos Vindobonensis* (1893), pp. 99–102 = CIJ II, no. 757; revised text in TAM II.2, no. 612). It runs: Πτολεμαῖος Λε[υ]κίου

Τλωεὺς κατεσκεύασεν ἐκ τῶν ἰδίων τὸ ἡρῷον ἀπὸ θεμελίων αὐτὸς καὶ ὑπὲρ τοῦ υἱοῦ αὐτοῦ Πτολεμαίου β' τοῦ Λευκίου ὑπὲρ ἀρχοντείας τελουμένας παρ' ἡμεῖν Ἰουδαίοις ὥστε αὐτὸ εἶναι πάντων τῶν Ἰουδαίων, καὶ μηδένα ἐξὸν εἶναι ἕτερον τεθῆναι ἐν αὐτῷ· ἐὰν δέ τις εὑρεθείη τινὰ τι[θ]ῶν, ὀφειλέσει Τλοέων τῷ δήμῳ... The end is missing. The word *heroon*, which strictly signifies the burial-place of a hero (G. Rohde, *Psyche* II, pp. 149 ff.), has in this case the meaning of a burial-place in general (see for examples J. Kubinska, *Les monuments funéraires dans les inscriptions grecques de l'Asie Mineure* (1968), index s.v.; also (for example) G. E. Bean, T. B. Mitford, *Journeys in Rough Cilicia in 1964–68* (1970), s.v. in Index 7d; cf. in general D. C. Kurtz, J. Boardman, *Greek Burial Customs* (1971), especially ch. 16. It is very common also on Christian epitaphs in Phrygia (see Ramsay, *Cities and Bishoprics* I.2, pp. 514–68). Thus Ptolemaeus built a burial-place for the Jews in Tlos in thanksgiving for his son's attainment to *archonteia*, the office of an *archon*, in the Jewish community. From the nature of the script and orthography, the inscription would appear to date from the end of the first century A.D.

From *Termessos* in Pisidia there is a third-century epitaph on a sarcophagus from the necropolis inscribed by a father τῇ θυγατρὶ αὐτοῦ Αὐρ. Ἀρτεμει (*sic*) Ἰουδέᾳ μόνῃ, TAM III, no. 448, see L. Robert, *Hell.* XI–XII (1960), p. 386.

For the spread of Judaism in *Pamphylia* we have the testimony of 1 Mac. 15:23 and Philo, *Legatio* 36 (281); cf. also Acts 2:10. Note in addition the puzzling epitaph from Beth She'arim, M. Schwabe and B. Lifshitz, *Beth She'arim* II: *The Greek Inscriptions* (1967), no. 203: Ἰακὼς (*sic*) Καισαρεὺς ἀρχισυνάγωγος Πανφυλίας. שלום. According to 1 Mac. 15:23, the town of *Side* in particular is to be regarded as a Jewish centre.

The following is an inscription from Side dating to the early Byzantine period (JIIS 28 (1908) p. 195, no. 29 = CIJ II, no. 7814 = DF, no. 36): [Ἰσά]κις φροντιστὴς τῆς ἁγιωτάτ[ης] συναγωγῆς ἔστην. εὐτ[υχῶ]ς καὶ ἀνεπλήρωσα τὴν μαρμάρωσιν ἀπὸ [τοῦ] ἄμβωνος ἕως τοῦ σῖμμα καὶ ἔσμηξα [τὰ]ς δύο ἐπταμφύξους καὶ τὰ δύο κιονοκέφαλα, ἰνδ(ικτιῶνος) ιε, μη(νὸς) δ'. Similarly from the late period (fifth-sixth centuries) comes another inscription from Side, published by A. M. Mansel, G. E. Bean, J. Inan, *Die Agora von Side* (1951), no. 69, and re-interpreted as Jewish by L. Robert, Rev. Phil. 32 (1958) pp. 36–47; Lifshitz, DF, no. 37: [ἐ]πὶ Λεοντίου πρεσβ. καὶ ζυγ. [κ]αὶ φροντιστοῦ, νείου Ἰακὼβ ἀρχ. καὶ ζυγ. ἐγένετον ἡ κρήνη σὺν τῷ μεσαύλῳ ἰνδ(ικτίονι) γ', μη(νὶ) ζ'. The reference to 'the fountain with the courtyard' is noteworthy.

Cilicia, too, is said by Philo, *Legatio* 36 (281), to have been inhabited by Jews. Jews from Cilicia lived in Jerusalem in considerable numbers (Acts 6:9). *Tarsus*, the capital of Cilicia, was, as is well-known, the home town of the apostle Paul (Acts 8:11; 21:39; 22:3). See C. B. Welles, 'Hellenistic Tarsus', MUSJ 38 (1962), pp. 41–75. A grave inscription from Jaffa refers to a certain Ἰούδας υἱὸς Ἰοσῆ Ταρσεύς, CIJ II, no. 925. For Jews in Tarsus in general, see also W. M. Ramsay, *Exp.* (July 1906), pp. 32–47; Aug., pp. 151–60. The name Ἰωσῆς also occurs on an epitaph from *Selinus* (BE 1965, no. 426). Epiphanius relates in passing that the Jewish patriarch Judah (fourth century A.D.) sent an *apostolos* to Cilicia to collect contributions from the Jews there (Epiphanius, *Haer.* 30, 11). He mentions also their *archisynagogi*, priests, elders and superintendents (ἀζανῖται = *hazzanim*).

From *Seleucia* on the Calycadnus there is one Jewish epitaph, identified as such by two menorahs (MAMA III, no. 23 = CIJ II, no. 783), and, engraved on the door of a funerary chamber, the words παραστατικὸν Ἑβρέων (MAMA III, no. 32 = CIJ II, no. 784), and from *Olba* the epitaph of two brothers described as Ἰουδέων (795).

From *Corycus* in Cilicia a number of Jewish funerary inscriptions are known. Collected in MAMA III (1931) by J. Keil and A. Wilhelm, they are reproduced by Frey, CIJ II. The MAMA number is given first: 205 = 785: σωματοθήκη Ἀβᾶ Σύμωνος τοῦ μακαρίου ἱερέων (menorah); 222 = 786: ἐνθάδε κεῖται Ἀλέξανδρος Ἀνεμουριεὺς Ἰουδαῖος; 237 = 787: σωματοθήκη Ἀναστασίου καὶ Ἰακώ(βου) καλιγαρίων (menorah); 262 = 788: σωματοθήκη Αὐρ(ηλίου) Εὐσανβατίου Μενάνδρου Κωρυκιώτου βουλευτοῦ (menorah); 295 = 789: [θήκη Δ]αμια[ν]ο[ῦ] Ἰουδέου; 344 = 790: θήκη Εὐσαμβατίου Ἰουδέου πρεσβυτέρου μυρεψοῦ (two menorahs); 440 = 791: ἐνθάδε κεῖτε Ἰούδας καὶ Ἀλεξᾶς Νισαίου [υἱ]εῖς Ἰουδαῖοι; 448 = 792: σωματοθήκη Ἰουλίου μυρεψοῦ υἱοῦ Ἰουλίου πρεσβυτέρου (menorah); 607 = 793: σωματοθήκη [Μ]ωσῖ προταυραρίου Ἑβρέος; 679 = 794: Σαμοῆ Κωπᾶ κ(αὶ) Αὐξέντιος Εἰουδέων (menorah).

There was a Jewish synagogue in *Iconium* in Lycaonia in the time of the apostle Paul (Acts 14:1). That in Steph. Byz. s.v. the Enoch legend is located in Iconium in association with the flood legend of Deucalion, is perhaps due to the influence of Phrygia, where the Enoch legend may first have been adopted (see above, p. 30). Cf. especially for Jews in Lycaonia ('South Galatia') in general, Ramsay, HDB II, 88b.

For *Galatia* proper the evidence is very sparse. It is significant that Jews are not discussed in the excellent analysis by S. Mitchell, 'Population and Land in Roman Galatia', ANRW II.7, 2 (1980), pp. 1053–81. The edict of Augustus in favour of the Jews, *Ant.* xvi 6, 2 (162–5), was previously regarded as such because of the instruction at its conclusion that the text should be exhibited in *Ancyra*, the capital city of Galatia. But Ἀγκύρῃ is no more than a conjecture on the part of Scaliger. The manuscripts all have αργυρη, and the context demands a reference to the site of the temple of Rome and Augustus in *Asia*, namely Pergamum.

Recently collected epigraphical evidence from N. Galatia, however, gives some indication of a Jewish presence, or at least Judaising influences. See S. Mitchell, *Regional Epigraphic Catalogues of Asia Minor* II : *The Ankara District. The Inscriptions of North Galatia* (*Br. Inst. Arch. Ankara. Monogr.* 4; BAR Int. Ser. 135, 1982) : no. 133 (= CIJ II, no. 796 with substantial revisions), from Kayakent near the *colonia* of Germa, has the names 'Jacob' and 'Estheras' (perhaps from the Byzantine period) ; 141, from the same place, has δύναμις 'Υψιστοῦ and may be Jewish ; 209B from Kalecik, NE of Ankara, has τῷ μεγάλῳ θεῷ 'Υψίστῳ καὶ 'Επουρανίῳ καὶ τοῖς 'Αγίοις αὐτοῦ 'Ανγέλοις καὶ τῇ προσκυνητῇ αὐτοῦ προσευχῇ, and is probably Jewish (third century A.D.?). See A. R. R. Sheppard, 'Pagan Cults of Angels in Roman Asia Minor', Talanta 12–13 (1980–1), pp. 77–101. Note also no. 418, from near Tavium, a dedication to Theos Hypsistos ; 509–12, gravestones, possibly Jewish, of the Byzantine period, from Evci, NE of Tavium.

It is to be assumed from 1 Mac. 15:22 (the letter of the Romans to King Ariarathes) that Jews lived in the region of the kingdom of *Cappadocia*. Cf. also Acts 2:9 ; m*Ket.* 13:11 (where it is debated in what money the *ketubah* is to be paid when a man marries in Palestine and dismisses his wife in Cappadocia, or vice versa marries in Cappadocia and dismisses her in Palestine, or finally, marries her in Cappadocia and dismisses her there). Jews from Cappadocia living in *Sepphoris* are mentioned in y*Sheb.* 9:5. Jewish scholars from Cappadocia also appear : R. Judah the Cappadocian, R. Jannai the Cappadocian, R. Samuel the Cappadocian. In *Caesarea Mazaca*, the capital of Cappadocia, twelve thousand Jews are alleged to have been put to death at the time of Sapor. See in general, A. Neubauer, *Géographie du Talmud*, pp. 317–19 ; Hamburger, RE s.v. 'Kappadocien' ; S. Krauss, *Griech. und lat. Lehnwörter im Talmud* II (1899), p. 558; Bacher, *Die Agada der paläst. Amoräer* III, pp. 106, 749; Krauss, 'Cappadocia', JE III (1902), cols. 558–9. From *Jaffa* comes the following Jewish epitaph τόπος Είακὼ⟨β⟩ Καπάδοκος κὲ 'Αχολίας συνβίου αὐτοῦ κὲ 'Αστερίου (PEFQSt (1893), p. 290 = CIJ II, no. 910). Equally from Jaffa comes the epitaph ἐν⟨θ⟩άδε κ⟨ί⟩τ⟨ε⟩ 'Ισάκις πρεσβύτερος τῆς Καπαδόκων Τάρσου λινοπώλου, or according to another reading λινοπωλὸν = λινοπωλῶν (PEFQSt (1900), p. 118, no. 122 = CIJ II, no. 931). The interpretation of this text is not clear.

From *Amastris* in Paphlagonia there is the dedication DF, no. 35 θεῷ ἀνεικήτῳ καὶ τῇ κυρίᾳ προσευχῇ εὐξάμενος, perhaps of the third century.

For *Bithynia* and *Pontus* we have Philo's evidence, *Legatio* 36 (281) : ἄχρι Βιθυνίας καὶ τῶν τοῦ Πόντου μυχῶν. It is just possible that

'Sampsame' in 1 Mac. 15:23 could be understood as *Amisus* in Pontus (p. 4 above).

Aquila, the companion of Paul, came from Pontus (Acts 18:2: Ἰουδαῖον.. Ποντικὸν τῷ γένει) and similarly the proselyte Aquila, the translator of the Old Testament (see pp. 493–9). Compare also Acts 2:9.

From *Nicomedia* in Bithynia we have an epitaph with a penalty payable τῇ συναγω[γ]ῇ τῶν Ἰουδέων (CIJ II, no. 799 = TAM IV.1, no. 377) and another, adorned with Jewish symbols, which is certainly Jewish (798, revised text in *Hell*. XI–XII, pp. 395–7. See now TAM IV.1, no. 374. More recently discovered grave-inscriptions include one with a penalty payable τῇ συναγωγῇ and another with the imprecation ἕξῃ κρίσιν πρὸς τὸν θεόν (L. Robert, *Hell*. XI–XII, pp. 386–9 = TAM IV.1, no. 375. All four appear to date to the mid-third century.

TAM IV.1, no. 376 has a grave-mult payable τῇ συγαγωγῇ, and 319, one payable τῇ ἀγειωτ[άτῃ...], almost certainly a reference to a Jewish community (see BE 1976, no. 684 and 1979, no. 557).

Also from Bithynia, in the neighbourhood of the Bosphorus, north-east of *Chalcedon*, comes a late Greek inscription which can be restored as ἐνθάδε κατάκ⟨ει⟩τ⟨αι⟩ Σανβάτι⟨ο⟩s, υ⟨ἱ⟩ὸs Γερ⟨ο⟩ντ⟨ί⟩ου πρ(εσβυτέρου), γραμ⟨μ⟩ατεὺs κ⟨αὶ⟩ ⟨ἐ⟩π⟨ι⟩οτά⟨τη⟩s τ⟨ῶ⟩ν παλ⟨αι⟩ῶν (REJ 26 (1893), pp. 167–71 = CIJ II, no. 800 = IK Kalchedon, no. 75, and from *Chrysopolis*, immediately opposite Istanbul, the epitaph of Εἰάκουβος πρεσβύτερος υεῖος Λεοντίου πρεσβυτέρου (CIJ II, no. 801 = IK Kalchedon, no. 76). Both are adorned with menorahs.

Jews were also living on the *North Coast of the Black Sea* from an early period. An organised Jewish community existed in *Panticapaeum* (modern Kerch) on the Cimmerian Bosporus (the Crimea) in, at the latest, the first century A.D., as is attested by an inscription dated 377 of the Bosporan era = A.D. 81 (CIG II, p. 1005, Addenda no. 2114^bb = IOSPE II, no. 52 = IGR I, no. 881 = CIJ I², no. 683 = CIRB, no. 70). In the inscription, a Jewish woman declares the manumission of a slave: ἀφείημι ἐπὶ τῆς π[ρο]σευχῆς θρεπτόν μου Ἡρακλᾶν... ἀνεπικωλύτως καθὼς η[ὐ]ξάμην, χωρὶς ἰς τ[ὴ]ν προσευχὴν θωπείας τε καὶ προσκα[ρτερ]ήσεω[s], συνεπινευσάντων δὲ καὶ τῶν κληρ⟨ο⟩νόμων μου Ἡρακλείδου καὶ Ἑλικωνιάδος, συνε[πιτ]ροπευούσης δὲ καὶ τῇ[s] συναγωγῆ[s] τῶν Ἰουδαίων. The purpose of the final remark, that the heirs have also assented and that the Jewish community is superintending the matter, is to render the legal effect of the act permanently secure (on the frequency of such indications see L. Mitteis, *Reichsrecht und Volksrecht in den östlichen Provinzen des römischen Kaiserreichs* (1891), pp. 372 ff.). On the formula χωρὶς ἰς τὴν προσευχὴν θωπείας τε καὶ προσκαρτερήσως see B. Nadel, VDI (1958), pp. 203–6 and below, p. 105. Of very similar content are three other, more damaged, inscriptions, also from Panticapaeum: a) CIRB, no. 71 = CIJ I², no. 683a (prol. p. 65), with bibliography; b) CIRB, no. 72 = CIJ I², no. 683b (prol., p. 66); c) CIG no. 2114b = IOSPE II, no. 53 = CIRB 73 = CIJ I², no. 684. Note in particular the concluding formula of a): συνεπιτροπευούσης τῆς συναγωγῆς τῶν Ἰουδαίων καὶ θεὸν σέβων, and for the issues raised by this and comparable expressions see H. Bellen, 'Συναγωγὴ τῶν Ἰουδαίων καὶ Θεοσεβῶν. 'Die Aussage einer bosporanischen Freilassungsinschrift (CIRB 71) zum Problem der "Gottesfürchtigen", JAC 8–9 (1965–6), pp. 171–6, and pp. 165–8 below.

No more than meagre fragments of names are recognizable on a few Jewish grave inscriptions found in Panticapaeum (IOSPE II, nos. 304–6 = CIJ I², nos. 687, 686, 685 = CIRB, no. 735; IOSPE IV, no. 405 = CIJ I², no. 689. More noteworthy is a bilingual epitaph in Hebrew and Greek of the third-fourth century, IOSPE IV, no. 404 = CIRB, no. 736 = CIJ I² no. 688. Cf. also from near Kerch, an epitaph adorned with a menorah ἐνθά κ(εῖται) (on opposite side) Σαμοηλ υἱ⟨ὸ⟩s Σεβέρο⟨υ⟩, CIRB, no. 743; CIJ I², no. 689a (p. 66). The Jewish character of two inscriptions from *Gorgippia* (modern Anape) on the Tuman peninsula, east of the Cimmerian Bosporus, dated to the year 338 of the Bosporan era = A.D. 41, is by contrast disputed. They are CIJ I², no. 690 = CIRB, no. 1123; CIJ I², no. 690a (p. 67) = CIRB, no. 1126. The formula θεῷ ὑψίστῳ παντοκράτορι εὐλογητῷ with which they begin suggests that they are Jewish. Doubt might be raised by the fact, shown by Latyschev, that the final oath-formula is to be read ὑπὸ Δία, Γῆν, Ἥλιον (IOSPE II, no. 400, cf. vol. I, note on no. 98). The formula ὀμνύω Δία, Γῆν, Ἥλιον is not rare, see e.g. OGIS, nos. 229, 60, 70; 266, 23, 51; 532, 8; for the declaration that a slave is to be freed ὑπὸ Δία, Γῆν, Ἥλιον see also IOSPE II, no. 54; P. Oxy., nos. 48, l. 6 and 49, l. 8. However, evidence from the Elephantine papyri shows that observing Jews might make use of pagan oath-formulas, which in this case will have been a legal necessity. Note also in CIJ I², no. 690, ll. 8–9, the expression ἀνέθηκεν (ἐν) τ[ῇ] [προσ]ευχῇ κατ' εὐχ[ή]ν. The inscriptions should therefore be regarded, on balance, as Jewish. The judaizing introductory formula can also be restored in the mutilated introduction of another inscription, equally from Gorgippia (IOSPE II, no. 401 = IGR I, no. 911 = CIRB, no. 1125). Note also CIJ I², pp. 68–9 (CIRB, no. 1124), a further manumission-inscription, probably from Gorgippia, dating to A.D. 59, and with (l. 10) [τὸ γένος] Ἰουδαί[ο]υ[s..], and CIRB, no. 1127, the end of a manumission-inscription from Gorgippia, with the words προσμέ[νου]σα τῇ προσευ[χῇ]. Less certain is the Jewish character of CIRB, no. 985 = CIJ I², no. 691 (and see prol. p. 69), a manumission-inscription certainly dated to A.D. 16, in which ll. 8–9 can hypothetically be restored ἐ[πὶ] τ[ῆς προσευχῆς], and of CIRB, no. 1128, where a similar restoration can be made. IGR I, no. 873 = CIRB, no. 64, from Panticapaeum, dated to A.D. 306, is a dedication to Theos Hypsistos Epekoos and records the building of a *proseuche*. Similarly, IOSPE I², no. 176 = CIJ I², no. 682 (cf. prol. p. 64), from Olbia, records the restoration of a *proseuche*.

In spite therefore of some uncertainty as to the significance of the terminology employed, it can be taken as certain that observant Jewish communities were established on the northern coast of the Black Sea by the first century A.D. See E. R. Goodenough, 'The Bosporus Inscriptions to the Most High God', JQR 47 (1956–7), pp. 1–44; B. Lifshitz, 'Le culte du Dieu Très Haut à Gorgippia', Riv. fil. 92 (1964), pp. 157–61, M. Tačeva-Hitova in VDI 1978, pp. 133–42, and p. 72 below.

Jewish settlement in *Egypt* is now known from documentary evidence to have begun not later than the sixth century B.C. The most important early evidence, in the form of Aramaic papyri of the Persian period, relates to the Jewish community of Elephantine in Upper Egypt. The main collections of documents are as follows:

Sachau, E., *Aramäische Papyrus und Ostraka aus einer Militär-Kolonie zu Elephantine* (1911) (APO).

Cowley, A., *Aramaic Papyri of the Fifth Century B.C.* (1923) (a re-edition of all the Aramaic papyri then known) (AP).

Kraeling, E. G., *The Brooklyn Museum Aramaic Papyri: New Documents of the Fifth Century B.C. from the Jewish Colony at Elephantine* (1953) (BP).

Note also: Bresciani, E., 'Papiri aramaici egiziani di epoca persiana presso il Museo Civile di Padova', RSO 35 (1960), pp. 11–24; R. Degen, 'Neue Fragmente aramäischer Papyri aus Elephantine', NESE 2 (1974), pp. 71–8; 3 (1978), pp. 15–31.

See further: Yaron, R., *Introduction to the Law of the Aramaic Papyri* (1961).

Porten, B., *Archives from Elephantine: The Life of an Ancient Jewish Military Colony* (1968).

Muffs, Y., *Studies in the Aramaic Legal Documents from Elephantine* (1969).

Porten, B., 'The Jews in Egypt', in Davies, W. D., Finkelstein, L. (eds.), *The Cambridge History of Judaism* I (1984), pp. 372–400.

Note especially Grelot, P., *Documents araméens d'Égypte* (1972), a substantial collection of Aramaic papyri and ostraca in translation with notes and commentary covering not only the Jewish military colony of Elephantine but the correspondence of the Persian administration, which used Aramaic (note especially Driver, G. R., *Aramaic Documents of the Fifth Century B.C.*, 1954, ²1957), and non-Jewish Aramaic-speaking persons settled in Egypt.

For preliminary notices of a papyrus of the late Persian or early Ptolemaic period written in demotic characters but containing a collection of non-Jewish literary texts in Aramaic see R. A. Bowman, 'An Aramaic Religious Text in Demotic Script', JNES 3 (1944), pp. 219–31; S. P. Vleeming, J. W. Wesselius, 'An Aramaic Hymn from the Fourth Century B.C.', BO 39 (1982), pp. 501–9. For nine Jewish-Aramaic grave-inscriptions of the Persian period, perhaps around 400 B.C., from Edfu in Upper Egypt, see W. Kornfeld, 'Jüdisch-aramaïsche Grabinschriften aus Edfu', ÖAW Anzeiger 110 (1973), pp. 123–37, with corrections by R. Degen, NESE 3 (1978), pp. 59–66.

Two Jewish names are now attested in the substantial group of largely fragmentary Aramaic (and Phoenician) papyri, apparently of the Persian period, found at the excavations at N. Saqqâra near Memphis, and published by J. B. Segal, *Aramaic Texts from North Saqqâra with some Fragments in Phoenician* (1983). In doc. 47. l. 8 there appears the name ‏יהור(ד)ם‎ = Yehoram, 'Yeho is lofty' (also already attested at Saqqâra in N. A. Giron, *Textes araméens d'Égypte* (1931), 33, l. 1); and doc. 54, l. 4, the name of a female slave, Yehomori, 'Yeho is my teacher, or guide'. It should be noted that the existence of a Jewish community at Memphis in the first half of the sixth century in already attested by Jeremiah (44:1).

Since the history of the Jewish community of Elephantine is now well known, and also falls outside the chronological limits with which we are concerned, only a few salient points need be mentioned.

The origins of the Jewish military colony on the island of Elephantine are unknown, but it is clearly attested in a document of 410 B.C. (AP, no. 30–1; Grelot, no. 102) that the Jews believed that their temple of 'Yaho' went back to 'the days of the Kings of Egypt', that is, as is explicitly stated, to before the conquest by Cambyses in 525. The colony was thus established at some point in the Saite period, and passed into the service of the Persian Empire. The document mentioned records the destruction of the temple (‏אגורא‎) at the instance of the local Egyptian priests. In the third year of Artaxerxes II (402), the temple had evidently been rebuilt, and the area was still under Persian control (BP, no. 10; Grelot, no. 51), as also in the fourth year, 401 (BP, nos. 11–12; Grelot, nos. 52–3). But by (probably) 400, a dating is made by 'the fifth year of Amyrtaeus' (AP, no. 35; Grelot, no. 7), namely, the Egyptian king who at the end of the fifth century established independence from Persia. The colony had presumably now passed into his service. The latest known document of the Jewish colony announces the accession of the rival Egyptian king Nepherites in 399 or 398 B.C. (BP, no. 13; Grelot, no. 103).

No attempt will be made to summarize the complex evidence on the nomenclature, family relations, law and business practice of this Jewish colony (see especially Porten, *opp. cit.*). Two points may however be stressed. Firstly the temple at Elephantine was clearly conceived of as a temple *in which* God dwelt. See e.g. BP, no. 12 = Grelot no. 53 : 'Yahu the god who dwells in Yeb the fortress' (יהו אלהא שכן יב בירתא); cf. AP, no. 30 = Grelot, no. 39: 'the Temple of Yahu the god who is in Yeb the fortress' (אגורא זי אלהא זי ביב זי בירתא), see Kraeling, *op. cit.*, p. 85. It thus provides a parallel to the later temple at Leontopolis (see pp. 145–7 below).

Secondly, the well known but unfortunately fragmentary papyrus of 419 B.C. seems to reveal that Darius II gave orders for some observance to last from the 15th to the 21st of Ni[san], which involved abstention from anything leavened or fermented (חמיר) (AP, no. 21 ; Grelot, no. 96). While certainty is impossible, especially in view of the damaged state of the text, it seems at least probable that this is a reference to Passover. If so, there is a clear parallel to the earlier royal backing for the reforming mission of Nehemiah.

Jewish settlement in Egypt in the early sixth century is also attested by Jer. 44:1 and 46:14, and for the Saite and Persian periods by the *Letter of Aristeas* 13 (the latter refers to mercenary services against the Ethiopians and thus, if in any way historical, may relate to the colony at Elephantine).

Finally, from the Persian period, what appear to be Jewish names are found on Aramaic documents from Memphis. See p. 39 above.

Evidence for Jewish settlement in Egypt for most of the fourth century, marked by Egyptian independence until the Persian re-conquest of 343 B.C., is thus entirely lacking. However, from the late fourth or early third century, after Alexander's conquest, we may note an Aramaic papyrus of no exact provenance which contains a list of payments and includes a significant number of both Jewish and Greek names (AP, no. 81 ; Grelot, no. 13 ; see especially J. Harmatta, 'Irano-Aramaica (zur Geschichte des frühhellenistischen Judentum in Ägypten)', AAAScHung 7 (1959), pp. 337–409, suggesting a date close to 310 B.C.). The papyrus attests the presence of Jews in Migdal in the N.E. Delta, Thmuis and Syene, and possibly in other places. Two priests are mentioned, one resident in Thmuis. The deduction from this that such a presence implies a temple in the same place (Kraeling, *op. cit.*, pp. 118–19; Harmatta, *op. cit.*, p. 406), possibly identical with that in Isaiah 19:19, is without foundation.

Another Aramaic papyrus, whose script is thought to be of a similar character, is therefore regarded as being of approximately the same date (AP, no. 82). Here too there is no exact provenance, but it possibly mentions Thebes (l. 3: בטבה). A number of Jewish names appear and there are allusions to judges (l. 1: דיניא), perhaps not Jewish, and to the 'heads of the congregation' (l. 5: [על ראשי עד[תא). The word תורה appears in l. 10, but its meaning is not quite certain.

It thus remains altogether unclear how far there was a continuity of Jewish settlement in Egypt from the Persian to the Ptolemaic period. Nevertheless, our evidence presupposes, without any doubt, that there was a substantial immigration of Jews in the early Hellenistic period, and from the late fourth century onward we are almost wholly dependent on documents and literary sources in Greek.[36]

The *Letter of Aristeas*, which reports Jewish mercenary service in the Saite period (above), also claims that Ptolemy I Lagus transported 100,000 Jews to Egypt, armed 30,000 of them and quartered them as occupation troops in the fortresses.[37] The old, the children and the women are said to have been handed over as slaves to his soldiers at their demand, for services rendered (14). Ptolemy II Philadelphus is then stated to have secured the liberation of all these Jewish slaves by paying twenty drachmas for each slave to their owners (15–27, cf. 37). As Josephus, when relating the same story, *C. Ap.* ii 4 (44–47), *Ant.* xii 1 (7–9), follows Aristeas (in the first passage this is clear, in the other probable), Aristeas is our only witness. But in spite of the fictional character of the narrative, it is at least credible that Ptolemy Lagus brought Jewish prisoners to Egypt and employed them on guard duties in the forts; for the fact that Ptolemy I captured Jerusalem is attested by Agatharchides, Jos. *C. Ap.* i 22 (209–11); *Ant.* xii 1 (4–6) = GLAJJ I, nos. 30a-b; cf. Appian, *Syr.* 50/252 = GLAJJ II, no. 343. Again, the statement about the transportation of Jewish prisoners of war to Egypt, *Ant.* xii 1 (7–8), appears to derive from a source independent of Aristeas. The employment of Jews in military roles in specific places is in any case confirmed by the existence still later, in different districts of Egypt, of 'Jews' camps' (Ἰουδαίων στρατόπεδα, *castra Iudaeorum*). See below p. 48. It is also possible that 'after the death of Alexander not a few Jews migrated of their own free will to Egypt on account of the unrest in Syria', as reported by Hecataeus, a contemporary source.[38]

36. On Jews in Egypt in the Graeco-Roman period, see J. Juster, *Les juifs dans l'empire romain* I (1914), 204–7; L. Fuchs, *Die Juden Ägyptens* (1924); H. I. Bell, *Jews and Christians in Egypt* (1924), and *Juden und Griechen im römischen Alexandreia* (1926); V. Tcherikover, *Hellenistic Civilization and the Jews* (1961), and CPJ I, pp. 1–111; A. Kasher, *The Jews in Hellenistic and Roman Egypt* (1978) (Hebrew).

37. Aristeas 3 (12–13). Cf. also 4 (35–6).

38. Hecataeus *ap.* Jos. *C. Ap.* i 22 (194), cf. also 22 (186 ff.); both passages in GLAJJ I, no. 12. The authenticity of these reports has often been questioned, but it seems probable

Military settlers also occur frequently in the Greek sources of the Ptolemaic period. Previously, these were taken for veterans to whom land had been assigned, but subsequent discoveries have long shown this interpretation to be untenable. The *katoikoi* were active soldiers of alien nationality, and their *kleroi* were passed on from father to son.[39] The Aramaic documents now show us that this system was practised as early as the Persian period, and at that period also could be applied to Jews. Even Alexander the Great is alleged to have transported Samaritan soldiers to Upper Egypt (the Thebaid), where he granted them plots of land and employed them on garrison duties.[40] Similarly, Idumeans are attested as serving in the Ptolemaic army.[41] It would therefore not be surprising if Jews fulfilled the same role.[42] A Jewish settler is probably attested in a Greek document of the twenty-sixth year of Ptolemy II Philadelphus (April 260 B.C.),[43] and another in a similar document from the time of Ptolemy III Euergetes.[44] It remains uncertain whether only an urban plot was allotted to the soldiers settled in the fortresses, or land outside as well; the Jews transported by Antiochus the Great to Phrygia and Lydia possessed both, see Jos. *Ant.* xii 3, 4 (151).

In Alexandria, so Josephus claims, already at the foundation of the city by Alexander Jewish settlers were accepted under the same rights

that they are, at least substantially, the work of Hecataeus of Abdera, rather than a later Jewish pseudepigraphical composition. See Stern, GLAJJ I, no. v. For the argument against authenticity see now J.-D. Gauger in JSJ 13 (1982), pp. 6–46.

39. The material as far as 1900 was edited by P. Meyer, *Das Heerwesen der Ptolemäer und Römer in Ägypten* (1900), and W. Schubart, *Questiones de rebus militaribus, quales fuerint in regno Lagidarum* (1900); see also A. Bouché-Leclercq, *Histoire des Lagides* IV (1907), pp. 1–69; J. Lesquier, *Les institutions militaires de l'Egypte sous les Lagides* (1911); more recently CPJ I (1957), pp. 11–15; see especially no. 37; P. M. Fraser, 'Inscriptions from Ptolemaic Egypt', Berytus 13 (1960), pp. 123–61, on pp. 147–52; F. Übel, *Die Kleruchen Ägyptens unter den ersten sechs Ptolemäern* (1968); A. Kasher, 'First Jewish Military Units in Ptolemaic Egypt', JSJ 9 (1978), pp. 57–67.

40. Jos. *Ant.* xi 8 (345). The authenticity of this narrative, which concerns the Jewish-Samaritan schism and the relation of both groups to Alexander, is however open to dispute. See Loeb *Josephus* vol. VI, App. B and C, and cf. A. Momigliano, 'Flavius Josephus and Alexander's Visit to Jerusalem', Athenaeum 57 (1979), pp. 442–8. There is no certain evidence of Samaritan *katoikoi* or *klerouchoi* in Ptolemaic Egypt; see Übel, *op. cit.*, pp. 189 and 198; M. Nagel, CE 49 (1974), pp. 356–65.

41. See p. 45 below.

42. Note also the publication by E. Breccia, BSAA 9 (1907), pp. 35–86 (cf. also 23 (1930), p. 108, for another posibly Jewish tomb) of the early Ptolemaic necropolis of El-Ibrahimiyye, Alexandria, see CPJ I, p. 3 and III, pp. 139–9 (inscriptions nos. 1424–31); Breccia regarded this as a necropolis for foreign mercenaries, including Jews, a characterisation which remains unproven.

43. P. Hib. no. 96 = CPJ I, no. 18. See further p. 50 below.

44. CPJ I, no. 19 (226 B.C.): Δωσί[θεος...]ίου Ἰουδαῖος τῆς ἐπιγονῆς. On this see below, p. 51.

as Greeks, as a reward for the military assistance (συμμαχία) which they had rendered, *B.J.* ii 18.7 (487); *C. Ap.* ii 4 (42–44). This has been widely contested by later critics and cannot be either fully substantiated or finally refuted. Supporting evidence seems to be provided by the edict of the emperor Claudius, quoted by Jos. *Ant.* xix 5, 2 (279–85), which indicates that the Jews in Alexandria settled there simultaneously with the Alexandrians. However, in the papyrus copy of Claudius' letter to the Alexandrians of A.D. 42, the Emperor expresses himself in much vaguer terms: 'to the Jews who have been dwelling in the same city for many years' (CPJ II, no. 153, ll. 83–4). This text is also relevant to the associated claim to equal rights, which was already controversial in Antiquity, and which will be discussed further below (pp. 127–9).

In the period of the Diadochi, the Jews in Alexandria are said to have been allotted their own quarter separate from the rest of the city, 'so that they could live a life of greater purity by mixing less with strangers'.[45] This Jewish quarter lay along the harbourless shore near the royal palace, that is, in the north-eastern part of the city.[46] Later this separation seems not to have been observed with absolute strictness. For according to Philo, Jewish houses of prayer were to be found in all parts of the city,[47] and there were quite a few Jews living in all the quarters.[48] But Philo also states that of the five city districts,

---

45. *B.J.* ii 18, 7 (488): (οἱ διάδοχοι) τόπον ἴδιον αὐτοῖς ἀφώρισαν, ὅπως καθαρωτέραν ἔχοιεν τὴν δίαιταν, ἧττον ἐπιμισγομένων τῶν ἀλλοφύλων. Strabo *ap* Jos. *Ant.* xiv 7, 2 (117) = GLAJJ I, no 105: τῆς ιῶν Ἀλεξανδρέων πόλεως ἀφώριστο μέγα μέρος τῷ ἔθνει τούτῳ. Jos. *C. Ap.* ii 4 (35) implies that Alexander the Great had allotted this quarter to the Jews. *B.J.* ii 18, 7 (488), however, states that this measure was first taken by the Diadochi. On Jews in Alexandria see especially H. I. Bell, *Jews and Christians in Egypt* (1924); idem, *Juden und Griechen im römischen Alexandreia* (1926); E. Breccia, *Juifs et Chrétiens de l'ancienne Alexandrie* (1927); CPJ I, pp. 1 ff.; V. Tcherikover, *Hellenistic Civilisation and the Jews* (1961), pp. 272–87; 410–15; P. M. Fraser, *Ptolemaic Alexandria* (1972), pp. 54 ff.; A. Kasher, *op. cit.*.

46. Jos. *C. Ap.* ii 4 (33, 36) (quoting from Apion): ἐλθόντες ἀπὸ Συρίας ᾤκησαν πρὸς ἀλίμενον θάλασσαν, γειτνιάσαντες ταῖς τῶν κυμάτων ἐκβολαῖς (Josephus himself adds): πρὸς τοῖς βασιλικοῖς ἦσαν ἱδρυμένοι. The great harbour of Alexandria, along which lay the greater part of the city, is bounded on the west by the island of Pharos and the dam connecting the island with the mainland, on the east by the headland Lochias which juts out into the sea from the mainland (see the map in H. Kiepert, *Zur Topographie des alten Alexandria* (1872)). On the headland of Lochias and nearby lay the palace (*basileia*) with the numerous buildings belonging to it, see Strabo xvii 1, 9 (794), which together accounted for a fifth of the city (Pliny, *N.H.* v 10/62); see especially T. D. Neroutsos-Bey, *L'ancienne Alexandrie* (1888); D. Puchstein, 'Alexandreia', in RE I, cols. 1376 ff., each with map; G. Lumbroso, *L'Egitto dei Greci e dei Romani* (²1895), pp. 154 ff.; RAC s.v. 'Alexandria', with map; Fraser, *Ptolemaic Alexandria*, ch. 1, with map. The Jewish Quarter therefore lay on the coast eastwards from the headland of Lochias.

47. Philo, *Legatio* 20 (132).

48. Philo, *In Flaccum* 8 (55). See following note.

which were known by the first five letters of the alphabet, two were called 'Jewish' because they were occupied mainly by Jews.[49] In the main, however, it is probable that some separation was maintained and that the main Jewish quarters at the time of Philo were still in the same area as before, that is in the east of the city.[50] According to an incidental reference by Josephus, the Jews lived especially in the 'so-called Delta', that is, in the fourth district.[51]

On the diffusion of the Jews throughout the rest of Egypt the literary sources give us only a few scanty reports. The most significant is Philo's assertion that the total number of Jewish inhabitants of Egypt amounted to a million, in that they lived 'from Katabathmos near Libya to the Ethiopian frontier'.[52] The 'Ethiopian frontier' is at Elephantine, where according to the Aramaic documents a Jewish community existed as early as the sixth century B.C. (pp. 38–40 above). While Philo's figure must be regarded as a rhetorical exaggeration, the documentary evidence now available does illustrate the presence of Jews throughout Egypt, from the late fourth or the third century B.C. onwards.[53]

It may be relevant at this point to note the evidence for other groups of Semitic origin who are attested in Graeco-Roman Egypt.

(a) *Phoenicians.* A colony of Phoenicians (Tyrians) had existed in the time of Herodotus at Memphis, Herod. ii 112.

What may be Phoenician names occur in a list of agricultural workers from January 240 B.C. (CPJ I, no. 36); here a farmer in the *nomos* of Bubastis gives for taxation purposes a list of his employees, among them: Ῥαγεσοβάαλ and Νατανβάαλ. Since names compounded with 'Baal' had at that time long been prohibited, the bearers of these

---

49. Philo, *In Flaccum* 8 (55): πέντε μοῖραι τῆς πόλεώς εἰσιν, ἐπώνυμοι τῶν πρώτων στοιχείων τῆς ἐπιγραμμάτου φωνῆς· τούτων δύο Ἰουδαϊκαὶ λέγονται, διὰ τὸ πλείστους Ἰουδαίους ἐν ταύταις κατοικεῖν. οἰκοῦσι δὲ καὶ ἐν ταῖς ἄλλαις οὐκ ὀλίγοι σποράδες. The division of Alexandria into five districts named after the first five letters of the alphabet is attested elsewhere, see Fraser, *Ptolemaic Alexandria*, pp. 34–5.

50. Josephus says expressly, *C. Ap.* ii 4 (35), that the Jews even later had not given up the place occupied by them.

51. *B.J.* ii 18, 8 (495). On the Jewish necropolis in Alexandria: T. D. Neroutsos, *L'ancienne Alexandrie* (1888), pp. 82–4; C. Clermont-Ganneau, *Rec. d'Arch. or.* 8, pp. 59–71, and see n. 42 above.

52. Philo, *In Flacc.* 6 (43): οὐκ ἀποδέουσι μυριάδων ἑκατὸν οἱ τὴν Ἀλεξάνδρειαν καὶ τὴν χώραν Ἰουδαῖοι κατοικοῦντες ἀπὸ τοῦ πρὸς Λιβύην καταβαθμοῦ μέχρι τῶν ὁρίων Αἰθιοπίας.

53. Subsequent discoveries of papyri and inscriptions have conclusively disproved the view of H. Willrich, *Juden und Griechen vor der makkabäischen Erhebung* (1895), that before the Maccabaean period there was virtually no Jewish diaspora in Egypt.

names were probably not Jews. But it is not always possible to distinguish Phoenician from other Semitic names in Greek transcription. For a brief sketch of the literature on Semitic theophoric names see J. Teixidor, *The Pagan God* (1977), pp. 156 ff. For Semitic names in papyri see H. Wuthnow, *Die semitischen Menschennamen in griechischen Inschriften und Papyri des vorderen Orients* (1930); S. M. Ruozzi Sala, *Lexicon Nominum Semiticorum quae in papyris graecis in Aegypto repertis ab anno 323 a. Ch. n. usque ad annum 70 p. Ch. n. reperiuntur* (1974).

(b) *Syrians.* 'Villages of Syrians' (Σύρων κῶμαι) are attested in a number of different parts of Egypt, as are Syrian quarters in towns; see CPJ I, pp. 4–5.

(c) *Samaritans.* On their settlement in Egypt from the third century B.C. onwards see below, p. 59. The references in Josephus (*Ant.* xi 8, 6 (345); 12, 1 (7–10)) are open to doubt; papyrus documents attest that there was a village Σαμαρεία in Middle Egypt already in the third century B.C., see CPJ I, no. 22, n. 6. The significance of this remains uncertain.

(d) *Idumaeans.* See in general U. Rapaport, 'Les Iduméens en Égypte', RPh 43 (1969), pp. 73–82 (speculative); note also Fraser, *Ptolemaic Alexandria*, pp. 280–1 and notes. A settlement of Idumaeans at Memphis is known to us from a decree which it passed in honour of a high-ranking official called Dorion (OGIS, no. 737 = SB, no. 8929). Its opening reads: ἔτους ἕκτου ἐπὶ συναγωγῆς τῆς γενηθείσης ἐν τῷ ἄνω Ἀπολλωνιείῳ τοῦ πολιτεύματος καὶ τῶν ἀπὸ τῆς πόλεως Ἰδυμαίων etc. The date of the decree is uncertain, though the first century B.C. may be slightly more probable than the second. The *politeuma* is certainly not that of the city of Memphis (which would be referred to as *polis* or *demos*), but the military colony of Idumaeans settled near Memphis, with whom the Idumaeans living in the city have associated themselves (on the frequent designation of such communities as *politeuma* see p. 88 below). The Idumaeans conclude by saying that Dorion should know how grateful the city (*polis*) was to him.

To much the same period as this honorific decree belongs a stele, also found in Memphis, on which are listed the names of those who contributed to the erection of a building, probably a temple (SB, no. 681). The nomenclature is predominantly Greek, but among them occur quite a few non-Greek, predominantly Semitic names. Among these there are a significant number which are compounds of 'Kos'. These are certainly Idumaean, for Kos was a high god of the Idumaeans; see T. C. Vriezen, *The Edomitic Deity Qaus* (1965). See also M. Sartre in IGLS XIII (1982), no. 9003 and commentary. These Idumaeans apparently belonged to the *politeuma* known to us from the previous inscription; note also that the Semitic names occur (with few exceptions) almost exclusively as patronymics. The second generation is hellenized.

(e) *Arabs* (?). Numerous Semitic names occur also on an inscription found in Hermupolis Magna, in the south of Middle Egypt, which like the foregoing gives a long list of those who have erected a building to the honour of the king and queen (SB, no. 4206), of between 80 and 69 B.C. The contributors in this instance are certainly soldiers. Alongside a great number of Greek names occur also a few Macedonian, Thracian and Egyptian, but especially Semitic names. See P. Meyer, *Das Heerwesen der Ptolemäer und Römer in Ägypten* (1900), pp. 95–7; C. Clermont-Ganneau, *Rec. d'Arch. or.* 6 (1905), pp. 213 ff.; M. Lidzbarski, *Eph. sem. Epigr.* II.3 (1908), pp. 338 ff. Some of the Semitic names (e.g. Zabinas) are Aramaic; Abdokos (i.e. 'Servant of Kos') is presumably Idumaean; most are probably to be regarded as related to Arabic. For a comparable list see SB, no. 8066, also from Hermupolis Magna.

For the geographical distribution of Jewish settlement in Egypt we have the following evidence. Only items of a reasonably clear date, location and character have been included. This survey is not intended as a general history of the Jews in Alexandria and Egypt, and does not consider in detail events (such as those of A.D. 38–41) recounted in literary sources.

I. *Lower Egypt*

Third Century B.C.

That Jews came to Egypt in considerable numbers, possibly already under Alexander the Great and certainly under Ptolemy I Lagus, is, from the evidence, scarcely in doubt. Under Ptolemy II Philadelphus (285–247 B.C.) Manetho wrote his historical work containing legendary material of an anti-Jewish character (Jos. *C. Ap.* i 26–7 (227–53) = GLAJJ I, no. 21, see below). It is perhaps unlikely that he would have engaged in this polemic if there had not been a significant Jewish settlement in Egypt.

From the reign of Ptolemy III Euergetes (247–221 B.C.) comes the following inscription found in Schedia near Alexandria: ὑπὲρ βασιλέως Πτολεμαίου καὶ βασιλίσσης Βερενίκης ἀδελφῆς καὶ γυναικὸς καὶ τῶν τέκνων τὴν προσευχὴν οἱ Ἰουδαῖοι (OGIS, no. 726 = CIJ II, no. 1440, cf. CPJ III, p. 141; cf. vol. II, p. 425). The inscription is certainly not later, for the only young consort of the king named Berenice (married successively to Ptolemy XI and Ptolemy XII) had no children and would have been called Cleopatra Berenice. Further, the orthography suggests Ptolemy III.

The existence of this inscription makes it possible that another, otherwise not so easy to date, also belongs to the time of Ptolemy III. If so, it has not survived in its original form but only as reinscribed in the Imperial period. This later inscription, found in Lower Egypt, now in the Aegyptisches Museum in Berlin, runs as follows: βασιλίσσης καὶ βασιλέως προσταξάντων ἀντὶ τῆς προανακειμένης περὶ τῆς ἀναθέσεως τῆς προσευχῆς πλάκος ἡ ὑπογεγραμμένη ἐπιγραφήτω. βασιλεὺς Πτολεμαῖος Εὐεργέτης τὴν προσευχὴν ἄσυλον. *Regina et rex iusser(un)t* (CIL III Suppl. no. 6583 = OGIS, no. 129 = CIJ II, no. 1449, cf. CPJ III, p. 144). On this evidence, a Ptolemy Euergetes had once granted the right of asylum to the *proseuche* in question, and the tablet concerned with the matter was later replaced by another 'at the command of the queen and king'. 'The queen and king' are perhaps, as Mommsen was the first to suggest, Zenobia and Vaballathus, during the brief Palmyrene occupation of Egypt c. A.D. 269–72 · (the formula βασιλέων προσταξάντων is found for example in the *Tebtunis Papyri* I (1902), no. 7; cf. M. T. Lenger, *Corpus des Ordonnances des Ptolemées* (^{2}1980), p. 357). However, J. Bingen, 'L'asylie pour une synagogue, CIL III Suppl. 6583 = CIL 1449', *Studia Paulo Naster Oblata* II (1982), pp. 11–16, argues that the original Greek inscription should be assigned to Cleopatra and Caesarion or Ptolemy XIV and that the Latin is contemporary, reflecting Roman influence at the end of the Ptolemaic period.

In a necropolis in Alexandria have been found, along with many anonymous gravestones, a few with inscriptions of persons from very different nationalities, which may suggest that mercenaries from the early Ptolemaic period, the third century B.C., were buried here. There are also Jews among them; on one gravestone (CIJ II, no. 1424) the name 'Aqabiah son of Elyōenai' can be read. See E. Breccia, 'La Necropoli de l'Ibrahimieh', BSAA 9 (1907), pp. 35–86; on the Jewish graves pp. 38–42, on the date, pp. 65–9; especially p. 67. On the Jewish graves see also: C. Clermont-Ganneau, CRAI 1907, pp. 234–43, 375–80 and *Rec. d'Arch. orientale* VIII, pp. 59–71 and plates II-V; cf. CIJ II, nos. 1424–31; cf. CPJ III, pp. 138–9.

Second Century B.C.

Under Ptolemy VI Philometor, in about 160 B.C., the Jewish High Priest Onias founded a Jewish temple at Leontopolis (Tell el-Yehudieh) in the *nomos* of Heliopolis on the eastern side of the Delta, in which sacrifice was regularly offered from then until it was destroyed on the orders of Vespasian, Jos. *Ant.* xii 9, 7 (387–8); xiii 3, 1–3 (62–73); 10, 4 (283–7 = Strabo, GLAJJ I, no. 99); xx 10, 3 (236), B.J. i 9, 4 (190); vii

10, 2–4 (421–36). See CIJ II, pp. 378–438; CPJ III, pp. 145–68, on the extensive group of Jewish epitaphs from the site (note CPJ, pp. 162–3, nos. 1530A-D, not included in CIJ). The place was called 'the land of Onias', ἡ 'Ονίου χώρα (*Ant*. xiv 8, 1 (131); *B.J.* i 9, 4 (190); cf. CIJ II, no. 1530: 'Ονίου γᾶ τρυφὸς ἀμετέρα in a metrical epitaph). The Jews living here must have represented a considerable force, since they later threatened to prevent the passage of an army marching from Palestine to the support of Caesar, *Ant*. xiv 8, 1 (131), cf. *B.J.* i 9, 4 (190–2). Willrich therefore argued that they were military settlers, Arch. f. Pap. 1 (1901), pp. 48–56. It was indeed by military exploits that two sons of Onias, Chelkias and Ananias, the generals of Cleopatra in the war against her son Ptolemy Lathyrus, distinguished themselves, *Ant*. xiii 10, 4 (285–7); 13, 1–2 (348–55). The son of a Chelkias (not Chelkias himself) is mentioned in a fragmentary inscription from the Heliopolite nome, in which the person concerned is referred to as *strategos* and is honoured by the award of a golden crown, CIJ II, no. 1450, see CPJ III, pp. 144–5; no secure conclusions can be based on this.

Some commentators have applied to the foundation by Onias the passage Isa. 19:18–19, where it says that Yahweh will have an altar in Egypt. In that case the passage must have been inserted into the text of Isaiah not before the second century, and the statement of Josephus, that Onias himself appealed to it, *Ant*. xiii 3, 1 (68), would be unhistorical. However, we know in any case from the Aramaic papyri that a Jewish shrine existed in Egypt as early as the sixth century B.C. A stronger argument for relating the texts to the Temple of Onias would be the mention of the 'City of the Sun' (i.e. Heliopolis) in Isa. 19:18, if this reading were certain. The statement that the language of Canaan was spoken at that time in five Egyptian towns (Isa. 19:18) could still be consistent with the Hellenistic period (see pp. 40–1 above).

With the settlement of Onias may reasonably be connected the *castra Iudaeorum* which, according to *Notitia Dignitatum* xxviii, 42, ed. Seeck, p. 60, lay within the province of Augustamnica, namely the territory east of the Delta, where in any case the colony of Onias was located. If, as is now generally agreed, it is identical with the modern Tell-el-Yehudieh, a little north of Heliopolis (see further below, pp. 145–6), the expression *castra Iudaeorum* would fit well with this, for Tell-el-Yehudieh has 'altogether the appearance of a fortress' (E. Naville, *The Academy* (1888), Pl. 49b; cf. the description by Flinders Petrie, *Hyksos and Israelite Cities* (1906), pp. 19–27).

The 'Jewish camp' (τὸ καλούμενον 'Ιουδαίων στρατόπεδον, Jos. *Ant*. xiv 8, 2 (133) = *B.J.* i 9, 4 (191)) on the western side of the Delta is in any case distinct from the above *castra Iudaeorum*. The army of Mithridates of Pergamon, hurrying from Palestine to the support of Caesar, came into contact with it after passing Memphis and the head of the Delta.

On this evidence, it is clear that this camp would have lain on the *west* side. There is no cause to assume an error on the part of Josephus (so W. Judeich, *Caesar im Orient* (1885), pp. 92–7) for it is very likely that there were several 'Jewish camps' (Judeich himself showed that the final campaigns of Mithridates must have taken place on the western side of the Delta).

The *Vicus Iudaeorum* may be also mentioned here. According to the *Itinerarium Antonini* it lay north-east of Heliopolis, on the eastern side of the Delta therefore (*Itinerarium Antonini* ed. O. Curtz, p. 23). It is certainly to be distinguished from the *castra Iudaeorum* of the *Notitia Dignitatum*.

It is presumably to the time of Ptolemy VI Philometor that two inscriptions belong testifying to the existence of a Jewish community in Athribis in the southern part of the Delta (OGIS, nos. 96, 101 = CIJ II, nos. 1443–4, cf. CPJ III, pp. 142 ff.). The first reads: ὑπὲρ βασιλέως Πτολεμαίου καὶ βασιλίσσης Κλεοπάτρας Πτολεμαῖος Ἐπικύδου ὁ ἐπιστάτης τῶν φυλακιτῶν καὶ οἱ ἐν Ἀθρίβει Ἰουδαῖοι τὴν προσευχὴν θεῷ ὑψίστῳ. The second reads: ὑπὲρ βασιλέως Πτολεμαίου καὶ βασιλίσσης Κλεοπάτρας καὶ τῶν τέκνων Ἑρμίας καὶ Φιλότερα ἡ γυγὴ καὶ τὰ παιδία τήνδε ἐξέδραν τῇ προσευχῇ.

Whether the ἐπιστάτης τῶν φυλακιτῶν called Ptolemy was himself a Jew is doubtful; perhaps he was only a friend to the Jews. He and the Jewish community built the *proseuche* 'to the most high God', while Hermias and his wife and children installed the *exedra* for this *proseuche*. Again, since there were four Ptolemies who had a wife named Cleopatra, Ptolemy V, VI, VII and VIII, the date is uncertain. The friendly attitude of Ptolemy VI to the Jews, however, makes it most natural to think of his time.

Two inscriptions of the period 143 to 117 B.C. attest the presence of synagogues in the western Delta (cf. vol. II, p. 425, n. 5): (a) from Xenephyris, CIJ II, no. 1441; (b) from Nitriai, 1442 (CPJ III, pp. 141–2).

First Century B.C.

An inscription from Alexandria (Gabbary), of uncertain date, but most probably 37 B.C., reads: [ὑπὲρ] βασ[ιλίσση]ς καὶ β[ασιλ]έως θεῷ [με]γάλῳ ἐ[πηκό]ῳ, Ἄλυπ[ος τὴν] προσε[υχὴν] ἐπόει [*vacat?*] (ἔτους) ιέ Με[χείρ..] (OGIS no. 742 = CIJ II, no. 1432, cf. CPJ III, p. 139).

A number of papyri of the late first century B.C. dated by the reign of Augustus (i.e. following the Roman acquisition of Egypt in 30 B.C.), name persons who *may* be Jewish: CPJ II, no. 144 (13 B.C.)—Apollonia daughter of Sambathion; 146 (13 B.C.)—Theodote daughter of Dositheos; 147 (14 B.C.)—Martha; 148 (10

B.C.)—Martha; 149 (10 B.C.)—Lysimachus son of Theodotos, his
wife Marion daughter of Isakis, and Tryphon son of Theodotos. No.
145 refers to the 'land of Helkias' in the Bousirite district. But the only
reliable papyrus evidence for a Jewish presence is firstly an allusion in
no. 143 to the will of Theodoros (also referred to in 142) which he had
deposited in the 'archive of the Jews': καθ' ἣν ἔθετο διαθήκ(ην) διὰ τοῦ
τῶν 'Ιουδαίων ἀρχείου (and even here the reading 'Ιουδαίων is not entirely
certain). Secondly there is a document of 5-4 B.C. which is of
considerable importance for the question of Jewish status in Alexandria
(see pp. 127–9 below). A complaint addressed to the Prefect of Egypt
by a Jew named Helenos, it is written by a scribe. The petitioner
appears as 'Helenos son of Tryphon an Alexandrian (crossed out)—a
Jew of those from Alexandria' (written above the line): παρὰ 'Ελένου
το(ῦ) Τρύφωνο(ς) [['Αλεξανδρέω(ς)]]—'Ιουδαίου τῶν ἀπὸ 'Αλεξανδ-
ρε(ίας) (CPJ II, no. 151). The same papyrus alludes to the
laographia, the poll-tax to which Alexandrian Jews, but not the Greek
citizens of Alexandria, became liable in the early Roman period (see
CPJ I, pp. 60 ff.).

First Century A.D.

The major document from the first century A.D. is the famous letter of
Claudius to the Alexandrians (PLond, no. 1912 = CPJ II, no. 153), to
be discussed further below (pp. 128–9). That apart, there is the striking
letter (CPJ II, no. 152) of the same year, A.D. 41, addressed by an Egyptian
Greek named Sarapion to his agent in Alexandria, in which he tells him
that, like everyone, he should keep clear of the Jews (ὡς ἂν πάντες καὶ
σὺ βλέπε σατὸν (*sic*) ἀπὸ τῶν 'Ιουδαίων). The significance of this remains
controversial, but it may be a reference to the current conflicts in the
city.

From Babylon in the district of Heliopolis, near the southern border
of Lower Egypt, a document of A.D. 59 (CPJ II, no. 417) shows a loan
made by a Roman soldier to Petos son of Helkias and his two sons,
Helkias and Dor[...]koas, 'all three Jews, Persians of the *epigone* from
the Syrian village' (οἱ τρῖς 'Ιουδαῖοι, Πέρσαι τῆς ἐπιγονῆς τῶν [ἀ]πὸ
Σύρων κώμης).

2. Middle Egypt

Third Century B.C.

Papyrus from the twenty-sixth year of Ptolemy II Philadelphus, April
260 B.C., found at Hibeh (the Greek name is unknown) in the *nomos* of
Heracleopolis, PHibeh I, no. 96 = CPJ I, no. 18. It is an agreement
between two persons with grievances against one another who now
come to terms to end their dispute. The text is written twice. From the

wording, which in both instances contains lacunae, the opening can be restored as follows: συγγραφὴ ἀποστασίου [Ἀνδρονίκου τοῦ — 15 letters — τῆς ἐπιγονῆ]ς καὶ Ἀλεξάνδρου τοῦ Ἀνδρονίκου Ἰουδαίου μετὰ [20 letters — τῶν Ζωίλου δεκανι]κοῦ. The name of the first party to the dispute, Andronicus, is supplied from the later part of the text. His opponent, Alexander son of Andronicus, is presumably not his son. The first is characterised as a military settler by the phrase, τῆς ἐπιγονῆς. In the case of the Jew Alexander, this addition is lacking; but he appears to have a partner who is a soldier, for the latter is classified with the people of the *dekanikos* Zoilus, and *dekanikos* is a military rank.

Papyrus from the tenth year of Ptolemy III Euergetes, i.e. 238 B.C., discovered in the *nomos* of Arsinoe, the present Fayûm, CPJ I, no. 126. A will of Philo son of Heraclides, who bequeaths to his wife and daughters, along with other things, also his slaves, among them (ll. 14–16) Ἀπολλ[ωνιον?] παρεπίδημον, ὃς καὶ Συριστὶ Ἰωναθᾶς καλεῖται. He is evidently a Jew.

According to a papyrus from the same period and district (the date has not survived), certain taxes were to be paid in the village of Psenyris εἰς τὰ ἀποδόχια τῆς κώμης παρὰ τῶν Ἰουδαίων καὶ τῶν Ἑλλήνων ἑκάστου σώματος, CPJ I, no. 33. *Sôma* is sometimes used for a slave, but in this case the expression means simply 'from each person'. Clearly the Jews and Hellenes formed a distinct group alongside the indigenous population.

On the village Psenyris see C. Wessely, *Topographie des Fayyum*, pp. 163 ff.

A papyrus from 226 B.C. in the reign of Ptolemy III Euergetes, in the *nomos* of Arsinoe, CPJ I, no. 19, contains a collection of legal decisions, among them a case of a complaint by a Jew against a Jewess, ll. 13–14. The description 'of the *epigone*' characterises the man concerned as a military settler, moreover one not of the first generation. The document is clear evidence of Jewish military settlers in the time of Ptolemy II Philadelphus at the latest (see e.g. CPJ I, p. 13). Compare the loan-contract of 228–21 B.C. from Tebtynis between Mousaios son of Simas, a Jew of the *epigone*, and Lasaites son of Iz[...]is, 'Jew of the *epigone*' (PTebt. no. 815 = CPJ I, no. 20), and the report by the village scribe of Apollonius (Fayûm) in 210 of a robbery by three 'Jews of the *epigone*' (CPJ I, no. 21).

A papyrus from 'the fifth year', probably of Ptolemy IV, therefore 218 B.C., in any case still from the third century B.C., found at Magdola in the *nomos* of Arsinoe, CPJ I, no. 129, contains a petition from a woman to the king about the theft of a cloak, which the thief refuses to hand over. At this point there occur the words [τὸ ἱμ]άτιον ἐν τῇ προσευχῇ τῶν Ἰουδαίων (the thief appears to have deposited the cloak with the warden of the *proseuche*). Mention of the *proseuche* makes it clear that there were not only individual Jews in Magdola but a Jewish community. CPJ I, no. 128, from the same place and year, also contains a complaint against a Jew, this time by his wife.

In another papyrus from Magdola, CPJ I, no. 37, complaint is made by three persons, Theodotus, Gaddaeus and Phanias, against a certain Demetrius concerning infringement of a lease contract. All three petitioners are probably Jews.

The name Magdola is itself Semitic (מגדול), but occurs frequently in Egypt. See C. Wessely, *Topographie des Fayyum* (1904), pp. 101–4; PTebt II (1907), p. 388. A *Migdol* in the neighbourhood of Pelusium is mentioned in Jer. 44:1; 46:14; also Exod. 14:2; Num. 33:7; Ezek. 29:10; 30:6.

An inscription from Arsinoe-Crocodilopolis of the reign of Ptolemy III (246–221 B.C.), unfortunately broken at the crucial point, appears to record a Jewish community and synagogue there: SB, no. 8939 = CPJ III, no. 1532A, not in CIJ II: οἱ ἐν Κροκ[ο]δίλων πόλει Ἰου[δαῖ]οι τὴν προ[σ]ε[υχήν] (cf. vol. II, p. 425, n. 5). In CPJ I, no. 38 (218 B.C.) a wool-dealer living in Arsinoe-Crocodilopolis complains of being wronged by a Jew named Seos. The six Jews who acted as witnesses to a contract in Samareia in the Fayûm (see p. 45 above) may also have been military settlers (CPJ I, no. 22).

Individual Jews, and other persons with Semitic names who may be Jewish, are also attested in the Fayûm in the Zenon papyri of the mid-third century B.C., see CPJ I, nos. 7–17. Those who are certainly Jewish are no. 8: Ἀντιγονῆς (*sic*) Ἰουδαῖος, and 9a-b: 'Pasis the Jew'; cf. also no. 13: παρὰ Ἰσμαήλου, and nos. 14–15 with the name Σαμοήλ.

Second Century B.C.

'Jews of the *epigone*' continue to be attested in the second century in the Fayûm. One makes a loan to another, witnessed by six others, in P. Tebt. 817 = CPJ I, no. 23 (182 B.C.); the last two witnesses are soldiers of the first hipparchy settled by Dositheos and holding eighty *arourai* of land. Another 'Jew of the *epigone*' appears on a contract of 172-1 B.C. (CPJ I, no. 26) and a Jewish watchman or policeman (*phylakites*) in a contract of 173 B.C. (CPJ I, no. 25). Jewish settlers are probably attested also in no. 28 from Samareia (see above) and 29–32.

Papyrus, end of the second century B.C. in Tebtynis, in the *nomos* of Arsinoe, PTebt I, no. 86 = CPJ I, no. 134, a land-survey in which a προσευχὴ Ἰουδαίων is twice mentioned, ll. 18 and 29, to which belongs a portion of ground described as 'sacred garden-land' (ἱερὰ παράδεισος). This is presumably to be explained on the basis of Egyptian usage, and thus means temple property. This may well be the same synagogue as that mentioned above.

On Tebtynis see C. Wessely, *Topographie des Fayyum*, pp. 146 ff.; PTebt II, p. 404.

Papyrus from the second century B.C., *nomos* of Arsinoe, CPJ I, no. 47, a fragmentary land tax account. The wording, with figures and signs omitted, is as follows:

τὰ λόγια γῆς α[...] διὰ Πτολεμαίο[υ]
Θεόδοτος Ἀλεξάνδρου Θεοδότ[ου]...
Θεοδώρα Λεόντις Μαρίου ...
Θεόμνηστος [Δ]ωσιθέου Θεοδώρου...
Μεσορὴ ά
Σαββάθιον Ἀριστίππου Ἰακούβιος...
Σαββάθιον Σαββαίου δ(?) καὶ Μαρίον..
Δωσιθέα Θεοδότου Θεοδώρου ...

Since Ἰακούβιος and Σαββάθιον are Hebrew names, and since a strikingly large number of names are compounded with *theos*, it is reasonable to assume that all these persons are Jews. But since on the recto of the papyrus the words τῶν περὶ Σαμαρείαν appear, all the persons mentioned here may be Samaritans.

A papyrus from Philadelphia (Fayûm), whose script indicates the second century B.C., contains a petition by 'Judas son of Dositheos, a Jew' who was a farmer in the area (CPJ I, no. 43). Note also CPJ I, no. 133 from the Fayûm, mid-second century B.C.

The letter-forms also indicate that the following inscription found in the Fayûm, CIJ II, no. 1531, cf. CPJ III, p. 163, is of the Hellenistic period: Ἐλεάζαρος Νικολάου ἡγεμὼν ὑπὲρ ἑαυτοῦ καὶ Εἰρήνης τῆς γυναικὸς τὸ ὡρολόγιον καὶ τὸ φρέαρ. The term *hegemon* here is presumably a military title.

A papyrus of the second or first century B.C. (BGU, no. 1282 = CPJ I, no. 46) contains an agreement for joint use of a pottery made by two Jewish potters from the 'village of Syrians' (see p. 45 above) with two Egyptians.

First Century A.D.

A papyrus of A.D. 3 from Philadelphia in the Fayûm records a loan of a quantity of barley to Sambathion son of Dionysius, a 'Persian of the *epigone*', who may be Jewish (CPJ II, no. 411); another Sambathion in no. 413 (Tebtynis, A.D. 16). The names Abramos, Sambataios and Dositheos appear on a list of owners of sheep and goats from Hermupolis Magna, A.D. 8-9 (412), a man named Josepos in an Oxyrhynchus papyrus of A.D. 21 (414), and tax-payers called Iosepos and Sambathion at Philadelphia in A.D. 25 (416). None of these is explicitly identified as Jewish (note however the isolated word Ἰουδαίου in no. 415, from Hawara, A.D. 24-5). For Jewish names on a papyrus probably relating to Oxyrhynchus in the first century A.D. see CPR VII, Griechische Texte IV (1979), no. 2.

Unambiguous evidence of the presence of Jews in Middle Egypt in the first century A.D. is supplied by parts of a large papyrus listing tax-payers and their respective liabilities in Arsinoe in the Fayûm in A.D. 73 (CPJ II, no. 421). The document contains the reports of the Amphodarches of a quarter of the town, in which he gives an exact list of those obliged to pay the Ἰουδαικὸν τέλεσμα, the two-drachma tax imposed after the destruction of the Temple (see also p. 122 below). Only the women and children are listed, since the men were entered in another register which is not preserved. However we can can obtain their names from the list of women. The list runs as follows:

Τρύφαινα, age 61.

Δωσάριον, daughter of Ἰακούβος and of Σαμβοῦς, wife of Σίμων, 22 years of age.

Φιλοῦς, daughter of [...] and Πτολλοῦς, wife of Θεόδωρος, 20 years of age.

Σαμβάθ[ιον], daughter of Σαβῖνος and of Ἡραῖς, wife of Θηγένης, 18 years of age.

Σ[..., daughter of ...] and Θευδοῦς, wife of Σαμβαθ(ίων?), 1[.] years of age.

Ἐ[ρώτιον, daughter of ...] and Εὐτέρπη, wife of Πτολλᾶς, 22 years of age.

Boys:

Φίλισκος, son of Πτολλᾶς and Ἐρώτιον, 4 years of age.

Σεύθης, son of Θεόδωρος and Φιλοῦς, 3 years of age.

Girls:

Πρωτοῦς, daughter of Θεόδωρος and Φιλοῦς, 5 years of age.

Πρωτοῦς, daughter of Σίμων and Δωσάριον, 4 years of age.

To these are added the five men, Σίμων, Θεόδωρος, Θεγένης, Σαμβαθ(ίων?), Πτολλᾶς: fifteen persons in all, as is specifically stated. (Φιλοῦς at the age of 20 already has a five-year-old daughter.) The tax amounted in each case to 8 drachmas, 2 obols. On its relation to the didrachma tax see pp. 122–3 below.

Incidental items of information include POxy, no. 276 = CPJ II, no. 422, a receipt from Oxyrhynchus of A.D. 77 mentioning someone who is the son of Iakoubos, and a papyrus of about A.D. 85, from Oxyrhynchus, POxy, no. 335 = CPJ II, no. 423, recording the sale of the sixth part of a house ἐπ᾽ ἀμφόδου Ἰουδα⟨ϊ⟩κ(οῦ), which was sold to Νικαίᾳ Σιλ[βα]νῷ Ψουβίου τῶν ἀπ᾽ Ὀξ(υρύγχων) πόλ(εως) Ἰουδαίων. Cf. also a somewhat later papyrus of A.D. 133 (POxy, no. 100 = CPJ III, no. 454) from Oxyrhynchus: ἐπ᾽ ἀμφόδου Κρητικοῦ καὶ Ἰουδαϊκῆς ⟨λαύρας⟩. The restoration of a feminine noun meaning 'alley' or 'lane' is conjectural. But it is evident that the adjective 'Jewish' is attached to some topographical feature.

There is also a letter of A.D. 87, addressed by a lady named Joanna to someone at Ptolemais Hermeiou (CPJ II, no. 424), and Jewish names on documents of A.D. 93 from Oxyrhynchus (no. 425) and of c. 94 from the *nomos* of Arsinoe (no. 426).

Second Century A.D.

Papyrus from the year A.D. 101–2 from the Fayûm, BGU III (1903), no. 715 = CPJ II, no. 428, a list of *sitologoi*, including Ἰωσῆς ὁ καὶ Τεύφιλο(ς), Στράτων ἐπικαλού(μενος) Ἰσάκ(ις), Ἐλεά[ζαρος] Πτ[ολεμ]- αίου, Ἀβράμ[ιος], and Σαμβαθ(ίων) Ἰακούβου.

Papyrus from the fourth year of Trajan, 10 February, A.D. 101, from Apollonias in the Fayûm, BGU IV, no. 1068 = CPJ II, no. 427. A father reports to the royal clerk the death of his son Joseph, who was still a minor and so had not been included in the last census (which took place only every fourteen years). The father asks therefore that he be registered among the dead. The names (Joseph—twice—and Sarra) show that the family was Jewish. Note the liability of the deceased for the poll-tax (*laographia*) and the oath taken by the name of the Emperor at the end of the declaration. Cf. the census-return of A.D. 105 from Arsinoe, with two Jewish names (CPJ II, no. 430).

Papyrus about A.D. 110, *nomos* of Arsinoe, i.e. the Fayûm, PFay, no. 123 = CPJ II, no. 431: a letter of a certain Harpocration to his brother Sabinus, in which he tells him among other things that the Jew Teuphilos has reported having been impressed for work in the fields (of uncertain character) and demands to be excused because he wants to go to Sabinus. The announcement seems to have been made suddenly that same day. Clearly Harpocration wishes to warn his brother against the untrustworthy worker.

Papyrus of A.D. 113, CPJ II, no. 432, which contains the accounts of the four commissioners for the waterworks of Arsinoe. In the long list of items of income for the supply of water the following are mentioned among others (ll. 57–61): ἀρχόντων Ἰ[ου]δαίων προσευχῆς Θηβαίων, 128 drachmas monthly. The same sum also for the *eucheion*. The amount is remarkably high; the explanation may perhaps lie in the need for a large amount of water for ritual purposes. The 'Proseuche of the Thebans' is of course the *proseuche* of the Jews from Thebes (in Upper Egypt). In Arsinoe these were apparently so numerous that they had their own *proseuche*, which perhaps implies that there were other Jewish *proseuchai* in the town. A *eucheion* distinct from the *proseuche* occurs here for the first time. The precise meaning of the term ('place of prayer') is not known.

The papyri (CPJ II, nos. 435–50) relating, or possibly relating to the Jewish revolt of A.D. 115–17 (see vol. I, pp. 529–34, and M. Pucci,

'C.P.J. II 158, 435 e la rivolta ebraica al tempo di Traiano', ZPE 51 (1983), pp. 95–103) give little precise evidence on the areas of Jewish settlement in normal times. An exception is no. 445, a letter of the *strategos* of the Herakleopolite *nomos* to the *strategos* of the Oxyrhynchite *nomos* (and mentioning one addressed to the *strategos* of the Kyriopolite *nomos*), referring to a register of property formerly held by Jews and now evidently confiscated. The date is presumably not long after A.D. 117. A document of A.D. 130 (no. 448) alludes to similar confiscations of land owned by Jews in the Athribite *nomos*.

A second-century document from the Oxyrhynchite *nomos* (CPJ II, no. 452b) makes a reference to a tax called ἐμπορία 'Ιουδαίων, not otherwise known, or explicable. Isakous, daughter of Herakleides, farming near Theadelphia in A.D. 132 (no. 455) may have been Jewish, as might the farmer Heras, also called Azakiel, at Soknopaiou Nesos (no. 464). At Karanis in the Arsinoite *nomos* the Jewish tax was being collected in the mid-second century (no. 460).

In Antinoopolis on the southern boundary of Middle Egypt a Hebrew grave inscription was found, CIJ II, no. 1534, cf. CPJ III, p. 165. The date, second century A.D. at the earliest, is quite uncertain. For a Greek grave inscription from Antinoopolis with names which *may* be Jewish, see CIJ II, no. 1535 = CPJ III, p. 165.

A papyrus of the late second or early third century records the existence at Hermupolis (as possibly at Arsinoe, p. 54 above) of a 'Jewish lane', 'Ιουδ(αϊκῆς) λαύρας (CPJ III, no. 468).

Papyrus of A.D. 199–200 from Oxyrhynchus, POxy, no. 705 = CPJ II, no. 450. It contains a petition from a certain Orion to the emperors Septimius Severus and Caracalla, in which he refers to the fact that the inhabitants of Oxyrhynchus had proved their loyalty to the Romans by fighting alongside them in the war against the Jews and by celebrating annually the day commemorating the victory (ll. 31–4). The reference is certainly to the war in the reign of Trajan of A.D. 115–17, which had extended over Middle Egypt where so many Jews lived, see vol. I, pp. 529–34.

A papyrus from Oxyrhynchus containing a nine-line lamentation in Hebrew is published by F. Klein-Franke, 'A Hebrew Lamentation from Roman Egypt', ZPE 51 (1983), pp. 80–4, and conjecturally related to the aftermath of the war of A.D. 115–17.

Third Century A.D.

A document which is considerably more revealing than most from the second and third centuries is a papyrus of A.D. 291 from Oxyrhynchus (POxy, no. 1205 = CPJ III, no. 473) concerning the manumission of some Jewish slaves. A sum has been paid to their owner 'by the community of the Jews' (παρὰ τῆς συναγω[γ]ῆς τῶν 'Ιουδαίων) through the agency of two or more men, one of whom was a town councillor of Ono in Palestine and also 'father of the (community?)'—πατρὸς τῆς [συναγωγῆς?].

Papyrus from A.D. 295, Oxyrhynchus, POxy, no. 43 = CPJ III, no. 475, verso col. ii, l. 13: six watchmen in the Serapeum, among them Jacob son of Achilles. The name Jacob perhaps suggests that this watchman in the temple of Serapis was by birth a Jew.

Jewish names occur also in the later sources from Middle Egypt. See e.g. CPJ III, nos. 474a-b; 477; 480; 503; 506-12; 517. Note also POxy, no. 3314 (fourth century). In view of the relatively large volume of evidence for Jews in Egypt in the period with which this book is mainly concerned it is not necessary to consider these references in detail.

3. *Upper Egypt*

Second Century B.C.

Among the mass of tax receipts on sherds of pottery (ostraca) which have been found in the neighbourhood of Thebes, there are some with Jewish names belonging to the second century B.C. See U. Wilcken, *Griechische Ostraka aus Ägypten und Nubien* I (1899), pp. 523-4, for the first systematic collection of Jewish (or Semitic) names from these sources. See now CPJ I, section V, pp. 194-226 (nos. 48-124): 'Jewish Tax-Collectors, Government Officials and Peasants in Upper Egypt'. The names which can be regarded with reasonable certainty as Jewish are now listed in CPJ I, pp. 200-2.

Following Wilcken's suggestion we should think of these persons to whom receipts are issued not as individual tax-payers but as contractors who brought in the taxes and paid the government an annual lump sum for them. We must reckon with the possibility that the bearers of these Hebrew names are not really Jews but Samaritans, for Alexander the Great is alleged to have settled Samaritan soldiers in the Thebaid, Jos. *Ant.* xi 8, 6 (345).

To the second century B.C. belongs also a letter, found in the Thebaid, written by a certain Menon to Hermocrates, in which a Jew is mentioned as having failed to hand over a horse and (?) carriage, CPJ I, no. 135.

First Century B.C.

A dining-association with Jewish members may be attested in CPJ I, no. 139, from Apollinopolis Magna (Edfu).

First Century A.D.

A continued Jewish presence in Upper Egypt is again attested by the appearance of Jewish names on ostraca (see above), this time from Apollinopolis Magna; they are collected and discussed in CPJ II, pp. 108–77 (nos. 160–408d). In particular the ostraca illustrate the payment of the two-drachma tax imposed on all Jews after the destruction of the Temple in A.D. 70 (see vol. I, p. 513); in these documents it is called 'Ιουδαϊκὸν τέλεσμα or τιμὴ δηναρίων δύο 'Ιουδαίων, and its payment is attested from A.D. 71-2 (no. 160) to A.D. 116 (nos. 227–9). Payment of other taxes is attested from A.D. 56 (no. 230) to 116 (no. 369); nos. 371–2 belong to uncertain dates in the reign of Trajan (A.D. 98–117). Whether the cessation is to be regarded as a side-effect of the revolt of A.D. 115–17, or ascribed to some other cause, or merely the accidents of discovery, remains unclear.

How numerous the Jews in the Thebes were is suggested by the fact that Jews from Thebes in Arsinoe had their own *proseuche*. See the papyrus from the reign of Trajan described above, p. 55.

Second Century A.D.

Some evidence for the existence of a substantial Jewish community in Upper Egypt is provided by the fact that the uprising in the time of Trajan is reported by later sources to have extended into the Thebaid (Euseb. *Chron.* ed. Schoene II, pp. 164 ff. on the eighteenth year of Trajan; Orosius vii 12).

As characteristic illustrations of the broadmindedness of this Egyptian Jewry there are two inscriptions in the temple of Pan at Apollonopolis Magna in Upper Egypt, OGIS, nos. 73–4; CIJ II, nos. 1538, 1537 (CPJ III, pp. 165–6). One reads: εὐλόγει τὸν θεὸν Πτολεμαῖος Διονυσίου 'Ιουδαῖος. The other reads: θεοῦ εὐλογία Θευόδοτος Δωρίωνος 'Ιουδαῖος σωθεὶς ἐκ πελ⟨άγ⟩ους. The second thus gives thanks for rescue from danger at sea; both pay homage to 'the god' without mention of his name. Whether this was Pan or Yahweh seems not to have been of great importance to them.

A further group of ostraca from Apollinopolis Magna dating to the 150s and 160s (CPJ II, nos. 375–403) has been regarded as revealing the presence of a Jewish family; but the positive evidence for this is not clear.

Consistent with their great numbers and importance, the Jews of Alexandria and Egypt were also involved in various major conflicts with the pagan inhabitants and with the Roman authorities; this was the case with the great persecution under Caligula (vol. I, pp. 390–4), with the conflicts under Nero and Vespasian,[54] and in the time of Trajan (vol. I, pp. 529–34). The very history of these conflicts is at the same time

54. *B.J.* ii 18, 7–8 (487–98); vii 10 (407–36).

proof of the continuing importance of Egyptian Jewry in the Roman period also.

Apart from Jews proper, however, Samaritans also lived in Egypt.[55] Alexander the Great himself is reported to have settled Samaritans in the Thebaid.[56] Ptolemy I Lagus, on his conquest of Palestine, took many prisoners of war, not only from Judaea and Jerusalem, but also 'from the inhabitants of Samaria and Mt. Gerizim', and settled them in Egypt.[57]

A village 'Samareia' in Middle Egypt occurs in papyrus sources as early as the middle of the third century B.C.[58] The inhabitants certainly included Jewish settlers in the Ptolemaic period, and the significance of the name is unclear (p. 45 above). At the time of Ptolemy VI Philometor, Jews and Samaritans in Egypt are alleged by Josephus to have brought their dispute on the true place of worship (Jerusalem or Gerizim) before the King's court.[59] In the fictional letter of Hadrian to Servianus given in the *Historia Augusta* the same is said of the Samaritans in Egypt as of the Jews and Christians there, that they are a bunch of 'astrologers, diviners and quack healers'.[60] This evidence is of no value as regards the second century A.D. A number of possible or probable Samaritans are attested in the papyri of the Roman period (PMilVogl, no. 212: Σαμαρείτης, Tebtynis, A.D. 109; PMich, no. 223–4: Gaius Iulius Maximus Σαμαρείτης, Karanis, A.D. 171-2), but identification is complicated by the possibility that all that is indicated is origin from the village Samareia; see M. Nagel, 'Un Samaritain dans l'Arsinoite au 2ᵉ siècle après J.-C.', CE 49 (1974), pp. 356–65. For the late Roman period there is the divorce-deed of A.D. 586 (CPJ III, no. 513 = SB, no. 9278) from Hermopolis Magna, in which the two parties are called 'Samaritans by observance' (Σαμαρῖται τὴν θρησκ⟨ε⟩ίαν). The existence of Samaritans in Egypt is also presupposed in a letter of the emperors Valentinian, Theodosius and Arcadius to the

---

55. Cf. T. G. J. Juynboll, *Commentarii in historiam gentis Samaritanae* (1846), pp. 38–41, 43–5; M. Nagel, CE 49 (1974), pp. 356–65.

56. *Ant.* xi 8, 6 (340–5).

57. *Ant.* xii 1 (7).

58. PPetrie II, pp. [14] 2, [88] 9, [93] 4, [94] 22, [96] 12. III, nos. 66b iv.3, 87b ii.2, 112e ii.4, 139b i.3. All these sources of the Petrie collection belong to the third century B.C. and were found in the Fayûm (*nomos* of Arsinoe). See also PTebt II, nos. 566, 609; III, no. 820 = CPJ I, no. 22; 882 − CPJ I, no. 28; PRyl. no. 71 (97–5 B.C.). The village was later also called Kerkesephis, and still existed five hundred years later, A.D. 289, BGU no. 94; it does not appear that the two places were identical in the Ptolemaic period, see PPetrie II, pp. 383–4.

59. *Ant.* xiii 3, 4 (74–9). Cf. xii 1 (10).

60. HA *Vita Saturnini* 8: 'nemo illic archisynagogus Iudaeorum, nemo Samarites, nemo Christianorum presbyter non mathematicus, non haruspex, non aliptes.'

praefectus Augustalis in 390.[61] The letter of a bishop Eulogius reports a synod which he has held against the Samaritans. If, as is now generally assumed, this is the well-known Eulogius of Alexandria (patriarch A.D. 581–607), it is natural to presume that there was a known Samaritan community in Egypt in the sixth century (as the divorce-deed of A.D. 581 also suggests).[62] Their existence there can however be proved for the Middle Ages and on into the seventeenth century A.D.[63] Compare the evidence cited below for Samaritans living in Delos in the second century B.C. (pp. 70–1) and for a Samaritan synagogue at Thessalonika (pp. 66–7).

The Jewish dispersion is also well attested further west along the North African coast. In *Cyrenaica*, which was settled by Greeks in the seventh century B.C., and remained Greek-speaking, Jews were very strongly represented. Already Ptolemy I Lagus is said to have sent Jewish settlers there.[64] The Roman letter mentioned in 1 Mac. 15:23 presupposes Jewish inhabitants of Cyrene. A certain Jason of Cyrene composed the work on which 2 Maccabees is based (2 Mac. 2:23). According to Strabo, at the time of Sulla (around 85 B.C.) the inhabitants of the city of *Cyrene* fell into four categories: 1) citizens; 2) farmers; 3) resident aliens; 4) Jews.[65] The Jews of that time played a prominent part in the disturbances in Cyrene which Lucullus himself, because of his accidental presence there, had to settle.[66] A Jewish

---

61. *Cod. Theod.* xiii 5, 18.

62. This work of Eulogius is known to us only from the report in Photius, *Biblioth.* cod. 230 s. fin. (ed. I. Bekker, p. 285; ed. R. Henry, vol. V (1967), pp. 60–1). Photius takes the author to be Eulogius of Alexandria (end of sixth century), but this is inconsistent with the textual report that the Synod was held in the seventh year of the emperor Marcianus (A.D. 450–7). It is normally accepted that Μαρκιανός should be emended to read Μαυρικιός, i.e. Mauricius, who reigned A.D. 582–602.

63. T. E. J. Juynboll, *Commentarii in historiam gentis Sam.*, pp. 43–5. A. Brüll, 'Die Samaritaner in Kairo', Jahrb. für jüdische Gesch. und Literatur 7 (1885), pp. 43–5; R. Gottheil, 'Egypt' in JE V, pp. 70 ff. No modern survey of the evidence for the Samaritan diaspora appears to be available.

64. Jos. *C. Ap.* ii 4 (44). For the history of Cyrenaica in general see F. Chamoux, *Cyrène sous la monarchie des Battiades* (1953); P. Romanelli, *La Cirenaica romana* (1943); R. G. Goodchild, *Cyrene und Apollonia* (1971); Beurlier s.v. 'Cyrène', in F. Vigouroux, DB II, cols. 1177–84. Note esp. S. Applebaum, *Jews and Greeks in Ancient Cyrene* (1979), and G. Luederitz, *Corpus jüdische Zeugnisse aus der Cyrenaika* (1983).

65. Strabo *ap.* Jos. *Ant.* xiv 7, 2 (115) = GLAJJ I, no. 105: τέτταρες δ᾽ ἦσαν ἐν τῇ πόλει τῶν Κυρηναίων, ἥ τε τῶν πολιτῶν καὶ ἡ τῶν γεωργῶν, τρίτη δ᾽ ἡ τῶν μετοίκων, τετάρτη δ᾽ ἡ τῶν Ἰουδαίων.

66. Strabo *ap.* Jos. *Ant.* xiv 7, 2 (115–18) = GLAJJ, *loc. cit.* On the activities of Lucullus in Cyrene see Plutarch, *Luc.* 2; MRR II, pp. 55–6. His main object was to requisition ships for Sulla. In doing so he had, however, also to settle internal disturbances, since conditions in Cyrene were still in great disorder. The last king, Ptolemy Apion of Cyrene, had died in 96 B.C., after naming the Romans as his heirs; but Cyrene was not incorporated as a province until 74 B.C.

politeuma in the city of *Berenice* in Cyrenaica is revealed in three important inscriptions of the first century A.D., recently re-edited by J. M. Reynolds in J. A. Lloyd (ed.), *Excavations at Sidi Khrebish, Benghazi (Berenice)* I (Libya Antiqua, Supp. VI. 1981), pp. 242–7 (henceforward Reynolds) : a) SEG XVII, no. 823 = AE 1960, no. 199 = Reynolds, no. 16 = CJZC, no. 72, of A.D. 55 recording a decision by the community (συναγωγή) of the Jews in Berenice to list the names of subscribers to the repair of the synagogue (also συναγωγή) ; of the subscribers, ten are described as ἄρχων and one as ἱερεύς, *cohen*, see also DF, no. 100 ; b) CIG III, no. 5361 = IGR I, no. 1024 = Reynolds, no. 17 = CJZC, no. 71, dating to either 41 B.C. or (more probably) A.D. 24, and recording a vote at Sukkot (ἐπὶ συλλόγου τῆς σκηνοπηγίας) by the *politeuma* of the Jews in Berenice in recognition of the services of a Roman official, M. Tittius ; c) CIG III, no. 5362 = SEG XVI, no. 931 = Reynolds, no. 18 = CJZC, no. 70, also an honorific decree passed by the *politeuma*, date not given.

The cemetery of *Teucheira* (Tokra) has also yielded a substantial number of Hebrew names transliterated into Greek, and of theophoric names ; the evidence, in spite of many difficulties of interpretation, indicates a significant Jewish population there in the first century A.D.[67] Some Jewish names are also attested on epitaphs from *Apollonia* (CJZC, nos. 1–2, possibly 3–5), as from *Ptolemais* (nos. 31–4 ; App., nos. 4–8). A catalogue of ephebes from the city of *Cyrene*, dating to A.D. 3–4, contains a few clearly Jewish names.[68] Similarly, a list of city officials (*nomophylakes*) from A.D. 60–1 includes 'Elazar son of Jason' (CJZC, no. 8). Augustus and Agrippa issued rulings in favour of the Jews of Cyrene.[69] References in the New Testament are many : Mt. 27:32 ; Mk. 15:21 ; Lk. 23:26 (Simon of Cyrene) ; Acts 2:10 (Cyreneans at the feast of Passover in Jerusalem) ; Acts 6:9 (Cyrenean synagogue in Jerusalem) ; Acts 11:20 (Cyreneans come to Antioch from Jerusalem) ; Acts 13:1 (Lucius of Cyrene in Antioch) ; cf. CJZC, no. 29, noting that such designations may indicate the region of Cyrenaica rather than the city of Cyrene itself. At the time of Vespasian, Jewish *Sicarii* found a following among their co-religionists in Cyrene, at least (according to Josephus) among the poor. As a result, as many as three thousand wealthy Jews lost their lives and property.[70] The great Jewish rebellion

---

67. See Applebaum, *Jews and Greeks*, pp. 144–60 ; CJZC, nos. 41–69, and App. nos. 9–25. The identification as Jewish is often very uncertain.

68. SEG XX, no. 741 = CJZC, no. 7 : e.g., col. I, l. 34, Βαρθύβας Βαρθύβρα (sic) ; l. 57, Ἰούλιος Ἰησοῦτος ; col. II, l. 47, Βαρθύβας Βαρθύβα ; l. 48, Ἐλάσζαρ Ἐλάζαρος. See Applebaum, *Jews and Greeks*, p. 177, and cf. CJZC, no. 6, with one certainly Jewish name. For Jewish epitaphs from the area of Cyrene see CJZC, nos. 10–12, and App., nos. 1–3.

69. Jos. *Ant.* xvi 6, 1 (161).

70. Jos. *B.J.* vii 11, 1–2 (437–46). *Vita* 76 (424) – 'two thousand' induced to join the rebellion.

in Cyrenaica during Trajan's reign was a formidable affair.[71] According to Procopius there was in *Boreum* (Bu-Grada, on the Gulf of Syrtis south of Berenice) a Jewish 'temple' (*naos*, meaning of course synagogue) which the emperor Justinian converted into a Christian church.[72]

Some evidence also exists of the presence of Jews in Latin-speaking North Africa in the Imperial period, from Tripolitania to the Atlantic coast.[73] There is nothing to indicate how and when this immigration took place, but as neighbouring Cyrenaica was colonized by Jews as early as the Ptolemaic period, it might be supposed that the settlement of Africa began then, in *Africa proconsularis* at any rate, followed by Numidia and Mauretania. But so far as our present evidence goes, there is in fact no clear sign of Jewish settlement in Latin-speaking North Africa until the second century A.D.[74]

a) *Africa proconsularis*. In *Carthage*, an extensive Jewish necropolis has been excavated, with more than one hundred tombs, each containing around fifteen to seventeen burial-places. The frequent representation of the seven-branched candlestick (menorah) testifies to its Jewish origin (see A. L. Delattre, *Gamart ou la nécropole juive de Carthage* (1895); Le Bohec, *op. cit.*, nos. 24–63. Latin inscriptions found in the same place (a little over a dozen) mostly give only the names of the dead, sometimes with the addition 'in pace' (CIL VIII, Suppl. nos. 14097–114, Monceaux, *RA* (1904), pp. 363–6). A small number of epitaphs have also been found elsewhere in Carthage (Le Bohec, *op. cit.*

71. Dio lxviii 32; Euseb. *Hist. Eccl.* iv 2, 4. For the substantial archaeological and inscriptional evidence see vol. I, pp. 531–2, and CJZC, nos. 17–25.

72. Procop. *de aedific.* vi 3. See R. G. Goodchild, 'Boreum of Cyrenaica', JRS 41 (1951), pp. 11–163, and CJZC, no. 76.

73. A Jewish object which may well have come to Carthage through Phoenician trade was the subject of a report by Ph. Berger, CRAI (1905), pp. 757–8. It is an engraved stone from a sarcophagus of the third century B.C., bearing the name Joab in Hebraic script and the image of a demon with outspread wings. From the script and other characteristics it must originate from the sixth or seventh century B.C. The Carthaginian interred in the sarcophagus therefore wore the stone as an antiquity by then already three to four hundred years old. This remains the sole identifiable Jewish object from North Africa of the Punic period, see Le Bohec, *op. cit.*, pp. 201–2.

74. Cf. especially P. Monceaux, 'Les colonies juives dans l'Afrique romaine', REJ 44 (1902), pp. 1–28, repr. in Les Cahiers de Tunisie 18 (1970), pp. 157–84. Also, the compilation of Jewish inscriptions from North Africa in Rev. Arch., 3 (1904), pp. 354–73. M. Rachmuth, 'Die Juden in Nordafrika bis zur Invasion der Araber', MGWJ (1906), pp. 25–58. Cf. J. Juster, *Les Juifs dans l'empire romain* I (1914), p. 207, n. 12; H. Z. (J. W.) Hirschberg, *A History of the Jews in North Africa* I (1974), pp. 21–86; J.–M. Lasserre, *Ubique Populus* (1977), pp. 413–26; Y. Le Bohec, 'Inscriptions juives et judaïsantes de l'Afrique romaine', Antiquités Africaines 17 (1981), pp. 165–207; cf. *idem*, 'Juifs et judaïsants dans l'Afrique romaine: remarques onomastiques', *ibid.*, pp. 209–29. Note?? ?also H. Solin, 'Juden und Syren im westlichen Teil der römischen Welt', ANRW II.29.2 (1983), pp. 587–789, 1222–1249, on pp. 771–5.

nos. 16–21), one of which (18) has a brief inscription in Hebrew. It has moreover often been asserted that Tertullian's *Adversus Iudaeos* presumes the presence of Jews in Carthage (the authenticity of 1–8 of this work may be regarded as certain, though 9–14 has raised doubts. See O. Bardenhewer, *Gesch. der altkirchl. Literatur* II (1903), pp. 357–9, A. Harnack, *Gesch. der altchristl. Literatur* II.2 (1904), pp. 288–92; B. Altaner, A. Stuiber, *Patrologie* ([8]1978), p. 153, accepting the whole as genuine.) But see T. D. Barnes, *Tertullian* (1971), pp. 90–3; 273–5; for a different view, C. Aziza, *Tertullien et le judaïsme* (1977). The fact that Tertullian writes about the Jews proves nothing; only concrete and localisable references have any value in this context (e.g., the anecdote concerning a lapsed Jew, apparently in Carthage, in *Ad. Nat.* i 14, 2).

At *Hammam-Lif* (Naro), not far from Carthage, the foundations have been found of a synagogue from the Roman period whose mosaic floors carry Jewish inscriptions in Latin (for the literature on this subject see vol. II, p. 434, and F. M. Biebel, 'The Mosaics of Hammam Lif', Art. Bulletin 18 (1936) pp. 541–51, and for the text of the inscriptions also CIL VIII, Suppl. no. 12457; P. Monceaux, RA (1904), pp. 366–8 (nos. 138–9); Le Bohec, *op. cit.*, nos. 13–15).

On an inscription in *Utica*, an *archon* appears, perhaps a Jewish synagogue official (CIL VIII, no. 1205, and Add. p. 931; Le Bohec, *op. cit.*, no. 65, with references and discussion).

From *Thaenae* there is the certainly Jewish epitaph of a boy named Abedo, with a Hebrew inscription and a menorah (Le Bohec, no. 7) and from *Sullecthum* another inscription with a menorah (8), as also from *Thagura* (67).

In *Oea* in Tripolitania, a Christian bishop during the time of Augustine consulted local Jews concerning a passage in the new translation of the Bible by Jerome (Augustine, *Ep.* 71, 3, 5; cf. Jerome, *Ep.* 112, 21–2).

From the same place there are a few probably Jewish epitaphs (Le Bohec, nos. 1–6), one of which comes from a small catacomb, adorned with the menorah, and mentions a lady named Μαζαζαυλα (possibly a Libyan name), described as a πρεσβετέρησα.

In *Lepcis Magna* in Tripolitania a Greek inscription contains the name Ioses Theodoros (*sic*) with a second line which may be transliterated Punic, F. Vattioni, Ant. Afric. 19 (1983), pp. 63–4.

On the Peutinger Map, a place appears in the same district named *locus Iudaeorum Augusti* (see Le Bohec, p. 171).

b) *Numidia*. The existence of Jews in *Hippo* is evident from Augustine, *Sermo* 196, 4.

In *Cirta*, modern Constantine, the following Jewish inscriptions have been found: CIL VIII, nos. 7150 = ILAlg II, no. 826 = Le Bohec, no. 69: *Iulius Anianus Iudaeus*; 7155 = ILAlg II, no. 827 = 70: *Pompeio*

Restuto Iudeo; 7530 = 19468 = ILAlg II, no. 828 = 71: *Iuliae Victoriae [Iu]deae.*

From *Henchir Fouara* near Tebessa, the brief Latin inscription, with a menorah, 'D[eus Abr]aham, Deus Isa(a)c', CIL VIII, no. 16701 = ILAlg I, no. 2912 = Le Bohec, no. 68.

(c) *Mauretania. Sitifis*, Latin inscriptions, CIL VIII, no. 8423 = Le Bohec no. 73: *Caelia Thalassa Iudaea*; 8499 = Le Bohec, no. 74: *Avilia Aster Iudea, M. Avilius Ianuarius pater sinagogae fil(iae) dulcissimae.* In the same place, Jewish converts appear in a Christian grave-inscription, CIL VIII, no. 8640 = 2034: *Memoria innocenti⟨um⟩ Istablici qui et Donati. P(osuit) frater ips⟨i⟩us Peregriniu(s) q(ui et) Mosattes de Iudeus (sic).* The plural *innocentium* instead of *innocentis* is undoubtedly a mistake on the part of the stonemason. Since it carries the Christian monogram, the inscription can only relate to converts from Judaism to Christianity.

From *Auzia*, CIL VIII, no. 20759 = Le Bohec, no. 76: *Furfanius Honoratus Iudeus.*

In *Tipasa* a Jewish synagogue was temporarily established in the late Roman period (*Passio Sanctae Salsae* 3). In *Caesarea*, the house of the president of a Jewish synagogue is mentioned (*Acta Marcianae* 4; see P. Monceaux, REJ 44 (1902), p. 8). Even in *Volubilis*, in the westernmost part of Mauretania, a number of Hebrew inscriptions have been found, see G. Vajda in *Inscriptions antiques du Maroc* (1966), ed. L. Galand, J. Février and G. Vajda, pp. 135–7. Of the six known inscriptions, one dates to the seventeenth and one to the early eighteenth century. It is impossible to determine whether any of the others go back to the Roman Imperial period. However, there is no doubt that there was then a Jewish community in Volubilis. The most important item of evidence is the third-century epitaph, R. Thouvenot, REA 71 (1969), pp. 357–9 = AE 1969-70, no. 748 = Le Bohec, no. 79: ὧδε κοιμᾶτε Καικιλιανὸς ὁ πρωτοπολίτες (*sic*), πατὴρ τῆς συναγωγῆς τῶν Ἰουδέον. For πρωτοπολίτης compare SEG XX, no. 1668 (Khirbet Zif, near Hebron), and see F. Vattioni in Studia Papyrologica 16 (1977), pp. 23–9. From *Sala* there is also the inscription (Le Bohec, no. 78) of Μαρεῖνος Πτολεμαῖος Ἰουδέος.

In the present state of our evidence it is therefore reasonable to regard Jewish settlement in Latin-speaking North Africa as having taken place during the Imperial period and on a small scale.

Jewish dispersion in *Macedonia* and *Greece* is attested in the first instance by the letter recorded by Philo, *Legatio* 36 (281), from Agrippa to Caligula. *Thessaly, Boeotia, Macedonia, Aetolia, Attica, Argos, Corinth* and finally the largest and best parts of the *Peloponnese* are the areas named by him as inhabited by Jews. If this general assertion is compared with the meagre individual items of documentary evidence, it becomes clear how patchy our information is.

Because of their date and content, an inscription from Oropus, and two from Delphi, are particularly important. The inscription from Oropus dates to the first half of the third century B.C. and records the manumission of a slave. It was put up in the shrine of Amphiaraos there by Μόσχος Μοσχίωνος 'Ιουδαῖος ἐνύπνιον ἰδὼν προστάξαντος τοῦ θεοῦ 'Αμφιαράου καὶ τῆς 'Υγιείας (CIJ I², prol. p. 82, see D. M. Lewis, JJS 11 (1957), pp. 264–6). Moschos son of Moschion is thus the earliest Jew known from the Greek mainland; it is noteworthy that he is prepared to receive instructions in a dream from two pagan deities. The two inscriptions from Delphi are concerned with the manumission of Jewish slaves in the second century B.C. and are among a large number of similar documents from that place. In one, a certain Atisidas declares free three female Jewish slaves (σώματα γυναικεῖα τρία αἷς ὀνόματα 'Αντιγόνα τὸ γένος 'Ιουδαίαν καὶ τὰς θυγατέρας αὐτᾶς Θεοδώραν καὶ Δωροθέαν), see C. Wescher et P. Foucart, *Inscriptions recueillies à Delphes* (1863), no. 57 = H. Collitz *et al.*, *Sammlung der griechischen Dialekt-Inschriften*, no. 1722 = CIJ I², no. 709. In the other, the person to be freed is described as σῶμα ἀνδρεῖον ᾧ ὄνομα 'Ιουδαῖος, τὸ γένος 'Ιουδαῖον, see Wescher et Foucart, no. 364 = Collitz *op. cit.*, no. 2029 = CIJ I², no. 710. The name 'Ιουδαῖος must = 'Ιούδας. Both documents belong to the same period, 170–156 B.C. The second dates to 162 B.C. They therefore possibly relate to prisoners of war from the Maccabaean period, sold as slaves and taken to Greece. A third manumission-inscription from Delphi dates to 119 B.C. and records the freeing of a slave by a man named 'Ιουδαῖος (CIJ I², no. 711). It is not clear whether this implies that he was Jewish.

In the time of the apostle Paul, there were Jewish synagogues in Philippi, Thessalonica, Beroea, Athens and Corinth (Acts 16:12–13; 17:1, 10, 17; 18:4, 7).

Jewish-Greek inscriptions have been found in the following places. *Athens*: IG III, nos. 3545–7 = CIJ I², nos. 712–3; (714?) 715; cf. *ibid.* nos. 2891–3 (Samaritan); IG II², nos. 8934; 10949; 12609 (of the second century B.C., see BE 1958, no. 211 and CIJ I², prol. p. 83); 8231–2; 8358; 9756; III, no. 3496 (pp. 84–5). *Piraeus*: CIJ I², no. 715i (prol. p. 85). Note L. B. Urdahl, 'Jews in Attica', Symb. Osl. 43 (1968), pp. 39–46, with numerous errors, discussed in BE 1969, no. 206. *Corinth*: A. Deissmann, *Licht vom Osten* (⁴1923), p. 12, no. 8; ET, *Light from the Ancient East* (1910), p. 13, no. 7 = *Corinth* VIII.1: *Greek Inscriptions*, no. 111 = CIJ I², no. 718: [συνα]γωγὴ 'Εβρ[αίων]; ?*Corinth* VIII.3, no. 304 = CIJ I², no. 718a (prol. p. 85). Two small but quite informative Jewish inscriptions from Corinth have recently been published, Arch. Ephemeris 1977, pp. 80–2, see BE 1980, no. 230.

No. 29, with the name [Ἄννα]ς and μισκάβ, 'tomb'; no. 30 (SEG XXIX, no. 300), perhaps to be restored διδάσ[καλος] καὶ ἀρχ-[ισυνάγωγ]ος τῆ[ς συναγωγῆς Κορίνθου?]. Five further fragmentary Hebrew inscriptions, of uncertain date, are to be found in Corinth Museum, see *Corinth* VIII.3 (1966), p. 214. *Patrae* in Achaea: CIG no. 9896 = CIJ I², no. 716. *Laconia*: REJ 10 (1885), p. 77 = IG V.1, no. 1349 = CIJ I², no. 721; CIJ I², no. 721b (prol. p. 86) = DF, no. 9a (perhaps third century A.D.). *Argos*: W. Vollgraff, BCH 27 (1903), p. 262, no. 4 = CIJ I², no. 719. *Messenia*, no. 721c, two persons named Αὐρ. Ἰωσῆς in an ephebe-list of A.D. 246. *Mantinea*: BCH 20 (1896), p. 159 = REJ 34 (1897), p. 148 = IG V.2, no. 295 = CIJ I², no. 720 = Lifshitz, DF, no. 9. ? *Tegea*: BCH 25 (1901), p. 281 = CIJ I², app. 101. *Taenarum*: IG V.1, no. 1256, see *Hell.* III, p. 100. *Corone*: IG V.1, no. 1398, ll. 91–2.

Larissa Pelasgiotis in *Thessaly*: IG IX.2, nos. 985–90, CIJ I², nos. 699–708, epitaphs with the formula τῷ λαῷ χαίρειν, among them one with Jewish names, no. 988, CIJ I², no. 701: Μαρία Ἰουδα. Accordingly, the others may also safely be regarded as Jewish. From *Larissa* note also CIJ I², nos. 697–8, and two epitaphs, nos. 708a-b (prol. p. 80), another, probably from Larissa, and not yet fully published (prol. p. 81), and a column inscribed with a name and a menorah, BE 1980, no. 291, SEG XXIX, no. 537. From *Almyra* in Thessaly, nos. 695–6. The formula λαῷ χαίρε[ιν] recurs in an epitaph from *Pherae* in Thessaly, CIJ I², no. 708d (prol. p. 81). From *Achaea Phthiotis* comes a magical amulet with Jewish angelic names, CIJ I², no. 717, see prol. p. 85; and from *Thebes* in Phthiotis, three epitaphs, *ibid.* p. 79 and BE 1980, no. 284, SEG XXIX, no. 556.

Macedonia now supplies material of considerable interest and of varied dates. From *Thessalonica* there is a late-Roman epitaph of 'Abrameos' and his wife 'Theodote' (CIJ I², no. 693 = IG X.2, 1, no. 633), which may however be Christian; two grave-inscriptions with the menorah (nos. 693b-c, prol. pp. 75–6; D. Feissel, *Recueil des inscriptions chrétiennes de Macédonie* (1983), p. 242, nos. 292–3); and much more significant, the bilingual (Greek and Samaritan) inscription of a Samaritan community (CIJ I², no. 693a, prol. pp. 70–5 = IG X.2, 1, no. 789). The Greek inscription includes the Samaritan version of the blessing of the priests in Numbers 6:22–7, while the Samaritan has the two blessings

l. 1 ברוך אלהינו לעולם
l. 2 ברוך שמו לעולם

For discussion see also B. Lifshitz and J. Schiby, 'Une synagogue samaritaine à Thessalonique', RB 75 (1968), pp. 368–78; BE 1969, no. 369; G. H. R. Horsley, *New Documents Illustrating Early Christianity* (1981), no. 69; D. Feissel, *op. cit.*, p. 240, no. 291. The inscription belongs to the late-Roman period but no more exact date has been assigned to it. See J. D. Purvis, 'The Palaeography of the Samaritan Inscriptions from Thessalonica', BASOR 221 (1976), pp. 121–3, suggesting fourth-sixth century. It does not prove the existence of an actual building, nor indeed of any communal organisation of Samaritans in Thessalonica.

Also from Thessalonica comes the inscription CIJ I², no. 693d, prol. p. 76 = IG X.2, 1, no. 72: Θεῷ Ὑψίστῳ κατ' ἐπιταγὴν *ΙΟΥΕΣ*, which is possibly Jewish. The last word may be an attempt to render the Tetragrammaton. For the question of syncretism and the worship of the 'Highest God', see pp. 32, 38, 68, 70–2, 169.

From *Beroea* in Macedonia there are two Jewish epitaphs of the late-Roman period (CIJ I², 694a-b, prol. pp. 77–8; Feissel, *op. cit.*, pp. 243–4, os. 294–5).

The most important evidence for a Jewish community in Macedonia is provided by a substantial Greek inscription from the inland town of *Stobi*, in the north of the province. The inscription probably dates from towards the end of the second or the third century A.D. The pillar on which it was inscribed was almost certainly incorporated later in its present architectural setting, apparently a Christian basilica of the fifth-sixth centuries (and therefore, contrary to various earlier interpretations, not to be regarded as the synagogue referred to in the inscription). CIJ I², no. 694 and prol., pp. 76–7; Lifshitz, DF, no. 10. The essential study is M. Hengel, 'Die Synagogeninschrift von Stobi', ZNW 57 (1966), pp. 145–83; reprinted in J. Gutmann (ed.), *The Synagogue* (1975), pp. oo–o. The inscription runs: [Ἔτους ΤΙΑ?] [Κλ.] Τιβέριος Πολύχαρμος, ὁ καὶ Ἀχύριος, ὁ πατὴρ τῆς ἐν Στόβοις συναγωγῆς ὃς πολειτευσάμενος πᾶσαν πολειτείαν κατὰ τὸν ἰουδαϊσμὸν εὐχῆς ἕνεκεν τοὺς μὲν οἴκους τῷ ἁγίῳ τόπῳ καὶ τὸ τρίκλεινον σὺν τῷ τετραστόῳ ἐκ τῶν οἰκείων χρημάτων μηδὲν ὅλως παραψάμενος τῶν ἁγίων, τὴν δὲ ἐξουσίαν τῶν ὑπερῴων πάντων πᾶσαν καὶ τὴν ⟨δ⟩εσποτείαν ἔχειν ἐμὲ τὸν Κλ. Τιβέριον Πολύχαρμον καὶ τοὺς ⟨καί τοὺς⟩ κληρονόμους τοὺς ἐμοὺς διὰ παντὸς βίου, ὃς ἂν δὲ βουληθῇ τι καινοτομῆσαι παρὰ τὰ ὑπ' ἐμοῦ δοχθέντα, δώσει τῷ πατριάρχῃ δηναρίων ⟨μ⟩υριάδας εἴκοσι πέντε. οὕτω γάρ μοι συνέδοξεν, τὴν δὲ ἐπισκευὴν τῆς κεράμου τῶν ὑπερῴων ποιεῖσθ(α)ι ἐμὲ καὶ κληρονόμους ἐμούς. The inscription seems to record the grant of part of a private house for use as a synagogue and other associated communal purposes, with the owner retaining possession of the upper floor and accepting responsibility for maintenance of the roof. The very large (and presumably unenforcible) fine payable 'to the patriarch' in case of contravention seems to reflect the period of the growth of the power of the Patriarch-Ethnarch-Nasi in Palestine, i.e., from the late second century onwards.

Further excavations conducted in 1970 on the site of the Christian basilica produced a number of fresco fragments, dated by associated pottery and coins to the third century, and containing several examples of a painted legend: Πολύχαρμος ὁ πατὴρ εὐχήν. A bronze plaque was also discovered, bearing the dedication Ποσιδονία θεῷ Ἁγίῳ εὐχήν. The evidence suggests that the synagogue associated with Polycharmos was built in the second or third century and replaced by a more elaborate building with a mosaic floor, itself destroyed before the end of the fourth century, and replaced by the Christian basilica. See J. Wiseman and D. Mano-Zissi, 'Excavations at Stobi, 1970', AJA 75 (1971), on pp. 406–11; A. T. Kraabel, 'Diaspora Synagogue', ANRW II.19.1 (1979), on pp. 494–7; W. Poehlman, 'The Polycharmos Inscription and Synagogue I at Stobi', *Studies in the Antiquities of Stobi* III, ed. B. Aleksova and J. Wiseman (1981), pp. 235–46.

A number of epigraphic references to the worship of 'Zeus Hypsistos' are known from Macedonia; it has to be determined in each case whether these are pagan or Jewish, and certainty is often unattainable; see further p. 72 below. a) IG X.2, 1, no. 62*, possibly from *Thessalonica*; b) *Beroea*, see J. M. R. Cormack, 'Dedications to Zeus Hypsistos at Beroea', JRS 31 (1941), pp. 19–23; c) *Edessa*, dedications to 'Zeus Hypsistos', S. Pelekides, Arch. Deltion 8 (1923), pp. 268–9; d) *Kozani*, SEG XXIV, nos. 481–2; e) The most striking find comes from near ancient *Pydna*, a dedication erected in A.D. 250 by a guild of worshippers of Zeus Hypsistos (οἱ συνελθόντες θρησκευταὶ ἐπὶ θεοῦ Διὸς Ὑψίστου) whose officials included an *archisynagogos*. Published by J. M. R. Cormack, 'Zeus Hypsistos at Pydna', *Mélanges helléniques offerts à Georges Daux* (1974), pp. 51–5, and reproduced by G. H. R. Horsley, *New Documents Illustrating Early Christianity* (1981), no. 5.

On the large islands of *Euboea, Cyprus* and *Crete*, Jews were very numerous. Philo names all three in the letter of Agrippa (*Legatio* 36 (282)).

For *Cyprus* cf. also 1 Mac. 15:23; Acts 4:36; 11:20; 13:4 ff.; Josephus, *Ant.* xiii 10, 4 (284–7), a late-Hellenistic Onias from Kourion, BE 1972, no. 583. At the time of Trajan, the Jews in Cyprus massacred thousands of the non-Jewish inhabitants and destroyed Salamis, the capital city; for this they were banned from the island (Dio lxviii 32, 1–3; Euseb. *Chron.* ed. Schoene II, pp. 164 ff. etc., see vol. I, pp. 529–34). The ban was not effective indefinitely, however, as is shown by a third-century inscription re-edited by Th. Reinach, REJ 48 (1904), pp. 191–6 = CIJ II, no. 736 = DF, no. 83, and a fourth-century inscription from Golgoi, CIJ II, no. 735 = DF, no. 82; also, from Salamis, Byzantion 20

(1950), p. 110, no. 3 (= DF, no. 85) and p. 141, no. 12 (= DF, no. 84).

For *Crete*, cf. 1 Mac. 15:23 (Gortyn); Josephus, *Ant.* xvii 12 (327); *B.J.* ii 7, 1 (103); *Vita* 76 (427).

For *Euboea* note the judaising formula in a second-century A.D. grave imprecation from Chalcis, discussed by L. Robert, CRAI 1978, pp. 245 ff.

Of the other islands, *Delos, Samos, Cos* and *Rhodes* are named in 1 Mac. 15:23. As the last three lie near the coast of Caria, the settlement of Jews there may have been associated with their movement into Caria. In *Cos*, Mithradates seized substantial funds from them (Strabo, *ap.* Josephus, *Ant.* xiv 7 (112) = GLAJJ, no. 102). The enormous size of the sum (800 talents) is explained by Josephus as owing to the fact that it was Temple money collected in Asia Minor and taken to Cos to escape Mithradates. Even so, the sum is still remarkably large. For this reason, Reinach considered it to have been the private capital of refugee Jews (REJ 16 (1888), pp. 204–10), and H. Willrich, that it constituted the capital of Alexandrian Jews, because Cleopatra's money is mentioned directly beforehand (*Hermes* 39 (1904), p. 250). In any case, it cannot be concluded from this passage that great Jewish bankers were living in Cos (as J. J. Herzog, *Koische Forschungen* (1899), p. 35; cf. also JE VII, col. 563 s.v. 'Cos'); on the source of the money, note also S. M. Sherwin-White, ZPE 21 (1976), p. 183, n. 3, suggesting that it came from mainland Asia Minor and that its being deposited on Cos implies a Jewish community there. Sherwin-White, *ibid.*, pp. 183–8, republishes three brief inscriptions from Cos originally published by Paton and Hicks, *Inscriptions of Cos* (1891): a) no. 303, the name Eutychos with qoppa and menorah; b) no. 323, epitaph with (?) representation of gabled Torah shrine; c) no. 63, a dedication to Theos Hypsistos. She also notes (p. 186) no. 278, 'Eirene *theosebes*', and (p. 184), Josephus, *Ant.* xiv 10, 15 (233), a letter from Gaius Fannius to the magistrates of Cos about the protection of Jewish ambassadors. For a summary of the evidence, S. M. Sherwin-White, *Ancient Cos* (1978), pp. 249–50.

From *Rhodes* there is virtually no significant evidence. In the first half of the first century B.C., two eminent authors living there wrote against the Jews, Posidonius and Apollonius Molon (both are attacked by Josephus in his work *Contra Apionem*; cf. GLAJJ, nos. xxxviii–ix). In Tiberius' time, a grammarian lived there called Diogenes, of whom it is said that he used to debate only on the sabbath (Suet. *Tib.* 32 = GLAJJ II, no. 305: 'Diogenes grammaticus, disputare sabbatis Rhodi solitus, venientem eum, ut se extra ordinem audiret, non admiserat ac per servolum suum in septimum diem distulerat'). A Menippus described as Ἰερ[οσυλ?]υμίτα[ς], i.e. (perhaps) from Jerusalem, appears on an inscription in Rhodes (IG XII.1, no. 11). Note however CIJ I², no. 731e (prol. p. 89), discussed by L. Robert, *Études anatoliennes* (1937), p. 441, n. 5: Εὐφρο⟨σ⟩ύνα θεοσεβὴς χρηστὰ χαῖρε.

Delos because of its political and commercial importance in the Hellenistic period was a place of assembly for oriental merchants. That Jews of Greek education lived there in, at the latest, around 100 B.C., is apparent, firstly, from two Greek inscriptions originating from the island of *Rheneia*, the burial-place of the inhabitants of Delos, which contain maledictions calling down God's vengeance on the unknown murderers of two girls. The prayers are undoubtedly Jewish, and from the orthography the inscriptions date to not later than the end of the second, or the beginning of the first, century B.C. (See A. Wilhelm, JOAI 4 (1901), Supp. cols. 10–18; A. Deissmann, *Philologus* 61 (1902), pp. 252–65; *Licht vom Osten* (1908), pp. 305–16, (⁴1923), pp. 351–62; ET *Light from the Ancient East* (1910), pp. 423–35; *Inscriptions de Délos*, no. 2532, CIJ I², no. 725.) Because of the remarkable interest of its content, almost exactly identical to the other, the wording of the better-preserved inscription is given here: Ἐπικαλοῦμαι καὶ ἀξιῶ τὸν Θεὸν τὸν ὕψιστον, τὸν κύριον τῶν πνευμάτων καὶ πάσης σαρκός, ἐπὶ τοὺς δόλωι φονεύσαντας ἢ φαρμακεύσαντας τὴν ταλαίπωρον ἄμρον Ἡράκλεαν ἐχχέαντας αὐτῆς τὸ ἀναίτιον αἷμα ἀδίκως, ἵνα οὕτως γένηται τοῖς φονεύσασιν αὐτὴν ἢ φαρμακεύσασιν καὶ τοῖς τέκνοις αὐτῶν, κύριε ὁ πάντα ἐφορῶν καὶ οἱ ἄγγελοι Θεοῦ, ᾧ πᾶσα ψυχὴ ἐν τῇ σήμερον ἡμέρᾳ ταπεινοῦται μεθ' ἱκετείας, ἵνα ἐγδικήσῃς τὸ αἷμα τὸ ἀναίτιον ζητήσεις καὶ τὴν ταχίστην. The day 'on which all humble themselves' is either the Day of Atonement or some other day of fasting.

The most important evidence for Jews in Delos in the Hellenistic period is however that which relates to the building now generally accepted as having been a synagogue. See A. Plassart, 'La synagogue juive de Délos', *Mélanges Holleaux* (1913), pp. 201–15; Ph. Bruneau, *Recherches sur les cultes de Délos* (1970), pp. 480–93. The following inscriptions are known from this building:

ID, no. 2328 = CIJ I², no. 728: Λυσίμαχος Θεῷ Ὑψίστῳ χαριστήριον.

2329 = 726: Ἀγαθοκλῆς καὶ Λυσίμαχος ἐπὶ προσευχῇ.

2330 = 728: Λαωδίκη Θεῷ Ὑψίστῳ σωθεῖσα ταῖς ὑφ' αὐτοῦ θεραπήαις εὐχήν.

2331 = 727: Ζωσᾶς Πάριος Θεῷ Ὑψιστῳ εὐχήν.

2332 = 730: Ὑψίστῳ εὐχὴν Μαρκία.

2333 = 731: [. .] γενόμενος ἐλεύθερος.

(also Lifshitz, DF, nos. 3–8). The first three date to the first century B.C., the last three to the Imperial period. So far as can be determined, the synagogue seems to have been in use also from some time in the first century B.C. to the second century A.D. (Bruneau, *op. cit.*, pp. 491–3). Note also the Πραῦλος Σαμαρεύς who appears in an inscription from Delos of the late second or early first century B.C., ID, 2616, col. ii, l. 53

(Bruneau, p. 486). This reference immediately gains added significance from the publication of two new Hellenistic inscriptions which explicitly attest the presence of a Samaritan community on Delos; see Ph. Bruneau, "'Les Israélites de Délos" et la juiverie délienne', BCH 106 (1982), pp. 465–504. Both inscriptions were discovered at a point just over 90 metres north of the synagogue. One (*op. cit.*, p. 471, no. 2) is considered to date to the first half of the second century B.C. and reads:

[οἱ ἐν Δήλῳ] Ἰσραηλῖται οἱ ἀπαρχόμενοι εἰς ἱερὸν ἅγιον Ἀργαριζεὶν ἐτίμησαν Μένιππον Ἀρτεμιδώρου Ἡρακλεῖον, αὐτὸν καὶ τοὺς ἐγγόνους αὐτοῦ, κατασκευάσαντα καὶ ἀνάθεντα ἐκ τῶν ἰδίων ἐπὶ προσευχῇ τοῦ θε[οῦ] ΤΟΝ[... (fragmentary). The other (*op. cit.*, p. 467, no. 1) is complete: οἱ ἐν Δήλῳ Ἰσραελεῖται οἱ ἀπαρχόμενοι εἰς ἱερὸν Ἀργαριζεὶν στεφανοῦσιν χρυσῷ στεφάνῳ Σαραπίωνα Ἰάσονος Κνώσιον εὐεργεσίας ἕνεκεν τῆς εἰς ἑαυτούς. The letter-forms suggest a date between 150 and 50 B.C. The 'Israelites who pay first fruits to sacred (holy) Gerizim' were beyond question Samaritans. The earlier inscription seems to date from before, and the later probably from after, the destruction of the temple on Mount Gerizim by John Hyrcanus *c.* 129 B.C. (vol. I, p. 207); but, as is well known, the site remained (and remains) sacred to them.

The two inscriptions seem to derive from a building (note also the reference to construction, κατασκευάσαντα, in the earlier inscription) presumably associated with the Samaritan community. This therefore leaves open various possibilities. Either a) the synagogue (whose identification as such is defended by Bruneau, *op. cit.*, pp. 489–95) was Samaritan. In this connection, note what is said by Pseudo-Eupolemus (Euseb. *Praep. Ev.* ix 17, 5 = FGrH 724 F 1 (5)), perhaps in the second century, speaking of Abraham: ξενισθῆναί τε αὐτὸν ὑπὸ πόλεως ἱερὸν Ἀργαριζίν, ὃ εἶναι μεθερμηνευόμενον ὄρος ὑψίστου. Alternatively b) the synagogue was Jewish, and the Jewish community either succeeded or co-existed with the 'Israelite' one. These questions cannot be decided; further light might be thrown by excavations of the area between and around the two sites, some ninety metres apart and both close to the sea.

Documents from the time of Caesar in favour of the Jews of Delos are given in Jos. *Ant.*, xiv 10, 8; 14 (213–16; 231–2).

Further reference may be found to Jews in *Paros*, *Ant.* xiv 10 (213) and *Melos*, *Ant.* xvii 12 (327), *B.J.* ii 7, 1 (103).

The epitaphs from *Thera*, which contain the word ἄγγελος and the name of the dead person in the genitive, or only ἄγγελος or ἀγγέλου, may as easily be Jewish or Christian (IG XII.3, nos. 933–74; for Christian origin see especially H. Achelis, ZNW (1900), pp. 87–100).

Three Jewish epitaphs are known from *Crete*, CIJ I², prol. pp. 87–91, no. 731b (Elyros): Σανβάθι(ς) Ἑρμῇ μνάμας χάριν (dubious); 731c

(Cisamus): Σοφία πρεσβυτέρα καὶ ἀρχισυναγωγίσσα Κισάμου... (fourth-fifth century); 731d, from Ins. Cret. I, p. 12, no. 17 (Arcades): 'Ιωσήφος Θεοδώρου 'Ιούδᾳ τῷ υἱῷ αὐτοῦ. From *Samos*, no. 731e (see G. Dunst, 'Eine jüdische Inschrift aus Samos', *Klio* 52 (1970), pp. 73–8); BE 1971, no. 508: [..κ]αὶ οἱ πρεσβύτεροι καὶ [.... τῶ]ν 'Ιουδαίων τῆς κατὰ [Σάμον?...συ]ν-αγωγῆς ἐτίμησαν ΑΡ[....πρεσβύ]τερον... (probably third century A.D.).

Finally, there are two well-known inscriptions on mosaic from the island of *Aegina*, CIJ I², nos. 722–3 (and prolegomenon, p. 87); Lifshitz, DF, nos. 1–2: Θεόδωρος ἀρχισυν[άγωγος φ]ροντίσας ἔτη τέσσερα [.....] ἐκ θεμελίων τὴν συναγ[ωγὴν] οἰκοδόμησα... The second refers to 'Theodorus the younger', and to the execution of the mosaic (ἐμουσώθη). The date is perhaps the fourth century.

Jewish inscriptions are also known from the Greek-speaking areas of the Balkan region. From *Moesia Inferior* there is a possibly Jewish inscription from *Tomi* (CIJ I², no. 681b, prol., p. 63), and a fragmentary dedication to Theos Hypsistos, SEG XXIV, no. 1065, see D. M. Pippidi, Studii Clasice 16 (1974), pp. 260–3, arguing against Jewish influence. There is also an inscription (surprisingly) in Latin from *Oescus* on the Danube: 'Ioses arcisina(go)gos et principal⟨e⟩s' (CIJ I², no. 681; corrections in prol. p. 63; A. Scheiber, CIHJ, no. 8 = JIH, no. 10). Also from Oescus a fragmentary Greek inscription accompanied by a menorah is reported (BE 1960, no. 233; CIJ I², prol., p. 63). In the province of *Thrace*, an inscription which may be Jewish comes from Asenovgrad near Sofia (Serdica):]ΕΙΑ 'Ελένη ἀνέθηκεν εὐλογητῷ εὐχήν (IG Bulg III, no. 1432; CIJ I², no. 681a, prol., p. 63), as may the dedication to Theos Hypsistos from the same place (IG Bulg III, no. 1431) and a similar dedication from Philippopolis (no. 937). The Jewish character of these and a number of other dedications to Theos Hypsistos is firmly denied by M. Tacheva-Hitova, 'Dem Hypsistos geweihte Denkmäler in Thrakien', *Thracia* IV (1977), pp. 271–301, eadem, 'Dem Hypsistos geweihte Denkmäler in den Balkanländern', Balkan Studies 19 (1978), pp. 59–75, and in her *Eastern Cults in Moesia Inferior and Thracia* (1983), pp. 190–215. From Bizye there is a Jewish epitaph, with menorah and ethrog (CIJ I², no. 692, see L. Robert, *Hell.* III, pp. 107–8) and from *Heraclea—Perinthos* another, with menorah, lulab, ethrog, shofar (?) and maḥtah (?), CIJ I², no. 692a (prol., p. 70).

The Latin-speaking (or at least Latin-writing) provinces of the Balkans and central Europe, namely *Dalmatia* and *Pannonia*, have also yielded a small number of Jewish inscriptions. From *Dalmatia* there is CIJ I², no. 680 (and prol., p. 61); from *Senia* (Zengg), see L. Robert,

Hell. III, p. 107, and a Jewish tomb of the third-fourth century from Dolcea (Duklju near Titograd), CIJ I², prol. p. 62; IL Iug., no. 131 (fourth century) *may* reflect a Jewish community in Salona. From *Pannonia*, apart from two Jewish epitaphs in Latin, but written (like the previous inscription) in Greek letters, CIJ I², no. 675 = CIHJ, no. 1 = Scheiber, JIH, no. 2 (Aquincum), and no. 676 (with prol. p. 59) = CIHJ, no. 3 (Solva) = I. Bilkei, 'Die griechischen Inschriften des römischen Hungarns', Alba Regia 17 (1979), nos. 9 and 8 = RIU III (1981), no. 787 = JIH, no. 1, and a Latin epitaph of 'Septima (sic) Maria Iudea' from Siklós (CIHJ, no. 2 = JIH, no. 7), there is a difficult Latin inscription from *Intercisa*, which seems to refer to a 'synagogue of the Jews', CIL III, no. 3327 = ILS, no. 3981 = CIJ I², no. 677 = CIHJ, no. 4. It has been re-studied by F. Fülep, 'New Remarks on the Question of the Jewish Synagogue at Intercisa', AArchAcScHung 18 (1966), pp. 93–8, whence AE 1966, no. 302. See now JIH, no. 3. This dedication for the safety of Severus Alexander and Iulia Mammaea (hence A.D. 222–35) is made by Cosmius, described as PR(aepositus?) STA(tionis) SPONDILL A SYNAG(ogae) IUDEOR(um) (last word inscribed separately on the side. The word 'spondilla?' is not otherwise known, and has been taken to be a place-name; but it may hypothetically, as Fülep argues, be interpreted as the name of an office or function in the synagogue. The A may perhaps go with the following word, hypothetically producing A(rchi)SYNAG(ogus). Persons with Semitic names are attested at Intercisa (see e.g., CIHJ nos. 5–7; JIH, nos. 4-6) but none can be proved specifically to have been Jewish. A Syrian auxiliary unit was stationed there, see J. Fitz, *Les Syriens à Intercisa* (1972).

At *Mursa* a damaged inscription (CIJ I², no. 678a, prol., p. 60 = JIH, no. 8) refers to a [pro?]SEUCHAM, which may mean a synagogue, but can hardly be assumed to do so, as by A. Mócsy, *Pannonia and Upper Moesia* (1974), p. 228.

In *Italy, Rome* itself was the centre of a Jewish community numbering thousands.[75] The first appearance of Jews there reaches back into the

75. Cf. in general for the Jews in Rome: A. Berliner, *Geschichte der Juden in Rom von der ältesten Zeit bis zur Gegenwart* I–II (1893); H. Vogelstein and P. Rieger, *Geschichte der Juden in Rom* I (from 139 B.C. to A.D. 1420) (1896), (ET *History of the Jews in Rome*, 1940); A. Bludau, 'Die Juden Roms im ersten christlichen Jahrhundert', Katholik 83 (1903), pp. 113–34, 193–229; S. Ochser, s.v. 'Rome' in JE X, pp. 444–67 (only briefly for the ancient period); J. Juster, *Les Juifs dans l'empire romain* I–II (1914), especially I, p. 180, n. 6; H. Gressmann, 'Jewish life in ancient Rome', *Jewish studies in memory of Israel Abraham* (1927), pp. 170–91; G. La Piana, 'Foreign Groups in Rome during the First Centuries of the Empire', HThR 20 (1927), pp. 183–403, especially 341–93; S. W. Baron, *A social and religious history of the Jews* I–II (²1952); H. J. Leon, 'The Jewish Community of Ancient Porto', HThR 45 (1952), pp. 165–75 (showing that the majority, at least, of the identifiably Jewish inscriptions from Porto had been brought there from Rome), and *The*

Maccabaean period. Already Judas Maccabaeus sent an embassy to the Roman senate to conclude an alliance with the Romans, or more precisely, to request an assurance of their friendship and support (1 Mac. 8:17–32; cf. vol. I, p. 171). His brother and successor, Jonathan, probably followed his example (1 Mac. 12:1–4, 16; vol. I, p. 184). Of greater significance was the embassy despatched to Rome in 140–139 by the third of the Maccabaean brothers, Simon, which saw the conclusion of a genuine alliance of protection and trust with the Romans (1 Mac. 14:24; 15:15–24; vol. I, pp. 194–7). During their rather lengthy stay in Rome, it is possible, but not securely attested, that people in the company of this embassy also attempted to make religious propaganda. According to the text preserved in the epitome made by Julius Paris, Valerius Maximus i 3, 2 reads: 'Idem (i.e., the praetor Hispalus) Iudaeos, qui Sabazi Iovis cultu Romanos inficere mores conati erant, repetere domos suas coegit'.[76] Jupiter Sabazius is in fact a Phrygian and Thracian deity corresponding to the Greek Dionysus.[77] But since the word *Iudaeos* is attested in this text, the presence of his name in the passage may be due to a confusion of the Jewish *Sabaoth* (*Ẓeba'oth*) with *Sabazius*, an error that occurs elsewhere.[78] However, another epitome, that of Ianuarius Nepotianus,

---

Jews of ancient Rome (1960), especially bibliography on pp. 347–64. CIJ I² (1975), especially introduction, pp. liii–cxliv, and prolegomena, pp. 25–39; U. M. Fasola, 'Le due catacombe ebraiche di Villa Torlonia', Riv. Arch. Cr. 52 (1976), pp. 7–62; A. T. Kraabel, 'Jews in Imperial Rome: More Archaeological Evidence from an Oxford Collection', JJS 30 (1979), pp. 41–58. Note the survey by R. Penna, 'Les Juifs à Rome au temps de l'apôtre Paul', NTS 28 (1982), pp. 321–47, and Solin, *op. cit.*, pp. 655–66.

76. The text of the first book of Valerius Maximus contains a considerable lacuna. Two extant epitomes from his works serve to restore this: those of Iulius Paris and Ianuarius Nepotianus (both published by A. Mai, *Scriptorum veterum nova collectio* III.3 (1828); for the lacuna see also Kempf's edition of Valerius Maximus (1854)). For this question, see H. Vogelstein, *The History of the Jews in Rome*, pp. 10–14; H. J. Leon, *The Jews of Ancient Rome*, pp. 2–4; GLAJJ I, no. 147a–b; S. Alessandri, 'La presunta caccia dei Giudei da Roma nel 138 a. Cr.', SCO 17 (1968), pp. 187–98; M. Simon, 'Jupiter-Yahve', Numen 23 (1976), pp. 40–66; E. N. Lane, 'Sabazius and the Jews in Valerius Maximus', JRS 69 (1979), pp. 35–8.

77. On Sabazius see F. Cumont, *Les religions orientales dans le paganisme romain* (⁴1929), pp. 60–2; M. P. Nilsson, *Geschichte der Griechischen Religion* II (²1961), pp. 658–67; Ch. Picard, 'Sabazios, Dieu thraco-phrygien', RA 1961, pt. 2, pp. 129–76; R. Fellmann, 'Der Sabazios-Kult', in M. J. Vermaseren (ed.), *Die orientalischen Religionen im Römerreich* (1981), pp. 316–40.

78. In itself, Zebaoth is of course not a proper name. Since however *Yahweh Ṣebaoth* is rendered κύριος Σαβαώθ (so the LXX, particularly in Isaiah, see the Concordances by Trommius and by Hatch and Redpath, and Σαβαώθ is the better-attested form, not Σαββαώθ), Σαβαώθ was treated by Jews, Christians and pagans as a divine name. See *Orac. Sibyll.* i 304, 316; ii 240; xii 132; Celsus quoted in Origen *C. Cels.* i 24; v 41, 45; the Gnostics quoted in Irenaeus i 30, 5; Origen *C. Cels.* vi 31–2; Epiphanius, *Haer.* 26, 10; 40, 2; see G. W. H. Lampe, *Patristic Greek Lexicon* s.v. Σαβαώθ. It is found frequently on gems (see W. Baudissin, *Studien zur semitischen Religionsgeschichte* I (1876), pp. 187 ff.; for

makes no reference to Sabazius: 'Iudaeos quoque, qui Romanis tradere sacra sua conati erant, idem Hispalus urbe exterminavit, arasque privatas e publicis locis abiecit.' Reconstructions based on a supposed syncretism of the Jewish God and Sabazius are therefore insecure. All that remains is the statement that the praetor of 139 B.C., which cannot be proved to be the exact year of Simon's embassy, expelled some Jews for proselytism. A connection with Simon's embassy is not indicated in our sources and remains hypothetical. It consequently also remains unclear from this whether Rome had as yet any permanent Jewish residents at that time. Such settlements appear nevertheless to have taken place already in the first third of the first century B.C., for Jewish money was being exported from Italy to Jerusalem even before 61.[79] Roman Jewry grew to greater importance after Pompey. When he conquered Jerusalem in 63, he brought back with him to Rome great numbers of Jewish prisoners of war who were sold there as slaves, but many of whom were manumitted soon afterwards, perhaps because they proved troublesome to their masters on account of their strict adherence to Jewish observances. Granted—in the case of freed slaves—the rights of Roman citizenship, they settled on the further bank of the Tiber and reinforced the Jewish community probably already established there.[80] From then on, the colony in Trastevere constituted a not insignificant element in Roman life. In 59 B.C., when Cicero spoke in defence of Flaccus, there was a considerable crowd of Jews in his audience.[81] At the death of Caesar, their great protector, a throng of Jews lamented throughout the night beside his funeral pyre.[82] In the reign of Augustus, Jews already numbered several thousands. Josephus, in any case, relates that eight thousand Roman Jews supported the embassy which came to Rome from Judaea in 4 B.C.[83] The reign of Tiberius saw the onset of repressive measures. The whole community was expelled from Rome in A.D. 19 because, according to

---

examples of its use in magical papyri see K. Preisendanz, *Papyri Graecae Magicae* ([2]1973), no. iv, ll. 981; 1485; 3052 f.; v, 352. There is certainly no question of any connection with the Hebrew *Sabbath*, for it is impossible to see how it could be conceived of as a divine name.

79. Cicero, *pro Flacco* 28/67 (GLAJJ I, no. 68): 'Cum aurum Iudaeorum nomine quotannis ex Italia et ex omnibus provinciis Hierosolyma exportari soleret, Flaccus sanxit edicto, ne ex Asia exportari liceret.' Flaccus was propraetor of Asia in 62 B.C. If Jewish money was being exported from *Italy* to Jerusalem, the settlement of Jews in Italy cannot be regarded as dating to after the triumph of Pompey (61 B.C.). See Leon, *The Jews of Ancient Rome*, pp. 4–9.

80. Philo, *Legatio* 23 (155).

81. Cicero, *pro Flacco*, 28/69.

82. Suetonius, *Div. Iul.* 84 (GLAJJ I, no. 302): 'In summo publico luctu exterarum gentium multitudo circulatim suo quaeque more lamentata est, praecipueque Iudaei, qui etiam noctibus continuis bustrum frequentarunt.'

83. *B.J.* ii 6, 1 (80–3); *Ant.* xvii 11, 1 (299–302). See vol. I, pp. 330–5.

Josephus, a few Jews had swindled a distinguished convert by the name of Fulvia out of large sums of money on the pretext of sending it to the Temple in Jerusalem. For this, four thousand Jews fit to bear arms were deported to Sardinia to combat the brigands there; the rest were banished from the city. On this point, the reports of Tacitus,[84] Suetonius[85] and Josephus[86] are essentially in agreement. According to Eusebius, Philo, a contemporary, had stated that these measures were carried out at the request of the then powerful Seianus.[87] Without giving details, Philo asserts in the surviving *Legatio* that Seianus was responsible for anti-Jewish measures, and that after his fall (A.D. 31), Tiberius had recognized that the Jews living in Rome had been slandered baselessly by him, and had ordered the officials in all areas not to oppress them or obstruct them in the practice of their religion.[88] Presumably, therefore, they were also permitted to return to Rome;

84. *Ann.* ii 85 (GLAJJ II, no. 284) : 'Actum et de sacris Aegyptiis Iudaicisque pellendis, factumque patrum consultum, ut quattuor milia libertini generis ea superstitione infecta, quis idonea aetas, in insulam Sardiniam veherentur, coercendis illic latrociniis et, si ob gravitatem caeli interissent, vile damnum; ceteri cederent Italia, nisi certam ante diem profanos ritus exuissent.'

85. *Tib.* 36 (GLAJJ II, no. 306) : 'Externas caerimonias, Aegyptios Iudaicosque ritus compescuit, coactis qui superstitione ea tenebantur religiosas vestes cum instrumento omni comburere. Iudaeorum iuventutem per speciem sacramenti in provincias gravioris caeli distribuit, reliquos gentis eiusdem vel similia sectantes urbe summovit, sub poena perpetuae servitutis nisi obtemperassent.'

86. Josephus, *Ant.* xviii 3, 5 (84), states definitely that four thousand Jews were impressed into military service and despatched to Sardinia. Tacitus gives the same number but writes of Egyptians and Jews. According to Tacitus, the rest were expelled from Italy; according to Josephus, from Rome only. Suetonius agrees more with Josephus.

The severe punishment (instead of simple expulsion) was explained by Mommsen on the grounds that as *libertini* the Jews in Rome were Roman citizens ('Der Religionsfrevel nach römischen Recht', *Ges. Schr.* III (1907), pp. 389–422).

Seneca, *Ep. Mor.* 108, 22 (GLAJJ I, no. 189) contains an allusion to this edict: 'his ego instinctus abstinere animalibus coepi ... quaeris, quomodo desierim? in primum Tiberii Caesaris principatum iuventae tempus inciderat. alienigena tum sacra movebantur, sed inter argumenta superstitionis ponebatur quorundam animalium abstinentia. patre itaque meo rogante, qui non calumniam timebat, sed philosophiam oderat, ad pristinam consuetudinem redii.'

87. Euseb. *Chron. ad ann. Abr.* 2050 (ed. Schoene II, p. 150) according to the Armenian version: 'Seianus Tiberii procurator, qui intimus erat consiliarius regis, universam gentem Iudaeorum deperdendam exposcebat. Meminit autem huius Philon in secunda relatione.' Cf. Syncellus, ed. Dindorf I, p. 621.

Jerome, *Chron.* (*ap.* Euseb. *Chron.* ed. Schoene II, p. 151; ed. Helm, p. 176: 'Seianus praefectus Tiberii qui aput eum plurimum poterat instantissime cohortatur, ut gentem Iudaeorum deleat. Filo meminit in libro legationis secundo.'

The same statement on the authority of the same work of Philo occurs also in Euseb. *Hist. Eccl.* ii 5, 7.

Cf. on this work of Philo, below, pp. 856–64.

88. Philo, *Legatio* 24 (159–61). See Smallwood *ad loc.*

and this would explain how Philo took for granted the renewed establishment of the Roman community as early as the reign of Gaius. Claudius' reign began with a general edict of tolerance towards the Jews, issued at the request of king Agrippa I and his brother king Herod;[89] but later, this emperor, too, found it necessary to bring measures into force against the Jews. According to brief reports in Acts and Suetonius, an actual expulsion of Jews from Rome took place on his orders.[90] But from Dio it appears that Claudius only forbade the Jews the right to assemble, for an expulsion would not have been enforceable without great disturbance.[91] But even this would have been equivalent to a ban on religious freedom and no doubt have led to many leave the city. The date of the edict cannot be determined with certainty; it probably belongs to the later part of Claudius' reign, perhaps A.D. 49.[92] Suetonius' words imply that it was caused by

89. Jos. *Ant.* xix 5, 3 (286–91). On Claudius' reign see Leon, *op. cit.*, pp. 21–7, with bibliography.

90. Ac. 18:2: διὰ τὸ διατεταχέναι Κλαύδιον χωρίζεσθαι πάντας τοὺς Ἰουδαίους ἀπὸ τῆς Ῥώμης. See Haenchen *ad loc.* Suet. *Claud.* 25 (GLAJJ II, no. 307) : 'Iudaeos impulsore Chresto assidue tumultuantes Roma expulit.'

91. Dio lx 6 (GLAJJ II, no. 422): τούς τε Ἰουδαίους πλεονάσαντας αὖθις, ὥστε χαλεπῶς ἂν ἄνευ ταραχῆς ὑπὸ τοῦ ὄχλου σφῶν τῆς πόλεως εἰρχθῆναι, οὐκ ἐξήλασε μέν, τῷ δὲ δὴ πατρίῳ βίῳ χρωμένους ἐκέλευσε μὴ συναθροίζεσθαι. The passage occurs in Dio at the beginning of the reign of Claudius, whereas the measure reported in Acts probably happened much later (see n. 92). However, Dio is not at this point writing chronologically but presenting a general characterisation of Claudius; for this feature of his treatment of the reigns of emperors compare F. Millar in JEA 48 (1962), pp. 124–5; *A Study of Cassius Dio* (1964), p. 40. With the words λέξω δὲ καθ' ἕκαστον ὧν ἐποίησε in chapter 3, Dio does not switch to chronological narrative, but to a description of Claudius' good features. An edict unfavourable to the Jews is not likely to belong to the earliest years of his reign for it was just then that he published an edict of tolerance in their regard. The edict referred to by Dio is therefore very likely identical with that of Suetonius. It would certainly be strange for one of them to mention only the latter edict, and the other, only the former. The word 'expulit' in Suetonius could be interpreted on the analogy of Suet. *Tib.* 36 : 'expulit et mathematicos, sed deprecantibus ... veniam dedit.' Expulsion was no doubt intended, but when it was realized that it would run into difficulties, it was abandoned. This might explain the silence of Tacitus and Josephus. However, the wording of Acts seems both to imply something more specific and more effective and to indicate a date in the late 40s. For a different view see Stern, GLAJJ cit. II, pp. 115–16.

92. The edict in question has been identified by many as that mentioned by Tacitus for the year 52, Tac. *Ann.* xii 52 : 'De mathematicis Italia pellendis factum senatus consultum atrox et irritum.' But 'mathematici' cannot possibly be taken to refer to the Roman Jewish community.

In the *Chronicle* of Eusebius and Jerome there is no allusion to an expulsion of the Jews by Claudius. Only Orosius vii 6, 15 (ed. Zangemeister, 1882) provides an exact date for the edict (the ninth year of Claudius A.D. 49): 'Anno eiusdem nono expulsos per Claudium urbe Iudaeos Iosephus refert. Sed me magis Suetonius movet, qui ait hoc modo ...' However, since Josephus does not discuss the matter at all, the notice is in any case erroneous and therefore unreliable. On the other hand, this date would fit with the implications of Acts (see above).

trouble stirred up by 'Chrestus' (? 'Christus'), within the Jewish community.[93] Its effects in any case were also not permanent. Even a measure such as this could not again uproot the firmly settled Jewish community or weaken it lastingly. Expelled from the city, some of its members may have moved into the surrounding district, in the direction of Aricia,[94] to return subsequently to Rome. Acts 28:17–28 reflects a stable Jewish community in Rome in the reign of Nero. The history of the Jews in the capital may be summarized in the words of Dio. 'Often repressed, they nevertheless increased most strongly, so that they themselves obtained the free practice of their observances'.[95] It is true that prominent Romans regarded them with suspicion, but the frequent allusions by the satirists themselves testify to the extent to which the Jews were taken note of in Roman society.[96] Also, from as early as the reign of Augustus, there was no lack of direct relations between them and the Imperial court; indeed, in the time of Nero the empress Poppaea herself may have been attracted to Judaism.[97]

---

93. On Chrestus = Christus see A. von Harnack, *Die Mission und Ausbreitung des Christentums* I ([2]1906), pp. 346, 348; ET *The Expansion of Christianity in the First Three Centuries* II (1905), p. 16. See GLAJJ II, pp. 116–17. Even in Tac. *Ann.* xv 44 the Mediceus has 'Chrestianos', see GLAJJ II, p. 92.

94. Such a move is indicated by the scholiast on Juvenal iv 117: 'qui ad portam Aricinam sive ad clivum mendicaret inter Iudaeos, qui ad Ariciam transierant ex Urbe missi' (Stern, GLAJJ II, no. 538). The story might alternatively refer to the expulsion under Tiberius, or to another event, or be fictional.

95. Dio xxxvii 17, 1 (GLAJJ II, no. 406): ἔστι καὶ παρὰ τοῖς 'Ρωμαίοις τὸ γένος τοῦτο, κολουσθὲν ⟨μὲν⟩ πολλάκις, αὐξηθὲν δὲ ἐπὶ πλεῖστον, ὥστε καὶ ἐς παρρησίαν τῆς νομίσεως ἐκνικῆσαι.

96. On the social position of Jews in Rome, see the literature cited in n. 74 above. Sources in GLAJJ I–II. M. Stern, 'The Jews in Greek and Latin Literature', JPFC II, pp. 1101–59; J. N. Sevenster, *The Roots of Pagan Anti-Semitism in the Ancient World* (1975).

97. The names Αὐγουστήσιοι and 'Αγριππήσιοι, used by two of the Jewish communities in Rome, point to the relationship that existed between the Jews and Augustus and Agrippa (see below, pp. 96).

The empress Livia owned a Jewish slave-girl named Akme, Jos. *Ant.* xvii 5, 7 (141); *B.J.* i 32, 6 (641); 33, 7 (661), and presented ornaments to the Temple in Jerusalem, Jos. *B.J.* v. 13, 6 (563); Philo, *Legatio* 40 (319).

The emperor Claudius had as friend the Jewish alabarch, Alexander, who had served his mother Antonia as *procurator*, *Ant.* xix 5, 1 (276). See CPJ II, nos. 418–20 and com.

An inscription from the time of Claudius mentions a '[Cl]audia Aster [Hi]erosolymitana [ca]ptiva', perhaps a Jewish slave-girl belonging to Claudius (CIL x, no. 1971 = ILS, no. 8193 = CIJ I[2], no. 556).

In the court of Nero there was a Jewish actor named Alityrus, Jos. *Vita* 3 (16).

Poppaea is herself described as θεοσεβής and was always ready to bring Jewish petitions to the notice of the emperor, Jos. *Ant.* xx 8, 11 (195); *Vita* 3 (16). Tacitus *Ann.* xvi 6 observes that after death she was not cremated in accordance with Roman tradition, but was embalmed 'after the custom of foreign kings'. It remains uncertain, however, whether this evidence can prove a specific attachment to Judaism. For a negative view see E. M. Smallwood, 'The Alleged Jewish Tendencies of Poppaea Sabina', JThSt 10 (1959), pp. 329–35.

Gradually they spread through the city. Trastevere did not remain the only quarter where they were to be found. Later, they were living also in Campus Martius, and in the middle of the business area of Rome, the Subura (cf. pp. 97 below). Juvenal jokes over the fact that the sacred grove of Egeria before Porta Capena is occupied by Jews and swarms with Jewish beggars (*Sat.* iii 12–16 = GLAJJ II, no. 296). Their presence in other parts of the city, and their continuing prosperity into the later Imperial period, is also attested by the discovery of Jewish burial-places, or catacombs, knowledge of which continues to increase. The following is a general list of those known so far.[98]

1) The oldest cemetery is probably that on the Via Portuensis, discovered in 1602 by Bosio but not further explored at that time.[99] Without doubt the burial-place of the Trastevere Jews, it remained lost to sight for a long time until various accounts of it were published in about the mid-eighteenth century. The inscriptions found then were dispersed among various collections.[100] Subsequently, it stayed

---

Josephus lived in Rome under Vespasian, Titus and Domitian, and was supported and honoured by all three emperors, Jos. *Vita* 76 (422–3).

Through Flavius Clemens, the cousin of Domitian, even the imperial family was affected by 'Jewish customs', understood as atheism; so Dio lxvii 14, 1–3 = GLAJJ II, no. 435, cf. Suet. *Dom.* 15. This is not to be taken as a reference to Christianity, see Stern *ad loc.*

Also to be noted is the lively relationship of Herod and his dynasty with Augustus and his successors. Most of Herod's sons were educated in Rome. Agrippa I spent the greater part of his life, until his nomination as king, in Rome. As a boy he was the friend of Drusus, the son of Tiberius, and later of Caligula, Jos. *Ant.* xviii 6, 1 (143). The close association of Agrippa II and Berenice with Vespasian and Titus is well known. (See e.g., J. A. Crook, 'Titus and Berenice', AJPh 62 (1951), pp. 162–75; cf. Z. Yavetz, 'Reflections on Titus and Josephus', GRBS 16 (1975), pp. 411–32.)

For Christians at the imperial court compare A. von Harnack, *Mission und Ausbreitung des Christentums* II ([2]1906), pp. 32–40; ET *The Expansion of Christianity in the First Three Centuries* II (1905), pp. 192–4; cf. W. Eck, 'Das Eindringen des Christentums in den Senatorenstand bis zu Konstantin d. Gr.', Chiron 1 (1971), pp. 381–406.

98. Cf. earlier surveys in H. Vogelstein and P. Rieger, *Gesch. der Juden in Rom* I (1896), pp. 49 ff. Also pp. 459–83, a compilation of inscriptions. See S. Krauss s.v. 'Catacombs', JE III, pp. 614–18.

The Greek-Jewish inscriptions from Rome as then known were collected in CIG IV, nos. 9901–26. See several Latin inscriptions in CIL VI, nos. 29755–63. See above Vol. I, pp. 15–16 for the literature on the inscriptions in general. On the catacombs, see J. Juster, *Les Juifs dans l'empire romain* (1914), I, pp. 477–85; E. R. Goodenough, *Jewish Symbols in the Greco-Roman Period* II (1953), ch. 1; CIJ I[2], pp. lvi–lxii and prolegomenon; H. J. Leon, *The Jews in Ancient Rome* (1961), pp. 46 ff. On inscriptions, CIJ I[2], nos. 1–531; Leon, *op. cit.*, pp. 67–74, 263–346. For a full account of the successive stages of discovery, H. J. Leon, 'The Jewish Catacombs of Rome: An Account of their Discovery and Subsequent History', HUCA 5 (1928), pp. 299–314.

99. A. Bosio, *Roma Sotterranea* II (1632), ch. 22, pp. 141–3.

100. See e.g. the description by R. Venuti in *Giornale dei letterati* (Rome, 1748). Most of the inscriptions went to the Museo Borgiano at Velletri, and from there to Naples and the

unknown for a further long period until it was re-discovered in October 1904. The excavation, very laborious because the site had been filled in, was carried out by N. Müller.[101]

2) An imposing cemetery was found in 1859 on the via Appia in the Vigna Randanini, now named Vigna San Sebastiano, somewhat further out than the Calixtus Catacombs. This, too, yielded a large number of Roman-Jewish epitaphs.[102]

3) In 1866, a Jewish cemetery was uncovered in the Vigna of Conte Cimarra, which is also on the via Appia, almost opposite the Calixtus catacombs. De Rossi published a brief notice of this.[103]

4) A Jewish cemetery on the via Labicana, now via Casilini, in the neighbourhood of the Esquiline and Viminal, dating to some time in the Antonine period. This was identified by Marucchi in 1883.[104]

5) A preliminary account was published by N. Müller of a Jewish cemetery discovered in 1885 on the via Appia, opposite the Vigna Randanini. No full report on this catacomb was ever published and no trace of it now remains.[105]

6) The latest significant Jewish catacomb to be discovered was that found in 1919 in the grounds of the Villa Torlonia. It was explored in the 1920s, and plans and a substantial number of inscriptions were published.[106] Renewed excavations carried out in 1973 and 1974 have revealed that the complex in fact consists of two separate catacombs at different levels. These researches have also yielded a substantial number of new inscriptions, including the striking epitaph of an

---

Capitol, some to the Museum Kircherianum, and to the collection of the Benedictines of San Paolo fuori (details in S. de Ricci, *op. cit.* in next note).

101. For the redicovery see S. de Ricci, CRAI (1905), pp. 245-7, and A. de Waal, RQCA 19 (1905), 1, pp. 140-2. See further N. Müller, *Die jüdische Katakombe am Monteverde zu Rom* (1912); N. Müller and N. A. Bees, *Die Inschriften der jüdischen Katakombe am Monteverde zu Rom* (1919); CIJ I², pp. 206-359, nos. 291-493; Leon, *op. cit.*, pp. 46-51, 68-73, 307-36.

102. Cf. R. Garrucci, *Cimitero degli antichi Ebrei scoperto recentemente in Vigna Randanini* (1862); *Dissertazioni archeologiche di vario argomento* II (1865), pp. 150-92. On the site of the cemetery see the plan in G. B. de Rossi, BAC 5 (1867), p. 3, with the explanation *op. cit.*, pp. 51, 70-1, 274-305. For a note on a number of largely fragmentary inscriptions mainly deriving from Vigna Randanini and not included in CIJ, see L. Moretti, 'Iscrizioni greco-giudaiche di Roma', RAC 50 (1974), pp. 213-19, on p. 215.

103. G. B. de Rossi, BAC 5 (1867), p. 16. For the inscriptions from this cemetery see CIJ I², pp. 194-7, nos. 277-81; Leon, *op. cit.*, pp. 51, 305.

104. O. Marucchi, 'Di un nuovo cimitero giudaicho scoperto sulla via Labicana', Diss. Pont. Acc. Rom. di Arch. ser. ii, 2 (1884), pp. 499-532; *idem, Le catacombe romane* (1903), pp. 279-97 (revd. ed. 1932, pp. 678-81); CIJ I², pp. 46-9, nos. 73-8; Leon, *op. cit.*, p. 52.

105. N. Müller, 'Le catacombe degli Ebrei presso la via Appia Pignatelli', MDAI (Rome) 1 (1886), pp. 49-56; CIJ I, pp. 50-3, nos. 79, 80; Leon, *op. cit.*, pp. 52-3, 274.

106. See R. Paribeni, 'Catacomba giudaica sulla Via Nomentana', Not. d. Sc. 17 (1920), pp. 143-55; H. W. Beyer and H. Lietzmann, *Die jüdische Katakombe der Villa Torlonia in Rom* (1930); CIJ I², pp. 9-46, nos. 6-72; Leon, *op. cit.*, pp. 53, 73, 265-73.

ἀρχιγερουσιάρχης (the only appearance of this term to date) and another of Γαϊανὸς γραμματέους *(sic)* ψαλμῳδὸς φιλόνομος, one of only two explicit references so far known to psalm-singing in the Diaspora synagogue of the classical period (for a parallel from Aphrodisias in Caria, see p. 26 above). The two catacombs seem to date to the third-fourth centuries.[107] The age of these cemeteries as a group, and of the inscriptions surviving in them, can only be stated approximately. For the most part, they probably belong to about the second-fourth centuries A.D., although those mentioned first, on the Via Portuensis, may be older.

Besides Jews proper, there were, as in Alexandria, Samaritans living in Rome.[108] One named Thallus, a freed slave of emperor Tiberius, once lent a large sum of money to Agrippa I in Rome.[109] The existence of Samaritans in the city as late as the time of the Ostrogothic king Theodoric is attested by a letter, incorporated in Cassiodorus' correspondence, from this king to Count Arigernus.[110] The Imperial legislation frequently directed at them indicated that the Samaritans, in the Roman Empire in general, were still not without importance in the later Imperial period.[111]

In the rest of *Italy*, Jews are mainly not traceable until the later Imperial period. The Jewish community in *Puteoli* (Dicaearchia), the main port for trade between Italy and the Orient, was however comparatively early. In addition to Phoenicians and other Orientals, Jews are found here around, at the latest, the beginning of our era (immediately following the death of Herod in 4 B.C.).[112] The most important evidence for a fairly early Jewish community in Italy relates, however, to *Ostia*, where excavations have brought to light the remains of a synagogue of the first century A.D., along with two very relevant inscriptions, covered by a more extensive synagogue of the fourth century.[113] The first of the two inscriptions comes from the

107. U. M. Fasola, 'Le due catacombe ebraiche di Villa Torlonia', Riv. Arch. Cr. 52 (1976), pp. 7–62. for the epitaph of Gaianos see pp. 19–20. The two epitaphs mentioned are reproduced and discussed by G. H. R. Horsley, *Documents Illustrating Early Christianity* (1981), nos. 73–4·(note also nos. 75–6 from the same catacomb).

108. See T. E. J. Jouynboll, *Commentarii in historiam gentis Samaritanae* (1846), pp. 47–9. For general surveys note also J. A. Montgomery, *The Samaritans* (1907; ²1968).

109. Jos. *Ant.* xviii 6, 4 (167).

110. Cassiodorus, *Var.* iii 45.

111. *C. Theod.* xiii 5, 18; xvi 8, 16 and 28; *Nov. Just.* 129 and 144.

112. Jos. *Ant.* xvii 2, 1 (23–5); *B.J.* ii 7, 1 (101–5). Note also CIJ I², no. 561, a *gerusiarches*. There was also a Christian community here as early as Nero's reign (Acts 28:13–14).

113. See F. Zevi, 'La sinagoga di Ostia', Rassegna mensile di Israel 38 (1972), pp. 131–45; M. F. Squarciapino, *La sinagoga di Ostia* (1964); R. Meiggs, *Roman Ostia* (²1973), pp. 587–8; Kraabel, 'Diaspora Synagogue', pp. 497–500.

site of the synagogue itself, is partly in Latin and partly in Greek, and
contains a reference to a shrine or Ark (*kibotos*) for keeping the scrolls of
the Torah (AE 1967, no. 77; see M. Guarducci, *Epigrafia greca* III
(1974), pp. 15–17, with photograph): 'Pro salute Aug(usti),
οἰκοδόμησεν κὲ αἰπόησεν (*sic*) ἐκ τῶν αὗτου δομάτων καὶ τὴν κειβωτὸν
ἀνέθηκεν νόμῳ ἁγίῳ Μίνδις Φαῦστος με[..]'. The second, from an area to
the south of Ostia, provides evidence of an *archisynagogus* named Plotius
Fortunatus:[114] 'Plotio Fortunato archisyn(agogo) fec(it *or* -erant)
Plotius Ampliatus Secundinus Secunda P. T. N. et Ofilia Basilia
co < n > iugi B. M.' (it is not certain how the names in ll. 2–4 should be
divided).

The existence of this new evidence makes it much more reasonable to
restore a long-known inscription from *Castel Porziano*, some ten
kilometres south-east of Ostia (CIJ I², no. 533) as alluding to the
community (*universitas*? cf. *Cod. Just.* i 9, 1 : 'universitati Iudaeorum qui
in Antiochensium civitate constituti sunt') of the Jews living in Ostia :
'[universitas] Iudeorum [in col. Ost. commor]antium ...'; it also
contains two references to a *gerusiarches*. The inscription is thought to
date to the first half of the second century A.D.

Note also a fragmentary Greek inscription, probably from *Portus*
near Ostia, with the words Θεοδώ[ρου κα]ὶ Ἑλλὴλ φροντιστῶν, G.
Sacco, *Arch. Class.* 31 (1979), p. 252, no. 4 = SEG XXIX, no. 981.

For further Jewish, and possibly Jewish, inscriptions from *Portus* see
now G. Sacco (ed.), *Iscrizioni greche d'Italia : Porto* (1984), nos. 84–94.

Pompeii supplies some very slight evidence for the presence of Jews, or
for Jewish influence in that city, before the moment of its destruction in
A.D. 79.[115] In the later Imperial period, Jews were widely dispersed,

---

114. This inscription appears only to have been published by M. F. Squarciapino, 'M.
Plotius Fortunatus, archisynagogus', Rassegna mensile di Israel 36, nos. 7–9 (1970), pp.
183–91, and has not apparently been reproduced in any standard collection, nor by
Lifshitz in CIJ I².

115. On the walls of a house is a graffito with 'Sodoma, Gomora', CIJ I², no. 567.
Besides 'Maria', which might be a Jewish name, 'Martha' also appears. There is in
addition a graffito which may be in Hebrew (no. 562), and an inscription of Felix (slave)
of Ioudaikos (CIL IV, no. 6990 = no. 563). On pottery : 'mur[ia] cast[a]' and 'gar[um]
cast[um]' or 'cast[imoniale]' ; compare with this, Pliny *N.H.* xxxi 95 (A. Mau, *Pompeii in
Leben und Kunst* (1900), pp. 15 ff.).

G. B. de Rossi proposed to interpret the 'princeps libertinorum' who recommends the
election of a certain Cuspius Pansa to the aedileship (CIL IV, no. 117 = ILS, no. 6419g,
'Cuspium Pansam aed. Fabius Eupor princeps libertinorum') as the head of a synagogue
of freedmen (Bull. arch. cr. (1864), pp. 70, 92 ff.). This suggestion has been revived
subsequently, e.g., by Della Corte (below), but can be confidently dismissed ; see P. Castrén,
Ordo Populusque Pompeianus (1975), p. 166. Cf. in general J. B. Frey, 'Les Juifs à
Pompei', RB 42 (1933), pp. 365–83 ; M. Della Corte, *Case ed abitanti a Pompeii* (³1965),
nos. 14 ; 18 ; 186–7 ; 217 ; 401 ; 462 ; 776 and p. 386 (speculative).

especially in southern Italy.[116] In some of the cities of *Apulia* and *Calabria* in the fourth century, the local offices could not be regularly filled because the Jewish inhabitants tried to claim immunity from them.[117] In *Venosa* (Venusia in Apulia, the birthplace of Horace), a Jewish catacomb has been discovered, with numerous Greek, Latin and Hebrew inscriptions, from about the sixth century A.D.[118] They are encountered also in this later period in *Taranto, Capua* and *Naples*, and in all the principal cities of Sicily—*Syracuse, Palermo* and *Agrigento*.[119] From Bruciano in the territory of *Nola* note two recently-published inscriptions of the third-fourth century: a) שלום ἔνθα κῖτε ὁ 'Ρεββι 'Αββα Μάρις ὁ ἔντιμος (shofar, menorah, palm-

116. See G. I. Ascoli, *Iscrizioni* etc. (1880), pp. 33–8; A. Neubauer, 'The early settlement of the Jews in Southern Italy', JQR 4 (1892), pp. 606–25; H. M. Adler, 'The Jews in Southern Italy', JQR 14 (1902), pp. 111–15 (inscriptions from the museum in Taranto). See J. Juster, *Les Juifs dans l'empire romain* I (1914), pp. 180–3, and esp. L. Levi, 'Ricerche di epigrafia ebraica nell'Italia meridionale', *Vol. spec. in memoria di F. Luzzatto*, Rass. mens. di Israel 38.3–4 (1962), pp. 132–53.

117. Letter of the emperors Arcadius and Honorius from A.D. 398 in *Cod. Theod.* xii 1, 158: 'Vacillare per Apuliam Calabriamque plurimos ordines civitatum comperimus, quia Iudaicae superstitionis sunt, et quadam se lege, quae in Orientis partibus lata est, necessitate subeundorum munerum aestimant defendendos.'

118. The catacomb was discovered already in 1853 and was described in two notes (by P. De Angelis, R. Smith and S. D'Aloe). Both, however, lay buried for some years in the archives of the museum at Naples. Their contents were made known 1) through G. I. Ascoli, *Iscrizioni inedite o mal note greche latine ebraiche di antichi sepolcri giudaici del Napolitano, Torino e Roma* (1880); and 2) in CIL IX (1883), pp. 660–5, nos. 6195–241; cf. 647, 648. Cf. also ThLZ (1880), pp. 485–8. H. Grätz, MGWJ (1880), pp. 433 ff.; J. Dérénbourg, REJ 6 (1883), pp. 200–7.

In addition to the catacomb inscriptions, dated ninth-century Hebrew epitaphs are known from Venosa, see Ascoli, *op. cit.*; ThLZ (1880), p. 485. On the Venosa catacomb see now CIJ I², pp. 420–43, nos. 569–619, and prol., pp. 46–8 (five further epitaphs); H. J. Leon, 'The Jews of Venusia', JQR 44 (1954), pp. 267–84; B. Lifshitz, 'Les Juifs à Venosa', Riv. fil. 40 (1962), pp. 367–71; Solin, *op. cit.*, pp. 734–5, 737–8 (noting a number of newly-published fragmentary inscriptions).

119. *Taranto*: Ascoli, *Iscrizioni* etc. (1880), p. 84; Notizie degli Scavi (1882), pp. 386, 387; (1883), p. 179 ff.; CIL IX, nos. 6400–2; H. M. Adler, JQR 14 (1902), pp. 111–15; CIJ I², nos. 620–31. *Capua*: CIL X, no. 3905 = CIJ I², no. 553. Note also a Jewish ossuary in Jerusalem with the inscription Μαρία 'Αλεξάνδρου γυνή, ἀπὸ Καπούης, CIJ II, no. 1284. *Naples*: Procop. *Bell.* v 8, 41 and 10, 24–5. For inscriptions from Naples, CIJ I², nos. 555–60, incorporating CIL X, nos. 8059⁴·⁶⁴ and 1971. *Syracuse*: CIG no. 9895; P. Orsi, 'Nuovi ipogei di Sette cristiane e giudaiche ai Cappuccini in Siracusa', Röm. Quartalschr. f. chr. Altertums. 14 (1900), pp. 187–209; CIJ I², nos. 651–3. *Palermo* and *Agrigento*: in letters of Gregory the Great contained in MGH, *Epistolae* I–II (index s.vv. 'Hebraeus' and 'Iudaeus'); see S. Katz, 'Pope Gregory the Great and the Jews', JQR 24 (1933), pp. 113 ff.; CIJ I²,no. 654. Further inscriptions in CIJ I² from *Southern Italy* (nos. 552; 554; 568; 632–5); *Sicily* (no. 650; 649a; 650a–b; prol., pp. 51–2; 653 = DF, no. 102), add Solin, *op. cit.*, pp. 746–7; *Malta* (no. 655); two Greek inscriptions from the catacomb of Rabat are now known, one mentioning a γερουσιάρχης, Solin, *op. cit.*, p. 747. *Sardinia* (nos. 656–60 and 660a–b, prol., p. 55).

branch); b) ἔνθα κῖτε Βενιαμὶν ὁ προστατη(ς) ὁ Κεσαρεύς.[120]
Jews do not seem to have settled so thickly in northern Italy, but there too, they are found in most of the larger cities— *Ravenna, Aquileia, Bologna, Brescia, Milan* and *Genoa*.[121]
In regard to the remainder of the western provinces, evidence similarly does not appear until the later Imperial period.[122] For *Spain*, evidence concerning the Jewish dispersion in about A.D. 300 is provided by the canons of the synod of Elvira.[123] For the period prior to that, a comprehensive recent review has produced no reliable testimony relating to settled Jewish communities.[124] Our most vivid evidence for

---

120. E. Miranda, 'Due iscrizioni greco-giudaiche della Campania', Riv. Arch. Cr. 55 (1979), pp. 337–41, see BE 1980, no. 585, SEG XXIX, nos. 968–9.

121. *Ravenna*: *Anonymus Valesianus* ii, ch. 81–2, printed in an appendix to most editions of Ammianus Marcellinus. *Aquileia*: CIJ I², no. 147 (from Rome): θυγάτηρ Οὐρσακίου ἀπὸ Ἀκουλείας γερουσιάρχου; no. 643 (Aquileia); 643a (epitaph of a Jew converted to Christianity). For a fourth-century building at Aquileia dedicated 'd(omi)no Sab(aoth)', with inscriptions by persons some of whom have Semitic, or specifically Jewish, names see CIJ I², prol., p. 50. Cf. Solin, *op. cit.*, pp. 739, 745. *Bologna*: Ambrose, *Exhortatio virginitatis* 1. *Brescia*: CIL V, no. 4411 = ILS, no. 6724 = CIJ I², no. 639; IG XIV, no. 2304 = CIJ I², no. 638. *Milan*: Cassiodorus, *Variae* v 37; CIL V, nos. 6294, 6251, 6310 = CIJ I², nos. 644–6. *Genoa*: Cassiodorus, *Variae* ii 27. For other inscriptions from *central* and *northern Italy*, CIJ I², nos. 636–7, 640–2, 647–9. See now L. Ruggini, 'Ebrei e orientali nell'Italia settentrionale fra il IV e il VI secolo d. Cr.', Stud. et. doc. hist. et iur. 25 (1959), pp. 186–308.

122. For the late appearance of Jewish communities in the Latin-speaking provinces of Western Europe see e.g., T. D. Barnes, *Tertullian* (1921), App. 28.

123. Text in K. J. Hefele, H. Leclerq, *Histoire des Conciles* I.1, pp. 212–64; A. C. Vega, *España sagrada* 56 (1957), pp. 196–222. Relevant are Canon 49: 'admoneri placuit possessores ut non patiantur fructus suos ... a Iudaeo benedici'; Canon 50: 'si vero quis clericus vel fidelis cum Iudaeis cibum sumpserit'; Canon 78: 'si quis fidelis habens uxorem cum Iudaea vel gentili fuerit moechatus'.

124. W. P. Bowers, 'Jewish Communities in Spain in the Time of Paul the Apostle', JThSt 26 (1975), pp. 395–402, and cf. Solin, *op. cit.*, pp. 749–52.

a) Trilingual (Hebrew, Latin?, Greek) inscription from *Tarragona*, of uncertain date, CIJ I², no. 660c (prol. pp. 55–6).

b) Trilingual (Hebrew, Latin, Greek) inscription from *Tortosa* of uncertain date between the second and sixth century, CIJ I², no. 661 = G. Alföldy, *Die römischen Inschriften von Tarraeo* (1975), no. 1076.

c) An early third-century inscription from *Adra* of a Jewish girl called Salo[mo]nida, CIJ I², no. 665.

d) A bilingual inscription from *Tarragona*, from about the end of the fifth century or later, referring to a local *archisynagogos*, Alföldy, *op. cit.*, no. 1075.

e) A Latin inscription from *Pallaresos* dated to the fourth century, and decorated with menorah and lulab, CIJ I², no. 660d = Alföldy, *op. cit.*, no. 1074: epitaph of 'Jonatus' and Axia: 'pauset anima eius in pace cum omne Israel, amen, amen, amen'.

f) The Latin inscription mentioning 'Rabbi Se[muel?]' and 'Rabbi Ja[cob]' from *Emerita* (Mérida) which may be as early as the fourth century (or as late as the eighth-tenth), CIJ I², no. 665a (Prolegomenon, p. 57).

g) Three very fragmentary inscriptions in Greek from the floor of what is taken to be a synagogue at *Elche*, CIJ I², nos. 662–4, see prol., p. 57 and DF, no. 101.

this area derives from a Christian account of the destruction of the community of Minorca in 417 or 418.[125] As for *Southern Gaul* it is possible that Jews resided there in the earlier Imperial period, since Christian communities were established in Lyon and Vienne already in the second century, and the Christian missions, at least in New Testament times, tended to follow in the traces of the Jews.[126] Apart from very scattered individual items of archaeological evidence, there is however no definite attestation of a Jewish settlement in Gaul until the fifth century.[127] In *Germany*, a Jewish community was certainly established in Cologne in 321.[128] The evidence relating to this later dispersion in the west cannot be pursued further here.[129]

125. See E. D. Hunt, 'St. Stephen in Minorca : An Episode in Jewish-Christian Relations in the Early 5th Century A.D.', JThSt 33 (1982), pp. 106–23 (based on the letter of Severus printed in PL XX, cols. 731–46 and XLI, cols. 821–32).

126. Th. Reinach, 'La communauté juive de Lyon au deuxième siècle de notre ère', REJ 51 (1906), pp. 245–50, is based on Eusebius, *Hist. Eccl.* v 1, 26: the martyred woman, Biblis, bears witness that Christians are not permitted to consume blood. From this it has sometimes been concluded that Jewish butchers traded in Lyon, otherwise the small Christian communities, dependent on pagan butchers, would have been unable to obey this prohibition. The fragility of this deduction is obvious.

127. See B. Blumenkranz, 'Les premières implantations des Juifs en France', CRAI 1969, pp. 162–74; *idem, Histoire des Juifs en France* (1972), pp. 13 ff.; 'Premiers témoignages épigraphiques sur les Juifs en France', *S. W. Baron Jubilee Volume* (1975), pp. 229–35; Solin, *op. cit.*, pp. 753–5. In the late Roman period, Jews settled in the greatest numbers in the commercial towns of Narbo, Arelate and Massilia. See H. Gross, *Gallia Judaica, Dictionnaire géographique de la France d'après les sources rabbiniques* (1897), pp. 73–90 (ארלי *Arles*), pp.366–84 (מרשילייה *Marseilles*), pp. 393 f. (ניצה *Nice*), pp. 401–30 (נרבונה *Narbonne*), pp. 489–93 (פרובינסא *Provence*).

Inscriptions: Latin inscriptions at Narbonne dated to A.D. 688, CIJ I², no. 670. Hebrew: D. Chwolson, *Corpus inscr. hebr.*, pp. 179 ff.; M. Schwab, 'Inscriptions hébraïques en France du VIIIᵉ au XVᵉ siècle', Bull. arch. (1897), pp. 178–217; and 'Rapport sur les inscriptions hébraïques de France', Nouvelles archives des missions scientifiques 12.3 (1904), pp. 143–402; pp. 169–89 give the inscriptions of the early Middle Ages. CIJ I², nos. 671–2, 672. Cf. J. Juster, *Les Juifs dans l'empire romain* I (1914), pp. 184–6.

128. *Cod. Theod.* xvi 8, 3: 'Imp. Constantinus A. Decurionibus Agrippiniensibus: Cunctis ordinibus generali lege concedimus, Iudaeos vocare ad curiam' (dated to A.D. 321). See Solin, *op. cit.*, p. 754.

129. On this see e.g. Juster, *Les Juifs* I, pp. 183–6; *idem, La condition légale des juifs sous les Rois visigoths* (1912); rev. ed. by A. M. Rabello, *The Legal Condition of the Jews under the Visigothic Kings* (1976); B. Blumenkranz, *Juifs et Chrétiens dans le monde occidental (430–1066)* (1960); *Juifs et chrétiens. Patristique et Moyen Age* (1977). Note *Gli Ebrei nell'Alto Medioevo* (Sett. de Stud. del Centro It. di St. sull' Alto Medievo, Spoleto, 26, 1980). Note also J. Caro, 'Die Juden des Mittelalters in ihrer wirtschaftlichen Betätigung', MGWJ (1904), pp. 423–39; 576–603. Pp. 423–9 are devoted to later antiquity. He refers *inter alia* to a passage in Jerome's Commentary on Isaiah 66:20, in which the latter argues against a literal interpretation of the biblical passage, according to which all the Jews are to be expected to return to the Holy Land, the prominent personalities among them, in carriages : 'qui senatoriae fuerint dignitatis et locum principum obtinuerint, de Britannis, Hispanis, Gallisque extremis hominum Morinis, et ubi bicornis finditur Rhenus, in

carrucis veniant ...' If Jerome is not merely allowing his imagination to run riot, there must already have been Jews in Britain and Belgium (the Morini are a Belgic people) who belonged to municipal senates. Note however S. Applebaum, 'Were there Jews in Roman Britain?', Trans. Jewish Hist. Soc. England 17 (1951–2), pp. 189–205, reviewing all the possible evidence and finding nothing concrete.

II

1. *Internal Organization of the Communities*

The survival of the Jewish religion and way of life among the various groups dispersed throughout the world was obviously possible only if the Jews, even among foreigners, in the midst of the pagan world, organized themselves into self-supporting communities within which the faith and law of the fathers could be observed as in the Holy Land. This may well have been the case even in earlier periods, but is certain from the beginning of the Hellenistic period onwards. The actual form of organization differed according to time and place, depending on whether these Jewish communities took on the character of purely private associations or, at other times, were strengthened by the enjoyment of considerable, or at least some, political rights. In all instances however an independent organization could be established only where Jews lived near one another in some numbers.[1]

From this point of view, least is known of the eastern Diaspora; indeed for the Diaspora in the land beyond the Euphrates no detailed evidence is available before the Talmudic period. Material is also scarce for the Diaspora even in the region of Greek civilization. However, some conclusions may be drawn in the first place from the different terms used for the notion 'community' which we meet in this connexion. They show how much the form of these communities varied.

1. The simple term οἱ Ἰουδαῖοι is used on some inscriptions from the earlier part of the period, and occasionally later.

(a) Inscription from Schedia near Alexandria, dating to the time of Ptolemy III Euergetes (247–221 B.C.): ὑπὲρ βασιλέως.. τὴν προσευχὴν οἱ Ἰουδαῖοι (see above, p. 46). 'The Jews' is here the term for the community of the locality.

---

1. P. Wesseling, *Diatribe de Judaeorum archontibus ad inscriptionem Berenicensem* (1738), is still of interest today. See J. Juster, *Les Juifs dans l'empire romaine* I (1914), pp. 409–96; S. Krauss, *Synagogale Altertümer* (1922); M. La Piana, 'Foreign groups in Rome', HTR 20 (1927), pp. 341–93; J. B. Frey, 'Les communautés juives à Rome aux premiers temps de l'Église', RSR 20 (1930), pp. 267–97 and 21 (1931), pp. 129–68; Frey, CIJ I (2 ed. Lifshitz, 1975), Introduction, pp. lxviii-cxi; V. Tcherikover, *Hellenistic Civilization and the Jews* (1961), pp. 296–343; B. Lifshitz, 'Fonctions et titres honorifiques dans les communautés juives. Notes d'épigraphie palestinienne', RB 67 (1960), pp. 58–64; H. J. Leon, *The Jews of Ancient Rome* (1961), pp. 167–194. Note also B. Brooten, *Women Leaders in the Ancient Synagogue* (1982).

(b) Inscription from Athribis in the southern part of the Delta (probably from the second century B.C.): οἱ ἐν 'Αθρίβει 'Ιουδαῖοι (see above, p. 48).

(c) Inscription of the second or third century A.D. from Ephesus, p. 23 above.

2. Πολίτευμα. For this term, as applied to Jewish communities, there are three attestations.

(a) Ps.-Aristeas 310: καθὼς δὲ ἀνεγνώσθη τὰ τεύχη (i.e. of the translation of the Pentateuch), στάντες οἱ ἱερεῖς καὶ τῶν ἑρμηνέων οἱ πρεσβύτεροι καὶ τῶν ἀπὸ τοῦ πολιτεύματος οἵ τε ἡγούμενοι τοῦ πλήθους εἶπον. Alongside the priests and elders of the translators, 'the elders τῶν ἀπὸ τοῦ πολιτεύματος' and the 'leaders' (ἡγούμενοι) are named. Οἱ ἀπὸ τοῦ πολιτεύματος is here the entire Jewish people in Alexandria, synonymous with τὸ πλῆθος.[2] The latter expression is used by Aristeas also in a previous passage, 308.

(b) Two inscriptions from Berenice in Cyrenaica: a) probably A.D. 24 (CIG, no. 5361 etc., see p. 61 above), lines 21 ff.: ἔδοξε τοῖς ἄρχουσι καὶ τῷ πολιτεύματι τῶν ἐν Βερενίκῃ 'Ιουδαίων. b) CIG, no. 5362 = SEG XVI, no. 931 (see p. 61 above), ll. 12–13: ἔ[δοξε τοῖς ἄ]ρχουσι καὶ τῷ πολιτεύματι τ[ῶν] ἐν Βερενικίδι 'Ιουδαίων (first century B.C. or A.D.). In later Greek *politeuma* can mean not only the administration and structure of the political body but also that body itself, or its members.[3] It can however also refer to quite a small civilian community, or group of mercenaries, which is organized like a city commune and enjoys a measure of independent existence alongside the city commune; in this sense the term always refers to a group of different nationality from the local community as a whole.[4] The

2. On this passage see P. Wendland, *Festschrift für Vahlen* (1900), p. 128, and the edition by A. Pelletier (1962), ad loc. On the basis of the free rendering of the passage in Josephus (*Ant.* xii 2.13 (108): τῶν ἑρμηνέων οἱ πρεσβύτεροι καὶ τοῦ πολιτεύματος οἱ προεστηκότες) one is tempted to erase οἱ ἡγούμενοι with Wilamowitz, omitting τε. It is read however not only in all the manuscripts of Aristeas but also in all those of Eusebius, *Praep. ev.* viii 5, 6 (354b), and is certainly to be retained (so Wendland, *op. cit.*). See V. Tcherikover, *Hellenistic civilization and the Jews* (1961), p. 297.

3. Πολίτευμα meaning 'political body' or 'citizens' occurs even earlier than Polybius and is frequent after him; OGIS, nos. 229, ll. 60, 72 (Magnesia); 332, l. 56 (Elana); O. Kern, *Die Inschriften von Magnesia am Meander* (1900), no. 100a, ll. 12–13: τῷ σύνπαντι πλήθει τοῦ πολιτεύματος, also no. 101, l. 14; 2 Mac. 12:7: Judas wished to return καὶ τὸ σύμπαν τῶν 'Ιοππιτῶν ἐκριζῶσαι πολίτευμα. Philo, *De conf. ling.* 23 (109): ἐφιέμενος ἐγγραφῆς τῆς ἐν τῷ μεγίστῳ καὶ ἀρίστῳ πολιτεύματι τοῦδε τοῦ κόσμου. Cf. *De Josepho* 14 (69). See also Paul, Phil. 3:20 and commentaries; ThWNT vi, 516 ff.; W. Tarn and G. T. Griffith, *Hellenistic Civilization* (³1952), pp. 147, 222.

4. For example, interesting material is offered by the epitaphs of mercenaries in Sidon discovered and published by Th. Macridy, RB 1904, pp. 547–56: p. 549: Καυνίων τὸ πολίτευμα; p. 551: Τερμησσέων τῶν πρὸς Οἰνοάνδοις Πισιδῶν τὸ πολίτευμα; p. 552: Πιναρέων τὸ πολίτευμα. According to the rest of the content of the epitaphs they are

significant feature of such a *politeuma* is that it has officials and can pass decrees independently of the rest of the community.

3. Κατοικία. Inscription from Hierapolis in Phrygia from the Roman period: on unauthorized use of a grave a fine is to be paid τῇ κατοικίᾳ τῶν ἐν Ἱεραπόλει κατοικούντων Ἰουδαίων (see above, p. 27). The terms *katoikos* and *katoikia* can have a wide variety of meanings.[5] A *katoikia* may be a separate settlement, whether established by royal authority or not, or a defined group within a larger city community, as is clearly the sense here; in a parallel inscription from Hierapolis the grave-mult is payable to the λαός of the Jews (see below).

4. Λαός. This word, in biblical Greek the main designation of the chosen people, occurs also as the designation of a local community.

(a) The inscription from Hierapolis in Phrygia of the Roman period, mentioned above: the unauthorized user of the grave must pay a fine τῷ λαῷ τῶν Ἰουδαί[ω]ν (see also p. 27 above).

(b) Mantinea: πατὴρ λαοῦ διὰ βίου.[6]

(c) Inscriptions from Larissa Pelasgiotis and elsewhere in Thessaly with the frequent formula, τῷ λαῷ χαίρειν (the dead person bids farewell to the community), see above p. 66. That these inscriptions are Jewish can be taken as virtually certain from the name of Μαρία Ἰούδα occurring on them.

(d) We can take as certain the Jewish origin of the inscription from Nysa given above, p. 24: a certain Menander has erected τὸν τόπον (presumably the synagogue) τῷ λαῷ καὶ τῇ συνόδῳ τ[ῶν περὶ]

---

unquestionably corporations of mercenaries who originate from various parts of Asia Minor, but are established in Sidon. The members call themselves πολῖται (pp. 551, 554). Part of the material also in L. Jalabert, Rev. Arch. 4 (1904), pp. 1–16. For the inscription of the mercenaries from Caunus, a town in Caria, see OGIS, no. 592. Corporations of a similar kind are for example: πολίτευμα τῶν Φρυγῶν on an inscription found in Pompeii and probably originating in Egypt, OGIS, no. 658; the *politeuma* of the Idumaeans in Memphis, OGIS, no. 737, see p. 45 above; the *politeuma* of Boeotians, SB, no. 6664; of Cilicians, no. 7270; the *politeuma* of the Cretans on a papyrus in Middle Egypt, PTebt I, no. 32 = Wilcken, *Chrestomathie*, no. 448. For further examples, and discussions of the term, see J. Lesquier, *Les institutions militaires de l'Égypte sous les Lagides* (1911), pp. 142–55; W. Ruppel, 'Politeuma. Bedeutungsgeschichte eines staatsrecht-lichen Terminus', Philologus 82 (1927), pp. 268–312; 433–54 (the fullest discussion of the term); M. Launey, *Recherches sur les armées hellénistiques* I-II (1949–50), pp. 1064–85; P. M. Fraser, Berytus 13 (1962), pp. 147–52.

5. For opinions on the possible uses of *katoikia* see e.g. F. Oertel in RE s.v. 'Katoikoi' (1922); L. Robert, *Études Anatoliennes* (1937), pp. 191–4; E. Bikerman, *Institutions des Séleucides* (1938), pp. 100–5; M. Rostovtzeff, SEHHW (1941), pp. 499–501; D. Musti, 'Lo stato dei Seleucidi', SCO 15 (1966), pp. 61–200, on pp. 178 ff. The use of the term *katoikos* for military settlers in Ptolemaic Egypt, from the second century B.C. onwards, is well-established, see J. Lesquier, *Les institutions militaires* (1911), esp. pp. 48 ff.; *katoikia* could also denote a Seleucid military settlement, see B. Bar-Kochva, *The Seleucid Army* (1976), pp. 22–7.

6. CIJ I², no. 720 (see p. 66 above).

Δωσίθεον Θεογένου. The double description is intended to indicate that the 'people' forms an association which is grouped round Dositheus, son of Theogenes (similar designations of associations are not infrequent). The inscription is presumably pre-Christian.

(e) Note also the '*grammateus* of the *laos* in Smyrna', p. 20 above.

5. Ἔθνος. Inscription from Smyrna, third century A.D. (see above, p. 20): the unauthorized user of the grave must pay a fine τῷ ἔθνει τῶν Ἰουδαίων. The use of the expression τὸ ἔθνος shows that there was no strict differentiation between the term ὁ λαός for the chosen people and τὰ ἔθνη for the gentile 'peoples'.

All the terms mentioned so far reflect the fact that the Jews lived as a foreign people among strangers. The two last-mentioned instances express this directly, while *politeuma* and *katoikia* indicate the fact that they occupied a position in some ways politically independent alongside the rest of the inhabitants.

6. Σύνοδος. The Jews from Sardis, who are simultaneously Roman citizens, assure L. Antonius (governor of the province of Asia in 50–49 B.C.) that they have their own σύνοδος, Jos. *Ant.* xiv 10, 17 (235): αὐτοὺς σύνοδον ἔχειν ἰδίαν κατὰ τοὺς πατρίους νόμους ἀπ᾽ ἀρχῆς καὶ τόπον ἴδιον ἐν ᾧ τά τε πράγματα καὶ τὰς πρὸς ἀλλήλους ἀντιλογίας κρίνουσιν. By this they mean that in spite of their special position as Roman citizens they abstain from seeking justice before the Roman assizes, or *conventus*. As the expression *synodos* occurs in opposition to this *conventus*, no certain conclusion can be drawn from the statement about the way in which the community designated itself. On the other hand *synodos* is used in this sense in the inscription from Nysa mentioned as no. 4 above. In connection with Greek cult-associations *synodos* occurs and means (i) a festive meeting of the association, (ii) an association itself. See E. Ziebarth, *Das griechische Vereinswesen* (1896), pp. 136–8. The former sense (an assembly for observing a feast) appears also in the Jewish inscription from Berenice (CIG, no. 5361, see p. 61 above and 94 below), ll. 23–4: καθ᾽ ἑκάστην σύνοδον καὶ νουμηνίαν.

7. Συναγωγή, the usual designation of the Jewish community in the later period. The documentary evidence includes:

(a) Inscriptions from Panticapaeum (see above, p. 36), containing declarations of the manumission of slaves. At the end they have the formula συνεπιτροπευούσης δὲ καὶ τῆς συναγωγῆς τῶν Ἰουδαίων. The significance is apparently that the manumission took place under the supervision of the community, which thereby at the same time guaranteed the permanence of the arrangement.

(b) Inscription from Phocaea (above, p. 19): συναγωγὴ ἐ[τείμη]σεν τῶν Ἰουδαίων...

(c) Inscription from Acmonia (above, p. 31): οὔστινας καὶ ἡ συναγωγὴ ἐτείμησεν ὅπλῳ ἐπιχρύσῳ etc.

(d) An inscription of A.D. 55 from Berenice in Cyrenaica (p. 61 above) where συναγωγή is used both of the community and of their synagogue.

(e) Note also 'the most sacred *synagoge* of the *Hebraioi*' attested at Deliler near Philadelphia, p. 22 above.

(f) A papyrus of A.D. 291 from Oxyrhynchus in Egypt records a sum paid 'by the *synagoge* of the Jews', p. 56 above.

The term *synagoge* is frequent, with the meaning 'community', on Roman epitaphs. On this see below pp. 96 ff. In the New Testament see especially Ac. 6:9; 9:2. On the later usage see vol. II, pp. 429–31. Originally *synagoge* like *synodos* is the assembly itself, and occurs in this sense also in connexion with Greek cult associations (examples vol. II, p. 430, n. 13). From the meaning 'assembly, gathering' the meaning 'community' develops, as with *synodos*. This is the term consistently used by the LXX for עדה, which means the assembled community of Israel. In the later period however *synagoge* is normally applied to a local community.

The suppression of the terms *politeuma*, *katoikia*, *laos* and *ethnos* by *synagoge* may have been facilitated by the fact that the latter was rendered familiar by the terminology of the LXX. But it may perhaps also have reflected a change of emphasis, from the characterisation of Jewish communities as ethnic groups to one which reflected their character as private religious associations.

8. In Latin the designation *universitas* also occurs. An imperial rescript of the year A.D. 213 is concerned with the legacy of a woman to the *universitas Iudaeorum, qui in Antiochensium civitati constituti sunt.*[7] This designation should probably also be restored in the mutilated inscription from Castel Porziano near Ostia (p. 82 above): '[universitas] Iudeorum [in col. Ost. commor]antium'; it also survived into the Middle Ages.[8]

The internal structures of the communities of course varied greatly in different times and places. The different external situations and the greater or more limited political rights of the communities were bound to exercise their influence on their internal structures. Two extremes are represented by Alexandria and Rome. In the former a united corporation of Jews, numbering many thousands, with significant political power, in the latter, in spite of considerable numbers, only isolated private associations without special political rights. These two cosmopolitan cities are incidentally the only ones about whose Jewish population we are informed in any detail. In these cases alone a more detailed analysis of their structure can be attempted. Some relatively

---

7. *Cod. Just.* i 9, 1.
8. E.g. in Marseilles in the fourteenth century, REJ 47 (1903), p. 73: 'Universitatis Iudaeorum ... civitatis Massiliae'. Ib. p. 63: 'Universitas Iudaeorum'.

detailed evidence also concerns Cyrenaica. For the rest, our evidence for Jewish communal structure consists of incidental and isolated evidence which can best be considered in conjunction with that concerning the Roman communities.

It can be presumed as probable that two categories of officials existed practically everywhere: (1) the ἄρχοντες, and (2) the ἀρχισυνάγωγοι.

In Alexandria, according to Pseudo-Aristeas, the Jewish community in the third century B.C. formed a *politeuma* at whose head stood elders (πρεσβύτεροι) and 'leaders' (ἡγούμενοι) (see above, p. 88). Since the Jews—at least in the time of Philo—are said to have made up about two-fifths of the inhabitants (see above, pp. 43 ff.), this must have been a community of considerable importance. *Hegoumenoi* is only a general designation, not a title; presumably it means the same as *archontes* (the office-holders among the *presbyteroi*?), but it remains an undecided question whether the latter were always headed by a single leader. At the time of Strabo there stood at the head of the Jews an *ethnarches*, 'who directs the people and enacts judgement and is concerned with the discharge of obligations and obedience to regulations, like the *archon* of an independent city-state'.[9] The Jews then formed in Alexandria, although they claimed to possess the Alexandrine citizenship, an autonomous organisation within or alongside the rest of the city, as in Cyrene. This autonomous position may have been made possible by the fact that Alexandria from Augustus until the time of Septimius Severus, in contrast with almost all other Hellenistic cities, had no city council.[10]

In the latter part of Augustus' reign some kind of modification seems to have appeared in the structure of Alexandrine Jewry. It is indeed stated in an edict of the emperor Claudius that Augustus himself, after the death of the ethnarch at the time of the Prefect Aquila (A.D.

9. Strabo *ap.* Jos. *Ant.* xiv 7, 2 (117) = Stern, GLAJJ I, no. 105: καθίσταται δὲ καὶ ἐθνάρχης αὐτῶν, ὃς διοικεῖ τε τὸ ἔθνος καὶ διαιτᾷ κρίσεις καὶ συμβολαίων ἐπιμελεῖται καὶ προσταγμάτων, ὡς ἂν πολιτείας ἄρχων αὐτοτελοῦς.

10. Cassius Dio li 17, 2: τοῖς δ' Ἀλεξανδρεῦσιν ἄνευ βουλευτῶν πολιτεύεσθαι ἐκέλευσε (sc. *Augustus*); HA, *v. Sept. Sev.* 17: 'Alexandrinis ius buleutarum dedit, qui sine publico consilio ita ut sub regibus ante vivebant, uno iudice contenti'. Cf. also OGIS, no. 709. From Cassius Dio it might be deduced that Augustus brought to an end the *boule* which had existed up to then (whereas the Historia Augusta states that none had ever existed). In fact there is just sufficient evidence from the Hellenistic period to show that a council had originally existed, and the probability is that it was indeed suppressed by Augustus, see P. M. Fraser, *Ptolemaic Alexandria* (1972), pp. 94–5. Under Augustus or one of his immediate successors an Alexandrian embassy petitioned the Emperor for the establishment of a council (SB, no. 7448 = Musurillo, *Acta Alexandrinorum*, no. 1 = CPJ II, no. 150); and Claudius' famous letter to Alexandria of A.D. 41 (PLond, no. 1912 = CPJ II, no. 153, ll. 66–72) shows that a further embassy had claimed (apparently with reason) that a council had existed under the Ptolemies. Claudius promises to have the matter investigated. But no change was in fact made until Severus' reign.

10–11), 'had not objected to the existence of ethnarchs'.[11] The sole concern of Claudius in this edict is to emphasize that under Augustus also the political rights and the religious freedom of the Jews in Alexandria had not been diminished. This principle might still have allowed a certain modification of the internal structure of the community. Such a thing had according to Philo been carried out by Augustus; for he says that the latter, on the death of the Jewish *genarch*, introduced a *gerousia* for the administration of Jewish affairs, through instructions addressed to Magius Maximus who was on the point of taking over the administration of Egypt, as he in fact did in A.D. 11.[12] On this evidence the difference between the previous and subsequent organization was either that the individual authority of the *ethnarches* was superseded by that of a *gerousia*, or that a *gerousia* was established alongside him. The latter view gains support from the fact that the edict of Claudius seems to presuppose the persistence of the Ethnarch even after the intervention of Augustus; but it is admittedly also possible that Claudius only means to state in general that the Jews continued to have their own communal officials (ἐθνάρχαι).[13] In any case the Jewish *gerousia* was first introduced by Augustus in the year A.D. 11, or more precisely, reintroduced; for Pseudo-Aristeas represents a *gerousia* as already in existence in the third century B.C.; if so, it had given way subsequently to a more monarchical regime. The *gerousia* and the *archontes* are mentioned by Philo several times in his narrative of events in A.D. 38.[14] The latter are presumably identical with (or include?) the πρωτεύοντες τῆς γερουσίας who occur in

11. Jos. *Ant.* xix 5,2 (283): καθ' ὃν καιρὸν Ἀκύλας ἦν ἐν Ἀλεξανδρείᾳ τελευτήσαντος τοῦ τῶν Ἰουδαίων ἐθνάρχου τὸν Σεβαστὸν μὴ κεκωλυκέναι ἐθνάρχας γίγνεσθαι. For the date of Aquila's prefecture see PIR² I 165.

12. Philo, *In Flacc.* 10 (74): τῆς ἡμετέρας γερουσίας, ἣν ὁ σωτὴρ καὶ εὐεργέτης Σεβαστὸς ἐπιμελησομένην τῶν Ἰουδαίων εἵλετο μετὰ τὴν τοῦ γενάρχου τελευτὴν διὰ τῶν πρὸς Μάγνον Μάξιμον ἐντολῶν μέλλοντα πάλιν (?) ἐπ' Αἰγύπτου [read Ἀλεξανδρείας καὶ τῆς χώρας ἐπιτροπεύειν]. In place of Μάγνον, the reading of the Philo manuscripts, Μάγιον should be read (CIL IX, no. 1125 = ILS, no. 1335: 'M. Magio M. f. Maximo praef. Aegypti'). The word πάλιν is dubious, since the manuscript reading in this entire phrase is disturbed, and there is no other evidence for iteration of the Prefecture, until a single case in the fourth century. J. R. Rea, CE 43 (1968), pp. 365–7, suggests hypothetically that the reading might be μέλλοντα πόλιν ⟨τὴν⟩ ἀπ' Αἰγύπτου καὶ τὴν χώραν ἐπιτροπεύειν. At any rate the only documentary evidence for the dates of any tenure of a Prefecture by Magius Maximus are A.D. 11–12 (SB, no. 5235) and the first Egyptian year of Tiberius, A.D. 14-15, see G. Wagner, BIFHO 70 (1971), pp. 21–9.

13. P. Wesseling, *De Judaeorum archontibus* (1738), ch. 8, pp. 65–9, supposed two different ordinances of Augustus, one when Aquila was governor of Egypt, and one later when Magius Maximus was governor. This view is rendered very unlikely by the chronology of the governors.

14. Philo, *In Flacc.* 10 (76): τῶν ἀπὸ τῆς γερουσίας τρεῖς ἄνδρες, and μεταπεμψαμένῳ πρότερον τοὺς ἡμετέρους ἄρχοντας. *Flacc.* 80: τοὺς ἄρχοντας, τὴν γερουσίαν. *Flacc.* 14 (117): τῶν μὲν ἀρχόντων.

Josephus.[15] With regard to the number of members of the *gerousia*, note that Flaccus at one point ordered thirty-eight members of it to be dragged into the theatre and to be fettered there.[16] It is not unlikely that the total number was seventy (more exactly, seventy-one) as rabbinic tradition presumes.[17]

That the Jews in Cyrene also occupied a special political position is suggested by the remark of Strabo that the inhabitants of the city were divided into four classes: (1) citizens, (2) farmers, (3) resident aliens, (4) Jews.[18] In spite of this special position the Jews are stated by Josephus to have enjoyed equal civil rights (ἰσονομία).[19]

Very valuable conclusions about communal structure in the Jewish Disapora are made possible by the Jewish inscriptions from the city of Berenice in Cyrenaica. One of these was found in Tripoli and from there was brought to Aix en Provence, and is now in Toulouse.[20] We see from this that the Jews in Berenice formed their own *politeuma* (lines 17 ff. and 21 ff.) at whose head stood nine (of course Jewish) *archontes* (lines 2–8, 21, 25). On *politeuma* see above pp. 88 ff. The inscription is dated to the year 55 of a local era which will have begun either from 96 B.C., giving 41 B.C. or, more probably, from 31 B.C. (the era of Actium), giving A.D. 24.[21]

A second, more damaged inscription from Berenice, now in the museum at Carpentras, also contains a decree of the *politeuma* of the Jews in Berenice, on this occasion for a Roman citizen who was

15. Jos. *B.J.* vii 10, 1 (412).

16. Philo, *In Flacc.* 10 (74).

17. tSuk. 4:6; ySuk. 5:1: in the great synagogue at Alexandria there stood 71 golden chairs corresponding to the 71 elders (cf. vol. II, p. 211).

18. Strabo *ap.* Jos. *Ant.* xiv 7, 2 (115) = Stern, GLAJJ I, no. 105.

19. Jos. *Ant.* xvi 6, 1 (160). See in general S. Applebaum, *Jews and Greeks in Ancient Cyrene.*

20. CIG III, no. 5361 = IGR I, no. 1024. Re-edited by G. and J. Roux, 'Un décret du politeuma des Juifs de Bérénikè en Cyrénaïque', REG 62 (1949), pp. 281–96; photograph on Pl. IV. Restudied by J. M. Reynolds (see p. 61 above); see now CJZC, no. 71:
[ἔ]τους νε΄ Φαῶφ κε΄ ἐπὶ συλλόγου τῆς σκηνοπηγίας ἐπὶ ἀρχόντων Κλεάνδρου τοῦ Στρατονίκου Εὐφράνορος τοῦ Ἀρίστωνος Σωσιγένους τοῦ Σωσίππου Ἀνδρομάχου τοῦ Ἀνδρομάχου Μάρκου Λαιλίου Ὀνασίωνος τοῦ Ἀπολλωνίου Φιλωνίδου τοῦ Ἀγήμονος Αὐτοκλέους τοῦ Ζήνωνος Σωνίκου τοῦ Θεοδότου Ἰωσήπου τοῦ Στράτωνος vac. Μᾶρκος Τίττιος Σέξτου υἱὸς Αἰμιλία ἀνὴρ καλὸς καὶ ἀγαθὸς παραγενηθεὶς εἰς τὴν ἐπαρχείαν αὐτῶν ἐποιήσατο φιλανθρώπως καὶ καλῶς ἔν τε τῇ ἀναστροφῇ ἡσύχιον ἦθος ἐνδικνύμενος ἀεὶ διατελῶν τυγχάνει οὐ μόνον δὲ ἐν τούτοις ἀβαρῆ ἑαυτὸν παρέσχηται ἀλλὰ καὶ τοῖς κατ᾽ ἰδίαν ἐντυγχάνουσι τῶν πολιτῶν υ. ἔτι δὲ καὶ τοῖς ἐκ τοῦ πολιτεύματος ἡμῶν Ἰουδαίοις καὶ κοινῇ καὶ κατ᾽ ἰδίαν εὔχρηστον προστασίαν ποιούμενος οὐ διαλείπει τῆς ἰδίας καλοκἀγαθίας ἄξια πράσσων ὧν χάριν ἔδοξε τοῖς ἄρχουσι καὶ τῷ πολιτεύματι τῶν ἐν Βερενίκῃ Ἰουδαίων ἐπαινέσαι τε αὐτὸν καὶ στεφανοῦν ὀνομαστὶ καθ᾽ ἑκάστην σύνοδον καὶ νουμηνίαν στεφάνωι ἐλαΐνωι καὶ λημνίσκωι τοὺς δὲ ἄρχοντας ἀναγράψαι τὸ ψήφισμα εἰς στήλην λίθου Παρίου καὶ θεῖναι εἰς τὸν ἐπισημότατον τόπον τοῦ ἀμφιθεάτρου.

21. For the date see J. M. Reynolds in J. A. Lloyd, *Excavations at Sidi Krebish, Benghazi* (Libya Antiqua, Supp. V), pp. 244–5.

apparently one of their members, and who had been responsible for the plastering of a floor and the painting of walls in the amphitheatre (also mentioned in the previous inscription). The names of (apparently) seven *archontes* are given. The date is missing, but the letter-forms suggest the Augustan period or not much later. See G. and J. Roux, REG 62 (1949), pp. 285 ff. and Pl. III; SEG XVI, no. 931; J. M. Reynolds, *op. cit.*, p. 245, no. 18; CJZC, no. 70.

In view of what is said above (p. 91) about the tendency for *synagoge* to replace other terms for a Jewish community in a Greek city, it is interesting to find this term in use in the third known decree of the Jews of Berenice [?], dated to 3rd December of the second year of Nero, A.D. 55 (G. Caputo, Parola del Passato 12 (1957), pp. 132–4; SEG XVII, no. 823; AE 1960, no. 199; Reynolds, *op. cit.*, p. 242, no. 16; CJZC, no. 72). The decree of the community is recorded in the following terms (ll. 3–6): ἐφάνη τῇ συναγωγῇ τῶν ἐν Βερενικίδι Ἰουδαίων τοὺς ἐπιδιδοντ < a > ς εἰς ἐπισκευὴν τῆς συναγωγῆς ἀναγράψαι αὐτοὺς εἰ < ς > στήλην λίθου παρίου. It is striking that *synagoge* is thus used here in the same sentence to refer to the community and to their building, or 'synagogue'. The *synagoge* of the Jews votes to inscribe on stone the names of those who have contributed to the repair of the *synagoge*. Eighteen names of contributors are listed before the text breaks off. Ten are described as *archon* and one as a priest (*hiereus*).

Our fullest information relates to the community structure of the Jews in Rome, and in Italy in general, through the numerous Jewish epitaphs discovered in the cemeteries in Rome and Venosa.[22] They suggest that here conditions remained essentially unchanged for hundreds of years; for the inscriptions in Venosa from the sixth century A.D. give much the same picture as the Roman, from which the oldest belong presumably to the first centuries of the Christian era. From the Roman inscriptions it becomes immediately clear that the Jews in Rome formed a large number of individual, independently-organized communities (*synagogai*), each with its own synagogue, its own *gerousia* and its own community officials. Of a union of all the Roman Jewish groups under one *gerousia* there is no trace. While by contrast the Jews in Alexandria formed a single major political corporation, here in

---

22. For what follows see: E. Schürer, *Die Gemeindeverfassung der Juden in Rom in der Kaiserzeit nach den Inschriften dargestellt* (1879); H. Vogelstein and P. Rieger, *Gesch. der Juden in Rom* I (1896), pp. 38 ff.; G. La Piana, 'Foreign Groups in Rome during the First Centuries of the Empire' HThR 20 (1927), pp. 183–403, on pp. 341–71; J. B. Frey, 'Les communautés juives à Rome aux premiers temps de l'Église' RSR 20 (1930), pp. 269–97; 21 (1931), pp. 129–68; CIJ I, p. liii-cxliv, and nos. 1–499; H. J. Leon, *The Jews of Ancient Rome* (1961), pp. 268–346; CIJ I², ed. B. Lifshitz (1975), prolegomenon, pp. 21–42. See also pp. 73–81 above. On the different organization of the Jewish community in the Talmudic period see M. Weinberg, MGWJ (1897), 588 ff., 639 ff., 673 ff. For the inscriptions from Venosa see CIJ I², nos. 569–619.

Rome they had to be content with the more modest situation of individual religious associations. The individual communities used different names, of which the following are attested on inscriptions: (1) a συναγωγή Αὐγουστησίων,[23] (2) a συναγωγή Ἀγριππησίων,[24] (3) a *synagoga Bolumni* (read *Volumni*) or Βολουμνησίων.[25] These three communities are all named after prominent persons. Since as well as the *Augoustesioi*, *Agrippesioi* are also found, the former will have taken their name from the first Augustus and the latter theirs from his friend and adviser, M. Agrippa. Augustus and Agrippa may perhaps have been patrons of the communities concerned, or the communities may have originally consisted of slaves and freedmen of Augustus or of Agrippa (cf. οἱ ἐκ τῆς Καίσαρος οἰκίας, Phil. 4:22). The latter is the more likely. Whether these small associations continued to exist even after the death of those whose names they bore we do not know. The *Augoustesioi* might also have derived their name from the current Augustus.[26] Other communities were named after the part of the city of Rome in which the members lived, such as (4) the Καμπήσιοι after the Campus

23. CIJ I², no. 284: 'Marcus Cuyntus Alexus grammateus ego (= ἐκ) ton AUGUSTHSION (= Augustesion) mellarcon ECCION Augustesion'. 301: γερουσ⟨ι⟩άρχης συναγωγῆς Ἀγουστεσίων. 368: γερουσιάρχης συναγωγῆς Αὐγουστησίων. 496: [μή]τηρ συνα[γωγῆς] Αὐγουστη[σίων]. See in general CIJ I², p. lxxi.

24. No. 365: προστάτης Ἀγριππησίων. 425: γερου[σιάρχ]ης συ[ναγωγ]ῆς Ἀγρι[ππησίων. 503: συναγωγῆς Ἀγριππησίων. See CIJ I², pp. lxxi-ii.

25. No. 343: ἄρχων ἀπὸ συναγωγῆς Βολυμνησίων. 402: μελλάρχων Βολουμνησίων. 417: συναγωγῆς Βολυμνήσων (sic). 523: 'mater synagogarum Campi et Bolumni'. See CIJ I², pp. lxxii-iii.

26. The following parallels may be cited: the *Traianesioi* in Ostia, IG XIV, no. 925: ἀγνῆς εὐσέμνοιο σπείρης Τραιανησίων οἴδε ἱερεῖς ἱέρειά τε θεοῦ μεγάλου Διωνύσου; according to a Latin inscription, CIL XIV, no. 4, these *Traianenses* also worshipped Diana. On Latin inscriptions there occur, for example: *Augustiani* (CIL VI, no. 8532), a *collegium Faustinianum* (CIL III, no. 6077 = ILS, no. 1505), *Aeliani* (CIL VI, no. 978). According to J. P. Waltzing (*Étude historique sur les corporations professionelles chez les Romains* IV (1900), pp. 153 ff.) these should be regarded as associations formed by persons within the imperial service. The following designations of Greek brotherhoods have another meaning: Διονυσιασταὶ Χαιρημόνειοι (P. E. Foucart, *Des associations religieuses chez les Grecs* (1873), p. 230), Ἀγαθοδαιμονιασταὶ Φιλόνειοι (ibid.), Διοσαταβυριασταὶ Εὐφρανόρειοι οἱ σὺν Ἀθηναίῳ Κνιδίῳ (ibid., p. 229), Διοσκουριασταὶ Θευδότειοι (BCH 10 (1886), p. 425). Foucart, probably rightly, regards Chaeremon, Philon, Euphranor etc. in these cases as the founders of the respective associations (BCH 10 (1886), pp. 203, 205). A different significance is to be attached to the designations *Pompeiastai* (worshippers of Pompeius in Delos, ID, nos. 1641, 1797) and *Agrippiastai* (worshippers of Agrippa in Sparta, IG V.1, no. 374 = CIL III, no. 494). Here it is a matter of a religious cult, analogous to the emperor cult. The word-formation is the same as in *Apolloniastai* (Syll.³, nos. 726; 746), *Asklepiastai* (Syll.³, no. 1114) etc. See E. Ziebarth, *Das griechische Vereinswesen* (1896); F. Poland, *Geschichte des griechischen Vereinswesens* (1909). See also P. Bruneau, *Recherches sur les cultes de Délos à l'époque hellénistique et à l'époque impériale* (1970), pp. 585 ff.; 621 ff., and L. Cracco Ruggini, 'La vita associativa nelle città dell'Oriente greco: tradizioni locali e influenze romane', in D. M. Pippidi (ed.), *Assimilation et résistance à la culture gréco-romaine dans le monde ancien* (1976), pp. 463–91.

Martius,[27] and (5) the *Σιβουρήσιοι* after the Subura, one of the most populous quarters of ancient Rome, well-known as a trading area.[28] Other synagogue names known to us are: (6) a *συναγωγή Ἑβρέων*.

Exactly what is implied by this, whether continued use of Hebrew or relatively recent immigration from Palestine (true at least of one 'Hebrew', identified as coming from Caesarea), remains uncertain;[29] (7) a *συναγωγή Βερνακλησίων* or *Βερνακλώρων*, i.e. *vernaculorum*, therefore (apparently) 'of the indigenous (Jews)';[30] (8) a *συναγωγή Ἐλαίας*—the significance of the name is quite uncertain;[31] (9) a *συναγωγή Καλκαρησίων*, which may have owed its name to the profession of its members (*calcarienses*, i.e. lime-burners), or alternatively have derived it from some locality;[32] (10) a *συναγωγή Τριπολειτῶν* is

---

27. No. 88: *πατρὸ[ς] συναγωγῆς Καμπησίων*. 319: *πατρὸς συναγωγῆς Καμπησίων Ῥώμης*. Cf. 433 and 523 (n. 25 above). See CIJ I², p. lxxiv.

28. No. 18: *γραμματεὺς Σιβουρήσων*. 22: *ἄρχ[οντος συναγωγ]ῆ[ς] Σιβουρή[σων]*. 37: *[ἄρχων Σιβουρ?]ησίων*. 67: *[γραμματ]έος Σιβουρησίων*. 140: *ἄρχων Σ[ιβο]υρησίων*. 380: *ἄρχων Σιβουρησίων*. On the Subura see RE VI, s.v.; S. B. Platner, T. Ashby, *Topographical Dictionary of Ancient Rome* (1929), pp. 500–1. In the city of Rome proper, within the *pomerium*, it is true that even in the beginning of the imperial period no foreign *sacra* could be performed, see J. Marquardt, *Römische Staatsverwaltung* III (1978), p. 35; O. Gilbert, *Geschichte und Topographie der Stadt Rom in Altertum* III (1890), pp. 65 ff., esp. 109–115. But from the second century onwards the situation was different. Cf. G. Wissowa, *Religion und Kultur der Römer* (²1912), pp. 373 ff. From then on even Jewish synagogues were probably permitted within the *pomerium*. On the community of the Suburenses see CIJ I², pp. lxxiii-lxxiv.

29. No. 291: *[ἄ]ρχοντος Ἑβρέων*. 317: *ἐξάρχων τῶν Ἑβρέων*. 510: *πατρὸς συναγωγῆς Αἰβρέων*. 535: *πατρὸς τῶν Ἑβρέων*. Individuals are also sometimes identified as Hebrews: nos. 354; 379. Note 370: *Μακεδόνις ὁ Αἰβρέος, Κεσαρεὺς τῆς Παλεστίνης*. A [συνα]γωγή Ἑβρ[έων] is also attested at Corinth (p. 65 above). For the 'synagogue of the Hebrews' see CIJ I², pp. lxxvi-vii.

30. No. 318: *γραμματεὺς συν[α]γωγῆς Βερνακλώρω[ν]*. 383: *ἀρχισυν[ά]γωγος [συ]ναγωγ[ῆς B]ερνάκλων*. 398: (*ἄρχων?*) *διὰ βίου Βερνακλησίων*. 494: *π[ατ]ὴρ συναγωγ[ῆς B]ερνάκλων*. CIJ I², p. lxxvii.

31. No. 281: *συνα[γωγ]ῆς Ἐλέας*. 509: *πατὴρ (sic) συναγωγῆς Ἐλαίας*. Frey, CIJ I², pp. lxxvii-viii, discusses various towns named 'Elea' which might provide an explanation for this name. But no convincing explanation is available.

32. No. 304: *ἄρχων Καλκαρ[ησ]ίων*. 316: *Καλκ[α]ρήσων δὶς ἄρχ[ων]*. 384: *ὁ δὶς ἄρχων τῆς συναγωγῆς Καλκαρήσις (sic)*. 433: *γραμ[μ]ατε[ὺς συναγ]ωγῆς Κα[λκαρησίων?]*. 504: *ἱερεύς, ἄρχων Καλκαρησίων*. 537: *θυγάτηρ Μηνοφίλου πατὴρ (sic) συναγωγῆς Καλκαρησίων, καλῶς βιώσασα ἐν τῷ Ἰουδαϊσμῷ*. See CIJ I², pp. lxxv-vi, rejecting the explanation based on the members' employment as *calcarienses* and preferring a (hypothetical) derivation from a locality in Rome. However, the former explanation cannot be strictly disproved. *Collegia*, or associations, whose members also observed the same cult, were of various forms in Roman antiquity (see the bibliography on the *collegia* below, p. 112; among these occur also *sodales calcareses* (CIL VI, no. 9224); *calcarienses* (CIL VI, no. 9223, *Cod. Theod.* xii 1, 37); *calcis coctores* (*Cod. Theod.* xiv 6; *Edict. Dioclet.* vii, 4); *exonerator calcariarius* (CIL VI, no. 9384). Cf. W. Liebenam, *Zur Geschichte und Organisation des römischen Vereinswesens* (1890), p. 120.

attested once,[33] as is (perhaps) a συναγωγή "Αρκης Λιβάνου.[34] The expression γραμμ[ατεὺς] Σεκηνῶν in no. 7 may refer to a 'synagogue', but if so any explanation (see e.g. CIJ I², p. lxxix) must be hypothetical. The supposed 'synagogue of the Herodians' (CIJ I², no. 173 and p. lxxii) depends on a quite uncertain restoration and should be rejected (see prolegomenon, p. 31).

Of the officials who are mentioned on the inscriptions the *gerousiarches* and the *archontes* should be specially noticed.

(1) A γερουσιάρχης occurs not only on the Roman inscriptions,[35] but also at Venosa[36] and elsewhere.[37] The title must indicate some position of importance within or in relation to the *gerousia*. From the formulae γερουσιάρχης συναγωγῆς Αὐγουστησίων (twice) and γερουσιάρχης συναγωγῆς Ἀγρι[ππησίων] it is clear however, as has already been emphasized above, that at least some of the Jewish communities in Rome had their own *gerousia* with their own officials. In view of this fact it is significant that the title *presbyteros* appears in the Roman inscriptions only on a single occasion. The text is unfortunately fragmentary (no. 378): [Μ]ητρό[δ]ωρος [πρεσβ]ύτερος. On this basis it is not possible to say whether *presbyteros* denoted a member of the *gerousia* or, if not, whether there was any term which referred to an 'ordinary' member of the *gerousia*, as opposed to a *gerousiarches*. Nor is it clear how we should understand the term *archigerousiarches*, now attested in a Jewish catacomb in Rome (p. 81 above). Nor do these texts, all referring to individuals, give any indication of the normal numbers of members or office-holders. (2) A very common title in the Roman epitaphs is *archon*.[38] It is met also elsewhere, scattered throughout the

33. No. 390: ἄρχων συναγωγῆς Τριπολειτῶν. Cf. 408: ἱεροσάρχης (= γερουσιάρχης) Τριπολίτης. The city referred to is probably Tripolis in Phoenicia. Cf. CIJ I², pp. lxxvii-ix, and prolegomenon, p. 36.

34. No. 501: ἀπὸ τῆς συναγ(ωγῆς) Ἀρκ[ου Λι]βάνου. For an alternative restoration and interpretation see Leon, *op. cit.*, pp. 163–5.

35. No. 368: Κυντιανὸς γερουσιάρχης συναγωγῆς Αὐγοστησίων. 95: Ἀστερίῳ γερουσιάρχῃ. 147: Οὐρσακίου ἀπὸ Ἀκουιλείας γερουσιάρχου. 106: Παγχάρις γερουσιάρχης. 119: Θαιόφιλ[ος γερο]υσιάρχης. 511: Σειλίκες γερουσιάρχης. 425: γερου[σιάρχ]ης συ[ναγωγ]ῆς Ἀγρι[ππησίων]. 301: γερουσάρχης (sic) συναγωγῆς Ἀγουστεσίων. 353: Ἰουλιανὸς γερουσιάρχης. 408: see n. 33. 355: [. .]ος ἱερου[σιάρ]χων. The orthography in both the last two cases is probably the result not of a mistake of the stone-cutter, but of phonetic changes.

36. CIJ I², no. 600: Φαυστῖνος γερουσιάρχον ἀρχίατρος. 613: *filius Viti ierusiarcontis*. Notice in both cases the form *gerousiarchon*, while the Roman inscriptions almost throughout have *gerousiarches*.

37. CIJ I², no. 533 (from Castel Porziano, probably referring to the Jewish community of Ostia), l. 6: '...]no gerusiarche'; l. 8: ...]stus gerusiarches fecit'. Cf. no. 561: 'Ti. Claudius Philippus dia viu et gerusiarches' (Puteoli). See also CIJ I², pp. lxxxv-vi; Leon, *op. cit.*, pp. 180–3; p. 14 above (Antioch and Apamea).

38. In this connection note no. 291: [ἄ]ρχ(οντος) Ἑβρέων and 304: Ἄπερ ἄρχων Καλκαρ[ησ]ίων. Note also 347: ἄρχοντες καὶ ἱερεῖς καὶ ἀδελφοί. No. 538 also belongs

Jewish Diaspora, in Syria, Asia Minor, Egypt, Cyrenaica.[39] It also occurs in Jewish epitaphs from elsewhere in Italy,[40] and Tertullian gives *archon* as well as *levites* and *sacerdos* as typical Jewish titles.[41] To judge by all other existing parallels (cf. especially Alexandria and Berenice), it may be taken for granted as true for the Roman communities that each had several *archontes* in office at any one time; there is however nothing to indicate their precise functions. From the frequently occurring title δὶς ἄρχων[42] one can see that the *archons* were appointed for a prescribed time, presumably a year. A late-Roman Christian homily records that Jewish *archontes* were elected in September, i.e. at the Jewish New Year: 'mensem Septembrem ipsum novum annum nuncupant, quo et mense magistratus sibi designant, quos Archontas vocant'.[43] Nevertheless, alongside appointment for a fixed period, election for life also appears to have occurred. At any rate it is probable that the frequently occurring enigmatic title διὰ βίου refers to lifelong *archons*.[44] From time to time an additional phrase is added to

among the Roman inscriptions (see p. 73 above). For further details see J. Juster, *Les Juifs dans l'empire romain* I (1914), pp. 443–7; CIJ I², pp. lxxxvii-ix; Leon, *op. cit.*, pp. 173–80.

39. Antioch in Syria: Jos. *B.J.* vii 3, 3 (47): ἦν γὰρ ἄρχων τῶν ἐπ' Ἀντιοχείας Ἰουδαίων; Tlos in Lycia, inscription (above, p. 33): ὑπὲρ ἀρχοντείας τελουμένας (*sic*) παρ' ἡμεῖν Ἰουδαίοις. Alexandria, see above, p. 93. Arsinoe in Middle Egypt (p. 55 above): ἀρχόντων Ἰουδαίων προσευχῆς Θηβαίων. Berenike in Cyrenaica: ἄρχοντες (pp. 94–5 above).

40. No. 553: *Alfius Iuda arcon arcosynagogus* (at Capua). For an *archon* (ארכון) at Dura-Europos in the third century A.D. see p. 11 above.

41. Tertullian, *De corona* 9, 1: 'Quis denique patriarches, quis prophetes, quis levites aut sacerdos aut archon, quis vel postea apostolus aut evangelizator aut episcopus invenitur coronatus?' The *archon* occurring in an inscription in Utica (CIL VIII, no. 1205, Addenda p. 931) may therefore be a Jewish *archon*; see Y. Bohec, Ant. Afric. 17 (1981), p. 189, no. 65.

42. No. 397: Σαββάτις δὶς ἄρχων. 289: Ἰάσων δὶς ἄρχων. 316: [Γα]υδέντις Κα[λκαρ]ήσων δὶς ἄρχων. 391: Πρώκουλος ὢ δὴς ἄρχων. 125: Μαρῶν β΄ ἄρχ(ων). 505: Καίλι⟨ο⟩ς Κυεῖντος.. β΄ ἄρχων. Note also nos. 15, 337, 384. It is noticeable that we have several examples of a single re-election but only one of a re-election repeated further (494: τρὶς ἄ[ρχ]ων). In the case of Roman *collegia* there occur: *magister iterum, ter, quater*. See Waltzing, *Étude historique sur les corp. profess.* I, p. 368; IV, p. 359.

43. The homily, on Luke's account of the birth of John the Baptist, is found in the older editions of the works of Chrysostom until that of Montfaucon, for example (according to Wesseling, *De Judaeorum archontibus*, ch. 10) in *Chrysostomi Opera* t. II, ed. Paris (1687); or in *Opp. Chrisostomi latine veris* (Paris, 1588), II, p. 1088. The passage is given as in Wesseling's version. See also DACL VII (1927), cols. 2173–4.

44. No. 416: Δατίβου τοῦ ζὰ (= διὰ) βίου ἀπὸ τῆς συναγωγῆς τῶν Αὐγουστησίων. 503: Ζώσιμος διὰ βίου συναγωγῆς Ἀγριππησίων. 398: Σαβεῖνος διὰ βίου Βερνακλησίων. 266: Ἀλια Πατρικια Τουλλιο Ειρηναιο κονιουγι βενεμερεντι φηκιτ δια βιο (Latin in Greek letters; it is highly uncertain whether this is a reference to an archonship). 561: 'Ti. Claudius Philippus dia viu et gerusiarches' (Puteoli). 480: 'Tettius Rufinus Melitius vixit annis LXXXV IA BI US (?)'. 575: Τάφος Ἄνα διὰ βίου. In the case of some of these inscriptions, especially where the formula διὰ βίου stands at the end, the explanation

archon, which signifies a higher honour.[45] No precise explanation can be offered for these, or for the titles *proarchon* (not certainly attested in a Jewish context) and *exarchon*.[46] There also occur additional phrases in honour of officials from distinguished families; the high status of such families may explain the occurrence of 'under-age *archon*' or 'future *archon*'.[47]

As in Palestine, so also in Rome and Italy, and indeed everywhere in the Diaspora, the office of *archisynagogos* is found.[48] The essential difference of this office from that of the *gerousiarches* and of the *archontes* has already been remarked (vol. II, pp. 435–6). The *archisynagogos* is not a kind of president of the community, but has the specific task of leading and supervising the congregation at divine service. He can of course be selected from among the *archontes* so that one and the same person was at the same time *archon* and *archisynagogos*; but in themselves

given is open to question. But in some cases (esp. nos. 398 and 561 above) this interpretation seems relatively certain. It is supported by the very common occurrence of διὰ βίου in this sense in Greek inscriptions: e.g. ἱερεὺς, ἀρχιερεὺς, ξυστάρχης or ἀγωνοθέτης διὰ βίου. In a non-Jewish cult association in Delos there occurs a συναγωγεὺς διὰ βίου, F. Durrbach, *Choix d'inscriptions de Délos* (1921), no. 162 = ID, no. 1641. Indeed we have two certain parallels from Jewish contexts: (1) a lifelong *archisynagogos* (inscription from Acmonia in Phrygia, see p. 31 above): Γ. Τυρρώνιος Κλάδος ὁ διὰ βίου συνάγωγος, and (2) a πατὴρ λαοῦ διὰ βίου from Mantinea, see p. 66 above. It remains uncertain whether we ought always to supply the word ἄρχων. The analogous title *magister perpetuus* (in an association of actors) is attested in CIL XIV, no. 2299 = ILS, no. 5206.

45. No. 470: 'L. Maecius archon <et>(?) alti ordinis' (for the sign before 'alti ordinis' which *may* signify 'et' see Leon, *op. cit.*, p. 176, n. 3). 324: Ἑρμογένης ἄρχων πάσης τιμῆς. 85: Ἀλέξανδρος ἄρχων πάσης τειμῆς. 265: 'Stafulo arconti et archisynagogo honoribus omnibus fu(n)ctus'.

46. No. 539: Μαρκιανε προάρχων. But see H. J. Leon, HThR 45 (1952), pp. 171–2, showing that there is no adequate reason to regard it as Jewish. 465: 'C. Furfanius Julianus exarchon'. 317: Γελάσις ἐξάρχων τῶν Ἑβρέων.

47. No. 88: Ἀννιανὸς ἄρχων [νή]πιος ... αἰτὼν η' Ἀννιανὸς ἄρχων [νή]πιος ... αἰτὼν η' (eight years old, and son of Iulianus, 'father of the synagogue of the Campesians'). 120: Ἰοκαθῖνος ἄρχων νήπιος. 85: Ἀλεξάνδρῳ μελλά⟨ρ⟩χοντι. 284: 'mellarcon eccion (read ἐκ τῶν) Augustesion an. XII' (twelve years old). 325: Ἐτήτος μελλά[ρ]χων. 402: Σίκουλος Σαβεῖνος μελλάρχων Βολουμνησίων ἐτῶν β' μηνῶν ι' (thus a child of two years!). There is an analogy in the occurrence of *decuriones* who are minors in the Roman municipalities; e.g. CIL V, no. 334 = ILS, no. 6679; IX, no. 1166; IX, no. 3573 = ILS, no. 2053; X, no. 846 = ILS, no. 6367; X, no. 1036 = ILS, no. 6365. See RE IV, cols. 2328–9.

48. In Rome: CIJ I², no. 504: Ἰουλιανοῦ ἀρχισυναγώγου. 265: 'Stafulo arconti et archisynagogo'. 336: Εὐφράσις ἀρχισυναγώγης (sic). 383: Πολύ[μ]νις ἀρχισυν⟨ά⟩γωγος (sic). In Capua: 553: 'Alfius Juda arcon arcosynagogus'. In Venosa: 587: τάφος Καλλίστου νιπίου ἀρχοσσιναγωγοῦ (sic). 596 (and prolegomenon, p. 45): τάφως Ασηλονονα ἀρχοσσηναγωγοῦ (sic). 584: τάφως Ἰοσὴφ ἀρχησυναγωγὼς υἱὸς Ἰωσὴφ ἀρχησυναγωγοῦ. In Brescia: 638: [ἀρ]χισυνάγωγο[ς]. For evidence on the occurrence of *archisynagogoi* in Egypt, Asia Minor, Greece and Africa see above, vol. II, pp. 435–6, and note Y. Bohec, Ant. Afric. 17 (1981), p. 178, no. 14 (Hammam Lif). Note also the recently published inscription of an *archisynagogus* from Ostia (p. 82 above). Cf. Juster, *op. cit.*, I, 450–3; CIJ I², pp. xcvii–ix; Leon, *op. cit.*, pp. 170–3. For Syria see p. 14 above.

the two offices are distinct, as the inscriptions clearly show. On the later usage of *archisynagogos* as (perhaps) a mere title for children still in infancy, and for women, see vol. II, p. 435. Note however that this presupposition is challenged by B. Brooten, *Women Leaders in the Ancient Synagogue* (1982). Besides the *archisynagogoi* a 'servant' (ὑπηρέτης) is mentioned once on a Roman epitaph.[49] Note also a *hazzan* and *diakon* from Apamea (p. 14), and persons concerned with psalm-singing, attested in Aphrodisias (p. 16) and Rome (p. 81). A 'scribe' or 'secretary' (*grammateus*) is attested at Smyrna (p. 20), as is the post of *phrontistes* ('superintendent'?) at Side (p. 33), as at Caesarea in Palestine (SEG XX, no. 462). Finally, the titles *pater synagogae* and *mater synagogae* are fairly frequent in the inscriptions.[50] The very fact that the last-named title occurs makes it possible that the position was a purely honorific one.[51] It was probably not identical with the role of *patronus* of the community,[52] but rather an honorary title for (elderly?) members

49. CIJ I², no. 172 : Φλάβιος Ἰουλιανὸς ὑπηρέτης. See Juster, *op. cit.*, I, p. 454 ; CIJ I², p. xcix.

50. Πατὴρ συναγωγῆς : CIJ I², nos. 88 ; 93 ; 319 ; 508 (πατὴρ συναγωγιῶν) ; 509–10 ; 537 (see prolegomenon, p. 40) ; AE 1969-70, no. 748 (Volubilis, Mauretania), see Y. Bohec, Ant. Afric. 17 (1981), p. 194, no. 79. *Pater synagogae*: CIL VIII, no. 8499, see Bohec, p. 192, no. 74; cf. *Cod. Theod.* XVI 8, 4 : 'Hiereos et archisynagogos et patres synagogarum et ceteros, qui synagogis deserviunt'. Note esp. the synagogue inscription from Stobi (p. 67 above), CIJ I², no. 694 (= Lifshitz, DF, no. 19) : ὁ πατὴρ τῆς ἐν Στόβοις συναγωγῆς. Note also CIJ II, no. 739: πατὴρ τοῦ στέμ(μ)ατος (Smyrna); 720 (= Lifshitz, DF, no. 9) : πατὴρ λαοῦ διὰ βίου, from Mantinea, see p. 66 above. *Pater* (without addition) : 271 ; 611–13 (Venosa). *Mater synagogae*: 523 : 'mater synagogarum Campi et Bolumni' (Rome) ; 639 : 'matri synagogae Brixianorum' ; 496 : [μή]τηρ συνα[γωγῆς]. Cf. Juster, *op. cit.*, I, pp. 448 ff. ; CIJ I², pp. xcv-vi ; Leon, *op. cit.*, pp. 186–8.

51. Such is probably the significance of the title πατὴρ συνόδου in inscriptions of a monotheistic (Jewish-influenced) cult-association in Tanais. See B. Latyschev, IOSPE II (1890), nos. 445, 451, 455 = V. V. Struve, CIRB (1965), nos. 1227; 1282; 1288. Cf. E. Ziebarth, *Das griechische Vereinswesen* (1896), p. 154; cf. C. Roberts, T. C. Skeat, A. D. Nock, 'The Guild of Zeus Hypsistos', HThR 29 (1936), pp. 39–88 = A. D. Nock, *Essays on Religion and the Ancient World* I (1972), pp. 414–43. A πατὴρ ὀργεωνικῆς συνόδου in Athens, Syll.³, no. 1111 = IG II-III², no. 2361. A προφήτης and πατὴρ τῆς .. τάξεως among the Παιανισταὶ τοῦ ἐν Ῥώμῃ Διὸς Ἡλίου μεγάλου Σαράπιδος, IG XIV, no. 1084 = IGR I, no. 144 = Moretti, IGUR I, no. 77. *Pater* is frequent in the Mithraic cult associations, both alone and in the combinations *pater sacrorum, pater patrum, pater et sacerdos, pater et antistes*, see the examples in F. Cumont, *Textes et monuments figurés relatifs aux mystères de Mithra* II (1896), Index p. 535.

52. As argued by Th. Mommsen, 'Der Religionsfrevel nach römischem Recht', HZ 64 (1890), pp. 389–429, on p. 428, in his comparison of the titles *pater collegi* and *mater collegi* in the professional and religious associations of the Romans (= *Ges. Schr.* III, p. 422). But *patronus* and *pater* should probably be distinguished (see Waltzing, *op. cit.* I, pp. 425 ff., 446 ff.). It is only the latter, not the former, which is comparable to the Jewish *pater*. On both titles see also E. Kornemann in RE IV, cols. 424 ff., 'collegium'. Examples of *pater* in Waltzing IV, pp. 372 f. ; for *patronus* and *patrona* : Waltzing IV, pp. 373–416.

who had deserved well of it.[53] For the patron the Greek term *prostates* also occurs.[54]

There is also evidence for the titular use of *presbyteros* among the Jews of the Diaspora. But the earliest clearly dated evidence is provided by the painted Aramaic and Greek inscriptions from the synagogue of Dura-Europos, from A.D. 244–5 (pp. 11–12 above), followed by imperial pronouncements from the fourth century onwards.[55] The inscriptions on which the title occurs all seem to be relatively late.[56] This does not of course prove that 'elders' as an institution did not exist; compare the *gerousia*, attested in Alexandrian and Roman communities, and note also the *presbyteroi* in the synagogue inscription of the first century A.D. from Jerusalem, CIJ II, no. 1404. But such a council of 'elders' cannot be regarded as identical with *presbyteroi* as officials. The attested officials from the earlier period are called everywhere in the Diaspora—as far as our knowledge goes—*archontes* (see pp. 98–100). It is also open to question whether *presbyteros* in the inscriptions is everywhere meant as a title, and not on occasion simply as a designation of age.[57]

53. Cf. the indications of age in CIJ I², no. 509: Παγχάριος πατὴρ συναγωγῆς Ἐλαίας ἐτῶν ἑκατῶν (sic) δέκα. 523: 'Beturia Paulina ... quae bixit an. LXXXVI meses VI ... mater synagogarum Campi et Bolumni'.

54. CIJ I², no. 100 (and prolegomenon, p. 28); 365; cf. pp. xciv-v. For a female *prostates* from Aphrodisias in Caria, mother of an *archon*, see p. 25 above. For the same title in Greek cult associations see P. Foucart, *Des associations religieuses chez les Grecs* (1873), p. 28. Much material in E. Ziebarth, *Das griechische Vereinswesen* (1896), Index, s.v.; F. Poland, *Geschichte des griechischen Vereinswesens* (1909), pp. 363–6.

55. *Cod. Theod.* xvi 8, 2 (A.D. 330): 'qui devotione tota synagogis Iudaeorum, patriarchis vel presbyteris se dederunt'; xvi 8, 13 (A.D. 397): 'archisynagogi sive presbyteri Judaeorum', *Cod. Just.* i 9, 15 (415): 'Si qua inter Christianos et Iudaeos sit contentio, non a senioribus Iudaeorum, sed ab ordinariis iudicibus dirimatur'; *Novell.* 146.1: οἱ παρ' αὐτοῖς ἀρχιφερεκῖται ἢ πρεσβύτεροι τυχὸν ἢ διδάσκαλοι προσαγορευόμενοι.

56. Inscriptions from Apamea in Syria, A.D. 391 (p. 14); a *presbyteros* from the Yemen attested at Beth Shēarim (p. 16); Smyrna (CIJ II, no. 739); Corycus in Cilicia (p. 34); Bithynia (p. 36); Joppa (epitaph of a Cappadocian, p. 35); Rome and Elche in Spain (p. 84). Attested for women at Bizye in Thrace (CIJ I², no. 692, see p. 72 above). Venosa, see CIJ I², nos. 581, 590, 597; cf. also no. 595, which gives the Greek text in Hebrew as well as in Greek script: πρεσβυτέρου- פרסוביטרו. The title does not seem to be attested as the name of an office in pagan cult associations, but it is with the monotheistic (Judaising) cult-association at Tanais at the beginning of the third century A.D. (Latyschev, IOSPE II, nos. 450, 452, 456 = V. V. Struve, CIRB, nos. 1285, 1283, 1286). On *presbyteroi* in the context of the Greek cities, A. Deissmann, *Bibelstudien* (1895), pp. 153–5; I. Lévy, REG 8 (1895), pp. 231, 240; J. H. Oliver, *The Sacred Gerusia* (1941), esp. p. 41. For a collection of references see F. E. Poland, *Geschichte des griechischen Vereinswesens* (1909), pp. 98–102.

57. Clermont-Ganneau took *presbyteros* in the epitaph of a Cappadocian in Joppa (see p. 35 above), for example, as referring to age (*Rec. d'arch. or.* IV, pp. 146 ff.); cf. two Palestinian inscriptions published by him in *Arch. des miss. sc.* II (1885): p. 206, no. 28, Τρύφωνος πρεσβυτέρου and p. 208, no. 32: βερουταρίου νεωτέρας. Note the Πλῆνις νεώτερος in A. Deissmann, *Licht vom Osten* (⁴1923), p. 78; ET *Light from the Ancient East* (1910), p. 98; and the catacomb inscription from Rome CIJ I², no. 400: Σάρα Οὐρ⟨σα⟩

The use of the expressions *archontes* and *gerousia* suggests that the Jewish organisation in the Diaspora tended to imitate the communal structure of the Greek cities.[58] The extent ofin which this example generally influenced the social structure of Jewish communities is also indicated by other evidence.

Note first the *Ioudaioi neoteroi* who are attested once, on an inscription from Hypaepa (see above p. 22). In the Greek communities the young men of the city (*neoi* or *neoteroi*) formed an association, chiefly for the purpose of gymnastic exercises. Related to these are the Latin *collegia iuvenum*.[59] The *Ioudaioi neoteroi* appear to have been a similar association of Jews, even if not formed for the same purpose.

In the Greek cities it was customary to honour benefactors by the bestowal of a wreath and sometimes of precedence (*proedria*) in the theatre and at the games.[60] This practice was taken over not only by Greek and Roman,[61] but also by Hellenized, or semi-Hellenized oriental associations, for example those of Tyrians and Egyptians in Delos, or Sidonians in Athens (see p. 109 below) and also those of the Jews themselves. In this connection we may also note the new inscription from Delos which records that the 'Israelites who pay first fruits to sacred Gerizim' (Samaritans) there voted to award a crown to someone in return for his benefactions (p. 71 above). The community of

---

πρεσβύτ⟨η⟩s, which is certainly to be understood as reference to her age, like νήπιος or παρθένος.

58. Compare the influence of city organisation on the structure of Greek and Roman *collegia* and associations, for which see E. Ziebarth, *Das griechische Vereinswesen*, pp. 133 ff.; 147 ff. and elsewhere. E. Kornemann in RE IV, cols. 418 ff.

59. Cf. L. M. Collignon, 'Les collèges de "Néoi" dans les cités grecques', Ann. Fac. lett. Bordeaux 2 (1880), pp. 135–51 (pp. 136 ff. gives a table of the inscriptions then known); Ziebarth, *Das griechische Vereinswesen* (1896), pp. 111–15; E. Kornemann in RE IV, col. 390; V. Chapot, *La province romaine proconsulaire d'Asie* (1904), pp. 153–8; Demoulin, 'Les collegia juvenum dans l'Empire romain', Le Musée Belge 1 (1897), pp. 114–36; 200–17; 3 (1899), pp. 177–92; material also in Dittenberger, *Syll.³*, Index p. 455, and for the Latin *collegia iuvenum* in Waltzing, *op. cit.* IV, pp. 216–22. M. Rostowzew, *Römische Bleitesserae* (1904), pp. 81 ff.; RE X, cols. 1357–8 s.v. 'Iuvenes'; C. A. Forbes, *Neoi* (1933); M. Della Corte, *Iuventus* (1934), A. H. M. Jones, *The Greek City* (1940), p. 225 and n. 30. Note esp. two inscriptions from Pergamum: (1) *Ins. v. Pergamon*, no. 274 = *Syll.³*, no. 831, a letter of Hadrian addressed to the *synodos* of the *neoi* in Pergamum. (2) no. 278: the gymnasium of the *neoi*; further the *corpus quod appellatur neon* in Cyzicus, CIL III, no. 7060 = ILS, no. 7190. *Epheboi* and *neoi* or *neoteroi* are frequently mentioned together, e.g. at Phintia in Sicily, IG XIV, no. 256.

60. S. Schmitthenner, *De coronarum apud Athenienses honoribus, Quaestiones epigraphicae* (Diss. Berlin, 1891); A. Dittmar, 'De Atheniensium more exteros coronis publice ornandi', Leipziger Studien zur class. Philol. 13 (1891), pp. 63–248. See in general K. Baus, *Der Kranz in Antike und Christentum* (1940); M. Blech, *Studien zum Kranz bei den Griechen* (1982). For *proedria* see Dittenberger, *Syll.³*, index s.v.; M. Bieber, *History of the Greek and Roman Theatre* (1961), pp. 63; 70–1; 114–15; 123, and Figs. 267–9.

61. See Ziebarth, *Das griechische Vereinswesen*, pp. 164 f.; Waltzing, *op. cit.* I, pp. 493 ff.; Poland, *op. cit.*, pp. 426 ff.

Phocaea honoured a woman, who had paid for the building of the synagogue from her own resources, with a gold wreath (χρυσῷ στεφάνῳ) and precedence (προεδρίᾳ), see above, p. 19; *proedria* here presumably means the right to sit in front at the synagogue. The community in Berenice passed a resolution to crown στεφανοῦν ὀνομαστὶ καθ' ἑκάστην σύνοδον καὶ νουμηνίαν στεφάνῳ ἐλαΐνῳ καὶ λημνίσκῳ—a Roman official in the province who had shown himself friendly to the Jews. This resolution was to be inscribed on a marble *stele* and set up in the most prominent part of the amphitheatre (see above, p. 61 for this and a second inscription with the same formula). Setting up an inscription in the amphitheatre does not seem to have been a usual custom for Jews; hence it has been suggested that the reference might be to a Jewish meeting-place of amphitheatral shape; see L. Robert, *Les gladiateurs dans l'Orient grec* (1940), p. 34, n. 1. But this has no clear parallels, and the reference must be presumed to be to the city amphitheatre. More often such honorific decrees were probably set up in the forecourts of synagogues; for Philo says that at the destruction of the Jewish *proseuchai* (synagogues) in Alexandria even the shields and golden wreaths and *stelai* and inscriptions erected in honour of the emperors had been destroyed along with them.[62] On another occasion he remarks that through the destruction of the *proseuchai* of the Jews the absence of sacred precincts rendered impossible the pious expressions of gratitude due to benefactors. The honorific dedications were, then, set up in the περίβολοι of the synagogues, that is in the open forecourts.[63]

Just as cities dedicated temples and other buildings 'for the salvation' (*soteria*) of kings and emperors, so also Jewish communities erected synagogues 'on behalf of' the king. We have two examples of this kind from the Ptolemaic period. Under Ptolemy III Euergetes (246–221 B.C.) the Jews erected a synagogue in Schedia in Alexandria 'on behalf of King Ptolemy and Queen Berenike ...' (p. 47) as in the same reign did those of Arsinoe-Crocodilopolis (p. 52). Under a later Ptolemy, probably Ptolemy VI Philometor, the Jews in Athribis in the southern Delta built their synagogue 'on behalf of King Ptolemy and Queen Kleopatra' (two inscriptions, see above, p. 49). A specially remarkable instance is the building at Casiun (Qasyun or Qatsyon) in northern Galilee from the second century A.D. In the ruins of this building

---

62. Philo, *Leg.* 20 (133): καὶ σιωπῶ τὰς συγκαθαιρεθείσας καὶ συμπρησθείσας τῶν αὐτοκρατόρων τιμὰς ἀσπίδων καὶ στεφάνων ἐπιχρύσων καὶ στηλῶν καὶ ἐπιγραφῶν.

63. Philo, *In Flacc.* 7 (48); the open-air courtyard (τὸν περίβολον τοῦ ὑπαίθρου) next to the synagogue building (*oikos*) is mentioned also by the inscription from Phocaea (see above, p. 19, and L. Robert, *Rev. Phil.* 32 (1958), pp. 45–7, mentioning also the courtyard (μέσαυλος) with a fountain attested at Side, p. 33 above). Cf. the large forecourt of the synagogue at Sardis, p. 21 above. Public inscriptions were put up also in the forecourt of the temple at Jerusalem, see 1 Mac. 11, 37; 14, 27 and 48; indeed even booty in the form of weapons was placed there, Jos. *Ant.* XV 11.3 (402).

Renan found the following inscription: ὑπὲρ σωτηρίας τῶν κ[υρί]ων ἡμῶν αὐτοκρατόρω[ν] (Septimius Severus, Caracalla and Geta) ..[προσ?]ευχῆς 'Ιουδαίων. The building may or may not be a synagogue.[64] The structure was built therefore 'on behalf of' the emperor Septimius Severus and his sons Caracalla and Geta. We may compare the synagogue-inscription from Ostia, beginning 'Pro salute Aug(usti)' (AE 1967, no. 77, see p. 82 above).

Influence from Greek legal forms connected with slave manumission is attested by the inscriptions from Panticapaeum (see above, pp. 36 ff.). The manumission takes place ἐπὶ τῆς προσευχῆς, 'in the synagogue' (presumably before the congregation).[65] Complete freedom is granted to the slave, but with one proviso, χωρὶς εἰς τὴν προσευχὴν θωπείας τε καὶ προσκαρτερήσεως, 'apart from respect towards the synagogue and regular attendance'.[66] Thus the manumitted slave is to remain under this obligation. A partial parallel to this manumission at the cult centre, with a specific obligation towards it, that is towards the deity, is provided by the well-attested form of manumission in ancient Greece which consisted either of the dedication of a slave to a god or of a fictitious sale to a god. The act is performed in the temple in accordance with a formula by which the owner, in most cases, sells the slave to the deity (and usually the slave himself has to contribute the purchase price). In reality however the purchased man does not now become a temple slave. He is made the property of the deity only in a formal sense and is actually free, though often subject to the obligation to remain with his former owner for a specified period.[67] Different as the pagan and Jewish forms are, the connexion is unmistakeable. See p. 65 above not only for the manumission of two Jewish female slaves at Delphi, but for a manumission by a Jew of the third century

64. E. Renan, *Mission de Phénicie*, pp. 774–6; IGR III, no. 1106; CIJ II, no. 972. For the archaeological evidence see F. Hüttenmeister, G. Reeg, *Die antiken Synagogen in Israel* I (1977), pp. 359–62.

65. CIRB, nos. 70–1; 73.

66. Προσκαρτερεῖν occurs also in the New Testament in a similar sense: Ac. 1:14; 2:42, 46; 6:4; Rom. 12:12; 13:6; Col. 4:2. The noun προσκαρτέρησις occurs in Eph. 6:18. On the inscriptions of Panticapaeum only sincere and constant zeal for the synagogue, i.e. regular attendance, can be meant.

67. See L. Mitteis, *Reichsrecht und Volksrecht in den östlichen Provinzen des römischen Kaiserreichs* (1891), pp. 374 ff. (referring also to the Christian *manumissio in ecclesia*, Cod. Theod. iv 7; Cod. Just. i 13, etc.). A selection of the inscriptions relating to this form of manumission is given in *Recueil des inscriptions juridiques grecques* by R. Dareste, B. Haussoullier and T. Reinach II.2–3 (1904), pp. 233–318 (p. 233 gives further references). See e.g. M. Bloch, *Die Freilassungsbedingungen der delphischen Freilassungsinschriften* (1914); R. Daux, *Delphes au IIᵉ et au Iᵉ siècles* (1936), pp. 46 ff.; W. L. Westermann, 'The Paramone as General Service Contract', JJP 2 (1948), pp. 3–50. For the clause indicating consent by heirs or relatives see W. L. Westermann, 'Extinction of Claims in Slave Sales at Delphi', JJP 4 (1950), pp. 49–61. Cf. also F. Pringsheim, *The Greek Law of Sale* (1950), pp. 184 ff.

B.C., carried out at the shrine of Amphiaraos at Oropos in Boeotia.
Especially if the Panticapaeum documents are held to imply an
obligatory conversion of the freed slave to Judaism at the moment of
manumission, this would provide a close parallel to the pagan form of
sale to a deity. An interesting intermediate case is the dedication to
Theos Hypsistos from Gorgippia (CIRB, no. 1123, cf. nos. 1124–8, see
p. 37 above), where it is stated of the owner that he has dedicated a
slave-woman to the *proseuche*. The Greek influence in the documents
from Panticapaeum also appears unmistakeably in the clause declaring
that the heirs also have given their assent (cf. n. 67).

Another parallel to motifs found on pagan Greek inscriptions is
provided by the Jewish epitaphs from Smyrna, Hierapolis, Tlos in
Lycia and Corycus in Cilicia (see above, pp. 19 ff.). They threaten the
unauthorized user of the grave with a fine which is payable in part to a
city or Imperial treasury, in part to the Jewish community. According
to the inscription from Smyrna (p. 20) the guilty party is obliged to
pay to the imperial treasury 1500 *denarii* and to the '*ethnos* of the
Ioudaioi' 1000 *denarii*. The inscription from Hierapolis (p. 27)
stipulates only those fines which are to be paid to the Jewish
community, the *laos* of the *Ioudaioi* or the *katoikia* of the *Ioudaioi* living in
Hierapolis; at the same time the second inscription from Hierapolis
orders a further compensation in favour of the informer. The inscription
from Tlos (p. 33) breaks off at the point where it is stated that a fine is
to be paid to the *demos* of the Tloans, therefore to the city treasury.
Thus we cannot say whether a further stipulation of a fine in favour of
the Jewish community treasury followed. According to the inscription
from Corycus in Cilicia (p. 34) damage to the grave is punished by a
fine of 2500 *denarii*, which is to be paid to the Imperial treasury.
Inscriptions of this kind are numerous everywhere in Asia Minor.[68]

As a parallel to Greek and Roman customs we must mention lastly

---

68. See G. Hirschfeld, 'Über die griechischen Grabinschriften, welche Geldstrafen
anordnen', Königsberger Studien 1 (1887), pp. 83–144; A. Merkel, 'Über die
sogenannten Sepulcralmulten', *Festgabe der Göttinger Juristenfakultät für Rud. von Jhering*
(1892), pp. 79–134; E. Rohde, *Psyche* II (²1898), pp. 340–4; Th. Mommsen, *Römisches
Strafrecht* (1899), pp. 812 ff.; W. Liebenam, *Städteverwaltung im römischen Kaiserreiche* (1900),
pp. 37–54. For further examples see IGR, index s.v. *multae sepulchrales* and FIRA² III, pp.
257 ff. See G. Wesenberg, *Verträge zugunsten Dritter* (1949), pp. 79 ff. Cf. a somewhat
different kind from the above inscriptions is that from Apamea which does not state a
fixed penalty but in an entirely general way refers any disturber of the grave to the known
law of the Jews: τὸν νόμον οἶδεν τῶν Εἰουδέων, see above, p. 28); but there are pagan
parallels also for this (Merkel, pp. 113–15). On Christian epitaphs in Phrygia the usual
formula is ἔσται αὐτῷ πρὸς τὸν Θεόν. But the threat of a fine also occurs, see W. Ramsay,
Cities and Bishoprics of Phrygia I.1–2 (1895–7), pp. 514–68, 717 ff. See L. Robert, *Hellenica*
XI–XII (1960), pp. 399–406; E. Gibson, 'A Unique Christian Epitaph from the Upper
Tembris Valley', BASP 12 (1975), pp. 151–7; T. Drew-Bear, *Nouvelles inscriptions de
Phrygie* (1978), pp. 106 ff., nos. 44, nos. 44–8.

also the bestowal of titles and offices on women. There are many examples of women receiving the title and office of *prytanis, stephanephoros gymnasiarchos, agonothetes,* or *dekaprotos.*[69] In Latin inscriptions there occurs the title *mater collegi.*[70] Indeed women are found as actual officials of associations.[71] These parallels are certainly relevant to use of titles *archisynagogos* (above, p. 101), '*presbytera* and *archisynagogissa*' (p. 72), *presbeteresa* (p. 63) and *mater synagoguae* (p. 101) among Jews.[72]

In other cases where there are clear parallels, it is not certain which of the two sides may claim the priority. In pagan cult associations there occurs from time to time the designation *proseuche* applied to a building for divine worship, and officials with the titles *synagogos* and *archisynagogos* (see vol. II, pp. 429–31; 436). But the evidence for this is so isolated and moreover so late that the possibility of borrowing from Judaism cannot be excluded.

The influence of pagan models on the structure of Jewish Diaspora communities should not be over-emphasized, in spite of what has just been said. It concerns almost exclusively external features; certainly the idea of the acceptance of Greek or Roman law on the part of the Jewish communities, to any significant extent, is to be rejected. On the contrary, the independent organization of the communities had as its specific object that not only Jewish worship but also Jewish law should be applied among Jews everywhere. As far as the authorities allowed it (and we shall see that this was to a great extent the case) the Jews enjoyed even in the Diaspora their own courts which functioned 'according to the ancestral laws', see Jos. *Ant.* xiv 10, 17 (235).

2. *Constitutional Position of the Communities*

Within the framework of the Graeco-Roman world the Jewish communities were not a wholly unique phenomenon. Overseas settlement and trade had been practised even in remote antiquity by Near Eastern peoples, above all by the Phoenicians, who were attracted to the west not only for fleeting journeys but for lasting settlement. The form of settlement varied however according to the level of culture in the western peoples. As long as the Phoenicians still appeared as the bearers of a dominant culture, they founded their own cities, which

---

69. See e.g. V. Chapot, *La province romaine proconsulaire d'Asie* (1904), pp. 158–63; R. MacMullen, 'Women in Public in the Roman Empire', Historia 29 (1980), pp. 208–18; R. van Bremen, 'Women and Wealth', in A. Cameron and A. Kuhrt (eds.), *Images of Women in Antiquity* (1983), pp. 223–42.

70. *ILS* III, index, p. 723. Cf. Waltzing, *op. cit.* IV, pp. 369 f.

71. CIL VI, no. 8639, or X, no. 6637 (list of the four annual officials of an association, among whom several women appear). Further material in Waltzing, *op. cit.* IV, p. 255.

72. See now the detailed study by B. Brooten, *Women Leaders in the Ancient Synagogue* (Brown Judaic Studies XXXVI, 1982).

functioned as permanent settlements from which agriculture, trade and military operations were conducted. This happened especially in the western half of the Mediterranean, in North Africa and Spain.[1] Later, and above all in places where a developed culture was already present, the easterners could settle only as aliens (non-citizens) within the political framework of the Graeco-Roman world. But even under these conditions they formed distinct units which fostered not only the material but also the spiritual interests of the group, above all in maintaining the form of worship of the homeland. The language of the homeland too they retained for a relatively long time.[2] Besides the Phoenicians it was particularly Egyptians who in the Greek and Roman period emigrated to all the chief centres of the Mediterranean Sea and formed communal organisations there. Thus, just as there were Jewish Diaspora communities, so there were also Phoenician, Egyptian, etc. Some illustrative evidence for this is as follows:[3]

1. In Delos an inscription of 154-3 B.C. attests a κοινὸν τῶν Τυρίων Ἡρακλεϊστῶν ἐμπόρων καὶ ναυκλήρων which held regular assemblies (*synodoi*) for worship, and also dealt with other concerns of the *koinon*.[4] Earlier connections of Tyrians with Delos are illustrated by a bilingual inscription (in Greek and Phoenician, fourth century B.C.) according to which traders from Tyre dedicated to Apollo in Delos statues symbolising the cities of Tyre and Sidon.[5] In the same way there was in Delos a *koinon* of traders and shippers from Berytus who worshipped Poseidon.[6] Another inscription, whose opening is lost, records the honours voted by a *synodos* to two of its benefactors. From the reference to the Egyptian month Mecheir it appears that this is an association of Egyptians settled in Delos.[7]

1. For this see the works cited in vol. II, p. 60, n. 183, and also C. R. Whittaker, 'The Western Phoenicians: colonisation and assimilation', PCPhS 200 (1974), pp. 58–79; H. G. Niemeyer (ed.), *Phönizier im Westen* (1982).

2. The Phoenician and Punic inscriptions published in CIS I extend beyond the time of Alexander the Great. Apart from those found in Phoenicia itself (nos. 1–9) they divide into the following regions: Cyprus (nos. 10–96); Egypt (nos. 97–113); Delos (no. 114); Athens (nos. 115–121); Malta and Gozo (nos. 122–132); Sicily (nos. 133–138); Sardinia (nos. 139–163); Praeneste in Italy (no. 164); Marseilles (no. 165); Carthage (nos. 166 ff.); see further KAI, nos. 30–173; M. G. Guzzo Amadasi, *Le iscrizioni fenicie e puniche delle colonie in Occidente* (1967), and cf. F. Millar, 'The Phoenician Cities: A Case-Study of Hellenisation', PCPhS 209 (1983), pp. 55–71.

3. Cf. also the collections made by W. Liebenam, *Zur Geschichte und Organisation des römischen Vereinswesens* (1890), pp. 89–97; E. Ziebarth, *Das griechische Vereinswesen* (1896), pp. 26–33, 121–3.

4. ID, no. 1519. See Ph. Bruneau, *Recherches sur les cultes de Délos à l'époque hellénistique et à l'époque impériale* (1970), p. 622.

5. CIS I, no. 114; ID, no. 50.

6. OGIS, no. 591; ID, nos. 1520; 1772–96; 2323–7; 2611. See esp. Bruneau, *op. cit.*, pp. 622–30.

7. P. Roussel, *Les cultes égyptiens à Délos* (1915–16), p. 204, no. 216; ID, no. 1521.

2. In Athens there lived aliens from all regions of the civilized world. In the standard collection the number of the epitaphs of aliens found there, dating to the period from the fourth century B.C. to the Roman empire, comes to 2649, which admittedly includes people from other Greek cities; but a very high proportion is furnished by people from Asia Minor and the Levant.[8] Here too the Phoenicians and Egyptians were organized in independent corporations, which were allowed to build temples in the Piraeus (not in the city). The most important evidence for the community of Sidonians is a Phoenician inscription which was discovered in the Piraeus in 1887.[9] It is dated from the fifteenth year of the Sidonians. If this is the Sidonian era known from other evidence, which began in 111 B.C., the inscription would belong to the year 96 B.C.; but according to the letter-forms of the Greek text it is certainly considerably older, and most probably dates to the mid-third century B.C. The Phoenician text records that the community of Sidonians has bestowed the honour of a golden crown upon a certain Samabaal, son of Magon, who as a communal official had built the forecourt of the temple of the god Baal-Sidon. The Greek text runs: 'The *koinon* of the Sidonians (honours) Diopeithes the Sidonian' (Diopeithes is the approximate Greek rendering of Samabaal). The Sidonians in Athens were, then, at that time organized as an association, and had their own temple in the Piraeus. Epitaphs of Sidonians have been found in considerable numbers in Athens. The earliest are bilingual and come from the fourth to third century B.C.[10] The relations of Sidon with Athens are shown by an Athenian decree honouring King Straton of Sidon, about 367 B.C.;[11]

8. IG II-III, nos. 7882–10530. We find here e.g. Antiochenes, Ascalonians, Berytians, Gadarenes, Kitieis and Salaminioi (both from Cyprus), Samaritans, Sidonians, Syrians, Tyrians. On the corporations of aliens in Athens see C. Wachsmuth, *Die Stadt Athen im Alterthum* II.1 (1890), pp. 151–64.

9. See G. A. Cooke, *Textbook of North Semitic Inscriptions* (1903), no. 33; KAI, no. 60; J. C. L. Gibson, *Textbook of Syrian Semitic Inscriptions* III: *Phoenician Inscriptions* (1982), no. 41. See F. Millar, *op. cit.* (n. 2 above), p. 61; J. Teixidor, 'L'assemblée législative en Phénicie d'après les inscriptions', Syria 57 (1980), pp. 453–64.

10. Note esp. the bilingual inscriptions of the fourth century B.C., CIS I, no. 116 = IG II-III², no. 10270 = KAI, no. 53 = Gibson, *op. cit.*, no. 40, and, from the third century, CIS I, no. 119 = IG II-III², no. 10271 = Cooke, *op. cit.*, no. 35. A Sidonian also erected a tombstone for an Ascalonite named Antipater in Athens, Cooke, *op. cit.*, no. 32 = IG II-III², no. 8788; cf. vol. II, p. 108, n. 115. Cf. for the Phoenician inscriptions in Athens and Piraeus in general, CIS I, nos. 115–21. For Greek epitaphs of Sidonians see IG II-III², nos. 10265a–06.

11. SIG³, no. 185 = IG II-III², no. 141 = M. N. Tod, *Greek Historical Inscriptions* II (1948), no. 139. See R. A. Moysey, 'The Date of the Strato of Sidon Decree (IG II², 141)', AJAH 1 (1976), pp. 182–9. By the decree King Strato of Sidon was granted *proxenia*; at the same time *symbola* were agreed upon by which Sidonian ambassadors to Athens and Athenian ambassadors to Sidon could establish their identity. In a rider it was decreed that Sidonians who had citizenship status in Sidon and visited Athens only

by the inscription on the base of a statue which was set up in Athens to Philocles 'King of the Sidonians' (about 300–280 B.C.),[12] and also by other incidental mentions of Sidonians in Athens.[13] Like the Sidonians, the merchants from Kition (in Cyprus) formed their own association. As early as 333 B.C. the Kitian merchants were allowed by a decree of the Athenians to build a temple to Aphrodite in the Piraeus.[14] Evidence for the existence of their community is afforded also by a votive inscription to Aphrodite Urania by a woman from Kition, as also by several epitaphs, of which two, Greek-Phoenician bilinguals, belong to the third century B.C., and a fragment perhaps to the fifth.[15] From a fragmentary inscription found in the Piraeus it can be seen that the Salaminioi (from Salamis in Cyprus) also maintained the cult of Aphrodite and Adonis in the same place. It seems that they too formed their own association.[16] Further, even before the Phoenicians, the Egyptians had obtained permission for the building of a temple of Isis in the Piraeus, as is shown by the decree of 333 B.C. in favour of the Kitians (above). This suggests that the Sidonians did not build their temple of Baal-Sidon until after 333 B.C.

3. In Italy, Puteoli was the main port for trade with the east and so also an important site for eastern communities.[17] A fragmentary inscription from the year A.D. 79 concerns the transfer of a deity, 'the

---

for the sake of trade should not be liable to the tax imposed on *metoikoi* or to other burdens.

12. IG II-III², no. 3425 = L. Moretti, *Iscrizioni storiche ellenistiche* I (1967), no. 17. For the complex and controversial evidence on his career see *Prosopographia Ptolemaica* VI (1968), no. 15085, and J. Seibert, 'Philokles, Sohn der Apollodoros, König der Sidonier', *Historia* 19 (1970), pp. 337–51.

13. IG II-III², nos. 343, 960, 1043, 2314, 2216. In a list of offerings from the second half of the fourth century B.C. there occurs a [ζωίδι?]ον ἐ[λεφ]άντιν[ον .. γράμματ]α φοινικικὰ ἔχο[ν], perhaps a votive gift offered by Phoenicians, IG II-III², no. 1456. The restoration γράμματα suggests itself from a similar inscription, no. 1485.

14. P. Foucart, *Des associations religieuses chez les Grecs* (1873), pp. 187–9; IG II-III², no. 337; Tod, *op. cit.*, no. 189. The cult of (the Phoenician) Aphrodite was served also by the *thiasotai* of Aphrodite, three of whose decrees are preserved on an inscription in the Piraeus from the years 302, 301 and 300 B.C., P. Foucart, BCH 3 (1879), p. 510, no. 726 = IG II-III², no. 1261 = SIG³, no. 1098. The formation of this *thiasos* is certainly closely connected with the settlement of the Phoenicians; but it would be incorrect to identify it with the community of the Kitieis.

15. The votive inscription is IG II-III², no. 4636. The epitaphs: IG II-III², nos. 9031–6. The bilingual ones are: no. 9034 = CIS I, no. 117 = KAI, no. 55, and no. 9035 = KAI, no. 57. The fragmentary 9031, with three surviving Phoenician letters, is thought to be of the fifth or fourth century.

16. II-III², no. 1290. For epitaphs of Salaminians in Athens see IG II-III², nos. 10216 and 10217-18.

17. See C. Dubois, 'Cultes et dieux à Pouzzoles', MEFR 22 (1902), pp. 23–68; *idem*, *Pouzzoles antique: histoire et topographie* (1907), pp. 83–110; RE s.v. 'Puteoli', XXIII.2 (1959), esp. cols. 2052–3.

holy god of Sarepta', from Tyre to Puteoli.[18] An extensive inscription of the year A.D. 174 contains a letter of the Tyrians settled in Puteoli to their home-town, in which the association, much reduced compared with formerly, begs for a subvention from the home-town for the maintenance of their ancestral worship.[19] On an inscription of the year A.D. 116 are mentioned *cultores Iovis Heliopolitani Berytenses qui Puteolis consistunt*, evidently a community of Berytians in Puteoli.[20]

Apart from associations of merchants and others from foreign countries there were within the boundaries of the Greek and Roman world also religious associations of local people. Like the Jews the easterners who had come to the west made propaganda for their beliefs among Greeks and Romans, sometimes with great success. From the earliest times Greek religion had of course been affected by influences from the east;[21] in the Hellenistic period cults originating in the Near East are attested with increasing frequency on inscriptions. The cults of Egyptian deities penetrated even to Rome in the last years of the republic; in the imperial period cults of Syrian and Persian origin followed, particularly that of Mithras (for details see pp. 155–8 below). These foreign cults were not as a rule maintained by the cities or the Roman state as the old indigenous cults were. It was an exception if a Greek city or Rome formally introduced a new cult. Such cults were normally observed by private associations which might be permitted by the city or state but which in their internal organization were independent, and therefore relied for finance on the contributions of their members. In Greece these associations are encountered from the fourth century B.C. under the names *thiasoi* or *eranoi*, which in spite of considerable diversity collectively manifest certain common characteristics.[22] In Rome there were *collegia* from ancient times for

18. IGR I, no. 420 = OGIS, no. 594, with restorations by C. C. Torrey, 'The Exiled God of Sarepta', Berytus 9 (1948–9), pp. 45–9. The inscription is dated A.D. 79. The text runs : κατέπλευσεν ἀ[πὸ] Τύρου εἰς Ποτι[ό]λοις (sic) θεὸς [ἅγ]ιος [Σ]αρεπτηνό[ς], ἤγαγεν [ἴς?] ἠλείμ κατ᾽ ἐπιτο[λὴν]. On this interpretation, dependent on a dedication published by Torrey, θεῷ ἁγίῳ Σαραπτηνῷ, ἴς = שׂרפת is supplied and the phrase is taken to mean 'a man of the Elim' (Phoenician priests).

19. IG XII, no. 830; IGR I, no. 421; OGIS, no. 595.

20. CIL x, no. 1634 = ILS, no. 300. In shorter form : *corpus Heliopolitanorum, ibid.*, no. 1579 = *ILS*, no. 4291. On Jupiter of Heliopolis see e.g. H. Drexler, s.v. 'Heliopolitanus' in Roscher's *Lex. der griech. und röm. Mythologie* I, cols. 1987–93 ; A. B. Cook, *Zeus* I (1914), pp. 549–76; III (1940), pp. 1093–5; IGLS VI (1967), p. 38; Y. Hajjar, *La triade d'Héliopolis-Baulbek* I-II (1977; ET, 1985).

21. Note the standard work by W. Burkert, *Griechische Religion der archaischen und klassischen Epoche* (1977).

22. For religious associations in Greece cf.: P. Foucart, *Des associations religieuses chez les Grecs, thiases, éranes, orgéons, avec le texte des inscriptions relatives à ces associations* (1873); E. Ziebarth, *Das griechische Vereinswesen* (1896); F. Poland, *Geschichte des griechischen Vereinswesens* (1909); M. P. Nilsson, *Geschichte der griechischen Religion* II[2] (1961), pp.

very varied purposes, especially unions of craftsmen for the purpose of mutual support, sometimes also to ensure decent burial for the members of the *collegium* (*collegia tenuiorum, collegia funeraticia*). These craft associations also maintained a common cult. There were however also associations for strictly religious purposes. All these associations enjoyed official toleration in Rome, only political clubs being forbidden from the time of Caesar and Augustus.[23]

A third parallel to the Jewish Diaspora communities is afforded, finally, by the corporations of Greeks and Romans in non-Greek or non-Roman countries. Given the wide diffusion of Hellenism, however, Greeks had little incentive for the formation of such corporations. But as a possible example the evidence from Tanais (on the NE point of the Palus Maeotis-Sea of Azov) may be mentioned. Here we find on the one hand both *archontes* of the people of Tanais and a *Hellenarches*. The nature of this distinction however remains unclear.[24] Associations of immigrant Romans are much more frequently attested. As the dominant power, the Romans outside Italy everywhere claimed a special position. They normally submitted neither to taxation by the cities nor to the jurisdiction of the city authorities; rather they formed independent bodies within or alongside the communities in which they lived. Examples of this are attested in great numbers for large parts of the Roman empire.[25]

117–19 (associations); 119–31 (foreign cults); pp. 672–79 (Roman period, foreign cults). See esp. Ph. Bruneau, *Recherches sur les cultes de Délos à l'époque hellénistique et à l'époque impériale* (1970).

23. For the Roman *collegia* see e.g. DA, s.v. 'collegium'; W. Liebenam, *Zur Geschichte und Organisation des römischen Vereinswesens, drei Untersuchungen* (1890) (rich in material, but different types not distinguished sharply enough); E. Kornemann, s.v. 'collegium' in RE IV, cols. 380–480 (copious synopsis of material); J.-P. Waltzing, 'Les colleges funéraires chez les Romains', *Musée Belge* 2 (1898), pp. 281–94; 3 (1899), pp. 130–57. On the craft associations: J.-P. Waltzing, *Étude historique sur les corporations professionelles chez les Romains depuis les origines jusqu'à la chute de l'Empire d'Occident* I-IV (1895–1900). This is a standard work. Supplementary material in J.-P. Waltzing, 'Recueil des inscriptions etc. Suppléments', *Musée Belge* 5 (1901), pp. 62–4; 127–35. A synoptic survey is given by J. Marquardt, *Römische Staatsverwaltung* III (1878), pp. 131–42. Note also F. M. de Robertis, *Il fenomeno associativo nel mondo romano* (1955); idem, *Storia delle corporazioni e del regime associativo nel mondo romano* I-II (1971). Much material is provided by the Indices to CIL. For the legal side note *Digest* xlvii 22 : *de collegiis et corporibus*.

24. CIRB, nos. 1237; 1242–3; 1245–8; 1250; 1251a; 1256; 1258?; 1260? For arguments against the common assumption that the *Hellenarches* is to be seen as an official of a distinct Greek community see V. F. Gajdukevič, *Das bosporanische Reich* (1971), pp. 362 ff.

25. Cf. W. Liebenam, *Zur Geschichte und Organisation des römischen Vereinswesens* (1890), pp. 89–97; L. Mitteis, *Reichsrecht und Volksrecht in den östlichen Provinzen des römischen Kaiserreichs* (1891), pp. 143–58; E. Kornemann, *De civibus Romanis in provinciis imperii consistentibus* (1892); A. Schulten, *De conventibus civium Romanorum sive de rebus publicis civium Romanorum mediis inter municipium et collegium* (1892); W. Liebenam, *Städteverwaltung im röm. Kaiserreiche* (1900), pp. 217–19; E. Kornemann s.v. 'Conventus civium Romanorum', RE

The constitutional position of Jewish Diaspora communities was certainly very different in different regions and periods.[26] No generalisation can be valid, firstly because the question concerns cities and local communities in different regions, and different cultures (in most cases either Greek or Latin) and over a wide range of time. Secondly, local laws and rights might be affected if the city or community in question was, or came to be, within one of the Hellenistic kingdoms, such as those of the Seleucids or Ptolemies, under the rule of the Roman Republic or (as was eventually true of all those west of the Euphrates), under the Roman Empire. The status of the Jews seems to have been more comparable now to one and now to another of the three forms of association mentioned. In Alexandria and Cyrene the Jews formed self-governing political groups. In this respect their position may have borne some resemblance to that of the *conventus civium Romanum* in cities outside Italy. The opposite extreme is provided by the position of the private religious guilds of the native inhabitants. Their members received no special political status; they were citizens or non-citizens, like other inhabitants, with all their rights and duties. Whether the Jewish communities in antiquity at any time stood within this category appears doubtful; for in the later imperial period they still, so far as our knowledge goes, enjoyed their own jurisdiction in civil actions involving their members. However, the position of Jews in Rome, where they had citizen rights as descendants of *libertini* and were not organized into a unity, but formed separate congregations (*synagogai*), cannot have been entirely different from that of other religious associations. In most areas however the position of the Jewish communities is perhaps more comparable with that of other associations of immigrants from the Near East. Jews, like Phoenicians and Egyptians, lived as aliens within a foreign city. Yet in this connexion two things are to be noted. On the one hand they placed great value upon their own jurisdiction. In that this was conceded to them, at any rate by the Romans in the course of the first century B.C. (which in the case of Phoenicians, Egyptians, etc. is unlikely), their privileged position bore some resemblance to that of the *conventus civium Romanorum*.[27] On the other hand they may have had citizen rights in

---

IV (1900), cols. 1179–1200; J. Hatzfeld, *Les trafiquants italiens dans l'Orient hellénique* (1919); A. J. N. Wilson, *Emigration from Italy in the Republican Age of Rome* (1966); P. A. Brunt, *Italian Manpower 225 B.C.—A.D. 14* (1971), pp. 159 ff.

26. Cf. e.g. J. Juster, *Les Juifs dans l'empire romain* I (1914), pp. 213–42; 391–408; II, pp. 1–27; S. Applebaum, 'The Legal Status of the Jewish Communities in the Diaspora', JPFC I (1974), pp. 420–63; A. M. Rabello, 'The Legal Condition of the Jews in the Roman Empire', ANRW II.13 (1980), pp. 662–762.

27. A. Schulten, *De conventibus civium Romanorum*, pp. 59–60 emphasized this similarity, but too strongly, p. 59: 'eiusdem fere rationis jurisque atque civium R. sunt Judaeorum conventus'. This formulation overlooked the freedom from local taxation enjoyed by the

some specific cities; in such instances they will presumably have ceased to be aliens (*metoikoi, peregrini*) and have taken their part in the rights and duties of citizens. That in spite of this they retained their special status led directly to conflicts in these cities.[28]

A factor which remained almost completely constant was the political tolerance of the Jewish religion, and above all that freedom of movement without which the Jewish communities could not have developed a life of their own. In the empires of the Ptolemies and Seleucids the religious freedom of the Jews was taken for granted. The early Ptolemies and Seleucids went further in conceding important political rights to Jews living within their empires (see pp. 126–30 below). Ptolemy II is even said to have initiated the translation of the Jewish Law into Greek, Ptolemy III to have offered sacrifice in Jerusalem.[29] Antiochus the Great gave orders for the granting of protection and privileges for the Temple in Jerusalem.[30] It seems clear

---

cives Romani.

28. Th. Mommsen, 'Der Religionsfrevel nach römischen Recht', HZ 64 (1890), pp. 389–429 on pp. 421–6, = *Ges. Schr.* III (1902), pp. 389–422, argued that only until the destruction of Jerusalem were the Jews regarded as 'a people' (*gens, ethnos*). From that moment on 'in the place of the privileged nation the privileged religion' appeared. While earlier constitutional privileges had been valid for all born Jews and only for these, from that time they were valid for all confessing Judaism, and only for these. There is no clear evidence that the year 70 formed so clear a boundary (except indeed in respect of the payment of the two-drachma tax, see pp. 122–3 below). For what it is worth the expression 'the *ethnos* of the Ioudaioi' can be found on inscriptions of the later period, e.g. CIJ II, no. 741 (Smyrna); no. 776: 'the *laos* of the Ioudaioi' (see above, p. 27); the nomenclature proves that it must be dated substantially after A.D. 70. Indeed it was precisely later emperors who tried to prevent the 'religion' extending beyond the boundaries of the people, so that belonging to the latter and not the former bestowed the privilege. Nevertheless Mommsen's position has some justification. Jewish communities in the earlier period can be seen as essentially associations of immigrants with specific privileges, while later—and increasingly with time—they are better understood as private associations whose special rights were continually shrinking, while on the other hand their members became citizens of city communities. Cf. above, p. 91.

29. For the pro-Jewish attitude of the early Ptolemies in general see Jos. *C. Ap.* ii 4–5 (37–64). Ptolemy III Euergetes (or a later Ptolemy) granted the right of asylum to a Jewish *proseuche* in the form possessed by pagan temples (CIL III, Suppl. no. 6583; OGIS, no. 129; see the text of the inscription, p. 47 above). On the tolerant religious policy of the Ptolemies in general see W. Otto, *Priester und Tempel im hellenistischen Ägypten* II (1908), pp. 261 ff.

30. Jos. *Ant.* xii 3, 3–4 (129–53). Antiochus, as conqueror of the country, had an interest in winning the good opinion of the Jews. The first of the two orders is contained in a letter (138–44), addressed to a certain Ptolemaeus, offering every kind of gift from the royal stores required for sacrifices and for the completion of the Temple, permitting the people to live according to their ancestral laws and exempting the priests from poll and crown tax. See Loeb, *Josephus*, vol. VII, App. D, and esp. the classic article by E. Bickerman, 'La charte séleucide de Jérusalem', REJ 100 (1935), pp. 4–35. In the second order, a general edict (*programma*), *Ant.* xii 3, 4 (145), it is forbidden for a foreigner to set foot in the forecourt of the Temple and for unclean animals to be brought into Jerusalem.

that Antiochus Epiphanes, at least, made a serious attempt to suppress the Jewish religion by force.[31] The resistance showed that the undertaking was impracticable; and on the whole tolerance remained the rule later as well as earlier. A particular friend of the Jews was found in Ptolemy VI Philometor, who even allowed a Jewish temple to be built in Egypt (see pp. 145–6 below). If Ptolemy VII Physcon adopted a hostile attitude to the Jews, this came about not on account of their religion but of their political associations.[32] Roman legislation

See on this E. Bickerman, 'Une proclamation séleucide relative au temple de Jérusalem', *Syria* 25 (1946-8), pp. 67–85. The Ptolemaeus to whom the first ordinance is addressed is Ptolemaeus son of Thraseas, who in 219 B.C. was still in the service of Ptolemy IV Philopator of Egypt (Polyb. v 65, 3); in 218 he was governor of Coele-Syria and Phoenicia, as a votive inscription originating from him proves, OGIS, no. 230. An extensive inscription from near Scythopolis, published by Y. H. Landau, 'A Greek Inscription found near Hefzibah', IEJ 16 (1966), pp. 54–70, emendations in BE 1970, no. 627, attests him again as *strategos* and High Priest in 202-1, receiving letters from and addressing memoranda to, Antiochus III. It is probable that he defected during, or just before, Antiochus' invasion. See J. E. Taylor, *Seleucid Rule in Palestine* (Diss. Duke Univ., 1979; University Microfilms, 1983), pp. 108 ff. A parallel to the privileges granted by Antiochus to the Jewish temple is the allowance granted by an Antiochus (which one is not quite certain, but most likely I or II) to the temple of Zeus in Baetokaeke, CIL III, no. 184; OGIS, no. 262; C. B. Welles, *Royal Correspondence in the Hellenistic Period* (1934), no. 70; revised text, translation and extensive commentary in IGLS VII, no. 4028. Note the important article by H. Seyrig, 'Arados et Baetocécé', *Syria* 28 (1951), pp. 193–206 = idem, *Antiquités Syriennes* IV (1953), pp. 172–85. Antiochus here grants to the temple of Zeus the village of Baetokaeke with all its revenues, freedom from market dues for the market on the fifteenth and last days of each month, the right of asylum for the temple, exemption for the village from liability to billeting and furnishing of post horses.

31. See vol. I, pp. 146–63: F. Millar, 'The Background to the Maccabean Revolution', JJS 29 (1978), pp. 1–22; cf. K. Bringmann, *Hellenistische Reform und Religionsverfolgung in Judäa* (1983).

32. For the political history of the Jews in Egypt in relation to the Ptolemies see CPJ I, pp. 19–25. Josephus tells the following story of Ptolemy VII Physcon, *C. Ap.* ii 5 (51–5). After the death of Ptolemy VI, Ptolemy VII tried to overthrow his widow, the successor of the first Cleopatra, whose army was commanded by the Jewish general Onias. While Ptolemy VII took the field against Onias he ordered the Jews living in Alexandria to be thrown bound to the elephants so that they would be trampled to death by them; but the elephants instead turned on the friends of the King, whereupon he desisted from the undertaking in remorse. In memory of this miraculous deliverance the Jews of Alexandria had celebrated an annual thanksgiving festival ever since. The story of the miraculous deliverance from the elephants forms the main content of the historical romance which is known as the Third Book of the Maccabees, where in the same way the remark is added that the Jews have ever since celebrated an annual thanksgiving festival (3 Mac. 6:36). The chief actor here however is called not Ptolemy Physcon (VII) but Ptolemy Philopator (IV). Both this parallel and the content itself make the story more than suspect; but if this much at least is historical, that Ptolemy VII showed a hostile attitude to the Jews, the cause of this was not religious denomination but their political position on the side of Cleopatra. H. Willrich, *Juden und Griechen vor der makkabäischen Erhebung* (1895), pp. 142–53; *Judaica* (1900), pp. 9–14, argued that Ptolemy Physcon was a friend of the Jews. He regarded the historical nucleus of 3 Maccabees as the events of the year 88–7 B.C., under Ptolemy Alexander, see *Hermes* 39 (1904), pp. 244–58. The existence of

also expressly recognized the Jews' right to free practice of their religion, and protected them against certain attempts at suppression by Greek cities. It was Caesar and Augustus in particular whom the Jews had to thank for their formal recognition in the Roman empire. Josephus has preserved for us a considerable number of official documents, *Ant.* xiv 10 (185–267); xvi 6 (160–79)—some *senatus consulta*, some exemptions by Caesar and Augustus, some similar documents from Roman magistrates or governors of the late Republic or early Empire—all of which have the purpose of assuring to the Jews the right to practice their religion and to retain their privileges.[33] Caesar's policy was in general repressive as regards associations in Rome, since at that time they served various political ends, and for this reason Caesar banned all *collegia* other than those existing from earlier times.[34] The Jewish communities were however expressly excepted from this ban: they were also not to be obstructed from making communal contributions or from holding assemblies.[35] It was by invoking this edict that, for example, a Roman official warned the authorities of Paros (or Parium) not to hinder the Jews in the performance of their religious customs.[36] Similarly it is to the influence of Caesar that we should no doubt trace the four official documents which Josephus has brought together in *Ant.* xiv 10, 20–4 (241–61). They all serve directly or indirectly to guarantee the Jews in Asia Minor the unobstructed practice of their religion.[37] After the death of

synagogue inscriptions 'on behalf of' Physcon (vol. II, p. 426) may perhaps lend some credence to the argument for friendly relations between him and the Jews (see CPJ I, p. 23).

33. On these documents cf.: L. Mendelssohn, 'Senati consulta Romanorum quae sunt in Josephi Antiquitatibus', *Acta societatis phil. Lips. ed. Ritschelius* 5 (1875), pp. 87–288; B. Niese, 'Bemerkungen über die Urkunden bei Josephus Archäol. B. XII, XIV, XVI', *Hermes* 11 (1876), pp. 466–88. For subsequent bibliography see Loeb, *Josephus*, vol. VII, App. J; H. Schreckenberg, *Bibliographie zu Flavius Josephus* (1968); E. M. Smallwood, *The Jews under Roman Rule* (1976), ch. 6 and App. B; cf. vol. I, pp. 272–5. See also C. Saulnier, 'Lois romaines sur les Juifs selon Flavius Josèphe', RB 88 (1981), pp. 161–98; T. Rajak, 'Was there a Roman Charter for the Jews?', JRS 74 (1984), pp. 107–23.

34. Suet. *Div. Iul.* 42: 'Cuncta collegia praeter antiquitus constituta distraxit'. The embargo was later upheld by Augustus, Suet. *Div. Aug.* 32: 'Collegia praeter antiqua et legitima dissolvit'.

35. *Ant.* xiv 10, 8 (215).

36. *Ant.* xiv 10, 8 (213–16). The text of these documents is so corrupt that the Roman names can often not be determined. The name of the official from whom the letter to the Parians was despatched reads in the text which has come down to us, Ἰούλιος Γάιος, which must be a corruption.

37. The four official documents are: (1) A letter of the authorities at Laodicea to the proconsul, presumably of Asia, in which they give assurances that they will not obstruct the existing order concerning the Jews in regard to celebration of the sabbath and the practice of their religious customs, *Ant.* xiv 10, 20 (241–3). The name of the proconsul is not Γάιος Ῥαβίλλιος or Ῥαβέλλιος, as the transmitted text of Josephus' text has it, but, according to an inscription found in Delos, Γάιος Ῥαβήριος (i.e. Rabirius). See Th.

Caesar the two contending parties rivalled one another in maintaining Jewish privileges. On one side P. Cornelius Dolabella, a supporter of Antonius, who in 43 B.C. made himself master of Asia Minor, confirmed to the Jews of Asia Minor the freedom from military service and the free religious practice which previous governors had preserved for them, and made this known to the authorities in Ephesus by a letter.[38] On the other side M. Iunius Brutus, who early in 42 B.C. was preparing for war against Antonius and Octavian, directed the Ephesians to pass a decree to the effect that Jews should not be obstructed in celebrating the sabbath or in the rest of their religious customs.[39] The effect of these measures, and further similar pronouncements by Augustus and Agrippa, was to secure a general toleration and protection of Jewish communities in the Roman Empire.[40] That even the Jews in the city of Rome enjoyed this

Homolle, BCH 6 (1882), pp. 608–12 ; Th. Mommsen, *Ephemeris epigr.* V, p. 68 ; CIL III, suppl. no. 7239 = I², no. 773 = *ID*, no. 1859 ; cf. MRR II, p. 481.

(2) A letter from the proconsul of Asia to the authorities in Miletus, in which the latter are warned not to hinder the Jews in celebrating the sabbath or in practising their religious customs or administering their assets according to their usual manner, *Ant.* xiv 10, 21 (244–6). The proconsul will almost certainly be P. Servilius Isauricus, well attested as proconsul in 46 to 44 B.C., see D. Magie, *Roman Rule in Asia Minor* (1950), ch. 17, nn. 41–2 ; MRR II, pp. 298 ; 309–10 ; 329.

(3) Decree of the Halicarnassians allowing the Jews τά τε σάββατα ἄγειν καὶ τὰ ἱερὰ συντελεῖν κατὰ τοὺς Ἰουδαϊκοὺς νόμους καὶ τὰς προσευχὰς ποιεῖσθαι πρὸς τῇ θαλάσσῃ κατὰ τὸ πάτριον ἔθος, *Ant.* xiv 10, 23 (256–8) ; on the recital of prayers on the seashore see above, Vol. II, pp. 441, 444. On the correction of the names in the letter to the Milesians and in the decree of Halicarnassus, Jos. *Ant.* xiv 10 (245–56), see also A. Wilhelm, JOAI 8 (1905), pp. 238–42.

(4) Decree of the city of Sardis that Jews are to be allowed to assemble on days listed in advance by them, for celebration of their religious customs ; further that a place be allotted specially to them by the city authorities 'for building and living' (εἰς οἰκοδομίαν καὶ οἴκησιν αὐτῶν), *Ant.* xiv 10, 24 (259–61). It seems however from the petition of the Jews previously mentioned here that it is a matter only of building a synagogue. These official documents seem to relate to a single legislative act in Rome, probably a *senatus consultum*. But its exact date and character cannot be recovered.

38. *Ant.* xiv 10, 11–12 (223–7). See *MRR* II, p. 344.

39. *Ant.* xiv 10, 25 (262–4). On this, Mendelssohn, *Acta* V, 251–4. In the transmitted text the name appears as Μάρκῳ Ἰουλίῳ Πομπηίῳ υἱῷ Βρούτου (Niese: Μάρκῳ Ἰουλίῳ Ποντίου υἱῷ Βρούτῳ). See MRR II, p. 461.

40. The expression *religio licita* is never found ; *only* Tertullian, *Apol.* 21, uses the phrase : 'insignissima religio, certe licita' ; it is not a technical term in Roman jurisprudence. This speaks rather of *collegia licita* (*Dig.* xlvii 22). Thus the crucial point was whether the adherents of a cult would be allowed to assemble themselves corporately and to assemble for the practice of their cult. Hence the formula, *coire, convenire licet*, which often recurs in edicts of toleration in favour of Jews. Cf. also Philo, *Leg.* 40 (311–20) ; cf. Cassius Dio lx 6 (ban by Claudius) ; see pp. 77–8 above. Material on the formula *coire licet* is collected by Waltzing, *Étude historique sur les corporations professionelles* IV, pp. 581–3. The right of assembly was a paramount matter also for the constitutional position of Christians, as is clear particularly from Tertullian, *Apol.* 38–9. See also Juster, *Les Juifs dans l'empire romain* I, pp. 338–90.

toleration and protection is attested by Philo for the time of Augustus.[41] Nevertheless it is possible, by analogy with other foreign cults, that the Jews in Rome until the second century A.D. were not allowed to practice their religion within the *pomerium*.[42]

Two important powers went along with public recognition of the Jewish communities and their religion: the right of administration of their own finances, and jurisdiction as it concerned their own members.[43] The former is emphasized several times in the documents from the time of Caesar.[44] It was of particular importance to the Jews because only thus could they discharge their obligations towards the Temple at Jerusalem and send there the dues required by the Law. It was precisely this export of money from the provinces which seems however to have been a special stumbling-block for the pagan authorities. We know from Cicero's speech on behalf of Flaccus that the latter during his administration of Asia (62–61 B.C.) ordered the confiscation of such Jewish temple money in various places.[45] The city authorities in Asia also appear to have proceeded in the same manner even after the edicts of Caesar's time and in spite of them. The official documents from the time of Augustus therefore concern themselves chiefly with this point. Just as Augustus allowed the export of such money from Rome itself,[46] so it was impressed on the cities of Asia Minor and Cyrene that they were to place no hindrance in the path of

---

41. Philo, *Leg.* 23 (156–7).

42. Cf. J. Marquardt, *Römische Staatsverwaltung* III, p. 35; O. Gilbert, *Geschichte und Topographie der Stadt Rom im Altertum* III (1890), pp. 109–15; and below, pp. 157–8. It remains uncertain whether Jewish synagogues should in this respect be classified with pagan cults, which required temples, priests and sacrifices.

43. On the parallel provided by Greek associations see E. Ziebarth, *Das griechische Vereinswesen* (1896), pp. 156–83. On administration of the finances of Jewish communities see J. Juster, *Les Juifs dans l'empire romain* I, pp. 377–88; on jurisdiction, Juster, *op. cit.*, II, pp. 93–214.

44. Caesar himself allowed the Jews χρήματα συνεισφέρειν, *Ant.* xiv 10, 8 (215). In the letter of the proconsul of Asia to the Milesians, *Ant.* xiv 10, 21 (245), the Jews are allowed τοὺς καρποὺς μεταχειρίζεσθαι καθὼς ἔθος ἐστὶν αὐτοῖς.

45. Cicero, *pro Flacco* 28-67-9: 'Cum aurum Iudaeorum nomine quotannis ex Italia et ex omnibus provinciis Hierosolyma exportari soleret, Flaccus sanxit ˈedicto, ne ex Asia exportari liceret ... Ubi ergo crimen est? quoniam quidem furtum nusquam reprehendis, edictum probas, iudicatum fateris, quaesitum et prolatum palam non negas, actum esse per viros primarios res ipsa declarat: Apameae manifesto deprehensum, ante pedes praetoris in foro expensum esse auri pondo centum paullo minus per Sex. Caesium, equitem Romanum, castissimum hominem atque integerrimum; Laodiceae viginti pondo paullo amplius per hunc L. Peducaeum, iudicem nostrum; Adramyttii per Cn. Domitium legatum; Pergami non multum.' See A. J. Marshall, 'Flaccus and the Jews of Asia (Cicero, *Pro Flacco* 28-67-9)', Phoenix 29 (1975), pp. 139–54. Earlier Mithradates had ordered the confiscation of Jewish money in Cos, *Ant.* xiv 7, 2 (112). Cf. p. 69 above.

46. Philo, *Leg.* 23 (156–7). The fact of export *ex Italia* is mentioned also by Cicero in the passage given above.

the Jews over this matter.[47] Embezzlement of such monies is to be punished as temple robbery.[48] That these rules were still in force at the time of the war of Vespasian is evident from an incidental utterance of Titus.[49]

Of equal importance for the Jewish communities was their own jurisdiction. Since the Mosaic Law is concerned not only with matters of cult but also with civil life, and places the latter under the direction of the divine Law, it was an intolerable situation for the Jewish conscience for Jews to be judged by any other but Jewish law.[50] Wherever Jews went they took with them their own law and held courts of justice according to its direction for the members of their community. Some reflections of this appear in the New Testament. The apostle Paul obtained full powers from the Sanhedrin in Jerusalem for the arrest of any Jews living in Damascus who believed in Christ (Ac. 9:2). He also had those in other places thrown into prison and flogged (Ac. 22:19; 26:11). Later, as a Christian, he himself was flogged five times by Jews (2 Cor. 11:24); this seems to refer not to Judaea but to Jewish communities in the Diaspora. In Corinth the proconsul Gallio instructs the Jews to take their complaint against Paul to their own forum, because he is willing to be judge only if Paul has committed a felony, but not if it is simply a matter of a breach of the Jewish law (Ac. 18:12–16). It can be seen from all this that the Jews in fact exercised

47. Jos. *Ant.* xvi 6, 2 and 7 (162–73); Philo, *Leg.* 40 (311–18). Of these documents, *Ant.* xvi 6, 5 (169–70) is concerned with Cyrene, the rest with the province of Asia. The chronology of the latter is as follows:

(1) The letter of Agrippa to Ephesus probably belongs to the year 14 B.C., *Ant.* xvi 6, 4 (167–8). When Herod himself in 14 B.C. visited Agrippa in Asia Minor, the Jews there complained about the oppressive acts which they had to suffer at the hands of the city authorities; they were robbed of their sacred monies, and were compelled to appear in court on the sabbath. Agrippa protected the rights of the Jews on both matters, *Ant.* xvi 2, 3–5 (27–65); cf. xii 3, 2 (125–8). See vol. I, p. 292. It is precisely with these points that the cited letter of Agrippa is concerned.

(2) In 12 B.C. in response to Jewish embassies Augustus proclaimed in an edict the right of the Jews to send money to Jerusalem, the proconsul at the time being C. Marcius Censorinus, *Ant.* xvi 2 (162–5). See G. W. Bowersock, 'C. Marcius Censorinus, Legatus Caesaris', HSCPh 68 (1964), pp. 207–10; cf. F. Millar, JRS 56 (1966), p. 161.

(3) The letter of Augustus to Norbanus Flaccus, *Ant.* xvi 6, 6 (171), probably belongs to soon after 12 B.C., as do the letters of Norbanus Flaccus to the magistrates of Sardis, *Ant.* xvi 6, 6 (171), and of Ephesus, Philo, *Leg.* 40 (315); for the date see Smallwood ad loc. See also F. Millar, JRS 56 (1966), p. 161.

(4) The proconsulate of Iullus Antonius, who again impressed the orders of Augustus and Agrippa upon the Ephesians, *Ant.* xvi 6, 7 (172–3) will belong some time between his consulate in 10 B.C. and 3 B.C., see PIR² A 800.

48. *Ant.* xvi 6, 2 and 4 (162–5; 167–8).

49. *B.J.* vi 6, 2 (335): δασμολογεῖν τε ὑμῖν ἐπὶ τῷ θεῷ καὶ ἀναθήματα συλλέγειν ἐπετρέψαμεν.

50. Cf. e.g. the rabbinic passages in J. J. Wetstein, *Nov. Test.*, on 1 Cor. 6:1, or Str.-B. *ad loc.*

not only a civil but even a kind of criminal jurisdiction towards their own members. Whether they were everywhere formally entitled to do this may be doubted. In any case, some restrictions will surely have been imposed in Corinth, as they probably were in Judaea during the period of the prefects and procurators.[51] But it is certain that Jewish communities enjoyed their own jurisdiction in civil matters not only in Alexandria (see above, pp. 92 ff.) but also elsewhere. This is expressly conceded even before the time of Caesar, for example to the Jews of Sardis in a letter of Lucius Antonius (50–49 B.C. proconsul of the province of Asia) to the authorities of Sardis.[52] Further, the legislation of the Christian emperors shows that even later this right was still granted to Jewish communities in general (see below at the end of this section).

Since adherence to the Jewish Law could easily bring the Jews of the Diaspora into conflict with the laws of pagan cities or states, a perfectly free observance of their religion was not assured until and unless the state demanded nothing of the Jews which was not disallowed by their law. Even in this regard Roman toleration granted important concessions to Jews. A critical point here was military service. For a Jew this was in principle impossible in non-Jewish armies, since on the sabbath he would neither carry weapons nor march further than 2000 cubits.[53] None the less, it seems clear (pp. 38–9 above) that Jews served as soldiers under the Ptolemies. How the problems mentioned above were solved is not known. The question again became particularly relevant when at the outbreak of the civil war between Caesar and Pompey in 49 B.C. the Pompeian party undertook vast recruiting campaigns in the whole of the Near East. In the province of Asia alone the consul Lentulus raised two legions of Roman citizens.[54] Since by now, as was revealed by this very process, many Jews in that area possessed Roman citizenship, they became liable to conscription; but at their request Lentulus exempted them from war service, and gave the appropriate instructions to the various officials carrying out

51. On the vexed problem of the capital jurisdiction of the Sanhedrin, see vol. II, pp. 218–23.

52. Jos. Ant. xiv 10, 17 (235): Ἰουδαῖοι πολῖται ἡμέτεροι (or ὑμέτεροι?) προσελθόντες μοι ἐπέδειξαν αὑτοὺς σύνοδον ἔχειν ἰδίαν κατὰ τοὺς πατρίους νόμους ἀπ᾽ ἀρχῆς καὶ τόπον ἴδιον ἐν ᾧ τά τε πράγματα καὶ τὰς πρὸς ἀλλήλους ἀντιλογίας κρίνουσιν.... On L. Antonius (a brother of the triumvir Marcus Antonius) as proquaestor pro praetore in Asia in 49 see MRR II, p. 260. The letter may have dealt only with Jews who possessed Roman citizenship. But the text is unfortunately uncertain, and it remains unclear whether Antonius calls the Jews 'our' citizens (Romans) or 'your' (of Sardis); the latter seems more likely.

53. Ban on carrying weapons: mShab. 6.2, 4. On Sabbath journeys see vol. II, p. 472; also Ant. xiii 8, 4 (251); xiv 10, 12 (225–7).

54. Caesar, Bell. Civ. iii 4: '(Pompeius) legiones effecerat civium Romanorum IX ..., duas ex Asia, quas Lentulus consul conscribendas curaverat.'

the levy.[55] Six years later (43 B.C.) Cornelius Dolabella confirmed to the Jews there their right of exemption from military service (*astrateia*) by express reference to the former edicts.[56] In Judaea also the same concession was made to them by Caesar.[57]

Of other privileges, which were the result of respect for Jewish legislation, it remains to mention the fact that the Jews, following a ruling by Augustus, could not be compelled to appear before a court on the Sabbath;[58] and the ruling by Augustus, according to which Jews living in Rome who were entitled to share in distributions of grain or money, could, if the appointed day fell on a Sabbath, collect their share on the following day;[59] lastly, the privilege granted to the Jewish community of Antioch and other cities by Seleucus I, and preserved, in the case of Antioch at least, by the refusal of Licinius Mucianus, as *legatus Augusti pro praetore* of Syria in A.D. 68–9, to revoke it although the pagan population wished to do so. This consisted in the right to receive a cash payment in lieu of the oil distributed free to the citizens for use in the gymnasia.[60]

This entire legal position was never substantially or permanently altered in the later period. Imperial legislation indeed introduced from time to time certain restrictions. Judaism suffered incidental persecution, see for instance Jos. *C. Ap.* i 8 (43); ii 30 (219); but a lasting and substantial alteration of the existing situation did not occur until the later imperial period. The measures of Tiberius against Roman Jews *en masse* (pp. 75–7 above) were confined to the city of Rome alone. In the time of Caligula it is true that a serious crisis developed; but this fact itself demonstrated how valuable it was for the Jews to possess already a long-established legal position. The religious freedom of the Jews was indeed potentially threatened by the introduction and constant evolution of the cults of emperors, living or deceased. The more this was officially practised, the more inevitably it seemed disloyalty for Jews not to take part in it. When Caligula peremptorily demanded adherence everywhere to the cult which from the reign of Augustus onwards had been introduced in various forms by the

---

55. *Ant.* 10, 13–14; 16; 18–19 (228–32; 234; 236–40).

56. *Ant.* xiv 10, 11–12 (223–27).

57. *Ant.* xiv 10, 6 (202–10).

58. *Ant.* xvi 6, 2 and 4 (162–5; 167–8). The technical expression ἐγγύας ὁμολογεῖν means to give security that one intends to appear before a court. On the occasion of these rulings see above, n. 47. On the Jewish prohibition of holding court on the sabbath see vol. II, p. 223.

59. Philo, *Leg.* 23 (158). On these distributions of money and grain see RE IV, col. 880 (s.v. 'congiarium'); W. Liebenam, *Städteverwaltung im römischen Kaiserreiche* (1900), pp. 109 ff.; D. van Berchem, *Les distributions de blé et d'argent à la plèbe romaine sous l'Empire* (1939).

60. Jos. *Ant.* xii 3, 1 (119–24); on the unacceptability of pagan oil for Jews see vol. II, p. 84. For Mucianus see PIR[2] L 216.

provincials, the religious freedom of the Jews would have been lost beyond hope of recovery if the demand had been consistently carried out in their case also. In the reign of Caligula, the attempt to do this was actually made; and it is a matter of history that this created a situation of extreme danger for the Jewish population of Judaea (see vol. I, pp. 394–7). Fortunately for them however the reign of Caligula did not last long. His successor Claudius immediately issued a general edict of toleration to resore the former situation.[61] From that time on no serious suggestion was ever made of compelling Jews to participate in the imperial cult. It counted as an ancient right that they were free from this obligation, a circumstance through which they enjoyed particular advantage by comparison with Christians. The subsequent measure of Claudius against the Roman Jews was, like that of Tiberius, confined to the city of Rome, and was probably not of lasting application. The reign of Nero was in general again favourable to the Jews, perhaps because of the influence of his wife Poppaea (cf. above, p. 78). The great Vespasianic war and the destruction of the Temple in Jerusalem did however bring as a consequence for the Jews in the Diaspora that what had hitherto been the Temple tax of two drachmas had to be paid to the temple of Jupiter Capitolinus.[62] This must indeed have represented a traumatic blow to Jewish sensibilities; but otherwise the religious freedom of the Jews suffered no encroachment through Vespasian. Their political rights, for example in Alexandria and Antioch, were even expressly protected by him.[63] Domitian exacted the two-drachma tax with vigour[64] and punished Romans who converted to Judaism.[65] The

---

61. *Ant.* xix 5, 2–3 (278–91).

62. Jos. *B.J.* vii 6, 6 (218); Cassius Dio lxvi 7, 2 = GLAJJ II, no. 430. For the history of this tax cf. O. Hirschfeld, *Die kaiserlichen Verwaltungsbeamten* (²1905), p. 73; CPJ I, pp. 80–2; II, pp. 111–16 (the most important treatment); see also C. J. Hemer, 'The Edfu Ostraka and the Jewish Tax', PEQ 105 (1973), pp. 6–12. The following inscription belongs to the time of the Flavian emperors (CIL VI, no. 8604 = ILS, no. 1519): 'T. Flavio Aug(usti) lib(erto) Euschemoni, qui fuit ab epistulis item procurator ad capitularia Iudaeorum, fecit Flavia Aphrodisia patrono et coniugi bene merenti.' By far the most important evidence for the tax is now provided by documents from Egypt, namely ostraka from Edfu (Apollinopolis Magna), CPJ II, nos. 160–229, covering the years A.D. 71–2 to 116, a papyrus from Arsinoe (no. 421) of A.D. 73 and another from Karanis (no. 460). Two of the ostraka (164, 166) show that payment was back-dated to the second year of Vespasian (A.D. 69-70). Unlike the didrachma paid to the Temple, the Jewish tax (called either τιμή δηναρίων δύο Ἰουδαίων or, more normally, Ἰουδαϊκὸν τέλεσμα) was paid by both males and females from age 3 to 60 or 62, as is shown by no. 421, where three columns of an extensive tax-roll concern the Jewish tax. Slaves and freedmen of a household were also included (CPJ II, p. 114). The rate here, as in the ostraka, is 8 Egyptian drachmae and 2 obols, plus 1 drachma labelled ἀπαρχαί ('first fruits'). One ostrakon (181) mentions a 'collector of the Jewish tax' (πράκτωρ [Ἰουδαϊκ]ου τελέσματος). No. 460 shows that the tax was still paid at the same rate in the mid-second century.

63. Jos. *Ant.* xii 3, 1 (119–24); *B.J.* vii 5, 2 (100–11); cf. pp. 127–9 below.

64. Suet. *Dom.* 12 = GLAJJ II, no. 320: 'Iudaicus fiscus acerbissime actus est; ad quem deferebantur, qui vel inprofessi Iudaicam viverent vitam, vel dissimulata origine imposita

existing rights of Jews were however not abolished, and under Nerva relaxations once more made their appearance. The two-drachma tax was not, it is true, abolished, but it was not permitted for anyone to be prosecuted for 'a Jewish way of life',[66] and thus the denunciations and malicious persecutions given pretext by the *fiscus Judaicus* were prevented.[67]

A fundamental threat to this privileged status, the most effective which the Jews had lived through since Caligula, will have resulted from the great conflicts under Trajan and Hadrian (vol. I, pp. 529–57). Hadrian is stated to have issued—and it was one cause of the revolt in his reign—a formal prohibition of circumcision,[68] which is not likely to have been cancelled after the successful suppression of the revolt. His immediate successor Antoninus Pius, however, allowed the resumption of circumcision for those born within Judaism, and restricted the prohibition to non-Jews.[69] Similarly Septimius Severus is alleged by a poor source to have forbidden only the formal act of going over to Judaism.[70] The same source says of Severus Alexander: 'Iudaeis privilegia reservavit'.[71] These passing references in the late fourth-century set of Imperial biographies known as the *Historia Augusta* cannot however be used as the basis for the history of the Diaspora Judaism at this time, a history which can only (if at all) be reconstructed

---

genti tributa non pependissent. Interfuisse me adulescentulum memini, cum a procuratore frequentissimoque consilio inspiceretur nonagenarius senex, an circumsectus esset.'

65. Cassius Dio lxvii 14, 2 = GLAJJ II, no. 435: καὶ ἄλλοι ἐς τὰ τῶν Ἰουδαίων ἔθη ἐξοκέλλοντες πολλοὶ κατεδικάσθησαν... See E. M. Smallwood, 'Domitian's Attitude towards the Jews and Judaism', *CPh* 51 (1956), pp. 1–13; L. A. Thompson, 'Domitian and the Jewish Tax', *Historia* 31 (1982), pp. 329–42.

66. Cassius Dio lxviii 1, 2 = GLAJJ II, no. 436: οὔτ' ἀσεβείας οὔτ' Ἰουδαϊκοῦ βίου καταιτιᾶσθαί τινας συνεχώρησε.

67. This is the sense of the legend on a coin of Nerva: FISCI JUDAICI CALUMNIA SUBLATA, see e.g. BMC Roman Empire III: Nerva, nos. 88, 98, 105–6. It cannot be concerned with the abolition of the tax, for the latter was still in existence later on (Appian, *Syr.* 50/253 = GLAJJ II, no. 343; Origen, *Epist. ad African.* 14; Tertullian, *Apol.* 18: 'vectigalis libertas' means freedom bought at the price of a tax). Also the wording itself would be against this, for *calumnia* is a hostile, malicious accusation, and so equivalent to 'denunciation' (see RE III, cols. 1414–21 s.v. 'calumnia'; Th. Mommsen, *Röm. Strafrecht* (1899), pp. 491 ff.). Such accusations had evidently occurred quite often under Domitian through occasions provided by the Jewish tax. Nerva prohibited them and thereby did away with the *calumnia fisci Judaici*, i.e. denunciation in the interest of the *fiscus Judaicus* and the malicious prosecution which went with it.

68. So HA, *v. Had.* 14, 2 = GLAJJ II, no. 511: 'moverunt ea tempestate et Iudaei bellum, quod vetabantur mutilare genitalia.' The prohibition of circumcision was general and not specially directed against Jews, but was felt by them most acutely. For details see vol. I, pp. 536–40.

69. *Dig.* xlviii 8, 11: 'Circumcidere Iudaeis filios suos tantum rescripto divi Pii permittitur: in non eiusdem religionis qui hoc fecerit, castrantis poena irrogatur.'

70. HA, *v. Sept. Sev.* 17, 1 = GLAJJ II, no. 515: 'Iudaeos fieri sub gravi poena vetuit.' By 'Iudaeos fieri' formal conversions involving circumcision should be understood.

71. *v. Sev. Alex.* 22, 4 = GLAJJ II, no. 520.

from fragmentary local evidence (pp. 1–85 above). In the fourth century there is at least a substantial body of Imperial legal rulings, preserved in the *Codex Theodosianus*. The policy of the Christian emperors was not always consistent, but even those most unfavourably inclined towards the Jews did not abolish existing rights. Their repressive measures were restricted to preventing any further expansion of Judaism, including intermarriage between Christians and Jews and the acquisition by Jews of non-Jewish slaves. For those born as Jews the existing legal situation was otherwise formally maintained.[72] Three points in connection with this are worth making.

(1) The Jewish religion remained in the later, as in the earlier period,[73] under the formal protection of the state. When on one occasion Callistus, the future bishop, in the time of Bishop Victor, A.D. 189–99, broke up a Jewish service in Rome, he was accused of this by the Jews before the city prefect, Fuscianus, and condemned by him to exile in the mines of Sardinia.[74] Of the Christian emperors, even those who were unfavourably inclined towards the Jews, and prohibited the building of new synagogues, still brought the existing ones under the increasingly necessary protection of the law.[75]

(2) The right of administering their own property was retained by the Jewish communities just as before. In certain cases they could even claim, or attempt to claim, fines from non-Jews, for example for the unauthorized use of a grave.[76] Specially important was the fact that the Jews could still (until towards the end of the fourth century) send their religious dues to the patriarchate in Palestine (the new central authority of the Jewish people which had arisen in the period since the destruction of Jerusalem). These dues were collected annually and brought to Palestine by the *apostoli* sent out by the patriarchs.[77] It was not until

72. See *Codex Theodosianus* xvi 8 and cf. Haenel, *Corpus Legum*, Index, pp. 211 ff. No adequate history of the Jews in the later Roman Empire exists. For brief histories, mainly concentrating on the Holy Land, see M. Avi-Yonah, *The Jews of Palestine. A Political History from the Bar Kochba War to the Arab Conquest* (1976); J. Maier, *Grundzüge der Geschichte des Judentums im Altertum* (1981); P. Schaefer, *Geschichte der Juden in der Antike. Die Juden Palästinas von Alexander dem Grossen bis zur arabischen Eroberung* (1983). For the gradually worsening legal position see J. E. Feaver, *Persecution of the Jews in the Roman Empire (300–438)* (1952). Note also A. Linder, *Roman Imperial Legislation on the Jews* (1983), giving the texts with Hebrew translation and commentary.

73. Cf. esp. the decree of the Halicarnassians, Jos. *Ant.* xiv 10, 23 (256–8): ἂν δέ τις κωλύσῃ ἢ ἄρχων ἢ ἰδιώτης, τῷδε τῷ ζημιώματι ὑπεύθυνος ἔστω καὶ ὀφειλέτω τῇ πόλει.

74. Hippolytus, *Philosophoumena* ix 12.

75. *C. Theod.* xvi 8, 9; 12; 20; 21; 25–7.

76. Inscription of Rufina at Smyrna, CIJ II, no. 741, and inscriptions at Hierapolis, cf. p. 106 above.

77. See for these *apostoli* and their functions: Euseb. *Comment. ad Isa.* 18:1 (PG XXIV, col. 213); Epiphanius, *Haer.* 30, 4 and 11; Jerome, *ad Gal.* 1:1 (PL XXVI, col. 311); *C. Theod.* xvi 8, 14; W. Seufert, *Der Ursprung und die Bedeutung des Apostolates in der christlichen Kirche* (1887), pp. 8 ff.; A. von Harnack, *Die Mission und Ausbreitung des Christentums* I (⁴1924), pp. 342–6, E.T. *The Expansion of Christianity in the first three centuries* I (1904), pp.

towards the end of the fourth century that the emperors gradually took steps against this.[78]

(3) Further, their own jurisdiction was conceded to the Jews even in the later imperial period, of course only for civil cases, and only if the two litigating parties were agreed on seeking a legal decision before Jewish courts.[79] A very extensive authority must have been enjoyed by the Jewish Ethnarch or Patriarch in Palestine who in the third and fourth centuries gained a position of considerable power not only within the Holy Land but outside it (note the allusion to the Patriarch in the inscription from Stobi, p. 67 above). His authority was so extensive that the church fathers were obliged to give serious attention to proving that nonetheless the sceptre had been taken away from Judah in the time of Christ.[80]

Perhaps nothing is more indicative of the guaranteed legal position of the Jews as we have described it than the circumstance that during pagan persecutions of Christians it had even happened that Christians converted to Judaism to protect themselves.[81]

409–14; JE II, pp. 20 ff. s.v. 'apostole', 'apostoli'; Juster, *Les Juifs* I, pp. 388–90. They seem to have had the primary function of acting as intermediaries between the Jewish communities. Note e.g. at Venosa, in an epitaph of a fourteen year-old girl, 'quei dixerunt t(h)r<e>nus (= θρήνους) duo apostuli et duo rebbites', CIJ I², no. 611. But it is not certain whether the *apostoli* mentioned in this fifth-century inscription are those sent by the Patriarch.

78. Cf. for a proposal to abolish the *apostole* (not carried out) : Julian, *Epist.* 25 Hertlein = Bidez-Cumont, no. 204 = Loeb III, no. 51. The authenticity of this letter is much disputed, and is rejected for instance by Bidez and Cumont. See the discussion by M. Stern, GLAJJ II, no. 486a. See *C. Theod.* xvi 8, 14 ; 17 ; 29.

79. *C. Theod.* ii 1, 10: 'Sane si qui per compromissum, ad similitudinem arbitrorum, apud Iudaeos vel patriarchas ex consensu partium in civili dumtaxat negotio putaverint litigandum, sortiri eorum iudicium iure publico non vetentur : eorum etiam sententias provinciarum iudices exsequantur, tamquam ex sententia cognitoris arbitri fuerint attributi' (Arcadius and Honorius, A.D. 398). Cf. also *C. Theod.* xvi 8, 8.

80. Pamphilus, *Apol. pro Orig.* in Routh, *Reliquiae sacrae* IV, p. 360; Cyril, *Cateches.* xii 17. In general also Origen, *ad African.* 14 (see the passage above, vol. II, p. 209). HA *v. Quadr. Tyr.* 8, 4 = GLAJJ II, no. 527. See on this passage R. Syme, 'Ipse Ille Patriarcha', *Bonner Historia-Augusta-Colloquium (1966-7)* (1968), pp. 119–30 = *Emperors and Biography* (1971), ch. 2. In 415 the patriarch Gamaliel was deposed by the emperor Theodosius II because he had misused his power against Christians (*C. Theod.* xvi 8, 22; cf. for this Gamaliel also Jerome, *Epist.* 57 *ad Pammachium* 3). He was probably the last patriarch, for in the year 429 the office is referred to as having been extinct for some time (*C. Theod.* xvi 8, 29). On the Patriarchs see J. Juster, *Les Juifs dans l'empire romain* I, pp. 391–400. For the earlier evolution of the office see L. I. Levine, 'The Jewish Patriarch (Nasi) in Third Century Palestine', ANRW XIX.2 (1981), pp. 649–88; M. D. Goodman, *State and Society in Roman Galilee A.D. 132–212* (1983), pp. 111–18.

81. Euseb., *HE.* vi 12, 1.

III. CIVIC RIGHTS

In most of the ancient cities of Phoenicia, Syria and Asia Minor, as in Greece itself, immigrant Jews certainly occupied the position of aliens (non-citizens).[1] Their communities were corporations of foreigners, recognized by the city and granted certain rights, but their members did not enjoy citizenship and therefore took no part in the conduct of city affairs. There were however also a number of cities in which it was claimed that Jews possessed rights of citizenship, namely the newly-founded cities of the Hellenistic age, and among them primarily the capital cities of the Seleucid and Ptolemaic empires, Antioch and Alexandria. It is possible that the Jews in these cities formed separate 'tribes' (*phylae*); since membership by individual Jews of the other city *phylae*, which had developed in close association with pagan cults, is scarcely conceivable in view of the special religious position of the Jews. If therefore Paul was in reality a citizen of Tarsus (Ac. 21:39), it is possible that in some other cities Jews as a group enjoyed citizenship.[2] The following evidence exists of cities where Jewish citizenship is claimed by our sources.

Seleucus I Nicator (d. 280 B.C.) is stated to have bestowed citizenship on the Jews in the cities which he founded in Asia Minor and Syria,[3] and Josephus claims that they still possessed it in all these

1. This is clear indirectly in particular from Jos. *C. Ap.* ii 4 (38–9), for here Josephus emphasizes as something of an exception the fact that the Jews in Alexandria, Antioch and the Ionian cities had the citizenship. It remains uncertain whether it could be claimed that those in all the cities founded by Seleucus I had the citizenship. However it is clear that its possession was not normal. Cf. Juster, *Les Juifs dans l'empire romain* II, pp. 1–40.

2. The view that in at least some cities Jews were citizens was supported by Ramsay, see Exp. (1902, Jan.), pp. 22–9: 'The Jews as Hellenic citizens'. On *phylae* in the Greek cities under the Roman Empire see W. Liebenam, *Städteverwaltung im römischen Kaiserreiche* (1900), pp. 220–5; E. Szanto, 'Die griechischen Phylen', SAW 144.5 (1902); see pp. 54 ff., 62–71 on the *phylae* in the cities of Asia Minor. Cf. A. H. M. Jones, *The Greek City* (1940), pp. 158 ff.; K. Latte, RE XX.1 (1941), cols. 994–1011, s.v. 'Phyle'; B. M. Levick, 'Two Inscriptions from Pisidian Antioch', AS 15 (1965), pp. 53–62. Further material on the *phylae* in the Greek cities of Egypt is given by a papyrus of the year A.D. 212 from Antinoopolis, PLond III (1907), pp. 154 ff. Cf. POxy 3053 (Tripolis); 3054 (Bostra). The *phylae* are frequently called after gods, e.g. in Magnesia: Apollonias, Dias, Hermeis, Areis, Aphrodisias, Poseidonias (Szanto, p. 62).

3. A list of them is offered by Appian, *Syr.* 57. On this see B. Niese, *Geschichte der griechischen und makedonischen Staaten seit der Schlacht bei Chaeronea* I (1893), pp. 393 ff.; V. Tscherikover, *Die hellenistischen Städtegründungen* (1927), esp. pp. 165 ff.; see also G. M.

places in his own time.[4] The most important among them was Antioch where the rights of the Jews were inscribed on bronze tablets.[5] In one passage Josephus implies that the Jews of Antioch first received citizenship from the successors of Antiochus Epiphanes.[6] Since it is very improbable that they should have gained so great a favour just at that time, we should perhaps prefer other passages of Josephus, and understand this as a restoration after the time of persecution by Antiochus Epiphanes. Under the Romans also these rights were not diminished. Even in the time of the war under Vespasian, Titus refused the request of the Antiochenes that Jews should be deprived of their citizenship by a simple appeal to their ancient rights.[7] It remains however quite uncertain whether Josephus' claims regarding Jewish citizenship in Seleucid foundations should be accepted. Tcherikover, for example, points out, firstly, that there is no confirmation outside the pages of Josephus for the claim that Jews enjoyed citizenship; and secondly, that some of the evidence Josephus adduces, e.g. the *dikaiomata* of the Jews in Antioch, *B.J.* vii 5, 2 (110), could just as easily refer to the privileges of an immigrant community; and thirdly, that he has to resort to weak indirect arguments, such as the entitlement of the Jews in Antioch to receive a cash payment in lieu of oil, *Ant.* xii 3, 1 (120).[8] These arguments do not however amount to a conclusive disproof of Josephus' claims. Without clear documentary evidence on either side, the question must be left open.

The same must be said for the question of Jewish citizenship in Alexandria, which was keenly disputed in Antiquity. Here too, it is repeatedly claimed by Josephus that Jews received citizenship already at the founding of the city.[9] Thus he states that Alexander the Great

Cohen, *The Seleucid Colonies* (1978).

4. *Ant.* xii 3, 1 (119): Σέλευκος ὁ Νικάτωρ ἐν αἷς ἔκτισε πόλεσιν ἐν τῇ Ἀσίᾳ καὶ τῇ κάτω Συρίᾳ καὶ ἐν τῇ μητροπόλει Ἀντιοχείᾳ πολιτείας αὐτοὺς ἠξίωσε καὶ τοῖς ἐνοικισθεῖσιν ἰσοτίμους ἀπέφηνε Μακεδόσιν καὶ Ἕλλησιν, ὡς τὴν πολιτείαν ταύτην ἔτι καὶ νῦν διαμένειν.

5. *B.J.* vii 5, 2 (110). Cf. for the whole subject, besides *Ant.* xii 3, 1 (119–24), also *C. Ap.* ii 4 (39): αὐτῶν γὰρ ἡμῶν οἱ τὴν Ἀντιόχειαν κατοικοῦντες Ἀντιοχεῖς ὀνομάζονται· τὴν γὰρ πολιτείαν αὐτοῖς ἔδωκεν ὁ κτίστης Σέλευκος.

6. *B.J.* vii 3, 3 (43): μάλιστα δ' αὐτοῖς ἀδεᾶ τὴν ἐκεῖ κατοίκησιν οἱ μετ' Ἀντίοχον βασιλεῖς παρέσχον. *Ibid.* (44): οἱ δὲ μετ' αὐτὸν τὴν βασιλείαν παραλαβόντες ... συνεχώρησαν αὐτοῖς ἐξ ἴσου τῆς πόλεως τοῖς Ἕλλησι μετέχειν.

7. *B.J.* vii 5, 2 (100–11); *Ant.* xii 31, 1 (121–2).

8. V. Tcherikover, *Hellenistic Civilization and the Jews* (1959), pp. 328–9.

9. On the citizenship of Jews in Alexandria see A. Bludau, *Juden und Judenverfolgung im alten Alexandria* (1906); J. Juster, *Les Juifs dans l'empire romain* II (1914), pp. 6–14; H. I. Bell, *Jews and Christians in Egypt* (1924), also *Juden und Griechen im römischen Alexandreia* (1926), esp. pp. 24–7; Th. Reinach, 'L'empereur Claude et les Juifs d'après un nouveau document', REJ 78 (1924); CPJ I, pp. 39–43 (esp. p. 39, n. 100) and 61–74; V. Tcherikover, *Hellenistic Civilization and the Jews*, pp. 320–8; P. M. Fraser, *Ptolemaic Alexandria* (1971), pp. 54–8; A. Kasher, *The Jews in Hellenistic and Roman Egypt* (1978) (Hebrew).

bestowed on them 'equal rights with the Macedonians' (these were the full Alexandrian citizens), and that the Diadochi allowed them also to call themselves Macedonians.[10] In the Roman period none of these rights were changed. They were expressly confirmed by Julius Caesar, as might still be read in the time of Josephus on a *stele* erected in Alexandria.[11] In the persecution under Caligula the rights of Alexandrian Jews were admittedly trampled on. Flaccus even promulgated an edict declaring them to be foreigners and aliens.[12] But as soon as Claudius came to the throne Josephus says that he took steps to reaffirm the privileges of the Jewish community.[13] In the edict which Josephus states that he then promulgated, he explicitly acknowledges that the Jews were called 'Alexandrians', had been fellow-settlers with the first Alexandrians and had received equal rights from the kings. Unfortunately, there must be some doubt as to the authenticity of these words of Claudius. For in his well-known letter of November A.D. 41, preserved on papyrus (CPJ II, no. 153), he speaks in rather different terms. Firstly he tells the Alexandrians to behave gently and humanely 'to the Jews who have for a long time been dwelling in the same city' (ll. 83–4): Ἰουδαίο⟨ι⟩ς τοῖς τὴν αὐτὴν πόλειν ἐκ πολλῶν χρόνων οἰκοῦσει (*sic*). Then, some lines later (ll. 92 ff.), he tells the Jews not to intrude themselves into the games presided over by Alexandrian magistrates 'as people who are able to draw benefit from their own property and in a city which belongs to others to enjoy an abundance of plentiful good things' (μηδὲ ἐπισπαίειν γυμνασιαρχικοῖς ἢ κοσμητικοῖς ἀγῶσει, καρπουμένους μὲν τὰ οἰκία ἀπολα⟨ύ⟩οντας δὲ ἐν ἀλλοτρίᾳ πόλει περιουσίας ἀπθόνων ἀγαθῶν).

Claudius' words clearly imply that he conceived of the Jews as being long-standing inhabitants of the city with a right to be there; but equally that he did not see them as possessing citizens' rights identical with those of the Greek inhabitants. What he says is not in itself

---

10. Jos. *C. Ap.* ii 4 (35–6): ἴσης παρὰ τοῖς Μακεδόσι τιμῆς ἐπέτυχον ... καὶ μέχρι νῦν αὐτῶν ἡ φυλὴ τὴν προσηγορίαν εἶχεν Μακεδόνες. *B.J.* ii 18, 7 (487): Ἀλέξανδρος .. ἔδωκεν τὸ μετοικεῖν κατὰ τὴν πόλιν ἐξ ἰσοτιμίας (Niese: ἴσου μοίρας, clearly corrupt for ἰσομοιρίας) πρὸς τοὺς Ἕλληνας. διέμεινε δὲ αὐτοῖς ἡ τιμὴ καὶ παρὰ τῶν διαδόχων, οἵ .. καὶ χρηματίζειν ἐπέτρεψαν Μακεδόνας.

11. *Ant.* xiv 10, 1 (188): Καῖσαρ Ἰούλιος τοῖς ἐν Ἀλεξανδρείᾳ Ἰουδαίοις ποιήσας χαλκῆν στήλην ἐδήλωσεν ὅτι Ἀλεξανδρέων πολῖται εἰσίν. *C. Ap.* ii 4 (37): τὴν στήλην τὴν ἑστῶσαν ἐν Ἀλεξανδρείᾳ καὶ τὰ δικαιώματα περιέχουσαν ἃ Καῖσαρ ὁ μέγας τοῖς Ἰουδαίοις ἔδωκεν. Philo, *In Flaccum* 10 (78) also emphasizes that the Jews had the legal position of Ἀλεξανδρεῖς and not of Αἰγύπτιοι.

12. Philo, *In Flaccum* 8 (54): τίθησι πρόγραμμα, δι' οὗ ξένους καὶ ἐπήλυδας ἡμᾶς ἀπεκάλει.

13. *Ant.* xix 5 (280–5) with a retrospective survey of the history of the citizenship of Jews in Alexandria: ἐπιγνοὺς ἀνέκαθεν τοὺς ἐν Ἀλεξανδρείᾳ Ἰουδαίους Ἀλεξανδρεῖς λεγομένους συγκατοικισθέντας τοῖς πρώτοις εὐθὺ καιροῖς Ἀλεξανδρεῦσι καὶ ἴσης πολιτείας παρὰ τῶν βασιλέων τετευχότας...

evidence for the original rights of the Jewish community, if for no other reason than the fact that elsewhere in the same papyrus (ll. 66–7) he confesses himself unable to say whether or not the city had possessed a council (*boule*) in the Ptolemaic period. But they do seem to compel the conclusion that the wording of the edict quoted by Josephus cannot be authentic. As in the other cases, there is no reason to doubt that the Jews enjoyed long-established rights in Alexandria. But whether these should be described as rights of citizenship was disputed in Antiquity (see the papyrus quoted on p. 50 above) and must remain in doubt today. Josephus however records that under Vespasian and Titus the rights of citizenship (τὰ δίκαια τὰ τῆς πολιτείας) of the Jews in both Alexandria and Antioch were preserved in the face of demands from the Greek inhabitants.[14]

Apart from the cities which were newly founded in the Hellenistic period, Jews were claimed to have enjoyed the right of citizenship in the cities of the Ionian coast, particularly in Ephesus. Whatever rights there were, were probably bestowed upon them there by Antiochus II Theos (261–246 B.C.); the long-accepted idea that this will have been in the course of a general process of granting democratic constitutions to these cities rests however on very slender foundations.[15] When the city

14. *Ant.* xii 3, 1 (121): δεηθέντες οἱ Ἀλεξανδρεῖς καὶ Ἀντιοχεῖς ἵνα τὰ δίκαια τῆς πολιτείας μηκέτι μένῃ τοῖς Ἰουδαίοις, οὐκ ἐπέτυχον. For discussions of Josephus' claims written before the publication of the papyrus containing Claudius' letter see e.g. Th. Mommsen, *Römische Gesch.* V, p. 491; H. Willrich, *Beiträge zur alten Geschichte* III (1903), pp. 403–7; J. Wellhausen, *Israelit. u. jüd. Gesch.* (⁴1901), pp. 239 ff.; F. Stähelin, *Der Antisemitismus des Altertums* (1905), p. 35.

15. *Ant.* xii 3, 2 (125) runs: τῶν γὰρ Ἰώνων κινηθέντων ἐπ᾽ αὐτοὺς καὶ δεομένων τοῦ Ἀγρίππου, ἵνα τῆς πολιτείας, ἣν αὐτοῖς ἔδωκεν Ἀντίοχος ὁ Σελεύκου υἱωνός, ὁ παρὰ τοῖς Ἕλλησι θεὸς λεγόμενος, μόνοι μετέχωσιν... The phrase τῆς πολιτείας, ἣν αὐτοῖς ἔδωκεν could be construed to mean 'the (democratic) constitution which he granted to them' (so e.g. Josephus Loeb vol. VII, App. C). But it is much more natural to read πολιτεία as meaning 'citizenship'; αὐτοῖς in that case would most naturally mean the Jews. The Milesians did however grant Antiochus II the additional name 'Theos' because he delivered them from the tyrant Timarchos (Appian, *Syr.* 65; confirmed by the inscriptions: OGIS, no. 226 = Ins. Didyma, no. 358; OGIS, no. 227 = Ins. Didyma, no. 493). Similarly, on an inscription from Smyrna it is stated of Seleucus II, son and successor of Antiochus II, that he upheld the city's *autonomia* and *demokratia* (ll. 10–11). Since directly preceding this there is an honorific allusion to Antiochus II, it seems that he was the real benefactor of the city. Seleucus II merely confirmed the rights bestowed by him. See OGIS, no. 229 = H. H. Schmitt, *Staatsverträge des Altertums* III (1969), no. 492 (with bibliography and discussion). Given the fluctuating boundaries of the power of the rival Hellenistic monarchies and the nature of the diplomatic vocabulary employed in relation to the king by the cities in their public decrees, these allusions are not of themselves enough to establish a general policy of the granting of democratic constitutions by Antiochus II. If however we take the allusion by Josephus to be to the granting of citizenship to the Jews there, there is some support for this in Jos. *C. Ap.* ii 4 (39): οἱ ἐν Ἐφέσῳ καὶ κατὰ τὴν ἄλλην Ἰωνίαν τοῖς αὐθιγενέσι πολίταις ὁμωνυμοῦσιν, τοῦτο παρασχόντων αὐτοῖς τῶν διαδόχων. But once again the exact nature of the right granted is

authorities demanded in the time of Augustus that the Jews should either be excluded from these rights, or be compelled to give up their own special cult, and worship the native gods, M. Agrippa, who at that time had overall charge of the Greek provinces, protected the ancient rights of the Jews, whose case was represented by Nicolaus of Damascus in the name of Herod (14 B.C.).[16] Jews in Sardis also enjoyed certain specific rights, but the text which attests these is not secure evidence for their having enjoyed the citizenship also.[17] Josephus similarly reports that under Augustus the Jewish communities not only of Asia but also of Cyrene took steps to protect the 'equality of rights' (*isonomia*) granted them by the Hellenistic kings.[18] Once again the exact content of the term remains unclear.

The situation created through the granting of all these rights to the Jews involved certain contradictions. On the one hand they formed in the pagan cities a community of strangers independently organized to take care of their religious affairs, and whose religion remained wholly incompatible with any kind of pagan worship. On the other hand they nevertheless shared in the rights and duties of the ordinary life of the cities; if it were the case, in some cities, that the Jews as a group also possessed the full citizenship, then they will have enjoyed the rights of voting in the city assemblies and of holding office.[19] It is however precisely at this point that our evidence becomes unclear. Firstly it contains no unambiguous proof that members of the Jewish community could vote in the *ekklesia* of any Greek city. For instance in A.D. 66, when the people of Alexandria met in the amphitheatre to debate sending an embassy to Nero, some Jews who entered with them were driven out as 'enemies' and 'spies', *B.J.* ii 18, 7 (490–1). As for more specific communal or political roles, documentary evidence from Ptolemais in Cyrenaica, for example, shows persons with Jewish names in lists of *epheboi* from various years in the first half of the first century A.D., and a city official (*nomophylax*) of A.D. 60-1 called Elazar son of

---

not clear. Caution is enjoined by the fact that in OGIS, no. 229 = Schmitt, *Staatsverträge* III, no. 492 of c. 240, Smyrna grants citizenship to persons living in Magnesia 'provided that they are free and Hellenes' (l. 45). For a discussion of the entire question see Tcherikover, *Hellenistic Civilization*, pp. 288–90 and 329–31, and for the most detailed recent treatment of the entire context see W. Orth, *Königlicher Machtanspruch und städtische Freiheit* (1977).

16. *Ant.* xii 3, 2 (126) ; xvi 2, 3–5 (27–65).

17. *Ant.* xiv 10, 24 (259–61), a decree of Sardis with the words οἱ κατοικοῦντες ἡμῶν ἐν τῇ πόλει Ἰουδαῖοι πολῖται, where the last word seems clearly to be an interpolation.

18. *Ant.* xvi 6, 1 (160) ; see e.g. J. Marquardt, *Staatsverwaltung* I (1881), p. 463 ; Tcherikover, *Hellenistic Civilization*, p. 331 ; S. Applebaum, *Jews and Greeks in Ancient Cyrene* (1979), pp. 176 ff.

19. The essence of citizenship lay in sharing the power of government. See e.g. E. Szanto, *Das griechische Bürgerrecht* (1892), pp. 2 ff.

Jason.[20] However the meaning of such items of evidence must remain uncertain, since we cannot ascertain its bearing on the collective rights of the Jewish community in a city, nor be certain that the persons concerned had not lapsed from Judaism, like Tiberius Iulius Alexander (see p. 137 below), or Antiochus, a member of the Jewish community of Antioch, *B.J.* vii 3, 3 (47–53).

On the other hand significant changes are attested from the early third century onwards. Septimius Severus and Caracalla allowed Jews to hold city offices (*honores*), while stating that they were exempt from obligations which infringed their religion (*Dig.* l 2, 3, 3). From approximately this period, note that Ti. Claudius Polycharmus in Stobi had 'performed all his political functions in accordance with Judaism' (p. 67 above); in the third century a 'father of the synagogue of the Jews' at Volubilis was described as a 'leading citizen', *protopolites* (p. 64 above). In the altered conditions of the late third and fourth centuries, when the distinction between local offices (*honores*) and obligations (*munera*) effectively disappeared, and the cities were seeking to distribute the functions imposed by the state over as many categories as possible, including non-citizen residents (*incolae*), the question became one of the strictly limited exemption of specific numbers of synagogue officials in each city. This situation is first attested in a ruling of Constantine addressed to the town council of Cologne in A.D. 321.[21] In the classical period, however, it does not appear to have been normal for Jews either to vote or to hold local office. None the less the existence within pagan Greek cities of Jewish minorities enjoying established rights was bound to lead to continuous friction. For a division between the spheres of religion and political life was utterly alien to classical antiquity: in the affairs of the city the cult of the city's gods had a central place. It will have been a constant cause of conflict to have among the citizens, as a permanent group enjoying defined privileges, people who persisted not only in worshipping their own god, as it were next door to the city gods, but also in rejecting every kind of pagan worship as an abomination. Tolerance of such fundamentally opposed religious systems side by side with one another was in reality possible only within the cosmopolitan framework of the Roman empire. There was thus room here for the Jews as well. By contrast, to the city

20. Ephebes: QAL 4 (1961), p. 20, no. 7: i, 34 and ii, 47 = CJZC, no. 7: Βαρθύβας Βαρθύβ(ρ)α. ii, 48: Ἐλάσζαρ Ἐλάζορος. i, 57: Ἰούλιος Ἰησοῦτος. ii, 49: Ἀγαθοκλῆς Ἐλάζαρος. *Nomophylax*: QAL 4 (1961), p. 16, no. 2 = CJZC, no. 8: Ἐλάζα[ρ Ἰ]άσωνος.

21. *C.Th.* xvi 8, 3. See, for a succinct treatment, A. H. M. Jones, *The Later Roman Empire* (1964), pp. 946–8. For the general background, F. Millar, 'Empire and City, Augustus to Julian: Obligations, Excuses and Status', JRS 73 (1983), pp. 76–91. In Minorca in the early fifth century Jews are found occupying prominent local offices including that of *defensor civitatis*. See E. D. Hunt, 'St. Stephen in Minorca', JThSt 33 (1982), pp. 106–24.

communities which held fast to the old way of life in the religious sphere
as well as in others, the existence of Jewish fellow-inhabitants must have
been a thorn in the flesh. It is therefore not surprising, but rather quite
consistent with the overall historical framework, that the Jews were
persecuted by the cities, while the higher authority of the Roman
imperium took them under its protection. Hatred against the Jews
repeatedly broke out in the cities, and of course especially where the
Jews had the most marked communal rights, as in Alexandria, Antioch,
many cities in Asia Minor, and even in Caesarea in Palestine, where
pagans and Jews had received equality of rights from Herod the
Great.[22] The central complaint was precisely that the Jews refused to
worship the gods of the city.[23] But it was always the Roman supreme
authority which protected the religious freedom of the Jews, so long as
the latter did not forfeit these rights (as in Judaea in A.D. 66) through
revolutionary action. It is very striking how Nicolaus of Damascus, in
the speech in which he pleaded the rights of Jews of Asia Minor before
Agrippa, emphasized it as something novel, as a benefaction first
brought into being by the Roman world-order, that men were
everywhere allowed 'to live by the worship of their own gods'.[24]

The more favourable the general attitude of the Roman world-power
to Judaism, the more worthwhile it was for many of the Jews in the
Diaspora, not only in Rome but also elsewhere, to possess Roman
citizenship. In Rome, according to Philo, most of the Jews living there
had it by virtue of their position as descendants of freedmen. Many of

---

22. In Alexandria Jews and pagans lived from the foundation of the city onwards in
continual disharmony, *B.J.* ii 18, 7 (487–93); at the time of Caligula it was the pagan
mob there who above all persecuted the Jews, even before the emperor himself proceeded
against them (Philo, *In Flaccum*). In the reign of Vespasian the Alexandrians addressed
the emperor with the request that the Jews there should be deprived of their rights, *Ant.*
xii 3, 1 (121). In Antioch in the time of Vespasian it came to bloodshed, *B.J.* vii 3, 3
(43–53); Titus received a request that the Jews should all be driven from the city, and
when Titus did not grant this, that at least they should be deprived of their rights, *B.J.* vii
5, 2 (100–11); *Ant.* xii 3, 1 (121). In Asia Minor the city communes continually renewed
their efforts to hinder the Jews in the practice of their religion, and thus necessitated the
Roman edicts of toleration, *Ant.* xii 3, 2 (125–7); xvi 2, 3–5 (27–65), and above all the
edicts in *Ant.* xiv 10 (186–267) and xvi 6 (160–78). The same happened in Cyrene, *Ant.*
xvi 6, 1 and 5 (160–1, 169–70). In Caesarea pagans and Jews were repeatedly involved in
bloody conflict, *Ant.* xx 8, 7, 9 (173–8, 182–4); *B.J.* ii 13, 7 (266–70); 14, 4–5 (284–92);
18, 1 (457). Even in cities where there is no evidence that the Jews enjoyed established
rights, the hatred of the pagan mob broke out against them from time to time, in
particular at the outbreak of the Jewish war in Ascalon, Ptolemais, Tyre, Hippos,
Gadara, *B.J.* ii 18, 5 (477–8) and Damascus, *B.J.* ii 20, 2 (559–61). Of the Ascalonites
Philo says that they bore implacable hostility towards Jews, *Leg.* 30 (205). Of the
Phoenicians, the Tyrians were, according to Josephus, especially hostile in their attitude
to Jews, *C. Ap.* i 13 (70).

23. *Ant.* xii 3, 2 (126). Cf. *C. Ap.* ii 6 (65).

24. *Ant.* xvi 2, 4 (36): ἐξεῖναι κατὰ χώραν ἑκάστοις τὰ οἰκεῖα τιμῶσιν ἄγειν καὶ διαζῆν.

the Jewish prisoners of war whom Pompey had brought to Rome and sold into slavery were liberated by their masters, and gained citizen rights along with their manumission, rights which their descendants retained from then onwards.[25] It even appears that such *libertini* returned again to Jerusalem from Rome and founded there their own community, for the 'Synagogue of *libertini*' mentioned in Act. 6:9 can scarcely be other than Roman freedmen and their descendants.[26] Even in Jerusalem, therefore, there lived Jews with the Roman citizenship; but we find them also elsewhere as early as the late Republic, particularly in Asia Minor.[27] A Roman citizen, Marcus Laelius Onasion, appears among the *archontes* of the Jewish *politeuma* of Berenice in a decree of (probably) A.D. 24 (p. 61 above). It is thus not wholly exceptional that the apostle Paul, from Tarsus in Cilicia, was in possession of the Roman citizenship (Ac. 16:37 ff.; 22:25–9; 23:27), though there is no way of determining how this came about.[28] How some Jews in the province of Asia obtained a right to it is also beyond our knowledge.[29] The fact itself is hardly questionable since it is also

25. Philo, *Leg.* 23 (155–7): Ῥωμαῖοι δὲ ἦσαν οἱ πλείους ἀπελευθερωθέντες. αἰχμάλωτοι γὰρ ἀχθέντες εἰς Ἰταλίαν ὑπὸ τῶν κτησαμένων ἠλευθερώθησαν, οὐδὲν τῶν πατρίων παραχαράξαι βιασθέντες .. ἀλλ' ὁ μὲν (Augustus) οὔτε ἐξῴκισε τῆς Ῥώμης ἐκείνους, οὔτε τὴν Ῥωμαϊκὴν αὐτῶν ἀφείλετο πολιτείαν. Cf. Tac. *Ann.* ii 85: 'quattuor milia libertini generis'. Manumission could take place in different ways. By the proper and formal manumission the freedman received Roman citizenship. See RE XIII, cols. 104 ff., s.v. 'Libertini'. This citizenship obtained by the freed slave himself was not however of full status; he was for instance able to vote, but not to hold public office. See Th. Mommsen, *Römisches Staatsrecht* III.1 (1887), pp. 420–57; E. von Herzog, *Gesch. und System der römischen Staatsverfassung* II.2 (1891), pp. 936 ff.; see also A. M. Duff, *Freedmen in the Early Roman Empire* (1928), pp. 12–35; S. Treggiari, *Roman Freedmen during the Late Republic* (1969), pp. 1–86; G. Fabre, *Libertus* (1981), pp. 5–68.

26. *Libertinus* is distinguished from *libertus* only in that the former indicates the social and legal status of the freed slave, the latter the same man as the freedman of a particular master (often with possessive genitive of a *praenomen* of possession). Children of freedmen were originally subsumed under the category of *libertini*, but this was no longer the case according to later usage (see Mommsen, *Römisches Staatsrecht* III.1, pp. 422 ff.). However, the Jerusalem congregation founded by freedmen appears to have retained its name συναγωγὴ Λιβερτίνων also among later generations. Cf. the commentaries on Ac. 6:2.

27. As in Ephesus, *Ant.* xiv 10, 13, 16, 19 (228, 234, 240); ?Sardis, xiv 10, 17 (235); Delos, *Ant.* xiv 10, 14 (232); in general: *Ant.* xiv 10, 18 (237).

28. Doubts were expressed with regard to the Roman citizenship of Paul by, for example, E. Renan, *Paulus* (1869), p. 442 = *Saint Paul* (*Oeuvres complètes* IV, ed. H. Psichari, 1949), p. 1063, and F. Overbeck, *Erklärung des Apostelgesch.*, pp. 266 ff., 429 ff. The only reason for these worth consideration is the frequent fettering of the apostle (2 Cor. 11:24–5); but such infringements of the law occurred not infrequently. See e.g. W. M. Ramsay, *St Paul: The traveller and the Roman Citizen* (1895); Th. Mommsen, 'Die Rechtsverhältnisse des Apostels Paulus', ZNW 2 (1901), pp. 81–96 = *Ges. Schr.* III (1907), pp. 431–46; A. N. Sherwin-White, *Roman Society and Roman Law in the New Testament* (1963), pp. 144 ff.

29. On the different ways in which Roman citizenship could be attained see RE, Suppl. I (1903), cols. 307 ff. s.v. 'civitas'; C. E. Goodfellow, *Roman Citizenship: A Study of its*

known that by the early first century B.C. many thousands of Roman citizens were living in Asia Minor.[30] The simultaneous possession of citizenship of Rome and (in some sense) of a Greek city, for which there is evidence in the case of the Jews in Ephesus and Sardis, as for the apostle Paul (Ac. 21:39: 'Ιουδαῖος, Ταρσεὺς τῆς Κιλικίας, οὐκ ἀσήμου πόλεω πολίτης), corresponds to the conditions of that period, in which it was not uncommon.[31]

The advantages granted along with the possession of the Roman citizenship were no doubt considerable. None the less it should be emphasised that almost all the evidence relating to the legal privileges of Roman citizens is ambivalent and controversial, and that few confident generalisations can be offered. The following can be said: (1) The third of the five edicts of Augustus from Cyrene (SEG IX, no. 8, iii) makes clear that Roman citizenship conferred immunity neither from direct Roman taxes on provincial land nor from personal obligations in a man's own city, unless such rights had been given by a specific grant. (2) The important document of the Triumviral period granting the Roman citizenship to Seleucus of Rhosus in Syria (IGLS, no. 718, ii) also grants freedom from tribute (*aneisphoria*), and the right, if accused, to choose to face trial in his own city, in a free city or before Roman magistrates or pro-magistrates. (3) It remains quite unclear to what extent a Roman citizen was normally considered to be subject to the laws of his own native city, or of any other city where he happened

---

Territorial and Numerical Expansion from the Earliest Times to the Death of Augustus (1935); F. Vittinghoff, *Römische Kolonisation und Bürgerrechtspolitik unter Caesar und Augustus* (1952); A. N. Sherwin-White, *The Roman Citizenship* ([2]1973); see also B. Holtheide, *Römische Bürgerrechtspolitik und römische Neubürger in der Provinz Asia* (1983).

30. The atrocity committed by Mithridates in 88 B.C. is well-known: he ordered the murder of all Roman citizens in Asia Minor, including women and children; see the evidence e.g. in E. Kuhn, *Die städtische und bürgerl. Verfassung des röm. Reiches* I, p. 25. The number of the victims is given by Valerius Maximus ix 2, ext. 3 as 80,000. This seems to have involved Italian-born citizens. Scarcely forty years later the number of Roman citizens in Asia Minor was so great that the consul Lentulus could raise two legions of Roman citizens there in 49 B.C. (Caesar, *B.C.* iii 4; see the passage on p. 120 above). In this case, however, they were certainly not only of Italian parentage. For the subject in general cf. also the literature mentioned above, n. 29.

31. According to earlier Roman notions 'simultaneous multiple citizenship or simultaneous membership of more than one community is logically as well as in practice impossible' (Mommsen, *Römisches Staatsrecht* III.1, p. 47). From Augustus, however, the opposite was the rule: 'Roman citizenship can be held along with that of any imperial municipality' (Mommsen, *op. cit.*, p. 699). It even happened not infrequently that one individual acquired citizenship in several cities; and a vain title hunter is attested as having spent considerable sums in order to be granted the *politeia* of a really large number of cities. See E. Szanto, *Das griechische Bürgerrecht* (1892), pp. 65–6. For the role of the citizenship of a city see e.g. L. Robert, *Hellenica* I (1940), pp. 37–42. Multiple citizenship is widely attested, e.g. in inscriptions honouring famous athletes, see L. Moretti, *Iscrizioni agonistiche greche* (1953), e.g. no. 79.

to be resident, and how the situation was affected if the city was a 'free' city, i.e. one formally exempt from the jurisdiction of the governor. All that is clear is that such cities might lose their freedom for flogging or executing Roman citizens.[32] (4) It can reasonably be accepted that Roman citizens were regarded as being in principle exempt from flogging by city magistrates or Roman officials, from torture and from cruel or humiliating forms of execution such as crucifixion.[33] (5) It is clear that there existed some right of appeal for Roman citizens against capital sentences. The earliest formal statement of a right of appeal, made formerly to the Roman *populus* and subsequently to the emperor, belongs however to the third century. Our evidence does not allow us to state, for the period in question, what were the exact workings of any such system of appeal, or how far it was exclusive to citizens.[34] (6) There is also some evidence of citizens being sent spontaneously by provincial governors to stand trial in Rome.[35]

Through possession of established rights in many Greek cities the Jews were given a degree of equality with the rest of the population, yet they do not seem generally to have filled any prominent public role there. On the contrary, possession of these rights gave rise to hostility and persecution, as we have seen. In some places, however, particularly in Egypt, Jews at certain periods played a prominent part in government and public life. The earlier Ptolemies are said to have been in the main favourably inclined towards them.[36] Individual Jews also secured important positions under some of the later Ptolemies. Ptolemy VI Philometor and his wife Cleopatra are said to have 'entrusted their whole kingdom to Jews, and the Jews Onias and Dositheus were commanders of the entire army'.[37] Even if this account by Josephus is

---

32. For various views see e.g. E. Kuhn, *Die städtische und bürgerl. Verfassung des römischen Reichs* II, p. 24; J. Marquardt, *Römische Staatsverwaltung* I (1881), pp. 75 ff.; A. H. M. Jones, *The Greek City* (1940), pp. 119; 130–1; see also J. Colin, *Les villes libres de l'Orient gréco-romain* (1965); A. J. Marshall, 'Romans under Chian Law', GRBS 10 (1969), pp. 255–71.

33. See Ac. 16:37 ff.; 22:25 ff.; RE s.v. 'crux'; U. Brasiello, *La repressione penale in diritto romano* (1937); P. Garnsey, *Social Status and Legal Privilege in the Roman Empire* (1970), esp. pp. 266 ff. Cf. P. A. Brunt, 'Evidence Given under Torture in the Principate', ZSS 97 (1980), pp. 256–65.

34. See RE s.v. 'appellatio' and 'provocatio'; Th. Mommsen, *Römisches Staatsrecht*[3] II, pp. 958 ff.; *idem*, *Römisches Strafrecht* (1899), pp. 242 ff.; see also H. Volkmann, *Zur Rechtssprechung im Prinzipat des Augustus* (1935); J. M. Kelly, *Princeps Iudex* (1957); A. H. M. Jones, *Studies in Roman Government and Law* (1960), ch. 4–5; Sherwin-White, *Roman Society and Roman Law* (1963), pp. 57 ff.; P. Garnsey, 'The Lex Iulia and Appeal under the Empire', JRS 56 (1966), pp. 167–89; F. Millar, *The Emperor in the Roman World* (1977), pp. 507–16.

35. See e.g. Pliny, *Ep.* x 96: 'Fuerunt alii similis amentiae, quos quia cives Romani erant adnotavi in urbem remittendos'.

36. Jos. *C. Ap.* ii 4 (44–7).

37. *C. Ap.* ii 5 (49).

exaggerated, it may be taken as certain that in the fraternal strife of
Ptolemy VI Philometor and his wife Cleopatra with Ptolemy VII
Physcon, the Jews, under the leadership of these two generals, took the
side of the former and earned their gratitude thereby.[38] Another
Cleopatra, daughter of the couple just mentioned, in the war against
her son Ptolemy Lathyrus, similarly appointed two Jews, Chelkias and
Ananias, to the command of her forces.[39] The name of Chelkias also
appears on the fragment of an honorific inscription according to which
the person concerned—perhaps not Chelkias himself but his son—was
honoured with the award of a golden crown as *strategos*.[40] Whether the
Ptolemaios son of Epikydes, *epistates* of the *phylakitai*, who helped the
Jews in Athribis to build their synagogue, was himself a Jew, remains
uncertain: he may have been a non-Jew friendly to the Jews.[41]
Tax-collectors with Jewish names occur on tax receipts of the Ptolemaic
period found in Egypt.[42]

In the Roman period also, some rich Jews in Alexandria still played
a prominent part in public life. In particular, we know that the office of
alabarch, i.e. probably, of customs superintendent on the Arabian side of
the Nile, was sometimes discharged by Jewish notables, as in the case of
Alexander, brother of the philosopher Philo, and later of a certain
Demetrius.[43] The *alabarch* Alexander was also the *epitropos*, or agent, of

---

38. The description by Josephus is on this point supported by the words of Apion which
he quotes, Jos. *C. Ap.* ii 5 (50) = GLAJJ I, no. 167: μετὰ ταῦτα, φησίν, 'Ονίας ἐπὶ τὴν πόλιν
ἤγαγε στρατὸν ⟨οὐκ⟩ ὀλίγον... Cf. also B. Niese, *Gesch. der griech. und makedon. Staaten* III,
pp. 213 ff.; CPJ I, pp. 20–1.

39. *Ant.* xiii 10, 4 (285); 13, 1–2 (348–55). In the first passage Josephus quotes a
passage from Strabo (GLAJJ I, no. 99, with Stern's comments) to support his account.
Chelkias and Ananias were the sons of the high priest Onias, builder of the temple at
Leontopolis.

40. CIJ II, no. 1450; cf. CPJ III, pp. 144–5. The text is fragmentary and the overall
meaning uncertain.

41. OGIS, no. 96 = SB V, no. 8872; CIJ II, no. 1443; see CPJ III, p. 142 (text on p.
41 above). On the title ἐπιστάτης τῶν φυλακιτῶν (probably distinct from ἀρχιφυλακίτης)
see Th. Reinach in REJ 17 (1888), pp. 235–58; and O. Hirschfeld, SAB 1891, p. 867
(taking these terms as synonymous). Since Jews in Egypt also rendered military service
(see above, pp. 41–2 f.) the Ptolemaeus mentioned may have been a Jew, as may
the *phylakitai* under him. See CPJ I, p. 17.

42. See CPJ I, pp. 18–19, and pp. 194–226. Cf. above, p. 57.

43. On Alexander, the brother of the philosopher Philo: *Ant.* xviii 6, 3 (159); 8, 1
(259); xix 5, 1 (276); xx 5, 2 (100). Demetrius: *Ant.* xx 7, 3 (147). U. Wilcken, *Griechische
Ostraka aus Ägypten und Nubien* I (1899), pp. 347–51. It is now generally accepted that the
term *alabarches* (OGIS, no. 570; inscription from Chalcis in Euboea, BCH 16 (1892), p.
119, no. 44, and later in Palladas, *Anth. Pal.* xi 383, 4) and the *arabarches* (OGIS, nos. 202;
674; 685; BGU II, no. 665; SEG IV, no. 520; *C. Theod.* iv 12, 9 = *C. Just.* iv 61, 9 (see
below); Cic. *ad Att.* ii 17, 3; Juvenal i 130, see Courtney ad loc.) are identical. See J.
Lesquier, *L'armée romaine d'Égypte* (1918), pp. 421 ff.; not accepted however by M.
Rostovtzeff, YCS 2 (1931), pp. 49–51. For proof that the 'Arabarch' was concerned with
the collection of taxes see esp. *C. Theod.* iv 12, 9 = *C. Just.* iv 61, 9 (Gratian, Valentinian

Antonia, mother of the emperor Claudius.[44] One of his sons, Marcus
Iulius Alexander, is known from a group of ostraka showing his agents
engaged in trade on the routes from Koptos to Berenike and Myos
Hormos.[45] The other brother, Tiberius Iulius Alexander, son of the
alabarch Alexander just mentioned, even attained the highest rank in
the Roman equestrian career, though at the price of apostasy from his
ancestral religion.[46] Jewish 'chief physicians' (*archiatroi*) occur on
inscriptions in Ephesus and Venosa (see above, pp. 23, 83). In Rome
itself individual Jews occasionally exercised some influence in upper
class society. But in the Empire in general the few cases of office-holding
known from Egypt in the early Empire remain wholly exceptional. It is
striking that some Jews in Judaea had attained equestrian rank by the
reign of Nero.[47] But in general it seems to have been only from around
A.D. 200 that Jews were able to hold even city offices (p. 131
above), and only for a brief period in the late fourth and early fifth
centuries that they might hold office in the imperial service. Both civic
and imperial posts were formally forbidden to Jews in the *Novella* 3 of
Theodosius II in A.D. 438.[48]

---

and Theodosius): 'Usurpationem totius licentiae summovemus circa vectigal
Arabarchiae per Aegyptum atque Augustamnicam constitutum, nihilque super
transductionem animalium, quae sine praebitione solita minime permittenda est,
temeritate per licentiam vindicari concedimus.' This interpretation is established by an
inscription from Coptos, OGIS, no. 674. This contains a tariff which states how much the
contractors for the tariff payable to the *arabarchia* in Coptos may levy. No explanation can
be offered of the appearance of the title on the brief inscription from Xanthos (OGIS, no.
570), the Christian epitaph from Chalcis (BCH 16 (1892), p. 119), or an inscription from
Alexandria Troas, J. M. Cook, *The Troad* (1973), p. 405, no. 31.

44. *Ant.* xix 5, 1 (276).
45. CPJ II, nos. 419a-c.
46. *Ant.* xx 5, 2 (100): τοῖς γὰρ πατρίοις οὐκ ἐνέμεινεν οὗτος ἔθεσιν. On Tiberius Iulius
Alexander see vol. I, p. 457, n. 9.
47. Among the Jews crucified in A.D. 66 by Florus in Jerusalem, there were some who
possessed the status of Roman *equites*, *B.J.* ii 14, 9 (308). Their execution by Florus is
rightly characterized by Josephus as a particularly serious infringement of the law.
48. See E. D. Hunt in JThSt 33 (1982), pp. 118–22. For a full collection of Imperial
legislative texts, with Hebrew introduction and commentary, see now A. Linder, *Roman
Imperial Legislation on the Jews* (1983).

IV. Religious Life

The Jews, though scattered throughout the ancient world, maintained their religious identity for the most part with remarkable tenacity. There were of course cases of defection to paganism or syncretism. If in Jerusalem itself at the time of Antiochus Epiphanes some circles were ready to take part in pagan cults, it is scarcely surprising that at Oropus in Greece in the first half of the third century a Jew freed a slave 'having seen a dream, at the orders of the god Amphiaraos and Hygieia' (p. 65 above); or that in Iasus in Caria, for example, one Niketas from Jerusalem was a patron of the festival of Dionysus (p. 25 above). In the Roman period, also, the example of Tiberius Iulius Alexander was not unique (if οἱ ποτὲ ’Ιουδαῖοι on an inscription from Smyrna (p. 20 above) means 'the former Jews'; A. T. Kraabel, JJS 33 (1982), p. 455, asserts that it means 'people formerly of Judaea'). Examples of syncretistic attitudes are also attested, especially in Egypt. A remarkable example is the Hellenistic Jewish author Artapanus, from whom some fragments have been preserved (see pp. 521–5 below). He thought to enhance the reputation of Judaism by representing the patriarchs and Moses not only as creators of all the world civilizations, but as founders of the Egyptian polytheistic cults, as he understood them. In the temple of Pan at Apollonopolis Magna (Edfu in Upper Egypt) are two inscriptions in which Jews express gratitude for a rescue they have experienced to 'the god' (the expression is no doubt deliberately unspecific).[1] Such traces of syncretism however never acquired the same extent or significance as with other religions of the East. On the whole, the resistant attitude of Judaism in the face of other religions remained a continuing characteristic.

Constant contact with Greek culture could admittedly not remain without influence on the internal development of Judaism in the Diaspora. Particularly in places where the Jews, through wealth and social status, were in a position to make use of the educational means of their time—as was specially the case in Alexandria (see esp. E. G. Turner in JRS 44 (1954), pp. 54 ff.)—Judaism struck out in a direction substantially different from that of Palestinian Judaism. The educated Jew of the Diaspora was not only a Jew but at the same time a Greek by language, education and customs, and he was compelled by the force of circumstances to try to reconcile and unite Judaism and Hellenism.

1. CIJ II, nos. 1537-8 (CPJ III, pp. 165–6). For the texts see p. 58 above.

Such external influences are clearly shown for instance in the use of pagan motifs in epitaphs, and especially of representation in art, extending in the case of the Dura-Europos synagogue to narrative frescoes of Old Testament scenes (see vol. I, p. 556, n. 192). There is also scattered evidence of Jews attending public shows in Greek cities (pp. 25, 128 above), and ample indications that Philo, at least, was familiar with Greek athletics; see H. A. Harris, *Greek Athletics and the Jews* (1976), ch. 3 (see further §§ 33 and 34).

Such a fusion of Greek and Jewish religiosity was possible to a certain degree, so long as the emphasis lay on general religious and ethical ideas, and the specifically Jewish, the cultic and ceremonial, elements were kept in the background; in other words, so long as the prophetic trends in Judaism were followed rather than the legal and Pharisaic. The Old Testament itself is after all familiar with the thought that obedience is better than sacrifice and heedfulness better than the fat of rams (1 Sam. 15:22); that God delights in love and not in sacrifice, and in the knowledge of God rather than in burnt-offerings (Hos. 6:6).[2] Even such a man as Jesus ben Sira, who so energetically urges his reader to keep the Law and holds the priestly cult in high regard, also says that sacrifice is of no avail if a man acts unjustly towards his neighbour (Ecclus. 7:9; 31:21–31), that God does not allow himself to be bribed by sacrifice (32:14–26), and that the true gift is to be good and to avoid evil (32:1–5). These views were very strongly emphasized, for instance, in the Greek verses quoted by Christian writers, who attribute them either to Menander or Philemon. If, as has often been claimed, they are of Jewish origin, it is significant that they express the view that it is an error if a man thinks that he will obtain God's favour by sacrifice and votive gifts. Man must be good and virtuous, do nothing evil. 'Sacrifice to God by being at all times upright.'[3]

This view was perhaps more widespread in the Diaspora than in the motherland in the post-Maccabean period. The influence of the Greek environment may have tended to suppress the extended observance of Jewish law and custom as taught by the Pharisees more than in the homeland. The Jew in the Diaspora may have felt himself more strongly directed to place in the forefront his general religious ideas, the

2. See e.g. G. F. Moore, *Judaism in the first centuries of the Christian Era* I (1927), pp. 497–534.

3. The verses are in Pseudo-Justin, *De monarchia* 4 (*Corpus Apologet.*, ed. Otto, 3rd ed., III, pp. 140 ff.), and with some variations in Clem. Alex., *Strom.* v 14, 119 ff. and in Euseb. *Praep. Evang.* xiii 13, 45–6. Pseudo-Justin ascribes them to Philemon, Clement to Menander. The following lines are particularly noteworthy (given according to the recension of Clement): εἴ τις δὲ θυσίαν προσφέρων, ὦ Πάμφιλε ... εὔνουν νομίζει τὸν θεὸν καθεστάναι, πεπλάνητ' ἐκεῖνος καὶ φρένας κούφας ἔχει. δεῖ γὰρ τὸν ἄνδρα χρήσιμον πεφυκέναι ... θεῷ δὲ θῦε διὰ τέλους δίκαιος ὤν. Note however that A. Koerte, *Menander, Reliquiae* II (1959), Fr. 683, accepts their attribution to Menander.

notion of a supreme God and of a future reward. Only with this presupposition could he to a certain extent harmonize Jewish and Greek culture, and only by emphasizing the universal elements may he have been able to rely on tolerance from his Greek surroundings. The task of apologetic and proselytism may itself have brought about a tendency towards an 'attenuated Judaism' (see p. 153 below).

Nevertheless, it was only a matter of differences of degree between Diaspora and Palestinian Judaism. In Palestine itself, on the one hand, the stream of prophetic religion was not entirely stopped by the strict observances emphasised by the Pharisees; and on the other, Hellenism exercised a profound influence (see esp. vol. II, pp. 29–81). Conversely, the Judaism of the Diaspora never abandoned Jewish observance.[4] The notion that in the Diaspora a strong and radical anti-legalistic current existed is in no way attested by the sources.[5] Attenuation was a tendency only, not an accomplished fact. Certainly, according to Philo there were those who, inasmuch as they understood the wording of the Law as a symbolic expression of supernatural truths, studied the latter scrupulously but had little opinion of the former.[6] But the number of these Jewish philosophers, who progressed from allegorical exegesis to a depreciation of the literal sense, or even to an actual disregard of it, can have been very small. Diaspora Judaism as a whole always maintained contact with Palestine; it sent every year to the Temple the dues required by the Law, it observed the Sabbath and the laws of diet and purity. There are no grounds for the conclusion that non-observance of the Law would have been tolerated anywhere in the synagogue-communities of the Diaspora. The mocking remarks of Roman satirists themselves show how steadfastly in Rome itself the average Jew kept to his way of life based on the Law; and for the educated circles of Alexandria we have the classical example of Philo. This learned philosopher, who was an expert in the art of allegorical interpretation of the Law, rejects most decidedly any neglect of the literal sense. Text

---

4. On 'The main trends of the spirit within Judaism' see e.g. G. Hoennicke, *Das Judenchristentum im ersten u. zweiten Jahrhundert* (1908), pp. 33–77.

5. This opinion was vigorously defended by M. Friedländer, who saw in this law-emancipated Judaism of the Diaspora the direct foundation of law-emancipated Christianity. His writings relevant to this subject were: *Zur Entstehungsgeschichte des Christentums* (1894); *Das Judentum in der vorchristlichen griechischen Welt* (1897); *Der vorchristliche jüdische Gnostizismus* (1898); *Der Antichrist in den vorchristlichen jüdischen Quellen* (1901); 'The "Pauline" emancipation from the law a product of the pre-Christian Jewish Diaspora', JQR 14 (1902), pp. 265–302; *Geschichte der jüdischen Apologetik als Vorgeschichte des Christentums* (1903); *Griechische Philosophie im Alten Testament* (1904); *Die religiösen Bewegungen innerhalb des Judentums im Zeitalter Jesu* (1905); *Synagoge und Kirche in ihren Anfängen* (1908). But cf. e.g. G. F. Moore, *Judaism* I (1927), pp. 93–121; 359–64; V. Tcherikover, *Hellenistic Civilization and the Jews* (1961), pp. 344–77.

6. Philo, *De migratione Abrahami* 16 (89): εἰσὶ γάρ τινες οἱ τοὺς ῥητοὺς νόμους σύμβολα νοητῶν πραγμάτων ὑπολαμβάνοντες τὰ μὲν ἄγαν ἠκρίβωσαν, τῶν δὲ ῥᾳθύμως ὠλιγώρησαν.

and higher meaning are for him related as body to soul. As care must be taken of the body only as the dwelling-place of the soul, so must the literal sense of the Law be carefully considered (οὕτω καὶ τῶν ῥητῶν νόμων ἐπιμελητέον).[7] In his representation of the Mosaic giving of the Law he shows throughout how these laws are the most reasonable and most humane, while he presupposes as self-evident the connection with their literal sense.[8]

The regular Sabbath services in the synagogue were an all-important means of maintaining the ancestral religion in the Diaspora communities.[9] There is no doubt at all that these took place wherever there was even only one congregation. According to Philo, 'on the sabbath days in all the cities thousands of houses of learning were opened, in which discernment and moderation and proficiency and righteous living and indeed all virtues were taught'.[10] The apostle Paul found Jewish synagogues everywhere on his journeys in Asia Minor and Greece: in Pisidian Antioch (Ac. 13:14), Iconium (Ac. 14:1), Ephesus (Ac. 18:19, 26; 19:8), Philippi (Ac. 16:13, 16), Thessalonica (17:1), Beroea (17:10), Athens (17:17), Corinth (18:4, 7). Josephus mentions synagogues in Caesarea and Dora on the Phoenician coast.[11] Jewish προσευχαί are found on inscriptions even in the Crimea.[12] In cities where Jews lived in greater numbers they also had several synagogues, e.g. in Damascus (Ac. 9:20) and in Salamis in Cyprus (Ac. 13:5). In Alexandria there were a considerable number.[13] Josephus refers to the synagogue in Antioch as being particularly magnificent (i.e. the main synagogue there, for there must have been several there too). The successors of Antiochus Epiphanes, he says, had granted to it the bronze (but not the valuable gold and silver) offerings which Antiochus had plundered from the temple at Jerusalem; and the Jews of Antioch themselves adorned their holy place (τὸ ἱερόν) with valuable

---

7. *De migratione Abrahami* 16 (93).

8. The latter point was given insufficient prominence in the account by L. Treitel, 'Der Nomos, insonderheit Sabbat und Feste, in philonischer Beleuchtung', MGWJ (1903), pp. 214–31, 317–21, 399–417, 490–514. Cf. also his essay 'Die religions- und kulturgeschichtliche Stellung Philos', ThStKr (1904), pp. 380–401. It is true that Philo throughout gives to the Jewish laws an interpretation which makes them appear acceptable to the educated citizen of the world; but even then they remain binding according to their literal meaning. See e.g. E. R. Goodenough, *An introduction to Philo Judaeus* (1940), and pp. 875–80 below.

9. Cf. M. Friedländer, *Das Judentum in der vorchristlichen griechischen Welt* (1897), pp 20–31; 'Die Synagoge der Diaspora'; G. F. Moore, *Judaism in the first centuries of the Christian era* (1927) I, pp. 281–307; II, pp. 12–15; 21–39; V. Tcherikover, *Hellenistic Civilization and the Jews* (1961), pp. 307–8.

10. Philo, *De spec. leg.* ii 15 (62), quoted in vol. II, p. 448, n. 102.

11. Caesarea: *B.J.* ii 14, 4–5 (285–90); Dora: *Ant.* xix 6.3 (300).

12. Pp. 36–7 above.

13. Philo, *Leg.* 20 (132).

offerings.[14] In Rome, there were already in the time of Augustus a large number of synagogues, as Philo testifies. Inscriptions preserve the names of the individual synagogue communities.[15]

Thus the Law and the prophets were read and expounded and religious assemblies were held on every Sabbath day wherever Jews lived. A shrine or Ark to house the scrolls of the Torah is now attested at Dura-Europos (p. 12) and Sardis (p. 22), and on an inscription from Ostia (p. 82).

The normal language of the liturgy however was probably Greek throughout the communities of the Graeco-Roman world.[16] The evidence from Dura-Europos on the Euphrates shows that there both Aramaic and Greek were in use. The Hebrew text of a benediction after meals suggests that it may have been generally used for sacred purposes. However, Hebrew was indeed so little in use among the Jews elsewhere in the Diaspora that it was rarely used even on epitaphs. Only the Roman catacomb inscriptions, almost exclusively Greek or Latin (the latter to a much lesser extent), are sometimes found with brief formulaic additions in Hebrew. It is not until we come to the late Roman period, for instance the epitaphs from Venosa (from about the sixth century A.D.) that Hebrew can be seen.[17] But even these are preponderantly Greek or Latin. If Hebrew was not employed for such monuments, it will have been used still less for recitation in divine service. The rabbis in Palestine expressly allowed the use of any language for the prayers, _Shemā_ and _Shemoneh-Esreh_, and for grace at meals. Hebrew was demanded only for the priestly blessing and certain individual scriptural passages such as the formula at the presentation of the first fruits and at the _ḥaliẓah_.[18] A certain R. Levi bar Haitha once heard in Caesarea the _Shema'_ recited in Greek (אלינסתין).[19] It was

---

14. _B.J._ vii 3, 3 (44–5).

15. Philo, _Leg._ 23 (155–8). Cf. p. 75. For the different names of the Roman synagogue congregations see above, pp. 96–8.

16. On this cf., partly for partly against, J. B. Lightfoot, _Horae hebr. in epist. I ad Corinthios_, Addenda ad Cap. XIV (Opp. II, pp. 933–40; he disputes the use of the LXX in divine service); M. Frankel, _Vorstudien zu der Septuaginta_ (1841), pp. 56 ff.; L. Herzfeld, _Gesch. des Volkes Israel_ III (1857), p. 472; C. P. Caspari, _Quellen zur Geschichte des Taufsymbols_ III (1869), pp. 269 ff.; L. Blau, _Zur Einleitung in die heilige Schrift_ (_Jahresbericht der Landes-Rabbinerschule in Budapest_, 1894), pp. 84 ff.; K. Friedmann, _Onkelos und Akylas_ (1896), pp. 25 ff.; M. Friedländer, _Das Judenthum in der vorchristl. griech. Welt_ (1897), pp. 32–8; V. Tcherikover, _Hellenistic Civilisation and the Jews_ (1961), pp. 347–8; M. Hengel, 'Proseuche und Synagoge', in J. Jeremias et al. (eds.), _Tradition und Glaube_ (1971), p. 159; C. Rabin, 'Hebrew and Aramaic in the First Century', JPFC II, p. 1007.

17. CIJ I², nos. 569–75; 578–9; 584; 586; 593–7; 599–600; 606–7; 609; 611; 613. Note also e.g. no. 650 (Catania, A.D. 383).

18. 7:1–2. Cf. above, vol. II.

19. _ySot_ 7.21b. For the passage, see, e.g. Buxtorf, _Lex. Chald._ col. 104 (s.v. אלינסתין); Lightfoot, _Opp._ II.937; J. Levy, _Neuhebr. Wörterb._ I, 88. Cf. also vol. II, p. 77, n. 261; S.

explicitly permitted to *write* scripture in Greek, and here again Hebrew
was required only for individual passages, written for particular needs,
like the *tefillin* and *mezuzoth*.[20] Accordingly, since Hebrew was
obligatory in oral and in written use for individual passages only, the
reading of Scripture during divine service must also, in the rabbinic
view, have been permissible in another language, presumably Greek. It
is in any case made absolutely clear by various church fathers that the
Greek translation of the Bible was used in synagogues, and therefore at
divine service.[21] For all that, it is possible that Scripture was read in
Hebrew as well as in Greek, as happened later at the time of the
emperor Justinian.[22] But when one considers that, for example, the
apostle Paul was familiar with the Old Testament only in Greek
translation,[23] such a concurrent use of Hebrew and Greek text cannot
be regarded as probable for the apostolic period. The mathematician
and Stoic philosopher Cleomedes mocks the bad Greek spoken in
synagogues.[24] An interesting proof of the way in which the language of
the Greek Bible dominated Jewish devotional expression in the

---

Lieberman, *Greek in Jewish Palestine* ([2]1965), p. 30.

20. *mMeg.* 1:8. 'The books [of Scripture] differ from phylacteries and *mezuzot* only in that
the books may be written in any language, while phylacteries and *mezuzot* may be written
in the Assyrian script (אשורית, i.e. in square Hebrew characters) only. Rabban Simeon b.
Gamaliel says: The books, too, are only permitted to be written in Greek.'

21. Justin, *Apol.* i 31, 5: ἔμειναν αἱ βίβλοι καὶ παρ' Αἰγυπτίοις μέχρι τοῦ δεῦρο, καὶ
πανταχοῦ παρὰ πᾶσίν εἰσιν Ἰουδαίοις, οἳ καὶ ἀναγινώσκοντες οὐ συνιᾶσι τὰ εἰρημένα. Cf. also
Dial. c. Tryph. 72; Tertullian, *Apol.* 18: 'Hodie apud Serapeum Ptolemaei bibliothecae
cum ipsis Hebraicis exhibentur. Sed et Iudaei palam lactitant. Vectigalis libertas; vulgo
aditur sabbatis omnibus'; Pseudo-Justin, *Cohort. ad Graec.* (third century A.D.?) 13: εἰ δέ
τις φάσκοι ... μὴ ἡμῖν τὰς βίβλους ταύτας ἀλλὰ Ἰουδαίοις προσήκειν, διὰ τὸ ἔτι καὶ νῦν ἐν ταῖς
συναγωγαῖς αὐτῶν σώζεσθαι... ibid.: ἀπὸ τῆς τῶν Ἰουδαίων συναγωγῆς ταύτας ἀξιοῦμεν
προκομίζεσθαι. In all these passages the subject is expressly the Greek translation of the
Old Testament. For the preservation of the holy scriptures in the synagogues see vol. II,
p. 446.

22. Justinian, *Novell.* 146. The emperor says here in the introduction that he has heard,
ὡς οἱ μὲν μόνης ἔχονται τῆς ἑβραΐδος φωνῆς καὶ αὐτῇ κεχρῆσθαι περὶ τὴν τῶν ἱερῶν βιβλίων
ἀνάγνωσιν βούλονται, οἱ δὲ καὶ τὴν Ἑλληνίδα προσλαμβάνειν ἀξιοῦσι, καὶ πόλυν ἤδη χρόνον
ὑπὲρ τούτου πρὸς σφᾶς αὐτοὺς στασιάζουσιν. See e.g. V. Colorni, 'L'uso del greco nella
liturgia del Giudaismo ellenistico e la Novella 146 di Giustiniano', Ann. Stor. Dir. 8
(1964), pp. 19 ff.

23. See e.g. H. St J. Thackeray, *The Relation of St Paul to Contemporary Jewish Thought*
(1900); A. von Harnack, 'Das Alte Testament in den Paulinischen Briefen und in den
Paulinischen Gemeinden', SAB, ph.-hist. Kl. (1928), pp. 124–41; O. Michel, *Paulus und
seine Bibel* (1929); J. Bonsirven, *Exégèse Rabbinique et Exégèse Paulinienne* (1939); E. E. Ellis,
Paul's Use of the Old Testament (1957).

24. Cleomedes, *De motu circulari corporum caelestium* (ed. Ziegler, 1891) ii 1, 91: Epicurus,
he says, uses ill-chosen words, which come in part ἀπὸ μέσης τῆς προσευχῆς καὶ τῶν ἐπ'
αὐλαῖς προσαιτούντων, Ἰουδαϊκά τινα καὶ παρακεχαραγμένα καὶ κατὰ πόλυ τῶν ἑρπετῶν
ταπεινότερα. Cleomedes probably lived later than Posidonius but earlier than Ptolemaeus,
thus between 50 B.C. and A.D. 150. See E. Zeller, *Philosophie der Griechen* III.1 ([5]1923), p.
715; GLAJJ II, no. 333.

Diaspora as early as 100 B.C. is afforded by the inscribed execrations from the island of Rheneia near Delos, which are cast largely in Septuagintal forms (see above p. 70). It is obvious how important this Hellenization of the Jewish liturgy was for the success of Jewish propaganda.[25]

Apart from the Sabbath, Diaspora Jews also celebrated the New Moon and annual festivals.[26] The way in which they did so was no doubt the same as in Palestine outside Jerusalem. The main characteristic was the replacement of the sacrificial system by the synagogue service. Since sacrifice could only be offered in Jerusalem, the essential for festivals outside the holy city was assembly in the synagogue for prayer and scripture readings.[27] Psalms also appear to have been sung. At any rate the Jewish catacomb of the Villa Torlonia in Rome has revealed a *psalmodos* (p. 81 above) and the major Jewish inscription from Aphrodisias in Caria a *psalmo(logos?)* (p. 26).

Yet worship was not entirely confined to this spiritual form. Just as with the pagan cult-associations, it was taken for granted that from time to time fellow-worshippers came together for a festival meal, and as in Jerusalem too the Jewish festival pilgrims held their common sacrificial repasts, so also the Jews in the Diaspora did not entirely

---

25. Cf. A. Deissmann, 'Die Hellenisierung des semitischen Monotheismus', Neue Jahrbb. für das class. Altertum 6 (1903), pp. 161–77.

26. The Jews of Berenice in Cyrenaica resolved ἐπὶ συλλόγου τῆς σκηνοπηγίας to crown their benefactor, a Roman official named M. Tittius, καθ' ἑκάστην σύνοδον καὶ νουμηνίαν. Note also CPJ III, no. 452a (second century A.D.; Edfu?), mentioning the παννυχὶς τῆς σκηνοπηγίας (cf. p. 58 above). The ἑορτὴ τῶν ἀζύμων and the ἑορτὴ πεντηκοστῆς appear on an inscription from Hierapolis (see p. 27 above). In the execrations from Rheneia (see p. 70 above) there is reference to a day on which 'everyone humbles himself before God with prayer' (ταπεινοῦται μεθ' ἱκετείας), evidently either the Day of Atonement or else a fast day. In Galatians Paul opposes the celebration of μῆνες and καιροί (Gal. 4:10), and in Colossians speaks against the celebration of any ἑορτή or νεομηνία (Col. 2:16). Further, in the well-known passage of Horace, *Sat.* i 9, 69 (GLAJJ I, no. 129), 'hodie tricesima sabbata', the subject is not some thirtieth sabbath (nothing is known of the celebration of any such day); *tricesima* is the new moon which according to him was kept also by Roman Jews ('today is the thirtieth, a feast day'). Also in Commodian *tricesima* occurs as a name for the new moon (Commodian, *Instr.* i 40, 3: 'Et sabbata vestra spernit et tricesimas Altus'; *Carmen apol.* 688 (695): 'Ac idolis servit, iterum tricesimam quaerit'). For the new moon offering see Num. 28:11–15; for the new moon festival in general; Philo, *De spec. leg.* ii 17 (140–4); Wellhausen, *Geschichte Israels* I, pp. 115 ff. or *Prolegomena*, pp. 110 ff.; R. de Vaux, *Ancient Israel* (1961), pp. 469–70; W. Nowack, *Lehrb. der hebr. Archäologie* II, pp. 138 f.; Hamburger, *Real-Enc.*, Suppl., III (1892), s.v. 'Neumondsgottesdienst'; JE IX, pp. 243 ff., s.v. 'New Moon'; EB III, cols. 3401–4, s.v. 'New Moon'; IDB III, pp. 543–4, s.v. 'New Moon'. See in general A. M. Rabello, 'L'osservanza delle feste ebraiche nell'Impero Romano', SCI 6 (1981-2), pp. 57–84. For the observance of the Sabbath and the major festivals in Antioch in the late fourth century see R. L. Wilken, *John Chrysostom and the Jews* (1983), esp. pp. 64, 66–8. Celebration of Purim: *CTh* xvi 8, 18 (A.D. 408).

27. The scriptural lections for the annual festivals and the new moons are exactly prescribed in the Mishnah, *Meg.* 3:5–6; see above, vol. II, pp. 450–1.

dispense with something of the kind. According to Josephus, Caesar allowed the Jews to arrange communal dinners (σύνδειπνα ποιεῖν), and another official permitted them 'to meet and feast in accordance with their ancestral customs and laws'—κατὰ τὰ πάτρια ἔθη καὶ νόμιμα συνάγεσθαί τε καὶ ἑστιᾶσθαι—Niese's correct emendation of Jos. *Ant.* xiv 10, 8 (216)—and these reports must certainly have had an authentic foundation. One has only to think of the analogy of the sacrificial meals in Jerusalem, above all of Passover.[28] At the Feast of Tabernacles (Sukkoth) people ate together in booths erected from fresh branches.[29]

Alexandrian Jews kept also a few special feasts. There was one to commemorate the translation of the Law into Greek,[30] and one in memory of their miraculous deliverance when Ptolemy VII Physcon (?) wished to have them killed by elephants.[31]

In view of the strict centralization of the Jewish cult, the Jewish temple at Leontopolis in Egypt is a remarkable phenomenon. At the time of Antiochus V Eupator (164–162 B.C.) a high priest's son, Onias IV (a son of Onias III), came to Egypt when he saw that he had no prospect of reaching the office of high priest in Palestine, and was readily accepted there by Ptolemy VI Philometor and his consort Cleopatra.[32] The king made over to him an old ruined temple at

28. In connection with the pagan cult associations cf. the literature mentioned above, pp. 111 ff. In Jerusalem corporate meals were an essential element in the זבחי שלמים; cf. above, vol. II, p. 258. That these εὐωχίαι were celebrated even in the last period of the Temple's existence, in particular by pilgrims to the annual festivals, is shown by Josephus, *Ant.* iv 8, 7 (205); 8, 19; 22 (226–7; 240–3). The Passover also belonged originally to the same category, but this feast received a unique status through the legislation of the Priestly Code. Of the Passover meal we know for certain that it was celebrated also in the Diaspora, in a modified form without the sacrifice; see J. B. Segal, *The Hebrew Passover* (1963), pp. 219 ff.

29. Cf. the description by Plutarch in *Qu. Conviv.* iv 6, 2 (*Mor.* 671 D = GLAJJ I, no. 258.) The feast of the Dedication of the Temple was kept in a similar manner; it was to this feast that the Egyptian Jews are bidden by the Palestinian Jews in the letter preserved in 2 Mac. 1–2.

30. Philo, *Vit. Mos.* ii 7 (42). A banquet was connected with this festival also (μετ' οἰκείων καὶ φίλων ἑστιῶνται).

31. Jos. *C. Ap.* ii 5 (55). In 3 Mac. also the institution of this festival is mentioned (6:36), but the event is placed in the time of Ptolemy IV. See above, pp. 115 ff.

33. In *B.J.* vii 10, 2 (423) Josephus calls this Onias 'the son of Simon', in which case he would be Onias III, the last officiating high priest of this family, as is also implied by *B.J.* i 1 (30–3). On the other hand in *Ant.* Josephus says more than once, xii 5, 1 (237); xiii 3, 1 (62), that it was a son bearing the same name as this Onias, thus Onias IV, who founded the Temple at Leontopolis. Clearly this is a deliberate correction of the earlier statement and therefore more trustworthy. Again, because of its legendary nature, the statement in the Talmud that the builder of the Onias Temple was a son of Simon the Just (bMen. 109b; yYom. 6:3; L. Herzfeld, *Gesch. des Volkes Jisrael* III, p. 557; A. Wünsche, *Der babylon. Talmud* II.4, pp. 53 ff.; *idem, Der jerus. Talmud*, pp. 114 ff.) cannot serve as support for the statement of *B.J.* Identical name for father and son is indeed not common among the Jews, but certainly attested (inscription from Tlos, above, p. 33:

Leontopolis in the *nomos* of Heliopolis which had earlier been a shrine of the ἀγρία Βούβαστις.³³ This was rebuilt by Onias as a Jewish shrine on the pattern of the Temple at Jerusalem, but smaller, less splendid and with many deviations in detail; cf. the description in *B.J.* vii 10, 3 (426–32). Since there were also priests there in sufficient numbers, a formal Jewish temple worship was established, which from then on (i.e., from about 160 B.C.) was continuously in operation until after the destruction of Jerusalem, when this temple too was closed by the Romans (A.D. 73).³⁴ The cult was admittedly never regarded as

Ptolemy son of Ptolemy; inscription from Berenice, above, p. 94: Andromachus son of Andromachus). Admittedly, the history of the Oniads, on account of the numerous inconsistencies between 2 Maccabees and Josephus, is so confused that it is quite impossible to take up a confident position in this area.

33. The locality is described most exactly in *Ant.* xii 3, 2 (70): τὸ ἐν Λεόντων πόλει τοῦ Ἡλιοπολίτου ἱερὸν συμπεπτωκός ... προσαγορευόμενον δὲ τῆς ἀγρίας Βουβάστεως. The same identification is suggested by *Ant.* xii 3, 1 (65). In all other passages Josephus says only in general terms that the Temple was situated 'in the *nomos* of Heliopolis', *Ant.* xii 9, 7 (388); xii 10, 4 (285); xx 10, 3 (236); *B.J.* i 1, 1 (33); vii 10, 3 (426). In one passage he adds that the place lay 180 stades from Memphis, *B.J.* vii 10, 3 (426). Since the Leontopolis known from elsewhere formed its own *nomos*, further north than Heliopolis (Strabo, xvii 1, 19, p. 802; Pliny, *N.H.* v 9/49; Ptolemy iv 5, 51 = Didot ed. (I.2, 1901), iv 5, 22), another otherwise unknown Leontopolis in the *nomos* of Heliopolis must be meant here. For a more detailed localisation the following may be noted. Memphis lay on the southern tip of the Delta. Northwards from here, at a distance of 24 Roman miles, and on the eastern side of the Delta, lay Heliopolis. This distance corresponds fairly precisely to the 180 stades given by Josephus, which are equivalent to 22? Roman miles. Somewhat further north lies, even today, Tel-el-Yehoudieh, thus an ancient Jewish settlement, which Naville and Petrie first suggested may be identified with the settlement of Onias. See E. Naville, *The mound of the Jew and the city of Onias* (1890). The remains of the Onias Temple itself are thought to have been identified here by Flinders Petrie, *Hyksos and Israelite cities* (1906), pp. 19–27. In favour of this supposition speak not only the approximate position and the name Tel-el-Yehoudieh, but also the circumstance that in the vicinity a necropolis has been found with Jewish-Greek epitaphs, CIJ II, nos. 1451–1530; CPJ III, pp. 145–63 (with nos. 1530a-d, not in CIJ), on which the name Onias perhaps occurs (Ονιου πατηρ, CIJ II, no. 1455). (Since the stone is very defective, a longer name may of course have been there originally.) Apart from this there are Βαρχίας Βαρχίου (1454), Ἐλεάζαρος (1453, 1466, 1473), Σομόηλος (1451, 1469), Μίκκος Νεθάνεως (1452), Ἰούδας Ἰούδου (1465). Again, the building remains described by Petrie correspond to Josephus' account relating to the Onias Temple that it was 'like a tower', *B.J.* vii 10, 3 (427). For a brief description see J. Baines and J. Málek, *Atlas of Ancient Egypt* (1980), p. 174. Cf. pp. 47–8 above.

34. See in general Jos. *Ant.* xii 9, 7 (387–8); xii 3, 1–3 (62–73); xiii 10, 4 (285); xx 10 (236–7); *B.J.* i 1, 1 (31–3); vii 10, 2–4 (420–36). *Or. Sib.* v ll. 492–511 is apparently not concerned with the Onias Temple. See J. Geffcken, *Komposition und Entstehungszeit der Oracula Sibyllina* (1902), p. 26. See H. Willrich, *Juden und Griechen vor der makkabäischen Erhebung* (1895), pp. 77 ff.; 126–42. A. Büchler, *Die Tobiaden und die Oniaden im Zweiten Makkabäerbuche* (1899), pp. 239–76.

See also Du Mesnil du Buisson, BIFAO 35 (1935), pp. 59–71 (subsequent excavations); DB Supp. V (1957), pp. 359–72; Tcherikover, *Hellenistic Civilization*, pp. 275–81; M. Delcor, 'Le Temple d'Onias en Égypte', RB 75 (1968), pp. 188–203; R. Hayward, 'The Jewish Temple at Leontopolis: a Reconsideration', JJS 33 (1982), pp.

legitimate by the Palestinian sages, and the sacrifices offered there were regarded as valid only to a very limited degree.[35] But the Egyptian Jews themselves showed no sign of paying any attention to this temple, and maintained contact with Jerusalem. They went on pilgrimage to Jerusalem just the same, like all the others,[36] and when their priests married, they always had the genealogy of their wives examined there.[37]

As with the Law in general, so also directions concerning taxes due to the Temple and festival journeys to Jerusalem were observed, as far as was possible, by the Jews of the Diaspora. This was especially true of the taxes. Josephus remarks in connection with the looting of the Temple by Crassus that it was not at all surprising that such riches were heaped up there since all the Jews and all the *sebomenoi* throughout the world, in Asia and Europe, had from ancient times sent contributions there.[38] Philo describes the collection and despatch of temple taxes in detail.[39] 'The revenues of the Temple are derived not only from landed estates but also from other and far greater sources which time will never destroy. For as long as the human race endures, and it will endure for ever, the revenues of the Temple also will remain secure, co-eternal with the whole universe. For it is ordained that everyone, beginning at

---

429–43.

35. Mishnah *Men.* 13:10: [If he said,] 'I must pledge myself to offer a Whole-offering', he must offer it to the Temple. And if he offered it in the House of Onias he has not fulfilled his obligation. [If he said,] 'I will offer it in the House of Onias', he should offer it in the Temple, but if he offered it in the House of Onias he has fulfilled his obligation. R. Simeon says: Such is not accounted a Whole-offering. [If a man said,] 'I will be a Nazirite', he must offer the Hair-offering in the Temple; and if he offered it in the House of Onias he has not fulfilled his obligation. [If he said,] 'I will offer the Hair-offering in the House of Onias', he should offer it in the Temple; but if he offered it in the House of Onias he has fulfilled his obligation. R. Simeon says: Such a one is not accounted a Nazirite. If priests have ministered in the House of Onias they may not minister in the Temple in Jerusalem ... Thus they are like them that have a blemish; they may share and they may eat [of the Holy Things] but they may not offer sacrifice' (Danby's transl.). The name Onias in the printed standard text is חוניו. Two of the best witnesses, *cod. de Rossi* 138 and the Cambridge manuscript published by Lowe in 1883, consistently have instead נחוניו. The form חניה occurs also in the epitaph of the Bene Ḥzyr in Jerusalem, CIJ II, no. 1394.

36. Philo, *De providentia* ii 107, from Euseb. *Praep. ev.* vii 14, 64, p. 398b (and in the Armenian version in Aucher, *Philonis Judaei sermones tres*, p. 116). Philo says here that he had been in Ascalon καθ' ὃν χρόνον εἰς τὸ πατρῷον ἱερὸν ἐστελλόμην, εὐξόμενός τε καὶ θύσων.

37. *C. Ap.* i 7 (30–2).

38. *Ant.* xiv 7, 2 (110): θαυμάσῃ δὲ μηδεὶς εἰ τοσοῦτος ἦν πλοῦτος ἐν τῷ ἡμετέρῳ ἱερῷ, πάντων τῶν κατὰ τὴν οἰκουμένην Ἰουδαίων καὶ σεβομένων τὸν θεόν, ἔτι δὲ καὶ τῶν ἀπὸ τῆς Ἀσίας καὶ τῆς Εὐρώπης εἰς αὐτὸ συμφερόντων ἐκ πολλῶν πάνυ χρόνων. On the question of what contributions were payable by Diaspora Jews, see vol. II, p. 269. For *sebomenoi* see pp. 165–8 below.

39. Philo, *De Spec. Leg.* i 14 (76–8).

his twentieth year, should make an annual contribution ... As the nation is very populous, the offerings of first-fruits are naturally exceedingly abundant. In fact, practically in every city there are banking places for the holy money where people regularly come and give their offerings. And at stated times there are appointed to carry the sacred tribute envoys selected on their merits, from every city those of the highest repute, under whose conduct the hopes of each and all will travel safely. For it is on these first-fruits, as prescribed by the Law, that the hopes of the pious rest.' It has already been mentioned that the transport of this money out of Roman provinces frequently met with opposition in earlier times. Thus Flaccus confiscated Jewish Temple-money in Apamea, Laodicea, Adramyttium and Pergamum. By contrast, from the time of Caesar onwards its export was permitted everywhere, from Rome[40] as also from Asia Minor[41] and Cyrenaica,[42] and of course from Egypt, as is clear from the Philo quotation. The money flowed in the greatest quantities from Babylon and the lands beyond the Euphrates. The collection and transport was well organized here. The main treasuries which received the contributions initially were to be found in the cities of Nisibis and Nehardea. From here they were transferred at a stated time to Jerusalem, and many thousands undertook the delivery in order to protect the sacred treasure from robbers.[43]

After the destruction of the Temple the contributions necessarily underwent a transformation. The *didrachma* was changed into a Roman tax; other contributions could *ipso facto* no longer be paid (cf. vol. II, pp. 269 ff.). But even now the Jewish people still expressed its inner cohesion through voluntary contributions. A new central authority, the patriarchate, eventually came into existence, to which at least part of the religious tribute demanded by the Law was delivered annually. The collections now took place through emissaries of the patriarchate, the so-called *apostoli* (see above, pp. 124 ff.).

The bond between the Diaspora and the motherland was tied most closely by the regular pilgrimages of Jews from all parts of the world to the festivals in Jerusalem. 'Multitudes from countless cities come, some overland, others over sea, from east and west and north and south at every feast.'[44] Josephus reckons the number of Jews who undertook to

---

40. Philo, *Leg.* 23 (156–7).

41. *Ant.* xvi 6, 2–4; 6–7 (162–8; 171–3); Philo, *Leg.* 40 (313).

42. *Ant.* xvi 6, 5 (169–70).

43. *Ant.* xviii 9, 1 (310–13); cf. Philo, *Leg.* 31 (216); mShek. 3:4 (didrachma tax from Babylon and Media).

44. Philo, *De Spec. Leg.* i 12 (69): μυρίοι γὰρ ἀπὸ μυρίων ὅσων πόλεων οἱ μὲν διὰ γῆς, οἱ δὲ διὰ θαλάττης, ἐξ ἀνατολῆς καὶ δύσεως καὶ ἄρκτου καὶ μεσημβρίας, καθ' ἑκάστην ἑορτὴν εἰς τὸ ἱερὸν καταίρουσιν. For the pilgrimages from Babylon cf. besides the passage quoted, *Ant.* xviii 9, 1 (310–13), also *Ant.* xvii 2, 2 (26); mYom. 6:4; mTaan. 1:3.

be present in Jerusalem at the festivals to have been 2,700,000, a number which certainly includes the inhabitants of Jerusalem. No reliance can be placed on the figure itself, but it can be taken as an indication of the substantial scale of pilgrimage.[45]

The destruction of the Temple must thus have been of profound significance for the Diaspora. Yet even the most concrete consequence, the payment of the Jewish tax, finds no reflection in the local evidence so far known, except in Egypt (pp. 122–3 above). However, as Hengel has argued, the major series of Jewish revolts in A.D. 115–17 (vol. I, pp. 529–34) must imply the presence of powerful messianic expectations in the Diaspora, at least in the formerly Ptolemaic territories of Egypt, Cyrenaica and Cyprus. The background to these revolts can be discerned from the *Fifth Sibylline Oracle* (see further pp. 643–5 below), which thus represents a further, and very little known, element in the religious life of the Diaspora.[46]

45. *B.J.* vi 9, 3 (425). The passage in Ac. 2:9–11 is not relevant here, since according to 2:5 it does not relate to pilgrims but to Jews from abroad who had settled in Jerusalem. For a detailed discussion see Haenchen *ad loc.* On pilgrimage to Jerusalem see above all J. Jeremias, *Jerusalem in the Time of Jesus* (1969).

46. See M. Hengel, 'Messianische Hoffnung und politischer "Radikalismus" in der "jüdisch-hellenistischen Diaspora". Zur Frage der Voraussetzungen des jüdischen Aufstandes unter Trajan 115–117 n.Chr.', D. Hellholm (ed.), *Apocalypticism in the Mediterranean World and the Near East* (1979), pp. 655–86.

V. Gentiles and Judaism:
'God-Fearers' and Proselytes

A question of considerable importance in any description of Judaism in the Diaspora is that of the gentiles who attached themselves to the Jewish communities, whether as full proselytes or 'God-fearers' (see below). No full and satisfactory study of proselytism in the Graeco-Roman period has yet been written, and fundamental uncertainties remain as to both the numerical scale and the conditions of acceptance of both proselytes proper and 'God-fearers'. Nothing more can be offered here than a consideration of various general factors and a collection of the scattered items of direct evidence for the attraction or conversion of gentiles to Judaism.

At first sight it seems strange that Jewish propaganda should have aimed at any serious success among pagan populations, since the attitude of the Graeco-Roman world to the Jews was generally unsympathetic. It has already been seen how the Jews in Hellenistic cities were almost everywhere regarded with ill-will; how not only the mob but the city authorities themselves made repeated efforts to hinder them in the free practice of their religion (see above, pp. 116 ff., 126 ff.). Judgements expressed in Greek and Roman literature are also in general derogatory.[1] For most educated men of the period the Jewish religion was a *barbara superstitio*.[2] People did not hesitate to repeat with credulity the absurd fables invented above all by Alexandrian *literati*. Many allegations sprang, it is true, from ignorance and not from malice, as for example when it was concluded from the name *Iudaei* that they came from Crete and took their name from Mount Ida.[3] Similarly,

---

1. On this cf. e.g. H. Grätz, 'Ursprung der zwei Verleumdungen gegen das Judenthum vom Eselskultus und von der Lieblosigkeit gegen Andersgläubige', MGWJ (1872), pp. 193–206; Th. Reinach, *Textes d'auteurs grecs et romains relatifs au Judaïsme* (1895); F. Stähelin, *Der Antisemitismus des Altertums in seiner Entstehung und Entwicklung* (1905); M. Radin, *The Jews among the Greeks and Romans* (1915); I. Heinemann, RE suppl. V (1931), cols. 3–43; M. Stern, GLAJJ I-II; *idem*, 'The Jews in Greek and Latin Literature', JPFC II, pp. 1101–59; J. N. Sevenster, *The Roots of Pagan Anti-Semitism in the Ancient World* (1975); H. Braunert, 'Jüdische Diaspora und Judenfeindschaft im Altertum', *Politik, Recht und Gesellschaft in den griechisch-römischen Antike* (1980), pp. 29–48; L. Cracco Ruggini, 'Pagani, Ebrei e Cristiani: Odio sociologico e odio teologico nel mondo antico', Sett. di Studi del Centro It. di Studi sull'Alto Medioevo 26 (1980), pp. 13–101.
2. Cicero, *pro Flacco* 28/67 = GLAJJ I, no. 68.
3. Tacitus, *Hist.* v 2 = GLAJJ II, no. 281.

the famous golden vine in the Temple[4] and certain customs connected with the Feast of Tabernacles led to the erroneous belief that they worshipped Bacchus, an opinion fully debated in Plutarch,[5] while Tacitus rejects it with the words: 'Liber festos laetosque ritus posuit, Iudaeorum mos absurdus sordidusque.'[6] But most of the characteristics attributed to the Jews were malicious slanders which owed their origin for the most part to the fruitful soil of Alexandria.

It was, however, above all around the exodus of the Jews from Egypt that there was woven in the course of time a completely fictitious tale for which Manetho had already laid the foundation, and which was subsequently elaborated by the Alexandrian *literati*, Chaeremon, Lysimachus and Apion, and repeated by Tacitus and Justin with various modifications and additions.[7] The essence of it is that a number of lepers were banished from the country by an Egyptian king — sometimes called Amenophis, sometimes Bocchoris—and sent into the quarries or the desert. Among them was a priest of Heliopolis named Moses (according to Manetho his real name was Osarsiph). Under his influence the lepers apostasized from the Egyptian gods and adopted a new religion which he gave them. They then left the country under his leadership and came, after various experiences and committing many shameful deeds, to the neighbourhood of Jerusalem, which they conquered and occupied for a long period. From the detailed circumstances which accompanied this exodus Tacitus was able to deduce almost all the Jewish manners and customs, some imaginary, some genuine. Before him the Alexandrian grammarian Apion had already maintained that the Jews paid divine honours to the head of an ass.[8] Tacitus repeats this as one who believes it (although he himself also mentions the fact that their cult was imageless), and traces it back to the fact that the Jews in the desert had been made aware of plentiful

---

4. *mMid.* 3:8; Josephus, *Ant.* xv 11, 3 (395); *B.J.* v 5, 4 (210–11); Tacitus, *Hist.* v 5.

5. Plutarch, *Sympos.* iv 5 (*Mor.* 699E–71C = GLAJJ I, no. 258); see A. Büchler, 'La fête des cabanes chez Plutarque et Tacite', REJ 37 (1898), pp. 181–202.

6. Tacitus, *Hist.* v 5 = GLAJJ II, no. 281.

7. Manetho in Josephus, *C. Ap.* i 26–7 (227–53) = GLAJJ I, no. 21; Chaeremon, *ibid.* i 32 (288–92) = no. 178; Lysimachus, *ibid.* i 34 (304–11) = no. 158; Apion, *ibid.* ii 2 (8–27) = no. 164–5; Tacitus, *Hist.* v 3 = no. 281; Justin, xxxvi 2 = no. 137; cf. also Diodorus, xxiv 1 = no. 63; for further details on the literary tradition see pp. 595–609 below.

8. Josephus, *C. Ap.* ii 7 (80) = no. 170. Another form of the legend is to be found in Diodorus, xxiv 1 = no. 63. See Stern *ad loc.* for discussions of the sources of this view. According to this version of the legend Antiochus Epiphanes found in the holy of holies a stone statue of a man with a long beard, sitting on an ass with a book in his hands. He took this to be Moses, founder of Jerusalem and Lawgiver of the Jews. See J. Gager, *Moses in Greco-Roman Paganism* (1972), pp. 174 ff.

springs of water by a herd of wild asses.[9] The reason given for Jewish abstention from pork is that the pig is specially liable to scabies, the disease on whose account the Jews had once been treated so cruelly. The frequent fasts take place in memory of the hunger endured during the march through the desert. The use of unleavened bread is a token of the theft of corn at the time of the exodus. Finally, the keeping holy of the seventh day occurs because this brought them the end of their misery; and because idleness suited them so well, they consecrated also the seventh year.[10]

Three points in particular attracted the mockery of the educated world: abstention from pork, strict observance of the Sabbath and image-less worship. Whereas there is earnest debate in Plutarch as to whether abstention from pork does not have its origin in the divine honour accorded to the pig,[11] Juvenal pokes fun at the land in which 'customary kindness bestows on pigs a ripe old age' and where 'pork is accounted as precious as human flesh'. In Sabbath observance the satirist sees nothing but indolence and laziness, and in Jewish divine service only worship of the clouds and the sky.[12] It seems that even philosophically-educated contemporaries could not appreciate an imageless form of worship. It was the literary controversialists of Alexandria who accused the Jews of not worshipping the emperor.[13] Even Tacitus alludes to this, though without expressing any overt censure:[14] 'Iudaei mente sola unumque numen intellegunt: profanos qui deum imagines mortalibus materiis in species hominum effingant; summum illud et aeternum neque imitabile neque interiturum. Igitur nulla simulacra urbibus suis, nedum templis s < is > tunt; non regibus haec adulatio non Caesaribus honor.' Pliny also calls the Jews a 'gens contumelia numinum insignis'.[15]

The indignation of the Graeco-Roman world was however aroused mostly by the barriers which the Jew erected between himself and other men. Precisely at the time when through Roman world-rule and the levelling effect of Hellenism there was a general tendency for local cultures either to be submerged or to be absorbed in the overall

---

9. Tacitus, *Hist.* v 3–4 (= no. 281). For the supposed worship of an ass, cf. also Plutarch, *Sympos.* iv 5 (n. 5 above); Damocritus, *ap.* The Suda (ed. Adler), s.v. Δαμόκριτος = no. 247; Tertullian, *Apol.* 16; *Ad Nationes* i 11; Min. Felix, *Oct.* 9; S. Krauss, s.v. 'Ass Worship', JE II (1902), pp. 222–4; J. Halévy, 'Le culte d'une tête d'âne', Rev. Sem. 11 (1903), pp. 154–64; S. Reinach, *Cultes, mythes et religions* I (1905), pp. 342–6; F. Stähelin, *Der Antisemitismus des Altertums* (1905), pp. 15 f., 54.
10. Tacitus, *Hist.* v 4 = no. 281.
11. Plutarch, *Sympos.* iv 5 (n. 5 above).
12. Juvenal, *Sat.* vi 160 = no. 298; xiv 96–106 = no. 301. See Courtney *ad locc.*
13. Josephus, *C. Ap.* ii 6 (73–8).
14. Tacitus, *Hist.* v 5 = no. 281.
15. Pliny, *N.H.* xiii 4/46 = no. 214.

Graeco-Roman culture, it must have been felt as doubly frustrating that only the Jews were unwilling to be thought of as taking part in the process of amalgamation. 'Apud ipsos fides obstinata, misericordia in promptu, sed adversus omnes alios hostile odium', says Tacitus;[16] and Juvenal alleges that Jews will show the way only to co-religionists, and will direct only the circumcized to a well.[17] When it was said in Alexandria that the Jews took an oath to be well-disposed towards no gentile,[18] or even that they annually offered a Greek in sacrifice,[19] these are of course ridiculous slanders. But a particle of truth nevertheless lies in Tacitus' statement that Jewish proselytes learned nothing so quickly as to despise the gods, to abjure their fatherland, and to regard parents, children and kindred as nothing.[20]

The general attitude towards Judaism expressed in Graeco-Roman literature was not so much hatred as aversion. Through the entire characterization which Tacitus gives of Judaism runs an undertone of the profoundest disdain which prominent Romans cherished towards this *despectissima pars servientium*, against this *taeterrima gens*.[21] This attitude found perhaps its sharpest expression in the words reported of Marcus Aurelius by Ammianus Marcellinus: 'Ille enim cum Palaestinam transiret, Aegyptum petens, Iudaeorum faetentium et tumultuantium saepe taedio percitus dolenter dicitur exclamasse: O Marcomanni, o Quadi, o Sarmatae, tandem alios vobis in < qui > etiores inveni!'[22]

It is fair to ask how, in view of the opinions manifested in Graeco-Roman literature, it was possible for Jewish propaganda to have any success at all. While no confident generalizations can or should be offered, three relevant points may be made.

(1) In the Jewish literature of the period there is evidence of efforts to represent Judaism in a form acceptable even to Greeks and Romans. Whatever was bound at first sight to appear peculiar and unpalatable was left in the background as inessential, and the main emphasis was laid on issues for which a sympathetic understanding could be counted

---

16. Tacitus, *Hist.* v 5 = no. 281.

17. Juvenal, *Sat.* xiv 103–4 = no. 301.

18. Josephus, *C. Ap.* ii 10 (121–4).

19. Josephus, *C. Ap.* ii 8 (89–96) = no. 171. Cf. also Damocritus, n. 9 above. See esp. E. Bickermann, 'Ritualmord und Eselskult', MGWJ 71 (1927), pp. 171–87; 255–64 = *Studies in Jewish and Christian History* II (1980), pp. 225–55. Christians, too, were accused of holding 'Thyestean feasts' (letters of the communities of Lugdunum and Vienna in Eusebius, *H.E.* v 1, 14; Athenagoras, *Embassy* 3; Justin, *Apol.* ii 12; Min. Felix, *Oct.* 9; Tertullian, *Apol.* 8; *Ad Nat.* i 7; Orig. *C. Cels.* vi 27).

20. Tacitus, *Hist.* v 5 = no. 281: 'contemnere deos, exuere patriam, parentes liberos fratres vilia habere.'

21. Tacitus, *Hist.* v 8 = GLAJJ II, no. 506.

22. Ammian Marc. xxii 5 = GLAJJ II, no. 506.

on from many at any rate, above all in regard to the concept of God. Judaism could be presented as the genuinely enlightened religion which does not acknowledge a multiplicity of gods limited to their own spheres of power, but worships the one Lord and Creator of all things, the all-powerful and righteous God, who rewards each man strictly according to his moral conduct. Again it does not, like short-sighted paganism, present the divine Being in the restricted form of a man or even of an animal, but rejects all pictorial representation of the Godhead, revering only the invisible Lord of heaven and earth who reigns over all and is exalted above all the limitations of sense experience. That the main emphasis may have been laid upon these points, and that it was in this form that Judaism may have been introduced to their pagan fellow-citizens by Hellenistic Jews, is suggested, for example, by the writings of Philo and the Jewish Sibyllines.[23] It is therefore understandable that Strabo, for example, speaks with a certain sympathy of Moses; for the Jewish source, whether written or oral, in which his account originates, had represented the Jewish Lawgiver as a genuine Stoic philosopher. Moses, on this view, taught that the Egyptians were mistaken in making the Deity in the image of animals; likewise the Libyans, and also the Greeks, who portrayed him in human form. For God is the One who comprehends us all, and the earth and the sea, the One whom we call 'heaven' and 'universe' and the 'nature of things' (τὴν τῶν ὄντων φύσιν). What reasonable person would dare to make of him an image similar to one of the things familiar to us? Rather one should renounce the making of all images and, having dedicated a worthy temple to him, should worship him without any image at all.[24] Varro, too, appears to have expressed approval of the imageless Jewish worship of God.[25] Admittedly, Strabo, in spite of his favourable description of

23. See pp. 617 ff., 871–80 below.
24. Strabo, xvi 2, 35 (760–1) = GLAJJ I, no. 115. It was evidently in a similar light that educated Jews in the time of Alexander and of the Diadochi represented their religion to foreigners. This can be seen from e.g. Hecataeus, the contemporary of Ptolemy I, who says of Moses: ἄγαλμα δὲ θεῶν τὸ σύνολον οὐ κατεσκεύασε διὰ τὸ μὴ νομίζειν ἀνθρωπόμορφον εἶναι τὸν θεόν, ἀλλὰ τὸν περιέχοντα τὴν γῆν οὐρανὸν μόνον εἶναι θεὸν καὶ τῶν ὅλων κύριον (Hecataeus, ap. Diodorus xl 3, 4 = GLAJJ I, no. 11. At the time, when Greeks were becoming acquainted with Judaism for the first time through individual educated representatives of it, the Jews ranked therefore as 'philosophers among the Syrians'; thus Aristotle according to the report of his pupil Clearchus, ap. Josephus, C. Ap. i 22 (179) = GLAJJ I, no. 15; similarly Theophrastus, the pupil of Aristotle, ap. Porphyry, De abstinentia ii 26 = GLAJJ I, no. 4, and Megasthenes, about 300 B.C. ap. Clement of Alexandria, Strom. i 15, 72 = GLAJJ I, no. 14; F. Stähelin, Der Antisemitismus des Altertums (1905), pp. 3 ff., emphasized rightly that in these accounts no hostile note can be detected.
25. Augustine, De civ. Dei iv 31 = GLAJJ I, no. 72a, says of Varro: 'Dicit etiam antiquos Romanos plus annos centum et septuaginta deos sine simulacro coluisse. "Quod

Moses, did not convert to Judaism, for he thought that the Jewish religion later deteriorated through the acceptance of superstitious elements.[26] But when Jewish apologists learnt how to discover beneath even these 'superstitious' elements a deeper sense and content, might not many have felt attracted?

(2) A further factor which may have helped to win adherents to Judaism lies in the practical direction of the Jewish religion towards training in the conduct of ordinary life. Of course, no religion entirely lacks this; but in Judaism it is much more definite and more comprehensive than in the ancient religions. This contrast is, for instance, present throughout Josephus' work *Contra Apionem*.

(3) Finally, it may also be relevant to point to the well-known fact that Graeco-Roman paganism exhibited not only many elements of stability and conservatism, as in the maintenance of particular cults on the same site over many centuries, but also simultaneously a significant degree of innovation. Though it would be wrong to say that the traditional cults of classical antiquity no longer played a central part in the communal life of the ancient world, it is none the less clear that there was a widespread readiness to adopt new cult forms, including ones which had their origin in various parts of the Near East; partially as a consequence of busy commercial life and expanding trade conditions these cults seem to have become known in ever widening circles.[27] To take only a few examples, in Greece, especially in Athens,

---

si adhuc, inquit, mansisset, castius dii observarentur." Cui sententiae suae testem adhibet inter cetera etiam gentem Iudaeam; nec dubitat eum locum ita concludere, ut dicat, qui primi simulacra deorum populis posuerunt, eos civitatibus suis et metum dempsisse et errorem addidisse.'

26. Strabo xvi 2, 37 (761) = GLAJJ I, no. 115.

27. No adequate study exists of the evolution of ancient paganism as it affected the beliefs and observances of the ordinary man. For older studies and collections of material, many of them embodying questionable presuppositions, see for example L. Friedländer, *Darstellungen aus der Sittengeschichte Roms* III, ed. G. Wissowa ([9]1920), pp. 118–242; M. Foucart, *Des associations religieuses chez les Grecs* (1873); M. C. A. G. Boissier, *La religion romaine d'Auguste aux Antonins* I–II ([2]1878); J. Marquardt, *Römische Staatsverwaltung* III (1878), pp. 71–112; O. Seeck, *Geschichte des Untergangs der antiken Welt* I ([2]1897); II (1901–2); S. Dill, *Roman society from Nero to Marcus Aurelius* (1904), pp. 384–626; F. Cumont, *Les religions orientales dans le paganisme romain* (1906; [4]1929), E.T. *Oriental Religions in Roman Paganism* (1911); P. Wendland, *Die hellenistisch-römische Kultur in ihren Beziehungen zu Judentum und Christentum* (*Handbuch zum N.T.* I.2, 1907, pp. 54–103; [2-3]1912; [4]with add. bibliography by H. Dörrie, 1972).

Among subsequent publications only the major standard works can be mentioned here: J. Toutain, *Les cultes païens dans l'Empire romain* I–III (1907–20); G. Wissowa, *Religion und Kultur der Römer* ([2]1912); U. von Wilamowitz-Moellendorff, *Der Glaube der Hellenen* I–II (1931–2); M. P. Nilsson, *Geschichte der griechischen Religion* II ([2]1961); K. Latte, *Römische Religionsgeschichte* (1960); W. Burkert, *Griechische Religion der archäischen und klassischen Epoche* (1977).

For works dealing with 'conversion', the adoption of new forms of religious observance, and the spread of 'oriental' cults note for example R. Reitzenstein, *Hellenistische*

already at the end of the fifth century B.C. the Phrygian cults of Sabazius (Dionysus) and of the Great Mother had been adopted.[28] Not much later, Egyptian and other Near Eastern cults followed. In 333 B.C., the merchants from Kition (Cyprus) were permitted by a decree of the people of Athens to build a temple of Aphrodite in the Piraeus, i.e., to the Semitic Astarte; and in that connection reference was made to the fact that the Egyptians (those resident in Athens) already had a temple of Isis there. The latter must therefore have been erected around the middle of the fourth century.[29] More than a hundred years later, in 215-214 B.C., an association of Serapis worshippers (_Sarapiastai_) existed also in the Piraeus.[30] The latter were apparently no longer merely immigrants but, as the Greek names of the members suggest, native inhabitants who formed a cult association. In general, Egyptian cults are widely attested in the Greek world from the third century onwards.[31] There is also evidence of other oriental cults, especially in the Greek islands and in Asia Minor.[32]

Mysterienreligionen ([3] 1927; repr. 1956); A. D. Nock, _Conversion: The old and the new in religion from Alexander the Great to Augustine of Hippo_ (1933), and his _Essays on Religion and the Ancient World_ I-II, ed. Z. Stewart (1972); C. Schneider, 'Die griechischen Grundlagen der hellenistischen Religionsgeschichte', ARW 36 (1939), pp. 300–47; M. P. Nilsson, 'Problems of the history of Greek Religion in the Hellenistic and Roman Age', HThR 36 (1943), pp. 251–79; A.-J. Festugière, _Personal Religion among the Greeks_ (1954); E. R. Dodds, _Pagan and Christian in an Age of Anxiety_ (1965); J. Ferguson, _The Religions of the Roman Empire_ (1970); J. A. North, 'Conservatism and Change in Roman Religion', PBSR 44 (1976), pp. 1–12; J. H. W. G. Liebeschuetz, _Continuity and Change in Roman Religion_ (1979); R. MacMullen, _Paganism in the Roman Empire_ (1981).

For the diffusion of oriental cults note the series _Études préliminaires aux religions orientales dans l'empire romain_, 1961–. Note especially the survey volume (93), edited by M. J. Vermaseren, _Die orientalischen Religionen im Römerreich_ (1981).

28. See especially M. Foucart, _Des associations religieuses chez les Grecs_, chs. 9–11; Burkert, _op. cit._, p. 278 (Sabazios); 276–7 (Great Mother).

29. See M. Foucart, _op. cit._, pp. 187–9. The inscription is IG II², no. 337 = SIG³, no. 280 = M. N. Tod, _A Selection of Greek Historical Inscriptions_ II (1948), no. 189: καθάπερ καὶ οἱ Αἰγύπτιοι τὸ τῆς Ἴσιδος ἱερὸν ἵδρυνται. Cf. above, p. 110. In the same year as this decree was passed (333 B.C.) another Athenian inscription refers to a temple to Ammon, established in the Piraeus earlier in the century. IG II², no. 338 = SIG³, no. 281. See H. W. Parke, _The Oracles of Zeus_ (1967), ch. 9.

30. IG II², no. 1292, republished by S. Dow, 'The Egyptian Cults in Athens', HThR 30 (1937), pp. 183–232, on pp. 188–9, whence P. M. Fraser, 'Two Studies on the Cult of Sarapis in the Hellenistic World', _Opusc. Ath._ 3 (1960), pp. 1–54, App. no. 2.

31. For Sarapis see e.g. Fraser, _op. cit._, and 'Current Problems concerning the Early History of the Cult of Sarapis', _Opusc. Ath._ 7 (1967), pp. 23–45; J. E. Stambaugh, _Sarapis under the Early Ptolemies_ (1972); for Isis see F. Dunand, _Le culte d'Isis dans le bassin oriental de la Méditerranée_ I-III (1973); cf. Ph. Bruneau, _Le sanctuaire et le culte des divinités égyptiennes à Érétrie_ (1975).

32. Foucart, chs. 11–13. For recent surveys and collections of evidence see e.g. Ph. Bruneau, _Recherches sur les cultes de Délos à l'époque hellénistique et à l'époque impériale_ (1970); R. Salditt-Trappmann, _Tempel der ägyptischen Götter in Griechenland und an der Westküste Kleinasiens_ (1970); cf. P. Debord, _Aspects sociaux et économiques de la vie religieuse dans_

In Rome and Italy, it was equally above all the Egyptian cults which
early found a firm foothold.[33] They appeared there from the second
century B.C. onwards, were repeatedly banned by the senate and
suppressed by force, but always found new adherents. In 43 B.C. the
triumvirs themselves built a temple of Serapis and Isis for the official
cult.[34] Worship of Egyptian gods was therefore no longer practised
merely by private societies, but also by the *res publica*. Under Augustus
there were in Rome already several temples for the Egyptian *sacra*,
though still outside the *pomerium*.[35] Under Tiberius an attempt was
made to suppress them entirely,[36] but many of the subsequent emperors
only favoured them the more. In the provinces they were widespread
during the whole of the imperial period.[37] Cults originating in Asia
Minor, Syria and Persia gained entrance into Rome, and were diffused
throughout the empire, a little later than the Egyptian cults. They are
most fully attested in the second century A.D., which is however the
period which produced the largest number of inscriptions of all kinds.
The worship of the Syrian sun-god, already widely practised, was
further promoted in Rome by various emperors of the third century.[38]
Still more popular throughout the entire Roman empire was the cult of
the Persian Mithras with its secret mysteries. On the inscriptions from
almost all the provinces of the Roman realm in the imperial period no
oriental cult is met with as frequently as this.[39] Related to it is the cult
of the Phrygian Magna Mater (Cybele) in its later developed form. The
taurobolia, which came to be connected with the latter, underwent in the

---

l'Anatolie gréco-romaine (1982).

33. See J. Marquardt, *Römische Staatsverwaltung* III, pp. 76 ff., and for a full study M.
Malaise, *Les conditions de pénétration et de diffusion des cultes égyptiens en Italie* (1972).

34. Dio xlvii 15, 1.

35. Dio liii 2, 4.

36. Josephus, *Ant.* xviii 3, 4 (65–80); Tacitus, *Ann.* ii 85; Suetonius, *Tib.* 36.

37. For recent surveys see R. E. Witt, *Isis in the Graeco-Roman World* (1971); L. Vidman,
'Isis und Sarapis' and G. Hölbl, 'Andere Ägyptische Gottheiten', in M. J. Vermaseren
(ed.), *Die orientalischen Religionen im Römerreich* (1981), chs. 5–6.

38. Cf. for the Syrian cults G. Wissowa, *Religionen und Kultus der Römer*, pp. 299–307; F.
Cumont, *Les religions orientales* ([4]1929), ch. 5. See also G. H. Halsberghe, *The Cult of Sol
Invictus* (1972), and the essential study by H. Seyrig, 'Le culte du Soleil en Syrie à
l'époque romaine', *Syria* 48 (1971), pp. 337–73. Note E. Schwertheim, 'Jupiter
Dolichenus', Y. Hajjier, 'Jupiter Heliopolitanus', and H. J. W. Drijvers, 'Die Dea Syria
und andere syrische Gottheiten im Imperium Romanum', in M. J. Vermaseren, *op. cit.*,
chs. 7–9.

39. On Mithras see F. Cumont, *Textes et monuments figurés relatifs aux mystères de Mithra* II
(1896); I (1899) (a major work with a full collection of the material); G. Wissowa,
Religion und Kultus der Römer, pp. 307–12; Cumont, *Religions orientales* ([4]1929), ch. 6; M. J.
Vermaseren, *Corpus Inscriptionum et Monumentorum Religionis Mithriacae* I-II (1956–60);
idem, Mithras, the Secret God (1963); J. R. Hinnells (ed.), *Mithraic Studies* I-II (1975); U.
Bianchi (ed.), *Mysteria Mithrae* (1979); M. J. Vermaseren, *Orientalische Religionen*, ch. 4:
'Mithras in der Römerzeit'.

later imperial period a transformation by which they became also a ritual of purification, and occur in this form also in the cult of Mithras.[40]

The attractiveness of all these cults seems to have resided essentially in three typical traits which they have in common; it should however be emphasized that both the factual material and the conceptual framework for any confident analysis of the religious changes sketched above is lacking.[41] First there appears in all of them some form of monotheistic element. Whether the deity be described as Isis or Serapis or Mithras, or however else, these cults ordinarily involved—at least in the period with which we are concerned—the conception either that the god worshipped was a single supreme deity, or that different divine names functioned as designations of the same deity. A second element is the emphasis on expiation of sins and ritual purification generally required of their adherents. Connected with this there then seems to have been a third element, the expectation of a happy after-life which, as has often been supposed, was offered by most of these forms of worship in one shape or another. As regards the established cults of the Graeco-Roman world, these claims cannot be made in the same way. Certainly there was a tendency in philosophic circles to adopt a monotheistic interpretation of paganism; but it did not generally provide the elements of personal initiation and purification, possibly with the expectation of an after-life, which seem to have characterized some of the 'oriental' cults.[42]

In spite of the many profound uncertainties which attend any attempt to define the meaning of the 'oriental' cults for those who participated in them, it remains possible that attachment to Judaism satisfied some of the same needs. Thus even this *taeterrima gens*

40. See Roscher's *Lex. der griech. und röm. Mythologie*, s.v. 'Kybele' and 'Meter'; S. Dill, *Roman Society from Nero to Marcus Aurelius*, pp. 547–59 (*mater magna*); Cumont, *Religions orientales* ([4]1929), ch. 3; M. J. Vermaseren, *Cybele and Attis: The Myth and the Cult* (1977); G. Sanders, 'Kybele und Attis' in M. J. Vermaseren (ed.), *Orientalische Religion*, ch. 10. See also R. Duthoy, *The Taurobolium: Its Evolution and Terminology* (1969).

41. For these aspects, and possible explanations of the change of religious mentality involved see, apart from the works mentioned in the preceding footnotes, e.g. R. L. Gordon, 'Mithraism and Roman Society. Social Factors in the Explanation of Religious Change in the Roman Empire', Religion 2 (1972), pp. 92–121; U. Bianchi and M. J. Vermaseren (eds.), *La soteriologia dei culti orientali nell'impero romano* (1982).

42. On pagan belief in survival after death see e.g. L. Friedländer, *Darstellungen aus der Sittengeschichte Roms* III ([9]1920), pp. 298–327; G. Rohde, *Psyche. Seelencult und Unsterblichkeitsglaube der Griechen* II ([9-10]1925), especially pp. 379–96 on popular belief in Late Antiquity; F. Cumont, *After Life in Roman Paganism* (1922); *Recherches sur le symbolisme funéraire des Romains* (1942); *Lux Perpetua* (1949). See also J. M. C. Toynbee, *Death and Burial in the Roman World* (1971). For a sceptical view of the state of our knowledge as regards the expectation of an after-life see R. MacMullen, *Paganism in the Roman Empire* (1981), pp. 53 ff.

nevertheless won converts to its religion. It may even be that its success would have been much greater but for the modest social status of the Jews, the lack of a form of worship involving formal rituals, and the obligations imposed by adherence to the Law.

As discussed above, Jewish propaganda in the Hellenistic-Roman period is clearly reflected in contemporary literary sources. How far this propaganda is to be taken as the product of a serious practical effort to win converts is not immediately clear. Strict Pharisaic Judaism cannot have aspired to gain adherents beyond the circle of fellow-Jews, for if the promise was valid only for the children of Abraham, what could pagans hope to obtain by the adoption of Jewish customs? However, this exclusiveness, which rests on the view of Yahweh as the God peculiar to Israel, was already fundamentally surmounted by the prophetic idea of God. For the one God, the Lord of heaven and earth, cannot be God and Father of one nation alone, so that he takes only this one for himself. If God is one, he is not only God of the Jews but also of the gentiles. This conclusion was not first drawn by Paul (Rom. 3:28–9), but appears clearly in the greatest and most profound of the Old Testament prophets, Deutero-Isaiah. The people of Israel is indeed chosen by God to be his servant, to whom he first gave his 'Law' and 'Judgement' (תורה and משפט). But Israel now has the task of proclaiming this to the nations (Isa. 42:1–4; 49:1–6). It has to become a light to the gentiles (Isa. 42:6; 49:6). The religion of Israel has to become a world religion.[43] And the gentiles will then also be accepted by God (Isa. 56:1–8). This universalism was admittedly not wholly consistent in Judaism. Side by side with it went the view of Yahweh as the God peculiar to Israel, who had chosen *only* this people for redemption. The concurrence of both viewpoints gave rise to a tension in which now one, now the other prevailed.[44] In theory, especially in Palestinian Judaism, particularistic thought undoubtedly

43. That the 'Servant of God' in Deutero-Isaiah is the Jewish people or the ideal Israel is recognized by many modern exegetes. See for example B. Stade, *Biblische Theologie des A.T.* I (1905), p. 133, and the works mentioned there. For more recent surveys, see C. R. North, *The Suffering Servant in Deutero-Isaiah* ([2]1956); H. H. Rowley, *The Servant of the Lord* ([2]1965). For other literature see O. Eissfeldt, *The Old Testament—An Introduction* (1965), pp. 330–41.

44. K. Siegfried in particular drew attention to this antithesis, 'Prophetische Missionsgedanken und jüdische Missionsbestrebungen', JPTh (1890), pp. 435–53. On the universalistic trend of Jewish monotheism see especially also J. Wellhausen, *Israelitische und jüdische Geschichte*, ([4]1901), pp. 224–6; A. Bertholet, *Die Stellung der Israeliten und der Juden zu den Fremden* (1896) (esp. pp. 91–122, 191–5); M. Löhr, *Der Missionsgedanke im Alten Testaments* (1896); Ed. Meyer, *Die Entstehung des Judenthums* (1896), pp. 119–21, 221 ff.; E. Stave, *Ueber den Einfluss des Parsismus auf das Judentum* (1898), pp. 90 ff.; M. Meinertz, *Jesus und die Heidenmission* (1908) (esp. pp. 17–49); G. Hoennicke, *Das Judenchristentum* (1908), pp. 44–7; G. F. Moore, *Judaism in the first three centuries of the Christian Era* I (1927), pp. 219–34; F. Hahn, *Mission in the New Testament* (1965), especially ch. 1.

predominated. In practice it was otherwise. The natural urge of every living religion to communicate the possession of its own good to others showed itself here to be stronger than dogmatic preconceptions. If gentiles by their conversion to Judaism did not become full Israelite citizens, they would nevertheless be removed from the multitude of the damned and at least affiliated to the people of the promise. Thus even the Pharisees in Palestine can be portrayed as eager to find converts: 'You traverse sea and land to make a single proselyte' (Mt. 23:15).

However, it may be that in the diaspora the theory was more broadminded than among the Palestinian Pharisees. The expansive tendencies of Judaism[45] were probably stronger here than among the Palestinians (see above, pp. 139 ff.). It is noteworthy that Philo (*Spec. Leg.* i 51–3) makes a particular point of the welcome, and subsequent equality of rights, extended to full proselytes. At any rate, as has been described above, a varied literature came into being, the direct aim of which was to convince pagans of the folly of idolatry, to win them over to belief in the one true God, and at the same time to convert them to a more serious and moral way of life by pointing towards a future reward (see §33A, especially sections VI and VII). This literature did not of course always aim at winning pagans over to a full acceptance of the Law and to joining the Jewish community. Its purpose was often only conversion to the fundamental viewpoints of Judaism (see further below). In one way or another, Israel felt itself to be the teacher of the peoples of the world. It is clear from Justin's *Dialogue with Trypho* that Isa. 49:6, τέθεικά σε εἰς φῶς ἐθνῶν etc., was understood in this sense.[46] The Sibyl says that Jews 'will be for all mortals leaders to life' (Sib. 3:195: πάντεσσι βρότοισι βίου καθοδηγοὶ ἔσονται). Paul describes this proud self-awareness of Judaism in Rom. 2:19–20: πέποιθας σεαυτὸν ὁδηγὸν εἶναι τυφλῶν, φῶς τῶν ἐν σκότει, παιδευτὴν ἀφρόνων, διδάσκαλον νηπίων, ἔχοντα τὴν μόρφωσιν τῆς γνώσεως καὶ τῆς ἀληθείας ἐν τῷ νόμῳ. And how active they were in actual practice is manifest if only from Horace's mockery of the Jewish eagerness to make converts.[47]

The success of these efforts was considerable.[48] There is clear

---

45. See A. von Harnack, *Die Mission und Ausbreitung des Christentums* I (⁴1924), pp. 14–23; E.T. *The Expansion of Christianity in the First Three Centuries* I (1904), pp. 11–18.

46. Justin, *Dial. c. Tryph.* 121–2.

47. Horace, *Sat.* i 4, 142–3 = GLAJJ I, no. 127: 'ac veluti te Iudaei cogemus in hanc concedere turbam'.

48. On proselytes cf. e.g. J. Bernays, *Gesammelte Abhandlungen* II (1885), pp. 71–80; W. Bacher, *Die Agada der Tannaiten* I–II (1884–90); idem, *Die Agada der palästinensischen Amoräer* I–III (1892–9), index s.v. 'Proselyten'; A. Bertholet, *Die Stellung der Israeliten und der Juden zu den Fremden* (1896); Ed. Meyer, *Die Entstehung des Judenthums* (1896), pp. 227–34; W. Bousset, *Die Religion des Judentums* (²1906; ³1926); G. F. Moore, *Judaism* I (1927), pp. 323–56; B. J. Bamberger, *Proselytism in the Talmudic Period* (1939); W. G. Braude, *Jewish Proselytising in the First Five Centuries of the Common Era* (1940); M. Simon,

evidence that in the Hellenistic-Roman period a large number of gentiles, who attached themselves more or less closely to Jewish communities, took part in the Jewish divine service and observed Jewish precepts sometimes more, sometimes less completely. Many of the Greeks, boasts Josephus, 'have agreed to adopt our laws; some of whom have remained faithful, while others, lacking the necessary endurance, have again seceded.'[49] 'The masses', he says in another passage, 'have long since shown a keen desire to adopt our religious observances; and there is not one city, Greek or barbarian, nor a single nation, to which our custom of abstaining from work on the seventh day has not spread, and where the fasts and the lighting of lamps and many of our prohibitions in the matter of food are not observed.'[50] In

---

Verus Israel (1948, ²1964), pp. 313–53; L. H. Feldman, '"Jewish Sympathisers" in Classical Literature and Inscriptions', TAPhA 81 (1950), pp. 200–8; K. G. Kuhn and H. Stegemann, 'Proselyten', RE Supp. IX (1962), cols. 1248–83; A. Paul, 'Prosélyte, prosélytisme', DB Supp. VIII (1972), cols. 1353–6 (excellent bibliography).

49. *C. Ap.* ii 10 (123): πολλοὶ παρ' αὐτῶν εἰς τοὺς ἡμετέρους νόμους συνέβησαν εἰσελθεῖν, καί τινες μὲν ἐνέμειναν, εἰσὶ δ' οἳ τὴν καρτερίαν οὐχ ὑπομείναντες πάλιν ἀπέστησαν.

50. *C. Ap.* ii 39 (282): καὶ πλήθεσιν ἤδη πολὺς ζῆλος γέγονεν ἐκ μακροῦ τῆς ἡμετέρας εὐσεβείας, οὐδ' ἔστιν οὐ πόλις Ἑλλήνων οὐδ' ἡτισοῦν οὐδὲ βάρβαρος, οὐδὲ ἐν ἔθνος, ἔνθα μὴ τὸ τῆς ἑβδομάδος, ἣν ἀργοῦμεν ἡμεῖς, τὸ ἔθος διαπεφοίτηκεν καὶ αἱ νηστεῖαι καὶ λύχνων ἀνακαύσεις καὶ πολλὰ τῶν εἰς βρῶσιν ἡμῖν οὐ νενομισμένων παρατετήρηται. Cf. Tertullian, *Ad Nat.* i 13, 3–4: 'Vos certe estis, qui etiam in laterculum septem dierum solem recepistis, et ex diebus ipsorum praelegistis, quo die lavacrum subtrahatis aut in vesperam differatis, aut otium et prandium curetis. Quod quidem facitis exorbitantes et ipsi a vestris ad alienas religiones: Iudaei enim festi sabbata et cena pura et Iudaici ritus lucernarum et ieiunia cum azymis et orationes litorales, quae utique aliena sunt a diis vestris.' Tertullian is admittedly speaking here only of gentiles who observed isolated Jewish customs. Josephus also may be alluding to the observance of Jewish customs outside the circle of Jewish communities. For the 'sabbath light', נר השבת, cf. *mShab.* 2:6–7; JE VII, 600 ff., s.v. 'Lamp'. See Seneca, *Epist.* 95, 47 (ed. Reynolds) = GLAJJ I, no. 188: 'Quomodo sint dii colendi solet praecipi. Accendere aliquam lucernas sabbatis prohibeamus', etc. The satirist Persius, *Sat.* v 179–84 = GLAJJ I, no. 190, gives a hostile representation of this: 'But when the day of Herod comes round, when the lamps wreathed with violets and ranged round the greasy window-sills have spat forth their thick clouds of smoke, when the floppy tunnies' tails are curled round the dishes of red ware, and the white jars are swollen out with wine, you silently twitch your lips, turning pale at the sabbath of the circumcized.' (Loeb translation, amended by Stern.) A remarkable illustration of the spread of the Jewish Sabbath at the beginning of the imperial period is afforded by an experience of Tiberius in Rhodes. He is reported not to have been admitted by a Greek *grammaticus* of the name of Diogenes, because the latter used only to debate on the Sabbath (Suetonius, *Tib.* 32 = GLAJJ II, no. 305: 'Diogenes grammaticus, disputare sabbatis Rhodi solitus, venientem eum, ut se extra ordinem audiret, non admiserat ac per servolum suum in septimum diem distulerat'). In the vicinity of Elaeusa in western Cilicia appears a sect of *Sabbatistai* who venerated τὸν θεὸν τὸν Σαββατιστήν (OGIS, no. 573). Since *sabbatizein* is the usual word for celebrating the Sabbath (Exod. 16:30; Lev. 23:32; 26:35; 2 Chr. 36:21; 2 Mac. 6:6), there seems to be little doubt that the term denotes those who observe the Sabbath. Cf. generally for the subject of the spread of Sabbath observance among non-Jews, e.g. M. Friedländer, *Das Judenthum in der vorchristlichen griechischen Welt* (1897), pp. 39–46; R. Goldenberg, 'The Jewish Sabbath in the Roman

A.D. 66, so Josephus reports, every city in Syria not only contained a number of Jews but a group of 'judaisers' (ἰουδαΐζοντας), who could be suspected of siding with them, *B.J.* ii 18, 2 (463). In Antioch the Jewish community were always attracting to their services a large crowd of Greeks, 'and had made these, in a certain way, part of their own community', vii 3, 3 (45). Comparable evidence, though from a different point of view, is given by Seneca,[51] and Cassius Dio.[52] In order to explain the accumulation of treasure in the Temple at Jerusalem, Josephus refers not only to the generous contributions of Jews throughout the world, but equally to those of 'God-fearers'.[53] These general observations are supported by various individual items of evidence. In Antioch and Syria, as Josephus says (above), large numbers of gentiles attended Jewish services.[54] In Pisidian Antioch Paul is reported to have addressed as follows those assembled in the synagogue: ἄνδρες 'Ισραηλεῖται καὶ οἱ φοβούμενοι τὸν θεόν (Ac. 13:16), and ἄνδρες ἀδελφοί, υἱοὶ γένους 'Αβραάμ καὶ οἱ ἐν ὑμῖν φοβούμενοι τὸν θεόν (Ac. 13:26). After the close of the service there followed him πολλοὶ τῶν 'Ιουδαίων καὶ τῶν σεβομένων προσηλύτων (Ac. 13:43; cf. also 13:50). In Thessalonica Paul converted τῶν σεβομένων 'Ελλήνων πλῆθος πολύ (Ac. 17:4). In Athens Paul preached in the synagogue τοῖς 'Ιουδαίοις καὶ τοῖς σεβομένοις (Ac. 17:17). These passages should, in spite of recent arguments to the contrary, be taken as reflecting the historical fact of the existence of substantial bodies of 'sympathisers' or 'God-fearers' attracted to at least some Jewish communities at some periods (see further p. 165 below). In Rome, too, Jewish propaganda was not without success, as is known from the satires of Horace and Juvenal. Here as elsewhere there is some indication that women proved the most responsive.[55] In Damascus, Josephus claims, almost the whole of the female part of the population was devoted to Judaism,[56] and it

---

World up to the time of Constantine the Great', ANRW II.19.1 (1979), pp. 414–47.

51. Seneca, *ap.* Augustine, *De civitate Dei* vi 11 = GLAJJ I, no. 186: 'Cum interim usque eo sceleratissimae gentis consuetudo convaluit, ut per omnes iam terras recepta sit, victi victoribus leges dederunt ... Illi tamen causas ritus sui noverunt; maior pars populi facit, quod cur faciat ignorat.'

52. Cassius Dio xxxvii 16, 5–17, 1 = GLAJJ II, no. 406: ἥ τε γὰρ χώρα 'Ιουδαία καὶ αὐτοὶ 'Ιουδαῖοι ὀνομάζαται. ἡ δὲ ἐπίκλησις αὕτη ἐκείνοις μὲν οὐκ οἶδ' ὅθεν ἤρξατο γενέσθαι, φέρει δὲ καὶ ἐπὶ τοὺς ἄλλους ἀνθρώπους ὅσοι τὰ νόμιμα αὐτῶν, καίπερ ἀλλοεθνεῖς ὄντες, ζηλοῦσι.

53. *Ant.* xiv 7, 2 (110): τῶν κατὰ τὴν οἰκουμένην 'Ιουδαίων καὶ σεβομένων τὸν θεόν.

54. *B.J.* vii 3, 3 (45): ἀεί τε προσαγόμενοι ταῖς θρησκείαις πολὺ πλῆθος 'Ελλήνων κἀκείνους τρόπῳ τινὶ μοῖραν αὐτῶν πεποίηντο.

55. Hor. *Sat.* i 9, 68–72 = GLAJJ I, no. 129 (where the observer of Jewish Sabbaths describes himself as 'unus multorum'); Juvenal, *Sat.* xiv 96–106 = GLAJJ II, no. 301 (see further p. 164 below). For female proselytes attested in the inscriptions from Rome see CIJ I², nos. 222, 462, 523 (Beturia (*sic*) Paulina, who took the name Sara).

56. *B.J.* ii 20, 2 (560).

was quite often women of higher social standing who followed this trend.[57] But individual examples of the conversion of high-ranking men are also reported.[58] A particularly notable conversion to Judaism was that of the royal house of Adiabene, to which Josephus returns again and again with obvious pride, *Ant.* xx 2–4 (17–96); *B.J.* ii 19, 2 (520); iv 9, 11 (567); v 2, 2 (55); 3, 3 (119); 4, 2 (147); 6, 1 (252); vi 6, 3 and 4 (355–6).[59] The kingdom of Adiabene, on the frontier of the Roman and Parthian empires, and in a position of some dependence on the latter, was ruled in the time of Claudius by a certain Izates who converted to Judaism along with his mother Helena and later also involved his brother Monobazus together with the rest of his relatives.[60] As a result of their conversion this royal family formed various connections with Jerusalem. Izates had five of his sons educated there.[61] Helena travelled there on a pilgrimage and during the famine under Claudius distributed food among the people.[62] According to rabbinic tradition, Helena was for fourteen years, according to other opinions even twenty-one years, a Nazirite.[63] Both Helena and Monobazus

57. Ac. 13:50; 17:4; Josephus, *Ant.* xviii 3, 5 (81–4). The latter passage relates how a pair of Jewish swindlers had cheated a prominent Roman lady named Fulvia, who had adopted the Jewish faith, of large sums of money under the pretext of sending them to the Temple at Jerusalem. On the Empress Poppaea see above, p. 78.

58. Ac. 8:26 ff. (the chamberlain of the Queen Candace), Josephus, *Ant.* xx 7, 1 and 3 (139, 145) (Azizus of Emesa and Polemon of Cilicia, the two brothers-in-law of Agrippa II). Mention may be made here of the consul Flavius Clemens and his wife Domitilla. On this see Cassius Dio lxvii 14, 1–2 = GLAJJ II, no. 435. See Stern, *ibid.*, for the rejection of the frequently argued view that the pair had converted to Christianity, in contradiction to Dio's clear statement that the charge was 'atheism', equated with 'Jewish customs'. Later Christian sources however allege that his niece Flavia Domitilla was exiled on a charge of Christianity. Eusebius, *Hist. Eccl.* iii 18, 4–5; Eusebius, *Chron.*, ed. Schoene, II, pp. 160, 163, *ad ann. Abr.* 2112 (where the chronographer Bruttius or Brettius is quoted as authority, see Müller, FHG IV, p. 352; Jerome, *Chron.*, ed. Helm, p. 152). At the time of Jerome, 'cellulas in quibus illa longum martyrium duxerat' were shown on the island of Pontia (*Ep.* 108, 7). Cf. also ILChr, no. 2150: '[... in coemeterio?] Domit[illae?]'.

59. For a full recent discussion see A. Oppenheimer, *Babylonia Judaica*, pp. 14–17. Cf. also J. Teixidor, 'The Kingdom of Adiabene and Hatra', Berytus 17 (1967), pp. 1–11.

60. Josephus, *Ant.* xx 2–4 (17–96). Izates is mentioned as king of Adiabene in the time of Claudius also by Tacitus, *Ann.* xii 13, 14; Monobazus in the time of Nero, Tacitus, *Ann* xv 1, 14; Cassius Dio lxii 20; 23; lxiii 1. For both, especially Izates, cf. also A. von Gutschmid, *Kl. Schr.* III, pp. 45, 73 ff., 80 ff., 88 ff., 90 ff., 186; see PIR² I 891; M 679.

61. *Ant.* xx 3, 4 (71).

62. *Ant.* xx 2, 5 (49–53).

63. *m.Naz.* 3.6: 'If a man vowed to be a Nazirite for a longer spell and he fulfilled his Nazirite-vow and afterward came to the Land [of Israel], the School of Shammai say: He need continue a Nazirite [only for] thirty days [more]. And the School of Hillel say: He must again fulfil his vow as from the beginning. It once happened that the son of Queen Helena went to war and she said, "If my son returns in safety from the war I will be a Nazirite for seven years", and her son returned from the war, and she was a Nazirite for seven years. At the end of the seven years she came up to the Land [of Israel], and the School of Hillel taught her that she must be a Nazirite for yet another seven years; and at

(who succeeded his brother as ruler) possessed palaces in Jerusalem.[64] Both donated valuable gifts to the Temple at Jerusalem.[65] When Izates and his mother had died, Monobazus had them buried in a splendid tomb in Jerusalem built by Helena herself.[66] In the Jewish War, relations of Monobazus fought on the side of the Jews against the Romans.[67]

The possible forms of the union of gentiles to Judaism, and the extent of their observation of the Jewish Law, were clearly very varied. Tertullian speaks of gentiles who worshipped their pagan gods as well as observing individual Jewish precepts (see p. 161 above). On the other hand, those who underwent circumcision presumably undertook thereby the obligation to observe the entire Law to its full extent (cf. Gal. 5:3: μαρτύρομαι παντὶ ἀνθρώπῳ περιτεμνομένῳ ὅτι ὀφειλέτης ἐστὶν ὅλον τὸν νόμον ποιῆσαι). Between these two extremes there were presumably various intermediate positions. Much light is shed on this question by the fourteenth satire of Juvenal, in which he pursues the thought of the harmful effect of the bad example of parents upon their children. The poor morals of the former are inherited by the latter,

the end of this seven years she contracted uncleanness. Thus she continued a Nazirite for twenty-one years. R. Judah said: She needed to remain a Nazirite for fourteen years only.'

64. *B.J.* v 6, 1 (252–3); vi 6, 3 (355). A relative of Izates by the name of Grapte also had a palace in Jerusalem, *B.J.* iv 9, 11 (567).

65. *mYom.* 3:10: 'King Monobaz made of gold all the handles for the vessels used on the Day of Atonement. His mother Helena set a golden candlestick over the door of the Sanctuary. She also made a golden tablet on which was written the paragraph of the Suspected Adulteress.'

66. *Ant.* xx 4, 3 (95); *B.J.* v 2, 2 (55); 3, 3 (119); 4, 2 (147). The monument consisted of three pyramids, *Ant.* xx 4, 3 (95). Eusebius, who knew the monument as it originally was, speaks of *stelai* to be seen in the suburbs (*Hist. Eccl.* ii 12, 3). It was so famous that Pausanias, *Descr. Graeciae* viii 16, 3, compares it with the monument of Mausolus. From the passages of *B.J.* it emerges that the monument lay to the north of the city, according to *Ant.* xx 4, 3 (95), three stades distant from the city. According to Jerome, *Ep.* 108, 6, it lay, if approached from the north, to the left (i.e. eastwards) of the road: 'ad laevam mausoleo Helenae derelicto ... ingressa est Hierosolymam'. From all this it seems very probable that it is identical with the 'Tombs of the Kings', the most extensive ancient tombs in the vicinity of Jerusalem. See L. H. Vincent and A. M. Stève, *Jérusalem de l'Ancien Testament* I (1954), pp. 346–62. A strong argument for identifying the 'Tombs of the Kings' with the monument of Helena is afforded by a two-line inscription in the sarcophagus found there by de Saulcy, the first of which reads: צדן מלכתא (Queen Zaddan) and the second צדה מלכתה (Queen Zadda). The language of both lines is Aramaic, but in the first instance the script is one related to Syriac (Estrangelo), and in the second, Hebrew square script. This may perhaps be explained on the assumption that the (in any case Jewish) Queen 'Zaddan' or 'Zadda' belonged to a Syrian royal house, which (so far as is known) can only be that of Adiabene. For the texts see D. Chwolson, CIH (1882), cols. 72 ff. and facsimile no. 8; CIS II, Aramaic part i, no. 156. See further J. Pirenne, 'Aux origines de la graphie syriaque', Syria 40 (1963), pp. 106–37, who suggests that 'Queen Zaddan-Zadda' may belong to a later period (pp. 102–9).

67. *B.J.* ii 19, 2 (520); vi 6, 4 (357).

usually in heightened measure. As an example he mentions in the sphere of superstition the leaning towards Judaism. If the father is idle on every seventh day and regards the flesh of pigs as being as precious as that of human beings, the son not only does the same but also allows himself to be circumcised, despises Roman laws, and studies and scrupulously observes the Jewish Law handed down by Moses; namely that one should show the way only to fellow-believers and lead only the circumcised to the well for which they seek.[68] This suggests that there were different standards of observance of the Jewish Law. Book 4 of the Sibylline Oracles, which was composed about A.D. 80 and is most probably of Jewish origin, sets in the forefront of its preaching to pagans only worship of the true God and belief in a future judgement, and demands of gentile converts, it seems, not circumcision but only a purificatory bath.[69] The story of the conversion of King Izates is also very informative. He was filled with zeal for the Jewish Law and wished to be circumcised; but it was a Jew named Ananias who advised him in the strongest terms against it. The Jew feared that he would be in danger if the story went round that he had influenced the king towards circumcision. He therefore pointed out to the king that he could worship God *(τὸ θεῖον σέβειν)* even without circumcision, provided that he observed the Jewish laws in general; this was more important than circumcision. God would pardon him if he omitted this out of nervousness before his subjects.[70] Izates, it is true, had himself circumcised all the same; and the views of the merchant Ananias do not represent Jewish orthodoxy.

None the less there is a significant volume of evidence to suggest that a body of 'God-fearing' pagans was attached to many Jewish communities in the diaspora, and thereby adopted the Jewish (i.e. monotheistic and imageless) form of worship. They attended Jewish synagogues, but as regards the observance of the Law restricted themselves to certain aspects, and so were not counted as belonging to the main body of each Jewish community. On this view, it is

---

68. Juvenal, *Sat.* xiv 96–106 = GLAJJ II, no. 301 (with a very valuable commentary): 'Quidam sortiti metuentem sabbata patrem / Nil praeter nubes et coeli numen adorant, / Nec distare putant humana carne suillam, / Qua pater abstinuit, mox et praeputia ponunt: / Romanas autem soliti contemnere leges, / Iudaicum ediscunt et servant ac metuunt ius, / Tradidit arcano quodcumque volumine Moses: / Non monstrare vias eadem nisi sacra colenti, / Quaesitum ad fontem solos deducere verpos. / Sed pater in causa, cui septima quaeque fuit lux / Ignava et partem vitae non attigit ullam.' E. Courtney, *ad loc.*, wrongly assumes that Feldman's view that *metuentes* is not to be taken as referring to gentile 'sympathisers' can be accepted without question (see further below).

69. Sib. 4:162 ff. On the Jewish origin of this work see R. Charles, *Apocrypha and Pseudepigrapha of the Old Testament* II (1913), pp. 368–406; O. Eissfeldt, *The Old Testament, An Introduction* (1965), pp. 615–17; pp. 641–3 below.

70. Josephus, *Ant.* xx 2, 5 (49–53).

God-fearing pagans of this kind who are referred to by the expressions φοβούμενοι τὸν θεόν or σεβόμενοι τὸν θεόν sometimes used in Josephus, and more often in the Acts of the Apostles.[71] The question of whether these expressions, and the parallel one θεοσεβεῖς found on inscriptions (see below), can in fact be taken as technical or semi-technical terms for gentile 'God-fearers' who were not full proselytes, has long been the subject of debate, and particularly since the publication in 1950 of an article by L. H. Feldman.[72] It has been denied that these terms refer specifically to such an intermediate group, and pointed out (correctly) that they can be applied also to observing Jews. Since the problem is of fundamental importance for Jewish-pagan relations the relevant evidence must be set out. Firstly, that which explicitly contrasts Jews with 'God-fearers' attached in some way to a Jewish community is as follows. (1) The passages of Acts and Josephus mentioned above (p. 162). (2) An inscription from Panticapeum (p. 37 above) recording a manumission 'under the guardianship of the synagogue of the Jews and the "God-fearers"' (συνεπιτροπευούσης τῆς συναγωγῆς τῶν Ἰουδαίων καὶ θεὸν σέβων). (3) The major new inscription from Aphrodisias, of the second or third centuries A.D. (pp. 25–6 above). In this inscription, on face a. there appears a list of subscribers to a Jewish institution. Among the names three are described as proselytes—προσήλ(υτος), προσήλυ(τος) or προσή[λ(υτος)]—and two as 'God-fearers'—θεοσεβ(ής). More important, there follows on face b., first what seems clearly to be a list of members of the Jewish community, some fifty-four persons, including a large number with Hebrew names and/or patronymics, as well as several called 'Eusabbathios'. There is then a break of one line, and a list of 'God-fearers' (καὶ ὅσοι θεοσεβῖς, sic). The first nine are described as 'town-councillor'—*bouleutes*—and the total of names is fifty. There are no Hebrew names, but one person is called 'Eusabbathios'. It would be difficult to imagine clearer evidence that *theosebeis* could be categorized as a formal group attached to a Jewish community, and distinguished both from Jews and from full proselytes.

71. Φοβούμενοι τὸν θεόν: Ac. 10:2, 22; 13:16, 26. Σεβόμενοι τὸν θεόν: Josephus, *Ant.* xiv 7, 2 (110); Ac. 13:43, 50; 16:14; 17:4; 17:17; 18:7. The formulae vary here between the fuller σεβόμενοι τὸν θεόν (Josephus, *Ant.* xiv 7, 2 (110): Ac. 16:14; 18:7) and the plain σεβόμενοι (Ac. 13:50; 17:4; 17:17). Once the combination occurs σεβόμενοι προσήλυτοι (Ac. 13:43).

72. L. H. Feldman, '"Jewish Sympathisers" in Classical Literature and Inscriptions', TAPhA 81 (1950), pp. 200–8; see especially also H. Bellen, 'Συναγωγὴ τῶν Ἰουδαίων καὶ θεοσεβῶν'. Die Aussage einer bosporanischen Freilassungsinschrift (CIRB 71) zum Problem der "Gottesfürchtigen"', JAC 8-9 (1965-6), pp. 171–6; B. Lifshitz, 'De nouveau sur les "sympathisants"', JSJ 1 (1970), pp. 77–84; F. Siegert, 'Gottesfürchtige und Sympathisanten', JSJ 4 (1973), pp. 109–64; H. Hommel, 'Juden und Christen im kaiserzeitlichen Milet. Überlegungen zur Theaterinschrift', Ist. Mitt. 25 (1975), pp. 167–95; M. Stern, GLAJJ II (1980), pp. 103–6; A. T. Kraabel, 'The Disappearance of the "God-Fearers"', Numen 28 (1981), pp. 113–26.

It does not of course follow that the relevant terms were always so used. (4) Two inscriptions from the mosaic floor of the synagogue at Sardis (p. 21 above) name persons, called Αὐρ(ήλιος) Εὐλόγιος and Αὐρ(ήλιος) Πολύιππος, who had fulfilled vows, and who are each described as θεοσεβής. The first name in particular could well be that of a Jew; but in fact in neither case is there any proof either way. There is no reason why a Jew, named individually, could not be described as 'God-fearing'; but equally the term could indicate that both persons belonged to a category of gentile 'God-fearers' attached to the Sardis synagogue. (5) No conclusions can be drawn from the fragmentary inscription from the catacomb of the vigna Randanini in Rome (p. 80 above): [...]ΥΔΕΑ ΠΡΟΣΗ [...-...] ΕΟΣΕΒΙ[...] (CIJ I², no. 202), or from that on a marble slab of unknown origin now in Rome describing one Agrippas from Phaena as theosebes (ibid., no. 500), or from the epitaph of 'Eparchia theosebes' from the Via Appia, CIJ I², no. 228. (6) An inscription from Deliler near Philadelphia in Lydia (p. 22 above) shows a water basin being dedicated 'to the sacred synagoge of the Hebraioi' by a man called Εὐστάθιος ὁ θεοσεβής (CIJ II, no. 754). There is again no clear indication as to whether he is Jewish or not; but in the light of numbers 2 and 3 above and the possible contrast between himself and the Hebraioi here, it must be slightly more probable that he is to be seen as a gentile 'God-fearer'. (7) The same problems arise over the inscription from Tralles (p. 24 above) in which a lady named Capitolina, described as ἀξιόλογ(ος?) καὶ θεοσεβ(ής), records her construction of parts of a building which may well be a synagogue. (8) The most complex issues are however presented by the well known inscription from the theatre at Miletus.[73] Roughly carved on one of the rows of seats, probably in the later second or early third century, the inscription reads ΤΟΠΟΣ ΕΙΟΥΔΕΩΝ ΤΩΝ ΚΑΙ ΘΕΟΣΕΒΙΟΝ. The expected form of the last word would naturally be θεοσεβῶν, but in the light of the parallels previously given its meaning is clear. But are the persons to whom seats are allotted one group (and if so, which?) or two? In view of the informal character of the inscription it is not impossible that the third and fourth words have been reversed. The meaning would then be quite clear: 'seats of the Jews and "God-fearers"' (compare the inscription from Panticapaeum above). But clearly such a correction is to be avoided if possible. As it stands, the inscription refers to 'Jews, those also (called) "God-fearers"'. It has thus often been taken to be an allusion to the Jewish community itself, as established in Miletus. On the other hand a specific reference to the piety of a Jewish group seems both superfluous in general and all the

73. Published by A. Deissmann, Licht vom Osten (1906; ⁴1923), pp. 391 ff. (E.T., Light from the Ancient East (1910), pp. 446 ff.; SEG IV, no. 441; CIJ II, no. 748). See especially H. Hommel, art. cit. (n. 72 above), with Pl. 33.1.

more puzzling in this purely pagan context. H. Hommel has suggested, alternatively, that the allusion is specifically and only to gentile 'God-fearers'. On this interpretation they will have been known in Miletus as 'Jews' (Ἰουδαῖοι—for this usage see Cassius Dio, quoted in n. 52 above), but in the context of the theatre seating will have been given also a more precise designation. The inscription would, on this interpretation, have the meaning 'place of the "Jews" who are also (more precisely called) "God-fearers"'. If this interpretation is correct, it must follow that in Miletus gentile 'God-fearers' continued to attend the theatre and were a significant and publicly-recognized group. It may be relevant to recall the nine town-councillors listed first among the *theosebeis* of Aphrodisias.

It will be evident that no wholly secure interpretation of the theatre inscription can be offered. None the less, in spite of the variations in terminology between Acts and Josephus, using *phoboumenoi* or *sebomenoi*, and Greek inscriptions, which use *theosebeis* or *theon sebeis*, it is clearly premature to proclaim the 'disappearance' of the 'God-fearers' (so A. T. Kraabel). On the contrary, the evidence of Acts and Josephus and of the inscriptions of Aphrodisias and Panticapeum shows that these expressions in Greek could be used to refer to a category of gentiles who were in some definite way attached to Jewish synagogues.

If this is correct, it may not be unreasonable to connect the use of *phoboumenoi* or *sebomenoi* in Greek literary sources with the term *metuens* found for instance in Juvenal, as quoted above ('sabbata metuentem patrem'), and in a scatter of Latin inscriptions.[74] A number of poems in the (probably) third-century *Instructiones* of Commodian are addressed to judaisers, in one title (i, 25) called 'Qui timent et non credent'.[75] The brief phrases on the inscriptions however do not in most cases allow any certainty as to whether the persons named were 'fearers' of the Jewish God, and none of the Latin evidence reveals any collective or organisational relationship to a Jewish community.

74. For this association see J. Bernays, 'Die Gottesfürchtigen bei Juvenal', *Ges. Abhandlungen* II (1885), pp. 71–80; see the inscription CIL V.1, no. 88 = CIJ I², no. 642 (Pola): 'Aur. Soteriae matri pientissimae religioni(s) iudeicae metuenti.' Relevant also are CIL VI, no. 31839 = CIJ I², no. 5: 'Aemilio Va[l]enti eq. Romano metu[e]nti', fifteen years old (found near Rome); CIL VI, no. 29759 = CIJ I², no. 285: 'Larciae Quadrati[llae natione] Romanae metue[nti]'; *ibid.*, 29760 = CIJ I², no. 524: 'Dis Manib. Maianiae Homeridi dae (deum?) maetuenti'; *ibid.*, 29763 = CIJ I², no. 529: '[De?]um metuens' (the last three in Rome); CIL VIII, no. 4321 and *Addenda*, p. 956, see Y. Le Bohec, Antiquités Africaines 17 (1981), p. 191, no. 72: '[fidel]is metu[ens]' (in Numidia). The formulae in Juvenal, to which Bernays refers in the same context ('metuentem sabbata … Iudaicum metuunt ius'), are however quite different. A stronger expression than *metuens* is *iuste legem colens*, which is said of a certain *Iul. Irene Arista* on a Roman inscription, CIL VI, no. 29758 = CIJ I², no. 72.

75. Commodian, *Inst.* i 24–5; 37. See K. Thraede, 'Beiträge zur Datierung Commodians', JAC 2 (1959), pp. 90–114.

By contrast, an organisational structure is revealed by the evidence for cult associations worshipping the 'Highest God', such as that attested in the imperial period at Tanais. The parallelism in vocabulary is striking: newly admitted converts are called εἰσποιητοὶ ἀδελφοὶ σεβόμενοι θεὸν ὕψιστον (see CIRB, nos. 1278–87). However, as in a growing number of cases of the worship of the 'Highest God' attested throughout the Greek world, we cannot tell here what degree of Jewish influence, if any, is involved.[76]

At any rate the evidence from both the Greek-speaking and (to a lesser extent) the Latin-speaking parts of the ancient world is, though scattered, sufficient to demonstrate that there were gentiles who judaised without becoming converts, and that in at least some places these 'God-fearers' formed a defined group. It was presumably from among these that there came the 'Greeks who go up to worship (in the Temple) at the time of the festival (Passover)', mentioned in John's Gospel (12:20).

If it is asked which items of the ceremonial law were probably observed by these pagans, some indication is given by the passages already cited from Josephus, Juvenal and Tertullian (see nn. 50 and 68). All three agree that in the first place came the Sabbath commandment and the dietary laws. Precisely these two items are emphasized by Juvenal in the case of the father of a man who subsequently becomes a full Jew by circumcision ('metuentem sabbata patrem ... carne suillam, qua pater abstinuit'). Beyond these, it will have been a matter of personal choice as to how much of the Law was observed.

As Juvenal implies, a clear distinction should be made between these persons (*phoboumenoi, sebomenoi, theosebeis,* or *metuentes*) and full proselytes who underwent circumcision. The idea, which has been canvassed, that a form of proselytism existed in which circumcision was not required, should almost certainly be rejected.[77]

In the Old Testament, it is true, in the Hebrew no less than in the Greek Bible, גרים or προσήλυτοι are persons of a status comparable to that of metics in Athens, that is, aliens who live continuously in the land of Israel without however belonging to the community of Israel. But

---

76. See especially E. Schürer, 'Die Juden im bosporanischen Reiche und die Genossenschaften der σεβόμενοι θεὸν ὕψιστον ebendaselbst', SAB (1897), pp. 200–25. Related to them are the *Hypsistarioi, Hypsistianoi* and *Theosebeis* mentioned by the Church Fathers (SAB, pp. 221–4). For an important discussion of Zeus/Theos Hypsistos see A. D. Nock, C. Roberts and T. C. Skeat, 'The Guild of Zeus Hypsistos', HTR 29 (1936), pp. 39–88 = (with omissions) A. D. Nock, *Essays on Religion and the Ancient World*, ed. Z. Stewart, I (1972), pp. 414–43.

77. For this argument N. J. McEleney, 'Conversion, Circumcision and the Law', NTS 20 (1973-4), pp. 319–41, and the reply by J. Nolland, 'Uncircumcised Proselytes?', JSJ 12 (1981), pp. 173–94.

later usage consistently employs both expressions, without further
addition, to denote such pagans as by circumcision and observation of
the Torah have entered fully into the religious community of Israel.[78]

78. For the history of the concept cf. A. Geiger, *Urschrift und Uebersetzungen der Bibel*
(1857), pp. 349 ff.; A. Bertholet, *Die Stellung der Israeliten und der Juden zu den Fremden*
(1896); J. Juster, *Les Juifs dans l'empire romain* I (1914), pp. 253–90; G. F. Moore, *Judaism*
I (1927), pp. 323–53; W. G. Braude, *Jewish Proselytising in the First Five Centuries* (1940); S.
Zeitlin, 'Proselytes and Proselytism during the Second Commonwealth and the Early
Tannaitic Period', *H. A. Wolfson Jubilee Volume* (1965), pp. 871–81; B. J. Bamberger,
Proselytism in the Talmudic Period ([2]1968); K.-G. Kuhn, 'προσήλυτος', TDNT VI (1968),
pp. 727–44; J. Jeremias, *Jerusalem in the Time of Jesus* (1969), pp. 320–34; E. E. Urbach,
The Sages I (1975), pp. 541–54; M. Stern, JPFC II (1976), pp. 622–4; J. R. Rosenbloom,
Conversion to Judaism from the Biblical Period to the Present (1978). In the Mishnah, גר occurs
in the sense suggested in the following passages: *mDem.* 6:10; *mShebi.* 10:9; *mHal.* 3:6;
mBik. 1:4–5; *mPes.* 8:8; *mShek.* 1:3, 6; 7:6; *mKet.* 9:9; *mKid.* 4:1, 6, 7; *mB.K.* 4:7; 9:11;
mB.M. 4:10; *mB.B.* 3:3; 4:9; *mEduy.* 5:2; *mHor.* 1:4; 3:8; *mHul.* 10:4; *mKer.* 2:1; *mNid.*
7:3; *mZab.* 2:1, 3; *mYad.* 4:4. The feminine form is גיורת, *mYeb.* 6:5; 8:2; 11:2; *mKet.* 1:2,
4; 3:1, 2; 4:3; *mKid.* 4:7; *mB.K.* 5:4; *mEduy.* 5:6; גירת also occurs on an
ossuary-inscription from Jerusalem, CIJ II, no. 1390; compare no. 1385: Ἰουδάτος
Λαγανίωνος προσηλύτου. At Qumran, the term גר appears in CD 14:4, where the
community is described as consisting of priests, Levites, Israelites and proselytes. The
latter are probably converted slaves who have entered Abraham's covenant (אשר
באו עמו בברית אברהם , CD 12:10–11). The meaning 'converted foreigner' is so well
established for גר that a verb is even formed from it: נתגייר, i.e. 'to be converted', *mPeah*
4:6; *mShebi.* 10:9; *mHal.* 3:6; *mPes.* 8:8; *mYeb.* 2:8; 11:2; *mKet.* 1:2, 4; 3:1, 2; 4:3; 9:9;
mGit. 2:6; *mKid.* 3:5; *mHul.* 10:4; *mBekh.* 8:1; *mNeg.* 7:1; *mZab.* 2:3. The Aramaic form of
גר is גיורא which occurs twice also in the LXX (γειώρας Exod. 12:19; Isa. 14:1); Philo
read the word also in Exod. 2:22, where our Septuagint has πάροικος (*De conf. ling.* 82; see
edition by J. G. Kahn, 1963, *ad loc.*); it occurs further in Justin, *Dial. c. Tryph.* 122
(γηόρας) and Iulius Africanus, *Ep. ad Arist.*, in Eusebius, *Hist. Eccl.* i 7, 13: τὸ γένος ἀνάγειν
ἐπὶ τοὺς πατριάρχας ἢ προσηλύτους, τούς τε καλουμένους γειώρας τοὺς ἐπιμίκτους. Cf. also J.
F. Schleusner, *Lexicon in LXX*, s.v. γειώρας, and Otto on Justin, *op. cit.* Josephus frequently
mentions ὁ τοῦ Γιώρα Σίμων or υἱὸς Γιώρα, *B.J.* ii 19, 2 (521); ii 22, 2 (652); v 1, 3 (11);
vii 5, 6 (154)—iv 9, 2 (503). To signify simply 'resident foreigner' in the Old Testament
sense the Mishnah uses the Biblical expression גר תושב: *mB.M.* 5:6; 9:12; *mMak.* 2:3;
mNeg. 3:1. The same variation in meaning as גר has also been the fate of the Greek
προσήλυτος. Cf. for its use in the LXX, A. Geiger, *Urschrift und Uebersetzungen der Bibel*, pp.
353–4; W. C. Allen, 'On the meaning of προσήλυτος in the Septuagint', Expos 4 (1894),
pp. 264–75; Bertholet, p. 260; T. J. Meek, 'The Translation of *Ger* in the Hexateuch ...',
JBL 49 (1930), pp. 172–80; Kuhn, TDNT VI, p. 731. The word is originally equivalent
to πάροικος, *advena*, but later a convert to Judaism—νομίμοις προσεληλυθὼς τοῖς
Ἰουδαϊκοῖς, *Ant.* xviii 3, 5 (82). The former meaning can still be observed in the LXX (see
Kuhn); very often however the occurrences seem to imply the latter meaning. Philo,
attributing the sense usual in his time to the Old Testament word, explains, *Spec. Leg.* i 9
(51): τούτους δὲ καλεῖ προσηλύτους ἀπὸ τοῦ προσεληλυθέναι καινῇ καὶ φιλοθέῳ πολιτείᾳ Cf.
also the catena fragment on Exod. 22:20 in Philo, ed. Mangey II, p. 677, or J. R. Harris,
Fragments of Philo (1886), pp. 49 ff.; in general the material from Philo in Bertholet, pp.
285–90; Kuhn, TDNT VI, pp. 731–2. The Suda, *Lex. s.v.* gives the following
explanation: οἱ ἐξ ἐθνῶν προσεληλυθότες καὶ κατὰ νόμον ποθήσαντεσ πολιτεύεσθαι. In the
New Testament: Mt. 23:15; Ac. 2:10; 6:5; 13:43 (in the last passage, owing to the
addition of σεβόμενοι, the nature of the allusions is confusing). Cf. Kuhn, TDNT VI, pp.
742–3. Justin, *Dial. c. Tryph.* 122; Irenaeus, iii 12, 1 (Theodotion and Aquila ἀμφότεροι

How great their number was is impossible to determine. It may at one stage have been very considerable; the immense expansion of Judaism is not easy to explain simply by natural increase (cf. above, p. 4). In the Roman period, on the other hand, formal conversions to Judaism may perhaps have been less frequent than the looser attachment in the form of 'God-fearers'. From the time of Hadrian, Roman legislation expressly forbade conversion to Judaism by acceptance of circumcision (see above, p. 123); it would however be quite wrong to conclude from this that conversion, including circumcision, thereby ceased.

Earlier scholars identified these two categories of 'God-fearers' and genuine proselytes with two other categories apparently related to them, encountered in rabbinic literature. The 'God-fearers' were equated with those called in rabbinic writings 'proselytes of the gate' (גרי השער), but the genuine proselytes with 'proselytes of righteousness' (גרי הצדק).[79] In reality the latter identification alone is correct; the 'God-fearers' and the גרי השער have nothing to do with one another. These terms are altogether alien to the vocabulary of the Mishnah, which distinguishes only between גר and גר תושב. The former is a pagan converted to Judaism, the latter is the Old Testament *ger*, that is, a foreigner living in the Land of Israel (see n. 78). For the sake of greater clarity, גר צדק (a 'righteous man', i.e. a foreigner observing the Law) was later also used for גר, and גר שער for גר תושב, i.e. a foreigner living 'within the gates' or in the Land of Israel (following Ex. 20:10; Deut. 5:14; 14:21; 24:14). Thus גר שער is synonymous with the biblical גר. Nevertheless the expression is still absent from Talmudic vocabulary. The גרי תושב referred to in the Talmud are, as in the Old Testament, non-Jews living in the Land of Israel. This is also confirmed by the demands made of them, namely, to observe 'the seven commandments of the sons of Noah'.[80] Talmudic sages collected under

'Ιουδαῖοι προσήλυτοι); Tertullian, *Adv. Jud.* i 1, 1; Clement of Alexandria, *Quis dives salvetur* 28, 2. Hilarius on Math. 15:3 (Migne, PL IX, col. 1004); in Roman epitaphs the designation *proselytus* or *proselyta* is attested five times (cf. n. 55 above). In place of προσήλυτος there also occur: ἐπήλυτος: LXX Job 20:26; Philo, *Spec. Leg.* iv 34 (176); ἐπηλύτης: Philo, *Spec. Leg.* i 9 (53); 57 (309); ii 23 (118); *Virt.* 20 (102); 34 (182); ἔπηλυς: *Praem. et poen.* 26 (152); *Fr. ad Exod.* 22:20, *ap.* Harris, *Fragments*, p. 50.

79. Cf. S. Deyling, *Observationes sacrae* II (1737), pp. 462–9. The phrase גרי השער is not attested before the Middle Ages. Cf. Str.-B. II, p. 723; G. F. Moore, *Judaism* I (1930), pp. 340–1. Moore quotes Nahmanides' commentary on Ex. 20:10 as the earliest evidence for *géor sha'ar.* Cf. also K. G. Kuhn, TDNT VI, p. 737 and n. 99.

80. *bAZ* 64b: 'Who is a *ger toshab*? Any [gentile] who undertakes in the presence of three *haverîm* not to worship idols. Such is the teaching of R. Meir; but the Sages declare: Any man who takes upon himself the seven precepts accepted by the sons of Noah. Others maintain: . . . A proselyte who eats of animals not ritually slaughtered, i.e. he who has undertaken to observe all the precepts mentioned in the Torah apart from the prohibition of [eating] non-ritually slaughtered meat.' Cf. TDNT VI, pp. 740–2; Str.-B. II, pp. 722–3.

this title those commandments which in their view are binding on pre-Abrahamic and non-Abrahamic humanity (the 'sons of Noah').[81] The duties of a גֵּר תּוֹשָׁב, i.e. a non-Jew permanently resident in the Land of Israel, thus consisted in the observance of at least those commandments which are binding on the whole of mankind. Of course this was a purely notional obligation, for Greeks and Romans living in Palestine will scarcely have subjected themselves to this Jewish law. The so-called proselyte laws had therefore no practical significance; they represented only a legal theory which never became a reality.[82] Thus *sebomenoi*, etc., are wholly distinct from the גרי תושב, and belong in a quite different historical context.

In regard to the instruction of proselytes before their reception, nothing is known. They will have received substantially the same training as those members of the community who grew up in it, differing according to time and place. The instruction was naturally not confined to religious and moral fundamentals, but extended quite substantially to include the ritual content of the Torah. Attempts to discover more detailed information from early Christian literature concerning proselyte instruction provide at best only a picture of certain aspects of it, that is, of its religious and moral content, but not of tuition in the laws governing Jewish life, which was certainly a cardinal point.[83] Even the 'God-fearers' were presumably bound to

81. *bSanh*. 56b: 'The sons of Noah were given seven commandments with regard to (1) דינין ("judgements"); (2) ברכת השם (i.e. blasphemy); (3) עבודה זרה (idolatry); (4) גלוי עריות (i.e. incest and adultery); (5) שפכות דמים (i.e. murder); (6) גזל (theft); (7) אבר מן החי ("part of a living creature", i.e. an interdiction on eating flesh "with the blood in it", Gen. 9:4).' Cf. also *tAZ* 8(9): 4–6 with slight variations. See Str.-B. II, p. 722; III, pp. 37–8; Moore, *Judaism* I, pp. 274–5. See also JE ('Laws, Noachian'), VII, pp. 648–50; Enc. Jud. 12, cols. 1189–91.

82. The theory, as *bAZ* 64b shows, is put forward casually, and not earnestly and systematically. A collection of the biblical utterances on גרים would have given other results (see in general Exod. 12:43–50; 20:10; 22:20; 23:9, 72; Lev. 17:8, 10, 13, 15; 18:26; 19:10, 33–4; 20:2; 24:16–22; Num. 15:14–16; 19:10; Dt. 5:14; 14:21; 24:14; Ezek. 14:7. Cf. A. Bertholet, *Stellung der Israeliten*, pp. 27–50; R. de Vaux, *Ancient Israel* (1961), pp. 74–6.

83. In various early Christian writings, especially in *Barnabas* 18–20, *Didache* 1–6, parallel sections appear which under the title, 'Two Ways' (δύο ὁδοί—'duae viae'), present a short catechism of ethics. The relationship of the parallel texts to one another makes it very probable that they both go back to a common older source, which was probably Jewish. The concept of the 'Two Ways' is biblical (Jer. 21:8) and Jewish (*TAsher* 1:3–5: δύο ὁδοὺς ἔδωκεν ὁ θεὸς τοῖς υἱοῖς τῶν ἀνθρώπων; *mAb.* 2:9: דרך ישוק—דרך רעה). On the basis of this observation A. von Harnack, *Die Apostellehre und die jüdischen beiden Wege* ([2]1896), following the example of C. Taylor, *The Teaching of the Twelve Apostles* (1886), supposed that the 'Two Ways' was 'a catechism composed especially for proselytes'. A full version of this doctrine of 'duae viae' has emerged from the Dead Sea Scrolls (1QS 3:13–4:26). There it is presented as a catechism for the sectaries, i.e. the 'sons of light' (1QS 3:13) and addressed to the משכיל, the instructor. Cf. J.-P. Audet, 'Affinités littéraires et doctrinales du "Manuel de Discipline"', RB 59 (1952),

observe the most basic of the ritual commandments. For the proselytes proper Paul's remark was applicable, namely that whoever accepted circumcision was obliged to keep the whole Law (Gal. 5:3), even if this was administered with a very varying degree of strictness.

For the acceptance of real proselytes into the Jewish community during the existence of the Temple three demands were to be made, according to the rabbis: (1) מילה, circumcision; (2) טבילה, baptism, i.e. a purificatory immersion; (3) הרצית קרבן an offering to the Sanctuary.[84] In the case of women only the last two come into consideration.[85] After the destruction of the Temple, sacrifice also ceased. All three are regarded as traditional already in the Mishnah;[86] indeed, they are so much taken for granted in rabbinic Judaism that even in the absence of definite proof they can be considered as prevailing in Second Temple period. For in the same way that it was only possible to enter into the community of Israel through circumcision, so it also went without saying that a pagan, who as such was

---

pp. 219–38; 60 (1953), pp. 41–82; J. Licht, 'An Analysis of the Treatise of the Two Spirits in DSD', *Scrip. Hier.* 4 (1958), pp. 88–100; H. W. Huppenbauer, *Der Mensch zwischen zwei Welten* (1959); P. Wernberg-Møller, 'A Reconsideration of the Two Spirits in the Rule of the Community', RQ 3 (1962), pp. 433–41; J. H. Charlesworth, 'A Critical Comparison of the Dualism in 1QS III,13-IV,26 and the Dualism in the Fourth Gospel', NTSt 15 (1969), pp. 389–418. Rabbinic sources contain no direct indication relating to the proselytes' instruction in halakhah. Indirect evidence may be gathered from Qumran (1QS 6:13–23; 1QSa 1:6–9; CD 13:1–16), where the training of a new member entailed not only teaching but also periodical tests. That abridged versions of the Torah, intended as manuals of initiation, existed in proselytizing circles is probable. For such accounts, see G. Vermes, 'A Summary of the Law by Flavius Josephus', NT 24 (1982), pp. 289–303. The rabbinic anecdote concerning a gentile's request that Shammai and Hillel should teach him the whole Torah while he stood on one foot (*bShab.* 31a) suggests that such summaries may have been available.

84. Cf. *Sifre on Num.* 15:14 (ed. Horovitz (1908), p. 112). Cf. Moore, *Judaism* I, pp. 331–2; Kuhn, TDNT VI, pp. 738–9; B. J. Bamberger, *Proselytism in the Talmudic Period* (²1968), pp. 42–52. See also *mKer.* 2:1; *bKer.* 9a; bYeb. 46a.

85. *bKer.* 9a, interpreting *mKer.* 2:1, reads: 'As your forefathers entered the Covenant only by circumcision, immersion and the sprinkling of the blood, so shall they (the proselytes) enter the Covenant only by circumcision, immersion and the sprinkling of the blood.' *bYeb.* 46a furnishes a detailed discussion of the relationship between circumcision and baptism. 'A man cannot become a proper proselyte unless he has been circumcized and has also performed ritual ablution; ... If a proselyte was circumcized but had not performed the prescribed ritual ablution, R. Eliezer said, "Behold he is a proper proselyte; for so we find that our forefathers were circumcized and had not performed ritual ablution." If he performed the prescribed ablution but had not been circumcized, R. Joshua said, "Behold he is a proper proselyte; for so we find that the mothers had performed ritual ablution but had not been circumcized." The Sages, however, said, "Whether he had performed ritual ablution but had not been circumcized or whether he had been circumcized but had not performed the prescribed ritual ablution, he is not a proper proselyte, unless he has been circumcized and has also performed the prescribed ritual ablution."'

86. Circumcision and baptismal bath: *mPes.* 8:8; *mEduy.* 5:2. Sacrifice: *mKer.* 2:1.

unclean because he had not observed the ritual laws of purity, had to take a purificatory bath on his entry into the Jewish community.[87] Similarly, however, a pagan was also מחסר לפרה, 'in need of atonement', and remained so 'until blood was sprinkled for him'.[88]

In regard to proselyte baptism, it is unmistakably presupposed by the Mishnah to be the established rule.[89] Equally, the oft-quoted saying of Epictetus, as reported by Arrian, can best be understood of proselyte baptism.[90] Again, the Fourth Book of the Sibylline Oracles demands that repentant pagans should wash their whole bodies in rivers as an outward sign of their conversion.[91] The two last items, if their link with proselyte baptism is confirmed, will acquire special significance because they speak only of a bath and not of circumcision. So even where full acceptance into the Jewish community did not take place, at least immersion in water was demanded.

Those who converted to Judaism have at times also taken a Hebrew name. A very remarkable and ancient example of this is offered by the Jewish-Aramaic documents from Elephantine of the Persian period (see above, pp. 38–41). In one of these documents, from the year 420 B.C. (Cowley, no. 20, l. 3), an Egyptian appears with the name Ashor son of Zeho. Four years later, 416 B.C., the same man is called Nathan (the

---

87. Circumcision and proselyte baptism on the eve of Passover were the subject of controversy between the schools of Hillel and Shammai. Cf. *mPes.* 8:8; *mEduy.* 5:2. The latter permitted participation in the Passover to a proselyte circumcized and purified on the previous day. The school of Hillel, however, demanded seven days between circumcision and baptism. Whether the purification by water mentioned in connection with the ritual of the entry into the Covenant at Qumran (1QS 5:13–14) resembled proselyte baptism remains a matter for debate. Cf. O. Betz, 'Die Proselytentaufe der Qumransekte und die Taufe im Neuen Testament', RQ 1 (1958), pp. 213–34.

88. *mKer.* 2:1.

89. Cf. Kuhn, TDNT VI, pp. 738–9. It is unclear when proselyte baptism first originated. All that is known is that it is post-biblical and pre-Mishnaic. Current opinion dates its introduction to the first century A.D., principally because of the silence of Philo and Josephus. Cf. Bamberger, *Proselytism*, p. xxii; W. F. Flemington, 'Baptism', IDB I, p. 348. However, the *argumentum e silentio* from Philo and Josephus would be valid only if it could be shown that reference to proselyte baptism is absent from passages where it should have appeared.

90. Epictetus ii 9, 20–1 = GLAJJ I, no. 254: καὶ ὅταν τινὰ ἐπαμφοτερίζοντα ἴδωμεν, εἰώθαμεν λέγειν. οὐκ ἔστιν Ἰουδαῖος, ἀλλ᾽ ὑποκρίνεται. ὅταν δ᾽ ἀναλάβῃ τὸ πάθος τὸ τοῦ βεβαμμένου καὶ ᾑρημένου, τότε καὶ ἔστι τῷ ὄντι καὶ καλεῖται Ἰουδαῖος. Epictetus wishes to demonstrate that a man is a true philosopher only if he really behaves in accordance with his basic principles. Let the same apply to Jews. If someone calls himself a Jew but does not live as one, let him not be counted as a Jew. 'But if a man adopts the manner of life of a man who has been baptized and has made his choice, then he really is, and is called, a Jew.' The metaphorical interpretation of βεβαμμένου ('dedicated') is here however just as improbable as the view that Epictetus is confusing Jews and Christians. See Stern, GLAJJ, *ad loc.*

91. Sib. 4:165. J. J. Collins notes that the best parallel to this passage is provided by the baptism of repentance preached by John the Baptist. Cf. OTP I, p. 388, n. e2.

identity is apparent from that of his wife and sons, see Cowley, no. 25, l. 3). He had obviously gone over to Judaism in the meanwhile and taken the name of Nathan. Another example is Beturia Paulina on a Roman epitaph, who as a proselyte is called Sarah (see above p. 162). The new Jewish inscription from Aphrodisias in Caria (p. 26) now attests *proselutoi* called 'Samouel', 'Ioses' and 'Eioseph son of Eusebios', as well as a *theosebes* called 'Eusabbathios'.

The duties and rights of proselytes were exactly determined in much detail by the rabbis.[92] In general, it was taken for granted that according to strict Pharisaic opinion, echoed in Gal. 5:3, they had to observe the whole Torah, particularly in connection with religious dues.[93] The rabbis, however, very carefully drew certain boundaries here, especially in regard to the *terminus a quo* from which the obligation began. Only that income of a proselyte was liable to tax which came to him in a taxable condition after his conversion.[94] Brothers born before their mother's conversion were not bound by the law of levirate marriage.[95] The regulation of Dt. 22:13–21 does not apply to girls born before their mother's conversion.[96] The last stipulation shows how a limitation of rights was bound up with that of duties. In some situations involving marriage laws, only female proselytes who at their conversion were not yet three years and one day old had equal standing with born Jewesses.[97] Female proselytes could not marry priests; and daughters of proselytes could do so only if one of the parents was an Israelite by birth, a regulation valid even to the tenth generation.[98] On the other hand, female proselytes might marry castrated or mutilated men, which is forbidden to born Jewesses in Dt. 23:2.[99] The legal stipulation that anyone who inadvertently strikes a woman so that she suffers a miscarriage has to pay damages, *prima facie* did not apply to female proselytes.[100] On the other hand, the regulation concerning drinking the 'water of bitterness' (Num. 5:11 ff.) was valid also for female proselytes.[101]

The very care with which these distinctions are drawn shows that in

---

92. For the passages of the Mishnah see above, n. 78. Cf. also the tractate *Gerim* in M. Higger, *Seven Minor Tractates* (1930), E.T. in A. Cohen (ed.), *The Minor Tractates of the Talmud* II (1965), pp. 603–13.

93. *mBik.* 1:4; *mShek.* 1:3, 6; *mPeah* 4:6; *mHal.* 3:6; *mHul.* 10:4.

94. *mPeah* 4:6; *mHal.* 3:6; *mHul.* 10:4.

95. *mYeb.* 11:2.

96. *mKet.* 4:3.

97. *mKet.* 1:2, 4; 3:1, 2.

98. *mYeb.* 6:5; *mKid.* 4:7; *mBik.* 1:5.

99. *mYeb.* 8:2.

100. *mB.K.* 5:4. The commentators limit this to the case of a widow whose husband was himself a proselyte. In such a case damages are not to be paid to the heirs who, as gentiles, have no right to inherit. Cf. W. Windfuhr, *Baba qamma* (1913), p. 39.

101. *mEduy.* 5:6.

essentials proselytes were regarded by the rabbis as of equal status with born Israelites in regard to duties and rights. Nevertheless, a proselyte might never call the ancestors of Israel his fathers,[102] and in the theocracy he is ranked after a *nathin*.[103] Although the humane Jewish law emphasizes, by appeal to Ex. 22:20, that a person should never in an unfriendly way remind the son of a proselyte of the former way of life of his fathers,[104] yet proselytes as a rule did not enjoy the trust accorded to born Jews. The opinion of Rabbi Judah concerning the proselytes in Rekem, that they were liable to err in observance of the Law,[105] is thought by some, in the light of the Talmudic complaints against proselytes, to reflect a general doubt concerning their reliability in halakhic matters. But this reconstruction must be seen against the larger number of positive rabbinic statements regarding converts to Judaism.[106]

According to the Deuteronomic law, two nations, the Ammonites and the Moabites, were never to be accepted into the community of Israel, not even in the tenth generation (Dt. 23:4). This rule was destined to be the starting-point of a controversy in the time of Gamaliel II as to whether an Ammonite proselyte who wished to enter the community could be allowed to do so. Gamaliel's decision was negative, but R. Joshua's positive, on the ground that the ancient Ammonites no longer existed. The opinion of R. Joshua received the assent of the sages.[107]

---

102. *mBik.* 1:4: 'These may bring the First-fruits but they may not make the Avowal; the proselyte may bring them but he may not make the Avowal since he cannot say, *Which the Lord swore unto our Fathers for to give us*. But if his mother was an Israelite he may bring them and make the Avowal. And when he prays in private he should say, "O God of the fathers of Israel", and when he is in the synagogue he should say, "O God of your fathers". But if his mother was an Israelite he may say, "O God of our fathers".'

103. *mHor.* 3:8: 'A priest precedes a levite, a levite an Israelite, an Israelite a *Mamzer*, a *Mamzer* a *Nathin*, a *Nathin* a proselyte, and a proselyte a freed slave.'

104. *mB.M.* 4:10.

105. *mNid.* 7:3: 'All blood-stains that come from Rekem are clean. R. Judah declares them unclean since they are proselytes there and liable to err.'

106. Favourable and unfavourable opinions are compared in I. Lévi, 'Les rabbins de l'époque talmudique étaient-ils favorables ou hostiles au prosélytisme?', REJ 51 (1906), pp. 1–29; Bamberger, *Proselytism*, pp. 149–73; cf. also Enc. Jud. 13, cols. 1185–6. Philo strongly enjoins the duty of accepting proselytes as brothers, *De virtutibus* 20 (103): κελεύει (Moses) δὴ τοῖς ἀπὸ τοῦ ἔθνους ἀγαπᾶν τοὺς ἐπήλυτας, μὴ μόνον ὡς φίλους καὶ συγγενεῖς ἀλλὰ καὶ ὡς ἑαυτούς... According to G. F. Moore's balanced judgement, 'the tone of the utterances about proselytes is friendly, though not unduly enthusiastic'. Cf. *Judaism* I, p. 342.

107. *mYad.* 4:4.

Preliminary Remarks

It is generally agreed that zeal for the study, teaching and practice of the Torah and an intense eschatological hope were the distinctive characteristics of Judaism in the inter-Testamental era. At the same time, it should not be overlooked that these interests expressed themselves in very varied ways, and that side by side with the aspirations belonging to the sphere of spiritual life went others not immediately connected with them. A glance at the Jewish literature of the period shows to what extent this was the case. These works are so diverse that it is difficult to unite all the individual features into a comprehensive picture. This holds good already of the corpus written in Hebrew or Aramaic, but it is all the more true when the literature of Hellenistic Judaism is also taken into account. There then comes into view a domain so extensive, and apparently so heterogeneous in composition, that it is *prima facie* almost impossible to recognize the inner coherence of these writings.

In this motley variety two main groups used to be distinguished, the Palestinian and the (Diaspora-) Hellenistic, but the borderline between them was ill-defined and the designations only approximate. By Palestinian Jewish literature was understood that which in the main represented the standpoint of what was believed to be Pharisaic Judaism; by Hellenistic Jewish literature, that which, whether in form or content, exhibited in any notable way the influence of Greek culture. Sensitive scholars of the nineteenth and the first half of the twentieth centuries were conscious of the problem of classification. There was, to begin with, often uncertainty concerning the original language, especially when a text was preserved only in translation, or worse still, in translation of a translation. But more importantly, it was distinctly possible that a Hebrew (let alone an Aramaic) book originated outside Palestine, and conversely that a Greek work was written in the Holy Land. Phrased differently, a 'Palestinian' Judaism may have existed in the Diaspora in the same way that a 'Hellenistic' variety existed in Palestine.

The discovery of Hebrew, Aramaic and Greek manuscripts and manuscript fragments, pertaining to inter-Testamental Jewish literature and composed between the third century B.C. and the first century A.D., has placed the whole issue in a new perspective. Positively, the

Qumran fragments of known Apocrypha and Pseudepigrapha (e.g. Tobit, Jubilees, Enoch, etc.) have settled—definitively or partially—the identity of the original language of these compositions. Negatively, the unquestionably sectarian (Essene) character of the deposit has destroyed once and for all any facile general definition of 'Palestinian' Jewish literary work as Pharisaic. Moreover, the Greek fragments found in the Qumran caves amount to documentary evidence of the possible, if not probable, redaction of Greek works or Bible translations in Palestine. Accordingly, it has been decided that a division solely on the basis of language should altogether replace the old geographical-cultural categories. Works produced in Hebrew and Aramaic (§32), including the sectarian documents from Qumran treated in a separate chapter (§32.VIII), will be followed here by writings in Greek (§33A). A further section (§33B) will contain books whose original language cannot be determined with certainty. (For the principles of establishing whether an extant Greek text is a translation, see pp. 705–6.) Finally, a brief appendix will deal with a limited number of compositions which may be either of Jewish or of Christian provenance.

All the surviving Hebrew and Aramaic Jewish works dating to the inter-Testamental epoch are religious documents. Their chief inspiration is a passionate concern for the ancestral faith and for the exact meaning of the Bible. Most of them possess a practical aim and seek to exhort readers to fidelity to the commandments, to perseverance and to firm belief in the coming fulfilment of promises, prophecies and blessings. In general, they reflect official teaching, but sporadically, evidence of astrological and magical works has survived among them (§32.VII and VIII E).

To start with historiography, the golden age of the Hasmonaean dynasty produced national-religious annals (1 Maccabees, Chronicle of Hyrcanus) testifying to a patriotic self-awareness. After the overthrow of the Hasmonaeans by the Romans, no further trace of this kind of historical writing can be found. Josephus, when treating this period, relies exclusively on non-Jewish sources; and Qumran 'historiography' is purely sectarian in outlook and exegetical in form (§32.VIII B).

Religious poetry of the era drew its inspiration from the Psalter and was intended as a supplement to it (Maccabaean Psalms, Apocryphal Psalms, Psalms of Solomon). Their common purpose was spiritual edification and to inculcate attachment to the Torah. (For Qumran sectarian hymnology, see §32.VIII C.)

Wisdom literature, too, aimed at strengthening the religious spirit. The proverbs of Jesus ben Sira, despite all their practical bias, begin and end on an identical note: the fear of God and the observance of the commandments. In the pre-sectarian wisdom fragments retrieved from the Qumran caves, as well as in the precepts stressed by the scribes and rabbis of the Mishnah tractate Aboth, the same voice of exhortation to a whole-hearted obedience to the Torah resounds.

The didactic or paraenetical narratives (Judith, Tobit, Ahiqar) also recount in a free, quasi-fictional compilation stories of heroic faith, exemplary virtue and piety leading to divine intervention and assistance. Although displaying a noticeable degree of narrative skill (e.g. Tobit), these books are not primarily intended for entertainment but for the proclamation of a religious message, viz. that the fear of God is the highest wisdom.

A much cherished literary genre was pseudepigraphic-apocalyptic prophecy, where exhortation is based on special revelations which the authors claim to have received concerning the future destinies of Israel. Pseudepigraphy, i.e. the placing of the revelations in the mouths of the great men of the past, endowed the admonitions and consolations with special prestige and great authority. These prophetic pseudepigrapha (Daniel, Enoch, Assumption of Moses, Apocalypse of Ezra, etc.) were meant to impart comfort in present sorrows and to encourage sincere conversion and perseverance by emphasizing the certainty of eternal reward and punishment.

The writings described so far, although of scriptural inspiration, continue and develop traditional literary genres rather than expound the Bible itself. A clear tendency was nevertheless manifest among Jewish writers (following the pattern set by the Books of Chronicles, see vol. II, pp. 346–7), to re-tell the stories of Scripture and even reformulate its laws, in a modernized form and in the spirit of the author's own age (Jubilees, the Genesis Apocryphon, Ps.-Philo's Book of Biblical Antiquities, etc.). There were also attempts at re-writing not a whole book or books, but at narrating the lives of individual biblical figures (e.g. Noah, Amram, Isaiah, etc.). The main purpose of these re-edited versions was not so much the embellishment and further elaboration of a familiar account as reinforcement of its doctrinal and moral impact in prefiguration of later rabbinic midrash.

The non-biblical manuscripts discovered in the Qumran caves have enriched considerably the Semitic half of inter-Testamental literature. Those among them that furnish the Hebrew or Aramaic originals of works previously extant in translation (Apocryphal Psalms, Ben Sira, Jubilees, Enoch, etc.) and other manifestly pre-sectarian compositions are discussed at the appropriate moments in the following chapters. §32.VIII is wholly devoted to sectarian rules, Bible interpretation, hymns, liturgical compositions and a few miscellanea, viz. to writings expressing the same religious and moral preoccupations as mainstream Jewish literature but characterized by the particular stand of a self-contained minority group. The Qumran texts which, unlike the rest of inter-Testamental literature, have been preserved in their original tongue and in scrolls dating to the inter-Testamental period, offer in consequence a unique contribution not only to the study of Essene ideas and customs, but to a fuller understanding of the non-sectarian Apocrypha and Pseudepigrapha.

These introductory remarks apply also to the works listed in §33B, which contains the same literary classes (pseudepigraphic-apocalyptic prophecy and Bible exegesis) as chapters 5 and 6 in the present section, the sole difference being uncertainty regarding their original language, Hebrew/Aramaic or Greek.

I. HISTORIOGRAPHY

1. The First Book of Maccabees

The sources of the First Book of Maccabees deserve pride of place in any complete enumeration of the historical writings of the period.

The First Book of Maccabees recounts coherently, graphically and in great detail, first the events which led to the Maccabaean uprising, then the course of the revolt itself, with special reference to the deeds and fortunes of Judas Maccabaeus. Next follows the further history of Jewish nationalism under the leadership of Jonathan brother of Judas, and the founding of the Hasmonaean High-Priesthood, symbolizing Jewish independence. Finally, the book reports the history of Simon, brother and successor of Jonathan, who through the establishment in the Hasmonaean family of a hereditary rulership and High-Priesthood, and through the complete liberation of the Jews from Syrian sovereignty, brought Jonathan's work to a triumphant conclusion. The narrative continues to the death of Simon, thus embracing a span of forty years (175–135/4 B.C.).

The author's standpoint is that of a Jewish believer, faithful to the Torah. It is nevertheless noteworthy that the Maccabaean successes are scarcely ever attributed to any direct, miraculous intervention on the part of God, but appear throughout as resulting from the military ability and political sagacity of the Maccabaean-Hasmonaean princes. These are, admittedly, represented as having constantly acted with unshakeable trust in God. Nevertheless the author, living in the Hellenistic era, expresses himself very differently from the earlier biblical historians. A whole-hearted supporter of the Maccabees, he seeks to bring into prominence their services in the cause of the freedom and independence of the Jewish people.[1] The description of the unsuccessful expedition of Joseph and Azarias (5:55–62) closes with the

---

1. As early as 1857, A. Geiger noted: 'The author of the First Book of the Maccabees is the state historian of the Maccabaean dynasty.' (*Urschrift und Übersetzungen der Bibel*, p. 206.)

remark that they were routed because they had gone into battle against the will of Judas (5:61 ; cf. 5:18–19). 'They were not, however, of that family to whom it was granted to bring deliverance to Israel.' Compare in addition 13:2–6 and 14:26. The dynastic interest is also expressed in the speech of the dying Mattathias, chap. 2, inasmuch as Simon is here (v. 65) brought to the foreground, whereas this was by no means the case at the beginning of the story.

The detailed information available to the author of 1 Mac., writing some two generations after the events connected with the Maccabee brothers, presupposes the existence of written sources.[2]

The style is soberly narrative, after the manner of Old Testament historical writing. The author has at his command such an abundance of particular data that there can be by and large no doubt as to his being well-informed, not only in regard to Jewish matters, but also concerning Seleucid institutions (Goldstein, p. 26). The freedom with which figures are treated, and the speeches placed into persons' mouths, can hardly count against his basic trustworthiness. Ancient historical writing was in general not very scrupulous in such matters. It is of especial value that all the more important events are chronologically established in accordance mostly with the Babylonian Seleucid era, beginning in the spring of 311 B.C. (On the question of an occasional use of the Macedonian Seleucid calendar, beginning in the autumn of 312 B.C., see vol. I, pp. 17–19. Cf. also Goldstein, pp. 24–5.)

The startling divergences between the First and Second Books of the Maccabees raise a particular problem. Whilst most scholars attribute priority to First Maccabees, B. Niese (*Kritik der beiden Makkabäerbücher*, 1900) attempted to establish the opposite conclusion. His interpretation encountered universal contradiction (cf. Eissfeldt, p. 579).

As regards the date of composition, it is generally agreed that the author must have written before the Roman conquest, i.e. before 63 B.C., for he knows the Romans only as friends and protectors of the Jewish people against the Syrian kings. On the other hand, since he is conversant with a chronicle of the history of John Hyrcanus, he must have written at the earliest towards the end of his reign or, more likely, shortly after its termination (104 B.C.). Accordingly, the first decades of the first century B.C. appear to be the most probable period of composition. (Cf. Goldstein, pp. 62–4, dating 1 Mac. to the reign of Alexander Jannaeus, though not later than 90 B.C.)

It is generally held that 1 Mac. was originally written in Hebrew or Aramaic. This is argued primarily from the linguistic character of the

---

2. Cf. 1 Mac. 9:22, a cliché patterned on the books of the Kings. For a full discussion see Abel, pp. xxvi-viii ; Schunck (1954) ; W. H. Brownlee, IDB III, pp. 204–5 ; Eissfeldt, *Introduction*, p. 578 ; J. A. Goldstein, *I Maccabees* (1976), pp. 37–61, 90–103.

Greek,[3] and supported by Origen and Jerome. The Hebrew (or Aramaic) title, quoted by Origen as Σαρβὴθ Σαβαναιέλ, continues to puzzle scholars. Only a Greek translation, which was probably known to Josephus, has been preserved. Incorporated into the Greek Bible, it was inherited by the Christian Church, which ensured its survival.

Origen, as quoted by Eusebius *Hist. Eccl.* vi 25, 2, remarks at the close of his list of the Hebrew canon: Ἔξω δὲ τούτων ἐστὶ τὰ Μακκαβαϊκά, ἅπερ ἐπιγέγραπται Σαρβὴθ Σαβαναιέλ. Hence he was acquainted with a Hebrew version of what must have been the First Book of Maccabees, a work which did not, however, belong to the Hebrew canon. Jerome, in his *Prologus Galeatus* to the Books of Samuel (PL XXVIII, cols. 593 ff.) writes: 'Machabaeorum primum librum Hebraicum reperi. Secundus Graecus est, quod ex ipsa quoque φράσει probari potest.' On the meaning of the title cited by Origen, the most varied hypotheses have been advanced. But nearly all of them depend on the reading Σαρβὴθ Σαρβαναεέλ, which has prevailed since Stephanus (Robert Estienne), whereas the manuscripts attest Σαρβὴθ Σαβαναιέλ. A possible, though not very likely, connection between Σαβαναιελ and Σαραμελ in 1 Mac. 14:27 may be noted. The first word, Σαρβηθ, is usually transliterated as ספר בית ('Book of the House of'), Σαρ being corrected into Σφαρ on the basis of Origen's Σφαρθελλειμ = ספר תהלים ('Book of Psalms'). The second half of the title appears in Robert Estienne's 1544 edition of Eusebius as Σαρβανεελ, the equivalent of שר בני אל, 'Prince of the Sons of God'. Another reconstruction points to סרבני אל, i.e. 'Resisters of God', signifying either 'rebels on God's behalf', or, with an anti-Hasmonaean bias, 'rebels against God' (cf. Goldstein, pp. 20–21). The least arbitrary, but still not wholly satisfactory, interpretation takes Σαβαναιελ, the spelling attested in the manuscripts, as the transliteration of the Hebrew name שבניאל (cf. שבניה: Neh. 9:4–5; 10:5, 11, 13; 12:3, 14—שבניהו: 1 Chron. 15:24), represented in the LXX as Σαβανει, Σεβανι Σαβανια, Σεβανια. The whole title would then read: 'Book of the House of Sabanaiel' (cf. Abel, p. v). Already G. Dalman, *Grammatik des jüd.-paläst. Aram.* ([2]1905), p. 7, conjectured that Σαβαναιελ was a corruption from חשמנאי (Hashmon, Hasmonaean). Abel points to the reference Ματταθίας—Σαβανναιοῦς in 1 Esd. 9:33 which he calls 'curious'. He notes also that Saadia refers to a

---

3. Cf. P. Joüon, 'Quelques hébraïsmes de syntaxe dans le premier livre des Maccabées', Bibl. 3 (1922), pp. 204–6; H. W. Ettleson, 'Integrity of I Maccabees', Transact. of Connecticut Acad. 27 (1925), pp. 249–384, esp. p. 254; Abel, p. xxiii; Eissfeldt, p. 578; Goldstein, p. 14: 'Our author wrote in elegant biblical Hebrew, taking as his model the historical books of the Bible.' On the other hand, Goldstein notes that 1 Mac.'s vocabulary is remarkably rich so that 'had he wished, the translator could have written in normal Hellenistic Greek' (*ibid.*).

a 'Scroll of the House of Hashmon', מגלת בית חשמנאי, or *kitâb benê Hašmonaï* (*ibid.*).

No fragment—Hebrew or Greek—of 1 Mac. has been found in the Qumran caves. On the other hand, the probable anti-Hasmonaean tendency of the Dead Sea sect would make the contrary very surprising. For the medieval *Megillath Antiochus*, see vol. I, p. 116.

Josephus' knowledge of the First Book of Maccabees is generally regarded as unquestionable. Nevertheless, whether he was acquainted with the closing section of the book is not so certain, bearing in mind the astonishing rapidity with which he passes over the reign of Simon. Cf. vol. I, p. 50; R. Marcus, *Josephus* (Loeb) VII, p. 334, n. *d*; Goldstein, pp. 55–6.

Christian use of 1 Mac. is attested from an early date. See Tertullian, *Adv. Iudaeos* IV, 10 (CCL II, p. 1349): 'Nam et temporibus Maccabaeorum sabbatis pugnando fortiter fecerunt', etc. (cf. 1 Mac. 2:41 ff.). Hippolytus, *Comment. in Daniel IV*, cap. 3 (ed. Bonwetsch, p. 194) refers to 1 Mac. 1:5–9, using the formula ἐν τῇ πρώτῃ τῶν Μακκαβαϊκῶν ἀναγέγραπται. Origen (in addition to the passage already mentioned in Eusebius, *Hist. Eccl.* vi 25, 2) explicitly writes in his *Comment. in epist. ad Rom.*, Book VIII, chap. 1 (PG 14, col. 1158): 'sicut Mathathias, de quo in primo libro Machabaeorum scriptum est, quia "zelatus est in lege Dei", etc.' (1 Mac. 2:24). Note the designation, the 'First Book of Maccabees', as in the passages quoted from Hippolytus and Jerome, and in Eusebius, *Demonstr. evang.* viii 2, 72, ἡ πρώτη καλουμένη τῶν Μακκαβαίων βίβλος. Cyprian cites several different passages in his *Testimonia*, always with the formula 'in Machabaeis' (*Testim.* III, 4, 15, 53).

The Greek text of 1 Mac. has been handed down in the manuscripts of the Greek Bible. It is absent, however, from the Vaticanus (as well as from the canon of Athanasius and the Ethiopic version which follows Athanasius). The most important manuscript witnesses are Codex Sinaiticus (fourth century), Alexandrinus (fifth century) and Venetus (eighth century). Cf. Abel, pp. liii-lv; Goldstein, pp. 175–7.

The text of 1 Mac. is printed, along with the other Apocrypha, in most editions of the Septuagint.

Editions

Swete, H. B., *The Old Testament in Greek according to the Septuagint* I-III ([4]1909).
Rahlfs, A., *Septuaginta* I-II (1935).
Kappler, W., *Maccabaeorum liber I* (1936, rev. 1967) [Septuaginta. Vetus Testamentum Graecum auctoritate Societatis Litterarum Göttingensis editum] (This is the most important edition).
See further:
Würthwein, E., *The Text of the Old Testament* (1979), pp. 72–4.

Versions

a) *Latin:*
de Bruyne, D., *Les anciennes traductions latines des Machabées*, Anecdota Maredsolana IV
(1932).
b) *Syriac:*
Lagarde, P.A. de, *Libri Veteris Testamenti Apocryphi syriace* (1861).
Ceriani, A.M., *Translatio Syra Pescitto Veteris Testamenti* (1876–83).
See further:
Schmidt, G., 'Über die beiden syrischen Übersetzungen des 1. Makkabäerbuches', ZAW
17 (1897), pp. 1–47, 233–62.

Modern translations of the Apocrypha with commentary or notes

Kautzsch, E. (ed.), *Die Apokryphen und Pseudepigraphen des Alten Testaments* I-II (1900).
Charles, R.H. (ed.), *The Apocrypha and Pseudepigrapha of the Old Testament* I-II (1912–13).
Kahana, A., *Ha-S⁀farîm ha-hizōnîm* (²1956).
Hartum, E.S., *Ha-S⁀farîm ha-hizōnîm* (1958-   ).

Commentaries to 1 Maccabees

Bévenot, H., *Die heilige Schrift des Alten Testaments* (1931).
Schötz, D., *Die heilige Schrift in deutscher Übersetzung* (1948).
Abel, F.-M., *Les livres des Maccabées* (1949). (A fundamental work.)
Dancy, J. C., *I Maccabees* (1954).
Abel, F.-M., and Starcky, J., *La Bible de Jérusalem* (³1961).
Tedesche, S. S., *The Books of the Maccabees* (1962).
Bartlett, J. R., *The First and Second Books of the Maccabees* (1973).
Goldstein, J. A., *I Maccabees— The Anchor Bible* (1976). (Up-to-date and excellent.)
Schunck, K.-D., *1. Makkabäerbuch* (1980).

Literature

Niese, B., *Kritik der beiden Makkabäerbücher* (1900).
Ettelson, H. W., *The Integrity of I Maccabees* (1925).
Kolbe, W., *Beiträge zur syrischen und jüdischen Geschichte* (1926).
Momigliano, A. D., *Prime linee di storia della tradizione maccabaica* (1930, ²1968).
Bickerman(n), E., *Der Gott der Makkabäer* (1937). E.T. *The God of the Maccabees* (1979).
Schunck, K.-D., *Die Quellen des I. und II. Makkabäerbuches* (1954).
Sachs, A. J., and Wiseman, D. J., 'A Babylonian King List of the Hellenistic Period', Iraq
16 (1954), pp. 202–12.
Schaumberger, J., 'Die neue Seleukiden-Liste BM 35603 und die makkabäische
Chronologie', Bibl. 36 (1955), pp. 423–8).
Lévy, Isidore, 'Les deux livres des Maccabées et le livre hébraïque des Hasmonéens',
Semitica 5 (1955), pp. 15–36.
Plöger, O., 'Die makkabäischen Burgen', ZDPV 71 (1955), pp. 141–72.
Farmer, W. R., *Maccabees, Zealots and Josephus* (1956).
Plöger, O., 'Die Feldzüge der Seleukiden gegen den Makkabäer Judas', ZDPV 74 (1958),
pp. 155–88.
Tcherikover, V., *The Hellenistic Civilization and the Jews* (1959).
Wibbing, S., 'Zur Topographie einzelner Schlachten des Judas Makkabäus', ZDPV 78
(1962), pp. 159–70.
Ravenna, A., 'I Maccabei nella letteratura rabbinica', RBibIt 10 (1962), pp. 384–91.
Kreissig, H., 'Der Makkabäeraufstand. Zur Frage seiner sozialökonomischen Zusammen-
hänge und Wirkungen', Studi classici 4 (1962), pp. 143–72.

Hanhart, R., 'Zur Zeitrechnung des I und II Makkabäerbuches', in A. Jepsen and R. Hanhart, *Untersuchungen zur israelitisch-jüdischen Chronologie* (1964), pp. 49–96.
Hengel, M., *Judentum und Hellenismus* (1969, ²1973). E.T. *Judaism and Hellenism* (1974).
Davies, P., 'A Note on 1 Macc. iii.46', JThSt 23 (1972), pp. 117–21.
Neuhaus, G. O., *Studien zu den poetischen Stücken im 1. Makkabäerbuch* (1974). *Idem*, 'Quellen im 1. Makkabäerbuch?', JSJ (1974), pp. 162–75.
Murphy-O'Connor, J., 'Demetrius I and the Teacher of Righteousness (1 Macc. x 25–45)', RB 83 (1976), pp. 400–20.
Davies, P., 'Hasidim in the Maccabean Period', JJS 28 (1977), pp. 127–40.
Millar, F., 'The Background of the Maccabean Revolution: Reflections on Martin Hengel's *Judaism and Hellenism*', JJS 29 (1978), pp. 1–21.
Vermes, G., *The Dead Sea Scrolls: Qumran in Perspective* (1977, ²1982), pp. 137–62.
Bickerman, E., *Studies in Jewish and Christian History. Part II* (1980), pp. 24–135.
Bar-Kochva, B., *The Battles of the Hasmonaeans: The Times of Judas Maccabaeus* (1980) [Hebr.].
Eisenman, R., *Maccabees, Zadokites, Christians and Qumran* (1983). (An idiosyncratic work.)
Martola, N., *Capture and Liberation: A Study in the Composition of the First Book of Maccabees* (1984).

2. The History of John Hyrcanus

The 'History of John Hyrcanus', a work similar in all probability to 1 Maccabees, is mentioned in 1 Mac. 16:23–4: 'The rest of the story of John, his wars and the deeds of valour he performed, the walls he built, and his exploits, are written in the annals of his high priesthood from the time when he succeeded his father.' Apart from this report, nothing is known of the work. Josephus was not acquainted with it. His meagre comments on the reign of John Hyrcanus are either, where they concern external political history, borrowed from Greek historians, or, where they relate to internal affairs, purely legendary in character. There is not the slightest evidence for the use of a contemporary Jewish source.

In view of the early date at which this chronicle of John Hyrcanus vanished, it is also inconceivable that it should still have existed in manuscript form as late as the sixteenth century, as was supposed by many according to the records of Sixtus Senensis.

In his *Bibliotheca Sancta* (1566), p. 61 f., Sixtus Senensis refers to a Fourth Book of Maccabees which he saw in the library of Santes Pagninus in Lyons, and quotes its opening phrase: 'And after the death of Simon, his son John became High-Priest in his place.' According to Sixtus Senensis, the book gives the history of John Hyrcanus in the same way as Josephus, but in a different, Hebraizing, style: 'Historiae series et narratio eadem fere est quae apud Josephum libro Antiquitatum decimo tertio; sed stylus, hebraicis idiotismis abundans, longe dispar.' He thus presumes that this is a Greek translation of the Chronicle of Hyrcanus mentioned in 1 Mac. 16:24. As the library in question was destroyed by fire, the manuscript can no longer be re-examined. However, from the summary provided by Sixtus it would seem that the book was in fact a reproduction of Josephus through the intermediary of a Hebrew text.

3. Josephus - History of the Jewish War

The historiographical impulse seems to have died away in Jewish circles in post-Hasmonaean times. There is at least no mention of any coherent historical chronicle having been undertaken.[1] The events of A.D. 66–70 provided the first renewed inducement for doing so. Joseph, son of Mattathias, or Flavius Josephus, wrote the history of this war, originally in his mother tongue, Aramaic, which he intended primarily for the ἄνω βάρβαροι, that is to say, for the 'Parthians and Babylonians and the most remote tribes of Arabia with our countrymen beyond the Euphrates and the inhabitants of Adiabene', *B.J.* i 2 (6). All we know of the Aramaic work consists in an allusion by Josephus himself in his Greek revision of the history of the Jewish War, *B.J.* i 1 (3): 'I propose to provide the subjects of the Roman Empire with an account of the facts by translating into Greek the narrative which I previously composed in my vernacular tongue, and sent to the barbarians in the interior.'

The Greek edition of this work, as in general all the extant writings of Josephus, will be dealt with below, pp. 545–46. See also vol. I, pp. 43–63.[2]

---

1. Four types of historical documents—the term being used in a broader sense—are attested in this period. (1) *Genealogies*, especially priestly registers, cf. Josephus, *Vita* 1 (6); *C. Ap.* i 7 (31). See vol. II, pp. 240, 242, n. 16, and I. Ta-Shma, 'Genealogy', Enc. Jud. 7, cols. 379–83. (2) *Megillath Taanith*, listing days unsuitable for fasting because they commemorate happy events of the past. Cf. vol. I, pp. 114–15. An as yet unpublished fragmentary liturgical calendar from Qumran Cave IV contains also historical allusions. Cf. J. T. Milik, *Ten Years of Discovery* (1959), p. 73. (3) Qumran biblical commentaries representing historical events as fulfilments of prophecy. Cf. below, pp. 420–51. (4) Chapter 1 of *mAboth*, a list of the predecessors of Hillel and Shammai. Cf. E. Bickerman, 'La chaîne de la tradition pharisienne', RB 59 (1952), p. 47. None of these compositions can be categorized as historical literature proper. On the problem of Jewish historiography, see A. D. Momigliano, 'Remarks on Eastern History Writing', *Terzo contributo alla storia degli studi classici e del mondo antico* I (1966), pp. 237–8. Cf. also G. Vermes, 'The Essenes and History', JJS 32 (1981), pp. 29–31 (= *Jesus and the World of Judaism* (1983), pp. 137–9).

2. A. Schalit suggests that Josephus' account of the history of Babylonian Jewry and the episode of the brothers Asinaeus and Asileus in *Ant.* xviii 9, 1–9 (310–79) are based on an Aramaic source. Whilst the theory is perfectly plausible, the philological evidence found in the difficult passage of xviii 9, 5 (343), namely ἀνὴρ ... κτιλίων = קטילא גברא, 'dead man', is unconvincing. Cf. 'Evidence of an Aramaic source in Josephus' "Antiquities of the Jews"', ASTI 4 (1965), pp. 163–88. Schalit's hypothesis has been adopted by L. H. Feldman in *Josephus* (Loeb) ix (1965), p. 533.

II. Religious Poetry

1. Maccabaean Psalms

The Maccabaean dating of a number of Psalms, much in vogue in the late nineteenth century—B. Duhm in his commentary first published in 1899 proposed a late origin for the majority of poems in the Psalter[1]—is increasingly losing popularity in contemporary scholarship. There is doubtless no a priori argument against Maccabaean psalms. Poetic activity continued among Jews during the inter-Testamental age, as is shown by the apocryphal Psalms, the Psalms of Solomon and the Qumran hymns (see below). Nor can the final closure of the biblical canon be safely invoked, since the book of Daniel, at least, entered it during the Maccabaean-Hasmonaean era (see below). On the other hand, most of the Psalm allusions associated in the past with Maccabaean events may equally be applied to an earlier period.[2] Also, 1 Mac. 7:17 itself contains a citation from Ps. 79:2–3 introduced with a formula indicating Holy Scripture (κατὰ τὸν λόγον ὃν ἔγραψεν αὐτόν). This would appear to imply that the Psalter was already part of the biblical canon.[3] It has also been pointed out that from the linguistic point of view the Psalms predate Chronicles, a fourth-century B.C. composition,[4] and there is a growing tendency to recognize the Psalter as complete by the end of the third century B.C. at the latest.[5] All in all, while no absolute denial of the Maccabaean dating of some Psalms can be advanced with total certainty,[6] the possibility of such late compositions must be restricted to a handful (Pss. 44, 74, 79 and 83 are among those most frequently proposed),[7] and even that possibility should be seen as remote. J. A. Soggin correctly echoes the common

---

1. B. Duhm, *Die Psalmen* (1899, [2]1922), pp. xxi–iv.
2. Cf. S. Mowinckel, *The Psalms in Israel's Worship* I (1962), p. 118; II, pp. 154–5.
3. Cf. Mowinckel, *op. cit.* II, p. 199.
4. M. Tsevat, *A Study of the Language of the Biblical Psalms* (1955), pp. 70–2.
5. Cf. J. Hempel, 'Psalms, Book of', IDB III, p. 943.
6. For a balanced evaluation of the arguments, see P. R. Ackroyd, 'Criteria for the Maccabean Dating of Old Testament Literature', VT 3 (1953), pp. 113–32.
7. Eissfeldt (*Introduction*, p. 113) would not admit more than 'one or two' Maccabaean Psalms, and notes that many of the post-exilic features exhibited in these poems may have resulted from a revision of older compositions (*ibid.*, p. 448). Mowinckel also points out that at the time of the institution of the Hanukkah festival by the Maccabees to celebrate the rededication of the Sanctuary, 'no new festal psalm was composed, but Ps. 30—the existing "canonical" psalm deemed to be most suitable—was used as a thanksgiving psalm for the deliverance and the consecration of the Temple' (*op. cit.* II, p. 155). The titular inscription, 'Song for the dedication of the Temple' (שיר חנכת הבית) was probably added to this Psalm in Maccabaean times. Cf. 1 Mac. 4:36.

opinion prevalent today when he declares the theory of a Maccabaean dating of Psalms to be 'obsolete'.[8]

2. *Apocryphal Psalms*

The discovery of an incomplete Psalms scroll in Qumran Cave 11,[1] with extra-canonical poems interspersed among the traditional compositions, has brought to the foreground the problem of apocryphal Psalms. One of these, Ps. 151, according to the superscription David's 'own', 'supernumerary' hymn, forms part of the Septuagint Psalter.[2] The same text, together with four further pieces, has survived in Syriac in two biblical manuscripts, and in eight copies of 'The Book of Investigation' (*k͑taba d͑ durrasha*) by the tenth century Nestorian bishop Elija of Anbar. First noted in 1759 by S. E. and J. S. Assemani in their description of Ms. Vat. sir. 183 in the catalogue of the Vatican Library, the Psalms were edited from a Cambridge manuscript by W. Wright in 1887, and, on the basis of further manuscripts and accompanied by a retranslation into Hebrew, by M. Noth in 1930. The latest critical edition of the Syriac text appeared in 1972 in the Leiden Peshitta project.[3]

11QPsᵃ cols. 28 supplies the Hebrew text of Ps. 151 (= Syr. I); cols. 18 and 24, that of Psalms 154 and 155 (Syr. IV and V). Pss. 152–3 (Syr. II and III) have not been retrieved, either because they were included in the lost part of the scroll, or because they never figured in it. By contrast, the Qumran manuscript (cols. 19, 22 and 26) yields three further unknown Hebrew poems, as well as (col. 27) a summary account of all the David Psalms (תהלים) and songs (שיר). Also, a fragmentary Psalms scroll from Cave 4 contains remains of *11QPsᵃ* col. 22, and two further apocryphal poems.[4] Since the Dead Sea manuscript provides the original Hebrew of all the texts apart from the Syriac Pss. II and III, it will be used as the main source for the presentation of the Apocryphal Psalms, and the individual pieces will be designated according to the symbols adopted in DJD IV.

11QPsᵃ 151 (= *Syr. Ps. I*) is a poetic midrash on 1 Sam. 16:1–13, in

8. *Introduction to the Old Testament* (1980), p. 364.

1. For the *editio princeps*, see J. A. Sanders, DJD IV (1965).

2. Cf. H. B. Swete and R. R. Ottley, *Introduction to the O.T. in Greek* (1914), pp. 252–3. Swete noted resemblances between this poem and various biblical passages, but felt unable to decide whether the original was Greek or Hebrew.

3. Bibliographical references are listed at the end of this chapter. The link between the apocryphal Psalms and Syrian Christianity lies in the late eighth century manuscript discovery in the Jericho region mentioned by the Nestorian Patriarch Timothy I, which included 'more than two hundred Psalms of David'. Cf. J. Strugnell, HThR 59 (1966), pp. 257–8. See also pp. 205–6 below.

4. Cf. J. Starcky, 'Psaumes apocryphes de la grotte 4 de Qumrân (4Q Psᶠ VII–X)', RB 73 (1966), pp. 353–71.

which the young shepherd, David, relates how he was chosen and anointed to be the ruler of his people. Both the Greek and the Syriac end with a mention of his victory over Goliath. The latter point is, however, the subject of a separate Hebrew poem designated as Ps. 151 B, of which only the title and the first verse have survived in col. 28, lines 13 and 14. Whilst the Syriac and the Greek are very close to one another, they represent an abridgement and a reworking of two Hebrew Psalms. The superscriptions are also suitably re-edited.[5] In verses 3 and 4, trees and flocks of sheep are said to have enjoyed David's music, a possible adoption and adaptation of the Orpheus myth.[6]

11QPs^a 154 (= *Syr. Ps. II*) is a sapiential hymn, the beginning and end of which may be reconstructed from the Syriac. Praise of God and meditation on his Torah are the essential acts of piety equal to sacrificial worship (verses 10–14). The vocabulary is biblical, free of any definite Qumran terminology.[7]

11QPs^a 155 (= *Syr. Ps. III*) is a mixture of an individual lamentation and thanksgiving. The final lines have been preserved only in Syriac. From line 9 onwards the poem is an alphabetic acrostic.[8]

Pss. 152 and 153 (*Syr. Pss. IV and V*), which lack a Hebrew original, are both ascribed to David, and depict him as the protector of his flock against wild animals. Ps. IV is a poetic complaint and appeal for divine help; Ps. V is a thanksgiving.

11QPs^a Plea for Deliverance (= *11QPs^b*). Fifteen verses survive, but the beginning is missing. This is an individual thanksgiving hymn celebrating the poet's escape from death. The terminology is biblical and recalls Isa. 38:18–19; Job 7:21; Ps. 6:4–5, etc.[9]

11QPs^a Zion (= *4Q Ps^f VII, 14-VIII, 16*), an irregular, but

---

5. The Hebrew title is 'Hallelujah. Of David son of Jesse' for 151 A and 'The beginning of David's power after God's prophet had anointed him' for 151 B. The LXX reads Οὗτος ὁ ψαλμὸς ἰδιόγραφος εἰς Δαυειδ καὶ ἔξωθεν τοῦ ἀριθμοῦ, ὅτε ἐμονομάχησεν τῷ Γολιάδ. The Syriac has either 'Of David. When he alone fought with Goliath', or 'Thanksgiving of David'.

6. See Sanders, DJD V, p. 61–3, noting also the Doura Europos painting of a musician? ?and two lions identified either as Orpheus, or more probably David. Cf. further Sanders,? ? *The Dead Sea Psalms Scroll* (1967), pp. 98–100; A. Dupont-Sommer, 'Le Psaume cli dans 11Q Ps^a et le problème de son origine essénienne', Semitica 14 (1964), pp. 25–62; I. Rabinowitz, 'The alleged Orphism of 11Q Pss col. 28, 3–12', ZAW 76 (1964), pp. 193–200; M. Smith, 'Psalm 151, David, Jesus and Orpheus', ZAW 92 (1980), pp. 247–53.

7. None of the terms alluded to by Sanders (DJD IV, p. 70) contradicts this judgement. The expression החבירו יחד, described as 'the most arresting phrase', does not seem to appear anywhere in the Scrolls.

8. The superscription for Syr. Pss. II and III speaks of a 'Prayer of Hezekiah'.

9. Another copy of the Plea of Deliverance, also from 11Q, has been published by J. van der Ploeg, 'Fragments d'un manuscrit des psaumes de Qumrân (11Q Ps^b)', RB 74 (1967), pp. 408–12.

complete, alphabetic acrostic, is a hymn of praise of Jerusalem, modelled on Isa. 54:1–8, 60:1–22 and 62:6–8. The language is mostly biblical.

11QPs^a Creat. is a sapiential hymn to the Creator, ending with expressions borrowed from Jer. 10:12–13 and Ps. 135:7.

4QPs^f IX, 1–15 preserves relics of an eschatological hymn alluding to the judgement of the wicked and the reward of the poor and those who fear God.

4QPs^f X, 3–5 is an eschatological glorification of Judah, victorious over her enemies, couched in terms heavily reminiscent of biblical poetry.

11QPs^a Dav Comp, although written in prose, may usefully be added to this list, as it consists of a catalogue of David's inspired poetry. Having received from God a 'discerning and enlightened spirit' and composing 'through prophecy', he was the author of 3,600 Psalms, 364 songs for the daily Tamid offering, 52 songs for the Sabbath offering, 30 songs for festival offerings and four songs to be performed for the stricken (על הפגועים), probably demoniacs: in all, 4,050 verse compositions.[10]

For the dating of the apocryphal Psalms from Cave 11, and by analogy the two Syriac Psalms without Hebrew original, it is to be recalled that on archaeological and palaeographical basis *4QPs^f* is assigned to the middle of the first century B.C., and *11QPs^a* to the beginning of the first century A.D.,[11] and that, on account of the inclusion of Ecclus 51 on cols. 21–22, the compilation itself cannot antedate the early second century B.C. It may therefore be safely assumed that all the apocryphal poems belong to the pre-Christian era, and since the Hebrew *Vorlage* of the LXX Ps. 151 represents an earlier version than the text used by the Greek (and Syriac) translator(s), a second century B.C. *terminus ad quem* may be postulated. A later date would suggest itself only if the Psalms were identified as Qumran

---

10. This list is clearly a sectarian product presupposing the solar calendar of the Qumran community (52 weeks, 364 days). The 'stricken', i.e. persons possessed by demons, are referred to in rabbinic literature (yShab. 8b; yErub 26c; bShebu. 15b) in connection with Ps. 91:1–9. In this connection, mention should be made of a badly damaged scroll from Cave 11 (*11QPsAp^a*) containing apocryphal Psalms *and* Ps. 91 in a curious recension. The fragments attest the root פגע, refer to demons (שדים, רשף) and to the 'Name of YHWH', no doubt as a means of exorcism. None of the fragments is large enough for translation. Cf. J. van der Ploeg, 'Le psaume xci dans une recension de Qumrân', RB 72 (1965), pp. 210–17 and plates VII–IX; 'Un petit rouleau de psaumes apocryphes (11Q PsAp^a)', *Tradition und Glaube—Festgabe für K. G. Kuhn* (1971), pp. 128–39 and plates II–VII. For 'striking' demons and 'the stricken', see also *4Q510* 1, 6; *4Q511* 11, 4 and 8 in M. Baillet, DJD VII, pp. 216, 227–8.

11. Cf. Starcky, *art. cit.* [in n. 4], p. 355; Sanders, DJD IV, pp. 6–9.

compositions,[12] but, apart from the definitely sectarian prose catalogue, nothing in the texts would justify such an attribution. Besides, they are not grouped in the scroll as a unit, but are dispersed among the canonical Psalms. On the whole, none of these poems is likely to be later than the first half of the second century B.C., but several may belong to the late Persian or early Hellenistic eras.[13]

Further apocryphal Psalms may have been preserved in inter-Testamental writings and the New Testament. Among the former, Pseudo-Philo's Book of Biblical Antiquities (see below) transmits several poems of 'David', one of which (LAB 59:1–7) has been retranslated into Hebrew by J. Strugnell.[14] Another candidate for recognition as a psalmic exorcism sung by David to Saul is LAB 60:2.[15] In the New Testament, Lk. 1:46–55 (Magnificat) and 1:68–79 (Benedictus) have been seen as re-adapted hymns of praise.[16]

Editions

Hebrew text
Sanders, J. A., *The Psalms Scroll of Qumran Cave 11* [DJD IV] (1965).
Idem, The Dead Sea Psalms Scroll (1967).
Starcky, J., 'Psaumes apocryphes de la grotte 4 de Qumrân (4Q Ps^f VII-X)', RB 73 (1966), pp. 353–71.
Ploeg, J. van der, 'Un petit rouleau de psaumes apocryphes (11Q PsAp^a)', *Tradition und Glaube—Festgabe K.-G. Kuhn* (1971), pp. 128–39 and plates II-VII.

Translations

English
Sanders, *op. cit.*

French
Dupont-Sommer, A., Annuaire du Collège de France 64 (1964/5), pp. 317–20; 66 (1966/7), pp. 358–67.

Italian
Moraldi, L, *I manoscritti di Qumrân* (1971), pp. 465–94.

Syriac Text
Wright, W., 'Some Apocryphal Psalms in Syriac', Proceed. Soc. Bibl. Arch. 9 (1887), pp. 257–66.
Noth, M., 'Die fünf syrisch überlieferten apokryphen Psalmen', ZAW 48 (1930), pp. 1–23.
Baars, W., 'Apocryphal Psalms', *Vetus Testamentum syriace* [Leiden Peshitta] IV, 6 (1972).

12. Cf. M. Delcor, 'Cinq nouveaux psaumes esséniens?', RQ 1 (1958), pp. 85–102; *Les Hymnes de Qumrân* (1962), pp. 299–319; M. Philonenko, 'L'origine essénienne des cinq psaumes syriaques de David', Semitica 9 (1959), pp. 35–48.
13. A. S. van der Woude, 'Die fünf syrischen Psalmen', JSHRZ IV, 1 (1974), p. 35.
14. 'More Psalms of "David"', CBQ 27 (1965), pp. 207–16.
15. On this poem, see M. Philonenko, 'Remarques sur un hymne essénien de caractère gnostique', Semitica 11 (1961), pp. 43–54. On the exorcistic traits, cf. G. Vermes, *Jesus the Jew* (1973), pp. 67, 240.
16. P. Winter, 'Magnificat and Benedictus—Maccabaean Psalms?', BJRL 37 (1954), pp. 328–47.

Translation

English
Wright, *art. cit.*

German
Woude, A. S. van der, 'Die fünf syrischen Psalmen', JSHRZ IV, 1 (1974), pp. 39–46.

Bibliography

Delcor, M., 'Cinq nouveau psaumes esséniens?', RQ 1 (1958), pp. 85–102.
Philonenko, M., 'L'origine essénienne des cinq psaumes syriaques de David', Semitica 9 (1959), pp. 35–48.
Delcor, M., *Les Hymnes de Qumrân* (1962), pp. 299–319.
Carmignac, J., 'La forme poétique du Psaume 151 de la grotte 11', RQ 4 (1963), pp. 371–8.
Brownlee, W. H., 'The 11Q Counterpart to Psalm 151, 1–5', RQ 4 (1963), pp. 379–87.
Skehan, P. W., 'The Apocryphal Psalm 151', CBQ 25 (1963), pp. 407–9.
Dupont-Sommer, A., 'Le psaume CLI dans le 11Q Ps^a et le problème de son origine essénienne', Semitica 14 (1964), pp. 25–62.
Strugnell, J., 'Notes on the Text and Transmission of the Apocryphal Psalms 151, 154 (= Syr. II) and 155 (= Syr. III)', HThR 59 (1966), pp. 257–81.
Delcor, M., 'L'Hymne à Sion du rouleau des Psaumes de la grotte 11 de Qumrân', RQ 6 (1967), pp. 71–88.
Magne, J., 'Recherches sur les Psaumes 151, 154, 155. Bibliographie chronologique', RQ 8 (1975), pp. 503–7.
Idem, 'Orphisme, pythagorisme, essénisme dans le texte hébreu du Psaume 151', RQ 8 (1975), pp. 508–47.
Idem, 'Les textes grec et syriaque du Psaume 151', RQ 8 (1975), pp. 548–64.
Idem, 'Le verset des trois pierres dans la tradition du Psaume 151', RQ 8 (1975), pp. 565–91.
Carmignac, J., 'Nouvelles précisions sur le Psaume 151', RQ 8 (1975), pp. 593–7.
Skehan, P. W., 'Again the Syriac Apocryphal Psalms', CBQ 38 (1976), pp. 143–58.
Magne, J., 'Le Psaume 154 et le Psaume 155', RQ 9 (1977), pp. 95–111.
Auffret, P., 'Structure littéraire et interprétation du Psaume 151 de la Grotte 11 de Qumrân', RQ 9 (1977), pp. 163–88.
Idem, 'Structure du Psaume 155', RQ 9 (1978), pp. 323–56.
Idem, 'Structure ... du Psaume 154 ...', RQ 9 (1978), pp. 513–45.
Skehan, P. W., 'Qumrân. Apocryphes. A.T.', DBS IX (1978), cols. 813–17, 821–2.
Smith, M., 'Psalm 151, David, Jesus and Orpheus', ZAW 92 (1980), pp. 247–53.
Vermes, DSS (²1982), pp. 58–61.
Wigtil, D. N., 'The Sequence of the Translations of Apocryphal Psalm 151', RQ 11 (1983), pp. 401–7.

3. The Psalms of Solomon

A collection of eighteen psalms preserved in Greek (and in a Syriac translation) have been known under the title of 'Psalms of Solomon' since the patristic era. In some of the ancient records of the biblical canon they are listed, together with the Apocrypha, such as Maccabees, Wisdom of Solomon, Ecclesiasticus, Judith, Tobit, etc., under the heading ἀντιλε-γόμενα (see below, p. 195). The Greek text was first published in 1626 by Johannes Ludovicus de la Cerda.

The attribution of the poems to Solomon is secondary, and no doubt derives from the tendency to accredit the legendary wise king with a number of anonymous compositions such as the book of Wisdom, the Odes, and various astrological and medico-magical works (cf. below, pp. 375–79). In fact, Solomon is never referred to in the Psalms themselves.

Not only is the identity of the poet unknown, but it is not even certain that all eighteen compositions were written by the same person. Nevertheless, while the majority of the Psalms contain no chronological pointers—they portray a conflict between saints and sinners—three of them (Pss. of Sol. 2, 8 and 17) display allusions that seem to be easily datable. The poems presuppose an autonomous Jewish rule established by a family by force of arms, without the warrant of a divine promise (17:6). Instead of praising God, its members seized David's throne and the royal crown (17:7–8). During their government, all Israel lapsed into sin. The king broke the law, the judge dishonoured the truth, and the people behaved sinfully (17:21–2). But God overthrew these princes, raising up against them from the end of the earth a powerful foreign conqueror who waged war on Jerusalem and its surroundings (17:8–9). The princes of the land foolishly went out to meet him with joy and said to him: 'Your coming is much desired! Enter in peace! They opened the gates of Jerusalem to him, they crowned its walls. As a father [enters] the house of his sons, so he entered Jerusalem in peace' (8:15–20). As soon, however, as he had secured a foothold in the city, he seized the citadel also, and destroyed the walls of Jerusalem with the battering ram (8:21; 2:1). The city was trampled underfoot by Gentiles (2:20); foreign soldiers ascended to the altar of God itself (2:2). All the leading citizens and sages were slain: the blood of the inhabitants of Jerusalem was shed like water of uncleanness (8:23). The Gentile conqueror led the Jews away to captivity in the West and humiliated their princes (17:13–14; 2:6; 8:24). In the end however, the 'Dragon' that had conquered Jerusalem was himself slain on the mountains of Egypt, by the sea shore, and his body was left unburied (2:29–31).

It is maintained almost unanimously among contemporary experts that Ps. 8 refers to the first conquest of Jerusalem by the Romans.[1] The stance adopted by the poet is clearly anti-Hasmonaean. He disapproves of the princes who usurped the kingdom of Israel and arrogated to themselves the throne of David. The Hasmonaeans assumed the royal title from the time of Aristobulus I. The last princes of this house, Alexander Jannaeus and Aristobulus II, openly favoured the Sadducean party, and were therefore in the eyes of the author (probably a Pharisee) sinful and lawless men. The 'foreigner' and the

---

1. Cf. F.-M. Abel, 'Le siège de Jérusalem par Pompée', RB 54 (1947), pp. 243–55.

'powerful conqueror' brought by God from the end of the earth was Pompey. The princes who went out to meet him were Aristobulus II and Hyrcanus II. It was Hyrcanus' party which opened the gates to Pompey, whereat, with the help of the battering ram (ἐν κριῷ, 2:1), he demolished the fortifications and took the remaining part of the city in which the party of Aristobulus were entrenched. All that follows, the profanation of the Temple, the massacre of the inhabitants, the execution of the leading citizens,[2] the deportation of captives to the West and the humiliation of the princes (17:14), corresponds to historical events. In particular, the fact that the captives were taken to the West (17:14) testifies that this can apply only to Pompey and Titus. But since there is no mention in the Psalms of the destruction of the Temple, the reference must be to the events of 63 B.C. Doubts finally disappear when we read that the conqueror was slain on the Egyptian coast, by the sea (ἐπὶ κυμάτων), and that his body lay unburied (2:31), for this is precisely what happened to Pompey in 48 B.C. Psalm 2 was therefore certainly composed shortly after this event, whilst Pss. 8 and 17 should be placed between 63 and 48 B.C. It is reasonable to date the whole collection to the same period, although some authors argue that the 'foreigner' who in 17:9 is said to have risen against the Hasmonaean princes was Herod the Great.[3] It is, however, more reasonable to interpret it of the same person who, in 17:14, is reported to have carried off the captives to the West, i.e. Pompey.

The Psalms are imbued with the spirit of traditional piety, and insist on the fulfilment of the commandments, the δικαιοσύνη προσταγμάτων (14:2). They attest belief in the hereafter and that the future fate of a man is determined by his present way of life. It lies within his own free choice to do right or wrong (cf. esp. 9:7). If he does the first, he will rise to everlasting life; if the latter, he will go down to everlasting destruction (3:16; 13:9–11; 14; 15). The Psalmist hopes that the illegitimate Hasmonaean rule already brought to an end by Pompey will soon be replaced by the reign of the Davidic Messiah (17:1, 5, 23–51; 18:6–10; cf. also 7:9; 11).

The stress on obedience to the law, the doctrine of free will and faith in an afterlife are seen by many scholars as pointers to a Pharisaic origin of the Psalms.[4] However, doubts have been voiced in recent years concerning an over-confident attribution of these poems to the

---

2. Ps. 8:23: ἀπώλεσεν ἄρχοντας αὐτῶν καὶ πάντα σοφὸν ἐν βουλῇ. Cf. *Ant.* xiv 4, 4 (73): τοὺς αἰτίους τοῦ πολέμου τῷ πελέκει διεχρήσατο. See also *B.J.* i 7, 6 (165).

3. Cf. Eissfeldt, *Introduction*, p. 612.

4. Cf. e.g. J. Wellhausen, *Die Pharisäer und die Sadducäer* (1874, ²1924), pp. 112–20, 131–7; H. E. Ryle and M. R. James, *The Psalms of the Pharisees* (1891), pp. xliv–lii; J. Viteau, *Les Psaumes de Salomon* (1911), pp. 46, 86, etc.; G. B. Gray, APOT II, p. 630; J.-B. Frey, 'Apocryphes de l'A.T.', DBS I, col. 2002.

Pharisees, because neither the doctrines listed, nor intense Messianism can be characterized as exclusively belonging to that group.[5] The association of the Psalms with the Qumran-Essene sect, summarily proposed by A. Dupont-Sommer (*The Essene Writings*, pp. 296, 337), has made no impression on scholarly opinion. In fact, whereas the anti-Hasmonaean-Sadducean stand is common to both of them, no typically Qumran traits are detectable in the Psalms. Neither is there, needless to say, any trace (so far) of the original of these poems among the Dead Sea Scrolls. All in all, bearing in mind the doctrinal peculiarities and the political bias, it is reasonable to conjecture that the Psalms of Solomon represent Pharisee ideology.[6]

No Christian editorial work can be discovered in these poems. The opposite view advanced by J. Ephron may safely be discarded.[7]

The original language of the Psalms is generally thought to be Hebrew. A. Hilgenfeld's theory that they were written in Greek has never found favour.[8] A detailed argument in favour of a Hebrew original is offered by J. Viteau.[9] In the circumstances, it is reasonable to recognize the Psalms as a Palestinian composition. Some verbal similarity exists between Ps. 11 and the Greek Baruch 4:36–5:9, and if the secondary nature of the extant Greek text of the Psalms is accepted, Baruch's dependence on it is a likely hypothesis.[10]

The Syriac version is made from the Greek, according to its editor J. Rendell Harris;[11] K.-G. Kuhn's hypothesis that it derives directly from the Hebrew has been refuted by J. Begrich.[12]

For the Odes of Solomon, see below, pp. 787–89.

Concerning the place of the Psalms of Solomon in the Greek canon of Scriptures, see Ryle-James, *op. cit.*, pp. xxi–vii; Viteau, *op. cit.*, pp. 186–91. They are listed among the ἀντιλεγόμενα in Ps.-Athanasius, *Synopsis scripturarum sacrarum*, between Maccabees and Susanna (PG 28, col. 432) and in the Stichometry of Nicephorus between Sirach and Esther (PG 100, col. 1057). Cf. H. B. Swete and R. R. Ottley,

---

5. Cf. Eissfeldt, *Introduction*, pp. 612–13; P. Winter, IDB III, p. 959; U. Rappaport, 'Solomon, Psalms of', Enc. Jud. 15, col. 116; J. H. Charlesworth, PMRS, p. 195.

6. For a similar conclusion, see A.-M. Denis, IPGAT, p. 64; Nickelsburg, JLBBM, p. 223 ('circles closely related to the Pharisees').

7. 'The Psalms of Solomon, the Hasmonean Decline and Christianity', Zion 30 (1965), pp. 1–30 (Hebr.).

8. *Messias Judaeorum* (1869), pp. xvi–xviii.

9. *Op. cit.* (in n. 4 above), pp. 105–25.

10. Cf. Ryle-James, *op. cit.* (in n. 4 above), pp. lxxii–vii. The opposite conclusion is claimed, however, by W. Pesch, 'Die Abhängigkeit des 11. salomonischen Psalms vom letzten Kapitel des Buches Baruch', ZAW 67 (1955), pp. 251–63.

11. *The Odes and Psalms of Solomon* (1909, [2]1911), pp. 38–40.

12. Kuhn, *Die älteste Textgestalt der Psalmen Salomos* (1937); Begrich, 'Der Text der Psalmen Salomos', ZNW 38 (1939), pp. 131–64.

Introduction to the Old Testament in Greek (1914), pp. 207–9. In the catalogue of writings contained in Codex Vaticanus, the Psalms of Solomon appear after the New Testament and the works of Clement of Rome. Cf. Viteau, *op. cit.*, p. 186.

For the Greek manuscripts of the Psalms, see R. R. Hann, *The Manuscript History of the Psalms of Solomon* (1982). Cf. also O. von Gebhardt's edition of the text (see below); Viteau, *op. cit.*, pp. 150–9; APOT II, 625–6; Denis, *Introduction*, pp. 60–2.

Editions

Greek Text:
Cerda, Johannes Ludovicus de la, *Adversaria sacra, accessit Psalterium Salomonis* (1626).
Ryle, H. E., and M. R. James, *Psalms of the Pharisees commonly called The Psalms of Solomon* (1891).
Swete, H. B., *The Old Testament in Greek* III (1894, [4]1912).
von Gebhardt, O., *Die Psalmen Salomos* (1895).
Viteau, J., *Les Psaumes de Salomon* (1911).
Rahlfs, A., *Septuaginta* (1935).
Baars, W., 'A new Greek Version of the Psalms of Solomon', VT II (1961), pp. 441–4.
[A new critical text is being prepared by R. B. Wright: cf. J. H. Charlesworth, PMRS, p. 196.]

Syriac Text:
Harris, J. R., *The Odes and Psalms of Solomon* (1909, [2]1911).
Harris, R., and Mingana, A., *The Odes and Psalms of Solomon* I-II (1916–20).
Baars, W., 'Psalms of Solomon', Peshitta, Part 4, fasc. 6 (1972) i-vi, 1–27.

Translations and Commentaries

Kittel, R., APAT II, pp. 127–48.
Viteau, *op. cit.* (1911).
Gray, G. B., APOT II, pp. 625–52.
Riessler, P., *Altjüdisches Schrifttum ausserhalb der Bibel* (1928), pp. 881–902, 1323–4.

Bibliography

Wellhausen, J., *Die Pharisäer und die Sadducäer* (1874, [2]1924), pp. 131–64.
Frankenberg, W., *Die Datierung der Psalmen Salomos* (1896).
Perles, F., 'Zur Erklärung der Psalmen Salomos', OLZ 5 (1902), pp. 269–82, 335–42, 365–72.
Toy, C. H., 'Psalms of Solomon', JE X (1905), 250–1.
Kuhn, K.-G., *Die älteste Textgestalt der Psalmen Salomos* (1937).
Begrich, J., 'Der Text der Psalmen Salomos', ZNW 38 (1939), pp. 131–64.
Aberbach, M., 'The Historical Allusions of Chapters iv, xi and xiii of the Psalms of Solomon', JQR 41 (1950–1), pp. 379–96.
Braun, H., 'Vom Erbarmen Gottes über den Gerechten. Zur Theologie der Psalmen Salomos', ZNW 43 (1950–1), pp. 1–54.
Pesch, W., 'Die Abhängigkeit des 11. salomonischen Psalm vom letzten Kapitel des Buches Baruch', ZAW 67 (1955), pp. 251–63.
O'Dell, J., 'The Religious Background of the Psalms of Solomon', RQ 3 (1961–2), pp. 241–57.
Winter, P., 'Psalms of Solomon', IDB III, pp. 958–60.

Ephron, J., 'The Psalms of Solomon, the Hasmonean Decline and Christianity', Zion 30 (1965), pp. 1–46 [Hebr.].

Jonge, H. dc, *De toekomsterwachting in de Psalmen vom Salomo* (1965).

Eissfeldt, O., *Introduction* (1965), pp. 610–13, 773–4.

Holm-Nielsen, S., 'Erwägungen zu dem Verhältnis zwischen den Hodayot und den Psalmen Salomos', *Bibel und Qumran*, ed. S. Wagner (1968), pp. 112–31.

Denis, A.-M., IPGAT, pp. 60–9.

Rappaport, U., 'Solomon, Psalms of', Enc. Jud. 15, cols. 115–16.

Wright, R. B., 'The Psalms of Solomon, the Pharisees and the Essenes', *1972 Proceedings IOSCS*, ed. R.A. Kraft (1972), pp. 136–54.

Charlesworth, J. H., PMR (1976, ²1981), pp. 195–7.

Schüphaus, J., *Die Psalmen Salomos. Ein Zeugnis Jerusalemer Theologie und Frömmigkeit in der Mitte des vorchristlichen Jahrhunderts* (1977).

Holm-Nielsen, S., 'Religiöse Poesie des Spätjudentums' VII. 'Die Psalmen Salomos', ANRW II 19.1 (1979), pp. 172–82, 186.

Dimant, D., 'A Cultic Term in the Psalms of Solomon in the Light of the LXX', Textus 9 (1981), pp. 28–51 [Hebr.].

Nickelsburg, G. W. E., JLBBM, pp. 203–12, 229.

Hann, R. R., *The Manuscript History of the Psalms of Solomon* (1982).

III. Wisdom Literature

1. Jesus Sirach or Jesus ben Sira

The practical tendency of inter-Testamental Jewish literature written in Hebrew or Aramaic manifests itself most clearly in the fact that even its speculative features are arranged with special reference to the aims and tasks of the everyday life. Judaism, when uninfluenced by foreign cultures, never produced metaphysics in the strict sense.[1] Jewish wisdom (חכמה) is either of a practical kind (advice based on experience handed down from father to son, and on a practical knowledge of the laws governing the world) or focuses on religious problems (e.g. creation, divine presence or justice). One of the forms in which such meditations are expounded is the proverb (משל), which succinctly and powerfully concentrates a single thought in poetic style, without elaboration or demonstration. But other well-attested literary forms are the riddle, the fable, the wisdom hymn, etc. The most characteristic collection of this kind included in the Hebrew Bible is the Book of Proverbs.[2] The Wisdom of Jesus Sirach is a similar

1. This statement refers of course to philosophical systems. For a type of subconscious metaphysical thought, see Claude Tresmontant, *Essaie sur la pensée hébraïque* (1953); *Etudes de métaphysique biblique* (1955); T. Boman, *Hebrew Thought compared with Greek* (1960). On supposed Greek influences on late Hebrew canonical literature, see M. Hengel, *Judaism and Hellenism*, pp. 109–10. Hengel accepts that the spiritual crisis of early Hellenism may have influenced the author of Koheleth (*ibid.*, p. 127), but he is of the opinion that direct Greek impact on Hebrew literature cannot be demonstrated prior to the second century B.C. (p. 110).

2. On Wisdom literature, see W. W. Baudissin, *Die alttestamentliche Spruchdichtung* (1893); K. Siegfried, 'Wisdom', HDB IV, pp. 924–8; C. H. Toy, 'Wisdom Literature', EB IV, pp. 5322–36; J. Meinhold, *Die Weisheit Israels in Spruch, Sage und Dichtung* (1908); O. Eissfeldt, *Der Maschal im Alten Testament* (1913); H. Torczyner, 'The Riddle in the Bible', HUCA I (1924), pp. 125–49; W. Baumgartner, *Israelitische und altorientalische Weisheit* (1933); O. Rankin, *Israel's Wisdom Literature* (1936, [2]1954); M. Noth and D. W. Thomas, *Wisdom in Israel and the Ancient Near East* SVT III (1955); W. G. Lambert, *Babylonian Wisdom Literature* (1960); N. H. Tur-Sinai, *'Ḥokhmah'*, Enc. Miq. III, pp. 127–33; H. H. Schmidt, *Wesen und Geschichte der Weisheit* (1966); H. J. Hermisson, *Studien zur israelitischen Spruchweisheit* (1968); C. Bauer-Kayatz, *Einführung in die alttestamentliche Weisheit* (1969); P. W. Skehan, *Studies in Israelite Poetry and Wisdom* (1971); R. B. Y. Scott, 'Wisdom, Wisdom Literature', Enc. Jud. 16, cols. 557–63; *The Way of Wisdom in the Old Testament* (1971); U. Wilckens and G. Fohrer, 'Sophia', TDNT VII, pp. 465–528; B. L. Mack, *Logos und Sophia. Untersuchungen zur Weisheitstheologie im hellenistischen Judentum* (1973); R. N. Whybray, *The Intellectual Tradition in the Old Testament* (1974); J. N. Crenshaw, 'Wisdom', *Old Testament Form Criticism*, ed. J. H. Hayes (1974); idem (ed.), *Studies in Ancient Israelite Wisdom* (1975); 'Wisdom in the Old Testament', IDBS, pp. 952–6; *Old Testament Wisdom: An Introduction* (1981); J. G. Williams, *Those Who Ponder Proverbs: Aphoristic Thinking and Biblical Literature* (1981); D. F. Morgan, *Wisdom in the Old Testament Traditions* (1981); J. Blenkinsopp, *Wisdom and Law in the Old Testament* (1983).

anthology. Indebted both in form and in content to the scriptural
model, it introduces nevertheless a substantial amount of fresh and
original thoughts.

The author's basic concept is that of wisdom. He wishes to show how
the wise man judges the things of this world, and how he conducts
himself in practical life. His book contains therefore an inexhaustible
number of rules for behaviour in joy and sorrow, good fortune and
adversity, wealth and poverty, in sickness and health, trial and
temptation; in the society of fellow citizens; in intercourse with friend
and foe, high and low, poor and rich, good and evil, intelligent and
foolish; in trade and commerce, business and profession; above all also
in one's own house and family—how children should be raised,
servants treated, and how one should behave towards one's wife, and
women in general. All these varied relationships are considered by the
author, and he gives penetrating advice in each case, mostly on the
grounds of serious ethical conviction, which changes only occasionally
into superficial worldly wisdom. Ben Sira's counsel is the ripe fruit of
earnest and deep reflection on things and a rich experience of life. By
entering into so much detail, it affords at the same time a lively picture
of the customs and usages, and of the culture in general, of his period
and of his nation. To what extent the thoughts expressed and the form
in which they are expressed are the author's own, and to what extent he
merely assembles what was already in circulation among the people by
word of mouth, cannot of course now be determined. To a certain
degree both will have been the case. But he is in any case no mere
compiler; his individuality comes much too clearly and distinctly to the
fore for this to be so. Despite the great diversity of the maxims, they are
nevertheless the product of a unified and coherent view of the world
and of life.

The background of this practical worldly wisdom is a vivid and
healthy piety. True wisdom comes from God. In creation, God
arranged all things marvellously and continues to rule the world with
the same wisdom (39:12–35). He sees all things and governs all things,
rewarding the good, and punishing the wicked. Happy is the person
who trusts in him; such a one is steadfast in sorrow (2:1–18),
courageous and unafraid in every situation (31:13–20; E.T. 34:13–17).
The supreme wisdom is therefore the fear of God.

Ben Sira is the first expressly to identify divine wisdom with the
Torah. God has established wisdom in Israel (24:8–22), and with the
Law of Moses it has come to expression (24:23–29).[3] Israel is the elect of

3. For an evaluation of Ben Sira's portrayal of Wisdom within the context of the
encounter between Jewish and Hellenistic thought, see Hengel, *Judaism*, pp. 157–62.
Whether the actual identification, Torah = Wisdom, can be traced to Ben Sira
personally, or to the Wisdom school of scribes attached to Simeon the Righteous, cannot

God (45); she has received through Moses 'the Law of life and knowledge' from God (45:5). Therefore one must hold fast to it, and do it, and not be ashamed of it (2:16; 15:1; 19:20; 21:11; 42:2); therefore knowledge of the Law is very important (35:24–36:6—chs. 32 and 33, E.T.), and the position of interpreters of the Law ranks among the first (38:24–39:11). Sacrifice is of no use if a person has acted wrongly against his neighbour (7:9; 31:21–31—E.T. 34:18–26). God is not to be bribed with offerings (32:14–26—E.T. 35:12–20); the correct gift is to be kind and to avoid evil (32:1–5—E.T. ch. 35). Nevertheless the author esteems sacrificial worship highly and recommends giving generously to God whatever is due to him. 'Do not appear before the Lord empty-handed; perform these sacrifices because they are commanded.' 'Give to the Most High as he has given, and as generously as your hand has found. For the Lord is the one who repays, and he will repay you sevenfold' (32:6–13—E.T. ch. 35). The priestly service of Aaron is an essential component of the glory of the Jewish people (45:6–22). After praising the righteous deeds of Israel's ancestors (44–9), an innovation in Wisdom literature which previously lacked historical perspective,[4] Ben Sira presents an enthusiastic and colourful portrait of the High-Priest Simeon, a faithful minister in the Temple, obedient to the prescriptions of the Law (ch. 50). He exhorts therefore also that the prescribed offerings should be paid to the priests (7:29–31), and emphasizes that the house of Phinehas is divinely elected for the High-Priesthood (45:23 ff.; 50:24, Hebrew text; cf. Num. 25:10 ff.). His sympathies are in favour of the 'Sons of Zadok' (51:12, 9, Hebrew).

This interest in the legitimate High-Priesthood reflects the historical circumstances under which the author wrote.[5] It was the time of the invasion of Hellenism. The writer belonged to the old, faithful core, in controversy with Hellenistic liberalism, and complains bitterly that

be decided, but it is worth noting that Simeon's saying reproduced in mAb. 1:2 envisages the Torah as the first of the three pillars on which the world rests (Torah, worship and deeds of loving-kindness). Cf. Hengel, *ibid.*, p. 161. For the Wisdom-Torah association in rabbinic Judaism, see *ibid.*, pp. 169–75. For a study of the Jewish, Hellenistic and Egyptian (Demotic) ingredients of Ben Sira's work, see J. T. Sanders, *Ben Sira and Demotic Wisdom* (1983).

4. Cf. E. Jacob, 'L'histoire d'Israël vue par Ben Sira', *Mélanges bibliques rédigés en l'honneur d'André Robert* (1957), pp. 288–94; T. Maertens, *L'éloge des Pères (Ecclésiastique XLIV-L)* (1956); R. T. Siebeneck, 'May their Bones return to Life: Sirach's Praise of the Fathers', CBQ 21 (1959), pp. 411–28; J. L. Duhaim, 'El elogio de los Padres de Ben Sira y el Cántico de Moisés (Sir 44–50 y Dt 32)', Est. Bibl. 35 (1976), pp. 226–8; J. Marböck, 'Das Gebet um die Rettung Zions. Sir 36:1–22 im Zusammenhang der Geschichtsschau Ben Siras', *Memoria Jerusalem. Freundesgabe Franz Sauer* (1977), pp. 93–115.

5. Cf. Hengel, *Judaism*, pp. 138–53. Cf. also V. Tcherikover, *Hellenistic Civilization and the Jews* (1959), pp. 143–5; T. A. Burkill, 'Ecclesiasticus', IDB II, pp. 15–16; Th. Middendorp, *Die Stellung Ben Siras zwischen Judentum und Hellenismus* (1973).

'ungodly men have forsaken the law of the Most High God' (41:8). He prays to God: 'Lift up thy hand against foreign nations, and let them see thy might' (33:3—E.T. ch. 36) ; 'Destroy the adversary and wipe out the enemy' (*ib.* 7) ; 'May those who harm thy people meet destruction. Crush the heads of the rulers of the enemy, who say "There is no one but ourselves"' (*ib.* 9–10 ; cf. 1–13). If it is permissible to take the congregation of Israel to be the subject of 51:1–12, she is denounced before the king by calumniators and liars, but rescued through the help of God. The High-Priest Simon is exalted (chapter 50) for his correct discharge of the priestly service, because since then it had no longer been ministered according to the prescriptions of the Law. The writer thus lived in a period when the priestly aristocracy turned more and more in the direction of Hellenism. He hoped for the triumph of that legitimate High-Priesthood which remained faithful to the Law.

The author names himself at the close, 50:27 (chap. 51, which follows, is an appendix), but the text varies. Most Greek manuscripts, including the Vaticanus, Sinaiticus and Alexandrinus, read 'Ἰησοῦς υἱὸς Σειρὰχ Ἐλεαζὰρ ὁ Ἱεροσολυμείτης.[6] The Hebrew text confirms however that the name is original, for it runs, both in the inscription to the whole book following chap. 51, and in Sāadya : שמעון בן ישוע בן אלעזר בן סירא.

According to the unanimous testimony of antiquity, beginning with the Prologue to the Greek version which refers to the author as 'my grandfather Jesus' (ὁ πάππος μου Ἰησοῦς), the name of the writer was not Simeon, but Jesus. Hence שמעון בן in the Hebrew text appears to be a gloss, or to form an inversion of Jesus and Simeon as the Syriac title would suggest (ישוע בר שמעון). The designation 'Jesus son of Sirach' or 'Sira', which has become common, names the author after his grandfather, and not after his father. The Hellenization of the names appears to have followed the establishment of this convention.[7]

It is generally thought that Sirach derives from סירא, coat of mail, armour, the appended χ apparently indicating that the name is indeclinable.[8]

The theory that Jesus ben Sira was a priest depends on the reading of

6. The variant in the Sinaiticus (ὁ ἱερεὺς ὁ Σολυμείτης) is no doubt a corruption. The undeclined Ἐλεαζάρ is corrected into Ἐλεαζάρου or Ἐλεαζάρος or is altogether omitted. Cf. R. Smend, *Die Weisheit des Jesus Sirach* (1906), pp. 492–3.

7. See R. Smend, *op. cit.*, pp. xiv-xv ; I. Lévi, *L'Ecclésiastique* (1898), p. 216 ; 'Sirach', EJ XI, p. 388 ; W. O. C. Oesterley, *Ecclesiasticus* (1912), pp. xiv-xv ; W. O. E. Oesterley and G. H. Box, APOT I (1912), pp. 270–1, 291 ; M. H. Segal, *Sefer Ben Sira ha-Shalem* (1953), p. 1 In rabbinic texts he is simply referred to as סירא (tYad. 2:13 ; ySanh. 28a ; Eccl. R. 12:11).

8. Cf. Ἀκελδαμάχ (= חקל דמא, χωρίον αἵματος) in Act. 1:19, Ἰωσηχ (= יוסי) in Lk. 3:26, as has been pointed out by G. Dalman, *Grammatik des jüdisch-palästinischen Aramäisch* (²1905), p. 202, n. 3.

the Sinaiticus (see n. 6), which is probably an inner-Greek corruption. His elevation to the status of High-Priest by Syncellus[9] is the result of a misinterpretation of the Chronicle of Eusebius, where Jesus Sirach is listed after the High-Priest Simeon, son of Onias II, but merely as the author of a book, and not as a Pontiff.[10]

The age in which Ben Sira lived can be fixed with reasonable accuracy. According to the Prologue attached to the work, his grandson[11] who translated the book into Greek arrived in Egypt ἐν τῷ ὀγδόῳ καὶ τριακοστῷ ἔτει ἐπὶ τοῦ Εὐεργέτου βασιλέως.[12] Since the first of the two Ptolemies, surnamed Euergetes, reigned only twenty-five years, the second, whose full name was Ptolemy Physcon VII Euergetes II, must be meant. He ruled conjointly with his brother (170–164 B.C.), then (from 145–117 B.C.) alone, but reckoned the years of his reign from the earlier date. Accordingly, the thirty-eighth year in which the grandson of Jesus ben Sira came to Egypt is 132 B.C. His grandfather must therefore have lived and written *circa* 190–170 B.C. This also accords with the fact that in his book he dedicates to the High-Priest Simon son of Onias II a reverential obituary (50:1–26). By this is to be understood, that is to say, not Simon I (beginning of the third century B.C.—see *Ant.* xii 2, 5 (43)), but Simon II (beginning of the second century—see *Ant.* xii 4, 10 (224)). Jesus ben Sira experienced the days of the later Simon and praises his fidelity to the Law compared to the Hellenizing current prevailing at the time when he wrote. Since the work presupposes the death of Simon II (still in office in 198 B.C.) but does not allude to the deposition of Onias III in 174 B.C., it is reasonable to conclude that Jesus ben Sira flourished between *c.* 190–175 B.C.[13]

The book was originally written in Hebrew, as is explicitly stated in the Prologue to the Greek translation. Jerome was acquainted with the Hebrew text—see *Praef. in vers. libr. Salom.* (PL XXVIII, cols. 1307–8): 'Fertur et πανάρετος Iesu filii Sirach liber et alius ψευδεπίγραφος, qui Sapientia Salomonis inscribitur. Quorum priorem Hebraicum reperi, non Ecclesiasticum, ut apud Latinos, sed Parabolas praenotatum, cui iuncti erant Ecclesiastes et Canticum Canticorum, ut similitudinem Salomonis non solum librorum numero, sed etiam materiarum genere

9. *Chron.*, ed. Dindorf, I, p. 525.

10. Eusebius, *Chron.* ad Ol. 137–8 (ed. Schoene II, p. 122).

11. Cf. H. J. Cadbury, 'The Grandson of Ben Sira', HThR 48 (1955), pp. 219–25.

12. The thirty-eighth year refers to king Euergetes' reign and not to his age. This interpretation is demonstrated by the close parallels of 1 Mac. 13:42; Hag. 1:1; 2:1; Zech. 1:7; 7:1, and further corroborated, with additional evidence, in A. Deissmann, *Bible Studies* (1901), pp. 339 ff. It is appropriate also to recall the coin of Agrippa II, with the inscription ἐπὶ βασ. Αργι. ετ(ους) κζ (cf. vol. I, p. 481, n. 45).

13. Cf. Eissfeldt, *Introduction*, p. 597; Hengel, *Judaism*, p. 131; Nickelsburg, JLBBM, p. 64.

coaequaret.' The Hebrew text is also quoted in the Talmud and other Rabbinic writings (see below).

Substantial remains of the Hebrew Ben Sira, regarded as lost for many centuries, were discovered in 1896 in the Genizah attached to the Ezra Synagogue in Cairo. Further Genizah fragments were published in the following years, and additional pages came to light more recently in the Cambridge Genizah holdings.[14] From Qumran Cave 2, minute scraps of a manuscript have been identified as belonging to the Hebrew Ben Sira, chapter 6.[15] The Psalms Scroll from Cave 11 (cols. xxi, ll. 11–17, xxii, l. 1) preserves the first half of the alphabetical acrostic poem from Sir. 51:13–20, 30.[16] Finally, the Masada excavations have yielded a fragmentary scroll representing Sir. 39:27–44:17.[17] As a result of these finds, about two-thirds of the Hebrew Ben Sira is now restored.

Prior to the Qumran and Masada discoveries, several important scholars argued that far from reflecting the original text of Ecclesiasticus, the Genizah fragments represent medieval retranslations into Hebrew from Syriac and Persian (D. S. Margoliouth);[18] from Syriac (G. Bickell, H. L. Ginsberg);[19] from the Greek (E. J. Goodspeed, M. Hadas, C. C. Torrey);[20] or from the Greek and Syriac (H. Duesberg and P. Auvray).[21] The protagonists of authenticity include the editors,[22] Israël Lévi,[23] R. Smend,[24] N. Peters,[25] G. H. Box and W. O.

14. See A. E. Cowley and A. Neubauer, *The Original Hebrew of a Portion of Ecclesiasticus* (1897); S. Schechter and C. Taylor, *The Wisdom of Ben Sira: Portions of the Book of Ecclesiasticus from Hebrew Manuscripts in the Cairo Genizah Collection* (1899); I. Lévi, 'Fragments de deux nouveaux manuscrits hébreux de l'Ecclésiastique', REJ 40 (1900), pp. 1–30; J. Marcus, *The Newly Discovered Original Hebrew of Ben Sira (Ecclesiasticus xxxii, 16-xxxiv, 1): The Fifth Manuscript and a Prosodic Version of Ben Sira (Ecclesiasticus xxii, 22-xxiii, 9)* (1931) = JQR 21 (1930–1), pp. 223–40; J. Schirmann, 'Daf ḥadash mittokh sefer Ben-Sîra' ha-ivri', Tarbiz 27 (1957–8), pp. 440–43; 'Dappîm nosefîm mittokh sefer Ben-Sîra'', ibid. 29 (1959–60), pp. 125–34.

15. M. Baillet, DJD III: *Les 'Petites Grottes' de Qumrân* (1962), pp. 75–7.

16. J. A. Sanders, DJD IV: *The Psalms Scroll of Qumran Cave 11* (1965), pp. 79–85; *The Dead Sea Psalms Scroll* (1967), pp. 74–6; 112–17.

17. Yigael Yadin, *The Ben Sira Scroll from Masada* (1965).

18. *The Origin of the 'Original Hebrew' of Ecclesiasticus* (1899).

19. G. Bickell, 'Der hebräische Sirachtext: eine Rückübersetzung', WZKM 13 (1899), pp. 251–6; H. L. Ginsberg, 'The Original Hebrew of Ben Sira 12:10–14', JBL 74 (1955), pp. 93 ff.

20. E. J. Goodspeed, *The Story of the Apocrypha* (1939), p. 25; M. Hadas, *The Apocrypha*, transl. by E. J. Goodspeed (1959), p. 222; C. C. Torrey, *The Apocryphal Literature* (1945), p. 97; 'The Hebrew Text of Ben Sira', *Alexander Marx Jubilee Volume* (1950), pp. 585–602.

21. *Le livre de l'Ecclésiastique [La Sainte Bible de Jérusalem]* (²1958), p. 20.

22. See e.g. C. Taylor, *The Originality of the Hebrew Text of Ben Sira* (1910).

23. *L'Ecclésiastique* I (1898), p. xviii; II (1901), pp. xx-xxi; *The Hebrew Text of the Book of Ecclesiasticus* (1904), pp. x-xi.

24. *Die Weisheit des Jesus Sirach* (1906).

25. *Das Buch Jesus Sirach oder Ecclesiasticus* (1913).

E. Oesterley,[26] M. H. Segal,[27] and Alexander A. di Lella.[28] In their view, the many doublets and clumsy phrases are attributable either to a popularizing revision of the classical style of Ben Sira (M. H. Segal),[29] or to the introduction of occasional retranslation from the Greek (J. Ziegler),[30] or the Syriac (A. A. di Lella).[31] In the words of H. P. Rüger, the authenticity of the older form of the text can be unconditionally affirmed while the more recent Hebrew version results from a Jewish revision rather than a retranslation.[32]

The Qumran and Masada fragments seem to have settled the debate. While the tiny remains from Cave 2 yield no independent argument, the Ben Sira extract from the Psalms Scroll, and especially the Masada manuscript, dated respectively on palaeographical grounds to the beginning of the first century A.D. and to the first half of the first century B.C.,[33] are sufficiently close to the Genizah fragments to render the theory of a medieval retranslation into Hebrew highly unconvincing. The precise relationship between the two sets of documents still awaits a thorough examination. The alphabetical character of Sir. 51:13 ff., gravely corrupt in the Genizah text in the *aleph* to *lamed* section, a fact recognized already by the editors,[34] can now be emended with the help of 11QPs[a] for the verses between *aleph* and *kaph*.[35] A careful comparison of the larger Masada document with the text and the marginal notes of Manuscript B of the Genizah has enabled Y. Yadin to draw the following general conclusions: (a) The Masada text is basically identical with the Genizah manuscripts. (b) The text of Manuscript B. and its marginal variants correspond to two recensions, already containing errors and editorial alterations, of the original work. (c) The Hebrew version used by the Greek translator is closer to that of the Masada manuscript than is any other recension. (d) The latter's

---

26. R. H. Charles, APOT I (1912), pp. 275–8; Oesterley, *Ecclesiasticus* (1912), p. xcv.

27. *Sefer Ben Sira ha-Shalem* (1953, ²1958).

28. *The Hebrew Text of Sirach: A Text-Critical and Historical Study* (1966).

29. *Op. cit.*, pp. 62–3. Cf. 'The Evolution of the Hebrew Text of Ben Sira', JQR 25 (1934–5), p. 118.

30. 'Zwei Beiträge zu Sirach', BZ 8 (1964), pp. 277–84.

31. *Op. cit.*

32. Hans Peter Rüger, *Text und Textform im hebräischen Sirach* (1970), p. 115. Rüger disagrees with both Ziegler and di Lella; cf. *op. cit.*, pp. 1–11.

33. di Lella, *op. cit.*, pp. 148–9.

34. Cf. Schechter and Taylor, *op. cit.* [in n. 14], p. lxxxvii.

35. Cf. J. A. Sanders, DJD IV, p. 79. 'There can be little doubt that Grk presents an interpretive recension of the canticle. While Q may possibly not represent the original text of the poem in all details, it is clearly superior to Syr-Cairo and Latin ... it is now clear that the canticle is totally independent of Sirach. If Jesus, son of Sira, of Jerusalem, had penned the canticle it would hardly be found in *11QPs[a]*, which claims Davidic authorship.' (*Ibid.*, p. 83.)

wording (apart from mistakes and lacunae) is nearest, and possibly identical, to Ben Sira's original.[36]

The complete text of Sirach is preserved in two translations: 1. the Greek version, prepared by the author's grandson, has passed into the Greek Bible; 2. the Syriac version, contained in the Peshitta, which in the judgement of all modern scholars derives not from the Greek, but directly from the Hebrew text.[37]

Ecclesiasticus is described as 'the worst piece of translation in the Syriac Bible', whose value for textual criticism is moreover limited by the translator's regular recourse to the Greek version too.[38] Despite all these strictures, it remains, along with the Hebrew fragments and the Greek translation, a valuable auxiliary means of arriving at Ben Sira's own meaning.

The existence of a Hebrew text in the time of Jerome, the quotations in Rabbinic writings, and finally the Hebrew fragments preserved from the tenth and twelfth centuries, all prove that the book was popular in Rabbinic circles.[39]

The presence in the Cairo Genizah of medieval copies of the Hebrew Ben Sira and of the Damascus Rule (CD), later discovered at Qumran (see below, pp. 389, 395), calls to mind the discovery, at the end of the eighth century, of Hebrew manuscripts in the Jericho area mentioned by the Nestorian Patriarch of Seleucia, Timothy I, in a Syriac letter to Sergius, Metropolitan of Elam.[40] According to the Patriarch, writing

---

36. Cf. Yadin, *op. cit.* [in n. 17], pp. 7–11. The Hebrew section of the volume contains three tables. The first lists the cases where the Masada scroll agrees with the marginal glosses of Manuscript B (pp. 7–8). The second indicates agreements between it and the text of Manuscript B against the marginal variants (p. 9). The third gives examples where Masada, Manuscript B and B marg all differ (pp. 11–13).

37. Cf. e.g. Smend, *op. cit.*, p. cxxxvi; Oesterley, *op. cit.*, p. c; Segal, *op. cit.*, p. 59; Eissfeldt, *Introduction*, p. 599. It has recently been conjectured by M. M. Winter ('The Origins of Ben Sira in Syriac. Peshitta Institute Communication XII', VT 27 (1977), pp. 237–53, 494–507) that the discrepancies of the Syriac version from the Hebrew as well as from the Greek and the Latin point to an Ebionite origin in the third or early fourth century A.D. The basic translation was revised in the late fourth century in orthodox Christian circles.

38. Cf. Smend, *op. cit.*, pp. cxxxvii, cxxxix.

39. A complete enumeration of rabbinic quotations from Ben Sira, or references to his writings, may be found in Smend, *op. cit.*, pp. xlvi–lvi; Segal, *op. cit.*, pp. 37–42. Cf. also S. Lieberman, 'Ben Sira à la lumière du Yerouchalmi', REJ 97 (1934), pp. 50–7. The earliest citation appears in mAb. 4:4a (R Levitas appropriating Sir. 7:17 in a slightly different form). Cf. G. Beer, *Abot* (1927), pp. 92–3. For Ben Sira quotations by Saadya Gaon (882–942) in his *Sefer ha-Galuy*, see Smend, *op. cit.*, pp. l–lvi; di Lella, *op. cit.*, p. 95. Twenty-five hemistichs cited (Sir. 3:21–2; 5:5–6; 6:6–8, 13; 11:28; 13:11) are identical to all intents and purposes with Manuscript A of the Genizah; another (Sir. 13:11) is reproduced freely (cf. di Lella, *ibid.*).

40. Cf. O. Braun, 'Ein Brief des Katholikos Timotheos I über biblische Studien des 9. Jahrhunderts', Oriens Christianus 1 (1901), pp. 299–313; R. S. Bidawid, *Les lettres du*

apparently in 796 or 797 (Bidawid, p. 71), trustworthy Jews (receiving instruction in Christianity) reported that ten years earlier, books of the Old Testament and other Hebrew documents, including more than two hundred Psalms of David, had been found in a cave in the vicinity of Jericho. There is a serious possibility that the Genizah manuscripts of Ecclesiasticus, the Aramaic Testament of Levi and the Damascus Rule are ultimately traceable to scrolls removed between 780 and 790 from a Qumran cave.[41]

On rabbinic attitudes to the canonical status of Ben Sira, see vol. II, p. 319. For a full list of relevant excerpts, see Sid Z. Leiman, *The Canonization of Hebrew Scripture: The Talmudic and Midrashic Evidence* (1976), pp. 92–7.[42]

The early medieval composition known as the *Alphabet of Ben Sira* is dependent in part on Talmudic quotations. It owes its title to two sets of twenty-two alphabetically arranged proverbs, the first in Hebrew, the second in Aramaic. Five out of the twenty-two are known from rabbinic sources as sayings of Ben Sira. These proverbs have been inserted in a vulgar and irreverent story of Ben Sira, who is said to have been the son of the prophet Jeremiah's daughter, who conceived him 'miraculously' in a public bath from floating semen which belonged to her father. The work has survived in four recensions showing traces of censorship practised by copyists in connection with irreligious or shocking passages.[43]

On the title of the book, see in particular the passage from Jerome on p. 202 above. The Hebrew text has a dual signature: דברי שמעון בן ישוע בן אלעזר בן סירא and חכמת שמעון בן ישוע בן אלעזר בן סירא בן סירא (cf. Segal, *op. cit.*, p. 358). In Rabbinic writings, the book is designated as

Patriarche nestorien, Timothée I (1956).

41. Cf. O. Eissfeldt, 'Der gegenwärtige Stand der Erforschung der in Palästina neu gefundenen hebräischen Handschriften', ThLZ 74 (1949), cols. 595–600; R. de Vaux, 'A propos des manuscrits de la Mer Morte', RB 57 (1950), pp. 417–29; P. Kahle, *The Cairo Geniza* ([2]1959), pp. 16–17; di Lella, *op. cit.*, pp. 81–105.

42. tYad. 2:13 ('the Books of Ben Sira do not defile the hands') indicates that the work is not canonical. ySanh. 28a, bSanh. 100b and Eccl. R. 12:12 forbid its reading. By contrast, the many quotations in the Talmud and the introductory formulae suggest that Ecclesiasticus was often used and interpreted as a biblical book. Cf. Leiman, *op. cit.*, p. 97. For the view that Ben Sira was read in the Jewish liturgy, see C. Roth, 'Ecclesiasticus in the Synagogue Service', JBL 71 (1952), pp. 171–8.

43. For the text, see M. Steinschneider, *Alphabetum Siracidis utrumque* (1858), containing the traditional version and additional material from a Leiden manuscript; D. Z. Friedman and D. S. Loewinger, *Alpha Betha de-Ben Sira* (1926), representing a different recension from a Kaufmann codex from Budapest; A. M. Haberman, "*Aleph-Betha de-Ben Sîra'-Nūsāḥ sh'lishit*', Tarbiz 27 (1957–8), pp. 190–202, editing a Jerusalem manuscript. For a general outline, see J. Dan, 'Ben Sira, Alphabet of', Enc. Jud. 4, cols. 548–50. Cf. also L. Ginzberg, 'Ben Sira, Alphabet of', JE II, pp. 678–81, where the Aramaic proverbs are translated into English. Peter the Venerable of Cluny quotes from the Alphabet; cf. I. Lévi, REJ 29 (1894), pp. 197–205.

ספרי בן ס׳, סיפרא דבן ס׳, סיפרא דבן ס׳, ספר בן סירא, and in Genizah fragments משלי בן ס׳ (cf. Segal, *op. cit.*, p. 12; S. Schechter, 'A Further Fragment of Ben Sira', JQR 12 (1899–1900), pp. 460 ff.). In the Greek manuscripts, the title runs Σοφία 'Ιησοῦ υἱοῦ Σιράχ. In the Greek Church, the designation ἡ πανάρετος σοφία, first customary for quotations from Proverbs (Clement of Rome, *I Cor.* 57:3; Clement of Alexandria, *Strom.* ii 22, 136; Euseb. HE iv 22, 8) was transferred to this book, too. It is first found in Eusebius, *Chron.*, ed. Schoene II, p. 122 (where the agreement of Syncellus and Jerome with the Armenian text proves that the expression is peculiar to Eusebius himself). *Demonstr. evang.* viii 2, 71: Σίμων, καθ' ὃν 'Ιησοῦς ὁ τοῦ Σιράχ ἐγνωρίζετο, ὁ τὴν καλουμένην πανάρετον Σοφίαν συντάξας. This designation does not yet appear in the numerous quotations in Clement and Origen. In the Latin church, the title 'Ecclesiasticus' has been current since the time of Cyprian (*Testim.* ii 1; iii 1, 35, 51, 95, 96, 109, 110, 111). Compare also the Latin translation of Origen's Eighteenth Homily on Numbers, chap. 3 (ed. Lommatzsch X, p. 221): 'in libro qui apud nos quidem inter Salomonis volumina haberi solet et Ecclesiasticus dici, apud Graecos vero sapientia Iesu filii Sirach appellatur'.

The work of Ben Sira has enjoyed high esteem in Christianity; both Greek and Latin church fathers frequently quote it as 'Scripture'. Already the Epistle of James includes a number of sayings reminiscent of Jesus Sirach, although these do not amount to actual citations.[44]

In patristic literature, the *Didache* uses Sirach without specifically quoting it.[45] By contrast, Clement of Alexandria often cites the book, most frequently with the formulae ἡ γραφὴ λέγει, φησίν, etc. (thirteen times: *Paedag.* i 8, 62; 8, 68; ii 2, 34; 5, 46; 8, 69; 8, 76; 10, 98; 10, 99; iii 3, 17; 3, 23; 4, 29; 11, 58; 11, 83); or with the formulae ἡ σοφία λέγει, φησίν, and the like (ten times: *Paedag.* i 8, 69; 8, 72; 9, 75; 13, 102; ii 1, 8; 2, 24; 7, 54; 7, 58; 7, 59; *Stromat.* v 3, 18); or even as words of the παιδαγωγός (*Paedag.* ii 10, 99.101.109). The book is only twice designated as the σοφία 'Ιησοῦ (*Stromat.* i 4, 27; 10, 47). Solomon is named as author four times, but only in the *Stromata*, never in the *Paedagogus*, to which most of the quotations belong (*Strom.* ii 5, 24, beginning and end; vi 16, 146; vii 16, 105, ed. O. Stählin, p. 46). On one occasion, a maxim from Sirach's σοφία is described as pre-Sophoclean (*Paedag.* ii 2, 24). Cf. in general especially O. Stählin,

44. Cf. J. B. Mayer, *The Epistle of St. James* ([3]1910), pp. lxxiii ff.; Oesterley and Box, APOT I, pp. 294–6; J. H. Ropes, *James* (ICC, 1916), p. 19 prefers to speak of 'a general similarity of ideas rather than proper literary dependence'. Similarly, M. Dibelius, *James* (1976), p. 27.

45. Cf. J.-P. Audet, *La Didachè* (1958), pp. 275–80 (at *Did.* 1:6); P. W. Skehan, '*Didache* 1, 6 and Sirach 12, 1', Bibl 44 (1963), pp. 533–6.

Clemens Alexandrinus und die Septuaginta (1901), pp. 46–58; also Stählin's edition of Clement of Alexandria in the Berlin corpus.

The situation is similar regarding the Sirach quotations of Origen, only here in many instances the introductory formulae cannot be established with certainty because the majority of Origen's writings are preserved only in Latin. Origen seems to have referred to the book most frequently as γραφή. In the Latin text, Solomon is occasionally named as author (*In Numer. homil.* xviii, 3 = ed. Baehrens, GCS 30, p. 170; *In Iosuam homil.* XI, 2 = *ibid.*, p. 363; *In Samuel. homil.* I, 13 = GCS 33, p. 21), but that this cannot be attributed to Origen himself is attested by *Contra Cels.* vi 7 (ed. Koetschau, GCS 2, p. 77): παραδείξωμεν ἀπὸ τῶν ἱερῶν γραμμάτων, ὅτι προτρέπει καὶ ὁ θεῖος λόγος ἡμᾶς ἐπὶ διαλεκτικήν· ὅπου μὲν Σολομῶντος λέγοντο ... ὅπου δὲ τοῦ τὸ σύγγραμμα τὴν σοφίαν [read τῆς σοφίας] ἡμῖν καταλιπόντος Ἰησοῦ υἱοῦ Σειρὰχ φάσκοντος. In the writing *De aleatoribus* c. 2, found amongst Cyprian's works but really pre-Cyprianic, Sirach is introduced as 'et alia scriptura dicit'. Cyprian himself cites the book throughout as the work of Solomon (*Testim.* ii 1; iii 6.12.35.51.53.95.96.97.109.113; *Ad Fortunam* c. 9; *De opere et eleemosynis* c. 5; *Epist.* iii 2). Other Latin writers do the same. See especially the passage already referred to from the Latin version of Origen, *In Numer. homil.* xviii, 3; cf. also Jerome's rendering of Eusebius, *Demonstr. evang.* viii 2, 71: 'Simon, quo regente populum Iesus filius Sirach scripsit librum, qui Graece πανάρετος appellatur et plerisque Salomonis falso dicitur' (*In Daniel.* 9). Thus many western canon indexes number without further ado *five* Solomonic writings (see Th. Zahn, *Geschichte des neutestamentl. Kanons* II, pp. 151, 245, 251, 272, 1007 ff. ; E. Nestle, ZAW 27 (1907), pp. 294–7).

For the further history of the use of the book, see Oesterley, *Ecclesiasticus* (1912), pp. lxxviii-lxxxvi.

A. Manuscripts and Editions

1. Hebrew
a) Qumran material
Baillet, M., Milik, J. T., Vaux, R. de, DJD III : *Les 'Petites Grottes' de Qumrân* (1962), pp. 75–7.
Sanders, J. A., DJD IV : *The Psalms Scroll of Qumran Cave 11* (1965), pp. 79–85.
b) Masada fragments
Yadin, Y., *The Ben Sira Scroll from Masada* (1965).
c) Genizah MSS A-E
Cowley, A. E., and Neubauer, A., *The Original Hebrew of a Portion of Ecclesiasticus* (1897).
Schechter, S., and Taylor, C., *The Wisdom of Ben Sira : Portions of the Book of Ecclesiasticus from Hebrew Manuscripts in the Cairo Genizah Collection* (1899).
Margoliouth, G., 'The Original Hebrew of Ecclesiasticus XXXI, 12–31 and XXXVI, 22-XXXVII, 26', JQR 12 (1899–1900), pp. 1–33.
Adler, E. N., 'Some missing Chapters of Ben Sira', JQR 12 (1899–1900), pp. 466–80.
Schechter, S., 'A further Fragment of Ben Sira', JQR 12 (1899–1900), pp. 456–65.

Lévi, I., 'Fragments de deux nouveaux manuscrits hébreux de l'Ecclésiastique', REJ 40 (1900), pp. 1–30.

Gaster, M., 'A new Fragment of Ben Sira', JQR 12 (1899–1900), pp. 688–702.

Marcus, J., *The Newly Discovered Original Hebrew of Ben Sira (Ecclesiasticus xxxii, 16-xxxiv, 1) : The Fifth Manuscript and a Prosodic Version of Ben Sira* (Ecclesiasticus xxii, 22-xxiii, 9) (Q 31) = JQR 21 (1930–31), pp. 223–40.

Schirmann, J., דף חדש מתוך ספר בן סירא העברי, Tarbiz 27 (1957–8), pp. 440–3.

Schirmann, J., דפים נוספים מתוך ספר בן סירא, *ibid.* 29 (1959–60), pp. 125–34.

B. Complete Editions

1. Hebrew

Facsimiles of the Fragments hitherto recovered of the Book of Ecclesiasticus in Hebrew (1901).

Lévi, I., *L'Ecclésiastique ou la Sagesse de Jésus, fils de Sira*, Parts I and II (1898, 1901).

Peters, N., *Der jüngst wiederaufgefundene hebräische Text des Buches Ecclesiasticus untersucht, herausgegeben, übersetzt und mit kritischen Noten versehen* (1902).

Strack, H. L., *Die Sprüche Jesus, des Sohnes Sirachs, der jüngst gefundene hebräische Text mit Anmerkungen und Wörterbuch* (1903).

Lévi, I., *The Hebrew Text of the Book of Ecclesiasticus* (1904).

Peters, N., *Liber Jesu filii Sirach sive Ecclesiasticus hebraice* (1905).

Smend, R., *Die Weisheit des Jesus Sirach hebräisch und deutsch* (1906).

Segal, M. H., ספר בן סירא השלם (1953, [2]1958).

The Book of Ben Sira : Text, Concordance and an Analysis of the Vocabulary (1973).

2. Greek

On the editions of the Greek Bible, see pp. 489–90. The most up-to-date text is:

Ziegler, J., *Sapientia Jesu Filii Sirach* [Göttingen Septuaginta XII, 2] (1965).

Two Greek minuscules 248 = Vaticanus Gr. 346 and 70 = München Gr. 493, formerly 551 contain additional verses especially in chaps. 1–26. Cf. J. H. A. Hart, *Ecclesiasticus : The Greek Text of Codex 248* (1909) ; J. Ziegler, *Die Münchener griechische Sirach-Handschrift 493* (1962).

3. Syriac (see above, p. 205).

4. Translations from the Greek text

a) Old Latin

Sabatier, P., *Bibliorum Sacrorum latinae versiones antiquae* (1739–49, [2]1751).

Lagarde, P. de, 'Die Weisheiten der Handschrift von Amiata', *Mitteilungen* I (1884), pp. 283–378.

Herkenne, H., *De veteris Latinae Ecclesiastici capitibus I-XLIII* (1899).

b) Vulgate

Biblia sacra juxta latinam vulgatam versionem ad codicum fidem XII : Liber Hiesu Sirach (1964).

Jerome did not revise the Old Latin: 'Porro in eo libro, qui a plerisque Sapientia Salomonis inscribitur et in Ecclesiastico quem esse Iesu filii Sirach nullus ignorat, calamo temperavi, tantummodo canonicas Scripturas vobis emendare desiderans' (*Praef. in edit. librorum Salomonis iuxta LXX interpretes*, ed. Vallarsi X, p. 436.

c) Syro-Hexaplaric version

Ceriani, A. M., *Codex Syro-Hexaplaris Ambrosianus* (1874).

d) Coptic (Sahidic)

Lagarde, P. de, *Aegyptiaca* (1883), pp. 107–206.

e) Ethiopic

Dillmann, A., *Biblia Veteris Testamenti Aethiopica* (1894), pp. 54–117.

Commentaries

Fritzsche, O. F., *Die Weisheit Jesus Sirachs* (1859).
Lévi, I., *L'Ecclésiastique ou la sagesse de Jésus fils de Sira* I-II (1898, 1901).
Ryssel, V., 'Die Sprüche Jesus des Sohnes Sirachs', APAT I, pp. 230–475.
Knabenbauer, J., *Commentarius in Ecclesiasticum cum appendice: textus Ecclesiastici hebreus* (1902).
Peters, N., *Der jüngst wieder aufgefundene hebräische Text des Buches Ecclesiasticus* (1902).
Smend, R., *Die Weisheit des Jesus Sirach* I-II (1906).
Peters, N., *Das Buch Jesus Sirach* (1913).
Box, G. H., and W. O. E. Oesterley, 'Sirach', APOT I, pp. 268–517.
Eberharter, A., *Das Buch Jesus Sirach* (1925).
Segal, M. H., *Sefer Ben Sira ha-Shalem* (1953, ²1958).
Schilling, O., *Das Buch Jesus Sirach* (1956).
Hamp, V., *Das Buch Sirach oder Ecclesiasticus* (1959).
Duesberg, H., and Auvray, H. P., *Le livre de l'Ecclésiastique* (²1958).
Vattioni, F., *Ecclesiastico* (1968).
Snaith, J. G., *Ecclesiasticus* (1974).
Sauer, G., *Jesus Sirach (Ben Sira)* [JSHRZ III, 5] (1978).

Bibliography

For an exhaustive bibliography until 1963, see A. A. di Lella, *The Hebrew Text of Sirach* (1966), pp. 154–68.
Bickell, G., 'Ein alphabetisches Lied Jesus Sirachs', ZKTh 6 (1882), pp. 319–33.
Nestle, E., 'Zum Prolog des Ecclesiasticus', ZAW 17 (1897), pp. 123–4.
Peters, N., *Die sahidische-koptische Uebersetzung des Buches Ecclesiasticus* (1898).
Bacher, W., 'Die persischen Randnotizen zum hebräischen Sirach', ZAW 20 (1900), pp. 308–10.
Grimme, H., 'Mètres et strophes dans les fragments du manuscrit parchemin du Siracide', RB 9 (1900), pp. 400–13. 'Mètres et strophes dans les fragments hébreux du manuscrit A de l'Ecclésiastique', RB 10 (1901), pp. 55–65, 260–7, 423–35.
Nestle, E., 'Sirach (Book of)', HDB IV, pp. 539–51.
Toy, C. H., 'Ecclesiasticus', EB II, pp. 1167–79. 'Sirach', EB IV, pp. 4645–51.
Lévi, I., 'Sirach, The Wisdom of Jesus the Son of', JE 11 (1905), pp. 388–97.
Ginzberg, L., 'Randglossen zum hebräischen Ben Sira', *Orientalische Studien Th. Nöldeke gewidmet*, ed. C. Bezold (²1906), pp. 609–25.
Smend, R., *Griechisch-Syrisch-Hebräischer Index zur Weisheit Jesus Sirach* (1907)
Marmorstein, A., 'Jesus Sirach 51, 12 ff.', ZAW 29 (1909), pp. 287–93.
Wellhausen, J., 'Reis im Buch Sirach', ZDMG 64 (1910), p. 258.
Baumgartner, W., 'Die literarischen Gattungen in der Weisheit des Jesus Sirach', ZAW 34 (1914), pp. 161–98.
Büchler, A., 'Ben Sira's Conception of Sin and Atonement', JQR 13 (1922–3), pp. 303–35, 461–502; 14 (1923–4), pp. 53–83.
Bruyne, D. de, 'Etudes sur le texte latin de l'Ecclésiastique', Rev. Bénédictine 40 (1928), pp. 5–48.
Idem, 'Le prologue, le titre et la finale de l'Ecclésiastique', ZAW 47 (1929), pp. 257–63.
Lieberman, S., 'Ben Sira à la lumière du Yerouchalmi', REJ 97 (1934), pp. 50–7.
Segal, M. H., 'The Evolution of the Hebrew Text of Ben Sira', JQR 25 (1934–5), pp. 91–149.
Driver, G. R., 'Ecclesiasticus: A New Fragment of the Hebrew Text', ET 49 (1937–8), pp. 37–8.
Torrey, C. C., 'The Hebrew of the Genizah Sirach', *Alexander Marx Jubilee Volume* (1950), pp. 585–602.

Trinquet, J., 'Les liens "sadocites" de l'Ecrit de Damas, des manuscrits de la Mer Morte et de l'Ecclésiastique', VT 1 (1951), pp. 287–92.

Driver, G. R., 'Ben Sira XXXIII, 4', JJS 5 (1954), p. 177.

Segal, M. H., 'Ben Sira', *Enz. Miqr.* II, pp. 162–9.

Cadbury, H. J., 'The Grandson of Ben Sira', HThR 48 (1955), pp. 219–25.

Mowinckel, S., 'Die Metrik bei Jesus Sirach', Stud. Theol. 9 (1955), pp. 137–65.

Winter, P., 'Ben Sira and the Teachings of the Two Ways', VT 5 (1955), pp. 315–18.

Auvray, P., 'Notes sur le prologue de l'Ecclésiastique', *Mélanges bibliques rédigés en l'honneur d'André Robert* (1957), pp. 281–7.

Ziegler, J., 'Zum Wortschatz des griechischen Sirach', BZAW 77 (1958), pp. 274–87.

Idem, 'Hat Lukian den griechischen Sirach recensiert?', Bibl. 40 (1959), pp. 210–29.

Idem, 'Die hexaplarische Bearbeitung des griechischen Sirach', BZ 4 (1960), pp. 174–85.

Carmignac, J., 'Le rapport entre l'Ecclésiastique et Qumrân', RQ 3 (1961), pp. 209–18.

Lehmann, M. R., 'Ben Sira and the Qumran Literature', RQ 3 (1961), pp. 103–16.

Hartman, L. F., 'Sirach in Hebrew and Greek', CBQ 23 (1961), pp. 443–51.

Burkill, T. A., 'Ecclesiasticus', IDB II, pp. 13–21.

di Lella, A. A., 'Qumran and the Genizah Fragment of Sirach', CBQ 24 (1962), pp. 245–7.

Idem, 'Authenticity of the Genizah Fragments of Sirach', Bibl. 44 (1963), pp. 171–200.

Gormann, H., 'Jesus ben Siras Dankgebet und die Hodajoth', ThZ 19 (1963), pp. 81–7.

Rivkin, E., 'Ben Sira and the non-Existence of the Synagogue', *In the Time of Harvest, Festschrift A. H. Silver* (1963), pp. 321–54.

Pautrel, R., 'Ben Sira et le stoïcisme', RScR 51 (1963), pp. 535–49.

Segal, M. H., ספר בן סירא בקומראן, Tarbiz 33 (1963–4), pp. 243–6.

Ziegler, J., 'Die Vokabel-Varianten der O-Rezension im griechischen Sirach', *Hebrew and Semitic Studies presented to G. R. Driver* (1963), pp. 172–90.

Snaith, J. G., 'The Importance of Ecclesiasticus', ET 75 (1963–4), pp. 66–9.

di Lella, A. A., 'The recently identified Leaves of Sirach in Hebrew', Biblica 55 (1964), pp. 153–67.

Eissfeldt, O., *Introduction*, pp. 595–9, 772.

Baars, W., 'On a Latin Fragment of Sirach', VT 15 (1965), pp. 280–1.

Milik, J. T., 'Un fragment mal placé dans l'édition du Siracide de Masada', Bibl. 46 (1966), pp. 425–6.

di Lella, A. A., *The Hebrew Text of Sirach* (1966).

Haspecker, J., *Gottesfurcht bei Jesus Sirach* (1967).

Strugnell, J., 'Notes and Queries on the Ben Sira Scroll', Eretz Israel IX (1969), pp. 101–19.

Rüger, H. P., *Text und Textform im hebräischen Sirach* (1970).

Marböck, J., *Weisheit im Wandel: Untersuchungen zur Weisheitstheologie bei Ben Sira* (1971).

Sanders, J. A., 'The Sirach 51 Actostic', *Hommages à André Dupont-Sommer* (1971), pp. 429–38.

Skehan, P. W., 'The Acrostic Poem in Sirach 51:13–30', HThR 64 (1971), pp. 387–400.

Rickenbacher, O., *Weisheitsperikopen bei Ben Sira* (1973).

Dommershausen, W., 'Zum Vergeltungsdenken des Ben Sira', *Wort und Geschichte—Festschrift K. Elliger* (1973), pp. 37–43.

Middendorp, T., *Die Stellung Jesu ben Siras zwischen Judentum und Hellenismus* (1973).

Barthélemy, D., and Rickenbacher, O. (eds.), *Konkordanz zum hebräischen Sirach mit syrisch-hebräischem Index* (1973).

McKeating, H., 'Jesus ben Sira's Attitude to Women', ET 85 (1973–4), pp. 85–7.

Ben-Hayyim, Z., 'From the Ben Sira Entries', Leshonenu 37 (1973), pp. 215–17 (Hebr.).

Skehan, P. W., 'Sirach 30:12 and Related Texts', CBQ 36 (1974), pp. 535–42.

Wright, R. B., and Hann, R. R., 'A New Fragment of the Greek Text of Sirach', JBL 94 (1975), pp. 111–12.

Rivkin, E., 'Ben Sira—The Bridge between the Aaronid and Pharisaic Revolutions', Eretz Israel 12 (1975), pp. 95*–103*.

Crenshaw, J. L., 'The Problem of Theodicy in Sirach: On Human Bondage', JBL 94 (1975), pp. 47–64.

Prato, G. L., *Il problema della teodicea in Ben Sira* (1975).

Snaith, J. G., 'Ben Sira's supposed Love of Liturgy', VT 25 (1975), pp. 167–74.

Couroyer, B., 'Un égyptianisme dans Ben Sira IV, 11', RB 82 (1975), pp. 206–17.

Löhr, M., *Bildung aus dem Glauben: Beiträge zum Verständnis der Lehrreden des Buches Jesus Sirach* (1975).

Weinfeld, M., 'Traces of *kedushat yozer* and *pesukey de-Zimra* in the Qumran literature and Ben Sira', Tarbiz 45 (1975–6), pp. 15–26 (Hebr.).

Marböck, J., 'Gesetz und Weisheit. Zum Verständnis des Gesetzes bei Jesus Ben Sira', BZ 20 (1976), pp. 1–21.

Skehan, P. W., 'Ecclesiasticus', IDBS, pp. 250–1.

Winter, M. M., *A Concordance to the Peshitta Version of Ben Sira* (1976).

Idem, 'The Origins of Ben Sira in Syriac', VT 27 (1977), pp. 237–53, 494–507.

Alonso Schökel, L., 'The Vision of Man in Sirach 16, 24–17, 14', *Israelite Wisdom (Festschrift S. Terrien)* (1978), pp. 235–45.

Jacob, E., 'Wisdom and Religion in Sirach', *ibid.*, pp. 247–60.

Sanders, J. T., 'A Hellenistic Egyptian Parallel to Ben Sira', JBL 97 (1978), pp. 257–8.

Idem, 'Ben Sira's Ethics of Caution', HUCA 50 (1979), pp. 73–106.

Lebram, J. C. H., 'Jerusalem, Wohnsitz der Weisheit', *Studies in Hellenistic Religion*, ed. M. J. Vermaseren (1979), pp. 103–28.

Noorda, S., 'Illness and Sin, Forgiving and Healing. The Connection of Medical Treatment in the Religious Beliefs in Ben Sira 38, 1–15', *ibid.*, pp. 215–24.

Marböck, J., 'Sir 38, 24–39, 11: Der schriftgelehrte Weise. Ein Beitrag zu Gestalt und Werk Ben Siras', Bibliotheca EThL 51 (1979), pp. 293–316.

Muraoka, T., 'Sira 51, 13–30: An Erotic Hymn to Wisdom?', JSJ 10 (1979), pp. 166–78.

Wolfgang, R., 'Between the Fear of God and Wisdom in the Book of Ben Sira', Bet Mikra 81 (1980), pp. 150–62 (Hebr.).

Stadelmann, H., *Ben Sira als Schriftgelehrter* (1980).

Harrington, D. J., 'The Wisdom of the Scribe according to Ben Sira', *Ideal Figures in Ancient Judaism* [SCS 12] (1980), pp. 181–8.

Roth, W., 'On the Gnomic-Discursive Wisdom of Ben Sira', Semeia 17 (1980), pp. 59–79.

Marböck, J., 'Henoch—Adam—der Thronwagen. Zu frühjüdischen pseudepigraphischen Traditionen bei Ben Sira', BZ 25 (1981), pp. 103–11.

Nickelsburg, G. W. E., JLBBM, pp. 55–69.

Saracino, F., 'La sapienza e la vita: Sir 4, 11–19', RBiblt 29 (1981), pp. 257–72.

Caquot, A., 'La Siracide a-t-il parlé d'une "espèce" humaine?', RHPhR 62 (1982), pp. 225–30.

Trenchard, W. C., *Ben Sira's View of Women: A Literary Analysis* (1982).

di Lella, A. A., 'The Poetry of Ben Sira', Eretz Israel XVI (1982), pp. 26*–33*.

Nelis, J. T., 'Sir 38, 15', in N. C. Delsman *et al.* (eds.), *Von Kanaan bis Kerala; Festschrift für J. P. M. van der Ploeg* (1982), pp. 173–84.

Jongeling, B., 'Un passage difficile dans le Siracide de Masada (Col. IV, 22a = Sir 42, 11e)', *ibid.*, pp. 303–10.

Kister, M., 'Bᵉṣūle Sefer Ben Sira', Lesonénu 47 (1983), pp. 125–46.

Sanders, J. T., *Ben Sira and Demotic Wisdom* (1983).

2. Wisdom Literature from Qumran

Although the Dead Sea Scrolls (e.g. the Exhortation in the Damascus Rule and the Thanksgiving Hymns from 1Q) comprise a large quantity of sapiential material, only two sufficiently well preserved (and published) documents fall primarily into the category of wisdom literature.[1]

(a) *4Q184*, using the familiar metaphor of the 'harlot' or the 'strange woman', depicts the dangers and attractions of false doctrine. The seductress, who is unnamed in the surviving text, is vividly portrayed in her actions ('prompt to oil her words'; 'a multitude of sins is in her skirts'; 'her couches are beds of corruption'; 'she lifts her eyelids naughtily to stare at a virtuous one and join him') and is described as ראשית כול דרכי עול , 'the beginning of all the ways of iniquity'.

This woman has been identified as symbolizing Rome,[2] or a group associated with Idumaeans and Macedonians (= Herodians and Hellen- ized Jews),[3] or a company of unfaithful members within the Community.[4] Another interpretation takes the poem to be a straightforward expression of Essene misogyny.[5] Although none of these exegeses is demonstrably impossible, the text itself includes nothing explicitly sectarian and makes perfect sense if understood simply as a fresh expression of the old biblical sapiential theme developed in Prov. 7:1–27.[6] Apart from the script which is probably from the first century B.C., the poem contains nothing specifically datable.

(b) *4Q185* is a poem three columns of which have survived, the third in a badly mutilated form. Palaeographically it is dated to the end of the Hasmonaean epoch.[7] The author exhorts a group, addressed as 'my people', 'the Simple', 'my sons', to seek wisdom and learn from the history of the patriarchal and Mosaic age.

It has been argued on linguistic grounds that the document antedates Qumran, a theory requiring further examination.[8]

---

1. Among fragments too small for translation but classified as sapiential, the following should be noted: *4Q485–7*, palaeographically assigned to the first century B.C. and described as 'Texte prophétique ou sapientiel' or 'Ouvrage sapientiel (?)' (Baillet, DJD VII, pp. 4–5); *4Q498*, 'Fragments hymniques ou sapientiels (?)', dated to the turn of the eras (DJD VII, pp. 73–4). On the other hand, although *4Q510–11* are entitled by Baillet 'Cantiques du Sage' (*ibid.*, pp. 215, 219), they appear rather to be akin to psalms of exorcism (cf. above p. 190, n. 10).

2. J. M. Allegro, PEQ (1964), pp. 53–5.

3. A. M. Gazov-Ginzberg, RQ 6 (1967), pp. 279–85 (a far-fetched theory).

4. J. Carmignac, RQ 5 (1965), pp. 361–71.

5. A. Dupont-Sommer, Annuaire du Collège de France 65 (1965/6), pp. 353–4.

6. Verbal connections between this document and Prov. 7:5, 9 and 12 have been noted by Allegro, DJD V, p. 84. J. Strugnell has advanced the view that the figure in *4Q184* is 'Dame Folly' (RQ 7 (1970), pp. 266–7).

7. Strugnell, RQ 7 (1970), p. 269.

8. H. Lichtenberger, *Qumrân* (ed. M. Delcor) (1978), pp. 161–2.

Editions

Allegro, J. M., and Anderson, A. A., *Qumrân Cave 4 I (4Q158–4Q186)* [DJD V] (1968), pp. 82–7, plates XXVIII-XXX.
Strugnell, J., 'Notes en marge du volume V des "Discoveries in the Judaean Desert of Jordan"', RQ 7 (1970), pp. 263–73.

Translations

English
Allegro, *op. cit.*
Strugnell, *op. cit.*
Vermes, DSSE[2], pp. 255–9.

Italian
Moraldi, L., MQ (1971), pp. 695–705.

Bibliography

Allegro, J. M., 'The Wiles of the Wicked Woman', PEQ (1964), pp. 53–5.
Carmignac, J., 'Poème allégorique sur la secte rivale', RQ 5 (1965), pp. 361–71.
Dupont-Sommer, A., 'Explication des textes hébreux et araméens découverts à Qumrân', Annuaire du Collège de France 65 (1965/6), pp. 353–5.
Gazov-Ginzberg, A. M., 'Double Meaning in a Qumran Work', RQ 6 (1967), pp. 279–85.
Lichtenberger, H., 'Eine weisheitliche Mahnrede in den Qumranfunden (4Q185)', in M. Delcor (ed.), *Qumrân : Sa piété, sa théologie et son milieu* (1978), pp. 137–62.

3. Pirqê Abôth

Gnomic wisdom did not die out in the age which followed Jesus Sirach. Jesus of Nazareth for example often taught in the form of proverbs. A collection of such sayings has also survived in Hebrew, and occasionally in Aramaic, the earliest elements of which no doubt belong to this period. This is the *Pirqê 'Abôth* or Sayings of the Fathers, called also simply *'Abôth*. Included among the tractates of the Mishnah, in the Fourth *Seder*, it stands out as a peculiar unit. While the rest of the Mishnah codifies the Jewish law, *'Abôth* is an anthology like the book of Jesus ben Sira. The principal difference is that *'Abôth* is not the work of a single individual, but a collection of sayings from some sixty named sages, most of whom are already known as prominent Torah scholars (cf. vol. II, pp. 356–80). As a rule, two or more typical maxims are preserved from each teacher, those which his disciples transmitted as his favourite counsels. Many are merely practical advice, but most of them are related in some way to the sphere of religious action and are regularly associated with the teaching, learning and practice of the Torah (cf. the examples listed in vol. II, p. 415). The masters whose pronouncements are assembled in this manner belong for the most part to the period of the Mishnah: i.e., approximately A.D. 70 to 200. But the most outstanding authorities of earlier times, from Simon the

Righteous to Hillel, Shammai and Gamaliel the Elder, are given pride of place.

'Abôth is divided into six chapters, the first four of which represent an earlier composition with 4:22 as a conclusion. Chapter 5 contains a group of numerical sayings (5:1–15), and several further words of wisdom none of which is attributed to a specific sage or rabbi. Only 5:20–3 are ascribed to named teachers; the last two (Ben Bag-Bag and Ben He-He) are pseudonyms. Chapter 6, known also as *Qinyan Torah* (Acquisition of the Torah) is a late addition to *'Abôth* probably for liturgical purposes (cf. Danby, *The Mishnah* (1933), p. 458, n. 12).

To the detailed bibliography of *'Abôth* printed in vol. I, pp. 81–2, must now be added the following:

Saldarini, A. J., 'The End of the Rabbinic Chain of Tradition', JBL 93 (1974), pp. 97–106.

Idem, The Fathers according to Rabbi Nathan (1975).

Sharvit, S., 'The Custom of Reading Abot on the Sabbath', Bar Ilan 13 (1976), pp. 169–87 (Hebr.).

Viviano, B. T., *Study as Worship: 'Aboth and the New Testament* (1978).

IV. DIDACTIC AND PARAENETICAL STORIES

1. The Book of Judith

A special kind of literature, didactic or paraenetical story-telling, was frequent in the period under review. On a more or less fictional basis, tales were told which the author intended to present as real history, yet not for the purpose of instruction in history, but to offer ethical and religious advice and encouragement. Readers were to learn from them—stories from Jewish history or from the lives of individuals re-arranged and altered as much as was necessary—that the fear of God is the highest wisdom, since in the end he always delivers his children even though they may temporarily experience need and danger.

The Book of Judith is a narration of this kind. The story is briefly as follows. Nebuchadnezzar, king of Assyria,[1] summoned the nations of the Near East, amongst them the inhabitants of Palestine, to join him in his fight against Arphaxad, king of Media. Since they disregarded his command, Nebuchadnezzar, after his victory over Arphaxad, sent his commander-in-chief Holophernes with powerful forces against these people of the West, to punish them for their disobedience. Holophernes carried out his order, devastated the lands and destroyed the holy places, so that Nebuchadnezzar alone would be worshipped as God (chaps. 1–3). When he had advanced as far as the plain of Esdraelon, the Jews, who had just returned from the captivity and re-established Temple worship (sic!), prepared to offer resistance. Under the command of the High-Priest Joakim, they barred the way to Holophernes at the fortress of Bethulia (Βαιτυλουα, Latin Bethulia) (chaps. 4–6) facing the plain of Esdraelon.[2] Whilst Holophernes was

---

1. Cf. J. Greenfield, 'Nebuchadnezzar's Campaign in the Book of Judith', Yediot (Bulletin of the Israel Exploration Society) 28 (1964), pp. 204–8 (Hebr.).

2. Bethulia is not mentioned anywhere outside Judith. It may be 'an imaginary city' endowed 'with a theophoric name for the purposes of a historical romance' (M. Avi-Yonah, 'Bethulia', Enc. Jud. 4, col. 749). Scholars who maintain that Bethulia actually existed have advanced two main theories. The first, placing the town in the extreme south of Palestine, twelve miles south of Raphia, probably arose from confusion with a real locality of similar name. But this can hardly be described as being 'opposite Esdraelon, facing Dothaim [i.e. Dothan]' (Jud. 4:6). Hence in the second theory Bethulia is situated further north, in Samaria. For the identification of Bethulia with Shechem, see C. C. Torrey, JOAS 20 (1899), pp. 160–72; id., The Apocryphal Literature (1945), pp. 91–3; cf. also G. Dalman, Sacred Sites and Ways (1935), p. 115, n. 2; F.-M. Abel, Géog. Pal. II, p. 283; C. Steuernagel, 'Bethulia', ZDPV 66 (1943), pp. 232–45. More recently Bethulia has been located at Qabatiya near Dothan: J. P. Free, 'Dothan', RB 69 (1962), pp. 266–70; Eissfeldt, Introduction, p. 586 and n. 4. In general, see F. Stummer, Geographie des

besieging Bethulia, and in the town distress was steadily mounting to a climax, Judith, a rich, beautiful and pious widow, resolved to save her people by an act of courage (chaps. 7–9). Accompanied by her maid, she went gorgeously clothed to the enemy encampment and, under the pretence that she was willing to show the enemy the way to Jerusalem, obtained access to Holophernes. Captivated by her beauty, Holophernes trusted her. After staying in the camp for three days she was summoned to a drinking party, at the end of which she was left alone with him in his tent. Holophernes however was so drunk that Judith was able to carry out her plan. She seized his sword and struck off his head. Then unmolested, she went away, leaving her maid to bring Holophernes' head in a sack. Thus she returned to Bethulia, where she was received with joy (chaps. 10–13). When the enemy forces discovered what had happened, they fled in all directions and were massacred with ease by the Jews. But Judith was extolled as saviour by all Israel (chaps. 14–16).

The book is a quasi-fictional narrative that exhorts readers to resist the enemies of their faith and freedom.[3] Motivated by traditional piety, the author depicts Judith as a 'religious woman' ($\theta\epsilon o\sigma\epsilon\beta\dot{\eta}s$) who 'worships the God of heaven night and day' and is very attentive to the observance of food and purity laws. But the story refers to a time when danger threatened not only the nation but also its religion, since Holophernes required that Nebuchadnezzar should be honoured as God. For this reason it is improbable that the work was occasioned by the enterprises against the Jews of Artaxerxes Ochus (359–338 B.C.) in 350 B.C. with which already Sulpicius Severus (*c.* 360–420) linked the tale of Judith, as have in modern times A. von Gutschmid, T. Nöldeke, W. Robertson Smith, J. Wellhausen, and O. Eissfeldt.[4] Such a

---

Buches Judith (1947); E. W. Saunders, 'Bethulia', IDB I, p. 403. H. Y. Priebatsch sees in Bethulia a conflation of 'Bethel and Ai': 'Das Buch Judith und seine hellenistischen Quellen', ZDPV 90 (1974), pp. 50–60.

3. Among contemporary students of Judith, A.-M. Dubarle suggests that a real episode from the Persian age lies at the origin of the Judith story, and that the event, whose date, place and circumstances are unidentifiable, was progressively idealised by the tradition. Cf. *Judith: Formes et sens des diverses traditions* I (1966), pp. 135–6. H. Haag (*Studien zum Buch Judith, 1963*) followed by G. E. W. Nickelsburg (JLBBM, pp. 107, 151, n. 7), define Judith as a 'parable' composed by means of a conflation of biblical characters: Judith reflects Miriam (Ex. 15:20–1), Deborah and Jael (Judg. 4–5), the woman of Thebez (Judg. 9:53–4) and the woman from Abel-beth-maacah (2 Sam. 20:14–22). She is modelled on Jewish heroes, among them her ancestor the patriarch Simeon (9:2–3; 9:8–10), David beheading Goliath with the Philistine's own sword, etc. She may also be portrayed as a female counterpart of Judas Maccabaeus (Nickelsburg, p. 152, n. 10).

4. In favour of the Artaxerxes III Ochus theory, see Sulpicius Severus, *Chron.* II, 14–16, CSEL I; A. von Gutschmid, *Kleine Schriften* V, p. 286; Th. Nöldeke, *Die alttestamentliche Literatur* (1868), p. 78; W. Robertson Smith, *The Old Testament in the Jewish Church* (²1892), p. 439; O. Eissfeldt, *Introduction*, pp. 586–7. Cf. also A. Alt, *Kleine Schriften zur*

hypothesis could be true only in a very general sense. Indeed it can scarcely be accidental that two generals, Orophernes and Bagoas, who participated in the campaigns of Artaxerxes Ochus against Egypt, Phoenicia and Judaea, should also play a rôle in the book of Judith. The story of Ochus therefore furnished the writer with his material, nomenclature, and also the general historical framework.[5] But so far as we know Ochus never demanded to be worshipped as God by the Jews, whilst this is precisely the central issue stressed in the Book of Judith.[6] Furthermore, the name Nebuchadnezzer proves that the author took his chief personages, not from the history of his own days, but from an earlier age. He wrote in a period during which the Jewish religion was specifically threatened, which brings to mind the Book of Daniel and the Maccabaean era. It is to this time therefore that the composition of

---

Geschichte des Volkes Israel II (1953), p. 359 (late Persian period); J. M. Grintz, *Sefer Yehudith* (1958) [c. 360 B.C.]; A.-M. Dubarle, *Judith: Formes et sens des diverses traditions* I (1966), pp. 126–36 [Persian epoch, p. 136, n. 23]. On the basis of two ostraca dating to the Persian period and containing the name Judith, M. Heltzer suggests that the book also should be assigned to the same era: cf. 'Eine neue Quelle zur Bestimmung der Abfassungszeit des Judith-buches', ZAW 92 (1980), p. 437. The first ostracon reads יהדת דלוי ברת. Cf. R. Degen, 'Die aramäischen Ostraka in der Papyrus-Sammlung der Österreichischen Nationalbibliothek', Neue Ephemeris für semitische Epigraphik 3 (1978), pp. 43–7. The second, originally edited by M. Lidzbarski in Ephemeris für semitische Epigraphik 3 (1915), p. 299 as ... ליה׳ רתב, is reinterpreted by Heltzer as ... ליהדת ברת. Be this as it may, the value of the argument is slight.

5. In an account of the history and genealogy of the Cappadocian kings, Diodorus (xxxi 19, 2–3) reports that Holophernes, brother of king (satrap) Ariarathes, was despatched by him to fight with the Persians against the Egyptians, and was then sent back invested with great honour by Artaxerxes III Ochus, king of the Persians. It is uncertain which Egyptian campaign of Ochus is intended, because Holophernes is not otherwise named in the history of the wars; cf. however Marquart, Philologus 54 (1895), pp. 507–10. In his account of the campaign of Ochus against Phoenicia and Egypt in 350 B.C., Diodorus also mentions (xvi 47, 4) amongst the commanders a certain Bagoas, who, according to xvii 5, 3, was a eunuch (cf. also RE, s.v.). The name Bagoas is common; the story of the profanation of the Jewish Temple by a certain Bagoses or Bagoas occurred under Artaxerxes II (*Ant.* xi 7, 1 (297)), considerably earlier therefore; see above, p. 6. On one of his Egyptian campaigns, Ochus took Jewish prisoners and settled them in Hyrcania, on the Caspian Sea (Eusebius, *Chron.*, ed. Schoene II, p. 112, *ad ann. Abr.* 1657; Syncellus, ed. Dindorf, I, 486; Orosius III, 7; Solinus 35, 4—for the exact quotations, see above, p. 6, note 12). Since therefore a Holophernes and a eunuch Bagoas play a role in the Book of Judith (12:11, 13, 15; 13:1, 3; 14:14) in campaigns of the Great King directed against the peoples of the West, and particularly against the Jews, it is probable that the history of Ochus provided the author with a part of his material. There was also about the middle of the second century B.C. a Cappadocian king called Ὀλοφέρνης or Ὀροφέρνης (Diodorus xxxi, 32; Justin xxxv, 1; Polybius iii 5, 2; xxxii, 20; xxxiii, 12; Appian, Syr. 47). The name itself is of Persian origin. The combination of the two names (Holophernes *and* Bagoas) possesses great evidential value; Bagoas alone would be less decisive because this name was common (Pliny, *Hist. Nat.* xiii, 41: 'Ita vocant spadones, qui apud eos etiam regnavere'). Cf. J. H. Hayes and J. M. Miller (eds.), *Israelite and Judaean History* (1977), pp. 499–503.

6. No further anti-Jewish activities of Artaxerxes Ochus are known.

the book is in all probability to be dated.[7] As the author's interest seems to focus as strongly on political as on religious freedom, it is perhaps not of the first stage of the rebellion, but of a somewhat later date that one should think. It is not advisable to go down to the Roman period, for the political background (the High-Priest as sovereign of the Jewish state, the Hellenistic towns as independent political entities under obligation to their overlord only for emergency military conscription) corresponds more closely to the Hellenistic than to the Roman epoch. Moreover, since Jamnia and Azotus are not yet represented as part of the Jewish territory (Jud. 2:28), the reign of Alexander Jannaeus should be seen as the *terminus ante quem.*

The identity of the author is unknown, but speculative scholars have located him in Syria (Antioch or the province of Apamea).[8] It is commonly held that the Book of Judith derives from a Hebrew original.[9]

There is no early attestation of a Semitic text of Judith. No trace of it has been found at Qumran, not even in Greek. In Origen's time no Hebrew text was known, nor was the book in use among Palestinian Jews. Ἑβραῖοι τῷ Τωβίᾳ οὐ χρῶνται οὐδὲ τῇ ᾿Ιουδήθ· οὐδὲ γὰρ ἔχουσιν αὐτὰ ἐν ἀποκρύφοις ἑβραϊστί· ὡς ἀπ' αὐτῶν μαθόντες ἐγνώκαμεν (*Ep. ad Africanum* 13). The original Hebrew—if it was the original—disappeared at an early date. By contrast, an Aramaic text was available to Jerome (Opp. ed. Vall. X, 21): 'Apud Hebraeos liber Iudith inter apocrypha (*al.* hagiographa) legitur ... Chaldaeo sermone conscriptus inter historias computatur.' He asserts that he employed it in producing the Vulgate (see below). The various medieval Hebrew midrashic recensions are generally believed not to reflect the original. Cf. Zunz, pp. 131–2; A. Jellinek, *Beth ha-Midrasch* I (1853), pp. 130–1; II (1854), pp. 12–22; M. Gaster, 'An Unknown Hebrew Version of the History of Judith', PSBA 16 (1893–4), pp. 156–63; M. Higger, *Halakhoth we-Aggadoth* II (1933), pp. 105–13; B. M. Levin, Sinai 3 (1940), pp. 68–72; D. S. Löwinger, *Yehudith-Shoshanah* (1940). The fullest edition of the Hebrew Judith is A.-M. Dubarle, *Judith: Formes et sens des diverses traditions* I (Etudes), II (Textes) (1966). Dubarle prints as Text B a twelfth-century Bodleian manuscript (Heb. d. 11, ff. 259–65); text C is represented in printed editions (Venice 1651; Mantova 1725) under the title מעשה יהודית; text D is a revision of C

---

7. Cf. Eissfeldt, *Introduction*, p. 587; P. Winter, 'Judith', IDB II, p. 1025.

8. Cf. S. Zeitlin in M. S. Enslin, *The Book of Judith* (1972), p. 32; B. Z. Luria, 'Jews of Syria in the Days of Antiochus Epiphanes and the Book of Judith', Beth Miqra 62 (1975), pp. 328–41 (Hebr.).

9. Cf. Eissfeldt, *Introduction*, p. 587, F. Zimmermann, 'Aids for the Recovery of the Hebrew Original of Judith', JBL 57 (1938), pp. 67–74; Y. M. Grintz, *Sefer Yehudith*, pp. 56–63.

and is printed in Jellinek II, and text E is attested in a Bodleian manuscript (Heb. d. 47) edited by Higger and Lewin (= E¹) and in a manuscript from the Kaufmann collection in Budapest, edited by Löwinger (E²). Although Dubarle ascribes priority to the Hebrew, especially Text B, over the Vulgate and the Greek (*op. cit.* I, pp. 48–74) and discards the theory of the Hebrew being a translation from the Aramaic (*ibid.* pp. 75–6), he has not been able convincingly to refute the theory that the medieval texts are retranslations into Hebrew probably from the Vulgate (cf. Y. M. Grintz, *Sefer Yehudith* (1957); 'Judith, Book of', Enc. Jud. 10, col. 461).¹⁰

Regarding patristic references to Judith, the earliest allusion comes from Clement of Rome (*c.* A.D. 96) who mentions Ἰουδὶθ ἡ μακαρία (1 Clem. 55:4). Tertullian, *De monogamia* 173 (PL 2, col. 952): 'Nec Iohannes aliqui Christi spado, nec Iudith filia Merari, nec tot alia exempla sanctorum.' Clement of Alexandria, *Stromata* ii 7, 35; iv 19, 118 (in the latter passage, Judith is expressly named). Origen's citation of a fragment from *Strom.* vi is reproduced by Jerome in *Adversus Rufinum* i: 'Homo autem cui incumbit necessitas mentiendi, diligenter attendat ut sic utatur interdum mendacio quomodo condimento atque medicamine; ut servet mensuram eius, ne excedat terminos quibus usa est Iudith contra Holophernem et vicit eum prudenti simulatione verborum.' Other quotations may be found in *Comm. in Ioannem* 2:16 (ed. Preuschen, GCS IV); *In lib. Iudicum homilia* 9:1 (Baehrens, CCS 30, p. 518); *In lib. Ieremiae homilia* 19:7 (GCS 6, p. 187); *De oratione* 29 (Koetschau, GCS 2, p. 382). For additional references, see Dubarle, *op. cit.* I, pp. 110–25.

The text of Judith is extant in Greek, Latin, Syriac and Ethiopic.

(1) The *Greek* text appears in four recensions. 1. The original text is that of the textus receptus (Vaticanus, Alexandrinus, and Sinaiticus, etc.). 2. A revised text underlies Codex 58. 3. Another recension is contained in Codices 19 and 108. 4. A further recension comes from Codices 106 and 107. The oldest attestation is an ostracon dating to the second half of the third century A.D. and representing fragments of Jud. 15:1–7 (J. Schwartz, 'Un fragment grec du livre de Judith', RB 53 (1946), pp. 534–7 and pl. VII). For a survey of the Greek texts, see Dubarle, *op. cit.* I, pp. 11–15. The most important work relating to textual criticism is R. Hanhart, *Text und Textgeschichte des Buchs Judith* (1978). For the editions, see under 1 Mac. The Greek text is now available in the Göttingen *Septuaginta* VIII.4: R. Hanhart, *Iudith* (1979).

(2) The *Latin* versions, and especially the *Old Latin*, exhibit such wide

---

10. The story of Judith is well attested in late midrashic literature and in connection with the Hanukkah liturgy. Cf. Dubarle, *op. cit.* I, pp. 80–102.

textual divergences one from another that they fully corroborate the stricture made by Jerome in his day concerning the 'multorum codicum varietas vitiosissima' (see below). For the *Vetus latina*, see P. Sabatier, *Bibliorum sacrorum latinae versiones antiquae* I (1745), pp. 746–90. Cf. Dubarle, *op. cit.* I, pp. 15–19. S. Berger records eleven manuscripts of the Old Latin text for the Book of Judith (*Notices et extraits des manuscrits de la Bibliothèque Nationale et autres Bibliothèques* XXXIV, 2 (1893), pp. 142 f.). On most of these, see further his *Histoire de la Vulgate* (1893), *passim*. The Vulgate, according to Jerome, is a somewhat hurriedly made, free revision of the Old Latin: 'Apud Hebraeos liber Judith inter apocrypha (al. hagiographa) legitur ... Chaldaeo tamen sermone conscriptus inter historias computatur. Sed quia hunc librum Synodus Nicaena in numero sanctarum scripturarum legitur computasse, acquievi postulationi vestrae, immo exactioni, et sepositis occupationibus, quibus vehementer arctabar, huic unam lucubratiunculam dedi, magis sensum e sensu quam ex verbo verbum transferens. Multorum codicum varietatem vitiosissimam amputavi: sola ea, quae intelligentia integra in verbis Chaldaeis invenire potui, Latinis expressi' (Preface, ed. Vallarsi X, pp. 21–2). For the text, see *Biblia sacre iuxta latinam vulgatam versionem* VIII: *Libri Ezrae, Tobiae, Iudith* (1950). Cf. Dubarle, *op. cit.* I, pp. 44–6.

(3) For the *Syriac* version, see above, under 1 Mac. Cf. further A. Rahlfs, in P. A. de Lagarde, *Bibliotheca Syriaca* (1892), pp. 32^c–32^i, cf. 19–21; E. Nestle, *Marginalien und Materialien* (1893), pp. 43 ff.

(4) The *Ethiopic* version is edited by A. Dillmann, *Biblia Veteris Testamenti Aethiopica* V (1894).

Commentaries

Scholz, A., *Commentar über das Buch Judith* ([2]1896).
Löhr, M., in E. Kautzsch, APAT I (1900), pp. 147–64.
Cowley, A. E., in R. H. Charles, APOT (1913), pp. 242–67.
Miller, A., in F. Feldmann and H. Herkenne, *Die Heilige Schrift des Alten Testaments* (1940).
Soubigou, L., in L. Pirot and A. Clamer, *La Sainte Bible* (1949).
Stummer, F., in *Die Heilige Schrift in deutscher Uebersetzung* (1950).
Barucq, A., in *Bible de Jérusalem* (1952, [2]1959).
Bückers, H., in Herder's *Bibelkommentar* (1953).
Simon, M., in A. Kahana, *Ha-Sefarîm Ha-ḥiṣônîm* ([2]1956).
Grintz, J. M., *Sefer Yehudith* (1957).
Enslin, M. S., *The Book of Judith* (1972).
Zenger, E., *Das Buch Judith* (JSHRZ I 6) (1981).

Studies

Gaster, M., 'Judith', EB II (1901), cols. 2642–6.
Meyer, C., 'Zur Entstehungsgeschichte des Buches Judith', Bibl 3 (1922), pp. 193–203.
Brunner, G., *Der Nabuchodonosor des Buches Judith* (1940, [2]1959).

Stummer, F., *Geographie des Buchs Judith* (1947).
Dubarle, A.-M., 'Les textes divers du livre de Judith', VT 8 (1958), pp. 344–73.
Idem, 'La mention de Judith dans la littérature ancienne juive et chrétienne', RB 66 (1959), pp. 514–49.
Winter, P., 'Judith, Book of', IDB II (1962), pp. 1023–6.
Haag, H., 'Die besondere Art des Buches Judith und seine theologische Bedeutung', Trierer ThZ 71 (1962), pp. 288–301. *Id.*, *Studien zum Buch Judith* (1963).
Skehan, P. W., 'Why leave out Judith?', CBQ 24 (1962), pp. 147–54.
Idem, 'The Hand of Judith', CBQ 25 (1963), pp. 94–110.
Grintz, J. M., 'Judith', Enz. Miq. III (1965), cols. 510–17.
Zenger, E., 'Der Judithroman als Traditionsmodell des Jahweglaubens', Trierer ThZ 83 (1974), pp. 65–80.
Luria, B. Z., 'Jews of Syria in the Days of Antiochus Epiphanes and the Book of Judith', Beth Miqra 62 (1975), pp. 328–41 (Hebr.).
Alonso-Schökel, L., 'Narrative Structures in the Book of Judith', The Center for Hermeneutical Studies in Hellenistic and Modern Culture, Colloquy 11 (1975), pp. 1–20.
Craven, T., 'Artistry and Faith in the Book of Judith', Semeia 8 (1977), pp. 75–101.
Nickelsburg, G. E. W., JLBBM, pp. 105–9, 151–2.

2. The Book of Tobit

The Book of Tobit is a work similar in type to that of Judith, except that its milieu is not the field of political history but that of biography, and it accordingly addresses its paraenesis not to the nation at large, but to individuals.

Tobit, the son of Tobiel of the tribe of Naphtali, who in the days of Shalmaneser king of Assyria was taken captive to Nineveh, relates (in the first person) how he, together with his wife Anna and his son Tobias, lived in strict conformity with the requirements of the ceremonial and dietary laws both before and after captivity, and also under kings Sennacherib and Esarhaddon. He had been particularly zealous in performing acts of charity; he fed hungry Jews, clothed the naked and buried the bodies of those of his countrymen killed by Sennacherib and left unburied. Once, when he was sleeping in his courtyard after performing one of these services of love, some sparrow droppings fell in his eyes, as a result of which he became blind (chapters 1:1–3:6). At the same time, a young Jewish woman lived in Ekbatana in Media, Sarah daughter of Raguel, who had already had seven husbands, all of whom had been killed by the evil spirit Asmodaeus on the nuptial night before consummating the marriage (3:7–17). The aged Tobit remembered in his distress that he had once deposited ten talents of silver with a fellow tribesman, Gabael, in Rages in Media. Since he expected to die, he therefore sent his son Tobias there with instructions to have the money, which he was to inherit, handed over. Tobias set out, taking with him a hired guide who was in actual fact the angel Raphael (chapters 4–5). On the way, Tobias bathed in the river Tigris, and caught a fish. At the command of the angel, he cut out its heart, liver and gall, and took these with him. They reached Ekbatana, and lodged with Raguel. Raguel recognized a kinsman in Tobias, and gave him his daughter Sarah as wife. As soon as the newlyweds entered the bridal chamber Tobias, acting on the angel's instructions, prepared smoke from the heart and liver of the fish and drove away with these fumes the demon Asmodaeus, who wished to kill him as he had killed Sarah's other husbands. The fourteen days of the wedding feast therefore passed undisturbed and the angel meanwhile went to Rages to receive the money from Gabael (chapters 6–9). The festivities over, Tobias returned with his wife Sarah to his parents at Nineveh, where he restored sight to the eyes of his blind father Tobit by treating them with the gall of the fish, according to the angel's instructions (chapters 10–12). Full of gratitude to God, Tobit sang a song of praise, and lived for almost another hundred years. Tobias, too, lived until he was 127 years old (chapters 13–14).

The tale is skilfully organized, the detail copious, and the various threads of the story dexterously interwoven. As a literary product this book therefore ranks considerably higher than Judith. The religious viewpoint is not unlike in both works. Here, too, stress is laid on the observance of ceremonial, dietary and purity laws, but the practice of acts of charity is given equal, if not greater, prominence. The work, incidentally, provides instructive glimpses into the superstitions of the period.

As the entire story takes place in Assyria and Media, the author seems to have written predominantly for Jews of the Diaspora. By means of the examples which he holds up before the readers' eyes, he wishes to work towards holding the members of the nation scattered in the pagan world true to Judaism, strictly and conscientiously faithful to the Law. Whether the book originated in Palestine or in the Dispersion continues to be debated.[1]

The date of composition can only be fixed within somewhat wide limits. It may be taken as tolerably certain that the book was written before Herod had begun the reconstruction of the Temple around 20 B.C. Reference to this operation (13:16–17; 14:4–5) does not imply a date posterior to A.D. 70. The most likely theory envisages the redaction of Tobit at a time when the Temple of Zerubbabel was still standing. The author imagines himself to be in the Assyrian age, and can therefore predict, first the destruction of the Temple by the Babylonians, and then its rebuilding after the return from exile. He foresees (1) the erection of an unpretentious building until a certain period had elapsed; and (2) the subsequent construction of a splendid

---

1. Cf. Eissfeldt, *Introduction*, p. 585; F. Zimmermann, *The Book of Tobit* (1958), pp. 15–21. In addition to the Eastern diaspora and Judaea, Egypt and Syria have been proposed. According to J. T. Milik, Tobit is a Samaritan work re-edited in Jewish circles: 'La patrie de Tobie', RB 73 (1966), pp. 523–30.

sanctuary: 'And they will rebuild the house of God, though it will not be like the former one until the times of the ages are completed. After this they will return from the place of their captivity, and will rebuild Jerusalem in splendour. And the house of God will be rebuilt there with a glorious building for all generations for ever, just as the prophets said of it' (14:5). The Temple which the author knew is also simpler than the earlier Solomonic Temple. He would therefore scarcely have expressed himself in these terms had he already known the magnificent Temple of Herod. That Temple forms the final *terminus ad quem* for the composition of the book. Since there is no allusion to the desecration of the sanctuary under Antiochus Epiphanes, it may reasonably be assumed that Tobit was written before the Maccabaean era, probably in the third century B.C. The absence of any resurrection hope appears to corroborate such a dating.[2]

The Semitic, Hebrew or Aramaic linguistic origin of Tobit has been generally accepted in modern times.[3] In fact, already in antiquity Jerome was acquainted with an Aramaic text of this book, in the same way that he knew also an Aramaic Judith (see above, p. 219). His preface to his version of Tobit reads: 'Exigitis ut librum Chaldaeo sermone conscriptum ad Latinam stylum traham, librum utique Tobiae' (ed. Vallarsi, X, p. 1). A full Aramaic recension, contained in a fifteenth century manuscript of various midrashim, was published in 1878 by A. Neubauer in *The Book of Tobit. A Chaldee Text from a Unique Manuscript in the Bodleian Library.* Jerome's version and the Aramaic text agree in presenting the whole story in a third person narrative, whereas the Greek text and the versions dependent on it transmit Tobit 1:1–3:6 in autobiographical style.[4] Neubauer's Aramaic version cannot, therefore, be recognized as the prototype of the Greek Tobit. Indeed, the stylistic simplification is more probably a secondary feature. (For the Hebrew versions, which are late, see below, p. 230.) The high quality of the Greek could be, and was, used in favour of considering it as original, and not a translation. Nevertheless, the Semitisms of the recension preserved in Sinaiticus and the presumed early date of the composition have been seen as arguments strongly in favour of a Hebrew or Aramaic original.[5] Since the discovery in Qumran Cave 4 of

2. Zimmermann, *op. cit.*, pp. 25, 27, argues for a post-A.D. 70 date.

3. Eissfeldt, *Introduction*, p. 585. Cf. also M. M. Schumpp, *Das Buch Tobias* (1933), p. xlvii.

4. The same switch from a first person memoir to a third person description is found in IQapGen. (see below, p. 320).

5. Among scholars favouring a Greek original we find O. F. Fritzsche, *Die Bücher Tobit und Judith* (1853), p. 8; T. Nöldeke, 'Die Texte des Buches Tobit', Monatschr. BAW (1879), p. 61; M. Löhr, 'Tobit', Kautzsch APAT I (1900), p. 136. Proposers of a Semitic original (H = Hebrew; A = Aramaic): H. Grätz, 'Das Buch Tobias oder Tobit' (H), MGWJ 27 (1879); I. Lévi, 'La langue originale de Tobit' (H), REJ 44 (1902), pp.

fragments from five Tobit manuscripts, the issue appears to be settled. They are still unpublished, but their prospective editor, J. T. Milik, reports that four are in Aramaic and one in Hebrew. In his opinion, priority is to be given to the Aramaic, but both Semitic versions attest the longer recension (i.e. Sinaiticus and Vetus Latina, see below, pp. 227–30).[6]

On the story of Ahiqar, to which allusion is made in 14:10, see pp. 232–39 below.

288–91; J. T. Marshall (A), HDB IV (1902), p. 788; D. C. Simpson, 'The Book of Tobit' (H or A), Charles, APOT I (1913) (H or A) pp. 180–2; P. Joüon, 'Quelques hébraïsmes du Codex Sinaiticus de Tobie' (H), Bibl 4 (1923), pp. 168–74; M. M. Schumpp, *Das Buch Tobias* (H or A) (1933); F. Zimmermann, *The Book of Tobit* (A), pp. 38, 139–49.

6. J. T. Milik, 'La patrie de Tobie', RB 73 (1966), p. 523, n. 3; cf. *Ten Years of Discovery in the Wilderness of Judaea* (1959), pp. 31–2; p. 60. Milik reports to have identified the following fragments (the four Aramaic manuscripts are designated as *a1* to *a4*, and the Hebrew as *h*):

	a1	*a2*	*a3*	*a4*	*h*
Tobit	*1:17*				
	1:19–2:2				
	2:3				
	3:5				
			3:6–8		*3:6*
	3:9–15				3:10–11
	3:17				
	4:2–3				
	4:5–7				*4:3–9*
	4:21–5:1	*4:21–5:1*			
	5:3				5:2
	5:9				
		5:12–14			
	6:6–8	5:19–6:12			
		6:12–18			
	6:13, 15–18				
	6:18–7:6	*6:18–7:10*		7:11	
	7:13				
		8:17–19			
		8:21–9:4			
					10:7–9
					11:10–14
	12:18–22				*12:20–13:4*
	13:4–6				
	13:6–12				
	13:12–14:3				*13:13–14*
				14:2–6, 8–11	*13:18–14:2*
	14:7				
			14:10		

References printed in italics are attested in more than one manuscript.

In many respects, the tale of the grateful dead, which appears in countless variations among many peoples, is analogous to the Book of Tobit. An Armenian story in particular is reminiscent of it. A wealthy man rides through a wood and sees people abusing a corpse. The reason, he discovers, is that the man died owing them money. The stranger pays the debt and buries the dead. In the meanwhile he becomes poor. In his native town lives a rich man with an only daughter who has already married five husbands; but every one of them had died on the bridal night. The impoverished one, on the advice of an unknown manservant, nevertheless dares to marry her. On the wedding night, a snake crawls out of the mouth of the bride, intending to bite the bridegroom to death. But the unknown manservant, who has kept guard, kills it, saves the bridegroom's life, and makes himself known as the dead person whom he once buried. In a Russian story, it is the survivor of two brothers who looks after the burial of the dead one. When this survivor marries a merchant's daughter who had already lost two husbands on the bridal nights, the dead brother keeps watch in the marriage chamber and slays the dragon which once again intends to kill the young husband.[7] Since in the case of Tobit, it is his zeal for burying the dead that is praised, and since the young Tobias undergoes experiences resembling those of the heroes of these stories, there are striking similarities—but also marked differences. The evidence, in fact, is not such that any firm conclusion can be reached regarding any influence of these legends on the Tobit story. In particular, the great antiquity of those forms of the story in which there are real contacts with Tobit cannot be established.[8]

An Egyptian story, the Tractate of Khons or Khonsu preserved on the Bentresh Stela dating to *c.* 500 B.C., is also often cited as having parallel features. A princess living in the town of Bakhtan or Bechtan[9] was possessed by a demon, and Khons(u), 'the executor of plans', was

7. Cf. K. Simrock, *Der gute Gerhard und die dankbaren Todten* (1856); A. F. von Haxtausen, *Transkaukasia* I (1856), pp. 333–4; R. Köhler, *Germania* 3 (1858), pp. 202–3; E. Cosquin, 'Encore l'histoire du sage Ahikar, vraies et fausses infiltrations d'Ahikar dans la Bible', RB 8 (1899), pp. 513–15; G. H. Gerould, *The Grateful Dead* (1908); S. Liljeblad, *Die Tobiasgeschichte und andere Märchen mit toten Helfern* (1927); L. Ruppert, 'Das Buch Tobias—Ein Modellfall nachgestaltender Erzählung', in J. Schreiner (ed.), *Wort, Lied und Gottesspruch* (1972), pp. 109–19.

8. Cf. in general D. C. Simpson, APOT I, p. 188; M. Schumpp, *Das Buch Tobias* (1933), pp. LXXIV-VI; A. Miller, *Das Buch Tobias* (1940), p. 10. According to Schumpp and Miller, the legends depend on Tobit, and not vice versa.

9. *Bkhtn* is probably a corrupted Egyptian rendering of Bactria (cf. G. Lefebvre, *Romans et contes égyptiens de l'époque pharaonique* (1949), p. 227) rather than of Ekbatana (H. Schneider, see n. 11). The stela is from Karnak. It is now in the Louvre (C 284).

sent by the god of Thebes to exorcize and heal her.[10] However, whilst there is no problem concerning the age of the legend, the similarity is too faint to permit any firm suggestion of direct dependence.[11]

According to Origen, the Book of Tobit was not in use amongst Palestinian Jews of his time, and no Hebrew text of it was known (*Epistola ad Africanum*, 13, quoted on p. 219 above; cf. also *De oratione*, 14 (ed. Koetschau, GCS 2, p. 331): τῇ δὲ τοῦ Τωβὴτ βιβλῳ ἀντιλέγουσιν οἱ ἐκ περιτομῆς ὡς μὴ ἐνδιαθήκῳ). That it soon became popular, however, is proved by the extant Aramaic and Hebrew texts, one of which was known already to Jerome.

The use of the book in the Christian Church is attested already in the Apostolic Fathers. Cf. 2 Clem. 16:4 and Tobit 12:8–9; Ep. Polycarp 10:2 and Tobit 4:10, 12:9. Irenaeus i 30, 11, writes that the Ophites reckoned Tobias among the Old Testament prophets. Clement of Alexandria mentions the story of Tobias and his father Tobit, *Strom.*, i, 21, 123 (ed. Stählin, p. 77), and cites the book several times as γραφή, *Strom.*, ii, 23, 139; vi, 12, 102 (ed. Stählin, pp. 190, 483). Hippolytus draws the story of Tobit into his commentary on Susanna as a parallel (*In Dan.* 1:28, ed. Bonwetsch, p. 40). Origen, *Epistola ad Africanum*, 13 (PG 11, col. 80), makes ample reference to the story of Tobit, adding the general remark: χρῶνται τῷ Τωβίᾳ αἱ ἐκκλησίαι. He also often cites it as γραφή: *Comment in epist. ad Rom.* 8:12 (PG 14, col. 1193); *De oratione* 11:1, 14:4 and 31:5 (ed. Koetschau, pp. 321, 331, 398–9); *Contra Celsum* 5:19 and 29 (ed. Koetschau, pp. 20, 31). Cyprian makes frequent use of the book (*Testimonia*, iii, 1, 6, 62; *Ad Fortunam* 11; *De opere et eleemosynis* 5 and 20). For further information, see Schumpp, *op. cit.*, pp. lxii–vi; J. Gamberoni, *Die Auslegung des Buches Tobias in der griechisch-lateinischen Kirche der Antike und der Christenheit des Westens bis 1600* (1969).

Of the Greek text, three recensions exist. (1) The so-called common text preserved in most manuscripts, amongst others the Vaticanus, Alexandrinus and Venetus. On the relationship of these two manuscripts see A. Schulte, 'In welchem Verhältnis steht der Codex Alexandrinus zum Codex Vaticanus im Buche Tobias?', BZ (1908), pp. 262–6. The Syriac version follows this recension as far as 7:9. (2) The text of Sinaiticus diverges very sharply from the common text. The Old Latin follows this, not absolutely, but in the main. (3) The text of

---

10. J. H. Breasted, *Ancient Records of Egypt* III (1906), pp. 429–47; G. Roeder, *Urkunden zur Religion des alten Ägypten* (1923), pp. 169–73; J. A. Wilson, 'The Legend of the Possessed Princess', J. B. Pritchard (ed.), ANET (1950), pp. 29–31; Miriam Lichtheim, *Ancient Egyptian Literature. A Book of Readings* III, *The Late Period* (1980), pp. 90–4.

11. The theory of Tobit being a reshaped version of the Tractate of Khons(u) was advanced by H. Schneider, *Kultur und Denken der Babylonier und Juden* (1910), pp. 638–9. However, there is no valid argument in favour of a western (Egyptian) origin of Tobit, and, characteristically, neither Wilson nor Lichtheim makes any reference to our apochryphon.

codices 44, 106, 107 and, for chapter 2, POxyrhynchus 1076, which is related to that of Sinaiticus. This applies however only to chapters 6:9–13:8; before and afterwards, the manuscripts follow the common recension. This text lies at the basis of the Syriac from chapter 7:10 onwards. In O. F. Fritzsche, *Libri Apocryphi Veteris Testamenti Graece* (1871), three texts are printed complete in parallel columns. H. B. Swete (*The Old Testament in Greek*, II, pp. 815–48) prints both the Vaticanus and the Sinaiticus, the one above the other. The text of Sinaiticus is separately edited by F. H. Reusch, *Libellus Tobit e codice Sinaitico editus et recensitus* (1870). A. E. Brooke, N. McLean, H. St. J. Thackeray, *The Old Testament in Greek*, III, part 1 (1940), give (pp. 85–122) the full Greek text of Vaticanus and Sinaiticus, with a copious critical apparatus; they also print (pp. 123–44) the Old Latin text of P. Sabatier (1751), with a full critical apparatus. The latest and best edition is that of the Göttingen Septuagint by R. Hanhart, *Tobit* (1983).

Whether the common text or that of Sinaiticus is the original is still subject to controversy, but opinion has tended in more recent times to favour the latter. The greater originality of the common text was still defended by such scholars as O. F. Fritzsche, Th. Nöldeke, M. Löhr, and J. Müller; that of Sinaiticus, by H. Grätz, E. Nestle, J. Rendell Harris, D. C. Simpson, F. Zimmermann, and A. Wikgren. But already prior to the Qumran finds (see above), a cogent case could be made out in favour of the priority of the Sinaiticus recension, at least in substance, if not in every detail. In many instances the common text no doubt exhibits the better reading, hence probably the more primitive form. But by and large the more detailed, prolix text of Sinaiticus is surely the original. Its prolixity is not an elaboration of a situation by real and meaningful features, but simply the long-winded style of the original author, whose text was polished and abbreviated by later redactors. The stylistic polish is in many cases so obvious that it was candidly acknowledged even by J. Müller (BZAW XIII (1908), pp. 35–53). The abbreviations seem in general to afford evidence that the common text is the later one. A confirmation of this occurs right at the beginning in the remarkable textual divergences in respect of the tributes prescribed by the Law which, Tobit assumes, he has conscientiously fulfilled (1:6–8). According to the text of Sinaiticus, he has amongst other things presented to the priests a tithe of cattle (τὰς δεκάτας τῶν κτηνῶν); in the common text this is deleted. The text of Sinaiticus corresponds to the older usage, which is founded on Lev. 27:32–3 and retained also in the Book of Jubilees, 32:15. According to the later ruling codified in the Mishnah, the tithe of beasts came to be treated as 'second tithe'—that is to say, not given to the priests but utilised by the worshipper himself at the sacrificial festival meals in

Jerusalem (see vol. II, p. 264). The common text of Tobit has been corrected to agree with this later usage. Another difference is that according to the text of the Sinaiticus, Tobit gave the second tithe every third year to the poor, whereas in the common text after mention of the second tithe it is said that he gave the third tithe to the poor. Here, too, the text of the Sinaiticus corresponds to the earlier, and the common text to the later usage; according to the former, the poor tithe took the place every third year of the second tithe, according to the latter, the poor tithe was added every third year to the second tithe. (See vol. II, p. 264, n. 23.) The text of Sinaiticus demonstrates its priority also by the allusion in Tobit 14:10 to the legend of Ahiqar. On Ahiqar, see pp. 232–39.

The thesis set out in the preceding paragraph appears as proven to all intents and purposes in the light of the reported characteristics of the Tobit fragments from Qumran Cave 4. According to J. T. Milik, both the Aramaic and Hebrew texts reflect the longer recension of the Sinaiticus and Vetus Latina type. The Sinaiticus text contains however two long omissions due to *homoeoteleuton*. There the 4Q evidence is said to be in line with the Old Latin translation, as is also the case with the reference to *seven* sons of Tobiah in Tobit 14:3 (Milik, *Ten Years*, pp. 31–2).

Of the ancient versions the following are to be mentioned.

(1) The Latin, and specifically (a) the Old Latin version, the text of which, in the four manuscripts collated by Sabatier, exhibits very considerable variations but in essence agrees with the Sinaiticus (P. Sabatier, *Bibliorum sacrorum Latinae versiones antiquae*, vol. I). Sabatier's four manuscripts represent two recensions, one contained in Codex Regius 3564 from Paris and Codex Sangermanensis 4 and 15, the other in Vaticanus 7. Quotations in *Speculum Augustini*, edited by A. Mai in *Nova Patrum Bibliotheca* (1852) and reissued by F. Weihrich in CSEL XII (1887), offer fragments of a third recension. S. Berger lists in all twelve further manuscripts of the Old Latin text of the Book of Tobit (*Notices et extraits des manuscrits de la Bibliothèque Nationale et autres Bibliothèques* 24 (1893), p. 142). For further information, see Berger, *Histoire de la Vulgate* (1893), *passim*. (b) The translation of Jerome, the *Vulgate*, came into being in the same way as his revision of the Book of Judith. See his preface to his version of Tobit: 'Exigitis, ut librum Chaldaeo sermone conscriptum ad Latinum stilum traham, librum utique Tobiae, quem Hebraei de catalogo divinarum Scripturarum secantes his quae apocrypha (al. hagiographa) memorant manciparunt. Feci satis desiderio vestro … Et quia vicina est Chaldaeorum lingua sermoni Hebraico, utriusque linguae peritissimum loquacem reperiens, unius diei laborem arripui, et quidquid ille mihi Hebraicis verbis expressit, hoc ego accito notario sermonibus Latinis exposui' (PL

29, col. 23). A comparison of the Vulgate with the Old Latin demonstrates that Jerome used the latter as his basis and freely reworked it, perhaps taking into account the Aramaic text. A fuller evaluation must await the publication of the Qumran fragments. For the text of the Vulgate, see *Biblia sacra iuxta latinam Vulgatam versionem* VIII, *Libri Ezrae, Tobiae, Iudith* (1950).

(2) The Syriac text is reconstructed from the fragments of two different versions, of which one, up to 7:9, followed the ordinary Greek text, the other, from 7:10 onwards, the text of codices 44, 106, 107. The first half is the Syriac Hexaplar translation, as A. Rahlfs demonstrated in P. de Lagarde, *Bibliotheca Syriaca* (1892), pp. 32b–32i. As far as is known, the existing manuscripts, like the printed editions, give only the combined text. The Book of Tobit is not included in the great Milan Peshitta manuscript.

(3) The Aramaic version edited by A. Neubauer agrees essentially with the Greek recension of the Sinaiticus, but the text as it stands is probably only the abbreviated and revised form of a more ancient Aramaic account. On its dating, and other matters, see G. Dalman, *Grammatik des jüd.-pal. Aramäisch* (^{2}1905), pp. 35 ff. Comparison with the Qumran Aramaic fragments is not yet available.

(4) The Ethiopic translation is edited by A. Dillmann, *Biblia Veteris Testamenti aethiopica* V (1894).

(5) Finally, the medieval Hebrew versions are to be mentioned, two of which have been frequently printed since the sixteenth century, namely: (a) *Fagius' Hebrew*, i.e. a Hebrew translation based on the common Greek text, first published in Constantinople in 1517, then by Fagius in 1542; and (b) *Münster's Hebrew*, i.e. a free Hebrew rendering which, according to Neubauer, p. xii, was first published in Constantinople in 1516, then in 1542 by Sebastian Münster. Until the publication of the Aramaic text, it was believed that the Old Latin was based on this Hebrew version. Since that time however, it must be taken as established that *Münster's Hebrew* is a derivative, not of the extant form of the Aramaic text, but of an older recension. There, as in the Greek text, in the first three chapters the first person was employed, a usage also retained in *Münster's Hebrew*. A good edition of the latter, with comparison of two manuscripts and an English translation, is to be found in A. Neubauer, *The Book of Tobit* (1878). Both Hebrew texts, with Latin translations, are contained also in Walton's London Polyglot, vol. IV.

(c) The *London Hebrew* comes from Manuscript Add. 11639 (ff. 736–53) of the British Library, dating to the thirteenth century. It was published by M. Gaster, *Two Unknown Hebrew Versions of Tobit* (1897), pp. i-xi.

(d) *Gaster's Hebrew* derives from a midrash preserved in a fifteenth century Spanish manuscript. See Gaster, *op. cit.*, pp. xi-xiv.

Commentaries

Fritzsche, O. F., *Die Bücher Tobi und Judith erklärt* (1853).
Scholz, A., *Commentar zum Buche Tobias* (1889).
Löhr, M., in Kautzsch, APAT (1900), pp. 135–47.
Simpson, D. C., in Charles, APOT I (1913), pp. 174–241.
Schumpp, M., *Das Buch Tobias* (1933).
Miller, A., in *Die Heilige Schrift des Alten Testaments*, ed. Feldmann and Herkenne (1940).
Clamer, A., in L. Pirot and A. Clamer, *La Sainte Bible* (1949).
Stummer, F., in *Die Heilige Schrift in deutscher Uebersetzung* (1950).
Buckers, H., in *Herders Bibelkommentar* (1953).
Heller, B., in A. Kahana, הספרים החצונים (²1956).
Pautrel, R., in *La Bible de Jérusalem* (²1957).
Zimmermann, F., *The Book of Tobit* (1958).
Estradé, M. M., and B. H. Girbau, in *Monserrat Bible* (1960).

Bibliography

Nöldeke, Th., 'Die Texte des Buches Tobit', Monatsschrift BAW 1879, pp. 45–69.
Grätz, H., 'Das Buch Tobias oder Tobit', MGWJ 27 (1879), pp. 145–63, 385–408, 433–55, 509–20.
Harris, J. R., 'The Double Text of Tobit', AJTh (1899), pp. 541–4.
Plath, Margarete, 'Zum Buch Tobit', ThStKr 74 (1901), pp. 377–414.
Lévi, I., 'La langue originale de Tobie', REJ (1902), pp. 288–91.
Marshall, J. T., 'Tobit', HDB iv (1903), pp. 785–9.
Sieger, J., 'Das Buch Tobias', Katholik (1904), pp. 367–77.
Müller, J., 'Beiträge zur Erklärung des Buches Tobit', BZAW xiii (1908), pp. 1–53.
Simpson, C., 'The Chief Recensions of the Book of Tobit', JThSt 14 (1913), pp. 516–30.
Torrey, C. C., '"Nineveh" in the Book of Tobit', JBL 41 (1922), pp. 237–45.
Joüon, P., 'Quelques hébraïsmes du Codex Sinaiticus de Tobie', Bibl 4 (1923), pp. 168–74.
Prado, J., 'La indole literaria del libro de Tobit', Sefarad 7 (1947), pp. 373–94.
Idem, 'Historia, enseñanzas y poesia en el libro de Tobit', *ibid*. 9 (1949), pp. 27–51.
Glasson, T. F., 'The Main Source of Tobit', ZAW 71 (1959), pp. 275–7.
Altheim, F., and R. Stiehl, 'Achikar und Tobit', in *Die aramäische Sprache unter den Achaimeniden* II (1960), pp. 182–95.
Wikgren, A., 'Tobit, Book of', IDB IV (1962), pp. 658–62.
Schazzochio, L., '"Ecclesiastico", "Tobias", " Sapienza di Salomone" alla luce dei testi di Qumran', RStOr 37 (1962), pp. 199–209.
Flusser, D., טוביה, Enẓ. Miq. III (1965), cols. 367–75.
Milik, J. T., 'La patrie de Tobie', RB 73 (1966), pp. 522–30.
Soden, W. von, 'Fischgalle als Heilsmittel für die Augen', AfO 21 (1966), pp. 81–2.
Vattioni, L. F., 'Studi e note sul Libro di Tobia', Augustinianum 10 (1970), pp. 241–84.
Ruppert, L., 'Das Buch Tobias—Ein Modellfall nachgestaltender Erzählung', *Forschungen zur Bibel I: Festschrift J. Ziegler* (1972), pp. 109–19.
Dion, P. E., 'Deux notes épigraphiques sur Tobie', Bibl 56 (1975), pp. 416–19.
Idem, 'Raphaël l'exorciste', *ibid*. 56 (1976), pp. 399–413.
Ruppert, L., 'Zur Funktion der Achikar-Notizen im Buch Tobias', BZ 20 (1976), pp. 232–7.
Gamberoni, J., 'Das "Gesetz des Mose" im Buch Tobias', in G. Braulik (ed.), *Studien zum Pentateuch—W. Kornfeld Festschrift* (1977), pp. 227–42.
di Lella, A. A., 'The Deuteronomic Background of the Farewell Discourse in Tob. 14:3–11', CBQ 41 (1979), pp. 380–9.

Greenfield, J. C., 'Ahiqar in the Book of Tobit', *De la Tôrah au Messie: Mélanges Henri Cazelles* (1981), pp. 329–36.

Deselaers, P., *Das Buch Tobit: Studien zu seiner Entstehung, Komposition und Theologie* (1982) [a detailed, literary-critical study combined with an analysis of the history of traditions and doctrines].

3. The Story of Ahiqar

In four passages of the Book of Tobit (1:21 f.; 2:10; 11:17; 14:10) mention is made of a nephew of Tobit named Ahiqar.[1] This man, as grand vizier of the Assyrian king Sarchedonus (Esarhaddon) enabled Tobit to return to Nineveh (1:21 f.); supported him in his blindness (2:10); took part in the wedding-feast of the young Tobias (11:18); and was held up by the dying Tobit to his son Tobias as an example of the triumph of righteousness; for Ahiqar had been 'taken down alive under the earth' (ζῶν κατηνέχθη εἰς τὴν γῆν, thus Codex Sinaiticus), by his foster-son Nadan, but had returned to the light, whereas Nadan sank into everlasting darkness (14:10). The foster-son Nadan mentioned here also appears with Ahiqar in 11:17, where they are both called cousins of Tobit.[2]

The story of Ahiqar, at which Tob. 14:10 merely hints, it being assumed that its contents were well known, is preserved in numerous texts—e.g. Aramaic, Syriac, Arabic, Armenian, Neo-Syriac, Slavonic, Rumanian etc., and in shorter form also in Greek (as part of the Life of Aesop). The texts differ considerably from each other in details, but all give basically the same account. The less developed version is contained in the fifth century B.C. fragmentary Aramaic papyrus scroll from Elephantine, first published by E. Sachau in 1911 (*Aramäische Papyrus und Ostraka aus einer jüdischen Militär-Kolonie zu Elephantine*, pp. 147–82). Despite the many gaps, the story given in cols. 1–5 may be reconstructed as follows.

Ahiqar, counsellor and seal-bearer of kings Sennacherib and Esarhaddon of Assyria, had no son. He therefore adopted his nephew Nadan, and educated him in the hope that he would succeed him, and Esarhaddon approved of this plan. Thereupon Ahiqar retired to his house. However, the ungrateful and wicked nephew falsely accused Ahiqar of plotting against the king, who in his rage despatched an

1. The name reads in Codex Sinaiticus 1:21 f. Ἀχείχαρος; 2:10 Ἀχειάχαρος; 11:17 Ἀχείκαρ; 14:10 Ἀχείκαρος; in the Old Latin, 'Achicarus'. The majority of manuscripts, along with Codex Vaticanus and Alexandrinus, have throughout predominantly Ἀχιάχαρος. The correct form is Ahiqar, as the other forms of the story indicate. See also p. 235 below.

2. The name appears in a variety of different forms in the manuscripts in 11:17 and 14:10 (Ναβαδ, Ναδαβ, Νασβας, Ἄμαν), but all would appear to be corruptions of Nadan (Ναδαν), the form that the name takes in the other Ahiqar texts.

officer, Nabusumiskun, with two men to kill the hero. Realizing the purpose of their visit, Ahiqar reminded Nabusumiskun that in similar circumstances in the past he had spared his life and had hidden Nabusumiskun in his house until he was able to re-introduce him to Esarhaddon. The officer was moved and decided to simulate Ahiqar's execution by killing one of his own eunuchs. He then took Ahiqar home with him and looked after him whilst the king imagined that his former seal-bearer and counsellor was dead.

The rest of the story is missing from the Aramaic source. The main points of the longer version (especially according to the Arabic and Syriac) are as follows. Ahiqar,[3] the minister of Sennacherib, is despite his sixty wives childless. The sacrifices which he offers to the gods do not help him either. To his prayer to the Most High God, Creator of heaven and earth, he receives the reply that this is the punishment for his idolatry. (On the various religious backgrounds, see below.) He will also himself remain childless and should take his nephew Nadan as a son. Ahiqar does so. When Nadan grows up, he is appointed successor of Ahiqar by Sennacherib and is instructed by his foster-father. The wise sayings by means of which Ahiqar does this are recorded. Their content is frequently reminiscent of Ben Sira. Since Nadan, in spite of this teaching, leads a dissolute life and squanders Ahiqar's fortune, the latter adopts Nadan's younger brother Nebuzardan instead. To avenge himself, Nadan writes two forged letters, allegedly from Ahiqar to the kings of Persia and Egypt, in which Ahiqar promises to hand over to them the kingdom of Sennacherib. Then he writes another forged letter from Sennacherib to Ahiqar in which the latter is commanded to come with an army to the place designated as a rendezvous in the letter to the king of Egypt. When Nadan reads to Sennacherib the forged letters to the foreign kings allegedly discovered by himself, and when Sennacherib actually meets Ahiqar at the rendezvous with an armed force, he becomes convinced of his guilt. By means of a cunning ruse, Ahiqar is then handed over to the king by Nadan, fettered, and condemned to death. He however persuades the executioner, to whom he had formerly rendered a service, not to kill him, but to execute in his place a slave already under sentence of death. An underground hiding-place is prepared for Ahiqar, where he remains concealed. Nadan then rules cruelly in the house of Ahiqar.

When the king of Egypt hears that the wise Ahiqar is dead, he writes a letter to Sennacherib requesting him to despatch a skilled man to build him a castle between heaven and earth. Should Sennacherib be able to send such a man, the king of Egypt would pay tribute to him for

---

3. This is the form given in the Syriac text; the Arabic is Haiqar, the Armenian and Neo-Aramaic Hiqar, the Slavonic Akyrios.

three years, otherwise Sennacherib would have to pay tribute for the same period. This places Sennacherib in considerable embarrassment and he laments the death of Ahiqar, who alone in his wisdom might have been able to proffer advice. Then the executioner confesses that Ahiqar is not dead. Sennacherib is overjoyed and commands that Ahiqar be summoned. (Why the king is immediately convinced of his innocence is not quite clear.) When Ahiqar hears what is going on, he has two young eagles trained to carry two small boys into the air while they themselves are held by cords. With these Ahiqar sets off for Egypt. When he is led before Pharaoh, he guesses from the various garments in which that monarch appears that he likes to resemble Bel, the sun, the moon, and the spring month of Nisan. Ahiqar however likens his own king, Sennacherib, to the God of heaven himself. When he is then ordered to build the castle between heaven and earth, he lets the two eagles rise into the air with the two boys, and the boys call out for plaster, lime, clay and stone so that they can proceed with the building. As Pharaoh is unable to provide this, he surrenders his claim. After Ahiqar has given further proofs of his wonderful wisdom, Pharaoh lets him go, giving him tribute for Sennacherib for three years. On his return, Ahiqar takes a fearsome revenge on Nadan. He also delivers a long and severe lecture, comparing Nadan's behaviour to the foolish conduct of various animals. When he begs for forgiveness, Ahiqar replies with further wise proverbs. But Nadan swells out like a wineskin, and bursts and dies. For whoever digs a pit for others, himself falls into it (Prov. 26:27; Ecclus. 27:26).

Prior to the discovery of the Aramaic source of the Ahiqar story, the origin of the work—Jewish, gentile (Babylonian, Persian, Greek, Indian) or Christian—was hotly debated.[4] The latter thesis has however become untenable since the publication of the Elephantine papyri.

The historical milieu of the story is the last century of the neo-Assyrian empire, and recent cuneiform finds mention a sage, by the

---

4. Among the protagonists of a Jewish origin are M. Lidzbarski ('Zum weisen Achikâr', ZDMG 48 (1894), pp. 671–5); J. R. Harris (*The Story of Ahikar* (1898, ²1913), Introduction); L. Ginzberg ('Ahikar', JE I, pp. 287–90); P. Vetter ('Das Buch Tobias und die Achikar-Sage', Theol. Quartalschr. 86 (1904), pp. 321–64, 512–39; 87 (1905), pp. 321–70, 497–546); R. Smend (*Alter und Herkunft des Achikar-Romans und sein Verhältnis zu Aesop*, BZAW 13 (1908), pp. 55–125). A Babylonian derivation was proposed by, among others, F. Nau (*Histoire et sagesse d'Ahikar l'Assyrien* (1909), pp. 118–19). Vetter also postulated a Babylonian Ahiqar as the basis of the Jewish work. B. Meissner ('Quellenuntersuchungen zur Haikârgeschichte', ZDMG 48 (1894), pp. 171–97) considered the Greek *Life of Aesop* as the source of the Jewish legend. W. Bousset ('Beiträge zur Achikarlegende', ZNW 6 (1905), pp. 180–93) favoured a Persian origin. Finally the authorship of the story was assigned to a Syrian Christian by G. Hoffmann (*Auszüge aus syrischen Acten persischer Märtyrer* (1880), p. 182) and B. Meissner, art. cit.

name of Ahuqar, at the court of Esarhaddon.[5] Bearing in mind the setting and occasional literary and philological features, an Akkadian original appears to be a distinct possibility;[6] but it is equally conceivable that both the story and the proverbs are genuine Aramaic compositions.

That the Aramaic Ahiqar is first attested in a Jewish military colony in Upper Egypt in the late fifth century B.C. does not make it *ipso facto* a Jewish document. In fact, it contains no mention of Judaism; on the contrary, it refers repeatedly to the Mesopotamian god of justice, Shamash (cf. lines 92, 93, 108, 138, 171). It is reasonable therefore to deduce that the original story was Babylonian and polytheistic.[7] Among the more recent recensions, the Armenian describes Ahiqar as praying to the deities 'Belshim and Shimil and Shamin' (1:4).[8] The Arabic and neo-Syriac accounts represent him as a convert to monotheism (cf. Arabic 1:3–6). On the other hand, the Syriac and Slavonic Ahiqar worships the one true God from the start, reflecting a prior adoption of the story by Jews. Indeed this judaization, which patently antedates the Book of Tobit (late third century B.C.), where the Ahiqar of the legend becomes the son of Anael, brother of Tobit (Tob. 1:21), is to be placed to the fourth to third centuries B.C.

Since the Elephantine finds and the consequent determination of the high antiquity of the Ahiqar story, it is generally agreed that the latter was used by the writer of Tobit,[9] although, as has been already suggested, in a judaized form. The motive for introducing Ahiqar into the Tobit account seems to be to enhance Tobit's prestige through his family link with the famous court official and sage.

5. A list of post-diluvian sages (*ummanu*) found at Uruk and dating to the Seleucid era, reads: 'In the time of Esarhaddon there was Aba-NINNU-dari, whom the Arameans (Aḫlamu) call Aḫuqar' (J. van Dijk in H. J. Lenzen, *XVIII vorläufiger Bericht über die Ausgrabungen in Uruk-Warka* (1962), pp. 45, 51–2; cf. *idem*, 'Ausgrabungen von Warka. Die Tontafelfunde der Kampagne 1959/60', AfO 20 (1963), p. 217). For the name *Aḫuqar*, see C. Saporetti, *Onomastica medio-assira* I (1970), p. 79. Note also that the names *Aḫiaqar* and *Nadinnu* figure also in a document of 698 B.C. (cf. A. T. Olmstead, 'Intertestamental Studies', JAOS 56 (1936), p. 243).

6. One of the proverbs (8:17 in Syriac) is paralleled in Akkadian; cf. R. H. Pfeiffer in ANET, p. 426 [V(1)]. See J. C. Greenfield, 'The Background and Parallel to a Proverb of Ahikar', *Hommages à A. Dupont-Sommer* (1971), pp. 49–59. The Akkadian term *arru* = decoy bird has been preserved in Syriac at 8:15 (S. P. Brock). There appear also to be Egyptian features in the development of the Aramaic Ahiqar story: cf. J. C. Greenfield, 'Studies in Aramean Lexicography', JAOS 82 (1962), pp. 293, 297–9; S. P. Brock, 'A Piece of Wisdom Literature in Syriac', JSS 13 (1968), pp. 214–15.

7. Cf. A. Cowley, *Aramaic Papyri of the Fifth Century* B.C. (1923), pp. 206–7; H. L. Ginsberg, ANET, p. 427. Because of the acceptance of a gentile origin, introductions to Jewish literature include no chapter on Ahiqar. Eissfeldt, for example, contains only two allusions (pp. 52, 584); see also Nicklesburg, JLBBM, pp. 23, 161.

8. Cf. Harris, *op. cit.*, pp. xxxvii-lx.

9. Cf. Cowley, *op. cit.*, p. 208; Altheim and Stiehl, *op. cit.* II, pp. 193–5.

In addition to the Elephantine papyri, the Akkadian allusions and Tobit, the figure of Ahiqar is represented in Greek literature also. Democritus of Abdera (460–361 B.C.) is said by Clement of Alexandria in *Strom.*, i, 15, 69, 4–6 (GCS 52, pp. 43,13–44,4), according to Eusebius, *Praep. ev.*, x, 4, 23–4, to have visited Babylonia, Persia and Egypt, and to have incorporated in his writings the stela of Akikaros. A few sentences attributed to Democritus by Shahrastani (eleventh to twelfth century) may be traced to the oriental recensions of the proverbs of Ahiqar.[10]

Theophrastus (died 264 B.C.) is credited by Diogenes Laertius (*Vitae*, v, 2, 50) with a work entitled *Akicharos*, and Strabo [xvi, 2, 39 (p. 762)] lists Achaikaros among the diviners (μάντεις) from the Bosporus, a probable misreading for Borsippa.[11]

A Greek *Life of Aesop*, extant in sundry versions (see below), reproduces in its central part what is simply the Ahiqar story in a shortened form; only the names are changed.[12] Aesop takes the place of Ahiqar, Nadan is here called Αἶνος or Ἔννος, and the king is not Sennacherib, but Λυκοῦργος or Λυκῆρος. The only real difference of meaning is found at the close: whereas Nadan is severely punished by Ahiqar, Ainos or Ennos is magnanimously forgiven by Aesop. Otherwise, the details are identical. Experts are unanimous in their contention that the oriental episodes in the *Life of Aesop* are drawn from the Ahiqar romance (see Smend, *op. cit.*, pp. 76, 96–100). But Smend brought the fables of Aesop within the range of his investigation and showed that many are identical with the parables from animal life which appear at the end of the book of Ahiqar (in Ahiqar's severe reprimand to Nadan), and that here too there are strong arguments for the priority of the book of Ahiqar. Aesop's date of birth is admittedly unknown. But the same fables are to be found also in Babrius, and he may plausibly be dated to about A.D. 200.[13] The results obtained from Pseudo-Democritus are thus approximately confirmed.

---

10. Cf. R. Smend, *Alter und Herkunft des Achikar-Romans und sein Verhältnis zu Aesop* (1908); Altheim and Stiehl, *Das aramäische Sprache* I, pp. 186–92; B. E. Perry, 'Demetrius of Phalerum and the Aesopic Fables', *Trans. Proceed. Am. Philol. Ass.* 93 (1962), pp. 287–346; Denis, IPGAT, pp. 202–3. According to Smend, the Semitic character of the sayings preserved in Arabic indicates that Shahrastani cites a Pseudo-Democritus (*op. cit.*, pp. 67–75), but Altheim and Stiehl, and Perry (*loc. cit.*), favour the real Democritus. For a comparison of the sayings, see Harris in APOT II, pp. 716–17.

11. Cf. J. R. Harris, *op. cit.*, pp. xxxix-xlv; RE III, col. 735.

12. R. Smend, *op. cit.*, pp. 76–102; B. E. Perry, *Aesopica: A Series of Texts relating to Aesop or ascribed to him* (1952), pp. 66–73; A. M. Denis, *op. cit.*, pp. 204–5. For the Greek text and parallel English translation, see Charles, APOT II, pp. 780–4.

13. On Babrius, see O. Crusius, RE II, cols. 2655 ff.; B. E. Perry, *Babrius and Phaedrus* (Loeb, 1965).

There is also sporadic attestation of the Ahiqar story in Egyptian demotic documents.[14]

The Ahiqar legend has survived in a number of languages.

(1) *Aramaic:* The earliest form of the Ahiqar story is represented by fragments of fourteen columns of a scroll written in Aramaic and dating to the late fifth century B.C. They were found on the island of Elephantine (modern Assuan) in 1906–8 and first published by E. Sachau, *Aramäische Papyrus und Ostraka aus einer jüdischen Militär-Kolonie zu Elephantine* (1911), pp. 147–82. The most convenient edition is that of A. Cowley, *Aramaic Papyri of the Fifth Century* B.C. (1923), pp. 204–48 (introduction, text, translation and notes). For translations, see J. R. Harris in APOT II, pp. 777–9; F. C. Conybeare, J. R. Harris and A. Smith Lewis, *The Story of Ahikar* (²1913), pp. 168–73; H. L. Ginsberg in ANET (1950, ²1955, ³1969), pp. 427–30; P. Grelot, 'Les proverbes araméens d'Ahiqar', RB 68 (1961), pp. 178–94; *Documents araméens d'Égypte* (1972), pp. 432–52; J. M. Lindenberger, *The Aramaic Proverbs of Ahiqar. Text with English Translation* (1983).

(2) *Syriac:* Among the later recensions, the Syriac is one of the most important. It probably renders an Aramaic text, and the translation has been assigned to the Parthian era (so A. T. Olmstead, 'Inter-testamental Studies', JAOS 56 (1936), p. 243); but a possible Greek original has also been proposed (B. E. Perry, 'Demetrius of Phalerum and the Aesopic Fables', *Transactions Proc. Am. Philol. Ass.* 93 (1962), p. 322). The stylistic influence of the Old Testament Peshitta has been noted (A. Yellin, 'Notes on the Syriac Versions of the Story of Ahikar', JQR 15 (1924/5), pp. 119–21). The most important editions are J. R. Harris, *The Story of Ahikar* (²1913), pp. 99–127 (transl.), 34*–72* (text = BM Add. 7200, f. 114ᵃ⁻ᵇ; Cambridge Add. 2020 ff. 66ᵃ–78ᵃ) and M. H. Goshen-Gottstein, *The Wisdom of Ahiqar* (1965), reprinting Harris's text and those published by F. Nau, 'Documents relatifs à Ahiqar', Rev. Or. Chrét. 21 (1918/19), pp. 149–55, 273–307. For an English translation, see J. R. Harris, *The Story of Ahikar*, pp. 99–127; APOT II, pp. 724–76; French translation in F. Nau, *op. cit.*; Italian translation, F. Pennachietti, in P. Sacchi (ed.), *Apocrifi dell'Antico Testamento* (1981), pp. 65–95. A neo-Syriac version, made from the Arabic, has been published by M. Lidzbarski, *Die neuaramäischen Handschriften der königlichen Bibliothek zu Berlin* (1896), I, pp. 3–77 (text); II, pp. 3–41 (translation).

(3) *Arabic:* The Arabic Ahiqar has been translated from the Syriac. The most important editions are by M. Lidzbarski, *Die neuaramäischen*

---

14. Cf. W. Spiegelberg, 'Achikar in einem demotischen Texte der römischen Kaiserzeit', OLZ 33 (1930), col. 961; K. T. Zanzich, 'Demotische Fragmente zum Achikar Roman', H. Franke et al. (eds.), *Folia Rara* (1976), pp. 180–5.

Handschriften I (1894) ; A. Smith Lewis, *The Story of Ahiqar* (1898, [2]1913), pp. 1–32 (for the sources, see pp. xxiii–iv), cf. APOT II, pp. 724–76; L. Leroy, 'L'histoire d'Haîkar le sage d'après les manuscrits arabes 3637 et 3656 de Paris', Rev. Or. Chrét. 13 (1908), pp. 367–88. The story, in a largely reshaped form, is part of the *Thousand and One Nights* (cf. Smend, *op. cit.*, pp. 59–61; Denis, *op. cit.*, pp. 206–7; G. Graf, *Geschichte christlicher arabischer Literatur* I (1944), pp. 217–19).

(4) *Ethiopic:* Translated from the Arabic, a number of axioms attributed to Haikar are contained in *The Book of the Wise Philosophers*; see C. H. Cornill, *Das Buch der weisen Philosophen* (1875), pp. 19–21, 40–4. For other translations, see J. R. Harris, *op. cit.*, pp. 128–9 (APOT II, p. 777); F. Nau, *Histoire et sagesse d'Ahikar l'Assyrien* (1909, pp. 89–92; F. Altheim and R. Stiehl, 'Mashafa falasfa tabiban', in M. Black and G. Fohrer (eds.), *In Memoriam Paul Kahle* (1968), pp. 3–9.

(5) *Armenian:* An abridged version from the Arabic dates to the tenth century. It has been edited by F. C. Conybeare, *The Story of Ahikar* (1898, [2]1913), pp. 24–55 (translation), pp. 125–62 (text). For other translations, see P. Vetter, 'Das Buch Tobias und die Achikar-Sage', Th. Quartalschr. 86 (1904), pp. 330–64; F. Nau, *op. cit.*, pp. 92–8; Conybeare, APOT II, pp. 724–76.

(6) *Slavonic:* Translated from the Greek, it is available in V. V. Jagič's edition: 'Der weise Akyrios', Byz. Z. 1 (1892), pp. 107–26. English translation by A. Smith Lewis in *The Story of Ahikar*, pp. 1–23. French translation, F. Nau, *op. cit.*, pp. 98–102.

(7) *Rumanian:* Also rendered from the Slavonic, this version has been published by M. Gaster, *Chrestomathie roumaine* II, pp. 134–6 ('Histoire d'Arghir et de son neveu Anadam') ; 'Contributions to the History of Ahikar and Nadan', JROS 32 (1900), pp. 301–19.

Bibliography

Wissowa, G., 'Akikaros', RE I, c. 1168.
Streck, M., 'Akikaros', RE suppl. I, cols. 43–4.
Ginzberg, L., 'Ahikar', JE I, pp. 287–90.
Vetter, P., Das Buch Tobias und die Achikar-Sage', Th. Quartalschr. 86 (1904), pp. 321–64, 512–39; 87 (1905), 321–70, 497–546.
Smend, R., *Alter und Herkunft des Achikar-Romans und sein Verhältnis zu Aesop* (1908).
Meyer, E., *Der Papyrusfund von Elephantine* ([3]1912), pp. 98–128.
Nöldeke, Th., *Untersuchungen zum Achikar-Roman* (1913).
Stummer, F., *Der kritische Wert der altaramäischen Achikartexte aus Elephantine* (1914).
Meissner, B., *Das Märchen vom weisen Achikar* (1917).
Pirot, L., 'Ahikar', DBS I (1928), cols. 197–207.
Altheim, F., and R. Stiehl, *Die aramäische Sprache unter den Achaimeniden* II (1960), pp. 182–95 ('Achikar und Tobit').
Kraeling, E. G., 'Ahikar, Book of', IDB I (1962), pp. 68–9.
Denis, IPGAT, pp. 201–14.
McKane, W., *Proverbs: A New Approach* (1970) ['Ahikar', pp. 156–82].

Gutman, Y., 'Ahikar, Book of', Enc. Jud. 1 (1971), cols. 460–1.

Greenfield, J. C., 'The Background and Parallel to a Proverb of Ahiqar', *Hommages à André Dupont-Sommer* (1971), pp. 49–59.

Niditch, S., and Doran, R., 'The Success Story of the Wise Courtier: A Formal Approach', JBL 96 (1977), pp. 179–93.

Pennachietti, F., 'Storia e massime di Achicar', in P. Sacchi (ed.), *Apocrifi dell'Antico Testamento* (1981), pp. 51–95 (full bibliography).

Charlesworth, J. H., *The Pseudepigrapha and Modern Research with a Supplement* (1981), pp. 75–7, 273.

Greenfield, J. C., 'Ahiqar in the Book of Tobit', *De la Tôrah au Messie: Mélanges Henri Cazelles* (1981), pp. 329–36.

V. Prophetic-Apocalyptic Pseudepigrapha

Bibliography

Hilgenfeld, A., *Die jüdische Apokalyptik in ihrer geschichtlichen Entwicklung* (1857).

Gunkel, H., *Schöpfung und Chaos in Urzeit und Endzeit* (1895).

Charles, R. H., 'Apocalyptic Literature', EB I (1899), cols. 213–50.

Torrey, C. C., 'Apocalypse', JE I (1901), pp. 669–75.

Bousset, W., *Die jüdische Apokalyptik, ihre religionsgeschichtliche Herkunft und ihre Bedeutung für das Neue Testament* (1903).

Volz, P., *Jüdische Eschatologie von Daniel bis Akiba* (1903).

Bousset, W., *Die Religion des Judentums im späthellenistischen Zeitalter* (1906, [3]1926 rev. H. Gressmann, [4]1966).

Lagrange, M. J., *Le messianisme chez les Juifs* (1909).

Burkitt, F. C., *Jewish and Christian Apocalypses* (1914).

Volz, P., *Die Eschatologie der jüdischen Gemeinde im neutestamentlichen Zeitalter* (1934).

Rowley, H. H., *The Relevance of Apocalyptic* (1944).

Idem, Jewish Apocalyptic and the Dead Sea Scrolls (1957).

Bloch, J., *On the Apocalyptic in Judaism* (1952).

Russell, D. S., *The Method and Message of Jewish Apocalyptic* (1964).

Hruby, K., 'L'influence des apocalypses sur l'eschatologie judéo-chrétienne', *Or. Syr.* 11 (1966), pp. 291–320.

Betz, O., 'Zum Problem des religionsgeschichtlichen Verständnisses der Apokalyptik', ZTK 63 (1966), pp. 391–409.

Osten-Sacken, P. von der, *Die Apokalyptik im ihren Verhältnis zu Prophetie und Weisheit* (1969).

Schmidt, J. M., *Die jüdische Apokalyptik : Die Geschichte ihrer Erforschung von den Anfangen bis zu den Textfunden von Qumran* (1969, [2]1976).

Schreiner, J., *Alttestamentlich-jüdische Apokalyptik : Eine Einführung* (1969).

Koch, K., *Ratlos vor der Apokalyptik* (1970) ; E.T. *The Rediscovery of Apocalyptic* (1970).

Flusser, D., 'Apocalypse', Enc. Jud. 3 (1971), cols. 179–81.

Hanson, P. D., 'Jewish Apocalyptic against its Near Eastern Environment', RB 78 (1971), pp. 31–58.

Schmithals, W., *Die Apokalyptik : Einführung und Deutung* (1973).

Collins, J. J., 'Apocalyptic Eschatology as Transcendence of Death', CBQ 36 (1974), pp. 21–43.

Delcor, M., 'Le milieu d'origine de l'apocalyptique juive', in W. C. van Unnik (ed.), *La littérature juive entre Tenach et Mischna* (1974), pp. 101–17.

Saldarini, A. J., 'Apocalyptic and Rabbinic Literature', CBQ 37 (1975), pp. 348–58.

Barr, J., 'Jewish Apocalyptic in Recent Scholarly Study', BJRL 58 (1975), pp. 9–35.

Hanson, P. D., *The Dawn of Apocalyptic* (1975).

Idem, 'Prolegomena to the Study of Jewish Apocalyptic', in F. M. Cross *et al.* (eds.), *Magnalia Dei* (1976), pp. 389–413.

Idem, 'Apocalypse, Genre', IDBS (1976), pp. 27–8; 'Apocalypticism', *ibid.*, pp. 28–34.

Collins, J. J., 'Cosmos and Salvation : Jewish Wisdom and Apocalypse in the Hellenistic Age', HR 17 (1977), pp. 121–42.

Idem, The Apocalyptic Vision of The Book of Daniel (1977).

Coppens, J., 'L'apocalyptique, son dossier, ses critères, ses éléments constitutifs, sa portée néotestamentaire', EThL 53 (1977), pp. 1–23.

Saldarini, A. J., 'The Uses of Apocalyptic in the Mishna and Tosephta', CBQ 39 (1977), pp. 396–409.
Gruenwald, I., *Apocalyptic and Merkavah Mysticism* (1978).
Idem, 'Jewish Apocalyptic Literature', ANRW II 19.1 (1979), pp. 89–118.
Charlesworth, J. H., 'Apocalyptic' (bibliography), PMRS, pp. 46–52, 253–9.
Koch, K., and J. M. Schmidt (eds.), *Apokalyptik* [Wege der Forschung, 365] (1982).
Rowland, C., *The Open Heaven: A Study of Apocalyptic in Judaism and Early Christianity* (1982).
Hellholm, D. (ed.), *Apocalypticism in the Mediterranean World and the Near East* (1983).
Hanson, P. D. (ed.), *Visionaries and their Apocalypses* (1983).
Collins, J. J., *The Apocalyptic Imagination* (1984).

The literary productions examined so far all correspond more or less in form to the prototypes in the older literature which became canonical, remaining very close to it in spirit and content. A new type of composition, and the best-loved and most influential in this period, is the prophetic-apocalyptic pseudepigrapha. Whereas the biblical prophets in their teachings and admonitions addressed themselves directly to the people, primarily by means of the spoken word, and only secondarily and occasionally through the written word, now, those who wished to influence their contemporaries do not step forward themselves, but speak to the nation on the borrowed authority of great names of the past—Enoch, Moses, Baruch, Ezra etc.—in the expectation that their influence will be that much more certain and powerful.

The choice of pseudonymity and pseudepigraphy reflects the literary fashion of the age both among Jews and in the Hellenistic world.[1] The phenomenon is prominent already in the Bible. Not only are whole sections that were composed in exilic and post-exilic times assigned to Isaiah, who flourished in the eighth century B.C., but the Psalter in general, and a large number of Psalms in particular, claim Davidic authorship, and collections such as Proverbs, the Song of Songs and, in cryptically pseudonymous manner, Ecclesiastes, are associated with the traditional wisdom writer par excellence, King Solomon. But in the domain of apocalypticism, where the central theme is often the revelation of the ultimate triumph of justice over the wicked secular powers, pseudonymous clandestinity serves a practical political aim by concealing the identity of the writer from hostile Jewish or gentile authorities.[2]

---

1. Cf. M. Smith, 'Pseudepigraphy in the Israelite Literary Tradition', in K. von Fritz (ed.), *Entretiens sur l'antiquité classique* 18 (1972), pp. 191–227; M. Hengel, 'Anonymität, Pseudepigraphie und "Literarische Fälschung" in der jüdisch-hellenistischen Literatur', *ibid.*, pp. 231–329; J. J. Collins, 'Pseudonymity, Historical Reviews and the Genre of the Revelation of John', CBQ 19 (1977), pp. 329–43; C. Rowland, *The Open Heaven: A Study of Apocalyptic in Judaism and Early Christianity* (1982), pp. 61–70.

2. Cf. I. Gruenwald, 'Jewish Apocalyptic Literature', ANRW II Principat 19.1, pp. 97–9.

The standpoint of pseudonymity is usually maintained with skill. The writings are composed as though they were really aimed at the contemporaries of the persons concerned. But the message conveyed to these fictitious contemporaries is of more interest to the contemporaries of the real author. From the artificial viewpoint that is adopted, glimpses are given into the future. The coming history of Israel and the world is predicted in detail, but invariably so that the prophecy breaks off in the real author's lifetime and judgement as well as the dawn of redemption is seen to apply to that very age, to warn sinners and to comfort and encourage the pious. The fact that the alleged prophecies have already been fulfilled in history serves to authenticate the prophet; there will be all the more confidence in what is predicted for the future of his real contemporaries.

The contents of the prophetic pseudepigrapha are very varied. As in the older prophetic books, two elements usually go hand in hand, i.e., instruction and exhortation. But on the whole, visions and the revelation of divine secrets predominate. And yet all these writings belong to the same category. In accordance with their hortatory purpose, the revelations are primarily concerned with the history of the Jewish people and of mankind in general, but secondarily also with problems of religious doctrine, such as the relationship between sin and affliction on the one hand, and righteousness and happiness on the other. Information is also given about the mysteries of nature, the supernatural, heavenly origin and background of natural earthly events. On all these matters, whether closely or distantly connected with the religious life, the teaching given claims to be authentic.

The form in which these instructions are expressed is that of apocalyptic.[3] They appear throughout as supernatural revelations

---

3. The concept has been the subject of much argument. In the strict sense it designates all that pertains to the literary genre of apocalyptic. Taken more broadly, however, apocalyptic can apply to a mode of thought, a religious tendency, regularly expressed in apocalypses, but capable also of being included in other types of literature. Cf. James Barr, 'Jewish Apocalyptic in Recent Scholarly Study', BJRL 58 (1975), pp. 15–16. On the word itself, see M. Smith, 'On the History of $A\Pi OKAA\Upsilon\Pi T\Omega$ and $A\Pi OKAA\Upsilon\Psi I\Sigma$', in D. Hellholm (ed.), Apocalypticism (1983), pp. 9–20. There is good reason for distinguishing further 'apocalyptic' from 'messianic' because the former kind of eschatology is conceivable with or without a christological figure. For an analysis of the notions of 'apocalyptic', 'apocalypse' and 'eschatology', see C. Rowland, The Open Heaven (1982), esp. 23–72. Rowland differentiates correctly between apocalyptic and eschatology, characterizing the former as revelation of heavenly mysteries, the latter as concern for the future age. But it is clearly undeniable that the flowering of apocalyptic occurred during an age of eschatological enthusiasm. The collective volume edited by D. Hellholm, Apocalypticism (1983), contains a number of important essays on apocalypticism in the Bible (J. Carmignac, pp. 163–70), at Qumran (M. Philonenko, pp. 211–18; H. Stegemann, pp. 495–530), in Palestinian Judaism (E. P. Sanders, pp. 447–59) and in Hellenistic Judaism (J. J. Collins, pp. 531–48).

imparted by the mouth of those men of God in whose names the writings are issued. A special characteristic of this later 'apocalyptic', compared with much of the older genuine prophecy, is that it gives its revelations mysteriously and enigmatically. What is to be communicated is wrapped in parables and symbols so that the content can only be conjectured. Yet the extent of the disguise varies. Sometimes it consists merely in the author neglecting to mention the names of persons otherwise clearly described. Sometimes the entire presentation is symbolical. Persons are represented in the guise of animals, events in human history in the guise of natural occurrences. If an interpretation is then added, this is as a rule only a lighter form, not a solution, of the puzzle.

The images themselves are not always the free creations of the author. They frequently inherit traditional concepts which are merely remodelled and made to serve the writer's purpose. Occasionally, the rudimentary remains of pagan mythology and other ancient near-eastern influences can be recognized in them.[4]

Most of these writings were occasioned by times of particular distress and hardship, or by the low circumstances of the people in general. It was the contradiction between ideal and reality, between promises which the Jews believed they had received from God, and their present subjugation and persecution by gentile powers, it was this contradiction that induced the authors to write. Even when there was no immediate hardship or oppression, a pessimistic assessment of affairs still constituted the motive for writing. The existing situation, the present condition of the chosen people, stood in glaring contrast to their true destiny. A complete revolution must come, and soon. Such is the conviction expressed in all these writings. They therefore owe their inception on the one hand to a gloomy appraisal of the present time, and on the other to a very energetic faith in the nation's glorious future. And their purpose is to awaken and animate this faith in others. It is not a question of despairing, but of holding fast to the belief that God will lead his people, through all the misfortunes which he sends to test and purify them, to brightness and glory. This faith is to comfort and encourage the people in the sufferings of the present time. But inasmuch as this reversal is proclaimed as close and imminent, it is meant also to serve as a warning to sinners to turn whilst there is still time. For the judgement is inexorable; to one it brings redemption, to another destruction.

4. Cf. H. Gunkel, *Schöpfung und Chaos in Urzeit und Endzeit* (1895); P. D. Hanson,? ?'Jewish Apocalyptic against its Near Eastern Environment', RB 78 (1971), pp. 31–58; J. J. Collins, 'Jewish Apocalyptic against its Hellenistic Near-Eastern Environment', BASOR 220 (1975), pp. 27–36; P. D. Hanson, 'Apocalypticism', IDBS (1976), pp. 31–2; W. G. Lambert, *The Background of Jewish Apocalyptic* (1978).

The actual effect of these enthusiastic proclamations was obviously strong and enduring. Through them, eschatological or messianic hope received new life; through them, the nation was fortified in the faith that it had been called, not to serve, but to rule. For this very reason, apocalypticism played an essential part in the development of Palestinian Jewish politics. From the census of Quirinius whereby Judaea was placed under direct Roman control, the revolutionary tendency amongst the people grew throughout the years until it finally led to the revolt of A.D. 66. This process, animated by religious, political, social and economic motives, was strengthened and accelerated by apocalyptic literature.

The viewpoint in all these writings is essentially the correct Jewish viewpoint. They exhort to a God-fearing change of conduct in accordance with the norm of the Scriptures, and deplore the lawlessness that manifests itself here and there. Yet it is not the Judaism of the Pharisaic Torah scholars that is expressed here. The main emphasis is placed, not on what the people have to do, but on what is in store for them, i.e. on what they have to expect, and how the future should affect their present disposition. In the realm of conduct as such, things are taken by and large without any special weight being attached to formal correctness. In the process, quite a few peculiarities are to be found, as is to be expected in such products of lofty religious enthusiasm. The actual circles from which these writings may have emanated nevertheless cannot be named with any confidence. The Qumran discoveries have confirmed earlier suspicions concerning a definite link between this type of literature and Essenism.[5] However, although the caves have yielded a number of fragments of a prophetico-apocalyptic nature (see below, pp. 306–7), several major compositions belonging to this class are absent from the Dead Sea scrolls. The literature under review cannot be identified as the monopoly of a single school, but as the fruit of the spirit of an age.[6]

5. Cf. in particular A. Dupont-Sommer, *The Essene Writings from Qumran* (1961). On the relationship between the Essenes and the Qumran community, see vol. II, pp. 575–85.

6. It has been argued that anonymous or pseudonymous prophecy reflects the anti-prophetic tendency of so-called official Judaism. But, whilst the extinction of the spirit of prophecy is commonly asserted in rabbinic circles in the post-destruction era (cf. *tSot.* 13:2; *bSot.* 48b), belief in, and constant expectation of, prophetic, charismatic and miraculous phenomena remained part of popular religion. Cf. G. Vermes, *Jesus the Jew* (1973), pp. 58–82; J. B. Segal, 'Popular Religion in Ancient Israel', JJS 27 (1976), pp. 1–22. Leaders known as prophets found an easy following in the first century A.D. Cf. *Ant.* xx 5, 1 (97): Theudas stated that he was a prophet—προφήτης γὰρ ἔλεγεν εἶναι; cf. Acts 5:36. *Ant.* xx 8, 6 (169): The Egyptian declared that he was a prophet—προφήτης εἶναι λέγων; cf. *B.J.* ii 13, 5 (261); Acts 21:38. See especially *Ant.* xx 8, 6 (169); *B.J.* ii 13, 4 (259); vi 5, 2 (285). It is noteworthy that when Jesus son of Ananias persisted in uttering prophetic cries in the Temple in A.D. 62, the Jewish ἄρχοντες and Josephus himself suspected that he was acting under a supernatural impulse (δαιμονιώτερον τὸ

1. The Book of Daniel

The oldest and most original of the writings belonging to this group—the prototype indeed of the later ones—is the canonical Book of Daniel. The unknown author of this apocalypse created the forms in which subsequent writers expressed themselves. The book is the direct product of the Maccabaean struggles, born in the very midst of them. Even as the storms of battle break around him, the author seeks to encourage and console his fellow-believers with the promise of speedy deliverance.

The book falls into two parts. The first half (chapters 1–6) comprises a string of paraenetic stories; the second (chapters 7–12), a series of prophetic visions. Chapter 1 recounts how the young Daniel was educated together with three companions at the court of Nebuchadnezzar, king of Babylon. In order not to be defiled by non-Jewish food, the four youths refuse to eat the fare provided by the king and nourish themselves instead on vegetables and water. In spite of this, they look better than the other young men who partake of the royal food. The paraenetic aim of this story is immediately clear. In chapter 2, King Nebuchadnezzar has a dream, and demands that the wise men tell him its content as well as its interpretation. None of the native sages is able to do so. Only Daniel can do what is asked. He is therefore richly rewarded by the king and appointed chief of all the wise men in Babylon. According to the interpretation of the dream, the kingdom of Nebuchadnezzar will be followed by three others, the last of which, the Greek kingdom, will be 'split' (into that of the Ptolemies and the Seleucids) and will be crushed by the hand of God. Chapter 3: Nebuchadnezzar erects a golden image and demands that it be worshipped. When Daniel's three companions refuse to comply, they are cast into a fiery furnace, but remain there uninjured, so that Nebuchadnezzar himself perceives his folly and promotes the three young men to high honours. Chapter 4: Nebuchadnezzar relates in an edict how he was attacked by madness in punishment for his godless arrogance, but that as soon as he honoured God he was restored to his former glory. Chapter 5: Belshazzar, king of Babylon, son of Nebuchadnezzar, prepares a sumptuous banquet at which the Temple

---

κίνημα). Recognition, full or partial, of prophecy was therefore not restricted to the uneducated.

On 'prophet' in Josephus, see J. Blenkinsopp, 'Prophecy and Priesthood in Josephus', JJS 25 (1974), pp. 239–62; D. E. Aune, 'The Use of ΠΡΟΦΗΤΗΣ in Josephus', JBL 101 (1952), pp. 419–21. On the notion of prophecy in the inter-Testamental era, see R. Meyer, 'Prophetes', TDNT VI (1968), pp. 812–28; Vermes, *Jesus the Jew*, pp. 86–99. On the holy spirit, see H. Gunkel, *Die Wirkungen des heiligen Geistes* (1888); P. Schäfer, *Die Vorstellung vom Heiligen Geist in der rabbinischen Literatur* (1972).

vessels carried away by his father from Jerusalem are used as drinking goblets. In punishment for this, he loses in that same night his kingdom and his life. Chapter 6: Darius the Mede, the victor and successor of Belshazzar, causes Daniel to be thrown into the lions' den when he prays to his God against the express prohibition of the king, but he remains quite unharmed. Darius in consequence perceives his folly, and publishes a command that Daniel's God should be worshipped throughout the whole realm.

In the second part of the book (chapters 7–12) all the visions agree in predicting that the last world kingdom will be that of the Greeks and will come to a final end in the godless reign of Antiochus Epiphanes. The history of the Ptolemaic and Seleucid dynasties (for these are the two that are to be understood as the kingdom of the north and the kingdom of the south), and of their interrelationships, is prophesied in great detail, particularly in the last vision (chapters 11–12). The most striking feature is that the prediction becomes more exact and detailed the nearer it approaches the time of Antiochus Epiphanes. The history of this monarch is related with the utmost precision without his name being so much as mentioned (11:21 ff.). The abrogation of Jewish worship is foretold, the profanation of the Temple, the erection of an altar for pagan sacrifice as well as the beginning of the Maccabaean uprising (11:32–5). Here, however, the prophecy suddenly breaks off and the author anticipates that immediately after those battles the end will be ushered in and the kingdom of God will dawn. Moreover, it is not only in the eleventh chapter that the prophecy comes to a halt at this point; the author's horizon never extends beyond it, not even in the visions of the four world kingdoms of Babylon, the Medes, the Persians and the Greeks.

The unity of Daniel has been much debated in modern scholarship. The work as preserved in the Hebrew Bible indicates a twofold duality. The court tales (chapters 1–6) are narrated in the third person, whereas Daniel's eschatological visions (chapters 7–12) are depicted from a Babylonian viewpoint, and told in the first person. Linguistically, chapters 1–2:4a and 8–12 have survived in Hebrew, while chapters 2:4b–7:28 are in Aramaic. Such a division is attested already in the Daniel fragments from Qumran for Dan. 2:4 and 7:28–8:1.[1] Whilst the attribution of all twelve chapters to a single author continues to be maintained, it is the majority opinion that the tales of the first half of the book, dating probably to the third century B.C., precede the visions, and that, in consequence, the Hebrew sections are more recent

---

1. Cf. 1Q Dan[a] in DJD I, p. 150, and 4Q Dan[a] and 4Q Dan[b] according to RB 63 (1956), p. 58. See also J. J. Collins, *The Apocalyptic Vision of the Book of Daniel* (1977), p. 7.

than the Aramaic.[2] In particular, Dan. 1:1–2:4a, ending with the very convenient transitional gloss, 'And the Chaldeans said to the king *in Aramaic* (ארמית)', is best seen as an introduction prefixed to the Aramaic portions at the stage of the final redaction.

In view of these facts, it is now admitted by all critical scholars that the apocalyptic visions and, for those who consider the court tales as pre-existent, the redaction of the book as a whole, date to the reign of Antiochus Epiphanes, or more precisely to between 167 and 163 B.C., if not to 167 to 165 B.C., since the re-dedication of the Temple by Judas Maccabaeus in 164 B.C. appears to be beyond the author's field of vision.[3] Since the court stories could then be read as conveying a message for the generation of the Hellenistic crisis, the whole composition could serve as a tract for the author's generation.

The high esteem which the book enjoyed among Jews right from the beginning is evident from the fact that it was accepted into the canon. Even the somewhat older book of aphorisms by Jesus Sirach, which in form and content is nearer to early Hebrew literature than Daniel, is not part of the biblical canon. Clearly, the reason in both cases is that the book of Jesus ben Sira went out under its author's true name, but that of Daniel under the name of an earlier authority. The most likely reason why such a late composition should have been granted canonical status by Palestinian Jews is its usefulness in providing a clear basis for the doctrine of resurrection (Dan. 12:2–3). The elevation of the work to the rank of Scripture occurred at a stage when its redaction was still fluctuating. The prayer in 9:4–20, though probably a later addition (Eissfeldt, *Introduction*, p. 529), is part of the Hebrew text, but the

2. For the unity, see especially the numerous publications of H. H. Rowley in the bibliography below. For the duality, see e.g. J. A. Montgomery, *The Book of Daniel* (1927), pp. 92–9; J. J. Collins, *op. cit.*, pp. 7–11.

3. Cf. Eissfeldt, *Introduction*, pp. 520–2; Montgomery, *op. cit.*, p. 96 (168–165 B.C.); O. Plöger, *Das Buch Daniel* (1965), p. 29; N. Porteous, *Daniel* (1965), p. 70 (167–164 or 169–164 B.C.); Nickelsburg, JLBBM, p. 90 (167–164 B.C.). According to L. F. Hartman and A. A. di Lella, *The Book of Daniel* (1978), the Hebrew sections derive from an Aramaic original, and the translator is responsible for the publication of the complete work in around 140 B.C. (p. 16). The weak point in this theory lies in the absence of any attempt at updating the story by alluding to the re-consecration of the sanctuary or the death of Antiochus IV. The dating of Daniel to the age of Antiochus IV was first proposed by the neo-Platonist writer Porphyry (died in *c.* A.D. 304) in Book XII of his *Contra Christianos* (cf. A. von Harnack, *Porphyrius 'Gegen die Christen'* (1916), pp. 66–74). The aim of Porphyry was to prove that the prophecies of Daniel were largely *vaticinia ex eventu*. Jerome in the preface to his Daniel commentary writes: 'Contra prophetam Danielem XII librum scripsit Porphyrius, nolens eum ab ipso cuius inscriptus est nomine esse compositum, sed a quodam qui temporibus Antiochi qui appellatus est Epiphanes fuerit in Iudaea, et non tam Danielem ventura dixisse, quam illum narrare praeterita. Denique quidquid usque ad Antiochum dixerit veram historiam continere; siquid autem ultra opinatus sit, quia futura nescierit, esse mentitum' (PL 25, col. 491). See P. M. Casey, 'Porphyry and the Origin of the Book of Daniel', JThSt 27 (1976), pp. 15–33.

various additions (Prayer of Azariah, Song of the three young men in the furnace, Bel and the Dragon, and Susanna) have survived only in the Greek Apocrypha (cf. below, pp. 706–45).

The first literary allusions to Daniel are contained in the oldest Sibylline Oracles (iii 396–400), only a few decades later than Daniel (cf. below, p. 632), as well as in 1 Mac. 2:59–60 and Bar. 1:15–18.

The earliest Daniel manuscripts come from Qumran Caves 1, 4 and 6. Fragments from 1 and 6Q have been published.[4] But Cave 4 contains three copies of the work said to be relatively well preserved and yielding a considerable proportion of the book.[5]

If F. M. Cross's palaeographical judgement is accepted, one of the Qumran Daniel manuscripts belongs to the late second century B.C., i.e. to an epoch that is only fifty years or so more recent than the actual composition of the book.[6] For further Qumran material classified as Pseudo-Daniel, i.e. belonging to the Danielic cycle but additional to the canonical and apocryphal Daniel, see below, pp. 442–3.

A small incidental contribution towards the exegesis of Dan. 9:24–7 may be inserted here. The writer gives an explanation of the seventy years of Jeremiah (Jer. 25:11–12), interpreting them as seventy weeks of years (7 x 70). He breaks them up, that is, into 7 + 62 + 1. He counts the first seven weeks of years (i.e. forty-nine years), as from the context can be hardly in doubt, from the destruction of Jerusalem to the appearance of Cyrus, which is very nearly right (587–538 B.C.). The following sixty-two weeks of years, on the other hand, he reckons from the appearance of Cyrus to his own day, and even more precisely to when 'an anointed one shall be cut off', by which is probably meant the murder of the high priest Onias III in 170 B.C. However, whereas there are only 368 years between 538 and 170 B.C., sixty-two weeks of years would amount to 434 years. The author has therefore overestimated to the extent of about seventy years. Conservative exegetes have considered this impossible, and have in consequence tried by various means to by-pass the only explanation consistent with the context. But that such an error can really happen is proved most strikingly by the fact that Josephus, for example, makes a similar mistake, as appears from the following three passages. (1) In *B.J.* vi 4, 8 (270), he reckons 639 years and 45 days from the second year of Cyrus to the destruction of Jerusalem under Vespasian (A.D. 70). Accordingly, the second year

---

4. Cf. D. Barthélemy, DJD I, pp. 150–2 (Dan. 1:10–17; 2:2–6; 3:22–30); M. Baillet, DJD III, p. 114 (Dan. 10:8–16; 11:33–8 and possibly 8:16–17, 20–1). See also J. C. Trever, 'Completion of the Publication of some Fragments from Qumran Cave I', RQ 5 (1963/4), pp. 323–44.

5. F. M. Cross, 'Le travail d'édition des fragments manuscrits de Qumrân', RB 63 (1956), p. 58. 4Q Dan[a] includes, among others, Dan. 2:19–35, almost intact.

6. Cross, *The Ancient Library of Qumran*, p. 33.

of Cyrus would fall in 569 B.C. (2) In *Ant.* xx 10, 2 (234), he counts 414 years from the return from exile (in the first year of Cyrus, 538 B.C.) to Antiochus V Eupator (164–162 B.C.). (3) In *Ant.* xiii 11, 1 (301), he reckons 481 years and three months from the return from exile (in the first year of Cyrus) until Aristobulus I (104–103 B.C.). The accession of Cyrus would therefore occur according to (1) in 570 B.C.; according to (2) in 578 B.C.; and according to (3) in 585 B.C., whereas in fact it occurred in 537 B.C. Hence Josephus counted forty to fifty years too many. The Jewish Hellenist Demetrius tallies still more closely with Daniel, reckoning 573 years and nine months between the exile of the ten tribes (722/1 B.C.) and Ptolemy IV (222/1 B.C.), therefore seventy years too many, exactly like Daniel. (See the passage in Clement of Alexandria, *Strom.* i 21, 141; for further information on Demetrius, see below, pp. 513–7.) It follows that Daniel shared a widely-held opinion in estimating more or less seventy years too many for this period. The means were then lacking for a more accurate chronology.[7] In Daniel's case, however, the miscalculation occasions little surprise because his fixing of sixty-two weeks of years for the period in question merely resulted from his interpretation of Jeremiah's prophecy.

Bibliography

For an introduction to Daniel, see Eissfeldt, pp. 512–29, 767–69; J. A. Soggin, *Introduction to the Old Testament* (1980), pp. 406–13.

Selected Commentaries

Driver, S. R., *Daniel* (1900).
Marti, K., *Das Buch Daniel* (1901).
Baumgartner, W., *Das Buch Daniel* (1926).
Montgomery, J. A., *Daniel* (1927, [2]1949).
Charles, R. H., *Commentary on the Book of Daniel* (1929).
Rinaldi, G., *Daniele* (1947, [2]1962).
Nötscher, F., *Das Buch Daniel* (1948).
Bentzen, A., *Daniel* (1952).
Schneider, H., *Das Buch Daniel* (1954).
Menasce, P.-J. de, *Daniel* (1954, [2]1958).
Heaton, E. W., *Daniel* (1956).
Porteous, N., *Daniel* (1965, [2]1979).
Plöger, O., *Das Buch Daniel* (1965).
Delcor, M., *Le livre de Daniel* (1971).

7. Cf. N. Walter, 'Fragmente jüdisch-hellenistischer Exegeten', JSHRZ III/2 (1975), p. 292. For a survey of the exegeses of the seventy years, see Montgomery, *op. cit.*, pp. 390–401; Charles, *op. cit.*, pp. 244–6; Hartman and di Lella, *op. cit.*, pp. 250–3; Koch, *op. cit.*, pp. 149–54. The figure of '390 years' from Nebuchadnezzar to the emergence of the Qumran Damascus community mentioned in CD 1:5 raises questions similar to that of Dan. 9. Cf. H. H. Rowley, *The Zadokite Fragments and the Dead Sea Scrolls* (1952), pp. 62–4; G. R. Driver, *The Judaean Scrolls* (1965), pp. 311–16; G. Vermes, DSS, pp. 158–9.

Hammer, R., *The Book of Daniel* (1976).
Lacoque, A., *Le livre de Daniel* (1976). E.T. *The Book of Daniel* (1979).
Hartman, L. F., and di Lella, A. A., *The Book of Daniel* (1978).

Monographs

Gall, A. von, *Die Einheitlichkeit des Buches Daniel* (1895).
Thilo, M., *Chronologie des Danielbuches* (1926).
Junker, H., *Untersuchungen über literarische und exegetische Probleme des Buches Daniel* (1932).
Rowley, H. H., *Darius the Mede and the Four World Empires in the Book of Daniel* (1935, ²1959).
Ginsberg, L. H., *Studies in Daniel* (1948).
Collins, J. J., *The Apocalyptic Vision of the Book of Daniel* (1977).
Koch, K., *Das Buch Daniel* (1980). [This volume contains full bibliographies.]

Survey Articles

Baumgartner, W., 'Ein Vierteljahrhundert Danielforschung', ThR 11 (1939), pp. 59–83, 125–44, 201–28.
Lebram, J., 'Perspektiven der gegenwärtigen Danielforschung', JSJ 5 (1974), pp. 1–33.

Daniel and Qumran

Bruce, F. F., 'The Book of Daniel and the Qumran Community', in E. E. Ellis (ed.), *Neotestamentica et Semitica*, Matthew Black Festschrift (1969), pp. 221–35.
Mertens, A., *Das Buch Daniel im Lichte der Texte vom Toten Meer* (1971).

2. *The Ethiopic Book of Enoch*

Amongst the men of God of the Hebrew Bible, Enoch, along with Elijah, occupies a singular position inasmuch as he is said to have been translated from earth directly to heaven. Such a man must appear especially fitted to impart to the world revelations of divine mysteries since he was accounted worthy of direct relation with God. Quite early therefore, probably in the second century B.C., an apocalyptic writing, which was later enlarged and revised, appeared under his name. This Book of Enoch was already known to the author of Jubilees, and was subsequently much loved among Christians. It is cited in the Epistle of Jude (14–15) and was unhesitatingly made use of by many Church Fathers as a genuine writing of Enoch, with authentic divine revelations, although, apart from Ethiopia, it was never officially recognized by the Church as canonical. In the West, where it circulated in Latin translation, its authority has been seriously questioned only since the end of the fourth century. In the Greek, and particularly the Alexandrian Church, it retained its prestige somewhat longer. It is admittedly unlikely that the Byzantine chronicler, George Syncellus (c. A.D. 800), quoted directly from it the two long passages which he gives (Syncellus, *Chronologia*, ed. Dindorf I, 20–3, 42–7; cf. M. Black, *Apocalypsis Enochi Graece* (1970)). As H. Gelzer has indicated (*Sextus Julius Africanus und die byzantinische Chronographie* II.1 (1885), pp. 262–4), he knew it through the Alexandrian chronicler Panodorus (c. A.D. 400). But the latter drew from Enoch itself. Also, the writer of the eighth century A.D. papyrus manuscript containing an extant large Greek fragment probably had the whole book lying in front of him (see below). In the Middle Ages, however, and at a more recent date, the book was presumed lost, until in the eighteenth century the information came to light that it had been preserved in the Abyssinian Church in Ethiopic translation. The traveller James Bruce brought three manuscripts to Europe in 1773. But it was not until 1821 that the whole work was made known through the English translation of R. Laurence (*The Book of Enoch the Prophet*). The Ethiopic text (*Libri Enoch versio aethiopica*) was published first by the same author in 1838, then, on the basis of five manuscripts, by A. Dillmann in 1851 (*Liber Enoch aethiopica*). There were high hopes of substantial progress in understanding the book when a small Greek fragment, comprising chapter 89:42–9, was published by A. Mai. This facsimile, taken from a copy of Vaticanus (cod. Gr. 1809), is equipped with abbreviated notes and was deciphered by J. Gildemeister.[1] But Mai's conjecture that the codex contained more than had been issued proved groundless. By contrast, the discovery in 1886–7 of a large Greek fragment taken from a Christian tomb at Akhmim, the ancient Panopolis of Upper Egypt, brought an unexpected enrichment of material. In addition to a fragment of the Gospel of Peter and one of the Apocalypse of Peter, the manuscript contains the Greek text of the first thirty-two chapters of the Book of Enoch, with a duplicate rendering of 19:3–21:9.[2]

In 1930, the University of Michigan and A. Chester Beattie acquired a fourth century Greek codex, six pages of which contain Enoch 97:6–104 and 106–7.[3]

The most recent and surprising novelty concerning the Book of Enoch was the discovery in 1952 of Aramaic fragments belonging to eleven leather scrolls in Qumran Cave 4. Though mostly very scrappy, these manuscripts cover all the sections of the Ethiopic book apart from

---

1. 'Ein Fragment des griechischen Henoch', ZDMG 9 (1855), pp. 621–4. Cf. S. Lilla, *Il testo tachigrafico del 'De divinis nominibus' (Vat. Gr. 1809) [Studi e Testi 263]* (1970), pp. 11–16.

2. U. Bouriant, 'Fragments grecs du Livre d'Enoch', Mémoirs publiés par les membres de la mission archéologique française au Caire 9 (1892), pp. 91–147 (text: pp. 111–36); A. Lods, 'L'Evangile et l'Apocalypse de Pierre. Le texte grec du Livre d'Enoch', *ibid.*, pp. 217–35, and 34 plates. The manuscript was dated to the eighth century by Bouriant, but to the sixth by F. G. Kenyon, *The Palaeography of Greek Papyri* (1899), p. 119; *The Text of the Greek Bible* (1937, (²1949), p. 135; or even to the late fifth century, cf. Campbell Bonner, *The Last Chapters of Enoch in Greek* (1937), p. 3.

3. Campbell Bonner, *The Last Chapters of Enoch in Greek [Studies and Documents VIII]* (1937).

chapters 37–71. They have been edited by J. T. Milik.[4]

To impart a clearer idea of the origin and character of this remarkable book, it is necessary to give a brief summary of the contents of the Ethiopic version, the fullest of the surviving recensions.

Title : Enoch's blessing of the elect and the righteous.

Book I (chapters 1–36) : *The Book of Watchers*. Chapters 1–5 : Introduction. Enoch reports that he has seen a vision which the angels disclosed to him, and that he has heard from them what is to happen—that God will visit the wicked in judgement but that peace and bliss will fall to the lot of the elect and the righteous. 6–11 : An account in the third person of the fall of the angels, based on Genesis 6 but with elaborate embellishments. God ordains which punishments the fallen angels are to experience, and how the earth is to be purged of their transgression and wickedness. The angels have to fulfil both commands. 12–16 : Enoch, who associates with the angels in heaven, is sent by them to earth to announce to the fallen angels the judgement of imminent punishment. (Here, from 12:13, Enoch speaks once again in the first person.) When he acquits himself of his task, the fallen angels persuade him to intercede on their behalf before God. But in another powerful vision, Enoch's intercession is rejected by God, and he is charged again with announcing their downfall. 17–36 : Enoch reports (in the first person) how he was carried away over mountains, waters and rivers, and everywhere learned to know the secret divine origin of all the things and events in nature. He was even shown the end of the earth and the place to which the wicked angels will be banished; and the dwelling-place of departed spirits, both righteous and unrighteous; and the Tree of Life, which will be bestowed on the elect righteous; and the place of punishment of men who are damned (Gehinnom, near Jerusalem) ; and Paradise, with the Tree of Knowledge, from which Adam and Eve ate.

Book II (chapters 37–71) : *The Book of Parables*. 'The second vision . . . the vision of wisdom, which Enoch the son of Jared . . . saw', consists of three parables. 38–44 : *First Parable*. Enoch sees in a vision the habitations of the righteous, and the resting places of the saints. He sees also the myriads upon myriads of those who stand before the Majesty of the Lord of Spirits, and the four archangels Michael, Raphael, Gabriel and Phanuel. He sees further the mysteries of heaven : the storehouses of the winds and the storehouses of the sun and the moon, and finally also the lightning and the stars of heaven, which are all called by names and pay heed to them. 45–57 : *Second Parable*. In a vision modelled on Daniel 7, Enoch is told about the 'Elect', the 'Son of Man', i.e., the Messiah,

---

4. J. T. Milik with the collaboration of M. Black, *The Books of Enoch. Aramaic Fragments of Qumran Cave 4* (1976). The passages preserved in Aramaic are listed on pp. 364–5.

his nature and calling, and how he is to exercise judgement over the
world. 58–69: *Third Parable*. This is concerned with the blessedness of
the righteous and the elect; with the mysteries of lightning and
thunder; with the judgement which the Elect, the Son of Man, will
exercise. Several sections are interpolated here from a Book of Noah,
which break the continuity. 70–1: The conclusion of the parables;
Enoch's ascension.

Book III (chapters 72–82): *The Astronomical Book*. 'The book of the
revolutions of the lights of heaven'. Enoch offers here a medley of
astronomical instructions which he himself had received from the angel
Uriel.

Book IV (chapters 83–90): *The Book of Dream-Visions*. (a) 83–4:
Enoch recounts to his son, Methuselah, a terrible vision of the
destruction which is to come upon the sinful world (through the flood)
and implores God not to exterminate the whole of mankind from the
earth. (b) 85–90: The second dream-vision of cattle, sheep, wild beasts
and shepherd, by means of which imagery the entire history of Israel is
predicted until the dawn of the Messianic era. As this historical vision is
the only passage offering anything approaching reliable evidence for
determining the date of its composition, its contents will be discussed
more thoroughly later.

Book V (chapters 91–105): *The Book of Admonitions*. The Greek
version (100:6) refers to it as Enoch's ἐπιστολή. (There has been some
dislocation of the Ethiopic text in chapters 91–3.) 92: Enoch's
exhortation to his children. 93 and 91:12–17: The Apocalypse of
Weeks. Enoch gives an explanation 'from the books' concerning the
world weeks. In the first week, Enoch lives; in the second, Noah; in the
third, Abraham; in the fourth, Moses; in the fifth, the Temple is built;
at the end of the sixth, it is destroyed; in the seventh, a faithless
generation arises; at the end of this week, the righteous receive
instruction concerning the mysteries of heaven; in the eighth,
righteousness receives a sword and sinners are delivered over into the
hands of the righteous, and a house is built for the great King; in the
ninth, judgement is revealed; in the tenth, in the seventh part of it,
there comes judgement for all eternity. 94–105: Lamentations over
sinners and the godless, proclamation of their certain downfall,
exhortation to joyful hope for the righteous (this is all very prolix and
repetitive).

Appendix from the Book of Noah (106–7). An account of the birth of
Noah and of what then took place. His wonderful appearance gives
Enoch an opportunity to prophesy the flood. *Second appendix* (108). This
is an excerpt from 'another book written by Enoch', in which he relates
how he received information from an angel concerning the fire of hell,
to which the spirits of sinners and blasphemers will be brought, and

concerning the blessings to be allotted to the humble and the righteous.

The surviving parts of the eleven Aramaic manuscripts from Qumran Cave 4, despite their very fragmentary state,[5] afford a valid insight into the structure of the Aramaic Enoch. They cover all the large units represented in the Ethiopic version, including Appendix I, with the exception of Book II, the Parables, a book missing from the extant Greek version as well. By contrast, various Qumran Caves (1, 2, 4, and 6; for precise references, see Milik, p. 365) contain six copies of a section of the Enochic corpus absent from the Ethiopic, which Milik proposes to identify as the Book of Giants, and to date to the end of the second century B.C.[6] All the Qumran fragments except one are insignificant in themselves, but can be set against the relics of the Manichaean work, 'The Book of Giants', published by W. B. Henning,[7] and the later Midrash of Shemhazai and Azael (Milik, pp. 321–39).

The Book of Enoch is not a homogeneous composition. Its constituent parts are likely to have come into being separately before being assembled into a single work. The Aramaic evidence, thought to be pre-Christian in date (Milik, p. 7), indicates that Book III in the Ethiopic version, i.e. the Book of the Heavenly Lights, existed independently in scrolls containing no other section of the corpus. The oldest of the four copies (Enastr^a) is dated to about 200 B.C.; the other three (Enastr^{b,c,d}) roughly to between 50 B.C. and the beginning of the Christian era. The Aramaic original contains elaborate calendric calculations (seeking to synchronise the lunar and solar years) which have not been preserved in Ethiopic, and even those sections which are common to the two reveal a longer Aramaic recension. If the palaeographical dating of Enastr^a can be relied on, the Book of the Heavenly Light may be taken as one of the earliest components of

---

5. Milik, *op. cit.*, pp. 365–6, gives a full list of the preserved passages, but his references indicate the maximum extent of sections covered, not the actually surviving extracts. The so-called 'Diplomatic Transcription' of seven copies of Enoch (pp. 340–62) and the material transcribed in the chapter on the Astronomical Book (pp. 273–97) yield a much clearer picture.

6. These are *1Q23, 6Q8, 4QEn Giants^{b,c}*, a manuscript assigned to J. Starcky, and *4QEn Giants^a*, published by Milik (pp. 310–17, plates XXX–XXXII). The earliest witness (*4QEn Giants^b*) is dated on palaeographical grounds to the first half of the first century B.C. (Milik, p. 57; F. M. Cross, 'The Development of the Jewish Scripts', *The Bible and the Ancient Near East* (1961), p. 149). Advancing the double conjecture that the Damascus Rule, written in *c.* 110–100 B.C., includes a quotation from the Book of Giants (CD 2:18), and that the silence of Jub. 4:17–24 suggests that at the time of the composition of Jubilees (*c.* 125 B.C. according to him) this particular work of Enoch did not exist yet, Milik believes he is entitled to place the Book of Giants to the last quarter of the second century B.C. (pp. 57–8).

7. BSOAS 11 (1943–6), pp. 52–74. Cf. J. T. Milik, 'Turfan et Qumrân. Livre des Géants juif et manichéen', *Festgabe K. G. Kuhn* (1971), pp. 117–27.

Enoch, belonging probably to the third century B.C.[8]

The Book of Watchers (chapters 1–36) is the best represented section at Qumran of I Enoch as it is attested in five of the manuscripts (Enoch[a-e]). The first two are said to come from the first half to the middle of the second century B.C. (Milik, p. 22). These oldest documents attest only Book I, but Enoch[d] and Enoch[e] contain also Book IV (chapters 83–90), whilst Enoch[c] (dated to the first century B.C.) consists of Books I, IV, V and Appendix I. Milik further suggests that fragments of *4QEn Giants*[a], copied by the same hand as Enoch[c], were detached from the latter scroll, which consequently included four Enochic compositions (Milik, p. 58).

The Book of Dreams (chapters 83–90) survives fragmentarily in four manuscripts, the oldest of which (Enoch[f]) is thought to belong to *c.* 150–125 B.C. (Milik, p. 41). Its historical perspective, discernible in chapters 85–90 in the full Ethiopic account of a zoomorphic history of mankind from Adam to the author's own time, reveals the likely date of composition of Book IV. The final stage of the history of Israel is marked by the birth of white lambs which opened their eyes and saw, but failed to convince the other deaf and blind white sheep. The flock was attacked by ravens which carried away one of the lambs. Then they began to grow horns and one of them produced a great horn. The ravens tried to humble it, but were unable to do so (90:6–12). It is the commonly held view that this allegory relates to the emergence of the Hasidim, the removal of the high priest Onias III, and the rise of the Maccabees, led by Judas. Since his death in battle, which occurred in 161 B.C., is not alluded to, it is logical to conclude that this section of Enoch was completed sometime in the second half of the 160s B.C.[9]

The Book of Admonitions or Epistle of Enoch (chapters 91–105) is fragmentarily extant in Enoch[c] and Enoch[g] (*c.* the final fifty years of the pre-Christian age). The Apocalypse of Weeks contained in it (93:1–10 followed by 91:12–17 according to the Ethiopic text) depicts the seventh week following the destruction of the first Temple as an apostate generation that culminates in the emergence of 'the chosen righteous from the eternal plant of righteousness'. The eighth week marks the beginning of the Messianic age, so the author's horizon stops

---

8. See Nickelsburg, JLBBM, p. 47.

9. Milik, pp. 43–4, identifies in chapter 90:13–15 an allusion to the battle of Beth-Zur (2 Mac. 11:6–12) and concludes somewhat rashly that the Book of Dreams was 'composed during 164 B.C., probably in the early months of the year, during the few weeks which followed the battle of Bethsur'. (For the dating of the victory at Beth-Zur to the autumn of 165 B.C., see vol. I, pp. 160–2.) For the less likely identification of the deliverer as John Hyrcanus I or Alexander Jannaeus, see M. Stern, 'The Relations between Judea and Rome during the Rule of John Hyrcanus', *Tarbiz* 26 (1961), pp. 1–22, and C. C. Torrey, 'Alexander Jannaeus and the Archangel Michael', VT 4 (1954), pp. 208–11.

before the Maccabaean era. In consequence, the *terminus ad quem* of the composition of this section must be around 170 B.C.[10]

In brief, four of the five books preserved in the Ethiopic version can safely be attributed to the first four decades of the second century B.C. The Book of Watchers and the Book of the Heavenly Lights could even be traced to the third century B.C. The Qumran Aramaic evidence shows that whereas Book III (chapters 72–82) was not yet merged with the rest, and that in the oldest manuscripts Book I (chapters 1–36) stands on its own, Enoch[c] combines at least Books I, IV and V and possibly the Book of Giants, and Enoch[d] and Enoch[e] also contain more than one section of what finally became I Enoch.

It can reasonably be conjectured from the data so far assembled that a composite work bearing a pseudepigraphic attribution to Enoch existed already in the second century B.C., and more precisely before the compilation of the Book of Jubilees.[11] Jub. 4:17–19, in depicting Enoch's writing activities, discloses the contents of the Book of Enoch known to the author of Jubilees. These comprise Books I, III and IV, and possibly V as well.[12]

Leaving aside the Book of Giants already mentioned (p. 254 and n. 6), and the Book of Noah to be described below, the one remaining major issue is the nature and status of Book II, the Parables. Even prior to the Qumran discoveries it was the most controversial of all the Enochic sections. A number of nineteenth century authors viewed it as a Christian work.[13] Schürer himself, in the final German edition (p. 279), expressed the opinion that chapters 37–71 came from a different author, and were characterized by a peculiar designation of God as well as a distinct messianic, eschatological and angelological teaching. He further suggested that this section was more recent that the rest of Enoch. The only passage susceptible of historical identification is chapter 56:5–7, foretelling an eschatological invasion of the Holy Land by Parthians and Medes. Their horsemen would not enter the city of

10. Cf. Eissfeldt, *Introduction*, p. 619; R. H. Charles, APOT II, p. 171; Nickelsburg, JLBBM, p. 150.

11. The following dates have been assigned to Jubilees. 100 B.C.: Eissfeldt, *Introduction*, p. 608; 109–105 B.C.: Charles, APOT II, p. 6; 128–125 B.C.: Milik, *op. cit.*, p. 58; 168–140 B.C.: J. C. VanderKam, *Textual and Historical Studies in the Book of Jubilees* (1977), pp. 207–85; Nickelsburg, JLBBM, pp. 78–9. Bearing in mind that Jubilees is cited in CD, for which the most likely time of composition is the end of the second century B.C., the earlier of the proposed datings of Jubilees acquires greater probability.

12. Charles, APOT II, p. 18; Nickelsburg, JLBBM, p. 150.

13. For a Christian origin of the entire I Enoch, see J. C. K. Hofmann, 'Ueber die Entstehungszeit des Buches Henoch', ZDMG 6 (1852), pp. 87–91; H. Weisse, *Die Evangelienfrage* (1856), pp. 214–24; F. Philippi, *Das Buch Henoch* (1868), *passim*. For a Christian origin of the Parables, see A. Hilgenfeld, *Die jüdische Apokalyptik in ihrer geschichtlichen Entwickelung* (1857), pp. 150–84. For a Christian origin of the 'Son of Man' passages, see J. Drummond, *The Jewish Messiah* (1877), pp. 60–73.

God's elect, but would fight and destroy one another. According to one school of thought, represented by R. H. Charles among others, the allusion must be to a period prior to the Roman conquest of Palestine, i.e. probably to 100–64 B.C.[14] For another group of scholars—E. Sjöberg among them—the allusion concerns the Parthian invasion of Palestine in 40 B.C.[15]

A new situation arose with the discovery of the Aramaic fragments from Qumran. The absence of any attestation of the Parables in Cave 4 has led J. T. Milik to conclude (pp. 89–96) that Book II (chapters 37–71) of the Ethiopic version was not part of the Aramaic Enoch; that it did not exist at all in pre-Christian times; that it was a Greek Christian composition inspired by the Gospels, and inserted by a Christian redactor into I Enoch to replace there the Book of Giants; that Enoch 56:5–7 hints at the mid-third century A.D. attacks on Syria and Palestine by the Persians and Palmyrenes; and that accordingly the composition of the Book of Parables should be dated to 'around the year A.D. 270 or shortly afterwards' (p. 96). As regards the insertion of this work into the Book of Enoch, Milik notes that no patristic reference to it is extant from the first four centuries (pp. 91–2), and that the complete Greek form of the Pentateuch of Enoch, from which the Ethiopic translation derives, does not antedate the sixth or the seventh century, about which time the stichometry circulating under the name of the Patriarch of Constantinople, Nicephorus, may have been first compiled (p. 77).

Scholarly opinion has so far shown little inclination towards accepting Milik's thesis. In particular, there is quasi-universal disagreement with the dating of the Parables to the late third century A.D. and their attribution to a Christian author. The use of the 'Son of Man' and 'Elect' imagery in the context of universal judgement common to the Parables and certain Gospel passages can scarcely reveal a Christian hand behind this section of Enoch in the absence of any typical trait relating to the New Testament representation of the life and teaching of Jesus. In this case, lack of reference in patristic literature to the Book of Parables has no evidential value proving a late, post–A.D. 400 date. The thesis of the Pentateuch form of Enoch is also purely conjectural. The Ethiopic version happens to contain five sections, but this fact does not justify the claim that from its inception the composite work was by definition fivefold, and to speculate on the substitution, by a Greek Christian redactor, of the Parables for the original Aramaic Book of Giants.

These flimsy theories apart, Milik's reconstruction includes one point

---

14. APOT II, p. 222.
15. *Der Menschensohn im äthiopischen Henochbuch* (1946), p. 39.

requiring serious consideration. It concerns, needless to say, the lack of attestation of the Parables at Qumran. Some scholars are prepared to declare this to be purely accidental and consequently devoid of significance.[16] But if it is borne in mind that the Qumran sect showed considerable interest in the Enoch literature, as is apparent from the quantity of manuscripts discovered in Cave 4, the total absence of material relative to the Parables is not without significance.[17] But to infer from the silence of Qumran, as Milik and some of his critics do, that the hypothesis that the Parables were composed after the end of the Essene occupation of Qumran means that we are dealing with a Christian composition, is a logical fallacy, a point well made by M. A. Knibb.[18]

The second topic requiring further examination before the date of origin of the Parables is determined concerns chapter 56:5–7, the allusion to the Parthian and Mede invasion. E. Sjöberg's theory that the event envisaged is the Parthian attack on Palestine in 40 B.C. has been re-stated by Greenfield and Stone (p. 60), and more tentatively by Nickelsburg (JLBBM, p. 221). Two further hypotheses have been added in recent years. According to the first, Enoch 56:5–7 is seen as referring to the Parthian defeat of Trajan in A.D. 115–17 and to a subsequent imaginary advance on the Holy Land.[19] In the second reconstruction, 'Parthian' stands as a sobriquet for 'Roman', and the episode hinted at is Petronius' mission to Jerusalem to install Caligula's effigy in the Jerusalem Temple.[20] None of these interpretations is convincing, for the picture outlined in 56:5–7 (invasion of Palestine by Parthians and Medes, halted by 'the city of my chosen ones' and turning into internecine strife) is very distant from any of the so-called applications. It is therefore preferable to consider the passage, which ends with the depiction of Sheol swallowing up the attackers, as essentially eschatological and consequently unfit for historical speculation.[21]

16. Cf. e.g. Nickelsburg, JLBBM, p. 221; J. C. Greenfield and M. E. Stone, 'The Enochic Pentateuch and the Date of the Similitudes', HThR 70 (1977), pp. 55–6; D. W. Suter, 'Weighed in the Balance: The Similitudes of Enoch in Recent Discussion', Rel. St. Rev. 7 (1981), p. 217.

17. The parallel of Esther proposed by Greenfield and Stone is an ill-chosen and facile argument (p. 55). Not only is the Book of Esther known to have existed during say the first century A.D., thanks to the Septuagint and Josephus, but its non-attestation among the Dead Sea Scrolls could be explained in many ways, some of which are listed by Greenfield and Stone.

18. 'The Date of the Parables of Enoch: A Critical Review', NTSt 25 (1980), p. 348.

19. J. C. Hindley, 'Towards the Date of the Similitudes of Enoch', NTSt 14 (1967/8), pp. 557–65.

20. D. W. Suter, *Tradition and Composition in the Parables of Enoch* (1979), pp. 29–32; art. cit. (in n. 55), p. 218.

21. See Knibb's pertinent remarks in art. cit. (in n. 18), p. 355. It is worth noting that from A.D. 70 onwards the only power capable of challenging Rome was the Parthian

In sum, whereas there is general agreement among contemporary students of Enoch in rejecting Milik's late dating and Christian attribution of the Parables, opinions regarding their time of origin and relationship to the 'Son of Man' terminology in the Gospels still vary greatly. Nevertheless there seems to be a growing tendency towards placing this section of Enoch in the first century A.D. The dates range from 'around the turn of the era' (Nickelsburg, p. 223); 'some time during the first century C.E.' (Greenfield and Stone, p. 60); 'not ... much before 70 C.E.' (Suter, p. 218); 'the end of the first century A.D.' (Knibb, p. 359). However, on account of the themes common to the Parables, 2 Baruch and 4 Ezra, noted by Knibb (pp. 358–9), the possible connections with the Gospel of Matthew,[22] and the concept of a pre-existent, concealed and revealed Messiah, attested in the late first and in the second century sources,[23] it is justifiable to suggest the last quarter of the first Christian century as the most likely period for the writing of the Parables of Enoch.[24]

Since the Parables are extant only in Ethiopic, their original language remains to some extent at least problematic. The linguistic background of Enoch in general (see below, p. 260), and the 'Son of Man' terminology in particular, strongly suggest an Aramaic *Vorlage*. This view was first advanced by N. Smith;[25] and more recently, Edward Ullendorff has argued in favour of the Parables and much further Enoch material having been translated into Ethiopic both from the Greek and from the Aramaic.[26] M. A. Knibb, whilst postulating the availability of a Greek version to the Ethiopic translator, also demonstrates that the reading of certain passages in the Parables depends on a Semitic, and more precisely Aramaic, original.[27]

---

empire. The ensuing upheaval was imagined, according to sayings attributed to second century rabbis, as a preparation for the days of the Messiah. 'There is not a single palm tree in Babylon to which a Persian horse (סוס של פרשים) will not be tied, and not a single coffin in the land of Israel from which a Median horse (סוס [של] מדי) will not be eating hay' (R. Yose ben Kisma in bSanh. 98ab). 'When you see a Persian horse tethered in the land of Israel, then look for the footsteps of the Messiah' (R. Simeon ben Yohai in Lam. R. 1:13 (41); cf. J. Neusner, *A History of the Jews in Babylonia* I (1965), p. 79).

22. Cf. J. Theisohn, *Der auserwählte Richter. Untersuchungen zum traditionsgeschichtlichen Ort der Menschensohngestalt der Bilderreden des äthiopischen Henoch* (1975), pp. 149–82; Suter, *op. cit.* (in n. 59), pp. 25–9; D. R. Catchpole, 'The Poor on Earth and the Son of Man in Heaven: A Re-Appraisal of Matthew XXV.31–46', BJRL 61 (1979), pp. 355–97.

23. G. Vermes, *Jesus the Jew* (1973, ²1983), p. 176. Cf. also vol. II, pp. 520–2.

24. G. Vermes, *The Dead Sea Scrolls: Qumran in Perspective* (1977, ²1982), p. 223; Knibb, *art. cit.*, pp. 358–9.

25. 'The Original Language of the Parables of Enoch', in R. E. Harper et al. (eds.), *Old Testament and Semitic Studies in memory of W. R. Harper* II (1908), pp. 329–49.

26. 'An Aramaic "Vorlage" of the Ethiopic Text of Enoch?', *Atti del Convegno Internazionale di Studi Etiopici* (1960), pp. 259–67; *Ethiopia and the Bible* (1968), pp. 61–2.

27. M. A. Knibb with the assistance of Edward Ullendorff, *The Ethiopic Book of Enoch. A New Edition in the Light of the Aramaic Fragments* II (1978), pp. 37–46.

Noachic Portions. Extracts from a Book of Noah have been inserted in various places of Enoch. The work is mentioned in Jub. 10:13 and 21:10, and fragments of this type have been identified at Qumran (see p. 332). Chapters 54:7–55:2, 60:65–69:25 and 106–7 definitely belong to such an earlier work. Charles adds to this list chapters 6–11 and 60 (APOT II, p. 168).[28] The appendix already attested in *4QEnoch^c* in Aramaic may be seen as a forward look towards the successor of Enoch in the transmission of antediluvian wisdom (Milik, p. 184).

In regard to the redaction of Enoch, judgement should be reserved concerning the status of the Book of Giants until the publication of the full evidence. Manuscript c from Cave 4 of Qumran suggests that by the first century B.C. at least three of the five sections (Books I, IV and V) were included in a single scroll. Characteristically, perhaps, these are also the three books extant in Greek translation.[29] The Book of the Heavenly Lights, with its calendric and astronomical lore, even though copied separately, seems to be presupposed in the rest of the Enochic corpus. The inclusion of the Book of Parables must have followed close on its completion, for there is no evidence of any Jewish work more recent than the late first to early second century A.D. having been recognized as common treasure and inherited by the Christian Church.

Apart from the Parables, surviving only in Ethiopic translation, the original language of the bulk of the Book of Enoch is no longer controversial. All the Qumran fragments are in Aramaic. It is interesting to record that among those nineteenth and early twentieth century scholars who have made the right choice, are, in addition to N. Smith already cited, Israël Lévi (REJ 26 (1893), p. 149); Julius Wellhausen (*Skizzen und Vorarbeiten* VI (1899), p. 241); and Emil Schürer (III, p. 283). R. H. Charles (*The Ethiopic Version of the Book of Enoch* (1906), pp. xxvii-xxxiii) correctly proposed Aramaic as the language of chapters 6–36, but considered the rest of the work to have originated in Hebrew.

For the legend of Enoch, see (beside Gen. 5:18–24) Ecclus. 44:16; 49:14; Heb. 11:5; Jude 14; Irenaeus v 5, 1; Tertullian, *De Anima* 50; Hippolytus, *De Christo et Antichristo* 43–7; *Gospel of Nicodemus* (= *Acts of Pilate*) 25; *History of Joseph the Carpenter* 30–2. See further art. Enoch, JE V, pp. 178–9; Enc. Jud. 6, cols. 793–5; H. Odeberg, art. 'Ενώχ, TDNT II, pp. 556–60.

28. Cf. Charlesworth, PMRS, pp. 166–7.
29. If Milik is correct in identifying fr. 3 of Oxyrhynchus Papyrus 2069 (published by A. S. Hunt, *The Oxyrhynchus Papyri* xvii (1927), pp. 6–8) as Enoch 77:7–78:1, 8, then a Greek recension of Book III (chapters 72–82) would also be documented. Cf. Milik, 'Fragments grecs du Livre d'Hénoch (P. Oxy. xvii 2069)', *Chronique d'Égypte* 46 (1971), pp. 321–43. Knibb (*Enoch* II, p. 21) rightly points out, however, that owing to the smallness of the fragment, its evidential significance is negligible.

On the use of Enoch in Jewish literature, see R. H. Charles, *The Book of Enoch* (²1912), pp. lxx-lxxix; F. Martin, *Le livre d'Henoch* (1906), pp. cvi-cxii.

A remark by a Jewish or Samaritan Hellenistic writer (referred to as Eupolemus) to the effect that Enoch was the inventor of astrology inasmuch as he learnt it from the angels, which was included by Alexander Polyhistor in his last work, *On the Jews*, and survives in an excerpt by Eusebius, probably rests upon acquaintance with our book. (On the identity of Eupolemus, see p. 519 below.) Cf. Eusebius, *Praep. ev.* ix 17, 8 (ed. K. Mras): τοῦτον εὑρηκέναι πρῶτον τὴν ἀστρολογίαν. Cf. *ibid.* 17, 9: τοῦ δὲ 'Ενὼχ γενέσθαι υἱὸν Μαθουσαλάν, ὃν πάντα δι' ἀγγέλων θεοῦ γνῶναι, καὶ ἡμᾶς οὕτως ἐπιγνῶναι. See Milik, *op. cit.*, pp. 6–9.

In the Book of Jubilees, the Book of Enoch is copiously used and indeed explicitly quoted, 4:17 24 (cf. R. H. Charles, *The Book of Jubilees* (1902), pp. 37–8; APOT II, pp. 18–19).

In the *Testaments of the Twelve Patriarchs* reference is expressly made to the Enoch writings in nine passages. In five instances the reference is found in all Greek manuscripts: *T. Simeon* 5:4; *T. Levi* 10:5; *T. Dan* 5:6; *T. Naphtali* 4:1; *T. Benjamin* 9:1 (not in the Armenian). In four passages the reference is found only in one group of manuscripts, β: *T. Levi* 14:1 and 16:1; *T. Juda* 18:1; *T. Zebulun* 3:4. In the last case, the other manuscripts have Μωυσέως instead of 'Ενώχ —but the anachronistic allusion to Moses is due probably to the inadvertence of a later copyist inspired by the mention of the 'Mosaic' ritual prescribed in the case of the refusal of Levirate marriage (Dt. 25:7 9). The quotations cannot be found in any of the extant versions of Enoch, neither in the Ethiopic text, nor in the Slavonic Book of Enoch mentioned below (pp. 746–50), and they appear to be the fabrication of the author or interpolator which he perpetrated because he wished to appeal to a written authority. Even so, it can be concluded from the quotations that by the time of the author written material concerning Enoch was already in existence. The mention of 'Εγρήγορες (watchers, angels) in *T. Reuben* 5:6–7 and *T. Naphtali* 3:5 would appear to derive from I Enoch.

For rabbinic works on Enoch, see 3 Enoch, below pp. 269–77.

Enoch in the New Testament: ἐπροφήτευσεν δὲ καὶ τούτοις ἕβδομος ἀπὸ 'Αδὰμ 'Ενὼχ λέγων (Epistle of Jude 14), citing Enoch 1:9. Jude 6 also goes back doubtless to Enoch 10. For a list of New Testament passages which may have been influenced by Enoch, see Charles, APOT II, pp. 180–1.

Patristic testimonia: Quotations from Enoch appear in the Epistle of Barnabas: τὸ τέλειον σκάνδαλον ἤγγικεν περὶ οὗ γέγραπται ὡς 'Ενὼχ λέγει (4:3); λέγει γὰρ ἡ γραφή (16:5), followed by an Enoch citation. Justin Martyr, *Apologia* ii 5 (ed. Otto), speaks of the fall of the angels, evidently referring to Enoch 7. Irenaeus, *Adversus Haereses* iv 16, 2 (ed. Harvey) : 'Sed et Enoch sine circumcisione placens Deo, cum esset homo, Dei legatione ad angelos fungebatur et translatus est et conservatur usque nunc testis iusti iudicii Dei.' Tertullian, *De cultu feminarum* i 3 : 'Scio scripturam Enoch, quae hunc ordinem angelis dedit, non recipi a quibusdam, quia nec in armarium Iudaicum admittitur. Opinor, non putaverunt illam ante cataclysmum editam post eum casum orbis omnium rerum abolitorem salvam esse potuisse ...' Tertullian goes on to point out how this was possible, and continues: 'Sed cum Enoch eadem scriptura etiam de domino praedicarit, a nobis quidem nihil omnino reiciendum est, quod pertineat ad nos. Et legimus omnem scripturam aedificationi habilem divinitus inspirari. A Iudaeis potest iam videri propterea reiecta, sicut et cetera fere quae Christum sonant ... Eo accedit, quod Enoch apud Iudam apostolum testimonium possidet.' The whole of the beginning of chapter 2 should also be compared, the subject of which is taken from Enoch. Cf. *ibid.* ii 10: (iidem angeli) 'damnati a Deo sunt, ut Enoch refert.' *De idolatria* 4: 'Antecesserat Enoch praedicens ...' *Ibid.* 15: 'Haec igitur ab initio praevidens spititus sanctus [!] etiam ostia in superstitionem ventura praececinit per antiquissimum propheten Enoch.' Concerning the testimony of Tertullian, see also the discussion in Th. Zahn, *Geschichte des neutestamentlichen Kanons* I, pp. 120–2.

Clement of Alexandria, *Eclogae prophetarum* 2, 1 (ed. Stählin): " Εὐλογημένος εἶ ὁ βλέπων ἀβύσσους, καθήμενος ἐπὶ Χερουβίμ" ὁ Δανιήλ λέγει ὁμοδοξῶν τῷ ᾿Ενὼχ τῷ εἰρηκότι "καὶ εἶδον τὰ ὕλας πάσας" *Ibid.* 53, 4 (ed. Stählin): ἤδη δὲ καὶ ᾿Ενώχ φησιν τοὺς παραβάντας ἀγγέλους διδάξαι τοὺς ἀνθρώπους ἀστρονομίαν καὶ μαντικὴν καὶ τὰς ἄλλας τέχνας. Celsus endeavours to show, according to Origen, *Contra Celsum* v 52 (ed. Koetschau) that Christians would contradict themselves if they said that Christ was the only ἄγγελος sent into the world by God. As evidence he quotes the following: ἐλθεῖν γὰρ καὶ ἄλλους λέγουσι πολλάκις καὶ ὁμοῦ γε ἑξήκοντα ἢ ἑβδομήκοντα· οὓς δὴ γενέσθαι κακοὺς καὶ κολάζεσθαι δεσμοῖς ὑποβληθέντας ἐν γῇ, ὅθεν καὶ τὰς θερμὰς πηγὰς εἶναι τὰ ἐκείνων δάκρυα... In the commentary on this passage, Origen remarks (*ibid.* v 54–5) that the story is taken from the Book of Enoch, but Celsus had obviously not read the book himself but knew it only by hearsay, for he does not mention the author by name. *Ibid.* v 54: ἐν ταῖς ἐκκλησίαις οὐ πάνυ φέρεται ὡς θεῖα τὰ ἐπιγεγραμμένα τοῦ ᾿Ενὼχ βιβλία. Origen, *De principiis* i 3, 3 (ed. Koetschau): 'Sed et in Enoch libro his similia describuntur.' iv, 35: 'Sed et in libro suo Enoch ita ait: "ambulavi usque ad imperfectum" [Enoch 21:1] ... scriptum namque est in eodem libello dicente Enoch: "Universas materias perspexi".' *In Numeros homilia* 28, 2 (ed. Baehrens): 'De quibus quidem nominibus plurima in libellis, qui appellantur Enoch, secreta continentur et nentur e arcana: sed quia libelli isti non videntur apud Hebraeos in auctoritate haberi, interim nunc ea, quae ibi nominantur, ad exemplum vocare differamus.' *In Iohannem* 6 42 (ed. Preuschen): ὡς ἐν τῷ 'Ενὼχ γέγραπται, εἴ τῷ φίλον παραδέχεσθαι ὡς ἅγιον τὸ βιβλίον. Anatolius, in Eusebius, *Historia ecclesiastica* vii 32, 19 (ed. Schwartz): τοῦ δὲ τὸν πρῶτον παρ' 'Εβραίοις μῆνα περὶ ἰσημερίαν εἶναι παραστατικὰ καὶ τὰ ἐν τῷ 'Ενὼχ μαθήματα. Hilarius, *Commentarius in Psalmum* 132, vi (ed. Zingerle) cites Enoch, without naming him, with the formula: 'fertur autem id, de quo etiam nescio cuius liber extat, quod angeli concupiscentes filias hominum ...' Priscillian (*c.* 380), *Tractatus* iii, 56–7 (ed. Schepss), justifies his use of the book as a prophetic work by appealing to the authority of Jude and Paul: 'Quis est hic Enoc quem in testimonium profetiae apostolus Iudas adsumpsit? ... Aut fortassis Enoc profeta esse non meruit quem Paulus in epistula ad Hebraeos facta ante translationem testimonium habuisse testatur ... De quo si non ambigitur et apostolis creditur quod profeta est ...' Augustine is obliged to acknowledge: 'Scripsisse quidem nonnulla divine illum Enoch septimum ab Adam, negare non possumus, cum hoc in epistula canonica Iudas apostolus dicat'; nevertheless he rejects 'illa quae sub eius nomine proferuntur et continent istas de gigantibus fabulas' (*De civitate Dei* xv 23; cf. xviii 38). Jerome, *De viris illustribus* 4: 'Iudas frater Iacobi parvam, quae de septem catholicis est, epistolam reliquit. Et quia de libro Enoch, qui apocryphus est, in ea assumit testimonium, a plerisque reiicitur ...' *Commentarius in Epistolam ad Titum* i 12: 'Qui autem putant totum librum debere sequi eum, qui libri parte usus sit, videntur mihi et apocryphum Enochi, de quo apostolus Iudas in epistola sua testimonium posuit, inter ecclesiae scripturas recipere.' John Cassian gives in his *Collationes* viii 20–1, via the mouth of a monk called Serenus, an exposition of Genesis 6 which is influenced by the presentation in the Book of Enoch (H. J. Lawlor, 'The Book of Enoch in the Egyptian Church', in *Hermathena* 30 (1904), pp. 178–83). George Syncellus quotes several lengthy passages (*Chronography*, ed. Dindorf, i, 20–3 and 42–7) with the following formulae of introduction: ἐκ τοῦ πρώτου βιβλίου τοῦ 'Ενώχ (i, 19); ἐκ τοῦ πρώτου βιβλίου 'Ενὼχ περὶ τῶν ἐγρηγόρων (i, 20); ἐκ τοῦ πρῶτου λόγου 'Ενὼχ (i, 42); ἐκ τοῦ πρώτου βιβλίου 'Ενὼχ περὶ τῶν ἐγρηγόρων (i, 47). H. Gelzer, in his *Sextus Julius Africanus und die byzantinische Chronographie* I, 1 (1885), pp. 262–4, has convincingly shown that Syncellus has taken the passages, not directly from Enoch, but from the Alexandrian chronicler Panodorus (*c.* A.D. 400). Cf. Denis, *IPGAT*, pp. 17–18; Milik, *op. cit.*, pp. 18–19. In the Stichometry of Nicephorus, and the Synopsis of Athanasius, the Book of Enoch stands amongst the Apocrypha. On these two works, see below, p. 297. This is true also of that anonymous inventory of the canon, on which see below, pp. 297–8. *Apostolic Constitutions* vi 16 (ed. Funk): καὶ ἐν

τοῖς παλαιοῖς δέ τινες συνέγραψαν βιβλία ἀπόκρυφα Μωσέως καὶ
Ἐνὼχ καὶ Ἀδὰμ Ἠσαΐου τε καὶ Δαβὶδ καὶ Ἠλία καὶ τῶν τριῶν πατριαρχῶν,
φθοροποιὰ καὶ τῆς ἀληθείας ἐχθρά. In spite of its rejection by the official
Church, the book has maintained its influence in some circles, not
only into the Middle Ages but right to the present day (thus in the
Ethiopian Church). See the beginning of the subsection and the notes
following on the extant texts. For further information on the Patristic
testimonia, see H. J. Lawlor, 'Early Citations from the Book of Enoch',
Journal of Philology 25 (1897), pp. 164–225; F. Martin, *Le livre d'Henoch*
(1906), pp. cxxiii-cxxxvi; Charles, APOT II, pp. 181–4; Denis,
IPGAT, pp. 15–30.

Editions

(1) Aramaic fragments
Milik, J. T., with the collaboration of Matthew Black, *The Books of Enoch: Aramaic
Fragments of Qumrân Cave 4* (1976).
Knibb, M. A., with the assistance of Edward Ullendorff, *The Ethiopic Book of Enoch. A new
edition in the light of the Aramaic Dead Sea Fragments* I-II (1978).

(2) Greek text
(a) *The Akhmim Codex* (Panopolitanus): Enoch 1–32
Bouriant, U., *Fragments grecs du livre d'Hénoch. Mémoires publiés par les membres de la mission
archéologique française au Caire* ix, 1 (1892), pp. 91–147.
Lods, A., *Le livre d'Hénoch. Fragments grecs découverts à Akhmim (Haute-Égypte)* (1892).
Charles, R. H., *The Book of Enoch* (1893, ²1912).
Fleming, J., and Radermacher, L., *Das Buch Henoch* (1901).
Swete, H. B., *The Old Testament in Greek* III (⁴1912).
(b) *The Chester Beatty-Michigan Papyrus*: Enoch 97:6–107:3
Bonner, Campbell, *The Last Chapters of Enoch in Greek* (1937).
(c) *Vaticanus Graecus 1809*: Enoch 89:42–9
Mai, A., *Nova Patrum Bibliotheca* II (1844).
Gildemeister, J. 'Ein Fragment des griechischen Henoch', ZDMG 9 (1855), pp. 621–4.
Gitlbauer, M., 'Die Ueberreste griechischer Tachygraphie im Codex Vaticanus graecus
1809', *Denkschrift der kaiserlichen Akademie der Wissenschaften—Philosophisch-historische
Classe* 28 (1878).
(d) *Syncellus*: Enoch 6:1–9:4; 8:4–10:14; 15:8–16:1
Dindorf, G., *Georgius Syncellus et Nicephorus Constantinopolitanus—Corpus Scriptorum Historiae
Byzantinae* (1829).
Swete, H. B., *The Old Testament in Greek* (⁴1912) III, pp. 788–809, 897–9.
Flemming, J., and Rademacher, L., *Das Buch Henoch*, GCS 5 (1901).
Charles, R. H., *The Book of Enoch* (1893), p. 12.
(e) *Oxyrhynchus Papyrus 2069*: Enoch 77:7–78:1, 8; 85:10–86:2; 87:1–3
Milik, J. T., 'Fragments grecs du livre d'Hénoch (P. Oxy. xvii 2069)', *Chronique d'Égypte*
46 (1971), pp. 321–43; cf. A. S. Hunt, *The Oxyrhynchus Papyri* xvii (1927), pp.
6–8 (a possible identification).
The most comprehensive edition (Akhmim, Chester Beattie and Syncellus) is *Apocalypsis
Henochi graece* by M. Black (1970).

(3) Ethiopic version
Laurence, R., *Libri Enoch Versio Aethiopica* (1838).
Dillmann, A., *Liber Enoch Aethiopice* (1851).

Flemming, J., *Das Buch Henoch* (1902).
Charles, R. H., *The Ethiopic Version of the Book of Enoch* (1906).
Knibb, M. A., *The Ethiopic Book of Enoch: A New Edition in the Light of the Aramaic Dead Sea Fragments* I-II (1978). [The most up-to-date edition, translation and commentary produced with the assistance of Edward Ullendorff.] For a list of Ethiopic manuscripts, see vol. II, pp. 23–7.

(4) *Latin version*: Enoch 106:1–18 (abridged)
James, M. R., *Apocrypha Anecdota* [Texts and Studies ii.3] (1893), pp. 146–50.

(5) *Syriac version*: Enoch 6:1–7
Brock, S. P., 'A Fragment of Enoch in Syriac', JThSt 19 (1968), pp. 626–31.

(6) *Coptic version*: Enoch 93:3–8
Donadoni, S., 'Un frammento della versione copte del "Libro di Enoch"', *Acta Orientalia* 25 (1960), pp. 197–202.

(7) *Middle-Persian version*: Manichaean fragment of the Book of Enoch
Henning, W., 'Ein manichäisches Henochbuch', SAB, Philos.-hist. Kl. (1934), pp. 27-35.

Translations

(1) *English*
Laurence, R., *The Book of Enoch the Prophet* (1821).
Charles, R. H., *The Book of Enoch* (1893; rev. 1912); APOT II, pp. 163–81.
Knibb, M. A., *The Ethiopic Book of Enoch* II (1978).

(2) *German*
Dillmann, A., *Das Buch Henoch übersetzt und erklärt* (1853).
Beer, G., in E. Kautzsch, APAT II (1900), pp. 217–310.
Flemming, J., in J. Flemming and L. Radermacher, *Das Buch Henoch* (1901).
Riessler, P., *Altjüdisches Schrifttum ausserhalb der Bibel* (1928), pp. 355–451; 1291–7.

(3) *French*
Martin, F., *Le livre de Hénoch, traduit sur le texte éthiopien* (1906).

(4) *Italian*
Fusella, L., Loprieno, A., and Sacchi, P., 'Libro di Enoc', in P. Sacchi (ed.), *Apocrifi dell'Antico Testamento* (1981), pp. 415–723.

(5) *Hebrew*
Goldschmidt, Lazarus, *Das Buch Henoch* (1892).
Kahana, A., and J. Feitlowitz, *Ha-Sᵉfarim ha-Hizonim* (²1956).

Bibliography

A judiciously selected bibliography is contained in M. A. Knibb, *The Ethiopic Book of Enoch* II (1978), pp. 48–52. For a fuller list, see J. H. Charlesworth, PMRS, pp. 98–103, 278–83.
Hilgenfeld, A., *Die jüdische Apokalyptik* (1857), pp. 91–184.
Volkmar, G., 'Beiträge zur Erklärung des Buches Henoch nach dem äthiopischen Text', ZDMG 14 (1860), pp. 87–134, 296.
Gelzer, H., *Sextus Julius Africanus und die byzantinische Chronographie* (1885).
Dillmann, A., 'Über den neugefundenen griechischen Text des Henoch-Buches', SAB (1892), pp. 1039–54, 1079–92.
Büchler, A., 'Das Zehnstämmereich in der Geschichtsvision des Henochbuches', MGWJ 39 (1895), pp. 11–23.
Charles, R. H., 'Enoch', HDB I (1898), pp. 705–8.
Gry, L., 'La composition des paraboles d'Hénoch', *Le Muséon* 9 (1908), pp. 27–71.

Schmidt, N., 'The Original Language of the Parables of Enoch', in R. F. Harper et al. (eds.), *Old Testament and Semitic Studies in Memory of W. R. Harper* II (1908), pp. 329–49.

Gry, L., *Les paraboles d'Hénoch et leur messianisme* (1910).

Kuhn, K. G., 'Beiträge zur Erklärung des Buches Henoch', ZAW 39 (1921), pp. 240–75.

Messel, N., *Der Menschensohn in der Bildreden des Henoch* (1922).

Dix, G. H., 'The Enochic Pentateuch', JThSt 27 (1926), 29–42.

Schmidt, N., 'The Apocalypse of Noah and the Parables of Enoch', *Oriental Studies dedicated to Paul Haupt* (1926), pp. 111–23.

Lods, A., 'La chute des anges', RHPhR 7 (1927), pp. 295–315.

Jeremias, J., 'Ein neuer Textfund: das Henochfragment der Chester-Beatty-Papyri', Theol. Bl. 18 (1939), cols. 145–6.

Torrey, C. C., 'Notes on the Greek Text of Enoch', JAOS 62 (1942), pp. 52–60.

Zuntz, G., 'Notes on the Greek Enoch', JBL 61 (1942), pp. 193–204.

Idem, 'Enoch and the Last Judgement (ch. cii, 1–3)', JThSt 45 (1944), pp. 161–70.

Sjöberg, E., *Der Menschensohn im äthiopischen Henochbuch* (1946).

Black, M., 'The Eschatology of the Similitudes of Enoch', JThSt 3 (1952), pp. 1–10.

Milik, J. T., 'The Dead Sea Scrolls Fragment of the Book of Enoch', Bibl. 32 (1951), pp. 393–400.

Idem, 'Hénoch au pays des aromates (Ch. xxvii à xxxii). Fragments araméens de la grotte 4 de Qumrân', RB 65 (1958), pp. 70–7.

Grelot, P. 'La géographie mythique d'Hénoch et ses sources orientales', RB 65 (1958), pp. 33–69.

Idem, 'La légende d'Hénoch dans les apocryphes et dans la Bible', RScR 46 (1958), pp. 5–26, 181–210.

Idem, 'L'eschatologie des Esséniens et le livre d'Hénoch', RQ 1 (1958/9), pp. 113–31.

Ullendorff, E., 'An Aramaic "Vorlage" of the Ethiopic Text of Enoch', *Atti del convegno internazionale di Studi Etiopici* (1960), pp. 259–68.

Kutsch, E., 'Die Solstitien im Kalender des Jubiläenbuches und im äthiopischen Henoch 72', VT 12 (1962), pp. 205–7.

Caquot, A., and Geoltrain, P., 'Notes sur le texte éthiopien des "Paraboles" d'Hénoch', Semitica 13 (1963), pp. 39–54.

Widengren, G., 'Iran and Israel in Parthian Times with Special Regard to the Ethiopic Book of Enoch', Temenos 2 (1966), pp. 139–67.

Eissfeldt, O., *The Old Testament. An Introduction* (1966), pp. 617–22, 774.

Vermes, G., 'The Use of *bar nash/bar nasha* in Jewish Aramaic', in M. Black, *An Aramaic Approach to the Gospels and Acts* (³1967), pp. 210–28 [cf. *Postbiblical Jewish Studies* (1975), pp. 147–65].

Hindley, J. C., 'Towards a Date for the Similitudes of Enoch: An Historical Approach', NTSt 14 (1967/8), pp. 551–65.

Gil, M., 'Enoch in the Land of the Living', Tarbiz 38 (1969), pp. 322–37 (Hebrew).

Denis, IPGAT, pp. 15–30.

Milik, J. T., 'Problèmes de la littérature hénochique à la lumière des fragments araméens de Qumrân', HThR 64 (1971), pp. 333–78.

Idem, 'Tutfan et Qumrân. Livre des Géants juif et manichéen', in G. Jeremias et al. (eds.), *Tradition und Glaube. Festgabe für K. G. Kuhn* (1971), pp. 117–27.

Müller, K., 'Beobachtungen zur Entwicklung der Menschensohnvorstellung in den Bildreden des Henoch und im Buche Daniel', in E. C. Suttner et al. (eds.), *Wegzeichen. H. M. Biedermann Festgabe* (1971), pp. 253–62.

Philonenko, M., 'Une citation manichéenne du livre d'Hénoch', RHPhR 52 (1972), pp. 337–40.

VanderKam, J., 'The Theosophy of Enoch I 3b–7,9', VT 23 (1973), pp. 129–50.

Black, M., 'The Maranatha Invocation and Jude 14, 15 (I Enoch 1:9)', B. Lindars et al.

(eds.), *Christ and Spirit in the New Testament* (C. F. D. Moule Festschrift) (1973), pp. 189–96.

Idem, 'Fragments of the Aramaic Enoch from Qumran', in W. C. van Unnik (ed.), *La littérature juive entre Tenach et Mishna* (1974), pp. 15–28.

Lührmann, D., 'Henoch und die Metanoia', ZNW 66 (1975), pp. 103–16.

Theisohn, J., *Der auserwählte Richter: Untersuchungen zum traditionsgeschichtlichen Ort der Menschensohngestalt der Bildreden des äthiopischen Henoch* (1975).

Caquot, A., 'Léviathan et Behémoth dans la troisième "Parabole" d'Hénoch', Semitica 25 (1975), pp. 111–22.

Grelot, P., 'Hénoch et ses écritures', RB 82 (1975), pp. 481–500.

Black, M., 'The "Parables" of Enoch (1 En. 37–71) and the "Son of Man"', ET 88 (1976), pp. 1–8.

Idem, 'The New Creation in 1 Enoch', in R. W. A. McKinney, *Creation, Christ and Culture* (1976), pp. 13–21.

Casey, M., 'The Use of the Term "Son of Man" in the Similitudes of Enoch', JSJ 7 (1978), pp. 11–29.

Lindars, B., 'A Bull, a Lamb and a Word: 1 Enoch XC, 38', NTSt 22 (1975/6), pp. 483–6.

Glasson, T. F., 'The Son of Man Imagery: Enoch 14 and Daniel 7', NTSt 23 (1976/7), pp. 82–90.

Nickelsburg, G. W. E., 'Enoch, Book of', IDBS (1976), pp. 265–8.

Idem, 'Enoch 97–104: A Study of the Greek and Ethiopic Texts', in M. E. Stone (ed.), *Armenian and Biblical Studies* [*Sion*, suppl. 1] (1976), pp. 90–156.

Dexinger, F., *Henochs Zehnwochenapokalypse und offene Probleme der Apokalyptikforschung* (1977).

Fitzmyer, J. A., 'Implications of the New Enoch Literature from Qumran', ThSt 38 (1977), pp. 332–45.

Greenfield, J. C., and Stone, M. E., 'The Enochic Pentateuch and the Date of the Similitudes of Enoch', HThR 70 (1977), pp. 51–65.

Hanson, P. D., 'Rebellion in Heaven, Azazel and Euhemeristic Heroes in 1 Enoch 6–11', JBL 96 (1977), pp. 195–233.

Nickelsburg, G. W. E., 'Apocalyptik and Myth in 1 Enoch 6–11', JBL 96 (1977), pp. 383–405.

Idem, 'The Apocalyptik Message of 1 Enoch 92–105', CBQ 39 (1977), pp. 309–28.

Barr, J., 'Aramaic-Greek Notes on the Book of Enoch', JSS 23 (1978), pp. 184–98.

Suter, D. W., 'Apocalyptic Patterns in the Similitudes of Enoch', in P. J. Achtemeier (ed.), *SBL 1978 Seminar Papers* I (1978), pp. 1–13.

VanderKam, J., 'Enoch Traditions in Jubilees and other Secondary Sources', *ibid.*, pp. 229–51.

Kraft, R. A., 'Philo (Josephus, Sirach and Wisdom of Solomon) on Enoch', *ibid.*, pp. 253–7.

Himmelfarb, M., 'A Report on Enoch in Rabbinic Literature', *ibid.*, pp. 259–69.

Hanson, P. D., 'A Response to John Collins' "Methodological Issues in the Study of I Enoch"', *ibid.*, pp. 307–9.

Nickelsburg, G. W. E., 'Reflections on Reflections: A Response to John Collins' "Methodological Issues …"', *ibid.*, pp. 311–14.

Collins, J. J., 'Methodological Issues in the Study of I Enoch: Reflections on the Articles by P. D. Hanson and G. W. E. Nickelsburg', *ibid.*, pp. 315–22.

Dimant, D., '1 Enoch 6–11: A Methodological Perspective', *ibid.*, pp. 323–39.

Black, M., 'The Apocalypse of Weeks in the Light of 4Q En^G', VT 28 (1978), pp. 464–9.

Klijn, A. F. J., 'From Creation to Noah in the Second Dream Vision of the Ethiopic Henoch', *Miscellanea Neotestamentica* (1978), pp. 147–59.

Milik, J. T., 'Écrits préesséniens de Qumrân: d'Hénoch à Amram', in M. Delcor (ed.), *Qumrân, sa piété, sa théologie et son milieu* (1978), pp. 91–106.

Stone, M. E., 'The Book of Enoch and Judaism in the Third Century B.C.E.', CBQ 40 (1978), pp. 479–92.
Nickelsburg, G. W. E., 'Riches, the Rich, and God's Judgement in I Enoch 92–105 and the Gospel according to Luke', NTSt 25 (1978/9), pp. 324–44.
Knibb, M. A., 'The Date of the Parables of Enoch: A Critical Review', *ibid.*, pp. 345–59.
Mearns, C. L., 'Dating the Similitudes of Enoch', *ibid.*, pp. 360–9.
Greenfield, J. C., and Stone, M. E., 'The Books of Enoch and the Traditions of Enoch', Numen 26 (1979), pp. 89–103.
Suter, D. W., *Tradition and Composition in the Parables of Enoch* (1979).
Idem, 'Fallen Angel, Fallen Priest: The Problem of Family Purity in I Enoch 6–16', HUCA 50 (1979), pp. 115–35.
Newsom, Carol A., 'The Development of I Enoch 6–19: Cosmology and Judgement', CBQ 42 (1980), pp. 310–29.
Collins, J. J., 'The Heavenly Representative: The "Son of Man" in the Similitudes of Enoch', in *Ideal Figures in Ancient Judaism* (1980), pp. 111–33.
Black, M., 'The Composition, Character and Date of the Second Vision of Enoch', *Text-Wort-Glaube* (Kurt Aland Festschrift) (1980), pp. 19–30.
Suter, D. W., 'Weighed in the Balance: The Similitudes of Enoch in Recent Discussion', *ibid.*, pp. 217–21.
Nickelsburg, G. W. E., 'The Books of Enoch in Recent Research', *ibid.*, pp. 210–17.
Idem, *Jewish Literature between the Bible and the Mishnah* (1981), pp. 46–55, 65–6, 90–9, 145–60, 214–23, 227–30.
Idem, 'Enoch, Levi and Peter: Recipients of Revelation in Upper Galilee', JBL 100 (1981), pp. 575–600.
Neugebauer, O., 'The "Astronomical" Chapters of the Ethiopic Book of Enoch, with Additional Notes on the Aramaic Fragments by M. Black', *Roy. Danish Ac. of Sc. and Lit.* (1981).
Black, M., 'The Twenty Angel Dekadarchs at I Enoch 6.7 and 69.2', JJS 33 (1982), pp. 227–35.
Levine, B. A., 'From the Aramaic Enoch Fragments: The Semantics of Cosmography', *ibid.*, pp. 311–26.
Nickelsburg, G. W. E., 'The Epistle of Enoch and the Qumran Literature', *ibid.*, pp. 333–48.
Wacker, M. T., *Weltordnung und Gericht: Studien zu I Henoch 22* (1982).
Isaac, E., 'New Light upon the Book of Enoch from newly-found Ethiopic Manuscripts', JAOS 103 (1983), pp. 399–411.
Stegemann, H., 'Die Bedeutung der Qumranfunde für die Erforschung der Apokalyptik. 3.1.1. Die Henoch-Literatur', in D. Hellholm (ed.), *Apocalypticism in the Mediterranean World and the Near East* (1983), pp. 502–8.
VanderKam, J. C., '1 Enoch 77, 3 and a Babylonian Map of the World', RQ 11 (1983), pp. 271–8.
Idem, 'Studies in the Apocalypse of Weeks (1 Enoch 93:1–10; 91:11–17)', CBQ 46 (1984), pp. 511–23.
Díez Merino, L., 'Los "vigilantes" en la literatura intertestamentaria', in N. Fernández Marcos *et al.* (eds.), *Simposio bíblico español* (1984), pp. 575–609.
Molenberg, C., 'A Study of the Roles of Shemihaza and Asael in Enoch 6–11', JJS 35 (1984), pp. 136–46.
VanderKam, J. C., *Enoch and the Growth of an Apocalyptic Tradition* (1984).
Black, M. [in consultation with VanderKam, J. C.], *The Book of Enoch or First Enoch: A New English Edition with Commentary and Textual Notes* [with an Appendix on the 'Astronomical' Chapters (72–82) by Neugebauer, O.] (1985).

3 Enoch or the Hebrew Book of Enoch is part of the so-called Hekhalot literature—a collection of early Rabbinic texts in Hebrew and Aramaic which are largely concerned with the mysteries of the heavenly world. The work, whether in whole or in part, goes under a number of different titles in the manuscripts, e.g. 'The Book of Enoch by Rabbi Ishmael the High Priest' (ספר חנוך לר׳ ישמעאל כ״ג), 'The Book of the Palaces' (ספר היכלות), 'The Chapters of the Palaces' (פרקי היכלות), 'The Chapters of Rabbi Ishmael' (פרקי דרבי ישמעאל), 'The Matter of the Elevation of Metatron' (ענין עליית מטטרון). It was Odeberg who designated it '3 Enoch', presumably because he saw it, with some justification, as developing the traditions of 1 (Ethiopic) and 2 (Slavonic) Enoch. 3 Enoch in the form discussed here is almost certainly a very late work, but, along with the remaining Hekhalot texts and late apocalypses such as Sefer Zerubbavel, it can perform a valuable service for the student of early apocalyptic by defining a 'horizon' within which he may work and indicating how Rabbinic Judaism adopted and transformed earlier ideas.

3 Enoch is extant in a number of versions, the longest of which is found in two manuscripts—Vaticanus 228 and Bodleian 1656. The differences between the manuscripts relate primarily to the length of the work, not to the content of its individual tradition-units (pericopae), nor to the order in which they occur. The relationship between the various forms of the text is highly problematic; it is far from clear whether the shorter forms represent previous stages in the growth of the final long version, or are abbreviations or anthologies. On the basis of the extreme fluidity of the major Hekhalot manuscripts, Schäfer has argued that it is misleading to talk of the Hekhalot texts as if these constituted clearly defined, carefully redacted works. He maintains that Hekhalot Rabbati, Hekhalot Zutarti, and most of the other so-called Hekhalot treatises are essentially artificial creations of modern scholarship. This view has important implications. If the Hekhalot treatises are redactional fiction, it makes little sense to discuss them individually, to date them separately and arange them in chronological order, to compare and contrast their redactional or theological tendencies, or to trace their literary evolution towards a putative final form. The focus of the analysis will have to be moved from the treatise to the individual pericopae, and to the body of traditions as a whole. Schäfer has successfully demonstrated that the redactional identity of

many of the Hekhalot treatises is weak, but there are arguably, as he himself admits, two exceptions to his general rule. The first is *Massekhet Hekhalot*; the second, 3 Enoch. In the present discussion, 3 Enoch means the form of the work attested in Vaticanus 228 and Bodleian 1656. Possessing a strong redactional identity, the standard form- and literary-critical questions can legitimately be applied to it. The nature of the shorter forms of the text, and their relationship to each other and to the long form, cannot be investigated here.

The structure of 3 Enoch may be analysed as follows.

(1) *Superscription.* At the head of 3 Enoch stands Gen. 5:24, 'Enoch walked with God, and he was not, for God took him.' This text is probably more than a decorative quotation to open the work. Rather it suggests that the redactor of 3 Enoch wished to present his material as a sort of 'midrash' on Gen. 5:24, as the full story behind the cryptic allusions of that verse. Gen. 5:24 serves to validate 3 Enoch by providing a point in sacred Scripture into which its traditions can be inserted.

(2) Chaps. 1–2 (Schäfer §§ 1–3),[1] *The Ascension of Ishmael.* 3 Enoch opens with a typical ascension story, the elements of which can easily be paralleled from other apocalyptic and Merkavah ascensions. The protagonist here is not a quasi-mythical figure from the biblical saga (such as Enoch, Moses, Elijah or Isaiah), but a concrete historical person of more recent times, viz., the second century A.D. Palestinian scholar, R. Ishmael b. Elisha. Having ascended to heaven, Ishmael finds himself confronted by hostile angels who wish to deny him access to God's presence. God rescues him by sending him the archangel Metatron who escorts him into the heavenly throne room. The angels finally accept him and, at the climax of his ecstasy, he joins them in chanting the celestial Qedushah.

(3) Chaps. 3–16 (Schäfer §§ 4–20), *The Elevation of Metatron.* (a) 3:1–4:2. Ishmael questions his angelic mentor Metatron about his names, and in particular about the name 'Youth' (נער) with which he had been addressed by the Merkavah angels (2:2). Metatron replies that he is, in fact, Enoch the son of Jared: as the youngest of all the angel-princes he is known as the 'Youth' (cf. 4:3, 10). The title נער was probably originally used in Hekhalot circles in the sense of 'servitor', and was given to Metatron in virtue of his role as minister of the heavenly temple. In 3 Enoch, the title has been re-interpreted in order

---

1. The usual chapter and verse divisions of 3 Enoch (e.g. 3 Enoch 4:3), used in the translations of Alexander, M. Angeles Navarro, and Hoffman, go back to Odesberg's edition. Schäfer in his *Synopses* however, divides the text into numbered sections. References to Schäfer's *Synopse* are in the form: Schäfer §§ 1–3. On pp. x–xvii of his *Synopses* Schäfer gives tables which correlate his reference system and that of the older printed editions of the Hekhalot texts.

to forge a link between Metatron and translated Enoch. This bold move was perhaps influenced by the Talmudic tradition that Ps. 37:25, 'I have been young (נַעַר) and now I am old', was uttered by the Prince of the World (= ? Metatron) (bYev. 16b). (b) 4:3–7:1. The identification of Metatron with translated Enoch created problems, because (in contrast to earlier apocalyptic) Rabbinic tradition is markedly reticent about the figure of Enoch. 3 Enoch tries rather desperately to validate the ascension of Enoch in terms of extant Rabbinic haggadah. First (4:3–10), it exploits a cluster of traditions about the Flood. Gen.R. 28:8 and bSanh. 108a raise the problem for theodicy of God's destruction of innocent creatures in the waters of the Flood. Alluding to this tradition, 3 Enoch suggests that Enoch was taken up to heaven to witness to future generations that God had acted justly (4:5). bSanh. 38b contains a tradition that the angels opposed the creation of man and felt themselves vindicated when the wicked generation of the Flood arrived and God was forced virtually to wipe out mankind. 3 Enoch adapts this tradition (against all reasonable chronology) into angelic opposition to Enoch's ascension to heaven at the time of the Flood. Second (5:1–7:1), 3 Enoch tries to use certain Rabbinic traditions about the commencement of idolatry in the time of Enosh (Gen.R. 23:6f; bSanh. 118b) to argue that the Shekhinah must have been removed from earth to heaven at that time, and that Enoch was taken up with it. (c) 8:1–15:2. Then follows a description of Enoch's physical and mental transformation into the angel Metatron, and his installation as 'the lesser YHWH' (12:5). A parallelism emerges between the elevation of Enoch and the ascension of Ishmael recounted in the previous section. This is probably deliberate and is intended to suggest that Enoch's experience is in some sense paradigmatic for every adept. (d) 16:1–5. The account of Metatron's exaltation is brought to an abrupt end with a story of how he was humbled by the archangel Anafiel. Another version of this story occurs in bḤag. 15a, and it is well nigh certain that that version has priority over the one in 3 Enoch. Once again 3 Enoch has drawn on extant Talmudic haggadah to validate its view, even though in this case the material was originally hostile to Metatron-speculation and leads in the context of 3 Enoch to a sudden reversal of his fortunes.

(4) Chaps. 17–40 (Schäfer §§ 21–58), *The Familia Caelestis—its Hierarchies and Activities*. Having established Metatron's credentials as an *angelus interpres*, 3 Enoch proceeds to recount the mysteries which he disclosed to R. Ishmael. First, Metatron tells Ishmael about the angelic hierarchies. Three originally independent angelologies are woven together, the first contained in chap. 17, the second in chap. 18, and the third in chaps. 19–29. Then follow two miscellanies of traditions about the composition and activities of the Heavenly Law Court (chaps.

30–34), and the rituals associated with the recitation of the celestial Qedushah (chaps. 35–40).

(5) Chaps. 41–48A (Schäfer §§ 59–70), *Miscellaneous Heavenly Wonders.* In chaps. 17–40, Metatron *tells* Ishmael about the angels—he offers him a series of discourses; in chaps. 41–48A, however, he shows him the wonders of heaven. The characteristic formula of this section is: 'Come and I will show you ... I went with him ... and he showed me ...' (e.g. 41:1, 3). The first of the marvels are cosmological in character. Ishmael sees the cosmic letters 'by which heaven and earth were created' (41:1), either the letters of the Hebrew alphabet (cf. Sefer Yeẓirah), or, more likely in view of what follows, the letters of the name of God (41). Ishmael is also shown the cosmic power of divine names to hold in balance opposing and incompatible natural forces (42). Then he is shown various categories of 'souls'—the souls of the righteous (43); the souls of the wicked and the intermediate (44:1–6); the souls of the patriarchs (44:7–10); the souls of all past and future generations embroidered on the heavenly Curtain, the *Pargod* (45); the souls of the stars (46); and the souls of the erring angels (47). The final wonder is eschatological in character: Ishmael sees the right hand of God waiting to redeem Israel (48A).

(6) Chaps. 48BCD (Schäfer §§ 71–80), *Appendix: The Alphabet of Akiba Traditions about Metatron.* 3 Enoch effectively ends at 48A:10, on a note of hope, with a quotation of Zech. 14:9, 'The Lord will be king of the whole world.' However, in order to make the collection of Metatron traditions as full as possible, the redactor has appended the Metatron material found in certain recensions of the Alphabet of Akiba. The core of this material (48C) gives, in the form of an acrostic on the letter *alef*, a short account of the elevation of Enoch, parallel to that contained in 3 Enoch 3–15. Three blocks of material have been added to this: (a) a list of the seventy names of God (48B)—relevant here because Metatron's names are supposed to correspond to the names of God (cf. 4:1; 48D:5); (b) a list of the seventy names of Metatron (48D:5); (c) a section on Metatron as the Prince of Torah (*Sar Torah*) (48D:2–4, 6–10).

Internal literary analysis discloses few grounds for questioning the integrity of this long version of 3 Enoch. The one major intrusion appears to be the two parallel lists of the winds and chariots of God in chaps. 22–23, which clearly interrupt the third angelology (chaps. 19–21, 24–29). However, their insertion is easily explained. Chap. 21 is concerned with the Cherubim; chap. 22 opens, 'How many winds blow from under the wings of the Cherubim?'; and the first of the chariots in chap. 23 is 'the chariots of the Cherubim'. The final redactor himself may have added this material in order to fill out the traditions on the Cherubim in chap. 21. At 4:1 there is suspicion of a lacuna: Ishmael questions Metatron about his seventy names but receives a reply about only *one* name—'Youth'. It is tempting to suppose that material on the seventy names of Metatron—perhaps a list of names (cf. 48D:1, 5)—has been omitted. However, once again we may be faced with the work of the final redactor: he himself could have omitted the seventy names of Metatron (if omission there was), simply because they did not concern him at this point. Even chap. 16 on the humbling of Metatron, which enters so abruptly against the trend of the preceding narrative, could have been introduced by the final redactor, if, as suggested earlier, he felt the negative impression created by this story was outweighed by its power to validate his Metatron traditions. Like all the Hekhalot texts, 3 Enoch, as contained in Vaticanus 228 and Bodleian 1656, clearly consists of a large number of originally independent pericopae which have equally clearly been thematically grouped and crafted into a firm redactional unity.

Though 3 Enoch presents itself as a midrash on Gen. 5:24, in broad outline it exhibits one of the standard patterns of apocalyptic literature: someone ascends to heaven and receives, with or without the mediation of an angel, a revelation of certain mysteries (relating to cosmology, the end-time, or the heavenly world) which would otherwise have been unknown to man. In respect both of its broad structure and its detailed motifs, 3 Enoch contains many parallels to works such as 1 Enoch, 2 Enoch, Testament of Levi 2:6–5:3, Ascension of Isaiah 6–11, and Apocalypse of Abraham 15–29. Seen from this angle, 3 Enoch may be classified as an example of late Jewish apocalyptic. However, by far its strongest affinities are with the Hekhalot texts, with which it is associated in the mediaeval manuscripts, belonging to a branch of esoteric lore known to the Rabbis as *Ma'aseh Merkavah*, 'the Account of the Chariot' (mHag. 2:1), which was concerned with speculating on Ezekiel's vision of God's throne-chariot (Ezek. 1 and 10). *Ma'aseh Merkavah* material may be found in early apocalyptic (e.g. 1 Enoch 14:8–25), and in the angelic liturgies from Qumran (4QShirShabb). However, certain peculiarities of language, style and motif mark off the Hekhalot texts as a highly distinctive body of literature. There is still no agreement among scholars as to the historical development or setting of this literature. Scholem argues that it emanated from conventicles of mystics who practised trance-ascent to heaven. (A séance of such a conventicle may be indirectly described in *Hekhalot Rabbati* 13–18, ed. Jellinek, *Bet ha-Midrasch* III, pp. 93–7, Schäfer §§ 198 ff.). He believed that these conventicles flourished from Tannaitic to Gaonic times, and that their teachings, which were in significant ways similar to Gnosticism, are hinted at in classic Rabbinic literature (especially in mHag. 2:1, tHag 2:1–7, yHag. 2, 77a-d, and bHag. 11b–16a). Urbach and Halperin, on the other hand, are inclined to see the Hekhalot texts as attesting to essentially a literary, rather than a mystical, movement, the Hekhalot treatises having arisen out of attempts to explain and to clarify the cryptic *Ma'aseh Merkavah* passages in the Talmud. The truth probably lies somewhere between these two positions. There can be little doubt that literary artifice and convention are to be found in the Hekhalot texts, and that in some instances 'midrashic' activity—attempts to explain earlier stages of the tradition—has generated new material. (Scholem himself points to examples.) On the other hand it seems equally undeniable that at many points powerful, fresh visionary experience lies behind the traditions.

Hekhalot texts were well known in the Gaonic period; they are mentioned by Saadya, Sherira and Hai, sometimes in terms which suggest that they are of considerable antiquity. The Karaites attacked their intense anthropomorphism and used it as a stick with which to beat their Rabbanite opponents. Jacob al-Qirqisani actually seems to have known the short account of the elevation of Enoch contained in 3 Enoch 48C and ultimately deriving from a recension of the Alphabet of Akiba (see his *Kitab al-Anwar* 1.4.2), ed. Nemoy, vol. I, p. 31, 15). The early Gaonic era, then, would seem to be a *terminus ante quem* for the composition of most, if not all, of the Hekhalot literature. It is very hard, however, to be more precise than this. Milik argued that 3 Enoch cannot have been composed earlier than the ninth or tenth century A.D., and that, in fact, the greater part was written in Germany in the twelfth to fifteenth centuries. This is much too late, and the German provenance is based on a misunderstanding of Scholem's remarks about the influence of the Hekhalot literature on the *Ḥaside Ashkenaz*. Odeberg, by way of contrast, maintained that what he believed to be the earliest stratum of 3 Enoch (9:2–13:2) is not later than the first century A.D., while the main body of the text (3–48A) was redacted in the latter part of the third century A.D. This is probably too early. The persistent re-use of Talmudic material in 3 Enoch points to a post-Talmudic date—possibly the fifth or sixth centuries (as suggested by Scholem and Alexander). As to provenance, there are only two serious possibilities—Palestine and Babylonia. In favour of the former is 3 Enoch's use of Palestinian apocalyptic traditions; in favour of the latter is the fact that the central figure of 3 Enoch—Metatron—is best attested in Babylonian sources. Perhaps the fact that 3 Enoch 16 makes use of the story of the humbling of Metatron which is found elsewhere only in the Babylonian Talmud (bḤag. 15a) tips the balance in favour of a final redaction of 3 Enoch in Babylonia.

The Rabbinic traditions relating to Enoch are summarized by Ginzberg, *Legends of the Jews* I (1925), pp. 125–40, and V (1925), pp. 153–66. Noteworthy is Targum Pseudo-Jonathan to Gen. 5:24: 'Enoch served in truth before the Lord, and behold he was no longer with the inhabitants of the earth, because he was carried away and ascended to heaven by a word from before the Lord, and his name was called Metatron, the great scribe.' The little tract *Ḥayye Ḥanokh*, derived from *Sefer ha-Yashar*, contains a rather feeble life of Enoch: see A. Jellinek, *Bet ha-Midrasch* IV (²1938), pp. 129–32; and the German translation by A. Wünsche, *Aus Israels Lehrhallen* I (1907), pp. 1–6.

The best available text of 3 Enoch, Vaticanus 228, is printed in P. Schäfer, *Synopse zur Hekhalot-Literatur* (1981), §§ 1–80. Schäfer also transcribes Munich 40 (§§ 882–938), and so renders obsolete the transcription of that manuscript in Jellinek, *Bet ha-Midrasch* V, pp. 170–90. Odeberg, *3 Enoch* (1928, reprinted with a prolegomenon by J. Greenfield 1973), offers Bodleian 1656 (which is not in Schäfer's *Synopse*), together with variants from a number of other manuscripts and printed editions. Unfortunately he did not use Vaticanus 228. Other 3 Enoch texts may be found in Schäfer, *Synopse*, §§ 387–8, 855–71; Schäfer, *Geniza-Fragmente zur Hekhalot-Literatur* (1984), pp. 135–9: T.-S. K 21.95.L = 3 Enoch 1:1–2 (Schäfer §§ 1–2) + 43:2–44:3 (Schäfer §§ 61–62). For the manuscripts of 3 Enoch see P. Schäfer, 'Handschriften zur Hekhalot-Literatur', *Frankfurter Judaistische Beiträge* 11 (1983), pp. 113–93, esp. pp. 178–89.

In addition to the Hebrew text, Odeberg provides an English translation, introduction and commentary. These remain valuable. See further P. S. Alexander, '3 Enoch', in J. H. Charlesworth (ed.), *The Old Testament Pseudepigrapha* I (1983), pp. 223–315 (introduction, translation, commentary); M. Angeles Navarro, 'Libro Hebreo de Henoc (Sefer Hekalot)', in A. Diez Macho (ed.), *Apocrifos del Antiguo Testamento* IV (1984), pp. 206–91 (introduction, translation and commentary); H. Hofmann, *Das sogenannte hebräische Henochbuch (3 Henoch)* (1984) (translation, with variants from Odeberg's apparatus criticus).

Bibliography

The older bibliography on 3 Enoch and related literature may be found in Odeberg, *3 Enoch*, pp. 11–17, and Scholem, *Kabbalah*, pp. 203–6. The more noteworthy recent literature is as follows.

Bietenhard, H., *Die himmlische Welt im Urchristentum und Spätjudentum* (1951).
Black, M., 'The Origin of the Name Metatron', VT 1 (1951), pp. 217–19.
Néher, A., 'Le voyage mystique des quatres', RHR 140 (1951), pp. 59–82.
Murtonen, A., 'The Figure of Metatron', VT 3 (1953), pp. 409–11.
Scholem, G. G., *Major Trends in Jewish Mysticism* (³1954).
Maier, J., 'Das Gefährdungsmotiv bei der Himmelsreise in der jüdischen Apokalyptik und in der "jüdischen Gnosis"', Kairos 5 (1963), pp. 18–40.
Smith, M., 'Observations on Hekhalot Rabbati', in A. Altmann (ed.), *Biblical and Other Studies* (1963), pp. 142–60.
Maier, J., *Vom Kultus zur Gnosis. Studien zur Vor- und Frühgeschichte der 'jüdischen Gnosis'* (1964).

Lieberman, S., "משנת שיר השירים", in Scholem, *Jewish Gnosticism*, pp. 118–26.

Scholem, G. G., *Jewish Gnosticism, Merkabah Mysticism and Talmudic Tradition* ([2]1965).

Gruenwald, I., 'Yannai and Hekhalot Literature', Tarbiz 36 (1966–7), pp. 257–77 [Hebrew].

Altmann, A., 'Moses Narboni's "Epistle on Shi'ur Qomah"', in Altmann (ed.), *Jewish Mediaeval and Renaissance Studies* (1967), pp. 225–88.

Urbach, E. E., 'The Traditions about Merkabah Mysticism in the Tannaitic Period', in *Studies in Mysticism and Religion Presented to G. G. Scholem* (1967), Hebrew section, pp. 1–28.

Bowker, J., '"Merkabah" Visions and the Visions of Paul', JSS 16 (1971), pp. 157–73.

Neusner, J., 'The Development of the Merkavah Tradition', JSJ 2 (1971), pp. 149–60.

Maier, J., 'Serienbildung und "numinoser" Eindruckseffekt in den poetischen Stücken der Hekhalot-Literatur', Semitica 3 (1972), pp. 36–66.

Goldberg, A., 'Der Vortrag des Ma'asse Merkawa: Eine Vermutung zur frühen Merkawamystik', Judaica 29 (1973), pp. 4–23.

Goldberg, A., 'Einige Bemerkungen zu den Quellen und redaktionellen Einheiten der Grossen Hekhalot', Frankfurter Judaistische Beiträge 1 (1973), pp. 1–49.

Gruenwald, I., 'Knowledge and Vision: Towards the Clarification of Two "Gnostic" Concepts in the Light of their Alleged Origins', Israel Oriental Studies 3 (1973), pp. 63–107.

Séd, N., 'Les traditions secrètes et les disciples de Rabban Yohanan b. Zakkaï', RHR 184 (1973), pp. 49–66.

Vajda, G., 'Recherches récentes sur l'ésotéricisme juif', RHR 184 (1973), pp. 49–66.

Goldberg, A., 'Der verkannte Gott: Prüfung und Scheitern der Adepten in der Merkawamystik', Zeitschrift für Religions- und Geistesgeschichte 26 (1974), pp. 17–29.

Gruenwald, I., 'The Jewish Esoteric Literature in the Time of the Mishnah and the Talmud', Immanuel 4 (1974), pp. 37–46.

Scholem, G. G., *Kabbalah* (1974). (A collection of Scholem's articles on Jewish mysticism from the *Encyclopaedia Judaica*.)

Goldberg, A., 'Rabban Yohanans Traum: Der Sinai in der frühen Merkawamystik', Frankfurter Judaistische Beiträge 3 (1975), pp. 1–27.

Schäfer, P., *Rivalität zwischen Engeln und Menschen* (1975).

Wewers, G. A., *Geheimnis und Geheimhaltung im rabbinischen Judentum* (1975).

Milik, J. T., *The Books of Enoch: Aramaic Fragments from Qumran Cave 4* (1976), pp. 125–35 ['Enoch in Cabbalistic Literature'].

Schiffmann, L. H., 'The Recall of Rabbi Nehuniah b. Ha-Qanah from Ecstasy in the Hekhalot Rabbati', Association for Jewish Studies Review 1 (1976), pp. 268–82.

Alexander, P. S., 'The Historical Setting of the Hebrew Book of Enoch', JJS 28 (1977), pp. 156–80.

Dan, J., 'The Chambers of the Chariot', Tarbiz 47 (1977–8), pp. 49–55 [Hebrew].

Gruenwald, I., 'Jewish Sources for the Gnostic Texts from Nag Hammadi?', *Proceedings of the Sixth World Congress of Jewish Studies* III (1977), pp. 45–56.

Schäfer, P., 'Prolegomena zu einer kritischen Edition und Analyse der Merkava Rabba', Frankfurter Judaistische Beiträge 5 (1977), pp. 65–99.

Blumenthal, D. R., *Understanding Jewish Mysticism: The Merkabah Tradition and the Zoharic Tradition* (1978).

Blumenthal, D. R., 'A Philosophical-Mystical Interpretation of a Shi'ur Qomah Text', in J. Dan and F. Talmage (eds.), *Studies in Jewish Mysticism* (1978), pp. 153–71.

Schäfer, P., 'Die Beschwörung des Sar ha-Panim. Kritische Edition und Übersetzung', Frankfurter Judaistische Beiträge 6 (1978), pp. 107–45.

Dan, J., 'The Concept of Knowledge in the *Shi'ur Qomah*', in S. Stein and R. Loewe (eds.), *Studies in Jewish Religious and Intellectual History Presented to A. Altmann* (1979), pp. 67–73.

Rowland, C., 'The Visions of God in Apocalyptic Literature', JSJ 10 (1979), pp. 137–54.

Vajda, G., 'Pour le dossier de Métatron', in S. Stein and R. Loewe (eds.), *Festschrift Altmann* (1979), pp. 345–54.

Dan, J., "פרקי היכלות רבתי ומעשה הרוגי מלכות", in G. Blidstein, R. Bonfil and Y. Salmon (eds.), *Eshel Beer-Sheva. Studies in Jewish Thought* II (1980), pp. 63–80.

Grözinger, K. E., 'Singen und ekstatische Sprache in der frühen jüdischen Mystik', JSJ 9 (1980), pp. 66–77.

Gruenwald, I., *Apocalyptic and Merkabah Mysticism* (1980).

Halperin, D. J., *The Merkabah in Rabbinic Literature* (1980).

Lieberman, S., 'Metatron, the Meaning of His Name and His Functions', in Gruenwald, *Apocalyptic and Merkavah Mysticism*, pp. 235–41.

Oron, M., "נוסחים מקבילים של סיפור עשרת הרוגי המלכות ושל ספר היכלות רבתי", in G. Blidstein, R. Bonfil and Y. Salmon (eds.), *Eshel Beer-Sheva. Studies in Jewish Thought* II (1980), pp. 81–95.

Schäfer, P., 'Engel und Menschen in der Hekhalot-Literatur', Kairos 22 (1980), pp. 201–25.

Chernus, I., 'Individual and Community in the Redaction of the Hekhalot Literature', HUCA 52 (1981), pp. 253–74.

Dan, J., Review of Gruenwald, *Apocalyptic and Merkabah Mysticism*, Tarbiz 51 (1981–2), pp. 685–91 [Hebrew].

Gruenwald, I., "שירת המלאכים, ה"קדושה" ובעיית חיבורה של ספרות ההיכלות', in פרקים בתולדות ירושלים בימי בית שני (1981), pp. 459–81.

Séd, N., *La mystique cosmologique juive* (1981).

Chernus, I., 'Visions of God in Merkabah Mysticism', JSJ 13 (1982), pp. 123–46.

Chernus, I., *Mysticism in Rabbinic Judaism* (1982).

Elior, R., *Hekhalot Zutarti* (1982). (A useful edition of the text with notes.)

Grözinger, K. E., *Musik und Gesang in der Theologie der frühen jüdischen Literatur* (1982), pp. 281–331 ['Die mystischen Traktate'].

Rowland, C., *The Open Heaven: A Study of Apocalyptic in Judaism and Early Christianity* (1982).

Schäfer, P., 'Aufbau und redaktionelle Identität der Hekhalot Zutrati', *Festschrift Yadin* = JJS 33 (1982), pp. 569–82.

Schlüter, M., 'Die Erzählung von Rückholung des R. Neḥunya ben Haqana aus der *Merkava*-Schau in ihrem redaktionellen Rahmen', Frankfurter Judaistische Beiträge 10 (1982), pp. 65–109.

Alexander, P. S., Review of Schäfer, *Synopse*, in JJS 34 (1983), pp. 102–6.

Cohen, M. S., *The Shi'ur Qomah: Liturgy and Theurgy in Pre-Kabbalistic Jewish Mysticism* (1983).

Dan, J., 'Anafiel, Metatron and the Creator', Tarbiz 52 (1983), pp. 447–57 [Hebrew].

Gruenwald, I., 'Manichaeism and Judaism in the Light of the Cologne Mani Codex', Zeitschrift für Papyrologie und Epigraphik 50 (1983), pp. 29–45.

Schäfer, P., 'Tradition and Redaction in Hekhalot Literature', JSJ 14 (1983), pp. 172–81.

Uchelen, N. A. van, *Joodse Mystiek, Merkawa, Tempel en Troon* (1983).

Alexander, P. S., 'Comparing Merkavah Mysticism and Gnosticism: An Essay in Method', JJS 35 (1984), pp. 1–18.

Halperin, D. J., Review of Schäfer, *Synopse*, JAOS 104 (1984), pp. 543–51.

Schäfer, P., 'New Testament and Hekhalot Literature: The Journey into Heaven in Paul and in Markavah Mysticism', JJS 35 (1984), pp. 19–35.

Schäfer, P., 'Merkavah Mysticism and Rabbinic Judaism', JAOS 104 (1984), pp. 537–41.

3. The Assumption or Testament of Moses

It has long been known from Origen's *De principiis* iii 2, 1 (ed. Koetschau, GCS 17, p. 244) that the story of a dispute of the Archangel Michael with Satan concerning the body of Moses, touched on in Jude 9, was taken from an apocryphal *Adscentio Mosis*. Extracts from this Ἀνάληψις Μωυσέως have been preserved in patristic writings and in 1861 considerable portions of the work were published by A. M. Ceriani from an Old Latin version identified in a manuscript of the Ambrosian Library (*Monumenta sacra et profana* I, fasc. 1, pp. 55–62). The title of the document has been lost but its identity with the ancient Ἀνάληψις Μωυσέως becomes clear from a quotation of Gelasius Cyzicenus, *Church History* ii 17, 17 (ed. G. Loescheke and M. Heinemann, GCS 28, p. 74; A. M. Denis, FPG, p. 63): Μέλλων ὁ προφήτης Μωσῆς ἐξιέναι τὸν βίον, ὡς γέγραπται ἐν βίβλῳ Ἀναλήψεως Μωσέως, προσκαλεσάμενος Ἰησοῦν υἱὸν Ναυῆ καὶ διαλεγόμενος πρὸς αὐτὸν ἔφη· καὶ προεθεάσατό με ὁ θεὸς πρὸ καταβολῆς κόσμου εἶναί με τῆς διαθήκης αὐτοῦ μεσίτην. These same words are found in the Latin version 1:14: 'itaque excogitavit et invenit me, qui ab initio orbis terrarum praeparatus sum, ut sim arbiter testamenti illius.'

The content of the writing is as follows.

Introduction. 1:1–9. An address delivered by Moses to Joshua when he nominates him as his successor in office. 1:10–17. Moses reveals to Joshua that the appointed span of his life has elapsed, and that he is about to depart to his fathers. As a legacy, he hands over to him certain books of prophecies, which Joshua is to store in jars in a place appointed by God. *Chapter 2.* Moses cryptically predicts to Joshua the history of Israel, from her entry into Palestine until the destruction of the kingdoms of Israel and Judah. *Chapter 3.* A king (Nebuchadnezzar) will come from the East and will destroy the city and Temple by fire and deport the inhabitants. The captives will then remember that all this had been already foretold by Moses. The exile is to last for seventy-seven years. *Chapter 4.* In answer to the prayers of their leader, Daniel, God will have mercy upon them again and will raise up a king (Cyrus) who will set them free to return to their own land. A few representative remnants of the tribes will return, and will restore the Holy Place, and will persevere in their religious faith, but sadly and full of sighs, because 'they will not be able to sacrifice to the God of their fathers' (4:8).[1] *Chapter 5.* Punishment will also fall on their kings, their

---

1. The validity of the sacrificial worship in the Second Temple seems to be queried. A similar point of view is manifest in Mal. 1:7 and 1 Enoch 89:73. Cf. Charles, *The Assumption of Moses* (1897), p. 15. The reason for the author's attitude may be that gentile domination interfered with the purity of the cult, post-exilic Temple history being viewed from stand of someone who has witnessed the activities of Hellenizing priests.

gentile rulers (or, *through* their kings, Latin: 'de reges'), and the Jews themselves will be divided with regard to the truth ('dividentur ad veritatem').[2] The altar will be defiled by such as are not priests but slaves born of slaves. And their scribes ('magistri et dictores eorum') will be biassed and will prevent justice. And their land will be full of unrighteousness. *Chapter 6.* Then kings will arise amongst them, and priests of the Most High God will be named who will nevertheless commit sacrilege from the Holy of Holies. (This clearly refers to the Hasmonaeans.) These will be followed by an insolent king, not of priestly lineage, a bold and godless man. He will judge his predecessors according to their deserts. He will exterminate their leading men with the sword, and will bury their bodies in unknown places so that no one knows where their bodies are.[3] He will slay old and young alike, and will not spare them. Then there will be great fear of him among them in his land; and he will inflict judgement upon them, as the Egyptians did for four-and-thirty years. (All this obviously points to Herod the Great.) And he will produce sons who will reign as his successors, but for briefer periods. Cohorts will come into their land, and a mighty king of the west (Quintilius Varus), who will defeat them and take them captive, and will destroy a part of their Temple by fire; some he will crucify around their city.[4] *Chapter 7.* Subsequently, the end of times will come about. Their course will cease when four hours have come ... (here follow several lines in the manuscript which are scarcely legible.) And pernicious and godless men will reign over them, who will say that they are just. They are deceitful men who live only to please themselves, dissemblers in all that they do and lovers at every hour of the day of feasts, gluttons [Latin: 'deuoratores gulae'] ... (another lacuna). They devour the possessions of the poor and say that they do this out of compassion. Their hands and minds practise impurity and their mouths speak monstrous things; and they say, 'Do not touch me, lest you make me unclean'. *Chapter 8.* A second visitation will come upon them and wrath such as never was from the beginning until the time when he will raise up for them ('suscitauit' = 'suscitabit') a king of the kings (i.e. Antiochus Epiphanes), who will crucify those who confess circumcision,

---

2. Schmidt and Merx have proposed the following retranslation into Greek: καὶ αὐτοὶ διαμερισθήσανται πρὸς τὴν ἀλήθειαν. Cf. Luke 11:17. For the use of אמת in the sense of religion, see *1QS* 1 (*passim*). The allusion seems to refer to the religious controversy culminating in the Hellenistic crisis.

3. For secret executions by Herod, see *Ant.* xv 10, 4 (366): πολλοὶ δὲ καὶ φανερῶς καὶ λεληθότως εἰς τὸ φρούριον ἀναγόμενοι, τὴν Ὑρκανίαν, ἐκεῖ διεφθείροντο.

4. With reference to the Temple burning, cf. *Ant.* xvii 10, 2 (261–2); *B.J.* ii 3, 3 (49); for the crucifixions, cf. *Ant.* xvii 10, 10 (295); *B.J.* ii 5, 2 (75). It may be deduced that the writer is dealing with the war of Varus in 4 B.C.

who will cause their children to obliterate the marks of circumcision, and will compel them to carry impure idols publicly and to revile the word.[5] *Chapter 9.* Then, when that king publishes an edict, a man will appear of the tribe of Levi, *Taxo* by name, with seven sons. He will say to them: 'Behold, my sons, a second ruthless (and) unclean visitation has come upon the people. For what nation of godless people has ever had to suffer as much as we have? Now listen, my sons, and let us do this. Let us fast for three days, and on the fourth enter a cave in the country and rather die there than transgress the law of our Lord, the God of our fathers.'[6] *Chapter 10* is an eschatological hymn. And then his kingdom will appear among all his creatures. Then the devil will meet his end and grief will depart with him. Then the Heavenly One will rise

---

5. The phrase 'blasfemare uerbum' is rendered by Charles (p. 32) as 'to blaspheme ... the name'. In fact 'uerbum' suggests the Targumic-Aramaic מֵימְרָא regularly associated with the Tetragram. Cf. E.-M. Laperrousaz, *Le Testament de Moïse* [Semitica 19] (1970), p. 124; J. J. Collins, 'The Date and Provenance of the Testament of Moses', in G. W. E. Nickelsburg, *Studies on the Testament of Moses* (1973), p. 20; S. R. Isenberg, 'On the Non-Relationship of the Testament of Moses to the Targumim', *ibid.*, p. 82. For the most recent studies of *Memra*, see D. Muñoz Leon, *Dios-Palabra: Memra en los Targumin del Pentateuco* (1974); R. Hayward, *Divine Name and Presence: The Memra* (1981).

6. The confusing sequence of the historical hints has been the subject of much controversy. Chapter 5 seems to concern the rise of Hellenizing priests. Then without mentioning the outrage caused by Antiochus Epiphanes or the Maccabaean liberation, the author immediately passes to the Hasmonaean priest-kings, depicted in hostile colours, and Herod and the Herodians with a specific allusion to Varus (chapter 6). This age is followed by the end ('ex quo facto finiuntur tempora') in chapter 7. Chapter 8 speaks of a second visitation sketched with traits indistinguishable from the persecution inflicted on the Jews by Antiochus Epiphanes and chapter 9 relates the story of Taxo and his sons, reminiscent of Assidaean martyrdom. Attempts at disentangling these matters will be presented below.

Caves generally served as hide-outs during persecutions as well as places where the Torah could be observed without hindrance. Cf. 1 Mac. 2:31; 2 Mac. 6:11; 10:6. See Collins, *art. cit.*, p. 25. On Simeon ben Yohai's concealment in a cave during the Hadrianic persecution, see W. Bacher, *Die Agada der Tannaiten* II, p. 73. There has been unending speculation on the name *Taxo*. Cf. H. H. Rowley, *The Relevance of Apocalyptic* (1963), pp. 149–56. Hypothetical corrections of presumed corruptions need only to be mentioned. Taxo = תקסא to be read הקנא, the Zealot (Charles, p. 36); Taxo(c) = תכסוק, a cryptogram in which each letter is to be replaced by the following one, giving אלעזר ('God helps'), the name of a pre-Maccabaean martyr in 2 Mac. 6:18–31 (F. C. Burkitt, HDB III, p. 449). Interpretation by means of *gematria* (Taxo = Hasmonaean) may also be dismissed; cf. C. C. Torrey, 'Taxo in the Assumption of Moses', JBL 62 (1943), pp. 1–7; 'Taxo once more', *ibid.* 64 (1945), pp. 395–7. The least fanciful theory derives Taxo from the Greek τάξων, orderer (C. Clemen, APAT II, p. 326; P. Volz, *Die Eschatologie der jüdischen Gemeinde im neutestamentlichen Zeitalter* (1934), p. 201; J. Licht, 'Taxo, or the Apocalyptic Doctrine of Vengeance', JJS 12 (1961), p. 95, n. 1). The Greek word is thought to reflect the Hebrew מחוקק (S. Mowinckel, 'The Hebrew Equivalent of Taxo in Ass. Mos. ix', SVT 1 (1953), pp. 78–87; M. Delcor, 'Le Mehoqeq du Document de Damas et Taxo dans l'"Assomption de Moïse" ix', RB 62 (1955), pp. 60–6; O. Eissfeldt, *Introduction*, p. 624). Taxo(n) may therefore simply mean 'leader'. On the various uses of מחוקק, see G. Vermes, *Scripture and Tradition* ([2]1973), pp. 49–55.

up from the throne of his kingdom. And the earth will tremble; the sun will not give its light, the horns of the moon will be broken, for God the Most High appears and chastises the nations. Then will you be happy, O Israel, and God will raise you up. And you, Joshua (with these words Moses turns to him again), preserve these words and this book. But I am going to my father's rest. *Chapter 11* relates how, after this address, Joshua turned to Moses and lamented his imminent departure and his own weakness and incompetence compared to the immense task laid upon him. Whereat *chapter 12* reports that Moses admonished Joshua not to underestimate his ability, and not to doubt the future of his people since it will, according to God's decree, be much punished on account of its sins, but can never be utterly destroyed.

Here the manuscript breaks off, but the foregoing material leads to the expectation, which the fragments confirm, that the sequel was concerned with the assumption of Moses. Hence the title for the composition as a whole: Ἀναλήψις Μωυσέως. There must also have been question in this concluding portion of the book of the dispute mentioned in Jude 9 between the Archangel Michael and Satan over Moses' body.

The problem of dating the document is best presented in two stages, the first concerned with its final composition and the second with the theory of two successive redactional layers.[7]

(1) Two theses placing the final composition to the second century A.D. are supported only by their authors, S. Zeitlin and K. Haacker.[8] However, almost all scholars agree in dating to the first century A.D. the latest identifiable historical allusions. These appear in chapter 6, with references to Herod and the thirty-four years of his reign, to Herodian princes succeeding their father, and in particular to an invasion by Varus in 4 B.C.[9] Yet, whereas the identity of the 'rex

---

7. For the various views, see Charles, pp. xxi-viii; Laperrousaz, pp. 88–99; Collins, *art. cit.*, pp. 15–30.

8. Zeitlin dates the composition to about A.D. 140: 'The Assumption of Moses and the Revolt of Bar Kokhba', JQR 38 (1947), pp. 1–45. For Haacker, the writer of this work is a Samaritan living in the second century A.D.: 'Assumptio Mosis—eine samaritanische Schrift?', ThZ 25 (1969), pp. 385–405. For a criticism of both, see Collins, *art. cit.*, p. 16.

9. The redaction is dated shortly after 4 B.C. by O. Eissfeldt, *Introduction*, p. 624; and especially J. J. Collins, *art. cit.*, pp. 15–32 and 'Some Remaining Traditio-Historical Problems in the Testament of Moses', in Nickelsburg, *op. cit.*, pp. 38–43. Other scholars link the production of the Assumption of Moses to the deposition of Archelaus in A.D. 6: F. C. Burkitt, *Jewish and Christian Apocalypses* (1914), p. 19, n. 3; J.-B. Frey, 'Apocryphes de l'Ancien Testament: Assomption de Moïse', DBS I (1926), cols. 403–9. C. Lattey ('The Messianic Expectation in the Assumption of Moses', CBQ (1942), pp. 9–21) and H. H. Rowley (*The Relevance of Apocalyptic* (1963), p. 108) place the completion of the document to the years immediately preceding A.D. 30. R. H. Charles (*The Assumption of Moses* (1897), pp. lv-lviii) prefers the period between A.D. 7 and 30, and his view has been adopted by E.-M. Laperrousaz (*op. cit.*, pp. 98–9). D. M. Rhoads, in turn, sees in

petulans' and 'occidentis rex potens' as Herod the Great and Varus is almost certain, the presence of these latest historical characters in the middle of the document raises further questions. Firstly, next to the mention of the Hellenizing priesthood in chapter 5, appears a summary reference to the Hasmonaean priest-kings ('reges imperantes et in sacerdotes summi Dei vocabuntur'), and to Herod in chapter 6. Antiochus Epiphanes and his desecration of the Temple, the Maccabaean uprising, victory and restoration, go unmentioned. Yet after the declaration that the end has arrived in 7:1, there is further criticism of wicked Jews, who are to be punished by 'the king of kings of the earth', the latter's actions being depicted in terms reminiscent of the persecution of Antiochus IV (chapter 8). Finally, the Taxo episode in chapter 9 recalls the Hasidic martyrs of the pre-Maccabaean epoch (1 Mac. 2; 2 Mac. 6–7). One way of settling this disorder is to adopt Charles's theory and transfer chapters 8 and 9 between chapters 5 and 6 (*op. cit.*, pp. li, 28–30). But this hypothetical rearrangement of the chapters is not without its own difficulties, as has been indicated by J. Licht.[10]

(2) The thesis of two successive redactions was initiated by Licht and more fully argued by G. W. E. Nickelsburg. On the basis of a form-critical analysis of the document, followed by a comparison of the contents of chapter 8 with Daniel 7 and 11, Jubilees 23, and 1 Enoch 89–90, he concludes that the author has Antiochus' persecution in mind. The Taxo figure is associated with the stories of Mattathias and his sons and the mother and her seven sons, and 1 Mac. 12, 2 Mac. 7 and the Taxo account are connected with with the last chapters of Deuteronomy. In fact, Nickelsburg accords priority to the Taxo story, on which the relevant passages from the Books of the Maccabees 'are in some sense dependent'. If this be the case, chapter 6 with the allusions to Herod and Varus is best explained as an interpolation.[11] The original composition is to be dated to the beginning of the persecution of Antiochus, prior to the appearance on the scene of the Maccabees.[12] The revision of the work by means of the insertion of chapters 6 and 7 took place in the opening years of the Christian era.[13] As a result,

---

the Assumption of Moses a reflection of the revolutionary spirit in Palestine between 4 B.C. and A.D. 48 ('The Assumption of Moses and Jewish History: 4 B.C. to A.D. 48', in Nickelsburg, *op. cit.*, pp. 44–52).

10. 'Taxo', JJS 12 (1961), pp. 100–3.

11. 'An Antiochan Date for the Testament of Moses', *op. cit.*, pp. 33–7. The dependence of Maccabees on the Taxo story is purely speculative. The priorities should be reversed as Collins has shown (*art. cit.*, p. 25).

12. Cf. JLBBM, p. 82.

13. *Ibid.*, pp. 213–14.

chapters 8 and 9, originally relating to the age of Antiochus, are transformed into an eschatological vision.[14]

On the whole, the latter theory seems to be more consonant with the admittedly cryptic data of the text. In particular, it may be pointed out that the omission of any hint at the defeat of the Hellenizers by Judas Maccabaeus makes better sense if a pre-Maccabaean composition is re-shaped in Herodian times by a reviser hostile to the Hasmonaeans, than is the hypothesis of a single redaction from which both Antiochus Epiphanes and the first Maccabees are absent.

The provenance of the Assumption of Moses is no less controversial than its literary composition. The work has been assigned to every known Jewish sect: Sadducees,[15] Pharisees,[16] Zealots,[17] Essenes,[18] and Samaritans,[19] or to an undefined group.[20] That it displays a number of affinities with the Qumran writings is undeniable, in particular a priestly stand, a peculiar eschatological outlook,[21] and a violent

14. Laperrousaz, p. 122; Nickelsburg, p. 213. The persecution of Antiochus Epiphanes provides also the pattern for the portrayal of the final upheaval in Mark 13. Cf. Eissfeldt, *Introduction*, p. 624; Collins, *art. cit.*, pp. 21–2.

15. R. Leszynsky, *Die Sadduzäer* (1912), pp. 267–73.

16. R. H. Charles, *op. cit.*, pp. li-liv. 'He was a Pharisee ... recalling in all respects the Chasid of the early Maccabaean times, and upholding the old traditions of quietude and resignation' (p. liv). Cf. also E. Schürer in his final edition, p. 300; J. Bonsirven, *La Bible apocryphe. En marge de l'Ancien Testament* (1953), pp. 222–6. J. A. Goldstein, 'The Testament of Moses: Its Contents, its Origin and its Attestation in Josephus', in Nickelsburg, *op. cit.*, p. 50, suggests that the author 'could well have been a proto-Pharisee'.

17. This theory was fairly popular among nineteenth century scholars such as K. Wieseler, 'Die jüngst aufgefundene Aufnahme Moses nach Ursprung und Inhalt aufgesucht', *Jahrbücher für deutsche Theologie* (1868), pp. 622–48; F. Rosenthal, *Vier apokryphische Bücher* (1885), pp. 13–38; E. Schürer, in the second ed.; W. J. Deane, *Pseudepigrapha* (1891), pp. 95–130; C. A. Briggs, *The Messiah of the Apostles* (1895), pp. 5–7, 18. For a criticism of an old-fashioned Zealot theory and yet a simultaneous association of the document with a rebellious milieu in the first half of the first century A.D., see D. M. Rhoads, *art. cit.*, pp. 53–8.

18. M. Schmidt and A. Merx, 'Die Assumptio Mosis', in A. Merx, *Archiv für wissenschaftliche Erforschung des Alten Testaments* I.ii (1868), pp. 111–52; O. Holtzmann, *Neutestamentliche Zeitgeschichte* ([2]1906), pp. 301–3; P. Riessler, *Altjüdisches Schrifttum ausserhalb der Bibel* (1928), p. 1301; A. Dupont-Sommer, *The Essene Writings from Qumran* (1961), p. 296; M. Delcor, 'Contribution à l'étude de la législation des sectaires de Damas et de Qumrân (suite)', RB 62 (1955), p. 54; E.-M. Laperrousaz, *op. cit.*, p. 95 ('un Essénien quiétiste').

19. Cf. K. Haacker, 'Assumptio Mosis—eine samaritanische Schrift?', ThZ 25 (1969), pp. 385–405.

20. Among the latest students of the book, neither Collins nor Nickelsburg is prepared firmly to assign the authorship to any of the traditional Jewish groups. Collins speaks of a 'sectarian group' (*art. cit.*, p. 32); Nickelsburg wonders whether the author was a priest (JLBBM, p. 83).

21. Chapter 10:9—'et altabit te deus et faciet te haerere coelo stellarum'—suggests that final redemption will entail a kind of exaltation to heaven. This imagery recalls *1QH*

rejection of the Maccabaean-Hasmonaean rulers. Nevertheless, the absence of any fragment of this apocalypse among the Dead Sea Scrolls (so far at least) militates against its attribution to an Essene milieu. The furthest one can go is to suggest that it derives from a writer sympathetic to Essene ideology.[22]

The Latin text, preserved in a sixth century A.D. palimpsest manuscript,[23] was probably translated from the Greek in the fifth century.[24] It is generally assumed that the Greek version was rendered from a Semitic language.[25] The most thorough case for a Hebrew original was made out by R. H. Charles.[26] Among those voting in favour of Aramaic may be mentioned M. Schmidt and A. Merx,[27] and C. C. Torrey.[28] In view of the precariousness of the available evidence (a poor Latin version, supposedly made from the Greek, itself allegedly rendered from a Semitic original), few recent writers are ready to commit themselves.[29] The direct impact apparently made on the author(s) by the Hellenistic crisis, the rule of the Herods and the war of Varus suggests that the book was written in Palestine.

The legend concerning the death of Moses appears in various forms in Jewish literature. In addition to the work under discussion, it is given in pre-Rabbinic writings in Philo, *De Vita Mosis* ii (288–92) ; Josephus, *Ant.* iv 7, 48–9 (323–31), and Pseudo-Philo, *Liber Antiquitatum Biblicarum* 19:6–16. No Qumran manuscript strictly belongs to this category. The closest parallel is the document designated 'Words of Moses' (DJD I, pp. 91–7), a farewell discourse addressed to Eleazar and Joshua, of which only the beginning has survived in a very fragmentary form. The

---

3:20–2, *1QM* 17:7 (see Vermes, DSS, pp. 187–8) as well as 1 Thes. 4:17. It may also be noted that just as in the Qumran War Rule the victory of truth over falsehood is effected, not with the help of a royal Messiah, but through the intervention of Michael, the angelic protector of Israel (cf. also Daniel 10:13, 21 ; 12:1), so in the hymn of chapter 10 the leader wreaking revenge over the enemies is 'nuntius ... in summo constitutus'. It is worth remarking that the eschatological vision granted to Moses before his death, according to Targ. Ps.-J. on Deut. 34:1–3, culminates in the arrival of the saviour Michael.

22. Cf. Collins, *art. cit.*, pp. 30–2.

23. Cf. Denis, IPGAT, pp. 134–5 ; Laperrousaz, *op. cit.*, pp. 3–16.

24. For the principal arguments in favour of a Greek basis for the Latin version, see Laperrousaz, *op. cit.*, p. 16. None of the surviving Greek fragments parallels the sections preserved in Latin and cannot strictly be used as evidence. According to Laperrousaz, the two groups represent two different documents. Cf. *ibid.*, p. 17.

25. Cf. D. H. Wallace, 'The Semitic Origin of the Assumption of Moses', ThZ 11 (1955), pp. 321–28.

26. *Op. cit.*, pp. xxxviii-xlv. See also S. Mowinckel, 'The Hebrew Equivalent of Taxo in Assumption of Moses IX', SVT 1 (1953), pp. 89–90 ; M. Delcor, *art. cit.* (in n. 18 above), p. 60. For a full list, see Laperrousaz, *op. cit.*, pp. 17–18.

27. *Op. cit.* (in n. 18 above).

28. *Art. cit.* (in n. 6 above). For further names, see Laperrousaz, *op. cit.*, p. 18.

29. See e.g. Laperrousaz, *op. cit.*, p. 25 ; Nickelsburg, JLBBM, p. 83.

editor (J. T. Milik) surmises that 'the composition ended with Moses' death and possibly his ascension' (*ibid.*, p. 91). In Rabbinic literature the following need to be listed: Sifre on Deut. 34 (357); Palestinian Targs. to Deut. 34; *Tanhuma* (ed. Buber) V, pp. 56 f.; Deut. R. 11:10; *Yalqut Shim'oni* Deut. 940; *Bereshith Rabbati* (ed. Ch. Albeck, 1940); and Midrash on the Death of Moses (*Peṭirath Mosheh*), preserved in two recension.[30] There are also Samaritan,[31] Ethiopic[32] and Armenian versions.[33]

On Jewish Moses-legends in general, see L. Ginzberg, *The Legends of the Jews* II, pp. 243–375 (Notes V, pp. 391–439); III, pp. 5–481 (Notes VI, pp. 1–168).

The Assumption of Moses is not to be confused with the Apocalypse of Moses or The Life of Adam and Eve (cf. below, pp. 757–60). Another somewhat obscure title is that of the Apocryphon of Moses from which St. Paul is said to have taken Gal. 6:16 (οὔτε γὰρ περιτομή τί ἐστιν οὔτε ἀκροβυστία ἀλλὰ καινὴ κτίσις).[34] But the borrowing is much more likely to have been the other way (Charles, *op. cit.*, p. xvii). There were also Gnostic books of Moses used by the Sethites, according to Epiphanius, *Haer.* xxxix 5 (ed. K. Holl). The Prayer of Moses published by M. R. James (*Apocrypha Anecdota*: Texts and Studies II (1893), pp. 172–3) is in fact an excerpt from Pseudo-Philo's LAB 19 (on LAB, see below, pp. 325–31).

The earliest quotation from the Assumption of Moses appears in the Epistle of Jude 9, according to Clement of Alexandria, *Fragmenta in Ep.*

---

30. Ed. by A. Jellinek, *Bet ha-Midrasch* I (1853), pp. 115–29; VI (1878), pp. 71–8. For translations, see A. Wünsche, *Aus Israels Lehrhallen* I (1907), pp. 134–76; M. Abraham, *Légendes juives apocryphes sur la vie de Moïse* (1925), pp. 93–113; cf. pp. 28–45; R. Bloch, 'Quelques aspects de la figure de Moïse dans la tradition rabbinique', in H. Cazelles *et al.*, *Moïse, l'homme de l'Alliance* (1955), pp. 131–8. Cf. also M. Gaster, *The Chronicles of Jerahmeel* (1899), pp. 144–9; J. Theodor, 'Midrash Petirat Mosheh', JE VIII, pp. 575–6. The various recensions may be assigned to the seventh to eleventh centuries: see H. L. Strack and G. Stemberger, *Einleitung in Talmud und Midrasch* ([7]1982), p. 301.

31. For a full account, see J. D. Purvis, 'Samaritan Traditions on the Death of Moses', in Nickelsburg, *op. cit.*, pp. 93–117. The two most important sources are *Memar Marqah*: *The Teaching of Marqah*, ed. by J. Macdonald, I–II (1963); and *The Asatir*, ed. by M. Gaster (1927); Z. Ben-Hayyim, 'ספר אסטיר', *Tarbiz* 14 (1943), pp. 104–25, 174–90; 15 (1944), pp. 71–87.

32. J. Faïtlovitch, *Mota Musē (La mort de Moïse)* (1906); Edward Ullendorff, 'The "Death of Moses" in the Literature of the Falashas', BSOAS 24 (1961), pp. 419–43 (text and translation).

33. M. E. Stone, 'Three Armenian Accounts of the Death of Moses', in Nickelsburg, *op. cit.*, pp. 118–21. The main document, 'The History of Moses', was published by S. Yousep'ianc', *Ankanon Girk' Hin Ktakaranac* (Uncanonical Writings of the Old Testament) (1898), pp. 204–6.

34. Cf. Euthalius (ed. L. A. Zaccagni, *Collectanea monumentorum veterum* (1698), p. 561); Photius, *Ad Amphil.* 151 (PG 101, col. 813); Syncellus, ἐκ τῆς Μωυσέως ἀποκαλύψεως (ed. Dindorf I, p. 48).

Iudae 9 (ed. O. Stählin, p. 207: 'hic confirmat assumtionem Moysi'). Further legendary traits relating to the death and ascension of Moses in Clement may have originated in this writing (*Strom.* i 23, 153, 1; vi 15, 132, 2–3, ed. Stählin). Origen, *De Principiis* iii 2, 1 (ed. Koetschau): 'Et primo quidem in Genesi serpens Evam seduxisse describitur, de quo in Adscensione Mosis, cuius libelli meminit in epistola sua apostolus Iudas, Michael archangelus cum diabolo disputans de corpore Mosis ait a diabolo inspiratum serpentem causam exstitisse praevaricationis Adae et Evae.' Origen, *Homilia II, 1 in Libro Iesu Nave* (ed. W. A. Baehrens): 'Denique et in libello quodam, licet in canone non habeatur, mysterii tamen huius figura describitur. Refertur enim, quia duo Moses videbantur: unus vivus in spiritu, alius mortuus in corpore.' Didymus of Alexandria, *In Epist. Iudae enarratio* (PG 39, col. 1815), finds evidence in Jude 9 for the view that the devil is not evil by nature or 'substantialiter', and asserts that 'adversarii huius contemplationis praescribunt praesenti epistolae et Moyseos assumptioni propter eum locum ubi significatur verbum Archangeli de corpore Moyseos ad diabolum factum.' Gelasius Cyzicenus, *Church History* ii 17, 17, above, p. 278. See also ii 21, 7 (ed. Loeschcke and M. Heinemann): ᾿Εν βίβλῳ δὲ ᾿Αναλήψεως Μωσέως Μιχαὴλ ὁ ἀρχάγγελος διαλεγόμενος τῷ διαβόλῳ λέγει· ἀπὸ γὰρ πνεύματος ἁγίου αὐτοῦ πάντες ἐκτίσθημεν· καὶ πάλιν λέγει· ἀπὸ προσώπου τοῦ θεοῦ ἐξῆλθε τὸ πνεῦμα αὐτοῦ καὶ ὁ κόσμος ἐγένετο. *Ibid.* ii 20, a philosopher answering the bishops: περὶ δὲ τῆς ῥηθείσης ᾿Αναλήψεως Μωσέως, περὶ ἧς ἀρτίως εἰρήκατε, οὐδὲ ἀκήκοά ποτε εἰ μὴ νῦν. Evodius, *In Augustinum op. epist.* 158, 6 (PL 33, cols. 695–6): 'Quanquam et in apocryphis et in secretis ipsius Moysi, quae scriptura caret auctoritate, tunc cum ascenderet in montem ut moreretur, vi corporis efficitur ut aliud esset, quod terrae mandaretur, aliud quod angelo comitanti sociaretur. Sed non satis urget me apocryphorum praeferre sententiam illis superioribus rebus definitis.' For further passages, see A.-M. Denis, FPG, pp. 66–7.

The absence of correspondence between the Latin Assumption and the Greek quotations raises an important question of literary history: do the Greek fragments belong to the same work as the Latin text, or are there two separate documents? In fact the ancient texts of apocryphal books, the Stichometry of Nicephorus, the Synopsis of Pseudo-Athanasius, the Armenian list of Mechithar, etc., record a 'Testament' and an 'Assumption of Moses' (Διαθήκη/᾿Ανάληψις Μωυσέως). At first sight, the extant Latin text seems to correspond to the former, and the Greek quotations, dealing with events subsequent to the death of Moses, to the latter. One possible explanation of the duality of titles is that 'Testament' and 'Ascension' designate the two halves of a single work (Schürer). Another solution assumes that two originally distinct books have been united into a composite document

(Charles, p. xiii). Nevertheless, it must also be borne in mind that, according to the Byzantine lists, 'Testament' and 'Assumption' continued to exist separately, the first consisting of 1,100 and the second of 1,400 lines (Stichometry of Nicephorus). It would in consequence be equally reasonable to accept that the Testament and the Assumption have always remained autonomous entities.[35] Not enough solid evidence exists to justify any firm conclusion except that, if the Latin version is to be identified with either traditional title, there is no doubt that it corresponds to the Testament of Moses.

Editions of the Latin Text

Ceriani, A. M., *Monumenta sacra et profana* I, 1 (1861), pp. 55–64.
Hilgenfeld, A., *Novum Testamentum extra canonem receptum* I (1866), pp. 93–115; ([2]1876), pp. 107–35.
Idem, 'Die Psalmen Salomos und die Himmelfahrt des Moses griechisch hergestellt und erklärt', ZWTh 11 (1868), pp. 273–309, 356.
Volkmar, G., *Mose Prophetie und Himmelfahrt* (1867).
Schmidt, M., and Merx, A., *Die Assumptio Mosis. Archiv für wissenschaftliche Erforschung des Alten Testaments* I, 2 (1869), pp. 111–52.
Fritzsche, O. F., *Libri apocryphi Veteris Testamenti graece* (1871), pp. 700–30.
Charles, R. H., *The Assumption of Moses* (1893).
Clemen, C., *Die Himmelfahrt des Mose* (1904).
Laperrousaz, E.-M., *Le Testament de Moïse (généralement appelé 'Assumption de Moïse')* [Semitica 19] (1970).

Greek Fragments

Denis, FPG, pp. 63–7.

Translations

(a) *English*
Charles, R. H., *op. cit.*
Idem, APOT II (1913), pp. 407–24.

(b) *German*
Volkmar, G., *op. cit.*
Clemen, C., APAT II, pp. 311–31.
Riessler, P., *Altjüdisches Schrifttum ausserhalb der Bibel* (1928), pp. 485–95, 1301–3.
Branderburger, E., *Himmelfahrt Moses* [JSHRZ 5] (1976), pp. 59–84.

(c) *French*
Laperrousaz, E.-M., *op. cit.*

Bibliography

Rosenthal, F., *Vier apokryphische Bücher aus der Zeit und Schule Akibas* (1885), pp. 13–38.
Hölscher, G., 'Über die Entstehungszeit der "Himmelfahrt Moses"', ZNW 17 (1916), pp. 108–27, 149–58.
Kuhn, K. G., 'Zur Assumptio Mosis', ZAW 43 (1925), pp. 124–9.
Lattey, C., 'The Messianic Expectation in the Assumption of Moses', CBQ 4 (1942), pp. 9–21.

---

35. For a thorough criticism of Charles's thesis, see Laperrousaz, *op. cit.*, pp. 41–62.

Torrey, C. C., '"Taxo" in the Assumption of Moses', JBL 62 (1943), pp. 1–7.
Idem, '"Taxo" once more', JBL 64 (1945), pp. 395–7.
Rowley, H. H., 'The Figure of "Taxo" in the Assumption of Moses', JBL 64 (1945), pp. 141–3.
Zeitlin, S., 'The Assumption of Moses and the Revolt of Bar Kokhba', JQR 38 (1947/8), pp. 1–45.
Mowinckel, S., 'The Hebrew Equivalent of Taxo in Ass. Mos. IX', SVT 1 (1953), pp. 88–96.
Wallace, D. H., 'The Semitic Origin of the Assumption of Moses', ThZ 11 (1955), pp. 321–28.
Delcor, M., 'Contribution à l'étude de la législation des sectaires de Damas et de Qumrân. IV. Le Mehoqeq du Document de Damas et Taxo dans l'Assomption de Moïse IX', RB 62 (1955), pp. 60–6.
Licht, J., 'Taxo and the Apocalyptic Doctrine of Vengeance', JJS 12 (1961), pp. 95–103.
Rist, M., 'Moses, Assumption of', IDB III (1962), pp. 450–1.
Rowley, H. H., The Relevance of Apocalyptic (³1963), pp. 149–56.
Denis, IPGAT, pp. 128–41.
Schultz, J. P., 'Angelic Opposition to the Ascension of Moses and the Revelation of the Law', JQR 61 (1971), pp. 282–307.
Nickelsburg, G. W. E., Resurrection, Immortality and Eternal Life in Intertestamental Judaism (1972), pp. 18–31, 43–5, 97.
Idem (ed.), Studies on the Testament of Moses [SCS 4] (1973), with contributions from J. J. Collins, G. W. E. Nickelsburg, J. A. Goldstein, D. M. Rhoads, D. J. Harrington, A. B. Kolenkow, R. W. Klein, S. R. Isenberg, D. L. Tiede, J. D. Purvis, M. E. Stone, H. W. Attridge.
Collins, A. Yarbro, 'Composition and Redaction of the Testament of Moses 10', HThR 69 (1976), pp. 179–86.
Nickelsburg, G. W. E., JLBBM, pp. 80–3, 212–14.
Carlson, D. C., 'Vengeance and Angelic Mediation in Testament of Moses 9 and 10', JBL 101 (1982), pp. 85–95.

4. The Apocalypse of Abraham

This composite work, preserved only in Slavonic, consists of a legendary narrative concerning Abraham's conversion from idolatry to monotheism (chapters 1–8), and of an apocalypse constructed on the story of the patriarch's sacrifice recounted in Genesis 15 (chapters 9–31).

In the first section, Abraham realizes the futility of the idols fabricated by his father Terah. One of them, Marumath (probably from the Hebrew מרמות, Micah 6:11), a stone idol, is broken then mended; another, Barisat (from the Aramaic בר אשתא?, son of the fire), made of wood, turned to ashes. After an argument with his father, he asks the Creator to reveal himself. God orders him to depart, and immediately Terah and his house are consumed by fire from heaven.[1]

In the Apocalypse, Abraham is instructed by the angel Yaoel, who

---

1. For the story of Abraham's conversion, see Jub. 12:12–14; LAB 6. Cf. G. Vermes, Scripture and Tradition (²1973), pp. 76–90.

bears God's name (10:4).[2] After the completion of the sacrifice—despite Azazel's attempt to spoil it—Abraham ascends to heaven on the wings of a dove, accompanied by Yaoel travelling on a turtle-dove, and sees the celestial court and the throne of God, the *merkavah*, described after Ezekiel 1.[3] He is shown the various heavens and is given the divine promise that his numerous descendants would become a chosen people. Then follows a vision of events from the fall of the giant Adam to the destruction of the Temple (27:2). The final age is depicted as divided into twelve parts (cf. 4 Ezra 14:11; 2 Baruch 27:1–13), at the end of which the posterity of Abraham will execute God's judgement over the gentiles. Abraham suddenly finds himself on the earth again and hears a final announcement of the destruction of the nations by the Elect One.

The content of the book makes it probable that it is essentially Jewish. Arguing in favour of this are the accumulated divine names in 17:11, 'Eternal, Mighty, Holy, Sabaoth, Most Glorious, El, El, El, El, Yaoel';[4] the continuous designation of God as 'Mighty before all worlds' (9:2; 20:1); the general interest in Israel as such: they are the chosen people (chapter 22); the righteous from Abraham's seed 'will be strengthened by sacrifices and gifts of righteousness and truth in the eternity of the righteousness and will destroy those who have destroyed them, and insult those who have insulted them' (29:16–17); God will burn with fire those who have insulted his people, and have ruled over them in this age (31:2). The only possible Christian addition or alteration is in 29:3–11, where the 'man mocked and beaten' by some descendants of Abraham but worshipped by others, who is to liberate Israel from the nations, is probably modelled on Jesus. The old Slavonic version is thought to derive from a Greek text, which was in turn made from a Semitic, probably Hebrew, original (Philonenko, 23; Rubinstein).[5]

---

2. Yahoel (Jael/Joel) is mentioned also in the Slavonic version of the Life of Adam and Eve 32:1–2 and the Apocalypse of Moses 43:4 as well as in *Sefer ha-Razim* (ed. M. Margolioth, 1966), 2:38, 140. He is no doubt identical with the angel referred to in Exod. 23:20–1, and is associated also with Metatron. See 3 Enoch 48 D:1; 12:5; bSanh. 38b. Cf. G. Scholem, *Kabbalah* (1974), p. 378; P. S. Alexander, 'The Historical Setting of the Hebrew Book of Enoch', JJS 28 (1977), p. 161; '3 (Hebrew Apocalypse of) Enoch', OTP I, p. 224.

3. On the *Merkabah*, see G. Scholem, *Jewish Gnosticism, Merkabah Mysticism and Talmudic Tradition* ([2]1965); 'Merkabah Mysticism', *Kabbalah* (1974), pp. 373–6; D. J. Halperin, *The Merkabah in Rabbinic Literature* (1980); I. Gruenwald, *Apocalyptic and Merkavah Mysticism* (1980); P. S. Alexander, 'Comparing Merkavah Mysticism and Gnosticism', JJS 35 (1984), pp. 1–18; P. Schäfer, 'New Testament and Hekhalot Literature: The Journey into Heaven in Paul and in Merkavah Mysticism', JJS 35 (1984), pp. 19–35.

4. The fourfold repetition of El followed by Yaoel, this time God's name, seems to designate the Tetragram. Cf. Philonenko, p. 75.

5. G. H. Box and I. Landsman, *The Apocalypse of Abraham* (1918), p. xv (Hebrew or Aramaic); A. Rubinstein, 'Hebraisms in the Slavonic "Apocalypse of Abraham"', JJS 4 (1953), pp. 108–15; 'Hebraisms in the "Apocalypse of Abraham"', JJS 5 (1954), pp.

Apart from a possible emphatic allusion to the destruction of the Temple as implying a relatively recent event, which would suggest a possible late first-century date for the original composition,[6] nothing in the text justifies arriving at a firm chronological conclusion. That it was taken over by Christians also points to a relatively early date. It is likely to have been used in the Clementine Recognitions (I, 32), and is perhaps identical with the apocryphal book Ἀβραάμ mentioned in the Stichometry of Nicephorus and the Synopsis of Pseudo-Athanasius together with Enoch, the Testaments of the Twelve Patriarchs and the Assumption of Moses.

No solid evidence permits an identification of the group responsible for this apocalypse. An Essene origin has been suggested,[7] but it is a hypothesis so far unconfirmed by the Qumran finds.

The Pseudo-Clementine Recognitions I, 32 reports of Abraham: 'Ex ratione et ordine stellarum agnoscere potuit conditorem eiusque providentia intellexit cuncta moderari. Unde et angelus adsistens ei per visionem plenius eum de his quae sentire coepit edocuit. Sed et quid generi eius ac posteritati deberetur ostendit et non tam eis danda haec loca quam reddenda promisit.' This goes beyond Genesis 15 and shows links with our book. According to the Stichometry of Nicephorus, the apocryphal book of Abraham contained only 300 lines, and was too short to be the Apocalypse. An Apocalypse of Abraham was in use amongst the Sethite Gnostics (Epiphanius, *Haer.* xxxix 5, 4). It seems to have been very heretical (πάσης κακίας ἔμπλεων), and is scarcely to be identified with ours.

Origen (Hom. 35 in Lucam, ed. Raner, p. 197, 14) was also acquainted with an apocryphal book which dealt with Abraham: 'Legimus, si tamen cui placet huiuscemodi scripturam recipere, iustitiae et iniquitatis angelos super Abrahami salute et interitu disceptantes, dum utraeque turmae suo eum volunt coetui vindicare.' The title *Inquisitio Abrahae*, borne by an apocryphal book known to Nicetas

132–5; J. Licht, 'Apocalypse of Abraham', Enc. Jud. I, col. 125; R. Rubinkiewicz, 'Les sémitismes dans l'Apocalypse d'Abraham', *Folia Orientalia* 21 (1980), pp. 141–8; B. Philonenko-Sayar, and M. Philonenko, *L'Apocalypse d'Abraham*, Semitica 31 (1981), p. 23 ('Un original hébreu, peut-être teinté, ici ou là, d'araméen'); Rubinkiewicz, 'Apocalypse of Abraham', OTP I, pp. 682–3 suggests that the Slavonic version was made directly from the Hebrew in the eleventh or twelfth century, probably in Bulgaria.

6. Cf. Box, *op. cit.*; Denis, IPGAT, p. 37; Charlesworth, PMRS, p. 68; Nickelsburg, JLBBM, pp. 288–9; Philonenko, *op. cit.*, p. 34; R. Rubinkiewicz, 'La vision de l'histoire dans l'Apocalypse d'Abraham', ANRW II.19.1 (1979), p. 137, n. 1; 'Apocalypse of Abraham', OTP I, p. 683.

7. Cf. Box, *op. cit.*, pp. xxi, xxiii, xxx–xxxi; P. Riessler, *Altjüd. Schrift.*, p. 1267. According to Philonenko, the author belonged to one of the Essene communities that survived the destruction of the Qumran centre. *Op. cit.*, pp. 34–5. Rubinkiewicz suggests that the writer was a Palestinian Jew very close to Essene circles. *Art. cit.*, p. 137.

(fourth and fifth centuries A.D.), is admirably suited to the events recounted here. In a treatise *De psalmodiae bono*, the complete text of which was made known by G. Morin, he says: 'Neque enim illud volumen temerarie recipiendum est, cuius inscriptio est Inquisitio Abrahae, ubi cantasse ipsa animalia et fontes et elementa finguntur, cum nullius sit fidei liber ipse nulla auctoritate subnixus' (see G. Morin, 'Deux passages inédits du "de psalmodiae bono" de Saint Nicéta, IVe-Ve siècle', RB 6 (1897), pp. 282–8; cf also Morin's edition of the complete text of *De psalmodiae bono* in Revue bénédictine 14 (1897), pp. 385–97; see p. 392 for the passage concerning *Inquisitio Abrahae*). In a contest between good and wicked angels *super Abrahami salute et interitu*, it will in fact amount to an *Inquisitio Abrahae*. Nothing of the sort is to be found in the Slavonic Apocalypse or in the Testament of Abraham to be considered below, pp. 761–7; and Nicetas' testimony confirms the independence of the *Inquisitio*, and therefore its difference from either of those works. In view of the relatively ancient attestation of the *Inquisitio*, one might be led to identify it with the apocryphal Ἀβραάμ of the Stichometry of Nicephorus. But this Ἀβραάμ stands among the Apocalypses, and Jewish Apocalypses have in general made a deeper impression on Christianity than Jewish legends. M. R. James (JThSt 7 (1906), p. 562) proposes to read *Dispositio Adae* in place of *Inquisitio Abrahae*, because in the Greek fragments of the Testament of Adam (edited by him in *Texts and Studies* II.3 (1893), pp. 138–45) there is mention of animals worshipping God. But this coincidence does not justify the forced alteration of the title. The subject may have been alluded to in various apocryphal writings.

For the Testament of Abraham, see below, pp. 761–7.

Editions

Rubinkiewicz, R., *L'apocalypse d'Abraham (en slave)*. *Édition critique du texte, traduction ed commentaire* [Diss. Pont. Bibl. Institute, 1977] I-II (unpublished).
Philonenko-Sayar, B., and Philonenko, M., *L'apocalypse d'Abraham. Introduction, texte slave, traduction et notes* [Semitica 31, 1981].

Translations and Commentaries

English
Box, G. H., and Landsman, I., *The Apocalypse of Abraham* (1918).
Rubinkiewicz, R., 'Apocalypse of Abraham', OTP I, pp. 681–705.
French
Rubinkiewicz, R., and B. and M. Philonenko, see under Editions.
German
Bonwetsch, N., *Die Apokalypse Abrahams* (1897).
Riessler, P., *Altjüd. Schrift.* (1928), pp. 13–39.

Bibliography

Ginzberg, L., 'Abraham, Apocalypse of', JE I, pp. 91–2.
Frey, J.-B., 'Abraham, Apocalypse d'', DBS I, cols. 28–38.

Bamberger, B. J., 'Abraham, Apocalypse of', IDB I, p. 21.

Licht, J., 'Abraham, Apocalypse of', Enc. Jud. I, cols. 125–7.

Denis, IPGAT, pp. 37–8.

Turdeanu, E., 'L'apocalypse d'Abraham en slave', JSJ 3 (1972), pp. 153–80.

Rubinkiewicz, R., 'La vision de l'histoire dans l'Apocalypse d'Abraham', ANRW II.19.1 (1979), pp. 137–51.

Charlesworth, J. H., PMRS, pp. 68–9.

Nickelsburg, G. W. E., JLBBM, pp. 294–9, 306, 308.

5. The Chronicles of Jeremiah

A writing probably of Jewish origin, and preserved in Greek, Ethiopic, Armenian and Slavonic, recounts events surrounding the first fall of Jerusalem, the exile, and the return from the captivity. The principal characters are Jeremiah, Baruch and the Ethiopian slave Abimelech. The story may be summarized as follows.

God announces to Jeremiah that Jerusalem is to be delivered into the hands of the Chaldeans. Jeremiah must therefore bury the sacred Temple vessels and depart with the people to Babylon, but leave Baruch in Jerusalem (chapters 1–4). Shortly before the catastrophe, an Ethiopian slave, Abimelech, is sent by Jeremiah to the vineyard of Agrippa to fetch figs and falls asleep there. After lying unconscious for sixty-six years, he returns to the city and is greatly astonished to see it totally altered. An old man informs him about what has happened (chapter 5). Abimelech finds Baruch, who is directed by God to write to Jeremiah. His letter, with the attached evidence of the figs, still fresh after sixty-six years, is carried to Babylon by an eagle (chapter 6). On receiving the message attached to the eagle's neck—its arrival in Babylon is marked by the resurrection of a dead man—Jeremiah leads the people back to Jerusalem. However, those who are unwilling to leave their Babylonian wives are not allowed to enter the holy city. They return to Babylon, but are not admitted there either, so they build the city of Samaria (chapters 7–8). Jeremiah, while offering sacrifice in Jerusalem, collapses and apparently dies; but he revives after three days and foretells salvation by the son of God. Thereupon the people decide to stone him to death. The execution is, however, delayed miraculously until the prophet has passed on all the mysteries to Baruch and Abimelech (chapter 9).

Despite the Christian ending, it is reasonable to consider the main body of the book as Jewish, in particular because of its emphasis on separation from gentiles ($\dot{\alpha}\phi o\rho\dot{\iota}\zeta\epsilon\sigma\theta\alpha\iota$), and especially from gentile wives (6:13–14; 8:2).

The original language is likely to be Hebrew or Aramaic (K. Kohler, G. D. Kilpatrick, J. Licht, G. Delling) rather than Greek (R. H. Charles, J.-B. Frey). The dating of the work on the basis of taking the destruction of Jerusalem as alluding to A.D. 70, and adding to this the sixty-six years of Abimelech's sleep (= A.D. 136), advanced by J. R. Harris, J. Licht and P. M. Bogaert, is both simplistic and improbable in the light of the Hadrianic events. Most scholars opt for the period between A.D. 70 and 130 (Kohler, G. Beer, Kilpatrick, Delling, A.-M. Denis, M. E. Stone). Since however the identification of the events of A.D. 70 with the story of the apocryphon is by no means compulsory—the sixty-six years may point to the eve of the end of the seventy years of captivity! —a late second Temple date cannot be ruled out of court.

The title of this work is Παραλειπόμενα Ἱερεμίου τοῦ προφήτου in most Greek manuscripts and is kept here in preference to the confusing recent trend calling the book 2, 3 or 4 Baruch. It was first printed in the *Menaeum graecum* in Venice in 1609, and re-edited by A. M. Ceriani, *Monumenta sacra et profana* V, 1 (1868), pp. 11–18.

Editions

(1) *Greek text*
Harris, J. R., *The Rest of the Words of Baruch. A Christian Apocalypse of the Year 136* A.D. (1889).
Kraft, R. A., and Purintum, Ann-Elizabeth, *Paraleipomena Jeremiou* [Texts and Translations 1—Pseudepigrapha Series 1—SBL] (1972).

(2) *Ethiopic text*
Dillmann, A., 'Reliqua verborum Baruchi', *Chrestomathia aethiopica* (1866), pp. viii-x, 1–15.

(3) *Armenian text*
Josepheanz, H. S., *Armenian non-canonical Jewish texts* (1896), pp. 349–63; [E.T.] J. Issaverdents, *The Uncanonical Writings of the Old Testament* (²1907).

(4) *Slavonic text*
Turdeanu, E., *Apocryphes slaves et roumains de l'Ancien Testament* (1981), pp. 348–63.

Translations

English
Kraft, R. A., and Purintum, A. E., *op. cit.*

German
Riessler, P., *Altjüdisches Schrifttum* (1928), pp. 903–19, 1323.

Bibliography

Kohler, K., 'The Pre-Talmudic Haggadah. B. The Second Baruch or rather the Jeremiah Apocalypse', JQR 5 (1893), pp. 407–19.
Huber, M., *Die Wanderlegende von den Siebenschläfern* (1910), pp. 408–9.
Frey, J.-B., 'Apocryphes de l'Ancien Testament. No. 16. Les Paralipomènes de Jérémie', DBS I (1928), cols. 454–5.
Kilpatrick, G. D., 'Acts vii.52', JThSt 46 (1945), p. 141.
Meyer, R., 'Paralipomena Jeremiae', RGG V (²1961), pp. 102–3.
Licht, J., *Pinkhos Churgin Memorial Vol.* (1963), pp. 66–72 (Hebr.).

Delling, *Jüdische Lehre und Frömmigkeit in den Paralipomena Jeremiae* [BZAW 100] (1967).

Bogaert, P., *L'apocalypse syriaque de Baruch* [SC 144] I (1969), pp. 177–221.

Denis, IPGAT, pp. 70–8.

Stone, M. E., 'Baruch, The Rest of the Words of', Enc. Jud. 4, cols. 276–7.

Wolff, C., *Jeremiah in Frühjudentum und Urchristentum* (1976).

Charlesworth, J. H., PMRS, pp. 88–91.

Nickelsburg, G. W. E., JLBBM, pp. 313–18.

Riaud, J., 'La figure de Jérémie dans les *Paralipomena Jeremiae*', in A. Caquot and M. Delcor (eds.), *Mélanges bibliques et orientaux en l'honneur de M. Henri Cazelles* (1981), pp. 373–85.

6. The Fourth Book of Ezra

Of all the Jewish apocalypses, none circulated so widely in the ancient and medieval Church as the so-called Fourth Book of Ezra. It was used as a genuine prophetic work by the Greek and Latin Church Fathers. Translations in Syriac, Ethiopic, Arabic, Armenian and Georgian, together with a Coptic fragment, attest its dissemination in the East. An Old Latin version has been preserved in many Bible manuscripts, which indicates that the book was also eagerly read in the medieval Church, which is why it was added as an appendix to the official Roman edition of the Vulgate. All the extant versions stem, directly or indirectly, from a Greek text which has not survived, and which in its turn is a translation from either Aramaic or (more probably) Hebrew.

The Latin Vulgate text consists of sixteen chapters. It is however generally admitted that of these, the first two and the last two, which are missing in the oriental translations, are later additions by a Christian hand. The original book therefore consists only of chapters 3–14.

The content of this original book is divided into seven episodes (three dialogues and four visions) narrated by Ezra himself.

First dialogue (3:1–5:20). In the thirtieth year after the destruction of Jerusalem, Ezra is in Babylon, where he prays to God, bewailing Israel's misfortune and the prosperity of the heathen nations (3:1–36). The angel Uriel is sent to him and begins by rebuking him for his complaints (4:1–21), then proceeds to advise him that wickedness has its appointed time (4:22–32), just as the dead have their appointed time to remain in the underworld (4:33–43). The greater part of the calamity is however already past, and its end will be heralded by definite signs (4:44–5:13). Ezra is so exhausted by the revelation that he has to be fortified by the angel. He prepares himself, by means of a seven-day fast, for a fresh revelation (5:14–20).

Second dialogue (5:21–6:34). Ezra renews his complaints and is again rebuked by the angel (5:21–40), who points out that in the history of mankind one event must follow another, and that beginning and end cannot come at once. Ezra should be able to perceive that the end is already approaching. It will be brought about by God himself, the Creator of the world (5:41–6:6). The signs of the end are expounded more fully than in the preceding vision (6:7–29). Uriel takes leave of Ezra with the promise of new revelations (6:30–4).

Third dialogue (6:35–9:25). Ezra complains again and is again reproached by the angel (6:35–7:25). He then receives the following revelation. When the signs expounded in the preceding vision begin to occur, then those who have been delivered from the calamities will see wonderful things, 'For my son the Messiah shall be revealed with those who are with him, and those who remain shall rejoice four hundred years. And after those years my son the Messiah shall die, and all who draw human breath. And the world shall be turned back to primeval silence for seven days as it was at the first beginnings; so that no one shall be left. Then the dead will rise; and the Most High will appear upon the judgement seat and Judgement will take place' (7:26–35). And the place of torment will be revealed, and over against it the place of rest. And the length of the judgement day will be a week of years (7:36–44). Only a few will be saved. Most will be handed over to destruction (7:45–74). Furthermore, the godless do not enter dwellings after death, but wander about and suffer sevenfold torture, part of which is that a turning is no longer possible for them and that they foresee their future damnation. But the righteous come into rest and experience sevenfold joy, part of which is that they foresee their bliss (7:75–101). But on the day of judgement each receives what he has earned, and none can alter the lot of another by intercession.[1] Ezra's objection that, according to the Scriptures, the righteous frequently made intercession for the godless, is rejected by the angel with the statement that what is valid for this world has no validity for eternity (7:106–15). When Ezra laments that all destruction has come through Adam, the angel reminds him of the godlessness of men, through which they have incurred their own ruin (7:116–39). Further explanations follow of why it is that, of the many created, so few are saved (8:1–62). In conclusion, the signs of the last times are once more expounded to Ezra (8:63–9:13), and the angel again calms him over the fact that so many are lost (9:14–25).

First vision (9:26–10:59). Whilst Ezra is again complaining, he sees on his right hand a woman bitterly lamenting. In answer to his questions, she tells him that after thirty years of infertility she had given birth to a son and had reared him with great difficulty and had taken a wife for him, but on entering the bridal chamber he had fallen down dead (9:26–10:4). Ezra chides her for mourning only her son, whereas

---

1. The Latin Vulgate text resumes at this point.

she should rather bewail the destruction of Jerusalem and the ruin of so many (10:5–24). Then her face suddenly shines; she utters a cry; the earth trembles; and in the place of the woman appears a strongly built city. Ezra is so dismayed by this vision that he calls to the angel Uriel, who immediately arrives and interprets it as follows. The woman is Zion. The thirty years of barrenness signify the three thousand years during which no sacrifice had been offered on Zion.[2] The birth of the son represents the building of the Temple by Solomon and the initiation of sacrifice on Zion. The death of the son refers to the destruction of Jerusalem. But the newly-built city was shown to Ezra in the vision in order to comfort him and to prevent him from despairing (10:25–59).

Second vision (11:1–12:51). In a dream Ezra sees rising up from the sea an eagle with twelve wings and three heads. And out of the wings grew eight secondary wings which became small and feeble winglets. The heads, however, were at rest, and the middle head was larger than the other two. Then the eagle flew and ruled over the land. And a voice came from the midst of its body ordering the wings to rule one after the other. And the twelve wings ruled one after the other (the second for more than twice as long as any of the others (11:17)), and then disappeared; likewise also two of the winglets, so that in the end only the three heads and six winglets remained. Two of these winglets separated from the rest and occupied a place under the head on the right. The remaining four wished to rule but the first two disappeared immediately and the other two were consumed by the heads. And the middle head ruled over the whole earth and then disappeared. And the other two heads ruled likewise. But the head to the right devoured that to the left (11:1–35). Thereupon Ezra sees a lion, and hears it address the eagle in a human voice as the fourth of the beasts to which God has committed dominion over the world. And the lion announces to the eagle its downfall (11:36–46). Whereat the remaining head disappeared. And the two winglets which had joined themselves to it began to rule.[3] But their command was weak and the whole body of the eagle was consumed by fire (12:1–3). The interpretation of the vision which Ezra receives is this. The eagle is the last of Daniel's world dominions, the fourth kingdom. The twelve wings are twelve kings who are to reign over it, one after another. The second will begin to rule, and will endure longer than the others. The voice which issues from the middle of the eagle's body means that during the period of that kingdom (if the Syriac and other oriental translations are followed rather than 'post tempus regni illius' in the Latin) bad disorders will

2. The oriental versions give the figure 3,000. The Latin manuscripts have III or 'tres', whereby, if the reading is correct, world years of 1,000 years each must be intended.

3. The oriental translations here provide the correct text.

arise and it will be brought into great distress; but it will not fall, indeed it will regain its power. The eight under-wings, however, represent eight kings whose times will be brief. Two of them will perish when the intermediate time approaches ('appropinquante tempore medio', i.e., the interregnum just mentioned). Four will be reserved for the time approaching the end, and two for the end-time itself. But the meaning of the three heads is this. In the end-time, the Most High will raise up three kings[4] who will rule the earth. They will bring godlessness to a climax and will precipitate the end. One (the middle head) will die in his bed, but in torment. Of the remaining two, one will be slain by the sword of the other, who will himself fall by the sword in the end-time. Finally, the two under-wings which joined the head on the right signify the last two kings of the end-time, whose rule will be weak and full of disorder (12:4–30). But the lion that proclaims to the eagle its downfall is the Messiah whom the Most High has reserved for the end. He will set them (the kings?), while still alive, before his judgement seat, convict them of their wickedness, and destroy them. But he will bring delight to the people of God (for four hundred years as prophesied in the third vision) until the day of judgement draws near (12:31–4). After these revelations, Ezra is charged with writing in a book what he has seen and with storing it away in a hidden place (12:35–51).

Third Vision (13:1–58). Once again he sees in a dream a man climb out of the sea. People without number gathered together to attack him. As they advanced on him, he emitted fiery breath and flames from his mouth so that they were all burned up. Others then approached him, some joyful, some sad, some in chains (13:1–13). At Ezra's request, the vision is explained to him as follows. The man who climbs out of the sea is he through whom the Most High will redeem his creatures. He will destroy his enemies, not with spear or weapon of war, but by means of the Law, which is like fire. The peaceful multitude who approach him are the Ten Tribes returning from captivity (13:14–58).

Fourth vision (14:1–50). Ezra, portrayed as a new Moses, is charged by God to instruct the people, to set his house in order, and to put away earthly concerns, for he will be taken from this world. Furthermore, he is to take for himself five men who for a period of forty days will write down what they are told to write. Ezra did this. And the men wrote ninety-four books (according to the Oriental versions) of which twenty-four (the Bible) were to be published, but the remaining seventy were to be reserved for the wise. Afterwards, Ezra was carried away, and taken to the place of those like himself (14:1–50).

In determining the date of composition of this remarkable book, the

---

4. So the oriental translations. The Latin has 'tria regna'.

vision of the eagle is of prime importance; other passages which have been adduced in this connection are of too uncertain a character to be of much use. Chapter 6:9, for example, observes that the present world will end with the rule of Esau, while the world to come will begin with the rule of Jacob ('finis enim huius saeculi Esau, et principium sequentis Iacob'). Esau/Edom may be an allusion to the Roman empire,[5] but it is more likely that Esau and Jacob merely symbolize the present and the future worlds.[6] Quite uncertain is the reckoning of world periods expounded in 14:11–12 ('Duodecim enim partibus divisum est saeculum, et transierunt eius decem iam et dimidium decimae partis, superant autem eius duae post medium decimae partis'). Considering the great variation in reading here—the Syriac and Armenian versions do not include the passage at all—the only safe conclusion is that for the author the end was relatively close. Thus apart from the general contents of the book, the chief clue to the date of composition is furnished by the eagle-vision alone. In its interpretation, the following points, all based on an internal survey of its contents, are to be kept in mind: the twelve principal wings, the eight secondary wings and the three heads represent twenty-three rulers who reign in succession in the following order. First come the twelve principal wings and two of the secondary wings. Then follows a period of disorder. After this, the four other secondary wings appear, and after them the three heads. During the reign of the third head the Messiah is revealed, and only after his advent occur the downfall of the third head and the short, weak reigns of the two last secondary wings. Both the fall of the third head and the appearance of the two last secondary wings lie, from the author's standpoint, in the future; from which it follows that he wrote during the reign of the third head, and that the two last secondary wings belong not to history, but to his eschatological imagination.

The following points should be particularly noted. (1) The second principal wing reigns more than twice as long as any of the others (11:17). (2) Many of the wings, especially the secondary ones, rise without really attaining to monarchy and are thus merely pretenders and usurpers. (3) All the rulers belong to one kingdom and are—or at least desire to be—rulers of that whole kingdom. (4) The first head dies

5. Cf. M. A. Knibb, *The Second Book of Esdras* (1979), p. 147. In Rabbinic literature, Edom is quite a common designation for Rome—see J. Levy, *Neuhebr. Wörterbuch*, vol. I, p. 29. Cf. also Jerome, *Comment. ad Iesai.* 21:11–12: 'Quidam Hebraeorum pro Duma Romam legunt, volentes prophetiam contra regnum Romanum dirigi, frivola persuasione qua semper in Idumaeae nomine Romanos existimant demonstrari.' See further C. H. Hunzinger, 'Babylon als Deckname für Rom und die Datierung des 1. Petrusbriefs', *Gottes Wort und Gottes Land* [H.-W. Hertzberg Festschrift] ed. H. Reventlow (1965), pp. 67–77. M. D. Herr, 'Edom', Enc. Jud. 6, cols. 379–80, argues, however, that the identification Edom = Rome does not antedate the Bar Kokhba revolt.

6. Cf. J. M. Myers, *I and II Esdras* (1974), p. 197.

a natural death (12:26); the second is assassinated by the third (11:35; 12:28).

Although a few nineteenth century authors attempted to identify the allusions of the eagle-vision as referring to the Greek rule from Alexander the Great to the Ptolemies or Seleucids,[7] or to Roman history from Romulus to Julius Caesar,[8] almost all scholars writing during the last century and a quarter have understood the eagle as designating the Roman empire. There is general agreement on recognizing in the second wing, said to have ruled double the length of time of any of the others, Augustus. This would imply that Julius Caesar was reckoned as the first wing.[9] There is disagreement, however, on the succession of rulers. A. von Gutschmid and A. M. Le Hir trace the line from Caesar to Diadumenianus, i.e. to A.D. 218. Both nevertheless consider the eagle vision to be a later Christian addition and date the basic Jewish document respectively to 31 B.C. and the last quarter of the first century. The majority opinion holds that the three heads are the Flavian emperors (Vespasian, Titus and Domitian).

These, inasmuch as they had brought about the destruction of Jerusalem, naturally represented for the Jews the quintessence of brute force and godlessness. Vespasian died, as it is reported, 'super lectum et tamen cum tormentis' (12:26); cf. Suetonius, *Vesp.* 24; Cassius Dio lxvi 17. It is true that Titus was not murdered by Domitian, as is presupposed in 11:35 and 12:28, but this was widely believed to have been the case and Domitian himself gave sufficient occasion for such a report by his behaviour at the death of his brother (Suetonius, *Domitian.* 2; Cassius Dio lxvi 26; Sib. 12:120–3). Aurelius Victor, *Caesar* 10 and 11, says explicitly that Titus was poisoned by Domitian. With this corresponds the fact that certain of the secondary wings, i.e., the usurpers, are actually destroyed by the great head with the assistance of the two other heads. But the accommodation of twelve plus eight wings presents almost unsurmountable difficulties. The twelve principal wings may be enumerated thus: (1) Caesar; (2) Augustus; (3) Tiberius; (4) Gaius Caligula; (5) Claudius; (6) Nero; (7) Galba; (8) Otho; (9) Vitellius; and with him the three usurpers, (10) Vindex (11) Nymphidius (12) Piso.[10] But what is to be made of the eight subordinate wings? They cannot be applied, as W. O. E. Oesterley

---

7. Cf. A. Hilgenfeld, *Die jüdische Apokalyptik* (1857), pp. 217–21.

8. R. Laurence, *Primi Ezrae libri, qui apud Vulgatam appellatur quartus, versio Aethiopica* (1820).

9. It is well known that he was seen by Jewish authors as an emperor: cf. *Ant.* xviii 2, 2 (32) and 6, 10 (224) naming Augustus as the second and Gaius as the fourth emperor of Rome; see also Sib. v 10–15).

10. Cf. Knibb, *op. cit.*, pp. 240–2; for a survey of the various interpretations, see Myers, *op. cit.*, pp. 299–302.

proposed, to Herod the Great, Agrippa I, Eleazar, John of Gischala, Simon Bar-Giora, John the Idumean, Agrippa II and Berenice.[11] The secondary wings are distinguished from the principal wings only in that their reigns are short and weak (12:20), or that they never actually rule at all (11:25–7). Moreover, like the principal wings, they are, or wish to be, lords of the entire kingdom. There is therefore no question of their being vassal princes. They are rather to be thought of as governors or generals; but their precise identity cannot be established.

If the three heads are recognized to be the three Flavian emperors, the date of composition is easy to determine. It has already been noted that the author wrote during the rule of the third head, knowing the manner of death of the second head, but expecting the fall of the third head only after the appearance of the Messiah. The date of composition, therefore, is to be placed towards the end of Domitian's reign (A.D. 81–96). A post-A.D. 70 date is indicated negatively by the absence of IV Ezra from the Qumran library. There is no need to postulate with G. H. Box (*The Ezra Apocalypse* (1912), pp. xxxii-iii) that the original composition, which he dates to A.D. 95, was re-worked by a second century redactor (in around A.D. 120) reinterpreting the original sequence of rulers to make it end with Trajan, Hadrian and Lusius Quietus.

The unity of the composition, rejected by some nineteenth and early twentieth century scholars,[12] is no longer questioned by the latest students of the apocalypse.[13]

The extant versions of the book are thought to depend on a Greek text which, apart from a fragment corresponding to 15:57–9, preserved in POxy 1010 and recently published by R. Rubinkiewicz,[14] has not survived. The original language is, however, assumed to be Aramaic,[15] or more probably Hebrew as J. Wellhausen was the first to argue in detail.[16]

IV Ezra is one of the most important sources of late first century A.D. Jewish religious thought as has been indicated in vol. II, pp. 514–47.[17]

---

11. *II Esdras* (1933), p. 147.

12. R. Kabisch, *Das vierte Buch Esra auf seine Quellen untersucht* (1889); Box, *The Ezra Apocalypse* (1912), pp. xxi-xxxiii; Oesterley, *II Esdras* (1933), pp. xi-xviii.

13. Myers, *op. cit.*, pp. 120–1; Knibb, *op. cit.*, pp. 109–10.

14. 'Un fragment grec du IVe livre d'Esdras', Le Muséon 89 (1976), pp. 75–87.

15. Cf. L. Gry, *Les dires prophétiques d'Esdras (IV Esdras)* I (1938), pp. xxiii-lxxvi.

16. 'Zur apokalyptischen Literatur', *Skizzen und Vorarbeiten* VI (1899), pp. 234–40. Cf. also Box, *op. cit.*, pp. xiii-xix; F. Zimmermann, 'Underlying Documents of IV Ezra', JQR 51 (1960/1), pp. 107–34; Myers, *op. cit.*, pp. 115–17.

17. For the theology of 4 Ezra, see further F. W. Schiefer, *Die religiösen und ethischen Anschauungen des IV. Esrabuches* (1901); G. H. Box, *The Ezra Apocalypse* (1912), pp. xxxiv-lvii; idem in R. H. Charles, APOT II (1913), pp. 554–9; J. Keulers, *Die eschatologische Lehre des vierten Esrabuches* (1922); W. O. E. Oesterley, *II Esdras* (1933), pp. xix-xliv; J. M. Myers, *I and II Esdras* (1974), pp. 121–9; A. L. Thompson, *Responsibility for*

The designation of this work as the Fourth Book of Ezra is only customary in the Latin Church. It rests on the fact that the canonical Books of Ezra and Nehemiah are numbered (i.e. in the Latin Bible) I and II Esdras, and the Ezra of the Greek Bible, III Esdras (Jerome, *Praef. in version. libr. Ezrae*: 'Nec quemquam moveat, quod unus a nobis editus liber est; nec apocryphorum tertii et quarti somniis delectetur'). This enumeration is retained also in the official Roman Vulgate, where III and IV Ezra follow as an appendix after the New Testament. In the Amiens manuscript, from which R. L. Bensly edited the Latin fragment, the canonical Books of Ezra and Nehemiah are reckoned together as I Ezra, the so-called Third Book as II Ezra, and Fourth Ezra is made to consist of three books, chapters 1–2 counting as III Ezra, chapters 3–14 as IV Ezra, and chapters 15–16 as V Ezra (Bensly, *The Missing Fragment*, p. 6). Similar, but even more complicated, is the arrangement in Codex Sangermanensis and its daughter manuscripts (cf. Bensly, pp. 85 ff.). The nomenclature is further confused when chapters 1–2 and 15–16, prefixed and appended to IV Ezra (chapters 3–14), are designated V and VI Ezra. In the English terminology, I Esdras corresponds to III Esdras, and II Esdras to IV Esdras of the Vulgate; i.e. IV Ezra plus its Christian supplements, chapters 1–2 and 15–16.

In the Greek Bible, I Esdras is III Esdras of the Vulgate; II and III Esdras designate the canonical Ezra and Nehemiah; whereas IV Ezra bears the Greek title of Ἔσδρας ὁ προφήτης and Ἔσδρα ἀποκάλυψις (cf. Clement of Alexandria, *Stromata* iii 16, 100).

The earliest Christian allusion to IV Ezra occurs in the Letter of Barnabas: Ὁμοίως πάλιν περὶ τοῦ σταυροῦ ὁρίζει ἐν ἄλλῳ προφήτῃ λέγοντι· Καὶ πότε ταῦτα συντελεσθήσεται; λέγει κύριος· Ὅταν ξύλον κλίθῃ καὶ ἀναστῇ, καὶ ὅταν ἐκ ξύλου αἷμα στάξῃ. Cf. 4 Ezra 4:33: 'quomodo et quando haec?'; 5:5: 'si de ligno sanguis stillabit'. It is likewise highly probable that the legend that the whole of Holy Scripture, which perished in the destruction of Jerusalem by Nebuchadnezzar, was miraculously restored by Ezra, stems from Ezra 14:19–26, 37–48. Thus Irenaeus III, 21, 2; Tertullian, *De cultu femin.* i 3; Clement of Alexandria, *Strom.* i 22, 149; Priscillian III, 68, ed. Schepss, p. 52.

The first specific quotation (IV Ezra 5:35) is Clement of Alexandria, *Strom.* iii 16, 100: "Διὰ τί γὰρ οὐκ ἐγένετο ἡ μήτρα τῆς μητρός μου τάφος, ἵνα μὴ ἴδω τὸν μόχθον τοῦ Ἰακὼβ καὶ τὸν κόπον τοῦ γένους Ἰσραήλ;" Ἔσδρας ὁ προφήτης λέγει. On the basis of the generally believed narrative of IV Ezra concerning the restoration of the Scriptures through Ezra,

Evil in the Theodicy of IV Ezra (1977); [R. J. Coggins and] M. A. Knibb, *The [First and] Second Book of Esdras* (1979), pp. 105–8; E. Brandenburger, *Die Verborgenheit Gottes im Weltgeschehen: Das literarische und theologische Problem des 4. Esrabuches* (1981). See also the bibliography at the end of the chapter.

Prisciallian argues for the recognition of this book as not canonical, but certainly a sacred work: 'Recte illi libro fidem damus, qui Hesdra auctore prolatus, etsi in canone non ponitur, ad elogium redditi divini testamenti digna rerum veneratione retinetur' (Tract. iii 68, ed. Schepss, p. 52).

IV Ezra is repeatedly used and cited as a prophetic book, particularly by Ambrose in *De bono mortis* x-xii, *Ep.* xxxiv. Cf. Bensly, *The Missing Fragment*, pp. 74–6; James, pp. xxxii ff. Only Jerome, who in general adopts a critical attitude towards the Apocrypha, expresses himself unfavourably. See the passage cited above (p. 301), and especially *Adv. Vigilantium* 6: 'Tu vigilans dormis et dormiens scribis et proponis mihi librum apocryphum, qui sub nomine Esdrae a te et similibus tui legitur, ubi scriptum est, quod post mortem nullus pro aliis audeat deprecari, quem ego librum numquam legi. Quid enim necesse est in manus sumere, quod ecclesia non recipit.' Although it remained excluded from the official canon, the book was widely disseminated, especially in the Middle Ages. It is, as has already been mentioned, printed in the official Vulgate as an appendix, and is included in many translations of the Bible, among them the Authorized Version, the Revised Version, the Revised Standard Version and the New English Bible.

It is important not to confuse the Fourth Book of Ezra with the Christian Apocalypse of Ezra, which C. Tischendorf edited in *Apocalypses apocryphae* (1866), pp. 24–33. Cf. also Denis, IPGAT, pp. 91–6; N. B. Müller, 'Die griechische Esra Apokalypse', JSHRZ 5 (1976), pp. 85–102. Related to it are (1) a Greek apocalypse of Sedrach edited by M. R. James in *Apocrypha Anecdota* = *Texts and Studies* II, 3 (1893), pp. 127–37; cf. Denis, IPGAT, pp. 97–9; J. H. Charlesworth, PMRS, pp. 178–82; S. Agourides, 'Apocalypse of Sedrach', OTP I, pp. 605–13; and (2) a Latin *Visio beati Esdrae* edited by G. Mercati in *Note di letteratura biblica e cristiana antica* (1901), pp. 70–3. Another short Latin work, *Revelatio quae facta est Esdrae*, was also issued by Mercati (*ibid.*, pp. 77–9). Cf. Denis, IPGAT, pp. 93–4. An Ezra Apocalypse on the duration of the rule of Islam was edited in Syriac, with a German translation, by F. Baethgen, 'Beschreibung der syrischen Handschrift "Sachau 131"', ZAW 6 (1886), pp. 199–213. The same work, in accordance with the manuscript Paris syr. 326, was published by J. B. Chabot, 'L'apocalypse d'Esdras touchant le royaume des Arabes', RSem 2 (1894), pp. 242–50, 333–46. Cf. Denis, IPGAT, p. 94. It is probably IV Ezra that is meant by the Ἔσδρα ἀποκάλυψις mentioned in the Apocrypha lists. Cf. Denis, IPGAT, pp. xiv-xv; see also below, §V.8.

On the later additions to The Fourth Book of Ezra (chapters 1–2 and 15–16), which are missing in the oriental versions but appear in the

Latin manuscripts as separate books of Ezra and become more closely connected to chapters 3–14 for the first time in the printed text, see A. von Gutschmid, *Kleine Schriften* II, 211–40; Bensly, *The Missing Fragment*, pp. 35–40; James, pp. xxxviii-lxxx; and modern commentaries. For the Greek fragment of chapter 15:57–9 from an Oxyrhynchus papyrus, cf. A. S. Hunt, *The Oxyrhynchus Papyri* VII (1910), no. 1010, pp. 11–15. For the inclusion of IV Ezra 2:42–8 in the Roman Catholic liturgy, see D. de Bruyne, 'Une lecture liturgique empruntée au quatrième livre d'Esdras', Revue Bénédictine (1908), pp. 358–60. On the use of IV Ezra in the liturgy, cf. also R. Basset, *Les apocryphes éthiopiennes. IX. Apocalypse d'Esdras* (1899), p. 22.

Versions

(1) *Old Latin*. This is the most literal and most important of them all. The oldest manuscripts dating from the seventh to the thirteenth century are listed and described by B. Violet, pp. xv-xxiv, and L. Gry. The most ancient witnesses are a seventh century palimpsest codex (no. 15 in the cathedral library of Leon), containing part of chapter 7, the Codex Sangermanensis dating to A.D. 822, and the Codex Ambianensis also from the ninth century. There are a further six manuscripts produced between *c*. 900 and the thirteenth century.[18] Further documents containing the confession of Ezra (8:20–36) range from the eighth to the fifteenth century. The Codex Sangermanensis was published by P. Sabatier, *Bibliorum sacrorum latinae versiones antiquae* III (1743), pp. 1038, 1069–84. For more recent evidence, see D. de Bruyne, 'Quelques nouveaux documents pour la critique textuelle de

---

18. Violet arranges the manuscripts in two groups, the French and the Spanish, designated as ϕ and ψ. X and Y are two unknown sources in the following scheme:

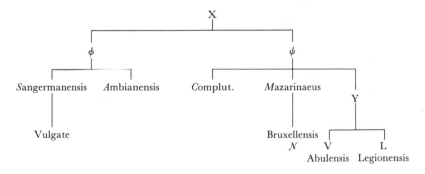

l'apocalypse d'Esdras', Rev. Bénédictine 31 (1920), pp. 43–7. The principal editions of the Latin text are: A. Hilgenfeld, *Messias Judaeorum* (1869), pp. 114–82; R. L. Bensly and M. R. James, *The Fourth Book of Ezra* (1895); B. Violet, *Die Esra Apokalypse (IV. Esra)* (1910).

(2) The *Syriac* translation, next to the Latin the best and the most reliable, is preserved in the Milan Peshitta manuscript (Codex Ambrosianus B.21 Inf.), dating to the sixth to seventh centuries. It was first published by A. M. Ceriani in *Monumenta sacra et profana* V, fasc. 1 (1868), 45–108. The best edition is by R. J. Bidawid, *4 Ezra* in *The Old Testament in Syriac according to the Peshitta Version—Sample edition : Song of Songs—Tobit—4 Ezra* (1966); *4 Esdras, Peshitta*, Part 4, fasc. 3 (1973), pp. i-iv, 1–50; S. P. Brock, 'Notes on some Texts in the Mingana Collection', JSS 14 (1969), pp. 210–11.

(3) The *Ethiopic* version is similarly of value for the reconstruction of the original text. It had already been edited by R. Laurence, with translations into Latin and English, but following one manuscript only, in *Primi Ezrae libri, qui apud Vulgatam appellatur quartus, versio Aethiopica, nunc primo in medium prolata et Latine Angliceque reddita* (1820). A. Dillmann was the first to provide a critical edition, in his *Biblia Veteris Testamenti aethiopica* V : *Libri apocryphi* (1894). Cf. Denis, IPGAT, p. 197.

(4) The two *Arabic* translations are of merely secondary importance owing to the liberties which their executors permitted themselves. (a) One translation, in a manuscript belonging to the Bodleian Library in Oxford, was first edited by H. Ewald in Abhandlungen der Göttinger Gesellschaft der Wissenschaft 11 (1862/3), pp. 133–230. H. Steiner furnished a German version in ZWTh 11 (1868), pp. 426–33. (b) Another Arabic translation was edited by J. Gildemeister, *Esdrae liber quartus arabice, e codice Vaticano 462 nunc primum edidit* (1877). There are further Arabic fragments: cf. Violet, p. xxxix, and L. Gry, *Les dires prophétiques de'Esdras* (1938), pp. xv-xvi.

(5) The *Armenian* version is very free. It may be found in the Armenian Apocrypha published by the Mekhitarists in Venice (1896). See also J. Issaverdens, *The Uncanonical Writings of the Old Testament* (1901). A critical edition has been issued by M. E. Stone, *The Armenian Version of IV Ezra* (1979). Cf. also *idem*, 'Manuscripts and Readings of Armenian IV Ezra', *Textus* 6 (1968), pp. 48–61 ; *Concordance and Texts of the Armenian Version of IV Ezra* (1971).

(6) A small portion of the *Coptic Sahidic* version was edited by J. Leipoldt and B. Violet in *Zeitschrift für ägyptische Sprache und Altertumskunde* 41 (1904), pp. 137–40. It contains only remains of chapter 13, yet it is of interest as furnishing proof that the book circulated in the Egyptian Church also.

(7) *Georgian*. Two manuscripts, one in Jerusalem and the other on

Mt. Athos, give a Georgian version. Cf. R. P. Blake, 'The Georgian Version of Fourth Esdras from the Jerusalem Manuscript', HThR 19 (1926), pp. 299–375 ; 'The Georgian Version of Fourth Esdras from the Athos Manuscript', HThR 22 (1929), pp. 57–105. See also C. K'urc'ikidze, *Georgian Version of Old Testament Apocrypha* I-II (1970–73) (in Russian).

Translations and Commentaries

English
Box, G. H., APOT II (1913), pp. 542–624.
Idem, The Ezra Apocalypse (1912).
Idem, The Apocalypse of Ezra (II Esdras III-XIV), translated from the Syriac text (1917).
W. O. E. Oesterley, *II Esdras* (1933).
Myers, J. M., *I and II Esdras* (1974).
Knibb, M. A. [and R. J. Coggins], *The [First and] Second Book of Esdras* (1979).
Metzger, B. M., 'The Fourth Book of Ezra', OTP I, pp. 517–59.

German
Gunkel, H., APAT II (1900), pp. 331–401.
Violet, B., *Die Apokalypsen des Esra und des Baruch in deutscher Gestalt* (1924).
Riessler, P., *Altjüdisches Schrifttum* (1929), pp. 255–309, 1282–5.
Schreiner, J., *Das 4. Buch Esra* [JSHRZ V/4] (1981), pp. 289–412.

French
Gry, L., *Les dires prophétiques d'Esdras* I-II (1938).

Bibliography

Hilgenfeld, A., *Die jüdische Apokalyptik* (1857), pp. 185–242.
Gutschmid, A. von, 'Die Apokalypse des Esra', ZWTh 3 (1860), pp. 1–81.
Volkmar, G., *Das vierte Buch Esra* (1863).
Kabisch, R., *Das vierte Buch Esra auf seine Quellen untersucht* (1889).
Clemen, C., 'Die Zusammensetzung des Buches Henoch, der Apokalypse des Baruch und des vierten Buches Esra', *Theol. St. und Krit.* 71 (1898), pp. 211–46.
Wellhausen, J., *Skizzen und Vorarbeiten* VI (1899), pp. 234–47.
Schiefer, F. W., *Die religiösen und ethischen Anschauungen des IV. Esrabuches* (1901).
Littmann, E., and K. Kohler, 'Esdras, Book of, II Esdras', JE V, pp. 220–2.
Bruyne, D. de, 'Quelques documents pour la critique textuelle de l'apocalypse d'Esdras', *Rev. Bénédictine* 32 (1920), pp. 43–7.
Keulers, J., *Die eschatologische Lehre des vierten Esrabuches* (1922).
Frey, J.-B., 'Le IVe livre d'Esdras ou l'Apocalypse d'Esdras', DBS I (1928), col. 412.
Montefiore, C. G., *IV Ezra : A Study in the Development of Universalism* (1929).
Kaminka, A., 'Beiträge zur Erklärung der Esra-Apokalypse und zur Rekonstruktion ihres hebräischen Urtextes', MGWJ 76 (1932), pp. 121–38, 206–12, 494–511, 604–7; 77 (1933), pp. 339–55.
Gry, L., 'La "Mort du Messie" en IV Esdras vii, 29', *Mémorial Lagrange* (1940), pp. 133–9.
Bloch, J., 'Was there a Greek Version of the Apocalypse of Ezra?', JQR 46 (1955/6), pp. 309–20.
Idem, 'The Ezra Apocalypse: Was it written in Hebrew, Greek or Aramaic?', JQR 48 (1957/8), pp. 279–84.
Idem, 'Some Christological Interpolations in the Ezra-Apocalypse', HThR 51 (1958), pp. 87–94.

Metzger, B. M., 'The "Lost" Section of II Esdras (= IV Ezra)', JBL 76 (1957), pp. 153–6.
Zimmermann, F., 'Underlying Documents of IV Ezra', JQR 51 (1960/1), pp. 107–34.
Turner, N., 'Esdras, Books of', IDB II (1962), pp. 140–2.
Eissfeldt, O., *Introduction* (1965), pp. 624–7.
Stone, M. E., 'Paradise in IV Ezra iv:8, vii:36 and viii:52', JJS 17 (1966), pp. 85–8.
Idem, 'Some Remarks on the Textual Criticism of IV Ezra', HThR 60 (1967), pp. 107–15.
Idem, 'The Concept of the Messiah in IV Ezra', *Religions in Antiquity*, ed. J. Neusner (1968), pp. 295–312.
Harnisch, W., *Verhängnis und Verheissung der Geschichte: Untersuchungen zum Zeit- und Geschichtsverständnis im 4. Buch Esra und in der syrischen Baruch Apokalypse* (1969).
Denis, IPGAT, pp. 194–200.
Stone, M. E., 'Ezra, Apocalypse of', Enc. Jud. 6, cols. 1108–9.
Philonenko, M., 'L'âme à l'étroit', *Hommages à A. Dupont-Sommer*, ed. A. Caquot and M. Philonenko (1971), pp. 421–8.
Hayman, A. P., 'The Problem of Pseudonymity in the Ezra Apocalypse', JSJ 6 (1975), pp. 47–56.
Gero, S., 'My Son the Messiah: A Note on 4 Ezra 7:28–9', ZNW 66 (1975), pp. 264–7.
Steck, O. H., 'Die Aufnahme von Genesis 1 in Jubiläen 2 und 4 Esra 6', JSJ 8 (1977), pp. 154–82.
Thompson, A. L., *Responsibility for Evil in the Theodicy of IV Ezra* (1977).
Charlesworth, J. H., PMRS, pp. 111–17.
Nickelsburg, G. W. E., JLBBM, pp. 287–94.
Knibb, M. A., 'Apocalyptic and Wisdom in 4 Ezra', JSJ 13 (1982), pp. 56–74.
Brandenburger, E., *Die Verborgenheit Gottes im Weltgeschehen: Das literarische und theologische Problem des 4. Esrabuches* (1981).
Stone, M. E., 'The Metamorphosis of Ezra: Jewish Apocalypse and Medieval Vision', JThSt 33 (1982), pp. 1–18.

7. *Qumran Pseudepigraphic Prophecies*

In addition to the Enoch manuscripts discussed above (pp. 251–2, 254), the Qumran Caves have yielded fragmentary remains of a 'prophetic' character. Most of them are too small for study.

1Q25 ['Une prophétie apocryphe (?)'] consists of only a few words 'prophetico-poetic' in style (DJD I, pp. 100–1). *2Q23* ['Une prophétie apocryphe'], said to be palaeographically Herodian, contains threatening words (DJD III, pp. 82–4). Likewise *3Q5*, dated to the first century A.D., may derive from a prophecy of doom: 'There is no peace; rather stroke upon stroke, trou[ble upon trouble ... misery] upon misery, bad news upon [bad] news ...' (DJD III, pp. 96–8). *6Q10*, a papyrus assigned to the first half of the first century B.C., is again hardly large enough for description, let alone identification, as a prophetic text. Yet it is claimed to possess a 'parenté évidente avec Ezéchiel' (DJD III, pp. 123–5). *6Q11* (first century A.D.?) is a tiny prophetic fragment containing the phrase: 'You will say, I will guard the vine that has been planted ...' The theme is familiar from Isa. 5, Jer. 8, Ezek. 17, 19, etc. *6Q12* (Herodian?) is an even smaller piece mentioning Israel, jubilees and dispersion among the nations. *6Q13* (first century A.D.) is another badly preserved fragment designated as 'Prophétie sacerdotale (?)' since it mentions 'the sons of Phinehas', 'the son of Jozedek', and possibly, 'And it will come to pass in those days'. (DJD III, pp. 123–7.)

The only document of sufficient length which can properly be classified as pseudepigraphic prophecy is *1Q27* or 'Book of Mysteries'. It has the appearance of a revelation uttered by an anonymous speaker concerning the destruction of wickedness and the triumph of righteousness. The presence of terms such as 'mystery' (רז), 'sign' (אות) and 'oracle' (משא) is indicative of the genre of the work (DJD I, pp. 102–7). Cave 4 has produced fragments belonging to two (or four) manuscripts of this work (cf. J. T. Milik, RB 63 (1956), p. 61). They still await publication.

Editions

Barthélemy, D., and J. T. Milik, DJD I (1955).
Baillet, M., J. T. Milik and R. de Vaux, DJD III (1962).

Translations (*1Q27*)

English
Vermes, DSSE[2], pp. 209–10 [The Triumph of Righteousness].

French
Milik, DJD I, *loc. cit.*
Dupont-Sommer, A., *Ecrits esséniens* ([2]1960), pp. 342–4.
Carmignac, J., E. Cothenet and H. Lignée, TQ II (1963), pp. 255–61.

German
Maier, J., TTM I (1960), pp. 171–2.

Italian
Moraldi, L., MQ (1971), pp. 631–7.

Bibliography

Rabinowitz, I., 'The Authorship, Audience and Date of the de Vaux Fragment of an Unknown Work', JBL 71 (1952), pp. 19–32.
Piper, O. A., 'The "Book of Mysteries" (Qumran I, 27)', JR 38 (1958), pp. 95–106.

VI. BIBLICAL MIDRASH

The authors of pseudepigraphic-apocalyptic prophecy sought to invest their writings with greater authority by ascribing them to the legendary personages of the past. In so doing, they reshaped and developed the biblical accounts. This tendency was central to inter-Testamental Jewish thought. The regular reading of Scripture and the constant meditation on it with a view to interpreting, expounding and supplementing its stories and resolving its textual, contextual and doctrinal difficulties, resulted in a pre-rabbinic haggadah which, once introduced into the scriptural narrative itself, produced a 'rewritten' Bible, a fuller, smoother and doctrinally more advanced form of the sacred narrative (cf. vol. II, pp. 346–55).

Examples of the 'rewritten' Bible relating mostly to Genesis are furnished by the Book of Jubilees and the surviving sections of the Qumran Genesis Apocryphon. The period of the Pentateuch is dealt with also by the Book of Biblical Antiquities erroneously attributed to Philo, but this work is more concerned with the stories from Joshua to David. Individual figures such as Noah, Kohath, Amram and Samuel in certain Qumran fragments, and the tribal ancestors in the Testaments of the Twelve Patriarchs, are given full treatment. The prophetic age, represented by the Martyrdom of Isaiah within the Christian composition of the Ascension of Isaiah, and the Life of the Prophets, exemplify the freer legendary trend with only sporadic contact with the scriptural text itself.[1]

1. The Book of Jubilees

Under the title τὰ Ἰωβηλαῖα or ἡ λεπτὴ Γένεσις, an apocryphal book dealing with patriarchal history is quoted by Didymus Alexandrinus, Epiphanius and Jerome. The Hebrew work referred to in the Damascus Rule (CD 16:3–4) as 'The Book of the Divisions of the Times into their Jubilees and Weeks' (ספר מחלקות העתים ליובליהם ובשבועותיהם) is almost certainly identical with it. Extensive quotations from the Greek writing appear also in the Byzantine chroniclers Syncellus, Cedrenus, Zonaras and Glycas from the beginning of the ninth to the twelfth century. It is however very probable that these were not taken directly from the Book of Jubilees but from intermediate sources, in particular

---

1. Because of the alterations to which they were subjected by Christian editors and copyists, the Testaments of the Twelve Patriarchs and the Life of the Prophets will be examined in §33B.

the Chronicles of Panodorus (*c.* 400 A.D.) and Aniacus (a little later). From then on the book disappeared until the nineteenth century, when it was rediscovered in an Ethiopic translation. It was first published by A. Dillmann in 1859. In addition to the Ethiopic version, there is also an old Latin rendering, a large section of which was found by A. M. Ceriani in a manuscript in the Ambrosian Library in Milan, and was published by him in his *Monumenta sacra et profana*, vol. I, fasc. 1 (1861). Another edition of the Ethiopic text was furnished by R. H. Charles (1895); and yet another was announced in 1964 by W. Baars and R. Zuurmond. Hebrew fragments of the work have been found at Qumran Caves 1, 2, 3, 4 and 11.[1]

In its essentials, Jubilees follows the canonical Genesis, and for that reason is also called 'Little Genesis', not because it is shorter (on the contrary, it is longer), but because it does not enjoy the same authority as the canonical book. Their relationship is similar to that of a haggadic commentary to Scripture. Jubilees is a free reworking of earliest biblical history, from the creation to the institution of the Passover (Exodus 12). The whole work is presented as a revelation given to Moses on Sinai by an 'angel of the Presence'. He addresses Moses in the second person singular (2:26 and 29; 4:26; 6:11–32, etc., and also in chapters 47–50) and usually speaks of himself in the first person plural, associating himself with the other angels,[2] but also sometimes in the first person singular.[3] This fiction that the work is an address to Moses by the angel is carried through to the end. The angel, for his part, draws his wisdom

---

1. The following fragments have so far been identified: *Jub. 3:25–7 (?)* = *11QJub.* 7 (J. T. Milik, 'A propos de 11QJub.', Bibl 54 (1973), pp. 77–8); *Jub. 4:7–11* = *11QJub.* 7 (A. S. van der Woude, 'Fragmente des Buches Jubiläen aus Qumran Höhle XI', *Tradition und Glaube-Festgabe für K. G. Kuhn* (1971), pp. 140–6); *Jub. 4:13–14* = *11QJub.M2* (Milik, *art. cit.*); *Jub. 4:16–17* = *11QJub.M3* (*ibid.*); *Jub. 4:17–24* = *4Q227* [ps.-Jub.] (Milik, *The Books of Enoch* (1976), p. 12); *Jub. 4:29–30* = *11Qfr.2* (van der Woude); *Jub. 5:1–12* = *11Qfr.3* (van der Woude); *Jub. 6:12 (?)* = *11QJub.6* (Milik, Bibl); *Jub. 12:15–17* = *11Qfr.4* (van der Woude); *Jub. 12:28–9* (van der Woude); *Jub. 21:22–4* = *4Q221* [4QJub[b]. 1] (Milik, 'Fragments d'une source du psautier et fragments des Jubilées', RB 73 (1966), pp. 94–106); *Jub. 23:6–7* = *3Q5fr.3* (M. Baillet, DJD III (1962), p. 98; R. Deichgräber, 'Fragmente einer Jubiläenhandschrift aus Höhle 3 von Qumran', RQ 5 (1965), pp. 415–22; A. Rofé, 'Further Manuscript Fragments of Jubilees in Qumran Cave 3', Tarbiz 34 (1965), pp. 333–6 [Hebr.]); *Jub. 23:7–8* = *1Q19 (2QJub[a].)* (Milik, DJD I, p. 83); *Jub. 23:10 (?)* = *3Q5fr.4* (Baillet, DJD III, p. 97); *Jub. 23:12–13* = *3Q5fr.1* (Baillet, Deichgräber, Rofé); *Jub. 25:12* = *4QJub.17* (Milik, DJD III, p. 226); *Jub. 27:19–21* = *1Q17* (Milik, DJD I, p. 83); *Jub. 36:12 (?)* = *1Q18fr.3* (*ibid.*); *Jub. 46:1–3* = *2Q20* [2QJub[b].] (Baillet, pp. 77–9). Another Jubilees fragment from Masada, without further specification, is alluded to in Y. Yadin, *Masada* (1966), p. 179.

2. The 'we' form is quite frequent in chapters 2–19: cf. 2:3, 17, 18, 19, 21, 28, 30; 3:1, 9, 12, 15; 4:6, 18, 23; 5:6, 8, 10; 10:7, 10–13, 23; 14:20; 16:1–4, 7, 15–19, 28; 18:14; 19:3. From then on, its use is sporadic and coincides with an anti-anthropomorphic tendency which substitutes angels for God. Cf. Jub. 30:20; 41:24; 48:10, 11, 16, 19.

3. Cf. Jub. 6:19, 22, 35, 38; 12:22, 26; 16:5; 18:9–11; 30:21; 48:4, 13; 50:13.

from the 'heavenly tablets' (1:29), to which he constantly refers (3:10, 31; 4:5, 32; 6:17, 29, 31, 35; 15:25; 16:28 f.; 18:19; 28:6; 30:9; 32:10, 15; 33:10; 39:6; 49:8; 50:13). By the choice of this form, the author seeks to endow the new teaching propounded by him with heavenly authority. He pays special attention to chronology in his shaping of the biblical story. The basis of his reckoning is the jubilee period of forty-nine years, i.e. seven year-weeks, or seven times seven years, and he determines precisely, for the occurrence of each event, the month of the year within the year-week of the relevant jubilee cycle. Hence the title 'Jubilees', τὰ 'Ιωβηλαῖα. As chronology in general is of special interest to him, the author also lays particular emphasis on the observance of the annual festivals, and seeks to prove that the main feasts were instituted already in the very earliest times: Pentecost or the Feast of Weeks (Jub. 6:17–22; cf. 15:1; 22:1; 44:4); the Feast of Tabernacles (16:21–31; 32:27–9, known simply as 'the Feast', in the seventh month); the Day of Atonement (34:18–19); and Passover (49). This explains why he finishes specifically with the institution of the latter festival (Exodus 12).[4]

Wishing to recount earliest history in the spirit of his own age, the author handles the biblical text very freely. Much of what was of no interest to him, or appeared scandalous, is omitted or altered; other passages are lengthened and enriched by the addition of numerous details. He explains how Gen. 2:17 was literally fulfilled,[5] and with whose help Noah brought the animals into the Ark (5:23); etc. He knows the names of the wives of all the patriarchs, from Adam to the twelve sons of Jacob; the number of the sons of Adam; the name of the peak on Ararat on which the Ark of Noah rested (5:28; 7:1, 17; 10:15); and many other matters of this sort.[6] All these embellishments and enrichments faithfully reflect the spirit of inter-Testamental Judaism. It is characteristic, in particular, that the patriarchs are made out to be,

---

4. The originality of Jubilees lies in the constant effort of the author to represent the yearly festivals of Judaism as memorials of events that occurred in the age of the patriarchs long before the time of Moses. Thus, for example, the feast of Weeks commemorates God's covenant with Noah (6:17); Sukkoth, the rejoicing of Abraham after the birth of Isaac (16:29). Passover coincides with the seven-day festival foreordained in the heavenly tablets in regard to the sacrifice of Isaac (17:15; 18:3, 19). The Day of Atonement was instituted as a reminder of Jacob's distress on seeing the blood-stained coat of Joseph (34:12, 18).

5. The divine threat that Adam would die on the day on which he ate the forbidden food was fulfilled when he died aged 930 years, i.e. 70 years short of the 1,000 years which are like one day in God's eyes. Cf. Jub. 4:30. See also 2 Pet. 3:8; Ep. of Barnabas 15:4; Gen. R. 19:22. Justin in *Dial.* 81, 3 appears to cite this passage. Cf. Charles, *Jubilees*, p. 41; Berger, *Jubiläen*, p. 347, n.a.

6. For further detail, see Charles, *Jubilees*. A theological discussion of the creation and the history of the world and of Israel may be found in M. Testuz, *Les idées religieuses du Livre des Jubilées* (1960), pp. 43–74.

even more than in the biblical story, paragons of virtue who already observe the Mosaic cultic laws, offer sacrifice and first-fruits, and celebrate the annual festivals as well as the New Moons and the Sabbaths.[7] It is also characteristic that the heavenly world stands everywhere in the background of earthly history. The angels, good and bad, continually intervene in the course of history. The angels in heaven were the first to observe the Law (cf. e.g. 6:18) for it was inscribed on heavenly tablets from the beginning and was only gradually communicated to men. Moreover, not all the teachings were openly proclaimed to Israel. Many were delivered to the patriarchs in secret books, which they bequeathed to later generations.

The *terminus ante quem* of the composition of Jubilees is indicated by the date of the Qumran fragments and the reference to the book in the Damascus Rule (CD 16:3–4), both pointing to around 100 B.C.[8] The *terminus a quo* is furnished by a quotation, in 4:17–24, of the first section of 1 Enoch, which is thought to date to the beginning of the second century B.C. (see p. 256 above) and the general historical background pointing to the Hellenistic crisis of the 170s B.C. Thus Jub. 3:31 prohibits Jews to 'uncover themselves as the gentiles uncover themselves' (cf. 1 Mac. 1:13–14). Jub. 15:33–4 alludes to a neglect of circumcision and thus of the covenant of God (cf. 1 Mac. 1:15, 63; 2:20, 27; 4:10). Large-scale apostasy is envisaged in Jub. 23:16. Jub. 50:12, by simply outlawing war on the Sabbath, echoes a pre-Maccabaean practice of the Hasidim (1 Mac. 2:31–8). Various commandments which are advanced with emphasis reflect the circumstances of the second century B.C. Thus the readers of Jubilees are enjoined not to eat with gentiles (22:16), and not to contract any marriage with them (25:1; 30:11–17). Furthermore, the expression of hatred of the Philistines (24:28–33) and the Amorites (34:2–9), as well as the account of the wars with the Amorites (34:2–9) and Edomites (37–8), may be seen to mirror the mood and the struggles of the Maccabaean period. The subjection of the Edomites to servitude by the sons of Jacob (38:10–14) probably echoes the defeat of the Idumaeans by Judas Maccabaeus or John Hyrcanus. As in the Testaments of the Twelve Patriarchs (see below, p. 768), the tribes of Levi and Judah are brought into the foreground in Jubilees in such a manner that Levi takes precedence; Isaac blesses Levi first (31:13–17), then Judah (31:18–20). Nevertheless, it is pointed out that from Judah will come a mighty Prince, i.e. the Messiah (31:18–20). But Levi is still the ruling tribe.

7. Cf. Testuz, *op. cit.*, pp. 101–19. The observance of ritual commandments, recorded in books by Enoch and Noah, is imposed by Abraham on Isaac (21:5–10).

8. For CD, see below, pp. 395–6. For the palaeographical argument, cf. J. C. VanderKam, *Textual and Historical Studies in the Book of Jubilees* (1977), p. 216; K. Berger, *Das Buch der Jubiläen* (1981), p. 300.

'And they [i.e. the children of Levi] will be princes and judges, and chiefs of all the seed of the sons of Jacob; they will speak the word of the Lord in righteousness, and they will judge all his judgements in righteousness' (31:15).

It also follows from the passage quoted (31:15) that the priestly circles are still the custodians of doctrine. According to 45:16, they are in addition the guardians of the sacred books: (Jacob) 'gave all his books and the books of his fathers to Levi his son that he might preserve them and renew them for his children until this day'.

Finally it is also very noteworthy that the halakhah attested in Jubilees antedates not only the Mishnah, but also Josephus and Philo, and definitely points to the pre-Christian era.

(1) According to Jub. 7:36, the fruit of the fourth year after planting is to be brought to God's altar, 'and what is left, let the servants of the house of the Lord eat before the altar which receives (it)'. Although the law of Lev. 19:24 can be understood in this sense, in the later halakhah voiced by Philo, *De virtutibus* 29 (150) and Josephus, *Ant.* iv 8, 19 (227), these fruits are not to be consumed 'by the servants of the house of God' but by the offerers themselves, before God, as second tithe (see vol. II, p. 264). (2) According to Jub. 15:1, 16:3, 44:4–5, the harvest festival (First-Fruits, identical with the Feast of Weeks, 6:21; 22:1) is to be celebrated 'in the middle' of the third month. There is no direct regulation on this matter in the Pentateuch. The calculation depends on the interpretation of the word 'Sabbath' in Lev. 23:11 and 15. The Sadducees understood by it the Sabbath proper; the Pharisees, the first festival day of Passover week, 15 Nisan (see vol. II, p. 410). The author of Jubilees, by contrast, seems rather to have interpreted Sabbath as the last day of Passover week, 21 Nisan. The Pharisee practice is however supported already in the Septuagint translation of Lev. 23:11 (τῇ ἐπαύριον τῆς πρώτης), and clearly prevailed in the time of Philo, *De spec. leg.* ii 29 (162), and Josephus, *Ant.* iii 10, 5 (248). (3) Jub. 21:12–15 pronounces that only certain kinds of wood are permitted for use on the altar of burnt-offering, amongst them the olive. According to mTamid 2:3, the olive tree and the vine are forbidden. (4) Jub. 32:15 prescribes that the tithe of cattle shall belong to the priests; thus also Tobit 1:6 according to the Sinaiticus, and Philo, *De virtutibus* 18 (95). According to the later halakhah, it is to be treated like the second tithe, and is therefore to be consumed by the offerers 'before God' (following mZebahim 5:8—see vol. II, p. 264). (5) According to Jub. 49:20, the Passover must be eaten in a courtyard of the Sanctuary. Later halakhah permits its consumption anywhere in Jerusalem (mZeb. 5:8; mMak. 3:3).

Whereas a second century B.C. dating is generally agreed today, some scholars see in Jubilees particular allusions to events during the rule of John Hyrcanus I (Charles, *op. cit.*, pp. lviii-lxvi; Milik, *Enoch*, p. 58), or to the period of Jonathan and Simon, 145–140 B.C. (K. Berger, *op. cit.*, p. 300). In turn, J. C. VanderKam is of the opinion that the last historical reference in Jubilees concerns Judas Maccabaeus' victory over Nicanor in 161 B.C. and he adopts therefore a high-Maccabaean date, 161–140 B.C., but more probably 161–152 B.C. (*op. cit.*, pp. 254, 284). The age of Judas (166–160 B.C.) is chosen also by G. L. Davenport (*The Eschatology of the Book of Jubilees* (1971), p. 15), whereas L. Finkelstein, prior to the Qumran discoveries, argued for a pre-Maccabaean dating: 175–167 B.C. ('The Date of the Book of Jubilees', HThR 36 (1943), pp. 19–24). Taking all these points into account, a date following closely the death of Judas Maccabaeus appears to be the most likely.[9]

The milieu from which Jubilees emerged was the object of much argument before the Dead Sea finds. It was assigned to the Samaritans (B. Beer), to the circle of Onias of Leontopolis (Z. Frankel), to the Essenes (A. Jellinek, J.-M. Lagrange), but mostly to the Pharisees (A. Dillmann, H. Rönsch, E. Schürer, R. H. Charles, etc.). Nevertheless, it was noted that in two areas the author parted company with the Pharisees. He adopted a solar calendric system (6:32–8) against that based on the moon, which was common currency, with consequent changes in the dates of festivals (cf. above, p. 312), and envisaged the after-life in the form of a survival of the spirit, while 'their bones will rest in the earth' (23:31), rather than as a bodily resurrection, the key teaching of the Pharisees. The identification of the author as an Essene was supported by the many allusions to angelology and to secret books, as well as his belief in a spiritual after-life common to Jub. 23:31 and the Essenes in *B.J.* ii 8, 11 (154–5). On the other hand, the absence of stress on purifications was underlined.

Since the publication of the Dead Sea Scrolls, however, the problem has appeared in a new perspective. As has been noted, the Qumran caves have yielded fragments of the original Hebrew text, and the Damascus Rule, a Qumran document, expressly advocates the calendar of Jubilees (CD 16:3–4). Moreover, the same solar calendar is integral to the doctrinal system of the Scrolls,[10] as is also belief in priestly

9. As for S. Zeitlin's theory placing Jubilees to the early part of the Second Commonwealth (the fifth or the fourth century B.C.), because of its discrepant halakhah and calendar reckoning it requires no serious refutation (JQR 30 (1939/40), pp.8–16; 36 (1945/6), pp. 187–9; 48 (1957/8), pp. 218–32).

10. On the Jubilees-Qumran calendar, see vol. I, pp. 599–601. For literature on the subject, see *ibid.*, p. 592, n. 15; M. Testuz, *Les idées religieuses du Livre des Jubilées* (1960), pp. 121–37; E. Kutsch, 'Der Kalender des Jubiläenbuches und das Alte und Neue Testament', VT 11 (1961), pp. 39–47; 'Die Solstitien im Kalender des Jubliäenbuches und in äth. Henoch 72', *ibid.* 12 (1962), pp. 205–7; B. Noack, 'The Day of Pentecost in Jubilees and Qumran', ASTI 1 (1962), pp. 73–95; J. M. Baumgarten, '4Q Halakha[a] 5,

supremacy. Similarities between Jubilees, the Damascus Rule, the Community Rule and the Thanksgiving Hymns have also been listed and examined,[11] and there are particularly close direct connections with the Genesis Apocryphon.[12] It is in consequence not surprising that there is a strong contemporary tendency to declare Jubilees to be a Qumran writing.[13] On the other hand, unlike the Dead Sea documents, Jubilees makes no mention of the schism within the Jewish priesthood out of which the Qumran-Essene community sprang. If all these conflicting data are borne in mind and if it is assumed that the work originated in the first half of the second century, around 160 B.C., its attribution to pre-Essene Hasidim would seem reasonable.[14]

The Ethiopic and Latin versions both stem from a Greek text (cf. Charles, p. xxx), alluded to by the Church Fathers and the Byzantine writers quoted above. The Greek, in turn, goes back to a Semitic original, which lay before Jerome (see below), and in effect fragments detached from a dozen or so Qumran manuscripts prove that Hebrew was the original language. It would be unwise to draw any conclusion from the fact that, unlike Enoch, the book makes its appearance in Christian literature only in the third century, suggesting, for example, that it was first translated into Greek at a rather late stage.

---

the Law of *Hadash* and the Pentecontad Calendar', JJS 27 (1976), pp. 36–46; L. Fusella, 'Giubilei', *Apocrifi del'Antico Testamento* [ed. P. Sacchi] (1981), pp. 202–6; K. Berger, *Jubiläen* (1981), pp. 283–4.

11. M. Testuz, *Les idées religieuses du Livre des Jubilées* (1960), pp. 33–4, 179–92; J. C. VanderKam, *Textual and Historical Studies in the Book of Jubilees* (1977), pp. 258–82.

12. Cf. N. Avigad and Y. Yadin, *A Genesis Apocryphon* (1956), p. 38 (possibly a development of the more concise Jubilees); G. Vermes, *Scripture and Tradition in Judaism* (1961, ²1973, 1983), p. 124 (Jubilees is a shortened, though doctrinally enriched, Essene recension of *1QGA*); J. C. VanderKam, *Textual and Historical Studies in the Book of Jubilees* (1977), pp. 277–80 (Jub. and *1QapGen* represent a common and distinctive exegetical tradition).

13. J. T. Milik, *Ten Years of Discovery in the Wilderness of Judaea* (1959), p. 32; M. Testuz, *op. cit.*, p. 33; A. Dupont-Sommer, *The Essene Writings from Qumran* (1961), pp. 298, 305; O. Eissfeldt, *Introduction*, pp. 607–8; J. A. Fitzmyer, *The Genesis Apocryphon of Qumran Cave I* (²1971), p. 10 (with reservation); J. C. VanderKam, *op. cit.*, p. 279; P. W. Skehan, 'Qumran et découvertes dans le désert de Juda', DBS IX (1978), col. 825. It should be noted, however, that the Genesis Apocryphon may not be a Qumran composition, but a pre-sectarian writing inherited by the Community. Cf. n. 12 above, and p. 323 below.

14. Similar views have been advanced by Charlesworth, PMRS, p. 143; Nickelsburg, JLBBM, p. 79 (Jubilees issued from an unnamed sect related to those responsible for Dan. 10–12, 1 Enoch 72–82, 85–90, and 93:1–109:1:12–17); K. Berger, *op. cit.*, p. 298 (the author belonged to an anti-Hellenistic, priestly reform group, closely linked to both the Assidaeans and to the Qumran community). According to VanderKam (*op. cit.*, p. 283), he was a 'proto-Essene'. An attempt to identify the author of Jubilees as a Sadducee is likely to fail, despite the leading role given to the tribe of Levi in 31:11–17, because the Sadducees, contrary to the views expressed in Jubilees, believed neither in angels nor in immortality.

The following titles are associated with the book: (a) Jubilees = τὰ Ἰωβηλαῖα; (b) The Little Genesis = ἡ λεπτὴ Γένεσις; ἡ Λεπτογένεσις; τὰ λεπτὰ Γενέσεως; ἡ Μικρογένεσις; (c) The Apocalypse of Moses = ἡ Μωϋσέως ἀποκάλυψις; (d) The Testament of Moses = ἡ διαθήκη τοῦ Μωϋσέως; (e) The Book of Adam's daughters = Liber de filiabus Adae; (f) The Life of Adam = βίος Ἀδάμ. Cf. Charles, *op. cit.* (1902), pp. xiv-xix,

where all the patristic sources are listed. See also H. Rönsch, *Das Buch der Jubiläen* (1874), pp. 461–82.

The Book of Enoch is evidently very much used in Jubilees. See in particular Jub. 4:17–24, but there are throughout numerous reminiscences of the same source. Cf. Charles, *The Book of Enoch*, pp. 34–5; *Jubilees*, pp. 36–7.

Parallels in rabbinic literature, in particular in Midrash *Wa-yissaʿu*, may be found in A. Jellinek, *Bet ha-Midrasch* III (1855), pp. ix-xiv, xxx-xxxiii; R. H. Charles, *The Ethiopic Version of the Hebrew Book of Jubilees* (1895), pp. 180–2. For the Chronicle of Yerahmeel, see A. Neubauer, *Medieval Jewish Chronicles* I (1887), pp. xix-xxi, 163–78, 190–1; M. Gaster, *The Chronicles of Jerahmeel* (1899). See further M. Epstein, 'Le livre des Jubilés, Philon, et le Midrasch Tadsché', REJ 21 (1890), pp. 80–97; 22 (1891), pp. 1–25; Charles, *Jubilees*, pp. lxxv-vii, 34, and 37–8. On the *Midrash Tadshe*, see also W. Bacher, *Die Agada der Tannaiten* II, p. 499.

The quotations in the Church Fathers and Byzantine writers are collected by Denis, FPG, pp. 70–102; cf. also Charles, *Jubilees*, pp. lxxvii-lxxxiii. For a systematic presentation of these texts, see Denis, IPGAT, pp. 150–62.

The earliest ecclesiastical writer who may have used the Book of Jubilees is Hippolytus in Διαμερισμὸς τῆς γῆς, the apportionment of the earth amongst the descendants of Noah. Cf. A. von Gutschmid, *Kleine Schriften* V (1894), pp. 587–971. A. Bauer, *Die Chronik des Hippolytus*, TU 29, 1 (1905), suggests, however, that this work is independent of Jub. 8–9.

Epiphanius, *Haer.* xxxix 6, 1–7 (ed. Holl, pp. 76–7): Ὡς δὲ ἐν τοῖς Ἰωβηλαίοις εὑρίσκεται, τῇ καὶ Γενέσει καλουμένῃ, καὶ τὰ ὀνόματα τῶν γυναικῶν τοῦ τε Κάϊν καὶ τοῦ Σὴθ ἡ βίβλος περιέχει... Cf. Jub. 4:9–11. Epiphanius, *De mensuris et ponderibus* 22 (PG 43, cols. 276B–77B) quotes Jub. 2:2–21 on the work of the creation. Cf. Denis, FPG, pp. 71–4.

Jerome, *Epistula 78 ad Fabiolam, mansio* 18 (PL 22, col. 711), on the place-name Rissah, Num. 33:21: 'hoc verbum quantum memoria suggerit nusquam alibi in scripturis sanctis apud Hebraeos invenisse me novi absque libro apocrypho qui a Graecis λεπτή id est parva genesis appellatur; ibi in aedificatione turris pro stadio ponitur, in quo exercentur pugiles et athletae et cursorum velocitas comprobatur.' *Ibid. mansio* 24, on the place-name Tarah, Num. 33:27: 'Hoc eodem vocabulo et iisdem literis scriptum invenio patrem Abraham, qui in supradicto apocrypho Geneseos volumine, abactis corvis, qui hominum frumenta vastabant, abactoris vel depulsoris sortitus est nomen.' The *Decretum Gelasii* names among the Apocrypha *Liber de filiabus Adae Leptogenesis* (see E. von Dobschütz, TU 38 (1910), p. 52). Cf. Denis, IPGAT, p. 160.

Syncellus, ed. Dindorf, I 5: ὡς ἐν λεπτῇ φέρεται Γενέσει, ἥν καὶ Μωϋσέως εἶναί φασί τινες ἀποκάλυψιν. I 7: ἐκ τῆς λεπτῆς Γενέσεως. I 13: ἐκ τῶν λεπτῶν Γενέσεως. I 49: ἐν τῇ Μωϋσέως λεγομένῃ ἀποκαλύψει. I 183: ἡ λεπτὴ Γένεσίς φησιν. I 185: ὡς ἐν λεπτῇ κεῖται Γενέσει. I 192: ὥς φησιν ἡ λεπτὴ Γένεσις. I 203: ἐν λεπτῇ Γενέσει φέρεται.

Cedrenus, ed. Bekker, I 6: καὶ ἀπὸ τῆς λεπτῆς Γενέσεως. I 9: ὡς ἐν λεπτῇ φέρεται Γενέσει, ἥν καὶ Μωσέως εἶναί φασί τινες ἀποκάλυψιν. I 16: ὡς ἡ λεπτὴ Μωυσέως Γένεσίς φησιν. I 48: ὡς ἐπὶ τῇ λεπτῇ κεῖται Γενέσει. I 53: ἐν τῇ λεπτῇ Γενέσει κεῖται. I 85: ἐν τῇ λεπτῇ Γενέσει κεῖται. Rönsch, pp. 302–12.

Zonaras, ed. Pinder (*Corpus scriptorum historiae Byzantinae* I, p. 18): ἐν τῇ λεπτῇ Γενέσει.

Glycas, ed. Bekker (p. 198): ἡ λεγομένη λεπτὴ Γένεσις. p. 206: ἡ δὲ λεπτὴ Γένεσις λέγει. p. 392: ἡ δὲ λεγομένη λεπτὴ Γένεσις, οὐκ οἶδ' ὅθεν συγγραφεῖσα καὶ ὅπως, φησίν.

For a detailed survey of the Byzantine sources, see Denis, IPGAT, pp. 152–7.

Editions

1. *Ethiopic Version*
Dillmann, A., *Mashafa Kufâlê sive Liber Jubilaeorum qui idem a Graecis Ἡ Λεπτὴ Γένεσις inscribitur, aethiopice* (1859).
Charles, R. H., *The Ethiopic Version of the Hebrew Book of Jubilees* (1895).

2. *Hebrew Fragments*
See p. 309, n. 1.

3. *Greek Fragments*
Charles, R. H., *The Book of Jubilees or the Little Genesis* (1902), pp. lxxvii–lxxxiii.
Denis, A.-M., *Fragmenta Pseudepigraphorum quae supersunt graeca* (1970).

4. *Latin Fragments*
Ceriani, A. M., *Monumenta sacra et profana* I, 1 (1861), pp. 15–54.
Rönsch, H., *Das Buch der Jubiläen, oder die Kleine Genesis, unter Beifügung des revidierten Textes der in der Ambrosiana aufgefundenen lateinischen Fragmente* (1874).
Charles, R. H., *op. cit.*
Denis, A.-M., *Concordance latine du Liber Jubilaeorum sive Parva Genesis* (1973).

5. *Syriac Fragments*
Ceriani, A.-M., *op. cit.* II, 1 (1863), pp. ix–x.
Charles, R. H., *op. cit.*, p. 183.
Rahmāni, I. E., *Chronicon civile et ecclesiasticum anonymi auctoris* (1904).
Tisserant, E., 'Fragments syriaques du Livre des Jubilées', RB 30 (1921), pp. 55–86, 206–32. Cf. *Recueil Card. Eugène Tisserant. Ab Oriente et Occidente* I (1955), pp. 25–87.

Translations

English
Charles, R. H., *The Book of Jubilees or the Little Genesis* (1902).
Idem, APOT II, pp. 1–82.

German
Dillmann, A., 'Das Buch der Jubiläen', Jahrbuch der biblischen Wissenschaft 3 (1851), pp. 72–96.
Rönsch, H., *op. cit.*
Littmann, E., in APAT II, pp. 31–119.
Riessler, P., *Altjüdisches Schrifttum ausserhalb der Bibel* (1928), pp. 539–666, 1304–11.
Berger, K., *Das Buch der Jubiläen* [JSHRZ II/3] (1981).

Italian
Fusella, L., 'Libro dei Giubilei', in P. Sacchi *et al.*, *Apocrifi dell'Antico Testamento* (1981), pp. 179–411.

Bibliography

Beer, B., *Das Buch der Jubiläen und sein Verhältniss zu den Midraschim* (1856).
Idem, *Noch ein Wort über das Buch der Jubiläen* (1857).
Bohn, F., 'Die Bedeutung des Buches der Jubiläen', ThStKr 73 (1980), pp. 167–84.
Finkelstein, L., 'The Book of Jubilees and the Rabbinic Halaka', HThR 16 (1923), pp. 39–61.
Büchler, A., 'Studies in the Book of Jubilees', REJ 82 (1926), pp. 253–74.
Idem, 'Traces des idées et des coutumes hellénistiques dans le Livre des Jubilées', REJ 89 (1930), pp. 321–48.
Albeck, Th., *Das Buch der Jubiläen und die Halacha* (1930).
Klein, S., 'Palästinisches im Jubiläenbuch', ZDPV 57 (1934), pp. 7–27.
Zeitlin, S., 'The Book of Jubilees, its Character and Significance', JQR 30 (1939/40), pp. 1–32.
Finkelstein, L., 'The Date of the Book of Jubilees', HThR 36 (1943), pp. 19–24.
Zeitlin, S., 'The Book of Jubilees', JQR 35 (1944/5), pp. 12–16.
Idem, 'Criteria for Dating the Book of Jubilees', JQR 36 (1945/6), pp. 187–9.
Rowley, H. H., 'Criteria for the Dating of Jubilees', JQR 36 (1945/6), pp. 183–7.
Torrey, C. C., 'A Hebrew Fragment of Jubilees', JBL 71 (1952), pp. 39–41.
Jaubert, A., 'Le calendrier des Jubilées et de la secte de Qumrân. Ses origines bibliques', VT 3 (1953), pp. 250–64.
Idem, 'Le calendrier des Jubilées et les jours liturgiques de la semaine', VT 7 (1957), pp. 35–61.
Idem, *La date de la Cène. Calendrier biblique et liturgie chrétienne* (1957).
Morgenstern, J., 'The Calendar of the Book of Jubilees, its Origin and its Character', VT 5 (1955), pp. 34–76.
Noack, B., 'Qumran and the Book of Jubilees', SEA 22/3 (1957/8), pp. 191–207.
Zeitlin, S., 'The Book of Jubilees and the Pentateuch', JQR 48 (1957/8), pp. 218–35.
Baumgarten, J. M., 'The Beginning of the Day in the Calendar of Jubilees', JBL 77 (1958), pp. 355–60.
Zeitlin, S., 'The Beginning of the Day in the Calendar of Jubilees', JBL 78 (1959), pp. 153–6.
Kutsch, E., 'Der Kalender der Jubiläenbuches und das Alte und Neue Testament', VT 11 (1961), pp. 31–41.
Testuz, M., *Les idées religieuses du Livre des Jubilées* (1960).
Wiesenberg, E., 'The Jubilee of Jubilees', RQ 3 (1961/2), pp. 3–40.
Cazelles, H., 'Sur les origines du calendrier des Jubilées', Bibl. 43 (1962), pp. 202–16.

Baars, W., and R. Zuurmond, 'The Project of a New Edition of the Ethiopic Book of Jubilees', JSSt 9 (1964), pp. 67–74.

Baillet, M., 'Remarques sur le manuscrit du livre des Jubilées de la grotte 3 de Qumrân', RQ 5 (1965), pp. 423–33.

Eissfeldt, O., *Introduction*, pp. 606–8.

Denis, IPGAT, pp. 150–62.

Davenport, G. L., *The Eschatology of the Book of Jubilees* (1971).

Milik, J. T., 'Recherches sur la version grecque du livre des Jubilées', RB 78 (1971), pp. 545–57.

Idem, 'A propos de 11Q Jub.', Bibl. 54 (1973), pp. 77–8.

Denis, A.-M., *Concordance latine du Liber Jubilaeorum sive Parva Genesis* (1973).

Skehan, P. W., '*Jubilees* and the Qumran Psalter', CBQ 37 (1975), pp. 343–7.

Steck, O. H., 'Die Aufnahme von Genesis 1 in Jubiläen 2 und 4 Esra 6', JSJ 8 (1977), pp. 154–82.

VanderKam, J. C., *Textual and Historical Studies in the Book of Jubilees* (1977).

Idem, 'Enoch Traditions in Jubilees and other Second-Century Sources', in P. J. Achtemeier (ed.), *SBL 1978 Seminar Papers* I (1978), pp. 229–51.

Hoenig, S. B., 'The Jubilees Calendar and the "Days of Assembly"', *Essays on the Occasion of the 70th Anniversary of the Dropsie University* (1979), pp. 189–207.

Caquot, A., 'Deux notes sur la géographie des Jubilées', in G. Nahon and C. Touati, *Hommages à Georges Vajda* (1980), pp. 37–42.

Grelot, P., 'Le livre des Jubilées et le Testament de Levi', P. Casetti *et al.* (eds.), *Mélanges Dominique Barthélemy* (1981), pp. 110–33.

VanderKam, J. C., 'The Putative Author of the Book of Jubilees', JSSt 26 (1981), pp. 209–17.

Idem, 'A Twenty-Eight-Day Month Tradition in the Book of Jubilees?', VT 32 (1982), pp. 504–6.

Caquot, A., 'Le livre des Jubilées, Melkisedeq et les dîmes', in G. Vermes and J. Neusner (eds.), *Essays in Honour of Yigael Yadin* [= JJS 33 (1982)], pp. 257–64.

Alexander, P. S., 'Notes on the "Imago mundi" of the Book of Jubilees', *ibid.*, pp. 197–213.

Rivkin, E., 'The Book of Jubilees—An Anti-Pharisaic Pseudepigraph', *Eretz Israel* 16 (1982), pp. 193–8.

Baumgarten, J. M., 'Some Problems of the Jubilees Calendar in Current Research', VT 32 (1982), pp. 485–9.

2. The Genesis Apocryphon from Qumran

The Genesis Apocryphon (*1QapGen*), earlier known as the Lamech Scroll,[1] is represented by a manuscript from Cave 1, of which twenty-two columns have survived. Five (cols. 2, 19–22) are reasonably well preserved, but the rest are very fragmentary. The tiny remains of a text, also from Cave 1, which still bears the title, 'Apocalypse of Lamech' (*1Q20* = DJD I, pp. 86–7), are thought to belong to the same scroll, although it is impossible to locate them within *1QapGen*.

The extant parts of the manuscript recount the biblical story from

---

1. When first discovered the manuscript could not be opened, but a fragment detached from it contained the name Lamech. Cf. J. C. Trever, 'Identification of the Aramaic Fourth Scroll from 'Ain Feshkha', BASOR 115 (1949), p. 9. In the Sixty Books of apocryphal writings, a work entitled 'Lamech' figures in third place between 'Enoch' and 'Patriarchs' (Denis, IPGAT, p. xiv).

Gen. 5:28 to 15:4, i.e. from Lamech to Abraham. The scroll is incomplete. The minute remains of col. 1 are unlikely to correspond to the beginning of the work; neither does it end on col. 22.

The story begins on col. 2 with Lamech expressing doubts (in the first person) concerning the legitimacy of Noah whom, he suspects, his wife Bathenosh[2] has conceived by one of the fallen angels. Despite her denials, he invites his father, Methuselah, to visit his father, Enoch, in Paradise to discover the truth. The badly damaged cols. 3–5 suggest that Enoch has given Methuselah a reassuring answer to Lamech's enquiry.

Cols. 6–11 furnish scraps of information on the life of Noah, again in autobiographical style, e.g.: 'I, Noah, ...' (6:6); 'I atoned for the whole earth' (10:12–13). The episode of Noah's planting of the vine on Mount Lubar[3] appears on col. 12. There is nothing readable on the next three columns, but they must also have dealt with Noah since cols. 16 and 17 present the division of the earth among his sons, mentioning the River Tina[4] and the Mount of the Bull.[5]

The Abraham story starts on col. 18; it is completely illegible but must have recorded the patriarch's life in Ur and Haran. With col. 19, Gen. 12:8 is reached, Abraham's arrival in Canaan, and from this point until col. 20:22, he is the narrator. He reports how he and Sarah entered Egypt by crossing the River Karmon;[6] how he was warned in a dream of the danger threatening him on account of his beautiful wife; how Sarah was abducted and how her virtue nevertheless remained intact in the royal palace because, at Abraham's prayer, God sent an evil spirit to afflict (i.e. render impotent) Pharaoh and all the men of his household for two full years. Lot, Abraham's nephew, then discloses to the Egyptian prince, Hyrcanus,[7] that Sarah is Abraham's wife. She is dismissed with presents after the patriarch has expelled the troublesome demon through prayer and the laying on of hands.[8]

2. The name appears also in Jub. 4:28 (*Bētēnōs*). On the problem of vocalization, cf. J. A. Fitzmyer, GAQ, p. 74.

3. Cf. Jub. 5:28; 7:1, 17; 10:15; *4QPsDan* (J. T. Milik, RB 63 (1956), p. 412). See also perhaps *6Q8* 21, 1 (DJD III, p. 119).

4. Cf. Jub. 8:12, 16, 25, 28; 9:2, 8.

5. תורא (cf. also 21:16), designating the Taurus-Amanus range known in Greek as Ταῦρος ὄρος. See Avigad and Yadin, GA, pp. 30–1.

6. Karmon is one of the seven branches of the Nile (19:11–12). It is no doubt identical with כרמין or כירמיך mentioned in mPar. 8:10; bB.B. 74b, as one of the four frontier rivers of the Land of Israel. Cf. Avigad and Yadin, p. 25; Fitzmyer, GAQ, pp. 97–8.

7. The spelling is חרקנוש, not the more common and correct הורכנוס. On the various speculations concerning the name, see Fitzmyer, GAQ, pp. 111–12.

8. The laying on of hands is non-biblical. D. Flusser ('Healing through the Laying-on of Hands in the Dead Sea Scrolls', IEJ 7 (1957), pp. 107–8) believes that this is the earliest attestation of the rite in Jewish literature. Cf. however the LXX on 2 Kings 5:11 (Vermes, *Scripture and Tradition*, p. 115, n. 2). For further details, see A. Dupont-Sommer,

On his return from Egypt, Abraham worships at Bethel and from the top of Ramath-Hazor is shown by God the land promised to his posterity. He takes symbolical possession of his territory by walking the boundaries. This leads him from the Mediterranean shore to the Taurus-Amanus range in the North, along the Euphrates to the Persian Gulf, and, following the coasts of the Arabian peninsula and of the Red Sea, to the Gihon River in the South.[9] He then settles at Mamre, outside Hebron.

At col. 21:23 the style of the narrative switches from autobiography to story-telling in the third person and continues in this style to the end. Cols. 21:23–22:26 recount the invasion of Canaan by the Mesopotamian kings, the capture of Lot and his rescue by Abraham, as well as the Melkizedek episode. The midrashic elaboration is less pronounced than in the earlier sections, but there is a trend towards modernizing the geographical data.[10]

Col. 22:27–34 paraphrases slightly, though with chronological supplements,[11] Gen. 15:1–4. These lines represent the beginning of God's promise of an heir to the patriarch. The remainder of the scroll is lost.

The language of the document is characterized as a transitional stage between the Aramaic of Daniel and 'Middle Aramaic' exemplified, *inter alia*, by the Palestinian Targums. The dialect is essentially western, though it includes some eastern Aramaic features as well as several Hebraisms. The most important philological study is by E. Y. Kutscher, 'The Language of the Genesis Apocryphon', Scrip. Hier. 4 (1958), pp. 1–35. J. A. Fitzmyer has appended the outline of a Qumran

'Exorcism et guérisons dans les écrits de Qoumrân', VTS 7 (1960), pp. 246–61; Fitzmyer, GAQ, pp. 124–5; M. Delcor, 'Qumrân. Apocryphe de la Genèse', DBS IX, col. 938.

9. For Gihon = Nile, see Jub. 8:15; Josephus, *Ant.* i 1, 3 (39). This identification is, however, not without difficulties in the geographical scheme of *1QapGen*. Cf. Vermes, *Scripture and Tradition*, p. 104, n. 2. See also Fitzmyer, GAQ, pp. 135–6.

10. 'Shinar' = Babylon as in Targums Onkelos and Neofiti. 'Ellasar' = *Kaptok*, Cappadocia. (Neofiti, Symmachus and Vulgate give Pontus.) 'King of the Goyim' = 'nations which lie between the rivers'. Josephus, *Ant.* i 9, 1 (171–2), identifies all the invaders as Assyrians. Cf. Vermes, *Scripture and Tradition*, p. 118; Fitzmyer, GAQ, pp. 141–4. 'The Valley of Shaveh, which is the Valley of the King' (Gen. 14:17) is described as the Valley of *Beth Karma* (*Beth ha-Kerem*) situated at 'Salem which is Jerusalem'. Cf. LXX Josh. 15:59; Jer. 6:1; Neh. 3:14; Copper Scroll (*3Q15*) 10:5 (DJD III, pp. 268, 295); Fitzmyer, GAQ, pp. 155–6. For an identification of Beth ha-Kerem with the modern Ramat Rahel, south of Jerusalem, see J. Aharoni, 'Excavations at Ramat Rahel', IEJ 6 (1956), pp. 152–6; *Excavations at Ramat Rahel: Seasons 1959 and 1960* (1962), p. 50. Note, however, that Hazezon-Tamar (col. 21:30), said to be Engedi already in 2 Chron. 20:2, in all the Targums on Gen. 14:7 and according to Jerome, *Hebr. Quaest. in Gen. in loc.* (CCL 72, p. 18), remains unidentified. Cf. Vermes, PBJS, pp. 17–18; Fitzmyer, GAQ, p. 148.

11. Cf. Gen. 16:3; Jub. 13 and GA col. 19:9–10. See Fitzmyer, GAQ, p. 161. In Jubilees, the chronology is set out in detail; here it is implicit.

Aramaic grammar to GAQ, pp. 173–206. For further references, see the bibliography.

The literary genre of *1QapGen* falls between the rabbinic categories of Targum and Midrash.[12] It would be true to say, however, that neither definition properly fits the Genesis Apocryphon. This work belongs just as well, if not better, to the genre represented by Jubilees, Josephus' Antiquities, Pseudo-Philo's *Liber Antiquitatum Biblicarum*; i.e. writings in which scriptural narrative and midrashic developments are amalgamated to form a 'rewritten Bible'.[13]

Nevertheless, even these broad categories are unable fully to accommodate *1QapGen*. Indeed, we can recognize in this composition, notwithstanding the fragmentary character of most of the columns, two distinct literary units. One of these, corresponding to the third person narrative (cols. 21:23–22:34), actually prefigures the Palestinian Targums to the Pentateuch. The other (i.e. all the earlier sections with stories told in the first person) may be defined as the 'memoirs' of Lamech, Noah and Abraham. They constitute therefore a genre cognate to midrash; but they are also akin to that special kind of fictional 'autobiography' which forms the substance of the pseudepigraphic testamentary literature (see below, p. 767).

The relationship between *1QapGen* and the Book of Jubilees—and, as far as col. 2 is concerned, the Book of Enoch 106–7—has been generally acknowledged.[14] The editors Avigad and Yadin conclude that 'the scroll may have served as a source for a number of stories told more concisely' in Enoch and Jubilees (p. 38). The opposite sequence, viz. that the author of *1QapGen* uses Enoch and Jubilees in combination with Genesis and supplements them with imaginative additions, is proposed by J. A. Fitzmyer (GAQ, p. 14). Both positions are perfectly tenable. Nevertheless, in favour of the priority of our document it can be argued that the parallels of Psalm 151 (cf. above, p. 189), the astronomical book of Enoch (cf. above, p. 254) and the Aramaic Testament of Levi (cf. below, p. 772) point towards an abbreviating tendency in inter-Testamental literature (which of course does not prove that early versions have never been enlarged). However, in practice, it is easier to account for the introduction of well-defined doctrinal peculiarities (e.g. Jubilees' specific calendric matters) into an unbiased story than for the creation of a fresh and simple narrative such

12. The Targum theory has been emphasized from an early stage onwards by M. Black, *The Scrolls and Christian Origins* (1961), pp. 193–8. For Midrash, see G. Vermes, *Scripture and Tradition*, p. 124. A mixture of both classes is preferred by M. R. Lehmann, '1Q Genesis Apocryphon in the Light of the Targumim and Midrashim', RQ 1 (1958/9), pp. 249–63.
13. Cf. Vermes, *Scripture and Tradition*, p. 95.
14. See Avigad and Yadin, p. 38. For a detailed list, cf. Fitzmyer, GAQ, pp. 222–3.

as our document at the end of a lengthy series of excisions.[15]

The dating of the Scroll itself is largely uncontroversial. On archaeological grounds, it belongs to the pre-A.D. 70 era, and palaeographically it is said to be 'Herodian'. Most scholars assign the copy to the late first century B.C. or the first half of the first century A.D.[16]

The dating of the composition has been attempted on the basis of (a) linguistic evidence, (b) the historical identification of names of persons and places, and (c) literary criticism.

(a) As far as the language is concerned, the above-mentioned detailed analysis by E. Y. Kutscher (p. 320) reaches the conclusion that *1QapGen* dates to 'the first century B.C.E. (—first century C.E.)'.[17] Kutscher prefers to be vague; others are more specific and opt definitely for the first century B.C. (Fitzmyer, p. 16; Delcor, DBS IX, col. 943, etc.). In fact the only conclusion that can strictly be drawn from Kutscher's study is that the Aramaic of *1QapGen* post-dates that of Daniel. However, the Aramaic Daniel does not necessarily indicate a second-century B.C. date, but may well go back to the third century B.C.[18] Consequently, on philological grounds, the Scroll may be assigned to the first *or* the second century B.C.

(b) No solid argument has been advanced for identifying historically any of the persons mentioned in the text. There is no reason why the Egyptian *Ḥarqenosh* or *Ḥirqanos* (col. 20:8) should be connected with Hyrcanus the Tobiad (*c.* 200 B.C.) or Hyrcanus II (63–40 B.C.).[19] The identification of Arioch and Tidal (col. 21:23–4) with Mithridates VI Pontus (121–63 B.C.) and Mithridates II, the Arsacid king of Upper Mesopotamia (126–86 B.C.), is equally speculative.[20]

(c) The literary critical argument is based essentially on the relationship between *1QapGen* and Jubilees (cf. above, p. 314 and J. C. VanderKam, *Textual and Historical Studies in the Book of Jubilees* (1977), pp. 277–80). If the Apocryphon is seen as dependent on Jubilees, it is bound to belong, at the earliest, to the end of the second century, and

15. Vermes, *Scripture and Tradition*, pp. 96, n. 2, 124.

16. N. Avigad, 'The Palaeography of the Dead Sea Scrolls and Related Documents', Scrip. Hier. 4 (1958), pp. 56–87, especially pp. 71–2; F. M. Cross, 'The Development of the Jewish Scripts', in G. E. Wright (ed.), *The Bible and the Ancient Near East* (1961), pp. 173–81; Fitzmyer, GAQ, p. 13.

17. Scrip. Hier. 4 (1958), p. 22.

18. Cf. J. A. Montgomery, *Daniel* (1927), p. 20; Eissfeldt, *Introduction*, p. 519; Fitzmyer, GAQ, p. 18, n. 56.

19. G. Lambert, 'Une "Genèse apocryphe" trouvée à Qumran', in *La secte de Qumrân et les origines du christianisme* (1959), p. 106; F. Altheim and R. Stiehl, 'Die Datierung des Genesis-Apokryphon vom Toten Meer', *Die aramäische Sprache unter den Achaimaniden* (1959), pp. 214–22.

20. Altheim and Stiehl, *ibid.*

more probably to the first century B.C. By contrast, if *1QapGen* precedes Jubilees, the beginning of the second century B.C. commends itself. The linguistic objection raised against this possibility has already been shown to be overstated. On balance, the earlier dating may be very slightly preferable.[21]

To determine the milieu in which *1QapGen* originated, the connections between this work and the sectarian compositions from Qumran must be investigated. So far, it should be remarked, no particular sectarian feature has been detected in the Apocryphon necessitating its attribution to a Qumran author. H. Lignée has proposed, in very reserved terms, that the apocalyptic traits of the Noah-Enoch passages and the use of dreams and visions as means of revelation would point towards the ideology dominant in the community of the Scrolls.[22] But none of these suggestions is impressive enough to demand serious refutation.[23] It is more likely that the Genesis Apocryphon is a 'haggadic' writing inherited by the Qumran group from pre-sectarian Judaism. Incidentally, this conclusion accords better with a second century B.C. origin than with a later dating of the document (see p. 322).[24]

Editions

Avigad, N., and Yadin, Y., *A Genesis Apocryphon: A Scroll from the Wilderness of Judaea* (1956).

Milik, J. T., 'Apocalypse de Lamech', DJD I, pp. 86–7.

Fitzmyer, J. A., *The Genesis Apocryphon of Qumran Cave I: A Commentary* (1966, [2]1971) [with detailed bibliography].

Jongeling, B., Labuschagne, C. J., and Woude, A. S. van der, *Aramaic Texts from Qumran* (1976), pp. 75–119.

Lignée, H., 'Concordance de 1Q Genesis Apocryphon', RQ 1 (1959), pp. 163–86.

21. To the arguments listed above it may be added in support of an early (i.e. second-century B.C.) date that two of the geographical terms, 'Ellasar' and 'Hazezon-Tamar', had not yet been modernized as 'Pontus' and 'Engedi' when *1QapGen* was written (cf. n. 10 above). Jews are likely to have become aware of Pontus after it has been conquered by Pompey in the first century B.C.; cf. Josephus, *Ant.* xiv 3, 4 (53). It is worth noting that earlier in *Ant.* ix 1, 4 (17), Josephus implies that Tarshish in 2 Chron. 20:36 refers to 'Pontus and the trading stations of Thrace'. Elsewhere, however, Tarshish is identified as Tarsus in Cilicia (*Ant.* i 6, 1 (127); ix 10, 2 (208)). Cf. also Tg. Ps.-Jon. and Neof. on Gen. 10:4 and Tg. 2 Chron. 20:36.

22. Cf. H. Lignée, 'L'apocryphe de la Genèse', in TQ II (1963), p. 211.

23. Fitzmyer, GAQ, p. 12; Delcor, DBS IX (1978), col. 942–3.

24. Although *1QapGen* is the only extant copy of this work, it would a priori be unsafe to assume that our manuscript represents the original composition. In fact, even if the palaeographical dating to the late first century B.C. is correct (cf. above, p. 322) internal evidence would militate against acknowledging the scroll from Cave 1 as the author's autograph copy (against R. de Vaux, RB 74 (1967), p. 101).

Translations

English
Avigad and Yadin, *op. cit.*
Fitzmyer, *op. cit.*
Jongeling *et al.*, *op. cit.*
Vermes, DSSE², pp. 215–24.

French
Dupont-Sommer, A., EE, pp. 291–306.
Lignée, H., TQ II, pp. 205–42.

German
Maier, J., TTM II, pp. 157–65.

Italian
Moraldi, L., MQ, pp. 603–32.

Bibliography

Trever, J. C., 'Identification of the Aramaic Fourth Scroll from 'Ain Feshkha', BASOR 115 (1949), pp. 8–10.
Kutscher, E. Y., 'Dating the Language of the Genesis Apocryphon', JBL 76 (1957), pp. 288–92.
Idem, 'The Language of the Genesis Apocryphon: A Preliminary Study', Scrip. Hier. 4 (1958), pp. 1–35.
Avigad, N., 'The Palaeography of the Dead Sea Scrolls and Related Documents', Scrip. Hier. 4 (1958), pp. 56–87.
Sarfatti, G., 'Notes on the Genesis Apocryphon', Tarbiz 28 (1958/9), pp. 254–9.
Idem, 'Supplement to "Notes ..."', *ibid.* 29 (1959/60), p. 192.
Lehmann, M. R., '1Q Genesis Apocryphon in the Light of the Targumim and Midrashim', RQ 1 (1959), pp. 249–63.
Grelot, P., 'Sur l'Apocryphe de la Genèse (XX, 26)', RQ 1 (1959), pp. 273–6.
Müller, W. W., 'Die Bedeutung des Wortes '*sprk* im Genesis-Apokryphon XXII, 31', RQ 2 (1960), pp. 445–7.
Osswald, E., 'Beobachtungen zur Erzählung von Abrahams Aufenthalt in Ägypten im Genesis-Apokryphon', ZAW 72 (1960), pp. 7–25.
Vermes, G., *Scripture and Tradition* (1961, ²1973), pp. 96–126.
Grelot, P., 'Parwaim des Chroniques à l'Apocryphe de la Genèse', VT 11 (1961), pp. 30–8.
Rowley, H. H., 'Notes on the Aramaic of the *Genesis Apocryphon*', in *Hebrew and Semitic Studies presented to G. R. Driver* (1963), pp. 116–29.
Grelot, P., 'Retour au Parwaim', VT 14 (1964), pp. 155–63.
Rüger, H. P., '1Q Genesis Apocryphon XIX, 19f. im Lichte der Targumim', ZNW 55 (1964), pp. 129–31.
Kuiper, G. J., 'A Study of the Relationship between A Genesis Apocryphon and the Pentateuchal Targumim in Gen. 14:1–12', *In Memoriam Paul Kahle* (1968), pp. 149–61.
Kutscher, E. Y., 'The Genesis Apocryphon of Qumran Cave I', Orientalia 39 (1970), pp. 178–83.
Grelot, P., 'Un nom égyptien dans *l'Apocryphe de la Genèse*', RQ 7 (1971), pp. 557–66.
Bardtke, H., 'Literaturbericht über Qumrân. VI.2. Das Genesis-Apokryphon 1Q Gen Ap.', ThR 37 (1972), pp. 193–204.
Muraoka, T., 'Notes on the Aramaic of the Genesis Apocryphon', RQ 8 (1972), pp. 7–51.
Dehandschutter, B., 'Le rêve dans l'Apocryphe de la Genèse', in W. C. van Unnik (ed.), *La littérature juive entre Tenach et Mischna* (1974), pp. 48–55.

Garbini, G., 'L'Apocrifo della Genesi nella letteratura giudaica', Annali dell'Instituto Orientale di Napoli 37 (1977), pp. 1–18.
Vermes, DSS, pp. 66–8.
Delcor, M., 'Qumrân', DBS IX, cols. 931–44.
VanderKam, J. C., 'The Poetry of 1Q Ap Gen XX, 2–8a', RQ 10 (1979), pp. 57–66.
Greenfield, J. C., 'The Genesis Apocryphon—Observations on some Words and Phrases', in G. B. Sarfatti *et al.* (eds.), *Studies in Hebrew and Semitic Languages* [E. Y. Kutscher Memorial Volume] (1980), pp. xxxii-ix.
Nickelsburg, JLBBM, pp. 263–5.
Weinfeld, M., 'Sarah in the House of Abimelek (Gen. 20)', Tarbiz 52 (1983), pp. 639–42 (Hebrew).

3. Pseudo-Philo's Book of Biblical Antiquities

The Latin version of a remarkable biblical history, the *Liber Antiquitatum Biblicarum*, wrongly ascribed to Philo of Alexandria, was first edited, together with the Latin translations of Philo's *Quaestiones et solutiones in Genesim, De Essaeis* (= a fragment of *De vita contemplativa*), *De nominibus hebraicis* and *De mundo*, by Johannes Sichardus in Basle in 1527. It was reprinted no less than four times before 1600,[1] but was soon forgotten and did not re-emerge until the end of the last century, when Leopold Cohn, editor of the Greek works of Philo, devoted to it an essay that turned out to be a landmark in Pseudo-Philo studies.[2] M. R. James, who in 1893 published four fragments of LAB without knowing their identity, further promoted research by issuing an annotated English translation with a substantial introduction in 1917. But it is only since the end of the second world war that this pseudepigraph has received the attention it deserves. The Latin text has been re-edited twice: first by Guido Kisch in 1949, then by Daniel J. Harrington in 1976.[3] It has also been translated into German[4] and French,[5] and is regularly used in the study of inter-Testamental Judaism.

The editio princeps of the Latin text resulted from the collation of two manuscripts, Fulda-Cassel (eleventh century) and Lorsch (now lost, but probably also dating from the eleventh century or earlier). Today, a further twenty manuscripts are completely or partly preserved, the oldest of them being Admont 359, Phillips 391, Munich

---

1. Cf. M. R. James, *The Biblical Antiquities of Philo* (1917; repr. 1971), p. 8. The 1971 reprint is preceded by a clxix-page *Prolegomenon* by Louis H. Feldman (cited as Feldman, *Proleg.*).

2. 'An Apocryphal Work ascribed to Philo of Alexandria', JQR 10 (1898), pp. 277–332.

3. Guido Kisch, *Pseudo-Philo's Liber Antiquitatum Biblicarum* (1949); Daniel J. Harrington, *Pseudo-Philon, Les antiquités bibliques* I [SC 229] (1976).

4. Christian Dietzfelbinger, *Pseudo-Philo: Antiquitates Biblicae* [JSHRZ II/2] (1975).

5. J. Cazeaux, *Pseudo-Philon, Les antiquités bibliques* I (1976). The second volume consists of a literary introduction and a full commentary by C. Perrot and P.-M. Bogaert [SC 230].

Lat. 18481 (all from the eleventh century); Budapest Cod. lat. med. aev. 23;⁶ Phillips 461; Vienna Lat. 446; Munich Lat. 17133 and 4569 (from the twelfth century). D. J. Harrington, in his 'Introduction critique', has attempted to determine the stemma of the extant witnesses, and in his reconstructed text the Fulda-Cassel manuscript of the editio princeps retains pride of place.⁷

The Latin text seems, from mistranslations and the retention of Greek words, to derive from the Greek. Greek is however unlikely to be the original language; in a number of passages the Latin postulates an underlying Hebrew idiom both in the author's own narration and in his citation of Scripture.⁸ The many haggadic developments embellishing the account also point to a close relation to rabbinic midrash. Nevertheless, the lengthy Hebrew extracts from LAB found in the fourteenth century Oxford manuscript of the *Chronicles of Yerahme'el* (Heb. d. 11) must not be regarded as relics of the Semitic original of this work, but rather as a medieval retranslation into Hebrew from the Latin, as L. Cohn and, more recently, D. J. Harrington have demonstrated.⁹

Pseudo-Philo retells biblical history from Adam to Saul and David. The first nineteen chapters deal with the Pentateuch; chapters 20–24 with Joshua; chapters 25–48 with Judges; chapters 49–65 with 1 Samuel. The genre of the composition is that of the 'rewritten Bible' (Vermes) or 'texte continué' (Perrot), i.e. a narrative that follows Scripture but includes a substantial amount of supplements and interpretative developments, its fullest example being the Jewish Antiquities of Josephus, and its prototype the biblical Chronicles.¹⁰

6. On this manuscript, see Ida Fröhlich, *Bibliai legendák a hellénisztikus zsidó történetírásban* (1973), pp. 14–57.

7. Cf. *op. cit.* [in n. 3] I, pp 15–57; especially p. 53.

8. Cf. Cohn, *art. cit.*; James, *op. cit.*, pp. 28–9; Kisch, *op. cit.*, p. 16; Dietzfelbinger, *op. cit.*, p. 92; Harrington, *op. cit.* II, pp. 75–8. Feldman, *Proleg.*, pp. xxvi-vii, considers the case unproven and a Greek original conceivable although noting that the use of the Hebrew Bible and LAB's affinity with Targumic tradition favour a Hebrew original. His own argument from Josephus' Antiquities, written in Greek, yet displaying similar Semitic features, would be valid only if he could demonstrate the existence of a wide Greek readership among Palestinian Jews, an unlikely hypothesis (cf. vol. II, pp. 79–80).

9. Cohn, 'Pseudo-Philo und Jerachmeel', *Festschrift zum 70. Geburtstage Jakob Guttmanns* (1915), pp. 173–85; Daniel J. Harrington, *The Hebrew Fragments of Pseudo-Philo's Liber Antiquitatum Biblicarum preserved in the Chronicles of Jerahmeel* (1974), pp. 2–7.

10. See Vermes, *Scripture and Tradition*, pp. 95, 124–6; C. Perrot, *Pseudo-Philo, Les antiquités bibliques* II, pp. 22–8. Apropos of the Chronicles, it has been pointed out that LAB ends exactly where, not counting the nine genealogical chapters, the story of 1 Chronicles begins, at the death of Saul (Riessler, *Altjüdisches Schrifttum*, p. 1315). The literary bond between Chronicles and LAB has been noticed by Cohn (*art. cit.*, p. 315). P. Riessler, A. Spiro and R. Le Déaut have conjectured that LAB was actually written as a supplementary introduction to Chronicles (Riessler, *Altjüdische Schriften* (1928), p. 1315; Spiro, 'Samaritans, Tobiads and Judahites in Pseudo-Philo', PAAJR 20 (1951), pp.

In his reworking of the biblical narration of the Torah, Pseudo-Philo often employs common haggadic themes (Abraham in the fiery furnace: 6:1–18; the sacrifice of Isaac: 18:5; 32:2–4; 40:2; the legends associated with the birth of Moses: 9:1–15; the Balaam story: 18:1–14).[11] He is more creative in the post-Mosaic sections. Nevertheless, he displays throughout unparalleled features, and occasionally so manipulates traditional material that the result is quite uncommon, as for instance when he portrays Balaam as a tragic hero rather than as the prototype of the sinner.[12]

A great variety of views have been expressed concerning the milieu to which Pseudo-Philo belonged and the consequent motivation of his work. LAB is defined as essentially a polemical, anti-Samaritan or anti-Mithraic Palestinian-Jewish writing on account of its silence regarding Samaritan sites and its criticism of foreign cults.[13] But such theses are scarcely tenable, firstly because LAB, although it may contain a certain amount of anti-Samaritanism common to inter-Testamental Judaism, is a didactic and not polemical-apologetic document. As for the anti-Mithraic traits, they are so vague as not to reach even the minimum level required for a conjecture to be respectable.[14] Neither is the Essene theory in its pre- or post-Qumran versions any more convincing.[15] In consequence, the most satisfactory

---

304–8; Le Déaut, *La nuit pascale* (1963), p. 188). The theory that the work is incomplete was first advanced by Sixtus Senensis, *Bibliotheca Sacra* (1566), p. 314, and has been echoed in more recent times by James, *op. cit.*, pp. 60–5; Kisch, *op. cit.*, p. 29; Dietzfelbinger, *op. cit.*, pp. 96–7 (arguing for the *terminus ad quem* of 587 B.C.). M. Delcor ('Philon, Pseudo-', DBS VII (1966), col. 1373), Feldman (*Proleg.*, p. lxxvii) and Perrot (*op. cit.* II, pp. 21–2) consider LAB to be complete.

11. These passages are examined in Vermes, *Scripture and Tradition*, pp. 85–90, 199–202, 174–5; 'La figure de Moïse au tournant des deux Testaments', *Moïse, l'homme de l'Alliance* (1955), pp. 86–92 (= *Cahiers Sioniens* 8 (1954), pp. 204–10).

12. See L. H. Feldman, *Proleg.*, pp. lxx–vi; for the Balaam episode, see Vermes, *Scripture and Tradition*, pp. 174–5.

13. Spiro, 'Samaritans, Tobiads and Judahites in Pseudo-Philo: Use and Abuse of the Bible by Polemicists and Doctrinaires', *passim*; Dietzfelbinger, *op. cit.*, pp. 97–8.

14. Cf. Feldman, *Proleg.*, pp. xxxiv–viii.

15. Riessler, *op. cit.*, p. 1315, sees in LAB's lack of emphasis on priestly matters and its apparent interest in precious stones (26:10 ff.) Essene characteristics, a theory hardly worth mentioning in the post-Qumran understanding of Essenism. M. Philonenko's attempts at connecting LAB with Qumran must also be declared a failure (cf. 'Remarques sur un hymne essénien de caractère gnostique', Semitica 11 (1961), pp. 43–54; 'Essénisme et gnose chez le Pseudo-Philon', *Studies in the History of Religions* 12 (1967), pp 401–10). Not only are the similarities in messianic terminology and mysticism too general, but LAB's definite assertion of the doctrine of resurrection in 3:10 ('Cum autem completi fuerint anni seculi, tunc quiescet lumen et extinguentur tenebre, et vivificabo mortuos et erigam dormientes de terra') conflicts with the Essene doctrine of purely spiritual survival (cf. vol. II, pp. 574, 582–3). Cf. also Feldman, *Proleg.*, pp. xxxviii–xliii. It goes without saying that no LAB fragment has turned up among the Qumran texts.

theory places Pseudo-Philo within mainstream Jewish thought, with non-sectarian Pharisaic colouring.[16] The date of composition of LAB cannot be determined exactly on the basis of the extant internal evidence. Since Cohn's study, the opinion has prevailed that the work belongs to the first century A.D., written probably after the destruction of Jerusalem by Titus. Although there is no direct allusion to this event, the author places the capture of the city by Nebuchadnezzar on 17 Tammuz, the day on which the tables of the Law were once broken.[17] In fact, Nebuchadnezzar's entry into Jerusalem took place on 9 Tammuz (Jer. 39:2; 52:6; 2 Kings 25:3), the destruction of the Temple on 10 Ab (Jer. 52:12), a date for which 9 Ab was later substituted. For this reason 9 Ab, and equally 17 Tammuz, were regarded as unpropitious days for Israel.[18] The cessation of the daily offering on this day during the siege by Titus seems to have initiated this tendency.

Relying on this datum, Cohn (p. 325) suggested that the redaction of the work followed shortly after A.D. 70, whereas James (*op. cit.*, pp. 32–3) opted for 'the closing years of the first Christian century'. This argument, impressive though it may appear, has been called into question.[19] For on the one hand, 17 Tammuz as a fast day, mentioned already in Zech. 8:19, was bound to appear as the memorial of some major calamity, such as the fall of either or both Temples; on the other hand, the seventeenth of Panemus (= Tammuz) in A.D. 70 was not the date of the destruction of the sanctuary but of the razing of the foundations of the fortress Antonia, coinciding with the accidental discontinuation of the *tamid* sacrifice [*B.J.* vi 2, 1 (93–4)].[20] P.-M.

---

16. Cf. Perrot, *op. cit.* II, p. 32. His three main reasons are: (1) absence of sectarian bias; (2) literary connections with 4 Ezra and the Apocalypse of Baruch; and (3) the main themes of LAB represent current, middle-of-the-way Jewish thinking.

17. Cf. Cohn, *art. cit.*, p. 326. 'Demonstrabo tibi locum, in quo mihi servient annos DCCXL, et post haec tradetur in manus inimicorum suorum, et demolientur eum et circumdabunt eum alienigenae. Et erit in illa die secundum diem illum, in quo contrivi tabulas legis quas disposui ad te in Oreb, et peccantibus illis evolavit ex eis quod erat scriptum; dies autem erat septima decima mensis quarti' (19:7).

18. 'On 17 Tammuz the tables of the Law were broken, and the daily offering (*tamid*) suspended, and Jerusalem captured by Nebuchadnezzar ... On 9 Ab, it was decreed against our fathers that they might not enter into the Holy Land; and the Temple was destroyed for the first time (by Nebuchadnezzar), and for the second time (by Titus); and Bethar was conquered, and Jerusalem was ploughed up' (mTaan. 4:6). The greater part of the passage will also be found in Jerome's Commentary on Zechariah 8:19 (CCL 76A, p. 820). Cf. especially 'Ieiunium quarti mensis ... die septima et decima eiusdem mensis, illud arbitrantur, quando descendens Moyses de monte Sina tabulas legis abiecerit atque confregerit, et iuxta Hieremiam muri primum rupti sunt ciuitatis.'

19. See Vermes, *Scripture and Tradition*, p. 6.

20. P.-M. Bogaert, *op. cit.* II, pp. 68–70. For a criticism of his handling of the evidence, see M. P. Wadsworth, 'A New Pseudo-Philo', JJS 29 (1978), pp. 189–91, who places the composition of LAB to the end of the first century A.D. (p. 188).

Bogaert argues in favour of a pre-A.D. 70 dating by stressing that the 'texte continué' (or rewritten Bible) disappeared with the Second Temple. Furthermore, LAB's attitude to sacrificial worship implies the existence of a sanctuary, as does also the phrase 'usque in hodiernum diem' in connection with the holocausts established by Joshua at Gilgal.[21] A further argument for an early (pre-70) dating for much of the material is advanced by J. Strugnell, who points out the presence in Pseudo-Philo's Hebrew Bible text of a large number of Septuagintal, proto-Lucianic and Palestinian readings.[22] Finally, it might well be asked whether a Palestinian Jewish book written during the last decades of the first century A.D. would not reveal some more obvious traces of the impact of the great national catastrophe? All in all, a first century A.D. date is *opinio communis*, but it is impossible to state categorically whether Pseudo-Philo completed his book before or after the capture of Jerusalem by the Romans.[23]

No direct references to Pseudo-Philo are to be found in patristic literature. The most interesting allusion is that by Clement of Alexandria, who knows that one of the names of Moses was Melchi: ἔσχεν δὲ καὶ τρίτον ὄνομα ἐν οὐρανῷ μετὰ τὴν ἀνάληψιν, ὥς φασιν οἱ μύσται, Μελχί (*Strom.* i 23, 153, ed. Stählin and Früchtel, p. 95; Denis, FPG, p. 64). LAB 9:16 ('Mater autem eius vocavit eum Melchiel') appears to be the only known Jewish parallel. See also Georgius Syncellus, *Chronographia* (ed. Dindorf, pp. 226–7): Μωϋσέα τε μετονομάζει ... τὸν Μελχίαν ὑπὸ τῶν γονέων πρὶν κληθέντα ... Μελχίας γὰρ βασιλεὺς ἑρμενεύεται. Georgius Cedrenus (PG 121, 104C): λέγουσι δὲ ὡς τοῦ Μωϋσέως γεννηθέντος Μελχίαν παρὰ τοῦ πατρὸς κληθῆναι, ὅπερ ἐστὶ βασιλεύς. Cf. S. Krauss, 'The Names of Moses', JQR 10 (1898), p. 726. Other possible allusions in Origen, Aphrahat, Ephraem, Ambrose and Theodoret may simply be due to common Jewish traditions. Cf. Feldman, *Proleg.*, pp. xi–xiii. On the quotations from LAB in the Hebrew *Chronicles of Jerahmeel*, see below.

No fragments of the original Hebrew or of the Greek translation have survived. The Latin version is dated to the fourth century. It circulated together with Philo's *Quaestiones et solutiones in Genesim*. On the latter see Françoise Petit, *L'ancienne version latine des Questions sur la Genèse de Philon d'Alexandrie* (1973).

Substantial sections of LAB have survived incorporated into the

---

21. *Ibid.*, pp. 71–2. For 'usque in hodiernum diem', see already Feldman, *Proleg.*, p. xxviii.

22. Strugnell, 'Philo (Pseudo) or Liber Antiquitatum Biblicarum', Enc. Jud. 13, col. 408.

23. Even if the post–70 hypothesis is adopted, most of the exegetical traditions used by the author should be traced back to the Second Temple era. The date of redaction of a work re-employing pre-existing material indicates the *terminus ante quem* of the latter.

Hebrew *Chronicles of Jerahmeel*, a fourteenth century manuscript of the Bodleian Library in Oxford (Ms. Heb. d. 11). These *Chronicles* recount human and Jewish history from the creation to the age of the Maccabees, and utilize, in so doing, LAB 1–7 (22^r–25^v), 9 (37^v), and extracts from 25–28, 31, 38, 39–40, 44, 46–48 (58^r–61^v). M. Gaster, *The Chronicles of Jerahmeel or The Hebrew Bible Historiale* (1899; repr. with a Prolegomenon by H. Schwarzbaum, 1971), offers an English translation of the *Chronicles*, and advances the thesis that Jerahmeel cites the original Hebrew text of Pseudo-Philo (pp. xxx-xxxix). L. Cohn (*art. cit.* [in n. 9 above]) and D. J. Harrington in his edition and translation of the Hebrew sections of LAB (cf. *op. cit.* [in n. 9 above], pp. 2–5) convincingly show that Jerahmeel used a retroversion of the Latin text into Hebrew.

For parallels between LAB, the Pseudepigrapha, Qumran, the New Testament and rabbinic literature, see Feldman, *Proleg.*, pp. li-lxxvi.

Editions

Latin text
Sichardus, Johannes, *Philonis Iudaei Alexandrini Libri Antiquitatum, Quaestionum et Solutionum in Genesim, De Essaeis, De Nominibus Hebraicis, De Mundo* (1527).
Kisch, G., *Pseudo-Philo's Liber Antiquitatum Biblicarum* (1949).
Harrington, D. J., *Pseudo-Philon, Antiquitates Biblicae* [SC 229] (1976).

Hebrew version
Harrington, D. J., *The Hebrew Fragments of Pseudo-Philo's Liber Antiquitatum Biblicarum* (1974).

Translations

English
James, M. R., *The Biblical Antiquities of Philo* (1917). Reprinted with a Prolegomenon by L. H. Feldman (1971).
Bowker, J., *The Targums and Rabbinic Literature*. Appendix I: 'The Biblical Antiquities of Philo: A Translation of the Passages related to Genesis' (1969), pp. 301–14.

German
Riessler, P., *Altjüdisches Schrifttum ausserhalb der Bibel* (1928), pp. 735–861, 1315–18.
Dietzfelbinger, C., *Pseudo-Philo: Antiquitates Biblicae* [JSHRZ II, 2] (1975).

French
Cazeaux, J., with C. Perrot and P.-M. Bogaert, *Pseudo-Philon, Les antiquités bibliques* I [SC 229] (1976).

Modern Hebrew
Hartom, A. S., *Ha-Sefarîm Ha-ḥiṣônîm* 7 (1967).

Bibliography

Cohn, L., 'An Apocryphal Work ascribed to Philo of Alexandria', JQR 10 (1898), pp. 277–332.
Gaster, M., *The Chronicles of Jerahmeel or The Hebrew Bible Historiale* (1899).
Cohn, L., 'Pseudo-Philo and Jerahmeel', *Festschrift zum siebzigsten Geburtstage Jakob Guttmanns* (1915), pp. 173–85.

James, M. R., 'Notes on Apocrypha (Pseudo-Philo and Baruch)', JThSt 16 (1915), pp. 403–5.

Kisch, G., 'Pseudo-Philo's Liber Antiquitatum Biblicarum: Postlegomena to the New Edition', HUCA 23/2 (1950/1), pp. 80–93.

Spiro, A., 'Samaritans, Tobiads and Judahites in Pseudo-Philo: Use and Abuse of the Bible by Polemicists and Doctrinaires', PAAJR 20 (1951), pp. 279–355.

Idem, 'Pseudo-Philo's Saul and the Rabbis' Messiah ben Ephraim', *ibid.* 21 (1952), pp. 119–37.

Idem, 'The Ascension of Phinehas', *ibid.* 22 (1953), pp. 91–114.

O. Eissfeldt, 'Zur Kompositionstechnik des pseudo-philonischen Liber Antiquitatum Biblicarum', NTT (1955), pp. 53–7.

Philonenko, M., 'Remarques sur un hymne essénien de caractère gnostique', Semitica 11 (1961), pp. 43–54.

Idem, 'Une paraphrase du cantique d'Anne', RHPR 42 (1962), pp. 157–68.

Winter, P., 'Philo, Biblical, Antiquities of', IDB III (1962), pp. 795–6.

Delcor, M., 'Philon (Pseudo-)', DBS VII (1966), cols. 1354–75.

Philonenko, M., 'Essénisme et gnose chez le Pseudo-Philon. Le symbolisme de la lumière dans le Liber Antiquitatum Biblicarum', *Le origini dello gnosticismo*, ed. U. Bianchi [Numen Suppl. XII] (1967), pp. 401–12.

Harrington, D. J., 'The Original Language of Pseudo-Philo's Liber Antiquitatum Biblicarum', HThR 63 (1970), pp. 503–14.

Strugnell, J., 'Philo (Pseudo-) or Liber Antiquitatum Biblicarum', Enc. Jud. 13 (1971), cols. 408–9.

Delling, G., 'Die Weise von der Zeit zu reden im Liber Antiquitatum Biblicarum', NT 13 (1971), pp. 305–21.

Idem, 'Von Morija zum Sinai. Pseudo-Philo Liber Antiquitatum Biblicarum 32, 1–10', JSJ 2 (1971), pp. 1–18.

Alexiou, Margaret, and Dronke, P., 'The Lament of Jephta's Daughter: Themes, Traditions, Originality', *Studi Medievali* 12 (1971), pp. 819–63.

Harrington, D. J., 'The Biblical Text of Pseudo-Philo's *Liber Antiquitatum Biblicarum*', CBQ 33 (1971), pp. 1–17.

Idem, 'The Text-critical Situation of Pseudo-Philo's *Liber Antiquitatum Biblicarum*', Rev. Bénédictine 83 (1973), pp. 383–8.

Bogaert, P.-M., 'Les Antiquités Bibliques du Pseudo-Philon', RThLouv 15 (1972), pp. 334–44.

Philonenko, M., 'Iphigénie et Sheila', *Le syncrétisme dans les religions grecque et romaine* (1973), pp. 165–77.

Feldman, L. H., 'Epilegomenon to Pseudo-Philo's Liber Antiquitatum Biblicarum', JJS 25 (1974), pp. 305–12.

Harrington, D. J., 'Biblical Geography in Pseudo-Philo's *Liber Antiquitatum Biblicarum*', BASOR 220 (1975), pp. 67–71.

Scheiber, A., 'Lacrimatoria and the Jewish Sources', IEJ 25 (1975), pp. 152–3.

Perrot, C., and P.-M. Bogaert, *Pseudo-Philon, Les antiquités bibliques* II: *Introduction littéraire, commentaire et index* [SC 230] (1976).

Wadsworth, M., 'A New Pseudo-Philo', JJS 29 (1978), pp. 186–91.

Zeron, A., 'The Swansong of Edom', JJS 31 (1980), pp. 190–8.

Nickelsburg, G. W. E., 'Good and Bad Leaders in Pseudo-Philo's *Liber Antiquitatum Biblicarum*', *Ideal Figures in Ancient Judaism: Profiles and Paradigms*, ed. J. J. Collins and G. W. E. Nickelsburg [SBLSCS 12] (1980), pp. 49–65.

Idem, JLBBM, pp. 265–8.

For a list of studies (up to 1975) making significant use of LAB, see Perrot and Bogaert, *op. cit.* II (1976), pp. 251–6.

4. The Book of Noah

Several groups of small fragments from Qumran Cave I ($1Q19$ and 19bis, DJD I, pp. 84–6, 152) attest the presence of a Hebrew Book of Noah in the Qumran library. They do not provide a continuous text, but fragments 3 and 13–14 reveal that the subject is the birth of Noah and the miraculous light phenomena which marked it.[1] The same story appears in I En. 106, minute Aramaic remains of which are extant (Milik, *Enoch*, p. 207), and in *1QapGen*, col. 2, equally in Aramaic (cf. above, p. 319). There are also a few Aramaic fragments from Cave 6 (*6Q8*) which may belong to a Noah story, alluding to his miraculous birth (fr. 1) and mentioning his maternal grandfather, Barakiel (cf. Jub. 4:28). Similarly *6Q19*, another Aramaic text written in 'Herodian' calligraphy, of which only a single small fragment is extant, deals with the sons of Noah. Moreover, two collections of Noachic fragments in Aramaic were announced by J. Starcky in 1955 (cf. RB 63 (1956), p. 66); they are however still unpublished.[2]

A Book of Noah is referred to in Jub. 10:13 and 21:10. In the first instance, Noah is said to have recorded secret angelic instructions relating to healing. In the second (Jub. 20:3–11), Abraham traces the rules concerning cultic worship (the ban on idolatry and on eating blood, and regulations affecting sacrificial offerings) to books written by Enoch and Noah. Similarly, the Greek supplement to the Testament of Levi 18:2 (from the Athos manuscript, cf. below, p. 776) mentions precepts concerning the use of blood ($\pi\epsilon\rho\grave{\iota}\ \tauο\hat{\upsilon}\ α\ddot{\iota}μ\alphaτος$) given in the Book of Noah ($\dot{\epsilon}\nu\ \tau\hat{\eta}\ γρ\alpha\phi\hat{\eta}\ \tau\hat{\eta}ς\ β\acute{\iota}βλου\ \tauο\hat{\upsilon}\ N\hat{\omega}\epsilon$).[3] Whether these derive from special medical or legal compositions attributed to Noah, or from a proper life-story of the patriarch, is impossible to decide. The latter alternative is supported by the Noachic excerpts incorporated into I Enoch, viz. chapters 6–11, 106–7 and several units in the Parables (54:7–55:2; 60; 65–69:25).[4] But whatever the case, the inference appears to be that an Aramaic 'midrashic' account, and its Hebrew

1. G. Vermes, *Scripture and Tradition*, pp. 91–2.

2. According to J. A. Fitzmyer ('The Aramaic "Elect of God" Text from Qumran Cave 4', *Essays on the Semitic Background of the N.T.* (1971), pp. 127–60), *4QMessar* (see below, p. 465) is not a messianic work—as has been argued by J. Starcky in 'Un texte messianique araméen de la grotte 4 de Qumrân' (*Mémorial du Cinquantenaire 1914–1964 de l'École des langues orientales anciennes de l'Institut Catholique de Paris* (1964), pp. 51–66)—but a narrative of the birth of Noah (cf. pp. 158–60). J. T. Milik (*Enoch*, p. 56) is of the same opinion, and adds that there are three further copies of the same document.

3. R. H. Charles, *The Greek Version of the Testaments of the Twelve Patriarchs* (1908), p. 252.

4. Cf. R. H. Charles, *The Book of Jubilees* (1902), pp. lxxi–ii; 'Book of Enoch', APOT II, p. 168; M. R. James, *The Lost Apocrypha of the O.T.* (1920), pp. 11–12; Denis, IPGAT, p. 17; Milik, *Enoch*, pp. 55–7; Charlesworth, PMRS, pp. 166–7.

version dealing with the life of Noah, circulated among Jews in the early inter-Testamental epoch. Thus assuming that the Aramaic Enoch and the Genesis Apocryphon echo this work, a Book of Noah, or a larger midrash, accommodating a section on Noah, is to be dated to the beginning of the second century B.C. at the latest, or more likely to the third century B.C.[5]

Medical and magical books continued to be associated with Noah by Jews even in medieval times.[6]

Editions

Milik, J. T., DJD I, pp. 84–6, 152.
Baillet, M., DJD III, pp. 116–19, 136.

Bibliography

See notes 3 and 4 above.

5. The Testament of Kohath

An Aramaic work, surviving in a single copy in Cave 4, introduces Kohath, the son of Levi and father of Amram, as the direct narrator. J. T. Milik has edited a small section from it (col. 2:9–12) in '4Q Visions de Amram et une citation d'Origène', RB 79 (1972), pp. 96–7. The fragment suggests that *4QTQahat* is another exemplar of patriarchal Testaments: Kohath entrusts to Amram all his books (כל כתבי) which he has received from Levi.

This extract is closely paralleled by Jub. 45:16 ('And he [Jacob] gave all his books and the books of his father to Levi his son that he might preserve them and renew them for his children until this day'). Milik (*art. cit.*) sees in the Qumran fragment the source of the Jubilees passage. No independent opinion can be expressed until the rest of *4QTQahat* is published.

Editions

Milik, J. T., *art. cit.* (with French translation).
Fitzmyer, MPAT no. 27, pp. 96–7, 205 (with English translation).

---

5. Whereas no certainty is attainable in historical reconstructions of this sort, the doubts expressed by J. P. Lewis concerning the existence of a Book of Noah derive largely from his inability to evaluate the Qumran evidence. Cf. *A Study of the Interpretation of Noah and the Flood in Jewish and Christian Literature* (1968), pp. 10–15.

6. For the *Sefer Noah*, see A. Jellinek, *Bet ha-Midrasch* III (1857), pp. xxx–xxxiii, 155–60. One of the recensions is known as the Book of Asaph the Physician (ספר אסף הרופא) : cf. L. Venetianer, *Asaf Judaeus* I–III (1915–17) ; Enc. Jud. 3, cols. 673–6. See also *Sefer Raziel* and *Sefer ha-Razim* (*ibid.*, cols. 1594–5). For a recent edition, see M. Margolioth, ספר הרזים (1966) ; *E.T.*: M. A. Morgan, *Sepher ha-Razim : The Book of Mysteries* [Texts and Translations 25—Pseudepigrapha Series 11] (1983).

6. The Testament of Amram

Fragments detached from five manuscripts of an Aramaic writing entitled 'Visions' or 'Testament of Amram' have been found in Qumran Cave 4 ($4QAmram^{a-e}$), and partly published by J. T. Milik (RB 79 (1972), pp. 77–97). The story is told in the first person. Fragment 1 from manuscript^c includes the complete title: 'Copy of the book of the Words of visions of Amram, son of Kohath, son of Levi. Al[l that] he declared and commanded to his sons on the day of his death . . . in the year 152 of Israel's exile in Egypt.'[1] Amram saw two spirits argue over his destiny, the prince of darkness, Melkiresha,[2] and the prince of light (probably Melkizedek). Fragment ^{e} expounds, it seems, the meaning of the vision.

Together with the Testament of Levi (see below, pp. 769–77) and the Testament of Kohath (see above, p. 333), *4QTAmram* belongs to the type of testamentary literature which appears to have flourished in the second century B.C.[3]

According to Milik, Origen in his thirty-fifth Homily on the Gospel of Luke (Lk. 12:58–9) alludes to the Testament of Amram: 'Legimus—si cui tamen placet huiuscemodi scripturam recipere—iustitiae et iniquitatis angelos super Abrahae salute et interitu disceptantes, dum utraeque turmae suo eum volunt coetu vindicare' (ed. M. Raner, GCS 49 (1955), pp. 197–8). The theory is based on two emendations: Amram is substituted for Abraham and 'utraeque turmae' is seen as the final stage of a series of corruptions which started from a conjectural Greek δύο ειρειν, two Watchers (עירין). Neither correction is impossible in itself, but the two, linked together, hardly constitute justification of the claim that the Aramaic Testament of Amram 'fut certainement traduit en grec et était utilisé par les écrivains chrétiens des premiers siècles' (*art. cit.*, p. 86).

Editions

Milik, J. T., '4Q Visions de 'Amram et une citation d'Origène', RB 97 (1972), pp. 77–97 (with a French translation).
Fitzmyer, MPAT nos. 24–6, pp. 94–7 (with an English translation).

Translations

English
Vermes, DSSE², pp. 260–1.

1. On the chronology, see J. Heinemann, '210 years of Egyptian Exile', JJS 22 (1971), pp. 19–30; P. Grelot, 'Quatre cent trente ans (Ex. 12, 40)', *Homenaje a Juan Prado* (1975), pp. 559–70.
2. On Melkizedek and Melkiresha, see below, pp. 449–50. Cf. J. T. Milik, '*Milkî-ṣedeq* and *Milkî-reša'* dans les anciens écrits juifs et chrétiens', JJS 23 (1972), pp. 95–144.
3. For the dating, see the *Testaments of the Twelve Patriarchs*, pp. 774–5 below.

Bibliography

Berger, K., 'Der Streit des guten und des bösen Engels um die Seele: Beobachtungen zu 4Q Amr^b und Judas 9', JSJ 4 (1973), pp. 1–18.

7. A Samuel Apocryphon

Seven fragments of a Hebrew composition centred on Samuel have been retrieved from Cave 4 and published under the slightly misleading title, 'The Vision of Samuel' (*4Q160*). Fragment 1, a paraphrase of 1 Sam. 3:14–17, represents, in a third person narrative, a conversation between Samuel and Eli. Fragments 3–6 contain a prayer, no doubt spoken by Samuel, for the deliverance of Israel, and fragment 7, a few words of an autobiographical discourse.

Palaeographically the script is assigned to the early or middle Hasmonaean period, i.e. to the second century B.C.

Editions

Allegro, J. M., DJD V, pp. 9–11 (with English translation).
Strugnell, J., 'Notes en marge ...', RQ 7 (1970), pp. 179–83.

8. The Martyrdom of Isaiah

An apocryphal work on the martyrdom of Isaiah is several times mentioned by Origen. He terms it simply an *apocryphon*, reports from it only that Isaiah was sawn in pieces, and characterizes it clearly as a Jewish writing. In the *Constitutiones apostolorum* vi 16, there is likewise merely a general mention of an apocryphal Isaiah. On the other hand, it is entered more precisely in the canonical list of Sixty Books as 'Ησαΐου ὅρασις (cf. above, p. 797). Epiphanius knows an ἀναβατικὸν 'Ησαΐου, which was in use amongst the heretical Archontics and Hierakites. Jerome speaks of an *Ascensio Isaiae*. It is very probable that not all these quotations refer to the same work; Origen appears to have had in mind a purely Jewish book, whereas the others were thinking of a Christian reworking of this, or of a Christian work quite independent of it. In effect, a Christian apocryphon concerning Isaiah has survived, the oldest part of which consists in a Jewish account of the prophet's martyrdom.

This apocryphon is preserved in its entirety only in an Ethiopic version, first edited by R. Laurence under the title *Ascensio Isaiae Vatis* (1819). The second half is available also in an old Latin translation, first issued in Venice in 1522 by A. de Fantis and re-edited by J. C. L. Gieseler in 1832 (*Vetus translatio latina Visionis Isaiae*). The material was brought together by A. Dillmann, *Ascensio Isaiae aethiopice et latine* (1877). B. P. Grenfell and A. S. Hunt published Greek papyrus fragments corresponding to the Ethiopic text (*The Amherst Papyri ... I*,

1 : *The Ascension of Isaiah*, 1900).[1] The fullest extant edition is by R. H. Charles, *The Ascension of Isaiah translated from the Ethiopic version, which, together with the new Greek fragment, the Latin versions and the Latin translation of the Slavonic, is here published in full* (1900).[2] The subject-matter of the whole work as it appears in the Ethiopic text is as follows. First Part: The Martyrdom (chapters 1–5). Isaiah prophesies to Hezekiah the future godlessness of his son Manasseh (chapter 1). After Hezekiah's death, Manasseh in fact gives himself over to the service of Satan, and as a result, Isaiah and his companions withdraw into solitude (chapter 2). A certain 'Belchîra',[3] a Samaritan, denounces Isaiah to Manasseh for prophesying against the king and the people of Israel (chapter 3:1–12). Belchîra's hostility towards Isaiah was incited by Satan (Beliar), who was angry with the prophet because he had predicted redemption through Christ. This affords an opportunity to relate the whole history of Jesus Christ and his community, as foretold by Isaiah, from the Incarnation to the Antichrist symbolized by Nero (4:2),[4] and to the Last Judgement (chapter 3:13–4:22). Manasseh, influenced by Beliar, orders the prophet to be cut in two with a wood-saw. Isaiah dies without

---

1. In addition to these Greek fragments, there is also extant a Christian medieval Greek legend noticeably dependent on the Ascension of Isaiah. Cf. O. von Gebhardt, 'Die Ascensio Isaiae als heilige Legende aus Cod. Gr. 1534 der Nationalbibliothek zu Paris', ZWTh 21 (1878), pp. 330–53.

2. The Slavonic versions represent the Vision of Isaiah (Asc. chapters 6–11), not the Martyrdom. Cf. Denis, IPGAT, pp. 173–4 and n. 16. See also W. Lüdtke, 'Beiträge zu slavischen Apokryphen. 3. Zur Ascensio Isaiae', ZAW 31 (1911), pp. 222–6, 235, n. 3; E. Turdeanu, 'Apocryphes bogomiles et apocryphes pseudo-bogomiles III. La Vision d'Isaïe', RHR 69 (1950), pp. 213–18; A. Vaillant, 'Un apocryphe pseudo-bogomile: La Vision d'Isaïe', Revue des Etudes Slaves 42 (1963), pp. 109–21.

3. The form, and consequently the etymology, of this name remains uncertain. The Ethiopic manuscripts give *Belchîra, Balchîra, Belachîra, Melâchîra, Mîlchîrâs, Îbchîra* and *Abchîra*. The Greek version displays Βελιχειάρ, Βελχειρά, Βεχειρά (Βεχειράς in the Greek legend). The Latin has *Bechira*. Note that in 1:8 the name borne by Satan is *Sammael Malchîrâ*. The two most likely Hebrew originals are בחיר רע (Βεχειρά, Βεχειράς, *Bechira*) = 'Elect of Evil' (D. Flusser, 'The Apocryphal Book of Ascensio Isaiae and the Dead Sea Sect', IEJ 3 (1953), p. 35), and מלכי רע or מלאכי רע = 'Evil king' or 'Evil angel' (Charles, APOT II, p. 159). מלכי רע is parallel to the name מלכי רשע, attested at Qumran as the designation of the chief demon opposed to מלכי צדק. Cf. J. T. Milik, 'Milkî-ṣedeq et Milkî-reša' dans les anciens écrits juifs et chrétiens', JJS 23 (1972), pp. 95–144; '4Q Visions de Amram et une citation d'Origène', RB 79 (1972), pp. 77–97. There seems to be a tendency to assimilate the Samaritan *Bechîr-ra'*, enemy of Isaiah, with the arch-devil *Malkhi-ra'*. The confusion is quasi-total in the Greek legend where the persecutor of Isaiah is called Μελχίας (3:5, 7, 8) as well as Βεχείρας (3:10). Cf. A. Caquot, 'Bref commentaire du Martyre d'Isaïe', Semitica 23 (1973), p. 75.

4. The epithet 'matricide' (μητραλῴας) refers to Nero. The following verse (4:3) alludes to the martyrdom of Peter (ὁ βασιλεὺς οὗτος τὴν φυτ(ε)ίαν ἣν φυτεύσουσιν οἱ δώδεκα ἀπόστολοι τοῦ ἀγαπητοῦ διώξε(ι) καὶ (τ)ῶν δώδεκα (εἷς) ταῖς χερσὶν αὐτοῦ (π)αραδωθήσεται). Cf. Charles, *op. cit.*, p. 25.

complaint while his lips continue to prophesy with the holy spirit.

Second Part: The Vision (chapters 6–11). In the twentieth year of Hezekiah, Isaiah sees the following vision, which he communicates to the king and also to his (the prophet's) son Josab (chapter 6). An angel conducts the prophet through the firmament and shows him the six lower heavens (chapters 7–8). They come at last to the seventh heaven, where Isaiah sees all the righteous dead from the beginning, and finally God himself (chapter 9). After hearing how God the Father charges his son to descend into the world, Isaiah returns in the company of the angel to the firmament (chapter 10). Here he sees the future birth of Jesus Christ, and the story of his earthly life to the crucifixion and resurrection, whereupon the angel returns to the seventh heaven, whilst Isaiah rejoins his earthly body (chapter 11).

This brief review is enough to indicate that the work is a composite one. The Vision is quite unconnected with the Martyrdom. Indeed, it is attached very clumsily to it, for it should have preceded the prophet's death. In general, the chronology of the events is given in a most haphazard manner (cf. Charles, p. xxxix). Since Charles's study it is accepted that the Jewish *Martyrdom* corresponds to 1:1–2a, 6b–13a; 2:1–8, 2:10–3:12; 5:1b–14, although more recently A. Caquot (*art. cit.*, pp. 92–3) has argued for a further restriction of the authentic Jewish substratum to 1:6–11; 2:1, 4–6, 12–16; 3:6–12; 5:1b–6, 8–10. As for the *Testament of Hezekiah* (3:13b–4:18) and the *Vision of Isaiah* (6:1–11:40), they both had an independent existence and are both of Christian origin. The three were finally put together by a Christian compiler whose hand is shown by a number of editorial additions (1:2b–6a, 13a; 2:9; 3:13a; 4:1a; 4:19–5:1a, 15–16; 11:41–3 (cf. Charles, pp. xl-xliii).[5] Moreover the account of the Martyrdom itself is interrupted by the passage 3:13–5:1, which is manifestly a later interpolation.

The Jewishness of the *Martyrdom of Isaiah* can scarcely be questioned. It is a typical haggadic story inspired by 2 Kings 20–21, and echoed in some way, as will be shown below (p. 338), by rabbinic literature. The *terminus ante quem* for its composition is provided by patristic quotations or allusions (*Opus imperfectum in Matth.*, Homil. I [Charles, *op. cit.*, pp. 8–9]; Jerome, *Comm. in Iesaiam* 64:4 [PL 24, col. 622C]; Origen, *Ep. ad Africanum* 9 [PG 11, col. 65BC]; *In Matth.* 13:57 [ed. Klostermann, p. 24, 9]; Justin, *Dial. c. Tryph.* 120, 5) and by a likely reference to it in Hebr. 11:37. Hence a first century A.D. date may be reasonably inferred (Charles, p. xliv), perhaps the last third of this century (E. Hammershaimb, JSHRZ II, 1 (1973), p. 19). On the more fragile basis

---

5. Charles disagrees with A. Dillmann in considering the greater part of chapter 1 as belonging to the Jewish composition and in holding 11:2–22 to be an integral part of the Vision. Against the originality of the latter, it may be noted that it is absent from the Old Latin and Slavonic versions.

of literary thematic parallels (attested in 2 Maccabees), an early first century B.C. date has been advanced (Eissfeldt, *Introduction*, p. 609), and since the discovery of the Dead Sea Scrolls, the hypothesis of a Qumran origin of the Martyrdom is also on record.[6] Neither of the two more specific theories is properly founded. Eissfeldt's thesis is no more than a possible coincidence. As for the Qumran theory, apart from the by no means exclusive motifs of dualism and desert mysticism, the correspondences between the Martyrdom and the Scrolls are forced and arbitrary.[7] The complete absence of Qumran fragments belonging to the Martyrdom of Isaiah further weakens this already weak hypothesis.[8]

The sawing of Isaiah in two had already been related by Justin Martyr, *Dial. c. Tryph.* 120; Tertullian, *De patientia* 14; *Scorpiace* 8 (see vol. II, p. 352 and n. 51). The author of the Epistle to the Hebrews was probably also familiar with the story (Heb. 11:37). For rabbinic legends concerning the death of Isaiah, see G. Beer in Kautzsch, *APAT* II, pp. 122–3; L. Ginzberg, *Legends* IV, p. 279; VI, pp. 374–5.

Fragments of the rabbinic account of Isaiah's death survive in both Talmuds. bYeb. 49b simply states that Manasseh slew the prophet (saying attributed to Simeon b. Azzai: מנשה הרג את ישעיה). The fuller narrative describes Isaiah fleeing from the king and concealing himself in a hole in a cedar tree. When he is discovered there, Manasseh orders the tree to be sawn through, thus killing him (*ibid.*; ySanh. 28c: נסרו לארזא ואיתחמי דמא גגד).

For the life and death of Isaiah, see further the *Vita Prophetarum*

---

6. Cf. D. Flusser, 'The Apocryphal Book of *Ascensio Isaiae* and the Dead Sea Sect', IEJ 3 (1953), pp. 30–47. Flusser conjectures that Isaiah, Manasseh and Beḥîr-raʿ of the Martyrdom represent the Teacher of Righteousness, the Wicked Priest and the Teacher of Lies in the Scrolls. He points to the dualistic outlook both in the *Ascension* and in the Qumran literature and to the withdrawal to the desert by Isaiah and his companions as well as by the Teacher of Righteousness and his followers. Both groups seek refuge in the North: Isaiah's colleagues are sent to the region of Tyre and Sidon (5:13), the Teacher's adepts to the land of Damascus. (The latter term is taken literally by Flusser; for a symbolical interpretation, see vol. II, p. 586). M. Philonenko, 'Le Martyre d'Esaïe et l'histoire de la secte de Qumrân' (*Pseudépigraphes de l'Ancien Testament et les manuscrits de la mer Morte*—Cahiers RHPhR 41 (1967), pp. 1–10) argues in the same direction as does also Nickelsburg, JLBBM, pp. 144–5.

7. Cf. V. Nikiprowetzky, 'Pseudépigraphes de l'Ancien Testament et manuscrits de la mer Morte. Réflexions sur une publication récente', REJ 128 (1969), pp. 5–13; A. Caquot, *art. cit.*, p. 93.

8. For the relative chronology of the three units of the Ascension, it should be noted that the *Testament of Hezekiah* is given the *terminus ante quem* of A.D. 100 and the *Vision of Isaiah* belongs probably to the second century A.D. Cf. Charles, pp. xliv-v. In consequence, the *Martyrdom* fits well into the first century A.D. The various sections were brought together to form the Christian *Ascension of Isaiah* probably in the third or fourth century (cf. Eissfeldt, p. 610).

(below, pp. 783–6). Cf. T. Schermann, *Propheten- und Apostellegenden* [TU III, 1] (1907); *Prophetarum vitae fabulosae, indices apostolorum discipulorumque Domini* (1907); C. C. Torrey, *The Lives of the Prophets* (1946).

Origen, in *Epist. ad Africanum* 9 (PG 11, col. 65BC), wishes to prove that the Jewish leaders discarded all the documents in which they appear in an unfavourable light. Nevertheless some of them survive in apocryphal writings (ὧν τινα σώζεται ἐν ἀποκρύφοις). He then continues: καὶ τούτου παράδειγμα δώσομεν τὰ περὶ τὸν Ἠσαΐαν ἱστορούμενα, καὶ ὑπὸ τῆς πρὸς Ἑβραίους ἐπιστολῆς μαρτυρούμενα, ἐν οὐδενὶ τῶν φανερῶν βιβλίων γεγραμμένα (the quotation Heb. 11:37 follows). Σαφὲς δ᾽ ὅτι αἱ παραδόσεις λέγουσι πεπρίσθαι Ἠσαΐαν τὸν προφήτην καὶ ἔν τινι ἀποκρύφῳ· τοῦτο φέρεται· ὅπερ τάχα ἐπίτηδες ὑπὸ Ἰουδαίων ῥεραδιούργηται, λέξεις τινὰς τὰς μὴ πρεπούσας παρεμβεβληκότων τῇ γραφῇ, ἵν᾽ ἡ ὅλη ἀπιστηθῇ.

Origen, *In Matth.* 13:57 (ed. Klostermann, CGS 40, p. 24, 9): καὶ Ἠσαΐας δὲ πεπρίσθαι ὑπὸ τοῦ λαοῦ ἱστόρηται· εἰ δέ τις οὐ προσίεται τὴν ἱστορίαν διὰ τὸ ἐν τῷ ἀποκρύφῳ Ἠσαΐα αὐτὴν φέρεσθαι, πιστευσάτω τοῖς ἐν τῇ πρὸς Ἑβραίους οὕτω γεγραμμένοις (Heb. 11:37).

Origen, *In Matth.* 23:37 (ed. Klostermann, CGS 38, p. 50): 'Propterea videndum, ne forte oporteat ex libris secretioribus, quo apud Iudaeos feruntur ostendere verbum Christi, et non solum Christi sed etiam discipulorum eius … Fertur ergo in scripturis non manifestis, serratum esse Esaiam, etc.'

Origen, *In Iesaiam homil.* I, 5 (ed. Baehrens, CGS 33, p. 247): 'Aiunt (Iudaei) ideo Isaiam esse sectum a populo, quasi legem praevaricantem et extra scripturas adnuntiantem. Scriptura enim dicit: "nemo videbit faciem meam et vivet", iste vero ait: "vidi Dominum Sabaoth". Moyses, aiunt, non vidit et tu vidisti? Et propter hoc eum secuerunt et condemnaverunt ut impium.' See *Martyrdom* 3:8–10. Cf. bYeb. 49b.

Origen, *Homilies on Jeremiah* (ed. Klostermann, 1901, p. 192): τοιοῦτόν τι πεποιήκασιν καὶ οἱ τὸν Ἠσαΐαν πρίσαντες· ὡς ἀδικηθέντες γὰρ (ἐπειδήπερ αἱ προφητεῖαι ἐπέστρεφον αὐτοὺς καὶ ἐκόλαζον αὐτούς, ἤλεγχον, ἐπετίμων) ἔπρισαν αὐτὸν καὶ κατεδίκασαν αὐτοῦ ψῆφον θανατικήν.

Ambrose, *Expositio in Ps. 118*, Sermo x, 32 (PL 15, col. 1444B), knows the story of Isaiah's steadfastness in martyrdom as it is told in chapter 5 of the apocryphon. Cf. also *Expositio in Lucam*, Lib. x, 25 (PL 15, col. 1891C).

The author of the *Opus imperfectum in Matthaeum*, Hom. I (under the works of Chrysostom) relates, in close agreement with chapter 1 of the apocryphon, that Isaiah foretold to Hezekiah the godlessness of his son Manasseh, whereupon Hezekiah would have had his son put to death, but was prevented by Isaiah. See PG 56, col. 626; Charles, pp. 8–9.

Epiphanius, *Haer.* xl 2, 2 [concerning the Archontics] (ed. K. Holl,

GCS 31, p. 82): λαμβάνουσι δὲ λαβὰς ἀπὸ τοῦ ἀναβατικοῦ 'Ησαΐα, ἐπὶ δὲ καὶ ἄλλων τινῶν ἀποκρύφων. *Haer.* lxvii 3, 4 [concerning the Hierakites] (GCS 33, p. 135): βούλεται δὲ (scil. Hierakas) τὴν τελείαν αὐτοῦ σύστασιν ποιεῖσθαι ἀπὸ τοῦ ἀναβατικοῦ 'Ησαΐου, δῆθεν ὡς ἐν τῷ ἀναβατικῷ λεγομένῳ ἐκεῖσε.

Jerome, *Comm. in Isa.* 64:4 (PL 24, col. 622C): 'Ascensio enim Isaiae et apocalypsis Eliae hoc habent testimonium'—namely 1 Cor. 2:9. On the *Apocalypse of Elijah*, see pp. 799–83.

Jerome, *Comm. on Isa.* 57:1–2 (PL 24, col. 568A): 'Iudaei ... arbitrantur ... Isaiam de sua prophetare morte quod serrandus sit a Manasse serra lignea, quae apud eos certissima traditio est.'

On the patristic quotations, cf. also E. Tisserant, *Ascension d'Isaïe* (1909), pp. 62–73.

Editions

(1) *Ethiopic version* (probably fifth century)

Laurence, R., *Ascensio Isaiae vatis* (1819).

Dillmann, A., *Ascensio Isaiae aethiopice et latine* (1877).

Charles, R. H., *The Ascension of Isaiah, translated from the Ethiopic Version, which, together with the new Greek fragment, the Latin versions and the Latin translation of the Slavonic, is here published in full* (1900).

(2) *The Greek version* (fifth-sixth century)

Grenfell, B. P., and Hunt, A. S., *The Amherst Papyri* I, 1: *The Ascension of Isaiah and other Theological Fragments* (1900) [2:4–4:4]. Cf. also Charles, above.

Gebhardt, O. von, 'Die Ascensio Isaiae als heilige Legende aus Cod. Gr. 1534 der Nationalbibliothek zu Paris', ZWTh 21 (1878), pp. 330–53 [second half of the tenth century].

Denis, A.-M., *FPG*, pp. 105–14 [Amherst Pap. and Legenda graeca].

(3) *Latin version* (fifth century?)

Mai, A., *Scriptorum veterorum nova collectio* III, 2 (1828), pp. 238–9. Cf. also Charles, above.

(4) *Coptic (Sahidic and Achmimic) versions* (fourth century)

Lefort, L. Th., 'Coptica Lovaniensia', Le Muséon 51 (1938), pp. 24–30 [Sahidic: 3:3–6, 9–12; 11:24–32, 35–40—Achmimic: 7:12–15; 8:16–17; 9:9–11; 10:9–11].

Lacau, P., 'Fragments de l'Ascension d'Isaïe en copte', *Mélanges L. Th. Lefort*, Le Muséon 59 (1946), pp. 453–67 [1:1–5; 3:25–8; 5:7–8; 6:7–11; 7:28–32; 9:28–30; 10:27; 11:14–16].

Translations

English

Charles, R. H., *op. cit.*

Idem, APOT II, pp. 159–62.

Flemming, J., and Duensing, H. [Hill, D.], ' The Ascension of Isaiah', in E. W. Hennecke, W. Schneemelcher and R. McL. Wilson (eds.), *New Testament Apocrypha* II (1965), pp. 642–3.

German

Beer, G., APAT II, pp. 119–27.

Riessler, P., *Altjüdisches Schrifttum* (1928), pp. 481–4, 1300–1.

Flemming, J., and Duensing, H., 'Die Himmelfahrt des Jesaja', E. W. Hennecke and W. Schneemelcher, *Neutestamentliche Apokryphen* II (³1964), pp. 454–68.
Hammershaimb, E., *Das Martyrium Jesajas* [JSHRZ II, 1] (1973), pp. 15–34.

French
Tisserant, E., *L'Ascension d'Isaïe. Traduction de la version éthiopienne avec les principales variantes des versions grecque, latines et slave avec introduction et notes* (1909).

Bibliography

Clemen, C., 'Die Himmelfahrt des Jesaja, ein ältestes Zeugnis für das römische Martyrium des Petrus', ZWTh 39 (1896), pp. 388–415.
Robinson, A., 'The Ascension of Isaiah', HDB II, pp. 499–501.
Littmann, E., 'Isaiah, Ascension of', EJ VI, pp. 642–3.
Charles, R. H., and Box, G. H., *The Ascension of Isaiah* (1919).
Burch, V., 'The Literary Unity of the Ascension of Isaiah', JThSt 20 (1919), pp. 17–23.
Idem, 'Material for the Interpretation of the Ascensio Isaiae', *ibid.* 21 (1920), pp. 249–65.
Schoeps, H. J., *Die jüdischen Prophetenmorde* (1943).
Flusser, D., 'The Apocryphal Book of Ascensio Isaiae and the Dead Sea Sect', IEJ 3 (1953), pp. 30–47.
Rist, M., 'Isaiah, Ascension of', IDB II, pp. 744–6.
Philonenko, M., 'Le martyre d'Ésaïe et l'histoire de la secte de Qumrân', *Cahiers de la RHPhR* 41 (1967), pp. 1–10.
Denis, IPGAT, pp. 170–6.
Stone, M. E., 'Isaiah, Martyrdom of', Enc. Jud. 9, cols. 71–2.
Caquot, A., 'Bref commentaire du Martyre d'Isaïe', Semitica 23 (1973), pp. 65–93.
Norelli, E., 'Il martirio di Isaia come *testimonium* antigiudaico', Henoch 2 (1980), pp. 37–57.
Charlesworth, J. H., PMRS, pp. 125–30, 289–90.
Nickelsburg, G. W. E., JLBBM, pp. 142–5, 157, 159.
Pesce, M. (ed.), *Isaia, il diletto e la chiesa—Visione ed esegesi profetica cristiano-primitiva nell'Ascensione di Isaia* (1983).

9. Apocryphal Fragments

Caves 2 and 6 have yielded small remains of works which seem to be apocryphal narratives in Hebrew.

2Q21 and *2Q22* are tentatively described as a Moses Apocryphon and a David Apocryphon. Both are said to represent 'Herodian' calligraphy. The former mentions two of the sons of Aaron and cites what may be a prayer of Moses. The second, which is related to an as yet unpublished manuscript from Cave 4, may derive from David's account of his fight with Goliath. *6Q9*, palaeographically assigned to the first half of the first century B.C., is judged to reflect the Samuel-Kings cycle with odd identifiable names such as David, Gath, the Philistines, the king of Moab, etc.

Editions

Baillet, M., DJD III, pp. 79–82, 119–23.

VII. Incantations and Books of Magic
by Dr P. S. Alexander
(University of Manchester)

To fail to consider magic would be to neglect an area of immense importance in the study of early Judaism. Incantations and books of magic, being intended for practical use, are not literature in the proper sense (though some contain passages of literary, even poetic, power), but belong essentially to the realm of folklore. Yet therein lies their significance, for they open up areas of popular religion which are often inadequately represented in the official literary texts, and which are in consequence frequently ignored by historians. As an indicator of the spiritual atmosphere in which large sections of the populace lived—rich and poor, educated and ignorant—their importance can hardly be overestimated.

Magic flourished among the Jews despite strong and persistent condemnation by the religious authority.[1] Healing by this means was especially common, sickness being widely diagnosed as caused by malevolent invading spirits which could only be driven out by the appropriate incantations and spells. In Jewish as in non-Jewish culture, the dividing-line between medicine and magic, doctor and magician, was extremely thin. Jubilees 10:10–14 accepts that demons cause disease. It asserts that the good angels instructed Noah how to bind them and that Noah inscribed the angels' remedies in a book which he passed on to his favourite son, Shem. Josephus traces healing magic back not to Noah but to Solomon, and regards it as part of the special wisdom vouchsafed to him by God. Josephus, *Ant.* viii 2, 5 (45–49), claims that some of Solomon's incantations were still being successfully used in his day. The best-attested form of magic among the Jews in the period before Bar Kokhba is, however, unquestionably exorcism. The story of how Tobias, on the advice of the angel Raphael, expelled the demon who threatened to ruin his wedding night, must surely reflect actual, contemporary magical practice (Tobit 6:3–9, 17–18; 8:1–3). The same may be said of the stories of how Abraham, by the laying on of hands, exorcized the spirit that afflicted Pharaoh (*1QapGen* 20:16–31), and of how David exorcized Saul's evil spirit (Ps.-Philo, *LAB* 60:1–3). Josephus, *Ant.* viii 2, 5 (46–48), gives a sharply observed account of an exorcism, which he himself witnessed, performed by a Jew called Eleazar in the presence of Vespasian and his officers. Eleazar

---

1. See Exod. 22:17 (Heb. 18); Lev. 19:26, 31; 20:6, 27; Deut. 18:10–11. Cf. 1 En. 7–8; 2 Mac. 12:40; Sib. iii 218–30; Ps.-Philo, *LAB* 34; mSanh. 6:6; 7:7, 11; 10:1.

may have belonged to the sect of the Essenes, whom Josephus elsewhere describes as specializing in the art of healing and as being expert in the medicinal properties of roots and stones (*B.J.* ii 8, 6 (136)).[2] Further evidence can readily be found in the New Testament. Jesus, his disciples, and other Jews perform numerous healing exorcisms.[3] According to Acts 19:13–20, 'certain itinerant Jewish exorcists' (τινες τῶν περιερχομένων Ἰουδαίων ἐξορκιστῶν) at Ephesus tried, with disastrous results, to drive out demons in the name of 'Jesus whom Paul preaches' (ὁρκίζω ὑμᾶς τὸν Ἰησοῦν ὃν Παῦλος κηρύσσει). Acts preserves the names of two Jewish magicians, Simeon (Acts 8:9) and Bar-Jesus, who was known in Greek as Elymas Magos (Acts 13:6–12), though precisely what form of magic they practised is not made clear. In a famous Rabbinic anecdote Yoḥanan b. Zakkai compares the ritual of the red heifer to exorcism; he gives a vivid description of a typical exorcism and seems to take its efficacy for granted.[4] Patristic evidence points in the same direction; Justin Martyr (*Trypho* 85) and Irenaeus (*Adv. Haer.* ii 6, 2), for example, both testify that Jews practised exorcism.

In regard to the content of early Jewish magic, there exist basically two lines of evidence. First, there are the testimonies to Jewish magical theory and practice embedded in literary texts—in the Bible, in intertestamental literature (e.g. apocrypha, pseudepigrapha, Josephus), in the earliest strata of Talmud and midrash, in the New Testament and other early Christian documents and in pagan authors. This material, some of which has been surveyed above, is crucially important since because it can be dated with some precision it provides a means of testing the chronologically dubious material to be considered presently. This indirect evidence is, however, hardly satisfactory on its own as a basis for the history of early Jewish magic. It is not really sufficient in quantity or exact enough in detail, and there is the added complication that it often occurs in works whose general outlook is hostile to magic.

The second line of evidence consists of actual Jewish magical texts, specimens of Jewish magical praxis. The problem here is that, apart from a few Dead Sea scrolls fragments, few such texts can be confidently dated to the period concerned with here (pre-135 A.D.). This does not necessarily mean that they do not exist. A considerable quantity of Jewish magical literature of uncertain date, and often of uncertain provenance, is extant comprising texts unearthed by archaeologists and

---

2. Note *B.J.* vii 6, 3 (180–85) where Josephus describes a root to be found near Baaras which could be used in exorcism.

3. Jesus: Mk. 1:25; 5:8; 9:25; Matt. 8:28–34. The disciples: Acts 5:16; 16:18. Other Jews: Mk. 9:38; Matt. 12:27.

4. Pesiqta deRav Kahana 4.7 (ed. Mandelbaum I, p. 74); Pesiqta Rabbati 14.4 (ed. Friedmann 65a); Tanḥuma Ḥuqqat 26 (ed. Buber IV, 118–19); Num. R. 19.8.

treasure-hunters (e.g. lead amulets and incantation bowls), as well as mediaeval manuscripts lodged in the Hebraica collections of the world's libraries. Among all this mass of material there could well be texts which in whole or in part go back to our period or close to it, or which if carefully used could throw light on the details of early magical theory and praxis. The intense conservatism of magic, the theory being that formulae and rituals retain their virtue only if reproduced without deviation, is a well-documented fact.[5] The famous late handbook of practical Kabbalah, *Sefer Raziel* (editio princeps Amsterdam 1701) appears to contain elements of an astonishingly early date.[6] The first task then must be to identify as precisely as possible the earliest surviving layers of Jewish magical literature, and to work back from these. The problems posed are very similar to those encountered in the study of early Jewish mysticism. But, unfortunately, early Jewish magic has not yet received the same attention as early Jewish mysticism;[7] the field is still largely unsystematized and all that can be attempted here is a preliminary clearing of the ground.

In sifting through the mediaeval Hebrew and Aramaic manuscripts with a view to separating the early from the late, Jewish writers of the Gaonic period provide some initial help. From time to time they mention, or even quote from, magical texts extant in their day. Particularly important are the testimonies of the Qaraites Daniel al-Qumisi, Salman b. Yeruḥam, Yefet b. 'Ali, and Yaqub al-Qirqisani. A standard element of the Qaraites' anti-orthodox polemic is the assertion that the Rabbanites subscribed to all kinds of fantastic and irrational ideas, and they list Rabbanite works which contain these notions.[8] These records mention Hekhalot tracts which have now been recovered from mediaeval manuscripts, and also refer to magical texts.[9] Works bearing the same name are also still extant among mediaeval manuscripts, but care must be exercised. Identity of title does not mean identity of content. However, in certain cases (e.g. *Ḥarba deMosheh*[10]), it is reasonably sure that the work referred to in the Gaonic period

---

5. See Origen's comments on this in *Contra Celsum* i 24–25. There is also astonishing continuity in the way magicians were tried. For example, in sixteenth and seventeenth century England, suspected witches were often 'swum' to establish their innocence or guilt (see K. Thomas, *Religion and the Decline of Magic* [1978], pp. 146, 658). Ordeal by water in cases of sorcery is attested as early as the Code of Hammurabi, sect. 2: see J. B. Pritchard, *Ancient Near Eastern Texts Relating to the Old Testament* ([2]1955), p. 166; further, G. R. Driver and J. C. Miles, *The Babylonian Laws* I (1952), pp. 61–5; II (1955), pp. 13–15.

6. See E. R. Goodenough, *Jewish Symbols in the Greco-Roman Period* II (1953), pp. 211–13.

7. L. Blau, *Das altjüdische Zauberwesen* ([2]1914), is still the only comprehensive survey.

8. J. Mann, *Texts and Studies in Jewish History and Literature* II (1972), pp. 55–7, 74–90.

9. See P. S. Alexander in Charlesworth, OTP I, pp. 228–9.

10. See below footnote 19.

(whether by Karaite or Rabbanite authors) is essentially the same as the one in existence, and the implication must be that such a work is from the early Gaonic or Amoraic periods at the latest. Works falling into this category (in whole or in part) are *Sefer haRazim, Ḥarba deMosheh, Havdalah deRabbi Aqiva, Sefer ha-Malbush,* the theurgic portions of the Hekhalot tracts (e.g. *Sar ha-Panim, Ḥotam Gadol, Shi'ur Qomah*), *Shimmushei Torah, Shimmushei Tehillim, Shimmusha Rabba* and *Mafteaḥ Shelomoh.*[11] It is in these and similar texts that one has to look if one is to recover the earliest stages of Jewish magic.

Other arguments besides Gaonic attestation may be used to support an early date. If a text contains a lot of Greek, and exhibits many precise parallels to the Greek magical papyri, then the chances are high that it belongs to the Talmudic era. *Sefer ha-Razim* is a case in point. The testimony of the early Jewish and non-Jewish literature referred to above also has its part to play. If there is a significant convergence between early external literary testimony and the later magical texts, then there would appear to be grounds for reading back (with due caution) the later material into the earlier period.

The problem with the Hebrew and Aramaic texts just mentioned is fundamentally one of date. Their Jewish identity or Jewish use is not in question. There exists, however, another body of material whose generally early date is not in dispute but whose Jewishness is uncertain. Goodenough has collected and worked over much of it in the section on charms and amulets in *Jewish Symbols,* vol. II.[12] The Greek papyri illustrate the problem of these texts very well. Many published by Preisendanz in *Papyri Graecae Magicae* (= PGM) clearly contain Jewish elements. Even Campbell Bonner, who unlike Goodenough was not given to exaggeration, concedes that there are few Greek magical texts from late antiquity without some sort of Jewish component.[13] But are they examples of Jewish magical literature? Not necessarily. Magic is notoriously syncretistic and non-Jewish magicians were prepared to draw on any religious tradition which offered them the chance of boosting their magical prowess. Some of these writings, though preserved in pagan sources, must nevertheless surely have originated with Jewish magicians. *Sefer ha-Razim* and other indisputably Jewish works demonstrate that such material was used by Jews. But the

---

11. Some of these are discussed below. For the others see H. Gollancz, *Sefer Mafteaḥ Shelomoh* (1914); G. Scholem, "סדרי דשומא רבא", Tarbiz 16 (1945), pp. 196–209; Scholem, *Major Trends in Jewish Mysticism* (³1954), pp. 68, 75–8, 155, 365, 368, 385; M. Margalioth, *Sepher Ha-Razim* (1966), pp. 29–46, 51–2; G. Scholem, *On the Kabbalah and its Symbolism* (1969), pp. 136–7; Scholem, *Kabbalah* (1974), p. 20 and passim; Scholem, "הבדלה דברי עקיבא — מקור למסורת המאגיה היהודית בתקופת הגאונים", Tarbiz 50 (1981), pp. 243–81.

12. E. R. Goodenough, *Jewish Symbols in the Greco-Roman Period* II (1953), pp. 153–295.

13. C. Bonner, *Magical Amulets* (1950), p. 28.

problem must be formulated with care. It is not yet possible to draw a hard and fast line between Jewish and pagan magic in late antiquity; in fact, given the fundamental syncretism of magic, it may be misguided in principle to try to do so. In many cases it is hard to label a given praxis or text as pagan or Christian or Jewish. It is simply magic, a conglomerate of motifs of diverse origin. A spectrum of texts can however be drawn up ranging from those with no, or almost no, Jewish elements at one extreme, to those with a high or totally Jewish content at the other. When this is done, it would seem obvious that texts towards the latter end of the spectrum are more entitled to be classified as Jewish than those towards the other end. Using such an approach it is certainly possible, as Goodenough has demonstrated, to extract from PGM materials with good claim to be regarded as Jewish in origin.

What follows is a survey of the earliest remains of Jewish magical literature. Only a representative selection of texts can be covered. They are not limited to exorcism or magic in any narrow sense of the term but take in most of the occult sciences. The justification for this broad perspective is twofold. First, the different forms of magic were clearly linked in the minds of many ancient writers; the ancients themselves (for whatever reason) tend to group them together. For example, Deut. 18:10–11, 1 En. 7–8, and Sibylline Oracles iii 218–30 offer comprehensive lists of the occult sciences—and damn them all without exception. Second, the occult sciences, then as now, were often intertwined. Physiognomy, for example, may be classified as a form of divination but is often linked with astrology; exorcism is connected with demonology and healing but may involve herbalism and astrology. Consequently, it is inadvisable, and indeed impossible, to treat the various forms of magic in isolation.

Bibliography

The following will serve for preliminary orientation on Jewish magic:
Blau, L., 'Magic', JE VIII (1904), pp. 255–7.
Blau, L., *Das altjüdische Zauberwesen* ([2]1914).
Daiches, S., *Babylonian Oil Magic in the Talmud and in the Later Jewish Literature* (1913).
Billerbeck, P., 'Zur altjüdischen Dämonologie', Str.-B. IV (1928), pp. 501–35.
Trachtenberg, J., *Jewish Magic and Superstition* (1939).
Lieberman, S., *Greek in Jewish Palestine* (1942), pp. 97–114.
Scholem, G. G., 'פרקים חדשים מעניני אשמדאי ולילית', Tarbiz 19 (1948), pp. 160–75.
Scholem, G. G., *Major Trends in Jewish Mysticism* ([3]1954), passim.
Simon, M., *Verus Israel* ([2]1964), pp. 394–431 ['Superstition et magie'].
Scholem, G. G., 'Some Sources of Jewish-Arabic Demonology', JJS 16 (1965), pp. 1–13.
Neusner, J., *A History of the Jews in Babylonia* II (1966), pp. 147–50; III (1968), pp. 110–26; IV (1969), pp. 330–62; V (1970), pp. 174–96, 217–43.
Dan, J., *et al.*, 'Magic', Enc. Jud. XI (1971), cols. 703–15.
Lieberman, S., 'Some Notes on Adjurations in Israel', in Lieberman, *Texts and Studies* (1974), pp. 21–8.
Scholem, G. G., *Kabbalah* (1974), passim.

Urbach, E. E., *The Sages: Their Concepts and Beliefs* I (1975), pp. 97–183 ['Magic and Miracle' / 'The Power of the Divine Name' / 'The Celestial Retinue'].

Maier, J., 'Geister (Dämonen)', RAC IX (1976), cols. 579–85, 626–39, 668–88.

Goldin, J., 'The Magic of Magic and Superstition', in E. S. Fiorenza (ed.), *Aspects of Religious Propaganda in Judaism and Early Christianity* (1976), pp. 115–47.

Hurwitz, H., *Lilith, die erste Eva* (1980).

For some further bibliography see

G. Delling and M. Maser, *Bibliographie zur jüdisch-hellenistischen und intertestamentarischen Literatur 1900–1970*, TU 106 (²1975), pp. 177 f. ['Zaubertexte'].

1. Sefer ha-Razim (The Book of Mysteries = ShR)

The most important early Jewish book of magic is the treatise known as *Sefer ha-Razim*. As reconstructed by M. Margalioth from diverse mediaeval fragments, it has a clear, logical structure. The introduction tells how the book was revealed by the angel Raziel to Noah, lists the benefits to be derived from studying it, and establishes a chain of tradition (similar to that in mAb.1) by which it was passed down through the ages. Then follow seven sections devoted in ascending order to the seven heavens. The whole is brought to a fitting climax by a long and solemn doxology to 'the One who sits upon the Throne of Glory' (7.7–40). ShR clearly consists of two distinct elements: (1) a framework comprising the descriptions of the seven heavens, plus the concluding doxology (this stratum of material contains many parallels to the Hekhalot literature); (2) a series of incantations woven into this framework, directed towards curing sickness, harming enemies, foretelling the future, influencing the authorities, interpreting dreams, and so forth. At first sight it is tempting to identify these two elements with literary sources and to suppose that ShR has been formed by combining a Merkabah tract with a collection of magical recipies. But this hypothesis does not really stand up to close analysis. ShR incorporates diverse materials, but what is remarkable is not its diversity but its unity. The general style of the work is uniform and distinctive, the descriptions of the various heavens are all similar in structure, and the incantation sections follow a common pattern throughout. The interweaving of the two strata is shown most plainly by the fact that the angels named in the hierarchies of the cosmological framework are the same as those invoked in the incantations.

The following passage is typical (2.57–72):

A. 'Upon the fourth step stand these: ṢGRY'L, MLKY'L, 'WNBYB, PGRY'L, 'NNY'L, KLNMYY', 'WMY'L, MPNWR, KWZZYB', 'LPY'L, PRYBY'L, ṢQMYH, KDWMY'L, 'SMD', HWDYH, YḤZY'L. As for these, their station is on the fourth step.

B. They are girded with storm and the sound of their steps is as the sound of bronze. They fly from the east and turn from the west towards the gate (πυλών). They are swift as lightning and fire is round about them. They withhold sleep from men and have the power to do good or ill.

C. If you wish to deprive your enemy of sleep, take the head of a black dog that has been blind from birth and take a strip of lead from a water-pipe (פסוכופורון ציץ = πέταλον ψυχροφόρον[14]) and write upon it [the names of] these angels, and say thus:

D. *I hand over to you, angels of disquiet who stand upon the fourth step, the life, soul and spirit of N son of N so that you may fetter him with chains of iron and bind him with bars of bronze. Do not grant sleep to his eyelids, nor slumber, nor drowsiness. Let him weep and cry like a woman in travail and do not permit anyone to release him [from this spell].*

E. Write thus and put [the lead strip] in the mouth of the dog's head. Put wax on its mouth and seal it with a ring which has a lion [engraved] upon it. Then go and conceal it behind his house, or in the place where he goes out and in.

F. If you wish to release him, bring up [the dog's head] from the place where it is concealed, remove its seal, withdraw the text and throw it into a fire. At once he will fall asleep. Do this with humility and you will be successful.'

A-B belong to the cosmological framework, C-E to the collection of magical recipes. But note how C refers back to A, thus locking the two elements together. A names the angels, B describes their general appearance and powers, as well as the purposes for which they may be invoked. C illustrates the *baqqashah*-formula which is common in ShR: 'If you wish to do such and such ... take such and such' (... אם בקשת קה ... inf. + ל). Cf. the ἐὰν δὲ θέλῃς formula of the Greek papyri, e.g. PGM IV 773: ἐὰν δὲ ἄλλῳ θέλῃς δεικνύειν, ἔχε κτλ. The praxis (C-E) involves a number of steps: the preparation and writing of the amulet (C), the invocation of the angels and the naming of the victim (D), the depositing of the amulet in an appropriate place (E). Finally (at F) a formula is given for reversing the spell.

Only one datable reference occurs in the text, viz. 1.27–8: 'These are the angels who are obedient in every matter during the first and second years of the fifteen year cycle of the reckoning of the Greek kings.' This is an allusion to the fifteen year indiction-cycle which began in A.D. 312.[15] ShR cannot, then, have been composed before A.D. 312. On the

14. Cf. A. Audollent, *Defixionum Tabellae* (1904), no. 155, A.28, B.23.

15. The discussion in M. Margalioth, *Sepher Ha-Razim* (1966), pp. 24–5, requires supplementation. There seems to be little doubt that the fifteen year indiction-cycle began in 312. A five year indiction-cycle may have been instituted in Egypt as early as A.D. 287. See O. Seeck, 'Die Entstehung des Indictionen-cyclus', *Deutsche Zeitschrift für Geschichtswissenschaft* 12 (1894–5), pp. 279 ff.; E. H. Kase, *A Papyrus Roll in the Princeton Collection* (1933), pp. 25–31; L. Amundsen, *Ostraca Osloensia* (1933), pp. 64–8; U.

other hand, it is unlikely to have been written close to that date. The indiction-cycle originally had to do with imperial taxation and was used only in tax matters. Apparently it was not until the second half of the fourth century that it began to be used (as in ShR 1.27–8) for dating in non-fiscal contexts.[16] So ShR can hardly have been put together before the end of the fourth century. It is impossible to be more precise because indiction-reckoning remained in use throughout the Byzantine era (and, indeed, down to the middle ages). The profusion of Greek loan words, the many exact parallels to the Greek magical papyri, taken with a *terminus a quo* of *c.* A.D. 350, point to the origin of the work in the Byzantine era. The nature of its Hebrew, as well as its Greek affinities, suggest ShR was composed in Palestine or (possibly) Egypt.

ShR contains many surprises which raise acutely the question of its orthodoxy. At 4.61–3 it gives a Greek prayer to Helios, transliterated into Hebrew. At 1.126 Aphrodite is invoked as the evening star; at 1.178 Hermes is invoked under his name Κριοφόρος, 'the ram-bearer'; and at 2.50–4 and 2.166–71 the moon is invoked. 1.176–85 gives a spell for necromancy, a form of divination expressly condemned in the Torah (Deut. 18:10–11; Lev. 19:31). At 3.35–43 there is a spell for success at the chariot races. To prevent a river or the sea flooding a town, 2.114–17 prescribes making an image of a type apparently forbidden in mAZ 3:1. Margalioth was convinced that the author of ShR was heretical and that the work emanated from the circles of the early *minim*,[17] but such a conclusion should not be jumped at too quickly. Doubtless, some early Rabbinic authorities would have condemned the subject-matter of ShR as *minut*, but there is good evidence to suggest that such material circulated at the very heart of Rabbinic society. The author of ShR was certainly no ignoramus. Although his work may reflect popular belief and practice, he writes good Hebrew and was patently a man of some learning.

Bibliography

The Hebrew text of ShR is printed in M. Margalioth, *Sepher Ha-Razim: A Newly Discovered Book of Magic from the Talmudic Period* (1966). Margalioth's introduction and notes are useful. Editorially, Margalioth exercised a very heavy hand and produced a highly eclectic, heavily corrected text. His *variae lectiones* at the back should not be ignored. However, he did not invent ShR: there is every reason to believe that a work of the form he postulates did once exist. M. A. Morgan, *Sepher Ha-Razim: The Book of Mysteries* (1983), gives an English version of Margalioth's text. On ShR see further: Merchavya, Ch., Review of Margalioth, *Sepher Ha-Razim*, Kirjath Sepher 42 (1966–7), pp. 297–303 [Hebrew].

Wilcken, *Archiv für Papyrusforschung* 11 (1955), pp. 313–14.

16. E. J. Bickerman, *Chronology of the Ancient World* ([2]1980), p. 78.

17. Margalioth, *Sepher Ha-Razim* (1966), pp. XV-XVI.

Kasher, M. M., *Torah Shelemah* XXII (1967), pp. 188–92 [Hebrew].
Dan, J., Review of Margalioth, *Sepher Ha-Razim*, Tarbiz 37 (1967–8), pp. 208–14 [Hebrew].
Maier, J., 'Das Buch der Geheimnisse', Judaica 24 (1968), pp. 98–111.
Maier, J., 'Poetisch-liturgische Stücke aus dem "Buch der Geheimnisse"', Judaica 24 (1968), pp. 172–81.
Merchavya, Ch., 'Sefer Ha-Razim', Enc. Jud. XIII (1971), cols. 1594–5.
Séd, N., 'Le Sēfer ha-Rāzim et la méthode de "combinaison des lettres"', REJ 130 (1971), pp. 295–304.
Niggemeyer, J. H., *Beschwörungsformeln aus dem 'Buch der Geheimnisse'* (1975).
Gruenwald, I., *Apocalyptic and Merkavah Mysticism* (1980), pp. 225–34 ['Sefer Ha-Razim'].
For fragments of mediaeval books of magical recipes from the Cairo Genizah see:
R. Gottheil and W. H. Worrell, *Fragments from the Cairo Genizah in the Freer Collection* (1927), no. XV (pp. 76–81), and no. XXIV (pp. 106–7); J. Mann, *Texts and Studies* II (1972), pp. 90–4; P. Schäfer, *Geniza-Fragmente zur Hekhalot-Literatur* (1984), no. 20; J. Naveh and S. Shaked, *Amulets and Magic Bowls* (1985), pp. 224–36.

2. Ḥarba deMosheh (The Sword of Moses = HdM)

This text, first published by Gaster in 1896 from a manuscript in his own possession (Cod. Hebr. Gaster 178), is, like ShR, a magical compendium. Part I (in Hebrew) provides a setting for the strictly practical sections which follow. It opens with an angelic hierarchy in which are disclosed the names of the angels in charge of the sword, and it explains how these angels revealed the sword to Moses. Instructions then follow concerning the elaborate preparations to be made if the adept is to use the sword effectively without danger to himself. Part II presents the sword itself, which consists of a long list of magical names. These are for the most part *nomina barbara* of indeterminate language. At the end, however, the text breaks into an Aramaic invocation of the angels of the sword. The sword is apparently regarded as a secret name of God (note the quotation from Is. 42:8 with which it concludes: 'I am the Lord, this is my Name'), but it contains obvious angelic names as well. It is not uncommon in early Jewish mystical and magical texts to find the same secret names applied both to God and the angels. The use of the term 'sword' for a magical composition can be paralleled in the Greek magical papyri; cf. Ξίφος Δαρδάνου as the title of PGM IV 1719 ff. The choice of the term may also have been influenced by Moses' final blessing of Israel in Deut. 33:29, 'Happy are you, O Israel, who is like unto you? A people saved by the Lord, the shield of your help, and that is the sword of your excellency!'

Part III (in Aramaic) gives instructions as to the specific purposes for which the sword may be employed. These are similar to the uses of the spells in ShR. It is notable, however, that a high proportion of HdM's incantations are directed towards healing and that often they employ *materia medica*. This links HdM with the ancient pharmacological tradition, as represented, for example, by Dioscorides, and entitles it to be regarded as an early Jewish work of 'science'.

The following are typical: 3.8: 'For croup (אסכרתא) recite over oil of roses from YY'H to 'WNṬW and put it in his mouth.' 3.10: 'For pains in the eyes recite over water for three days in the morning from HWTMY'S to MSWLS and wash the eye with it.' 3.33: 'For piles take tow, put salt on it, dip it in oil, recite over it from TPSMT to YGLWNY', and sit on it.'

These recipes are in a form common in HdM: 'For X (= an illness) do Y (= a medical preparation + appropriate incantation).' The *baqqashah*-formula is also found, or rather its Aramaic equivalent: אם ... סב ... inf. + בעית ל . E.g.: 3.68: 'If you wish to kill a man, take mud from the two banks of a river, make an image and write his name on it. Take seven thorns from a withered palm tree and make a bow from reed with the string of horse-sinew (?).[18] Put the image in a hollow, aim at it with the bow, and shoot it, saying at every shot from 'QTDS to PRSWSY, "May N son of N be destroyed!"'

Sometimes the formula is shortened by the omission of the initial 'If you wish'. E.g.: 3.54: 'To catch fish (נוניך) take a white potsherd, put leaves of the olive tree in it, and recite over them from 'NTShWRMY to 'TQNG on the bank of the river.'

The question of the date and provenance of HdM is complicated by its composite nature. The Hebrew introduction is presumably a later addition to the Aramaic sections. A *terminus ad quem* is provided by the clear reference to HdM in the famous responsum of Hai Gaon (d. 1038) to Kairwan: 'As for the texts you have seen which state, "He who wants to do such and such, let him do such and such", we have very many of them, such as the book called *Sefer ha-Yashar*, or the one known as *Ḥarba deMosheh* which begins, "Four angels are appointed over the sword", and in which are exalted and wonderful things; or there is the book called *Raza Rabba*, as well as separate, individual formulae which are innumerable.'[19] The provenance of HdM is very uncertain. The Aramaic of parts II and III is Babylonian, which points to Babylonia as the place of origin. This would also be supported by the fact that Greek elements are not so prominent in HdM as in ShR (though note the reference to χάρτης ἱερατικός[20] in 3.106). The Hebrew of part I,

---

18. The vocabulary of HdM is extremely difficult. I simply accept Gaster's guesses here. The general sense is clear enough.

19. See *Ta'am Zeqenim* 56b; Lewin, *'Oṣar ha-Ge'onim* IV, Ḥagigah 20–21.

20. The ἱερατικὸς χάρτης was a choice quality of papyrus; see Strabo xvii 1, 15 and Pliny, *N.H.* xiii 74. Further, N. Lewis, *Papyrus in Classical Antiquity* (1974), pp. 43–4. It was much favoured for the writing of spells: see PGM II 60f, γράφε ζμύρνῃ διπλοῦν εἰς

however, appears to be of a Palestinian variety.[21]

Bibliography

For text, translation and introduction to HdM see M. Gaster, *Studies and Texts* (1925–8), I pp. 288–337, III pp. 69–103 (reprinted New York, 1971, with a new prolegomenon by T. Gaster). Unfortunately, Cod. Hebr. Gaster 178 is a rather poor manuscript, and Gaster's transcription of it is somewhat careless. Sassoon 290 offers the same version of HdM, but in a better text. For this manuscript see M. Benayahu, 'ספר שושן יסוד העולם לרבי יוסף תירשום', Temirin 1 (1972), pp. 187–218, esp. pp. 197 and 202. Other versions of HdM are known. These have the same general form as the Gaster version (i.e. a list of magical names plus recipes as to their use), but show little overlap of specific content. Note the following: (a) Oxford 1531, fols. 61a–63b, בשם ייי חרבא דמשה. Schäfer, *Synopse* §§ 598–622 supersedes Gaster's transcription of this text (*Studies and Texts* III, pp. 88–91). New York, JTS 8128, fols. 35a–36b, דין חרבא דמשה (Schäfer, *Synopse* §§ 598–622) gives the same text with minor variations. Though the superscription is in Aramaic, this version of HdM is largely Hebrew. The sword is identified as the name of God revealed to Moses at the bush (§§ 598, 606). The New York manuscript claims the sword was revealed to R. Ishmael b. Elisha (§ 598). This ties the work into the Merkabah tradition in which Ishmael plays a prominent part. (b) New York, JTS 8128, fols. 38a–38b, הדין הוא חרבא דמשה (Schäfer, *Synopse* §§ 640–50). This is in Aramaic throughout. § 646 refers to the use of χάρτης ἱερατικός.

3. Incantation Bowls and Amulets in Hebrew and Aramaic

ShR and HdM are magical handbooks of the kind a practising magician would have consulted regularly in the course of his business. They tell him how to write amulets for all kinds of situations and they provide him with 'blank' charms in which 'N son of N' marks the spot where the client's name was to be inserted. But there also survive from the Talmudic era actual amulets and charms, in which the theory of the handbooks has been put into practice, and the client's name filled in.

(a) Incantation Bowls

These are ordinary, unglazed earthenware bowls on which spells have been inscribed in ink. The spell is normally written on the inner surface of the bowl, but sometimes, when the text is very long, it spills over onto the back. The bowls vary in size; the average are around 16 cm max. in diameter by 5 cm max. in depth, but one of the largest (Naveh-Shaked Bowl 13, p. 204) measures 34 cm by 15 cm. They come from a wide area of Iraq and western Iran, but the most important single collection is undoubtedly that unearthed at Nippur by the University of Pennsylvania Expedition in 1888–9. The Nippur group is

---

χάρτην ἱερατικόν; PGM IV 2363: γράφε εἰς χάρτην ἱερατικὸν τὰ ὀνόματα ταῦτα; PGM V 305, λαβὼν χάρτην ἱερατικὸν κτλ. Further, M. Margalioth, *Sepher Ha-Razim* (1966), pp. 1–2.

21. M. Margalioth, *Sepher Ha-Razim* (1966), p. 30.

significant not only because of its quantity (40 bowls), but because the bowls were found *in situ* in a well stratified archaeological context which gives vital clues as to their date and use. On the basis of the stratification, the bowls can be assigned to *c.* A.D. 300–600. Script and language point to the same period. With few exceptions, it seems likely that most of those that survive, not only those from Nippur or other known sites but also those of uncertain provenance, were written before A.D. 600.

The bowls are domestic phylacteries, designed to protect the persons named in them from various ills and disasters; from demons that cause sickness, domestic discord, damage to cattle or property, from ghosts that might haunt the house. There are love-charms (Montgomery 13 and 28), as well as charms to protect unborn children and women in childbirth (Montgomery 39). One long text (Naveh-Shaked Bowl 9) cursing an enemy consists largely of a catena of Scriptural verses. Liliths and their male counterparts, Lilis, are often identified as the source of the trouble and exorcized. The bowls were found mostly inside the houses, usually more than one to a house. A common practice appears to have been to bury a bowl at each corner of the house in order to establish a protective cordon round it. This explains why several copies of the same bowl were made out for the same client (cf. Montgomery 21, 22, 23). Bowls may also have been placed at the threshold (Montgomery 6.4, 6; Naveh-Shaked Bowl 5.1), and in the bed-chamber (Montgomery 7.1; 8.5; 19.3). Some bowls were intended for use in the cemetery, presumably to lay the ghosts of the dead.[22]

The bowls are in three languages: Aramaic, Syriac and Mandaean. The Aramaic is of the type well known from the Babylonian Talmud. Some bowls are patently of Jewish origin, but here too syncretism prevails and it is hard to draw a dividing line between Jewish and non-Jewish magic. The problem is well illustrated by one Mandaean bowl (McCullough D) which, though evidently written for a Mandaean client, contains striking and specific references to elements of Merkabah mysticism (lines 5–6). It is a problem to know whether this text was written by a Jewish magician who happened to know Mandaean, or by a Mandaean who drew on Jewish sources.[23]

---

22. J. A. Montgomery, *Aramaic Incantation Texts from Nippur* (1913), pp. 14, 43. Some bowls published by Pognon were inscribed דבית קבוריא, 'for the cemetery'; see further J. Naveh and S. Shaked, *Amulets and Magic Bowls* (1985), p. 16. Note Naveh-Shaked Bowl 4.2, הדין א (א) א א איסרא דקברא, 'This is ' ' ' ' the spell of the tomb'.

23. Note the judgement of J. Naveh and S. Shaked, *Amulets and Magic Bowls* (1985), pp. 17–18. In the light of the specifically Jewish elements, 'one must come to the conclusion that the writers of these Jewish-Aramaic bowls were in all probability practitioners of magic who belonged to the Jewish community. This conclusion does not necessarily apply to the clients, who ordered the bowls written for healing, protection or other purposes. There is, in fact, a combination of two factors which makes it likely that not a few of these

The incantations themselves are not in any standard literary form, though certain motifs and elements recur. The text, which is always careful to name the client or clients on whose behalf it was written, normally describes the demon or demons, and their activities, against whom the incantation is directed. Sometimes they are specifically named and their genealogy given. They are adjured not to harm the client in a variety of ways. Sometimes they are restrained by the use of *nomina barbara*; sometimes more powerful, beneficent spiritual forces (God, the good angels) are summoned against them; sometimes a famous and potent spell is employed ('the charm of Enoch', Montgomery 4.2; 'the spell of the monster Leviathan', Montgomery 2.4; 'the ban [אחרמתא] which fell on Mt. Hermon', Montgomery 2.6; 'the seal of Solomon', Montgomery 39.10–11); sometimes a verse of Scripture provides the word of power (e.g. the *Shema'*, Montgomery 26.1, Naveh-Shaked Bowl 11.6; Num. 10:35, Naveh-Shaked Bowl 3.5; Zech. 3:2, Naveh-Shaked Bowl 11.5–6). Of special interest is the magical *get* of Joshua b. Peraḥya, which is used on several occasions to divorce the demon from the client. E.g. Naveh-Shaked Bowl 5:

> 'I bind, tie and suppress all demons and harmful spirits that are in the world, whether male or female, from the greatest of them to the least, from the young to the old, whether I know his name or do not know his name. In case I do not know the name, it has already been explained to me at the seven days of creation. What has not been disclosed to me at the time of the seven days of creation, was disclosed to me in the *get* that came here from across the sea, which was written and sent to[24] Rabbi Joshua bar Peraḥya. Just as there was a Lilith who strangled people, and Rabbi Joshua sent a ban against her, but she did not accept it because he did not know her name; and her name was written in the *get*, and an announcement

---

customers were indeed non-Jews. First, there is the fact that Jewish bowls constitute the great majority of inscribed earthenware bowls from Mesopotamia and Iran, while Jews certainly did not form more than a minority of the population; and secondly, there is the fact that the names of most of the clients were not Jewish, and some of them are theophoric names of Zoroastrian significance. The second fact would not be particularly significant on its own, since there can be no doubt that many Jews carried Persian and other non-Jewish names. However, when it is combined with the first consideration, it adds some weight to the supposition that magic may have been considered to some extent a Jewish specialization, and that pagans and Zoroastrians often turned to Jewish practitioners when they sought an effective remedy, protection or curse.'

24. The situation envisaged appears to be this: Joshua bar Peraḥya issues a *get* to the Lilith who refuses to accept it because she is not specifically named in it. Heaven then intervenes by sending down a *get*, duly naming the Lilith, which Joshua uses. This heavenly *get* falls into the legal category of 'a bill of divorce from beyond the sea'. It is this *get* which the writer of the bowl invokes against the demons. Perhaps lines 5–6, דכתבו ושדרו לה לרבי יהושוע בר פרחיה, should be translated, 'which they wrote and dispatched *for* R. Joshua bar Peraḥya'.

was made against her in heaven by a *get* that came here from across the sea; so you are bound, tied and suppressed all of you beneath the feet of the said Marnaqa son of Qala. In the name of Gabriel, the mighty hero, who kills all heroes who are victorious in battle, and in the name of Yaho'el, who shuts the mouths of all [heroes]. In the name of Yah, Yah, Yah, Sabaoth. Amen, Amen, Selah.' Cf. Montgomery 8.7–10 and 17.1–11.

(b) Amulets

Bowl-magic appears to have been a distinctively Mesopotamian phenomenon. Even the bowls of uncertain provenance appear to have originated in the east. In the west a different practice prevailed in that incantations in Aramaic, or in a mixture of Hebrew and Aramaic, were incised with a stylus on thin metal sheets (gold, silver, copper, lead), which were then rolled up and inserted into a metal container, rather like a *mezuzah*-case. This could be worn on the body, hung in the house, or buried in a suitable spot in the ground. Some seventeen such metal amulets are known (far fewer in number than the bowls[25]) deriving from Syria, Palestine, Egypt and Turkey. To these may be added the love-charm on potsherd from Ḥorvat Rimmon (13 km north of Beer-Sheba) (Naveh-Shaked Amulet 10). The choice of potsherd in this case was integral to the praxis of the charm. The incantation, written on unbaked clay, was 'activated' by the clay being fired.

Several of the amulets were found by archaeologists in well-stratified remains. Three from Nirim in the north-west Negev (Naveh-Shaked Amulets 11–13) can be dated to the sixth century A.D.; two from Ḥorvat Kanaf in the Golan (Naveh-Shaked Amulets 2–3) belong to the sixth or early seventh centuries; the Ḥorvat Rimmon sherd just mentioned is from the fifth to sixth centuries. In other words, the evidence indicates that these amulets are from the same period as the bowls.[26] It seems that the same sort of magic was practised by Jews throughout the whole of the middle east, and that the substance on which the amulet or incantation was written was rather secondary. Jews in the Talmudic period doubtless wrote amulets on papyrus, cloth, and other less durable materials, but apart from an Aramaic papyrus fragment from Oxyrhynchus these have not survived.

Bibliography

C. D. Isbell gathered all (or most) of the Aramaic bowls together in his *Corpus of Aramaic Incantation Bowls* (1975). He gives full details of the original publications, which should always be consulted. The following works have appeared since 1975:
Isbell, C. D., 'Two New Aramaic Incantation Bowls', BASOR 223 (1976), pp. 15–23.

25. Over seventy bowls in Jewish Aramaic have been published to date.
26. Note Naveh-Shaked Amulet 13.12–22 which uses Exod. 15:26 as a charm, contrary to mSanh. 10:1. Cf. 3 En. 48D:10.

Geller, M. J., 'Two Incantation Bowls Inscribed in Syriac and Aramaic', BSOAS 39 (1976), pp. 422–7.
Gordon, C. H., 'Two Aramaic Incantations', in G. A. Tuttle (ed.), *Biblical and Near Eastern Studies: Essays in Honour of W. S. LaSor* (1978), pp. 231–44.
Geller, M. J., 'Four Aramaic Incantation Bowls', in J. Rendsburg *et al.* (eds.), *The Bible World: Essays in Honour of Cyrus H. Gordon* (1980), pp. 47–60.
Harviainen, T., 'An Aramaic Incantation Bowl from Borsippa. Another Specimen of Eastern Aramaic "Koiné"', *Studia Orientalia*, edited by the Finnish Oriental Society, 51:14 (1981).
Naveh, J., and Shaked, S., *Amulets and Magic Bowls: Aramaic Incantations of Late Antiquity* (1985). Thirteen new bowls.

In general on the bowls see:
Montgomery, J. A., *Aramaic Incantation Texts from Nippur* (1913).
Epstein, J. N., 'Gloses babylo-araméennes', REJ 73 (1921), pp. 27–58; 74 (1922), pp. 40–72.
Rossell, W. H., *A Handbook of Aramaic Magical Texts* (1953).
Yamauchi, E. M., 'Aramaic Magic Bowls', JAOS 85 (1965), pp. 511–23.
Yamauchi, E. M., *Mandaic Incantation Texts* (1967).
McCullough, W. S., *Jewish and Mandaean Incantation Bowls in the Royal Ontario Museum* (1967).
Levine, B. A., 'The Language of the Magical Bowls', in J. Neusner, *A History of the Jews in Babylonia* V (1970), pp. 343–75.
Hamilton, V. P., *Syriac Incantation Bowls*, PhD Brandeis University (University Microfilms, Ann Arbor Michigan 1971).
Kaufmann, S. A., 'A Unique Magic Bowl from Nippur', JNES 32 (1973), pp. 170–4.
Schiffman, L. H., 'A Forty-two Letter Divine Name in the Aramaic Magic Bowls', Bulletin of the Institute of Jewish Studies 1 (1973), pp. 97–102.
Greenfield, J. C., 'Notes on Some Aramaic and Mandaic Magic Bowls', The Journal of the Ancient Near Eastern Society of Columbia University 5 (= The Gaster Festschrift) (1973), pp. 149–56.
Isbell, C. D., 'The Story of the Aramaic Magical Incantation Bowls', BA 41 (1978), pp. 5–16.

All the Aramaic and Hebrew amulets from Syria-Palestine and adjacent regions have been collected and thoroughly re-edited in J. Naveh and S. Shaked, *Amulets and Magic Bowls* (1985), pp. 40–122. Their only omissions are the texts published by J. A. Montgomery in 'Some Early Amulets from Palestine', JAOS 31 (1911), pp. 272–81. Naveh and Shaked give full references to the earlier publications. The Aramaic papyrus amulet from Oxyrhynchus (Bodleian Ms. Heb. d. 83(P) S.C. 37016) was first edited by A. E. Cowley in 'Notes on Hebrew Papyrus Fragments from Oxyrhynchus', JEA 2 (1915), p. 209–13. See now M. J. Geller, 'An Aramaic Incantation from Oxyrhynchus', ZPE 58 (1985), pp. 96–8. Naveh and Shaked, *Amulets and Magic Bowls*, pp. 216–40, edit a number of mediaeval amulets from the Cairo Genizah. On these later amulets, and on Jewish amulets in general, consult the following:
Blau, L., 'Amulet', JE I (1901), pp. 546–50.
Gaster, M., 'Charms and Amulets (Jewish)', HERE III (1910), pp. 451–5.
Casanowicz, I. M., 'Jewish Amulets in the United States National Museum', JAOS 36 (1917), pp. 154–67.
Gaster, M., *Studies and Texts* I–III (1925–8; reprinted 1971), passim.
Budge, E. A. W., *Amulets and Superstitions* (1930), pp. 212–38 ['Hebrew Amulets'].
Trachtenberg, J., *Jewish Magic and Superstition* (1939), pp. 132–52 ['Amulets'].
Schrire, T., *Hebrew Amulets—Their Decipherment and Interpretation* (1966).
Kaplan, J., 'Two Samaritan Amulets', IEJ 17 (1971), pp. 158–62.

Schrire, T., 'Amulet', Enc. Jud. II (1971), cols. 906–15.

Naveh, J., 'A Nabatean Incantation Text', IEJ 29 (1979), pp. 111–19.

Naveh, J., 'A Recently Discovered Palestinian Jewish Aramaic Amulet', in M. Sokoloff (ed.), *Arameans and Aramaic Literary Tradition* (1983), pp. 81–8.

See also the bibliography under the Hadrumetum tablet in the next section.

4. *Jewish Magical Texts Preserved in Greek*

The following two texts will serve to illustrate the nature of the Jewish magical material which has apparently been transmitted through pagan Greek sources. The first is from a famous Greek book of magical recipes similar to ShR; the second is an actual amulet resembling the Aramaic metal amulets discussed earlier.

(a) The 'Hebraikos Logos' of the Great Magical Papyrus of Paris (PGM IV 3009–3085)

The opening words describe the text as 'an approved charm of Pibeches for those possessed by demons' (πρὸς δαιμονιαζομένους Πιβήχεως δόκιμον). The demon is adjured by 'the God of the Hebrews' (3019), 'by him who appeared to Osrael [*sic*] in the pillar of light and in the cloud by day' (3034–5), and by 'him who is in Jerusalem' (3069). Many allusions are made to sacred history (e.g. the ten plagues, the parting of the Red Sea and the River Jordan), and numerous verbal echoes of the Septuagint. At one point the demon is adjured by 'the seal which Solomon laid upon the tongue of Jeremiah and he spoke' (3039 f.: Κατὰ τῆς σφραγῖδος, ἧς ἔθετο Σολομὼν ἐπὶ τὴν γλῶσσαν τοῦ Ἰηρεμίου, καὶ ἐλάλησεν)—apparently an allusion to an otherwise unknown *haggadah*. God is invoked: 'Let your angel descend, the implacable one, and let him draw into captivity the demon as he flies round this creature [i.e. the demoniac] whom God formed in his holy paradise.' The situation envisaged is that the demon, having been expelled from the victim's body by the use of the potion and the amulet (φυλακτήριον) described earlier, has to be 'bound' by a heavenly agency to prevent it from re-entering. Cf. how, when Tobias had smoked the demon out of his bridal chamber, the angel Raphael pursued it to Upper Egypt and bound it to stop it from returning (Tobit 8:2–3).[27] Despite the many explicit Jewish references, the text can hardly have been written by a Jew (or for that matter a Christian) in the form in which it is now. The deformation of 'Israel' into 'Osrael', the reference to 'Jesus' as 'the God of the Hebrews' (3019), the Egyptian name Pibeches, and the very description of the text at the end as a '*Hebraikos logos*' (3085: ὁ γὰρ λόγος

---

27. Note the interesting haggadic reference in 3061: ὃν ὑμνοῦσι τὰ πτερυγώματα τοῦ χερουβίν. The idea here is that the cherubim sing to God by moving their wings. Cf. 3 En. 24:15, 'They [the cherubim] spread their wings to sing with them the song to him who dwells in clouds, and to praise with them the glory of the King of kings.' See Alexander's note *ad loc.* in Charlesworth, OTP I, p. 279.

358   §32. Jewish Literature in Hebrew or Aramaic

ἐστὶν Ἑβραϊκός), all tell against this. It is probably a pagan copy (perhaps with some re-working) of originally Jewish magical material. PGM IV is a large collection of magical recipes from diverse sources. The manuscript is likely to have been written around A.D. 300, but the contents are generally agreed to have been composed much earlier. Dieterich argued that the work must have been put together before the time of Diocletian.[28]

(b) The Hadrumetum Tablet

At Hadrumetum in north Africa, a third-century A.D. amulet was unearthed containing a Greek love-charm. Written on a sheet of lead, this had been rolled up and placed in a tomb in the town's necropolis. The text opens: *Horcizo se daemonion pneumn to enthade cimenon to onomati to agio*[29] *Αωθ Αβ[α]ωθ, τὸν θεὸν τοῦ Αβρααν* [=Αβρααμ] *καὶ τὸν Ιαω τὸν τοῦ Ιακου* [=Ισακου], *Ιαω Αω[θ Αβ]αωθ θεὸν τοῦ Ισραμα* [=Ισραηλ], 'I adjure you, demonic spirit who rests here (i.e. in the tomb), by the sacred name Aoth, Abaoth, the God of Abraham, and the Iao of Isaac, Iao Aoth Abaoth the God of Israel'. The client for whom the amulet was written is named as 'Domitiana whom Candida bore', and her purpose was to secure the undying love of 'Urbanus whom Urbana bore'. The text of the adjuration contains many verbal echoes from various parts of the Old Testament, and are in a form that suggests that the writer was quoting from memory. That he was someone who knew his Bible well and was not simply copying a sacred text for magical purposes points to a Jewish origin for the adjuration.[30] However, once again the text in its extant form must have been copied and perhaps adapted by a pagan. No Jew (or Christian) is likely to have misspelled, not once but twice (see also 38f), the names Abraham, Isaac and Israel. There is no need to suppose that Domitiana, or even the magician who probably wrote the amulet for her, were Jewish. The adjuration may have been taken from a syncretistic book of magical recipes, like PGM IV, containing both 'Jewish' and 'non-Jewish' material.

Text of the 'Hebraikos Logos': K. Preisendanz, *Papyri Graecae Magicae* I ([2]1973), pp. 170–2. For discussion of PGM IV in general, and the *'Hebraikos Logos'* in particular, see the following:

Wessely, C., *Griechische Zauberpapyrus von Paris und London* (1888). Cf. Patrologia Orientalis IV (1908), pp. 187–90.

Blau, L., *Das altjüdische Zauberwesen* ([2]1914), pp. 112–17.

Dieterich, A., *Eine Mithrasliturgie* ([3]1923).

Deissmann, A., *Light from the Ancient East* ([2]1927), pp. 254–64.

Festugière, A.-J., *La révélation d'Hermès Trismégiste* I ([2]1950), pp. 303–8.

28. A. Dieterich, *Eine Mithrasliturgie* ([3]1923), p. 44.
29. Sic! = Ὀρκίζω σε δαιμόνιον πνεῦμα τὸ ἐνθάδε κείμενον τῷ ὀνόματι τῷ ἁγίῳ κτλ.
30. Cf. the adjurations in Naveh-Shaked Geniza 4.6 ff. and Geniza 7.8 ff.

Smith, Morton, 'Observations on *Hekhalot Rabbati*', in A. Altmann (ed.), *Biblical and Other Studies* (1963), pp. 142–60, esp. 158 ff.
Meyer, H. W., *The 'Mithras' Liturgy* (1976).

E. R. Goodenough, *Jewish Symbols in the Greco-Roman Period* II (1953), pp. 190–205, attempts to identify other Jewish texts in 'pagan sources'. His more convincing examples are as follows:
PGM IV 1166–1225a; PGM V 97–173: note 109f, ἐγώ εἰμι Μοϋσῆς ὁ προφήτης σου, ὦ παρέδοκας τὰ μυστήρια σου τὰ συντελούμενα Ἰσραήλ;
PGM V 460–88, ἐπικαλοῦμαι σε τὸν κτίσαντα γῆν κτλ.
PGM VII 594–618; PGM VII 1017–1022, Χαῖρε ῞Ηλιε ... χαῖρε Γαβριήλ κτλ;
PGM XIII 254–259: note 254f, ἐγώ εἰμι ὁ ἐπὶ τῶν δύο χερουβείν;
PGM XIII 334–337, ἐγώ εἰμι ὁ ἐπὶ τῶν δύο χερουβείν;
PGM XXIIa 17–27; PGM XXIIb 1–28, Προσευχὴ Ἰακώβ;
PGM XXXV 1–42, Ἐπικαλοῦμαι σε, ὁ καθήμενος ἐπὶ τῆς ἀβύσσου κτλ.
PGM XXXVI 36–67; PGM XXXVI 187–204; PGM XXXVI 295–311.
Moses is mentioned frequently in the Greek magical papyri, but few of the texts are identifiably Jewish. He was clearly revered as a great master by magicians of all persuasions. A cluster of references to him occurs in PGM XIII. Note the following:
XIII 3–4: Βίβλος ἱερὰ ἐπικαλουμένη Μονὰς ἢ Ὀγδόη Μοϋσέως περὶ τοῦ ὀνόματος τοῦ ἁγίου.
XIII 21 : ὁ δὲ λέγει ἐν τῇ Κλειδί Μοϋσης.
XIII 344 : Μοϋσέως ἱερὰ βίβλος ἀπόκρυφος ἐπικαλουμένη ὀγδόη ἢ ἁγία.
XIII 971 : ὡς δὲ Μωϋσῆς ἐν τῇ Ἀρχαγγελικῇ.
XIII 1059 : Μοϋσέως ἀπόκρυφος Σεληνιακή.
XIII 1078 : Μοϋσέως ἀπόκρυφος ἡ Δεκάτη.

Note also PGM VII 620–627, Ἐκ τοῦ Διαδήματος Μοϋσέως; and PGM V 109f quoted above. For Moses amulets from Amisos (Pontus) and Acre (Sicily), see below. Further, J. G. Gager, *Moses in Greco-Roman Paganism* (1972), pp. 134–61 ['Moses and Magic'].

Magical papyri published since PGM :
Bell, H., Nock, A., and Thompson, H., *Magical Texts from a Bilingual Papyrus* (1931).
Wortmann, D., 'Neue magische Texte', *Bonner Jahrbücher* 168 (1968), pp. 56–111.
Parassoglu, G. M., 'Artificial Scripts and Magical Papyri', *Studia Papyrologica* 13 (1974), pp. 57–60.
Daniel, R., 'Two Love Charms', *ZPE* 19 (1975), pp. 249–64.

In general on the Greek magical papyri see :
Griffith, F. L., and Thompson, H., *The Demotic Magical Papyrus of London and Leiden* (1904).
Eitrem, S., *Papyri Osloenses*, Fasc. I (1925).
Nock, A. D., 'Greek Magical Papyri', *JEA* 15 (1929), pp. 219–35; reprinted in Nock, *Essays on Religion and the Ancient World* I (1972), pp. 176–94.
Festugière, A.-J., *L'idéal religieux des Grecs et l'Évangile* (1932), pp. 281–328 ['La valeur religieuse des papyrus magiques'].
Eitrem, S., 'Aus "Papyrologie und Religionsgeschichte" : Die magischen Papyri', in W. Otto and L. Wenger (eds.), *Papyri und Altertumswissenschaft* (1934), pp. 246–63.
Nilsson, M., 'Die Religion der griechischen Zauberpapyri', in Nilsson, *Opuscula Selecta* III (1960), pp. 129–66.
Gundel, H. G., 'Vom Weltbild in den griechischen Zauberpapyri : Probleme und Ergebnisse', in D. H. Samuel (ed.), *Proceedings of the Twelfth International Congress of Papyrology* = American Studies in Papyrology 7 (1970), pp. 183–93.
Betz, H. D., 'Fragments from a Catabasis Ritual in a Greek Magical Papyrus', *HR* 19 (1980), pp. 287–95. Text of the Hadrumetum tablet: A. Audollent, *Defixionum Tabellae* (1904), pp. 373–7. Further :

Deissmann, A., *Bible Studies* (1901), pp. 271–300 ['An Epigraphic Memorial to the Septuagint'].
Wünsch, R., *Antike Fluchtafeln* ([2]1912), pp. 21–6.
Blau, L., *Das altjüdische Zauberwesen* ([2]1914), pp. 112–17.

The following Greek amulets are probably Jewish:
(1) Frey, CIJ 673 : Regensburg (Germany).
(2) Frey, CIJ 674 : Badenweiler (Germany).
(3) Frey, CIJ 717 : Achaea (Greece).
(4) Frey, CIJ 802 : Amisos (Pontus) ; see further R. Wünsch, 'Deisidaimoniaka', Archiv für Religionswissenschaft 12 (1909), pp. 24–32 ; J. G. Gager, *Moses in Greco-Roman Paganism* (1972), pp. 157–9.
(5) A. Vogliano and K. Preisendanz, ' Laminetta Magica Siciliana', Acme : Annali della Facoltà di Filosofia e Lettere della Università Statale di Milano 1 (1948), pp. 73–85. A φυλακτήριον Μωσέως from Acre in Sicily. See further E. Peterson, *Frühkirche, Judentum und Gnosis* (1959), pp. 346–54 ['Das Amulett von Acre'].
(6) P. Perdrizet, 'Amulette grecque trouvée en Syrie', REG 41 (1928), pp. 73–82.

For other *defixionum tabellae* see :
Wünsch, R., *Sethianische Verfluchungstafeln aus Rom* (1889).
Wünsch, R., *Defixionum Tabellae Atticae* (1893).
Pradel, F., *Griechische und süditalienische Gebete, Beschwörungen und Rezepte des Mittelalters* (1907).
Jordan, D. R., 'A Curse Tablet from a Well in the Athenian Agora', ZPE 19 (1975), pp. 245–8.

For general discussion of the *defixionum tabellae* see :
Eitrem, S., and Herter, H., 'Bindezauber', RAC II (1954), cols. 380–5.
Preisendanz, K., 'Fluchtafel (Defixion)', RAC VIII (1972), cols. 1–29.

The problems of identifying the Jewish examples among the surviving small amulets and magical gems (which often have only one or two words of inscription) seem almost insurmountable. For discussion see Goodenough, *Jewish Symbols* II, pp. 208–95. Further :
Bonner, C., *Studies in Magical Amulets chiefly Graeco-Egyptian* (1950), esp. pp. 27–32, 100–1, 208–11, 226.
Bonner, C., 'A Miscellany of Engraved Stones', Hesperia 23 (1954), pp. 138–57.
Delatte, A., and Derchain, P., *Les intailles magiques gréco-égyptiennes* (1964), esp. pp. 261–4 ['Salomon cavalier'] and pp. 311–13.
Wortmann, D., 'Neue magische Texte', Bonner Jahrbücher 168 (1968), pp. 102–6.
Wortmann, D., 'Neue magische Gemmen', Bonner Jahrbücher 175 (1975), pp. 63–82.
Parassoglu, G. M., 'A Christian Amulet against Snakebite', Studia Papyrologica 13 (1974), pp. 107–10.

A good general introduction to Greek amulets is F. Eckstein and J. H. Waszink, 'Amulett', RAC I (1950), cols. 397–411.

Goodenough, *Jewish Symbols* II, pp. 164–90 discusses the possibility of Jewish magical texts surviving in Christian Syriac and Coptic sources. For these see:
Gollancz, H., *The Book of Protection being a collection of charms edited from Syriac MSS* (1912). See further above the bibliographies under 'Incantation Bowls and Amulets in Hebrew and Aramaic'.
Kropp, A. M., *Ausgewählte koptische Zaubertexte* I-III (1930–1).
Stegemann, V., *Die koptische Zaubertexte der Sammlung Papyrus Erzherzog Rainer in Wien* (1934).
Quecke, H., 'Ein Fragment eines koptischen Zaubertextes', Studia Papyrologica 8 (1969), pp. 97–100.

The following will serve to introduce the whole field of Greek magic:

Dieterich, A., *Abraxas: Studien zur Religionsgeschichte des späteren Altertums* (1891).

Hubert, H., 'Magia', Daremberg-Saglio, *Dictionnaire des antiquités grecques et romaines* III/2 (1904), pp. 1494–1521.

Bousset, W., 'Zur Dämonologie der späteren Antike', Archiv für Religionswissenschaft 18 (1915), pp. 134–72.

Hopfner, T., *Griechisch-ägyptischer Offenbarungszauber* I-II (1921–4).

Hopfner, T., 'Mageia', RE XIV.1 (1928), cols. 301–93.

Barb, A., 'The Survival of Magic Arts', in A. Momigliano (ed.), *The Conflict between Paganism and Christianity in the Fourth Century* (1963), pp. 100–25.

Brown, P., 'Sorcery, Demons and the Rise of Christianity from Late Antiquity to the Middle Ages', in M. Douglas (ed.), *Witchcraft, Confessions and Accusations* (1970), pp. 17–46.

Hull, J. M., *Hellenistic Magic and the Synoptic Tradition* (1974).

Colpe, C., *et al.*, 'Geister (Dämonen)', RAC IX (1976), cols. 546 ff.

Smith, Morton, *Jesus the Magician* (1978).

Smith, J. Z., 'Towards Interpreting Demonic Powers in Hellenistic and Roman Antiquity', in H. Temporini and W. Haase (eds.), ANRW II.16.1 (1978), pp. 425–39.

Aune, D. E., 'Magic in Early Christianity', *ibid.* II.23.2 (1980), pp. 1507–57.

Segal, A. F., 'Hellenistic Magic: Some Questions of Definition', in R. van den Broek and M. J. Vermaseren (eds.), *Studies in Gnosticism and Hellenistic Religions presented to G. Quispel* (1981), pp. 349–75.

5. Theurgy in the Hekhalot Texts

The so-called Hekhalot literature, produced by the Merkabah mystics of the Talmudic and early Gaonic periods, abounds in magic of a theurgic nature. The adepts were interested in acquiring secret knowledge about various subjects—the heavenly world, the mysteries of nature, the esoteric meanings of Torah, the future course of human history—and they used theurgic techniques to obtain this knowledge. Sometimes, by means of ritual and incantation, they ascended to heaven, at others they conjured a powerful angel down to earth and compelled him to impart the desired information. Some of their incantations take the form of hymns or prayers which they believed to be part of the angelic liturgy. By reciting these the adepts put themselves into a trance in which they supposed their souls were transported, by a kind of sympathetic magic, into heaven. They also used magical names of great power by which the angels could be controlled and forced to do their will. The Hekhalot tracts are full of *nomina barbara* and other unintelligible magical formulae (see e.g. 3 En. 48B:1, 48D:1 in the Alphabet of Akiba recension, Wertheimer, *Batei Midrashot* II, pp. 350–5). The mystics were deeply interested in the 'science' of names. The names, as well as the rituals they practised in their conventicles, are very similar to those found on Jewish amulets and incantation bowls, in Sefer ha-Razim, and in the Greek magical papyri. The following passages are typical:

(a) The Great Séance in Hekhalot Rabbati (Schäfer §§ 198 ff.)
R. Ishmael describes how Neḥunyah b. Ha-Qanah rose in a trance to
heaven. The text takes every opportunity to stress the dangers of such
an ascent: only those free from certain vices should attempt it, and
then only in the right setting, after due preparation, and in the right
company (among the ḥaverim, the members of the fellowship). The
ascent is achieved by invoking Suryah, Prince of the Divine Presence,
and conjuring 112 times, neither more nor less, counting on the
fingers, by a magical nomen barbarum. On going up, the adept passes
through seven concentric palaces (היכלות) guarded by angels, whose
fearsome, warlike appearance is described in detail. The only way
past them is to show them 'seals' (חותמות) consisting of magical
names which somehow 'neutralize' their power. The names of the
gatekeepers and the seals appropriate to each are carefully listed. If
the adept does everything right, he is finally conducted before the
Throne of Glory and seated with the cherubim and the other angels.
Besides giving the praxis of the ascent, the account of the Great
Séance contains an elaborate technique by which the ḥaverim could
bring the adept back to earth. This involved putting him into a state
of very marginal ritual impurity, enough to cause the angels to dismiss
him from the pure regions of heaven, but not sufficient to provoke
them into attacking and destroying him. Such a technique would
have had great practical importance if the adepts themselves were
unable to break their trances or seemed to the bystanders to be in
psychological distress.

(b) The Conjuration of the Prince of the Divine Presence (שר
הפנים) (Schäfer §§ 623–39; Schäfer, Geniza-Fragmente no. 1)
R. Eliezer instructs R. Aqiva on how to conjure the Śar ha-Panim to
earth and make him reveal the mysteries of the upper and lower
worlds. The adept prepares himself for seven days, then on the actual
day of the conjuration, fasts and immerses himself in water up to his
neck. Before reciting the conjuration he must protect himself with a
forty-two letter magical name. The immense dangers of the ritual are
again stressed. The Prince of the Divine Presence is invoked first by
the fourteen names by which he revealed himself to the prophets and
seers, then by his five names which correspond to the name of God,
and finally, at the climax, by the one special name that is 'the greatest
of his names'. The passage ends with an ἀπόλυσις —a formula for
dismissing the angel after he has done the adept's will. This is a
standard and essential element of magical praxis. It is vitally
important to ensure that the spirits called up return to the realms
from which they came. As in a number of the spells in ShR and in
PGM, the adept is meant to 'personalize' the incantation by inserting
his own name into it at the point marked 'N son of N'.

(c) The Great Seal (חותם גדול) and the Terrible Crown (כתר נורא)
(Schäfer §§ 318–21, 651–4)

R. Ishmael learns from Neḥunyah b. Ha-Qanah 'the Great Seal by which the heavens and the earth were sealed' and 'the Crown by which the Princes of Wisdom are conjured'. The Seal and the Crown are two especially potent magical formulae consisting of *nomina barbara* of the type familiar from the incantation bowls and amulets. So potent are they that the adept must protect himself before reciting them. The two liturgical compositions given for this purpose consist of straight-forward hymns of praise to God which would not look out of place in the *Siddur*.

Bibliography

Texts of these passages may be found at the points indicated in P. Schäfer, *Synopse zur Hekhalot-Literatur* (1981), and Schäfer, *Geniza-Fragmente zur Hekhalot-Literatur* (1984).

On Merkabah mysticism and Hekhalot literature see §32.V.2 Appendix on 3 Enoch, where full bibliographies are given. Of the works there listed note the following:
(a) On the Great Séance: Smith, in Altmann, *Biblical and Other Studies* (1963), pp. 144–6; Scholem, *Jewish Gnosticism* (²1965), pp. 9–13; Schiffmann, AJS Review 1 (1976), pp. 268–82; Alexander, JJS 28 (1977), pp. 169 73; Gruenwald, *Apocalyptic and Merkavah Mysticism* (1980), pp. 160–7; Schlüter, FJB 10 (1982), pp. 65–109. Add S. Lieberman, 'The Knowledge of Halakha by [sic] the Author (or Authors) of the Heikhaloth', in Gruenwald, *Apocalyptic and Merkavah Mysticism*, pp. 241–4; P. S. Alexander, *Textual Sources for the Study of Judaism* (1984), pp. 120–5 ['*Heikhalot Rabbati* 15:1–22:2. The Ascent to God's Heavenly Throne'].
(b) On the Šar ha-Panim: Schäfer, FJB 6 (1978), pp. 107–45. Add: M. Gaster, *Studies and Texts* (1925–28), I pp. 332–6; III pp. 91–3.
(c) Keter Nora / Ḥotam Gadol: Schäfer, FJB 5 (1977), pp. 94–9.

For other examples of theurgy in the Hekhalot texts see Schäfer, *Synopse* §§ 418–21, 422–4, 498–517, 825–31; Schäfer, *Geniza-Fragmente* nos. 4, 6, 13, 14, 15, 16, 17, 19. And in general consult Scholem, *Jewish Gnosticism* (²1965), pp. 75–83, and Cohen, *The Shi'ur Qomah* (1983).

Many parallels exist between Greek theurgy (as found, e.g., in the Chaldaean Oracles) and the theurgy of the Merkabah mystics. Cf. Porphyry's description of the séance at the Iseum which Plotinus attended (*Vita Plotini* 10) with the account of the Great Séance in Hekhalot Rabbati.

On Greek theurgy see:
Hopfner, T., 'Theurgy', RE VIA.1 (1936), cols. 258–70.
Eitrem, S., 'La théurgie chez les néo-platoniciens et les papyrus magiques', Symbolae Osloenses 22 (1942), pp. 49–79.
Dodds, E. R., *The Greeks and the Irrational* (1966), pp. 283–311 ['Theurgy'].
Lewy, H., *Chaldaean Oracles and Theurgy*, new ed. by M. Tardieu (1978).

There are interesting parallels between the Great Séance and the so-called 'Mithras Liturgy' (PGM IV 475–830), on which see the bibliography above under 4. 'Jewish Magical Texts Preserved in Greek'. Note in particular Smith, in Altmann, *Biblical and Other Studies* (1963), pp. 158–60. Comparison with Gnostic texts is also instructive, e.g. Origen's account of the teachings of the Ophians (*Contra Celsum* vi 24–38), on which see Alexander, JJS 35 (1984), pp. 2–3. For apocalyptic antecedents to the Great Séance see M. Dean-Otting, *Heavenly Journeys: A Study of the Motif in Hellenistic Jewish Literature*

(1984). Consult further A. F. Segal, 'Heavenly Ascent in Judaism, Early Christianity and their Environment', in H. Temporini and W. Haase (eds.), ANRW II.23.2 (1980), pp. 1333–94.

6. The Dead Sea Scrolls

(a) 4QCryptic (*4Q186*)

4QCryptic tries to establish a way of discovering a man's inner spiritual natural from two external indicators: (1) the shape of certain parts of his body; and (2) his date of birth and the astrological conditions prevailing then. Strictly speaking the text is not a horoscope, or series of horoscopes, but a piece of astrological physiognomy based on the common astrological doctrine that a person's temper, physical features and luck are determined by the configuration of the heavens at the time of his birth. Cf. the astrological text ridiculed by Hippolytus in *Refutatio* 4.15–27. The mixture of physiognomy and astrology is reminiscent of one of the Cairo Genizah physiognomies (Fragment A; see section 7, below).

A proportion of each man's spirit is assigned (on a scale of one to nine) to the 'House of Light' (בית האור) and to the 'Pit of Darkness' (בור החושך). These two expressions have no obvious astrological reference, but recall the 'Fountain of Light' (מעין אור) and the 'Source of Darkness' (מקור חושך) in the Sermon on the Two Spirits (*1QS* III), the purpose of which, according to its preamble, was to instruct the Sons of Light regarding 'the nature of all the children of men (בתולדות כול בני איש),[31] according to the kind of spirit which they possess, the signs identifying their works during their life-time, their visitation for chastisement, and the time of their reward'. The 'signs' (אותות) actually mentioned in the body of the sermon are virtues and vices, such as humility, charity, greed, deceit. However, it is not impossible that at some point in the history of the Qumran sect someone tried to set out physiognomic criteria for deciding who belonged to the two spirits. The leadership could have used such criteria to determine who was allowed to join the sect, or to assign rank within it (though no hint of this can be found in the Manual of Discipline).[32]

It is hard to know what to make of the fact that the text is written in code. Obviously someone did not want it to be readily intelligible. This could be consonant with the theory that physiognomy was applied as a

31. The language echoes Gen. 5:1, זה ספר תולדות אדם, a verse given physiognomic significance by the mediaeval Jewish physiognomists. See section 7 below, and G. G. Scholem in *Sefer Assaf* (1953), pp. 477–9.

32. Apart from 4QMess ar (on which see below), no hints of physiognomy appear elsewhere in the Dead Sea scrolls. The description of Sarah's beauty in *1QapGen* XIX-XX is very general. Note, however, that her slender fingers are praised. 4QCryptic III regards short, fat fingers as a negative feature.

secret test within the community (hence the silence about it in the Manual of Discipline). On the other hand the scribe of 4QCryptic may have employed cipher because he was aware that its contents were somehow contrary to the teachings of the sect. It is really not possible to decide between these alternatives.[33]

(b) 4QMess ar

This fragmentary Aramaic text describes the wonderful career of someone referred to as 'the elect of God' (I 10). At his birth he will have certain distinguishing marks on his body, two of which are of particular interest: (1) טלופחין (I 2) = 'lentils'. Gaster suggested the reference is to freckles, which are called 'lentils' in Greek and Latin.[34] 'Lentils' (Aram. טלופחא; Heb. עדשה) are mentioned a number of times in later Rabbinic physiognomies (see section 7 below).[35] (2) שומן (I 3) = 'moles'. שומא = 'mole' in the Talmud, and there seems to be no good reason for not giving the word this sense here too. The medieval Jewish physiognomies sometimes regard moles in a positive light.[36] 4QMess ar has no astrological content, and so can hardly be the horoscope of the Messiah (or of anyone else for that matter). Nor, strictly speaking, is it physiognomy, since it does not relate physical appearance to moral character or luck. The physical marks mentioned are probably intended as 'signs' by which the wondrous child would be identified. Cf. the description of the antichrist's physical appearance in Apoc. Elijah 3:14–18. However, the fact that these particular features are singled out as significant throws indirect light on physiognomy at Qumran. Cf. below, p. 465.

(c) 4QBrontologion

Milik describes this unpublished text as follows: 'Two fragmentary columns from Cave IV give the signs of the Zodiac distributed over the days of the month. "On the 13th and 14th (of the month of Tebet)", we read, "Cancer ..." Then follow predictions that can be drawn from thunder. "If it thunders in the sign of the Twins, terror and distress caused by foreigners and by ..."'[37] He correctly classifies the text as a

33. There are a number of Greek magical texts in code, but so far they have resisted decipherment. See G. M. Parassoglu, 'Artificial Scripts and Magical Papyri', Studia Papyrologica 13 (1974), pp. 57–60.

34. T. H. Gaster, *The Dead Sea Scriptures* (³1976), pp. 448, 475. The Greek is φακός (e.g. Plutarch, *Mor.* 563A, 800E), the Latin 'lenticula' (e.g. Pliny, *N.H.* xxvi 7).

35. E.g. Sefer Re'iyyat ha-Yadayim (ed. Scholem, *Sefer Assaf*, p. 491): ומן אותות בטופרין אית זמנין, דנהרין בהו; Zohar, *Yitro*, II 76a: יש דומות לעדשה ויש דומות לזרע קשואין, ואינן שקיעין כהאי ממסרא על לוחא ;ככבין חוורין דקיקין, ואלין אינון כתולדה דטלופחין. See further Scholem, *Sefer Assaf*, p. 491, footnote 41.

36. E.g. Sefer Re'iyyat ha-Yadayim (ed. Scholem, *Sefer Assaf*, p. 489): וכל אשר בכף ידו ג אותיות שחורות או שומות יהיה לו מזל טוב וגדולה ועושר וכבוד הרבה. Note also Cairo Genizah Fragment A: B/1, 11–12 (ed. Gruenwald p. 313). On שומא in the Talmud see J. Preuss, *Biblical and Talmudic Medicine* (1978), pp. 200–1.

37. J. T. Milik, *Ten Years of Discovery in the Wilderness of Judaea* (1959), p. 42.

brontologion, a type of composition well attested in Byzantine literature. Jews, like their neighbours, believed in prodigies, omens and signs. Josephus (*B.J.* vi 5, 3–4 (288–315)) gives a long list of portents which foretold the destruction of the Temple in A.D. 70, and references to omens are common in apocalyptic scenarios of the end-time.[38] The interpretation of prodigies required skill: Josephus (*B.J.* vi 5, 3 (291)) regards it as a task belonging to the province of the sacred scribes (ὁ τοῖς μὲν ἀπείροις ἀγαθὸν ἐδόκει, τοῖς δ' ἱερογραμματεῦσι πρὸς τὸν ἀποβεβηκόπων εὐθέως ἐκρίθη). The Qumran text, if Milik's report is accurate, represents an attempt to systematize augury, and to raise it to a scientific level by linking it with the highest of the occult 'sciences', astrology.

Bibliography

For magic at Qumran, the exorcisms described in *1QapGen* 20:16–31 and in the Prayer of Nabonidus (*4QPrNab*) are of considerable interest. See A. Dupont-Sommer, 'Exorcismes et guérisons dans les écrits de Qoumrân', SVT 7 (1960), pp. 246–61.

On Qumran in general and on 4QCryptic and 4QMess ar in particular, see below, pp. 464–6.

For Jewish physiognomy see section 7, 'Rabbinic Physiognomy'; and for Jewish astrology, section 8, 'Treatise of Shem'.

Milik compares 4QBrontologion with the brontologion attributed to Zoroaster in Geoponica I 10 (cf. J. Bidez and F. Cumont, *Les mages hellénisés* II [1938], pp. 182–3). For other examples of this genre see *Catalogus Codicum Astrologorum Graecorum* (= CCAG) III (1901), ed. A. Martini and D. Bassi, pp. 50–2; CCAG IV (1903), ed. D. Bassi *et al.*, pp. 128–31 (ἐὰν ἐν τῷ Κριῷ βροντήσῃ ἀπὸ τῆς ἀνατολῆς κτλ.); CCAG VII (1908), ed. F. Boll, pp. 163–7; CCAG VIII.3 (1912), ed. P. Boudreaux, pp. 122–5; 168–9 (Βροντολόγιον Δαβὶδ τοῦ προφήτου); 169–71; 193–7; CCAG IX.2 (1953), ed. S. Weinstock, pp. 120–3; CCAG X (1924), ed. A. Delatte, pp. 58–9 (ταύτας τὰς ἡμέρας ἐφανέρωσεν ὁ Θεὸς Ἐσδρᾷ τῷ ἱερεῖ κτλ.); 60–2; 140–2; CCAG XI.1 (1932), ed. C. O. Zuretti, pp. 145–6; 155–7. Note also the medieval Hebrew texts described by M. Steinschneider, *Die hebräischen Übersetzungen des Mittelalters und die Juden als Dolmetscher* (1893), pp. 905–6. Further A. Bouché-Leclercq, *Histoire de la divination dans l'antiquité* I (1879), pp. 198 ff.; K. Krumbacher, *Geschichte der byzantinischen Literatur* (²1897), p. 603; P. Händel, 'Prodigium', RE XXIII.2 (1959), cols. 2283, 2296; K. Berger, 'Hellenistisch-heidnische Prodigen und die Vorzeichen in der jüdischen und christlichen Apokalyptik', in H. Temporini and W. Haase (eds.), ANRW II.23.2 (1980), pp. 1428–96; S. J. Scherrer, 'Signs and Wonders in the Imperial Cult', JBL 103 (1984), pp. 599–610.

7. Rabbinic Physiognomy

Physiognomy was studied by the medieval Qabbalists; the Zohar, for example, treats it as one of the 'secrets of the Torah', and devotes considerable space to elucidating it.[39] Rabbinic interest in the subject,

---

38. See e.g. 4 Ezra 4:51–5:13; 6:20–26; Mk. 13:1–37; Rev. 6:12–14. Note also the late Hebrew text 'The Signs of the Messiah', Jellinek, *Bet ha-Midrasch* II, pp. 58–63.

39. See Zohar, *Yitro*, II 70a–78a; II 272a–275a (*Raza deRazin*); Tiqqunei Zohar, no. 70 (towards end).

however, began well before the middle ages, perhaps as early as the Talmudic era. Manuscripts exist containing physiognomic treatises which emanated from the circles of the Merkabah mystics. These, like the Neopythagoreans and (possibly) the Qumran covenanters, may have employed physiognomic criteria to determine who should be allowed to join their conventicles.[40] Or physiognomy may simply have been part of the esoteric lore studied in the conventicles. Like their cosmological speculations, the study of physiognomy may evince an interest on the part of the mystics in 'scientific' subjects. Gruenwald has argued that there are significant correspondences between the later Rabbinic physiognomies and the Dead Sea texts (4QCryptic and 4QMess ar) which point to direct continuity of tradition.[41] The parallelism is perhaps not quite strong enough to make such a conclusion inevitable. However, the Dead Sea discoveries have proved beyond any doubt that Jews were involved in speculation on physiognomy at a very early date. In some of the Rabbinic texts (as in 4QCryptic) the physiognomy is linked with astrology; in others, astrology is totally absent and a purely intuitive approach is adopted. The following texts are noteworthy:

(a) 'The Physiognomy of R. Ishmael' (הכרת פנים לר' ישמעאל). This opens: 'This is the book of the generations of men (תולדות אדם), to distinguish between the righteous and the wicked.' However, it is not concerned so much with men's inner moral natures as with their luck, with whether they will be fortunate or unfortunate. Two methods are used to discover a man's fate: (1) metoposcopy (reading the lines on his forehead); and (2) chiromancy (palmistry). The preamble classifies physiognomy as esoteric doctrine which should not be disclosed to unsuitable people.

(b) 'The Book of the Reading of the Hands by an Indian Sage' (ספר ראיית הידים מאחד מחכמי הודו) is largely concerned with palmistry, but it also considers the significance of other parts of the body (including the testicles). The physical indicators are taken to reveal luck, rather than inner character.

(c) 'The Secret of Physiognomy' (סוד הכרת פנים) is very brief and deals mainly with the theory of physiognomy. It does, however, touch on the relationship between certain specific physical features (such as the shape of the eyes) and a man's character and physical qualities.

(d) Genizah Fragment A (T.-S. K 21.88) contains general physiognomy, chiromancy and metoposcopy, in which physical attributes are related both to moral character and destiny. Combined

---

40. Lewin, 'Oṣar ha-Ge'onim IV, Ḥagigah, Responsa section p. 12; P. S. Alexander, 'The Historical Setting of the Hebrew Book of Enoch', JJS 28 (1977), pp. 168–9.

41. I. Gruenwald, 'Further Jewish Physiognomic and Chiromantic Fragments', Tarbiz 40 (1970–1), pp. 304–6 [Hebrew]. See above footnotes 35 and 36.

368   §32. *Jewish Literature in Hebrew or Aramaic*

with this is astrological material in which the day on which a man is born, and the astrological conditions prevalent then, are related to his physical characteristics and his fate. From the way the physiognomy and the astrology alternate, without any direct connection, Gruenwald argues that the text has drawn on two quite distinct sources.

(e) Genizah Fragment B (T.-S. NS 252.2) deduces a man's luck and fate from the shape of different parts of his body, including his testicles. It overlaps partially with Sefer Re'iyyat ha-Yadayim, above (b).

(f) Genizah Fragment C (T.-S. K 21.95L). This contains 3 En. 1:1–2 (Schäfer §§ 1–2) + 3 En. 43:2–44:3 (Schäfer §§ 61–2) + a fragment of astrological physiognomy in which the time of a man's birth and the astrological influences dominant then are linked with his physical appearance and his fate. The fragment opens with the words סימן טוב, 'a good omen', and at 2b/3 it quotes Gen. 5:1, 'This is the book of the generations of men etc.', perhaps to indicate the beginning of a new section. Cf. text (a) above.

Bibliography

Texts: (a) 'Physiognomy of R. Ishmael': see G. G. Scholem, 'הכרת פנים וסדרי שרטוטין', in M. D. Cassuto, J. Klausner and J. Guttmann (eds.), *Sefer Assaf* (1953), pp. 480–7; German translation Scholem, 'Ein Fragment zur Physiognomik und Chiromantik aus der Tradition der spätantiken jüdischen Esoterik', in *Liber Amicorum: Studies in Honour of C. J. Bleeker* (1969), pp. 182–6. (b) 'Book of the Reading of the Hands by an Indian Sage': see Scholem, *Sefer Assaf*, pp. 488–92. (c) 'The Secret of Physiognomy': see Scholem, *Sefer Assaf*, pp. 492–5. (d) Genizah Fragment A: see I. Gruenwald, 'Further Jewish Physiognomic and Chiromantic Fragments', Tarbiz 40 (1970–1), pp. 306–17. (e) Genizah Fragment B: see Gruenwald, Tarbiz 40 (1970–1), pp. 317–19. (f) Genizah Fragment C: see P. Schäfer, *Geniza-Fragmente zur Hekhalot-Literatur* (1984), no. 12 (pp. 135–9).

Scholem, *Sefer Assaf*, pp. 45–95, *Festschrift Bleeker*, pp. 175–93, and Gruenwald, Tarbiz 40 (1970–1), pp. 301–19, give good general accounts (in Hebrew) of early Rabbinic physiognomy.

See further:
Scholem, G. G., 'Chiromancy', Enc. Jud. V (1971), cols. 477–9.
Gruenwald, I., *Apocalyptic and Merkavah Mysticism* (1980), pp. 218–24 ['Physiognomy Chiromancy and Metoposcopy'].

Note also the chapter on physiognomy (הכרת הפרצוף) in the Hebrew version of the *Secretum Secretorum* published by M. Gaster, *Studies and Texts* (1925–28) II, pp. 799–803; III, pp. 268–72. Further on the *Secretum Secretorum*: M. Manzalaoui, 'The pseudo-Aristotelian *Kitāb Sirr al-Asrār*', Oriens 23–24 (1974), pp. 147–257.
The standard collection of Greek and Latin physiognomic texts is R. Förster, *Scriptores Physiognomici Graeci et Latini* I-II (1893). Note also the text and translation of Pseudo-Aristotle, *Physiognomica*, in W. S. Hett, *Aristotle: Minor Works*, Loeb Classical Library (1936). *Catalogus Codicum Astrologorum Graecorum* VII (1908), ed. F. Boll, pp. 236–44, prints the text of a treatise of chiromancy from the Byzantine era.

On ancient physiognomy in general see:
Förster, R., *Die Physiognomik der Griechen* (1884).
Förster, R., *De Polemonis Physiognomicis dissertatio* (1886).

Förster, R., *Quaestiones physiognomicae* (1890).
Gundel, W., 'Individualschicksal, Menschtypen und Berufe in der antiken Astrologie', Jahrbuch der Charakterologie 4 (1927), pp. 135–93.
Schmidt, J., 'Physiognomik', RE XX.1 (1941), cols. 1064–74.
Evans, E. C., *Physiognomics in the Ancient World*, Transactions of the American Philosophical Society 59/5 (1969).

8. Treatise of Shem (= TrShem)

This Syriac astrological tract, preserved in a unique fifteenth century manuscript in the John Rylands University Library, Manchester, contains prognostications regarding crops, political events, personal health, and climate, deduced from the constellation in which the year begins (lit. 'is born'). Mingana, its first editor, suggested (very tentatively) that it was composed by a Jew in Palestine, or in Egypt, in the aftermath of the disastrous first and second Jewish wars against Rome. Charlesworth, however, argues very emphatically that it originated in Alexandria in the late twenties B.C., shortly after the battle of Actium, that the author was a Jew, and that the original language was Jewish Aramaic. An Egyptian provenance for the document is a reasonable assumption in view of its constant predictions about the Nile-flood, and its frequent references to Egypt and Alexandria.[42] The date, however, is much more problematic. Charlesworth's case is very far from proved. His argument depends on identifying a number of precise historical allusions in the text. For example, 3:6, 'The Romans [and the Parthian]s will make severe wars on each other', is taken by him as pointing to a date shortly after Antony's victory over the Armenians, Medes and Parthians, and the celebration of his triumph in Alexandria (not in Rome as tradition demanded) in the fall of 34 B.C. But there is a lacuna in the text: Charlesworth supplies *Parthwaye* on the grounds that 'the Romans fought ... the Parthians'. *Rhomaye*, however, can just as easily refer to the Byzantines as the Romans, and *Parsaye*, 'Persians', is as satisfactory as supplement as *Parthwaye*. Charlesworth takes 12:4, 'Egypt (will rule) over Palestine', as an allusion to Antony's grant of Palestine to Cleopatra in 34 B.C., but once again the text is problematic. Though there is no lacuna, a verb has evidently gone astray. There seem to be no good grounds for assuming, as Charlesworth does, 7:19, that 'There will be in Galilee a severe earthquake', refers precisely to the earthquake which Josephus says struck Palestine in 31 B.C. (*B.J.* i 19, 3 (370); *Ant.* xv 5, 2 (121)). The fact is that none of the alleged historical

---

42. The Coptic and Arabic almanacs published by 'Abd al-Masiḥ (Les Cahiers Coptes, 1956 no. 10, pp. 5–9), both written (one assumes) in Egypt, show a similar interest in the Nile-flood.

allusions is anywhere near clear enough to make the dating certain. It should be remembered that TrShem is not an apocalypse, in which cryptic references are made to contemporary events, which we might still have a chance of decoding. It is an almanac, and it is the very nature of such literature to be extremely vague.[43]

There is not much religious content in TrShem, and little beyond its title to suggest that it might be of Jewish origin. The expression 'the living God' occurs twice (8:4 and 12:9), but this could have been used by either a Jew or a Christian (cf. Deut. 5:26; 1 Sam. 17:26; Matt. 26:63; Rom. 9:26). Charlesworth translates 1:8, 'From Passover (*Pesḥa*) [until the New Year] produce will have a blight.'[44] But *Pesḥa* can be 'Easter' as well as 'Passover', so a Christian interpretation of the passage cannot be ruled out. There are no clear examples of Jewish almanacs of precisely the type of TrShem, but that Jews indulged in the kind of speculation that it contains is shown by the physiognomic Fragment A from the Cairo Genizah discussed above (section 7). TrShem 2:1 states: 'If the year begins in Taurus, everyone whose name contans a Beth, or Yudh, or Kaph will become ill.' Cf. with this Cairo Genizah Fragment A: A/2, 9–12 (ed. Gruenwald p. 310): 'He who is born on the third day of the week in the constellation Scorpio or Leo . . .

43. S. Brock, JJS 35 (1984), p. 204, comments: 'Attention should be paid to the mention of rice at 5:3, by implication a staple crop: this is hardly appropriate for a document allegedly written in Egypt in the late first century B.C.E., for rice seems only to have been imported into Roman and Byzantine Egypt, and not cultivated.' It is not, however, absolutely clear that the text refers to the *growing* of rice (Syriac *ruza* = Hebrew אורז, Jewish Aramaic אורזא/ארוזא/אוריזא, Greek ὄρυζα). It simply states that 'wheat and rice and dried peas will be expensive'. It is also a moot point whether or not rice was grown in Egypt. The *loci classici* on the subject in Pliny probably do imply that *Indian* rice was imported, but they also seem to suggest that Pliny recognizes a *local* variety of rice in Egypt; see *N.H.* xviii 93: 'adiciuntur his genera bromos et tragos, externa omnia, ab oriente invectae oryzae similia. tiphe et ipsa eiusdem est generis, ex qua fit in nostro orbe oryze'; xviii 81: 'arinca Galliarum propria copiosa et Italiae est; Aegypto autem ac Syriae Ciliciaeque et Asiae ac Graeciae peculiares zea, <olyra>, <oryza> <sive> tiphe' (Rackham's text in the Loeb Classical Library edition). Strabo xv 1, 18 says that rice was grown in Babylonia and lower Syria (φύεσθαι δὲ καὶ [sc. τὴν ὄρυζαν] ἐν τῇ Βακτριανῇ καὶ Βαβυλωνίᾳ καὶ Σουσίδι, καὶ ἡ κάτω δὲ Συρία φύει), a statement corroborated by Rabbinic sources: see e.g. mSheb. 2:10, 'One may flood a rice-field in the Sabbatical Year. R. Simeon says: But one may not cut [the rice-plants]' (,ממרסין באורז בשביעית ר' שמעון אומר, אבל אין מכסחין). See further Stadler, 'Reis', RE IA.1 (1914), cols. 517–19; A. C. Johnson, in Tenney Frank (ed.), *An Economic Survey of Ancient Rome* II (1936), p. 2; F. M. Heichelheim, in Frank, *Economic Survey* IV (1938), p. 129; *Encyclopaedia Talmudit* I (1951), pp. 176–8 (*sub* אורז); V. Hehn, *Cultivated Plants and Domesticated Animals in their Migration from Asia to Europe* (new ed. 1976), pp. 379–83.

44. Charlesworth notes *ad loc.*: 'A lacuna of 50 mm, room for approximately 14 letters', and he proposes restoring [*'admt lwt ryš š]nt*'. This implies -*nt*' is visible after the gap, which would certainly suggest that *šnt*' was the final word. These letters, however, are not visible. What can be seen is probably to be read as -*ṭ*', which suggests the restoration *'dm*' *lpntyqwsṭ*', '(from Easter) to Pentecost'. This makes rather better agricultural sense.

will at the age of nineteen marry a woman whose name begins with He, Yod.'

Bibliography

S. Brock, JJS 35 (1984), p. 203, rightly assigns TrShem to the genre of astrological almanac known as a 'Dodekaeteris Chaldaica', many examples of which survive in Greek, Latin, Syriac, Coptic and Arabic. Note in particular *Catalogus Codicum Astrologorum Graecorum* (= CCAG) VI (1903), ed. G. Kroll, p. 45, Cod. 4 (= Vindobon. gr. 262), fols. 158–62; and CCAG XI.1 (1932), ed. C. O. Zuretti, pp. 159–64. Both these texts cast their predictions, like TrShem, in the form: ἐὰν γεννᾶται ἐν Κριῷ ὁ χρόνος κτλ. On the second, Zuretti comments: 'Haec est "Dodekaeteris Chaldaica" recentior, fortasse ex Arabico vel Persico exemplare versa.' For other related materials see: (a) Greek: CCAG II (1900), ed. F. Boll *et al.*, pp. 144–52 (Boll demonstrates, pp. 139–44, that the first of the two dodekaeterides printed here was written in Syria in the time of Augustus); CCAG V.1 (1904), ed. F. Cumont and F. Boll, pp. 172–9, 241–2;: CCAG IX.2 (1953), ed. S. Weinstock, pp. 170–5; Geoponica I 12 (ed. Beckh, Teubner [1895], p. 21; cf. J. Bidez and F. Cumont, *Les mages hellénisés* II [1938], pp. 183–7). (b) Latin: *Revelatio Esdrae de qualitatibus anni*; see D. A. Fiensy, 'Revelation of Ezra', in Charlesworth, OTP I, pp. 601–64. (c) Syriac: Rylands Syriac 44, fols. 74b–81b (immediately before the text of TrShem!); Mingana 266, fols. 4–18b (Mingana, *Catalogue* I [1933], cols. 524–5); BL Add. 14,173, fol. 164b (Wright, *Catalogue* I [1870], p. 152 = CCCCXXXVII/6); E. A. W. Budge, *Syrian Anatomy, Pathology and Therapeutics, or 'The Book of Medicines'* II (1913), pp. 522–3 ('If the year is born in the sign of the Ram etc.'). Further G. Furlani, 'Astrologisches aus syrischen Handschriften', ZDMG 75 (1921), pp. 122–8; A. Baumstark, *Geschichte der syrischen Literatur* (1922), p. 352. (d) Coptic: Y. 'Abd al-Masiḥ, 'A Fragmentary Farmer's Almanac', Les Cahiers Coptes, 1956 no. 10, pp. 5–9. 'Abd al-Masiḥ lists other Coptic examples. (e) Arabic: 'The Vision of Daniel', ed. 'Abd al-Masiḥ, *op. cit.* Further, G. Graf, *Geschichte der christlichen arabischen Literatur* I (1944), p. 216.

The *locus classicus* on the dodekaeteris Chaldaica is Censorinus, *de Die Nat.* xviii 6–7: 'proxima est hanc magnitudinem quae vocatur δωδεκαετερίς ex annis vertentibus duodecim. huic anno Chaldaico nomen est, quem genethliaci non ad solis lunaeque cursus, sed ad observationes alias habent adcommodatum, quod in eo dicunt tempestates frugumque proventus ac sterilitates, item morbos salubritatesque circumire.' Cf. Manilius, *Astron.* 3.510–59. Further A. Bouché-Leclercq, *L'astrologie grecque* (1899), pp. 489–91; F. Boll, *Sphaera* (1903), pp. 328 ff.; Boll, 'Dodekaeteris', RE V.1 (1903), cols. 1254–5; J. Bidez and F. Cumont, *Les mages hellénisés* I (1938), pp. 122–3; W. Gundel and H. Gundel, *Astrologoumena: Die astrologische Literatur in der Antike und ihre Geschichte*, Sudhoffs Archiv, Beiheft 6 (1966), p. 49.

The text of TrShem is edited by A. Mingana in 'Some Early Judaeo-Christian Documents in the John Rylands Library', BJRL 4 (1917–18), pp. 59–118. Mingana gives also an English version and a brief introduction. For introduction, translation and commentary see J. H. Charlesworth, 'Treatise of Shem', in Charlesworth, OTP I, pp. 473–80.

Further:

Charlesworth, J. H., PMR (1976), pp. 182–4 ['Treatise of Shem'].

Charlesworth, J. H., 'Rylands MS 44 and a New Addition to the Pseudepigrapha: The Treatise of Shem Discussed and Translated', BJRL 60 (1977–78), pp. 376–403.

In general on Jewish astrology see:

Steinschneider, M., *Die hebräischen Übersetzungen des Mittelalters und die Juden als Dolmetscher* (1893), *passim*, esp. pp. 3–4, 525–7, 599–604, 666, 846–7, 856–9.

Rosin, D., 'Die Religionsphilosophie Abraham ibn Esra's', MGWJ 42 (1898), pp. 247–52, 305–15, 345–62, 394–407.

Blau, L., and Kohler, K., 'Astrology', JE II (1902), pp. 241–5.
Gaster, M., 'The Wisdom of the Chaldeans: An Old Hebrew Astrological Text', in Gaster, *Studies and Texts* (1925–28) I, pp. 338–55, III, pp. 104–8.
Marx, A., 'The Correspondence between the Rabbis of Southern France and Maimonides about Astrology', HUCA 3 (1926), pp. 311–58.
Levy, R., *Astrological Works of Abraham ibn Ezra* (1928).
Altmann, A., 'Astrology', Enc. Jud. III (1971), cols. 788–95.
Kennedy, E. S., and Pingree, D., *The Astrological History of Máosháo'alláoh* (1971).
Charlesworth, J. H., 'Jewish Astrology in the Talmud, Pseudepigrapha, the Dead Sea Scrolls, and Early Palestinian Synagogues', HThR 70 (1977), pp. 183–200.

For introduction to ancient astrology see:
Bouché-Leclercq, A., *L'astrologie grecque* (1899).
Boll, F., *Sphaera* (1903).
Cumont, F., *Astrology and Religion among the Greeks and Romans* (1912).
Boll, F., Bezold, C., and Gundel, W., *Sternglaube und Sterndeutung: Die Geschichte und das Wesen der Astrologie* ([1]1918; [7]1977).
Gundel, W., *Dekane und Dekansternbilder* (1936).
Gundel, W., 'Astrologie', RAC I (1950), cols. 817–31.
Festugière, A.-J., *Le révélation d'Hermès Trismégiste* I ([2]1950) ['L'astrologie et les sciences occultes'].
Cramer, F. H., *Astrology in Roman Law and Politics* (1954).
Neugebauer, O., and Van Hoesen, H. B., *Greek Horoscopes* (1959).
Gundel, W., and Gundel, H. G., *Astrologoumena: Die astrologische Literatur in der Antike und ihre Geschichte*, Sudhoffs Archiv, Beiheft 6 (1966).
Gundel, H. G., *Weltbild und Astrologie in den griechischen Zauberpapyri* (1968).
Neugebauer, O., and Parker, R. A., *Egyptian Astronomical Texts* I-III (1960–69).
Gundel, H., and Böker, R., 'Zodiakos', RE XA (1972), cols. 462–709.
Goold, G. P., *Manilius Astronomica*, Loeb Classical Library (1977), pp. xvi-cxxii. A good, brief introduction.

9. Testament of Solomon (= TSol)

The textual history of the Greek Testament of Solomon, like that of so much popular magical literature, is very complex. The sixteen or so manuscripts so far identified contain at least four different recensions of the text. The majority of manuscripts classify the work as a 'testament' (διαθήκη), and in testament-style it is narrated by Solomon in the first person. Solomon tells how, using a magical ring (δακτυλίδιον) given to him by the archangel Michael, he called up various demons and compelled them to assist him in building the Temple. TSol has two basic components: (1) a haggadic framework which recounts, in the manner of a folktale, how Solomon forced the demons to help him; and (2) a detailed demonology giving precise descriptions of the various demons and their powers. McCown held that the haggadic framework once existed as an independent work, prior to the insertion of the detailed demonology. He believed his manuscript D (Dionysius Monastery, Mt. Athos no. 132) contains a reworking of that original haggadic narrative. However, it is equally possible that manuscript D was created by extracting the haggadah from a full version of TSol and adding embellishments.[45] Whatever the relationship between the haggadah and the demonology, TSol in its full forms must be treated as a serious work on magic; it is a mistake to read it simply as a folktale or literature of entertainment. Its seriousness is indicated by the care with which the physical appearance of each demon is described, its powers defined, and the angel who 'inhibits' it identified. There is a strong astrological element in TSol: both demons and men 'reside' in a star, a sign of the Zodiac, or a phase of the moon, and, as McCown notes, 'mortals seem to be particularly liable to injury from demons who are συναστροί with them, that is, belong to the same star.'[46] Chap. 18 contains an important list of the thirty-six decans who cause sickness to various parts of the body. The surrounding haggadic material, some of which can be paralleled in Rabbinic sources,[47] has been used simply as a means of systematizing, and contextualizing, demonological lore of great practical use to magicians. It serves precisely the same purpose as the seven-heaven schema in ShR (see section 1 above). TSol in its full forms was intended as a sort of encyclopaedia of demonology.

TSol's complex textual history naturally makes it difficult to date. The reference to 26:5 in the Dialogue of Timothy and Aquila shows that it was current in some form around A.D. 400.[48] Part of the section on the *decani* (18:34–40) is extant in a sixth century papyrus fragment (Pap. gr. Vindobon. 330), but little can be deduced from this as to the date of the work as a whole because the list of the decans is the one part sure to have circulated independently, before its incorporation into TSol.[49] McCown argued that the basic haggadic narrative (which he believed once formed a separate little Jewish tract) may be as early as the first century A.D. However, the archetype of all the full versions (incorporating the demonology) cannot have been put together before the early third century A.D. He points to clear linguistic and

45. As a parallel to the second possibility M. R. James (JTSt 24 [1923] p. 468) cites 'the treatment meted out to the *Ascension of Isaiah* by the author of the "Greek Legend of Isaiah", who has cut about and rearranged the old text, with large omissions, and put in matter from the Epiphanian Lives, producing a result very much like D.'

46. *Testament of Solomon* (1922), p. 46.

47. See L. Ginzberg, *Legends of the Jews* VI (1928), p. 292 note 54. Note in particular bGit. 68a–68b.

48. *The Dialogue of Timothy and Aquila*, ed. F. C. Conybeare (1898), p. 70: ὁ Χριστιανὸς εἶπε... γνῶθι δὲ 'Ιουδαῖε, ὅτι προσεκύνησεν [sc. Σολομῶν], καὶ ἀκρίδα ἔσφαξεν τοῖς γλυπτοῖς. ὁ 'Ιουδαῖος εἶπεν; οὐκ ἔσφαξεν ἀλλὰ ἔθλασεν ἐν τῇ χειρὶ ἀκουσίως. ταῦτα δὲ οὐ περιέχει ἡ βίβλος τῶν βασιλέων, ἀλλ' ἐν τῇ διαθήκῃ αὐτοῦ γέγραπται. ὁ Χριστιανὸς εἶπεν; ἐν τούτῳ γὰρ ἔστην πιστοποιῶν, ὅτι οὐκ ἐν χειρὶ ἱστοριογράφου ἐφανερώθη τοῦτο, ἀλλ' ἐκ τοῦ στόματος αὐτοῦ τοῦ Σολομῶντος ἐγνώσθη τοῦτου. Cf. TSol 26:5: οὐδὲν ἐνόμισα τῶν ἀκρίδων τὸ αἷμα καὶ ἔλαβον αὐτὰς ὑπὸ τὰς χεῖράς μου καὶ ἔθυσα εἰς τὸ ὄνομα 'Ραφὰν καὶ Μολόχ τοῖς εἰδώλοις.

49. W. Gundel dates the archetype of the list of the decans in TSol 18 to the first century B.C. (*Dekane und Dekansternbilder* [²1969], p. 45).

text-critical evidence that TSol went on being re-worked down to the middle ages (possibly to as late as the twelfth or thirteenth centuries). Allusions to Jesus (15:10 ff.; cf. 11:6; 22:20), and to the Virgin (22:10; cf. 15:10) show that at some point in its history it passed through Christian hands. Its obvious Jewish content led Conybeare to the conclusion that it was originally a Jewish work which had been (only slightly) re-edited by a Christian. It is hard to tell whether or not this was so, or whether a Christian composed the whole but used some Jewish materials. Much of the Jewish colouring of TSol is derived from canonical, or semi-canonical, sources. For example, the section of Asmodeus in chap. 5 is largely dependent on the book of Tobit, which circulated among Jews and Christians alike. These references to Asmodeus may be classified as 'Jewish', but they no more point to a Jewish origin for the work than do the references to King Solomon. In a case such as TSol there is nothing to be gained by trying to demarcate sharply between 'Jewish' and 'Christian' elements, at least as far as the magic is concerned. The eclecticism of early magic has already been well illustrated. TSol, even if not a Jewish work in the forms in which it now lies before us, or even if not based on a Jewish work, clearly contains much Jewish material, and can surely be used to throw light on early Jewish demonology.

TSol is in fluent *Koinē* Greek, and that appears to have been its original language. Evidence for translation from Hebrew or Aramaic is inconclusive.[50] Its provenance is very uncertain. Its closest literary and magical affinities are with Egyptian texts (note, again, chap. 18 on the decans), so Egypt is most probably its place of origin.

Bibliography

The standard edition of the Greek text of TSol is C. C. McCown, *The Testament of Solomon* (1922). Manuscripts not used by McCown have been published by A. Delatte, 'Testament of Solomon', *Anecdota Atheniensia* I = Bibliothèque de la faculté de philosophie et lettres de l'Université de Liège 36 (1927), pp. 211–27 (Paris BN 2011); and by K. Preisendanz, 'Ein Wiener Papyrusfragment zum Testamentum Salomonis', Eos: Commentarii Societatis Philologae Polonorum 48/3 (1956) = *Festschrift Taubenschlag* III, pp. 161–7 (Pap. gr. Vindobonensis 330). An Arabic version of TSol is extant in a seventeenth century Vatican manuscript (Vat. ar. 448, fols. 39–54), on which see G. Graf, *Geschichte der christlichen arabischen Literatur* I (1944), p. 210. According to J. H.

50. M. Gaster, *Studies and Texts* (1925–28), I p. 294, suggests that TSol 13:6 (ms P), τῷ ἀγγέλῳ τοῦ θεοῦ τῷ καλουμένῳ ἀφαρώφ, ὃ ἑρμενεύεται ῥαφαὴλ, points to a mistranslation of Hebrew, but his argument is far from clear. However, his comparison (see p. 309) of the double angelic name here with the double names in the Merkabah texts is to the point. Note in particular the following passage from the Conjuration of the Śar ha-Panim (Schäfer § 628, Oxford 1531): שוב אני קורא לך בי׳ד׳ שמותיך שאתה גלה להם לנביאים וחתים ... וכך פירושם וכינויים ... מפורש אטמון כינוי צצמס ניהו הי הוה... The linguistic correspondence between מפורש/פירוש and ὃ ἑρμενεύεται is striking.

Charlesworth, PMRS, pp. 197, 201, the sixteenth century Karshuni manuscript, Paris BN, fonds syriaque 194, fols. 153a–156b, contains 'a recension of portions of the Testament of Solomon'. However, Graf, *Geschichte* I p. 209, appears to describe precisely the same text as follows: 'Mahnrede Salomons an seinem Sohn Roboam zu einem rechtschaffenen Leben, in der Hss. "Testament" (Gebot, waṣiya) genannt.' He lists several other manuscripts of the same work.

Translations

Conybeare, F. C., 'The Testament of Solomon', JQR 11 (1899), pp. 15–45. This is based on Paris BN, anciens fonds grecs no. 38 (Colbert 4895) = McCown siglum P, as printed in F. F. Fleck, *Wissenschaftliche Reise durch das südliche Deutschland, Italien, Sicilien und Frankreich* II.3 (1837), pp. 111–40; cf. PG CXXII (1889), cols. 1315–58.

Duling, D. C., 'Testament of Solomon', OTP I (1983), pp. 960–87.

Whittaker, M., 'The Testament of Solomon', in H. D. F. Sparks (ed.), *The Apocryphal Old Testament* (1984), pp. 737–51 [only summarizes chaps. 7–18].

The introductions in McCown (pp. 1–136), Conybeare (pp. 1–15), Duling (pp. 935–59), and Whittaker (pp. 733–7) provide general discussion of the problems of TSol. Duling offers the most extensive commentary. See further:

Toy, C. H., 'Solomon, Testament of', JE XI (1905), pp. 448–9.

Frey, J.-B., 'Apocryphes de l'Ancien Testament: Le Testament de Salomon', DBS I (1928) ed. L. Pirot, cols. 455–6.

Preisendanz, K., 'Salomo (Testament)', RE Suppl. VIII (1956), cols. 684–90.

Naldini, M., 'Un frammento esorcistico e il Testamento di Salomone', in *Studia Florentina Alexandro Ronconi sexagenario oblata* (1970), pp. 281–7.

Charlesworth, J. H., PMRS, pp. 197–9 ['Testament of Solomon].

Celsus, quoted in Origen, *Contra Celsum* viii 58, explains the idea of the decans, listed in TSol 18, as follows: 'They [sc. the Egyptians] say that the human body has been put in charge of thirty-six daemons, or ethereal gods of some sort (δαίμονες ἢ θεοί τινες αἰθέριοι), who apportion it between them, that being the number of parts into which it has been divided (though some claim that there are many more). Each daemon is in charge of a different part. And they know the names of the daemons in their own tongue, such as Chnoumen, Chnachoumen, Knat, Sikat, Biou, Erou, Erebiou, Rhamanoor, and Rheianoor, and all the other names which they use in their language. By invoking these they heal the infirmities of the various parts of the body.' Cf. Manilius, *Astronomica* iv 294–407, with G. P. Goold's note in the Loeb Classical Library edition (1977), pp. lxxxv-lxxxvii. On the decans see further:

Bouché-Leclercq, A., *L'astrologie grecque* (1899), pp. 215–35.

Scott, W., *Hermetica* I (1924) pp. 410–20 [Stobaei *Hermetica*, Excerptum VI]; III pp. 363–73.

Festugière, A.-J., *La révélation d'Hermès Trismégiste* I (²1950), pp. 139–43 ['Plantes décaniques'].

Gundel, W., *Dekane und Dekansternbilder* (²1969), esp. pp. 49–62 on TSol.

Gundel, H. G., *Weltbild und Astrologie in den griechischen Zauberpapyri* (1968), pp. 17–24 ['Die Dekane'].

Neugebauer, O., and Parker, R. A., *Egyptian Astronomical Texts* I (1960) ['The Early Decans'], and III (1969) ['Decans, Planets, Constellations and Zodiacs'].

Appendix : Solomon and Magic

In Jewish, Christian and Muslim magic and folklore Solomon is regarded as one of the great magicians, and numerous treatises on magic are attributed to him. The roots of this tradition lie in 1 Kings

4:29–34 (Hebrew 5:9–14), where Solomon's wisdom is said to surpass 'the wisdom of all the people of the east, and all the wisdom of Egypt'. Note how this passage is interpreted in Sap. Sol. 7:15–22. Unquestionably, the most important early reference to Solomon and magic is Josephus, *Ant*. viii 2, 5 (45–49). There, Josephus asserts that Solomon 'composed incantations (ἐπῳδάς) by which illnesses are relieved, and left behind forms of exorcism (τρόπους ἐξορκώσεων) with which those possessed by demons drive them out never to return'. Compare with this Origen on Matt. 26:63 (PG XIII 1757C): 'Quaeret aliquis, si convenit vel daemones adiurare; et qui respicit ad multos, qui talia facere ausi sunt, dicet non sine ratione fiere hoc. Qui autem adspicit Iesum imperantem daemonibus, sed etiam potestatem dantem discipulis suis super omnia daemonia, et ut infirmitates sanarent, dicet quoniam non est secundum potestatem datam a Salvatore, adiurare daemonia; Iudaicum est enim. Hoc etsi aliquando a nostris tale aliquid fiat, simile fit ei, quod a Salomone scriptis adiurationibus solent daemones adiurari. Sed ipsi, qui utuntur adiurationibus illis, aliquoties nec idoneis constitutis libris utuntur; quibusdam autem et de Hebraeo acceptis adiurant daemonia.'

Josephus, in the passage just cited, describes how he saw the Jewish exorcist Eleazar draw out a demon by using a 'ring which had beneath its seal one of the roots prescribed by Solomon' (τὸν δακτύλιον ἔχοντα ὑπὸ τῇ σφραγῖδι ῥίζαν ἐξ ὧν ὑπέδειξε Σαλομών). This is the earliest known reference to the magical ring of Solomon which became so famous in later magic and folktale. As Josephus' language shows, Solomon's ring is not to be distinguished from Solomon's seal, which is also frequently referred to in magic: the ring is a signet ring, bearing a seal-stone. Cf. TSol 1:6, δακτυλίδιον ἔχον σφραγῖδα γλυφῆς λίθου τιμίου. According to bGit. 68b, Solomon's ring was engraved with the Tetragram (עזקתא דחקוק עליה שם ...). However, in Arabic tradition, the hexagram, nowadays popularly known as the 'Magen David', is called 'Solomon's Seal' (see G. G. Scholem, *The Messianic Idea in Judaism and Other Essays* [1971], pp. 257–81; Scholem, *Kabbalah* [1974], pp. 362–8).

The name of Solomon appears frequently in magical papyri and on amulets. Like Moses (see section 4 above), he was respected by magicians of all religious persuasions. PGM IV 850–929 contains a text entitled Σαλομῶνος κατάπτωσις, καὶ ἐπὶ παίδων καὶ τελείων ποιοῦσα. PGM IV 3039f refers to 'the seal which Solomon placed on the tongue of Jeremiah' (section 4(a) above). PGM P17,10 (a Christian text): Ἐκξορκισμὸ⟨ς⟩ Σαλομῶνος πρὸς πᾶν ἀκάθαρτον πν(εῦμ)α; C. Wessely, *Neue griechische Zauberpapyri*, Denkschriften der kaiserl. Akad. d. Wiss., philos.-hist. Cl., Wien, XLII.2 (1894), p. 66, line 29; R. Heim, 'Incantament magica graeca latina', Jahrbücher für classische Philologie, Suppl. 19 (1983), pp. 463–576: No. 56 = 169, 'recede ab illo Gaio Seio, Solomon te sequitur'; 61, Σφραγὶς Σολομῶνος, Σολομών σε διώκει; 62, σφραγὶς Σολομῶνος; 236, 'ter incanto in signo Solomonis et signo domna Artemix'; 237, Σολομωνε. A common type of amulet shows *recto*, under the legend Σολομών, a horseman spearing a recumbent female figure, and *verso*, the inscription Σφραγὶς θεοῦ. This type of amulet was, presumably, invented by Jews: the female figure probably originally represented a Lilith; however, when the amulet became popular among non-Jews, its iconography was doubtless subject to reinterpretation. See G. Schlumberger, 'Amulettes byzantines anciens', REG 5 (1892), pp. 73–93; P. Perdrizet, 'ΣΦΡΑΓΙΣ ΣΟΛΟΜΩΝΟΣ', REG 16 (1903), pp. 42–61; E. Peterson, ΕΙΣ ΘΕΟΣ (1926), pp. 96–109; C. Bonner, *Studies in Magical Amulets* (1950), pp. 208–21; E. R. Goodenough, *Jewish Symbols in the Greco-Roman Period* II (1953), pp. 227–35; A. Delatte and P. Derchain, *Les intailles magiques gréco-égyptiennes* (1964), pp. 261–4; B. Bagatti, 'Altere medaglie di Salomone cavaliere e loro origine', Rivista di Archeologia Christiana 47 (1971), pp. 331–42. An interesting example published by A. Sorlin Dorigny, 'Phylactère Alexandrin', REG 4 (1891), pp. 287–96, bears the extended inscription: Ἄγγελος Ἀραάφ, φεῦγε μεμισημένι, Σολομών σε διώκει. Cf. the amulet from the region of Smyrna published by T. Homolle, Bulletin de Correspondence Hellénique 17 (1893), p. 638: Φεῦγε μισιμένι, Ἀραάφ ὁ ἄγγελος σε διόκι ⟨κι⟩ κὲ Σολομὸν ἀπὸ τοῦ φοροῦντ(ος).

The Bordeaux Pilgrim (A.D. 333–4) contains the following description: 'Interius vero civitati sunt piscinae gemellares, quinque porticos habentes, quae appellantur Betsaida. Ibi aegri multorum annorum sanabantur. Aqua autem habent hae piscinae in modum coccini turbatam. Est ibi et crepta, ubi Solomon daemones torquebat' (ed. P. Geyer, CSEL XXVIII [1898], p. 21).

Solomon is associated with demons three times in the Nag Hammadi texts: On the Origin of the World NH II,5:107; Apocalypse of Adam NH V,5:78–9; Testimony of Truth NH IX,3:70. For interpretation of these passages see S. Giversen, 'Solomon und die Dämonen', in M. Krause (ed.), *Essays on the Nag Hammadi Texts in Honour of Alexander Böhlig* (1973), pp. 16–21.

Nicetas Choniates, de Manuele Comneno iv 7 (PG CXXXIX 489A), tells how an official at the court of Manuel Comnenus, Aaron by name, was caught red-handed with a book of Solomonic magic which could be used to call up the demons: ἑάλω δὲ καὶ βίβλον Σολομώντειον ἀνελίττων ἥτις ἀναπτυσσουμένη τε καὶ διερχομένη κατὰ λεγεῶνας συλλέγει καὶ παρίστησι τὰ δαιμόνια συχνάκις ἀναπυνθανόμενα, ἐφ' ὅτῳ προσκέκληνται· καὶ τὸ ἐπιταττόμενον ἐπισπεύδοντα περατοῦν, καὶ προθύμως δρῶντο τὸ κελευόμενον. The reference may be to one of the versions of the Hygromanteia of Solomon—a work sometimes titled, or subtitled, τὸ κλειδίον τῆς πασῆς τέχνης τῆς ὑγρομαντείας, or ἡ κλεὶς τοῦ Σολομῶντος. Cf. Κλεὶς Μοϋσῆς, PGM XIII 21, 36. See J. Heeg, *Catalogus Codicum Astrologorum Graecorum* VIII.2 (1911), pp. 139–43. The Latin *Clavicula Salomonis*, while not directly translated from any known form of the Hygromanteia, clearly belongs to the same tradition. The Clavicula was one of the most popular books of magic in the middle ages, and was translated into a number of European languages. See S. L. M. Mathers, *The Key of Solomon* (1889). The relationship of the Hebrew *Mafteaḥ Shelomoh* (ed. H. Gollancz, 1914) to the Clavicula and the Hygromanteia is a matter of dispute. See Scholem, *Kabbalah* (1974), pp. 186, 324; contrast Enc. Jud. XI (1971), col. 706.

The Zohar's references to various books of Solomon (Ginzberg, *Legends* VI, p. 302 note 93) should be treated with some reserve, even when quotations are given. It seems the Zohar is not above 'quoting' from non-existent works purely for effect.

Decretum Gelasianum V.8 (ed. E. von Dobschütz, TU XXXVIII/4 [1912], pp. 57–8): 'Scriptura quae appellatur Salomonis Interdictio [v.l. Contradictio] apocrypha. Phylacteria omnia quae non angelorum, ut illi confingunt, sed daemonum magis nominibus conscripta sunt apocrypha.' The mention of the Interdictio in the context of amulets may indicate it was a magical work. M. R. James, *The Lost Apocrypha of the Old Testament* (1920), p. 52, identifies it with *The Dialogue of Salomon and Saturn*.

mPes. 4:9, 'Six things did king Hezekiah: with three they consented and with three they did not consent ... He hid away the Book of Cures (ספר רפואות) and they consented.' Cf. bPes. 56a; bBer. 10b. Maimonides, in his commentary to mPes. 4:9, records a tradition that this Book of Cures had been composed by Solomon. The Yerushalmi version of this mishnah refers, not to a Book of Cures, but to a 'Tablet of Cures'—טבלא של רפואות (ySanh. 18d; yNed. 40a; yPes. 36c bottom line). This is probably the original text of the mishnah: the allusion in the unexpected word טבלא is to the tradition, found e.g. in Syncellus (see below), that Solomon's cures were inscribed on a plaque affixed to the Temple gate. The tradition that Hezekiah tried to suppress Solomon's magic is found in George Syncellus, *Chronographia*, ed. Dindorf, CSHB XX (1829), pp. 376–7: ἦν δὲ καὶ Σολομῶντος γραφή τις ἐγκεκολαμμένη τῇ πύλῃ τοῦ ναοῦ παντὸς νοσήματος ἄκος περιέχουσα, ᾗ προσέχων ὁ λαὸς καὶ τὰς θεραπείας νομιζόμενος ἔχειν κατεφρόνει τοῦ θεοῦ· διὸ καὶ ταύτην Ἐζεκίας ἐξεκόλαψεν ἵνα πάσχοντες τῷ θεῷ προσέχωσιν. The version of this tradition given in the Suda sub Ἐζεκίας (Suidae *Lexicon*, ed. Adler II p. 208) replaces γραφή by βίβλος ἱμάτων. Cf. Michael Glycas, *Annales* II (PG CLVIII 349B); and Josephus, *Hypomnesticum*, c. 74 (PG CVI 89C): εἰσὶ δὲ καὶ ἕτεροι πλεῖστοι λόγοι, οὓς ἀπέκρυψεν ὁ εὐσεβὴς βασιλεὺς Ἐζεκίας... τοὺς δὲ δαιμόνων ἐκφευκτικοὺς καὶ παθῶν ἰατρικοὺς καὶ κλεπτῶν φωρατικοὺς οἱ τῶν Ἰουδαίων ἀγύρται παρ' ἑαυτοῖς φυλάσσουσιν ἐπιμελέστατα. Note the present tense, suggesting direct, personal observation. A. von Gutschmid, *Kleine Schriften* V (1889), p. 618, dates Josephus to the tenth century; F. Diekamp, *Hippolytus von Theben* (1898), pp. 145–51, would place him at the latest around the turn of the eighth or ninth centuries, but perhaps considerably earlier. On the Greek tradition about Hezekiah's attempt to suppress Solomonic magic see further McCown, *Testament of Solomon*, pp. 96–100; Ginzberg, *Legends* VI, p. 369 note 90.

In general on Solomon and magic see:

Fabricius, J. A., *Codex Pseudepigraphus Veteris Testamenti* I (1722), pp. 1013–70. Still valuable despite its great age.

Montgomery, M. W., 'Solomon, in Arabic Literature', JE XI (1905), pp. 444 ff.

Seligsohn, M., 'Solomon, in Rabbinical Literature and Legend', JE XI (1905), pp. 438–44.

Seligsohn, M., 'Solomon, Apocryphal Works', JE XI (1905), pp. 446–8.

Salzberger, G., *Die Salomonsage in der semitischen Literatur* (1907).

Ginzberg, L., *Legends of the Jews* IV (1913), pp. 149–54 ['Solomon Master of the Demons']; 165–9 ['Asmodeus'].

James, M. R., *Lost Apocrypha of the Old Testament* (1920), pp. 51–3.

McCown, C. C., 'The Christian Tradition as to the Magical Wisdom of Solomon', JPOS 2 (1922), pp. 1–24.

McCown, C. C., *Testament of Solomon* (1922), pp. 90–104.

Delatte, A., *Anecdota Atheniensia* I = Bibliothèque de la faculté de philosophie et lettres de l'Université de Liège 36 (1927). A collection of magical texts attributed to Solomon.

Preisendanz, K., 'Salomo', RE Suppl. VIII (1956), cols. 660–704.

Denis, A.-M., IPGAT (1970), pp. 67–9.

Rothkoff, A., 'Solomon, in the Aggadah', Enc. Jud. XV (1971), cols. 106–8.

Hirschberg, H. Z., 'Solomon, in Islam', Enc. Jud. XV (1971), col. 108.

Löfgren, O., 'Der Spiegel des Salomo: Ein äthiopischer Zaubertext', in *Ex Orbe Religionum: Studia G. Widengren* I (1972), pp. 208–23.

Bagatti, B., 'I Giudeo-Cristiani e l'Anello di Salomone', RSR 60 (1972), pp. 151–60.

Pritchard, J. B. (ed.), *Solomon and Sheba* (1974).

Duling, D. C., 'Solomon, Exorcism and the Son of David', HTR 68 (1975), pp. 235–52.

Charlesworth, J. H., PMRS, pp. 199–202.

VIII. The Writings of the Qumran Community

Thanks to the manuscript discoveries at Qumran between 1947 and 1956, the total of extant inter-Testamental Jewish literature has grown beyond all expectation.[1] Dead Sea Scrolls evidence relating to the Apocrypha and Pseudepigrapha, and Qumran material of a non-sectarian character, have been dealt with in earlier chapters. The titles examined here are those which may be assigned, either with complete assurance or with a high degree of probability, to the Qumran (Essene) movement.[2] They will be arranged in five categories: A. Rules; B. Bible interpretation; C. Hymns; D. Liturgical texts; E. Miscellaneous compositions. Fragments too small for meaningful treatment will be ignored. As is hardly necessary to recall, a large proportion of the fragments, found in Cave 4 more than thirty years ago, is still unpublished. The present chapter will consequently be in need of updating for years to come.

1. A select bibliography relating to the Dead Sea Scrolls, up-to-date until 1972, is given in vol. I, pp. 118–22. For more recent works, see J. A. Fitzmyer, *The Dead Sea Scrolls: Major Publications and Tools for Study* (1975, [2]1977). The following editions of Qumran texts have been published in the meanwhile: J. T. Milik, *The Books of Enoch: Aramaic Fragments of Qumran Cave 4* (1976); R. de Vaux and J. T. Milik, *Qumrân Grotte 4 II (4Q128–4Q157)* [DJD VI] (1977); Y. Yadin, *Meͤgillat ha-Miqdash* [The Temple Scroll] I-III (1977) (in Hebrew) [*The Temple Scroll* I-III (1983)]; M. Baillet, *Qumrân Grotte 4 III (4Q482–4Q520)* [DJD VII] (1982). For recent general introductions or surveys, see G. Vermes, *The Dead Sea Scrolls: Qumran in Perspective* (1977, with revisions 1981, 1982); E.-M. Laperrousaz *et al.*, 'Qumrân et découvertes au désert de Juda', DBS IX (1978), cols. 737–1014; H. Bietenhard, 'Die Handschriftenfunde vom Toten Meer (Ḥirbet Qumran) und die Essenerfrage. Die Funde in der Wüste Juda', in H. Temporini and W. Haase (eds.), *Aufstieg und Niedergang der römischen Welt* XIX, 1 (1979), pp. 704–78; D. Dimant, 'Qumran Sectarian Literature', in M. E. Stone (ed.), *Jewish Writings of the Second Temple Period* [*Compendia Rerum Iudaicarum ad Novum Testamentum* II.2] (1984), pp. 483–550. Cf. also M. Delcor (ed.), *Qumrân. Sa piété, sa théologie et son milieu* (1978).

Among the Qumran finds belonging to the section, 'Sources' (vol. I, §3), the following are to be added to subsection III, 'The Targums': Tg. Lev. 16:12–15, 18–21; Tg. Job 3:5–9; 4:16–5:4 *(4Q156–7*; J. T. Milik, DJD VI, pp. 86–90). The references indicate the maximum extent of the biblical pericopae covered by the Targum fragment. In fact, the surviving text is minute. Nevertheless, the Leviticus Targum (which represents a non-midrashic, translation type) is not without interest insofar as it includes expressions linking *4Q156*, not with Onkelos, but with Neofiti (cf. Vermes, JJS 29 (1978), p. 194). The Job fragments are not represented in *11QTgJob* which begins at 17:14. For supplementary bibliography on the latter, see M. Sokoloff, *The Targum to Job from Qumran Cave XI* (1974); T. Muraoka, 'The Aramaic of the Old Targum of Job from Qumran Cave XI', JJS 25 (1974), pp. 425–43; 'Notes on the Old Targum of Job from Qumran Cave XI', RQ 9 (1977), pp. 117–25; J. A. Fitzmyer, 'The First-Century Targum of Job from Qumran Cave XI', *A Wandering Aramean* (1979), pp. 161–82.

2. The problem of identity of the Dead Sea Community is discussed in vol. II, §30, pp. 555–90, especially pp. 575–85.

A. The Rules:

1. *The Community Rule or Manual of Discipline*

Five documents somewhat different in nature fall under the heading of Rules. They all consist, either wholly or substantially, of precepts governing the life of all the members of the Community, or of certain groups within it. Some contain legislation relating to their own time; others seem to have in view the eschatological era. Besides legal and administrative matters, the Rules accommodate also liturgical, paraenetical and poetic sections.

The Community Rule (*1QS*) is attested by a scroll from Cave 1 and by fragments from Caves 4 and 5. The title, *Serekh ha-Yaḥad*, figures in the manuscript itself (*1QS* 1:1, 16; cf. 5:1).[3] *1QS* comprises eleven reasonably well preserved columns, the last of which, with the bottom third left blank, contains the end of the document. Col. 1 is nevertheless not the beginning, nor col. 11 the end of the primitive scroll, for seams of thread at both extremities indicate that originally other strips of skin were attached to the manuscript. It is in effect reasonably certain that the Community Rule Annexe or Messianic Rule (*1QSa*) and the Blessings (*1QSb*) followed col. 11 of *1QS*.[4] Fragments detached from ten copies of the Rule await publication among the texts from Cave 4,[5] and a further *Serekh* manuscript may be identified with the help of tiny fragments from Cave 5 (*5Q11*), corresponding perhaps to *1QS* 2:4–7.[6]

3. The remains of the title formerly attached to the beginning of the Scroll have been published by D. Barthélemy, DJD I, p. 107 and plate 28. Cf. also Milik, RB 67 (1960), p. 412, quoting the phrase ספר סרך from *4QSᵃ*.

4. Cf. DJD I, pp. 107–8.

5. Cf. J. T. Milik, 'Le travaille d'édition des manuscrits de Qumrân', RB 63 (1956), pp. 60–1; 67 (1960), pp. 411–16. According to RB 63, two of the manuscripts are attested by a single small fragment each and another two manuscripts are written on papyrus. There are variants and somewhat differing recensions, especially in col. 5 where the abbreviated text of two manuscripts begins with מדרש למשכיל על אנשי התורה המתנדבים. In RB 67, Milik releases a number of variant readings from the 4Q manuscripts numbered from *a* to *j*, and appends the following list of *1QS* passages identified in the 4Q fragments:

1:1–5 (Sᵃ)	4:4–10 (Sᶜ)	6:10–13 (Sᵇ)	8:6–17 (Sᵈ)	10:3–8 (Sᵇ)
1:1–3 (Sᶜ)	4:13–15 (Sᶜ)	6:16–18 (Sᵇ)	8:19–21 (Sᵈ)	10:9–11 (Sᶠ)
1:15–19 (Sᵇ)	4:24–25 (Sᶜ)	6:22–25 (Sᵍ)	8:24–9:10 (Sᵈ)	10:4–12 (Sᵈ)
1:21–3 (Sᵇ)	5:1–20 (Sᵇ)	6:27–7:3 (Sᵍ)	9:15 (Sᵈ)	10:12–18 (Sᵈ)
2:4–5 (Sᵇ)	5:1–21 (Sᵈ)	7:8–15 (Sᶜ)	9:12–20 (Sᵉ)	10:13–18 (Sᵇ)
2:4–11 (Sᶜ)	5:21–6:7 (Sᵈ)	7:10–14 (Sᵍ)	9:15–10:3 (Sᵈ)	10:15–20 (Sᶠ)
2:6–11 (Sᵇ)	5:22–24 (Sᵍ)	7:13 (?) (Sᵈ)	9:20–24 (Sᶜ)	10:20–24 (Sᶠ)
2:26–3:10 (Sᶜ)	6:1–3 (Sⁱ)	7:16–18 (Sᵍ)	9:18–22 (Sᵇ)	11:7 (Sᵈ)
3:4–5 (Sʰ)	6:3–5 (Sᵍ)	7:20–8:10 (Sᶜ)	9:23–24 (Sᶠ)	11:14–22 (Sᵈ)
3:7–12 (Sᵃ)	6:9–12 (Sᵈ)	8:11–15 (Sᶜ)	10:1–5 (Sⁱ)	11:22 (Sᵈ)

6. Cf. Milik, DJD III, pp. 180–1; see also *5Q13, ibid.*, pp. 181–3.

Palaeographically *1QS* is dated to the Hasmonaean period, possibly to the early first century B.C.[7] No information is available concerning the script of the Cave 4 manuscripts; *5Q11* is vaguely described by J. T. Milik as 'écriture tardive' (DJD III, p. 180), which no doubt means mid-first century A.D.

The manuscript of *1QS* has been revised by a second hand, or perhaps by several later scribes. Some of the corrections eliminate simple copyist's mistakes; others, especially on cols. 7 and 8, introduce variant readings. Their significance cannot be assessed until the proper publication of the material from Cave 4.

The text of the Community Rule may easily be divided into six sections.

The opening unit (1:1–18) delineates the aims of the community (*yahad*) whose members are joined together through their entry into the Covenant. The second section (1:18–3:12) sketches the yearly Covenant ritual, reproducing a formula of general confession by the participants as well as priestly blessings and levitical curses pronounced on the sons of light and the sons of darkness respectively. Insincere converts are condemned by both priests and Levites.

Section 3 (3:13–4:26) concerns the doctrine of the two spirits of truth and falsehood, whose continuing struggle with one another governs the life of each individual and the history of all mankind.[8]

Section 4, the main body of *1QS* (5:1–9:11), proclaims the rules relating to the common life, and describes the stages of initiation and the organization of the Community. It includes, moreover, a detailed penal code believed to remain in force until the coming of 'a Prophet and the Messiahs of Aaron and Israel' (*1QS* 9:11).

Section 5 (9:12–10:8) lists directives to be followed by the *maskil* or Master, of the sect 'in his commerce with all the living', and expounds the Community's particular teaching on the proper times of worship.

The final section (10:9–11:22), a thanksgiving hymn intended for the Master, shares the same inspiration and voices the same ideas as the poems of the *Hodayoth* Scroll (see below, pp. 452–6).

No agreed opinion has been reached on the original structure and composition of *1QS*. If on the one hand the work in its final form appears to be carefully arranged in four sections between a clearly defined introductory paragraph and a poetic finale, on the other hand a painstaking analysis reveals signs of a lack of original unity. The first theory, elaborated in detail by P. Guilbert, depicts the Rule as consistent in plan, language and style.[9] The second, i.e. that *1QS* is a

7. Cf. F. M. Cross, *The Ancient Library of Qumran*, p. 89 (first quarter of the first century B.C.); N. Avigad, Scrip. Hier. IV, p. 71; M. Delcor, 'Qumrân', DBS IX, cols. 851–2.

8. On the doctrine of the 'Duae viae', see above p. 172, n. 83 [Proselytism].

9. 'Le plan de la "Règle de la Communauté"', RQ 1 (1959), pp. 323–44.

composite document, has been combined with an attempt to distinguish in the four layers of the Rule successive stages of a historical development of the sect. The principal protagonist of this thesis is J. Murphy-O'Connor, followed by J. Pouilly. They divide *1QS* into the following segments: 1. The earliest unit (8:1–16a; 9:3–10:8a) representing a pre-Qumran stratum, a kind of priestly manifesto (9:7), seeking to establish a community. 2. The section 8:16b–9:2, with its primitive penal code, already testifies to an autonomous group. 3. A new stage, 5:1–7:25, in which lay members of the community begin to share the authority originally enjoyed only by 'the sons of Aaron', i.e. the priests. 4. The central body of the Rule (sections 1–3), enlarged by the addition of a preface (cols. 1–4) and the concluding hymn (10:9–11:22).[10]

Whilst the precise literary and historical reconstruction of the Rule is bound to be speculative, a careful scrutiny of *1QS* itself points to the use of independent sources by the compiler of the document. In particular, the unity of *1QS* 8:1–16; 9:3–11, the section generally recognized as reflecting the most primitive concept of the Community, is patently disturbed by the skeletal penal code of 8:16–9:2, which itself follows naturally after the more detailed code of 6:24–7:25. It should also be noticed that the ritual of entry into the Covenant reveals itself to be a shortened version of a proper liturgy. See especially *1QS* 1:18–24 which, instead of recording the words to be recited by the priests and the Levites, simply provides the relevant rubrics. In short, while it can safely be argued that the Community Rule incorporates pre-existing literary materials, as might be expected from a document of this sort, it would be hazardous, and in the absence of the evidence from Cave 4 also unsound, to advance more developed historico-literary conjectures.

The main importance of *1QS* lies in the field of the institutions and practices of the Qumran community, its eschatological expectations and complex messianic beliefs. Its testimony is moreover vital for the identification of the Dead Sea sectaries as Essenes. For a discussion of these matters, see vol. II, pp. 550–4, 575–85 and the literature quoted there.

The Community Rule is devoid of any internal chronological pointers. Its dating depends on archaeology and palaeography and on the establishment of its relationship to other Qumran documents. In regard to the writing used by the scribe of *1QS*, even if the rather precise table of palaeographical sequences proposed by Qumran experts is taken with a pinch of salt, there can be little doubt that the manuscript belongs to the initial stages of the development of the

---

10. Cf. J. Murphy-O'Connor, 'La genèse littéraire de la Règle de la Communauté', RB 76 (1969), pp. 528–49; J. Pouilly, *La règle de la Communauté de Qumrân. Son évolution littéraire* (1976).

Qumran Hebrew script. Consequently, its attribution to the first half of the first century B.C. seems to be unobjectionable. An early dating is further supported by the nature of the document, fundamental as it is to the life and organization of the Community, its importance being witnessed by the presence of a dozen manuscripts in the various Caves. Moreover, it should also be noted that *1QS* 3:4–5 is cited in *5Q13* (DJD III, p. 183),[11] and that it is also used in the Damascus Rule.[12]

The facts that the Rule, as has been shown, is a composite work with a prehistory,[13] and that it reflects a fully developed organizational structure, militate against too early a setting in the second century B.C. Hence a reasonable dating appears to be around 100 B.C.[14]

The Community Rule belongs to a type of literature for which it is inappropriate to speak of a single author. Its attribution to the Teacher of Righteousness *in toto*, or as far as the section 8:1 ff. is concerned, must be declared purely speculative.[15]

Editions

Burrows, M., Trever, J. C., and Brownlee, W. H., *The Dead Sea Scrolls of St. Mark's Monastery*, vol. II, Fasc. 2 (1951).
Lohse, E., TQHD, pp. 1–43.

Translations with Introductions

English
Dupont-Sommer, A., *Essene Writings*, pp. 68–103.
Vermes, DSSE², pp. 71–94.

French
Dupont-Sommer, EE, pp. 83–127.
Guilbert, P., TQ I, pp. 9–80.

German
Maier, J., TTM I, pp. 21–45.

Italian
Moraldi, L, MQ, pp. 113–72.

11. Another 4Q Hebrew document, inspired by *1QS* and CD, is mentioned by J. T. Milik in DJD III, p. 188.

12. Cf. P. Wernberg-Møller, 'Some Passages in the "Zadokite" Fragments and their Parallels in the Manual of Discipline', JSS 1 (1956), pp. 110–28; Vermes, DSS, pp. 195–6.

13. The correction 'one year', substituted for 'six months' in *1QS* 7:8, suggests that the penal regulations were subject to change whilst the manuscript was in use, unless of course the corrector considered the original text to be erroneous.

14. Cf. Milik, RB 67 (1960), p. 411.

15. Cf. J. T. Milik, *Ten Years of Discovery in the Wilderness of Judaea* (1959), p. 37; A. Dupont-Sommer, *Essene Writings*, pp. 71–2: 'The *Rule* may, basically, very easily derive from the Teacher of Righteousness himself.' G. W. E. Nickelsburg, JLBBM, p. 132: 'Very possibly [the nucleus of the work, 8:1–16 and 9:3–10:8] is the product of the Teacher of Righteousness himself.'

Commentaries

Brownlee, W. H., *The Dead Sea Manual of Discipline* [BASOR Suppl. Stud. 10–12] (1951).
Wernberg-Møller, P., *The Manual of Discipline* (1957).
Siedl, S. H., 'Qumran, eine Mönchgemeinde im Alten Bund', *Studie über Serek ha-Yaḥad* (1963).
Licht, J., מגילת הסרכים (1965).
Leaney, A. R. C., *The Rule of Qumran and its Meaning* (1966).

Bibliography

Burrows, M., 'The Discipline Manual of the Judaean Covenanters', Oudtest. Stud. 8 (1950), pp. 156–92.
Audet, J.-P., 'Affinités littéraires et doctrinales du "Manuel de Discipline"', RB 59 (1952), pp. 219–38; 60 (1953), pp. 41–82.
Baumgarten, J. M., 'Sacrifice and Worship among the Jewish Sectaries of the Dead Sea Scrolls', HThR 46 (1953), pp. 141–59.
Talmon, S., 'The Sectarian Yaḥad: A Biblical Noun', VT 3 (1953), pp. 133–40.
Yadin, Y., 'A Note on DSD IV,20', JBL 74 (1955), pp. 40–3.
Wernberg-Møller, P., 'Some Reflections on the Biblical Material in the Manual of Discipline', StTh 9 (1955), pp. 40–66.
Idem, 'Some Passages in the "Zadokite" Fragments and their Parallels in the Manual of Discipline', JSS 1 (1956), pp. 110–28.
Otzen, B., 'Some Textual Problems in 1QS', StTh 11 (1957), pp. 89–98.
Driver, G. R., 'Three Difficult Words in Discipline (III, 3–4; VII, 5–6, 11)', JSS 2 (1957), pp. 247–50.
Licht, J., 'Analysis of the Two Spirits', Scrip. Hier. 4 (1958), pp. 88–101.
Carmignac, J., 'Conjecture sur la première ligne de la Règle de la Communauté', RQ 2 (1959), pp. 85–7.
Guilbert, P., 'Le plan de la Règle de la Communauté', RQ 2 (1959), pp. 323–44.
Sutcliffe, E. F., 'The First Fifteen Members of the Qumran Community: A Note on VIII.1 ff.', JSS 4 (1959), pp. 134–8.
Weise, M., *Kultzeiten und kultischer Bundesschluss in der 'Ordensregel' vom Toten Meer* (1961).
Wernberg-Møller, P., 'A Reconsideration of the Two Spirits in the Rule of the Community', RQ 4 (1961), pp. 413–41.
Stendahl, K., 'Hate, Non-Retaliation, and Love: 1QS X,17–20 and Rom. 12:19–21', HThR 55 (1962), pp. 343–55.
Priest, J. F., 'Mebaqqer, Paqîd and the Messiah', JBL 81 (1962), pp. 55–61.
Hunzinger, C.-H., 'Beobachtungen zur Entwicklung der Disziplinarordnung der Gemeinde von Qumrân', in H. Bardtke (ed.), *Qumran-Probleme* (1963), pp. 231–48.
Baer, Y., '*Serek ha-Yaḥad*', Zion 29 (1964), pp. 1–60 (Hebr.).
Murphy-O'Connor, J., 'La genèse littéraire de la Règle de Qumrân', RB 76 (1969), pp. 528–49.
Wernberg-Møller, P., 'The Nature of the Yaḥad according to the Manual of Discipline and Related Documents', ALUOS 6 (1969), pp. 56–81.
Osten-Sacken, P. von der, *Gott und Belial* (1969).
Bardtke, H., 'Literaturbericht über Qumran VII. Die Sektenrolle 1QS', ThR 38 (1974), pp. 257–91.
Pouilly, J., *La règle de la Communauté de Qumrân* (1976).
Duhaime, J.-L., 'L'instruction sur les deux esprits et les interpolations dualistes à Qumrân (1QS III,13-IV,26)', RB 84 (1977), pp. 566–94.
Delcor, M., 'Qumrân. Règle de la Communauté', DBS IX (1978), cols. 851–7.
Wernberg-Møller, P., 'Priests and Laity in the *Yaḥad* of the Manual of Discipline', in *Sefer M. Wallenstein* (1979), pp. 72*–83*.

Puech, E., 'Remarques sur l'écriture de 1QS VII-VIII', RQ 10 (1979), pp. 35–43.
Allison, D. C., 'The Authorship of 1QS III,13-IV,14', RQ 10 (1980), pp. 257–68.
Nickelsburg, G. W. E., JLBBM, pp. 132–7.
Thorion, Y., 'The Use of Preposition in 1Q Serek', RQ 10 (1981), pp. 405–33.
Kruse, C. G., 'Community Functionaries in the Rule of the Community and the Damascus Document', RQ 10 (1981), pp. 543–51.
Dohmen, C., 'Zur Gründung der Gemeinde von Qumran (1QS VIII-IX)', RQ 11 (1982), pp. 81–96.

2. The Rule of the Congregation or Messianic Rule

Two columns of a document (*1QSa*) have been reconstructed from fragments originally part of the scroll containing the Community Rule (cf. above, p. 381). Copied by the same scribe and dating to the same period as *1QS*, the title, Rule of the Congregation, is borrowed from the opening line: זה סרך לכול עדת ישראל ('This is the Rule for all the congregation of Israel'—*1QSa* 1:1). The alternative designation corresponds to the subject-matter, which concerns the 'last days' and introduces two eschatological figures, 'the Priest' and 'the Messiah of Israel' (*1QSa* 2:12, 14, 19–20).

The work lays down regulations for the eschatological integration of the 'congregation of Israel'—men, women and children—into the Community led by 'the sons of Zadok, the priests, and the men of their Covenant'. Their association is to begin with a general assembly at which 'the precepts of the Covenant' and 'the statutes' are proclaimed and expounded (1:1–5).

Children introduced into the group are to receive education and training until the age of twenty years[1] when the young men are to be individually enrolled, allowed to marry and to participate in community business (1:6–11).

By the age of thirty, the lay member may be allotted various offices under the supreme direction of the priests. Duties and tasks are to depend on age and intelligence. Liaison between the lay units and the priests is to be provided by the Levites who are to be also responsible for ensuring that a three-day purification takes place before important events such as trials, council meetings or departure to war (1:12–27).

The Rule lists as qualified to attend council meetings conducted by the priests, the sages of the congregation, the lay leaders and the Levites. Excluded are the impure, those with bodily defects and the senile. These are also pronounced unfit to participate in the war

1. The statute is based on Ex. 30:14; 38:26. The enrolment, without specifying the age, is referred to in CD 15:6; cf. 10:1. See S. B. Hoenig, 'On the Age of Mature Responsibility in 1QSa', JQR 48 (1957–58), pp. 371–5; 'The Age of Twenty in Rabbinic Tradition and 1QSa', JQR 49 (1958–59), pp. 209–14; J. M. Baumgarten, '1QSa 1,11: Age of Testimony or Responsibility', JQR 49 (1958–59), pp. 157–60; P. Borgen, 'At the Age of Twenty in 1QSa', RQ 3 (1961), pp. 267–77.

destined to vanquish the nations (1:27–2:11).

The final section of the document deals with the council meeting summoned by the priestly Messiah[2] and attended by the Messiah of Israel, and with the subsequent ritual of the messianic banquet represented as the model for all communal meals with a minimum quorum of ten men (2:11–22).

1QSa possesses a number of distinctive traits linking it both to the Community Rule with reference to the Sons of Zadok and the men of their Covenant (*1QS* 5:2, 9); the divisions of Thousands, Hundreds, etc. (*1QS* 2:21); and especially the common meal (*1QS* 6:4–5), and to the Damascus Rule, with which it has in common not only the social setting of married members and their children, but more particularly the mention of the 'Book of Meditation' (*1QSa* 1:7—CD 10:6; 13:2).[3] The allusion to the army and the fight against the Gentiles connects this work with the War Rule.

The dating of this writing cannot be established independently of the Community Rule since, *qua* manuscript, it has the same origin, its two columns having been copied immediately after col. 11 of *1QS* (see above, p. 381). Hence, if the original scroll is placed in the first half of the first century B.C. (p. 384), *circa* 50 B.C. must be the *terminus ante quem* for the composition of this annexe to the Rule.

As for the relative sequence, D. Barthélemy places *1QSa* before *1QS*, considering the former as applying to the Hasidim prior to the Maccabaean uprising (DJD I, p. 108). This theory is based on the

---

2. The sentence relating to 'the Priest-Messiah' is very obscure partly due to the bad state of preservation of *1QSa* 2:11–12. For the various readings and interpretations see DJD I, pp. 117–18; R. Gordis, 'The "Begotten" Messiah in the Qumran Scrolls', VT 7 (1957), pp. 191–4; A. S. van der Woude, *Die messianischen Vorstellungen der Gemeinde von Qumran* (1957), pp. 96–104; Y. Yadin, 'A Crucial Passage in the Dead Sea Scrolls (1QSa II,11–17)', JBL 78 (1959), pp. 238–41; E. F. Sutcliffe, 'The Rule of the Congregation (1QSa) II,11–12: Text and Meaning', RQ 2 (1960), pp. 541–7; M. Smith, 'God's Begetting the Messiah in 1QSa', NTSt 5 (1959), pp. 218–24; O. Michel and O. Betz, 'Von Gott gezeugt', *Judentum—Urchristentum—Kirche* [*Festschrift für J. Jeremias*] (1960), pp. 3–23; W. Grundmann, 'Die Frage nach der Gottessohnschaft des Messias im Lichte von Qumran', in H. Bardtke (ed.), *Qumran-Probleme* (1963), pp. 86–111; Vermes, DSS, p. 196.

3. The nature and identity of this work are still debated. The editor of *1QSa* is content with describing it as a 'livre populaire' (DJD I, p. 113). Others have sought to identify it with the Community Rule (A. Dupont-Sommer, *Essene Writings*, p. 70), a 'written corpus of Torah exegesis' (P. Wernberg-Møller, 'The Nature of the *Yahad* ...', ALUOS 6 (1969), pp. 79–80, n. 32; a sectarian writing for basic instruction (J. M. Baumgarten, 'The Unwritten Law in the Pre-Rabbinic Period', *Studies in Qumran Law* (1977), pp. 15–16 and n. 13); or the Temple Scroll (Y. Yadin, *The Temple Scroll* I, p. 301 [Hebrew]). It is more likely, however, that the book in question is the Bible, or the Pentateuch (N. Wieder, *The Judean Scrolls and Karaism* (1962), pp. 215–51; J. Licht, *Megillat ha-Serakhim* (1965), pp. 255–6; L. H. Schiffman, *The Halakhah at Qumran*, p. 44; Vermes, DSS, p. 113).

totally subjective evaluation of the term עדה = συναγωγή, hence συναγωγή 'Ασιδαίων (1 Mac. 2:42), and on the equally subjective view that *1QSa* compared to *1QS* reveals an evolution corresponding to that between Hasidim and Essenes.

In fact, as has been indicated earlier, the author of *1QSa* looks towards the final stage of the eschatological future, whereas the Community Rule is pre-Messianic in outlook. Indeed, the great assembly of initiation alluded to in the opening lines corresponds, no doubt, to the ultimate phase of 'conversion' before the dividing-line between the party of God and that of Satan is finally drawn. In the circumstances, the date of origin of the Rule of the Congregation may well be approximately the same as that of the Community Rule, i.e. *circa* 100 B.C.

The attribution of authorship to the Teacher of Righteousness is no more demonstrable in the case of *1QSa*[4] than it is for the Community Rule (cf. above, p. 384).

Editions

Barthélemy, D., and Milik, J. T., DJD I, pp. 108–18.
Lohse, E., TQHD, pp. 45–51.

Translations

English
Vermes, DSSE[2], pp. 118–21.

French
Barthélemy, *op. cit.*
Dupont-Sommer, A., EE, pp. 119–23.

German
Maier, J., TTM I, pp. 173–6.
Lohse, *op. cit.*

Italian
Moraldi, L., MQ, pp. 173–91.

Bibliography

North, R., 'Qumran "Serek a" and Related Fragments', Orientalia 25 (1956), pp. 90–9.
Rost, L., 'Die Anhänge der Ordensregel (1QSa und 1QSb)', ThLZ 82 (1957), cols. 667–70.
Carmignac, J., 'Quelques détails de lecture dans la Règle de la Congrégation, le Recueil des Bénédictions . . .', RQ 4 (1962), pp. 83–8.
Rinaldi, G., 'L'"ultimo periodo" della storia. Considerazioni sulla Regola a (1QSa) di Qumran', Biblia e Oriente 7 (1965), pp. 161–85.
See also the references in notes 1 and 2 above.

4. J. Carmignac, TM II, p. 11.

3. The Damascus Rule or Zadokite Fragments

Together with the Hebrew Ben Sira and the Aramaic Testament of Levi, the Damascus Rule testifies to a bond between the Dead Sea Scrolls and the Cairo Genizah. It is, in fact, the only Qumran Essene composition known prior to 1947.

Remains of two medieval manuscripts of the Damascus Rule were discovered in the Genizah attached to the Ezra Synagogue in Old Cairo in 1896. Acquired by the Cambridge University Library, they were edited in 1910 by Solomon Schechter. Manuscript A (T.-S. 10K6), dating to the tenth century, consists of eight leaves written on both sides, i.e. pages 1–16; Manuscript B (T.-S. 16 311), from the eleventh or twelfth century, is represented by a single leaf also inscribed recto and verso, designated as pages 19–20. Text B partly overlaps Text A: p. 7, line 6 to p. 8, line 21 runs parallel, with variants, to p. 19, line 1 to line 34. Page 19, line 34 to page 20, line 34 furnishes the continuation of the document missing from Manuscript A. The text is generally well preserved apart from the bottom lines of pages 13–16.

The publication of the Community Rule from Qumran Cave 1 revealed immediately its close relationship with the Cairo document and proved that the latter was in some way related to the Dead Sea Scrolls. The recognition that it was an integral part of Qumran literature resulted from the discovery of Damascus Rule fragments in Caves 4, 5 and 6. Of these M. Baillet edited five small scraps from Cave 6 (*6Q15*) corresponding to CD 4:19–20; 5:13–14; 5:18–6:2; 6:20–7:1 and a passage unattested in the Cairo manuscripts, presumed to be from the first century A.D. on palaeographical grounds (DJD III, pp. 128–31). Another fragment, dated to the second half of the first century B.C., which echoes CD 9:7–10, has been published among the Cave 5 materials (*5Q12*), by J. T. Milik (DJD III, p. 181). According to the same scholar, Cave 4 yielded seven manuscripts of the Damascus Rule. They are still unavailable but are said to correspond to the Text A of the Genizah, though representing a different recension (or recensions) and to contain sections missing from the Cairo version (RB 63 (1956), p. 61). Milik further indicated in 1959 (but the evidence is still unpublished) that on the basis of the 4Q material the original Damascus Rule consisted of the following sections:

1. Initial columns absent from the Cairo text.
2. CD 1–8 and parallel from 19–20.
3. A missing part from CD on ritual purity, laws of diseases (Lev. 13:29 ff.), sexual impurities (Lev. 15), marriage laws, agricultural laws, tithes, contact with Gentiles, relation between men and women, magical practices, etc.

4. CD 15–16.
5. CD 9–14.
6. End of the document missing from the Cairo manuscripts, dealing with the penal code, and the liturgy of the feast of the Renewal of the Covenant.[1]

The Genizah version of the Damascus Rule falls into two distinct parts, an Exhortation (1:1–8:21 and 19:1–20:34) and a collection of Statutes (9:1–16:19).

The Exhortation takes the form of a sermon, or extracts from several sermons,[2] in which a teacher admonishes his 'sons' (2:14), who 'enter the Covenant' (2:2), to consider and understand God's conduct towards the good and the evil. A moral teaching is preached with the help of examples borrowed from the history of the sect (1:3–2:1),[3] and from biblical history, beginning with the fall of the heavenly Watchers until the foundation of a group of converts, the forerunners of the Qumran community (2:14–4:12).

At the centre of the sermon is an explanation of the three chief spiritual threats of the age, the 'three nets of Belial' (4:15), 'fornication', 'riches' and 'profanation of the Sanctuary', each being given a particular sectarian definition (4:12–6:1).[4] To escape these dangers and save the faithful, a group of priests and Israelites separated themselves from the Temple and established a 'new Covenant in the Land of Damascus',[5] whose essential tenets are set out in CD 6:11–7:9.

1. See Milik, *Ten Years of Discovery*, pp. 151–2.

2. There are three openings: 'Hear now, all you who know righteousness' (1:1); 'Hear now all you who enter the Covenant' (2:2); 'Hear now, my sons' (2:14).

3. On the origins of the Essenes, see vol. II, pp. 586–7. For special studies on Qumran history, using the CD evidence, see H. H. Rowley, 'The History of the Qumran Sect', BJRL 49 (1966), pp. 203–32; J. Murphy-O'Connor, 'The Essenes and the History', RB 81 (1974), pp. 215–44; M. Delcor, 'Qumran. Document de Damas', DBS IX (1978), cols. 836–8; G. Vermes, 'The Essenes and History', JJS 32, (1981), pp. 18–31.

4. The first 'net of Belial', fornication, is diversely interpreted as alluding probably to polygamy alone (P. Winter, 'Sadoqite Fragments IV,20, 21 and the Exegesis of Gen. I,27 in Late Judaism', ZAW 68 (1956), pp. 74–7; Y. Yadin, 'L'attitude essénienne envers la polygamie et le divorce', RB 79 (1972), pp. 98–9 [cf. J. Murphy-O'Connor, 'Remarques sur l'exposé du professeur Y. Yadin', *ibid.*, pp. 99–100]; G. Vermes, 'Sectarian Matrimonial Halakhah in the Damascus Rule', PBJS, pp. 50–6. Cf. also J. A. Fitzmyer, 'The Matthean Divorce Texts and some new Palestinian Evidence', ThStud 37 (1976), pp. 197–226.

5. The 'Land of Damascus' has been understood either as a straightforward geographical noun (cf. H. H. Rowley, *The Zadokite Fragments and the Dead Sea Scrolls* (1952), pp. 75–6; A. Dupont-Sommer, EE, p. 135; S. Iwry, 'Was there a Migration to Damascus?', Eretz-Israel 9 (1969), pp. 80–8), or as a symbolical designation of the Community's exile, possibly at Qumran (F. M. Cross, *The Ancient Library of Qumran* (1958), pp. 81–2; R. de Vaux, *Archaeology and the Dead Sea Scrolls* (1973), pp. 113–14; G. Vermes, *Scripture and Tradition*, pp. 43–9; DSS, pp. 159–60). R. North, 'The Damascus of Qumran Geography', PEQ 87 (1955), argues that both Qumran and Damascus were parts of the Nabataean kingdom: hence the designation. For a survey, see P. R. Davies,

The final section of the Exhortation (7:9–20:34) sketches the respective destinies of the faithful and the wicked members of the Community. Those who persevere 'shall prevail over the sons of the earth. God will forgive them and they shall see his salvation because they took refuge in his holy Name' (CD 20:33–4).

The second half of the Damascus Rule, the Statutes (pages 9–16), combines legal and moral precepts determining the way of life of the members of the Community in the 'assembly of the towns' (12:19), and sectarian constitutional and organizational regulations of the 'assembly of the camps' (12:22–3) in the pre-Messianic age.[6] They are set out in discrete units according to their subject-matter.

The general halakhic and ethical commandments cover, in the existing order of the Cairo Manuscript A, the following topics: 1. The use of Gentile law courts (9:1). 2. The duty to warn transgressors before laying charges against them (9:2–8). 3. The judicial oath (9:8–16). 4. The ritual bath (10:10–13). 5. Sabbath observances (10:14–11:18). 6. Purity laws concerning the place of worship (11:18–12:2). 7. The case of the man preaching apostasy (12:2–3) or profaning the Sabbath by error (12:3–6). 8. Contact with Gentiles (12:6–11). 9. Laws relating to ritual uncleanness (12:11–18). 10. Cancellation of vows made by men and women (16:6–12). 11. Rules concerning free-will offerings (16:13–16).

The remaining statutes belong to sectarian legislation proper: 1. Rules concerning witnesses (9:16–10:3) and judges (10:4–10). 2. Regulations for the camps (12:22–13:7). 3. The functions of the Guardian of the camp (13:7–14:2). 4. The general assembly of the camps (14:3–6). 5. The chief Priest (14:6–8). 6. The Guardian General (14:8–12). 7. Rules relating to communal charity (14:12–16). 8. An incomplete penal code (14:20–2). 9. Oath of the Covenant (15:1–5). 10. Entry into the Community (15:5–16:6).

This outline of the Statutes shows that the Damascus Rule, following the model set by the final chapters of Jubilees (see chapters 49–50), constitutes an early effort to construct a systematically arranged legal code, even employing specific headings: 'Concerning the oath' (9:8); 'This is the Rule for the judges of the Congregation' (10:4); 'Concerning purification by water' (10:10); 'Concerning the Sabbath' (10:14); 'The Rule of the assembly of the Towns of Israel' (12:18); 'This is the Rule of the Assembly of the Camps' (12:22–3); 'This is the Rule of the Guardian of the Camp' (13:7); 'This is the Rule for the

---

The Damascus Covenant (1983), pp. 16–17, 207.

6. Like *1QS* 9:10–11, and in contrast to *1QSa*, the laws of CD are definitely intended for the then present age: 'This is the exact statement of the statutes in which [they shall walk until the coming of the Messi]ah of Aaron and Israel' (14:18–19). For a recent attempt to describe the life of the 'Damascus' Community, see Vermes, DSS, pp. 97–105.

assembly of all the Camps' (14:3); 'This is the Rule for the Congregation by which it shall provide for all its needs' (14:12); 'Concerning the oath of a woman' (16:10); 'Concerning the Statute for free-will offerings' (16:13).

Both the Exhortation and the Statutes include a considerable amount of citations from Scripture, and produce characteristic examples of sectarian haggadic and halakhic Bible exegesis.[7] There are also allusions to a work ascribed to Levi, the son of Jacob (CD 4:15), possibly an unknown passage of the Testament of Levi (cf. below, p. 777) and to the 'Book of the Divisions of the Times into their Jubilees and Weeks', i.e. the Book of Jubilees (cf. above, p. 308). For the Book of *Hagu* or *Hagi*, see above, p. 387, and for the 'Sealed Book of the Law' (CD 5:5), identified as the Temple Scroll by Y. Yadin and B. Z. Wacholder, see below, p. 417.[8]

The literary composition and the purpose of the Damascus Rule are still hotly debated issues, as the latest detailed survey by P. R. Davies demonstrates.[9]

In respect of the composition, the first problem concerns the relationship between the Exhortation and the Statutes. Scholars whose main interest lies in the complex literary structure of the Exhortation (e.g. Murphy-O'Connor and Davies) are not particularly bothered by this primary issue. In fact, both the Cairo Manuscript A and the evidence from Cave 4 testify to the joint existence of the two sections,

7. The most important haggadic examples are found in CD 1:13–14 (Hos. 4:16); 3:20–4:6 (Ezek. 44:15); 4:10–12 (Mic. 7:11); 4:12–21 (Isa. 24:17); 5:7–11 (Lev. 18:13); 6:2–11 (Num. 21:18; Isa. 54:16); 6:11–14 (Mal. 1:10); 7:9–21 (Isa. 7:17; Am. 5:26–7; Am. 9:11; Num. 24:17); 19:5–13 (Zech. 13:7; Ezek. 9:4); 8:1–18 (Hos. 5:10; Dt. 32:33; Ezek. 13:10; Mic. 2:11; Dt. 9:5; Dt. 7:8).

The following halakhic interpretations are noteworthy: CD 4:20–5:2 (Gen. 1:27; 7:9; Dt. 17:17); 9:2:8 (Lev. 19:18; Nah. 1:2; Lev. 19:17); 9:8–10 (1 Sam. 25:26); 11:17–18 (Lev. 23:38); 11:18–21 (Prov. 15:8); 12:2–3 (Lev. 20:27); 12:17–18 (Lev. 11:32); 16:6–9 (Dt. 23:24); 16:10–11 (Num. 30:9); 16:14–15 (Mic. 7:2). It is remarkable that not only prophetic passages, but even a verse from the Writings (Prov. 15:8), are employed in legal arguments.

For further information, see the commentaries on CD and studies of Qumran Bible exegesis, e.g. F. F. Bruce, *Biblical Exegesis in the Qumran Texts* (1959); O. Betz, *Offenbarung und Schriftforschung in der Qumransekte* (1960); G. Vermes, *Scripture and Tradition* (1961, [2]1973); S. Lowy, 'Some Aspects of Normative and Sectarian Interpretation of the Scriptures', ALUOS 6 (1969), pp. 84–163; Vermes, PBJS (1975); 'Interpretation (History of) at Qumran', IDBS, pp. 438–41; H. Gabrion, 'L'interprétation de l'Ecriture dans la littérature de Qumrân', ANRW 19.1 (1979), pp. 779–848.

For a special study of CD 4:20–5:2, see the references in note 4 above; CD 6:2–11, see Vermes, *Scripture and Tradition*, pp. 53–4; CD 7:9–21, see H. Kosmala, 'Damascus Document 7,9–21', in *Essays in the Dead Sea Scrolls in Memory of E. L. Sukenik* (1961), pp. 183–90.

8. Cf. Yadin, *Megillat ha-Miqdash* I (1977), p. 302; B. Z. Wacholder, *The Dawn of Qumran: The Sectarian Torah and the Teacher of Righteousness* (1983), pp. 119–29.

9. *The Damascus Covenant: An Interpretation of the 'Damascus Document'* (1983), pp. 3–47.

and there is no reason to doubt the originality of their juxtaposition, at least as far as the history of their text can be followed. (For speculations on the prehistory of the document, see below.) The presentation, side by side, of hortatory and legal elements in a single writing may be seen as an adoption of biblical precedents, in particular, that offered by Deuteronomy.[10] Further considerations will be formulated presently when the purpose or *Sitz im Leben* of CD is discussed.

The unity of the Exhortation has often been questioned in various ways. Some of the objections, e.g. that prose passages are interpolated into a poetic admonition,[11] or that there are midrashic elements additional to the basic text,[12] fail to carry conviction because of the uncertainty, in the first case, concerning the poetic character of the sections in question and because of the normalcy and basic acceptability, in the second, of exegetical sections in a homiletic address.

Other, more influential theories seek to distinguish in the Exhortation several independent literary units and associate these with various stages of the prehistory and history of the Qumran sect. A.-M. Denis, taking the theme of knowledge as his yardstick, postulates a pre-sectarian stage dating to the time of the composition of Daniel in CD 1:1–4:6a, and two sectarian stages in 4:6b–6:11 and 7:4b–20:34 belonging to later periods.[13]

A weightier and more ambitious thesis has been put forward by J. Murphy-O'Connor.[14] For him, CD 2:14–6:1 represents the original nucleus of the Exhortation. It is a 'Missionary Document' intended to win converts to the Essene community. The latter is seen as a movement of Babylonian origin and the 'Missionary Document' represents their return and proselytizing activity in Palestine. This section has a historical and a theological preface (CD 1:1–2:1 and 2:2–14). A second layer is represented by a 'Memorandum' (6:11–8:3) reflecting the stand of a group, withdrawn from the Temple, which under the leadership of the Teacher of Righteousness embraces a separatist existence. The two sections are joined by means of a

---

10. Cf. E. Cothenet, TQ II, p. 132.

11. I. Rabinowitz, 'A Reconsideration of "Damascus" and "390 Years" in the "Damascus" (Zadokite) Fragments', JBL 73 (1954), pp. 11–35.

12. J. Becker, *Das Heil Gottes* (1964), p. 57.

13. *Les thèmes de connaissance dans le Document de Damas* [Studia Hellenistica 15] (1967). For the conclusions, see pp. 208–13.

14. 'An Essene Missionary Document? CD II,14-VI,1', RB 77 (1970), pp. 201–29; 'A Literary Analysis of Damascus Document VI,2-VIII,3', RB 78 (1971), pp. 210–32; 'The Critique of the Princes of Judah (CD VIII,3–19)', RB 79 (1972), pp. 200–16; 'A Literary Analysis of Damascus Document XIX,33-XX,34', RB 79 (1972), pp. 544–64. Among the forerunners of this thesis the following deserve to be noted: I. Rabinowitz, *art. cit.* in n. 10; A. Jaubert, 'Le pays de Damas', RB 65 (1958), pp. 214–48; S. Iwry, *art. cit.* in n. 5.

'Midrash' (6:2–11). The third unit (8:3–19) consists of a criticism of the Jewish authorities unwilling to support the Essene cause. This 'Critique of the Princes of Judah' is associated with the period of Jonathan Maccabaeus. Finally, the fourth section (19:33–20:34) reproaches unfaithful members of the Community and stresses the need for loyalty and perseverance. Apart from paragraph 20:1–8, which Murphy-O'Connor assigns to the lifetime of the Teacher of Righteousness, the whole pericope is judged to have originated shortly after the Teacher's death.

Not unlike it in basic approach, but differing from the foregoing thesis in some of its major conclusions, is P. R. Davies's redaction-critical theory.[15] He, too, distinguishes a fourfold structure in the Exhortation, but defines them somewhat differently from Murphy-O'Connor, viz. 'History' (1:1–4:12a); 'Laws' (4:12b–7:9); 'Warnings' (7:9–8:19); and 'The New Covenant' (19:33b–20:34). The principal novelty in Davies's reconstruction of the history of the Exhortation is that he declares the whole work to be pre-Qumran and pre-Essene, and to have been produced by 'an organised, well-developed community with a clearly-expressed ideology and historical traditions' (p. 202). The roots of this ideology 'may antedate the middle of the fifth century B.C.E.' (p. 203), and the work itself is conjectured to be of Babylonian diaspora origin. The Qumran community sprang from this group—and not from the second century B.C. Palestinian Hasidim—after the appearance of the Teacher of Righteousness (p. 203). This implies that mention of him in the historical scheme of CD 1:1–11 may not be original, but 'a product of Qumranic redaction' (p. 200).

The last two theories offer not only a fully-argued literary and redaction-critical analysis, but also a tentative explanation of the purpose and *Sitz im Leben* of the various units, as well as an attempt to mark out their historical setting. If proved correct, they might necessitate a number of readjustments regarding the prehistory and early history of the Essenes.[16] Their principal weakness—apart from the innate fragility of historical reconstructions dependent on literary analysis alone—lies in the questionable reliability of the Cairo

15. Cf. n. 8 above.
16. The reconstruction of the origins of the Community in vol. II, pp. 575–85 is based on a combination of information from CD, the Qumran *pesher* literature and Josephus. The principal difficulty under which it has laboured lies in the dearth of historical data. To claim, as Davies does, that the Damascus Document should be given priority over the Commentaries, because the latter have possibly been 'a hindrance rather than a help in the elucidation of the origins ... of the Qumran community' (p. 204), is likely to lead to an unnecessary diminution of the already scarce evidence. The dangers entailed in his method are revealed by the fact that he is compelled to relegate the passage dealing with the Teacher of Righteousness in CD 1, an essential link between the Damascus Rule and the *pesharim*, among the later Qumran interpolations into the original CD text.

manuscripts as the sources of far-reaching critical conclusions before they have been compared to the fragments, unedited so far, containing recensional differences. As has been rightly stated, 'Little can be done on this text that is of lasting value before the full publication of the Cave IV material.'[17]

Scholars who consider the Damascus Rule as essentially a unitary document, and not one composed of several autonomous units, believe that the focus around which the Exhortation and the Statutes are construed is the Qumran Feast of the Renewal of the Covenant. Bearing in mind that the Cave 4 material explicitly deals with this feast, it can be argued that the preacher of the Exhortation is the מבקר or Guardian or possibly the Guardian of all the camps addressing those who enter into or renew the Covenant, and that the Statutes were intended to be proclaimed in the same way as the Torah was read out to the assembly of the Jews in the days of Ezra (Neh. 8:2–3), or 'the precepts of the Covenant' to the congregation of the Messianic Rule (*1QSa* 1:4–6).[18]

As regards the date of the Damascus Rule, the medieval Cairo manuscripts, probably deriving from the scrolls discovery at the end of the eighth century referred to above (pp. 188, 205–6), are of no assistance. The Qumran fragments, or at least some of them, belong to the pre-Christian era.[19] Those from Cave 4 have not yet been assigned to any precise period. At the upper end of the scale, P. R. Davies suggests that this writing should be placed before the occupation of Qumran which, in his view, may have occurred as late as the beginning of the first century B.C., but after the composition of Jubilees, which may have existed before 200 B.C.[20] Most other authors propose a date falling between the second half of the second century and the middle of the

17. J. A. Fitzmyer, 'Prolegomenon' to S. Schechter, *Fragments of a Zadokite Work* (1970), p. 24. P. R. Davies, conscious of this warning which he quotes in his Introduction (p. 1), tries to counter the difficulty by reducing the import of the fragments to the domain of textual criticism. As he has deduced from the study of the Cairo text that '*the document as a whole is basically older than the Qumran community*', he is obliged to assume that all the 'manuscripts (from Cairo and presumably also from the Qumran caves) represent a Qumranic recension' and 'can only attest the *post-redactional* history of the document' (pp. 2–3). But even if this were so, would as full a knowledge as possible of the 'Qumranic recensions', the only factual evidence available, not be an essential requisite for any hypothetical reconstruction of the literary prehistory of the Damascus Rule?

18. Cf. G. Vermes, DSSE, pp. 95, 97; E. Cothenet, TQ II, pp. 137–8; L. Moraldi, MQ, p. 213.

19. Cf. above, p. 389. J. T. Milik declares that the oldest manuscript of this work (*4QD^b*) dates to 75–50 B.C. Cf. *Ten Years of Discovery*, pp. 38, 58.

20. *Damascus Covenant*, p. 203. The latter point is purely speculative, and is immediately weakened by a cautionary comment: 'the possibility that Jubilees existed in an earlier form before the second century B.C.E. cannot be discounted. (Nor can we be certain that the reference to Jubilees in CD XIV is not secondary.)' (*ibid.*).

first century B.C. and generally consider CD to be somewhat younger than the Community Rule.[21] In fact, there is no compelling argument against suggesting that the composition of the Damascus Rule is roughly contemporaneous with it, originating perhaps shortly after 100 B.C.

Since CD 19:13–15 alludes to the death of the Teacher of Righteousness as having taken place nearly forty years earlier, the Damascus Document is one of the few texts which cannot be attributed to him.

Editions

Cairo manuscripts
Schechter, S., *Documents of Jewish Sectaries : Fragments of a Zadokite Work* (1910). Reprinted with a Prolegomenon and detailed bibliography by J. A. Fitzmyer (1970).
Rost, L., *Die Damaskusschrift neu bearbeitet* (1933).
Rabin, C., *The Zadokite Documents* (1954).
Lohse, E., QT, pp. 63–107 (printed Hebrew text).
Davies, P. R., *The Damascus Covenant* (1983), pp. 232–67.
Zeitlin, S., *The Zadokite Fragments* (1952). [A facsimile edition of the Genizah manuscripts from the Cambridge University Library.]

Qumran fragments
Baillet, M., and Milik, J. T., DJD III, pp. 128–31, 181.

Translations

English
Charles, R. H., APOT II, pp. 785–834.
Vermes, DSSE², pp. 95–117.
Davies, P. R., *op. cit.*, pp. 232–67.

French
Dupont-Sommer, A., EE, pp. 129–78.
Cothenet, E., TQ II, pp. 129–204.

German
Maier, J., TTM I, pp. 46–70.
Lohse, E., *op. cit., ibid.*

Italian
Moraldi, L., MQ, pp. 205–70.

Bibliography

Pre-Qumran
Lévi, I., 'Un écrit sadducéen antérieur à la destruction du Temple', REJ 61 (1911), pp. 161–205; 63 (1912), pp. 1–19.

---

21. Cf. F. M. Cross, *Ancient Library*, p. 60; A. Dupont-Sommer, *Essene Writings*, p. 120 (before 48 B.C.); E. Cothenet, TQ II, pp. 140–3 (*c.* 60 B.C.); L. Moraldi, MQ, p. 217 (from John Hyrcanus to Pompey). Among writers who hold CD to be older than *1QS* may be listed H. H. Rowley, *From Moses to Qumran* (1963), p. 260, and the authors named in n. 1, and G. Vermes in his earlier publications (*Les manuscrits du désert de Juda* (1953), pp. 53, 66; *Discovery in the Judean Desert* (1956), pp. 48, 61).

Lagrange, M.-J., 'La secte juive de la Nouvelle Alliance au pays de Damas', RB 9 (1912), pp. 213–40, 321–60.

Büchler, A., 'Schechter's "Jewish Sectaries"', JQR 3 (1912–13), pp. 429–85.

Meyer, E., *Die Gemeinde des Neuen Bundes im Lande Damaskus* (1919).

Ginzberg, L., *Eine unbekannte jüdische Sekte* (1922). E.T.: *An Unknown Jewish Sect* (1976).

Post-Qumran

(*N.B.* Fitzmyer's *Prolegomenon* pp. 25–34 [see 'Editions'] contains a detailed bibliography up to 1969 and Davies, *op. cit.*, pp. 27–31 [see 'Editions'] a select bibliography up to 1982.)

Brownlee, W. H., 'A Comparison of the Covenanters of the Dead Sea Scrolls with pre-Christian Jewish Sects', BA 13 (1950), pp. 50–72.

Segal, M. H., 'The Habakkuk Commentary and the Damascus Fragments', JBL 70 (1951), pp. 131–47.

Rowley, H. H., *The Zadokite Fragments and the Dead Sea Scrolls* (1952).

Rubinstein, A., 'Urban Halakhah and Camp Rules in the Cairo Fragments of the Damascus Covenant', Sefarad 12 (1952), pp. 283–96.

Delcor, M., 'Contribution à l'étude de la législation des sectaires de Damas et de Qumrân', RB 61 (1954), pp. 533–53; 62 (1955), pp. 60–75.

Rabin, C., 'Notes on the Habakkuk Scroll and the Zadokite Document', VT 5 (1955), pp. 148–62.

Wiesenberg, E., 'Chronological Data in the Zadokite Fragments', VT 5 (1955), pp. 284–308.

Wernberg-Møller, P., 'Some Passages in the "Zadokite" Fragments and their Parallels in the Manual of Discipline', JSS 1 (1956), pp. 110–28.

Kahle, P., 'The Community of the New Covenant and the Hebrew Scrolls', *Opera Minora* (1956), pp. 96–112.

Carmignac, J., 'Comparaison entre les manuscrits "A" et "B" du Document de Damas', RQ 2 (1959–60), pp. 53–67.

Betz, O., 'Zadokite Fragments', IDB IV, pp. 929–33.

Baltzer, K., *Das Bundesformular* (²1964), pp. 117–27.

Eissfeldt, O., *Introduction*, pp. 649–52.

Schwarz, O. J. R., *Der erste Teil der Damaskusschrift und das Alte Testament* (1965).

Denis, A.-M., *Les thèmes de connaissance dans le Document de Damas* (1967).

Murphy-O'Connor, J., see n. 14 above.

Hoenig, S. B., 'An Interdict against socializing on the Sabbath', JQR 62 (1971), pp. 77–83.

Bardtke, H., 'Literaturbericht über Qumran. VIII. Die Damaskusschrift', ThR 39 (1974), pp. 189–221.

Schiffman, L. H., *The Halakhah at Qumran* (1975).

Vermes, DSS, pp. 48–51, 87–115.

Rosso-Ubigli, L., 'Il Documento di Damasco e la Halakah sectaria', RQ 9 (1978), pp. 357–99.

Osten-Sacken, P. von der, 'Die Bücher der Tora als Hütte der Gemeinde-Amos 5,26f in der Damaskusschrift', ZAW 91 (1979), pp. 423–35.

Brooke, G. J., 'The Amos-Numbers Midrash (CD 7,13b–8,1a) and Messianic Expectation', ZAW 92 (1980), pp. 397–404.

Schwartz, D. R., 'To join oneself to the House of Judah (Damascus Document IV,11)', RQ 10 (1981), pp. 435–46.

Nickelsburg, G. W. E., JLBBM, pp. 123–6.

Milikowsky, C., 'Again: *Damascus* in the Damascus Document and in Rabbinic Literature', RQ 11 (1982), pp. 97–106.

Davies, P. R., 'The Ideology of the Temple in the Damascus Document', JJS 33 (1982), pp. 287–301.

Schiffman, L. H., *Sectarian Law in the Dead Sea Scrolls: Courts, Testimony and Penal Code* (1983).

Idem, 'Legislation concerning Relations with non-Jews in the Zadokite Fragments and Tannaitic Literature', RQ 11 (1983), pp. 379–89.

Derrett, J. D. M., '*Beḥuqey Hagoyim*: Damascus Document IX, 1 again', RQ 11 (1983), pp. 409–15.

4. The War Rule

Among the documents discovered in Cave 1 figures a nineteen-column scroll devoted to 'The War of the Sons of Light against the Sons of Darkness' (*1QM*). It was published posthumously by E. L. Sukenik in '*Ozar ha-Megillot ha-genuzot* or *The Dead Sea Scrolls of the Hebrew University* in 1954/1955. The bottom lines of each column have been destroyed, and col. 19 is particularly badly mutilated. The end of the work is not extant, but the contents of the last two columns would suggest that only a small amount of the text is missing. Two small fragments detached from the scroll are included in DJD I, pp. 135–6. The script is thought to belong to the Herodian era.[1]

Remains of six further manuscripts (M^a-M^f) have been retrieved from Cave 4 (*4Q491–496*) which also contained papyrus fragments representing a cognate work (*4Q497*). They have all been edited by M. Baillet in DJD VII in 1982. Of the Cave 4 manuscripts, M^b (*4Q492*) corresponds to parts of *1QM* 19:1–14; M^d (*4Q494*) to the missing end of *1QM* 1–2:3; M^e (*4Q495*) to *1QM* 10:9–10 and 13:9–12; and the 122 tiny papyrus fragments of M^f (*4Q496*) appear to have preserved small portions of the first four columns of the War Rule. There are also further scraps which cannot be located into the framework of *1QM*. By contrast to M^b, M^d, M^e and M^f which reflect the same type of text as *1QM*, M^a (*4Q491*), the most extensive of the fragments, and M^c (*4Q493*) testify to a different recension of the War Rule.[2] Palaeographically the fragments are assigned to the first century B.C.-first century A.D.[3]

---

1. Cf. F. M. Cross, *The Ancient Library of Qumran* (1958), p. 89, n. 20; 'The Development of Jewish Script', in E. G. Wright (ed.), *The Bible and the Ancient Near East* (1961), pp. 137–91. N. Avigad (Scrip. Hier. 4, p. 74) places the script of *1QM* after *1QIsa*[b] among the Herodian group (mid-first century B.C.-A.D. 70). Similarly, Y. Yadin is content with a vague second half of the first century B.C. or first half of the first century A.D. (*The Scroll of the War of the Sons of Light against the Sons of Darkness* (1962), p. 243). J. T. Milik (*Ten Years of Discovery*, p. 40) declares by contrast all the War manuscripts to be 'post-Herodian', i.e. belonging to the first century A.D. In turn, M. Baillet (DJD VII, p. 45) opts for the middle of the first century B.C.

2. M. Baillet conjectures that the two manuscripts represent the same recension (DJD VII, p. 50).

3. M. Baillet dates M^a to the turn of the eras or slightly earlier (DJD VII, p. 12); M^b to the middle of the first century B.C. (*ibid.*, p. 45); M^c to the first half of the first century B.C. (*ibid.*, p. 50); M^d to the beginning of the first century A.D. (*ibid.*, p. 53); M^e to the mid-first century B.C. (*ibid.*, p. 55); and M^f to a little before 50 B.C. (*ibid.*, p. 58). The document related to the War Rule (*4Q497*) is also assigned to the mid-first century B.C. Since some of Baillet's dates depend on that of *1QM*, it should be noted that he puts the

The Cave 1 recension of the War Rule may be divided into eleven sections.

1. An introduction (col. 1) deals with the circumstances of the proclamation of the eschatological war in which the Sons of Light, identified as the 'exiles of the desert' recruited from the tribes of Levi, Judah and Benjamin, confront the Sons of Darkness or army of Belial, led by the Kittim of Assyria and their allies the Edomites, Moabites, Ammonites, Philistines (i.e. Israel's traditional enemies), and 'the ungodly of the Covenant', or wicked Jews. The Sons of Light fight a battle in 'the Desert of Jerusalem' and with the help of the angelic forces defeat their opponents.

2. This victory, entailing the capture of Jerusalem, enables the Community to re-enter the Sanctuary and re-organize its cultic worship (col. 2:1–6).[4]

3. The restoration of the Temple service occurs in the seventh year of the war, i.e. a sabbatical year during which no fighting may take place. The remaining period of a forty-year war, not counting the subsequent years of release, is devoted to a planned conquest of all the foreign nations, the children of Shem, Ham and Japheth (2:6–14).

4. The battle time-table is followed by rules for the trumpets, and for the inscriptions to be engraved on them (2:15–3:11).

5. Likewise, the document prescribes the measurements and inscriptions on the various standards, and the legend to appear on the shield of the commander in chief (3:13–5:2).

6. Next the battle divisions each numbering one thousand men, together with their weapons of spear, sword and scabbard, are depicted in great detail (5:3–14).

7. Here the War Rule lays down regulations for the movements of three divisions of foot-soldiers, the first armed with javelins, the second with spears and shields and the third with shields and swords (5:4–6:6). The foot-soldiers are to be supported by cavalrymen on either wing, whose horses must conform to specific requirements. Their riders are to be furnished with breast-plates, helmets, greaves, bucklers, spears, javelins, bows and arrows. The ages of officers and men are defined (horsemen: 30–50 years old; foot-soldiers: 40–50; camp inspectors: 50–60; officers: 40–50; auxiliaries: 25–30) with, curiously, the middle-aged assigned to fighting, and the younger men to non-combatant duties (6:8–7:3).

8. A small paragraph concerns the holiness of the army. To protect it

---

script of the latter to *c.* 50 B.C., while most other scholars are inclined towards a later date.

4. The link between section 1 and section 2 is lost in the lacuna created by the missing lines at the bottom of col. 1, only very partially restored with the help of *4QM*[d] *(494)*, lines 1–3 (DJD VII, p. 53).

from uncleanness, the Rule excludes women, boys, persons with bodily defects from the camp, and forbids men suffering from temporary ritual impurity to participate in battle. Latrines are to be sited at a considerable distance from the camps 'for the holy angels will be with their hosts' (7:3–7).

9. The leading roles in the eschatological conflict are played, not by the fighting men, but by the priests and Levites. Seven chief priests, wearing war vestments, are to lead the combat, the first delivering an exhortation and the others blowing the various trumpets to direct the battle and signal its phases. They are accompanied by seven Levites each holding a shofar whose sound is intended 'to terrify the heart of the enemy' (7:9–9:9).

10. A brief section outlines a special battle formation, called 'towers', each consisting of three hundred soldiers holding shields. These bear the names of the four archangels, Michael, Gabriel, Sariel and Raphael (9:10–18).

11. In the lacuna at the bottom of col. 9, the words of the battle liturgy begin. They include Bible quotations (Dt. 20:2–4; Num. 10:9; Num. 24:17–19; Isa. 31:8) together with hymns, a recitation of God's saving acts in Israel's history, and they aim at bringing about God's triumph over the nations[5] (10:1–12:18). As the conflict reaches its climax, the High Priest, the priests, Levites and the elders of the army pronounce blessings and curses, and rejoice because God's 'mighty hand' achieves salvation and peace (13:1–14:1). The final act of worship is a thanksgiving ceremony on the battlefield after the annihilation of the enemy (14:2–18).

12. The last five columns of *1QM* (cols. 15–19) repeat the rules set out in the previous sections for the battle against the king of the Kittim and the host of Belial. These include a priestly admonition before the fight; regulations for the use of trumpets; an exhortation by the High Priest before the battle, fought in seven phases, in the last of which 'the great hand of God' deals a mortal blow to Belial and the Kittim. Col. 19 ends with an unfinished thanksgiving ritual where once more the Kittim are expressly mentioned.

The only wholly unparalleled material among the fragments from Cave 4 consists of two incomplete hymns in *4Q491* (= M[a]), fragments 11 and 12. Baillet (DJD VII, pp. 26, 29) designates them as 'Song of Michael' (frag. 11, lines 8–18 and frag. 12), although the name of the archangel appears nowhere in it, and 'Song of the Righteous' (frag. 11, lines 20–24). The text of *4Q493* (M[c]) provides another account of battle movements governed by the priests' trumpet signals. In line 13, it

5. In 11:11, the enemies are identified as 'the Kittim', interpreting 'Assyria' in Isa. 31:8.

mentions the Sabbath trumpets; these are unknown to *1QM*.

Study of the structure of the War Rule has generated divergent theories. Authors of the earliest monographs, Y. Yadin and J. Carmignac, considered the work to be a coherent unity, composed by a single author who no doubt relied on literary sources.[6] However, the majority of subsequent scholars have judged *1QM* to be a composite work. J. van der Ploeg, relying on the repetitive character of cols. 15–19 compared with the preceding sections, has advanced the thesis that *1QM* includes an original work, inspired by Dan. 11:40–12:3 and Ezek. 38–39, corresponding roughly to *1QM* 1, 10–12 and 15–19, and possibly to 13–14. He suggests that it is centred on a war against the Kittim in 'seven lots' or stages and that this primitive composition was subsequently enlarged by another writer to accommodate the concept of a forty-year war against all the nations of the world (cols. 2–9).[7]

J. Becker similarly argues against a unitary conception of the War Scroll, accepting C.-H. Hunzinger's theory that a published fragment of *4QM*[a] testifies to an older version of the text.[8] He, too, has adopted van der Ploeg's view concerning a first collection comprising cols. 1, 15–19 to which he adds 7:9 to 8:19; the rest, he believes, belongs to a second composition, the two having been subsequently brought together to form a single work.[9] P. von der Osten-Sacken is responsible for an almost identical analysis of *1QM*.[10]

The most complex literary theory has been advanced by P. R. Davies, for whom *1QM* consists of three original documents (cols. 2–9, 15–19, 10–12); two independent fragments (cols. 13 and 14); and a preface intended to unify the independent sections (col. 1). Of the three major units, Davies considers cols. 2–9 to be a little older than cols. 10–12, followed much later by cols. 15–19.[11]

No detailed study has appeared since the publication of the Cave 4 material in 1982, but in the light of M[a] and, to a lesser extent, of M[c], it seems to be incontestable that the War Rule had a prehistory and that

---

6. Y. Yadin, *The Scroll of the War of the Sons of Light against the Sons of Darkness* (1962), pp. 3–17; J. Carmignac, *La Règle de la Guerre* (1958), p. xiii. The latter attributes *1QM* to the same author (the Teacher of Righteousness) as *1QS*, *1QSa* and *1QH*. More nuanced, Yadin envisages a single (anonymous) author employing a number of sources, biblical, apocryphal, pseudepigraphic, and sectarian.

7. J. van der Ploeg, *Le rouleau de la Guerre* (1959), pp. 11–22.

8. 'Fragmente einer älterer Fassung des Buches Milḥāmā aus Höhle 4 von Qumran', ZAW 69 (1957), pp. 131–51.

9. J. Becker, *Das Heil Gottes* (1964).

10. *Gott und Belial* (1969).

11. P. R. Davies, *1QM, the War Scroll from Qumran : Its Structure and History* (1977). This author concluded that the relevance of the poetic fragment, corresponding to *1QM* 14, of *4QM*[a] edited by Hunzinger is doubtful, since it may derive from 'a psalter rather than an earlier recension of 1QM' (p. 84). The full publication of *4QM*[a] has proved this assumption to be groundless.

1QM, and possibly *4QM^b*, *M^d-f*, represent the final stage of a literary evolution.

Regarding the structure of *1QM*, there is no doubt that the theory of a composite work, clearly divisible at least into col. 1, cols. 2–14 and cols. 15–19, is definitely to be preferred. By contrast, no decisive argument favours any of the literary theses advanced so far. Nevertheless, the familiar theme, from the Book of Daniel onwards, of a single great eschatological event presided over by the heavenly Prince Michael, has all the appearances of antedating the uncommon concept of a progressive conquest of the world by the Jews, culminating in a final battle against the chief enemy. Hence, until the contrary is proved, it can be reasonably maintained that cols. 15–19 have priority over cols. 2–14. Col. 1 may be seen as partly reflecting the same ideas as cols. 15–19 (a universal fight in seven stages against the Kittim and their allies), and partly as an editorial preface to account for the first six years of the forty-year war. The regulations, both military and liturgical, set out in cols. 2–14 should in consequence be understood, when parallels exist, as modelled on those in cols. 15–19. It has been noted, in particular, that the term 'Kittim' in cols. 15–19 corresponds in cols. 2–9 to the generic 'enemy' (אויב),[12] an abstraction required to fit the scheme of consecutive battles against the nations listed in col. 2:10–14.

The purpose of the War Rule has been defined in semi-practical terms by Y. Yadin. According to him the author seeks to answer four questions. 1. When and against whom will the war be waged? 2. What are the biblical laws concerning warfare? 3. How do the secular rules of war relate to the Torah? 4. How will the battle be fought in practice?[13] Taken too literally, such an understanding of the War Rule is likely to mislead. In fact, set against the warlike symbolism of the eschatological canvas drawn by the author of the Community Rule in the section of the 'Two Spirits' (*1QS* 3:13–4:26), the War Rule may be seen as an elaborate dramatization of a final spiritual conflict, an apocalyptic teaching presented in the form of a liturgy.[14] Eph. 6:10–17 attests a similar military imagery within a strictly religious context.[15]

Apart from the *terminus ante quem* furnished by palaeography, viz. *c.* the turn of the eras, the dating of the War Rule essentially depends on

---

12. Cf. Davies, *op. cit.*, p. 71. He may also be correct in suggesting that the hymns and prayers included in cols. 10–12 originally formed a separate collection (p. 123).

13. Yadin, *op. cit.*, p. 6.

14. Cf. J. Carmignac, TQ I, p. 84. See also J. van der Ploeg, *op. cit.* [in n. 7 above], p. 20.

15. K. G. Kuhn, 'πανοπλία', TDNT V, pp. 298–300.

the historical identification of military data.[16] A few scholars, writing in the early years of Qumran research, one of them relying only on preliminary publications of *1QM*, have associated the contents of this work with Hellenistic warfare.[17] Others prefer to point to the Maccabaean army as the source on which the author of the battle sections of the War Rule drew.[18] But both kinds of argument fade into insignificance when compared to the precise coincidences between the data of the scroll and what is known of Roman weaponry, army divisions and manoeuvres. This thesis has been associated with the names of A. Dupont-Sommer, and especially Y. Yadin.[19] Yadin has furnished a full comparison between the weapons, battle formations and tactics described in the scroll and their Roman equivalents (e.g. מגן = 'scutum', מגן עגלה = 'clipeus' or 'parma', כידון = 'gladius', זרקה = 'iaculum' or 'hasta velitaris', רומח = 'pilum', מגדל = 'turris' or 'testudo', etc.).[20] He concludes that the evidence as a whole points towards a Roman model dating to the second half of the first century B.C.: 'after the Roman conquest but before the end of Herod's reign' (*op. cit.*, pp. 244–6).[21] On this basis, the composition of the War Rule must be dated to a period corresponding to, or following, the Herodian era.

The reference in *1QM* 15:2 to the 'King of the Kittim' may also be used for chronological purposes. Bearing in mind that in the Nahum Commentary from Cave 4 (cf. below, p. 431), Antiochus and Demetrius are called '*kings* of Greece' (מלכי יון: DJD V, p. 38), but the leaders of the Kittim '*rulers*' (מושלי כתיים: *ibid.*) here as well as in the Habakkuk Commentary (see below), the terminological variant in *1QM* is most likely to reveal a governmental change among the Kittim. In other words, if 'rulers' allude to republican Rome, מלך refers to the emperor. In that case, *1QM* cannot predate Augustus, and should be assigned to the final decades of the first century B.C.; or, if the

16. J. Carmignac stands out among the students of *1QM* for completely disregarding the evidence relating to weapons and tactics. He dates *1QM* to 110 B.C. and defines it as one of the late works of the Teacher of Righteousness, posterior to *1QS* and *1QSa*, but preceding some of the psalms of *1QH*. Cf. TQ I, pp. 85–6; *La Règle de la Guerre* (1958), p. xiii.

17. Cf. J. G. Février, 'La tactique hellénistique dans un texte de 'Ayin Fashkha', Semitica I (1950), pp. 53–9; K. M. T. Atkinson, 'The Historical Setting of the War of the Sons of Light and the Sons of Darkness', BJRL 40 (1958), pp. 272–97.

18. Cf. M. H. Segal, 'The Qumran War Scroll and the Date of its Composition', Scrip. Hier. 4 (1958), p. 140; P. R. Davies, *op. cit.* [in n. 11], pp. 58–67.

19. Dupont-Sommer, 'Règlement de la guerre des fils de lumière', RHR 148 (1955), pp. 25–43, 141–80; *Essene Writings*, pp. 177–83. Yadin, *op. cit.* [in n. 6].

20. Yadin, *op. cit.*, pp. 114–97.

21. Cf. also G. R. Driver, *The Judaean Scrolls* (1965), pp. 180–97: 'Roman army ... of the imperial period' (p. 193).

palaeographical data may be stretched a little, to the early decades of the first century A.D.[22]

No individual author of the War Rule can be identified. J. Carmignac's attribution of it, together with a number of other major Qumran compositions, to the Teacher of Righteousness, is totally baseless.[23]

In addition to the Hebrew Bible, from which he quotes frequently,[24] the compiler of the War Rule appears to have had at his disposal other written sources. One is mentioned in *1QM* 15:5 as ספר סרך עתו (the Book of God's Time) which included 'the Prayer in the Time of War' and 'all their Hymns'. Several scholars think that this work has found its way into *1QM* itself.[25] The ספר תהלים (Book of Psalms), referred to in frag. 17, line 4 of *4QM*ᵃ, may be either the biblical book or a sectarian collection.[26]

The War Rule may have been used by the author of the Thanksgiving Hymns (*1QH* 6:29–35).[27]

Editions

(a) *1QM*

Sukenik, E. L., *The Dead Sea Scrolls of the Hebrew University* (1954/55).

Lohse, E., TQHD, pp. 177–225.

Yadin, Y., *The Scroll of the War of the Sons of Light against the Sons of Darkness* edited with *Commentary and Introduction* (1962; Hebrew ed. 1955).

(b) *4QM* (*4Q491–497*)

Baillet, M., DJD VII, pp. 12–72.

Hunzinger, C.-H., 'Fragmente einer älterer Fassung des Buches Milḥāmā aus Höhle 4 von Qumrân', ZAW 69 (1957), pp. 131–51.

Baillet, M., 'Les manuscrits de la Règle de la Guerre de la grotte 4 de Qumrân', RB 79 (1972), pp. 217–26.

22. Cf. Vermes, DSSE², p. 123; DSS, p. 149; see also Driver, *op. cit.*, p. 202. Yadin, *op. cit.*, p. 331, suggests without any justification that from 44 B.C. (*sic*!) onwards Julius Caesar 'was to all intents and purposes a king'. P. R. Davies's comment on this point (*op. cit.*, p. 89) seems to be prejudiced. *1QM* 15:2 is the only known passage where the phrase 'king of the Kittim' appears. Note, however, that J. T. Milik proposes to restore line 1 of frag. 9–10 in the Commentary on Psalm 68 to read מל]כי כתיאים] (DJD I, p. 82) and that Vermes inserts the word 'King' into the lacuna preceding 'Kittim' in *1QM* 1:4 (DSSE², p. 124).

23. Cf. TQ I, p. 86.

24. Cf. J. Carmignac, 'Les citations de l'Ancien Testament dans "la Guerre des fils de lumière contre les fils de ténèbres"', RB 63 (1956), pp. 234–60, 375–90.

25. Cf. Yadin, *op. cit.*, p. 322; C. Rabin, 'The Literary Structure of the War Scroll', in *Essays on the Dead Sea Scrolls in Memory of E. L. Sukenik* (1961), pp. 31–47 (Hebr.); B. Jongeling, *Le Rouleau de la Guerre des manuscrits de Qumrân* (1962), p. 327.

26. M. Baillet, DJD VII, pp. 40–1.

27. Cf. J. Carmignac, TQ I, pp. 86, 224–7.

Translations [with Commentary]

English
Yadin, *op. cit.*
Vermes, DSSE², pp. 122–48.

French
Carmignac, J., *La Règle de la Guerre des fils de lumière contre les fils de ténèbres* (1958).
Ploeg, J. van der, *Le Rouleau de la Guerre* (1959).
Carmignac, J., 'La Règle de la Guerre', TQ I, pp. 81–125.
Dupont-Sommer, A., EE, pp. 179–211.

German
Maier, J., TTM I, pp. 123–48.

Italian
Moraldi, L., MQ, pp. 271–326.

Bibliography

Avi-Yonah, M., 'The "War of the Sons of Light against the Sons of Darkness" and the Maccabean Warfare', IEJ 2 (1952), pp. 1–5.
Carmignac, J., 'Les Kittîm dans la "Guerre des fils de lumière contre les fils de ténèbres"', NRTh 87 (1955), pp. 737–48.
Idem, 'Précisions apportées au vocabulaire de l'hébreu biblique par la guerre des fils de lumière contre les fils de ténèbres', VT 5 (1955), pp. 345–65.
Rost, L., 'Zum "Buch der Kriege der Söhne des Lichtes gegen die Söhne der Finsternis"', ThLZ 80 (1955), cols. 205–8.
Carmignac, J., 'Les citations de l'Ancien Testament dans la Guerre des fils de lumière contre les fils des ténèbres', RB 63 (1956), pp. 234–60, 375–90.
Kuhn, K. G., 'Zum Verständnis der Kriegsrolle von Qumran', ThLZ 81 (1956), cols. 25–30.
Stegemann, H., 'Die Risse in der Kriegsrolle von Qumran', ThLZ 81 (1956), cols. 205–10.
Ploeg, J. van der, 'La guerre sainte de la "Règle de la guerre" de Qumrân', in *Mélanges bibliques rédigés en l'honneur d'André Robert* (1957), pp. 326–33.
Treves, M., 'The Date of the War of the Sons of Light', VT 8 (1958), pp. 419–24.
Segal, M. H., 'The Qumran War Scroll and the Date of its Composition', Scrip. Hier. 4 (1958), pp. 138–43.
North, R., '"Kittim" War or "Sectaries" Liturgy?', Bibl 39 (1958), pp. 84–93.
Carmignac, J., 'Concordance hébraïque de la Règle de la guerre', RQ 1 (1958), pp. 7–49.
Ploeg, J. van der, 'La composition littéraire de la "Règle de la guerre" de Qumrân', in J. Coppens *et al.* (eds.), *Sacra Pagina* II (1959), pp. 13–19.
Grintz, J. M., 'The War Scroll, Its Time and Authors', in *Essays on the Dead Sea Scrolls in Memory of E. L. Sukenik* (1961), pp. 19–30 (Hebr.).
Rabin, C., 'The Literary Structure of the War Scroll', *ibid.*, pp. 31–47 (Hebr.).
Ploeg, J. van der, 'Zur literarischen Komposition der Kriegsrolle', in H. Bardtke (ed.), *Qumran-Probleme* (1963), pp. 293–8.
Becker, J., *Der Heil Gottes* (1964).
Ginsberg-Gazov, A. M., 'The Structure of the Army of the Sons of Light', RQ 5 (1965), pp. 163–76.
Osten-Sacken, P. von der, *Gott und Belial* (1969).
Vermes, G., 'The Archangel Sariel: A Targumic Parallel to the Dead Sea Scrolls', in J. Neusner (ed.), *Christianity, Judaism and other Greco-Roman Cults. Studies for Morton Smith at Sixty* III (1975), pp. 159–66.
Duhaime, J.-L., 'La rédaction de 1QM XIII et l'évolution du dualisme à Qumrân', RB 84 (1977), pp. 210–38.

Davies, P. R., *1QM, the War Scroll from Qumran. Its Structure and History* (1977).
Idem, 'Dualism and Eschatology in the Qumran War Scroll', VT 28 (1978), pp. 28–36.
Delcor, M., 'Qumrân. Le livre de la guerre', DBS IX, cols. 919–31.
Hurvitz, A., 'The Garments of Aharon and his Sons according to 1QWar VII,9–10', in
    Studies in Bible and the Ancient Near East (1978), pp. 139–41 (Hebr.).
Collins, J. J., 'Dualism and Eschatology in 1QM', VT 29 (1979), pp. 212–16.
Davies, P. R., 'Dualism and Eschatology in 1QM. A Rejoinder', VT 30 (1980), pp. 93–7.
Flusser, D., 'Apocalyptic Elements in the War Scroll', in A. Oppenheimer *et al.* (eds.),
    Jerusalem in the Second Temple Period (1980), pp. 434–52 (Hebr.).

5. The Temple Scroll

The Temple Scroll was discovered in one of the Qumran caves (in Cave
11, it is thought, in 1956)[1] and remained in the hands of an Arab
antique dealer until the Israeli military government confiscated it in
June 1967. It was first published in Hebrew under the title מגילת
המקדש by Yigael Yadin in 1977. A revised English edition appeared in
1983: *The Temple Scroll*: I. Introduction, II. Text and Commentary,
III. Plates and Text (hence *TS* I, II, III). The story of its recovery and
acquisition is recounted in *TS* I, pp. 1–5.

The manuscript containing the Temple Scroll is the longest of all the
Qumran scrolls, measuring 8.148 m. The first column is lost, and the
next four survive only in fragments. They add another 60 cm to the
length of the manuscript. The scroll is made from nineteen sheets of
thin skin. The first includes five columns of text; ten sheets have four
columns, and a further seven, three columns each. The last sheet had
only a few lines (now lost) of a single column, the remainder of the
leather being left blank. Originally the columns consisted of twenty-two
or twenty eight lines, of which, not counting the first and the last
column, between six and twenty-one lines have been preserved.

Further Temple Scroll fragments retrieved from Caves 4 and 11 are
housed in the Rockefeller Museum in Jerusalem. Thirty-six of them
have been reproduced by Yadin as supplementary plates 35*–40*, and
all but thirteen are, firmly or hypothetically, located in the main
manuscript.[2]

The scroll is the work of two scribes. Scribe A was responsible for
cols. 1–5; scribe B, for the rest of the manuscript. Both are said to be
Herodian hands, scribe B being placed to the turn of the eras, and

---

1. Cf. J. A. Fitzmyer, *The Dead Sea Scrolls. Major Publications* ... ([2]1977), p. 37. The
Scroll is generally designated as *11QT* or *11QTemple*.

2. For the 11Q material, see J. van der Ploeg, 'Une halakha inédite de Qumrân', in M.
Delcor, *Qumrân* (1978), pp. 105–13; cf. in particular pp. 112–13; Y. Yadin, 'Le Rouleau
du Temple', *ibid.*, p. 119, n. 2; *The Temple Scroll* I, pp. viii-ix. Cf. also L. van den
Bogaard, 'Le Rouleau du Temple. Quelques remarques sur les petits fragments', in W. C.
Delsman *et al.* (eds.), *Von Kanaan bis Kerala. Festschrift für Prof. Mag. Dr. Dr. J. P. M. van
der Ploeg* (1982), pp. 285–94.

scribe A a little later. The 11Q fragments are also middle or late Herodian, but the texts listed under the symbol Rockefeller 43.366 are considerably older, representing the middle-Hasmonaean semi-formal script. Yadin proposes that it should be dated to the end of the second century B.C.[3] On account of their textual variations, these fragments, as well as the remains of the unpublished 4Q manuscript alluded to by J. Strugnell, may testify to an earlier form, or a source, of the Temple Scroll.

The scroll may be defined as Temple law, arranged systematically, apparently in the framework of a Covenant or of its renewal. It adopts and adapts the relevant statutes relating to the desert tent-Sanctuary, with its priesthood and sacrifices as described in various chapters of Exodus, Leviticus and Numbers. But it incorporates also large sections of Deuteronomy from chapter 12 onwards, and especially chapters 17 to 23:1. Scriptural laws are sometimes reproduced literally, sometimes re-worded, and often supplemented by non-biblical regulations.

The contents of the Temple Scroll are set out in detail in *TS* I, pp. 39–70. They may be summarized thematically as follows.

The work opens with an account, borrowed from Exod. 34:10–16, of a Covenant struck between God and Israel (cols. 1(?)–2). This is followed by a general outline of the Temple and its furniture according to Exod. 35:5–16 (col. 3), which in turn leads to more detailed regulations concerning the building of the Temple specifying, among other things, the dimensions of the various architectural units such as the Sanctuary, the Holy of Holies, the upper chamber, the colonnades (cols. 4–7). Subsequently, the sacred furniture is described: the mercy seat, the cherubim, the golden veil, the table for the bread of Presence, the frankincense, the golden lampstand, etc. (cols. 7–11).

A substantial section is devoted to cultic laws, viz. the offering of the

---

3. *TS* I, pp. 20, 386. However, his claim that the manuscript designated as Rockefeller 43.366, of which three fragments are reproduced (III, pp. 38*, 5 and 40*, 1–2), belongs to TS, remains doubtful. For, if the first of these fragments actually corresponds to cols. 41:5–42:3, the other two are unidentified. Moreover, as B. A. Levine has already noted (BASOR 232 (1978), p. 6), Fr. 40*, 1 lines 3 and 4 include the phrases וידבר מושה (Lev. 23:44) and וידבר יהוה אל מושה (*ibid.* 24:1). Cf. *TS* II, p. 46. This style, as will be shown presently, is alien to the Temple Scroll. Furthermore, according to a letter written by J. Strugnell to B. Z. Wacholder on 28 April 1981, and published by the latter (*The Dawn of Qumran* (1983), pp. 205–6, 278), 'the 4Q fragments improperly labelled Rockefeller 43.366 do not pertain to a copy of the Temple Scroll', but to 'a Pentateuch with frequent non-biblical additions'. The fragments are dated palaeographically, not to the late second century B.C. as Yadin states, but to 'ca. 75 B.C.'. This peculiar Pentateuch may be a source of the Temple Scroll or alternatively, it may borrow from it. Another piece of revolutionary information supplied by Strugnell concerns a group of unpublished 4Q fragments, which were unknown to Yadin, containing 'quotations from, or the text of, the Temple Scroll, or at least one of its sources'. The script of this document can scarcely be placed to 'much later than 150 B.C.'.

various sacrifices and the construction of the altar (cols. 11–12). A series of statutes relates to the perpetual burnt-offering and to sacrifices for the Sabbath, the beginning of the months, the first day of the first month, the seven days of ordination, the Passover, the feast of Unleavened Bread and the festival of the Waving of the Sheaf (cols. 13–18).

The next section deals with the festivals of the First Fruits of Wheat, Wine and Oil (cols. 18–23). The Wood Offering festival was to be celebrated six days after that of the Oil and to be accompanied by several sacrifices (cols. 23–25).

The autumn high holidays were to start with the Day of Memorial on the first day of the seventh month, followed by the Day of Atonement and the Feast of Tabernacles, together with all their rituals (cols. 25–29). In conclusion, it is stated that these sacrifices were to be offered in the Temple to be built by the Israelites and were to continue until the day of blessing when a new Temple would be constructed by God in conformity with the Covenant which he made with Jacob in Bethel (cols. 29–30).

The buildings in the Temple courts are next described: the stairhouse, the house of ablutions, the house of the sacred utensils, and the slaughterhouse with its equipment. At this point, the Scroll introduces regulations concerning burnt-offerings (cols. 30–35).

Because of its extreme holiness, the area surrounding the altar was to be reserved for the priests alone, provided that they were ritually pure; access by all others was to be forbidden under the pain of death. A colonnade on the west side of the Sanctuary was to house the guilt and sin-offerings of the priests, which were to be kept separate from those of laymen (col. 35).

Of the three courts of the Temple, the inner court, similarly open only to priests, was to be furnished with four gates and an inner colonnade. The middle court, with twelve gates named after the sons of Jacob, was to admit men aged twenty or over, but not women or boys. The outer court, also possessing twelve gates, contained chambers for the Levites and booths for the lay leaders. Presumably, women and children were to be allowed to enter there (cols. 35–46).

The purity of the Temple was to be protected by bird-scarers and by a terrace before the gates of the outer court. A ditch around the Temple, 100 cubits wide, was to prevent any sudden approach to it. Further purity regulations excluded from the Temple and from its city men unfit on account of nocturnal emissions, sexual intercourse, blindness, venereal discharge, contact with a dead body and leprosy. Latrines were to be built at a distance of 3,000 cubits north-west of the city, and to the east, three separate reserves were to be established for men suffering from leprosy, venereal discharge and for those who had had a nocturnal emission. Only containers made of the skins of animals sacrificed in the Temple could be used inside the Temple city (cols. 46–47). A list of clean and unclean animals is supplied here (col. 48).

Special provisions are made to guard the purity of the cities of Israel. Four were to share a single cemetery, and places of quarantine were to be erected, not only for lepers and persons afflicted with a venereal disease, but also for women during menstruation and after childbirth. Laws are next listed concerning the house as a source of uncleanness when it contains a dead body. A woman carrying a dead child in her womb is declared analogous to a grave and declared ritually impure. Contact with animal carcasses is also said to cause uncleanness (cols. 48–51).

The remainder of the Scroll mostly follows Deuteronomy, first legislating on judges and officers (Deut. 16:18–19), and explicitly imposing the death penalty on a judge who takes bribes (col. 51). Laws against idolatry are listed according to Deut. 16:21–22, etc. (cols. 51–52).

Special rules relating to sacrificial and other animals include a ban on slaughtering blemished or pregnant animals and on the simultaneous sacrifice of a mother and her young. There follow laws concerning the offering of the first-born of the herd and the flock. The deuteronomic prohibition to muzzle a treading ox (Deut. 25:4) or to harness an ox and an ass together when ploughing (Deut. 22:10) is repeated. Clean animals were to be killed in the Temple; their slaughter was forbidden in an area within three days' journey from the city. Blemished clean animals were not to be killed within thirty stadia from the Temple and were not to be eaten in the city of the Temple (cols. 52–53).

Various commandments on vows, oaths and pledges, including those made by women, and the special conditions under which they might be cancelled form a short section (cols. 53–54). After it come laws aimed at the false prophet (Deut. 13:2–6), the seducer (Deut. 13:7–12), the apostate city (Deut. 13:13–19) and the idol worshipper (Deut. 17:2–7) (cols. 54–55).

Deut. 17:8–13 defines the function of the priests, Levites and judges, and Deut. 17:14–20 is considerably enlarged to provide the statutes of the Jewish king, with regulations dealing with the organization of the army, the royal bodyguard of 12,000 men, the king's council, the law of monogamy, and in general royal duties in peace and war (cols. 56–59).

Deut. 18:1–8 provides the framework for the determination of the priestly and Levitical dues and 18:9–14 bans the idols of the Gentiles (cols. 60–61). This leads on to legislation concerning witnesses, including the treatment of false witness (Deut. 19:15–21) (col. 61), the conduct of war (Deut. 20:1–21:14), and the treatment of a rebellious son (Deut. 21:18–21).

Deut. 21:22–23 provides a basis for the introduction of new laws in regard to crimes punishable by 'hanging', namely treason and the cursing of the Jewish people among Gentiles (col. 64). The Scroll ends with miscellaneous laws modelled on Deut. 22:1–29, and an incomplete list of rules against incest (Deut. 21:1, etc.) (cols. 64–66). The end of the document figured in the few lost lines at the top of col. 67. The surviving part of the final sheet of the manuscript is blank.[4]

Apart from the many scriptural citations, the Temple Scroll may be described as written in imitation biblical Hebrew coloured by syntactic and terminological features characteristic of inter-Testamental and rabbinic language.[5] Its bond with the Dead Sea literature is attested by the presence of typical Qumran words and idioms (TS I, p. 38). The linguistic aspects of the document will be touched on again in the discussion of the origin and date of the Temple Scroll (cf. pp. 412, 415).

Whereas the sequence of the subjects generally follows the Pentateuch, starting with Exodus and finishing with Deuteronomy, the structure of the Temple Scroll manifests an effort at systematization in that a law is freely combined with further rules on the same topic appearing elsewhere in the Torah. For example, legislation against incest begins with Deut. 23:1 and is completed by Deut. 27:22 and Lev. 18:12–13, 17; 20:13, 17, 19, 21 (col. 66:11–17).

The grouping of precepts may result in a legislation that is more developed, but it may also endeavour to harmonize duplicate commandments. Thus the obligation to pour away the blood of a slaughtered animal (Deut. 12:23–24) and the additional duty of covering it with earth (Lev. 17:13) are merged: 'Only be sure that you do not eat the blood; you shall pour it on the ground like water and cover it with dust' (col. 53:5–6). Perhaps the most striking illustration derives from the combination of Deut. 22:28–29 (a rapist must marry his unmarried or unbetrothed victim whom he cannot divorce later) with Exod. 22:16 (a seducer must marry the girl he has seduced) with the further specification that the law applies only if no legal

---

4. In addition to Yadin's Introduction and Commentary, the following studies may be consulted: J. Milgrom, 'Studies in the Temple Scroll', JBL 97 (1978), pp. 501–23; B. A. Levine, 'The Temple Scroll', BASOR 232 (1978), pp. 5–23; J. M. Baumgarten, Review of TS, JBL 97 (1978), pp. 584–9; 'The Pharisaic-Sadducean Controversies about Purity and the Qumran Texts', JJS 31 (1980), pp. 157–70.

5. In addition to TS I, pp. 34–8, see E. Qimron, 'The Language of the Temple Scroll', Lešonénu 42 (1978), pp. 83–98; 'The Text of the Temple Scroll', ibid., pp. 136–45 (both in Hebr.); G. Brin, 'Linguistic Comments on the Temple Scroll', ibid. 43 (1978), pp. 20–8 (Hebr.); L. H. Schiffman, 'The Temple Scroll in Literary and Philological Perspective', in W. S. Green (ed.), Approaches to Ancient Judaism II (1980), pp. 143–58; E. Kimron, 'The Vocabulary of the Temple Scroll', Shnaton 4 (1980), pp. 239–62 (Hebr. with English summary).

impediment opposes the union (col. 66:8–11). Elsewhere, the purpose of a supplement is to clarify the halakhic meaning of a scriptural passage. E.g. the addition of a reference to the blood of a dead person as a source of defilement to the text of Num. 19:16 renders explicit the import of Num. 19:13 where, on the basis of Lev. 17:14 and Deut. 12:23, 'soul' (נפש) is identified as 'blood' (דם);[6] hence the 'soul' causing uncleanness is understood as the dead man's blood.

Moreover, the sense of a biblical commandment may be substantially altered through affixing an extra clause. Deut. 21:10–14 enjoins the capturer of a woman prisoner to grant her a month's respite before cohabiting with her. However, once sexual intercourse has taken place she becomes his wife and may not be sold as a slave. The Temple Scroll nevertheless specifies that, although she may share his bed, she may not have any contact with his pure food or partake in sacrificial meals for another seven years (col. 63:13–15).

In addition to modifications such as these, the Scroll also includes whole complementary sections. The most important are (1) the Temple legislation proper, inspired by the rules of the desert tabernacle (Exod. 25–31, 35–40) and hinted at in 1 Chron. 28:11–12 (cols. 3–12, 30–46); (2) laws regulating the festivals (cols. 17–29); (3) purity rules relating to the Temple and its city (cols. 46–47); and (4) the much enlarged deuteronomic statutes of the king (cols. 56–59).

The literary genre of the document cannot easily be determined for, whereas the bulk of the material is concerned with the Temple, the last twenty columns of the manuscript deal with more general issues. Thus although the title, Temple Scroll, can be justified, the alternative designation of Qumran Torah, advanced by B. Z. Wacholder,[7] and indirectly by Yadin himself,[8] is no less appropriate. In favour of the thesis that the document enjoyed the status of Scripture in the Dead Sea community is the fact that the additional legislation consistently presents God as the speaker and that the quotations from Deuteronomy 12–23:1 are similarly re-phrased in columns 53–57 and 60–66. Therefore, notwithstanding that the grouping of parallel or related laws from diverse parts of Scripture and the insertion of explanatory comments into the biblical account itself point towards ancient Jewish exegesis (cf. Josephus' *Antiquities* or the Palestinian Targums), the adoption of the pronoun 'I' for God by the author of the Temple Scroll

6. *TS* I, pp. 335–6. For the interpretation of נפש as דם, see Tg. Ps.-Jon. on Num. 19:13. mOhol. 2:2 lists the blood of a dead man among the sources of uncleanness.
7. B. Z. Wacholder, *The Dawn of Qumran: The Sectarian Torah and the Teacher of Righteousness* (1983), p. 31.
8. *TS* I, p. 392: 'It is difficult to avoid the conclusion that the author—and *a fortiori*, the members of the sect—regarded (the Scroll) as a veritable Torah of the Lord.' Yadin's popular book is entitled *The Temple Scroll: The Hidden Law of the Dead Sea Sect* (1985).

can only stress that the contents of the writing represent a divine revelation to Moses[9] more immediate than the biblical recension, which contains only a Mosaic re-wording of the commandments of God. A comparison between Deut. 21:5 and its re-edited version in col. 63:3 may illustrate this point.

And the priests, the sons of Levi,   And the priests, the sons of Levi,
shall come forward,   shall come forward,
for *YHWH your God* has chosen them   for *I* have chosen them
to minister to *him*   to minister to *me*
and to bless in the name of *YHWH*.   and to bless in *my* name.[10]

The origin of the Temple Scroll is the subject of unresolved controversy among scholars. A non-Qumran derivation is argued on linguistic and doctrinal grounds by B. A. Levine,[11] L. A. Schiffman,[12] and H. Stegemann.[13] The opposite view is championed, also on ideological and philological grounds, by Yadin and most other writers. The linguistic evidence is presented summarily in *TS* I, p. 38, but Yadin's thesis is confirmed by G. Brin's study.[14]

The doctrinal kinship between the Temple Scroll and other Dead

---

9. The name of Moses does not appear in the extant document; neither does it figure in Yadin's concordance. However, in col. 45:5, God qualifies Aaron as 'your brother'. Whether the introduction of the first person style is due exclusively to the author of the Temple Scroll will not be known until the relevant 4Q material is published, but the evidence quoted in n. 3 suggests that this may well have been the case.

10. Yadin sees an additional argument in favour of the canonical status of the document in its use of square Hebrew letters for writing the Tetragram, a peculiarity common to the Scroll and to the biblical manuscripts from Qumran. By contrast, in the non-canonical *pesharim* the divine name is spelled with proto-Hebraic characters (*TS* I, p. 392; cf. *The Temple Scroll: The Hidden Law* ..., p. 224). This argument is, however, unconvincing, for on the one hand the Psalms Scroll from Cave 11, a biblical manuscript, employs archaic letters for the Tetragram; on the other hand, several *pesher* fragments from Cave 4, published in DJD V, display square characters for YHWH (cf. index). Yadin was not unaware of these facts (cf. *TS* I, p. 392, n. 10). For the scribal evidence concerning the divine name prior to the Temple Scroll, see J. P. Siegel, 'The Employment of Palaeo-Hebrew Characters for the Divine Names at Qumran in the Light of Tannaitic Sources', HUCA 42 (1971), pp. 159–72.

11. B. A. Levine, 'The Temple Scroll: Aspects of its Provenance and Literary Character', BASOR 232 (1978), pp. 5–23. See rejoinders by J. Milgrom, 'Sabbath and Temple City in the Temple Scroll', *ibid.*, pp. 25–7, and by Y. Yadin, 'Is the Temple Scroll a Sectarian Document?', *Thirty Years of Archaeology in Eretz-Israel 1948–1978* (1981), pp. 152–71 (Hebr.).

12. L. H. Schiffman, *art. cit.* [in n. 4], pp. 143–58. This article, written soon after the first appearance of the Hebrew edition of the Temple Scroll, contains some hasty generalizations.

13. 'Die Bedeutung der Qumranfunde für die Erforschung der Apokalyptik', in D. Hellholm (ed.), *Apocalypticism in the Mediterranean World and the Near East* (1983), pp. 515–16.

14. 'The Bible as reflected in the Temple Scroll', Shnaton 4 (1980), p. 223 (Hebr.).

Sea documents, in particular the Damascus Rule, strongly favours recognition of the former as part of Qumran literature. The solar calendar to which they both testify (*TS* I, pp. 116–19) may admittedly serve only as background, since the same system of reckoning time also underlies Jubilees and 1 Enoch, neither of which is likely to have originated in the sect. On the other hand, the feast of the new oil (col. 21:12), a feast peculiar to the Temple Scroll and dated to the twenty-second day of the sixth month, appears in an unpublished calendar fragment from Cave 4 quoted by J. T. Milik.[15]

The most important ideological overlap with the Damascus Rule relates to the ban on royal polygamy, on marriage between uncle and niece, and on sexual intercourse in the city of the Sanctuary (CD 4:20–5:11; 12:1–2). The case of obligatory monogamy, of general application in the Damascus Rule though particularly associated with King David, figures explicitly in col. 57:16–18 among the Scroll's statutes of the king: 'He shall take for himself a wife from the family of his father. And he shall not take another wife in addition to her, for she alone shall be with him all the days of her life.'[16] The prohibition of matrimony between uncle and niece is stated formally in col. 66:15–17 in the section dealing with incest: 'No man shall marry his brother's daughter or his sister's daughter.'[17] As for the ban on sexual intercourse in the holy city,[18] it is not given as a formal statute as in CD 12:1–2 but may be deduced from col. 45:11–12 by means of an *a fortiori* reasoning: 'If a man lies with his wife and ejaculates, he shall not enter any part of the city of the Sanctuary ... for three days.'[19]

Features common to the Temple Scroll and the War Rule are equally noteworthy. The exclusion of women and under-age boys from the camps of the Sons of Light during the eschatological war (*1QM*

---

15. 'Le travail d'édition des manuscrits du Désert de Juda', *Volume du Congrès Strasbourg 1956* (1957), p. 25; *Ten Years of Discovery*, p. 109.

16. *TS* I, pp. 355–7. Cf. Vermes, PBJS, pp. 40–1, 50–6; J. A. Fitzmyer, 'The Matthean Divorce Texts and some new Palestinian Evidence', Theol. Studies 37 (1976), pp. 197–226; 'Divorce among First-Century Palestinian Jews', Eretz-Israel 14 (1978), pp. 103–10; J. B. Mueller, 'The Temple Scroll and the Gospel Divorce Texts', RQ 10 (1980), pp. 247–56.

17. Cf. L. Ginzberg, *An Unknown Jewish Sect* (1970), pp. 23–4; Vermes, PBJS, pp. 40–1; Wacholder, *op. cit.* [in n. 6 above], p. 126.

18. I.e. Jerusalem (*pace* Levine who limits it to the area surrounding the Temple). Cf. Ginzberg, *op. cit.*, pp. 73–4; J. M. Baumgarten, *Studies in Qumran Law* (1977), p. 41.

19. In other words, if the sex act performed elsewhere rendered a man unfit to enter the Temple city for three days afterwards, *a fortiori* no intercourse could ever be licit within that city's boundaries. In fact, the establishment of areas reserved for ritually unclean men, but none for women (col. 46:16–18), indicates that there were no permanent female residents in the Temple city. The other Jewish towns catered for women during their periods and after childbirth by creating quarters for them outside the inhabited area (col. 48:14–17).

7:3–4) is parallel to the ban on women in the city of the Temple implicit in the absence of special restricted areas outside for those who were ritually unclean. As has been seen, such places of segregation existed in the other towns of Israel (cf. col. 48:16 contrasted with 46:16–18). Similarly, the building of latrines (מקום יד) 3,000 cubits north-west of the Temple city (col. 46:13–16) recalls a similar arrangement for מקום היד at 2,000 cubits' distance from the camps (*1QM* 7:6–7).[20]

Finally both the Temple Scroll and the Nahum Commentary from Cave 4 refer to the uncommon form of death penalty by 'hanging men (alive) on the tree'. In *4QpNah* (see vol. I, pp. 224–5), the Furious Young Lion (Alexander Jannaeus) is said to have taken revenge of his enemies in such a way. In its turn, the Temple Scroll prescribes this form of execution in the case of a traitor or of one who, guilty of a capital crime, has fled abroad and cursed Israel, his own people (col. 64:6–13).[21]

Taken together, all these common elements seem to recommend the theory that the Temple Scroll in its final shape sprang from the same source as the other sectarian writings from Qumran, above all the Damascus Rule.

Still in connection with the genre and the purpose of the Temple Scroll, the question arises whether it is to be regarded as a historical code of law or as an eschatological legislation intended for the age of the new creation rather than for the present world. The basic answer is not in doubt. The wording of the commandments concerning the Sanctuary indicates that the author of the Scroll envisaged throughout a this-worldly edifice and worship. In fact, in col. 29:8–10, he expressly points to another everlasting Temple which God would create in the age to come: 'And I will consecrate my Sanctuary by my glory, and I will cause my glory to dwell on it until the day of Blessing[22] on which I will create my Sanctuary, establishing it for myself for all days according to the Covenant which I made with Jacob at Bethel.'[23]

Both the general context, postulating Mosaic antiquity, and the divergence of the architectural plan in the Scroll from that of Ezekiel's Temple, as well as from the Second Temple and the Herodian Sanctuary,[24] suggest that the document speaks of the edifice which

20. Cf. *TS* I, pp. 294–304. For a different rendering of the phrase, see Wacholder, *op. cit.* [in n. 6], p. 7.

21. Cf. *TS* I, pp. 373–9. On the literature on 'hanging', cf. below, p. 431.

22. Qimron reads הברית instead of Yadin's הברכה. Cf. Lešonénu 42 (1978), p. 142.

23. Cf. *TS* I, pp. 182–7. The notion of a Temple made by God as part of a new creation is well attested in Jub. 1:15–17; 26–9.

24. *TS* I, pp. 188–200. For the apparently Hasmonaean features of the slaughterhouse, see below, p. 415.

Solomon was to build. The First Temple, as is well known, is not described in detail in the Bible, but it is not without interest to note that Josephus' picture of Solomon's Sanctuary displays notable similarities to the Qumran scroll.[25]

The dating of the Temple Scroll in the absence of apparently important 4Q material cannot but be conjectural. The earliest date advanced is that of the fourth or third century B.C. The theory is that of H. Stegemann who in a summary notice denies the Qumran origin of the document.[26] B. Z. Wacholder also champions a relatively early date, 200 B.C., although he tries to reconcile this with a sectarian origin within the framework of his own reconstruction of the early chronology of Qumran.[27]

Since the Temple Scroll contains no uncontroversial chronological data, scholars have had to rely on indirect evidence furnished by palaeography, philology, the contents of the document and its relationship to other Qumran writings. The latter point envisages the Scroll in its final form irrespective of its possible or probable prehistory.

As regards the script of the main manuscript and of the fragments from Cave 11, it is considered to be Herodian, i.e. late first century B.C. or early first century A.D. The turn of the eras therefore appears to be the *terminus ad quem*. The use of the Cave 4 fragments (Rockefeller 43.366 and the document mentioned by Strugnell in n. 3) cannot safely serve for dating purposes as they probably reflect a source, or a pre-Qumran recension, of the Temple Scroll. The linguistic features yield little in the way of positive evidence either beyond indicating that they belong to the latter part of the second Temple period. The 'mishnaic' traits would definitely militate against an early, pre-second century B.C., dating.

Nor are the contents of the Scroll particularly helpful, though Yadin has selected three data which in his opinion suggest a Hasmonaean origin for the composition. References to rings in the slaughterhouse, as well as to pillars and wheels (col. 34:1–7), imply that the author envisaged the existence of equipment intended to immobilise the sacrificial victims. The Mishnah describes a similar system (Mid. 3:5), but it alludes also (M.Sh. 5:15; Sot. 9:10) to an innovation in the slaughter ritual. Yohanan, the High Priest (thought to be John Hyrcanus I) is said to have dismissed the נוקפים or 'stunners', Temple functionaries whose task it was to render the animals unconscious by pole-axing them (tSot. 13:10). Yohanan apparently decreed that this practice blemished the victims and thus rendered them unfit for the

25. See *Ant.* viii 3, 1–9 (61–98).
26. *Art. cit.* [in n. 13], p. 516.
27. *Op. cit.* [in n. 6], pp. 171–229.

altar, and introduced rings (and chains) instead to which they were tied (ySot. 24a).[28] Yadin considers this concatenation of data sufficiently reliable to conclude that the Scroll must have originated during the reign of John Hyrcanus (135/4–104 B.C.), if not slightly earlier.[29] More sceptical students of rabbinic literature are less inclined to accept this argument as constituting solid evidence. Besides, the notorious hostility between the Dead Sea sectaries and the Hasmonean rulers weakens further the evidential value of these texts. If Yadin's conjecture were accepted as being at least probable, viz. that the Hyrcanus reform was inspired either by the Temple Scroll itself or by the sect's ideas underlying it, this objection would be eliminated. But it remains pure speculation.

Furthermore, Yadin finds the regulations concerning offensive and defensive war particularly well suited to the conditions prevailing in the time of Hyrcanus I (cf. cols. 58–59). Again, the author's insistence on the Jewish ethnicity and the religious qualities of the royal bodyguard (col. 57:5–11) may be seen as a criticism of the employment of foreign mercenaries by the same Hasmonaean ruler (*Ant.* xiii 8, 4 (249)). In a more general sense, the Scroll's royal statutes are associated by M. Weinfeld[30] and D. Mendels[31] with Hellenistic royal ideologies. If so, the second half of the second century B.C. would form an appropriate historical background.

Hanging as a special form of capital punishment, referred to earlier (p. 414) and mentioned again apropos of the Nahum Commentary (p. 431), is the third historical pointer cited by Yadin (*TS* I, pp. 373–8, 389). If, as is likely, the execution in question, practised also by the Romans (עושה שהמלכות כדרך),[32] is crucifixion, the only known Jewish parallel is furnished by the gruesome episode when Alexander Jannaeus crucified 800 Pharisees who were his political opponents.[33]

28. Cf. *TS* I, pp. 230–1. See also S. Lieberman, *Hellenism in Jewish Palestine* (1962), pp. 140–1.

29. But would the Qumran Community have approved of a custom invented by a Hasmonaean? Yadin tacitly overcomes this objection by assuming 'that it was the commands of the scroll—or the concept behind them favoured by the author and his sect—that influenced John Hyrcanus to make the changes in the Temple in their spirit' (*TS* I, p. 388).

30. '"Temple Scroll" and "King's Law"', Shnaton 3 (1978–9), pp. 214–37; 'The Royal Guard according to the Temple Scroll', RB 87 (1980), pp. 394–6.

31. '"On Kingship" in the "Temple Scroll" and the Ideological *Vorlage* of the Seven Banquets in the "Letter of Aristeas to Philocrates"', Aegyptus 59 (1979), pp. 127–36.

32. Sifre on Deut. 21:22 (221); bSanh. 46b.

33. *Ant.* xiii 14, 2 (380): ἀνασταυρῶσαι; *B.J.* i 4, 6 (97): ἀνασταυρώσας. The episode of eighty women 'hanged' by Simeon ben Shetah in Ashkelon according to mSanh. 6:4 is historically unreliable. Cf. vol. I, p. 231. See also M. Hengel, 'Rabbinische Legende und frühpharisäische Geschichte: Schimeon b. Schetach und die achtzig Hexen von Askalon', AWH, Philos.-hist. Kl. (1984/2).

Moreover, crucifixion does not seem to have been current during the reign of Herod, but became common during the Roman administration of Judaea and consequently an abomination in Jewish eyes.[34] In the circumstances, the Hasmonaean age appears to be the only convenient chronological framework for the Temple Scroll passage.

Yadin's argumentation falls short of proving that the Temple Scroll was actually composed in the days of John Hyrcanus. It offers, nevertheless, a reasonably strong hypothesis for an early Qumran dating. Study of the literary interrelations between the Scroll and the Damascus Rule (cf. above, p. 413) as well as the War Rule and the Nahum Commentary also suggest that priority belongs to the Temple Scroll. If therefore the Damascus Rule is to be dated to 100 B.C. or a little later (cf. p. 396), the same period would provide a likely *terminus ante quem* for the Scroll.[35] Needless to say, if it had a prehistory, as seems to be the case, it could date back to the first half of the second century B.C. or even earlier.

The authorship of the Temple Scroll is no more ascertainable than any of the other Qumran writings, but because of its probable early date and authoritative nature it is bound to be associated with the name of the Teacher of Righteousness. Yadin proposes this cautiously. He identifies the Temple Scroll as 'the Sealed Book of the Law'[36] which Zadok, i.e. the founder of the community (the Teacher of Righteousness) discovered according to CD 5:2–5. He further conjectures that this was the Torah sent by the Teacher to the Wicked Priest (*4QpPs* on Ps. 37:32–33).[37] B. Z. Wacholder goes much further in his elaborate reconstruction of Qumran history, dating the Temple Scroll to 200 B.C. and the life-span of the Teacher of Righteousness to 240–170 B.C., a rather large mouthful to swallow.[38]

The only definite sources of which the author of the Temple Scroll availed himself are the books of the Bible. The publication of the fragments from Cave 4 may however modify this judgement. Even so, a document purporting to be direct divine revelation is unlikely to contain literary quotations. By contrast, it is probable that the Scroll

---

34. Cf. M. Hengel, *Crucifixion in the Ancient World* (1977), pp. 84–5.

35. The absence of any reference to the Feast of the Renewal of the Covenant in the Temple Scroll is interpreted by T. Elgvin as indicating that it is earlier than *1QS* or CD. He dates the Temple Scroll to mid-second century B.C. Cf. 'The Qumran Covenant Festival and the Temple Scroll', *JJS* 36 (1985), pp. 103–6.

36. *TS* I, pp. 394–5. Yadin further suggests that it is connected with the 'Book of Hagu' (CD 10:6; 13:2; 14:7; *1QSa* 1:7) and 'the Book of the Second Torah' (ספר התורה שנית) from *4Q177*, line 14 (DJD V, p. 67). Cf. *TS* I, pp. 393–4, 396–7.

37. *TS* I, p. 396.

38. *Op. cit.* [in n. 6], pp. 99–140, 202–12.

418 §32. *Jewish Literature in Hebrew or Aramaic*

influenced the Damascus Rule, and indirectly perhaps the War Rule and the Nahum Commentary.

Its impact on non-sectarian writers remains highly problematic. Yadin's hypothesis concerning Josephus' dependence on the Temple Scroll in his description of Solomon's Sanctuary is wildly speculative (cf. I, p. 194). Equally fragile is Wacholder's theory in regard to Eupolemus' use of the Temple Scroll.[39] The Qumran parallels are too flimsy, largely because of the bad state of conservation of the relevant passages. Furthermore, the date of the completion of Eupolemus' work (157 B.C. according to Wacholder) would necessitate an early second century or third century B.C. origin for the Temple Scroll.

For rabbinic allusions to a Temple Scroll, linked to 1 Chron. 28:11–12, see *Midrash Shemuel* (ed. S. Buber, 1893) 15:3 (p. 92), where מגילת בית המקדש is said to have been transmitted from God to Moses, to Joshua, to the elders, to the prophets, to David and finally to Solomon. Cf. also Yalq. Shim'oni 115. See also yMeg. 70a; ySanh. 29a; Agad. Bereshith (ed. Buber) 38:1 (pp. 75–6). See *TS* I, pp. 403–4.

Editions

Yadin, Y., מגילת המקדש I-III (1977).
Idem, The Temple Scroll I-III (1983).

Translations

English
Yadin, Y., *op. cit.*

French
Caquot, A., 'Le Rouleau du Temple', Et. Théol. Rel. 53 (1978), pp. 443–500.

German
Maier, J., *Die Tempelrolle vom Toten Meer* (1978).

Spanish
García, F., 'El Rollo del Templo', Est. Bibl. 36 (1977), pp. 247–92.

Bibliography

Yadin, Y., 'The Temple Scroll', BA 30 (1967), pp. 135–9 [repr. in D. N. Freedman and J. C. Greenfield (eds.), *New Directions in Biblical Archaeology* (1971), pp. 139–48].
Idem, 'The Gate of the Essenes and the Temple Scroll', *Jerusalem Revealed: Archaeology of the Holy City 1968–1974* (1976), pp. 90–1.
Idem, 'Le Rouleau du Temple', in M. Delcor (ed.), *Qumrân* (1978), pp. 115–19.
Ploeg, J. van der, 'Une halakha inédite de Qumrân', *ibid.*, pp. 105–13.
Levine, B. A., 'The Temple Scroll: Aspects of its Historical Provenance and Literary Character', BASOR 232 (1978), pp. 5–23.
Milgrom, J., 'Sabbath and Temple City in the Temple Scroll', *ibid.*, pp. 25–7.
Idem, 'Studies in the Temple Scroll', JBL 97 (1978), pp. 501–23.
Lehman, M. R., 'The Temple Scroll as Source of Sectarian Halakhah', RQ 9 (1978), pp. 579–87.

39. *Ibid.* pp.62–77. Eupolemus' text is preserved in Eusebius, *Praep. ev.* ix 34, 4–16. Cf. in general, Wacholder, *Eupolemus: A Study of Judeo-Greek Literature* (1974).

Kimron, E., 'New Readings in the Temple Scroll', IEJ 28 (1978), pp. 161–72.
Idem, 'The Language of the Temple Scroll', Lešonénu 42 (1978), pp. 83–98.
Idem, 'The Text of the Temple Scroll', IEJ 28 (1978), pp. 161–72.
Weinfeld, M., '"Temple Scroll" and "King's Law"', Shnaton 3 (1978–9), pp. 213–47 (Hebr.).
Mendels, D., '"On Kingship" in the "Temple Scroll" and the Ideological *Vorlage* of the Seven Banquets in the "Letter of Aristeas to Philocrates"', Aegyptus 59 (1979), pp. 127–36.
Bernstein, M. J., 'Midrash Halakhah at Qumran? 11Q Temple 64:6–13 and Deuteronomy 21:22–23', Gesher 7 (1979), pp. 145–66.
Baumgarten, J. M., 'The Pharisaic-Sadducean Controversies about Purity and the Qumran Texts', JJS 31 (1980), pp. 157–70.
Milgrom, J., 'Further Studies in the Temple Scroll', JQR 71 (1980), pp. 1–17.
Maier, J., 'Die Hofanlagen im Tempel-Entwurf des Ezechiel im Lichte der "Tempelrolle" von Qumran', in J. Emerton (ed.), *Prophecy: Essays presented to G. Fohrer* (1980), pp. 55–68.
Schiffman, L. H., 'The Temple Scroll in Literary and Philological Perspective', in W. S. Green, *Approaches to Ancient Judaism* II (1980), pp. 143–58.
Mueller, J. B., 'The Temple Scroll and the Gospel Divorce Texts', RQ 10 (1980), pp. 247–56.
Weinfeld, M., 'The Royal Guard according to the Temple Scroll', RB 87 (1980), pp. 394–6.
Jongeling, B., 'A propos de la Colonne xxiii du Rouleau du Temple', RQ 10 (1981), pp. 593–5.
Thiering, B. E., '*Mebaqqer* and *Episkopos* in the Light of the Temple Scroll', JBL 100 (1981), pp. 59–74.
Delcor, M., 'Le statut du roi d'après le Rouleau du Temple', Henoch 3 (1981), pp. 47–68.
Thorion, Y., 'Zur Bedeutung von גבורי חיל למלחמה in 11QT LVII,9'—'Zur Bedeutung von חטא in 11QT', RQ 10 (1981), pp. 597–9.
Laperrousaz, E. M., 'Note à propos de la datation du Rouleau du Temple', RQ 10 (1981), pp. 447–52.
Schwartz, D., 'The Contemners of Judges and Men (11QTemple 64:12)', Lešonénu 47 (1982), pp. 18–24 (Hebr.).
Tov, E., 'The Temple Scroll and Old Testament Textual Criticism', Eretz-Israel 16 (1982), pp. 100–11 (Hebr.).
Bogaard, L. van den, 'Le Rouleau du Temple. Quelques remarques concernant les "petits fragments"', in W. C. Delsman *et al.* (eds.), *Von Kanaan bis Kerala. Festschrift für ... J. P. M. van der Ploeg* (1982), pp. 285–94.
Wilson, A. M., and Willis, L., 'Literary Sources of the Temple Scroll', HThR 75 (1982), pp. 287–8.
Sweeney, M. A., 'Sefirah at Qumran: Aspects of the Counting Formulas for the First-Fruit Festivals in the Temple Scroll', BASOR 251 (1983), pp. 61–6.
Thorion, Y., Die Sprache der Tempelrolle und die Chronikbücher', RQ 11 (1983), pp. 423–6.
Idem, 'Tempelrolle lix, 8–11 und Bablî, Sanhedrin 98a', *ibid.*, pp. 427–8.
Wacholder, B. Z., *The Dawn of Qumran: The Sectarian Torah and the Teacher of Righteousness* (1983).
Rokéah, D., 'The Temple Scroll, Philo, Josephus, and the Talmud', JThSt 34 (1983), pp. 515–26.
Bernstein, M. J., "כי קללת אלהים תלוי" (Deut. 21:23): A Study of Early Jewish Exegesis', JQR 74 (1983), pp. 21–45.
Dimant, D., 'Qumran Sectarian Literature', JWSTP II (1984), pp. 526–30.

Elgvin, T., 'The Qumran Covenant Festival and the Temple Scroll', JJS 36 (1985), pp. 103–6.

Hengel, M., Charlesworth, J. H., and Mendels, D., 'The Polemical Character of the "On Kingship" in the Temple Scroll: An Attempt at Dating 11Q Temple', JJS 37 (1986) (forthcoming).

VIII B. Bible Interpretation

The surviving manuscript evidence proves that scriptural exegesis was one of the chief literary activities of the Qumran Community.[1] From the structural point of view, it may be divided into three classes. (1) Interpretative extracts figure in the Rules, especially in the Damascus Rule, as supports of doctrinal claims. (2) There are also paraphrastic re-wordings, altering the original significance of a text, inserted e.g. into the Temple Scroll. These two non-autonomous units require no special treatment here. (3) The Dead Sea manuscripts include also a proper exposition of Scripture reflecting two types of exegetical procedure: (i) interpretation of a particular book; and (ii) midrash devoted to a theme, and utilising several works of the Bible. The former may take the shape of a quasi-verse-by-verse exegesis (the prime example is the Habakkuk Commentary), or a more or less free recasting of the biblical account in the style of Jubilees and the Qumran Genesis Apocryphon (cf. pp. 318–25 above). The latter (i.e., exegesis of a combination of scriptural passages) may develop legal or doctrinal topics (Ordinances— Florilegium, etc.), or present simply a set of proof texts (Testimonia, Catenae).

As far as exegetical method is concerned, the Qumran documents reflect the peculiarities of the halakhic and haggadic midrash (cf. vol. II, pp. 337–55), as well as those of the 're-written Bible', that is, a reformulation of the scriptural text in which Bible and interpretation merge into a single new narrative. The most characteristic type of

---

1. For a study of Qumran exegesis, the following works may be consulted: W. H. Brownlee, 'Biblical Interpretation among the Sectaries of the Dead Sea Scrolls', BA 14 (1951), pp. 54–76; F. F. Bruce, *Biblical Exegesis in the Qumran Texts* (1959); O. Betz, *Offenbarung und Schriftforschung in der Qumransekte* (1960); G. Vermes, *Scripture and Tradition in Judaism—Haggadic Studies* (1961, [2]1973); J. Carmignac, 'Notes sur les Pesharim', RQ 3 (1962), pp. 505–38; J. D. Amusin, 'Bemerkungen zu den Qumran-Kommentaren', in *Bibel und Qumran—Festschrift H. Bardtke* (1968), pp. 9–19; E. Slomovic, 'Toward an Understanding of the Exegesis in the Dead Sea Scrolls', RQ 7 (1969), pp. 3–15; G. Vermes, *Post-biblical Jewish Studies* (1975), pp. 35–56; L. H. Schiffman, *The Halakhah at Qumran* (1975); G. Vermes, 'Interpretation (The History of) at Qumran', IDBS (1976), pp. 438–41; J. M. Baumgarten, *Studies in Qumran Law* (1976); P. M. Horgan, *Pesharim: Qumran Interpretation of Biblical Books* (1979); H. Gabrion, 'L'interprétation de l'Écriture à Qumrân', ANRW II.19.1 (1979), pp. 779–848; G. J. Brooke, 'Qumran Pesher: Towards a Redefinition of a Genre', RQ 10 (1981), pp. 483–503; L. H. Schiffman, *Sectarian Law and the Dead Sea Scrolls* (1983); D. Dimant, 'Qumran Sectarian Literature: Biblical Interpretation', in M. Stone (ed.), JWSTP II, pp. 503–8.

Qumran exegesis is known as *pēsher*.[2] It exemplifies the genre which may be designated as fulfilment interpretation, i.e. an exposition in which the meaning of an oracle, or of a presumed prophecy, is determined by the historical event or personality which the biblical author is thought to have predicted. According to Qumran belief, the key to the solution of the mysteries of the sacred words was entrusted by God to the Teacher of Righteousness and through him to his disciples (*1QpHab.* 6:14–7:5). In other words, in the sect's teaching, divine revelation regarding the end-time was transmitted in two stages: the prophets received and conveyed it in an imperfect form, but the Teacher was granted full knowledge and passed it on to his immediate followers who, in their turn, disclosed it to the initiates of the Qumran Community.

Another interpretative genre explicitly named is *midrash* (*4QFlor* 1:14; cf. CD 20:6) in connection with the exegesis of a combination of biblical passages.

The individual Qumran Bible commentaries will be presented in the order of the books of Scripture in the Hebrew Canon. The composite works, on the other hand, will be arranged thematically, as devoted to law, messianism, eschatology, etc.

i. Interpretation of Particular Books

1. The Genesis Apocryphon (1QapGen)

This important work, preserved among the Dead Sea Scrolls but probably of pre-sectarian origin, has already been analysed on pp. 218–25.

2. The Ages of the Creation (4Q180)

A Hebrew fragment from Cave 4 has been edited under this misleading title by J. M. Allegro in DJD V, pp. 77–9. A less controversial description is provided by the opening line of the text, פשר על הקצים, 'Interpretation of the Ages'. The script is characterized by J. Strugnell as 'late Herodian', i.e. no doubt belonging to the first century A.D.

The text alludes, in the context of a chronology of seventy weeks of years, to the birth of Isaac, the fall of Azazel and the other angels, and the birth of the giants (cf. *4Q181*, fr. 2, line 3; cf. *4Q180*, fr. 1, line 5). There seem to be further hints at Abraham and his three visitors at Mamre, and possibly at the sacrifice of Isaac on Mt. Moriah, identified as Zion or Jerusalem.

---

2. The introductory formulae appearing between the text and its interpretation use phrases such as 'Its interpretation concerns' (פשרו על), 'The interpretation of the saying concerns' (פשר הדבר על), etc. A repeated part of a longer quotation is preceded by 'And that which he said' (ואשר אמר). Cf. *1QpHab, passim*. For a full description, see M. P. Horgan, *Pesharim* (1979), pp. 239–44.

The nature of this document cannot be established with any degree of confidence beyond the generalities already stated. Strugnell wonders whether *4Q180* might be a commentary on *4Q181*, a sectarian wisdom composition.[1] J. T. Milik, in turn, associates not only these two fragments from Cave 4, but also the Melkizedek document from Cave 11.[2]

Edition

Allegro, J. M., DJD V (1968), pp. 77–9; cf. pp. 79–80 for *4Q181*.

Translation

English
Allegro, *op. cit.*
Vermes, DSSE², pp. 259–60.

French
Milik, *art. cit.* [in n. 2], pp. 112, 119–21.

Italian
Moraldi, L., MQ, pp. 685–91.

Bibliography

Allegro, J. M., 'Some Unpublished Fragments of Pseudepigraphical Literature from Qumran's Fourth Cave', ALUOS 4 (1962–3), pp. 3–6.
Hoenig, S. B., 'The New Qumran Pesher on Azazel', JQR 56 (1966), pp. 248–53.
Strugnell, J., *art. cit.* [in n. 1], pp. 254–6.

3. The Blessings of Jacob (4QPBless)

A small section of a Cave 4 document, devoted to a commentary on Gen. 49, and corresponding to the classic messianic verse, Gen. 49:10, has been available in a preliminary edition since 1956, but failed to be included in DJD V.

The main emphasis of the interpretation lies on the necessity, 'whenever Israel rules', of the Davidic descent of the king until and including 'the Messiah of Righteousness', called also the 'Branch of David'.[1] The exegesis probably discloses an anti-Hasmonaean sentiment, and is best assigned to the pre-Herodian epoch.

The full edition, entrusted apparently to J. T. Milik, is still to come.

Editions

Allegro, J. M., 'Further Messianic References in Qumran Literature', JBL 75 (1956), pp. 174–6.

1. 'Notes en marge du volume V des *Discoveries in the Judaean Desert of Jordan*', RQ 7 (1970), pp. 252, 254.
2. 'Milkî-ṣedeq et Milkî-reša' dans les anciens écrits juifs et chrétiens', JJS 23 (1972), pp. 109–24. In her yet unpublished 'Pesher on the Periods' D. Dimant rejects this combination on material and structural grounds. Cf. 'Qumran Sectarian Literature', JWSTP II, p. 521, n. 185.
1. Cf. vol. II, pp. 550–1; Vermes, DSS, pp. 184–5, 195.

Lohse, E., TQHD, pp. 245–7.

Translations

English
Vermes, DSSE², p. 224.

French
Dupont-Sommer, A., EE, pp. 327–8.
Carmignac, J., TQ II, pp. 285–8.

German
Maier, J., TTM I, pp. 182–3.
Lohse, *op. cit.*

Italian
Moraldi, L., MQ, pp. 570–1.

Bibliography

Wieder, N., 'Notes on the new Documents from the Fourth Cave of Qumran', JJS 7 (1956), pp. 72–4.
Yadin, Y., 'Some Notes on Commentaries on Genesis XLIX and Isaiah from Cave 4', IEJ 7 (1957), pp. 66–8.
Vermes, G., *Scripture and Tradition* (1961, ²1973), pp. 52–3.
Stegemann, H., 'Weitere Stücke von 4QpPs37, von 4Q Patriarchal Blessings ...', RQ 6 (1967–9), pp. 193–227.
Vermes, DSS, p. 69.
Schwartz, D. R., 'The Messianic Departure from Judah (4Q Patriarchal Blessings)', TZ 37 (1981), pp. 257–66.

4. *Pentateuch Anthology* (4Q158)

Fourteen fragments (written by a 'Herodian' hand, according to J. Strugnell) of a work entitled 'Biblical Paraphrase: Genesis-Exodus' have been published by J. M. Allegro in DJD V. The designation is misleading because the extracts are neither restricted to Genesis or Exodus, nor generally paraphrastic. In fact, they mostly reproduce the biblical text without real exegetical additions. The passages appear in the following somewhat haphazard order: Gen. 32:25–32; Exod. 4:27–8 (Frs. 1–2); Gen. 32:31 (?) (Fr. 3);[1] Exod. 3:12; 24:4–6 (Fr. 4); Exod. 19:17–23 (Fr. 5); Exod. 20:12, 16, 17, 21, 22–26; 21:1, 3, 4, 6, 8, 10 (Frs. 7–8); Exod. 21:15, 16, 18, 20, 22, 25 (Fr. 9); Exod. 21:32, 34, 35–37; 22:1–11, 13 (Frs. 10–12); Ex. 30:32, 34 (Fr. 13); Apocryphal discourse of God after the exodus (Fr. 14).[2]

The only notable exegetical supplement, in addition to Fr. 14, appears in Frs. 1–2, lines 7–12, and represents the blessing of Jacob by the angel, alluded to in Gen. 32:29: 'And he said to him: May the Lo[rd] make you fruitful [and multiply] you ... [kno]wledge and

---

1. Strugnell, RQ 7 (1970), p. 170, wonders whether this passage derives from Jacob's death-bed speech.

2. For a fresh reading of Fr. 14, see Strugnell, *art. cit.*, pp. 175–6.

understanding, and may he deliver you from all violence and ... until this day and for everlasting ages ...' The blessing is followed by the proclamation of a ritual precept: 'And when he had blessed him there, he went on his way ... on that day and he said, "Do not eat ..."'

Edition

Allegro, J. M., DJD V, pp. 1–6.

Bibliography

Strugnell, J., 'Notes en marge ...', RQ 7 (1970), pp. 168–75.

5. The Words of Moses (1QDM = 1Q22)

Fragments belonging to four very poorly preserved columns of a manuscript have been pieced together by J. T. Milik in DJD I, pp. 91–7. They form an anthological account of a divine revelation to Moses and his message to the Israelites. Since the inspiration of the work is mainly deuteronomic, Milik proposes the title, 'Little Deuteronomy', modelled on 'Little Genesis', the secondary designation of the Book of Jubilees (cf. above, p. 315).

If the heavily reconstructed text of the editor is accepted, the document consists, in addition to the date of the event (1:1–2: the first day of the eleventh month in the fortieth year after the exodus from Egypt: cf. Dt. 1:3) of a speech by God (1:2–11), followed by Moses' address to Eleazar and Joshua, exhorting them to faithfulness to the commandments (1:11–2:5). He then enjoins the Israelites to appoint sage interpreters of the Law (2:5–11). The work includes also instruction regarding the sabbatical year (3:1–7; cf. Lev. 25 and Dt. 15) and the Day of Atonement (3:8–4:12; cf. Lev. 16 and 23).

There are two particularly noteworthy exegetical additions. The first appears in col. 1:3, where the verb [ר]שׁפ (to interpret) is employed in connection with the transmission of the words of God to the Levites and priests, as against צוה (to command) apropos of the Israelites, indicating the specific teaching role of the former. The second (col. 3:9–10) concerns the origin of the Day of Atonement, associated with the wanderings of the Israelites in the wilderness until the tenth day of the seventh month.[1]

Edition

Milik, J. T., DJD I, pp. 91–7.

Translations

English
Vermes, DSSE², pp. 225–6.

1. Cf. Milik, DJD I, p. 95. See Jub. 34:18–19.

French
Dupont-Sommer, A., EE, pp. 220–3.
Carmignac, J., TQ II, pp. 247–53.
German
Maier, J., TTM I, pp. 168–70.
Italian
Moraldi, L., MQ, pp. 597–9.

Bibliography

Carmignac, J., 'Quelques détails de lecture dans ... les Dires de Moïse', RQ 4 (1963), pp. 88–96.
Delcor, M., 'Qumrân. Dires de Moïse', DBS IX, cols. 910–11.

6. Commentaries on Isaiah

Remains of six *pesharim* of the Book of Isaiah have been retrieved from Caves 3 and 4. They are mostly badly mutilated and the explanatory sections rarely offer large enough contexts for translation. The fragments will be presented in the sequence of the biblical chapters.

(a) *3Q4*

Cave 3 has yielded a small fragment corresponding to Isa. 1:1. The script is considered to be 'Herodian'. Of the surviving part of the exposition, only the phrase 'day of judgement' can be deciphered.

(b) *4QpIsa[a] or 4Q161*

The first of five severely damaged Isaiah interpretations from Cave 4 deals with Isa. 10:21 (Fr. 1); 10:22, 24–7 (Frs. 2–4); 10:28–32 (Frs. 5–6); and 10:33–11:5 (Frs. 8:10). The Tetragram is written with archaic letters in Frs. 2–4, line 9 and Frs. 8–10, line 13.

Fragments of exegesis survive in Frs. 5–6, lines 2–3, where the message of deliverance of Isa. 10:27 is linked with the 'Prince of the Congregation' and dated to the period following the Community's return from 'the desert of the peoples' (cf. *1QM* 1:2–3); and in lines 10–13, where events taking place at the end of days are referred to, and the march of the 'invader' (?) towards Jerusalem is said to start in the north, in 'the Vale of Acco'.

The 'pesher' of Isa. 10:33–4 in Frs. 8–10 applies the oracle to the defeat of the Kittim. The latter are identified in verse 34 with Isaiah's 'Lebanon',[1] and the victor (the Prince of the Congregation?) with the biblical אדיר.

The messianic prophecy of Isa. 11 introduces 'the [Branch] of David arising in the last [days] to defeat the nations and Magog' (Frs. 8–10, lines 17–19). His judicial wisdom is attributed to the instruction he has received from the priests (lines 22–4).

The reference to the Vale of Acco has been seen as an allusion to the

---

1. Cf. Vermes, *Scripture and Tradition*, pp. 32–5.

advance of Ptolemy Lathyrus from Acre to Judaea, mentioned by Josephus in *Ant.* xiii 12, 2 (324)–13, 3 (364) and *B.J.* i 412 (86–7).[2] The basic weakness of this theory lies in its automatic equation of the Kittim with the Seleucids, although such an identification finds no support in the less fragmentary commentaries (cf. below, pp. 431, 434–5). It should also be noted that any invader of Palestine approaching Jerusalem from Syria was expected to pass through the coastal plain by way of Acre and Caesarea.[3]

(c) *4QpIsa*[b] or *4Q162*

The three columns of the second Cave 4 Isaiah *pesher*, with only the second column containing any continuous exposition, is devoted to Isa. 5:5–6, 10–14, 24–25, 29–30. The script, according to Strugnell, may be slightly pre-Herodian (RQ 7 (1970), p. 186). The interpretative context is eschatological, and the Jewish group criticized in verses 11–14 and 24–25 consists of 'the scoffers in Jerusalem' (cf. CD 20:11; 1:14), i.e. the doctrinal opponents of the Qumran sect.

(d) *4QpIsa*[c] or *4Q163*

Palaeographically the oldest of the *pesharim*, according to J. Strugnell, dating to the beginning of the first century B.C. (RQ 7 (1970), p. 188), the third Isaiah commentary, a papyrus document, deals with Isa. 8:7–8; 9–11 (?), 14–20; 10:12–13, 19(?)–24; 14:8, 26–30; 19:9–12; 29:10–11, 15–16, 19–23; 30:1–5, 15–18, 19–21; 31:1 and 32:5–6. The interpreter seems also to have introduced quotations from other prophets, Zechariah (Frs. 8–10, line 8; Fr. 21, line 7) and Hosea (Fr. 23 II, line 14a). The *pesher* refers to 'the seekers of smooth things in Jerusalem', a well known cryptic name for the sect's adversaries (cf. *1QH* 2:15, 32; CD 1:8; *4QpNah* Frs. 3–4, 1:2), who flourish in 'the last days'.

(e) *4QpIsa*[d] or *4Q164*

This *pesher* contains, in fragmentary form, a small part of an exegesis of Isa. 54:11–12. The various precious stones appearing in the biblical text are all identified. The 'antimony' is Israel; 'the sapphires', God's elect, i.e. 'the Council of the Community', founded by the priests and the people; 'the pinnacles of agate' are 'the twelve [chief priests]' and 'the gates of carbuncles' represent 'the chiefs of the tribes of Israel'.

The script, in Strugnell's opinion, probably belongs to an early Herodian date (RQ 7 (1970), p. 196).

(f) *4QpIsa*[e] or *4Q165*

The fifth Cave 4 *pesher* is gravely mutilated. Tiny scraps from Isa.

2. J. D. Amusin, 'A propos de l'interprétation de 4Q161', RQ 8 (1974), pp. 381–92; 'The Reflection of Historical Events of First Century B.C.E. in Qumran Commentaries', HUCA 48 (1977), pp. 123–34.

3. M. Hengel, for instance, expresses the view that the allusion concerns Cestius Gallus' march from Ptolemais to Jerusalem in A.D. 66. Cf. *Die Zeloten* ([2]1976), pp.289–90.

14:19; 15:4–6; 21:11–15 and 32:5–7 have been identified, but the exegetical remains convey no connected meaning: 'The interpretation of the saying ... revealed the teaching of ri[ghteousness]' (Frs. 1–2, line 3); 'the elect of Israel' (Fr. 6, line 1); 'men of the Commu[nity]' (Fr. 9, line 3).

Editions

Baillet, M., DJD III, pp. 95–6.
Allegro, J. M., DJD V, pp. 11–30.

Translations

English
Vermes, DSSE², pp. 226–9.

French
Carmignac, J., TQ II, pp. 65–76.
Dupont-Sommer, A., EE, pp. 286–8.

German
Maier, J., Q-E, pp. 308–11.

Italian
Moraldi, L., MQ, pp. 525–36.

Bibliography

Vaux, R. de, 'Exploration de la région de Qumrân', RB 60 (1953), pp. 555–6.
Allegro, J. M., 'Further Messianic References in Qumran Literature', JBL 75 (1956), pp. 177–82.
Idem, 'More Isaiah Commentaries from Qumran's Fourth Cave', JBL 77 (1958), pp. 215–21.
Yadin, Y., 'Some Notes on the newly published Pesharim on Isaiah', IEJ 9 (1959), pp. 39–42.
Flusser, D., 'The Pesher of Isaiah and the Twelve Apostles', Eretz-Israel 8 (1967), pp. 52–62 (Hebrew).
Strugnell, J., 'Notes en marge ...', RQ 7 (1970), pp. 183–99.
Amusin, J. D., 'A propos de l'interprétation de 4Q161', RQ 8 (1974), pp. 381–92.
Horgan, M. P., *Pesharim: Qumran Interpretation of Biblical Books* (1979), pp. 70–148.
Dimant, D., 'Qumran Sectarian Literature', JWSTP II, pp. 513–14.

7. The New Jerusalem

Fragments of an Aramaic composition, reworking the eschatological description of Jerusalem contained in Ezekiel 40–48, have been discovered in Caves 1, 2, 4, 5 and 11. Apart from two large pieces from Cave 4, which are still unpublished, they are available in definitive or provisional editions.

The only available manuscript affording a long enough text is 5Q15, published by J. T. Milik, who was able also to consult the Cave 4 material. According to his summary of the latter, the visionary of the document visits the heavenly city and Temple in the company of an angelic surveyor, whose work it is to measure every architectural unit in the New Jerusalem. First they observe the walls with their twelve gates. Then they enter the city and measure its blocks of houses. From this point onwards, the account is available from the texts found in Cave 5.

(a) *5Q15*

The remains of two columns in a Herodian script have been completed by Milik with the help of the *4Q* fragments. The narrative opens with a description of the square blocks of houses (357 cubits on each side), and continues with that of the thoroughfares (three situated in an east-west and three in a north-south direction) and streets, paved with white stones, marble and jasper.

The author describes the side portals (14 cubits wide) and the entrance gates (21 cubits) with their two towers. Next the door leading into an block of houses is measured (14 cubits wide) and the interior of the blocks described in detail. Small houses (21 cubits long, 14 cubits high and 14 cubits wide) stand one next to the other. There are also dining halls containing twenty-two couches.

Of the rest of the manuscripts, *1Q32*, published also by J. T. Milik, consists of twenty-two unconnected fragments with occasional architectural terms (column, door, wall) and measurements.

The eleven fragments of *2Q24*, edited by M. Baillet, are somewhat larger, but unless set against a better preserved text, they can indicate only the general topic of the passage. Fr. 1 appears to correspond to the beginning of *5Q15*, when the visionary enters the city. Frs. 3 and 4 treat of the bread of presence, the two loaves offered on the Feast of Weeks and the ram. Frs. 5–8 have for object the altar of burnt offerings, describing its dimensions and purpose.

The fragment of *11QJérNouvAr*, published by B. Jongeling, corresponds to lines 9–16 of Fr. 4 of *5Q15*. Its main contribution is that the mention of לברא מן היכלא (outside the Temple) renders improbable Baillet's hypothesis that Fr. 3 refers to the table of the bread of presence, since the latter was situated within the Sanctuary.

Apart from Ezek. 40–48, the Heavenly Jerusalem document shows similarities to the eschatological city described in Isa. 54:11–12 and Tob. 13:17 (gold and precious stones used as building material). There are connections also with the Temple Scroll.

The document discloses, moreover, strong resemblances to the Jerusalem descending from heaven in Revelation 21:10–27 in the New Testament. There is, nevertheless, a fundamental difference, viz. the presence of a Temple in the new City (21:22).

Editions

Milik, J. T., DJD III, pp. 184–93 (*5Q15*).
Idem, DJD I, pp. 134–5 (*1Q32*).
Baillet, M., DJD III, pp. 84–9 (*2Q24*).

Jongeling, B., 'Publication provisoire d'un fragment provenant de la grotte 11 de Qumrân (11QJér Nouv ar)', JSJ 1 (1970), pp. 58–64.

Translation

English
Vermes, DSSE², pp. 260–4.

French
Milik, *op. cit.*

Italian
Moraldi, L., MQ, pp. 723–31.

Bibliography

Baillet, M., 'Fragments araméens de Qumrân. 2. Description de la Jérusalem nouvelle', RB 62 (1955), pp. 222–45.
Jongeling, B., 'Note additionelle', JSJ 1 (1970), pp. 185–6.
Licht, J., 'An Ideal Town Plan from Qumran. The Description of the New Jerusalem', IEJ 29 (1979), pp. 45–59.
Dimant, D., 'Qumran Sectarian Literature', JWSTP II, pp. 531–2.

8. *Commentaries on Hosea* (4QpHos = 4Q166–167)

Two fragmentary manuscripts, copied by different scribes using the 'Rustic Semi-formal Herodian' writing, represent small sections of a Hosea *pesher* (or possibly two commentaries?). The identifiable passages are Hos. 2:8–14 (*4Q166*); 5:13–15; 6:4, 7, 9–10; 8:6–7, 13–14 (*4Q167*).

The surviving interpretative material alludes to wicked Jews who rejected the divine commandments because they listened to seducers in the age of wrath. They were punished and humiliated by God before the nations, and their enjoyment of Gentile feasts would be changed to mourning (*4Q166*).

The quotation of Hos. 5:13–15 (*4Q167*) is followed by cryptic historical references to 'the furious young lion' (cf. *4QpNah* Frs. 3–4, i 5–6 below) and to 'the last Priest' who will smite 'Ephraim' (cf. CD 7:12–13; 14:1; *4QTest* 27; *4QpPss^a*, Frs. 1–2, ii 17–19; *4QpNah* Frs. 3–4, i 12; ii 2, 8; iii 5; iv 5).

Although insignificant in itself, *4QpHos* yields a few clues to use in connection with the better preserved text of the Nahum and Psalm 37 commentaries.

Edition

Allegro, J. M., DJD V, pp. 31–6.

Translations

English
Vermes, DSSE², p. 230.

French
Carmignac, J., TQ II, pp. 77–81.

Italian
Moraldi, L., MQ, pp. 537–40.

Bibliography

Allegro, J. M., 'Further Light on the History of the Qumrân Sect', JBL 75 (1956), pp. 89–95.
Idem, 'A recently discovered Fragment of a Commentary of Hosea from Qumrân's Fourth Cave', JBL 78 (1959), pp. 142–7.
Strugnell, J., 'Notes en marge . . .', RQ 7 (1970), pp. 199–203.
Horgan, M. P., *Pesharim* (1979), pp. 138–58.
Carlson, D. C., 'An Alternative Reading of 4Q p Osea^a II, 3–6', RQ 11 (1983), pp. 417–21.

9. Commentary on Micah (1QpMic = 1Q14)

Twenty-three very small fragments, found in Cave 1 and representing a *pesher* on Micah, have been edited by J. T. Milik in DJD I. The passages correspond to Mic. 1:2–5, 5–7, 8–9; 4:13 (?); 6:14–16; 7:8–9, 17. The exegesis is eschatological in character: Samaria is seen as alluding to 'The Spouter of Lies' (see *1QpHab* 10:9; CD 8:13; cf. 19:25); Juda and Jerusalem are associated with the Teacher of Righteousness and the Council of the Community.

Remains of Mic. 4:8–12 (*4Q168*) may attest another Micah commentary, possibly part of a complete *pesher* on the minor prophets, unless, of course, the fragment simply belongs to a biblical scroll. No exegetical content has survived.

Editions

Milik, J. T., DJD I, pp. 77–80.
Allegro, J. M., DJD V, p. 36.

Translations

English
Vermes, DSSE², pp. 230–1.

French
Milik, *op. cit.*
Carmignac, J., TQ II, pp. 82–4.

Italian
Moraldi, L., MQ, pp. 541–3.

Bibliography

Carmignac, J., 'Notes sur les Pesharim', RQ 3 (1962), pp. 515–19.
Strugnell, J., 'Notes en marge . . .', RQ 7 (1970), p. 204.
Horgan, M. P., *Pesharim* (1979), pp. 55–63.

10. Commentary on Nahum (4QpNah = 4Q169)

Substantial fragments of a Nahum *pesher* from Cave 4, palaeo-graphically dated to the second half of the first century B.C.

(Strugnell), preserve the text and a good portion of the exegesis of Nah. 1:3–6; 2:12–14; and 3:1–14.

In the large fragments 3–4, representing four mutilated columns of the manuscript, the prophetic metaphors 'lion' and 'young lion' are applied by the exegete to kings, Gentile and Jewish. Among the former, two are actually named: Demetrius (דמי[טרוס]) and Antiochus (אנטיכוס), kings of Greece (מלכי יון), a novelty in Qumran literature. Demetrius is said to have failed to invade Jerusalem, which had remained unconquered by Gentile monarchs since Antiochus, and would be taken only by the rulers of the Kittim (מושלי כתיים). Their eschatological discomfiture seems to be foretold in the mutilated *pesher* on Nah. 1:4 (Frs. 1–2), in connection with God's punishment of 'the sea' (on the association between the Kittim and the sea, see below, p. 434).

The Demetrius episode resulted in the punishment of the 'seekers of smooth things', the Jewish group that had invited the Seleucid monarch to Jerusalem, by 'the Furious Young Lion' who 'hanged men alive'.[1] His punishment is alluded to in a damaged part of the text. Next the commentator deals with 'the seekers of smooth things', called also 'Ephraim' (cf. *4QpHos* above). They are indicted as false teachers and their continuous chastisement and final annihilation by 'the sword of the nations' are predicted. There would, however, be a partial conversion of 'the simple of Ephraim' who are to join the true Israel 'when the glory of Judah shall arise'.

The 'Amon' of Nah. 3:8 is identified as 'Manasseh', to whose 'great men' the unfaithful defected. This group is also threatened with captivity and the sword in the final age.

The oracle of Nahum is expounded as a prophecy foretelling the retribution of the sect's opponents, of whom 'Ephraim', the doctrinal adversaries, are usually identified as the Pharisees, and 'Manasseh', the representatives of political power, as the Sadducees. The historical

1. The rabbinic parallels relevant to תלה, in contexts different from hanging a corpse (cf. Targum on Dt. 21:22), are to be found in mSanh. 6:4 (ySanh. 23c; yHag. 77d): Simeon b. Shetah 'hanged' eighty women in Ashkelon, i.e. no doubt executed them (cf. vol. I, p. 231, n. 7). Similarly TgRuth 1:17 where צליבת קיסא is substituted for חנק (strangulation) as the fourth mode of judicial execution (cf. J. Heinemann, 'The *Targum* of Ex. xxii, 4 and the Ancient *Halakha*', Tarbiz 38 (1968–9), pp. 294–6 (Hebrew). The Temple Scroll 64:6–13, paraphrasing Deut 21:22, twice uses the sequence: 'you shall hang him on the tree and he shall die' (lines 8, 10–11). None of these texts defines precisely the meaning of תלה. Cf. J. M. Baumgarten, *Studies in Qumran Law* (1977), pp. 172–82. On the other hand, Sifre on Dt. 21:22 (221) [cf. also bSanh. 46b] specifically contrasts the biblical 'hanging' of a dead body with 'hanging someone alive' (תולין אותו חי) as the Roman imperial authority does (כדרך שהמלכות עושין). See N. Wieder, 'Notes on the New Documents from the Fourth Cave of Qumran', JJS 7 (1956), pp. 71–2; D. N. Halperin, 'Crucifixion, the Nahum Pesher and the Penalty of Strangulation', JJS 32 (1981), pp. 32–46. For fuller bibliography see n. 4 below.

event cryptically portrayed is generally recognized as the conflict between Demetrius III Eucaerus (95–88 B.C.) and Alexander Jannaeus, 'the Furious Young Lion'. The charge that the latter hanged men alive recalls the crucifixion by Jannaeus of eight hundred Pharisees (the 'seekers of smooth things'), allies of Demetrius, after his withdrawal from Judaea.[2]

Although there is general agreement on the chronological setting of the Nahum *pesher*, controversy persists in regard to the interpretation of אשר יתלה אנשים חיים. In the light of the available evidence no certainty is possible concerning the significance and precise halakhic status of execution by 'hanging'. J. M. Baumgarten,[3] while agreeing that the event alluded to in the *pesher* is likely to be identical to the Jannaeus episode, considers תלה חי to mean 'to hang' by the neck, but the majority of the scholars who have written on the topic have understood it to mean 'to crucify',[4] especially since Y. Yadin has shown that in the Temple Scroll (64:6–13) 'hanging' is the form of execution reserved for traitors.[5] His theory concerning the commentator's approval of Jannaeus' act fails to take into account the inherent improbability that any Qumran spokesman should have adopted a positive attitude towards one of the chief enemies of the Community.

Editions

Allegro, J. M., DJD V, pp. 37–42.
Lohse, E., TQHD, pp. 261–7.

2. For Alexander Jannaeus' vengeance on the Pharisees, see Josephus, *Ant.* xiii 15, 2 (380–3); *B.J.* i 4, 6 (96–8); cf. vol. I, p. 224 and n. 22. Among scholars identifying the Furious Young Lion as Jannaeus, note J. M. Allegro, 'Thrakidan, the "Lion of Wrath" and Alexander Jannaeus', PEQ 91 (1959), pp. 47–51 (cf. however M. Stern, Tarbiz 29 (1959–60), pp. 207–9); J. T. Milik, *Ten Years of Discovery* (1959), p. 73; A. Dupont-Sommer, *Essene Writings*, pp. 268–70; Vermes, DSSE, p. 65; J. Carmignac, TQ II, pp. 53–4; A. Dupont-Sommer, 'Observations sur le Commentaire de Nahum', Journal des Savants (1963), pp. 201–27; Y. Yadin, 'Pesher Nahum (4QpNahum) reconsidered', IEJ 21 (1971), pp. 1–12; J. D. Amusin, 'The Reflection of Historical Events in the First Century B.C.E. in Qumran Commentaries', HUCA 48 (1977), pp. 134–46; G. Vermes, DSS, pp. 114, 152; D. Dimant, 'Qumran Sectarian Literature', JWSTP II, pp. 511–12. For a second-century B.C. framework with Demetrius identified as Demetrius I Soter (162–150 B.C.), see the speculative essay by I. Rabinowitz, 'The Meaning of the Key ("Demetrius") Passage in the Qumran Nahum Pesher', JAOS 98 (1978), pp. 394–9.

3. 'Does TLH in the Temple Scroll refer to Crucifixion?', *Studies in Qumran Law* (1977), pp. 172–82. Originally published in JBL 91 (1972), pp. 472–81.

4. Cf. Yadin, 'Pesher Nahum ...', IEJ 21 (1971), pp. 1–12; Vermes, DSS, p. 114; Yadin, *Temple Scroll* I (1977), p. 289 (Hebr.); M. Hengel, *Crucifixion* (1977), pp. 84–5; J. A. Fitzmyer, 'Crucifixion in Ancient Palestine, Qumran Literature and the New Testament', CBQ 40 (1978), pp. 493–513; D. N. Halperin, 'Crucifixion, the Nahum Pesher and the Penalty of Strangulation', JJS 32 (1981), pp. 32–46.

5. Cf. *Temple Scroll* I, pp. 285–90 (Hebr.).

Translations

English
Allegro, *op. cit.*
Vermes, DSSE², pp. 231–5.

French
Dupont-Sommer, A., EE, pp. 280–2.
Carmignac, J., TQ II, pp. 85–92.

German
Maier, J., TTM I, p. 180.
Lohse, E., *op. cit.*

Italian
Moraldi, L., MQ, pp. 545–52.

Bibliography

Allegro, J. M., 'Further Light on the History of the Qumran Sect', JBL 75 (1956), pp. 89–95.

Idem, 'Thrakidan, the "Lion of Wrath" and Alexander Jannaeus', PEQ 91 (1959), pp. 47–51.

Idem, 'More unpublished Pieces of a Qumran Commentary on Nahum (4QpNah)', JSS 7 (1962), pp. 304–8.

Dupont-Sommer, A., 'Observations sur le Commentaire de Nahum découvert près de la Mer Morte', Journal des Savants (1963), pp. 201–27.

Amusin, J. D., 'Ephraïm et Manassé dans le Péshèr de Nahum', RQ 4 (1964), pp. 389–96.

Hoenig, S. B., 'Dorshé Halakot in the Pesher Nahum Scroll', JBL 83 (1964), pp. 119–38.

Idem, 'Pesher Nahum "Talmud"', JBL 86 (1967), pp. 441–5.

Strugnell, J., 'Notes en marge . . .', RQ 7 (1970), pp. 204–10.

Dupont-Sommer, A., 'Observations nouvelles sur l'expression "Suspendu vivant sur le bois" dans le Commentaire de Nahum (4QpNah II, 8) à la lumière du Rouleau du Temple (11Q Temple Scroll LXIV, 6–13)', CRAI 1973, pp. 709–20.

Amusin, J. D., 'The Reflection of Historical Events in the First Century B.C.E. in Qumran Commentaries', HUCA 48 (1977), pp. 134–46.

Vermes, DSS, pp. 114, 152.

Yadin, Y., *The Temple Scroll* I (1977), pp. 285–90 (Hebr.).

Rabinowitz, I., 'The Meaning of the Key ("Demetrius") Passage in the Qumran Nahum Pesher', JAOS 98 (1978), pp. 394–9.

Fitzmyer, J. A., 'Crucifixion in Ancient Palestine, Qumran Literature and the New Testament', CBQ 40 (1978), pp. 493–513.

Halperin, D. N., 'Crucifixion, the Nahum Pesher and the Penalty of Strangulation', JJS 32 (1981), pp. 32–46.

Garcia Martínez, F., '4QpNah y la Crucifixión', EstBib 38 (1979–80), pp. 221–35.

Dimant, D., 'Qumran Sectarian Literature', JWSTP II, pp. 511–12.

11. Commentary on Habakkuk (1QpHab)

The longest and best preserved of all the Qumran *pesharim*, *1QpHab*, includes, in a 'Herodian' script and with the Tetragram written in archaic letters, the first two chapters of the biblical prophecy and most of the accompanying expositions. The scroll consists of thirteen columns of text. The first is badly worn, the final couple of lines being absent throughout, except in col. 13, where the writing stops at line 4, corresponding to the end and indicating that the Commentary did not cover chapter 3 of Habakkuk.[1]

The document, despite its cryptic style, proves to be one of the most important sources not only for sectarian Bible interpretation but also for the study of the history of Qumran origins, and for the understanding of the Community's ideas relating to prophecy. The conflict of the righteous and the wicked and the mission of the Chaldeans, as instruments of divine punishment recorded in Hab. 1–2, are understood by the commentator as foreshadowing the struggle between the Teacher of Righteousness and the Wicked Priest and the subsequent rise of the Kittim. This powerful Gentile nation is commissioned by God to execute revenge on the 'last priests of Jerusalem', the lawless successors of the 'Wicked Priest', who ill-treated 'the Teacher of Righteousness' and his followers.

The direct chronological order of the events appears to be as follows. A leading religious authority, designated as 'the Liar' / 'the Spouter of Lies' (2:1–2; 5:11; 10:9), defected from the group headed by the Teacher of Righteousness to found a rival congregation. This opponent *may* have been 'the Wicked Priest', or 'the Priest who rebelled', or 'the ignominious Priest' (8:8, 16; 9:8; 11:4, 12; 12:2, 8), but this identity is not assured. The 'Wicked Priest' fell from grace only after he became Israel's ruler. Prompted by greed, he seized the wealth of the nations (8:12) and robbed 'the riches of the Poor', i.e. the Community (12:10). He also sinned against the Teacher of Righteousness and his men (9:9–10), chastised him (5:10), and pursued him to his exile on the Community's Day of Atonement (11:5). He was to be punished first by unnamed 'enemies' (9:10) and later by God (10:3–5; 11:14–15). His successors and imitators, 'the Last Priests of Jerusalem', would lose all their unjust gains to the Kittim, 'the remnant of the peoples' (9:4–7).

Two of the cryptograms, viz. 'Kittim' and 'the Wicked Priest', appear to be more easily decipherable than the rest. 'Kittim', originally designating the inhabitants of Kition, a Phoenician colony on Cyprus, acquired in later Jewish parlance the generic sense of people living on islands and sea shores,[2] especially powerful maritime conquerors, such

---

1. The most likely reason for the omission of the last chapter is that the Psalm contained in it does not furnish suitable material for the kind of exegesis the author intended to produce. To deduce from the absence of chap. 3 from the Commentary that at the time of the redaction of *1QpHab* it had not yet been joined to the scriptural book (cf. A. Dupont-Sommer, *Observations sur le Commentaire d'Habacuc* (1950), p. 4) is wholly unwarranted. The Psalm of Habakkuk is extant in the LXX, and is also partly attested (3:9–15) in col. 14 of the Greek Minor Prophets from Nahal Hever (cf. D. Barthélemy, *Les devanciers d'Aquila* (1963), p. 176).

2. Cf. Josephus, *Ant.* i 6, 1 (128): 'Chethimos held the island of Chethima—which is now called Cyprus—whence all the islands and most maritime regions are named *Chethim*

as the Greeks or the Romans.[3] There is now quasi-general agreement that the Qumran references are to the latter.[4] It is to be stressed that the Kittim are nowhere linked with the Teacher of Righteousness or the Wicked Priest and appear to belong to a somewhat later period. From this it may be inferred that the struggle between the Teacher and his opponent dates to the Hellenistic era.

The 'Wicked Priest', seen by almost all scholars as a historical personage[5] (a man who ruled Israel, conquered and looted neighbouring nations and fell in the end into enemy hands), must correspond to one of the High Priests of the second or early first century B.C. The majority opinion assigns the title to Jonathan and/or Simon Maccabaeus.[6] Various identities have been suggested for the Teacher of

by the Hebrews (καὶ ἀπ' αὐτῆς νῆσοί τε πᾶσαι καὶ τὰ πλείω τῶν παρὰ θάλατταν Χεθὶμ ὑπὸ Ἑβραίων ὀνομάζεται) ... one of the cities of Cyprus ... even in its Hellenized form Kition (Κίτιον), is not far removed from the name Chethimos.' Cf. *1QpHab* 3:10–11 interpreting Hab. 1:8 (the Chaldeans coming from afar = מרחוק) as alluding to the Kittim advancing 'from the islands of the sea' (מאיי הים). Cf. also *4QpNah*, on p. 431 above.

3. For Alexander the Great portrayed as proceeding ἐκ γῆς Χεττιμ, or Perseus described as Κιτιέων βασιλεύς, see 1 Mac. 1:1; 8:5. The 'ships of Kittim' (ציים כתים) in Dan. 11:30 are explicitly rendered in the LXX as Ῥωμαῖοι (Κίτιοι in Theodotion). The association of the Kittim with the final foreign conqueror is based on Num. 24:24 (וצים מיד כתים). The distinction between Greece and Kittim is manifest in *4QpNah* Frs. 3–4 i 3 where reference is made, on the one hand, to מלכי יון, and on the other hand to מושלי כתיים. Cf. above, p. 431.

4. One of the principal arguments invoked for the Roman identity of the Kittim is the allusion in *1QpHab* 6:3–4 to their sacrificing to their standards (אותות). For a striking example of the Roman practice, see Josephus, *B.J.* vi 6, 1 (316), depicting the worship of the *signa* by the legionaries in the burning Temple of Jerusalem–in A.D. 70 (κομίσαντες τὰς σημαίας εἰς τὸ ἱερὸν ... ἔθυσάν τε αὐταῖς αὐθότι). For a discussion of the problem of the Kittim, see R. Goossens, 'Les Kittim du Commentaire d'Habacuc', La Nouvelle Clio 4 (1952), pp. 137–70; Vermes, *Les manuscrits du désert de Juda* (1953), pp. 84–9 (= *Discovery in the Judean Desert*, pp. 79–85); G. R. Driver, *The Judaean Scrolls* (1965), pp. 197–216. For the Seleucid identity of the Kittim, see H. H. Rowley, *The Zadokite Fragments and the Dead Sea Scrolls* (1952), pp. 62–88; I. Rabinowitz, 'The Meaning of the Key ("Demetrius") Passage of the Qumran Nahum Pesher', JAOS 98 (1978), pp. 394–9.

5. The opposite theory, viz. that 'the Wicked Priest' represents, not a single person, but a succession of priestly figures from Judas Maccabaeus to Alexander Jannaeus, has been recently argued by A. S. van der Woude, 'Wicked Priest or Wicked Priests?', JJS 33 [*Essays in Honour of Yigael Yadin*] (1982), pp. 349–59.

6. For the Jonathan/Simon thesis see G. Vermes, *Les manuscrits du désert de Juda* (1953), pp. 92–100 [= *Discovery*, pp. 89–97]; J. T. Milik, *Dix ans de découvertes dans le désert de Juda (1957)* [= *Ten Years of Discovery*, pp. 84–7]; F. M. Cross, *The Ancient Library of Qumran* (1958), pp. 135–53; R. de Vaux, *L'archéologie et les manuscrits de la Mer Morte* (1961), pp. 90 1 [= *Archaeology and the Dead Sea Scrolls* (1973), pp. 116–17; G. Vermes, DSSE, pp. 63–4; G. Jeremias, *Der Lehrer der Gerechtigkeit* (1963); L. Moraldi, MQ, p. 107; H. Stegemann, *Die Entstehung der Qumrangemeinde* (1971); M. Hengel, *Judaism and Hellenism* I (1974), pp. 224–7; J. Murphy-O'Connor, 'The Essenes and their History', RB 81 (1974), pp. 215–44; idem, 'Demetrius I and the Teacher of Righteousness', RB 83 (1976), pp. 400–20; idem, 'The Essenes in Palestine', BA 40 (1977), pp. 100–24; G. Vermes, DSS, pp. 137–62; H. Burgmann, 'Gerichtsherr und Generalankläger: Jonathan und Simon', RQ

Righteousness, but none of them is based on sufficiently convergent argument.[7] The 'House of Absalom', a friendly group which failed to support the Teacher of Righteousness against 'the Liar' (5:9–12), also remains undefined.[8]

Editions

Burrows, M., Trever, J. C. and Brownlee, W. H., *The Dead Sea Scrolls of St. Mark's Monastery* I (1950), pl. LV-LXI.
Lohse, E., TQHD, pp. 227–43.

Translations

English
Vermes, DSSE[2], pp. 235–43.

French
Dupont-Sommer, A., EE, pp. 270–80.
Carmignac, J., TQ II, pp. 93–117.

German
Maier, J., TTM I, pp. 149–56.
Lohse, *op. cit.*

Italian
Moraldi, L., MQ, pp. 553–69.

Bibliography

Dupont-Sommer, A., *Observations sur le Commentaire d'Habacuc découvert près de la Mer Morte* (1950).

---

9 (1977), pp. 3–72; J. Starcky, 'Le Maître de Justice et la chronologie de Qumrân', in M. Delcor (ed.), *Qumrân* (1978), pp. 249–56; H. Burgmann, 'Das umstrittene inter-sacerdotium in Jerusalem 159–152 v. Chr.', JSJ 11 (1980), pp. 135–76; G. Vermes, 'The Essenes and History', JJS 32 (1981), pp. 18–31 [= *Jesus and the World of Judaism* (1983), pp. 128–39, 182–4]; D. Dimant, 'Qumran Sectarian Literature', JWSTP II, p. 510. For the identification of the Wicked Priest as Menelaus, cf. H. H. Rowley, *The Zadokite Fragments and the Dead Sea Scrolls* (1952), pp. 68–70. For Alexander Jannaeus, see J. Carmignac, TQ II (1963), pp. 48–55.
  7. The following identifications of the Teacher have been advanced: Onias III (H. H. Rowley, *Zadokite Fragments*, pp. 67–8); Yose ben Yoezer (E. Stauffer, 'Der gekreuzigte Thoralehrer', ZRGG 8 (1956), pp. 250–3); anonymous successor of Alcimus as High Priest (J. Murphy-O'Connor, 'The Essenes and their History', RB 81 (1974), pp. 229–30); Eleazar the Pharisee (H. H. Brownlee, 'The Historical Allusions of the Dead Sea Habakkuk Midrash', BASOR 126 (1952); the Essene Judas (J. Carmignac, 'Qui était le Docteur de Justice?', RQ 10 (1980), pp. 235–46, 585–6); Onias the Righteous (R. Goossens, 'Onias le Juste, le Messie de la Nouvelle Alliance', La Nouvelle Clio 1–2 (1949–50), pp. 336–53; John the Baptist (B. E. Thiering, *Redating the Teacher of Righteousness* (1979), p. 212); Jesus of Nazareth (J. L. Teicher, 'Jesus in the Habakkuk Scroll', JJS 3 (1952), pp. 53–5); Menahem, son of Judas the Galilean (G. R. Driver, *The Judaean Scrolls* (1965), pp. 267–81).
  8. Unless Absalom is simply taken as symbolizing a rebellious son, the commentator may refer to various historical characters of the Maccabaean age (1 Mac. 11:70; 13:11 or 2 Mac. 11:17; cf. D. N. Freedman, 'The House of Absalom in the Habakkuk Scroll', BASOR 114 (1949), pp. 11–12) or to an associate of Menahem son of Judas the Galilean (Josephus, *B.J.* ii 17, 9 (448); cf. Driver, *Judaean Scrolls*, p. 281).

Delcor, M., *Essai sur le Midrash d'Habacuc* (1951).
Dagut, M. B., 'The Habakkuk Scroll and Pompey's Capture of Jerusalem', Bibl 32 (1951), pp. 542–8.
Segal, M. H., 'The Habakkuk Commentary and the Damascus Fragments', JBL 70 (1951), pp. 131–47.
Stauffer, E., 'Zur Frühdatierung des Habakukmidrasch', ThLZ 76 (1951), cols. 667–74.
Talmon, S., '*Yom Hakkippurim* in the Habakkuk Scroll', Bibl 32 (1951), pp. 549–63.
Brownlee, W. H., 'Historical Allusions in the Dead Sea Habakkuk Midrash', BASOR 126 (1952), pp. 10–20.
Elliger, K., *Studien zum Habakuk-Kommentar vom Toten Meer* (1953).
Wieder, N., 'The Habakkuk Scroll and the Targum', JJS 4 (1953), pp. 14–18.
Teicher, J. L., 'The Habakkuk Scroll', JJS 5 (1954), pp. 47–59.
Rabin, C., 'Notes on the Habakkuk Scroll and the Zadokite Documents', VT 5 (1955), pp. 148–62.
Brownlee, W. H., 'The Habakkuk Midrash and the Targum of Jonathan', JJS 7 (1956), pp. 169–86.
Osswald, E., 'Zur Hermeneutik des Habakuk-Kommentar', ZAW 58 (1956), pp. 243–56.
Ploeg, J. van der, 'L'usage du parfait et de l'imparfait, comme moyen de datation dans le Commentaire d'Habacuc', in *Les manuscrits de la Mer Morte* (1957), pp. 25–35.
Bruce, F. F., 'The Dead Sea Habakkuk Scroll', ALUOS 1 (1958–9), pp. 5–24.
Atkinson, K. M. T., 'The Historical Setting of the Habakkuk Commentary', JSS 4 (1959), pp. 238–63.
Brownlee, W. H., *The Text of Habakkuk in the Ancient Commentary from Qumran* (1959).
Winter, P., 'Two Non-Allegorical Expressions in the Dead Sea Scrolls', PEQ 91 (1959), pp. 38–46.
Silberman, L. H., 'Unriddling the Riddle: A Study of the Structure and Language of the Habakkuk Pesher', RQ 3 (1961), pp. 328–64.
Vermes, G., 'Lebanon', *Scripture and Tradition*, pp. 26–39.
Williamson, H. G. M., 'The Translation of 1 Q pHab V, 10', RQ 9 (1977), pp. 263–5.
Delcor, M., 'Qumrân', DBS IX, cols. 904–8.
Brownlee, W. H., *The Midrash Pesher of Habakkuk* (1979).
Horgan, M. P., *Pesharim* (1979), pp. 10–55.

12. Commentaries on *Zephaniah* (1Q15 and 4Q170)

Insignificant fragments of two expositions of Zephaniah have been discovered in Caves 1 and 4. The former covers Zeph. 1:18–2:2. The divine name is written in archaic characters. In line 4, the term פשר can be read but only the words 'land of Judah' are preserved from the commentary. Similarly, the two minute scraps of *4Q170* indicate that Zeph. 1:12–13 is followed by the introductory formula, פשרו.

Editions

Milik, J. T., DJD I, p. 80.
Allegro, J. M., DJD V, p. 42.

Bibliography

Carmignac, J., TQ II, p. 118.
Strugnell, J., 'Notes en marge ...', RQ 7 (1970), pp. 210–11.
Moraldi, L., MQ, p. 544.
Horgan, M. P., *Pesharim* (1979), pp. 63–5.

13. Commentaries on the Psalms (4QpPss^{a-b} *or* 4Q171, 173)

Two 'Herodian' manuscripts containing *pesher*-type commentaries on the Psalms have emerged from Cave 4 and have been edited by J. M. Allegro in DJD V. The first of these, originally known as *4QpPs37*, consists of thirteen fragments and represents the text and substantial remains of the exegesis of Ps. 37:7–40; 45:1–2 and 60:8–9. The Tetragram appears in archaic script eight times. The second manuscript survives in five fragments according to its editors, but Fr. 5 appears to have been copied by a different, somewhat later hand.[1] They are all tiny, but it is possible to recognize Ps. 127:2–3, 5; 129:7–8, and Fr. 5 contains a reference to Ps. 118:26–7. Fr. 3 mentions the Teacher of Righteousness.

The four columns of *4Q171* dealing with Ps. 37 apply a description of the destiny of the righteous and the wicked to the sectaries and their opponents. The first are portrayed as 'those who return to Torah' (2:2–3); 'the congregation of (God's) elect' (2:5; 3:5); 'the Poor' (2:9; 3:10); 'the Council of the Community' (2:14); 'the penitents of the desert' (3:1); 'the congregation of the Community' (4:19). They are led by 'the Interpreter of Knowledge' (1:19); 'the Priest, the Teacher of Righteousness' (3:15; 4:8). The enemies of the sect are 'the wicked of Ephraim and Manasseh' (2:17); 'the violent . . . who plot to destroy those who practise the Torah' (2:13–14). They are the followers of 'the Liar' (1:18; 4:14); of 'the Wicked Priest' (4:8) who seeks (unsuccessfully, it seems) to eliminate the Teacher of Righteousness and his associates (2:18–19; 4:8–9), and is destined to be delivered into the hands of the violent of the nations (4:9–10; cf. 2:19).

The historical allusions usefully supplement the information gathered from the prophetic *pesharim*, especially those of Habakkuk and Nahum, in particular by the clear statement regarding the priestly character of the Teacher of Righteousness, and by specifying that the enemies who punished the Wicked Priest were Gentiles and not Jews. This feature appears to weigh heavily in favour of the identification of Jonathan Maccabaeus as the chief adversary, since he was captured and murdered by the Seleucid general, Tryphon.[2] It is worth noting once more that the Kittim are not mentioned in the age of the Teacher of Righteousness and the Wicked Priest.

There is no clear dating criterion in the extant material, but it may be assumed that, like other *pesharim*, *4QpPss* also originated in the first century B.C.

Ps. 37 is followed, after a single blank line, by Ps. 45 (4:23–7). Only five non-continuous words of the *pesher* to verses 1–2 are extant, with a

1. J. Strugnell, 'Notes en marge', RQ 7 (1970), p. 219.
2. Cf. vol. I, pp. 186–8; vol. II, p. 587.

possible mention of the 'Teach[er of Righteousness]'. Similarly, all that can be deduced from Fr. 13 is that it belongs to a commentary on Ps. 60:8–9. Col. 4 in which Psalms 37 and 45 are juxtaposed proves that the commentary deals, not with the whole Psalter, but only with a selection of Psalms.

$4QpPs^b$ (4Q173) contains two mentions of the Teacher of Righteousness (Fr. 1, line 4 and Fr. 2, line 2) without any meaningful context. Fr. 4 contains the quotation of Ps. 129:7–8.

Fourteen tiny remains of unidentifiable *pesher* texts (4Q172) may belong, because of the apparent identity of the script, either to $4QPss^a$ = 4Q171, or $4QpIsa^a$ = 4Q161, or $4QpHos^a$ = 4Q166.[3]

Editions

Allegro, J. M., DJD V, pp. 42–53.
Lohse, E., TQHD, pp. 269–75.

Translations

English
Allegro, *op. cit.*
Vermes, DSSE², pp. 243–5.

French
Dupont-Sommer, A., EE, pp. 282–5.
Carmignac, J., TQ II, pp. 119–28.

German
Maier, J., Q-E, pp. 302–4.

Italian
Moraldi, L., MQ, pp. 517–24.

Bibliography

Allegro, J. M., 'A newly discovered Fragment of a Commentary on Psalm 37 of Qumrân', PEQ 86 (1954), pp. 69–74.
Idem, 'Further Light on the History of the Qumran Sect', JBL 75 (1956), pp. 94–5.
Carmignac, J., 'Notes sur les Pesharim', RQ 3 (1962), pp. 505–38.
Stegemann, H., 'Der Pešer Psalm 37 aus Höhle 4 von Qumrân', RQ 6 (1963), pp. 235–70.
Dupont-Sommer, A., 'Explication des textes hébreux …: Commentaire du Psaume XXXVII', Annuaire du Collège de France 64 (1964), pp. 320–3.
Stegemann, H., 'Weitere Stücke von 4QPsalm 37', RQ 6 (1967), pp. 193–227.
Dupont-Sommer, A., '4QpPs37', Ann. du Coll. de France 69 (1969–70), pp. 395–404.
Strugnell, J., 'Notes en marge', RQ 7 (1970), pp. 211–20.
Coote, R. B., 'MWD HT'NYT in 4Q171', RQ 8 (1972), pp. 81–5.
Pardee, D., 'A Restudy of the Commentary on Psalm 37 from Qumran Cave IV', RQ 8 (1973), pp. 163–94.
Horgan, M. P., *Pesharim* (1979), pp. 192–226.
Dimant, D., 'Qumran Sectarian Literature', JWSTP II, pp. 512–13.

3. Allegro, *op. cit.*, p. 50 adds ?$4QHos^b$ to this list, but Strugnell, ?*art. cit.*, p. 218 believes to be able to ?distinguish there another hand. ? ?

14. Prayer of Nabonidus (4QprNab)

Three Aramaic texts related in some way to the Book of Daniel have been discovered in Cave 4 and issued in preliminary editions. Some may belong to the pre-Essene period, but until further evidence is forthcoming it is safer to classify them as sectarian.

The first, and so far the most important, document is the Prayer of Nabonidus (*4QprNab*) which pertains to the manuscript lot entrusted to J. T. Milik, who dates it palaeographically to the second half of the first century B.C.

The document is furnished with a heading: 'The words of the prayer uttered by Nabunai, king of [the] l[and of Ba]bylon, [when he was afflicted] with an evil ulcer in Teiman by the decree of the [Most High] G[od].' The title is followed by the actual prayer composed in the first person. The king relates that after he had suffered from a disease for seven years, a Jewish exorcist (גזר)[1] pardoned his sins, and ordered him to record the story of his recovery to honour the Most High God who, unlike man-made gods, was able to restore him to health.

The account is parallel to that of the illness and miraculous cure of Nebuchadnezzar in Dan. 4. The principal difference between the two is that in the Qumran version the Jewish exorcist plays a prominent role.

Milik conjectures that *4QprNab*, or the tradition on which it depends, is the source of the scriptural story.[2] His main reason is that the replacement of the less well known Nabonidus by the more famous Nebuchadnezzar is more likely than vice versa.[3] In the absence of a fuller account of the work, this argument, though attractive, remains unconvincing, as it is conceivable that the apocryphal story concerned *two* healing miracles, one with Nabonidus, the other with Nebuchadnezzar as the patient.

The link attested in this passage between sickness, forgiveness of sins and physical cure is an important landmark in post-biblical Jewish religious thought.[4]

In regard to the date of *4QprNab*, if Milik's hypothesis is accepted, the document must belong to the pre-Daniel, and consequently

1. Cf. A. Dupont-Sommer, 'Exorcismes et guérisons dans les écrits de Qoumrân', *Congress Volume Oxford 1959* (1960), pp. 256–9.
2. 'Prière de Nabonide et autres écrits d'un cycle de Daniel', RB 63 (1956), p. 411.
3. *Ten Years of Discovery*, p. 37.
4. Cf. Vermes, *Jesus the Jew*, pp. 65–9; *Jesus and the World of Judaism*, pp. 6–10. P. Grelot, 'La prière de Nabonide (4 Q Or Nab)', RQ 9 (1978), pp. 483–95, attempts to reconstruct the damaged text so that the healing is attributed to God: 'Et ap[rès cela,] D[ieu] dirigea [sa face vers moi et il me guérit,] et mon péché, il le remit. Un devin—et celui-ci [était un homme j]uif . . .' (p. 485). The weakness of the hypothesis is that Grelot overlooks the ideological link between healing and forgiveness of sins. His new reading creates also an unnatural division between שבק לה and גזר. It is much smoother to end the phrase with the latter, and start a new sentence with והוא.

pre-Qumran, era and may be assigned to the beginning of the second century, or perhaps the third century B.C., if not earlier.[5] But if it is not considered as a source of the biblical composition—the reference to healing/forgiveness of sins may be seen as an Essene characteristic[6]—a late second century or first century B.C. date would seem appropriate. The choice of Aramaic rather than Hebrew would favour the earlier period.

Editions

Milik, J. T., 'Prière de Nabonide et autres écrits d'un cycle de Daniel: Fragments araméens de Qumrân 4', RB 63 (1956), pp. 407–11.
Fitzmyer, J. A. and Harrington, D. J., MPAT, no. 2, pp. 2–4, 191–3.
Jongeling, B., Labuschagne, C. J. and Woude, A. S. van der, *Aramaic Texts from Qumran* I (1976), pp. 123–31.

Translations

English
Vermes, DSSE[2], p. 229.
Fitzmyer and Harrington, *op. cit.*
Jongeling *et al.*, *op. cit.*

French
Dupont-Sommer, A., EE, pp. 336–41.
Carmignac, J., TQ II, pp. 289–94.

German
Meyer, R., *Das Gebet des Nabonid. Eine in den Qumranschriften wiederentdeckte Weisheitserzählung* (1962).

Italian
Moraldi, L., MQ, pp. 671–6.

Bibliography

Vogt, E., 'Precatio regis Nabonid in pia narratione iudaica', Bibl 37 (1956), pp. 532–4.
Dupont-Sommer, A., 'Exorcismes et guérisons dans les écrits de Qumrân', *Congress Volume Oxford 1959* [VTS 7] (1960), pp. 246–61.
Meyer, R., *Das Gebet des Nabonid: Eine in den Qumran-Handschriften wiederentdeckte Weisheitserzählung* (1962).
Dommershausen, W., *Nabonid im Buche Daniel* (1964), pp. 68–76.
Delcor, M., 'Le Testament de Job, la prière de Nabonide et les traditions targoumiques', in *Bibel und Qumran* (H. Bardtke Festschrift) (1968), pp. 57–74.
Mertens, A., *Das Buch Daniel im Lichte der Texte vom Toten Meer* (1970), pp. 34–42.
Kirchschläger, W., 'Exorcismus in Qumran?', Kairos 18 (1976), pp. 135–53.
Grelot, P., 'La prière de Nabonide (4Q Or Nab). Nouvel essai de restauration', RQ 9 (1978), pp. 483–95.
Woude, A. S. van der, 'Bemerkungen zum Gebet des Nabonid', in M. Delcor, *Qumrân* (1978), pp. 121–9.

5. R. Meyer, *Das Gebet des Nabonid* (1962), places it in the Persian period, and is followed by Nickelsburg (JWSTP II, p. 36). Grelot, *art. cit.*, p. 495, prefers a third century B.C. date during the reign of Antiochus III.
6. Cf. Vermes, PBJS, pp. 8–29.

García Martínez, F., '4Q OrNab. Nueva sintesis', Sefarad 40 (1980), pp. 5–25.
Nickelsburg, G. E. W., 'Stories of Biblical and Early Post-Biblical Times', JWSTP II, pp. 35–7.
Cross, F. M., 'The Prayer of Nabonidus', IEJ 34 (1984), pp. 260–4.

15. Pseudo-Daniel Cycle (4QpsDan ar^{a-c})

Small Aramaic fragments detached from two manuscripts of the same work (Manuscripts *a* and *b*, divided into sections A-F), and possibly from a third manuscript (*c*), have been retrieved from Cave 4. The script is described as 'Herodian' by the editor, J. T. Milik.

The work represents a history of mankind, beginning in section A with Noah's descent from Mount Lubar (cf. above, p. 319) after the flood and the building of the tower. In the next episode (section B), reference is made to Egypt and the crossing of the Jordan, no doubt following the exodus. The third section (C) alludes to the wickedness of the Israelites (sacrificing their sons to demons), for which they were punished by Nebuchadnezzar. Section D appears to introduce the Danielic concept of the four kingdoms, explicitly referring (if the reconstruction [מלכותא קד[מיתא] is correct) to the first of these, no doubt that of Babylon, as the mention of 'seventy years' suggests. Section E has preserved the name בלכרוס, and two further endings in רהוס... and וס... Hence the passage must deal with the kingdom of the Greeks. Section F and Manuscript *c* relate to the eschatological era.

Owing to the fragmentary nature of the document, it is impossible to assert with any degree of confidence whether its world powers are the same as Daniel's, viz. Babylon, Media, Persia, and Greece. But since there is no evidence of the presence of the Kittim-Romans, it is reasonable to end history with the Seleucids.

If the absence of the Romans is not fortuitous, the work would antedate 63 B.C. If, moreover, Milik's suggestion that Balakros is Alexander Balas, a contemporary of Jonathan Maccabaeus (cf. vol. I, pp. 130, 181), a mid-second century B.C. *terminus a quo* would be needed. The date of composition, proposed by the editor, is *circa* 100 B.C.[1]

---

1. Another fragment of the Pseudo-Daniel cycle, designated *4QpsDanA^a* (= *4Q246*),was presented by J. T. Milik in a public lecture at Harvard University in 1972, and was published, no doubt on the basis of a hand-out, by J. A. Fitzmyer in 'The Contribution of Qumran Aramaic to the Study of the New Testament', NTSt 20 (1973–74), pp. 382–407 (= *A Wandering Aramean* (1979), pp. 85–113; esp. 90–3). The Aramaic text is contained in a badly mutilated two-column fragment which Milik assigns, on palaeographical grounds, to the last third of the first century B.C.

The document appears to speak of the eschatological distress preceding the triumph of God's people. The 'king of Assyria' and 'Egypt' are mentioned. The better preserved section consists of a prophetic announcement of someone called 'Son of God' (ברה די אל), and 'Son of the Most High' (בר עליון). Milik offers a historical interpretation and, oddly, proposes to identify the personality as Alexander Balas. Fitzmyer, by contrast, prefers a

Editions

Milik, J. T., 'Prière de Nabonide et autres écrits d'un cycle de Daniel. Fragments araméens de Qumrân 4', RB 63 (1956), pp. 411–15.

Fitzmyer, J. A., and Harrington, D. J., MPAT no. 3, pp. 4–9.

Translations

English
Fitzmyer, *op. cit.*

French
Milik, *op. cit.*

Bibliography

Mertens, A., *Das Buch Daniel im Lichte der Texte vom Toten Meer* (1970), pp. 42–50.

ii. Interpretation of Diverse Biblical Texts

1. Ordinances or Commentaries on Biblical Laws (4Q159, 513, 514)

Three 'Herodian' manuscripts found in Cave 4 preserve parts of a re-interpretation of scriptural commandments. *4Q159* and *4Q513* partly overlap. It is less certain that *4Q514* also belongs to the same halakhic complex.

The first section (*4Q159* 2:1–5) deals with Dt. 23:25–6. Whereas the Bible permits a traveller to pluck ears of corn in another's field as long as he does not use a sickle, the Qumran exegete, applying the law to a destitute Israelite, stipulates that he may eat in the field, but must not collect grain to store it in his home.

The second section (2:6–17 and *4Q513*, Frs. 1–2) relates to the half-shekel tax imposed by Exod. 30:11–16 on every Israelite man from the age of twenty years. This is interpreted to mean a single payment, according to the shekel of the Sanctuary, and not a yearly tribute as was the general rule from Neh. 10:32 onwards.[1]

The third exegetical complex (*4Q159*, Frs. 2–4) expounds Lev. 25:39–46 concerning the prohibition to sell an Israelite as a slave to Gentiles. Next, the document introduces a court consisting of ten

---

Jewish ruler. It is useless to speculate further whether in fact the character in question should be recognized as eschatological or messianic until more authoritative information is made available.

J. T. Milik has also published three small fragments of an Aramaic manuscript which 'appears to date to the second half of the first century B.C.' and comes from Cave 4. He conjectures that they are from the Daniel cycle and represent the background of the Susannah story: *4QDanSus(?)*. However, as no specific traits are discernible in the text, the identification must remain highly problematic. Cf. 'Daniel et Susanne à Qumrân?', in J. Doré *et al.* (eds.), *De la Tôrah au Messie. Mélanges Henri Cazelles* (1981), pp. 337–59, esp. 355–7.

1. Cf. J. Liver, 'The Half-Shekel ?Offering in Biblical and Post-Biblical ?Literature', HThR 56 (1963), pp. 173–98; G. ?Vermes, PBJS, pp. 41–2. ?

Israelites and two priests,[2] endowed with capital jurisdiction. In the following section, Dt. 22:5, outlawing any interchange of garments between the sexes, is restated in general terms in regard to women, but as far as men are concerned it is specified that they must wear neither the mantle nor the tunic of a woman. Finally, the law of Dt. 22:13–21, concerning a virginity suit, is summarized.

4Q513, Frs. 2–4 treat of purity rules regarding food, and of feasts mentioned in Lev. 23. Fr. 12 seems to refer to uncleanness caused by oil;[3] Fr. 18 to the sabbatical year. The rest is so broken that no interpretation is possible.

4Q514 also legislates on ritual purification in connection with common meals.[4]

Editions

Allegro, J. M., DJD V, pp. 6–9.
Baillet, M., DJD VII, pp. 287–98.

Translations

English
Allegro, *op. cit.*
Vermes, DSSE[2], pp. 249, 252.

French
Carmignac, J., TQ II, pp. 295–7.

Italian
Moraldi, L., MQ, pp. 653–7.

Bibliography

Allegro, J. M., 'An Unpublished Fragment of Essene Halakhah (4Q Ordinances)', JSS 6 (1961), pp. 71–3.
Liver, J., 'The Half-Shekel Offering in Biblical and Post-Biblical Literature', HThR 56 (1963), pp. 173–98.
Yadin, Y., 'A Note on 4Q159 (Ordinances)', IEJ 18 (1968), pp. 250–2.
Strugnell, 'Notes en marge . . .', RQ 7 (1970), pp. 175–9.

2. Cf. J. M. Baumgarten, 'The Duodecimal Courts of Qumran, the Apocalypse, and the Sanhedrin', *Studies in Qumran Law* (1977), pp. 145–71.
3. Cf. J. M. Baumgarten, 'The Essene Avoidance of Oil and the Laws of Purity', *op. cit.*, pp. 88–97.
4. A small fragment of a halakhic document (*4QHalakhah[a]5*), developing the law regarding the offering of new grain and wine (Lev. 23:15–21; Dt. 26:1–11), has been appended to the Copper Scroll by J. T. Milik (DJD III, p. 300). It has been subjected to a fuller analysis by J. M. Baumgarten, '*4QHalakah[a]5*, the Law of *Ḥadash*, and the Pentecostal Calendar', JJS 27 (1976), pp. 36–46 = *Studies in Qumran Law* (1977), pp. 131–42.
   The halakhic composition from Cave 11, summarily described by J. van der Ploeg, 'Une *halakha* inédite de Qumrân', in M. Delcor, *Qumrân* (1978), pp. 107–13, belongs to the Temple Scroll. Cf. *ibid.*, pp. 112–13, and Y. Yadin, 'Le Rouleau du Temple', *ibid.*, p. 119, n. 2.

Weinert, F. D., '4Q159: Legislation for an Essene Community outside of Qumran', JSJ 5 (1974), pp. 179–207.
Vermes, G., PBJS, pp. 41–2.
Idem, DSS, pp. 79–80.
Weinert, F. D., 'A Note on 4Q159 and a New Theory of Essene Origins', RQ 9 (1977), pp. 223–30.

2. *Florilegium or Midrash on the Last Days* (4QFlor = 4Q174)

Twenty-six fragments of an 'early Herodian' manuscript, the first ten of which are large enough to be meaningful, transmit a selection of biblical texts with expository comments.

The scriptural citations include 2 Sam. 7:10–14, combined with Exod. 15:17–18 and Amos 9:11; Ps. 1:1 together with Isa. 8:11 and Ezek. 44:10; Ps. 2:1; Dan. 12:10 and various excerpts from Dt. 33 (8–11, 12?, 19–21).

The main text in the first section, 2 Sam. 7:10–14, immediately introduces an eschatological slant by applying the words of 2 Sam. 7:10, in the light of Exod. 15:17–18, to the Temple 'in the last days', which shall not be profaned by Gentiles as was the historical building. A third Temple concept appears in the phrase מקדש אדם, 'Sanctuary of men', where the 'works of the Torah' form the sacrificial offerings. The biblical reference to Solomon is interpreted here as announcing 'the Branch of David' and 'the Interpreter of the Torah', the royal and (probably) the priestly Messiahs.[1]

The מדרש composed of Ps. 1:1, Isa. 8:11 and Ezek. 44:10 appears to identify the 'wicked' as the unfaithful members of the sect and the 'blessed' as the Council of the Community.

The opening verse of Psalm 2 is understood to allude to the enmity between the elect and the Gentiles, and to the eschatological trial foretold by Daniel. The final excerpt contains the blessing of Moses in Deuteronomy 33 concerning Levi, perhaps also Benjamin, Zebulun and Gad, but no translatable remains of the exegesis are extant.

Although in 1:17 the commentator applies the prophetic words to the 'sons of Zadok', the style of the exegesis differs from that of a *pesher*. Indeed in 1:14 the actual term *'midrash'* is used, implying no doubt an interpretative method whereby the meaning of the text under consideration is derived from other biblical quotations. Scriptural works are cited as 'the Book of Isaiah the prophet' (1:15); 'the Book of Ezekiel the prophet' (1:16); 'the Book of Daniel the prophet' (2:3); and probably 'the Book of [Moses]' (1:2–3), introducing Exod. 15. The 'Sanctuary of men' no doubt corresponds to the idea of an intermediary spiritual centre of worship formed by the members of the

---

1. For צמח דויד see *4QpIsaᵃ*, Frs. 8–10, line 17; *4QPBless*3–4; for דורש התורה, cf. *1QS* 6:6; CD 6:7; 7:18. See Vermes, DSS, pp. 184–5, 195–6.

sect after their secession from the Jerusalem sanctuary, but prior to the restoration of the Temple cult in the seventh year of the final war.[2]

Editions

Allegro, J. M., DJD V, pp. 53–7.
Lohse, E., TQHD, pp. 255–9.

Translations

English
Allegro, *op. cit.*
Vermes, DSSE[2], pp. 245–7.

French
Dupont-Sommer, A., EE, pp. 325–7.
Carmignac, J., TQ II, pp. 279–84.

German
Maier, J., TTM I, pp. 185–6.
Lohse, *op. cit.*

Italian
Moraldi, L., MQ, pp. 572–6.

Bibliography

Allegro, J. M., 'Further Messianic References in Qumrân Literature', JBL 75 (1956), pp. 174–6.
Idem, 'Fragments of a Qumrân Scroll of Eschatological Midrashim', JBL 77 (1958), pp. 351–4.
Yadin, Y., 'A Midrash on 2 Samuel VII (4Q Florilegium)', IEJ 9 (1959), pp. 95–9.
Flusser, D., 'Two Notes on the Midrash on 2 Sam. VII (4Q Florilegium)', IEJ 9 (1959), pp. 99–109.
Strugnell, J., 'Notes en marge . . .', RQ 7 (1970), pp. 220–5.
Vermes, DSS, p. 80.
Delcor, M., 'Qumrân', DBS IX, col. 912.
Schwartz, D. R., 'The Three Temples of 4Q Florilegium', RQ 10 (1979), pp. 83–91.
Ben-Yashar, M., 'Noch zum Miqdaš Adam in Florilegium', RQ 10 (1981), pp. 587–8.
Dimant, D., 'Qumran Sectarian Literature', JWSTP II, pp. 518–21.

3. Testimonia or Messianic Anthology (4QTest = 4Q175)

A nearly complete column of a 'mid-Hasmonean' manuscript (first quarter of the first century B.C.)[1] lists three biblical citations (Dt. 5:28–9; 18:18–19 [= Samaritan Exod. 20:21b];[2] Num. 24:15–17; Dt. 33:8–11) and a quotation from the sectarian Psalms of Joshua, combined with Josh. 6:26. None of the extracts is accompanied by an exposition, but the first three clearly point to eschatological characters:

---

2. Cf. Vermes, *Scripture and Tradition*, pp. 26–39; PBJS, pp. 84–5. See also D. R. Schwartz, 'The Three Temples of 4Q Florilegium', RQ 10 (1979), pp. 83–91.

1. Cf. Strugnell, RQ 7 (1970), p. 225. See also F. M. Cross, *Ancient Library*, p. 114; J. T. Milik, *Ten Years of Discovery*, p. 124.

2. Cf. Strugnell, *art. cit.*, p. 172 apropos of *4Q158*.

(a) a prophet like Moses, i.e. a messianic prophet, or the prophetic Messiah; (b) the Star arising from Jacob according to Balaam's prophecy, or the royal Messiah; and (c) the eschatological representative of Levi, or the priestly Messiah.[3]

The Psalms of Joshua quotation is usually taken to refer to an anti-Messiah.[4] However, the mention of '*two* instruments of violence' (line 25) seems to imply that the writer bears in mind not one but two, if not three, wicked men, viz. a father and his two sons, on the model of Josh. 6:26. If the latter hypothesis is correct, the document would portray three messianic characters set against three antichrists.[5]

The only solid pointer for dating is the identity of the theological outlook regarding an eschatological trio between *4Q175* and *1QS* 9:11. Together with the palaeographical evidence, it would favour the early first century B.C.

On the literary genre of Testimonia in relation to the New Testament, see J. A. Fitzmyer, *Essays on the Semitic Background of the New Testament* (1971), pp. 59–89.

Editions

Allegro, J. M., DJD V, pp. 57–60.
Lohse, E., TQHD, pp. 249–53.

Translations

English
Allegro, *op. cit.*, p. 60.
Vermes, DSSE², pp. 247–9.

French
Dupont-Sommer, A., EE, pp. 328–33.
Carmignac, J., TQ II, pp. 273–8.

German
Maier, J., TTM I, pp. 183–5.
Lohse, *op. cit.*

Italian
Moraldi, L., MQ, pp. 593–6.

3. Cf. vol. II, pp. 550–3; Vermes, DSS, pp. 184–5, 195–6.
4. Cf. J. T. Milik, *Ten Years of Discovery*, p. 125; D. Flusser, 'The Hubris of the Antichrist in a Fragment from Qumran', Immanuel 10 (1980), pp. 31–7.
5. For historical identifications, see Milik, *op. cit.*, pp. 63–4 (Mattathias, Jonathan and Simon); Cross, *op. cit.*, p. 113 (Simon Maccabaeus and his two sons); A. Dupont-Sommer, EE³, pp. 366–7 (John Hyrcanus I, Alexander Jannaeus and Aristobulus I). Vermes, DSS, p. 144 suggests that the phrase 'instruments of violence', borrowed from Gen. 49:5, brings to mind two murderous brothers and would refer to Jonathan and Simon.

Bibliography

Allegro, J. M., 'Further Messianic References in Qumran Literature', JBL 75 (1956), pp. 182–7.
Strugnell, J., 'Notes en marge . . .', RQ 7 (1970), pp. 225–9.
Amusin, J. D., '4Q Testimonia 16–17', *Hommages à André Dupont-Sommer* (1971), pp. 357–61.
Fitzmyer, J. A., '4Q Testimonia and the New Testament', *Essays on the Semitic Background of the New Testament* (1971), pp. 59–89.
Vermes, DSS, pp. 80–1.
Delcor, M., 'Qumrân', DBS IX, cols. 912–13.
Dimant, D., 'Qumran Sectarian Literature', JWSTP II, p. 518.

4. Tanhumim or Words of Consolation (4QTanh = 4Q176)

Fifty-seven fragments, about a quarter of which can be identified, represent an anthology of biblical passages with consolation as their common theme. They were originally followed by exegeses, but most of these are either completely missing or damaged beyond recovery.

The majority of the quotations are borrowed from Deutero-Isaiah (Isa. 40:1–5; 41:8–9; 43:1–2, 4–6; 49:7, 13–17; 51:22–3; 52:1–3; 54:4–10). From the exegetical material only the introductory formula, 'And consolations from the Book of Isaiah' (ומן ספר ישעיה תנחומים), and the very fragmented commentary attached to 54:10, survive. The latter also contains the phrase דברי תנחומים (Frs. 8–11, line 13). Citations apart from Isaiah include Zech. 13:9 and Psalm 79:2–3 (Frs. 1–2, lines 1–4) with scraps of exegesis where the phrase 'bodies of your servants' in verse 2 is replaced by 'bodies of your priests' (כוהניה).

Edition and Bibliography

Allegro, J. M., DJD V, pp. 60–7.
Strugnell, J., 'Notes en marge . . .', RQ 7 (1970), pp. 229–36.
Moraldi, L., MQ, pp. 588–92.

5. Catena A or Midrash on the Psalms (4Q177)

Under the generic title Catena, thirty fragments of various sizes, detached from an 'early Herodian' manuscript, attest a composite exegetical writing. Edited by J. M. Allegro in DJD V, it has been re-examined by J. Strugnell who has shown that the theme is eschatological (cf. Frs. 1–4, lines 5, 7; 9, line 2; 12–13, col. 1:2; col. 2:3), and that in a number of passages the basic text is taken from Psalms 6–16: Ps. 6:2–3, 6 (Frs. 12–13, col. 1:2–3, 5); Ps. 11:1 (Frs. 5–6, line 7); Ps. 12:1 (*ibid.*, line 12); Ps. 12:7 (Frs. 10–11, line 1); Ps. 13:2–3, 5 (*ibid.*, lines 8–9, 11–12); Ps. 16:3 (Frs. 1–4, line 2); Ps. 17:1 (*ibid.*, line 4). Strugnell further notes that the structure of the work, with the quotation of the opening verses of at least Pss. 11, 12 and 17, resembles that of the *Midrash* on Psalms 1 and 2 in *4QFlor* or *4Q174* (cf. above, p. 445).

The commentary is far too broken to be comprehensible, but several typical phrases such as 'seekers of smooth things' (Fr. 9, line 4); 'his angel of Truth' and 'sons of Light' (Frs. 12–13, line 7); 'men of the Community' and especially 'Council of the Community' (Frs. 5–6, line 1; 14, line 5) are incontrovertibly sectarian.[1]

Edition

Allegro, J. M., DJD V, pp. 67–74.

Translations

English
Allegro, *op. cit.*

Italian
Moraldi, L., MQ, pp. 582–6.

Bibliography

Strugnell, J., 'Notes en marge . . .', RQ 7 (1970), pp. 179–83.

6. The Melchizedek Midrash (11QMelch)

An eschatological *pesher*, thirteen fragments of which, in 'late Hasmonaean or early Herodian' book hand, have survived, has as its principal character the heavenly prince Melchizedek, and final salvation as its main theme. The biblical text on which the exposition is based is Leviticus 28.[1] Since both Lev. 25:13 in line 2, and Lev. 25:9 in line 25, are introduced with ואשר אמר, a formula used in *1QpHab* to repeat part of a quotation given in full earlier in the document, it would be logical to infer that the lost section preceding line 1 must have contained at least Lev. 25:8–13, and possibly even all the verses relating to the jubilee legislation.

The Leviticus material is linked to Dt. 15:2, dealing with the remission of debts in the sabbatical year, and Isa. 61:1, proclaiming the liberation of captives, no doubt because they are envisaged as owing a debt to God. The composite *pesher* identifies Melchizedek as the agent of redemption, and places the events described in the first week of the tenth jubilee cycle, the eschatological Day of Atonement followed by ultimate salvation being expected at the end of that cycle (lines 6–7).[2]

---

1. *4Q182*, designated as Catena B, and *4Q183* are historico-exegetical fragments, the former referring to 'the Book of Jerem[iah]' and to 'the end of d[ays]', and the latter to the profanation of the sanctuary. In col. 2, both the term אל and the Tetragram are written in archaic characters. Cf. Allegro, DJD, pp. 80–2; Strugnell, RQ 7 (1970), pp. 256, 263; Moraldi, MQ, p. 587.

1. Cf. J. A. Fitzmyer, 'Further Light on Melchizedek from Qumran Cave 11', *Essays on the Semitic Background of the New Testament* (1971), p. 251.

2. If the jubilee is a period of 49 (7 x 7) years, the end of the tenth jubilee in the year 490 coincides with the completion of seventy weeks of years.

Melchizedek is depicted as the final judge in fulfilment of Ps. 82:1–2, coupled with Ps. 7:7–8; and those condemned by him are the spirits of Belial, alluded to in Ps. 82:2. Isa. 52:7 is explained as proclaiming the great day of redemption, and the four key words in 'How beautiful upon *the mountains* are the feet of *the messenger* ... who says to *Zion*, Your *Elohim* reigns' are explained as referring to 'the prophets' (*mountains*); 'the Anointed of the spirit' (*the messenger*), associated with Daniel (no doubt 9:25: 'an anointed one, a prince');[3] 'those who uphold the Covenant' (*Zion*); and almost certainly ['Melkizedek who will save them from] the hand of Belial' (*Elohim*).

Since the chief character is said to be the leader of the heavenly host, of 'the sons of God', who shall execute vengeance over the spirits of Belial, it is scarcely possible to avoid concluding that Melchizedek = Prince of Light (*1QS* 3:20; CD 5:18; *1QM* 13:10) = the archangel Michael (*1QM* 17:6–7). This deduction acquires further substance from the parallel name Melchiresha given to Belial/Satan in the Testament of Amram (cf. above, p. 334) and in *4Q280–282* (cf. below, p. 459).

For the legend of Melchizedek, see 2 Enoch (p. 749 below) and the Epistle to the Hebrews 7:1–10. Cf. V. Aptowitzer, 'Malkizedek: Zu den Sagen der Agada', MGWJ 70 (1926), pp. 93–103; O. Michel, Μελχισεδέκ, TDNT IV, pp. 568–71; J. A. Fitzmyer, *Essays on the Semitic Background of the N.T.* (1971), pp. 221–43; M. Delcor, 'Melchizedek from Genesis to the Qumran Texts and the Epistle to the Hebrews', JSJ 2 (1971), pp. 115–35; F. L. Horton, *The Melchizedek Tradition* (1976); P. J. Kobelski, *Melchizedek and Melchireša'* (1981).

Edition

Woude, A. S. van der, 'Melchisedek als himmlische Erlösergestalt in den neugefundenen eschatologischen Midraschim aus Qumran Höhle XI', OTS 14 (1965), pp. 354–73.

Translations

English
Jonge, M. de, and Woude, A. S. van der, '11Q Melchizedek and the New Testament', NTSt 12 (1966), pp. 301–26.
Fitzmyer, J. A., 'Further Light on Melchizedek from Qumran Cave 11', JBL 86 (1967), pp. 25–41 [= *Essays on the Semitic Background*, pp. 245–67].
Vermes, DSSE², pp. 265–8.

French
Milik, J. T., '*Milkî-ṣedeq* et *Milkî-reša'* dans les anciens écrits juifs et chrétiens', JJS 23 (1972), pp. 95–144.

German
Woude, A. S. van der, *art. cit.*

---

3. It would seem that this 'Anointed one' is the royal Messiah. Cf. also Fitzmyer, *op. cit.*, p. 266.

Italian
Moraldi, L., MQ, pp. 577–80.

Bibliography

Yadin, Y., 'A Note on Melchizedek and Qumran', IEJ 15 (1965), pp. 105–8.
Dupont-Sommer, A., 'Explication des textes hébreux découverts à Qoumrân ... 11QMelch', Annuaire du Coll. de France 68 (1968–9), pp. 426–30.
Carmignac, J., 'Le document de Qumrân sur Melkisédeq', RQ 7 (1970), pp. 343–78.
Delcor, M., 'Melchizedek from Genesis to the Qumran Texts and the Epistle to the Hebrews', JSJ 2 (1971), pp. 115–35.
Laubscher, F. du T., 'God's Angel of Truth and Melchizedek. A Note on 11QMelch 13b', JSJ 3 (1972), pp. 46–51.
Aune, D. E., 'A Note on Jesus' Messianic Consciousness and 11Q Melchizedek', Evang. Quart. 45 (1973), pp. 161–5.
Sanders, J. A., 'The Old Testament in 11Q Melchizedek', J. of the Anc. N. East Soc. of Columbia Univ. 5 (1973), pp. 373–82.
Woude, A. S. van der, 'Melchizedek', IDBS, pp. 585–6.
Vermes, DSS, pp. 82–3.
Skehan, P. W., 'Qumran. Apocryphes. A.T.', DBS IX, cols. 826–8.
Kobelski, P. J., *Melchizedek and Melkireša'* (1981).

C. Poetry

Among the poetic (or quasi-poetic)[1] compositions of the Qumran sect, pride of place belongs to the Thanksgiving hymns or *Hodayoth* (*1QH*) from Cave 1. To these are to be added a hymn incorporated into the Community Rule (*1QS* 10:9–11:22); another into the War Rule (*1QM* 12:10–18, repeated at 19:2–8); the remains of two Lamentations (*4Q179* and *4Q501*); and a number of small poetic fragments, painstakingly edited, but devoid of independent meaning.[2] Material still awaiting publication includes six fragmentary manuscripts of the *Hodayoth* Scroll from Cave 4,[3] and five further Cave 4 manuscripts containing poems other than those known from *1QH*.[4] Various other passages in the Community Rule, the Damascus Rule, the War Rule, etc. have been translated as hymnic or poetic, but since there is not even a minimum degree of agreement among scholars, it is advisable not to include them in this section.

---

1. Owing to the difficulty in defining Hebrew poetry, it is not surprising that for certain scholars *1QH* represents no more than rythmic prose. Cf. D. Dombkowski Hopkins, 'The Qumran Community and the 1Q Hodayot: A Reassessment', RQ 10 (1981), p. 331.

2. Cf. J. T. Milik, DJD I (*1Q35, 1Q36, 1Q37–40*) and M. Baillet, DJD III (*3Q6; 6Q18; 8Q5*) and DJD VII (*4Q498–9*).

3. J. Strugnell, 'Le travail d'édition', RB 63 (1956), p. 64. The oldest of the 4Q manuscripts is dated to the beginning of the first century B.C. (100–80 B.C.): J. Starcky, 'Les quatre étapes du messianisme à Qumrân', RB 70 (1963), p. 483, n. 8.

4. Strugnell, *art. cit.* (in n. 3), p. 64.

452   §32. Jewish Literature in Hebrew or Aramaic

1. The Hodayoth or Thanksgiving Hymns (1QH)
The text of eighteen columns together with sixty-six further unplaced
fragments was edited by E. L. Sukenik under the title *Hodayoth* in *The
Dead Sea Scrolls of the Hebrew University* in 1954/5. *1QH* survives in two
originally separate manuscripts, written by two different 'Herodian'
hands. The arrangement of the columns by Sukenik will be followed to
avoid confusion, although J. Carmignac's careful examination of the
material, including the fragments, suggests the following order:[5]

> *Manuscript A*
> Cols. 13–16 (Sukenik)
> Frs. 15, 18, 22
>
> *Manuscript B*
> Cols. 1–3 lost
> Col. 4 = Sukenik 17
> Cols. 5–16 = Sukenik 1–12
> Col. 17 = Fr. 5
> Col. 18 = Frs. 1, 46, 58
> Col. 19 = Sukenik 18
> Col. 20 = Frs. 6, 9, 50
> Col. 21 = Frs. 2, 8
> Col. 22 = Frs. 3, 7
> Col. 23 = Fr. 4
> Col. 24 lost.

The mutilated state of the scrolls makes it impossible to determine the
precise number of poems included in them. Since most Hymns open
with 'I thank you, O Lord' (אודכה אדוני): *1QH* 2:20, 31; 3:19, 37; 4:5;
5:5, 20; 7:6, [26], 34; 8:4; 11:3, 15; 14:23) or 'Blessed are you, O Lord'
(ברוך אתה אדוני: [5:20, variant] 10:14), it would seem that there are
at least thirteen units. In fact, without counting the fragments,
estimates vary between twenty-five (Vermes, Carmignac), thirty-two
(Dupont-Sommer, Licht), thirty-three (Moraldi), etc.
    All the psalms are written in imitation biblical Hebrew with a very
large number of borrowings from Scripture.[6] They may be classified as
individual thanksgiving hymns,[7] since the poet always speaks in the first

5. TQ I, p. 129. Cf. also *idem*, 'Remarques sur le texte des Hymnes de Qumrân', Bibl 39
(1958), pp. 139–58; 'Localisation des fragments 15, 18 et 22 des Hymnes', RQ 1 (1959),
pp. 425–30; 'Compléments au texte des Hymnes de Qumrân', RQ 2 (1960), pp. 267–76,
549–58.
    6. Cf. J. Carmignac, 'Les citations de l'Ancien Testament dans les Hymnes de
Qumrân', RQ 2 (1960), pp. 357–94 [673 borrowings]. For a list of biblical texts used in
1QH see S. Holm-Nielsen, *Hodayot : Psalms from Qumran* (1960), pp. 354–9.
    7. On this type of poems in the Bible, see Eissfeldt, *Introduction*, pp. 121–4.

person singular, except apparently in Frs. 10:6–8; 18:2 and 47:1, where the subject is 'we'.

The principal reasons for thanksgiving, stated at the opening of each hymn, are the following. The psalmist's life has been saved, protected or strengthened by God (2:20–1; 2:31; 3:19; 3:37; 5:15; 5:20; 7:6). He has been enlightened by the divine truth of the Covenant (4:5; 7:26; 11:15; 14:23). He has not been placed among the wicked (7:34), but beside a spring of water (8:4). He has been graciously and marvellously treated by God (10:14; 11:3). In short, a dual theme dominates: deliverance from evil, persecution, oppression and the divine gift of election and knowledge within the Covenant of the Community.

The second group of Hymns is associated in various ways with entry into the sect. A number of them would apply to any member. Others would fit better a teacher of the sect, such as the מבקר of the Community Rule (e.g. *1QH* 7:6 ff.; 12:3 ff.; 14:8 ff.; 17:26 ff.).[8] Among the poems in which deliverance plays a leading part, there are a few (in particular 2:3–18 and 4:5–40) that appear to depict a persecuted leader, betrayed and abandoned by some of his disciples. 'For I am despised by them (the teachers of lies) ... They have banished me from my land like a bird from its nest; all my friends and brethren are driven far from me and hold me for a broken vessel' (4:8–9). The destiny of this psalmist resembles that of the Teacher of Righteousness as portrayed in *1QpHab* (cf. p. 334). Indeed, he is thought by some scholars to be the author of these hymns, if not of all the *Hodayoth* (see below).

As far as their purpose is concerned, some *Hodayoth* are understood by many as expressing the sentiments and experiences of their author. This would apply first and foremost to 'the psalms of the Teacher of Righteousness'.[9] For others, the Hymns are primarily didactic poems. Containing much wisdom material, they are intended to be read and meditated on by individuals. They are meant to serve private piety.[10] Yet another theory claims that the function of the poems was, from the outset, cultic: they were to be recited by individuals in the context of communal worship.[11]

---

8. See in particular 7:20–1 (אב לבני חסד and אמון לאנשי מופת).Cf. also משכיל in 12:11, a term used in connection with the person in charge of instruction in *1QS* 3:13; 9:12, 21; CD 12:21; 13:22. It should further be noted that *1QSb* 1:1 and 3:22 are dedicated to the *maskil* and that למשכיל appears also in *1QH*, fr. 8:10.

9. Cf. M. Delcor, 'Qumran. Les Hymnes', DBS IX, col. 897.

10. Cf. H. Bardtke, 'Considérations sur les cantiques de Qumran', RB 63 (1956), pp. 220–33.

11. Cf. B. Reicke, 'Remarques sur l'histoire de la forme (Formgeschichte) des textes de Qumrân', *Les manuscrits de la Mer Morte. Colloque de Strasbourg* (1957), pp. 38–44. Reicke sees the model for the *Sitz im Leben* of the *Hodayoth*, the liturgy of the Therapeutae, described by Philo in *De vita contemplativa* 10 (80). (On the Therapeutae, see vol. II, pp.

Of the three theories, the last appears to make the best overall sense. Indeed, even if it could be substantiated that several of the poems are genuine lyric compositions by the Teacher of Righteousness, the bulk of them do not belong to this category, and the stylistic arguments advanced in favour of a single author[12] appear to be far too flimsy when the paramount biblical colouring of the language and the stereotyped form of the majority of the hymns are borne in mind. Neither can Bardtke's stress on the sapiential character of the *Hodayoth* be justified. The psalmist's insistence on the disproportion between the frailty of man—a creature of clay—and his supernatural destiny, rather than providing food for wisdom meditation, serves to heighten his sense of gratitude for his election.

In support of the cultic hypothesis, it may be pointed out that the Qumran feast of the Renewal of the Covenant (cf. above, p. 395) offers an ideal setting for the *Hodayoth*. These would have been recited by the Guardian and the sectaries individually as was the case with the president and the members of the religious banquet of the Therapeutae, referred to above. This hypothesis is strengthened by a reminder that before the communal meal mentioned in the Messianic Rule, the benediction pronounced by 'the Priest' and 'the Messiah of Israel' is followed by prayers recited by *each* participant.[13] Furthermore *1QH* 14:17–18 alludes to an oath which is no doubt the same as that in *1QS* 5:8.[14] Finally, the hymn which begins at 14:23 may well be described as a poetic commentary on the liturgy of the entry into the Covenant.[15]

In the absence of clear evidence, it would be unwarranted to advance definitive claims regarding the authorship of the *Hodayoth*. The attribution of the whole collection to a single poet on stylistic grounds is based on specious reasoning (see above pp. 453–4 and n. 12), and whereas it is impossible categorically to deny that some of the hymns might have been the work of the Teacher of Righteousness, their firm ascription to this author is manifestly unprovable.[16] S. Holm-Nielsen's conclusion formulated a quarter of a century ago is still worth repeating: 'There is evidence that (these psalms) are not all of the same cast, but that they

---

591–7.)

12. Cf. J. Carmignac, TQ I, p. 132. For a similar, but less emphatic view, see A. Dupont-Sommer, *Le Livre des Hymnes découvert près de la Mer Morte* [Semitica 7] (1957), pp. 11–12. See also J. Licht, *The Thanksgiving Scroll* (1957), pp. 22–4 (Hebrew).

13. וברכו כול עדת היחד אנ‫יש‬ לפ‫י‬ן כבודו (*1QSa* 2:21).

14. Compare ובשבועה הקימותי על נפשי (*1QH* 14:17) to ויקם על נפשו בשבועת אסר (*1QS* 5:8) and בשבועת הברית יקימו עליהם (CD 15:6).

15. Cf. Vermes, DSSE², pp. 149–50; DSS, pp. 56–7. See also Carmignac, TQ I, p. 135.

16. For a refutation of the authorship of the Teacher of Righteousness, see Licht, *op. cit.* (in n. 12), pp. 25–6. The use of *Hodayoth* evidence for the reconstruction of the history of Qumran seems therefore highly unsafe *pace* G. Jeremias, *Der Lehrer der Gerechtigkeit* (1963), pp. 36–78; H. Stegemann, *Entstehung der Qumrangemeinde* (1971), pp. 95–113, 198–252.

form a collection of different poems, possibly from different authors and from different times. Nothing can be said definitely of the authors themselves, and the question of their identity is of minor significance.'[17]

If, in the light of these considerations, the authorship of the Teacher of Righteousness is not allowed to play any part in dating the *Hodayoth*, and if it is furthermore admitted that the poems may have originated from several writers, palaeography remains the sole evidence for determining the age of the collection. Therefore, the least objectionable conjecture is to assign the various hymns to the first century B.C.

Of the two hymns incorporated in other Qumran scrolls, *1QS* 10:9–11:22 represents the same genre of poetry as the *Hodayoth*, possibly a teacher's psalm. By contrast, that from the War Scroll (*1QM* 12:10–18; 19:2–8) is a hymn of victory, celebrating God's prowess and Jerusalem's future glory.

The first of the two Lamentations from Cave 4 (*4Q179*) is attested by two damaged fragments and three further scraps, dated by J. Strugnell on palaeographical grounds to the mid-first century B.C. Inspired by the biblical book of the same name, it portrays Jerusalem as a forsaken woman who has lost all her children.[18]

The second Lamentation (*4Q501*), a 'Herodian' manuscript assigned by M. Baillet to the third quarter of the first century B.C., voices the complaints of God's children, sons of his Covenant, because of the slanderous attacks directed towards them by the wicked. The tone of the poem and some of its vocabulary are reminiscent of *1QH*, except that *4Q501* is a communal, not individual, lament.[19]

Editions

Sukenik, E. L., *The Dead Sea Scrolls of the Hebrew University* (1954/5).
Licht, J., *The Thanksgiving Scroll* (1957) (Hebrew).
Delcor, M., *Les Hymnes de Qumrân. Texte hébreux, introduction, traduction, commentaire* (1962).
Lohse, E., TQHD, pp. 109–75.

Translations

English
Mansoor, M., *The Thanksgiving Hymns translated and annotated with an Introduction* (1961).
Vermes, DSSE[2], pp. 149–201.

French
Dupont-Sommer, A., *Le Livre des Hymnes découvert près de la Mer Morte* [Semitica 7] (1957).
Idem, EE, pp. 213–66.

17. *Op. cit.* (in n. 6 above), p. 331.
18. *4Q179* has been edited by J. M. Allegro, DJD V, pp. 75–7. Cf. J. Strugnell, RQ 7 (1970), pp. 250–2. See also Vermes, DSSE[2], pp. 254–5; L. Moraldi, MQ, pp. 693–4; M. P. Horgan, 'A Lament over Jerusalem (4Q179)', JSSt 17 (1972), pp. 222–34; H. Pabst, 'Eine Sammlung von Klagen in den Qumranfunden (4Q179)', in M. Delcor, *Qumrân* (1978), pp. 137–49.
19. See M. Baillet, DJD VII, pp. 79–80, containing also a French translation.

Carmignac, J., TQ I, pp. 129–280.
Delcor, M., *op. cit.*

German
Maier, J., TTM I, pp. 71–122.
Lohse, E., *op. cit.*

Italian
Moraldi, L., MQ, pp. 329–463.

Bibliography

Baumgarten, J. M., and Mansoor, M., 'Studies in the new Hodayot', JBL 74 (1955), pp. 115–24, 188–95; 75 (1956), pp. 107–13.
Licht, J., 'The Doctrine of the Thanksgiving Hymns', IEJ 6 (1956), pp. 1–13.
Silberman, L. H., 'Language and Structure in the Hodayot', JBL 75 (1956), pp. 96–106.
Mowinckel, S., 'Some Remarks on Hodayoth 39 (V, 2–20)', JBL 75 (1956), pp. 265–76.
Bardtke, H., 'Considérations sur les cantiques de Qumrân', RB 63 (1956), pp. 220–33.
Idem, 'Das "Ich" des Meisters in den Hodajoth von Qumrân', Wissenschaftliche Zeitschrift der Karl-Marx Universität 6 (1956–57), pp. 93–104.
Betz, O., 'Die Geburt der Gemeinde durch den Lehrer. Bemerkungen zum Qumranpsalm 1QH III, 1 ff.', NTSt 3 (1957), pp. 314–26.
Reicke, B., 'Remarques sur l'histoire de la forme (Formgeschichte) des textes de Qumrân', *Les manuscrits de la Mer Morte. Colloque de Strasbourg* (1957), pp. 38–44.
Morawe, G., *Aufbau und Abgrenzung der Loblieder von Qumrân* (1960).
Holm-Nielsen, S., '"Ich" in den Hodayoth und die Qumrângemeinde', in H. Bardtke (ed.), *Qumran-Probleme* (1963), pp. 217–29.
Jeremias, G., *Der Lehrer der Gerechtigkeit* (1963).
Thiering, B., 'The Poetic Forms of the Hodayot', JSSt 8 (1963), pp. 189–209.
Stegemann, H., *Rekonstruktion der Hodayot. Die ursprüngliche Gestalt der Hymnenrolle aus Höhle I von Qumrân* (1964).
Wernberg-Møller, P., 'Contribution of the Hodayot to Biblical Textual Criticism', Textus 4 (1964), pp. 133–75.
Eissfeldt, O., *Introduction*, pp. 654–7.
Holm-Nielsen, S., 'Erwägungen zu dem Verhältnis zwischen den Hodajot und den Psalmen Salomos', in *Bibel und Qumran* (Festschrift Bardtke) (1966), pp. 112–31.
Ringgren, H., 'Die Weltbrand in den Hodajot', *ibid.*, pp. 177–82.
Sanders, E. P., 'Chiasmus and the Translation of 1Q Hodayot VII, 25–27', RQ 6 (1968), pp. 427–32.
Hübner, H., 'Anthropologischer Dualismus in den Hodayoth', NTSt 18 (1972), pp. 268–84.
Nielsen, E., '1 Q H V, l. 20–27: An Attempt at Filling out some Gaps', VT 24 (1974), pp. 240–3.
Vermes, DSS, pp. 56–8.
Delcor, M., 'Qumrân. Les Hymnes', DBS IX, cols. 861–4, 897–904.
Dombrowski Hopkins, D., 'The Qumran Community and 1 Q Hodayot: A Reassessment', RQ 10 (1981), pp. 323–64.
Kittel, B. P., *The Hymns of Qumran: Translation and Commentary* (1981).
Thorion, Y., 'Der Vergleich in 1 Q Hodayot', RQ 11 (1983), pp. 193–217.
Dimant, D., 'Qumran Sectarian Literature', JWSTP II, pp. 522–4.

D. Liturgical Texts

A large number of fragments found in Caves 1, 2, 4 and 6 represent benedictions and prayers which were no doubt used in the framework

of the Community's worship. The best preserved compositions will be
followed here by smaller units belonging to the same literary genre.

1. The Master's Blessings (1QSb)

As has been noted earlier (cf. p. 381), the Community Rule (*1QS*) is
accompanied in the same scroll by two supplementary sections, The
Messianic Rule or Rule of the Congregation (*1QSa*) and a series of
liturgical benedictions (*1QSb*). The latter have been published by J. T.
Milik in DJD I. Like the rest of the manuscripts, they are assigned
palaeographically to the beginning of the first century B.C. Remains of
five very damaged columns survive out of an original six-column
document. The sequence of the blessings is not certain.

Three units are provided with an *incipit*: 'Words of blessing. For the
master to bless ...'—דברי ברכ[ה] למשכיל לברך (1:1 ; 3:22) and 'For
the master to bless ...'—למשכיל לברך (5:20). These relate to the
faithful of the Covenant (1:1–20), to the High Priest (1:21?–3:21),[1] to
the priests, sons of Zadok (3:22–5:19), and to the Prince of the
Congregation (5:20–29).

The blessing of the members of the Covenant is to enable them to
persevere; that of the High Priest (if his blessing is separate from that of
the priests in general) is to render his office one of everlasting peace.
The priests are to be blessed that they may serve in the Temple of the
Kingdom in the company of the angels and glorify God's name.
Finally, the blessing of the Prince of the Congregation foresees him as
destroyer of the ungodly, fortified by God's name and filled with his
spirit.

Like the Rule of the Congregation, these blessings also appear to
envisage the messianic age. Again, if *1QS*—of which *1QSb* is an
appendix—is accepted as a guide, a distinct blessing of the High Priest
appears probable. If so, the High Priest is the Messiah of Aaron of *1QS*
9:11 and 'the Priest' of *1QSa* 2:12, 19, and the Prince of the
Congregation is the Messiah of Israel, or Branch of David (*1QS* 9:11 ; CD
7:20 ; *4QPBless* ; *4QFlor*).

According to Milik, this liturgical document was not meant for use
by the sectaries, but was to await the dawn of the messianic era.[2] Yet if
the rubric appended to *1QSa*, enjoining the members of the sect to
imitate in advance the programme of the eschatological banquet 'at
every meal', is taken as indicative of sectarian practice, the actual
recitation of the messianic benedictions may also have been intended as

---

1. R. Leivestad has advanced the thesis that the scroll consists of three blessings only:
those of the people (1:1–3:21), the priests (3:22–5:19), and the Messiah (5:20 ff.). Cf.
'Enthalten die Segenssprüche 1QSb eine Segnung des Hohenpriesters der messianischen
Zeit?', ST 21 (1977), pp. 137–45.

2. DJD I, p. 120.

a ritual anticipation of the coming Kingdom.[3]
Because of their link with the Community Rule, the Blessings of *1QSb*
are best dated to around 100 B.C.
Five insignificant papyrus fragments from Cave 6 (*6Q16*), dated by
M. Baillet to the first century A.D., appear to have derived from
benedictions similar to *1QSb*.[4] Another small piece, entitled by him
'Bénédiction' (*4Q500*), has preserved allusions to an orchard and a vine-
yard, but it may be just as well a psalm as a blessing.[5]

Editions

Milik, J. T., DJD I, pp. 118–30.
Lohse, E., TQHD, pp. 53–61.

Translations

English
Vermes, DSSE², pp. 206–9.

French
Milik, *op. cit.*
Dupont-Sommer, A., EE, pp. 124–7.
Carmignac, J., TQ II, pp. 31–42.

German
Maier, J., TTM I, pp. 176–9.

Italian
Moraldi, L., MQ, pp. 193–204.

Bibliography

Rost, L., 'Die Anhänge des Ordensregel (1QSa und 1QSb)', ThLZ 82 (1957), cols.
    667–72.
Talmon, S., 'The "Manual of Benedictions" of the Sect of the Judaean Desert', RQ 2
    (1960), pp. 475–500.
Carmignac, J., 'Quelques détails de lecture dans ... le "Recueil de Bénédictions"', RQ 4
    (1963), pp. 83–96.
Leivestad, R., 'Enthalten die Segenssprüche 1 Q Sb eine Segnung des Hohenpriesters der
    messianischen Zeit?', ST 21 (1977), pp. 137–45.
Vermes, DSS, p. 61.
Delcor, M., 'Qumrân. Recueil des Bénédictions', DBS IX, cols. 859–60.

2. Blessings and Curses

Two fragmentary documents from Cave 4 were issued in a preliminary
publication by J. T. Milik in 1972 in JJS 23. Both echo the liturgical
blessings and curses forming part of the ritual of the renewal of the
Covenant according to *1QS* 2:1–18, with a further parallel in *1QM*
13:4–6.

---

3. Vermes, DSSE², p. 206.
4. M. Baillet, DJD III, pp. 131–2.
5. M. Baillet, DJD VII, pp. 78–9.

The first text, provisionally entitled *4QBerakot*, exists in two manuscripts, *a* and *b*, or *4Q286* and *4Q287*. Its first line ends the blessing of the Council of the Community. This is followed by repeated maledictions of Belial, the Wicked One, the Angel of Perdition and the Spirit of Destruction and all his realm.

The second composition, *4QTeharotD* or *4Q280*, also echoes *1QS* 2:4 ff., but is distinguished by its identification of Satan as 'Melchiresha' (cf. above, p. 450).

Edition and Bibliography

Milik, J. T., '*Milkî-ṣedeq* et *Milkî-reša'* dans les anciens écrits juifs et chrétiens', JJS 23 (1972), pp. 126–35 (texts and French translations).
Vermes, DSSE², pp. 252–4.

3. Daily Prayers

Two substantial compositions from Cave 4 offer prayers for the days of the week and of the month. The first, the Words of the Heavenly Lights or *Dibre Ha-Me'oroth*, exists in three manuscripts (*DibHam*$^{a\ b\ c}$ = *4Q504–6*). *4Q504* consists of forty-eight fragments, about a dozen of which are fairly large, written by a 'Hasmonaean' hand. M. Baillet's dating, the mid-second century B.C., may be exaggeratedly high. *4Q505* includes ten small fragments with 'late Hasmonaean' calligraphy ('circa 70–60 B.C.') and *4Q506* is a papyrus made up of fifty-eight tiny pieces dated on a palaeographical basis to mid-first century A.D.

The second work, entitled by M. Baillet 'Prières quotidiennes' (*4Q503*), is also written on papyrus by a 'Hasmonaean' scribe apparently in 100–75 B.C. Altogether 225 fragments are extant.

(a) The Words of the Heavenly Lights (4Q504–6)

The title is said to appear on Fr. 8 verso as דברי המֿאֿרֿוֿתֿ, with the last five letters marked as uncertain. The work represents collective prayers with biblical reminiscences, e.g. Israel called God's first-born son, David chosen as 'princely shepherd', Israel banished in exile. Since the second unit (col. 7, line 4) is entitled הודות ביום השבת, Hymns on the Day of Sabbath, it may safely be inferred that it is preceded by prayers intended for Friday. A further reference appears to 'the fourth [da]y' on Fr. 3 (col. 2, line 5). The prayer mentions how God carried his people on an eagle's wings (Fr. 6, lines 6–7) and how Adam was created in the Garden of Eden (Fr. 8 recto, lines 4–6). According to the editor, the latter passage is to be connected with Sunday. It would seem reasonable to conclude that the complete document contained hymns or prayers for each day of the week.

(b) Daily Prayers (4Q503)

In this poorly preserved document, evening and morning blessings are listed for each day of an unspecified month. The first date, 'the fifth' of the month, appears on col. 3, line 6, and the last, 'the [twenty-]sixth', on col. 12, line 23. The prayers, none of which is extant in full, are relatively short and stereotyped, beginning with 'Blessed be the God of Israel' (ברוך אל ישראל) and ending with 'Peace be on you, Israel' (שלום עליכה ישראל). The fifteenth of the month appears to be a joyous feast day (col. 7, Frs. 24–5, line 5).

The fact that, contrary to the arrangement underlying for example *1QS* 10:1–3, where light comes before darkness, here evening precedes morning, presupposes not a solar but a lunar time reckoning. The editor, M. Baillet, wonders, however, whether the month is meant to be an ideal model for a combined lunar and ancient priestly solar calendar, the festival celebrated in the middle of it being Passover (DJD VII, pp. 105–6).

Editions

Baillet, M., DJD VII, pp. 105–36 ['Prières quotidiennes']; 137–75 ['Paroles des Luminaires], both with French translation.

Translations

English
Vermes, DSSE², pp. 202–5.

French
Baillet, *op. cit.*
Carmignac, J., TQ II, pp. 299–310.

Italian
Moraldi, L., MQ, pp. 643–51.

Bibliography

Baillet, M., 'Un recueil liturgique de Qumrân, grotte 4: Les Paroles des Luminaires', RB 68 (1961), pp. 195–250.
Idem, 'Remarques sur l'édition des Paroles des Luminaires', RQ 7 (1964), pp. 23–42.
Lehmann, M. R., 'A Re-Interpretation of 4Q Dibrê ham-me'oroth', RQ 7 (1964), pp. 106–10.
Rinaldi, G., 'Una "Supplica" da Qumrân (4Q Dib Ham)', Bibbia e Oriente 14 (1972), pp. 119–31.

4. Prayers for Festivals

Three extremely worn manuscripts from Cave 4 (*4Q507–9*), together with fragments from Cave 1 (*1Q34* and *1Q34^{bis}*), represent liturgical prayers intended for various festivals. Of the Cave 4 texts, *4Q507* and *4Q508* are assigned by M. Baillet, on the basis of their script, to the beginning of the first century A.D., while *4Q509* is said to be 'late Hasmonaean' (70–60 B.C.).

The prayers are in the first person plural with the customary beginnings ('Blessed be the Lord', or 'Remember, Lord') and endings ('Amen, amen'). There is explicit reference only to תפלת ליום כפורים

('Prayer for the Day of Atonement': *1Q34*^{bis}, Frs. 2 + 1, line 6; *4Q508*, Fr. 2, line 1), but the editor assumes that *4Q509* starts with the New Year, continues with the Day of Atonement, Tabernacles, and no doubt others (Passover, etc.), and finally with תפלה ליום ה]בכורים ([Prayer for the Day of] First-fruits', or Feast of Weeks: Frs. 131-2, col. 2, line 5).

Editions

Milik, J. T., DJD I, pp. 136, 152-5.
Baillet, M., DJD VII, pp. 175-215.

Translations

English
Vermes, DSSE², pp. 205-6 (*1Q34*^{bis}).

French
Milik, *op. cit.*
Baillet, *op. cit.*
Dupont-Sommer, A., EE, pp. 345-6.
Carmignac, J., TQ II, pp. 263-7.

Italian
Moraldi, L., MQ, pp. 639-42.

Bibliography

Carmignac, J., 'Le recueil de prières liturgiques de la grotte 1', RQ 4 (1963), pp. 271-6.

5. Marriage Ritual (?) (4Q502)

Three hundred and forty-four minute papyrus scraps attest a liturgical work from Cave 4 dated palaeographically by M. Baillet to the beginning of the Christian era. The contents appear to belong to the hymnic genre with benedictions recited by a community which includes both sexes and various age groups. Joy is the dominating feature, the noun שמחה and the verb שמח occurring eighteen times.

Baillet conjectures that the ceremony is that of a wedding on the basis of allusions to '[man] and his wife' (Fr. 1, line 3: Gen. 2:25) and to 'producing seed' (לעשות זרע: *ibid.*, line 4). Fr. 16 appears to be a quotation from the Community Rule's section concerning the Two Spirits (*1QS* 4:4-6). However, the editor's identification of the document as a marriage ritual has been questioned,[1] and an alternative theory has been proposed by J. M. Baumgarten, who notes the frequency of references to 'men of mature age' (אשישים: Fr. 9, lines 3, 9, 11, 13), to 'old men' (זקנים) and 'old women' (זקנות), and even to an 'assembly (סוד) of old men and women' (Fr. 24, line 4). Such an emphasis on the elderly of both sexes does not, in his opinion, suggest a

---

1. See G. Vermes, Review of DJD VII in TLS, 1 Oct. 1982, p. 1082.

wedding-feast, but recalls the worshipping assembly of the Therapeutae of Philo (cf. vol. II, pp. 591–7), and possibly also the joyful celebration in the Temple courtyards at the feast of Tabernacles alluded to in the Tosefta (tSuk. 4:2).[2]

Edition

Baillet, M., DJD VII, pp. 81–105 (with French translation).

Bibliography

Baillet, M., 'Débris de textes sur papyrus de la grotte 4 de Qumrân', RB 71 (1964), pp. 353–71.

6. The Angelic Liturgy or Serekh Shiroth 'olath ha-Shabbath

A liturgical document describing angelic worship in the heavenly Temple has been discovered in six copies in Cave 4 (*4Q400, 400', 401, 402, 403*, and *405*). Further small fragments have been found in Cave 11, and a large piece at Masada. They are all the work of 'Herodian' hands. None of the texts has yet been published in any 'official' edition, but parts of *4Q402* and *403* were issued in a preliminary study by J. Strugnell in 1960. The Masada fragment was discussed by Y. Yadin in 1965, and all the Cave 4 manuscripts have been subjected to a thorough scrutiny, including edition, translation and interpretation, by Carol Ann Newsom in a Harvard Ph.D. dissertation under the supervision of J. Strugnell.[1]

Dedicated to 'the Instructor' (למשכיל),[2] the songs convey angelic praises to God. The title specifies the place of the sabbath in question in the sequence of the fifty-two weeks of the solar year and its date within one of the twelve months. The first, sixth, seventh, eighth and eleventh sabbaths are mentioned in the surviving passages.

The best preserved heading is at *4Q402* 1 i 30: 'For the Instructor. Song of the sacrifice of the seventh Sabbath, on the sixteenth of the month: Praise the God of heaven, O you elevated ones among the gods of knowledge!'

The songs in general are concerned not so much with God as with

2. '4Q502, Marriage or Golden Age Ritual?', JJS 34 (1983), pp. 125–35.

1. J. Strugnell, 'The Angelic Liturgy of Qumran', VTS VII (1960), pp. 318–45; Y. Yadin, 'The Excavations at Masada: 1963–1964. A Preliminary Report', IEJ 15 (1965), pp. 105–8; Carol A. Newsom, *4Q Serek Šîrôt 'ôlat HaŠŠabbat (The Qumran Angelic Liturgy). Edition, Translation and Commentary* (1982). The editors are particularly grateful to Carol Newsom for kindly providing a copy of her thesis.

The Masada fragment (*MasŠirŠabb*) has now been published by Y. Yadin and Carol Newsom, 'The Masada Fragment of the Qumran Songs of the Sabbath Sacrifice', in IEJ 34 (1984), pp. 77–88. The text represents the conclusion of the song for the Fifth Sabbath and the first half of that of the Sixth Sabbath. There are overlaps with *4Q402, 403, 404* and *405*. *4Q400* preserves a closely related version.

2. Cf. *4Q400* 1–2, line 1; *4Q402* 1 i, line 30.

heavenly worship: with psalms and blessings sung by the seven angelic princes (*4Q402*), with the description of the celestial Temple and the throne-chariot, with angels and spirits and their special garments (*4Q403*). Although the headings refer to Sabbath *burnt offerings* (עולות), the poems include no pointers to sacrificial worship or to a heavenly altar.

The main source of inspiration of the Angelic Liturgy is Ezekiel chs. 1 and 10, regarding the throne-chariot, and chs. 40–48, for the heavenly sanctuary. Indeed, this document constitutes an important landmark for the study of the history of *Merkabah* mysticism and of the so-called Hekhaloth hymns.[3]

The composition contains nothing directly datable. Bearing in mind the palaeographical evidence and general considerations on Qumran literature, the Angelic Liturgy may best be assigned to the first century B.C.

Three explanations are possible for the presence of this Qumran work in the fortress of Masada. (1) The Qumran sectaries were Zealots. (2) A group of the Qumran-Essenes embraced the Zealot cause and brought with them some of their literature. (3) The Qumran site was seized by the Zealots after it had been evacuated by the Community and they transferred the contents of one of the caches to Masada. The first of these hypotheses is unlikely on general historical grounds.[4] The second is favoured by Y. Yadin,[5] but the third appears equally probable.

Editions

Strugnell, J., 'The Angelic Liturgy at Qumran—4Q Serek Šîrôt • *Ôlat Hassabbat*', *Congress Volume Oxford 1959* [VTS VII] (1960), pp. 318–45.

Newsom, C. A., *4Q Serek Šîrôt 'Ôlat HaŠŠabbat (The Qumran Angelic Liturgy) : Edition, Translation and Commentary* [University Microfilms International] (1982).

Translations

English
Strugnell, *op. cit.*
Newsom, *op. cit.*
Vermes, DSSE[2], pp. 210–13.

French
Dupont-Sommer, A., EE, pp. 427–33.
Carmignac, J., TQ II, pp. 311–20.

Italian
Moraldi, L., MQ, pp. 659–69.

3. Cf. G. Scholem, *Jewish Gnosticism, Merkabah Mysticism and Talmudic Tradition* (1965), p. 128, and, in particular, ch. VII of Carol Newsom's dissertation (pp. 79–92).
4. Vermes, DSS, pp. 122–5.
5. Cf. *Masada : Herod's Fortress and the Zealots' Last Stand* (1966), p. 174.

Bibliography

Carmignac, J., 'Quelques détails de la lecture dans la Règle des chants pour l'holocauste du Sabbat', RQ 7 (1964), pp. 563–6.
Yadin, Y., 'Excavations at Masada: 1963–1964. Preliminary Report', IEJ 15 (1965), pp. 1–120, esp. 105–8.
Vermes, DSS, pp. 63–4.
Delcor, M., 'Qumran. Liturgie', DBS IX, cols. 915–16.
Dimant, D., 'Qumran Sectarian Literature', JWSTP II, pp. 524–5.
Newsom, C. and Yadin, Y., 'The Masada Fragment of the Qumran Songs of the Sabbath', IEJ 34 (1984), pp. 77–88.

7. Small Liturgical Fragments

There remain a few exiguous pieces, apparently liturgical in character, but too broken for proper evaluation.

(a) *1Q29* consists of sixteen scraps of leather on which 'tongues of fire' and 'three tongues of fire' are mentioned, together with a 'priest' addressing a group of Israelites and pronouncing prayers over them.

(b) *1Q30* appears to be a prayer but includes also the word 'their interpretations' (פשריהם).

(c) *1Q31* speaks of 'the men of the Community', of 'the elect' and of 'camps'. It may belong to a battle liturgy.

(d) *2Q26*, an Aramaic fragment from a 'Herodian' hand, seems to allude to the ritual washing of a לוחא, a tablet or board.

(e) *4Q181* includes two 'Herodian' fragments which may represent a sectarian liturgical work, the first dealing with unfaithful members of 'the assembly of the sons of h[eaven] and earth' and the election of the members of 'the holy congregation', and the second containing allusions to biblical history.

Editions

Milik, J. T., DJD I, pp. 130–4.
Baillet, M., DJD III, pp. 90–1.
Allegro, J. M., DJD V, pp. 79–80.

E. Miscellaneous Texts

To complete the presentation of the Qumran material, consideration is to be given to a few documents which, for various reasons, do not fall within any of the previous categories. They may be grouped under three headings: (1) 'horoscopes'; (2) calendars; and (3) the Copper Scroll.

1. 'Horoscopes' (4QCryptic = 4Q186)

Two 'Herodian' fragments from Cave 4, both written from left to right and using irregularly letters of the archaic alphabet mixed with

Greek characters, contain 'horoscopes'.[1] The fragmentary state of the documents does not allow a full grasp of the meaning but it would seem that physical characteristics are associated with spiritual qualities, as well as with the birthday of the individual and his Zodiacal symbol. Each person is seen as consisting of nine parts, and in the extant examples light and darkness are variously mixed. As the number is uneven, either good or evil is bound to dominate. The first 'horoscope' refers to a lean man with a six to three ratio of light and darkness, and Taurus as his animal. The second is fat, with uneven teeth, thick fingers and thick, hairy thighs. The proportion of light to darkness is one to eight. The third 'horoscope' describes a black-eyed, bearded man, with a gentle voice and fine, straight teeth, medium height, having thin, elongated fingers and smooth thighs. His spirit consists of eight parts of light and one of darkness.

For astrology among Jews in general, see above, pp. 369–72, and in Hellenistic Judaism and Eupolemus, in particular, see below, p. 529.

(2) *Horoscope of the Elect of God or Birth of Noah*

Two badly damaged columns of a manuscript from Cave 4, dated on palaeographical grounds to around the turn of the eras, were issued in a preliminary publication by J. Starcky in 1964. His title, 'Un texte messianique araméen', reveals that in Starcky's opinion the subject of the work, designated as בחיר אלהא (the Elect of God) is a messianic figure. He is said to have red hair and various birthmarks, some of these on his thighs. He is full of wisdom and learned in the 'three books'.[2]

Although the messianic interpretation is possible, an alternative explanation, advanced by J. A. Fitzmyer,[3] is gaining momentum, according to which the text relates the marvellous birth of Noah (cf. above, pp. 319, 332). More recently J. T. Milik and F. García Martínez have declared themselves in favour of this theory.[4]

Needless to say, if the work is a life of Noah, it is likely to date to an earlier period, possibly to the second century B.C., and may be pre-sectarian (cf. above, p. 333). If, by contrast, it continues to be recognized as a messianic horoscope, the composition may be assigned to the late first century B.C. or the beginning of the first century A.D., which is the date suggested for the manuscript itself.

1. Otto Neugebauer (*Ethiopic Astronomy and Computus* (1979), p. 21) queries whether these documents are properly described as horoscopes, and suggests that they may be fragments of astrological treatises.
2. The 'three books' are variously interpreted as referring either to Torah-Prophets-Writings, or to three sectarian works.
3. *Essays on the Semitic Background of the New Testament* (1971), pp. 158–60.
4. Milik, *The Books of Enoch* (1976), p. 56; García Martínez, '4Q Mes Ar y el libro de Noé', *Escritos de Biblia y Oriente* (1981), pp. 195–232.

Editions (Horoscopes)

Allegro, J. M., DJD V, pp. 88–91.

Translations

English
Allegro, *op. cit.*
Vermes, DSSE², pp. 268–70.
Italian
Moraldi, L., MQ, pp. 677–84.

Bibliography

Allegro, J. M., 'An Astrological Cryptic Document from Qumran', JSS 9 (1964), pp. 291–4.
Carmignac, J., 'Les horoscopes de Qumrân', RQ 5 (1965), pp. 199–206.
Dupont-Sommer, A., 'Deux documents horoscopiques esséniens découverts près de la Mer Morte', CRAI (1965), pp. 239–53.
Gordis, R., 'A Document in Code from Qumran', JSS 11 (1966), pp. 37–9.
Delcor, M., 'Recherches sur un horoscope en langue hébraïque provenant de Qumrân', RQ 5 (1966), pp. 521–42.
Lehmann, M. R., 'New Light on Astrology in Qumran and the Talmud', RQ 8 (1975), pp. 599–602.
Vermes, DSS, pp. 84–5.

Editions (Elect of God)

Starcky, J., 'Un texte messianique araméen de la grotte 4 de Qumrân', *Mémorial du cinquantenaire de l'École des langues orientales anciennes de l'Institut Catholique de Paris* (1964), pp. 51–66.
Fitzmyer, J. A., *Essays on the Semitic Background of the New Testament* (1971), pp. 127–60.

Translations

English
Fitzmyer, *op. cit.*
Vermes, DSSE², p. 270.

Bibliography

García Martínez, F., '4Q Mes Ar y el libro de Noé', *Escritos de Biblia y Oriente* [Bibliotheca Salmanticensis 38] (1981), pp. 195–232.

2. Calendars

Several calendric fragments from Cave 4 have been mentioned by J. T. Milik in various publications, but they are still awaiting edition.

A first group, designated *4QMishmaroth*, offers a concordance between the lunar and the solar month, combined with the name of the priestly class officiating in the Temple. Thus the document reads: 'On the sixth day (= Friday) in (the service period of) Ezekiel, the 29th (day of the lunar month) = on the 22nd of the eleventh month (Shebat of the luni-solar calendar)': ב(6) ביחזקאל ל(29) ב(22) לעשתי עשר. A three-year cycle permits the two calendars to synchronize: 3 times 364 = 3 times 354 plus thirty.

The same manuscript lists also the festivals in the consecutive years of the cycle. E.g. 'The first year—its feasts: On the third day (Tuesday) in (the service of) Me'ozyah: Passover ... On the first day (Sunday) in (the service of) Yeshua': Feast of Weeks', etc.

Another similar work, contained in two very damaged manuscripts, sets out the order of the priestly groups according to the sabbaths of the year, but occasionally alludes also to historical events such as 'Salome killed ...': הרן]ג שלמציון. Other historical personalities named are Hyrcanus (הרקנוס) and Aemilius (אמליוס), no doubt Aemilius Scaurus, governor of Syria (cf. vol. I, pp. 244–5). The latter document has some link with *Megillath Ta'anith* (cf. vol. I, pp. 114–15).

A further minute calendar fragment comes from Cave 6 (6Q17).

Editions and Bibliography

Milik, J. T., 'Le travail d'édition des manuscrits du Désert de Juda', *Volume du Congrès, Strasbourg 1956* (1957), pp. 24–6.
Idem, Ten Years of Discovery, pp. 107–9.
Baillet, M., DJD VII, pp. 132–3.

3. The Copper Scroll (3Q15)

A scroll of heavily oxidized copper was discovered in Cave 3 in 1952. As it could not be unrolled, it was divided into longitudinal strips at the Manchester College of Science and Technology in 1956 and subsequently edited by J. T. Milik in DJD III in 1962. The text represents twelve columns and the script is said to be Herodian.

In all, the document lists sixty-four underground hiding places, in Jerusalem and in various regions of Palestine, where gold, silver, aromatics and scrolls, including another copy of the inventory with complete details (col. 12, lines 11–13), have been deposited. Each cache is semi-cryptically described. E.g. 'At Horebbeh, in the Vale of Achor, under the steps going eastwards, forty cubits' (col. 1, lines 1–3). The treasure described represents colossal wealth. According to J. M. Allegro, it totals approximately sixty-five tons of silver and twenty-six tons of gold.[1]

Scholarly opinion is neatly divided between those who accept the reality of the hidden treasure, which is thought to have belonged either to the Essenes (A. Dupont-Sommer), or to the Temple of Jerusalem (K. G. Kuhn, J. M. Allegro), or to have represented a sum of money collected after the destruction of the sanctuary to finance its rebuilding (B. Z. Lurie, M. R. Lehmann), or to have been the hidden treasure of Bar Kokhba (E.-M. Laperrousaz). If the reality of the deposit is

---

1. *The Treasure of the Copper Scroll* (1960), p. 59.

assumed—and the prosaic style of the description engraved on durable material may be cited in its favour—the Copper Scroll will be classified as a historical document and not as a literary work, and consequently requires no discussion here.

By contrast, if it is decided that the contents of the Copper Scroll are closer to fiction than to reality—and this is Milik's opinion—then it may be recognized as the prototype of a literary genre represented by the medieval Jewish Tractate concerning the Temple Vessels or מסכת כלים , describing the concealment of the treasures of the Sanctuary at the time of its destruction by Nebuchadnezzar.[2]

In the present state of research, the problem of the Copper Scroll is still insoluble. The folkloristic genre to which it should be ascribed according to the second hypothesis scarcely concurs with the choice of copper rather than leather or papyrus. Nor does it fit the dry realism of the description instead of the colourful style suitable to a legendary account.

Editions

Milik, J. T., DJD III, pp. 199–302.
Allegro, J. M., *The Treasure of the Copper Scroll* (1960).

Translations

English
Allegro, *op. cit.*

French
Milik, *op. cit.*

Italian
Moraldi, L., MQ, pp. 707–22.

Bibliography

Kuhn, K.-G., 'Les rouleaux de cuivre de Qumrân', RB 61 (1954), pp. 193–205.
Dupont-Sommer, A., 'Les rouleaux de cuivre trouvés à Qumrân', RHR 151 (1957), pp. 22–35.
Milik, J. T., 'Le rouleau de cuivre', RB 66 (1959), pp. 321–57, 567–75.
Idem, and Jeremias, J., 'Remarques sur le rouleau de cuivre de Qumrân', RB 67 (1960), pp. 220–23.
Ullendorff, E., 'The Greek Letters of the Copper Scroll', VT 11 (1961), pp. 227–8.
Laperrousaz, E.-M., 'Remarques sur l'origine des rouleaux de cuivre découverts dans la grotte 3 de Qumrân', RHR 159 (1961), pp. 157–72.
Lurie, B. Z., *The Copper Scroll from the Wilderness of Jerusalem* (1963) [Hebrew].
Lehmann, M. R., 'Identification of the Copper Scroll based on its Technical Terms', RQ 5 (1964), pp. 97–105.

---

2. A. Jellinek, *Bet ha-Midrasch* II (1853), pp. xxvi-vii, 88–91. Milik further cites a popular Arab literary work, *The Book of the Buried Pearls*, published by Ahmed Bey Kamal in Cairo in 1907.

Jeremias, J., 'Die Kupferrolle von Qumran und Bethesda', in *Abba* (1966), pp. 361–4.

Vermes, G., DSSE[2], pp. 271–3.

Idem, DSS, pp. 83–4.

Laperrousaz, E.-M., *Qumrân. L'établissement essénien des bords de la Mer Morte. Histoire et archéologie du site* (1976), pp. 131–47.

Pixner, B., 'Unravelling the Copper Scroll Code: A Study on the Topography of 3Q15', RQ 11 (1983), pp. 323–65.

§ 33 A. JEWISH LITERATURE COMPOSED IN GREEK

INTRODUCTORY REMARKS

The Jewish literature of this period written in Greek is as varied as the Semitic Jewish literature. Biblical Judaism and an oral midrashic tradition, on the one hand, Greek philosophers, poets, and historians, on the other, combined to produce a literature of the most mixed variety, diverse not only in its literary forms but also with regard to the points of view which the authors represented and the purposes which they pursued.

Generally, this literature shared the intellectual and literary character of the time, namely *the Hellenistic era*, during which Greek literature spread beyond Greece itself and became a world literature.[1] The nations around the Mediterranean Sea did not merely adopt Greek culture but also contributed to the literary production of the period. In every country, men with Greek education appeared as authors who took part in all kinds of literary enterprise and through their collaboration imprinted a cosmopolitan stamp on Greek literature, cosmopolitan both from the point of view of origin and of effect. The intellectual achievements of the East now entered increasingly into Greek literature. Religion and philosophy thus received new stimuli, and poets and historians new material. By the same token, the effect was also cosmopolitan in that whoever took up his pen might have an audience not only within the small Greek nation but among the educated of the whole world.

Hellenistic Jews also took part in this literary productivity. Indeed, the above remarks apply to them to a special degree, primarily because they introduced an entirely new element into Greek literature. The religious knowledge of Israel, which until then had belonged to only a small circle, now began to exercise an influence within Greek literature. The religious faith of Israel, its history, and its sacred antiquity were represented in the forms and with the media offered by Greek literary

---

1. See F. Susemihl, *Geschichte der griechischen Litteratur in der Alexandrinerzeit* I-II (1891–2); Knaack, 'Alexandrinische Litteratur', RE I.1 (1893), cols. 1399–1407; *idem*, RE suppl. I (1903), cols. 53–4; Beloch, *Griechische Geschichte* III.1 (1904), pp. 408–556; W. v. Christ, O. Stählin and W. Schmidt, *Geschichte der griechischen Litteratur etc.*[6] II.1 (1920); H. N. Fowler, *A History of Ancient Greek Literature* ([2]1923); J. G. Droysen and E. Bayer, *Geschichte des Hellenismus* (1952–3); W. W. Tarn and G. T. Griffith, *Hellenistic Civilization* ([3]1952); H. J. Rose, *A Handbook of Greek Literature from Homer to the Age of Lucian* ([4]1957), pp. 313–94; F. C. Grant, 'Hellenismus', RGG III ([3]1959), cols. 209–12; V. A. Tcherikover, *Hellenistic Civilization and the Jews* (1961), pp. 344–77; A. Lesky, *A History of Greek Literature* (1965), pp. 642–806.

culture, and thereby made accessible to the whole world. This effect was also certainly intended by a part of Jewish-Hellenistic literature. Some Jewish authors no longer wrote simply for their own people and co-religionists, but wished to acquaint the world with Israel's distinguished history and its superior religious knowledge. Other authors, however, wrote to provide those of their fellow Jews who had been attracted by their non-Jewish environment with a modern, i.e. hellenized, dress for accepted Jewish religious ideas.

A question of continuing and fruitful debate has been whether, for the Jews as for other Oriental peoples, the combination of their own national culture with that of the Greeks was merely an external one. Some have argued that Judaism and Hellenism really entered into a process of inner fusion with one another.[2] According to this view, Judaism, which appeared so unapproachably exclusive in its strict, proto-Pharisaic form launched by Ezra, proved itself open to change and accommodation on the soil of Hellenism; it allowed the powerful Greek spirit to exercise a far-reaching influence upon it. That which was the common property of the educated world, the great poets, philosophers, and historians of the Greeks, the Hellenistic Jews also wished to enjoy. They too drew from the fresh source of the Greek classical authors what appeared to the ancient world to be the highest good, i.e., human culture. Unnoticed, however, Judaism changed under this influence. It cast aside its more particularistic character and developed its universalizing tendencies. It discovered true and godly thought also in the literature of the Gentile world and appropriated it. It embraced all men as brothers, and wished to lead to the knowledge of the truth those who were still in darkness.

Others, however, have preferred to argue that no such fusion and no drastic change within Judaism took place. While the Jews moved comfortably within Greek culture, like other Oriental peoples, it became apparent at the same time that Judaism was something

2. On Hellenistic Judaism in general, cf. P. Wendland, 'Alexandrian Philosophy', JE I (1901), cols. 368–71; *idem, Die hellenist.-röm. Kultur in ihren Beziehungen zu Judentum und Christentum* (*Handbuch zum N.T.*, ed. H. Lietzmann and G. Bornkamm, I.2, 3rd ed., 1912; 4th ed., with additional bibliography by H. Dörrie, 1972); J. Juster, *Les Juifs dans l'Empire romain etc.* (1914), 2 vols.; G. H. Box, *Judaism in the Greek Period* (1932); O. Stählin, 'Die Hellenistisch-Jüdische Litteratur' in W. v. Christ, O. Stählin and W. Schmidt, *op. cit.*[6] II.1 (1920), pp. 535–656; E. R. Goodenough, *By Light, Light!* (1935); P. Dalbert, *Die Theol. der jüd. hellenist. Missionslit.* (*Theologische Forschung* 4, 1954); E. R. Goodenough, *Jewish Symbols in the Greco-Roman Period*, 13 vols. (1953–68); S. Cohen, 'Jüdische Philosophie', RGG III (³1959), cols. 1001–6; K. Galling, 'Judentum (Vom Exil bis Hadrian)', RGG³ III (1959), 978–86; V. A. Tcherikover, *Hellenistic Civilization and the Jews* (1961); O. Eissfeldt, *The O.T., An Introduction etc.* (ET 1965), pp. 571 ff.; S. Sandmel, *Judaism and Christian Beginnings* (1978), pp. 255–301. For further bibliography, see G. Delling, *Bibliographie zur jüdisch-hellenistischen und intertest. Literatur, 1900–1970* (²1975), pp. 20–3.

different from pagan religions. Its inner power of resistance was incomparably greater. While the other Oriental religions disappeared in the general religious fusion of the time, Judaism remained essentially unaltered. It adhered strictly to the unity of God and his worship without images, as well as to faith in the Law and to the belief that God's ways with man lead to a blessed end. It proved its superior religious strength against the pressures of Hellenism in this firm adherence to its central concepts.[3]

It is nonetheless reasonable to assume that it was at least possible that the very fact that such ideas were expressed in Greek will have affected their content, which is the justification for treating here the Jewish writings in Greek separately from those in Semitic languages. There are, however, considerable problems in attempting valid generalizations about Hellenistic Judaism as a whole. Most of the authors whose work has survived are represented only by small fragments of their writings. Those fragments were selected in the main by the early Christian writers in whose works they are preserved. It is impossible to tell whether the surviving authors are representative of a much larger Jewish literature or whether the number of Greek works composed by Jews in this period was meagre compared to those in Semitic languages.[4] In either case, if much midrash was orally transmitted, the extant writings may be of only partial relevance in reconstructing religious attitudes.

It can be said, however, that consciousness of religious superiority has stamped its character on the surviving Jewish literature. The authors largely pursued the practical goal not only of strengthening fellow-believers and familiarizing them with its great past but also of convincing non-Jewish readers of the foolishness of paganism and of persuading them of the greatness of the history of Israel and of the groundlessness of all attacks on its people. It is thus largely apologetic in the most comprehensive sense of the word. In this predominantly practical purpose, all the Jewish literature is alike, but while the works in Semitic languages mainly pursued the goal of strengthening and enlivening fidelity to the Law, the chief preoccupations of the Hellenistic Jewish authors whose works survive lay in the praise and

---

3. The argument against extensive changes in Jewish religious beliefs can be found most clearly stated in H. A. Wolfson, *Philo* (1947). Cf. also, Collins, BAAJ, p. 9.

4. In favour of scepticism about claims regarding the existence of a much larger corpus of Hellenistic Jewish literature, see G. Vermes and M. Goodman, 'La Littérature juive intertestamentaire à la Lumière d'un Siècle de Recherches et de Découvertes', in R. Kuntzmann and J. Schlosser, eds., *Études sur judaïsme hellénistique* (1984), pp. 30–9. The main reason for scepticism is the fact that such Jewish writings in Greek were likely to have been of great use to the apologists in the early Church and would have been easily accessible to early Jewish writers. Failure to use more than a handful suggests that only a few ever existed.

aggrandisement of Jewish religion and the history of the Jewish people. The size and wide spread of the Jewish diaspora in the eastern Mediterranean (see above, pp. 1–85) make it impossible to assert that any one place was the centre of Greek-speaking Judaism and the origin of this literature. Some of the surviving authors certainly wrote in Alexandria which, as the capital of the Ptolemaic kingdom, had been raised by the efforts of the Ptolemies into the principal centre of scholarship during the Hellenistic era. Since Alexandria also housed the largest Jewish community outside Palestine, and since that community spoke Greek, it was inevitable that some of the Jewish writings in that language should derive from there. It is however unlikely and certainly unprovable that all, or even most, of such writings came from Egypt. The Jewish texts are not the product of great learning and as such could have been produced in any Greek city; it is certainly wrong to assume that an Alexandrian origin should be stipulated unless indications to the contrary are found. It is probable that some, though perhaps not many, of these works were produced in Palestine.[5]

The diversity of literary forms and of theological standpoints of the writings to be discussed here is mainly due to the fact that they sometimes follow biblical examples and sometimes Greek. But between these two extremes there is a large variety of phenomena difficult to classify. Some writings cannot be clearly designated as Greek rather than Semitic compositions, and these works of dubious origin will be discussed in 33 B. Other works are now so thoroughly incorporated into later Christian texts that the original Jewish writing is beyond full recall. These texts will be considered in an appendix. The writings which are certainly Greek compositions by Jews cannot be usefully separated into either Greek or biblical genres, and are best discussed in the following general categories.

---

5. On Hellenistic Judaism in Palestine, cf. J. Freudenthal, *Alexander Polyhistor* (1875), 127–9; W. Bousset and H. Gressmann, *Die Religion des Judentums* ([3]1926); E. R. Bevan, *Jerusalem under the High Priests* (1904); S. Lieberman, *Hellenism in Jewish Palestine* (*Texts and Studies of the Jew. Theol. Sem. of America*, 18, 1950); S. Lieberman, *Greek in Jewish Palestine* (1942); F. M. Abel, *Hist. de la Palestine depuis la conquête d'Alexandre jusqu'à l'invasion arabe*, 2 vols. (1952); W. R. Farmer, *Maccabees, Zealots and Josephus. An Inquiry into Jewish Nationalism in the Greco-Roman Period* (1956); V. A. Tcherikover, *Hellenistic Civilization and the Jews* (1961), pp. 39–265; M. Hengel, *Judaism and Hellenism* (ET 1974); B. Z. Wacholder, *Eupolemus: A Study of Judaeo-Greek Literature* (1974), pp. 259–306 (ESJL); and further bibliography in G. Delling, *Bibliographie*, pp. 29–32.

§33A. Jewish Literature Composed in Greek

I. TRANSLATIONS OF THE CANONICAL BIBLE

1. The Septuagint

The basis of all Jewish-Hellenistic culture is the old, anonymous Greek Bible translation known as the Septuagint or LXX (οἱ ἑβδομήκοντα, septuaginta interpretes) and preserved for us mainly by Christian tradition. Without it the religion of Greek-speaking Jews was as unthinkable as the Church of England without the Authorised Version.[6] The uniform name should not lead to the idea that this is the work of a single hand. What was brought together under this name at a later time is not only the work of different translators, it also came about at different times. The oldest part is the translation of the Pentateuch. The so-called Letter of Aristeas purports to give detailed information of its origin. King Ptolemy II Philadelphus (283–246 B.C.) was persuaded by his librarian Demetrius of Phalerum to have the Jewish Law transcribed and translated into Greek for his library. At his request, the Jewish high priest Eleazar sent him seventy-two qualified men, six from each tribe, who finished the whole work in seventy-two days (cf. further under section VII). The detailed historicity of this account cannot be maintained and many of the embellishments are fanciful.[7] It is at first sight at least possible, however, that a genuine historical tradition was known to the author of the letter, according to which the translation of the Jewish Law into Greek was made at the command of Ptolemy, at the suggestion of Demetrius of Phalerum.[8] It would be conceivable and in keeping with the learned, literary zeal of the Ptolemies, and especially of Ptolemy Philadelphus, that he should have wanted to include in his library the Jewish Law.[9] Also the probability of Ps.-Aristeas having invented the whole story himself is lessened by the fact that the Jewish philosopher Aristobulus, at the time of Ptolemy VI Philometor, related the main elements of Ps.-Aristeas' narrative about Philadelphus and Demetrius without betraying any knowledge of the other elements of the Ps.-Aristeas' work. Although arguments have been put forward for the direct reliance of Aristobulus on Ps.-Aristeas

---

6. The name 'Septuagint' first referred to the translation of the Pentateuch only, but was later applied to that of the other (O.T.) books as well.

7. The objections to the purported authorship and date are given by M. Hadas, Aristeas to Philocrates (1951), pp. 5–9.

8. So e.g. L. Valckenaer, Diatribe de Aristobulo Judaeo (1806), pp. 49–58. Cf. G. Zuntz, 'Aristeas Studies II: Aristeas on the Translation of the Torah', JSS 4 (1959), p. 125.

9. On the Alexandrian libraries, see Dziatzko, s.v. 'Bibliotheken', RE III.1 (1899), cols. 409–14; Leclercq, 'Alexandrie', Dictionnaire d'archéologie chrétienne I.1 (1907), cols. 1098–1182; E. A. Parsons, The Alexandrian Library, Glory of the Hellenic World (1952); A. Pelletier, Lettre d'Aristée à Philocrate (1962), pp. 64 f., 66–71; P. M. Fraser, Ptolemaic Alexandria (1972), ch. 6.

and (less plausibly) vice-versa, it is most likely that both writers recorded independently a common tradition.[10] The role of Demetrius of Phalerum cannot, however, be historical since he was never in charge of the library, was early at variance with Ptolemy Philadelphus and was banished by him immediately after the death of Ptolemy I.[11] The role of the king is not necessarily also fictional, but it is in fact improbable that he was involved to any greater degree than in the acquiring of copies for the royal library or in some similar connivance in, or encouragement of, the translation project without being directly involved. The translation most likely came about through the needs of the Alexandrian Jews themselves. The work of Ps.-Aristeas makes it clear that the Pentateuch translation was accepted as an official version by the Alexandrian Jewish populace. The production of such a work by the Jewish community is entirely plausible. Jews for whom continued study of the Law was dear reacted to the decreased knowledge of the holy language in the Mediterranean diaspora and the adoption of Greek as the main spoken language by translating the Law into Greek. It was natural that they should begin with the Pentateuch, and the evidence of Ps.-Aristeas to this effect should be accepted. The translation may well have been made for a private purpose at first, perhaps for synagogue worship and instruction, and it is possible that the story in Ps.-Aristeas was produced in order to lend it the status of an official version.[12] At any rate, however obscure the origin of this translation may be, it is most unlikely that Ps.-Aristeas would have claimed an origin in Alexandria if this was not the case, and Alexandrian involvement is confirmed both by linguistic evidence and

---

10. The passage from Aristobulus is given in Eusebius, *Praep. ev.* xiii 12, 1–2. Aristobulus says here that Plato knew the Jewish Law. To prove it, he asserts that its essential contents had already been translated into Greek before Demetrius of Phalerum. He continues: 'Η δ' ὅλη ἑρμηνεία τῶν διὰ τοῦ νόμου πάντων ἐπὶ τοῦ προσαγορευθέντος Φιλαδέλφου βασιλέως, σοῦ δὲ προγόνου, προσενεγκαμένου μείζονα φιλοτιμίαν, Δημητρίου τοῦ Φαληρέως πραγματευσαμένου τὰ περὶ τούτων. This passage is reproduced freely in Clement of Alexandria, *Strom.* i 22, 148, where, through insertion of a καί in front of πραγματευσαμένου, enthusiasm for the matter and the organization of the translation are ascribed to Demetrius; but the καί is put in square brackets by Mondésert (SC (1951), p. 152) and Stählin and Früchtel (GCS, 52, p. 92).
11. The authority for this is Hermippus of Smyrna, a follower of Callimachus who lived under Ptolemy III and IV. Cf. the passage from Diogenes Laertius, v 78 in Müller, FHG, III, p. 47; on Hermippus, cf. S. Heibges, 'Hermippos (6)', RE VIII (1913), cols. 845–52. On Demetrius, see RE IV.2 (1901), cols. 2817–41, s.v. 'Demetrios' (85).
12. This was certainly the function of the legend at later times, see below.
It has been suggested that Pseudo-Aristeas wished to promote a new translation into Greek in opposition to earlier versions (P. Kahle, CG, p. 217), but it is more likely that Aristeas was concerned to assert the authority of the LXX translation over against inadequate copies of the Hebrew text currently available in Alexandria, cf. D. W. Gooding, 'Aristeas and Septuagint Origins: A Review of Recent Studies', VT 13 (1963), pp. 158–80, and below, note 278.

by the survival to the time of Philo of a festival on Pharos commemorating the completion of the project.[13] Nonetheless, there is no reason to deny the participation of the Jerusalem authorities that is described by Ps.-Aristeas.[14] This translation or something very similar to it was already written before the end of the third century B.C. when it was used by the historian Demetrius (see below, p. 514).

Whether the need for a Greek version of the Torah in the Hellenistic diaspora was filled by a unique effort of translation, i.e. *the* LXX, or by several, possibly local, attempts which were later given a unified and standard form, still remains an open question and a subject for fruitful debate.[15] All agree however that some sort of translation of the Pentateuch was extant in the early third century B.C., and that this still survives in later witnesses to the LXX. This is guaranteed by the use of early third century B.C. Greek word forms in the extant LXX text,[16] by Demetrius' use of *a* Greek version of the Hebrew Bible in the late third century[17] and by the presupposition of the Pentateuch translation in the LXX of Isaiah and Psalms.[18]

What has been said so far is true only of the translation of the Pentateuch, which is the only part of the Hebrew Bible to which the Aristeas legend refers. After the sacred Torah had been made available to Hellenistic Jews, the need was felt to have the other parts of the Scriptures in Greek as well. Translations into Greek of the *Prophets* and finally of the *Hagiographa* followed.[19] These too probably originated mainly in Egypt. Since some of the Writings, such as parts of Daniel, were themselves written in the Maccabaean period, the Greek translations of these later Writings cannot be dated earlier than the

---

13. Philo, *Vita Mosis* ii 7 (41). See Swete and Ottley, IOTG, pp. 9 ff., 16 ff., 289–314; Fraser, PA I, p. 689.

14. M. Gaster, *The Samaritans* (1925), pp. 112 ff., claims that the translation came entirely from Palestine, which is most unlikely, but Wacholder, ESJL, pp. 274–6, points out rightly that the accuracy of the LXX translation suggests greater knowledge of Hebrew than, *ex hypothesi*, was available among Alexandrian Jews at this time.

15. Kahle, CG, argued for the LXX as a Greek targum put together from unofficial versions, with the Pentateuch being given a 'standard' form only *c.* 100 B.C., this standardization being the act to which the Letter of Aristeas refers. But there is no evidence for such a *revision* of the text and most scholars still assume an original official translation, cf. Jellicoe, SMS, pp. 59–63.

16. Wackernagel, J., 'Die griechische Sprache', *Kultur der Gegenwart* I.8 ([3]1924), pp. 371–97, esp. p. 388.

17. Holladay, FHJA, I, pp. 52–3.

18. O. Eissfeldt, *The O.T., An Introduction etc.* (ET 1965), p. 703.

19. F. X. Wutz, *Die Transkriptionen von der Septuaginta bis Hieronymus* (1933); *idem*, *Systematische Wege von der Septuaginta zum hebräischen Urtext* (1937), argued for an intermediate stage of the transcription of the Hebrew characters into Greek letters. This hypothesis is however unproven and unnecessary.

middle of the second century B.C.[20] But it seems in fact that the main body of the Writings together with the Prophets were available in Greek translation at around this time. This is reflected in the remarks of the grandson of Jesus son of Sira, who came to Egypt in 132 B.C. and must have written before the death of Ptolemy VII Euergetes Physcon in *c.* 116 B.C. He excuses the imperfection of his translation by stating that the meaning of Hebrew sentences is not quite the same when they are translated into another language, as is the case not only with his work, but also with the Law, the Prophets, and the remaining writings (Ecclus., prologue: 'For what was originally expressed in Hebrew does not have exactly the same sense when translated into another language. Not only this work, but even the Law itself, the prophecies and the rest of the books differ not a little as originally expressed.'). He manifestly already also knew a translation of the Prophets and of the 'remaining writings'. A Greek translation of Chronicles, either that of the LXX or a 'Theodotionic' version, was possibly available to Eupolemus, who wrote about the middle of the second century B.C. (cf. J. Freudenthal, *Alexander Polyhistor*, p. 119; but note also the doubts expressed by B. Z. Wacholder, ESJL, pp. 252–4); that of Job was probably known to the historian Aristeas the Exegete, whose date is admittedly uncertain, though he must have lived at the latest in the first half of the first century B.C., because he is quoted by Alexander Polyhistor (cf. below, part III, and Freudenthal, *Alexander Polyhistor*, p. 139). Even if, as Kahle has denied, but the consistent patristic tradition of a single LXX version of the Hebrew Bible renders probable, there was one original 'official' Septuagint translation, it is still likely that all these books were translated at different times. The Pentateuch, the minor prophetical books and some of the apocrypha are attested in pre-Christian fragments, but these are even so too late to do more than confirm the *termini ante quem* already suggested.

That all these translations have a Jewish origin needs no further proof. The nature of the translation varies greatly in the different books,

---

20. Dating the translation of individual books is very difficult and depends almost entirely on internal evidence, and on possible interdependence among the books themselves. Cf. Redpath, 'A Contribution towards settling the dates of the translation of the various books of the Septuagint', JThSt 7 (1906), pp. 606–15 (dividing the books of the LXX in groups on the basis of different renderings of the divine names). It may be that the extremely unequal translation of individual books outside the Pentateuch indicates differences in date, cf. Hermann and Baumgärtel, 'Beiträge zur Entstehungsgeschichte der Septuaginta', BWAT new series, v (1923), but this too is disputed, cf. J. Ziegler, 'Die Einheit der Septuaginta zum Zwölfprophetenbuch', *Vorlesungsverzeichnis Braunsberg* (1934); H. St. J. Thackeray, *The Septuagint and Jewish Worship* ([2]1923); E. Tov, 'The impact of the LXX translation of the Pentateuch on the translation of the other books', in P. Casetti, O. Keel and A. Schenker, eds., *Mélanges Dominique Barthélemy* (1981), pp. 578–92.

sometimes rather free, sometimes awkwardly literal, predominantly the latter. A more detailed investigation has so far been undertaken only for some of the books.[21] Judgement about the competence of translations has too often been vitiated by preconceptions about the aims of the translators. Whether the intention was to reproduce the mood or simply the sense of the original was a difficult choice for the LXX, as for all, translators. If, as some have argued, the translations were intended for synagogal liturgy in the diaspora,[22] the qualities desired will have been much more rhetorical than a pedestrian word-for-word version could provide. The task of examining translation technique is especially difficult because frequently the translators' Hebrew text must be reconstructed first. Although fragments from Qumran Cave 4 have definitely proved the existence of a LXX-type Hebrew text, it nonetheless remains clear that some of the peculiarities of the Greek Bible need to be seen against the background of the historical, social, and religious conditions in which and for which they came about. With some reservation the words of Bertram still hold true: 'The Septuagint belongs more to the history of Old Testament exegesis than to that of the Old Testament text';[23] and the LXX deserves study as a Greek composition in its own right and not just as a means for correcting the Hebrew text. The language of all these writings is the common Greek as it was spoken in Egypt, only somewhat influenced by Hebrew.[24]

21. For general studies of translation techniques, see M. L. Margolis, 'Complete Induction for the Identification of the Vocabulary in the Greek Versions of the Old Testament with its Semitic Equivalents. Its Necessity and the Means of Obtaining it', JAOS 30 (1910), pp. 301–12; *idem*, 'The Mode of Expressing the Hebrew'*a'id* in the Greek Hexateuch', AJSL 29(1912/13), pp. 237–60; E. J. Bickermann, 'The Septuagint as a Translation', PAAJR 28 (1959), pp. 1–39 = *Studies in Jewish and Christian History* I (1976), pp. 167–200. For references to studies on individual books, see Jellicoe, SMS, pp. 269–313. The most relevant of these for the study of translation method are: A. Rahlfs, *Studie über den griechischen Text des Buches Ruth* (1922); M. L. Margolis, *The Book of Joshua in Greek*, parts I-IV (1931–8), part V and the introduction not published; H. M. Orlinsky, 'The Treatment of Anthropomorphisms and Anthropopathisms in the LXX of Isaiah', HUCA 29 (1956), p. 200; *idem*, 'Studies in the Septuagint of the Book of Job', HUCA 29 (1958), pp. 229–71; 30 (1959), pp. 153–67; 32 (1961), pp. 239–68; M. Dahood, *The Psalms* I (1966), pp. xxiv-xxx.

22. H. St. J. Thackeray, *The Septuagint and Jewish Worship* ([2]1923).

23. G. Bertram, 'Das Problem der Umschrift und die religionsgeschichtliche Erforschung der Septuaginta', BZAW 66 (1936), p. 109.

24. A. Deissmann emphasized the Koine Greek basis, cf. Deissmann, 'Hellenistisches Griechisch', Herzog and Hauck, *Realencyclopädie etc.*[3] VII, cols. 627–39, and 'Die Hellenisierung des semitischen Monotheismus', Neue Jahrbücher für das klassische Altertum 6 (1903), pp. 161–77. From studies of the papyri in secular Koine Greek, it has become clear that the Hebraisms and Aramaisms in the Greek of the LXX are considerably fewer than was once assumed. The Greek of each book or section must be dealt with separately, however, because the LXX is not a unified translation: the Greek of 2 Kings, for example, reflects a marked Semitic stamp in its syntax, whereas that of Job is relatively free from any Hebrew influence. Cf. E. Würthwein, *The Text of the O.T. etc.*

Occasionally, however, the Hebraisms are so predominant, for example in the syntax, that an educated Greek would hardly have understood them, and the Hebrew also had a considerable influence on the development of the meaning of some words. Not a few Greek words which correspond to *one* meaning of a Hebrew word were equated to *the whole range* of its meanings, so that they were given meanings which they do not have in Greek at all (one need only think of δόξα, εἰρήνη, δικαιοσύνη and others).[25] To what extent the colloquialisms of the Hellenistic Jews paved the way for the translators cannot be determined. Presumably the influence was reciprocal. Many of the translators' renderings were found by them in colloquial language. But equally strong at least must have been the influence which the translation, having passed into common use, exercised on the development of Jewish Greek, as is manifest in the idiom of the N.T.[26]

The translations in question were not only united into a whole, but were also generally received by the Jews of the diaspora as their Bible. If the patristic extracts in which his writings have survived are reliable, it seems that one of the oldest Hellenists, Demetrius, already based his works on biblical history entirely on the LXX; Philo and Josephus assumed it predominantly.[27] It is remarkable that, despite the variant readings in circulation in his time, Philo accepted the LXX of the Pentateuch as a sacred text to such an extent that he argued from

---

([2]1980), p. 48. The Hebraic character of LXX Greek is re-emphasized in opposition to Deissmann by H. S. Gehman, 'The Hebraic Character of Septuagint Greek', VT 1 (1951), pp. 81–90; for a partial rehabilitation of Deissmann's views, see M. Silva, 'Bilingualism and the character of Palestinian Greek', Bibl. 61 (1980), pp. 198–219, especially pp. 209–13 on Alexandria. For grammars, cf. H. St. J. Thackeray, *A Grammar of the O.T. in Greek According to the LXX* I (1909); F.-M. Abel, *Grammaire du grec biblique, suivie d'une choix de papyrus* (1927); E. Mayser, *Grammatik der griech. Papyri aus der Ptolemäerzeit, mit Einschluss der gleichzeitigen Ostraka und der in Ägypten verfassten Inschriften* I (1936); II (1926–34).

25. G. Bertram, 'Zur Septuaginta-Forschung', ThR 3 (1931), 283–96; 5 (1933), 173–86; 10 (1938), 69–80, 133–59; A. Descamps, 'La Justice de Dieu dans la Bible grecque', *Stud. Hell.* V (1948), pp. 69–92; D. Hill, *Greek Words and Hebrew Meanings* (SNTS Monograph 5) (1967); E. Repo, *Der Begriff 'Rhema' im biblisch-griechischen*, part I: *'Rhema' in der Septuaginta* (1951); N. M. Watson, 'Some Observations on the use of δίκαιος in the Septuagint', JBL 79 (1960), pp. 255–66; J. Barr, *Semantics of Biblical Language* (1961); M. Silva, *Biblical words and their meaning: an introduction to lexical semantics* (1983). Cf. the many useful examples given in TDNT.

26. Cf. M. Johannessohn, 'Das biblische καὶ ἐγένετο und seine Geschichte', Zeitschrift für vergleichende Sprachforschung 53 (1925), pp. 161–212; A. D. Nock, 'The Vocabulary of the New Testament', JBL 52 (1953), p. 138; M. Johannessohn, 'Das biblische καὶ ἰδού in der Erzählung samt seiner hebräischen Vorlage', Zeitschrift für vergleichende Sprachforschung 66 (1939), pp. 145–95; 67 (1942), pp. 30–84.

27. P. Katz, *Philo's Bible: The Aberrant Text of Bible Quotations in some Philonic Writings and its Place in the Textual History of the Greek Bible* (1950), argues that some LXX quotations in Philo were imported by later (Christian) copyists. The question of Philo's knowledge of Hebrew should be left open, cf. E. von Dobschütz, 'Philo', *Dict. Ap. Chr.* II (1918), 229a.

occasional details in it, and that this translation was not only generally in private use but also served as Holy Scripture in the synagogue service (cf. above, pp. 142 ff.). On the island of Pharos in Alexandria, where, according to tradition, the translation was produced, an annual celebration of thanksgiving like that of the Feast of Booths took place in remembrance of 'the ancient gift of God, so old yet ever new'.[28] Even in Palestine it achieved considerable prestige, being freely used by Josephus. The popularity of the LXX in Jewish circles means that it should not be studied only as a witness to the underlying Hebrew Bible but, as has been demonstrated in a number of recent studies, as a prime source of Hellenistic Jewish religious, social and exegetical ideas.[29] From Jewish hands it passed to Christianity, where it was directly accepted as the authentic text of Scripture. However, the triumph of the proto-Masoretic codification of the Hebrew Bible in Palestine and perhaps, indirectly, the fact that the Christians and other Jewish non-conformists had used the LXX as a polemical weapon in disputes, contributed to its gradual discrediting among Jews and, after first century A.D. Jewish attempts at revising it according to a Masoretic type Hebrew text,[30] to Aquila's new translation which at the time of Origen was held in higher esteem by the Jews than the LXX.

In the history of the LXX text the learned efforts of Origen were epoch-making though, through no fault of his, they led ultimately to confusion in the text. Because of the uncertainty of the text of the LXX and its marked differences from the Hebrew text available to him (i.e.,

28. Philo, *Vita Mosis* ii 41–4.

29. See the literature cited in S. P. Brock, C. T. Fritsch and S. Jellicoe, *A Classified Bibliography of the Septuagint* (1973), sections 12 (Particular Concepts), 13 (Anthropomorphism/-pathism), 14 (Hellenistic Exegesis), 39 (Individual Books). Particularly fruitful have been studies of the conception of God in the LXX (e.g. T. Wittstruck, 'The so-called anti-anthropomorphisms in the Greek text of Deuteronomy', CBQ 38 (1976), pp. 29–34; B. M. Zlotowitz, *The Septuagint translation of the Hebrew terms in relation to God in the book of Jeremiah* (1981)) and analysis of exegetical methods in the light of exegesis at Qumran, in Josephus, in the rabbinic writings, and in the Aramaic targumim. See for example G. Vermes, STJ, pp. 178–92 and passim; E. Tov, 'Midrash-type exegesis in the LXX of Joshua', RB 85 (1978), pp. 50–61.

30. D. Barthélemy, 'Redécouverte d'un chaînon manquant de l'histoire de la Septante', RB 60 (1953), pp. 18–29, argues from the evidence of the Leather Scroll of the Twelve Prophets found in the Judaean Desert that the LXX was subjected to revision by Jews in the first century A.D. Kahle, 'Die in August 1952 entdeckte Lederrolle mit dem griechischen Text der Kleinen Propheten', *Op. Min.* (1956), pp. 113–28, took the same evidence to indicate that the LXX had not yet reached a final form, but this view is not widely accepted. For pre-Origen assimilation of the LXX to the Hebrew text, cf. H. A. Sanders and C. Schmidt, *The Minor Prophets in the Freer Collection and the Berlin Fragment of Genesis* (1927), pp. 25 ff., 265; J. Ziegler, *Duodecim Prophetae* (1943), pp. 33 f.; *idem*, 'Die Bedeutung des Chester Beatty-Scheide Papyrus 967 für die Textüberlieferung der Ezechiel-LXX', ZAW 61 (1945/8), pp. 76–94. See especially D. Barthélemy, *Les devanciers d'Aquila* (1963); below, pp. 501–2.

the proto-Masoretic text), Origen prepared a large edition of the Bible with six parallel columns which would make clear those differences.

The contents of the first four of these columns are generally accepted to have been, in order, (1) a Hebrew text in Hebrew script, (2) a Hebrew text in Greek script, (3) the translation of Aquila, (4) the translation of Symmachus. Column (5) was *probably* Origen's own critical reconstruction of the 'standard' LXX text with reference to the Hebrew and the use of diacritical marks to show divergences from the Hebrew text. However, it has been noted correctly by Kahle that there is no evidence for diacritical signs being used actually *in* the Hexapla, so that the columns may have been intended as the *foundation* of Origen's criticism of the LXX text rather than its culmination (JBL 79 (1960), pp. 111–18). If Kahle is correct, the Origenian recension will have been a work quite separate from the Hexapla, and the fifth column of the Hexapla was presumably a transcription of a text in current circulation, probably the Alexandrian Jewish revision of the LXX text with the use of 'Theodotionic' readings (cf. Jellicoe, SMS, pp. 89, 123, for this text as the κοινή of Palestine, and below, p. 502). Column (6) contained mainly, but not exclusively, the translation of Theodotion. For the Psalter this column contained the translation named 'Quinta' (cf. Mercati, *Studi e Testi* 5 (1901), pp. 28–56; H.-J. Venetz, *Die Quinta des Psalteriums. Ein Beitrag zur Septuaginta- und Hexaplaforschung* (1974)), while for the minor prophets this column contained a recension 'tardive, éclectique et pseudépigraphe' according to Barthélemy on the basis of the Qumran Dodekapropheton scroll (*Les Devanciers d'Aquila* (1963), p. 269). Cf. the testimony of Jerome, *Comment. in Tit.*, 3, 9; Epiph. *De mens. et pond.*, 19, and the remaining witnesses given in Field, *Origenis Hexaplorum quae supersunt, prolegom* p. L. The attention of most ancient Christian users was naturally focused on the four last columns of the Hexapla because they were in Greek, to such an extent that Eusebius refers to them, almost certainly incorrectly, as a separate work of Origen (*Hist. Ecc.* vi 16, 4; cf. H. M. Orlinsky, 'Origen's Tetrapla—a Scholarly Fiction?', *Proceedings of the First World Congress of Jewish Studies, 1947* I (1952), pp. 173–82). One result of this interest in the four Greek versions was that three other, anonymous, translations added to the Hexapla at a later date were referred to by Eusebius as the 'Fifth', 'Sixth', and 'Seventh' versions, i.e., Quinta, Sexta and Septima (*Hist. Ecc.* vi 16, 1–3, as emended by Kahle, CG, p. 241, in the light of G. Mercati, 'D'alcuni frammenti esaplari sulla v^a e vi^a edizione greca della Bibbia', Studi e Testi 5 (1901), pp. 28–60). Of these, so little is known about Septima that it probably either never existed or is now lost to knowledge (Field, *op. cit.* I, p. xlvi, but, *contra*, J. Ziegler, *Duodecim Prophetae* (1943), pp. 107 ff.). In contrast the readings of Quinta and Sexta evidently differed considerably from the other translations and may have survived quite extensively (so, especially, Mercati, *Psalterii Hexapli Reliquiae* I (1958), pp. xix-xxxv, on Quinta in the sixth column of the Hexapla; cf. the Hexapla apparatus of the Göttingen LXX). Cf. generally about the whole work, the *Prolegomena* in F. Field, *Origenis Hexaplorum quae supersunt*, 2 vols. (1875, repr. 1964); also C. Taylor, 'Hexapla', DCB III, cols. 14–23; M. L. Margolis, 'Hexapla and Hexaplaric', AJSL 32 (1915–16), pp. 126–40; Swete and Ottley, IOTG, pp. 59–78; Jellicoe, SMS, pp. 100–33. See also the introductions to the O.T., e.g. O. Eissfeldt, *The O.T., An Introduction etc.* (ET 1965).

Disastrously, however, either in the fifth column of the Hexapla or in a separate recension based on the Hexapla, Origen was not content to set the text of the LXX parallel to the others, but, to facilitate its reading, marked in the text of the LXX itself the divergences from the Hebrew, in that he (a) supplied with an obelus (the sign of cancelling) words, sentences, or paragraphs absent from the Hebrew; and (b) included from other translations, generally from Theodotion, words, sentences or paragraphs found in the Hebrew but lacking in the LXX, marking them with an asterisk (cf. Origen's own description of his methods in *Comment. in Matth.* xv, c. 14, PG 13, 1293, GCS, Origen X, p. 388; and Jerome's specific assertion that the inserted passages were from Theodotion in *Praef. in vers. Paralipom.* PL XXVIII, 1324 ff.). He often proceeded similarly in cases of inexact translations in the LXX, in that he added behind the reading of the LXX marked with an obelus the reading parallel to the Hebrew from another version, marked with an asterisk, assimilating the LXX to the Hebrew text with the help of the other Greek translations. Because Origen's LXX text was frequently copied after Eusebius (cf. Field, *Proleg.*, p. xcix), and often circulated in a form in which the critical signs had been treated negligently, and because furthermore the common LXX text (the κοινή ἔκδοσις) was also corrected on the basis of the hexaplaric one, a large number of 'hexaplaric' readings found their way into the text of the LXX. This process may well have been aided if, as is possible, Origen himself produced, separately from the Hexapla, a critical edition of the LXX based on his own researches and *without* the critical marks which were naturally confined to his notes on the *old* text.[31] The elimination of

---

31. P. Kahle, review of I. Soisalen-Soininen, *Der Charakter der asterisierten Zusätze in der Septuaginta* (1959), ThZ 84 (1959), pp. 743–5. This view is based on the Mercati fragments but is still controversial; see above, p. 481. For the text used by Origen when preaching, see P. Nautin, introduction to Origen, *Hom. in Ieremiam* I (SC 232 (1976), pp. 112–25), who shows that Origen sometimes quoted (and misquoted) from memory but that he frequently made a point from the presence or absence of particular readings in the translations other than the Septuagint, presumably in such cases using a text which contained this information.

the hexaplaric additions is therefore one of the chief tasks of septuagintal research. It is generally possible to do this, at least for most books of the O.T., because Origen's critical notes have been preserved for the largest part of the O.T. The signs are found partially but imperfectly preserved in some Greek mss. (the Greek Codex Colberto-Sarravianus and the Chigi ms. 88) and partly in mss. of other text-families with hexaplaric readings in their margins, e.g. Codices Coislinianus and Marchalianus, cf. Jellicoe, SMS, p. 146, but most importantly in the Syriac translation of the hexaplaric LXX text (Syrohexapla), although the accuracy of the reproduction of the signs in the Syrohexapla should not always be trusted, cf. C. T. Fritsch, 'The Treatment of the Hexaplaric Signs in the Syro-Hexaplar of Proverbs', JBL 72 (1953), pp. 169–81. The fullest collection of pertinent material was made by Field, *Origenis Hexaplorum quae supersunt, sive veterum interpretum Graecorum in totum Vetus Testamentum fragmenta*, 2 vols. (1875). Cf. A. Möhle, 'Ein neuer Fund zahlreicher Stücke aus den Jesaiaübersetzungen des Akylas, Symmachos und Theodotion. Probe eines neuen "Field"', ZAW, new series, 11 (1934), pp. 176 ff.; for the material in Eusebius, *Comment. in Isaiam* discussed by Möhle, see now GCS Eusebius IX (1975). Since Field, the material has been significantly expanded by the finds of Morin, Mercati, and Taylor.[32]

32. See the list of sources and editions of Hexaplaric materials in Swete and Ottley, IOTG, p. 76, including C. Taylor, *Hebrew-Greek Cairo Genizah Palimpsests from the Taylor-Schechter Collection including a fragment of the twenty-second Psalm according to Origen's Hexapla* (1900). Noteworthy additional material can be found in L. Lütkemann and A. Rahlfs, *Hexaplarische Randnoten zu Isaias I-16 aus einer Sinai-Handschrift (MSU i, 6)* (1915) and, especially, G. Mercati, *Psalterii Hexapli Reliquiae, Pars Prima: Codex Rescriptus Bybliothecae Ambrosianae O 39 sup. phototypice expressus et transcriptus* (1958). In this latter publication, a palimpsest of the Ambrosiana library contains five of the six columns of the Hexapla of the Psalms: (1) Hebrew in Greek script, (2) Aquila, (3) Symmachus, (4) Septuagint without critical signs, (5) Quinta; the total vocabulary of this palimpsest is included in Hatch and Redpath, *Concordance to the Septuagint*, supplement fasc. II (1906). Cf. A. Schenker, *Hexaplarische Psalmenbruchstücke: Der hexaplarische-Psalmenfragmente der Handschriften Vaticanus graecus 752 und Canonicianus graecus 62* (1975). For research on the Hexapla, see bibliography in S. P. Brock, C. T. Fritsch and S. Jellicoe, *A Classified Bibliography of the Septuagint* (1973), pp. 88–92. Note especially the work on the transcription of the Hebrew text in the second column: H. M. Orlinsky, 'The columnar order of the Hexapla', JQR n.s. 27 (1936/7), pp. 137–49, suggesting that the whole Hexapla was intended as a teaching aid for learning Hebrew; G. Mercati, 'Il problema della colonna II dell'Esaplo', Bibl. 28 (1947), pp. 1–30, 173–215; J. A. Emerton, 'The purpose of the second column of the Hexapla', JThSt n.s. 7 (1956), 79–87, suggesting that the transliteration was intended to help with the vocalization of the consonantal Hebrew text, cf. also idem, 'A further consideration of the purpose of the second column in the Hexapla', JThSt 22 (1971), pp. 15–28. On the Syro-Hexapla, see bibliography in Brock, Fritsch and Jellicoe, *Bibliography*, pp. 191–3; W. Baars, *New Syro-hexaplaric texts, edited, commented upon and compared with the LXX* (1968); A. Vööbus, *Discovery of very important manuscript sources for the Syro-Hexapla* (1970); idem, *The Hexapla and the Syro-Hexapla* (1971); idem, *The Pentateuch in the version of the Syro-Hexapla: a facsimile edition of a Midyat Ms.*

Elimination of the passages marked with an asterisk from the Hexaplaric LXX by no means signifies, however, that one arrives at the original LXX text. The manuscripts already varied greatly at the time of Origen (cf. Origen, *Comment. in Matth.* xv, c. 14, PG 13, 1293, GCS Origen X, p. 388). From these, he himself first constructed a LXX text. Even though there are good grounds to believe that he was scrupulous in his scholarship in including the purest available form of the Greek text under obelus when inserting a reading from another version (Fritsch), and that the changes to accord with the Hebrew made by him in the LXX text, apart from the additions (which are easily recognizable) were relatively few and minor (cf. H. M. Orlinsky, 'Studies in the Septuagint of the Book of Job', HUCA 28 (1957), p. 56), nonetheless only the *recension of Origen* is obtained in this way.[33]

Other Christian scholars besides Origen also worked on the text of the LXX in the third and fourth centuries A.D. Despite the support of Eusebius and Pamphilus for Origen's version, there were at least two other recensions, and recent attempts to distinguish groups among the extant manuscripts have almost certainly revealed a third recension, identified as recension 'C' by Rahlfs when working on the text of Ruth, and by Margolis in the text of Joshua, cf. M. L. Margolis, 'Specimen of a New Edition of the Greek Joshua', in *Jewish Studies in Memory of Israel Abrahams* (1927), p. 309, with the suggestion that this recension 'was at home in Constantinople and Asia Minor'. The versions of Hesychius and Lucian are explicitly mentioned by Jerome; that of Hesychius apparently circulated in Egypt, whereas that of Lucian was preferred from Antioch to Constantinople (Jerome, *In Evangelistas ad Damasum praefatio*, PL 29, 557–62, cf. 559). The view that *Hesychius* was the same person as the Egyptian bishop of this name who was martyred in A.D. 312 during the persecution under Maximinus (Eusebius, *Hist. Eccl.* viii 13, 7) remains probable but unprovable, cf. Jellicoe, SMS, pp. 146–8. Nothing much is known about the nature of his recension, although the text of Codex Vaticanus (B) has been widely supposed to be Hesychian in many of its books, and readings in various other manuscripts have been plausibly assigned to this recension, cf. S. Jellicoe, 'The Hesychian Recension Reconsidered', JBL 82 (1963), pp. 409–18, and *idem*, SMS, 154–8, *contra* the scepticism of H. Dörrie, 'Zur Geschichte der

---

discovered 1964 (1975); *idem*, *The Book of Isaiah in the Version of the Syro-Hexapla : a facsimile edition of Ms St Mark 1 in Jerusalem* (1983).

33. On Origen's treatment of the LXX text, arguing that Origen changed it only little apart from the additions and deletions, and that all such changes were purely mechanical insertions of the text in the other extant versions when they seemed closer to the Hebrew, cf. M. L. Margolis, 'The Mode of Expressing Hebrew'a'id in the Greek Hexateuch', AJSL 29(1912/13), pp. 237–60; I. Soisalon-Soininen, *Der Charakter der asterisierten Zusätze in der Septuaginta* (1959). Cf. Jellicoe, SMS, pp. 134–46.

Septuaginta im Jahrhundert Konstantins', ZNW 39 (1940), pp. 57–110. Overwhelmingly probable is the identity of *Lucian* with the presbyter of that name martyred in A.D. 312 during the same persecution after acting as leader of the school in Antioch (Eusebius, *Hist. Eccl.* viii 13, 2; ix 6, 3). A link with Adoptionist theology made his orthodoxy at least dubious, cf. G. L. Prestige, *Fathers and Heretics* (1940), p. 104. According to the suda, s.v. Λουκιανὸς ὁ μάρτυς, Lucian emended the LXX on the basis of the Hebrew, but since there is no other evidence for his knowledge of Hebrew, it must be admitted more likely that the changes inserted into his recension came from older Greek versions (Jellicoe, SMS, pp. 160–3). Presumably he used Origen's Hexapla without recourse to the hexaplaric version. Despite difficulties in correctly identifying the Lucianic text in extant manuscripts (see below), much can be said about his distinctive version of the LXX. Lucian apparently aimed at a comprehensive, and sometimes conflating, inclusion of all possibly genuine, i.e. well-attested and ancient, readings and showed a marked preference for Attic Greek forms over Hellenistic forms. See, based on the Lucianic text of the N.T., remarks in K. Lake, *The Text of the N.T.* ([6]1928), p. 69; Jellicoe, SMS, p. 159. Cf. on Lucian in general, Field, *Prolegom.*, ch. 9; G. F. Moore, 'The Antiochian Recension of the Septuagint', AJSL 29 (1912–13), pp. 37–62; G. Bardy, *Recherches sur Saint Lucien d'Antioche et son école* (1936); J. Ziegler, 'Hat Lukian den griechischen Sirach rezensiert?', Bibl. 40 (1959), pp. 210–29; B. M. Metzger, 'The Lucianic Recension of the Greek Bible', *Chapters in the History of New Testament Textual Criticism* (1963), pp. 1–41; Barthélemy, *Les Devanciers d'Aquila* (1963), pp. 126 f.; N. Fernandez-Marcos, 'The Lucianic text in the Books of Kingdoms', in A. Pietersma and C. Cox (eds.), *De Septuaginta: Studies in Honour of J. W. Wevers* (1984), pp. 161–74. Cf. also Swete and Ottley, IOTG; E. Würthwein, *The Text of the O.T., etc.* ([2]1980), pp. 41 f.; Eissfeldt, *The O.T., An Introduction*, p. 712.

The recension of Lucian has been preserved in several manuscripts, though in all cases Lucianic readings are found mixed with readings from other recensions. The text published by P. Lagarde as 'Lucianic' in *Librorum Veteris Testamenti Canonicorum Pars Prior Graece* (1883) is in fact not always what it purports to be since Lagarde assumed quite wrongly that a Lucianic reading in one part of a manuscript would classify the whole manuscript as Lucianic. More reliable information on the Lucianic text can be found in the Göttingen editions of the LXX (see below, p. 490). See also on the transmission of the text, Field, *Origenis Hexaplorum etc.* I, pp. lxxiv f.; A. Rahlfs, *Septuaginta-Studien* i: *Studien zu den Königsbüchern* (1904); J. Dahse, 'Textkritische Studien', ZAW 28 (1908), pp. 1–21, 161–73; O. Procksch, *Studien zur Geschichte der Septuaginta: die Propheten* (BWAT VII) (1910); A. Rahlfs, *Septuaginta*

Studien III: *Lucians Rezension der Königsbücher* (1911); Kahle, CG, pp. 231 ff.; Jellicoe, SMS, pp. 163–8.[34]

The labours of Hesychius and Lucian caused still further confusion in the extant manuscripts of the LXX for now not only the hexaplaric text, but also that of Hesychius and Lucian were mixed with the standard text that had formed the basis of Origen's recension. And since the latter was very uncertain already in Origen's time, it is very difficult to recover one *original* text of the LXX. It is nevertheless possible, since the main recensions are still known, to judge which manuscripts are relatively most free of the peculiarities of these later recensions. An important aid in this is provided by the *Old Latin texts*, and the *Oriental* secondary translations, as well as the quotations in Philo and the older Church Fathers. Cf. about the ancient versions, H. B. Swete and R. R. Ottley, IOTG; R. H. Pfeiffer, *Introduction to the O.T.* (²1948), pp. 114–19; Jellicoe, SMS, pp. 243–68. Variant readings in the patristic sources and the earliest extant manuscripts, in particular the newly found papyri and leather documents, can also be used to cleanse the text of later editorial accretions.

All this assumes that *one* original version of the LXX did in fact exist, as argued above, p. 477. The contrary view, strongly maintained by Kahle, that numerous different Greek translations were made of a Hebrew text, which itself existed in various versions as proved by Qumran, would make pointless the attempt to discover one original form of the LXX. On the analogy of the Aramaic targumim, all the Greek versions of the Bible would, on this view, deserve equal prominence as part of the continuing exegesis of the Hebrew text.[35] It

---

34. This Lucianic recension embodies readings which are also found in very much older quotations. Thus 'Lucianic' readings are to be found in Philo (P. Katz, *Philo's Bible* (1950), p. 12) and in Josephus (A. Mez, *Die Bibel des Josephus, untersucht für Buch v-vii der Archäologie* (1895); P. Wendland, *Philologus* 57 (1898), pp. 283–7; H. St. J. Thackeray, 'Note on the evidence of Josephus', in *The Old Testament in Greek* II.i, *I and II Samuel* (1927), p. ix; *idem, Josephus, the Man and the Historian* (1929), pp. 81 ff.). They also appear in the Old Latin and therefore presumably in the Greek text from which that translation was made (S. R. Driver, *Notes on the Hebrew text ... of the Book of Samuel* (²1913), pp. lxxi, lxxxvii; J. A. Montgomery, *Daniel*, p. 45). Confirmation that the Lucianic text is sometimes based on materials considerably earlier than Lucian himself has come from the alleged discovery of Lucianic readings in P. Ryl. Gk. 458, a papyrus fragment of a part of Deuteronomy dating to the second century B.C., cf. Kahle, CG, pp. 220–2, in the Leather Scroll of the Greek Minor Prophets from Qumran, which dates probably to the beginning of the first century A.D. (Kahle, CG, pp. 226 f.), and in *4QSam*ᵃ. Cf. G. Howard, 'Lucianic readings in a Greek Twelve Prophets scroll from the Judaean desert', JQR 62 (1971/2), pp. 51–60. Cf., in general, E. Tov, 'Lucian and proto-Lucian: Toward a new solution of the problem', RB 79 (1972), pp. 101–13; A. Pietersma, 'Proto-Lucian and the Greek psalter', VT 28 (1978), pp. 66–72; T. Muraoka, 'The Greek text of 2 Samuel 11 in the Lucianic manuscripts', Abr Nahrain 20 (1981/2), pp. 37–59.

35. P. E. Kahle, ThStKr 88 (1915), pp. 410 ff.; *idem*, in *Festschrift O. Eissfeldt* (1947), pp. 161–80; *idem*, CG, pp. 209–264. See, *contra*, P. Katz, ThZ 5 (1949), pp. 1 ff.; *idem*,

must be said however that, although other unofficial Greek translations doubtless existed, the hypothesis of one original LXX text, of which the present manuscripts preserve more or less edited recensions, remains much the most likely, and the attempt to reconstruct that text remains a valid endeavour.

The number of mss. of this Greek translation is very large, not far from two thousand. Cf. A. Rahlfs, *Verzeichnis der griechischen Handschriften des Alten Testaments* (1914); Swete and Ottley, IOTG; B. J. Roberts, *The O.T. Text and Versions* (1951), pp. 144–61; F. G. Kenyon and A. W. Adams, *Our Bible and the Ancient Manuscripts* (⁵1958); F. G. Kenyon and A. W. Adams, *The Text of the Greek Bible* (²1961); Jellicoe, SMS, pp. 176–242.

The oldest mss. are the papyri and leather documents. *Papyrus Greek 458 of the John Rylands Library* in Manchester, with a fragment from Dt., dated in the middle of the second century B.C., is the oldest extant text of the Greek O.T. (C. H. Roberts, *Two Biblical Papyri in the John Rylands Library* (1936); cf. Kahle, CG, pp. 220 ff.; J. W. Wevers, 'The earliest witness to the LXX Deuteronomy', CBQ 39 (1977), pp. 240–4). The *Cairo Papyrus Fouad 266*, with fragments from Gen. and Dt., is dated to the mid-first century B.C. (Z. Aly and L. Koenen, *Three Rolls of the Early Septuagint: Genesis and Deuteronomy* (1980)). Fragments from Qumran 4 include a papyrus with fragments of Lev., a fragmentary leather scroll with parts of Num., both of which have been dated about the end of the first century B.C. or the beginning of the first century A.D., and a fragment of a leather scroll of Lev., dated towards the end of the second century B.C. (P. W. Skehan, 'The Qumran Manuscripts and Textual Criticism', *Suppl. to VT*, IV (1957), pp. 155–60; cf. J. W. Wevers, 'An early revision of the LXX of Numbers', Eretz Israel 16 (1982), pp. 235–9). Some fragments have been found in cave 7, e.g. of Ex., and have been published in M. Baillet, J. T. Milik, and R. de Vaux, *Discoveries in the Judaean Desert of Jordan* III (1962), pp. 142 ff., pl. xxx. Cf. E. Ulrich, 'The Greek mss. of the Pentateuch from Qumran', in A. Pietersma and C. Cox (eds.), *De Septuaginta: Studies in Honour of J. W. Wevers* (1984), pp. 71–82, with a collation of all the fragments. The *Leather Scroll of the Greek Minor Prophets*, discovered by Bedouin in 1952, in the subsequently identified 'Cave of Horror' in Nahal Hever, of which an additional thirteen fragments were recovered in 1961 by Y. Yadin, is dated between 50 B.C. and A.D. 50 (D. Barthélemy, 'Redécouverte d'un chaînon manquant de l'histoire de la Septante', RB 60 (1953), pp. 18–29; *Les devanciers d'Aquila: Première publication intégrale du texte des fragments du Dodécaprophéton trouvés dans le désert de Juda, précédée*

Philo's Bible. The aberrant Text of Bible Quotations in some Philonic Writings and its Place in the Textual History of the Greek Bible (1950); D. Barthélemy, *Les devanciers d'Aquila* (1963), p. 272.

d'une étude sur les traductions et recensions grecques de la Bible réalisée au premier siècle de notre ère sous l'influence du rabbinat palestinien in *Suppl. to VT* X, 1963; the 1961 fragments have been published by B. Lifshitz, 'The Greek Documents from the Cave of Horror', *Israel Exploration Journal* 12 (1962), pp. 201–7). Of later papyrus texts the most important are: (1) the *Chester Beatty-John H. Scheide Papyri*, from the second to the fourth centuries A.D., contain e.g. parts of nine O.T. books (F. G. Kenyon, *The Chester Beatty Biblical Papyri*, 7 vols., 1933–7; and A. C. Johnson, H. S. Gehman, E. H. Kase, *The John H. Scheide Biblical Papyri: Ezekiel* (*Princeton Univ. Stud. in Papyrology* III (1938)); cf. A. Allgeier, *Die Chester Beatty Papyri zum Pentateuch* (*Studien zur Geschichte und Kultur des Altertums* XXI.2 (1938)); A. Pietersma, 'F. G. Kenyon's text of Papyrus 963 (Numbers and Deuteronomy)', *VT* 24 (1974), pp. 113–18; *idem, Chester Beatty Biblical Papyri IV and V. A new edition with text-critical analysis* (1977); (2) the *Berlin Genesis fragments*, from the middle to the end of the third century, which were published together with the *Freer Minor Prophets Papyrus* of the same date (H. A. Sanders and C. Schmidt, *The Minor Prophets in the Freer Collection and the Berlin Fragment of Genesis*, 1927); (3) *Amherst Papyrus 3*, of the late third century, which contains a fragment of Genesis 1:1–5 in Aquila's version preceded by the LXX parallel in a hand of the first half of the fourth century (B. P. Grenfell and A. S. Hunt, *The Amherst Papyri* I (1900), pp. 30 ff.; cf. A. Deissmann, *Light from the Ancient East* (1910), pp. 192 ff.); (4) *The Antinoopolis Papyri*, with second- to third-century fragments of Psalms, Proverbs, Wisdom, Ben Sira and Ezekiel (C. H. Roberts, *The Antinoopolis Papyri* I (1950)).

Cf. further C. H. Roberts, JThSt 50 (1949), p. 155, n. 2; Jellicoe, SMS, pp. 224–42, and further bibliography in *idem*, SMS, pp. 326–88 and S. P. Brock, C. T. Fritsch and S. Jellicoe, *A Classified Bibliography of the Septuagint* (1973), pp. 69–74. Cf. also J. O'Callaghan, 'Lista de los papiros de los LXX', Bibl. 56 (1975), pp. 74–93; J. van Haelst, *Catalogue des papyrus littéraires juifs et chrétiens* (1976); K. Aland, *Repertorium der griechischen christlichen Papyri* I. Biblische Papyri (1976).

Among the Greek manuscripts which contain the whole O.T. or at least a large part of it, *Codex Vaticanus 1209* (B), from the fourth century, is the most important. Photographic edition in *Vetus Testamentum iuxta LXX Interpretum versionem e Codice omnium antiquissimo Graeco Vaticano 1209 phototypica repraesentatum* ..., 5 vols. (1889–90), reissued in 4 vols. as *Bibliorum sacrorum graecorum codex vaticanus 1209 denuo phototypice expressus* (1905–7).

Of hardly less importance is the *Codex Sinaiticus* (ℵ or S), also from the fourth century, discovered in the Convent of St. Catherine by Tischendorf in 1845 and now in the British Museum. About half of the O.T. has been preserved in this manuscript. Photographic edition by

H. and K. Lake, *Codex Sinaiticus Petropolitanus* ... 2 vols., N.T. 1911, O.T. 1922. This edition supersedes that by Tischendorf, *Bibliorum Codex Sinaiticus Petropolitanus*, 4 vols. (1862), with other fragments published separately in 1846, 1855, 1857, 1867 and 1875.

The third major manuscript is the *Codex Alexandrinus* (A), which dates to some time between the late fourth and the sixth century. This text is eclectic, with hexaplaric, Lucianic and Hesychian readings all represented. Photographic editions: autotype facsimile published by the British Museum as E. M. Thompson, ed., *Facsimile of the Codex Alexandrinus ... published by order of the Trustees*, 4 vols., N.T. 1879, O.T. 1881–3; reduced collotype facsimile published as F. G. Kenyon and H. J. M. Milne, eds., *The Codex Alexandrinus of the British Museum*, 5 vols., N.T. 1909, O.T. 1915–57.

Other important manuscripts available in photographic editions are: *Codex Marchalianus* (Q), a complete text of the Prophets written in the sixth century, published as J. Cozza, ed., *Prophetarum codex Graecus Vaticanus 2125 heliotypice editus* (1890); *Codex Colberto-Sarravianus* (G), sometimes described more simply as *Codex Sarravianus*, a late fourth or early fifth century manuscript which retains the Hexaplaric diacritical signs, published as *Codices graeci et latine photographice depicti duce G. N. du Rieu* I, 1897; *Codex Purpureus Vindobonensis* (L), a fifth-sixth century manuscript, published as W. Ritter von Hartel and F. Wickhoff, eds., *Die Wiener Genesis* (1895).

Transcriptions of other important manuscripts may be found in:

von Tischendorf, C., *Monumenta sacra inedita, nova collectio* I (1885), II (1857), III (1860), IV, VI (1869), IX (1870).
von Tischendorf, C., *Codex Ephraemi syri rescriptus sive fragmenta veteris testamenti* ... (1845); a new edition of this ms. is in preparation, cf. R. W. Lyon, 'A Re-examination of Codex Ephraemi Rescriptus', NTSt 5 (1958–9), pp. 260–72.
Abbott, T. K., *Par Palimpsestorum Dublinensium ... Fragments of the Book of Isaiah in the LXX Version* (1880).
Sanders, H. A., *Facsimile of the Washington manuscript of Deuteronomy and Joshua in the Freer Collection* (1910).
Tisserant, E., *Codex Zuqninensis rescriptus veteris testamenti* (1911).
Gerhäuser, W., and A. Rahlfs, *Münchener Septuaginta-Fragmente* (1913).
Vaccari, A., *Codex Melphictensis rescriptus Ezechielis fragmenta graeca* (1918).
Bieler, L., *Psalterium graeco-latinum Codex Basiliensis A vii.3* (1960).
Pietersma, A., *Two manuscripts of the Greek Psalter in the Chester Beatty Library Dublin* (1978).

See further about the mss.: Swete and Ottley, IOTG; F. G. Kenyon and A. W. Adams, *Our Bible and the Ancient Manuscripts* ([5]1958), pp. 113–27; Jellicoe, SMS, pp. 175–242; E. Würthwein, *The Text of the Old Testament* ([2]1980), pp. 68–72; B. M. Metzger, *Manuscripts of the Greek Bible: an introduction to Greek palaeography* (1981). See also the introductions to the separate volumes of the Göttingen Septuagint, cf. below, p. 490.

Editions of the Septuagint

(See for bibliographical references: Nestle in HDB IV, cols. 437–54, for older books;

S. P. Brock, C. T. Fritsch and S. Jellicoe, *A Classified Bibliography of the Septuagint* (1973), pp. 4–7, for modern editions.)

Editions of the Whole O.T.

(1) Holmes, R., and J. Parsons, *Vetus Testamentum Graecum cum variis lectionibus*, 5 vols., 1798–1827 (based on the Sixtine edition, *Vetus Testamentum iuxta Septuaginta ex auctoritate Sixti V Pont. Max. editum* (1587), which was itself based on Codex Vaticanus (B), but with a still unrivalled collection of critical material).

(2) Swete, H. B., *The Old Testament in Greek according to the Septuagint* I (⁴1909); II (²1907); III (⁴1912). (A manual edition based on Codex Vaticanus (B) with lacunae supplied from A and א (S) but with many other manuscripts collated.)

(3) Brooke, A. E., N. Mclean and H. St. J. Thackeray, *The Old Testament in Greek according to the text of Codex Vaticanus, supplemented from other uncial manuscripts with a critical apparatus containing the variants of the chief ancient authorities for the text of the LXX*, 9 parts (1906–40). (The Larger Cambridge edition, based on Codex Vaticanus (B) with lacunae supplied from A and א (S) and a rich collection of variants. Incomplete.)

(4) Göttingen Septuagint: *Vetus Testamentum Graecum Auctoritate Societatis Litterarum Gottingensis editum* (1931-). (The text here is a composite, critical reconstruction of the earliest attainable text, in which at each variant the reading is chosen which appears best in the light of the manuscript tradition as a whole. A critical apparatus gives the variants in text groups. So far published are: vol. I, *Genesis*, ed. J. W. Wevers (1974); III.1 *Numeri*, ed. J. W. Wevers (1982); III.2, *Deuteronomium*, ed. Wevers (1977); VIII.1, *Esdrae liber I*, ed. R. Hanhart (1974); VIII.3, *Esther*, ed. Hanhart (1966); VIII.4, *Iudith*, ed. Hanhart (1979); VIII.5, *Tobit*, ed. Hanhart (1983); IX.1, *Maccabaeorum liber 1*, ed. W. Kappler (1936); IX.2, *Maccabaeorum liber 2*, ed. W. Kappler and R. Hanhart (²1976); IX.3, *Maccabaeorum liber 3*, ed. Hanhart (²1980); X, *Psalms cum Odis*, ed. A. Rahlfs (1931); XI.4, *Iob*, ed. J. Ziegler (1982); XII.1, *Sapientia Salomonis*, ed. J. Ziegler (²1980); XII.2, *Sapientia Iesu Filii Sirach*, ed. Ziegler (²1980); XIII, *Duodecim Prophetae*, ed. Ziegler (²1967); XIV, *Isaias*, ed. Ziegler (²1967); XV, *Ieremias, Baruch, Threni, Epistula Ieremiae*, ed. Ziegler (²1976); XVI.1, *Ezechiel*, ed. Ziegler (²1977); XVI.2, *Susanna, Daniel, Bel et Draco*, ed. Ziegler (1954).

(5) Rahlfs, A., *Septuaginta. Id est Vetus Testamentum Graece Iuxta LXX Interpretes*, 2 vols. (1935). (A critical, manual edition, based mainly on the three major uncials, B, (S) and A.)

Important Editions of Single Books

Ottley, R. R., *The Book of Isaiah according to the Septuagint (Codex Alexandrinus)*, 2 vols., I (²1909), II (1906).
Rahlfs, A., *Das Buch Ruth griechisch als Probe einer kritischen Handausgabe der Septuaginta* (1922).
Idem, Genesis (Septuaginta Societatis Scientiarum Gottingensis Auctoritate I) (1926).
Margolis, M. L., *The Book of Joshua in Greek*, Parts I-IV (1931–8). (Incomplete.)
Nestle, E., ed. J. Dahse and E. Nestle, *Das Buch Ieremia griechisch und hebräisch* (²1934).
Tov, E., *The Hebrew and Greek Texts of Samuel* (1980).

Concordance

Hatch, E., and H. A. Redpath, *A Concordance to the Septuagint and the other Greek Versions of the O.T. (including the Apocryphal Books)*, 2 vols. (1897, with Supplement, 1900–6, reprinted in 2 vols., 1954). Cf. E. Tov, 'The use of concordances in the reconstruction of the *Vorlage* of the LXX', CBQ 40 (1978), pp. 29–36. Cf. also X. Jacques, *Index des mots apparentés dans la Septante* (1972); E. C. Dos Santos, *An expanded

Hebrew Index for the Hatch-Redpath Concordance to the LXX (n.d. 1977?); T. Muraoka, *A Greek-Hebrew/Aramaic Index to 1 Esdras* (1984).

General Works on the Septuagint

See the thorough bibliographies in G. Delling, *Bibliographie zur Jüdisch-Hellenistischen und Intertestamentarischen Literatur* (²1975), pp. 98–114 and especially S. P. Brock, C. T. Fritsch and S. Jellicoe, *A Classified Bibliography of the Septuagint* (1973). For works published since 1970, see the *Bulletin of the International Organization for Septuagint and Cognate Studies* and, for a more complete list, *Elenchus* (the bibliographical supplement to Bibl.). See also below, 33A.II.2 on Aquila and Theodotion, 33A.VII.5 on Ps.-Aristeas. Mentioned here are only the most important widely applicable studies. See also the studies listed in E. Tov, *A classified bibliography of lexical and grammatical studies in the language of the Septuagint* (1980).

Introductions to the Septuagint

Nestle, E., 'Septuagint', in HDB IV, cols. 437–54.

Swete, H. B., and R. R. Ottley, *An Introduction to the O.T. in Greek* (1914), repr. 1968 (IOTG).

Orlinsky, H. M., *The Septuagint : the oldest translation of the Bible* (1949).

Metzger, B. M., art. 'Versions, Ancient', in IDB IV, cols. 749–60.

Wevers, J. W., art. 'Septuagint', in IDB IV, cols. 273–8.

Kenyon, F. G., revised H. S. Gehman, art. 'Greek versions of the O.T.', in HDB (²1963), cols. 347–54.

Jellicoe, S., *The Septuagint and Modern Study* (1968) (SMS).

Tov, E., and R. Kraft, art. 'Septuagint', in IDBS, cols. 807–15.

O'Connell, K. G., art. 'Greek versions (minor)', IDBS, cols. 377–81.

Fernandez-Marcos, N., *Introduccion a las versiones griegas de la Biblia* (1979).

Brock, S. P., art. 'Bibelübersetzungen' I, in G. Krause and G. Müller, *Theologische Realenzyklopädie* VI (1980), pp. 161–9.

General Bibliography on Problems in the Study of the Septuagint

Burkitt, F. C., *The Rules of Tyconius* (1894).

Rahlfs, A., *Septuaginta-Studien* I-III (1904–11, repr. 1965).

Rahlfs, A., *Verzeichnis der griechischen Handschriften des Alten Testaments* (1914).

Thackeray, H. St. J., *The Septuagint and Jewish Worship* (²1923).

Gaster, M., *The Samaritans* (1925), pp. 112 ff.

Wutz, F. X., 'Ist der hebräische Urtext wieder erreichbar?', ZAW N.F. 2 (1925), pp. 115–19.

Wutz, F. X., *Die Transkriptionen von der Septuaginta bis zur Hieronymus* (BWAT II.9), Part 1 (1925), Part 2 (1933).

Margolis, M. L., 'Transliteration in the Greek O.T.', JQR n.s. 16 (1925), pp. 117–25.

Thackeray, H. St. J., *Some Aspects of the Greek Old Testament* (1927).

Bertram, G., 'Zur LXX-Forschung', ThR 3 (1931), pp. 283–96; 5 (1933), pp. 173–85; 10 (1938), pp. 69–80, 133–59.

Kenyon, F. G., *Recent Developments in the Textual Criticism of the Greek Bible* (1933).

Kenyon, F. G., rev. A. W. Adams, *The Text of the Greek Bible* (1937, ³1975).

Wutz, F. X., *Systematische Wege von der Septuaginta zum hebräischen Urtext* (1937).

Seeligmann, I. L., 'Problemen en perspectieven in het moderne LXX-onderzoek', Jaarbericht ... Ex Oriente Lux 2, 7 (1940), pp. 359–90, 763–6.

Orlinsky, H. M., 'On the Present State of Proto-Septuagint Studies', JAOS 61 (1941), pp. 81–91.

Orlinsky, H. M., 'Current progress and problems in LXX research', in H. R. Willoughby, ed., *The Study of the Bible Today and Tomorrow* (1947), pp. 144–61.

Soisalon-Soininen, I., *Die Textformen der Septuaginta-übersetzung des Richterbuches* (*Annales Acad. Scient. Fennicae* LXXII, 1951).

Wevers, J. W., 'LXX-Forschungen', ThR 22 (1954), pp. 85–137, 171–90.

Katz, P., 'Septuagint Studies in the Mid-Century, Their Links with the Past and their Present Tendencies', in W. D. Davies and D. Daube, eds., *The Background to the N.T. and its Eschatology* (1956).

Jouassard, G., 'Requête d'un patrologue aux biblistes touchant les Septante', *Studia Patristica* I (1957), pp. 307–27.

Kahle, P., 'Problems of the Septuagint', *Studia Patristica* I (1957), pp. 328–38.

Soisalon-Soininen, I., *Der Charakter der asterisierten Zusätze in der Septuaginta* (1959).

Kahle, P., *The Cairo Geniza* (²1959) (CG).

Kahle, P., 'LXX-Forschung', in RGG³ V, cols. 1404–7.

Kenyon, F. G., rev. A. W. Adams, *Our Bible and the Ancient Manuscripts* (⁵1958).

Ziegler, J., *Beiträge zur Jeremias Septuaginta* (MSU VI, 1958).

Kahle, P., 'The Greek Bible and the Gospels. Fragments from the Judaean Desert', Studia Evangelica 73 (1959), pp. 613–21.

Kahle, P., 'The Greek Bible Manuscripts used by Origen', JBL 79 (1960), pp. 111–18.

Gooding, D. W., 'Aristeas and Septuagint Origins: a Review of Recent Studies', VT 13 (1963), pp. 357–79.

Barthélemy, D., *Les Devanciers d'Aquila* (1963).

Jellicoe, S., 'The LXX today', ET 77 (1965/66), pp. 68–74.

Wevers, J. W., 'LXX-Forschungen seit 1954', ThR 33 (1968), pp. 18–76.

Jellicoe, S., 'LXX Studies in the Current Century', JBL 88 (1969), pp. 191–9.

Ziegler, J., *Sylloge: Gesammelte Aufsätze zur LXX* (1971).

Brock, S. P., 'The phenomenon of the Septuagint', Oudtestamentische Studien 17 (1972), pp. 11–36.

Orlinsky, H. M., *Essays in biblical culture and Bible translation* (1973).

Janzen, J. G., *Studies in the text of Jeremiah* (1973).

Walters (Katz), P., ed. D. W. Gooding, *The text of the Septuagint: its corruptions and their emendations* (1973).

Klein, R. W., *Textual criticism of the Old Testament: from the Septuagint to Qumran* (1974).

Jellicoe, S., *Studies in the Septuagint: origins, recensions and interpretations* (1974).

Orlinsky, H. M., 'The Septuagint as Holy Writ and the philosophy of the translators', HUCA 46 (1975), pp. 89–114.

Gooding, D. W., *Relics of Ancient Exegesis* (1976).

Barthélemy, D., *Études d'histoire du texte de l'Ancien Testament* (1978).

Ulrich, E. L., *The Qumran text of Samuel and Josephus* (1978).

Wevers, J. W., *Text History of the Greek Deuteronomy* (MSU XIII, 1978).

Hanhart, R., *Text und Text-geschichte des Buches Judith* (1979).

Sollamo, R., *Renderings of Hebrew Semiprepositions in the LXX* (1979).

Bodine, W. R., *The Greek text of Judges: recensional developments* (1980).

Tov, E., *The text-critical use of the Septuagint in biblical research* (1981).

Tov, E., *Lexical and grammatical studies on the language of the Septuagint and its revisions* (²1982).

Wevers, J. W., *Text History of the Greek Numbers* (MSU XV, 1982).

Aejmelaeus, A., *Parataxis in the LXX* (1982).

Silva, M., *Biblical words and their meaning* (1983).

Lee, J. A. L., *A lexical study of the Septuagint version of the Pentateuch* (1983).

Greenspoon, L, *Textual studies in the Book of Joshua* (1983).

Hanhart, R., *Text und Textgeschichte des Buches Tobit* (1984).

Pietersma, A., and C. Cox (eds.), *De Septuaginta: Studies in Honour of J. W. Wevers* (1984).

See also the introductions to the O.T. especially:

Eissfeldt, O., *The O.T., An Introduction etc.* (ET 1965), pp. 701–15.

Roberts, B. J., *The Old Testament Text and Versions* (1951), pp. 101–87.
Würthwein, E., *The Text of the Old Testament* (²1980), pp. 49–74.

2. Aquila and Theodotion

The translation of the Septuagint prevailed among Jews of the Greek-speaking diaspora as the main sacred version of the Bible until the beginning of the second century A.D. The period of its predominance coincided with the golden age of the Jewish community in Alexandria. In the second century A.D., however, it suffered near extinction and the translation of the Bible which it had championed fell into disfavour among Jews. This process was aided by two factors: an increase in the prestige of rabbinic commentators outside Palestine and the successful advance of Christianity. An important symptom of this change is to be found in the new Greek translations of the Bible, which were intended to provide Greek-speaking Jews with a translation based on the authoritative Hebrew text. On the one hand, the fact that these translations were undertaken is evidence of the existing strength and importance of Greek-speaking Judaism. But on the other hand, they indicate that the Hebrew was progressively attaining a position of increasing influence and recognition also among Hellenistic Jews, which may in turn have encouraged a decline in the production of a distinctively Greek Jewish literature. These translations are also a memorial of the struggle between Judaism and Christianity, since they were to provide the Jews with a polemical weapon in the battle against Christian theologians, who exploited the uncertain text of the LXX in their own interest (cf. especially Justin, *Dial. c. Tryph.* 68, 71, and elsewhere).

Of the three Greek translations of the Bible which Origen placed parallel to the LXX in his Hexapla (Aquila, Symmachus, and Theodotion, cf. above, p. 481), only Aquila and Theodotion are discussed here, because Symmachus, although he was both acquainted with earlier Jewish recensions, including that represented in the Leather Scroll of the Minor Prophets found at Qumran, and was capable of using the Hebrew text independently (cf. D. Barthélemy, *Les Devanciers d'Aquila* (1963), pp. 261 f.), was not himself Jewish. The testimony of Eusebius, *Hist. Eccl.* vi 17, that he was an Ebionite Christian should be accepted. Cf. H. J. Schoeps, *Symmachus-Studien* I–III (= I. *Ebionitisches bei Symmachus* (1942); II. 'Mythologisches bei Symmachus', *Bibl.* 26 (1945), pp. 100–11; III. 'Symmachus und der Midrasch', *Bibl.* 29 (1948), pp. 31–51; D. Barthélemy, 'Qui est Symmaque?', *CBQ* 36 (1974), pp. 451–65. It is however certain that Theodotion and Aquila were Jewish and that Aquila was a proselyte. It is likely that these translations were preceded by a number of Jewish hebraizing recensions along the same lines. The names of two such recensionists have been preserved as Ben La'ana and Ben Tilga, cf. S. Krauss, 'Two hitherto unknown Bible Versions in Greek', BJRL 27 (1942–3), pp. 97–105. It has also been claimed by Barthélemy that at least the Quinta if not the Sexta and Septima versions used by Origen were also of Jewish origin (cf. *Les Devanciers d'Aquila* (1963), pp. 215–20, on the Quinta as possibly to be identified with the text of the leather scroll of the Minor Prophets, which is certainly Jewish). This, however, is speculative, and the only strong assertion that should be put forward about these translations is that they existed.

According to Irenaeus, who is the first to mention Aquila, he was a Jewish proselyte from Pontus. The information relating to Aquila's homeland is a little suspect because of the striking parallel with Act. 18:2, although Epiphanius goes even further and names Sinope in Pontus as Aquila's native place. The tradition should nonetheless probably be accepted. In view of the nature and purpose of his undertaking, however, and especially if he is to be identified with the 'Onkelos' mentioned in rabbinic texts as the man to whom an Aramaic targum was assigned (see above, vol. I, pp. 100–1, 109–10), it is much more probable that the translation itself was made in Palestine, cf. A. E. Silverstone, *Aquila and Onkelos* (1931), p. 160. On the other hand, it seems certain that Aquila was a proselyte, in spite of his thorough knowledge of Hebrew, for he is described as such not only by all Church Fathers but also in the Jerusalem Talmud and in rabbinical literature generally, as אקלס הגר. Of the fantastic stories told about him by Epiphanius, *De mens. et pond.* 14—that he was a relation (πενθερίδης) of the Emperor Hadrian and became a Christian but was then excluded from the Christian congregation because of his inclination toward astrology, and that he finally became a Jew—the only credible point is that he lived during the time of Hadrian. Rabbinical tradition also (yKidd. 59a) places him in the time of R. Eliezer, R. Joshua, and R. Akiba, i.e. in the first third of the second century A.D.

The purpose of his translation was to imitate the Hebrew text as closely as possible. There can be no doubt that he worked directly from the Hebrew, though the survival of characteristic readings from before his time in, e.g., Philo makes it likely that he used either a Hebrew version different from that used for the LXX, or that he adopted some renderings from earlier recensions of the LXX. Thus, he not only ventured a number of new, daring word-formations in order to obtain Greek words which corresponded exactly to the Hebrew, but also rendered Hebrew particles slavishly by Greek particles, producing a quite idiosyncratic Greek style. The translation has been ridiculed since Jerome for translating in the very first sentence of Gen. the *nota accusativi* 'et by σύν (σὺν τὸν οὐρανὸν καὶ σὺν τὴν γῆν). Ridicule may however be misplaced if this usage was in fact not a grammatical absurdity but imitation of the Homeric use of σύν as an adverb rather than a preposition, cf. Barthélemy, *Les Devanciers*, pp. 15–21, in keeping with Aquila's style elsewhere, where he also tries to be Homeric (Field, *Origenis Hexapla*, p. xxiii). This attention to the smallest detail may perhaps be traced to the influence of Akiba, whose pupil Aquila is said to have been.

Jerome frequently mentioned a *prima* and a *secunda* edition of Aquila. The numerous passages where two different translations have been traced back to Aquila (collected by Field) suggest that either this work existed in two different recensions or other Jewish translations were attributed to him because of his growing prestige. Because of his close correspondence to the Hebrew, which made his work fully comprehensible only to someone already acquainted with that language, his text was approved as soon as it appeared by the most esteemed rabbinical authorities, R. Eliezer and R. Joshua, and became quickly preferred to the LXX by Hellenized Jews, as was already indicated by Origen and still confirmed in A.D. 533 by Justinian in his *Novella 146* (cf. Kahle, CG, pp. 315–17, for translation). About a dozen passages are quoted from it in rabbinical literature also.

The work as a whole disappeared with Greek-speaking Judaism. We owe that part of it which survives mainly to its inclusion in Origen's Hexapla. From this, numerous notes have been preserved concerning Aquila's translation, partly through quotations by Eusebius, Jerome, and other Church Fathers, who still used the original edition of the Hexapla in Pamphilus' library in Caesarea (Jerome, *Comment. in Tit.* 3, 9, PL XXVII, 630; *Comment. in Psalm.*, CCL LXXII, p. 185), and partly through marginal notes in manuscripts of the hexaplaric LXX text. The publication of Mercati's find (cf. above, n. 32) has provided larger fragments of Aquila's translation of the Psalms; the *Amherst Papyri* contain a small fragment (Gen. 1:1–5). But besides these fragments from Christian tradition, some of Jewish origin have also been known since 1897. Sixth-century A.D. palimpsest leaves with fragments from Aquila have been found among the manuscript treasure from the Cairo genizah (cf. above, under ben Sira, p. 203).

Irenaeus, iii 21, 1 (Greek in Eusebius, *Hist. Eccl.* v 8, 10: ἀλλ' οὐχ ὡς ἔνιοί φασιν τῶν νῦν τολμώντων μεθερμηνεύειν τὴν γραφήν· 'ἰδοὺ ἡ νεᾶνις ἐν γαστρὶ ἕξει καὶ τέξεται υἱόν', ὡς Θεοδοτίων ἡρμήνευσεν ὁ 'Εφέσιος καὶ 'Ακύλας ὁ Ποντικός, ἀμφότεροι 'Ιουδαῖοι προσήλυτοι. Eusebius, *Demonstr. evang.* vii 1, 32, ed. Heikel, GCS Eusebius VI, p. 304: προσήλυτος δὲ ὁ 'Ακύλας ἦν, οὐ φύσει 'Ιουδαῖος. Epiphanius, *De mensuris et ponderibus*, 14–15.

Jerome, *Epist. 57 ad Pammachium*, 11 (ed. Bartelink (1980), pp. 19–20) : 'Aquila autem proselytus et contentiosus interpres, qui non solum verba, sed etymologias verborum transferre conatus est, iure proicitur a nobis. Quis enim pro frumento et vino et oleo possit vel legere vel intelligere χεῦμα, ὀπωρισμόν, στιλπνότητα, quod nos possumus dicere "fusionem", "pomationem" que et "splendentiam"; aut, quia Hebraei non solum habent ἄρθρα, sed et πρόαρθρα, <ut> ille κακοζήλως et syllabus interpretetur et litteras dicatque σὺν τὸν οὐρανὸν καὶ σὺν τὴν γῆν, quod Graeca et Latina lingua omnino non recipit?' In general, Jerome approved of Aquila's accuracy and trustworthiness. Cf. *Epist. 32 ad Marcellam* (ed. Hilberg, CSEL LIV, p. 252), *Comm. in Esaiam*. xiii 49, 5–6 (CCL LXXIIIA, p. 537), *Comm. in Hoseam* 2:16–17 (CCL LXXVI, p. 29), *Comm. in Habak*. 3:11–13 (CCL LXXVIA, p. 641). The passages where Jerome mentions the *prima* and *secunda editio* of Aquila can be found in Field, *Origenis Hexapl. quae supersunt*, proleg. pp. xxv f.

yMeg. i 11, 71c: 'Aquila the proselyte translated the Law in the time of R. Eliezer and R. Joshua; and they praised him and said to him, You are the most beautiful among the children of men' (יפיפית מבני אדם), Ps. 45:3, with an allusion to the translation of the Torah into 'Japhetic', i.e. Greek. yKidd. i 1, 59a: 'Aquila the proselyte translated in the time of R. Akiba.' Jerome, *Comment. in Esaiam*. 8:11 ff. (CCL LXXIII, p. 116): 'Akibas quem magistrum Aquilae proselyti autumant.' Cf. above, vol. II, p. 378. A collection of rabbinical passages where Aquila's translation is quoted was already given by Azariah de Rossi, *Meor Enajim*, 45; cf. also R. Anger, *De Akila* (1845), pp. 12–25. The identification of Aquila with Onkelos, the reputed compiler of the Aramaic targum of the Pentateuch, is now widely accepted because of the close parallels in the traditions recorded respectively of Onkelos in the Babylonian Talmud and Tosefta and of Aquila in the Jerusalem Talmud, cf. A. E. Silverstone, *Aquila and Onkelos* (1931). The knowledge of Hebrew evident in Aquila's Greek translation would render it quite possible that he would also have been competent to produce the targum in a cognate Semitic language, though the alternative, that rabbinic references to *both* names concern a translation into Greek and not Aramaic, and that the extant targum was not produced by Onkelos at all, is quite possible (Barthélemy, *Les Devanciers*, pp. 148–54).

Origen, *Epist. ad African*. 4(2) (ed. De Lange, SC 302, p. 526) : Ἀκύλας ... φιλοτιμότερον πεπιστευμένος παρὰ Ἰουδαίοις ἡρμηνευκέναι τὴν γραφήν· ᾧ μάλιστα εἰώθασιν οἱ ἀγνοοῦντες τὴν Ἑβραίων διάλεκτον χρῆσθαι, ὡς πάντων μᾶλλον ἐπιτετευγμένῳ. It is mentioned in Justinian's *Novella 146* that there was conflict among the Jews themselves about whether the Bible was to be read in the synagogue worship service in Hebrew only, or in Hebrew and Greek. Justinian directs that the latter should not be impeded, and as a Christian emperor recommends above all the use of the LXX, but also permits Aquila's translation (which was therefore evidently preferred by at least some of the Jews).

For a collection of the fragments to be found in descriptions and citations in patristic and talmudic literature and incorporated in the texts or margins of LXX manuscripts, see F. Field, *Origenis Hexaplorum quae supersunt*, 2 vols. (1875).

An important enrichment of the material since Field's collection resulted from (1) Mercati's discovery of a sixth-century ms. containing the Hexapla of some 150 verses of the Psalter, including the version of Aquila (see above, p. 483, n. 32);

(2) The find in the Genizah of the synagogue in Cairo. (a) Among the mass of fragments which Schechter brought to Cambridge from this treasury were three palimpsest leaves with the upper writing in Hebrew and the lower writing in Greek uncials of the fifth or sixth century, containing the text, admittedly often difficult to read, of 1 Kg. 20:7–17 and 2 Kg. 23:11–27, evidently in Aquila's translation. Cf. the edition by F. C. Burkitt, *Fragments of the Books of Kings according to the Translation of Aquila* (1897).

(b) Similarly from the Cairo Genizah is the Hexapla fragment of Ps. 22, edited by Taylor, containing Aquila's translation of Ps. 22:20–28 (cf. above, p. 483, n. 32).

(c) Of considerably larger extent are the fragments of Aquila's translation of the Psalms communicated in the same publication by C. Taylor (*Hebrew-Greek Cairo Genizah Palimpsest*, 1900). There are three leaves, with writing similar to the Greek script of Burkitt's fragments of Kings. They contain Aquila's translation of Ps. 90–17; 91:1–16 (the last four verses defective); 92:1–10 (the first four verses defective); 96:7–13; 97:1–12 (defective); 93:3; 102:16–29; and 103:1–13 (defective).

(d) New fragments of the text of Malachi and Job have recently been identified, cf. N. R._M. de Lange, 'Some new fragments of Aquila on Malachi and Job?', VT 30 (1980), pp. 291–4; 31 (1981), p. 126.

(3) *The Amherst Papyri*, ed. by Grenfell and Hunt, I (1900), contain, amongst others, a letter with on the reverse side the text of Gen. 1:1–5 of the LXX and Aquila in handwriting from the time of Constantine (p. 31). The beginning reads: ἐν κεφαλέῳ ἔκτισεν θεὸς σὺν τὸν οὐρανὸν καὶ τὴν γῆν. (cf. A. Deissmann, *Light from the Ancient East* (1910), pp. 192 ff.).

(4) A few further Aquilanic readings have been identified since Field, sometimes in pre-Aquilanic contexts. Cf. P. Katz, 'Notes on the LXX. II. A fresh Aquila fragment recovered from Philo', JThSt 47 (1946), pp. 31–3; A. Rahlfs, 'Über Theodotion-Lesarten im Neuen Testament und Aquila-Lesarten bei Justin', ZNW 20 (1921), pp. 182–99; H. P.

Rüger, 'Vier Aquila-Glossen in einem hebräischen Proverbien-Fragment aus der Kairo-Geniza', ZNW 50 (1959), pp. 275–7. Cf. the index to Aquila's version: J. Reider, *Prolegomena to a Greek-Hebrew and Hebrew-Greek Index to Aquila* (1916); N. Turner, *An Index to Aquila* (suppl. to VT, 12) (1966) (revision and completion of Reider's Prolegomena); E. Tov, 'Some corrections to Reider-Turner's *Index to Aquila*', Textus 8 (1973), pp. 164–74.

The LXX translation of *Ecclesiastes* recalls Aquila's characteristic translation so strongly that one is tempted to assume that it is the latter (so Freudenthal, *Alexander Polyhistor*, 65; Grätz, *Koheleth* (1871), pp. 481 ff.; A. H. McNeile, *An Introduction to Ecclesiastes* (1904); H. St. J. Thackeray, *A Grammar of the Old Testament in Greek* (1909), p. 13, n. 2. Cf. also Barthélemy, *Les Devanciers*, pp. 21–30, dealing with the objections of, e.g., C. H. H. Wright, *The Book of Koheleth* (1883), p. 52). On the other hand, the translation actually attributed to Aquila in the hexaplaric notes frequently differs from the LXX text; cf. Jerome's reference to the two works, *Praef. in Ecclesiasten*, PL XXIII, 1062, CCL LXXII, p. 249. One text might be called *editio prima* of Aquila and the other *editio secunda* (so Grätz and McNeile), but it is more likely, although only hypothetical, that the Aquila version had been so firmly established in the LXX canon by the time of Origen that the version placed in the 'Aquila' column of the Hexapla had in fact no connection at all with Aquila but was simply inserted from another extant version to fill the gap, cf. Barthélemy, *op. cit.*, p. 30.

Bibliography

Field, F., *Proleg.*, pp. xvi–xxvii.
Krauss, S., 'Akylas der Proselyt', *Festschrift zum 80. Geburtstage M. Steinschneiders* (1896), pp. 148–63.
Friedmann, M., *Onkelos und Akylas* (1896).
Burkitt, F. C., and L. Ginzberg, 'Aquila', in JE (1902), pp. 34–8.
Swete, H. B., and R. R. Ottley, IOTG, pp. 31–42.
Abrahams, M., *Aquila's Greek Version of the Hebrew Bible* (1919).
Rahlfs, A., 'Über Theodotion-Lesarten im N.T. und Aquila-Lesarten bei Justin', ZNW 20 (1921), pp. 182–99.
Blondheim, D. S., 'Échos de judéo-hellénisme. Influence de la LXX et d'Aquila sur les versions néo-grecques des Juives', REJ 78 (1924), pp. 1–14.
Silverstone, A. E., *Aquila and Onkelos* (1931).
Möhle, A., 'Ein neuer Fund zahlreicher Stücke aus den Jesajaübersetzungen des Akylas, Symmachus und Theodotion', ZAW 52 (1934), pp. 176–83.
Walker, N., 'The Writing of the Divine Name in Aquila and the Ben Asher Text', VT 3 (1953), pp. 103 f.; cf. comments by P. Katz, VT 4 (1954), pp. 428 f.
Vaccari, A., 'S. Augustin, S. Ambrosius et S. Aquila', in *Augustinus Magister* (1955), pp. 473–82.
Katz, P., and J. Ziegler, 'Ein Aquila-Index in Vorbereitung', VT 8 (1958), pp. 264–85.
Kahle, P., CG, pp. 191–5.
Barthélemy, D., *Les Devanciers d'Aquila* (suppl. to VT, 10) (1963).

Smit Sibinga, J., *The O.T. Text of Justin Martyr*, i : *The Pentateuch* (1963).
Jellicoe, S., SMS, pp. 76–83.
Jellicoe, S., 'Aquila and his Version', JQR 59 (1968/9), pp. 326–32.
Soininen-Soisalon, I., 'Einiger Merkmale der Übersetzungsweise von Aquila', in *Wort, Lied und Gottesspruch (Festschrift für Joseph Ziegler)*, ed. J. Schreiner (1972), I, pp. 177–84.
Hyvärinen, H., *Die Übersetzung von Aquila* (1977).
Cf. also the introductions to the O.T., e.g., O. Eissfeldt, *The O.T., An Introduction etc.* (ET 1965), pp. 715 f., and other works cited above, pp. 491–3.

It may appear questionable whether *Theodotion* should be mentioned here at all since, like Symmachus, he is in one passage characterized by Jerome as an Ebionite. But Jerome himself in another passage describes him as a Jew and elsewhere explains that the Ebionite identification was only held by some. The opinion that Theodotion was a Jew, and more particularly a Jewish proselyte, is confirmed by Irenaeus, whose evidence cannot be discounted. Irenaeus' statement that Theodotion came from Ephesus is also likely to be correct, given the former's own Asiatic origins. Epiphanius' description of Theodotion as a Marcionite from Pontus who later proselytized to Judaism is of no independent value. The divergent testimonies of Irenaeus and Jerome may be due to confusion with Symmachus, but they would also be partially explained if Theodotion was a Jew who became temporarily attached to Jewish Christianity—hence the Ebionite tradition—before returning to Judaism. Modern identification of Theodotion with the first century A.D. Jonathan ben Uzziel to whom a targum, usually assumed to be into Aramaic, is ascribed in rabbinic texts (so Barthélemy, *Les Devanciers*, pp. 148–54), has little to recommend it. Even though Epiphanius' information is not in itself very trustworthy, his ascription to Theodotion of a date during the time of Commodus (A.D. 180–92) should probably be followed (see below, p. 500). In that case his work was carried out after Aquila but before that of the Jewish Christian Symmachus. In asserting this order, no weight should be put on the order of the columns in Origen's Hexapla, in which Theodotion was placed last, since this provides no evidence of the order of the translations themselves. The order of the Hexapla, whatever its rationale, was clearly not intended to provide a sort of historical survey of the development of the Bible in Greek.[36] Similarly, the fact that

36. There is no consensus on the reasons for the order of the Hexaplar columns. They may have been arranged solely on the basis of content, with Aquila next to the Hebrew text because it was most similar to it and Theodotion next to the LXX for the same reason, though the position of Symmachus next to Aquila would then be strange since this translation was in some cases not dependent at all on Aquila. H. M. Orlinsky, 'The Columnar Order of the Hexapla', JQR n.s. 27 (1936/7), pp. 139–49, has suggested that the order was intended to provide Christians with a textbook for learning Hebrew, but in such a scheme the sixth (Theodotionic) column would be redundant. It may be best to allow the possibility of chance in the order of columns three to six.

Irenaeus lists Theodotion before Aquila is mentioned is irrelevant for the dates of their translations. Theodotion's work generally had the same purpose as that of Aquila, i.e., to render a translation closer to the Hebrew text than the LXX, but he paid somewhat more attention to literary elegance than Aquila. A peculiarity of his work is his habit of transliterating Hebrew words into Greek, rather than providing translations, even more than Aquila and Symmachus did (Field, *Proleg.*, pp. xi ff., for instances of this). Theodotion, however, began his work with an already existing Greek translation before him, which he corrected after the Hebrew. In some cases, that translation will have been the Alexandrian LXX text, but in others it is clear that he used a different Greek version altogether which came into existence in the late pre-Christian era and is the source of 'Theodotionic' readings in first century A.D. texts that preceded Theodotion himself. (See below, pp. 501–2, on 'Ur-Theodotion'.)

No evidence exists concerning the use of this translation by the Jews. Some of his translation of Daniel has been preserved within the LXX tradition, although it cannot be assumed to be complete.[37] Probably through the editorial decision of Origen Theodotion's version of Daniel supplanted the Alexandrian text that had been in common use before. The original LXX version of Daniel has only survived in the following: in the tenth century Chigi cursive *Cod. Chisianus*, in a fragment among the Chester Beatty papyri covering about one third of Daniel,[38] and in the Syrohexapla (cf. above, p. 483; below, p. 503). Otherwise, many Theodotionic fragments have been preserved in the same way as those of Aquila. The publication of Mercati's find of the Hexaplaric Psalter in the Ambrosian library in Milan has also brought new Theodotionic material (cf. above, p. 483, n. 32).

Jerome, De viris illustr. 54 (PL XXIII, 702): 'Aquilae scilicet Pontici proselyti et Theodotionis Hebionei et Symmachi eiusdem dogmatis.' *Idem, Comment. in Habak.*, 3:11–13 (CCL LXXVIA, p. 64): 'Theodotio autem vere quasi pauper et Ebionita, sed et Symmachus eiusdem dogmatis, pauperem sensum secuti Iudaice transtulerunt ... Isti Semichristiani Iudaice transtulerunt, et Iudaeus Aquila interpretatus est, ut Christianus.' *Idem, Praef. in vers. Iob* (PL XXVIII, 1141–2): 'Judaeus Aquila, Symmachus et Theodotio, judaizantes haeretici.' However, elsewhere Jerome simply calls Theodotion a Jew. Cf. *Epist. 112 ad Augustin.* 19 (CSEL LV, p. 389): 'hominis Judaei atque

---

37. In Theodotion's revision of Daniel, the apocryphal additions were retained. From this they were translated by Jerome (PL XXVIII, 1386). Cf. further J. Ziegler, ed., *Susanna, Daniel, Bel et Draco* (²1977), pp. 28 ff., 61 ff. Against Theodotion as author of *any* of the 'θ' text in Daniel, cf. A. Schmitt, *Stammt der Sogenannte 'θ'-Text bei Daniel wirklich von Theodotion?* (NAG I.8 *Phil.-hist. Klasse*, no. 8) (1966).

38. F. G. Kenyon, *The Chester-Beatty Biblical Papyri* VII (1937), p. x.

blasphemi'. Jerome expresses himself most carefully in the *prol.*, *Comment. in Daniel* (CCL LXXVA, p. 774): 'Illud quoque lectorem admoneo, Danielem non juxta LXX interpretes sed juxta Theodotionem ecclesias legere, qui utique post adventum Christi incredulus fuit, licet eum quidam dicant Ebionitam, qui altero genere Judaeus est.' Irenaeus, iii 21, 1 (= Euseb., *Hist. eccl.* v 8, 10) ; cf the passage above, p. 495. Epiphanius, *De mensuris et ponderibus* 17–18.

As far as chronology is concerned, the conclusive point is that Theodotion was certainly older than Irenaeus, who mentions him explicitly. He therefore worked before the end of the second century A.D., cf. *Oxford Dict. Christ. Church* (²1974), s.v. 'Irenaeus'. The existence of Theodotionic readings before this date cannot be taken as evidence for the date of his recension, given the existence of an earlier translation ('Ur-Theodotion') from which he evidently worked. Indeed, the use of Theodotionic details within a basically Alexandrian version of Daniel by Justin Martyr in a long section of Daniel quoted in *Dial. c. Tryph.* 31, might reasonably be taken to suggest that no Theodotionic recension of Ur-Theodotion was yet available to Justin (see below, p. 502; cf. the study by J. Smit Sibinga, *The O.T. Text of Justin Martyr I: The Pentateuch* (1963). On both Irenaeus and Justin Martyr, see Swete and Ottley, IOTG, pp. 47, 414–24; Barthélemy, *Les Devanciers*, pp. 203–12. It is in fact the case that many Theodotionic readings are found widely scattered at a much earlier date.

Dan. 6:23 is found in the *Shepherd of Hermas, Vis.* iv 2, 4, in a form which agrees remarkably with Theodotion against the LXX (cf. Hort in *Johns Hopkins University Circular*, Dec. 1884, and Harnack, ThLZ, 1885, 146) ; the same passage occurs in *Clement of Rome* and *Barnabas* (cf. Schlatter, *Gesch. Israels,* ², 294).

That Theodotion is used in the Greek *Baruch*, c. 1–2, is almost unquestionable (cf. J. A. Montgomery, *The Book of Daniel* (1927), pp. 49 f.).

Already many contacts with Theodotion appear in *the New Testament* as well. The same passage from Dan. which is used in Hermas, *Vis.* iv 2, 4, is alluded to also in Heb. 11:33, in a text that agrees with Theodotion against LXX, cf. K. J. Thomas, 'The O.T. Citations in Hebrews', NTSt 11 (1965), pp. 303–25.

In Rev. sentences and expressions from Daniel are frequently used in a text more reminiscent of Theodotion than of the LXX (9:20; 10:6; 12:7; 13:7; 19:6; 20:4; 20:11). Cf. G. Salmon, *A Historical Introduction to the Study of the Books of the N.T.* (¹⁰1913), pp. 548–50; A. Bludau, 'Die Apokalypse und Theodotions Danielübersetzung', ThQ (1897), 1–26; H. B. Swete and R. R. Ottley, IOTG, p. 48. Cf. also R. H. Charles, *A Critical and Exegetical Commentary on the Revelation of St. John*, in the ICC series (1920), I, pp. lxvi-lxxxii. Most striking are the following two N.T.

passages: (1) 1 Cor. 15:54: κατεπόθη ὁ θάνατος εἰς νῖκος = Isa. 25:8, in exact agreement with Theodotion and marked departure from LXX (κατέπιεν ὁ θάνατος ἰσχύσας). Cf. here Barthélemy, *Les devanciers*, p. 148.
(2) Jn. 19:37: ὄψονται εἰς ὃν ἐξεκέντησαν = Zech. 12:10, similarly Rev. 1:7, correctly following the original text. The LXX translates ἐπιβλέψονται πρὸς μὲ ἀνθ' ὧν κατωρχήσαντο having read rkdw in place of dkrw. Jerome comments on this in his commentary on Zech. 12:10, CCL LXXVIA, p. 868. The correct ἐξεκέντησαν is also found in Justin, *Apol.* i 52 fin., *Dial. c. Tryph.* 14 fin. (in the first example the quotation from Zech. is more extensive, so that it cannot be from Jn. 19:37). It is reminiscent of Barnabas 7:9 (κατακεντήσαντες). But precisely this ἐξεκέντησαν is present in *Theodotion* and *Aquila*. Cf. for this passage generally: Böhl, *Die alttestam. Citate im N.T.*, pp. 110–12; Resch, *Ausserkanon. Paralleltexte* IV (1896), pp. 184 ff. In addition to these traces in the N.T., there are also some in Josephus, cf. A. Mez, *Die Bibel des Josephus* (1895), pp. 83 f.

A number of explanations may be given for these early Theodotionic readings. Theodotion may himself have worked before the apostles, as is asserted by Barthélemy, *Les devanciers*, pp. 144 ff., who identifies him with Jonathan ben Uzziel of the first half of the first century A.D. If so, however, the patristic evidence for his second century date would have to be discounted, and this is not warranted. Furthermore, against so early a date for Theodotion's recension is the *rarity* of Theodotionic traces in the N.T. and the tendency for such traces to be mixed up with readings from the LXX. Others have supposed, more plausibly, that there existed a 'Theodotion' before Theodotion. The exact nature of this 'Ur-Theodotion' is still disputed. It is possible that a revision of the LXX which was itself later revised by Theodotion existed before his time, cf. Mez, *op. cit.* It is more likely that a complete Greek version of the Bible quite separate from the main Alexandrian LXX tradition circulated in pre-Christian times and formed the basis of Theodotion's version in the second century A.D. (so J. Gwynn in *Dict. Christ. Biog.* IV (1887), cols. 970 ff.; H. St. J. Thackeray, *The Septuagint and Jewish Worship* (²1923), pp. 24 ff.). It has even been claimed that this version predates the LXX, cf. Kahle, CG, pp. 252–8. The later suppression of so much of this version would however be remarkable. Alternatively, Theodotionic readings of specific texts may have circulated in oral form as a sort of Hellenistic targum, cf. J. A. Montgomery, *The Book of Daniel* (1927), pp. 46 f. Finally, a quite full reconstruction of the transmission history of the Ur-Theodotionic version has been proposed by Barthélemy, who assigns it to Theodotion himself in the first century A.D. Barthélemy has made out a strong case for the identification of the καίγε recension represented in the Greek scroll of the Minor Prophets found in Qumran with that of Ur-Theodotion (cf. *Les devanciers*, pp.

33–47 on the καίγε group, but see also the cautious note about the inclusion of Theodotion in this group sounded by F. M. Cross, HThR 57 (1964), p. 283, n. 11). Cf. S. Jellicoe, 'Some reflections on the καίγε recension', VT 23 (1973), pp. 15–24. Barthélemy's claim that this was a *Palestinian* recension under the influence of the rabbis is however hypothetical,[39] and an origin in Alexandria or, given the use of this version by Asiatic writers, Western Asia Minor is likely, cf. Jellicoe, SMS, pp. 89–94; though a Syrian or Mesopotamian milieu has also been proposed, cf. K. Koch, 'Die Herkunft der Proto-Theodotion-Übersetzung des Danielbuches', VT 23 (1973), pp. 362–5. The fact that much of Theodotion's revision was apparently nonetheless based on the LXX rather than Ur-Theodotion or any other version (so Rahlfs, acc. to Würthwein, *The Text of the O.T.* ([2]1980), p. 54) may be explained either by supposing that in some books the LXX and Ur-Theodotion differed little (Swete), or that Ur-Theodotion was only a partial translation of the Bible intended to cover those books that the LXX covered badly or not at all (Jellicoe), so that Theodotion himself naturally had recourse to both versions. Whatever the materials with which he worked, there are no strong grounds for putting Theodotion's own work before that of Aquila (*contra* both H. M. Orlinsky, JQR n.s. 27 (1936–7), p. 143, n. 14, who ignores altogether the evidence of Epiphanius, and Barthélemy, *Les devanciers*, pp. 144–57, with the identification of Theodotion with the first-century A.D. Jonathan ben Uzziel). The order in which Irenaeus cites their work is irrelevant to their dating. It is true that Theodotion's work is much less laboriously faithful to the Hebrew than that of Aquila, and it is also true that its disappearance from Jewish tradition could be explained as a result of this. But there is no reason to assume *a priori* that any surviving less literal translation must mark a point in a progression towards acceptance of the stilted Greek of Aquila, and Theodotion's compromise between literalness and elegance may be accepted as a later work.

On the relation of Theodotion to the LXX, Jerome says in *Comment.*

---

39. D. Barthélemy, *Les devanciers d'Aquila* (1963), pp. 154–6. It should be seen that objections to the Theodotionic recension itself being of the first century A.D. do not preclude acceptance of the circulation of Theodotionic *readings* in an earlier form in the καίγε group. Barthélemy's arguments should therefore be accepted to this extent. On the other hand, identification of Ur-Theodotionic readings in later texts, including the Theodotion version in Origen's Hexapla, may well be impossible given the number of text revisions which may have taken place in the interim, cf. Barthélemy, *op. cit.*, pp. 253 ff., 267. Barthélemy's sole grounds for asserting the involvement of Palestinian rabbis in the translation seems to be the fact that the Minor Prophets scroll was found at Qumran. There is no reason to believe that this is particularly significant for the place of composition. The text of the Qumran scroll is similar to that in the Quinta, cf. G. Howard, 'The Quinta of the Minor Prophets: a first century Septuagint text?', Bibl. 55 (1974), pp. 15–22.

in Ecclesiasten 2:2 (CCL LXXII, p. 262): 'Septuaginta vero et Theodotion, sicut in pluribus locis, ita in hoc quoque concordant' (i.e. against Aquila and Symmachus).

The acceptance by the Christian church of Theodotion's translation of Daniel in place of the LXX is repeatedly affirmed by Jerome. Cf. *Contra Rufin.* ii 33 (CCL LXXIX, pp. 69–70; ed. Lardet, SC 303, p. 192); *Praef. comment. in Daniel* (CCL LXXVA, p. 774); *Praef. in version. Daniel* (PL XXVIII, 1357). One main reason for the rejection of the LXX was probably its false rendering of the important passages about the weeks of years, so Bludau, *Die alex. Uebersetzung des B. Daniel* (1897), p. 24; cf. Jellicoe, SMS, pp. 84–7, with the suggestion that the substitution of Theodotion's version for the LXX was made by Origen.

Bibliography

Hody, H., *De Bibliorum textibus* (1705), pp. 579–85.
Field, F., *Orig. Hexapl.*, proleg. pp. xxxviii-xlii.
Gwynn, J., 'Theodotion', DCB IV (1887), pp. 970–9.
Salmon, G., *A Historical Introduction to the Study of the Books of the N.T.* (⁸1897), pp. 538–51.
Torrey, C. C., 'The Apparatus of the Textual Criticism of Chronicles-Ezra-Nehemiah', *O.T. and Semitic Studies in Memory of William Rainer Harper* II (1908), pp. 55–111.
Swete, H. B., and R. R. Ottley, IOTG, pp. 42–9.
Charles, R. H., *A Critical and Exegetical Commentary on the Revelation of St. John*, in the ICC Series (1920).
Rahlfs, A., 'Über Theodotion-Lesarten im Neuen Testament und Aquila-Lesarten bei Justin', ZNW 20 (1921), pp. 182–99.
Wutz, F., *Die Transkriptionen von der Septuaginta bis zu Hieronymus*, I (1925), II (1933).
Montgomery, J. A., *A Critical and Exegetical Commentary on the Book of Daniel*, in the ICC Series (1927), pp. 46–50.
Möhle, F., 'Ein neuer Fund zahlreicher Stücke aus dem Jesajaübersetzungen des Akylas, Symmachos und Theodotion', ZAW 52 (1934), pp. 176–83.
Orlinsky, H. M., 'The Columnar Order of the Hexapla', JQR, new series, 27 (1936–7), p. 143.
Johnson, S. E., 'The biblical quotations in Matthew', HThR 36 (1943), pp. 135–55.
Cooper, C. M., 'Theodotion's influence on the Alexandrian text of Judges', JBL 67 (1948), pp. 63–8.
Roberts, B. J., *The O.T. Text and Versions etc.* (1951), 123–6.
Barthélemy, D., 'Redécouverte d'un chaînon manquant de l'histoire de la LXX', RB 60 (1953), pp. 25 ff.
Barthélemy, D., *Les devanciers d'Aquila* (1963).
Kahle, P. E., CG, 252–8.
Gil, L., 'Theodotion', EB VI (1965), cols. 934–5.
Jellicoe, SMS, pp. 83–94.
O'Connell, K. G., *The Theodotionic revision of the Book of Exodus* (1972).
Würthwein, E., *The Text of the O.T. etc.* (²1980), pp. 38 f.
Saiz, J. R. B., 'El texto Teodociónico de Daniel y la traducción de Simaco', Sefarad 40 (1980), pp. 41–55.

Note also the introductions to the O.T. by, e.g., O. Eissfeldt, *The O.T., An Introduction etc.* (ET 1965), pp. 715 ff. Cf. also above under the general bibliography on the LXX and Aquila.

II. Translations into Greek of Non-Scriptural Semitic Texts

The work of translating religious texts into Greek was not confined among Jews in the Hellenistic and Roman periods to the books of Scripture. Many other writings were also translated in this period. Of works of historiography, I Maccabees and Josephus *B.J.* were both put into Greek by a Jew soon after their original composition. Greek versions were also produced of the following: the Psalms of Solomon; the gnomic wisdom of Jesus ben Sira; the narratives of Judith, Tobit and Ahiqar; the pseudepigraphic prophecies in 1 (Ethiopic) Enoch, Assumption of Moses (Testament of Moses), 4 Baruch (The Chronicles of Jeremiah), 4 Ezra, and the Life of Adam and Eve; and the biblical midrash in Jubilees, the Martyrdom of Isaiah, and the Lives of the Prophets.[40] If, as is quite possible, many or most of the texts discussed below in 33 B and Appendix were also originally semitic compositions, they should also be added to the list of Jewish Greek translations.

Explicit external evidence of the origin of the translator is rarely to be found for these texts any more than for the Septuagint. The non-historicity of Ps.-Aristeas' account of the production of the Greek Pentateuch has been discussed above, p. 474. Of all the books of the Greek Bible only the book of Esther preserves a note about its translator. A colophon at the end of some of the manuscripts shows that it was the work of Lysimachus, the son of Ptolemy from Jerusalem, and that it had been brought to Egypt during the fourth year of King Ptolemy and Cleopatra by the priest Dositheus and his son Ptolemy. The trustworthiness of this information is probably not to be doubted,[41] but it does not yield a certain chronological result since there were several occasions when Egypt was ruled by a Ptolemy and a Cleopatra.

---

40. For the Greek text of the pseudepigraphic prophecies and the biblical midrashic works, see Denis, FPG, pp. 61–114, 118–20, 129–48. See also above, pp. 250, 278, 294, etc.

41. B. Jacob, 'Das Buch Esther bei dem LXX', ZAW 10 (1890), pp. 280–7, denied that the translation was made in Jerusalem on the grounds of Egyptian influence on the Greek, but close contacts with Egypt can be admitted without rejecting the colophon, since the names anyway imply this. More seriously, the colophon describes Dositheus as a 'priest and a Levite', cf. R. Marcus, 'Dositheus, Priest and Levite', JBL 64 (1945), pp. 269–71, *contra* E. J. Bickermann, 'The Colophon of the Greek Book of Esther', JBL 63 (1944), p. 348 = *Studies in Jewish and Christian History* I (1976), pp. 225–45, who proposes to read the personal name 'Leveites'; this must indicate some confusion. C. A. Moore, *Daniel, Esther and Jeremiah: The Additions* (1977), pp. 250–2, discusses the colophon and suggests that the repeated ἔφη indicates the colophonist's scepticism about Dositheus' claims about his origins. Nonetheless, the colophon is more likely to be genuine in its essentials than not.

A date in either *c.* 114 B.C., *c.* 77 B.C. or *c.* 48 B.C. would be possible; 114 B.C. is probably to be preferred.[42] It is quite striking that Esther should have been singled out in this way and it is possible that the need for a colophon asserting the authenticity of the translation is connected with the fact that the Greek text is extant in two widely differing versions, neither of which is at all close to the Masoretic Hebrew text.[43] The usual LXX text is represented by the main manuscripts, Vaticanus, Alexandrinus and Sinaiticus. A much shorter Greek text is found in Codd. 19, 93a and 108b. This shorter text may represent the 'Lucianic' recension of the LXX text, cf. P. de Lagarde, *Librorum Vet. Test. canonicorum pars prior graece* (1883), but it is impossible to prove dependence on the LXX text and it may be that it was a separate translation from the Hebrew, in which case the Hebrew text on which it depended presumably differed considerably from that which survives in the M.T.[44] If variant texts of Esther were in circulation at the time of Lysimachus' translation, that would explain the colophon concerning the authenticity of his version. It is likely, but not certain, that his text is the longer one since, although the colophon is appended to one of the three manuscripts of the short version, it is missing in the other two, although it is found in all the manuscripts of the long text.[45] Unfortunately, the possibility that the Hebrew text which he translated was not the one now extant makes it hard to judge the nature of his translation, as of much of the Septuagint.

Of the translations of the apocryphal books only the rendering of Ben Sira's work by his grandson can be similarly assigned a date and place. The preface to Ecclus. states that the translator came to Egypt in the thirty-eighth year of King Euergetes, i.e., Ptolemy VII Euergetes

---

42. B. Jacob, *art. cit.*, pp. 279 ff., proposes Ptolemy IX Soter II in *c.* 114 B.C.; E. J. Bickermann, *art. cit.*, pp. 339–62, suggests Ptolemy XII, *c.* 77 B.C.; J. B. Schildenberger, *Das Buch Esther* (1941), p. 21, suggests Ptolemy XIV in *c.* 48 B.C.; cf. also H. Willrich, *Judaica* (1900), p. 4.

43. Cf. C. C. Torrey, 'The Older Book of Esther', HThR 37 (1944), p. 1.

44. C. A. Moore, 'A Greek Witness to a Different Hebrew Text of Esther', ZAW 79 (1967), pp. 351–8; H. J. Cooke, 'The *A*-text of the Greek Version of the Book of Esther', ZAW 81 (1969), pp. 369–76; E. Tov, 'The "Lucianic" text of the canonical and the apocryphal sections of Esther: a rewritten biblical book', Textus 10 (1982), pp. 1–28. For further bibliography on these texts, see Brock, Fritsch and Jellicoe, pp. 112–13; Delling, *Bibliographie* 147–8.

45. C. A. Moore, *Daniel, Esther and Jeremiah: The Additions* (1977), p. 252. Whichever text contained the colophon is likely to have also contained some of the additions, but the differences between the additions in the two versions are too small to help in the present discussion, see below, §33B.I.2, p. 721. In favour of the antiquity of the shorter text is the presence of readings agreeing with it in the Old Latin, but both the Old Latin itself elsewhere and all the other ancient versions are based on the longer (LXX) text, apart from the Syriac and the Vulgate, which are based on the Hebrew, cf. Moore, *op. cit.*, p. 167.

Physcon, and, finding great scope for education, thought it very necessary to spend some energy and labour on the translation of his grandfather's book 'to publish it for the use of those who have made their home in a foreign land and wish to become scholars by training themselves to live according to the law'. His translation was therefore made in Egypt before the death of Euergetes in *c.* 116 B.C. Again, however, despite discoveries of Hebrew fragments at Qumran and Masada and a large part of a Hebrew version in a medieval manuscript from the Cairo Genizah, the relation of these texts to the Hebrew archetype is itself unclear (see above, p. 204) so that the nature of the text used by the Greek translator cannot be determined and only very general remarks can be made about his translation techniques. It is, however, salutary to note his own awareness that it is impossible for a translator to find precise equivalents for the original Hebrew in another language (Ecclus. *Prologue*).[46]

For all the other books translated into Greek in this period it is only possible to use the style and vocabulary as evidence for provenance. So, for example, the Greek text of the History and Maxims of Ahiqar, preserved as a section of the Life of Aesop, may derive from Egypt between 30 B.C. and A.D. 100 because of the use of Latin terms which presumably post-date Roman occupation (so B. E. Perry, *Aesopica* I, *Greek and Latin Texts* (1952), pp. 4–5).

Despite the problems in comparing these translations to their originals, enough can be discerned to suggest that they should be treated as compositions in their own right. The Septuagint is not always a literal translation, but sometimes a theological or haggadic commentary on the Hebrew text, sometimes a literary paraphrase, sometimes an amplification or curtailment (cf. Jellicoe, SMS, pp. 314–18, 321–2; E. J. Bickermann, 'The LXX as a Translation', PAAJR 28 (1959), pp. 1–39; C. Rabin, 'The Translation Process and the Character of the LXX', Textus 6 (1968), pp. 1–26; for further bibliography, see S. P. Brock, C. T. Frisch and S. Jellicoe, *A Classified*

---

46. On the translator and his work see: P. Auvray, 'Notes sur le prologue de l'Ecclésiastique', in *Mélanges A. Robert* (1957), pp. 281–7; H. J. Cadbury, 'The Grandson of Ben Sira', HThR 48 (1955), pp. 219–23; L. F. Hartmann, 'Sirach in Hebrew and in Greek', CBQ 23 (1961), pp. 443–51; D. de Bruyne, 'Le Prologue, le titre et la finale de l'Ecclésiastique', ZAW 47 (1929), pp. 257–63; J. H. A. Hart, 'The Prologue to Ecclesiasticus', JQR 19 (1907), pp. 284–97.

For the Greek text, see J. Ziegler, ed., *Sapientia Jesu Filii Sirach* (1965; ²1980).

For studies on that text, see especially J. Ziegler, 'Hat Lukian den griechischen Sirach rezensiert?', Bibl. 40 (1959), 210–29; *idem*, 'Ursprüngliche Lesarten im griechischen Sirach', in *Mélanges E. Tisserant* (*Studi e Testi* 231, 1964), pp. 461–87; Jellicoe, SMS, pp. 306–10.

Further bibliography in Brock, Fritsch and Jellicoe, *op. cit.*, pp. 129–32; Delling, *Bibliographie*, pp. 131–6.

Bibliography of the Septuagint (1973), pp. 34–7, and bibliography on individual books; E. Tov, 'Midrash-type exegesis in the LXX of Joshua', RB 85 (1978), pp. 50–61, with further references at note 1; cf. also above, note 29). All these aims combined with the special resonances of particular Greek words to produce a document with its own meaning quite different from the Semitic original (cf. C. H. Dodd, *The Bible and the Greeks* (1934, rp. 1954), pp. 3–95, and the numerous scholarly works on particular concepts in the LXX cited in Brock, Fritsch and Jellicoe, *op. cit.*, pp. 18–23). In just the same way, the translation of non-scriptural books by Jews in this period should be noted as a powerful means of spreading religious ideas among the Jews themselves, and perhaps also a gentile audience. In terms of literary output such translations may well have been just as influential among Greek-speaking Jews as independent compositions. Indeed, the fact that many such writings survive entire through preservation by early Christian authors who probably knew them only in their Greek form argues for a popularity greater than that enjoyed by the original Greek compositions which in many cases would have been entirely lost if they had not been quoted fragmentarily by pagan authors such as Alexander Polyhistor.

III. Prose Literature about the Past

The literary productions discussed so far are translations of Semitic works in which the Hellenistic elements imported by the use of Greek, though evident even in the LXX, are nonetheless not great. Potentially different are those Jewish-Hellenistic writings which in form are modelled on non-biblical, Greek compositions, in the field therefore of historical, poetical, and philosophical literature. First we deal with the historical writings. Biblical writers were less interested in history as such than as a pattern disclosing divine intervention in the world and as a source of instruction indicating how God should be served. For Hellenistic Judaism, however, a knowledge of past history was part of contemporary culture. A people could claim to be counted among the civilized nations only when it could point to a long and imposing history. Hence even nations earlier regarded as barbarian now hellenized their history in order to make it accessible to the civilized world. Hellenistic Jews also shared these aspirations. They too compiled their sacred history both for themselves and for the gentiles. It is reasonable to assume an apologetic tendency in all the history of this genre, even though it is often kept in the background. The most comprehensive work of this kind which we have is the great history of Josephus. He had however a number of predecessors who worked at sometimes larger and sometimes shorter periods of Jewish history in various forms, some in the sober style of annals (Demetrius), others with legendary midrashic embellishments *in maiorem Iudaeorum gloriam* (Eupolemus, Artapanus). Others, again, adopted a philosophizing manner to present the great Jewish Lawgiver as the best philosopher, indeed even as the father of all philosophy (Philo).

Hellenistic Jews did not, however, only compile accounts of biblical history in a style similar to and partly dependent on Palestinian midrash, they also recorded contemporary events (Jason of Cyrene, Philo, Josephus, Justus of Tiberias). Some writers worked in both areas. It is useful to consider in each case the extent to which the Jewish view of the past has been affected by the Greek literary genre. That genre, however, although well established by the Hellenistic period, was itself notable during that period for the diversity of approaches taken by historians, from the dry and antiquarian to the more common romantic and rhetorical history centred on individuals. It is sometimes hard to see anything Greek in the works of the Hellenistic Jewish historians apart from the language of composition. In such cases they are best understood within the midrashic traditions familiar from contemporary Semitic texts.

Most of the oldest Jewish-Hellenistic historians have been saved from complete oblivion only in the excerpts made by *Alexander Polyhistor*. Polyhistor's responsibility was not total, for a few texts may have been preserved through a different late first century B.C. chronographer, possibly Ptolemy of Mendes (see below, p. 520), and, since it is unlikely that his work was itself available to the main surviving authors (cf. N. Walter, 'Zur Überlieferung einiger Reste früher jüdisch-hellenistischer Literatur bei Josephus, Clemens und Euseb', *Studia Patristica* VII (1966), pp. 314–20), the role of other intermediaries was also crucial. At any rate, Alexander was a voluminous author, who lived about 80–40 B.C. (according to the statements of the Suda, s.v. Ἀλέξανδρος, and Sueton., *De gramm.* 20, cf. C. Müller, FHG III, p. 206, and the works mentioned below, especially Susemihl, Schwartz, Jacoby, FGrH III A, pp. 248 ff., and Stern, GLAJJ I, p. 157). He wrote among others a work entitled περὶ Ἰουδαίων, in which he strung together excerpts from non-Jewish authors about the Jews, apparently with only minor additions and critical comments of his own. Eusebius in turn included a large portion of this collection in his *Praeparatio evangelica* (ix 17–39). It is almost entirely to this circumstance that we owe our knowledge of the oldest Jewish-Hellenistic and Samaritan compilations of biblical history in prose and poetry: those by Demetrius, Eupolemus, Artapanus, Aristeas, Cleodemus, Philo, Theodotus, and Ezechiel. Besides Eusebius, Clement of Alexandria also once quotes Alexander's περὶ Ἰουδαίων (*Strom.* i 21, 130); and he probably uses it when he quotes from the authors of whom Alexander gave excerpts: Demetrius, Philo, Eupolemus, Artapanus, Ezechiel (*Strom.* i 21, 141; 23, 153–6). Josephus' quotation of Alexander in *Ant.* i 15, 1 (240) may also have come from περὶ Ἰουδαίων, since he probably betrays acquaintance with the work elsewhere, *C. Ap.* i 23 (218), although it is possible that this quotation came from Alexander's *Libyca*. There are a number of other possible traces in the *Antiquities*, and it is argued by some that Josephus uses Alexander very extensively, though this is still disputed, cf. Stern, GLAJJ I, p. 157, n. 2. But this is all that has come down of Alexander's writing in independent quotations.

Eusebius' excerpts are in chronological order of subject matter. They begin with fragments of the history of Abraham from Eupolemus, Artapanus, Molon, Philo, and Kleodemus. There follow parts of the history of Jacob from Demetrius and Theodotus; and finally of Joseph from Artapanus and Philo, etc. The nature of the text indicates that this order does not derive from Eusebius, but was followed before him by Alexander Polyhistor himself, for the individual sections are joined by means of connecting words by Alexander. This is confirmed by comparison with the quotations in Clement of Alexandria. As in Eusebius, that is to say, excerpts in Clement of the history of Moses directly follow one another:

Eupolemus = Euseb. ix 26 = Clement, *Strom.* i 23, 153.
Artapanus = Euseb. ix 27 = Clement, *Strom.* i 23, 154.
Ezechiel = Euseb. ix 28 = Clement, *Strom.* i 23, 155–6.

It is thus clear that this was the original order of Alexander Polyhistor.

The authenticity of Alexander's writing has been disputed, since it has been thought inconceivable that a gentile author such as Alexander should have had such a special interest in Jewish affairs. It has also been thought strange that he describes the O.T. Scriptures as ἱεραὶ βίβλοι (Euseb. ix 24, 29; 15 = Jacoby, FGrH IIIC 729 F3; 722, F2 and 4) and gives such detailed accounts here of Jewish history, whereas elsewhere he betrays a most peculiar ignorance of it. All this however can be seen to stem from Alexander's verbal dependence on his Jewish sources, cf. Freudenthal, pp. 174–84. The question is anyway of minor importance, since it does not really matter whether the excerpts were compiled by Alexander himself or by someone else. The extraordinary differences in form and content in these fragments guarantees in any case that these are extracts from works which really existed and not the unified work of a forger. It would nevertheless be of concern in determining the date if it could really be proved that the compilation was not made by Alexander Polyhistor, for then his lifetime could be dropped as a dating criterion. But since the fragments themselves give no cause for dating them to a later time, Alexander's responsibility for the compilation should be accepted. The most recent among the authors from whom excerpts are made and whose time can be determined independently of Alexander is Apollonius Molon (Euseb. ix 19), a Greek orator of the first half of the first century B.C. (cf. below, section VI).

It needs always to be kept in mind in the study of the Jewish Greek historians that this selection of material, first by Alexander Polyhistor and then by the early Church fathers, is likely to have produced a great distortion in the content of the surviving fragments. It should also be noted that Alexander seems to have made no distinction between Jewish and Samaritan writers. In this his decision has been helpful to modern scholarship since it is clear that the Samaritan authors often wrote within the same midrashic traditions and for similar reasons to their Jewish contemporaries, and an account of their work has therefore been included here.

Another work of Alexander Polyhistor was also concerned with biblical history, i.e., a *History of the Chaldeans*, in which he follows essentially Berossus (the title is not known exactly). Eusebius in particular makes much use of the work in his Chronicles. Cf. H. Gelzer, *Julius Africanus* II.1, pp. 24 ff.; Jacoby, FGrH IIIA, pp. 79, 109–14. In this work Alexander also quoted the Jewish Sibyl (Euseb., *Chron.*, ed. Schoene, I, col. 23; Cyrill., *Adv. Julian.*, ed. Spanh., 9c; Syncell., ed. Dindorf, I, p. 81; cf. Josephus, *Ant.* i 4, 3 (118); Freudenthal, pp. 25 f.; Jacoby, FGrH IIIA, pp. 110–11). According to the Suda, a work by him on Rome contained the strange assertion that the Jewish Law derived from a woman named Moso (Suda, s.v. Ἀλέξανδρος; Müller, FHG, no. 25; Jacoby, FGrH IIIA 273, F70; Stern, GLAJJ I, p. 163). It is possible that this work, otherwise unknown, was identical with his history of Italy (Jacoby, FGrH 273, F20). Also, the information that Judaea takes its name from Juda and Idumea, the children of Semiramis, probably springs either from his work on the Jews or his Chaldaean history (Steph. Byz., s.v. Ἰουδαία; Müller, FHG, nos. 98–102; Jacoby, FGrH, 273 F121; Stern, GLAJJ I, p. 164). It was these odd statements that gave rise to the denial of Alexander's authorship of περὶ Ἰουδαίων on the grounds that they are anti-Jewish. But it is unnecessary to assert any difficulty for Alexander in including in his works statements both friendly and hostile to the Jews. He simply copied what he found in the earlier documents. The value of his information therefore varies according to the quality of his sources.

The apparent ascription by Ps.-Justin, *Cohort. ad Graec.* 9, to Alexander of a statement about the date of Moses rests on a confusion and is not to be taken seriously.

Editions of the fragments περὶ Ἰουδαίων can be found in the following:

Eusebius, *Praeparatio Evangelica* (ed. Mras, GCS 43, 1954–6).
Clement of Alexandria, *Stromata* (vol. I, ed. Stählin and Treu, GCS 56 (³1972); vol. II, ed. Stählin and Früchtel, GCS 52 (³1960); vol. III, ed. Stählin, Früchtel and Treu, GCS 17² (²1970)). Also, ed. C. Mondésert et al., *Strom.* i (SC 30, 1951), *Strom.* ii (SC 38, 1954), *Strom.* v (SC 278, 1981).

Prose Fragments in:

Müller, C., FHG III, pp. 211–30.
Freudenthal, J., *Alex. Polyh.*, pp. 219–36.
Jacoby, FGrH III A, 273, F19.
Stern, GLAJJ I, pp. 159–63.

Bibliography

Müller, C., FHG III, pp. 206–44.
Vaillant, V., *De historicis qui ante Josephum res scripsere, nempe Aristea, Demetrio, Eupolemo, Hecataeo Abderita, Cleodemo, Artapano, Justo Tiberiensi, Cornelio Alexandro Polyhistore* (1851), pp. 88–98.
Freudenthal, J., *Alexander Polyhistor und die von ihm erhaltenen Reste jüdischer und samaritanischer Geschichtswerke* (1875). (Still the most important work.)

Susemihl, F., *Gesch. der griech. Litteratur in der Alexandrinerzeit* II (1892), pp. 356–64.
Schwartz, E., 'Alexander von Milet', RE I.2 (1894), cols. 1449–52.
Jacoby, FGrH IIIA Komm., pp. 248–313.
Denis, IPGAT, pp. 244–8.
Stern, GLAJJ I, pp. 157–64.
Wacholder, ESJL, pp. 44–52.

1. Demetrius

About sixty years after Berossus wrote the ancient history of the Chaldeans and Manetho that of the Egyptians, in *c.* 220–204 B.C., the Jewish Hellenist Demetrius compiled a brief chronological history of Israel following the sacred scriptures and producing, in his reworking of the biblical accounts, a dry but authentic version of native tradition. Clement of Alexandria (*Strom.* i 21, 141) gives the title of the work as περὶ τῶν ἐν τῇ Ἰουδαίᾳ βασιλέων and there is very little reason to doubt this. It is true that the fragments deal almost exclusively with the very early history of Israel, but this provides insufficient grounds to suppose this name to be incorrect since Justus of Tiberias, for example, also dealt with the time of Moses in his Chronicle of the Jewish kings, and Philo as well describes Moses as βασιλεύς (*Vita Mosis* ii 3–6). On the other hand, it is quite possible that Demetrius wrote more than one work, or that Clement quotes a title that applied only to the section of Demetrius' history that he was using. The first fragment in Eusebius, *Praep. ev.* ix 21, treats of the history of Jacob from his emigration to Mesopotamia until his death. It concludes with the genealogy of the tribe of Levi taken to the birth of Aaron and Moses. In this, the main interest is in chronology rather than in a history of the Greek type. The aim seems to have been to provide by chronological analysis a faithful confirmation of the text of Scripture, an aim which paradoxically led Demetrius occasionally to alter the Scriptural text to fit in with his chronological schemes, cf. Wacholder, ESJL, pp. 99–104. The precise time is established for every single occurrence in Jacob's life, e.g. for the birth of each of his twelve sons, etc. Naturally, many dates had to be postulated for which Scripture provides no clue. Nevertheless, a large part of the chronology is based on combinations, sometimes very complicated combinations, of real dates in Scripture. A second fragment (Euseb., *Praep. ev.* ix 29, 1–3), from the life of Moses, adds an interest in genealogy to that in dates, mainly attempting to prove that Zippora, the wife of Moses, was a descendant of Abraham and Keturah. This fragment is also used in *Chronicon paschale*, ed. Dindorf, I, p. 117, and is quoted with specific reference to Eusebius' *Chronicle* by Leo Grammaticus (*Cramer Anecdota Paris.*, II, p. 256 = Leo Grammaticus, ed. Bekker, 24: καθὼς ἱστορεῖ Δημήτριος, ὡς φάσκει Εὐσέβιος ἐν τῷ Χρονικῷ) and Georgius Cedrenus (ed. Bekker, I, p. 76, with exactly the same formula of quotation as in Leo Grammaticus). In a third fragment (Euseb., *Praep. ev.* ix 29, 15), the story is told of the bitter waters (Ex. 15:22 ff.). A fourth, brief, fragment, in Euseb., *Praep. ev.* ix 29, 16, concerns the problem of the origin of the weapons possessed by the Israelites in the desert. A fifth fragment in Euseb., *Praep. ev.* ix 19, 4, about Abraham's near-sacrifice of Isaac, is tentatively ascribed to Demetrius by Freudenthal, cf. Jacoby, FGrH 722, F7; Holladay, FHJA I, p. 62. Finally, the chronological fragment preserved in Clement of Alexandria's *Strom.* i 21, 141, defines precisely the time-span between the deportations into exile of the ten tribes and the tribes of Juda and Benjamin and until the reign of Ptolemy IV.

Clement of Alexandria, *Strom.* i 21, 141: Δημήτριος δέ φησιν ἐν τῷ περὶ τῶν ἐν τῇ Ἰουδαίᾳ βασιλέων τὴν Ἰούδα φυλὴν καὶ Βενιαμεὶν καὶ Δευὶ μὴ αἰχμαλωτισθῆναι ὑπὸ τοῦ Σεναχηρείμ, ἀλλ' εἶναι ἀπὸ τῆς αἰχμαλωσίας ταύτης εἰς τὴν ἐσχάτην, ἣν ἐποιήσατο Ναβουχοδονόσορ ἐξ Ἱεροσολύμων, ἔτη ἑκατὸν εἴκοσι ὀκτὼ μῆνας ἕξ. ἀφ' οὗ δὲ αἱ φυλαὶ αἱ δέκα ἐκ Σαμαρείας αἰχμάλωτοι γεγόνασιν ἕως Πτολεμαίου τετάρτου (221–205 B.C.) ἔτη πεντακόσια ἑβδομήκοντα τρία μῆνας ἐννέα, ἀφ' οὗ δὲ ἐξ Ἱεροσολύμων ἔτη τριακόσια τριάκοντα ὀκτὼ μῆνας τρεῖς.

The text of this fragment may be corrupt at a number of places, cf. Jacoby, FGrH 722, F6, *ad. loc.* (1) It is strange that Demetrius, so painfully accurate in his biblical chronology, could have reckoned the interval between the deportation of the ten tribes and the deportation of the tribes of Juda and Benjamin as 235 years (573, less 338), since it was in fact about a hundred years less. Hence the number 573 should perhaps either be reduced by one hundred, or 338 increased by one hundred. The latter is more likely to be correct for it can be shown that other ancient chronologists also made the post-exilic period too long (cf. above, under Daniel, pp. 249 f.). Accordingly, if Demetrius counted seventy years too many for this period, it is unjustified, precisely on that basis, to remove the error by changing 'Ptolemy IV' into 'Ptolemy VII' (Mendelssohn), for such a mistake in the post-exilic time, even by the careful Demetrius, cannot surprise us since the biblical dates completely let him down here.

(2) Through a shortening of the text the absurdity has arisen that Demetrius first denies a captivity on the part of 'Senachereim' and then reckons on the basis of this captivity. The meaning of the original text was undoubtedly that the tribes of Juda and Benjamin were not captured by Sennacherib, but only pillaged by him, and that 128 years elapsed between this plundering expedition and the deportation of Juda and Benjamin. It then agrees best with this calculation to count 135 years (573–438) from the deportation of the ten tribes to the deportation of Juda and Benjamin. For the deportation of the ten tribes by Shalmanezer actually took place about seven or eight years prior to Sennacherib's invasion of Judaea (2 Kg. 18:9–13). For a full discussion

of the chronological problems in the text, cf. E. J. Bickerman, 'The Jewish Historian Demetrios', in J. Neusner, ed., *Christianity, Judaism and other Greco-Roman Cults* III (1975), pp. 72–84. Bickerman's conclusion (pp. 80–4), that Demetrius may well have been totally confused about the duration of the exile as well as the post-exilic period, and that it is therefore wrong to amend any of the figures on the basis of our chronological knowledge, may be correct.

This fragment, which may well have been found by Clement in some compilation other than that of Alexander Polyhistor, also indicates when Demetrius lived. He clearly chose the time of Ptolemy IV (221–205 B.C.) as the terminus for his calculations because he himself lived during the reign of that monarch.

This fixed date is of great importance in ascertaining those of other Jewish writings in Greek.[47] Not least important, Demetrius' use of a translation of the Pentateuch similar to the LXX proves the existence of such a translation or something like it before the end of the third century B.C. Demetrius' methods show probable Hellenistic influence in, e.g., the characteristic literary technique of posing ἀπορίαι (but cf., *contra*, Wacholder, ESJL, p. 280, for a Jewish origin for this). Nonetheless, it is entirely obvious from the contents of the fragments that their author was a Jew. It would not have occurred to a gentile to take such pains in calculating and completing biblical chronology. As Eusebius says correctly, quoting Clement of Alexandria (*Hist. Eccl.* vi 13, 7), Demetrius was one of the Jewish writers who tried to show to the Greeks the antiquity of Moses and the Jewish people. The subject matter is entirely Jewish, Demetrius failing even to attempt any synchronization of biblical chronology with that of other peoples, but engaging in biblical criticism for its own sake. Josephus nevertheless may have thought him to be a gentile, perhaps because he identified him with Demetrius of Phalerum and took his information straight and uncritically from Alexander Polyhistor (*C. Ap.* i 23 (218) = Euseb., *Praep. ev.* ix 42), cf. Freudenthal, p. 170, note; but cf. Jacoby, FGrH 722 T1 = 723 T3, who suggests the excision of Φαλερεύς from the text. Eusebius, *Hist. Eccl.* vi 13, 7, and after him Jerome, *De vir. illustr.* 38 (PL XXIII, 687) however made the correct judgement. The intended

---

47. It is not at all implausible that a Jew should have reached such a level of literary sophistication in the third century B.C. in the Ptolemaic kingdom. The case of Dositheos b. Drimylus is instructive. The man is mentioned in 3 Mac. 1:3 as a renegade Jew of the time of Ptolemy IV Philopator. It appears from the papyri not only that the tradition in 3 Mac. is correct but also that Dositheos rose to become the royal ὑπομνηματογράφος, i.e. head of one of the two branches of the royal secretariat (CPJ I, no. 127). Such a position will have required literary expertise, which there is no reason to suppose was entirely confined to Jews who apostasized.

audience of the work cannot be known for certain, but it is hard to imagine any people other than Jews being tempted to read about biblical chronology in this form, and no polemic against gentile nations is ever made explicit (*contra* Fraser, PA I, p. 693, who argues that Demetrius intended to counter hostile Egyptian versions of the Exodus). The place of writing is also uncertain. Somewhere within the Ptolemaic kingdom is indicated by the reference to Ptolemy IV. That could as well be Palestine or Cyrene as the more commonly assumed origin, Alexandria. It cannot be taken for granted that Demetrius' use of a Greek Bible was occasioned by ignorance of Hebrew (cf. Wacholder, ESJL, pp. 281–2; *contra* Holladay, FHJA, vol. I, pp. 53, 55–6).

Editions

Fragments collected in:
Jacoby, FGrH 722, III C, pp. 666–7.
Denis, FPG, pp. 175–9.
Holladay, FHJA I, pp. 51–91.

Translations

English:
Holladay, FHJA, *loc. cit.*
Hanson, J. S., in Charlesworth, OTP II (forthcoming).

German:
Riessler, P., *Altjüd. Schrift.* (1928), pp. 241–5, 1280 ff.
Walter, N., *Fragmente jüdisch-hellenistischer Exegeten* (JSHRZ III.2) (1975), pp. 284–92.

Bibliography

Freudenthal, J., *Alexander Polyhistor* (1875), pp. 35–82, 205 ff., 219 ff.
Mendelssohn, L., *Anzeige Freudenthals in der Jenaer Lit.-Ztg.* (1875), no. 6.
Gutschmid, A. von, *Kleine Schriften* II, pp. 186 ff.
Gelzer, H., *Julius Africanus* (1880), pp. 87–9 (conjectured that Africanus used Demetrius).
Susemihl, F., *Gesch. der griech. Litt. in der Alexandrinerzeit* II (1891–2), pp. 647 ff.
Schwartz, E., 'Demetrios', in RE IV.2 (1901), cols. 2813–14.
Schlatter, A., *Geschichte*, pp. 72–5.
Gaster, M., 'Demetrius und Seder Olam. Ein Problem der hellenistischen Literatur', in *Studies and Texts in Folklore, Magic etc.* II (1928), pp. 650–9.
Dalbert, P., *Die Theologie der hellenistisch-jüdischen Missionsliteratur* (1954), pp. 27–32.
Gutman, Y., *The Beginning of Jewish-Hellenistic Literature* I (1958), pp. 132–9 (Heb.).
Hadas, M., *Hellenistic Culture, Fusion and Diffusion* (1959), pp. 94–5.
Walter, N., *Der Toraausleger Aristobulos* (1964), pp. 41–51, 97–9.
Wacholder, B. Z., 'How long did Abram stay in Egypt? A Study in Hellenistic, Qumran and Rabbinic Chronography', HUCA 35 (1964), pp. 43–56.
Walter, N., 'Untersuchungen zu den Fragmenten der jüdisch-hellenistischen Historiker' (Habilitationsschrift, Halle) (1967–8), pp. 15–36, 141–55.
Wacholder, B. Z., 'Biblical Chronology in the Hellenistic World Chronicles', HThR 6 (1968), pp. 452–8.
Denis, IPGAT, pp. 248–51.

Fraser, PA, vol. I, pp. 510, 690–4.
Bickerman, E. J., 'The Jewish Historian Demetrius', in J. Neusner, ed., *Christianity, Judaism and other Greco-Roman Cults : Studies for Morton Smith at Sixty* (1975) III, pp. 72–84 (repr. in *Studies in Jewish and Christian History* (1980) II, pp. 347–58).
Walter, N., *Fragmente jüdisch-hellenistischer Exegeten* (JSHRZ III.2) (1975), pp. 280–3.
Wacholder, ESJL, pp. 98–104, 280–2.
Holladay, C. R., 'Demetrius the Chronographer as Historian and Apologist', in *Christian Teachings : Studies in Honor of Lemoine G. Lewis* (1981), pp. 117–29.
Collins, BAAJ, pp. 27–30.

2. Eupolemus

In Eupolemus we find, instead of the dry, chronological calculations of Demetrius, a colourful narrative which deals freely with the biblical account, rewriting Scripture and embellishing it with various midrashic additions culled from his own imagination and Greek sources, including Herodotus and Ctesias as well as Jewish tradition. Here too, however, the main aim is to show the internal harmony of the biblical account, including its chronology, while demonstrating the magnificence of the past history of the Jewish people and its kings. Two titles of works by this author are mentioned in the ancient sources: (1) περὶ τῆς ʾΗλίου προφητείας, and (2) περὶ τῶν ἐν τῇ ʾΙουδαίᾳ βασιλέων.

However, the fragment assigned by Alexander Polyhistor to a work περὶ τῆς ʾΗλίου προφητείας (Eusebius, *Praep. ev.* ix 30–4) clearly belongs in fact to the history of the Jewish kings, cf. Jacoby, FGrH 723, F2, with the tentative emendation ἐν τινι πρὸ τῆς ῞Ηλει προφητείας and the suggestion that this passage is quoted from an early part of the history before Eupolemus dealt with the career of the young Samuel. There are, then, no grounds for positing more than one work.

A further large fragment assigned in Eusebius, *Praep. ev.* ix 17 to Eupolemus is generally attributed to a totally different writer, whose attitudes are seen as incompatible with those of Eupolemus. It is by no means certain that Eusebius was wrong in giving Eupolemus as the author, but the fragment will nonetheless be discussed separately (see below, no. 6, p. 528, on Ps.-Eupolemus).[48] If Eupolemus did indeed write this fragment, his work must have been more varied and syncretistic than is revealed by the rest of the surviving passages of his history. A

---

48. Identification of Pseudo-Eupolemus as a distinct historian, on the grounds of his divergent attitude towards the Samaritan site on Mount Gerizim and towards Abraham rather than Moses as the originator of knowledge, is now generally but not universally accepted. A. Schlatter, *Geschichte Israels* (³1925), pp. 187–92, denies any distinction between Eupolemus and Pseudo-Eupolemus and assigns both sets of fragments to an Alexandrian Jewish historian. Both W. G. Lambert, *The Background of Jewish Apocalyptic* (1978), p. 14, and F. Millar, 'The Background to the Maccabean Revolution: Reflections on Martin Hengel's "Judaism and Hellenism"', JJS 29 (1978), p. 6, n. 12, argue that the reference to Mount Gerizim is perfectly possible for a Palestinian Jew of the mid-second century B.C.

fragment, given in nearly identical form in Euseb. *Praep. ev.* ix 26, and Clement of Alexandria, *Strom.* i 23, 153, presents Moses as the 'first philosopher', who gave the knowledge of alphabetical writing to the Jews, which was then transmitted by them to the Phoenicians, and by the Phoenicians to the Greeks. The *Chronicon paschale*, ed. Dindorf, I, p. 117, and *Georgius Cedrenus*, ed. Bekker, I, p. 87, have this fragment as in Eusebius, and Cyril of Alexandria, *Adv. Julian.*, ed. Spanh., 231d, as in Clement. The large fragment in Euseb., *Praep. ev.* ix 30–4, refers to the history of David and Solomon. It begins with an account—much truncated, though this may have been due to the excerptor Alexander Polyhistor—of the chronology from Moses to David, then briefly relates the main events of the history of David (Euseb. ix 30), and after this gives, in the style traditional in Hellenistic historiography, an 'official' correspondence between Solomon and King Vaphres of Egypt and King Suron of Phoenicia concerning assistance in the building of the temple (Euseb. ix 31–4; cf. Clement of Alexandria, *Strom.* i 21, 130, *Chron. pasch.*, ed. Dindorf, I, p. 168). Finally, it describes in detail the building of the temple itself (Euseb. ix 34). The correspondence with Suron (= Hiram) is taken from 2 Chr. 2:2–15, cf. 1 Kg. 5:15–25 ; that with Vaphres is a free imitation of this model. Probably, the fragment in Euseb. ix 39, in which the story is told of how Jeremiah predicted the exile, and how this prediction was fulfilled in Nebuchadnezzar's conquest of Jerusalem, also belongs to Eupolemus. The fragment is anonymous according to some of the mss., but can be ascribed to Eupolemus on internal grounds (Freudenthal, pp. 208 ff. It is accepted tentatively by Jacoby, FGrH 723, F5, without hesitation by Holladay, FHJA I, p. 132).

Information concerning the date of Eupolemus is given in a chronological fragment in Clement of Alexandria, *Strom.* i 21, 141, which summarily calculates the time from Adam and Moses respectively to the fifth year of Demetrius or the twelfth year of Ptolemy. By this Demetrius is probably (cf. below) meant Demetrius I Soter (162–150 B.C.), so that Eupolemus probably wrote in 158/7 B.C., or shortly after. A date after 145 B.C. is proposed by W. Bousset and H. Gressmann, *Die Religion des Judentums* (³1926), p. 20, n. 2. He is almost certainly therefore identical with the Eupolemus mentioned in 1 Mac. 8:17 and 2 Mac. 4:11.

In that case he was from Palestine and may well be making a point about contemporary politics in his friendly attitude towards Egypt (Wacholder, ESJL, pp. 135–9), about Hasmonaean expansion in Palestine by his references to Solomon's expanded kingdom (M. Hengel, *Judaism and Hellenism* I (ET 1974), p. 93), and about the Maccabaean repurification of the Temple by his detailed account of Solomon's building (Hengel, p. 94). Furthermore, his writings may well have been one of the common sources of 1 and 2 Maccabees. A Palestinian origin is supported by the fact that, although he may have used the LXX of the Book of Chronicles (though this is dubious, see above, p. 477), he certainly also made use of a Hebrew text (Wacholder, ESJL, p. 252). Furthermore his Greek style is pompous, crude and poor, and the literary structure is Hebraic. It is certainly unlikely, on these grounds alone, that he came from Alexandria (Jacoby, RE VI, 1229). The hypothesis that he was a Palestinian who studied in Alexandria, cf. V. A. Tcherikover, *Eos* 48 (1956), p. 187, is not implausible, but unnecessary. As to whether he was a Jew or a gentile, ancient opinions vary as in the case of Demetrius. Josephus, *C. Ap.* i 23 (218) (= Euseb., *Praep. ev.* ix 42) suggests that he, like Demetrius, was a gentile, but since he is bracketed here with the elder Philo this may be intentionally misleading by Josephus. Eusebius, *Hist. eccl.* vi 13, 7, and Jerome, *De viris illustr.* 38, here dependent on Clement of Alexandria, *Strom.* i 23, 153, took him for a Jew and were undoubtedly correct, cf. Freudenthal, pp. 83–5, 109 ff. In general, the Jewish heritage is stronger in Eupolemus' writing than the Hellenistic. Even if his identity with the Eupolemus mentioned in 1 Mac. is not accepted, his interest in the Temple suggests that he was a priest, and the title 'On the kings of Judaea' has more Jewish than gentile parallels, cf. Wacholder, ESJL, p. 25.

Clement of Alexandria, *Strom.* i 21, 141 (= Jacoby, FGrH, 723, F4):

Ἔτι δὲ καὶ Εὐπόλεμος ἐν τῇ ὁμοίᾳ πραγματείᾳ τὰ πάντα ἔτη φησὶν ἀπὸ Ἀδὰμ ἄχρι τοῦ πέμπτου ἔτους Δημητρίου βασιλείας, Πτολεμαίου τὸ δωδέκατον βασιλεύοντος Αἰγύπτου, συνάγεσθαι ἔτη ͵εϱμθ. ἀφ᾽ οὗ δὲ χρόνου ἐξήγαγε Μωυσῆς τοὺς Ἰουδαίους ἐξ Αἰγύπτου ἐπὶ τὴν προειρημένην προθεσμίαν συνάγεσθαι ἔτη [δισ]χίλια πεντακόσια ὀγδοήκοντα. (ἀπὸ δὲ τοῦ χρόνου τούτου ἄχρι τῶν ἐν Ῥώμῃ ὑπάτων Γαΐου Δομετιανοῦ Κασιανοῦ συναθροίζεται ἔτη ἑκατὸν εἴκοσι).

In this fragment, as well, the text is defective. The number 2580 should perhaps be emended to 1580 by changing δισχίλια to χίλια (Clinton), which would bring the date of the Exodus closer to the actual date and to that given in the LXX, but the unemended text leaves Eupolemus in closer harmony with the date of the Exodus in the proto-Masoretic tradition, cf. Wacholder, ESJL, pp. 112, 250–4; Holladay, FHJA I, p. 155, n. 120. There are difficulties with the synchronization of the fifth year of Demetrius and the twelfth year of Ptolemy. The fifth year of Demetrius I (158/7 B.C.) coincided with the twelfth year of Ptolemy VIII Euergetes II Physcon (159/8 B.C.), but Ptolemy VIII Physcon was at that time only ruler of Cyrenaica, not of Egypt as Eupolemus states, while his brother, Ptolemy VI Philometor, who reigned at the same time in Egypt, had begun his rule at most seven years earlier. The whole statement about Ptolemy may be a gloss by Clement or an intervening source, or the number may be corrupt (Gutschmid; cf. Jacoby, RE VI.1 (1907), 1228). However this may be, the hypothesis that Demetrius I Soter is meant is supported by the fact that this was the view of Clement of Alexandria, and it should be accepted. Clement, or the source from which he quotes Eupolemus, counted from the fifth year of Demetrius to the consulship of Cn. Domitius Calvinus and C. Asinius Pollio (these names are certainly to be read instead of the corrupt reading Γαΐου Δομετιανοῦ Κασιανοῦ; cf. Freudenthal; Jacoby, FGrH 723, F4, with other suggested emendations *ad loc.*), i.e. to 40 B.C., when Herod was named king (Jos. *Ant.* xiv 14, 5 (389)), a total of 120 years which necessarily reaches back to Demetrius I, even though the calculation is not quite accurate. This closing sentence cannot have been written by Eupolemus himself but was added by a later writer, presumably in 40 B.C. since the end date is otherwise hard to understand. Gutschmid's restoration of these words as Γναΐου Δομετίου καὶ Ἀσινίου ὑπὸ Κασιανοῦ συναθροίζεται, indicating that they were derived from the second century A.D. Gnostic chronographer Julius Cassianus, has been correctly challenged by N. Walter, 'Der angebliche Chronograph Julius Cassianus', in *Stud. zum Neuen Testament und zur Patristik: Erich Klostermann zum 90 Geburtstag* (1961), pp. 177–92. The name of the chronographer who added the 40 B.C. date is therefore uncertain. It may have been Alexander Polyhistor, or Ptolemy of Mendes (Wacholder), or an unknown author.

Editions

Jacoby, FGrH III C, 723, pp. 671–8.
Denis, FPG, pp. 179–86.
Holladay, FHJA I, pp. 112–35.

Translations

English:
Wacholder, ESJL, Appendix A.
Holladay, *loc. cit.*
Fallon, F., in Charlesworth, OTP II (forthcoming).

German:
Riessler, P., *Altjüd. Schrift.* (1928), pp. 328–33, 1287 f.
Walter, N., *Fragmente jüdisch-hellenistischer Historiker* (JSHRZ I.2) (1976), pp. 99–108.

Bibliography

Freudenthal, J., *Alex. Polyh.*, pp. 82 ff., 105–30, 208 ff., 225 ff.
Gutschmid, *Jahrbb. f. prot. Theol.* (1875), 749 ff. = Gutschmid, *Kleine Schriften* II (1890), pp. 191 ff.
Schlatter, A., 'Eupolemus als Chronolog und seine Beziehungen zu Josephus und Manetho', ThStKr (1891), 633–703 (very hypothetical).
Susemihl, F., *Gesch. der griech. Litt.* II (1891–2), pp. 648–51.

Krauss, S., 'Eupolemus', JE V (1903), p. 269.
Jacoby, F., 'Eupolemos', RE VI.1 (1907), cols. 1227–9.
Schnabel, P., *Berossos und die babylonische-hellenistische Literatur* (1923), pp. 67–9.
Schlatter, A., *Geschichte Israels* (³1925), pp. 187–92.
Bousset, W., and H. Gressmann, *Die Religion des Judentums* (³1926), pp. 20, 494–5.
Weinreich, O., 'Gebet und Wunder. Zwei Abhandlungen zur Religions- und Literatur-geschichte', *Tübinger Beiträge zur Altertumswissenschaft* (Genethliakon Wilhelm Schmidt) (1929), pp. 298–309.
Dalbert, P., *Die Theologie der hell.-jüd. Missionsliteratur* (1954), pp. 35–42.
Schunck, K. D., *Die Quellen des I. und II. Makkabäerbuches* (1954), pp. 70–4.
Vermes, G., 'La figure de Moïse au tournant des deux testaments', *Moïse, l'homme de l'Alliance* (1955), p. 68.
Hadas, M., *Hellenistic Culture* (1959), pp. 95–6.
Gutman, Y., *The Beginnings of Jewish-Hellenistic Literature* II (1963), pp. 75–94.
Giblet, J., 'Eupolème et l'historiographie du Judaïsme hellénistique', EThL 39 (1963), pp. 539–54.
Walter, N., 'Untersuchungen zu den Fragmenten der jüdisch-hellenistischen Historiker' (Habilitationsschrift, Halle) (1967–8), pp. 37–56, 156–75.
Wacholder, B. Z., 'Biblical Chronology in the Hellenistic World Chronicles', HThR 61 (1968), pp. 451–81.
Denis, IPGAT, pp. 252–5.
Fraser, PA, vol. I, p. 694; vol. II, p. 962.
Hengel, M., *Judaism and Hellenism* I (ET 1974), pp. 92–5.
Momigliano, A., *Alien Wisdom : The Limits of Hellenization* (1975), pp. 93, 113.
Wacholder, B. Z., *Eupolemus : A Study of Judaeo-Greek Literature* (1974) (ESJL).
Walter, N., *Die Fragmente jüd.-hell. Hist.* (JSHRZ I.2) (1976), pp. 93–8.
Collins, BAAJ, pp. 40–2.
Holladay, FHJA I, pp. 93–156.

3. Artapanus

Artapanus in his colourful historical romance περὶ 'Ιουδαίων is still further removed from the sober style of Demetrius than Eupolemus. In his hands, biblical history is embellished, or rather remodelled, in a haggadic style with the purpose of glorifying the Jewish people. Special attention is directed to proving that the Egyptians owed all useful knowledge and institutions to the Jews. Thus the first fragment (Euseb. *Praep. ev.* ix 18) recounts that when Abraham immigrated into Egypt he taught King Pharetothes (or Pharetones) astrology. A second fragment (Euseb. ix 23) tells how Joseph, raised by the king to be chief governor of the country, provided better cultivation of the land. But the whole of the large section on Moses (Euseb. ix 27) gives detailed evidence that he was the real founder of all culture in Egypt, even of the worship of the gods. It seems clear that this life of Moses was intended as the central motif of the work and that the sections on Abraham and Joseph were only intended as introductory. Moses is the hero whom the Greeks called Musaeus,[49] the teacher of Orpheus, the author of many useful

---

49. The name Μουσαῖος for Moses is found in the second century A.D. pagan philosopher Numenius of Apamea, quoted in Eusebius, *Praep. ev.* ix 8, 2. Otherwise the

inventions and skills: navigation, architecture, military science, and philosophy. He also divided the land into thirty-six provinces, and commanded each province to worship God. He gave the priests the sacred writing-characters. He set right the affairs of state. Therefore he was loved by the Egyptians and called Hermes, 'because of the interpretation (ἑρμηνείαν) of the sacred writings'. But the king was envious and wanted to be rid of him. Yet none of the methods which he chose were successful. When King Chenephres contracted elephantiasis and died, Moses was commanded by God to free his people from Egyptian slavery. Then the story of the exodus and of all the events preceding it, especially the miracles which procured it, are recounted in detail, following the biblical narrative but with many trimmings and embellishments.

Some elements of this fragment are also found with explicit reference to Artapanus in Clement of Alexandria, *Strom.* i 23, 154, in *Chron. pasch.*, ed. Dindorf, I, p. 117, in *Chron. anonym.* by Cramer, *Anecdota* II, p. 176, by Georgius Cedrenus, ed. Bekker, I, pp. 86–7 (here without mention of Artapanus). Traces can also be found in Ps.-Dionysius of Telmahre (cf. Gelzer, *Julius Africanus* II, 1, p. 400), and later Syriac sources, cf. S. P. Brock, 'Syriac legends concerning Moses', JJS 33 (1982), pp. 237–55. Traces of the use of this work can be seen especially in Jos. *Ant.* ii 9, 1—16, 6 (201–349) (cf. Freudenthal, pp. 169–71). This influence may have been direct or through a later tradition taken by an intervening writer from the quotations of Artapanus in Alexander Polyhistor or elsewhere, but at any rate it is helpful in the clarification of the Artapanus narrative when that is fragmentary.

The clearer it becomes that Artapanus was, a Jew, the more surprising it may appear that Moses and the patriarchs are represented as the founders of the Egyptian cult of the gods. Jacob and his sons are said to have founded the sanctuaries at Athos and Heliopolis (Euseb. ix 23, 4), Moses to have instructed each province to worship its special god (27, 4), and to have prescribed the consecration of the Ibis (27, 9) and the Apis (27, 12). In short, the Egyptian cult is traced back to Jewish authorities. Freudenthal explained this fact by assuming that the author was indeed a Jew but wished to be taken for a gentile, and indeed for an Egyptian priest (149 ff., 152 ff.), which is incorrect. Nowhere is there any clear evidence of such an attempt. The knowledge of Egyptian religion displayed by Artapanus is mediated through Hellenistic sources as in the equation of Thoth with Hermes. In particular, an unknown name such as Artapanus would not have been

---

Greek forms of the name of Moses varied, cf. J. G. Gager, *Moses in Greco-Roman Paganism* (1972), p. 20 and *passim*.

chosen as a cover for this purpose.[50] Also, the phenomena themselves are not explained by this hypothesis, for, if the work appeared under a heathen mask, it would be expected to inveigh energetically against the horror of idol-worship in the name of the acknowledged authority, as is actually the case with the Sibyl (iii 30) and Ps.-Aristeas 134–9. Therefore the surprising fact remains that a Jewish writer represented Moses as the founder of Egyptian religion. Yet however strange this may seem, it can be explained from the trend of the whole, and is not impossible for a Jew with this sort of apologetic intent. Moses introduced *all* culture, even religious culture: this is the meaning and nothing else. It should be noted also that the gentile cult is basically represented in a fairly harmless light—Artapanus is not a polytheist, nor an assimilationist. The sacred animals were not so much worshipped as 'consecrated' to God on account of their usefulness. Nevertheless, if the narrative excerpted by Polyhistor is a sufficient guide, it seems that this Jewish author was more interested in the glory and honour of the Jewish nation than in the purity of divine worship. Perhaps, also, an apologetic purpose played a part here, i.e. to represent the Jews, who had been decried as mockers of the gods, as founders of religious cults, and in the case of Moses to offer a positive denial of slanders by gentile writers, particularly Manetho, of the name of the Lawgiver, though in the form of a general panegyric rather than specific apologetic. No further proof is needed that the author was Egyptian than the marked prominence of Egyptian references, and in particular his portrayal of Moses as an Egyptian patriot. It is possible that, given his interest in native Egyptian traditions, he came from one of the Jewish settlements in Egypt other than Alexandria. His probable reliance in Euseb. *Praep. ev.* ix 18, 1, on a tradition based on a Hebrew text of Gen. 14:13 for the claim that the Jews were called 'Hebrew' after Abraham (cf. Holladay, FHJA I, p. 226, n. 5) does not show that he himself knew any Hebrew.

With regard to his date we can only say with certainty that he, like most of the other historians examined here, must have lived before Alexander Polyhistor. His use of the LXX suggests a date after *c.* 250 B.C. More precise dating is only speculative. The latest date suggested has been *c.* 100 B.C. (Walter). The argument of Wacholder, HThR 61 (1968), p. 460, n. 34, that Artapanus' form of non-assimilationist syncretism would be unthinkable after the Maccabaean revolt is, even if true, not applicable to the Egyptian Jewish community. The much earlier dating, to the end of the third century B.C., rests on parallels between the attempt of Ptolemy IV Philopator (221–205 B.C.) to

---

50. The name is Persian, like Artabazus, Artaphernes, Artavasdes, Artaxerxes, and also occurs in the form Artabanus. No Persian by this name who was an authority on religious matters is known, cf. Fraser, PA II, p. 985, n. 199.

organize the cult of Dionysus and the treatment of Moses by the Pharaoh according to Artapanus, cf. L. Cerfaux, *Recueil L. Cerfaux* I (1954), pp. 81–5, who suggests that Artapanus reflects an attempt by Ptolemy IV to promote a Jewish Dionysiac cult. However, the evidence for such an attempt is still uncertain. Dates based on the mention of elephantiasis (Wacholder), the inclusion of Egyptian farmers in Moses' army (Collins), the reference, at Euseb. *Praep. ev.* ix 23, 4, to a temple not explicitly connected to the Oniad Jewish temple at Leontopolis (Holladay), or alleged dependence on Hecataeus, Ps.-Hecateus or Eupolemus (cf. Holladay, FHJA I, p. 190), are all too speculative to be useful.

Editions

Jacoby, FGrH 726, III A, pp. 680–6.
Denis, FPG, pp. 186–95.
Holladay, FHJA I, pp. 189–243.

Translations

English:
Holladay, *ad loc.*
Collins, J. J., in Charlesworth, OTP II (forthcoming).

German:
Riessler, P., *Altjüd. Schrift.* (1928), pp. 186–91, 1276 f.
Walter, N., *Die Fragmente jüdisch-hellenistischer Historiker* (JSHRZ I.2) (1976), pp. 127–36.

Bibliography

Freudenthal, J., *Alex. Polyh.* (1875), pp. 143–74, 215 ff., 231 ff.
Susemihl, F., *Gesch. der griech. Litt.* II (1892), pp. 646 ff.
Schwartz, 'Artapanus', RE II.1 (1895), 1306. Lévi, I., 'Moïse en Ethiopia', REJ 53 (1907), pp. 201–11.
Schlatter, A., *Gesch. Israels* ([3]1925), pp. 193–6.
Halévy, M. A., *Moïse dans l'histoire et dans la légende* (1927), pp. 54–5, 61.
Goodenough, E. R., *By Light, Light!* (1935, repr. 1969), p. 291.
Heinemann, I., 'Moses', RE XVI.1 (1935), 365–9.
Bieler, L., *ΘΕΙΟΣ ANHP. Das Bild des 'Göttlichen Menschen' in Spätantike und Frühchristentum* II (1936, repr. 1967), pp. 26, 30–3.
Braun, M., *History and Romance in Greco-Oriental Literature* (1938), pp. 26–31, 99–102.
Dalbert, P., *Die Theologie der hell.-jüd. Missionsliteratur* (1954), pp. 42–52.
Vermes, G., 'La figure de Moïse au tournant de deux testaments', in *Moïse, l'homme de l'alliance* (1955), pp. 63–92 (= STJ, pp. 80–2).
Tonneau, R. M., 'Moïse dans la tradition syrienne', in *Moïse, l'homme de l'alliance* (1955), pp. 245–65.
Hadas, M., *Hellenistic Culture* (1959), pp. 96 ff.
Merentitis, K. I., *Ho Ioudaios Logios Artapanos kai to Ergon autou* (1961).
Gutman, Y., *The Beginning of Jewish-Hellenistic Literature* II (1963), pp. 109–35.
Georgi, D., *Die Gegner des Paulus im 2. Korintherbrief* (1964), pp. 147–51, 201.
Denis, IPGAT, pp. 255–7.
Schalit, A., 'Artapanus', Enc. Jud. (1971), 645–6.
Tiede, D. L., *The Charismatic Figure as Miracle-Worker* (1972), pp. 146–77.
Fraser, PA I, pp. 704–6, 714.

Hengel, M., *Judaism and Hellenism* I (ET 1974), pp. 90–4.
Walter, N., *Die Fragmente jüd.-hell. Historiker* (JSHRZ I.2) (1976), pp. 121–6.
Holladay, C. R., *THEIOS ANER in Hellenistic Judaism* (1977), pp. 199–232.
Rajak, T., 'Moses in Ethiopia: Legend and Literature', JJS 29 (1978), pp. 111–22.
Conzelmann, H., *Heiden, Juden, Christen* (1981), pp. 149–52.
Brock, S. P., 'Syriac legends concerning Moses', JJS 33 (1982), pp. 237–55.
Collins, BAAJ, pp. 32–8.
Holladay, FHJA I, pp. 189–201.
Runnalls, D., 'Moses' Ethiopian campaign', JSJ 14 (1983), pp. 135–56.

4. Aristeas the Exegete

Eusebius, *Praep. ev.* ix 25, gives a fragment from the work περὶ 'Ιουδαίων of the otherwise unknown author Aristeas. 'Concerning Jews', which may be a title or a description of the work, briefly tells the history of Job following the biblical account. The story itself contains nothing noteworthy except that particulars concerning Job and his friends are added from other biblical material in an attempt to elucidate the original account in a way similar to that used by Demetrius. Thus it is said of Job that he used to be called Jobab, the son of Esau. In the Genesis account, Jobab is a son of Zerah (Gen. 36:33), and the latter a grandson of Esau (Gen. 36:10 and 13). Admittedly, according to the excerpt of Alexander Polyhistor, Aristeas is said to have related that Esau himself 'married Bassara in Edom and begot a son Job of her'. But most probably this is based on an inaccurate reference of Alexander Polyhistor, and Aristeas may have got the relationship of Esau to his great-grandson right. In that case υἱόν should perhaps be omitted, following one manuscript (Freudenthal) or, if retained, put down to Polyhistor's carelessness. The name of Bassara as Job's mother (Ἰωβὰβ υἱὸς Ζαρὰ ἐκ βοσόρρας) also comes from Gen. 36:33. Actually Bozrah in the Hebrew is not the mother but Jobab's home. It is noticeable that Aristeas' mistake is only possible from a Greek version of the Bible such as the LXX, as indeed is the connection of Job with Jobab, but it is remarkable that the epilogue to Job in the LXX compiles personal information about Job in exactly the same way as Aristeas. Freudenthal considered that this supplement certainly depended on Aristeas, but this is hard to reconcile with the LXX's reference to 'the Syrian book' as the source of the appendix. It is probable that Aristeas used the LXX of Job, though possible that both versions depend upon a common oral exegetical tradition. The identification of Job and Jobab appears also in the Testament of Job and elsewhere (cf. below, p. 552). The date of Aristeas therefore lies before the time of Polyhistor and probably after *c.* 250 B.C., the date of a Greek translation of Genesis. The place of origin is unknown and cannot be suggested even tentatively. There are no grounds for postulating any relation between this Aristeas and the pseudonymous author of the Letter of Philocrates, despite the reference in the Letter, c. 6, to an earlier work by the author. The two writings are of quite different style and this Aristeas, unlike the other, is quite openly Jewish.

Editions

Müller, C., FHG III, pp. 207 ff.
Jacoby, FGrH 725, III C, p. 680.
Denis, FPG, pp. 195–6.
Holladay, FHJA I, pp. 261–75.

Translations

English:
Holladay, *loc. cit.*
Doran in Charlesworth, OTP II (forthcoming).

German:
Riessler, P., *Altjüd. Schrift.* (1928), pp. 178, 1275.
Walter, N., *Die Fragmente hell.-jüd. Exegeten* (JSHRZ III.2) (1975), pp. 295–6.

Bibliography

Schwartz, E., RE II.1 (1895), 879.
Wendland, P., 'Aristeas the Historian', JE II (1902), p. 92.
Gray, G. B., 'The Addition in the Ancient Greek Version of Job', *The Expositor* 19 (1920), pp. 422–38, esp. 431–4.
Schlatter, A., *Geschichte Israels* (³1925), pp. 75–7.
Ginzberg, L., *The Legends of the Jews* V (1925, repr. 1968), p. 384.
Dalbert, P., *Die Theologie der hell.-jüd. Missionsliteratur* (1954), pp. 67–70.
Walter, N., 'Untersuchungen zu den Fragmenten der jüd.-hell. Historiker' (Habilitationsschrift, Halle) (1967–8), pp. 86–92, 216–21.
Denis, IPGAT, pp. 258–9.
Wacholder, B. Z., 'Aristeas', Enc. Jud. II (1971), pp. 438–9.
Hengel, M., *Judaism and Hellenism* I (ET 1974), p. 169.
Collins, BAAJ, pp. 30–1.

5. Cleodemus or Malchus

The mythology of a certain Cleodemus or Malchus, on which we unfortunately possess only a short note, appears to have presented a classic example of the mixture popular throughout the field of Hellenism of native (Oriental) and Greek traditions. The relevant report by Alexander Polyhistor can be found in Euseb. *Praep. ev.* ix 20, who quotes Josephus, *Ant.* i 15, 1 (240), who in turn quotes Alexander Polyhistor literally. Here the author is described as 'Cleodemus the prophet also called Malchus, in his history of the Jews relates in conformity with the narrative of their lawgiver Moses'. Both the Semitic name Malchus, and the content of his work, prove that the author was not a Greek by origin, but either a Semitic pagan, or a Jew or a Samaritan. A pagan origin is proposed by Wacholder, ESJL, p. 54, n. 114; p. 55, n. 119, on the grounds that Moses is referred to as 'their' lawgiver, the designation 'prophet' is unlikely for a Jew in this period, and Josephus quotes him as if he were a pagan author, cf. *idem*, Enc. Jud. V (1971), 603. None of these arguments is strong, given the implausibility of pagan interest in producing such an account. Reference to 'their' language may be due to the transmission of the text by Alexander Polyhistor, and Josephus quotes other Jewish authors as if they were gentile (see above, p. 514, on Demetrius). Freudenthal preferred a Samaritan origin, mainly because of the fusion of Greek and Jewish traditions, and he is followed by Fraser, PA II, p. 963, who accordingly also agrees with Freudenthal in identifying Herakles in the Cleodemus fragment with Melkart, to whom the Samaritans dedicated the Mount Gerizim temple. Such a fusion of traditions was however just as possible for a Jew after *c.* 200 B.C. as for a Samaritan, and it is reasonable to accept the implication of the title given to his work by Alexander Polyhistor that he was a Jew. This Malchus relates in his work that Abraham had three sons by Keturah, Ἀφέραν, Ἀσουρειμ, and Ἰάφραν (the precise names vary considerably in the mss., cf. Jacoby, FGrH 727, apparatus; Holladay, FHJA I, pp. 252, 254), from whom the Assyrians, the town of Aphra, and the land of Africa received their names. These are obviously identical with the names in Gen. 25:3–4 of Asshurim, Ephah and Epher. But, whereas Arab tribes are intended in Gen. 25, our author derives from them entirely different nations known to him. He records further that the three sons of Abraham went with Heracles to Libya and Anteus, and that Heracles married the daughter of Aphra and had a child called Diodorus, whose son was Sophonas, after whom the Sophaki were named.

The latter legends are also found in Plutarch, *Sertor.*, 9, except that the genealogical relation of Diodorus and Sophax is reversed: Sophax is the child of Heracles and Tinge, the widow of Anteus, and Diodorus the son of Sophax.[51]

Cleodemus-Malchus presumably wished to win for the Jews a share in the Phoenician glory of the colonization of Africa, prompted perhaps by the problems of the Punic colonies, especially Carthage, from the third century B.C. onwards, and the resulting change in attitude to their Phoenician neighbours by the North African Jews (so Gutman; no Jews are actually attested, even in Cyrenaica, until the first century B.C., see pp. 60–2 above). The general tendency to assert a relationship with other peoples is found also, e.g. in the relationship with Sparta claimed in 1 Mac. 12:5–23. This suggests perhaps an African or Egyptian background for Cleodemus. Walter believes Cleodemus to

---

51. It cannot be proved that Plutarch depended on a work of King Juba, as held by Müller, FHG III, p. 471, but it is likely, cf. R. Flacelière and E. Chambry, *Plutarque Vies* VIII (1973), pp. 6–7, *contra* H. Peter, *Die Quellen Plutarchs in den Biographien der Römer* (1865), pp. 61–5.

have come from the Jewish community in Carthage itself, which is not impossible; but none are attested there until the Roman Imperial period, p. 62 above. In favour of an origin in Syria or Palestine is only the Semitic name Malchus. There is no hint that Cleodemus knew or used the Hebrew text of the Bible, though his spelling of proper names is so odd that it is impossible to show use of the LXX. For the date it is only certain that Cleodemus must have written before Alexander Polyhistor.

Editions

Müller, FHG III, pp. 207 ff.
Jacoby, FGrH 727, IIIC pp. 686–7.
Denis, FPG, pp. 196–7.
Holladay, FHJA I, pp. 245–59.

Translations

English:
Holladay, *loc. cit.*
Doran in Charlesworth, OTP II (forthcoming).

German:
Riessler, P., *Altjüd. Schrift.* (1927), pp. 667, 1311.
Walter, N., *Die Fragmente jüd.-hell. Historiker* (JSHRZ I.2) (1976), pp. 119–20.

Bibliography

Freudenthal, J., *Alex. Polyh.* (1875), pp. 130–6, 215, 230.
Susemihl, F., *Gesch. der griech. Litt.* II (1892), p. 652.
Broydé, I., 'Malchus/Cleodemus the Prophet', JE VII, 277.
von Christ, W., O. Stählin and W. Schmidt, *Gesch. der griech. Litt.* II ([6]1920), p. 591.
Jacoby, F., 'Kleodemus', RE XI.1 (1921), 675.
Dalbert, P., *Die Theologie der hell.-jüd. Missionsliteratur* (1954), p. 11.
Gutman, Y., *The Beginnings of Jewish-Hellenistic Literature* II (1963), pp. 136–43 (Heb.).
Walter, N., 'Untersuchungen zu den Fragmenten der jüd.-hell. Historiker' (Habilitations-schrift, Halle) (1967–8), pp. 97–107, 224–33.
Denis, IPGAT, pp. 259–61.
Hengel, M., 'Anonymität, Pseudepigraphie und "Literarische Fälschung" in der jüd.-hell. Literatur', *Pseudepigrapha* I (Entretiens Hardt, 18) (1972), pp. 231–329.
Hengel, M., *Judaism and Hellenism* I (ET 1974), pp. 69, 74, 302; II, pp. 50, 52.
Walter, N., *Die Fragmente jüd.-hell. Historiker* (JSHRZ I.2) (1976), pp. 115–18.
Collins, BAAJ, p. 40.

6. An Anonymous Writer (Pseudo-Eupolemus)

Among the excerpts of Alexander Polyhistor are two in Eusebius, *Praep. ev.* ix 17 and 18, which are obviously identical in content, though the second is much shorter than the first. The longer excerpt (Euseb. ix 17) presents itself as taken from Eupolemus, who records that Abraham was a tenth- (or thirteenth-, cf. Jacoby, FGrH 724, F1, l. 19, apparatus) generation descendant of the giants who built the tower of Babel after the flood. Abraham himself is said to have emigrated from Chaldea to

Phoenicia, and to have taught the Phoenicians 'the course of the sun and the moon and all other things'. He also proved useful to them in war (a midrash on Gen. 14). He then because of famine migrated to Egypt, where he lived with the priests in Heliopolis, and taught them much, instructing them in 'astrology and the like'. Enoch, however, was the real discoverer of astrology; he received it from the angels and transmitted it to men (cf. Enoch, c. 72–82 and Jubilees 4:17–21).

The second excerpt, Euseb. ix 18, which Alexander Polyhistor took from an anonymous work (ἐν δὲ ἀδεσπότοις εὕρομεν), is essentially the same, though much shorter. To the fact that this parallel is remarkable must be added another, namely that the longer excerpt may not be from Eupolemus. Eupolemus was a Jew who gave primacy to the Jewish Temple; in the excerpt, however, Argarizim (i.e., Mount Gerizim) is described as 'the mountain of the Most High (*Hypsistos*)', and Abraham's encounter with Melchizedek is specifically located there. Furthermore, the syncretistic use of pagan mythology, e.g. Belus, Atlas, is much more marked in this excerpt than in Eupolemus. It is less significant that in Eupolemus Moses was said to have been the first sage, whereas in the excerpt Abraham is glorified as father of all knowledge, for even within Ps.-Eupolemus there is a contradiction between the roles of Abraham and Enoch. Freudenthal's hypothesis is therefore plausible, that these two sections depend on the same original and that the longer Alexander excerpt is erroneously ascribed to Eupolemus.[52] It is possible that the author of the fragments was a Jew,[53] but, given the emphasis on Mount Gerizim, it is also possible that this is an anonymous work of a Samaritan, in which Greek and Babylonian legends have been fused with biblical history with the apologetic intention of showing that the Jews had brought culture to all western peoples, including the Greeks. This is a work entirely within the genre of Hellenistic historiography in its historicizing of myths and interest in the spread of culture. The anti-Egyptian tendency of the writing suggests that the Samaritan author may have lived in Egypt. He will

52. The fragments are still ascribed to ?the Jewish Eupolemus by W. Bousset and H. Gressmann, *Die Religion des Judentums im späthellenistischen Zeitalter* ([3]1926), p. 21, n. 2; W. G. Lambert, *The Background of Jewish Apocalyptic* (1978), p. 14; F. Millar, 'The Background to the Maccabean Revolution', JJS 29 (1978), p. 6, n. 12. They are assigned to an Alexandrian Jewish writer by Schlatter (see above, note 48). If the ascription to Eupolemus is erroneous, so too, almost certainly, is the title of the book given by Alexander Polyhistor, namely 'Concerning the Jews of Assyria' (Eusebius, *Praep. ev.* ix 17, 2). 'Of Assyria' in this context probably modifies πόλιν Βαβυλῶνα, and 'concerning the Jews' is descriptive only, cf. B. Z. Wacholder, 'Pseudo-Eupolemos' Two Greek Fragments', HUCA 34 (1963), p. 85; Holladay, FHJA I, p. 178, n. 3.

53. The anonymous, shorter, fragment is attributed by Müller, FHG III, p. 212, to Artapanus, cf. also P. Riessler, *Altjüd. Schrift.* (1928), p. 186. However J. Freudenthal, *Alexander Polyhistor* (1875), pp. 14, 90, notes that this fragment cites its sources and that this is contrary to the practice of Artapanus.

then have come into contact with Jewish midrashic traditions through the Jews there. He is however equally likely to have written in Samaria itself, which would explain his acquaintance with Palestinian haggada and the Enoch tradition. It is not clear whether he was acquainted with Hebrew (cf. Walter, Klio 43/5 (1965), pp. 284–6; *contra*, Wacholder, ESJL, pp. 87–8). He used the LXX, but this was as possible in Palestine as in Egypt. For the date, his failure to mention the destruction of the Gerizim temple in 129 B.C. suggests a time earlier than that year. A date in the first half of the second century B.C. is likely, given the close contact with Jewish traditions which suggests that the schism had not yet become final, as it was to do in the Hasmonaean period.[54]

Editions

Müller, FHG III, pp. 207 ff.
Jacoby, FGrH, 724, III C, pp. 678–9.
Denis, FPG, pp. 197–8.
Holladay, FHJA I, pp. 157–87.

Translations

English:
Wacholder, ESJL, Appendix B.
Holladay, *loc. cit.*
Doran, R., in Charlesworth, OTP II (forthcoming).

German:
Riessler, P., *Altjüd. Schrift.* (1927), pp. 11 ff., 186, 1266 ff.
Walter, N., *Die Fragmente jüd.-hell. Historiker* (JSHRZ I.2) (1976), pp. 141–3.

Bibliography

Freudenthal, *Alex. Polyh.* (1875), pp. 82–103, 207 f., 223 ff.
Schnabel, P., *Berossos und die babylonisch-hellenistische Literatur* (1923), pp. 67–93, 246.
Vermes, G., STJ, pp. 77–83, 97, 115, 124.
Wacholder, B. Z., 'Pseudo-Eupolemus' Two Greek Fragments on the Life of Abraham', HUCA 34 (1963), pp. 83–113.
Gutman, Y., *The Beginnings of Jewish-Hellenistic Literature* II (1963), pp. 95–108.
Walter, N., 'Zu Pseudo-Eupolemus', Klio 43/5 (1965), pp. 282–91.
Walter, N., 'Untersuchungen zu den Fragmenten der jüd.-hell. Historiker' (Habilitationsschrift, Halle) (1967–8), pp. 112–27, 236–57.
Denis, IPGAT, pp. 259–61.
Kippenberg, H. G., *Garizim und Synagoge* (1971), pp. 80–3.
Hengel, M., *Judaism and Hellenism* I (ET 1974), pp. 88–92.

54. It is claimed by A. Peretti, *La Sibilla Babilonese* (1942), pp. 123–52, that there are close contacts between Pseudo-Eupolemus and the third Sibyl, to the extent that the Sibyl should be seen as writing polemic against Pseudo-Eupolemus. The similarities are however insufficient for any literary dependence to be shown, cf. V. Nikiprowetzky, *La Troisième Sibylle* (1970), pp. 127 ff. Pseudo-Eupolemus must at any rate have written after 293–292 B.C. because he makes use of the *Babyloniaca* of Berossus, cf. B. Z. Wacholder, HUCA 34 (1963), p. 85.

Wacholder, ESJL, pp. 287–93, 313 f.
Denis, A. M., 'L'historien anonyme d'Eusèbe (Praep. Ev. 9, 17–18) et la crise des Macchabées', JSJ 8 (1977), pp. 42–9.
Collins, BAAJ, pp. 38–9.

7. Jason of Cyrene and the Second Book of Maccabees

The work of Jason of Cyrene, on which the Second Book of Maccabees is based, is an example of how some Hellenistic Jews dealt also with important periods of later Jewish history which they themselves had experienced. 2 Mac. is in effect, as the author informs us, no more than an abridgement (2 Mac. 2:26, 28) from the larger work of a certain Jason of Cyrene (2 Mac. 2:23). The original consisted of five volumes, which are condensed into one in 2 Mac. (2 Mac. 2:23). The contents of the former therefore seem to have been parallel with the latter. The condensed version which has been preserved first recounts the story of an unsuccessful attack on the Temple treasury made during the time of Seleucus IV (187–175 B.C.) by his minister Heliodorus. It then tells of the religious persecution by Antiochus Epiphanes and the apostasy of some of the Jews. Finally, it gives an account of the Maccabaean revolt until the decisive victory of Judas over Nicanor (161 B.C.). The book thus covers a period of fifteen years (175–161 B.C.).

The events related are for the most part the same as in 1 Mac., except that 2 Mac. provides the only detailed extant account of the situation just before and during the hellenizing of Jerusalem (chapters 3–5). But the narrative differs in a great many particulars, partly even in the order of events, from the account of 1 Mac. (cf. above, vol. I, pp. 151–3).

The explanations offered for such differences are varied. It has been suggested that 1 Mac. represents a rewriting of the work of Jason of Cyrene along with other sources (Schlatter and Kolbe), so that the explanation of the differences must come from study of 1 Mac. Alternatively, 2 Mac. may rely on a written source ignored by 1 Mac. for political reasons, such as a hypothetical propagandistic history written by Onias IV; other sources unique to 2 Mac., such as a legendary history which acted as the foundation of 2 Mac. 13, can also be postulated, though not demonstrated (Goldstein). Thirdly, and most plausibly, either the epitomator of Jason of Cyrene's work or the still later reviser who added the two letters to 2 Mac. 1:1 and 2:18 may have changed the order of events which were placed in their correct position (i.e. like 1 Mac.) in the original work of Jason. If this latter hypothesis is correct, it can be assumed that both 1 Mac. and Jason of Cyrene used largely the same sources. These will have included a Seleucid chronicle and Hasmonaean documents and also, according to Wacholder, ESJL, pp. 38–40, 239, Eupolemus, as well as oral tradition. 2 Mac. is therefore as likely to be historically accurate as 1 Mac. whenever there is no good reason within the *tendenz* of the epitomator to suspect tampering with Jason's original version. Certainly there can be no doubt that Jason was extremely accurate on the institutions of the Seleucid monarchy and the royal administration. Most if not all the official documents quoted within 2 Mac. are now generally agreed to be genuine.[55]

If the assumption is correct that Jason of Cyrene based his history partly on oral reports of contemporaries, he probably wrote not long after 161 B.C. There is no compelling reason to posit a date much later, and, if 2 Mac. was itself composed in 124 B.C. (see below), every reason to suppose that Jason must have written quite some time before then, cf. 2 Mac. 2:23. Only if the anti-Hasmonaean bias of 2 Mac. is to be attributed to a deliberate attempt by Jason himself (rather than by the epitomator) to refute the Hasmonaean propagandist who composed 1 Mac. does it become necessary to argue that Jason wrote around 90 B.C. (Goldstein). In favour of a much earlier date it can be said that the legendary nature of many narratives (e.g. the martyrdom of Eleazar and his seven brothers, 2 Mac. 6–7) does not speak against an early origin since it needs only a few decades for the formation of such legends, especially far away from the scene of the events. The notice of 15:37, that Jerusalem remained in the hands of the Hebrews after the victory over Nicanor, is misleading given the extent of later Seleucid interference and can only have been written by someone very distant from there, but it derives not from Jason, but from his summarizer. Generally speaking, we do not know how much is due to the reviser and how much to the original author.

Why the narrative breaks off precisely with the victory over Nicanor is somewhat puzzling. Possibly this ending was not contemplated by Jason.

It may be that none of the 'pathetic' elements of 2 Mac. go back to Jason's original work and that he himself was a sober historian. Given his name he must have come from Cyrenaica, but it is likely that his narrative shows him to have spent some time in Judaea. There is no evidence about Jason outside 2 Mac., cf. above, vol. I, pp. 19–20; Jacoby, RE IX.1 (1914), 778–80; *idem*, FGrH 182, T1 with commentary.

The summarizer is likely to have worked in 124 B.C. (Niese, Momigliano) and certainly before Pompey in the 60s B.C., cf. 2 Mac. 15:37. The rhetorical Greek style of 2 Mac. must be largely his work. He himself declares his intention of producing an edifying and pleasing account in contrast to the mass of material more suited to real

---

55. See C. Habicht, 'Royal Documents in Maccabees II', HSCPh 80 (1976), pp. 1–18, with citations of earlier literature.

historians (2:23 ff.). The result is 'pathetic' history, for which the conventions are entirely Hellenistic although they defy rigid classification, cf. R. Doran, '2 Maccabees and "Tragic History"', HUCA 50 (1979), pp. 107–14. There is no reason to expect much of Jason's Greek style to survive so drastic, and in places incompetent, a compression. The epitomator explains that his work is intended to entertain and edify. It does so by combining a traditional view of the Maccabees as old Hebrew warriors, and the Temple service as central to Judaism, with rather different theological beliefs from those of 1 Mac. These new ideas are most concerned with supernatural intervention and, especially, martyrdom, which is closely associated with belief in individual bodily resurrection for the pious. It has been suggested that the concentration of 2 Mac. on Judas, to the exclusion of his brothers, reflects an anti-Hasmonaean bias (Goldstein), but this is unlikely.

Argument continues over the relation between the two letters prefixed to the book (2 Mac. 1:1–2:18) and the book itself. The editor who added the letters was not the author of the summary since they are not fully integrated into the text, which starts afresh with a new prologue in 2:19–32 and contains minor discrepancies with the letters. These are letters of Palestinian Jews to Egyptian Jews, in which the latter are summoned to the festival of the rededication of the Temple. The origin of the letters is dubious. Some believe that they were incorporated by an editor later than the author of the summary, and who tried to promote the epitome as a liturgical work in Alexandria for the feast of Hannukah sometime in the mid-first century B.C. In this case, the editor is likely to have been an Alexandrian who wrote to encourage continued loyalty to the Temple in Jerusalem. In favour of this hypothesis is the fact that, although the first letter (1:1–9) is firmly dated to 124/3 B.C. (cf. E. Bickermann, 'Ein jüdischer Festbrief vom Jahre 124 v. Chr. (II Mac. 1:1–19)', in *Studies in Jewish and Christian History* II (1980), pp. 136–58), the second letter (1:10–2:18) is impossible to date and could have been written much later (but probably not after 67 B.C., cf. Goldstein, *II Maccabees*, pp. 540–5). If so, the correspondence in the order of events described between the letters and 2 Mac., in opposition to the order in 1 Mac., will have been the work of this later editor (Eissfeldt). A second hypothesis, proposed in essence by Momigliano, is simpler. According to this version, the second letter, perhaps with some later interpolations in the legend about the Temple fire, was written before 124/3 B.C., as was the first letter. The whole work was prepared by the Jerusalem authorities in 124 B.C. to persuade Egyptian Jews to remain within the fold of the Jerusalem Temple. It is possible but not necessary to view this as polemic against the Leontopolis Jews, who were involved in this period as mercenaries in the dynastic struggles of the Ptolemies. The epitome will then have been prepared for the authorities by a writer acquainted with the techniques of pathetic historiography in order to become a festal book like the Book of Esther and thus fulfil the propaganda purpose of the whole work. The Jerusalem authorities then added their letters to the authorized epitome. This hypothesis has the advantage of explaining the apparent excesses in the second letter (1:18–2:16) in which the miracles and holiness of the Jerusalem Temple are emphasized. It has the disadvantage that it is hard to explain why there is no evidence that 2 Mac. was indeed ever read as a festal book. Neither hypothesis is entirely satisfactory.

Philo's book *Quod omnis probus liber*, 89–91, describes the way in which many tyrants persecuted the pious and virtuous. The individual features of this description are quite reminiscent of the portrait drawn of Antiochus Epiphanes in 2 Mac. They are not however sufficient for certainty that Philo knew this book.

Josephus has a few notices in common with our book, and lacking in 1 Mac., but it is improbable that he knew 2 Mac (*contra* Goldstein, *I Maccabees*, pp. 55–61 ; *II Maccabees*, p. 549).

On the other hand, the philosophical exhortations known as the Fourth Book of Maccabees depend entirely on the contents of 2 Mac. The same is true of the later treatments of the history of the Maccabaean martyrs in Jewish haggadah, cf. I. Lévi, 'Le martyre des septs Machabées dans la Pesikta Rabbati', REJ 54 (1907), pp. 138–141.

Christian evidence begins with Heb. 11:35,, for ἐτυμπανίσθησαν evidently depends on 2 Mac. 6:19, 28 (ἐπὶ τὸ τύμπανον προσῆγε, ἐπὶ τὸ τύμπανον εὐθέως ἦλθε), while other allusions, e.g. in Heb. 11:35 f., recall 2 Mac. 6–7.

The oldest citation is by Clement of Alexandria, *Strom.* v 14, 97 (cf. 2 Mac. 1:10).

Hippolytus refers to the book in *De Christo et Antichristo* 49 (ed. Achelis, GCS Hippolytus I, p. 33). In the commentary on Daniel also use is made of the book, cf. 2:20; 3:4 (ed. Bonwetsch, GCS Hippolytus I, pp. 80, 124; ed. Lefèvre, pp. 111, 134).

Origen appeals to the book repeatedly to prove important doctrines: (1) to 2 Mac. 7:28 for the doctrine of creation *ex nihilo*: *Comment in Joann.* i 17 (GCS, Origen IV, p. 22); *De principiis* ii 1, 5 (GCS, Origen V, p. 111; ed. Crouzel and Simonetti, SC 252, p. 244); (2) to 2 Mac. 15:14 for the doctrine of the intercession of the saints: *Comment. in Joann.* xiii 58 (57) (GCS, Origen IV, p. 289); *Hom. in Cant.*, *lib.* iii (GCS, Origen VIII, p. 191); *De oratione* 11, 1 (GCS, Origen II, p. 322); (3) he also makes particular mention of the story of Eleazar and the seven Maccabaean brothers (2 Mac. 6:18–7:*fin.*) as glorious examples of the courage of martyrs in *Exhortatio ad martyrium* 22–7 (GCS, Origen I, pp.

19–23); cf. also *Comment. in epist. ad Rom.* 1, iv 10 (PG XIV, 999).

(4) For other quotations in Origen see *Fragm. in Exod.* (PG XII, 267); *Contra Cels.* viii 46 (GCS, Origen II, p. 261; cf. H. Chadwick, *Origen : Contra Celsum* (1953), p. 486).

Cyprian, too, mainly cites the story of the Maccabaean martyrs of 2 Mac. 6–7 (*Ad Fortunatum* 11, and *Testim.* iii 17).

The Church Fathers in general liked to refer to these Maccabaean martyrs (often using the Fourth Book of Maccabees); indeed they were even finally given a place among Christian saints. Cf. W. H. C. Frend, *Martyrdom and Persecution in the Early Church* (1965), especially pp. 20–2.

The designation, Second Book of the Maccabees, is first found in Euseb. *Praep. ev.* viii 9, 38, and Jerome, *Prol. galeatus* to the books of Samuel (PL XXVIII, 602–3).

Presumably Hippolytus and Origen already followed the same numbering, since they name the other book 1 Mac. (cf. above, p. 183).

With regard to manuscripts, editions, and ancient translations, essentially the same applies as for 1 Mac. (cf. above, pp. 183 ff.). Cf. especially *LXX, VT Graecum Auct. . . . Gottingensis ed.* IX.2, *Maccabaeorum liber 2*, ed. W. Kappler and R. Hanhart (²1976). For the text, cf. E. Nestle, *Septuagintastudien IV* (1903), pp. 19–22; D. De Bruyne, 'Le texte grec des deux premiers livres des Macchabées', RB 31 (1922), pp. 31–54; *Idem*, 'Le texte grec du deuxième livre des Machabées', RB (1930), pp. 503–19; P. Katz, 'The Text of 2 Maccabees Reconsidered', ZNW 51 (1960), pp. 10–30; R. Hanhart, *Zum Text des 2. und 3. Makkabäerbuches. Probleme der Überlieferung, der Auslegung and der Ausgabe* (MSU VII) (1961), pp. 427–86.

It should be noted further (1) that Codex Sinaiticus has not preserved 2 Mac.; and (2) that, besides the recension of the Old Latin translation which passed into the Vulgate, a number of Old Latin texts survive which frequently based on a form of the Greek not found in the Greek manuscripts, cf. the edition of these texts in D. De Bruyne, *Les anciennes traductions latines des Macchabées* (Anecdota Maredsolana IV) (1932). The value of these for correcting the Greek manuscripts is emphasized by De Bruyne but minimized by Hanhart. On the Syriac and Armenian versions, see Goldstein, *II Maccabees*, p. 127.

The exegetical and critical literature for this book is also mainly the same as that for 1 Mac. (cf. above, pp. 184 ff.).

For commentaries, see:

Kamphausen in E. Kautzsch, *Die Apokryphen und Pseudepigraphen des A.T. etc.* I (1900; reprinted 1921), pp. 81–119.
Moffatt, J., 'The Second Book of Maccabees', in Charles, APOT I, pp. 125–54.
Bévenot, H., in F. Feldmann and H. Herkenne, *Die Heilige Schrift des A.T.* (1931).
Abel, F.-M. (= L.-F.), *Les Livres des Maccabées* (Ét. Bibliques) (1949) (full text and commentary).

Grandclaudon, M., in L. Pirot and A. Clamer, La Sainte Bible (1951).
Tedesche, S. S., S. Zeitlin in S. Zeitlin, Jewish Apocryphal Literature (1954).
Kahana, A., הספרים החיצונים (²1956).
Hartum, E. S., הספרים החיצונים (1958).
Laconi, M., La Sacra Bibbia (1960).
Abel, F.-M. (= L.-F.) and J. Starcky, Les Livres des Maccabées (Jerusalem Bible) (1961; ET 1966).
Bartlett, J. R., The First and Second Books of the Maccabees (Cambridge Bible Commentary) (1973).
Habicht, Chr., 2 Makkabäerbuch (JSHRZ, I.3) (1976).
Goldstein, J. A., II Maccabees (Anchor Bible) (1983).

General Introductions

Eissfeldt, O., The O.T., An Introduction etc. (ET 1965), pp. 579–81.
Nickelsburg, G. W. E., Jewish Literature between the Bible and the Mishnah (1981), pp. 118–21.
Collins, BAAJ, pp. 76–81.

Bibliography

(See also the books listed in G. Delling, Bibliographie zur jüd.-hell. und intertestamentarischen Literatur, 1900–1970 (²1975), pp. 141–6.)
Willrich, H., Juden und Griechen vor der makkabäischen Erhebung (1895), pp. 64 ff.
Idem, Judaica (1900), pp. 131–76.
Büchler, A., Die Tobiaden und die Oniaden im II. Makkabäerbuche und in der verwandten jüdisch-hellenistischen Litteratur (1899), pp. 277–398.
Niese, B., 'Kritik der beiden Makkabäerbücher nebst Beiträgen zur Gesch. der makkabäischen Erhebung', Hermes 35 (1900), pp. 268–307, 453–527.
Lévi, I., 'La date de la rédaction du IIe livre des Machabées', REJ 43 (1901), pp. 222–30 (against Niese).
Krauss, S., 'Jason of Cyrene', JE VIII, col. 75.
Barton, G. A., 'II Maccabees', JE VIII, cols. 240–1.
Abrahams, I., 'II Maccabees', JE VIII, cols. 243–4.
Torrey, C. C., 'Second Maccabees', EB III (1902), cols. 2869–79.
Laqueur, R., Kritische Untersuchungen zum zweiten Makkabäerbuch (1904).
Wellhausen, J., 'Ueber den geschichtlichen Wert des zweiten Makkabäerbuchs, im Verhältniss zum ersten', Nachrichten der Göttinger Gesellsch. der Wissensch., philol.-hist. Kl. (1905), pp. 117–63.
Jacoby, F., 'Iason von Kyrene', RE IX.1 (1914), cols. 778–80.
Juster, J., Les Juifs dans l'Empire romain etc. I (1914), pp. 1–3.
Stählin, O., in W. v. Christ-W. Schmidt, Gesch. der griech. Lit. II.1 (⁶1920), pp. 367–8.
Bickermann, E., 'Makkabäerbücher. Buch I und II', RE XIV.1 (1928), cols. 779–97.
Kappler, W., De memoria alterius libri Maccabaeorum (1929).
Tcherikover, V. A., 'Documents in II Maccabees', Tarbiz 1 (1929–30), pp. 31–45 (Heb.).
Kraeling, C. H., 'The Jewish Community at Antioch', JBL 51 (1932), pp. 130–60 (on 2 Mac. 4:9).
Bickerman(n), E. J., Der Gott der Makkabäer (1937); ET The God of the Maccabees (1979).
Surkau, H.-W., Martyrien in jüdischer und frühchristlicher Zeit (FRLANT 54, 1938), pp. 9–29.
Cavaignac, E., 'Remarques sur le deuxième livre des "Macchabées"', RHR 130 (1945), pp. 42–58.
Lévy, I., 'Notes d'histoire hellénistique sur le second livre des Maccabées', AIPhHOS 10 (1950), pp. 681–99.
Dagut, M. G., 'II Maccabees and the Death of Antiochus IV Epiphanes', JBL 72 (1953), pp. 149–57.

Schunck, K.-D., *Die Quellen des I und II Makkabäerbuches* (1954).

Lévy, I., 'Les deux livres des Maccabées et le livre hébraïque des Hasmonéens', *Semitica* 5 (1955), pp. 27–32.

Manson, T. W., 'Martyrs and Martyrdom', BJRL 39 (1956/7), pp. 463–84.

Gil, Luis, 'Sobre el estilo del Libro Secundo de los Macabeos', *Emerita Revista de linguistica y filologia classica* 26 (1958), pp. 11–32.

Hadas, M., *Hellenistic Culture* (1959), pp. 126–7.

Katz, P., 'Eleazar's Martyrdom in 2 Maccabees: The Latin Evidence for a Point of the Story', *Studia Patristica* IV (1961), pp. 118–24.

Adinolfi, M., 'Le apparizioni de 2 Mac. v, 2–4 e x, 29–30', *Rivista Biblica* 11 (1961), pp. 167–85.

Brownlee, W. H., 'Maccabees, Books of', IDB III (1962), cols. 201–15.

Zambelli, M., 'La Composizione del secondo libro dei Maccabei e la nuova cronologia di Antioco IV Epiphane', *Miscellanea Greca e Romana* (1965), pp. 195–299.

Arenhoevel, D., *Die Theokratie nach dem 1. und 2. Makkabäerbuch* (1967).

Bunge, J. G., 'Untersuchungen zum Zweiten Makkabäerbuch', diss. Bonn (1971).

Schmuttermayr, G., '"Schöpfung aus dem Nichts" in 2 Makk. 7,28?', BZ 17 (1973), pp. 203–22.

Momigliano, A., 'The Second Book of Maccabees', CPh 70 (1975), pp. 81–8.

Momigliano, A., *Alien Wisdom* (1975), pp. 103–6.

Habicht, Chr., 'Royal Documents in Maccabees II', HSCPh 80 (1976), pp. 1–18.

Doran, R., '2 Maccabees and "Tragic History"', HUCA 50 (1979), pp. 107–14.

Kellermann, U., *Auferstanden in der Himmel. 2 Makkabäer 7 und die Auferstehung der Märtyrer* (1979).

Doran, R., *Temple Propaganda: the Purpose and Character of 2 Maccabees* (1981).

On the two letters at the beginning of the book, cf. (in addition to the literature mentioned above):

Grätz, H., 'Das Sendschreiben der Palästinenser an die ägyptisch-judäischen Gemeinden wegen der Feier der Tempelweihe', MGWJ (1877), pp. 1–16, 49–60.

Büchler, A., 'Das Sendschreiben der Jerusalemer an die Juden in Aegypten in II Makkab. 1, 11–12, 18', MGWJ 41 (1897), pp. 481–500, 529–54.

Torrey, C. C., 'Die Briefe 2 Makk. 1, 1–2, 18', ZAW 20 (1900), pp. 225–42.

Winckler, 'Die Juden und Rom', *Altorientalische Forschungen*, 3rd series, I.2 (1902), pp. 97–134 (pp. 97–112g. on 2 Mac. 1:10 ff.).

Mercati, RB (1902), pp. 203–11 (on the text of 2 Mac. 1:7).

Kolbe, W., *Untersuch. z. jüd. und syr. Gesch.* (1925).

Bi(c)kerman(n), E., 'Ein jüdischer Festbrief vom Jahre 124 v. Chr. (II Macc. I.1–9)', ZNW 32 (1933), pp. 233–54 (reprinted in *Studies in Jewish and Christian History* II (1980), pp. 136–58).

Torrey, C. C., 'The Letters Prefixed to Second Maccabees', JAOS 60 (1940), pp. 119–50.

Idem, The Apocryphal Literature etc. (1945), pp. 78–9.

Wacholder, B. Z., 'The Letter from Judah Maccabee to Aristobulus: Is 2 Maccabees 1:10–2:18 Authentic?', HUCA 49 (1978), pp. 89–133.

8. The Third Book of Maccabees

Besides 2 Mac., the so-called Third Book of Maccabees may also be mentioned here, since it has at least the form of a historical narrative concerning an alleged episode of later Jewish history. In fact it is a romantic fiction, founded on at the most vague reminiscences of historical events, of which only a few occurred in the time and place described by the book. It recounts how Ptolemy IV Philopator

(221–205 B.C.) came to Jerusalem after his victory over Antiochus the Great at Raphia (217 B.C.) and wished also to enter the inner part of the Temple. Since nothing could deflect him from his purpose, the Jews cried in their distress to God, who answered their prayers and struck Ptolemy so that he fell stunned to the ground (1–2:24). Enraged, he returned to Egypt and planned revenge. He divested the Alexandrian Jews of their civil rights and commanded all the Jews of Egypt, with their wives and children, to be brought in chains to Alexandria, where he locked them up in the hippodrome. Their numbers were so great that the scribes who were to record their names had still not finished after forty days and were obliged to stop for lack of writing material (2:25–4:*fin.*). Ptolemy then commanded that 500 elephants be intoxicated with incense and wine and incited against the Jews in the hippodrome. The preparations were made, but the plan was left until a day later because the king slept till dinner time. On the second day, again nothing happened, because through God's providence the king suddenly forgot everything and was very angry that hostile plots had been made against the Jews, his most faithful servants. But on the very same day at mealtime he repeated his earlier command that the Jews be exterminated. When on the third day, matters at last appeared to become serious and the king was approaching the hippodrome with his troops, two angels appeared from heaven in answer to the Jews' prayer, and the troops and the king became transfixed with terror. The elephants, however, threw themselves on the king's troops, trampled on them, and destroyed them (5–6:21). The king was now very irate with his counsellors and commanded that the Jews be freed from their chains, indeed that they even be entertained for seven days at his expense. They therefore celebrated their deliverance with feasting and rejoicing and determined to keep these days forever as a festival. The king issued letters of protection for the Jews to all the governors in the provinces and permitted the Jews to put to death apostates among their people. Over 300 of these were killed in one day and the Jews returned home happily (6:22–7:*fin.*).

This story is mostly fictional, being closest in genre to Hellenistic romance. Certain elements may reflect genuine problems of the Alexandrian Jews under Ptolemy IV Philopator. Thus the account of the battle of Raphia (1:1–5) is not inaccurate. It is quite possible that Ptolemy IV did, as he is made to claim, try to initiate Jews with others into the mysteries of Dionysus and to give them citizen rights (3:21). Emphasis on the imposition of a census by Ptolemy IV is not implausible (2:28). It is however not justified to claim that 3 Mac. is therefore a good historical source for the period (Kasher). On the contrary, the author seems to delight in accumulating psychological impossibilities. His style is also correspondingly pretentious, bombastic and involved.

The main basis for the author's fiction seems rather to have been an older legend contained in Josephus. According to this (*C. Ap.* ii 5 (50–5)) Ptolemy VIII Physcon (145–116 B.C.) wished to cast the Jews of Alexandria, who as supporters of Cleopatra were his political enemies, before the intoxicated elephants. These, however, turned instead against the king's friends, whereat he gave up his plan. In remembrance, the Jews of Alexandria have since then celebrated this day as a festival.

According to this the celebration of the festival, also mentioned in 3 Mac. (6:36), appears at least to be historical. There may after all be some fact as the basis of the legend. The threat to the Jews during Physcon's rule was genuine enough because of their support for Cleopatra II. The older form of the legend seems to be that of Josephus because everything is much simpler here and psychologically more understandable, and he evidently did not know 3 Mac. Thus when 3 Mac. associates this story with Ptolemy IV instead of Ptolemy VIII, its author departs from the older legend. Other additions with which the author enriches his story increase the divergences still further. It is for instance possible though unprovable that he has conflated yet another episode of persecution with those under Ptolemy IV and Ptolemy VIII, namely the little-known troubles of the Alexandrian Jews in 88/87 B.C. known from Jordanes, *Romana* 81, ed. Mommsen (so Willrich). What seems to have occurred is that 3 Mac. intentionally conflated legends from different periods. So, for instance, Dositheus, who is mentioned in 1:3 as a companion of Ptolemy IV, is known to have existed, and to have been alive in 222 B.C. (P. Hibeh 90, cf. H. Willrich, Klio 7 (1907), pp. 293 ff.); but the name is also perhaps intentionally reminiscent of the general of Ptolemy Philometor mentioned in *C. Ap.* ii 5 (49). The author aimed to explain an already existing festival and to provide the Jews of Alexandria with ammunition in their struggle against the resident Greeks which occupied them from the late Ptolemaic into the Roman period.

On the date of the author, estimates have varied from the earliest part of the first century B.C. to the late first century A.D. The earliest possible date is fixed by the author's knowledge of the Greek additions to Daniel (3 Mac. 6:6), which belong in their present form to the second century B.C., but may have circulated separately earlier (see below, p. 725). The latest possible date is A.D. 70 because the Temple is assumed to be still standing and the book passed into Christianity. More precise dates have been suggested. If the royal edict included in the present Greek text of Esther was included in the original translation completed probably in 114 B.C. but possibly in 77 or 48 B.C. (see above, p. 506; below, p. 719) and if it was based on 3 Mac., then the latter work must date to before 114 (or 77 or 48) B.C. (cf. B. Motzo, 'Il

Rifacimento Greco di Ester e il III Mac.', in *Saggi di Storia e Letteratura Giudeo-Ellenistica* (1924), pp. 272–90). However, although some literary connection with the Greek Esther is certain, the relationship may plausibly be reversed, so that 3 Mac. will have used the Greek Esther and can be dated *after* 114 B.C. at the earliest. Furthermore if the edict was inserted into the Greek translation after the translation by Lysimachus had been completed, it could have been composed at any time before its first citation by Josephus (see below, p. 719). Wilcken, Tcherikover and Hadas maintain that a Roman date is assumed by the term used for the census, *laographia* (2:28), and, more specifically, that the concern expressed for Jewish civil rights is likely to go back to the years 25–15 B.C. and the census of 24/23 B.C., in which a special poll tax was imposed on the Jews to their considerable distress. The term is not a decisive indicator of composition in the Roman period, cf. A. Kasher, *The Jews in Hellenistic and Roman Egypt* (1978), pp. 207–8 (Heb.), but it makes a Roman date likely. Dating specifically to the time of Caligula because of the general atmosphere of state oppression is hypothetical given the lack of any references specific to that period, *contra* Collins, BAAJ, pp. 105–11. In fact, no specific persecution is needed to explain the composition of an aetiological historical romance of this sort in the constantly tense Jewish community of Alexandria at any time after the mid-second century B.C.

The subject matter makes it certain that the work was written in Alexandria. The verbose, rhetorical Greek style points clearly to an original Greek composition rather than a translation.

The oldest Christian evidence is that of Eusebius, for it may be concluded, from the agreement between them, that the references in Syncellus and Jerome come from Eusebius (Euseb., *Chron.*, ed. Schoene, II, cols. 122 ff.: Syncell.: ἡ τρίτη τῶν Μακκαβαίων βίβλος περὶ τοῦ Φιλοπάτορος τούτου Πτολεμαίου ἱστορεῖ; Jerome, ed. Helm, GCS Eusebius VII, 2nd ed., p. 134: 'Ea quae in tertio Maccabaeorum libro scripta sunt, sub hoc principe gesta referuntur').

The *Apostolic Canons* have in canon 84, Μακκαβαίων τρία (Zahn, *Gesch. des neutestamentl. Kanons*, ii, 184–93; Swete and Ottley, IOTG, p. 209).

The stichometry of Nicephorus also counts Μακκαβαϊκὰ γʹ (Zahn II, p. 299; Swete and Ottley, p. 208).

The *Synopsis Athanasii* reads instead of this, Μακκαβαϊκὰ βιβλία δʹ Πτολεμαϊκά (Zahn II, p. 317; Swete and Ottley, p. 207). According to Credner's conjecture καί should be read instead of the number δʹ, so that Πτολεμαϊκά would refer to 3 Mac. Zahn II, p. 309, proposed that we should read πολεμικά, 'of a hostile content', i.e. 'not canonical'. Since Syncellus (I, p. 516) cites the Letter of Aristeas with the formula καθὼς ἐν τοῖς Πτολεμαϊκοῖς γέγραπται it is possible that 3 Mac. was sometimes included with the Letter under the not inappropriate title of Πτολεμαϊκά. Apparently the book never became known in the Latin Church, and for that reason is also lacking in the Vulgate. On the other hand, it was accepted in the Syrian Church, as is proved by the extant old Syriac translation. The name 'Book of Maccabees' has been given to it quite improperly only because it deals with the persecution of faithful Jews.

The book has been preserved in only some of the LXX manuscripts. It is found in the Codex Alexandrinus (A) but not in Vaticanus or Sinaiticus. The main check on A is provided by the Codex Venetus. It appears therefore in most editions of the LXX, cf. especially *LXX, V. T. Graecum Auct. ... Göttingensis ed.* XI.3, *Maccabaeorum liber 3,* ed. R. Hanhart (²1980), and in the separate editions of the Greek Apocrypha (cf. above, p. 184).

Of the ancient translations, mention need only be made of the old Syriac (cf. above, p. 184). Cf. R. Hanhart, *Zum Text des 2. und 3. Makkabäerbuches. Probleme der Überlieferung, der Auslegung und der Ausgabe* (MSU, VII) (1961); W. Baars, 'Eine neue griechische Handschrift des 3 Makkabäerbuches', VT 13 (1963), pp. 82–7.

Commentaries

Grimm, C. L. W., *Das zweite, dritte und vierte Buch der Maccabäer: Exegetisches Handbuch zu den Apokryphen des A.T.s,* 4 parts (1857).

Kautzsch, E., in E. Kautzsch, APAT I (1900; repr. 1921), pp. 119–35.

Emmett, C. W., 'The Third Book of Maccabees', in Charles, APOT I (1913), pp. 155–73.

Riessler, P., *Altjüdisches Schrifttum ausserhalb der Bibel, übersetzt und erläutert* (1928), pp. 682–99, 1312–13.

Hadas, M., 'The Third and Fourth Books of Maccabees', in S. Zeitlin, *Jewish Apocryphal Literature* (1953).

Gaster, T. H., in A. Kahana, הספרים החיצונים (²1956).

Hartum, E. S., הספרים החיצונים (1958).

Bibliography

Grätz, H., *Gesch. der Juden* III (⁴1888), pp. 613–15.

Torrey, C. C., EB III (1902), cols. 2879 ff.

Willrich, H., 'Der historische Kern des III. Makkabäerbuches', *Hermes* 39 (1904), pp. 244–58.

Emmett, C. W., *The Third and Fourth Book of Maccabees* (1918).

Harris, J. R., 'Metrical Fragments in III Maccabees', BJRL 5 (1919), pp. 195–207.

Motzo, B., 'Il Rifacimento Greco di Ester e il III Mac.', *Saggi di Storia e Letteratura Giudeo-Ellenistica* (1924), pp. 272–90.

Bickermann, E., 'Makkabäerbücher (III)', RE XXVII (1928), cols. 797–800.

Tracy, S., 'III Maccabees and Pseudo-Aristeas', YCS 1 (1928), pp. 241–52.

Cohen, J., *Judaica et Aegyptiaca. De Maccabaeorum Libro III, Quaestiones Historicae* (1941).

Moreau, J., 'Le troisième livre des Maccabées', Chronique d'Égypte 16 (1941), pp. 111–22.

Hadas, M., 'III Maccabees and Greek Romance', Review of Religion 13 (1949), pp. 155–62.

Lévy, I., 'Ptolémée Lathyre et les Juifs', HUCA 23.2 (1950/1), pp. 127–36.

Jesi, F., 'Notes sur l'édit Dionysiaque de Ptolémée IV Philopator', JNES 15 (1956), pp. 236–40.

Loewe, R., 'A Jewish Counterpart to the Acts of the Alexandrians', JJS 12 (1961), pp. 105–22.

Tcherikover, V. A., 'The Third Book of Maccabees as a Historical Source of Augustus' Time', *Scripta Hieros.* VII (1961), pp. 1–25.

Kasher, A., 'Anti-Jewish Persecutions in Alexandria in the Reign of Ptolemy Philopator according to III Maccabees', in *Studies in the History of the Jewish People and the Land of Israel*, ed. U. Rappaport, IV (1978), pp. 59–76 (Heb.).

Kasher, A., *The Jews in Hellenistic and Roman Egypt* (1978), pp. 194–211 (Heb.).

Nickelsburg, G. W. E., JLBBM (1981), pp. 169–72.

Collins, BAAJ, pp. 104–11.

9. Philo's Historical Writings

As the author of historical works on Jewish history, the philosopher Philo also needs to be named here. Indeed, he has left us accounts not only on biblical subjects but also of events of his own time.

(1) With regard to the first, one large work must be mentioned above all, one that is almost completely preserved, namely a comprehensive presentation of the giving of the Mosaic Law. It is admittedly not a true historical record but a systematic description of the essential contents of the Pentateuch. Yet it is historical in so far as Philo surveys in it the legislative work of Moses. It is clear that he is influenced in this task by inherited traditions (cf., e.g., G. Vermes, STJ, pp. 127–77) and even more by his own philosophical views. But his main purpose is simply to offer as a historian a review of the giving of Mosaic legislation. The individual parts of this work have come down in the manuscripts and editions as separate books with special titles. It will be shown below (pp. 840–1) that the plan of the whole is as follows. (a) The first book deals with the creation of the world, for Moses apparently discussed this at the beginning of his exposition of the Law in order to make it clear that his legislation corresponded to the will of nature. (b) The following books treat of the lives of Enos, Enoch, Noah, Abraham, Isaac, Jacob, and Joseph, but in such a way that the first three are dealt with only briefly in the introduction to the life of Abraham, whereas a special book is devoted to the other four. The lives of Abraham and Joseph have been preserved. The story of all these men is told because they represented in their lives universal types of morality, the 'living, unwritten laws'. (c) Only now follows the actual giving of the Law, first the ten main commandments in one book, and then the special laws arranged in four books according to the rubrics of the ten main commandments (further details on pp. 847–54). In this way, the essential contents of the Pentateuch are presented really lucidly. The

tendency of the work is everywhere to represent the Jewish Law as the wisest and the most humane. The ritual and ceremonial laws are not omitted, but Philo always knew how to make them appear reasonable, so that whoever observed them perfectly was not only the best but also the most cultured person—the true philosopher.

In a separate composition which does not, as many have assumed, belong to this whole work, Philo also wrote a life of Moses. The method and purpose are the same here as in the systematic work. Moses is described as the greatest and wisest lawgiver, whose mighty deeds and miraculous experiences raised him above all others.

(2) The Jewish history of his own time is dealt with in a work in which Philo describes in detail how the persecutors of the Jews came to a violent end (for this, as far as can be ascertained from the sections preserved, is the essential theme; making it thus analogous to that of Lactantius' *De mortibus persecutorum*). According to Eusebius, the whole consisted of five books. The second dealt with Sejanus, the following with Flaccus and Caligula. But the complete work on Flaccus has been preserved and part of the history of Caligula missing here is the description of the downfall of Caligula by God's avenging hand. The sections preserved probably formed the third and fourth books of the total work (further details on pp. 859–64). Since Philo was to a great extent an eye-witness of the events recounted, indeed as leader of a Jewish delegation to Caligula took a prominent part in them, his work is a foremost source for the history of his time.

10. Thallus

It has become evident that Samaritan authors such as Ps.-Eupolemus may have been worked within the same framework as the Jewish authors who wrote in Greek. Since many have argued for a Samaritan origin for the historian Thallus, it is also appropriate to mention him here. His work was apparently a 'world-chronicle' from primitive times to the present, similar to that of Castor (cf. above, vol. I, p. 43), and, like the latter, it was one of the sources on which Iulius Africanus and Eusebius relied. Eusebius mentions it among his sources as follows (Eusebius, *Arm. Chron.*, ed. Karst, GCS 20, p. 125): 'From the three books of Thallus in which he collects [material] from the fall of Troy to the 167th Olympiad [112–109 B.C.].' Thallus, according to Iulius Africanus, mentioned a solar eclipse which Africanus identified with that at Jesus' crucifixion (Jul. Africanus in Georgius Syncellus, ed. Dindorf, I, p. 610), so either Eusebius did not hand down correctly the number of Olympiads or Thallus' work must have been extended at a later date. That the work goes back to a time earlier than Eusebius says is also suggested by the fact that the remaining fragments and notes are mostly concerned with the mythological primeval age, the story of Bel, Kronos, and Ogygus and the relation of Moses to them;[56] others relate to the story of Cyrus.[57] The reasons for believing Thallus to have been a Samaritan are two-fold. First, he wrote about the history of Syria according to Africanus, in Eusebius, *Praep. ev.* x 10, 8. Second, and more significantly, if Thallus is correctly reported by Africanus as having written about the eclipse of A.D. 29, his work goes up to at least the time of Tiberius, and it may therefore be possible to identify him with a Samaritan Thallus, whom Josephus may (depending on the text; see below) have mentioned as a freedman of Tiberius who once loaned a large sum of money to Agrippa when the latter was in debt (Jos. *Ant.* xviii 6, 4 (167)): καὶ δή τις ἦν θάλλος Σαμαρεὺς τὸ γένος Καίσαρος δὲ ἀπελεύθερος). However, θάλλος in Josephus' text is only a conjecture from ἄλλος in the manuscripts, and, although the original ἄλλος is difficult to understand in context because no other Samaritan has just been mentioned, nonetheless it is possible and has seemed to some preferable to keep the text unamended (cf. L. H. Feldman, Loeb ed., *ad loc.*). In that case the evidence for Thallus as a Samaritan historian would disappear, and he could be assumed to be Jewish or, more probably, pagan, since an interest in Moses of the sort displayed in the extant fragments is found in other gentile authors, and nothing in the fragments positively requires Jewish or Samaritan authorship. In favour of identification with Josephus' Samaritan Thallus is the fact that the name occurs many times on Roman inscriptions among the employees of Claudius' house.[58] The conjecture is certainly reasonable and should be accepted with caution. It is no argument against it that Josephus does not mention this Thallus more than he does since he had no need to do so. The mixture of Oriental and Greek legends in a demythologizing, euhemeristic fashion which is found in the fragments contains nothing specifically Samaritan but would not be at all incongruous in a Samaritan author any more than a Jewish one.[59]

<hr>

56. Theophilus, *Ad Autolycum*, 3, 29 (ed. Grant, p. 144), cf. also Lactantius, *Div. Inst.* i 23; Tertullian, *Apologet.* 10, cf. also Tertullian, *Ad Nat.* ii 12; Lactantius, *Div. Inst.* i 13; Minucius Felix, *Octav.* 21, 4; Julius Africanus in Eusebius, *Praep. ev.* x 10, 7; Georgius Syncellus, ed. Dindorf, I, p. 172. Moses is mentioned in Pseudo-Justin, *Cohortatio ad Graecos* 9, which is directly derived from Julius Africanus, cf. Eusebius, *Praep. ev.* x 10, 7–8.

57. Julius Africanus in Eusebius, *Praep. ev.* x 10, 4. John Malalas, ed. Dindorf, p. 157 (which should read θάλλος instead of θάλης).

58. A 'Ti(berius) Cl(audius) Thallus praepositus velariorum domus Augustanae' in CIL VI 8649. Others in Rome with the same name are listed in CIL VI, pp. 6987–8.

59. Willrich (Lehmann and Kornemann, eds., *Beiträge zur alten Geschichte* III, p. 106) identified the Samaritan Thallus with the mint official C. Iulius Thallus, who was a freedman of the imperial house, probably of Augustus. This is possible but unlikely, cf. Hirschfeld (*Die Kaiserlichen Verwaltungsbeamten bis auf Diokletian* (²1905), p. 181. The name is also far too common to connect our author with the secretary of Augustus by this name mentioned in Suetonius, *Div. Aug.* 67, *contra*, E. Täubler, 'Der Chronograph Thallos',

Editions

Müller, C., FHG, III, pp. 517–19.
Jacoby, FGrH 256, II B, pp. 1156–8 (komm. in II D, pp. 835–7).
Holladay, FHJA I, pp. 343–69.

Bibliography

Freudenthal, *Alexander Polyhistor* (1875), pp. 100 ff.
Goguel, M., 'Un nouveau témoignage non-chrétien sur la tradition évangélique d'après M. Eisler', RHR 98 (1928), pp. 1–12.
Laqueur, R., 'Thallos (1)', RE VA,1 (1934), cols. 1225–6.
Stein, A., 'Thallus (4) and (5)', RE VA,1 (1934), cols. 1226–7.
Rigg, H. A., 'Thallus: the Samaritan?', HThR 34 (1941), pp. 111–19.
Denis, IPGAT, pp. 267–8.
Wacholder, B. Z., 'Thallus', EJ XV, col. 1045.
Kippenberg, H. G., *Garizim und Synagoge* (1971), p. 84.
Bruce, F. F., *Jesus and Christian Origins Outside the New Testament* (1974), pp. 29–30.
Hengel, M., *Judaism and Hellenism* I (ET 1974), p. 89; II, pp. 60–1.

11. Josephus

The best known historical writer on Jewish affairs in the Greek language is the Palestinian Josephus, more precisely Joseph the son of Matthias, a priest from Jerusalem (*B.J.* i praef. (3)). Of his two main works, one, the Ἰουδαϊκὴ Ἀρχαιολογία, is a comprehensive presentation of the whole of Jewish history from the beginning until his own time. It is the most extensive work on Jewish history in the Greek language of which we know, and has therefore been lastingly popular among Jewish, pagan, and Christian readers, with the result that it has been preserved complete in many manuscripts (cf. vol. I, pp. 43–63; add also to the bibliography T. Rajak, *Josephus: the Historian and his Society* (1983); L. H. Feldman, *Josephus and Modern Scholarship* (1984)). Its trend is apologetic. With his whole representation Josephus wishes not only to instruct his gentile readers, for whom the book was intended in the first place, in the history of his people, but also to inspire in them an esteem for the Jewish people by showing that they had a very ancient history and a great number of outstanding men both in war and peace, and that in regard to their laws and institutions they compared favourably with other peoples (cf. particularly *Ant.* xvi 6, 8 (174–8)).

The other chief work of Josephus, the *History of the Jewish War* of A.D. 66–74, presents history more for its own sake. The occurrences of those years are so important in themselves that they seemed worthy of a detailed account. For the motivation of Josephus in composing this work, see now T. Rajak, *op. cit.*, pp. 78–103. Although probably not written at the direct command of Vespasian, it apparently pleased him when delivered as soon as it had been completed (*C. Ap.* i 9 (51); *Vita*

65 (361)). In this work, incidentally, the apologetic tendency refers more to Josephus' own person and to the Romans than to the Jews and their religion.

12. Justus of Tiberias

Justus of Tiberias was a contemporary and fellow-countryman of Josephus. Like him, he applied himself to writing after the defeat of his nation in A.D. 70, but, although a man of good Greek education (Josephus, *Vita* 9 (40)), he was less successful than Josephus in that his works were less read, at least after Eusebius helped to make Josephus popular, and have therefore been lost. Like him also, Justus dealt with Jewish history as a whole as well as with the events of his own time, each in a separate work. His *Chronicle of the Jewish Kings from Moses to Agrippa II* was, according to the statements of Photius who still knew it (*Biblioth. cod.* 33), 'very brief in expression and omitting much that is necessary'. Since it was used by Iulius Africanus in his *Chronicle*, this work was presumably in the form of a chronicle with an interest in chronography. Perhaps the material concerning the *Jewish Kings* which Photius had was merely an excerpt from a larger work, viz. a world-chronicle, for, according to Diogenes Laertius ii 5, 41, the history of Socrates was discussed by Justus as well. If so, this correlation of Jewish with universal history is found in other Jewish writers composing in Greek.

In another work, Justus presented the *History of the Jewish War* in such a way that Josephus felt himself compromised and engaged in consequence in a sharp controversy against him in his *Vita* (cf. vol. I, pp. 34–7; to the bibliography given there, add T. Rajak, 'Justus of Tiberias', CQ n.s. 23 (1973), pp. 345–68; Wacholder, ESJL, esp. pp. 123–7, 298–306; S. J. D. Cohen, *Josephus in Galilee and Rome* (1979), esp. pp. 114–43).

Editions

Jacoby, FGrH, 734, III C, pp. 695–9.
Holladay, FHJA I, pp. 371–89 (with translation and commentary).

13. Joseph and Asenath

Joseph and Asenath is a romantic love story in which the author has put a midrashic elaboration of Genesis 41:45, 50–2 and 46:20 into the form of a Hellenistic romance. All the normal ingredients of that genre are included in the story. The protagonists are of extraordinary beauty and virtue and they undergo many adventures in exotic locations; even the epic tone of the end of the book is appropriate to the genre.[60] It is not a work of great literary quality but it is no worse than some of the other romances that have survived. The contents can be divided into two parts. The first, and longer, section (Philonenko 1–21) describes the love affair between Joseph and Asenath. Joseph, travelling round Egypt collecting corn during the years of plenty, arrives at Heliopolis where Asenath, daughter of the local priest Pentephres, is voluntarily immured in a tower to avoid marriage despite her great beauty. Asenath's parents try to persuade her to marry Joseph. At first she refuses, preferring the son of Pharaoh, but, impressed by Joseph's appearance, she changes her mind only to be spurned by Joseph on the grounds of her paganism. Returning in grief to her tower she repents vehemently of her idolatry and is as a result entirely transformed after a visit by an angel. Joseph comes back to Heliopolis, kisses Asenath and, with Pharaoh's blessing, marries her. From their union Manasseh and Ephraim are born. The second section (Philonenko 22–9) takes place later, during the years of famine, and details the jealousy of Pharaoh's son and the failure of his attempt to get Asenath for himself during a visit by Joseph and his wife to Jacob in Geshem. Pharaoh's son tries to enlist some of Joseph's brothers on his side and succeeds with Dan and Gad, but Levi and especially Benjamin resist him and he is eventually killed, despite the attempts of Levi to preserve his life. Pharaoh is moved by Levi's compassion for his son, but he too dies and Joseph succeeds to the throne.

The origin of this story in earlier, probably oral, Jewish midrash about Joseph is very likely.[61] However, in the present form of the earliest recension of the text, in so far as it can be recovered (see below), the work is clearly a Greek composition, as is evidenced not only by the language, which is full of Septuagintalisms, but also the presence of characteristically Greek ideas.[62] The work seems to have filled a

60. M. Philonenko, ed., *Joseph et Aséneth* (1968), pp. 43–8. If K. Kerényi, *Die griechisch-orientalische Romanliteratur in religionsgeschichtlicher Beleuchtung* ([2]1962) and R. Merkelbach, *Roman und Mysterium in der Antike* (1962), are correct in asserting that all or most Greek romances carry a religious message connected with the mystery religions, the genre was particularly appropriate for the author to choose, but this association is in fact very dubious, cf. R. Turcan, 'Le roman "initiatique" : À propos d'un livre récent', RHR 163 (1963), pp. 149–99; B. E. Perry, *The Ancient Romances* (1967), p. 336, n. 17.

61. Cf. the other similar Jewish legends collected in Philonenko, *op. cit.*, pp. 32–40, and below, p. 798, on the Prayer of Joseph; *direct* influence on our text from any of these stories in the form in which they survive is not likely, but they attest the growth of traditions about Joseph. The strongest evidence of a semitic source can be found in the play on the name of Asenath (cf. Philonenko 15, 6: 'You will no longer be called Aseneth, but your name will be City of Refuge') which presupposes knowledge of Hebrew (Philonenko, *op. cit.*, pp. 30–2).

62. On the language as Greek, based on analysis of the shortest recension, see Philonenko, *op. cit.*, pp. 27–32. See also G. Delling, 'Einwirkungen der Sprache der

number of different purposes apart from its primary function as midrash, and it may well have been intended to convey different messages to Jewish and to gentile readers; both audiences were probably intended. The love story in the first section seems to have been designed to promote and to praise the repentance of gentiles and their conversion to Judaism, and to reassure Jews about the desirability of mixed marriage with converts and its compatibility with pious acceptance of the religious separation of Jew from gentile which is enjoined by the Law.[63] To some considerable extent, however, the story is also symbolical, with Asenath at the start a representative of paganism through her depiction as the goddess Neith, but possibly also including an allegory of the search for wisdom and an astrological meaning.[64] The epic struggle against the Pharaoh's son in the second part of the work may have carried a political meaning but, if so, it cannot now be recovered.

The place of writing of the book was almost certainly Egypt since the attacks on specifically Egyptian idolatry and the detailed allegorical references to the goddess Neith would have been incomprehensible elsewhere.[65] There is no reason to believe that the author belonged to a sect of any sort since the ideas expressed would be perfectly possible for

---

Septuaginta in "Joseph and Aseneth"', JSJ 9 (1978), pp. 29–56. On the extent to which the ideas are identifiably Greek, see Philonenko, *op. cit.*, pp. 56–7, on Repentance as a hypostasis; on the use of motifs from the Hellenistic romances, see further, C. Burchard, *Untersuchungen zu Joseph und Aseneth* (1965), pp. 84–96; *idem, Der dreizehnte Zeuge* (1970), pp. 59–86; S. West, 'Joseph and Asenath: A Neglected Greek Romance', CQ 24 (1974), pp. 70–81.

63. Cf. Philonenko, *op. cit.*, pp. 48–61. That Asenath is regarded as converted is evident, despite the lack of references to the rituals associated with conversion in other texts, cf. Philonenko, *op. cit.*, p. 52.

64. The precise references of the symbolism are naturally debated. For these suggestions, of which the reference to the golden Neith must be regarded as the most convincing, see Philonenko, *op. cit.*, p. 61–89, and *ibid.*, pp. 107–8, for the correct insistence that there is no reason to deny a number of different meanings on various levels to a single text. The suggestion that the romance is an allegory for a particular mystical rite of initiation should however be treated with great caution since there is no reason to posit any such rite beyond Asenath's acceptance of the laws of Judaism in general. Cf. Collins, BAAJ, pp. 213–16, *contra* Philonenko, *op. cit.*, pp. 89–98. Cf. also D. Sänger, *Antikes Judentum und die Mysterium* (1980). U. Fischer, *Eschatologie und Jenseitserwartung im Hellenistischen Diasporajudentum* (1978), pp. 115–23, argues that Asenath is identified with the heavenly Jerusalem but, though the transference of some Jerusalem salvation imagery to Asenath is correctly noted, there is nothing sufficiently specific to show a deliberate reference. Note also the hypothesis of D. Sänger, 'Bekehrung und Exodus. Zum jüdischen Traditionshintergrund von "Joseph und Aseneth"', JSJ 10 (1979), pp. 11–36, that the conversion of Asenath is an allegory of the exodus.

65. Philonenko, *op. cit.*, pp. 40–1, has also pointed out literary similarities between Joseph and Asenath and an Egyptian story of the nineteenth Dynasty. Suggestions of origin elsewhere presume wrongly a sectarian or Christian origin for the work; for references see Burchard, *Untersuchungen*, pp. 140–3.

any Jew.[66] The date of composition can only be fixed with some probability to before A.D. 117, if the work is indeed of Egyptian origin, since the eirenic attitude expressed towards gentiles would be unlikely there after that date, and to some time after the translation of the prophetic books in the LXX which have influenced the author's language, i.e. after *c.* 100 B.C.[67]

The work is clearly of Jewish origin, both because the whole subject of conversion and the midrash on Genesis would have lacked interest for a Christian author and because the earliest recensions show great use of the LXX but no obvious use of the New Testament. This is not to deny that the later recensions have been reworked by a Christian, cf. Philonenko, *op. cit.*, pp. 100–1, but, against the attempt by T. Holtz, 'Christliche Interpolationen in "Joseph und Asenath"', NTS 14 (1967–8), pp. 482–97, to establish Christian authorship of parts of the earlier recensions, cf. C. Burchard, *Der dreizehnte Zeuge* (1970), p. 59; see also *idem, Untersuchungen zu Joseph und Asenath* (1965), pp. 99–107 for a detailed refutation of earlier arguments for Christian authorship.

The Greek text is preserved in a number of manuscripts, of which the earliest dates from the tenth century A.D., cf. list in C. Burchard, *Untersuchungen*, pp. 4–7. These manuscripts fall into four groups (Burchard, *op. cit.*, pp. 18–23), whose relationships are still not clear, so that no complete critical edition of the text has yet been produced. In the production of such a text the ancient versions will be of primary importance. For the Slavic version, which seems to have kept close to its Greek original, see V. M. Istrin, 'Apokrif ob Josifye i Asenefye', *Trudy Slavianskoy komissii pri Imperat. Moskovskom Archeologicheskom Obschestvye* (1898), pp. 189–99. For the Syriac version of the sixth century A.D., which survives in two manuscripts in the British

66. Cf. Collins, BAAJ, p. 218. For an Essene origin, see P. Riessler, 'Joseph und Asenath. Eine altjüdische Erzählung', ThQ 103 (1922), pp. 4–8; for an attribution to the Therapeutae, see K. G. Kuhn, 'The Lord's Supper and the Communal Meal at Qumran', in K. Stendahl, *The Scrolls and the New Testament* (1958), p. 76; M. Delcor, 'Un roman d'amour d'origine thérapeute: Le Livre de Joseph et Aséneth', Bulletin de Littérature Ecclésiastique 63 (1962), pp. 3–27; for attribution to an otherwise unknown Jewish sect, cf. Philonenko, *op. cit.*, p. 105.

67. C. Burchard, *Untersuchungen zu Joseph und Aseneth* (1965), p. 146, favours a date in the first century B.C. because of the lack of reference to proselyte baptism, but the history of this practice is too obscure for its use as a dating criterion, cf. the conflicting views in J. Jeremias, *Die Kindertaufe in den ersten vier Jahrhunderten* (1958), pp. 29–34, and G. Delling, *Die Taufe im Neuen Testament* (1963), pp. 30–8. G. D. Kilpatrick, 'The Last Supper', ET 64 (1952), p. 5, asserts a date in the first century B.C. because of lack of references to the Romans, but the literary conventions of the romance account for this fact sufficiently. Philonenko, *op. cit.*, p. 109, dates the work to the early second century A.D., primarily because of similarities to other Greek romances, but the dating of all the works of this genre is itself very difficult and quite uncertain, cf. B. E. Perry, *The Ancient Romances* (1967), pp. 96–8, 173; T. Hägg, *The Novel in Antiquity* (1983), p. 5.

Museum, see J. P. N. Land, *Anecdota Syriaca* III (1870), pp. 18–46; E. W. Brooks, *Historia ecclesiastica Zachariae Rhetori vulgo adscripta* III.5 (1919), pp. 21–55; cf. Philonenko, *op. cit.*, pp. 12–13 for the date. For the other versions, especially the Armenian and the Latin, which, though late, may often preserve better readings than the Greek manuscripts, see Burchard, *Untersuchungen*, pp. 24–45; *idem*, 'Joseph und Aseneth 25–29, Armenisch', JSJ 10 (1980), pp. 1–10; Philonenko, *op. cit.*, pp. 13–16.

The present editions are not satisfactory. The text given in P. Battifol, 'Le Livre de la Prière d'Aseneth', in *Studia Patristica* I-II (1889–90), pp. 1–115 is that of the eleventh to twelfth century manuscript in the Vatican, Vat. Gr. 803, fol. 133r–147v, with variants noted from three other manuscripts and the Syriac. V. M. Istrin, *op. cit.*, recognized the existence of two separate recensions, one long and the other short, and gives the text of the short recension from Vatican manuscript, Pal. Gr. 17, f. 118v–134v, with variants from one other Greek manuscript and the versions. M. Philonenko, *Joseph et Aséneth* (1968), pp. 128–221, gives a careful critical edition of this same short recension from a greater number of Greek manuscripts and giving considerable weight to the older versions, cf. pp. 23–7 for his justification of this procedure. Philonenko's text assumes, however, that the short recension of the text is the oldest one extant. This is disputed by C. Burchard, 'Zum Text von Joseph und Aseneth', JSJ 1 (1970), pp. 3–34, who believes that the short recension is an abridgement and that the best and oldest text is preserved in the manuscript group described by Philonenko as the first long recension, and who argues further that an even better text based on this manuscript group can be reconstructed by taking readings when necessary from the other three groups since they developed independently from the primary group. See his preliminary edition produced on this basis in Dielheimer Blätter 14 (1979), pp. 1–53.

Translations and Commentaries

Brooks, E. W., *Joseph and Asenath* (1918) (English translation of the text in Battifol, with occasional readings from the versions).

Riessler, P., *Altjüdisches Schrifttum ausserhalb der Bibel* (1928), pp. 497–538 (German translation based on Battifol's text).

Philonenko, M., *Joseph et Aséneth* (1968) (text of short recension, French translation, and good introduction).

Burchard, C., 'Joseph and Asenath', in Charlesworth, OTP II (forthcoming) (English translation).

Bibliography

For a full list of works see the edition by M. Philonenko.

Massebieau, L., Annales de Bibliographie Théologique 11 (1899), pp. 161–72.

Perles, J., 'La légende d'Asnath, fille de Dina et femme de Joseph', REJ 22 (1891), pp. 87–92.

Krumbacher, K., Byzantinische Zeitschrift 8 (1899), pp. 228–9.
Kohler, K., 'Asenath', JE II (1902), col. 172.
Riessler, P., 'Joseph und Asenath. Eine altjüdische Erzählung', Theologische Quartalschrift 103 (1922), pp. 1–22, 145–83.
Aptowitzer, V., 'Asenath, the Wife of Joseph', HUCA I (1924), pp. 239–306.
Jeremias, J., 'The Last Supper', ET 64 (1952), pp. 4–8.
Joly, R., 'Note sur μετάνοια', RHR 160 (1961), pp. 149–56.
Delcor, M., 'Un Roman d'amour d'origine therapeute: Le Livre de Joseph et Asénath', Bulletin de Littérature Ecclésiastique 63 (1962), pp. 3–27.
Burchard, C., *Untersuchungen zu Joseph und Asenath* (1965).
Philonenko, M., 'Initiation et mystère dans Joseph et Aséneth', in C. J. Bleeker, ed., *Initiation* (Suppl. to Numen, 10) (1965), pp. 147–53.
Jeremias, J., *Abba. Studien zur neutestamentlichen Theologie und Zeitgeschichte* (1966), pp. 292–8.
Holtz, T., 'Christliche Interpolationen in "Joseph und Aseneth"', NTS 14 (1967/8), pp. 482–97.
Burchard, C., *Der dreizehnte Zeuge* (1970), pp. 59–88.
Burchard, C., 'Zum Text von "Joseph und Asenath"', JSJ 1 (1970), pp. 3–34.
Denis, IPGAT, pp. 40–8.
Burchard, C., 'Joseph et Aséneth: Questions Actuelles', in W. C. van Unnik, ed., *La Littérature juive entre Tenach et Mischna* (1974), pp. 77–100.
West, S., 'Joseph and Asenath: A Neglected Greek Romance', CQ 24 (1974), pp. 70–81.
Pines, S., 'From Darkness into Great Light', Immanuel 4 (1974), pp. 47–51.
Smith, E. W., Jnr., *Joseph and Asenath and Early Christian Literature: A Contribution to the Corpus Hellenisticum Novi Testamenti* (Claremont Ph.D., 1974).
Smith, E. W., Jnr., 'Joseph Material in Joseph and Asenath and Josephus relating to the Testament of Joseph', in G. W. E. Nickelsburg, ed., *Studies on the Testament of Joseph* (1975), pp. 133–7.
Philonenko, M., 'Un mystère juif', EHR 2 (1975), pp. 65–70.
Stehly, R., 'Une Citation des Uphanishads dans Joseph et Aséneth', RHPR 55 (1975), pp. 209–13.
Berger, K., 'Jüdisch-Hellenistische Missionsliteratur und apokryphe Apostelakten', Kairos 17 (1975), pp. 232–48.
Pervo, R. I., 'Joseph and Asenath and the Greek Novel', *Soc. Bib. Lit. Abstracts and Seminar Papers* (1976), pp. 171–81.
Kee, H. C., 'The Socio-Religious Setting and Aims of "Joseph and Aseneth"', *Soc. Bib. Lit. Abstracts and Seminar Papers* (1976), pp. 183–92.
Kan, G. V., 'Illustrated Manuscripts of the Romance of Joseph and Asenath', *Soc. Bib. Lit. Abstracts and Seminar Papers* (1976), pp. 193–208.
Burchard, C., 'Joseph und Aseneth Neugriechisch', NTS 24 (1977), pp. 68–84.
Fischer, U., *Eschatologie und Jenseitserwartung im Hellenistischen Diasporajudentum* (1978), pp. 115–23.
Delling, G., 'Einwirkungen der Septuaginta im "Joseph und Asenath"', JSJ 9 (1978), pp. 29–56.
Sänger, D., 'Bekehrung und Exodus. Zum jüdische Traditionshinterrund von "Joseph und Aseneth"', JSJ 10 (1979), pp. 11–36.
Sänger, D., *Antikes Judentum und die Mysterien. Religionsgeschichtliche Untersuchungen zu Joseph und Aseneth* (1980).
Burchard, C., 'Joseph und Aseneth 25–29, Armenisch', JSJ 10 (1980), pp. 1–10.
Nickelsburg, JLBBM pp. 258–63.
Collins, BAAJ, pp. 89–91, 211–18.
Kee, H.C., 'The socio-cultural setting of *Joseph and Aseneth*', NTSt 29 (1983), pp. 394–413.

Delling, G., 'Die Kunst des Gestaltens in "Joseph und Aseneth"', NT 26 (1984), pp. 1–42.

14. Testament of Job

Much like the retelling of the story of Joseph in Joseph and Asenath is the midrashic development of the story of Job which is found in the Testament of Job. It is distinguished from most other extant Jewish Greek narratives about biblical history by being couched in the external form of a testament similar to the Testaments of the Twelve Patriarchs. The dying father exhorts his children by telling them about his life. The genre provides however little more than the framework to the narrative, which predominates (16–44) almost to the exclusion of the other sections, such as the exhortation and apocalypse, which come to the fore in the other Jewish testamentary literature.

Job, portrayed as Jobab, a descendant of Esau (1:1), but also as an Egyptian king (28:8), gathers his children around his death-bed to tell them the events of his life and to exhort them to follow his example (1:1–5). He narrates in detail his conversion from paganism through insight granted by an angel after he had already begun to doubt the power of idols, his destruction of the idolatrous temple of Satan and, in a long elaboration of Job 1:13–21 ; 2:7–10, his patience, endurance and charitable piety in his successful and deliberately self-inflicted athletic contest with Satan, the prince of evil (1:6–27:10). Job's debate with his friends is similarly amplified in 28–43. The friends are portrayed as fellow monarchs whose sorrowful opposition, like that of Job's wife Sitidos (39–40), is put down to their ignorance of reality, which lies in heaven and not in the instability of earthly life, as opposed to Job's revealed knowledge, cf. 35–38, 40. The wisdom of Job's loyalty to God is confirmed by divine intervention and his friends are reconciled to God through his mediation (42), except for Elihu, who is filled with Satan, and condemned (43). Job's fortunes and health are restored (44). A brief exhortation to follow his loyalty and piety (which here includes also avoidance of inter-marriage with foreign wives) (45:1–4) is followed by his distribution of his inheritance, which is remarkable for the grant of heavenly gifts in the form of magical phylacteric sashes to his three daughters, who immediately join in the heavenly chorus in the language of the angels (45:5–51:3). The work concludes (51:4–53) with Job's death, the ascension of his spirit to heaven on a chariot, and the burial of his body.

The story as a whole seems calculated to appeal to gentiles in describing the advantages of loyalty to God and the limitations of idolatry. It can therefore be reservedly described as missionary literature (Rahnenführer). The non-Jewish audience is however forgotten in the summary exhortation at 45:1–4, where Job's sons are warned against inter-marriage with strangers. For the Jewish reader, the Testament urges an eclectic piety, emphasizing charity and the burial of the dead (39:1–10; 40:6–14; 53:5–7) as well as the prime virtue of endurance.

The place and date of the work cannot be fixed with certainty. It is clear that the work was composed in Greek.[68] In favour of Egyptian origin is only the description of Job as king of all Egypt (28:8), which should not be taken as decisive. There is nothing indisputably Christian in any of the work, and its Jewish origin should be accepted.[69] If the work is dependent on the LXX of Job, it must date after *c.* 100 B.C., when that translation was made, but such dependence is not certain. It is unlikely to have been written after *c.* A.D. 200, but even that would be possible.[70] Despite similarities to the Therapeutae, there are also differences, and there is insufficient reason to postulate a sectarian origin for the book.[71] The mystical tendencies

68. A Hebrew original was suggested by M. R. James, *Apocrypha Anecdota* (1897), pp. lxxii-cii, because of alleged semiticisms in the hymnic portions of the text, and an Aramaic original was alleged by C. C. Torrey, *The Apocryphal Literature* (1945), p. 145, on similar grounds. However, no manuscript evidence of a semitic origin survives and a Greek original is confirmed by the close relationship of the Testament to the LXX of Job, cf. B. Schaller, *Das Testament Hiobs* (JSHRZ, III.3) (1979), p. 307; R. P. Spittler, in Charlesworth, OTP I, pp. 830–83. It remains quite possible that the midrash was developed orally in one or other of the semitic languages before being written down in Greek.

69. *Contra* M. R. James, *Apocrypha Anecdota* (1897), pp. xciii-xciv, who saw it as a work of a 'Jewish Christian', cf. Schaller, *op. cit.*, p. 311. In favour of the more complex hypothesis put forward by R. P. Spittler, 'The Testament of Job' (Diss. Harvard, 1971), pp. 53–83 (cf. *idem* in Charlesworth, OTP I, p. 834), that an originally Jewish text has been reworked by a Montanist Christian in the second century A.D., is the fact that the sections which he regards as later (46–53) are indeed tacked on rather awkwardly to the main body of the Testament. Nonetheless, the hypothesis is unnecessary. Spittler suggests it only to explain the prominence of ecstatic women in Testament of Job 46–53, which he regards (correctly) as implausible for Therapeutae and therefore (incorrectly) as a late addition. But if the Jewish but non-Therapeutan origin of the whole Testament is accepted, this last passage can quite well be Jewish also.

70. The suggestion by M. Delcor, 'Le Testament de Job, la prière de Nabonide et les traditions targoumiques', in S. Wagner, ed., *Bible et Qumran* (1968), pp. 72–3, that Satan's guise as the king of the Persians in 17:1 refers to the Parthian King Pacorus and therefore dates the work to *c.* 40 B.C., should not be taken seriously. There is no reason to suspect any historical allusion. A date in the first century B.C. or A.D. is commonly given, cf. R. Spittler, in Charlesworth, OTP I, p. 833, but this depends only on the existence of other similar literature probably from that date, such as Joseph and Asenath or the Testament of Abraham. For a date after A.D. 200, see J.-B. Frey, DB suppl. I (1928), col. 455.

71. *Contra* M. Philonenko, 'Le Testament de Job et les Therapeutes', Semitica 8 (1958), pp. 41–53; 'Le Testament de Job', Semitica 18 (1968), pp. 9–24, who suggests an origin among the Egyptian Therapeutae because of the use of hymns and the inclusion of women in religious choirs. Neither criterion is very strong, but the similarity of the Testament of Job's cosmological dualism (cf. 33:3) and the hymn of Elihu (43:4–17) to

such as the chariot are paralleled in the Hekhalot literature.[72]

The Testament was virtually ignored both by early Christians and by Jews. The suggestion that it was used and redacted by Montanist Christians in the second century A.D. is very hypothetical (see above, note 69). It is possible that Tertullian, *De Patientia* 14:2–7 (ed. J. Borleffs, pp. 42 f.) uses a form of *Test. Job* 20:8 f., but he does not quote the extant text directly, cf. Spittler in Charlesworth, OTP I, p. 847.

The Greek text survives in four manuscripts of which the best, despite some Christian intrusion, is Paris Fonds grec 2658 of the eleventh century A.D., edited by M. R. James, *Apocrypha Anecdota* (1887), and (best) S. P. Brock, *Testamentum Iobi* (PVTG 2) (1967). Brock gives all significant variations in the other Greek manuscripts and the Slavonic. Paris fonds grec 938 is a sixteenth-century copy of the same text. A separate textual tradition is represented by the early fourteenth-century manuscript Messina, San Salvatore 29, edited by A. Mancini, 'Per la critica del "Testamentum Job"', Rendiconti della Reale Accademia dei Lincei, Classe di Scienzi Morali, Storiche e Filologiche Serie Quinta 20 (1911), pp. 479–502. The same tradition is probably that found in the twelfth-century manuscript Vaticanus Gr. 1238, published by A. Mai, *Scriptorum veterum nova collectio* (1833), vol. VII, cols. 180–91. The two latter manuscripts are edited together in R. A. Kraft, *The Testament of Job According to the S.V. Text* (1974).

On the manuscripts in general, cf. Brock, *op. cit.*, pp. 3–16. It is likely that the history of the text is associated with that of the LXX book of Job, but the relationship has not yet been clarified, cf. Denis, IPGAT, p. 102.

Ancient Versions

(1) An incomplete Coptic version is preserved, rather unevenly, in Papyrus Cologne 3221 of the fifth century A.D. Of considerable importance for the production of a critical text, this papyrus is as yet unpublished. It is being edited by M. Weber of the Institut für Altertumskunde at the University of Köln. Cf. M. Philonenko, 'Le Testament de Job', Semitica 18 (1968), pp. 9, 61–3 on differences between this version and the Greek.

(2) Old Church Slavonic survives in two complete manuscripts and one partial one. It is published by G. Polívka, 'Apokrifna priča o Jovu', Starine 24 (1891), 135–55. It is close to the Greek but often paraphrases it.

---

the material at Qumran should be noted.

72. H. C. Kee, 'Satan, Magic and Salvation in the Testament of Job', *Soc. Bibl. Lit. 1974 Seminar Papers* I, pp. 53–76.

Translations and Commentaries

French:
Philonenko, M., 'Le Testament de Job. Introduction, traduction et notes', Semitica 18 (1968), pp. 1–75.

German:
Riessler, P., *Altjüd. Schrift.* (1928), pp. 1104–34 (1333–4).
Schaller, B., *Das Testament Hiobs* (JSHRZ III.3) (1979), pp. 303–74.

English:
Kraft, R. A., ed., *The Testament of Job According to the S.V. Text* (1974).
Spittler, R. P., in Charlesworth, OTP I, pp. 829–68.

Bibliography

Conybeare, F. C., 'The Testament of Job and the Testaments of the XII Patriarchs', JQR 13 (1900–01), pp. 111–27.
Spitta, F., 'Das Testament Hiobs und das Neue Testament', *Zur Geschichte und Literatur des Urchristentums* III.2 (1907), pp. 139–206.
Mancini, A., 'Per la critica del "Testamentum Job"', Rendiconti della Reale Accademia dei Lincei 20 (1911), pp. 479–502.
Torrey, C. C., *The Apocryphal Literature* (1945), pp. 140–5.
Philonenko, M., 'Le Testament de Job et les Thérapeutes', Semitica 8 (1958), pp. 41–53.
Meyer, R., 'Hiobtestament', RGG (³1959), vol. III, col. 361.
Delcor, M., 'Le Testament de Job, la prière de Nabonide et les traditions targoumiques', in S. Wagner, ed., *Bibel und Qumran* (1968), pp. 57–74.
Jacobs, I., 'Literary Motifs in the Testament of Job', JJS 21 (1970), pp. 1–10.
Denis, IPGAT, pp. 100–4.
Rahnenführer, D., 'Das Testament des Hiob und das Neue Testament', ZNW 62 (1971), pp. 68–93.
Spittler, R. P., 'The Testament of Job' (Harvard Ph.D., 1971).
Collins, J. J., 'Structure and Meaning in the Testament of Job', in G. MacRae, ed., *Society of Biblical Literature : 1974 Seminar Papers* I (1974), pp. 35–52.
Kee, H. C., 'Satan, Magic, and Salvation in the Testament of Job', *ibid.*, pp. 53–76.
Glatzer, N. N., 'Jüdische TJob-Deutungen in den ersten christlichen Jahrhunderten', Freiburger Rundbrief 26 (1974), pp. 31–4.
Nickelsburg, JLBBM pp. 241–8.
Collins, BAAJ, pp. 220–4.
Schaller, B., 'Das Testament Hiobs und die Septuaginta Übersetzung des Buches Hiobs', Bibl. 61 (1980), pp. 377–406.
Nordheim, E. von, *Die Lehre der Alten* I (1980), pp. 119–35.
Nicholls, P. H., 'The Structure and Purpose of the Testament of Job' (Ph.D. diss. Jerusalem, 1982).

15. Philo the Elder

A historian Philo is quoted by Clement of Alexandria, *Stromata* i 21, 141, between Demetrius and Eupolemus, as also by Josephus in *C. Ap.* i 23 (218). According to Clement this Philo wrote about the kings of the Jews. Josephus took him for a gentile, since he gave him as one of the authorities that showed some gentiles to have had a fairly accurate knowledge of Jewish history. However, the fact that both Clement and Josephus named this Philo together with Demetrius and Eupolemus shows that both drew from the same source, which was probably but not necessarily Alexander Polyhistor. Association with Demetrius and Eupolemus in that source makes it likely that Philo was Jewish since those two writers certainly were. It is possible that this Philo was identical with Philo the epic poet (see below, p. 559) but this Philo, whose exact chronological king lists were quoted by some source in the mid-first century B.C., is rather unlikely to have written such lists in the epic hexameters favoured by the epic poet, though of course he could have composed in two different genres. If a separate historian existed he could have written at any time before the compilation was made from which Josephus and Clement drew, i.e. before the mid-first century A.D. at the latest. It has been argued that the citation of Philo between Demetrius and Eupolemus makes it likely that he wrote at a time between those two authors, i.e the second century B.C. (Dalbert), but it is preferable to leave the date undecided.

Bibliography

Laqueur, R., 'Philon (46)', RE XX (1941), pp. 51 f.
Dalbert, P., *Die Theologie der hell.-jüd. Missionsliteratur* (1954), pp. 33–5.
Jacoby, FGrH 729, T1–2, III C2, p. 689 (assuming the identity of the two Philos).
Walter, N., 'Zur Überlieferung einiger Reste früher jüdisch-hellenistischer Literatur bei Josephus, Clemens und Euseb', *Studia Patristica* VII (1966), pp. 314–20.
Walter, N., 'Untersuchungen zu den Fragmenten der jüdisch-hellenistischen Historiker' (Habitationsschrift, Halle) (1967–8), pp. 108–11, 234.
Denis, IPGAT, pp. 270 ff.
Walter, N., *Die Fragmente jüdisch-hellenistischer Historiker* (JSHRZ I.2) (1976), pp. 112–14.

16. Theophilus

A single short fragment of this author is cited by Alexander Polyhistor as a witness to corroborate the statement in Eupolemus that Solomon sent a golden pillar to be exhibited in the temple of Zeus in Tyre (Euseb., *Praep. ev.* ix 34, 19). Alexander Polyhistor gives no indication about his origin. He may, however, be the same Theophilus who is listed by Josephus in *C. Ap.* i 23 (216) as among those who testified to the antiquity of the Jews. Josephus states explicitly that the authorities he cites are gentile (*C. Ap.* i 23 (215)), but it is notorious that in *C. Ap.* i 23 (218) he includes among those authorities the elder Philo and Eupolemus, who were quite certainly Jewish, and it is therefore at least possible that Theophilus too was a Jew. This is rendered the more likely if he is identified with the author cited by Alexander Polyhistor because of his evident interest in Jewish history. The name is frequently attested among Jews. In favour of the identification of Theophilus as a hellenistic Jewish historian is N. Walter, *Die Fragmente der jüd.-hell. Historiker* (JSHRZ I.2) (1976), pp. 109–10. His case, however, is very hypothetical, as can be seen. It is significant that all the other historians quoted in *C. Ap.* i 23 (215) (as opposed to 218) are definitely gentile.

Most would accept the more sceptical view that he was a gentile historian who preceded Alexander Polyhistor, cf. Stern, GLAJJ I, pp. 126–7.[73]

Editions

Jacoby, FGrH, 733, III C, pp. 694–5.
Stern, GLAJJ I, pp. 126–7.
Holladay, FHJA I, pp. 337–42.

Translations

English:
Stern, *loc. cit.*
Holladay, *loc. cit.*

German:
Walter, N., *Die Fragmente der jüd.-hell. Historiker* (JSHRZ I.2) (1976), p. 111.

Bibliography

Freudenthal, *Alex. Polyh.*, pp. 117–18.
Laqueur, R., 'Theophilus', RE V A (1934), cols. 2137–8.
Walter, N., 'Untersuchungen zu den Fragmenten der jüd.-hell. Historiker' (Habilitationsschrift, Halle) (1967–8), pp. 93–6, 222–3.

17. Lost Greek Histories Written by Jews

Some histories written in Greek by Jews are so completely lost that no more is known about them than that they existed. For a full picture of Hellenistic Jewish writing about the past they should, however, be included here.

(1) *The Memoirs of Herod*. These are mentioned once by Josephus, *Ant.* xv 6, 3 (174) (see vol. I, pp. 26–7).

(2) *A History of the visit to Jerusalem of Alexander the Great*. Preserved in Jos. *Ant.* xi 8, 1 (304–5); 8, 3–7 (313–47), is a romantic account of a fictional visit to Jerusalem by Alexander the Great. The interest in Alexander makes it probable that it was written in Greek. It was written after the accession of Simon to the high-priesthood in 143 B.C., but before the destruction of the Samaritan shrine by John Hyrcanus in 129 B.C.

Bibliography

Büchler, A., 'La relation de Josèphe concernant Alexandre le Grand', REJ 34 (1898), pp. 1–26.
Marcus, R., in Loeb, ed., vol. VI, pp. 512–32.

---

73. Some scholars have also suggested that the Menander of Ephesus (or, according to Clement of Alexandria, *Strom.* i 21, 114, Pergamum), to whom Josephus refers in *C. Ap.* i 18 (116–26) (which is loosely repeated by Theophilus of Antioch, *Ad Autolycum* 22–3) was a Jewish author, but there is no good reason to believe this. Cf. J. H. Charlesworth, *The Pseudepigrapha and Modern Research* (1976), p. 159.

Motzo, B., 'Una fonte sacerdotale antisamaritana di Giuseppe', in *Saggi di storia e letterature giudeo-ellenistica* (1924).
Wacholder, B. Z., ESJL, pp. 293–5.
Momigliano, A. D., 'Flavius Josephus and Alexander's Visit to Jerusalem', Athenaeum 57 (1979), pp. 442–8.

(3) *The Saga of the Tobiads*. Preserved in Jos. *Ant.* xii 4, 1–11 (154–236) is a saga recounting the adventures of Josephus the son of Tobias and Joseph's son Hyrcanus in the Ptolemaic court. The story is entertaining fiction about historical personages who were figures of great power in Transjordan during the latter half of the third century B.C. The interest in, and favourable attitude towards, the Ptolemaic court makes it likely that this was written in Greek. The entirely favourable picture given of Joseph and Hyrcanus makes it likely that the work was written by a Tobiad descendant in Transjordan, which suggests a date in the middle or late second century B.C.

On the historical core to the story, see M. Hengel, *Judaism and Hellenism* I (ET 1974), pp. 270–7.

Bibliography

Willrich, H., *Juden und Griechen* (1892), pp. 91–106.
Tcherikover, V. A., *Hellenistic Civilization and the Jews* (1959), pp. 127–42.
Stern, M., 'Notes on the Story of Joseph the Tobiad', *Tarbiz* 32 (1962), pp. 35–47 (Heb.).
Hengel, M., *Judaism and Hellenism* (ET 1974), vol. I, pp. 269–70.
Goldstein, J. A., 'The Tales of the Tobiads', in J. Neusner, ed., *Christianity, Judaism and other Greco-Roman Cults : Studies for Morton Smith at 60* III (1975), pp. 85–123.
Wacholder, B. Z., ESJL, pp. 295–6.
Collins, BAAJ, pp. 73–5.

(4) *Saga of the Oniads (?)*. The activities of the High Priestly family of the Oniads before the Maccabaean revolt are so fully recounted in Jos. *Ant.* xii 6, 1 (265)-xiii 10, 7 (300) and in 2 Maccabees that Goldstein has tried to reconstruct a propagandistic history allegedly written by Onias IV from these accounts. His attempt must, however, be reckoned a failure and there is not sufficient reason to believe that such a work ever existed.

Bibliography

Goldstein, J. A., 'The Tales of the Tobiads', in J. Neusner, ed., *Christianity, Judaism and other Greco-Roman Cults* III (1975),. pp. 85–123.
Goldstein, J. A., *I Maccabees* (1976), pp. 55–61, 90–103.
Doran, R., *Temple Propaganda : The Purpose and Character of 2 Maccabees* (1981), pp. 17–19.
Collins, BAAJ, pp. 73, 76.
Goldstein, J. A., *II Maccabees* (1983), pp. 35–7.

IV. Epic Poetry and Drama

1. Philo the Epic Poet

The appropriation of Greek forms of literature by Hellenistic Jews did not stop with prose. Experiment was made with the Greek forms of epic poetry and drama, in that biblical history was composed in the form of the Greek epos and even presented in the form of Greek drama. For what has been preserved of this remarkable literature, we are indebted to the excerpts of Alexander Polyhistor included by Eusebius in his *Praeparatio evangelica* (cf. above, pp. 510 ff.). [74]

From the Greek poem of a certain Philo, 'About Jerusalem' (Περὶ τὰ Ἱεροσόλυμα), three small fragments are imparted by Eusebius (Euseb., *Praep. ev.* ix 20; 24; 37). The first fragment is concerned with Abraham, the second with Joseph, and the third with the springs and the water conduits of Jerusalem, whose abundance is praised. The first and the third are taken from the first book of the work cited (ix 20: Φίλων ἐν τῷ πρώτῳ τῶν Περὶ τὰ Ἱεροσόλυμα; ix 37: Φίλων ἐν τοῖς Περὶ Ἱεροσολύμων... ἐν τῇ πρώτῃ); the second ostensibly from the fourteenth book (ix 24: Φίλων ἐν τῇ ιδ' τῶν Περὶ Ἱεροσόλυμα). It is too improbable, however, that, if Philo dealt with events in chronological order, it should have taken him fourteen books to get as far as the history of Joseph. It can therefore be assumed with Freudenthal (*Alex. Polyh.*, p. 100, note) that ἐν τῇ δ' (the fourth book) should be read instead of ἐν τῇ ιδ', or even ἐν τῇ [ι]α' (the first book), cf. Jacoby *ad loc.*, tentatively, or that the poem followed some structure other than chronology, cf. Nickelsburg in JWSTP, p. 120. If the poet Philo is to be identified with the historian Philo the elder (see below), the reference to the latter in Clement of Alexandria, quoted by Eusebius, *Hist. eccl.* vi 13, 7, suggests that Philo may have reached as far as Moses in this or another work. The language is that of Greek epic poetry. Philo's

---

74. A reference which survives apart from the Polyhistor tradition in the *Excerpta Latina Barbari* (in *Chronica Minora*, ed. Frick (1892), p. 278), mentions a certain Sosates, who is described as 'Ebraicus Omirus', the 'Jewish Homer', and as flourishing in Alexandria in the reign of Ptolemy XII Auletes, i.e. the mid-first century B.C. Unfortunately the dating of the chronicle entry is confused, since Sosates is also said to have coincided with the high priesthoods of Simon and John, i.e. the second half of the second century B.C. Either date is possible, or it may be that the chronographer has moved the entry from somewhere else entirely since he apparently did so in other cases. At any rate, nothing at all is known about the content of his poetry, and it is not unlikely that it contained nothing specifically Jewish, like the rhetorical theory of Caecilius of Calacte (see below, p. 701). On Sosates, see Fraser, PA II, pp. 986–7; S. J. D. Cohen, 'Sosates, the Jewish Homer', HThR 74 (1981), pp. 391–6.

hexameters are however written without full control of Greek prosody, although the fact that his diction is pompous and stilted to the point of being unintelligible is in keeping with the purposeful obscurity of other Hellenistic epics. The title 'About Jerusalem' is also typical of such epics since many other poems about cities are known. Attempts to trace in Philo parallels with other Greek genres, e.g. the Orphic hymns (Gutman), are however too speculative to be useful.

The Philo mentioned by Clement of Alexandria (*Strom.* i 21, 141) and by Josephus (*C. Ap.* i 23 (218) = Euseb., *Praep. ev.* ix 42), whom Josephus designates 'the older Philo' (Φίλων ὁ πρεσβύτερος) in distinction from the younger philosopher, may possibly be identical with the author of the epic on Jerusalem, though this identity has been denied by Walter (see above, p. 556). In favour of identity is the fact that, if a separate historian called Philo existed, Alexander Polyhistor might have been expected to quote from him, but that, so far as is known in the extant quotations of Polyhistor, he did not do so. If the two Philos are in fact identical, Philo must have celebrated Jerusalem in verse in a way that provided at the same time a history of the Jewish kings, as we may suppose from the fragments of Eusebius. The hypothesis of two Philos remains however most probable.

In regard to the date of Philo, it can only be said that he was earlier than Alexander Polyhistor. Although there is no direct evidence for it, from the contents of the poem he was almost without doubt a Jew.

It is likely that the eulogy of Jerusalem indicates that the work was written there (Freudenthal). An Egyptian origin has been asserted (Hengel) on no very good grounds, but in fact a poem in praise of Jerusalem could have been written anywhere in the Diaspora.

Editions

Ludwich, A., *De Philonis carmine graeco-judaico* (1900).
Jacoby, FGrH 729, III C, pp. 689–91.
Denis, FPG, pp. 203–4.
(Emendations proposed by Y. Gutman in Script. Hier. 1 (1954), p. 40, should be rejected.)

Translations

English:
Attridge, H. W., in Charlesworth, OTP II (forthcoming).

German:
Ludwich, *loc. cit.*
Riessler, P., *Altjüd. Schrift.* (1928), pp. 733 f., 1315.
Walter, N., *Fragmente jüdisch-hellenistischer Epik* (JSHRZ IV.3) (1983), pp. 148–53.

Bibliography

(See works under Philo the Elder, above, p. 556.)
Gutman, Y., 'Philo the Epic Poet', Script. Hier. 1 (1954), pp. 36–63.
Gutman, Y., *The Beginnings of Jewish-Hellenistic Literature* I (1958), pp. 221–44 (Heb.).

Hadas, M., *Hellenistic Culture* (1959), pp. 99–100.
Denis, IPGAT, pp. 270 f.
Wacholder, B. Z., 'Philo (The Elder)', EJ XIII (1971), cols. 407–8.
Wacholder, B. Z., ESJL, pp. 282–3.
Collins, BAAJ, pp. 43–6.

2. Theodotus

Similar in kind to Philo's poem on Jerusalem appears to have been that of Theodotus on Shechem, from which Eusebius imparts a long fragment in *Praep. ev.* ix 22, partly in a literal quotation and partly in a description of its contents. The whole piece relates to the history of the town of Shechem. Its situation is first described, then the story of its capture by the Hebrews following Gen. 34. It tells how Jacob first lived in Mesopotamia, married there and had children, then moved with them to the neighbourhood of Shechem and obtained a plot of land from Hamor, King of Shechem; how Shechem the son of Hamor raped Dinah, Jacob's daughter, and subsequently how Jacob declared himself ready to give Dinah as wife to Shechem on the condition that all the Shechemites were circumcised; and finally how Simeon and Levi, two of the sons of Jacob, murdered Hamor and Shechem, and together with their brothers destroyed the town of the Shechemites.

Since Jacob's sojourn in Mesopotamia is not mentioned until after the description of the town of Shechem and only as an introduction to the subsequent story of the capture of Shechem by the Hebrews, the history of the town may have constituted the theme proper of the poem; and since, in addition, Shechem is designated 'holy city' (ἱερὸν ἄστυ), it is possible that Theodotus was a Samaritan. In that case, the title which Eusebius gave to the poem, i.e. Περὶ 'Ιουδαίων, would hardly be correct. The possible alternative title Σικίμων κτίσις is accordingly proposed by Jacoby, FGrH 732, III C, p. 692. It would not be surprising if Alexander Polyhistor and after him Eusebius proved to have mistaken a Samaritan for a Jew.

These arguments for a Samaritan origin are not however decisive.[75] The phrase ἱερὸν ἄστυ could be a Hebraism meaning 'splendid city', cf. Y. Gutman, *The Beginnings of Jewish-Hellenistic Literature* I (1958), p. 248 (Heb.), or could refer to the traditional holiness of the site in biblical

---

75. A. Ludwich already held that the description of Shechem as ἱερὸν ἄστυ is not decisive (note 8), and emphasized, against the Samaritan character of the section, that Jacob's wish to Judaize the Shechemites, and the atrocity committed against them by his sons, are told 'with objective calm' (therefore with approval) (note 22).

history. It is possible that the rest of the poem was about some topic other than Shechem. The surviving fragment concentrates on the town only because it was the origin of the city's name that Eusebius was concerned to elucidate (Eusebius, *Praep. ev.* ix 22). Some have therefore argued that the Jewish identity of Theodotus should be retained (Ludwich, Gutman, Collins). In favour of this is the title given by Eusebius. Furthermore, the thoroughly positive light in which is portrayed the atrocity of Jacob's sons in killing the 'impious' inhabitants of Shechem seems strange in a Samaritan work, even though Samaritans by the Hellenistic period doubtless identified as much with the descendants of Jacob as with the ancient inhabitants of the town. If the work is Jewish, the assumption made by Jacob that it was desirable that gentiles should be Judaized by circumcision points to a Hasmonaean date, perhaps the time of John Hyrcanus.

At the beginning of the excerpt it is said that the town of Shechem received its name from Sikimios, the son of Hermes (ἀπὸ Σικιμίου τοῦ Ἑρμοῦ). If this reading is correct, Theodotus must have embellished Jewish history with details from Greek mythology, following other Hellenistic writers.[76]

The linguistic form, quite different from Philo's, is simple, lively and clear; the construction of the hexameters is Homeric. Whether the writer was Jewish or Samaritan, it can be certain that he worked before Alexander Polyhistor. Identification of this author with the Theodotus cited by Josephus in *C. Ap.* i 23 (216) as a gentile witness to the antiquity of the Jews is very implausible. The same arguments apply against such an identification as in the case of Theophilus (see above, p. 556). There is no indication of the place of origin and Jerusalem is as possible as Alexandria or other places in the Greek-speaking diaspora.

Editions

Ludwich, A., *De Theodoti carmine graeco-judaico* (1899).
Jacoby, FGrH 732, III C, pp. 692–4 (with emendations proposed by Y. Gutman, *The Beginnings of Jewish-Hellenistic Literatur* I (1958), pp. 247–58).
Denis, FPG, pp. 204–7.

76. The transmitted reading Ἑρμοῦ is accepted by Jacoby, FGrH, 723, III C, p. 692. The emendation to Ἐμμώρ at the beginning of the fragment in its place (Ludwich, followed by Gifford, Mras, Collins) is unnecessary. It is characteristic of such euhemeristic literature to project biblical figures back into an even more remote past as part of the mythological legend of a city's foundation. Ἐμμώρ, i.e. Hamor, is given as the father of a man called Shechem later in Theodotus' account, where it is said that Hamor was ruler of the city (Jacoby, FGrH, III C, p. 692, line 26). This follows Genesis 34. The Σικίμιος who is said to have given his name to the city as its founder (lines 14–16) must be a different man whose father could well have been named by Theodotus as Hermes. The proof of this is that it is highly improbable that Σικίμιος in line 15 and Shechem in line 26 are identical because, if they were, Hamor would be portrayed as ruler of the town of Shechem after it had been founded by his own son.

Translations

English:
Fallon, F. T., in Charlesworth, OTP II (forthcoming).

German:
Ludwich, *loc. cit.*
Riessler, P., *Altjüd. Schrift.* (1928), pp. 1263–5, 1339.
Walter, N., *Die Fragmente jüdisch-hellenistischer Epik* (JSHRZ IV.3) (1983), pp. 164–71.

Bibliography

Freudenthal, *Alex. Polyh.* (1875), pp. 99 ff.
Susemihl, F., *Gesch. d. griech. Litt. i. d. Alexandrinerzeit* II (1892), p. 655.
Laqueur, R., 'Theodotus (21)', RE VA 2 (1934), cols. 1958–9.
Gutman, Y., *The Beginnings of Jewish-Hellenistic Literature* I (1958), pp. 245–61 (Heb.).
Bull, R. J., 'A Note on Theodotus' Description of Shechem', HThR 60 (1967), pp. 221–8.
Wacholder, B. Z., 'Theodotus', EJ xv, 1102 ff.
Wacholder, B. Z., ESJL, p. 285.
Collins, J. J., 'The Epic of Theodotus and the Hellenism of the Hasmonaeans', HThR 73 (1980), pp. 91–104.
Collins, J. J., BAAJ, pp. 47–8.
Walter, N., *Die Fragmente jüdisch-hellenistischen Epik* (JSHRZ IV.3) (1983), pp. 154–63 (a full discussion).
Pummer, R., and M. Roussel, 'A note on Theodotus and Homer', JSJ 13 (1982), pp. 177–82.
Pummer, R., 'Genesis 34 in Jewish writings of the Hellenistic and Roman periods', HThR 75 (1982), pp. 177–88.

3. Ezekiel the Tragic Poet

The most remarkable phenomenon in the field of Jewish-Hellenistic poetry is the conversion of biblical material into Greek dramas. We know of course of only one such Jewish dramatist, Ezekiel, and it remains uncertain whether he had predecessors or successors. His mastery of the form has suggested to some that he was working within an established tradition, but there is no explicit evidence of other such writers. (A drama about Susanna by ὁ Δαμασκηνός should probably be attributed not to Nicolaus of Damascus but to the fourth-century Christian writer John of Damascus, cf. Jacoby, FGrH IIC, p. 290, Komm. on 90, F132.) It is likely in any case that he composed other dramas besides the one known to us in excerpts, for he was named 'the poet of Jewish tragedies', in the plural (Clement of Alexandria, *Strom.* i 23, 155; Euseb., *Praep. ev.* ix 28). Since the Eusebius citation was taken from Alexander Polyhistor it is likely to be accurate, *contra* Fraser, PA II, p. 987. One of these dramas, entitled 'The Exodus', 'Εξαγωγή, and concerned with the history of the exodus of the Jews from Egypt, is well known through extensive excerpts in Eusebius (after Alexander Polyhistor) and Clement of Alexandria (Clement of Alexandria, *Strom.* i 23, 155; Euseb., *Praep. ev.* ix 29, 14).

The moment chosen as the point of departure seems to have been that in which Moses fled to Midian on account of the murder of the Egyptian (Exod. 2), for this is the time in which the first excerpt places us (Euseb., *Praep. ev.* ix 28 = Clement of Alexandria, *Strom.* i 23, 155–6). It consists in a long monologue by Moses, in which he recounts his life story until that point, and concludes by saying that he must in consequence now wander in a foreign land. He then sees the seven daughters of Reuel approaching (Exod. 2:16 ff.) and asks them who they are; whereat Zipporah informs him. The further course of the story is only indicated in the excerpt in that there is then question of the watering of the flocks, and of the marriage of Zipporah and Moses (Exod. 2:16 ff.).

In the second excerpt (Euseb. ix 29, 4–6), Moses tells his father-in-law of a dream, which the latter interprets to mean that Moses will attain to a ruling position and will know things present, past, and future.

A further scene (Euseb. ix 29, 7–11) represents, on the basis of Exodus 3–4, how God spoke with Moses from a burning bush and charged him with the mission of freeing the people of Israel from Egyptian slavery. Since God speaks invisibly from the bush, he does not himself appear on the stage; only his voice is heard. The details are more or less in agreement with Exodus 3–4.

In the following excerpt (Euseb. ix 29, 12–13), God gives exact instructions concerning the exodus and the celebration of the Passover according to Exodus 11–12. It is likely that the first half of this excerpt still belongs to the scene of the burning bush (up to line 174, ed. Jacobson = Euseb. ix 29, 12 *fin.*), while the second half belongs to the conference between Moses and the elders of the people.

In a further scene (Euseb. ix 29, 14), an Egyptian who has escaped the catastrophe in the Red Sea appears and relates how the Israelites successfully passed through, whereas the Egyptian army perished there.

Finally in the last fragment (Euseb. ix 29, 15–16), a messenger, conceived as a scout sent on ahead of the Israelite column, reports to Moses the discovery of an excellent camping place near Elim, with twelve springs and seventy palm trees (Exod. 15:27 = Num. 33:9). Nearby, says the messenger, there appeared a wondrously mighty bird, almost twice as large as an eagle, which all the other birds followed as their king. The description of this bird, described explicitly as a phoenix but without the mention of Ezekiel's name, also occurs in Eustathius, *Comm. in Hexaemeron* 25 ff. (PG XVIII, 729).

It is clear from these fragments that the story stays fairly close to the biblical narrative, but many midrashic embellishments have been added. Many of these can be paralleled in other midrashim of later date, cf. H. Jacobson, *The Exagoge of Ezekiel* (1983), pp. 20–3, including elements of Merkabah speculation in Moses' dream-vision, cf.

P. W. van der Horst, 'Moses' Throne Vision in Ezekiel the Dramatist', JJS 34 (1983), pp. 21–9. The author's poetry is quite prosaic. On the other hand, it is impossible to deny a certain skill in imagery and in the dramatization of the material. The diction and versification are tolerably fluent. His language has many affinities with Euripides and, to a lesser extent, with some other fifth century tragedians. It is likely that the drama was intended for performance like the Medieval passion plays, for the education of a Jewish audience and as alternative entertainment to pagan Greek drama. The failure to observe unity of scene between the five episodes has suggested to some that the play was read as pamphlets, as was not uncommon in Alexandria in this period (M. Hadas, *Hellenistic Culture* (1959), p. 100). However, too little is known about non-Jewish Hellenistic tragedy for any certainty about such dramatic conventions. In either case, a gentile audience was probably expected alongside the Jews who were the tragedian's main objective. In this connection, the choice of the Exodus theme of redemption was doubtless deliberate.

Ezekiel was clearly Jewish or Samaritan, as his name implies. A Samaritan origin was suggested by K. Kuiper, 'Le poète juif Ezéchiel', REJ 46 (1903), pp. 174 ff. and should not be entirely discounted given the conspicuous parallel between Ezekiel and the Samaritan Pentateuch, cf. van der Horst, *art. cit.* p. 28, n. 47. A Jewish origin is however more likely since nothing forbids it. His place of writing is uncertain. The common opinion is that he wrote in Alexandria (Fraser, Jacobson), but this is based on nothing stronger than the suitability of the Alexandrian Jewish community for such writings. The Exodus theme was important enough for all Jews for its use to indicate no special relation to Egypt in the author. The reference to 'Libya, held by diverse tribes of dark-skinned Ethiopians' (lines 60–62, ed. Jacobson, = Euseb. ix 28, 4), may possibly indicate a non-Egyptian, perhaps Cyrenaican, environment (Gutman); nor is it impossible that the play was composed in Palestine (Hadas). The date of writing was before Alexander Polyhistor. Since he knew the LXX and possibly Demetrius, cf. Wacholder, ESJL, p. 243, he must have written after the mid-third century B.C., but no more precise date can be fixed.

Ten trimeters in Epiphanius, *Panarion*, 64.29.6, were ascribed to Ezekiel by J. J. Scaliger and, following him, many others including A.-M. Denis, cf. FPG, p. 216, but this ascription is probably incorrect since the tenor of the passage is Christian, cf. H. Jacobson, 'Ezekiel the Tragedian and the primeval serpent', AJPh 102 (1981), pp. 316–20.

Editions

Eusebius, *Praep. ev.* ix 28 (ed. Mras, GCS Eusebius VIII.1, pp. 524–38).
Denis, FPG, pp. 207–16.

Snell, B., *Tragicorum Graecorum Fragmenta* I (1971), no. 128.
Jacobson, H., *The* Exagoge *of Ezekiel* (1983).

Translations

English:
Jacobson, *loc. cit.*
Robertson, J., in Charlesworth, OTP II (forthcoming).

German:
Riessler, P., *Altjüd. Schrift.* (1928), 337 ff.
Vogt, E., *Tragiker Ezechiel* (JSHRZ IV.3) (1983), pp. 121–33.

Bibliography

Delitzsch, *Zur Gesch. der jüdischen Poesie* (1836), pp. 28, 209, 211–19.
Susemihl, F., *Gesch. d. griech. Litt. i. d. Alexandrinerzeit* II (1892), pp. 653 ff.
Kuiper, K., 'Le poète juif Ezéchiel', REJ 46 (1903), pp. 48–73, 161–77 (includes reconstructed text).
Kuiper, K., 'Ad Ezechielem poetam judaeum curae secundae', Rivista di storia antica 8 (1904), pp. 62–94.
Dieterich, 'Ezechiel', RE VI.2 (1909), cols. 1701 ff.
Christ, W. v., O. Stählin and W. Schmidt, *Gesch. der griech. Lit.* II.1 (⁶1920), pp. 607 ff.
Wienecke, J., *Ezechielis Judaei poetae Alexandrini fabulae, quae inscribitur ΕΞΑΓΩΓΗ fragmenta* (Phil. Diss. Münster, 1931).
Wienecke, J., EJ VI, cols. 885 ff.
Dalbert, P., *Die Theologie der jüd.-hell. Missionsliteratur* (1954), pp. 52–65.
Strugnell, J., 'Notes on the Text and Metre of Ezekiel the Tragedian's *Exagoge*', HThR 60 (1957), pp. 449–57.
Hadas, M., *Hellenistic Culture* (1959), pp. 99–101.
Gutman, Y., *The Beginnings of Jewish-Hellenistic Literature* II (1964), pp. 9–69 (Heb.).
Snell, B., 'Die Jamben in Ezechiels Moses-Drama', Glotta 44 (1966), pp. 25–32.
Zwierlein, O., *Die Rezitationsdrama Senecas* (1966), pp. 138–46.
Kraus, C., 'Ezechiele Poeta tragico', Rivista di Filologia 96 (1968), pp. 164–75.
Denis, IPGAT, pp. 273–7.
Fraser, PA I, pp. 707 ff.; vol. II, p. 987.
Starobinski-Safran, E., 'Un poète judéo-hellénistique: Ezechiel le tragique', Museum Helveticum 31 (1974), pp. 216–24.
Holladay, C. R., 'The Portrait of Moses in Ezekiel the Tragedian', *Soc. Bib. Lit. Seminar Papers* (1976), pp. 447–52.
Jacobson, H., 'Two studies on Ezekiel the Tragedian', GRBS 22 (1981), pp. 167–78.
Jacobson, H., 'Mysticism and apocalyptic in Ezekiel's Exagoge', Illinois Classical Studies 6 (1981), pp. 272–93.
Jacobson, H., *The* Exagoge *of Ezekiel* (1983) (with extensive citations of previous scholarship).
van der Horst, P. W., 'Moses' Throne Vision in Ezekiel the Dramatist', JJS 34 (1983), pp. 21–9.
Vogt, E., *Tragiker Ezechiel* (JSHRZ, IV.3) (1983), pp. 115–20.

V. Philosophy

Whereas in the domains of historiography and poetry, it was mainly the external form only that was borrowed from the Greeks, it is debatable whether this is also true in the field of philosophy, or whether a real, internal blending of Jewish and Greek thought, a strong influence on the content of the Jewish faith by Greek philosophy, took place. If such a fusion of Judaism and Greek philosophy is to be found, it will be seen most clearly in the extensive works of Philo. Even in his case, however, the extent to which his thought is Hellenized cannot be readily decided, and argument continues, cf. § 34. Nor is it clear whether he should be taken as an isolated phenomenon in the history of his people in this period. Some have contended that he is a classic example of an intellectual influence which was felt throughout the period, and was an essential part of the nature of Hellenistic Judaism. According to this view, it was also part of Greek culture to know the great thinkers of the Greek people, and when the Hellenistic Jews accepted the former, they also subjected themselves to the influence of Greek philosophy. One would therefore expect to find evidence of such an impact from the very beginning of Jewish contact with Greece. Aristotle, then, should be taken seriously when he claims that the Jew whom he met in Asia Minor was already Ἑλληνικὸς οὐ τῇ διαλέκτῳ μόνον ἀλλὰ καὶ τῇ ψυχῇ (cf. above, p. 17).

However, the Jewish features of much Hellenistic Jewish philosophy remain so patent that it is also possible to argue that such fusion was very rare indeed and that, like Jewish history and poetry, the use of Greek had only a marginal effect on the content of what was written. Jewish Greek philosophy pursued essentially practical goals in the same way as the Palestinian ḥkmh. Its main content was not logic or physics, but ethics. This ethics was, of course, often based on the theoretical philosophy of the Greeks, but the latter was only a means to an end. The real purpose of Jewish philosophers was a practical one: to educate people in true morality and piety.

This Jewish foundation can also still be recognized in the choice of literary forms. Although much influenced by the genres of Greek literature, the basic literary form of these philosophical works derives from the Old Testament and the later traditions of Palestinian Judaism. The author of the Wisdom of Solomon chose the form of the proverb; Philo gives his debates in the form of the midrash, i.e. in prolix, learned commentaries on the text of the Pentateuch, from which the most heterogeneous philosophical ideas are developed with the aid of allegorical exegesis. He opted in only a few shorter compositions to choose the form of enquiry and dialogue following Greek examples. On the other hand, there is no obvious Jewish genre into which Aristobulus' work can be fitted, and even Wisdom, Philo and 4 Maccabees can only be properly understood as examples of Greek literary form as well as Jewish.

Whatever the general conclusion, it is clear that in these writers the mixture of Jewish and Greek ideas takes a variety of forms. In some the effect of Greek ideas is stronger than in others. But even those most deeply penetrated by them are essentially still rooted in Judaism, for they insist not only on the unity and transcendence of God, and on the rule of divine providence which chastises the wicked and rewards the good; they also firmly maintain that in the Mosaic revelation was given the most perfect knowledge of divine and human matters, so that Judaism is the way to true wisdom and true virtue.

Moreover, not only the degree of Greek influence varies, but different Greek systems are preferred by different authors. Plato, Aristotle, the Stoics, and the Pythagoreans furnished the ideas for these Jewish philosophers. In Platonic-Pythagorean and Stoic teachings, in particular, Jewish thinkers found many elements which could be used to support certain tenets of the Jewish faith. That this appropriation was always eclectic is self-evident. In this characteristic, however, Jewish philosophy merely shared the predominant character of later Greek philosophy in general.

1. The Wisdom of Solomon

The relationship between Jewish and Greek thought in Hellenistic Jewish philosophy is well exemplified in the so-called Wisdom of Solomon. Its surface form resembles that of the ancient Palestinian proverbial wisdom. Like Jesus ben Sira, the author praised true wisdom, which can only be found with God and can only be received by men from God; but the execution is quite different from that of Jesus ben Sira. The latter demonstrates how the truly wise man conducts himself in the various circumstances of practical life; the Wisdom of Solomon, however, is rather a warning against the foolishness of godlessness, particularly of idolatry. The contents of the whole book revolve around this one theme, which is why the proverbial form is not always maintained, but often passes into that of philosophical rhetoric. The author has synthesized Hebraic and Greek traditions in a quite original fashion.

According to chapters 7–9, the king himself is to be regarded as the speaker, and those he addresses are the judges and kings of the earth (1:1; 6:1). It is therefore really a hortatory address of the king (presumably Solomon, cf. 9:8, though he is never named) to his royal colleagues, the gentile rulers. He, the wisest of all kings, holds up to them the foolishness of godlessness and the value of true wisdom.

The contents fall into three parts which, despite varying aims, are demonstrably a unity, although some scholars have argued that they are the work of different authors or the same author at different times.[77] It is first shown (chapters 1–5) that the ungodly and the evildoer, although they may appear to be happy for a time, will not escape the judgement of God, but the pious and righteous, after they have been tried by suffering for a time, will obtain happiness and eternal life . In the second section, the book of Wisdom proper (chapters 6–9), the king, writing in the first person, directs the attention of his royal colleagues to his own example. It is because he has loved high, divine wisdom and taken her to be his bride, that he has achieved glory and honour. For that reason he still prays for such wisdom. The third section (chapters 10–19) sees in the history of Israel, particularly from the different fates of the Israelites and the Egyptians, the blessing of godliness and the curse of ungodliness. A lengthy diatribe on the foolishness of idolatry is inserted here (chapters 13–15).[78]

77. Many different arguments have been put forward in favour of multiple authorship, all of them based on the clear differences between different parts of the work as described here. Earlier arguments were effectively ended by a demonstration of the unity of style, expression and thought of the whole book by C. L. W. Grimm, *Das Buch der Weisheit erklärt* (1860). In this century however L. Lincke, *Samaria und seine Propheten* (1903), pp. 19–44, argued that 1:1–12:8 was written by a Samaritan, whereas 12:19–19:22 was the work of an Alexandrian Jew. W. Weber, 'Die Komposition der Weisheit Salomos', *ZWTh* 47 (1904), pp. 145–69, proposed four authors. F. Focke, *Die Enstehung der Weisheit Salomos* (1913), suggested that the first part of the book (1–5) was translated into Greek from the Hebrew by the author of the second part (6–19). It is indisputable that the parts of the book *could* have been written by different authors, but there are sufficient repetitions of vocabulary to make it unlikely, cf. J. Fichtner, *Weisheit Salomos* (1938). Since the book can be understood without difficulty as a structural unity (see below), the simpler assumption of a single author is to be preferred, cf. D. Winston, *The Wisdom of Solomon* (1979), pp. 12–14. Note should however be taken of the view of C. C. Torrey, *The Apocryphal Literature* (1948), pp. 100 ff., that Wisdom of Solomon 1–10 is a translation of a Hebrew original, particularly since this opinion is in accord with the syntax of these chapters compared to the rest of the book, cf. R. A. Martin, 'Some Syntactical Criteria of Translation Greek', *VT* 10 (1960), p. 307. The possibility of multiple authorship is greater if all or some of the book has been translated from a semitic original as Torrey argued. Cf. also C. E. Purinton, 'Translation Greek in the Wisdom of Solomon', *JBL* 47 (1928), pp. 276–304, suggesting a Hebrew original; F. Zimmermann, 'The Book of Wisdom: Its language and character', *JQR* 57 (1966), pp. 1–27, 101–35, positing Aramaic. Composition in Greek is, however, most probable.

78. This analysis of the structure of the Wisdom of Solomon has been questioned by a number of scholars, but all attempts to divine the subdivisions of such a work are necessarily speculative. The main alternative suggestion is that the first part, on Wisdom's gift of immortality, ends at 6:21, and the second part, on the nature of Wisdom and Solomon's quest for it, ends at 10:21. For alternative analyses, cf. A. G. Wright, 'The

The essential contents of the book are a warning against the foolishness of godlessness. It was intended for Jewish readers to the extent that godlessness or a tendency towards godlessness could be found among them, but it is surely correct to suppose that the author addressed his attack on idolatry to gentile readers also. However, the numerous partially veiled allusions to biblical history seem to presuppose Jewish readers or gentiles knowledgeable about Judaism. The framework of an address to the kings and rulers of the earth suggests the Hellenistic genre of the ethical kingship tract, especially since the author occasionally forgets the literary framework and applies his advice to all men (e.g. 9:13). The complexity of the book places it also in the Hellenistic category of protreptic (Reese), a form of elaborate, rhetorical, didactic exhortation in which a teacher of philosophy was expected to adopt a firm stand on a particular topic and attract students to his position by the deliberate display of a wide range of knowledge, or perhaps the equally common genre of encomium (Beauchamp). The skilful use of Hellenistic rhetorical devices (diatribe, syncrisis, aporia, paradeigma) presupposed an audience with Greek education. Only Jewish intellectuals could have appreciated both all the biblical allusions and all the Greek science and philosophy. The work was presumably intended to reassure such intellectuals of the value of Jewish wisdom in contrast to that provided by pagan competitors. Doubtless however other Jews and gentiles were expected to read it, with benefit even if only partial understanding. For such readers the deliberate obscurity of some of the allusions will have been a literary attraction, for this device is often to be found in other, non-Jewish works of the Hellenistic period.

The author's theological point of view agrees with that of Palestinian proverbial wisdom as we know it from Proverbs and Ecclesiastes. For him, too, divine wisdom is the supreme good, the source of all truth, virtue, and happiness. But whereas, like the author of Proverbs (chapters 8–9) and Jesus ben Sira, he starts from the assertion that this wisdom is first of all present in God, in his conception it almost, but not entirely, becomes an independent hypostasis side by side with God. Although his statements do not appear to go beyond those in Proverbs 8–9, a poetical personification provides, in his case, the rudiments of a philosophical theory. Wisdom is for him a breath of God's power, a pure emanation of the glory of the Almighty, a reflection of the eternal light (7:25–6). It is given to her to live with God. She has been initiated

Structure of the Book of Wisdom', Bibl. 48 (1967), pp. 165–84; J. M. Reese, 'Plan and Structure in the Book of Wisdom', CBQ 27 (1965), pp. 391–9; D. Winston, *The Wisdom of Solomon* (1979), pp. 8–12; G. W. E. Nickelsburg, JLBBM, pp. 175–84; and further literature cited by J. J. Collins, 'Cosmos and Salvation: Jewish Wisdom and Apocalyptic in the Hellenistic Age', History of Religions 17 (1977), pp. 123–4.

into the knowledge that belongs to God. She is arbiter of his works, i.e. she chooses from among the works whose idea God has conceived those which are to be executed (8:3–4). She is the associate on the throne of God (9:4); she understands God's works and was present when he created the world; she knows what is pleasing in his eyes and what is right according to his commandments (9:9). Accordingly, wisdom is represented not only as God's own possession, but also as God's helper, sprung from his own being. Moreover, 'the almighty word of God' is also personified in a way that is close to hypostasization (18:15 f.). Thus we already have here in an unworked form the same elements from which Philo formed his doctrine of the *logos* (= reason and word of God) as a hypostasis mediating between God and the world; for our author, wisdom has a relation to the world similar to that of Philo's *logos*. She has a spirit which moves easily, superintending everything, penetrating everything (7:22–4). She effects all things (8:5), orders all things (8:1), and renews all things (7:27). 'In every generation she passes into holy souls, and makes them friends of God and prophets' (7:27). It is also wisdom that reveals itself in the history of Israel, e.g. in the pillar of cloud and fire which led the Israelites through the wilderness (10:17, and in chapter 10 in general). In sum, wisdom is the medium through which God works in the world. The trend of this whole speculation is apparently the same as in Philo, namely to secure, through the insertion of such an intermediary, the absolute transcendence of God, who cannot be thought of as being in direct contact with a sinful world. It should not, nevertheless, be forgotten that it is not our author's purpose to emphasize this thought; he is not a theologian or a philosopher intent on making a systematic statement of fundamental Jewish beliefs. It is much more his aim to concentrate on the figure of divine wisdom and to exhibit it as the supreme good through which alone man may achieve real immortality. He does not wish to show that this wisdom is different from God, but on the contrary, how near it is to him. It is possible that this view of wisdom reflects traditions which are also found elsewhere.[79]

The influence of Greek philosophy is clear in the details of execution. The formulae in which the rule of wisdom in the world is described (7:24: διήκει δὲ καὶ χωρεῖ; 8:1: διοικεῖ) recall the Stoic doctrine of the world-spirit, of God as the world-reason, immanent in and pervading the world.[80] Even the enumeration of the four cardinal virtues (8:7: self-control, prudence, justice, courage) can be traced back to Stoic influence. The author's anthropology, on the other hand, is both Semitic and Greek, and the Greek element is eclectic either through his own efforts or the influence of Middle Platonism, in which many Stoic

---

79. Cf. on this doctrine of Wisdom in general the literature referred to above, pp. 198 f.
80. E. Zeller, *Die Philosophie der Griechen* III.2 (³1881; repr. 1963), p. 271.

notions were incorporated. Man is said to consist of both body and soul, both of which have an important role, but the soul is the determining element. At times (though not always, cf. 15:11) the author seems to subscribe to the notion that the soul is pre-existent (8:20), but his real meaning here seems to be that the good man possesses a fine soul which enters an unblemished body whose purpose is to serve as an 'earthly tent' for the *νοῦς* (9:15). He may at any time have to return the soul like a loan and then become dust (15:8). In this anthropology the Hebrew view, though not abandoned, is subordinated to the Greek: instead of the hope for a resurrection of the body, we have here the Greek view of the possible immortality of the soul.[81] Far from being a dualistic view of the soul, however, this is a moralizing image that insists that moral behaviour comes about through the soul, and that eternal happiness of the soul is God's gift through wisdom. The relationship of the just man to wisdom has changed from that in the Hebrew wisdom texts. Whereas there, the man is the pupil of wisdom, who personifies the Torah through which divine rewards may be achieved in this life, in the present work wisdom is the object of an intimate, personal religious experience that blossoms into the state of being near God in eternal happiness. This new emphasis largely results from the use of the language of contemporary Isis literature. The borrowing of such language may be part of a deliberate challenge to such non-Jewish cults.[82]

With regard to the date of the author, or authors if it is a composite work, the book provides no firm indication in either its language or its content, nor are there clear allusions to contemporary political conditions. The author used some books of the LXX and therefore must have written after *c.* 200 B.C. The *terminus ante quem* may be as late as the mid-first century A.D., a date during the rule of Caligula (A.D. 37–41) being favoured by some scholars on the grounds that, if the work is Alexandrian, the vicious attack on wicked idolaters (5:16–23) and comments on ruler cult (14:16–20) fit well into that period

---

81. Cf. W. Weber, 'Die Unsterblichkeit der Weisheit Salomos', ZWTh 48 (1905), pp. 409–44; F. C. Porter, 'The Pre-existence of the Soul in the Book of Wisdom and in the Rabbinical Writings', *Old Testament and Semitic Studies in Memory of W. R. Harper* I (1908), pp. 205–69 (= Am. Journ. Theol. (1908), pp. 53–115); Weber, 'Die Seelenlehre der Weisheit Salomos', ZWTh (1909), pp. 314–32; *idem*, 'Der Auferstehungsglaube der Weisheit Salomos', ZWTh (1912), pp. 205–39; H. Bückers, *Die Unsterblichkeitslehre des Weisheitsbuches* (1938); M. Delcor, 'L'immortalité de l'âme dans le Livre de la Sagesse et dans les documents de Qumrân', NRTh 77 (1955), pp. 614–30; G. W. E. Nickelsburg, *Resurrection, Immortality and Eternal Life in Intertestamental Judaism* (1972), pp. 48–92; J. J. Collins, 'The Root of Immortality: Death in the Context of Jewish Wisdom', HThR 71 (1978), pp. 177–92; D. Winston, *The Wisdom of Solomon* (1979), pp. 25–32, emphasizing the coherence of the attitude in Wisdom with that in Middle Platonism.

82. For pagan parallels to the attitude of Wisdom here, cf. D. Winston, *op. cit.*, pp. 159–218, and literature cited there.

(Winston). The hypothesis puts too much weight onto this polemic, which is in fact subordinate to the main themes of the book, but it has the merit of demonstrating that so late a date is not impossible. General linguistic evidence is not decisive for dating given the paucity of comparative material, although it should be said that such evidence as there is suggests the Roman period rather than earlier times, cf. L. Robert, *Études épigraphiques et philologiques* (1938), pp. 226–35 on the word θρησκεία, and note other words in Wisdom which do not appear in secular Greek literature before the first century A.D., listed by Winston, p. 22, note 33. Nor are literary comparisons helpful. Despite clear literary connections with Ben Sira, Posidonius and Philo, no reliance of Wisdom upon them or vice versa can be demonstrated, nor can the failure of Wisdom to use ideas put forward in the other authors be taken to indicate its priority (D. Georgi, *Weisheit Salomos* (JSHRZ III.4) (1980), pp. 396–7) since such omissions may be due solely to the different purposes of the authors. Since the Greek used by the author contains many more Hebraisms than are found in Philo (E. G. Clark, *The Wisdom of Solomon* (1973), pp. 7–8), and since his purpose is different from Philo's, so that, for instance, he altogether ignores the use of allegory as found in Philo and Aristobulus, there is no need to posit that he came from the same milieu despite the linguistic and thematic parallels with Philo that can be pointed out (cf. D. Winston, *The Wisdom of Solomon* (1979), pp. 59–63). He could have produced his relatively unsophisticated wisdom philosophy either before or after Philo had written.

For the place of origin, it is usually assumed that the author wrote in Alexandria because of the prominence of references to Egyptian matters and the intensity of the attacks on the Egyptians for their wickedness. The traditions of the Exodus were however an important subject for all Jews and an origin elsewhere is quite possible (cf. Georgi, *op. cit.*, pp. 395–6, whose own suggestion of a Syrian origin because of Wisdom's acquaintance with Palestinian apocalyptic is however not convincing). It is certainly wrong to assume that Philo himself was the author, which Jerome, *Praef. in vers. libr. Salom.* (PL XXVIII, col. 1308), mentions as the view of some of his contemporaries and which was followed by a number of later authors including Luther.

The book was used from the beginning by Christians, cf. C. Larcher, *Études sur le Livre de la Sagesse* (1969), pp. 11–84. It is probable that Paul was acquainted with it because there are echoes of it in Pauline letters, cf. Larcher, *op. cit.*, pp. 14–20, who points out however that these echoes may also be explained by a common training of Paul and the author of Wisdom.

It is fairly certain that it was known by Clement of Rome (Clement of Rome 27, 5 = Wisdom 12:12 and 11:21; cf. also Clement 60, 1 = Wisdom 7:17).

Tatian, *Oratio ad Graecos* 7 *init.*, says the same of Christ as the author of Wisdom 2:23 says of God. Echoes of Wisdom which may, but need not, reflect direct borrowing can be found in other patristic writers of the second century, cf. Larcher, *op. cit.*, pp. 36–8.

Irenaeus does not quote Wisdom in his large work on heresy, but at iv 38, 3 he borrows the phrase ἀφθαρσία δὲ ἐγγὺς εἶναι ποιεῖ θεοῦ from Wisdom 6:19. With reference to this, Eusebius, *Hist. eccl.* v 8, 8 says of Irenaeus: καὶ ῥητοῖς δέ τισιν ἐκ τῆς Σολομῶνος σοφίας κέχρηται, μονον-ουχὶ φάσκων· Ὅρασις δὲ θεοῦ περιποιητικὴ ἀφθαρσίας, ἀφθαρσία δὲ ἐγγὺς εἶναι ποιεῖ θεοῦ. According to Eusebius, Irenaeus explicitly quotes from Wisdom in βιβλίον διαλέξεων διαφόρων which has not come down to us (*Hist. eccl.* v 26).

The Muratori Canon, lines 68–70, reads: 'Sapientia ab amicis Salomonis in honorem ipsius scripta.' Cf. T. Zahn, *Gesch. des neutestamentl. Kanons* II, pp. 95–105; E. Hennecke and W. Schnee-melcher, eds., *New Testament Apocrypha*, trans. R. McL. Wilson, I (1963), pp. 44–5. The suggestion that 'ab amicis' represents a mistranslation of ὑπο Φίλωνος, i.e. 'by Philo', is quite probable since that would explain the listing of Wisdom in a New Testament canon, cf. Larcher, *op. cit.*, p. 40.

Tertullian, *Adv. Valentinianos* 2, refers to Wisdom 1:1 in the words: 'ut docet ipsa Sophia, non quidem Valentini sed Salomonis.'

Clement of Alexandria quotes and uses it frequently, treating it as Scripture, cf. O. Stählin, *Clemens Alexandrinus und die Septuaginta* (1901), pp. 45 ff. The explicit quotations are introduced either as sayings of Solomon (thus *Strom.* vi 11, 92; 14, 110; 14, 114; 15, 120–1), or of the σοφία (*Paedag.* ii 1, 7; *Strom.* ii 2, 5; iv, 16, 103–4; v, 14, 89), especially of the θεία σοφία (*Strom.* iv 16, 103–4), or as words of the γραφή (*Paedag.* ii 10, 99 *fin.*; *Strom.* v 14, 108; vi, 11, 92), or with the formula εἴρηται (*Strom.* vi 14, 113) or φησί, φασί (*Strom.* vi 11, 92–3). He may also have used Wisdom 7:25 in a fragment (Fr. 23) of his lost *Hypotyposes*, where, according to Photius, *Bibl.* 109, he supports his use of the word ἀπόρροια in his Christological speculations by quoting 'some expression of Scripture', cf. Winston, *op. cit.*, p. 68.

In the pseudo-Hippolytan *Remonstratio adversus Judaeos*, the book is repeatedly quoted as a genuine προφητεία Σολομῶν περὶ Χριστοῦ (*Adv. Judaeos* 9, 10, PG X, col. 793), particularly the passage 2:12:20, which is also frequently interpreted messianically by later authors (cf. above, vol. II, p. 500).

After the author of the Muratori Canon, Origen was the first to intimate doubt about Solomonic authorship. He cites it with such sceptical formulas as ἡ ἐπιγεγραμμένη τοῦ Σολομῶντος σοφία (*Comment. in*

Joann. xx 4 = GCS, Origen IV, p. 331), ἡ Σοφία ἡ ἐπιγεγραμμένη Σολομῶντος (*In Jerem. homil.* viii 1 = GCS, Origen III, p. 56; ed. Nautin, SC 232, p. 354), ὁ περὶ τῆς σοφίας εἰπών (*Selecta in Jerem.* c. 29 = PG XIII, col. 577), ἐν τῇ ἐπιγεγραμμένῃ Σολομῶντος Σοφίᾳ (*Contra Cels.* v 29 = GCS, Origen II, p. 30), 'in Sapientia, quae dicitur Salomonis, qui utique liber non ab omnibus in auctoritate habetur' (*De principiis* iv 4, 6 (33) = GCS, Origen V, p. 357; ed. Crouzel and Simonetti, SC 268, p. 414). But he cites it almost as often simply as the work of Solomon; and that he regarded it as a canonical book is shown in particular by the whole section *De principiis* i 2, 5–13, where he uses Wisdom 7:25–6 together with Col. 1:15 and Heb. 1:3 as fundamental passages from which he developed his Christology. The whole section *De principiis* i 2, 9–13 is nothing other than an exegetical discussion of the Christological meaning of Wisdom 7:25–6. There are in all about forty citations from this book in Origen.

Cyprian used Wisdom as canonical in the fullest sense. He quotes it as 'Sapientia Salomonis' (*Testim.* ii 14; iii 16, 53, 58, 59, 66; *Ad Fortunatum* 1), 'scriptura divina' (*De habitu virginum* 10; *Epist.* vi 2), 'scriptura sancta' (*Ad Demetrianum* 24), or with formulas such as 'scriptum est' (*De zelo et livore* 4; *Epist.* iv 1; lv 22), 'per Salomonem docet spiritus sanctus', and the like (*De mortalitate* 23; *Ad Fortunatum* 12).

He quotes passages a few times from Proverbs with the formula 'in Sapientia Salomonis' (*Testim.* iii 1, 6, 16, 56); and once, a passage from Wisdom with the formula 'in Ecclesiastico' (*Testim.* iii 112); both certainly as an oversight as elsewhere he distinguishes carefully between Proverbs, Ecclus., and Wisdom.

In the *Teachings of Silvanus* 113, a non-Gnostic document from Nag Hammadi dated to the late second or early third century, there is an explicit allusion to Wisdom 7:25–6, cf. J. M. Robinson, ed., *The Nag Hammadi Library* (1977), p. 359.

The Greek manuscripts, editions, and ancient translations (together with their editions) are mainly the same for Wisdom as for Ecclus. (cf. above, pp. 203 ff.). Cf. especially *LXX, VT Graecum Auct.* ... *Gottingensis ed.* XII.1: *Sapientia Salomonis*, ed. J. Ziegler (²1980), for the critical text as well as a full and careful listing of the Greek witnesses. A fragment of the Greek text of Wisdom has been found in Khirbet Mird, but has not yet been published (Ziegler, *op. cit.*, p. 11). Further papyrus fragments are in Pap. Ant. 8 (third century A.D.), cf. C. H. Roberts, *The Antinoopolis Papyri* Part I (1950), pp. 12 ff.; Pap. Wien. Rainer, Litt. theol. 5 (fourth-fifth century A.D.), cf. C. Wessely, *Studien zur Paläographie und Papyruskunde* IX (1909), p. 4, no. 4. See also I. A. Sparks, 'A Fragment of Sapientia Salomonis from Oxyrhynchus', JSJ 32 (1972), pp. 149–52. Note also F. Feldmann, *Textkritische Materialen zum Buch der Weisheit, gesammelt aus der sahidischen, syrohexaplarischen und armenischen Übersetzung* (1902).

Cf. further on the editions:

Dahse, J., 'Zur Herkunft des alttestamentlichen Textes der Aldina', ZAW 29 (1909), pp. 177–86.

Rahlfs, A., 'Die Abhängigkeit der sixtinischen Septuaginta-Ausgabe von der aldinischen', ZAW 33 (1913), pp. 30–46.

Ziegler, J., 'Der griechische Dodekapropheton-Text der Complutenser Polyglotte', Bibl. 25 (1944), pp. 297–310.

Idem, 'Der Text der Aldina im Dodekapropheton', Bibl. 26 (1945), pp. 37–51.

On the versions, see J. Ziegler, ed., *Sapienta Salomonis*, pp. 15–35. See also on the Peshitta, J. A. Emerton, *The Peshitta of the Wisdom of Solomon* (Stud. Postbibl. 2) (1959). On the Old Latin, which dates to the second half of the second century A.D. and therefore represents the reading of very early Greek manuscripts, see O. de Bruyne, 'Études sur le texte latin de la Sagesse', *Rev. Bénedict.* 41 (1929), pp. 230–43; J. Ziegler, 'Zur griechischen Vorlage der Vetus Latina in der Sapientia Salomonis', *Junker Festschrift* (1961), pp. 275–91; W. Baars, 'A Little-Known Latin Fragment of the Wisdom of Solomon', VT 20 (1970), pp. 230–3; W. Thiele, ed., *Sapientia Salomonis*, in P. Sabatier, ed., *Vetus Latina* XI (1977-). About the Bohairic, Ethiopic, and Arab translations, cf. *LXX, VT Graecum Auct. ... Gottingensis ed.* XII.1, *Sapientia Salomonis*, ed. J. Ziegler ([2]1980), pp. 27–32.

For the exegetical works in general, cf. above, pp. 000 f., and the extensive bibliography given in G. Delling, *Bibliographie zur jüdisch-hellenistischen und intertestamentarischen Literatur* ([2]1975), pp. 125–31; D. Winston, *The Wisdom of Solomon* (1979), pp. 70–96.

Commentaries

Grimm, C. L. W., *Das Buch der Weisheit, erklärt* (*Exegetisches Handbuch zu den Apokryphen*, part 6, 1860).

Siegfried, K., in E. Kautzsch, APAT I (1900; reprinted 1921), pp. 476–507.

Gregg, J. A. F., *The Wisdom of Solomon* (1909).

Heinisch, P., *Exegetisches Handbuch zum A.T.* (1912).

Holmes, S., 'The Wisdom of Solomon', in Charles, APOT I, pp. 518–68.

Goodrick, A. T. S., *The Book of Wisdom. With Introduction and Notes* (1913).

Feldmann, F., *Das Buch der Weisheit* (1926).

Fichtner, J., *Weisheit Salomos* (1938).

Fischer, J., in *Die Heilige Schrift in deutscher Übersetzung* (Echter-Verlag, 1950).

Stein, M. (= E.), in A. Kahana, הספרים החיצונים[2] (1956).

Reider, J., *The Book of Wisdom* (1957).

Clarke, E. G., *The Wisdom of Solomon* (1973).

Winston, D., *The Wisdom of Solomon* (1979) (with detailed commentary and introduction).

Georgi, D., *Weisheit Salomos* (JSHRZ, III.4) (1980).

Larcher, C., *Le Livre de la Sagesse* (1983).

Bibliography

Kohler, K., 'Wisdom of Solomon, Book of the', JE XII, cols. 538–40.

Lincke, *Samaria und seine Propheten* (1903), pp. 119–44.

Weber, W., 'Die Komposition der Weisheit Salomos', ZWTh 47 (1904), pp. 145–69.
Weber, W., 'Die Unsterblichkeit, die Seelenlehre, Heimat und Zeitalter, den Auferstehungsglauben der Weisheit Salomos', ZWTh 48 (1905), pp. 409–44; 51 (1909), pp. 314–32; 53 (1911), pp. 322–45; 54 (1912), pp. 205–39.
Friedländer, M., *Griechische Philosophie im A.T.* (1904), pp. 182–208.
Lagrange, 'Le livre de la Sagesse, sa doctrine des fins dernières', RB (1907), pp. 85–104.
Mariès, L., 'Remarques sur la forme poétique du livre de la Sagesse', RB (1908), pp. 251–7.
Heinisch, P., *Die griechische Philosophie im Buche der Weisheit* (1908).
Porter, F. C., 'The Pre-existence of the Soul in the Book of Wisdom and in the Rabbinical Writings', *American Journal of Theology* 12 (1908), pp. 53–118.
Feldmann, F., 'Zur Einheit des Buches der Weisheit', BZ (1909), pp. 140–50.
Gärtner, E., *Komposition und Wortwahl des Buches der Weisheit* (Diss. Würzburg, 1912).
Focke, F., *Die Entstehung der Weisheit Salomos (Forschungen zur Religion und Literatur des A. und N.T.*, 22, 1913).
Heinemann, I., 'Die griechische Quelle des Buches der Weisheit', in I. Heinemann, *Poseidonios metaphysische Schriften* I (1921), pp. 136–53.
Speiser, E. A., 'The Hebrew Origin of the First Part of the Book of Wisdom', JQR 14 (1923/4), pp. 455–82.
Motzo, B. R., 'L'età e l'autore della Sapienza', *Ricerche Religiose* 2 (1926), pp. 39–44.
Purinton, C. E., 'Translation Greek in the Wisdom of Solomon', JBL 47 (1928), pp. 276–304.
Kuhn, K. G., 'Beiträge zur Erklärung des Buches der Weisheit', ZNW 28 (1929), pp. 334–41.
Idem, 'Exegetische und textkritische Anmerkungen zum Buche der Weisheit', ThStKr 103 (1931), pp. 445–52.
Stein, M. (= E.), 'Ein jüdisch-hellenistischer Midrasch über den Auszug aus Ägypten', MGWJ 42 (1934), pp. 558–75.
Dupont-Sommer, A., 'Les "impies" de Livre de la sagesse sont-ils des Épicuriens?', RHR 3 (1935), pp. 90–109.
Macdonald, D. B., *The Hebrew Philosophical Genius* (1936; reprinted 1965).
Lange, S., 'The Wisdom of Solomon and Plato', JBL 55 (1936), pp. 293–302.
Blakeney, E. H., *The Praises of Wisdom; being Part I of the Book of Wisdom* (1937).
Fichtner, J., 'Die Stellung der Sapientia Salomonis in der Literatur- und Geistesgeschichte ihrer Zeit', ZNW 36 (1937), pp. 113–32.
Bückers, H., *Die Unsterblichkeitslehre des Weisheitsbuches* (1938).
Robert, L., *Études epigraphiques et philologiques* (1938), pp. 226–35.
Fichtner, J., 'Der A.T.-Text der Sapientia Sàlomonis', ZAW 57 (1939), pp. 155–92.
Skehan, P. W., 'Notes on the Latin Text of the Book of Wisdom', CBQ 4 (1942), pp. 230–43.
Torrey, C. C., *The Apocryphal Literature etc.* (1945), pp. 98–103.
Heinemann, I., 'Synkrisis oder äussere Analogie in der "Weisheit Salomos"', ThZ 4 (1948), pp. 241–51.
Pfeiffer, R. H., *History of N.T. Times with an Introduction to the Apocrypha* (1949).
Weisengoff, J.P., 'The Impious in Wisdom 2', CBQ 11 (1949), pp. 40–65.
Eising, H., 'Die theol. Geschichtsbetrachtung des Weisheitsbuches', in *Festschrift M. Meinertz* (1950), pp. 24–80.
Colombo, D., 'Pneuma Sophia eiusque actio in mundo in Libro Sapientiae', SBFLA 1 (1950–1), pp. 107–60.
Eising, H., 'Die Theologische Geschichtsbetrachtung im Weisheitsbuch', *Neutestamentliche Abhandlungen*, suppl. vol. I (1951), pp. 28–40.
Dubarle, A.-M., 'Une source du livre de la Sagesse', RSPhTh 37 (1953), pp. 425–43.
Dalbert, P., *Die Theol. der hellenist.-jüd. Missionslit.* (1954), pp. 70–92.

Delcor, M., 'L'immortalité de l'âme dans le livre de la Sagesse et dans les documents de Qumrân', NRTh 77 (1955), pp. 614-30.

Williams, C. S. C., 'Armenian Variants in the Book of Wisdom', JThSt 7 (1956), pp. 243-6.

Ziener, G., *Die theologische Begriffssprache im Buche der Weisheit* (BBB 11, 1956).

Suggs, M. J., 'Wisdom of Solomon 2:10-ch. 5: A Homily Based on the Fourth Servant Song', JBL 76 (1957), pp. 26-33.

Ziener, G., 'Die Verwendung der Schrift im Buche der Weisheit', Trierer Theologische Zeitschrift 66 (1957), pp. 138-51.

Philonenko, M., 'Le Maître de justice et la Sagesse de Salomon', ThZ 14 (1958), pp. 81-8.

des Places, É., 'Un emprunt de la "Sagesse" aux "Lois" de Platon?', Bibl. 40 (1959), pp. 1016 f.

Dulière, W. L., 'Antinoüs et le Livre de la Sagesse', ZRGG 11 (1959), pp. 201-27.

Finan, Th., 'Hellenistic Humanism in the Book of Wisdom', *Irish Theological Quarterly* 27 (1960), pp. 30-48.

Siebeneck, R. T., 'The Midrash of Wisdom x-xix', CBQ 22 (1960), pp. 176-82.

Vellas, B. M., *Η επιδρασις της Ελληνικης φιλοσοφιας επι του βιβλιου της σοφιας Σολομωντος* (1961).

Grelot, P., 'L'eschatologie de la Sagesse et les apocalypses juives', *Memorial Albert Gelin* (1961), pp. 165-80.

Idem, 'Sagesse x 21 et le Targum de l'Exode', Bibl. 42 (1961), pp. 49-60.

Brockington, L. H., *A Critical Introduction to the Apocrypha* (1961), pp. 67 ff.

Hadas, M., 'Wisdom of Solomon', in IDB IV, cols. 861-3.

Jaubert, A., *La notion d'alliance dans le Judaïsme aux abords de l'ère chrétienne* (1963).

Murphy, R. E., '"To Know your Might is the Root of Immortality" (Wis. xv, 3)', CBQ 25 (1963), pp. 88-93.

Beauchamp, P., 'Le salut corporel des justes et la conclusion du livre de la Sagesse', Bibl. 45 (1964), pp. 491-526.

Wright, A. G., 'The Structure of Wisdom 11-19', CBQ 27 (1965), pp. 28-34.

des Places, É., *De Libro Sapientiae* (1965).

Reese, J. M., 'Plan and Structure in the Book of Wisdom', CBQ 27 (1965), pp. 391-9.

Emerton, J. A., 'Commentaries on the Wisdom of Solomon', *Theology* 68 (1965), pp. 376-9.

Taylor, R., 'The Eschatological Meaning of Life and Death in the Book of Wisdom 1-5', EThL 42 (1966), pp. 72-137.

Zimmermann, F., 'The Book of Wisdom: Its language and character', JQR 57 (1966), pp. 1-27, 101-35.

Wright, A. G., 'The Structure of the Book of Wisdom', Bibl. 48 (1967), pp. 165-84.

Wright, A. G., 'Numerical Patterns in the Book of Wisdom', CBQ 29 (1967), pp. 524-38.

des Places, É., 'Le Livre de la Sagesse et les influences grecques', Bibl. 50 (1969), pp. 536-42.

Larcher, C., *Études sur le Livre de la Sagesse* (1969) (a very full study).

Gilbert, M., 'La structure de la prière de Salomon (Sg. 9)', Bibl. 51 (1970), pp. 301-33.

Reese, J. M., *Hellenistic Influence on the Book of Wisdom and its Consequences* (1970).

Beaucamp, E., trans. J. Clarke, *Man's Destiny in the Books of Wisdom* (1970).

Winston, D., 'The Book of Wisdom's Theory of Cosmogony', *History of Religions* 11 (1971), pp. 185-202.

Gilbert, M., *La critique des dieux dans le Livre de la Sagesse* (1973).

Mack, B. L., *Logos und Sophia. Untersuchungen zur Weisheitstheologie im hellenistischen Judentum* (1973).

Perrenchio, F., 'Struttura e analisi letteraria di Sapienzia 1,1-15 nel quadro del suo contesto letterario immediato', Salesianum 37 (1975), pp. 289-325.

Jacobson, H., 'Wisdom XVIII 9', JSJ 7.2 (1976), p. 204.

des Places, É., 'Épithètes et attributs de la "Sagesse" (Sg. 7,22–33 et *SVF* I 557 Arnim)', Bibl. 57 (1976), pp. 414–19.

Schmitt, A., 'Struktur, Herkunft und Bedeutung der Beispielreihe in Weish 10', BZ 21 (1977), pp. 1–22.

Amir, Y., 'The Wisdom of Solomon and the literature of Qumran', *Proceedings of the Sixth World Congress of Jewish Studies* III (1977), pp. 329–35.

Collins, J. J., 'Cosmos and Salvation: Jewish Wisdom and Apocalyptic in the Hellenistic Age', *History of Religions* 17 (1977), pp. 121–42.

Collins, J. J., 'The Root of Immortality: Death in the Context of Jewish Wisdom', HThR 71 (1978), pp. 177–92.

Beauchamp, P., 'Épouser la Sagesse—ou n'épouser qu'elle? Une énigme du Livre de la Sagesse', in M. Gilbert, ed., *La Sagesse de l'Ancien Testament* (1979), pp. 347–69.

Pelletier, A., 'Ce n'est pas la Sagesse mais le Dieu sauveur qui aime l'humanité', RB 87 (1980), pp. 397–403.

Nickelsburg, G. W. E., JLBBM, pp. 175–85.

Offerhaus, U., *Komposition und Intention der Sapientia Salomonis* (1981).

Perrenchio, F., 'Struttura e analisi letteraria di Sapienzia 1,16–2,24 e 5,1–23', Salesianum 43 (1981), pp. 3–43.

Collins, BAAJ, pp. 182–6.

Schaberg, J., 'Major midrashic traditions in Wisdom 1,1–6, 25', JSJ 13 (1982), pp. 75–101.

Gilbert, M., 'La figure de Salomon en Sg 7–9', in *Études sur le judaïsme hellénistique*, ed. R. Kuntzmann and J. Schlosser, pp. 225–49.

Kloppenborg, J. S., 'Isis and Sophia in the Book of Wisdom', HThR 75 (1982), pp. 57–84.

Gilbert, M., 'Wisdom literature', in JWSTP, pp. 301–13.

Cf. also O. Eissfeldt, *The O.T., An Introduction etc.* (ET 1965), pp. 600–3.

2. Aristobulus

The views of the author of the Wisdom of Solomon are predominantly those of Palestinian proverbial wisdom, which he partially modified under the influence of Greek philosophy. The Alexandrian Aristobulus, by contrast, although also in touch with contemporary Palestinian wisdom literature, was a Hellenistic scholar in the real sense of the word and possibly even a member of the Alexandrian Museum. He knew and specifically quoted the Greek philosophers Pythagoras, Socrates, and Plato, and was acquainted with their views as a professional philosopher.

Ancient authors are, it is true, not wholly in agreement regarding his date, but it may still be accepted as probable that he lived during the time of Ptolemy VI Philometor, i.e. towards the middle of the second century B.C. (about 180–145 B.C.). He himself states in his work addressed to a Ptolemy that the Greek translation of the Pentateuch was made 'under King Philadelphus, your ancestor' (Euseb., *Praep. ev.* xiii 12, 2). He therefore wrote under a descendant of Ptolemy II Philadelphus. However, Clement of Alexandria and Eusebius (in the

Chronicle) definitely mention Philometor[83] and their testimony should be accepted, not least because the same chronology was also assumed when Clement of Alexandria and Eusebius identified this Aristobulus with the one mentioned at the beginning of 2 Maccabees (2 Mac. 1:10).[84] These witnesses should be followed rather than Anatolius, a Christian author of the third century A.D. who, probably under the influence of late legends about the formation of the Septuagint, places Aristobulus under Ptolemy II Philadelphus,[85] and also against the only manuscript of the *Stromata* of Clement of Alexandria, which incorrectly reads Philadelphus instead of Philometor in one passage.[86]

83. Clement of Alexandria, *Strom*. i 22, 150: Ἀριστόβουλος ἐν τῷ πρώτῳ τῶν πρὸς τὸν Φιλομήτορα. The reading is certain here since in all manuscripts Eusebius also, who quotes this passage in *Praep. ev.* ix 6 from Clement, has Φιλομήτορα. Note also Eusebius, *Chron. ad Olymp*., 151 (ed. Schoene, II, pp. 124 ff.). The Greek text, which has been preserved in *Chronicon paschale*, ed. Dindorf, I, p. 337, reads: Ἀριστόβουλος Ἰουδαῖος περιπατητικὸς φιλόσοφος ἐγνωρίζετο, ὃς Πτολεμαίῳ τῷ Φιλομήτορι ἐξηγήσεις τῆς Μωϋσέως γραφῆς ἀνέθηκεν. So also the Armenian and Jerome (ed. Helm, GCS Eusebius VII, 2nd ed., p. 139). The 151st Olympiad, with regard to which Eusebius included this information about Aristobulus' *floruit*, lasted from 176–172 B.C., which has suggested to E. J. Bickermann, 'The Septuagint as a translation', PAAJR 28 (1959), p. 3, n. 2, that the years 176–170 B.C. are the most appropriate for Aristobulus' dedication to Ptolemy by himself, since at all other stages of his reign he ruled in conjunction with others. However, there is no reason to expect every monarch in power in Egypt at a particular time to be included in every dedication of this sort, and a powerful Jewish figure would be more likely in Philometor's court towards the end of his reign after the Maccabaean revolt (Fraser, PA II, p. 965).

84. Clement of Alexandria, *Strom*. v 14, 97. Eusebius, *Praep. ev.* viii 9 *fin*. It is possible that the dating of the fragments by Clement and Eusebius was done by them only in order to agree with 2 Mac. 1:10 (Walter), but more likely that the letter in 2 Mac. was attributed by its author to a well known Alexandrian of the appropriate period, i.e. the rule of Ptolemy Philometor, cf. E. J. Bickermann, ZNW 32 (1933), pp. 233–54.

85. Anatolius in Eusebius, *Hist. eccl.* vii 32, 16.

86. Clement, *Strom*. v 14, 97. Codex Laurentianus, the only manuscript in which Clement's *Stromata* are preserved (for Parisinus, saec. 15, is only a copy of it), reads here Φιλάδελφον. However, modern editors have correctly replaced it by Φιλομήτορα, cf. Le Boulluec, SC 278, *ad loc*. Further arguments about date have centred on the relationship . of Aristobulus to the Letter of Pseudo-Aristeas. Both authors refer to an alleged role of Demetrius of Phalerum in the translation of the Torah. It has been argued that the concentrated account in Aristobulus compared to the scattered references in Pseudo-Aristeas makes Aristobulus likely to be prior (N. Walter, *Der Thoraausleger Aristobulus* (1964), pp. 92–100; cf. A. Momigliano, Aegyptus 12 (1932), pp. 164–5), but it is also arguable that the much greater detail in Pseudo-Aristeas, and the fact that all later authors attribute to him the story about Demetrius of Phalerum, makes Pseudo-Aristeas likely to have written first (Fraser, PA I, p. 694; II, p. 964). It is of course also possible that both authors used a common oral tradition. Arguments for dating based on the comparative unsophistication of the allegorical exegesis in Aristobulus compared to Pseudo-Aristeas (e.g. Walter, *op. cit.*, pp. 146–7) are invalid, given both the possibility that Aristobulus' work survives only in too fragmentary a form to be judged by what it lacks, and the possibility that a less sophisticated author could nonetheless be later than a more sophisticated one. The whole question of priority is rendered less important by

According to Clement of Alexandria, *Strom.* v 14, 97, this Aristobulus wrote βιβλία ἱκανά. Presumably Clement does not mean by this that Aristobulus wrote several works, but that the one work which Clement knew was an extensive one in numerous volumes. Further information concerning it is to be found in Clement of Alexandria (*Strom.* i 15, 72; 22, 150; v 14, 97; vi 3, 32), Anatolius (in Euseb., *Hist. eccl.* vii 32, 16–19; Anatolius was an older contemporary of Eusebius), and Eusebius (*Praep. ev.* vii 14; viii 10; xiii 12). Origen also briefly mentions Aristobulus (*Contra Cels.* iv 51). The only two passages preserved literally are in Euseb., *Praep. ev.* vii 32, 16–18 (from Anatolius); viii 10 and xiii 12. Whatever else there is of literal citation (e.g. Clement, *Strom.* i 22, 150 = *Praep. ev.* ix 6; Clement, *Strom.* vi 3, 32 = Euseb., *Praep. ev.* vii 14) is to be found anyway in the text of these larger fragments.[87] The passage ascribed by Cyril of Alexandria to Aristobulus (*Contra Julian.* 134, ed. Spanh.) is not relevant since it actually derives from the third book of the *Indica* of Megasthenes and is assigned to Aristobulus by Cyril only on account of his careless reading of Clement of Alexandria, *Strom.* i 15, 72.

The work which lay before these Church Fathers was characterized as an elucidation of the Book of Moses.[88] From the preserved fragments, however, it is not to be considered as a proper commentary but as a free reproduction of the contents of the Pentateuch, in which it is at the same time philosophically explained. It is thus not analogous to Philo's allegorical commentaries on particular passages, but rather to his systematic discussion of the Mosaic legislation described above on pp. 542 ff. In the same way as Philo, Aristobulus gives a coherent description of the contents of the Pentateuch in order to show the cultivated world that the Mosaic Law, correctly understood, contains already everything that the best Greek philosophers learned subsequently. The work is dedicated to King Ptolemy Philometor,[89] who is thus also addressed in the text (Euseb., *Praep. ev.* viii 10, 1 ff.; xiii 12, 2).

doubts about the correct date of Pseudo-Aristeas, see below, p. 679. There is anyway no reason to doubt a date for Aristobulus during the rule of Ptolemy Philometor.

87. I.e.: (1) Clement, *Strom.* i 22, 150 = Eusebius, *Praep. ev.* ix 6 = Eusebius, *Praep. ev.* xiii 12, 1. (2) Clement, *Strom.* vi 3, 32 = Eusebius, *Praep. ev.* viii 10, 14. (3) Eusebius, *Praep. ev.* vii 14 = Eusebius, *Praep. ev.* xiii 12, 10–11. On the *Praeparatio evangelica* of Eusebius, cf. above, pp. 510–1, under Alexander Polyhistor. See the collection of the fragments by Denis, FPG, pp. 217–28.

88. Eusebius, *Praep. ev.* vii 13, 7: τὴν τῶν ἱερῶν νόμων ἑρμηνείαν. Eusebius, *Chron. ad Olymp.*, 151 (ed. Schoene, II, pp. 124 ff.): ἐξηγήσεις τῆς Μωυσέως γραφῆς (this Greek reading, preserved by *Chron. paschale*, ed. Dindorf, I, 337, is confirmed by the Armenian (*enarrationem librorum Moysis*) and by Jerome (*explanationum in Moysen commentarios*) (ed. Helm, GCS Eusebius VII, 2nd ed., p. 139)). Anatolius in Eusebius, *Hist. eccl.* vii 32, 16: βίβλους ἐξηγητικὰς τοῦ Μωϋσέως νόμου.

89. Clement, *Strom.* i 22, 150 = Eusebius, *Praep. ev.* ix 6, 6. Eusebius, *Praep. ev.* vii 13 *fin.* Anatolius in Eusebius, *Hist. eccl.* vii 32, 16.

It is likely, therefore, that it was directed at least partly to gentile readers and sought to appeal to them through the use of Hellenistic literary categories; but it would also have served a didactic purpose for conservative Jews by showing the sophisticated ideas that could be culled from the Torah, cf. Eusebius, *Praep. ev.* viii 10, 5. Its main object, according to Clement, was to demonstrate 'that peripatetic philosophy was dependent on the Law of Moses and the other prophets' (*Strom.* v 14, 97). The preserved fragments essentially confirm this, except that instead of peripatetic philosophy Greek philosophy in general should have been mentioned. Aristobulus is not content to point out the essential agreement between the Law of Moses and Greek philosophy, but asserts plainly that the Greek philosophers, e.g. Pythagoras, Socrates, Plato, derived their doctrines from Moses, and even that poets such as Homer and Hesiod borrowed much from him, since the essential contents of the Pentateuch had already been translated into Greek long before the Greek translation made under Ptolemy Philadelphus.[90] This bold assertion that Moses was the father of Greek philosophy and culture was also maintained by later Jewish Hellenists. It is re-encountered, in particular, in Philo (*Vita Mosis* ii 2–3) and Josephus, *C. Ap.* ii 16 (168).[91]

The preserved fragments give at least an approximate idea of its character. A majority of the passages are concerned with determining the true meaning of the biblical anthropomorphisms. Thus the long piece in Euseb., *Praep. ev.* xiii 12, 1–8, which, according to the parallel in Clement of Alexandria, *Strom.* i 22, 150 = Euseb., *Praep. ev.* ix 6, is taken from the first book of Aristobulus' work, and evidently belonged to an elucidation of the creation story, shows that the words, 'God said, and it was so', means no more than that all was made by God's power (δυνάμει), which was also taught by the Greek philosophers Orpheus and Aratus.

The next passage (*Praep. ev.* xiii 12, 9–16), which still belongs to the interpretation of the creation story, discusses the seventh day as a day of rest, and explains its significance by appealing, amongst others, to alleged verses from Hesiod, Homer, and Linus.[92]

A further passage (Euseb. *Praep. ev.* viii 10) indicates how allusions to

---

90. Cf especially Eusebius, *Praep. ev.* xiii 12, 1 = Clement, *Strom.* i 22, 150 = Eusebius, *Praep. ev.* ix 6, 6–8. Pythagoras, Socrates, and Plato: Eusebius, *Praep. ev.* xiii 12, 4. Homer and Hesiod: Eusebius, *Praep. ev.* xiii 12, 13.

91. Cf. G. Vermes, 'Bible and Midrash', *Camb. Hist. of the Bible* I (1970), pp. 199–231, 532 = PBJS, pp. 59–91; T. Rajak, 'Moses in Ethiopia: Legend and Literature', JJS 29 (1978), pp. 111–22.

92. A small fragment of this (Eusebius, *Praep. ev.* xiii 12, 10–11) is also found in *Praep. ev.* vii 14.

God's hands, arms, face, and feet should be understood in the Mosaic Law.[93]

Finally, the excerpt given by Anatolius (Euseb. *Hist. eccl.* vii 32, 17–18) deals with the Passover, celebrated when both the sun and the moon are in the equinox, that is, when the sun is in the vernal equinox and the moon opposite it in the autumnal equinox. It is this fragment that reveals that Aristobulus by no means confined himself to reinterpreting the text of the Pentateuch philosophically, but really provided a description and explanation of the Mosaic Law. Nevertheless, while attempting to determine its sense he often enters the domain of allegorical interpretation, as Origen in particular indicates (*Contra Cels.* iv 51).

With regard to Aristobulus' philosophical viewpoint, the fragments give no specific information. He was undoubtedly an eclectic. The fragment on the meaning of the Sabbath discusses the power of the numeral seven by means of a Pythagorean-like exposition.[94] Elsewhere, Aristobulus appeals in general to Pythagoras, Socrates, and Plato, as well as more specifically in particular cases to peripatetic doctrine.[95] Despite the unanimous witness of the Church Fathers in calling him a peripatetic, there is no reason from the extant writings to suppose that he had particularly close affinities with that philosophy.[96]

It is difficult to understand why many scholars have disputed the authenticity of the whole of Aristobulus' work, e.g. Willrich, Wendland, Bousset and especially Elter.[97] The picture which we obtain from the preserved fragments of this writing is perfectly possible for a Jew in the Hellenistic period, cf. in particular N. Walter, *Der Thoraausleger Aristobulus* (TU, 86) (1964), especially pp. 35–123.

A series of arguments have been formulated against its genuineness, but they are not compelling.

First, Aristobulus makes good use of forged verses of Greek poets which he could hardly expect a Ptolemaic king to accept as authentic if he had invented them himself for his apologetic. It is however likely that these verses were taken by Aristobulus from florilegia into which Jewish forgeries had already been inserted, and which Aristobulus himself would have had neither reason nor incentive to doubt. There is

93. A small sentence from it (Eusebius, *Praep. ev.* viii 10, 14) is also found in Clement of Alexandria, *Strom.* vi 3, 32.

94. N. Walter, *Der Thoraausleger Aristobulus* (1964), pp. 73, 166–71.

95. Eusebius, *Praep. ev.* xiii 12, 10–11 = vii 14.

96. Fraser, PA I, p. 695. There was no formal peripatetic school in Alexandria at this date and Aristobulus uses Platonic, Pythagorean and Stoic as well as Aristotelian ideas.

97. *De gnomologiorum graecorum historia atque origine*, part VIII (Bonn, *Universitäts-Progr.*, 1895), col. 226: 'etenim Aristobulum Judaeum Alexandrinum ecquis homo sanus etiamnunc Philonem Judaeum Alexandrinum antecessisse et tamquam huic praecursorem fuisse judicabit?'

nothing implausible in such florilegia having been produced in the
early Hellenistic period (see below, p. 659) and Aristobulus' use of them
is therefore no argument for a late (i.e. Roman) date for his work (cf.
Bousset) any more than it argues against his Jewish identity. The
practice of quoting such verses is a natural one for apologetic of any
period, and it is unduly sceptical to assume that either Aristobulus or
his audience (Jewish or gentile) was aware of the spurious origins of the
proof texts used (see below, section VII.3).

Secondly, Aristobulus is not mentioned by any writer before Clement
of Alexandria in the second century A.D. Again, this is not really
surprising. The failure of Josephus to mention Aristobulus is only a
reflection of Josephus' own interests. Josephus only mentions other
authors when they either support his case for the antiquity of the Jews
because they are, or he believes them to be, independent gentile
witnesses to that antiquity, or when they take part, as did Philo, in
some historical event which Josephus wishes to describe. It is salutary to
recall how much information about Jewish literature in Greek is only
preserved through the lists of authors in Clement and Eusebius, and
Alexander Polyhistor before them. With so scanty a tradition, specific
arguments from the omission of a particular work are perilous.

Thirdly, the recension of the forged Orphic poems used by
Aristobulus is, in its present form in the text of Eusebius, less original
than the recension used by Ps.-Justin, *De monarchia*, and even the
different recension used by Clement of Alexandria. It has therefore
been suggested that the Orphic forgery in Aristobulus dates the whole
of Aristobulus' work to the third century A.D. (Elter).[98] A complex
series of recensions both of Aristobulus' text and that of the Orphic
poems, as well as an implausibly late date in the second century A.D.
for Ps.-Hecateus who quoted other forged verses of Greek poets, has to
be stipulated for this theory to stand, but it is anyway unnecessary. The
original authorship of the Orphic poem may quite well be assigned to
the early Hellenistic period. It is perverse to assume that its first
recorded use, in the late second to early third century A.D., coincided
with its creation. The hazards of textual transmission account for the
preservation of a more correct text in a later author (Ps.-Justin) than an
earlier one (Aristobulus). See below, section VII.3.

Fourth, a general argument against the genuineness of the
Aristobulus fragments is that their content is unthinkable for a Jew
before Philo. The assertion that the Greek philosophers and poets
depended on Moses is particularly singled out (Elter).[99] This is a
curiously circular argument: Aristobulus' work would be part of the

98. Elter, A., parts V-VI (1894), cols. 152–87, with a summary of the results, p. vi,
cols. 177–87; p. vii (1895), col. 206: 'Theophili fere aetate.'
99. Elter, A., parts VIII-IX (1895), cols. 219–39. Cf. part VI (1894), col. 186.

evidence for such thought before Philo. Similarities to Philo are evident, but neither can direct dependence be shown nor can it be demonstrated that any idea found in Aristobulus is based solely on Philo's philosophy.[100] Similarly, Aristobulus' use of Greek philosophical terms otherwise first attested in Posidonius in the early first century B.C. (Pohlenz) does not prove a post-Posidonian date since each writer may be giving his own special meaning to terms already in common use.

Fifth, the picture of Aristobulus as treating the king Ptolemy as his student has struck some scholars as implausible (Bousset).[101] It is true enough that Clement and Eusebius probably inferred this description of Aristobulus with no better warrant than the letter in 2 Mac. 1:10, where the claim is made directly in this form, even though it is quite possible that Aristobulus only figured in the testimonial in 2 Mac. in the first place because he was well-known to the forger of the letter as a prominent Alexandrian Jew of the reign of Philometor (Walter). Nonetheless, Aristobulus' teachings addressed to the king involve quite unexceptional remarks about the way to understand anthropomorphic expressions in the Pentateuch, and would be quite possible as apologetic addressed to pagans to defend the Jewish view of God.[102]

---

100. The notion that Greek philosophy stemmed from Jewish sources is certainly pre-Philonic. On the Jewish side, the Jewish Sibyl, who wrote under Ptolemy VIII about 140 B.C., also accused Homer of stealing her verses (*Sib.* iii 419 32). Furthermore, there is a tendency in some Greek authors to believe something similar a long time before Aristobulus, cf. A. Momigliano, *Alien Wisdom: The Limits of Hellenization* (1975), pp. 83–7. Megasthenes, who lived about 300 B.C. (at the time of Seleucus I), admittedly does not assert Greek dependence, but affirms a relationship between Greek philosophy and that of the Brahmans and the Jews (fragment from the third book of his Ἰνδικά in Clement of Alexandria, *Strom.* i 15, 72: ἅπαντα μέντοι τὰ περὶ φύσεως εἰρημένα παρὰ τοῖς ἀρχαίοις λέγεται καὶ παρὰ τοῖς ἔξω τῆς Ἑλλάδος φιλοσοφοῦσι, τὰ μὲν παρ' Ἰνδοῖς ὑπὸ τῶν Βραχμάνων, τὰ δὲ ἐν τῇ Συρίᾳ ὑπὸ τῶν καλουμένων Ἰουδαίων. In explanation of these words, it may be noted that Aristotle, according to the report of his student Clearchus, already designated the Ἰουδαῖοι as the φιλόσοφοι παρὰ Σύροις: Jos. *C. Ap.* i 22 (179); cf. on this Stern, GLAJJ I, pp. 45–52). Hermippus Callimachius, who lived during the second half of the third century B.C. (under Ptolemy III and IV), already believed that Pythagoras borrowed from the Jews and the Thracians the summons not to pass by a place where an ass had sunk to its knees, to abstain from thirst-producing water, and to avoid all blasphemy (Josephus, *C. Ap.* i 22 (164–5); cf. Stern, GLAJJ I, pp. 93–6 and further details below, §33A.VII.8, in the section on Hermippus). The claims of a Pseudo-Hecataeus and Aristobulus are comprehensible after such precedents.

101. *Die Religion des Judentums* (²1906), p. 32.

102. The passage reads (Eusebius, *Praep. ev.* viii 10, 1–2): 'When, however, we had said enough in answer to the questions put before us, you also, O King, did further demand, why by our law there are intimations given of hands, and arm, and face, and feet, and walking, in the case of the divine power: which things shall receive a becoming explanation, and will not at all contradict the opinions which we have previously expressed. But I would entreat you to take the interpretations in a natural way (φυσικῶς), and to hold fast the fitting conception of God, and not to fall off into the idea of a fabulous anthropomorphic constitution.' It is clear that Aristobulus does not wish to

This sort of portrayal of writer and monarch as teacher and pupil is a common Hellenistic literary fiction, but it is also quite possible that the Jewish philosopher had a personal relationship with the king given all that we know of Philometor's relations to the Jews. When the king permitted Onias to found a Jewish temple in Egypt, and even had Jewish commanders in his army (cf. above, pp. 47–8), it is not impossible that a Jewish philosopher might have attempted to transmit to the king a correct understanding (i.e. correct from the point of view of the philosophers) of the Jewish religion.

The opponents of authenticity have never given a satisfactory answer to the question of the motives and purpose of the forgery. This would in fact only have had meaning if Aristobulus had been a distinguished person from the king's gentile circle, upon whom a later person foisted this apology for Jewish opinions. But the author describes himself quite honestly and unmistakeably as a Jew (Euseb. *Praep. ev.* xiii 12, 1: κατηκολούθησεν ὁ Πλάτων τῇ καθ' ἡμᾶς νομοθεσίᾳ; cf. 12, 8; 11; 13; viii 10, 1; 3; 8). Such a forgery would have been without meaning or purpose, for if the forger had wished to accomplish something for the benefit of the Jews, he would have put on a gentile mask, as others frequently did (cf. section VII). The hypothesis that the author wrote under a distinguished Jewish name for his fellow-believers is contradicted both by the dedication to King Ptolemy, and by the fact that the whole work apparently seeks to justify Judaism in the forum of Greek philosophy.

Aristobulus was, then, a distinguished Alexandrian Jew who combined his own Jewish tradition with the ideas of Greek philosophy in order to demonstrate that the Jews were basically a nation of philosophers. The allegorical interpretation of myth, as practised by the Stoa and the Alexandrian philologists, and the attribution of Greek philosophical concepts to Moses and the Torah, are similar to the ideas of Philo but much less sophisticated.

Editions

Denis, FPG, pp. 217–28.

Translations

English:
Collins, A. Yarbro, in Charlesworth, OTP II (forthcoming).

German:
Riessler, P., *Altjüd. Schrift.* (1928), pp. 179–85, 1275 f.

impart a philosophical doctrine about the nature of God to the king at all. He asks him only to take the symbolical language of the Bible as an expression of the true spiritual contemplation of God. He begins with this general request before going on to explain the individual metaphorical expressions.

Walter, N., *Fragmente jüdisch-hellenistischer Exegeten* (JSHRZ III.2) (1975), pp. 261–79.

Bibliography

Valckenaer, L., *Diatribe de Aristobulo Judaeo, philosopho peripatetico Alexandrino* (1806).
Lobeck, C. A., *Aglaophamus* I (1829), p. 448.
Zeller, E., *Die Philosophie der Griechen* III.2 ([4]1903), pp. 277–85.
Binde, R., *Aristobulische Studien*, 2 parts (*Gymnasialprogr.*, 1869–70).
Freudenthal, J., *Alexander Polyhistor* (1875), pp. 166–9.
Elter, A., *De gnomologiorum graecorum historia atque origine*, parts v–ix (*Universitätsprogramme*, 1894–5).
Willrich, H., *Juden und Griechen vor der makk. Erhebung* (1895), pp. 162–8.
Gercke, A., 'Aristobulus' (15), RE II.1 (1895), cols. 918–20.
Schlatter, A., *Das neu gefundene hebräische Stück des Sirach etc.* (1897), pp. 163–89.
Wendland, P., 'Aristobulus', JE II (1902), cols. 97 f. (Aristobulus is here wrongly called Aristobulus of Paneas).
v. Christ, W., O. Stählin and W. Schmidt, *Gesch. der griech. Lit.*[6] II.1 (1920), pp. 603 ff.
Schlatter, A., *Gesch. Israels* ([3]1925), pp. 81–90.
Bousset, W., and H. Gressmann, *Die Religion des Judentums* ([3]1926), pp. 28–9.
Heinemann, I., 'Hellenistica', MGWJ 73 (1929), pp. 425–43.
Bauer, L., 'Aristobulus', LThK I (1930), pp. 646–7.
Bickermann, E., 'Zur Datierung des Pseudo-Aristeas', ZNW 29 (1930), pp. 280–95.
Heinemann, I., *Philons griechische und jüdische Bildung* (1932).
Goodenough, E. R., *By Light, Light!* (1935), pp. 277–82.
Keller, R., *De Aristobulo Judaeo* (Diss., Bonn, 1948).
Dalbert, P., *Die Theologie der jüd.-hell. Missionsliteratur* (1954), pp. 102–6.
Kahana, A., הספרים החיצונים I ([2]1956), pp. 176 f.
Tcherikover, V. A., 'Jewish Apologetic Literature reconsidered', *Eos* 48, 3 (1956), pp. 169–93.
Gutman, Y., *The Beginnings of Jewish-Hellenistic Literature* I (1958), pp. 186–220, 276–86 (Heb.).
Lohse, E., 'Aristobul', RGG I ([3]1957), 597.
Bickerman(n), E., 'The Septuagint as a Translation', PAAJR 28 (1959), pp. 2 ff. = *Studies in Jewish and Christian History* I (1976), pp. 167–200.
Walter, N., 'Anfänge alexandrinisch-jüdischen Bibelauslegung bei Aristobulus', *Helikon* 3 (1963), pp. 353–72.
Walter, N., *Der Thoraausleger Aristobulus*, TU 86 (1964) (a full discussion with bibliography).
Denis, IPGAT, pp. 277–83.
Fraser, PA I, pp. 694–6; II, pp. 963–9.
Hengel, M., *Judaism and Hellenism* I (ET 1974), pp. 163–9.
Sandelin, K.-G., 'Zwei Kurze Studien zum alexandrinischen Judentum', *Studia Theologica* 31 (1977), pp. 147–52.
Sabugal, S., 'La exégesis biblica de Aristóbulo y del seudo-Aristeas', *Revista Agustiniana de Espiritualidad* 20 (1979), pp. 195–202.

3. Philo

The same policy as that of Aristobulus was followed by a fellow-countryman who lived two centuries later than him, Philo. It was his main endeavour, also, to prove that the views derived from Greek philosophy were genuinely Jewish; which he did, possibly occasionally for gentile but certainly usually for Jewish readers. His intention was to instil respect for Judaism in the former audience, and to educate the latter in the Judaism that he himself preferred. It cannot safely be assumed that there were other representatives of this tendency between Aristobulus and Philo. In favour of the existence of such philosophers is the fact that this philosophical position is presented with such certainty and in such a developed form in Philo that many scholars have found his achievement unthinkable without antecedents. But nothing has been preserved of the possible literary productions of these men, and there are sufficient differences between Philo, Aristobulus and the Wisdom of Solomon to make it unwise to assume without evidence that they all belonged to a single, developing tradition of which Philo is the peak.[103]

Since Philo, because of his great importance and the extent of his preserved works, demands a separate presentation (§34), we give here no more than a brief note of those of his works which deal mainly with philosophical instruction and discussion. These include firstly two of his principal works on the Pentateuch: (1) *Quaestiones et solutiones*, a short explanation of Genesis and Exodus in question and answer form, and (2) *De Legum allegoria*, the extensive allegorical commentaries on selected passages of Genesis in the form of rabbinical midrash. Also to be noted here are (3) *Quod omnis probus liber*; (4) *De Providentia*; (5) *Alexander*. The last two of these are also of interest on account of their literary form, viz. the Greek dialogue.

4. The Fourth Book of Maccabees

The so-called Fourth Book of Maccabees also belongs within the genre of philosophical literature to the extent that the Judaism recommended by its author is expressed entirely within the framework of Greek philosophy.

In form this document is a discourse, i.e. a *diatribe*, although at times it also verges into panegyric. The author addresses his readers or

---

103. Among the more recent attempts to depict a 'Philosophical Judaism' on the assumption of a continuous tradition, see Collins, BAAJ, pp. 175–94. See also many of the works on Philo cited below, § 34. Contrast the more reserved comments of Fraser, PA I, p. 696, who warns against assuming connections for which there is no evidence. Anatolius, in Eusebius, *Hist. eccl.* vii 32, 16, mentions three Jewish authors in addition to Aristobulus, after he has mentioned Philo and Josephus. These are Musaeus and two men called Agathobulus. These writers are cited as authorities for the calendrical fixing of the Passover and apparently wrote about the exodus (vii 32, 17: τὰ ζητούμενα κατὰ τὴν Ἔξοδον ἐπιλύοντες...). Of Musaeus nothing more can be said, but the two Agathobuli were apparently surnamed the Teachers of Aristobulus the Great (vii 32, 16, ed. Schwartz, GCS Eusebius II, p. 724: ἀμφοτέρων Ἀγαθοβούλων, τῶν ἐπίκλην διδασκάλων Ἀριστοβούλου τοῦ πάνυ). They presumably wrote biblical commentaries of some sort, but this testimony does not show that they were philosophers or indulged in allegory since they could have taught Aristobulus many other things.

hearers directly (1:1; 18:1). Since the aim of the book is religious edification, some have wished to call it a sermon, but the occasion for such an address based on a philosophical proposition rather than a scriptural text is hard to find in Jewish synagogal liturgy so far as it is known at this period. It is however quite possible that the work was delivered orally at some commemorative festival in honour of the martyrs, even though no direct record of such a festival survives (Hadas). On the other hand, there is no way to decide the preliminary question of whether the work was intended to be spoken, or was a fictive discourse that carefully imitated such speeches but was intended to be read. Either mode of composition would be fully comprehensible in Hellenistic literature.

As readers or listeners, the author had in view exclusively Jews (18:1: 'O Israelites, children born of the seed of Abraham'). He wished to show them that it was not difficult to lead a pious life if they only followed the precepts of 'religious reason'. For 'the inspired reason is supreme ruler over the passions' (1:1). This proposition is the theme proper of the discourse and may well have provided the original title of the book, 'On the Sovereignty of Reason' (Euseb. *Hist. eccl.* iii 10, 6). Its meaning is expounded, and its truth then substantiated from Jewish history, especially through the admirable martyrdom of Eleazar and the seven Maccabaean brothers. The author therefore devotes a large part of the contents to the rewriting of the martyrdom of these heroes of the faith, with detailed description of individual tortures, and rhetorical commentary, to emphasize the philosophical courage of the sufferers. 2 Mac. was apparently his source. It is possible that he had direct contact with the larger work of Jason of Cyrene from which 2 Mac. itself was epitomized (Freudenthal, pp. 72–90), but discrepancies between 2 and 4 Maccabees can be fully explained by their different purposes in recounting the same events, so that the hypothesis of separate recourse to Jason's work is unnecessary.

The author's own standpoint was influenced by a variety of Greek philosophical schools, especially Middle Platonism and Stoicism (cf. Breitenstein, pp. 132–3). It is possible that this eclecticism was the work of the source of the author's philosophy rather than of the author himself, since much Platonic philosophy of the late Hellenistic period was eclectic in this way. The fundamental idea of the whole discourse is that of Stoic ethics: the rule of reason over the passions. The list of the four cardinal virtues (1:18: prudence, justice, courage, self-control) could have been derived from Stoicism or Plato or both. But this influence of Greek philosophy has not in any way penetrated more deeply than this. Even the basic idea is a Jewish one recast, for the reason to which he ascribes command over the passions is not reason in the sense used by the Greek philosophers but religious reason, ὁ εὐσεβὴς λογισμός (1:1; 7:16; 13:1; 15:20; 16:1; 18:2), i.e. reason that follows the norm of the divine law (cf. also 1:15–17). He also goes his own way in describing and dividing the emotions (cf. 1:18 ff.). It would be misleading, however, to designate him an eclectic philosopher in his own right. Whether or not he worked within an existing philosophical school, he was only a dilettante *in philosophicis*, somewhat like Josephus, who also knew how to give his Judaism a philosophical veneer. The philosophy of the book is by no means consistent and it is quite probable that the author simply used ideas from all sources, in the fashion of contemporary rhetoric, to support his case wherever appropriate. Of all the known Jewish philosophers, he is remarkable for his uncompromising assertion that distinctively Jewish religious practices could, and should, be considered by the Greeks as wisdom. For in the Maccabaean martyrs, it is precisely their rigid adherence to the Torah that he praises.

Two of his Jewish views in particular are noteworthy. The first is his belief in immortality, which does not refer to the Pharisaic doctrine of bodily resurrection but assumes faith in an eternal and blessed life in heaven for the pious immediately after death (13:17; 15:3; 17:5, 18; 18:23); it is striking, however, that this doctrine does *not* dominate 4 Maccabees, in contrast to the author's probable source in 2 Mac. 7, but is included only to justify the reasonableness of the martyrs by introducing the doctrine of retribution. The second is his belief that the martyrdom of the righteous served as atonement and purification for the sins of the people (1:11; 6:29: 'Make my blood their purification, and take my soul to ransom their souls'; 17:21: 'having become a ransom for our nation's sin').[104]

Eusebius and other Church writers name Josephus as the author but the book is anonymous in many manuscripts, and was therefore certainly first issued as such. Against Josephus is the entirely different style, as well as the fact that he does not use 2 Maccabees at all in *Antiquities*, and thus apparently did not know it, whereas 4 Maccabees is completely based on it.

There are no certain indications of the place where the book was written. Later Church tradition put the graves of the martyrs at Antioch, cf. U. Kellermann, *Auferstanden in dem Himmel. 2 Makkabäer 7 und die Auferstehung der Märtyrer* (1979), p. 17. In favour of accepting this tradition is the fact that Antiochus, the Seleucid king, is portrayed as being present at the tortures, which would be most natural in the Seleucid capital (5:1; cf. Hadas, pp. 110–13); but this may be only a dramatic convention. Nothing specifically suggests Alexandrian

---

104. Cf. R. B. Townshend in Charles, APOT II, pp. 663 f.; A. Dupont-Sommer, *Le Quatrième Livre des Machabées* (1939), pp. 41–3; M. Hadas, *The Third and Fourth Books of Maccabees* (1953), pp. 121–2; G. Vermes, STJ, p. 198.

authorship. Against Palestinian provenance is the author's topo-graphical mistake (4:20) about the position of the Jerusalem gymnasium.

A date in the mid-first century A.D. is the most likely. Linguistic considerations point to a time after the end of the first century B.C., cf. E. Bickermann, 'The Date of Fourth Maccabees', in *Studies in Jewish and Christian History* vol. I (1976), pp. 276–7. Composition before A.D. 70 is likely, given the adoption of the work by the Christian Church, and appears to be confirmed by the title given to Apollonius in 4 Mac. 4:9, where he is called *strategos* of Syria, Phoenicia and Cilicia, an area put under one governor only for a brief period between A.D. 20 and 54 (Bickermann, *art. cit.*, pp. 279–80). Suggestions of a date in the early second-century A.D. (Dupont-Sommer; Breitenstein) should be dismissed. Lack of references to the Temple cult is due to the interests of the author, not to the non-existence of the Temple. Similarities between the Asianic style of 4 Maccabees and that in the early second-century author, Dio Chrysostom, simply demonstrate the long survival of that style of rhetoric.

When Eusebius speaks of the writings of Josephus, he says of the title and author (*Hist. eccl.* iii 10, 6): '[Josephus] has also produced another work of lofty character on the supremacy of reason designated by some as Maccabaean, etc.'

Jerome, *De viris illustr.* 13 (PL XXIII, col. 662): 'Another book of his, entitled "On the Supremacy of Reason", is an extremely polished work; it also deals with the martyrdom of the Maccabees'; cf. *idem, Contra Pelagianos* ii 6 (PL XXIII, col. 567): 'Unde et Josephus Machabaeorum scriptor historiae frangi et regi posse dixit pertur-bationes animi non eradicari' (= 4 Mac. 3:5). All later authors who ascribe the work to Josephus do so solely on the authority of Eusebius and Jerome.

The designation of the book as the Fourth Book of Maccabees (Μακκαβαίων δ'), without mention of Josephus as its author, is found in the fourth-century Codex Sinaiticus (ℵ or S), the fifth-century Alexandrinus (A) and eighth-ninth-century Venetus (V).

On the use of the book in Christian ascetic literature, cf. above, p. 535, on 2 Maccabees.

For rabbinic tradition about the death of a mother and her seven sons in the time of Hadrian, cf. Hadas, pp. 127–35.

The manuscripts in which this book has been preserved are partly biblical manuscripts and partly manuscripts of Josephus. The first are not very numerous, since as a rule only three books of Maccabees were received as canonical. The three most important witnesses are the already quoted biblical manuscripts A, ℵ and V. Cf. above, p. 489, on the editions of A and ℵ (S). These biblical manuscripts are more valuable than the versions given in the Josephus manuscripts. More can be found about the manuscripts from the apparatus in A. Rahlfs, ed., *Septuaginta* I (1935), pp. 1157–84.

Editions

Swete, H. B., *The O.T. in Greek according to the LXX* III (³1907).
Rahlfs, A., *Septuaginta* I (1935), pp. 1157–84.
Fritzsche, O. F., *Libri Apocryphi Veteris Testamenti Graeci* (1971).
There are also independent comments on the text in the commentaries of A. Deissmann (1900) and A. Dupont-Sommer (1939) (see below).

Versions

For the fourth century Latin paraphrase used by Erasmus in his own paraphrase, see H. Dörrie, *Passio SS. Machabaeorum. Die antike lateinische Übers. des IV. Makkabäerbuches* (*Abhandlungen der Akademie der Wissenschaften in Göttingen* III, 22, 1938).
Syriac translation: facsimile in A. Ceriani, *Translatio SyraPescitto ... photolithographice edita* II (1876–83). Translation and introduction in R. L. Bensly, *The Fourth Book of Maccabees and Kindred Documents in Syriac, First Edited on Manuscripts Authority by the Late R. L. Bensly, with an Introduction and Translations by Barnes* (1895).
On a Slavonic text, cf. Bonwetsch in Harnack, *Gesch. der altchristl. Literatur* I p. 917.

Commentaries

Grimm, C. L. W., *Viertes Buch der Maccabäer* (Exeg. Handbuch zu den Apocryphen), 4 parts (1857).
Deissmann, A., in E. Kautzsch, *Die Apocryphen und Pseudepigraphen der A.T.* II (1900), pp. 149–77.
Townshend, R. B., 'The Fourth Book of Maccabees', in Charles, APOT II, pp. 653–85.
Emmet, C. W., *The Fourth Book of Maccabees* (1918).
Riessler, P., *Altjüdisches Schrifttum ausserhalb der Bibel* (1928), pp. 700–28, 1313–14.
Dupont-Sommer, A., *Le quatrième livre des Machabées* (1939).
Gutman, J., 'The mother and her seven sons in aggadah and in II and IV Maccabees', in M. Schwabe and J. Gutman, eds., *Commentationes Iudaico-Hellenisticae in Memoriam Iohannis Lewy* (1949), pp. 25–37 (Heb.).
Hadas, M., 'The Third and Fourth Books of Maccabees', in S. Zeitlin, *Jewish Apocryphal Literature* (1953).
Schur, A., in A. Kahana, הספרים החיצונים (²1956).

Bibliography

Freudenthal, J., *Die Flavius Josephus beigelegte Schrift ueber die Herrschaft der Vernunft (IV Makkabäerbuch), eine Predigt aus dem ersten nachchristlichen Jahrhundert, untersucht* (1869).
Bacon, B. W., 'The Festival of Lives Given for the Nation in Jewish and Christian Faith', *The Hibbert Journal* 15 (1916–17), pp. 256–78.
Stählin, O., 'Die Hellenistisch-Jüdische Literatur', in W. v. Christ, O. Stählin and W. Schmidt, *Geschichte der Griechischen Litteratur etc.*⁶ II.1 (1920), pp. 570 ff.
Harris, J. R., 'Some Notes on IV Maccabees', ET 2 (1920/1), pp. 183–5.
Heinemann, I., *Poseidonios metaphysische Schriften* I (1921), pp. 154–9.
Norden, E., *Die antike Kunstprosa* (⁴1923), pp. 416–20.
Heinemann, I., RE XIV.1 (1928), cols. 800–5.

Günther, E., *Μάρτυς. Die Geschichte eines Wortes* (1941), pp. 90–4.

Torrey, C. C., *The Apocryphal Literature etc.* (1945), pp. 103–6.

Bickermann, E. J., 'The Date of Fourth Maccabees', *Louis Ginzberg Jubilee Volume* I (1945), pp. 105–112 (= *Studies in Jewish and Christian History* I (1976), pp. 276–81).

Zeitlin, S., 'The Legend of the Ten Martyrs and its Apocalyptic Origin', JQR 36 (1945/6), 1–16.

Perler, O., 'Das Vierten Makkabäerbuch, Ignatius von Antiochen und die ältesten Märtyrerberichte', Rivista di Archeologia Cristiana 25 (1949), pp. 47–72.

Bammel, E., 'Zum jüdischen Märtyrerkult', ThLZ 78 (1953), pp. 119–26.

Lauer, S., 'Eusebes Logismos in IV Macc.', JJS 6 (1955), pp. 170–1.

Vilar Huesoi, V., 'La recompensa de los justos immediata a su muerte en IV Macabeos y en las parábolas de Enoc', Anthologica Annua 3 (1955), pp. 521–49.

Thyen, H., *Der Stil der jüdisch-hellenistischer Homilie* (1955), pp. 6–48.

Günther, E., 'Zeuge und Märtyrer', ZNW 47 (1956), pp. 145–61.

Gelin, A., 'Les origines bibliques de l'idée de martyre', Lumière et Vie 36 (1958), pp. 123–9.

Brownlee, W. H., 'IV Maccabees', IDB III (1962), cols. 212–15.

Renehan, R., 'The Greek Philosophic Background of Fourth Maccabees', RhM 115 (1972), pp. 223–38.

O'Hagan, A., 'The Martyr in the Fourth Book of Maccabees', SBFLA 24 (1974), pp. 94–120.

Verme, M. del, 'L'apocrifo giudaico IV Maccabei e gli atti dei martiri cristiani del II secolo', Revista de scienze teologiche 23 (1976), pp. 287–302.

Lebram, J. H. C., 'Die literarische Form des vierten Makkabäerbuches', Vigiliae Christianae 28 (1974), pp. 81–96.

Williams, S. K., *Jesus' Death as Saving Event. The Background and Origin of a Concept* (1975).

Breitenstein, U., *Beobachtungen zu Sprache, Stil und Gedankengut des Vierten Makkabäerbuchs* (1976).

Fischer, U., *Eschatologie und Jenseitserwartung im hellenistischen Diasporajudentum* (1978), pp. 85–9.

Nickelsburg, G. W. E., JLBBM, pp. 223–7.

Collins, BAAJ, pp. 187–91.

Redditt, P. L., 'The concept of *Nomos* in Fourth Maccabees', CBQ 45 (1983), pp. 249–70.

VI. Apologetics

The Jews, more than other Oriental peoples, were an anomaly in the framework of the Greco-Roman world because of the exceptional number of their co-religionists who lived outside their original homeland, and because they denied all authority to other religions. They were at times paid back in the same coin, and their right of existence on the soil of Hellenistic culture was accordingly disputed. Cities sometimes attempted to get rid of these troublesome inhabitants; the mob was always ready in times of crisis to lift its hand against them and some of the educated people despised and derided them (cf. above, pp. 144 f., 150 ff.). Hellenistic Jews thus lived in a continual state of potential tension with the rest of the Hellenistic world, and often had to take measures in their own defence. A large part of the whole of Hellenistic-Jewish literature therefore serves apologetic aims in defence against gentile attacks, even when the prime purpose of a particular work lies in the edification of a Jewish audience. Historical and philosophical literature, in particular, tried to show that the Jewish nation was at least equal to other peoples, if not superior, because of the length of its history and the purity of its teaching. These works are indirectly apologetical; but there are also some which attempt to refute systematically the reproaches made against the Jews. They were evoked by the sometimes absurd fables propagated by certain Greek writers concerning the Jews, and in general by the direct accusations made against them in Greek and Roman literature. These accusations originated in Egypt (Jos. *C. Ap.* i 25 (223–6)), and Alexandrian authors were the first to write against the Jews. Non-Egyptian writers in the Hellenistic period, such as Apollonios Molon, added further libels of their own. The precise relationship between such literary antisemitism and the social, economic and cultural status of Diasporan Jews is complex and not always fully clear.[105] From these turbid waters later writers then drew, particularly Tacitus. In what follows, the literary opponents of Judaism will first be discussed and then the apologetic works themselves.

---

105. See M. Radin, *The Jews among the Greeks and Romans* (1915); I. Heinemann, 'Antisemitismus', RE suppl. V (1931), cols. 3–43; J. N. Sevenster, *The Roots of Pagan Anti-Semitism in the Ancient World* (NT suppl. 41) (1975); J. L. Daniel, 'Anti-Semitism in the Hellenistic-Roman Period', JBL 98 (1979), pp. 45–65. See also above, pp. 144–55.

1. The Literary Opponents[106]

1. Manetho (cf. Jos. C. Ap. i 26–31 (227–87)).

During the rule of Ptolemy II Philadelphus (283–246 B.C.), the Egyptian priest Manetho composed a learned work in Greek on Egyptian history, basing his account on the Egyptian priestly records themselves (*C. Ap.* i 14 (73) ; *ibid.* i 26 (228)). From these Αἰγυπτιακά of Manetho, Josephus gives in two places (*C. Ap.* i 14–16 (73–105) ; i 26–7 (227–253)) long fragments, quite different in character, with explicit attribution to Manetho. The passages in i 14–16 (73–105) deal with the rule of the Hyksos in Egypt (from the second book of the *History of Egypt*). Uniquely among ancient authors, they assert that the Jews and the Hyksos were identical. These passages are both informative and concise, and there is no reason to doubt that their contents do in fact depend on the ancient records although, given the likelihood that Josephus found these fragments of Manetho in an abridgement made by an earlier Jewish apologist, it is quite likely that some elements have been interpolated.[107] The passages in i 26–27 (227–53) are of quite another kind. They do not set out to be authentic history but, according to Manetho himself, give current legends concerning the Jews (i 16 (105) : 'The additional statements which Manetho derived not from the Egyptian records but, as he himself admits, from fables of unknown authorship (ἐκ τῶν ἀδεσπότως μυθολογουμένων) ...'; i 26 (228–9) : 'So far he followed the chronicles. But at this point, under the pretext of recording fables and current reports about the Jews, he took the liberty of introducing some incredible tales (λόγους ἀπιθάνους) ...'). He tells the story here of how King Amenophis of Egypt caused all the lepers from the whole country, a total of 80,000 persons, to assemble in one place, and sent them to work in the stone quarries east of the Nile. After they had laboured there for a long time, they petitioned the king to assign to them Avaris, where the Hyksos had formerly lived, as a place of residence. The king granted their request. However, when they had possession of the town, they deserted the king and chose as their leader the priest Osarsiph from Heliopolis, who gave them new laws which especially commanded

---

106. For a general introduction to Greek and Latin authors on Jews and Judaism see M. Stern, 'The Jews in Greek and Latin Literature', JPFC I.2, pp. 1101–59; *idem*, GLAJJ I–III. Cf. also I. Heinemann, 'Antisemitismus', RE suppl. V (1931) cols. 25–37; J. G. Gager, *Moses in Greco-Roman Paganism* (1972); A. Momigliano, *Alien Wisdom: The Limits of Hellenization* (1975), pp. 74–122.

107. Precisely which of the lines quoted by Josephus contain the genuine views of Manetho is very difficult to decide. It was suggested by Ed. Meyer that *C. Ap.* i 14–15 (84–97), on the meaning of the word 'Hyksos', was largely spurious. See discussion in Ed. Meyer, *Aegyptische Chronologie* (1904), pp. 71 ff. ; Fraser, PA II, pp. 730–2 ; Sevenster, *op. cit.*, pp. 184–8.

them to worship no gods and to kill the animals sacred to Egyptians. Osarsiph also summoned the Hyksos from Jerusalem as allies, and with their help the lepers drove out King Amenophis and ruled Egypt for thirteen years. The priest Osarsiph then adopted the name of Moses. After thirteen years, King Amenophis drove the Hyksos and the lepers out of Egypt.

Either Josephus or an intermediary source evidently read this history of the origin of the Jews in his text of Manetho. It has been questioned, however, whether it originated with Manetho. Bousset, among others, regarded the whole passage as a later insertion.[108] Others have accepted the main story as Manetho's but have assigned the identification of Osarsiph with Moses (*C. Ap.* i 26 (250)) to an antisemitic interpolator.[109] Neither view is impossible, since it is likely that Josephus possessed different recensions of Manetho or the intervening source from which he worked.[110] Neither, however, is probable. An enemy of the Jews who interpolated the passage later would surely not have been so truthful as to indicate explicitly that he was not giving authentic history but only τα μυθευόμενα καὶ λεγόμενα περὶ τῶν 'Ιουδαίων. These are the words of a rigorous scholar who, as an enemy of the Jews, cannot refrain from giving the stories but expressly distinguishes them as legends from authentic history. Josephus or his source must in any case have read this section in all the copies of Manetho known to him, since he does not mention any variant version.[111]

Editions

Müller, C., FHG II, pp. 512–616.
Jacoby, FGrH 609, III C, pp. 5–112.
Waddell, W. G., Loeb ed. published with Ptolemy, *Tetrabiblos* (1940) (with English translation).
Stern, GLAJJ I, pp. 62–86 (fragments in Josephus only, with English translation).

108. W. Bousset and H. Gressmann, *Die Religion des Judentums* (³1926), pp. 91, 493.

109. R. Laqueur, 'Manethon', RE XIV (1928), col. 1071. This compromise, though not impossible since the sentence which contains the identification does seem artificially connected to the rest of the account, would not alter the intention of Manetho in the rest of the passage to identify the Jews with the lepers.

110. This is suggested by the passage i 14 (82 ff.), where Josephus gives a long section from Manetho in which the name Hyksos is explained as 'Shepherd Kings'. Josephus remarks about this that 'in another copy' (ἐν ἄλλῳ ἀντιγράφῳ) another explanation was given. A similar note (εὑρέθη ἐν ἑτέρῳ ἀντιγράφῳ οὕτως) is found in a marginal gloss in Codex Laurentianus of Josephus, i 15 (98), which may suggest that the phrase in i 14 (83) should be similarly be ignored as the work of a copyist. However, when Josephus proffers in i 14 (91) an explanation of the Hyksos identical to that given in the first passage and introduces his statement in this latter place as being found ἐν ἄλλῃ δέ τινι βίβλῳ, this phrase cannot also be understood to mean 'in another copy', which in turn casts some doubt on the earlier phrase, cf. Stern GLAJJ I, p. 72.

111. In favour of genuineness, cf. Stern, GLAJJ I, p. 64.

Bibliography

Böckh, A., *Manetho und die Hundssternperiode, ein Beitrag zur Geschichte der Pharaonen* (1845).
Krall, J., 'Die Composition und die Schicksale des Manethonischen Geschichtswerkes', SAW 95 (1879), pp. 123–226, esp. 152–69.
Susemihl, F., *Gesch. der griech. Litteratur in der Alexandrinerzeit* I (1891), pp. 608 ff.
Wachsmuth, C., *Einleitung in das Studium der alten Geschichte* (1895), pp. 333–40.
Meyer, Ed., *Aegyptische Chronologie* (1904; Nachträge 1907).
Weill, R., *La fin du moyen empire Egyptien* (1918).
Laqueur, R., 'Manethon', RE XIV.1 (1928), cols. 1060–1101.
Heinemann, I., 'Antisemitismus', RE suppl. V (1931), cols. 26 ff.
Momigliano, A., 'Intorno al *Contra Apione*', Rivista di Filologia n.s. 9.4 (1931), pp. 490 ff = *Quinto Contributo* (1975), pp. 770 ff.
Schwartz, J., 'Le "Cycle de Petoubastis" et les commentaires égyptiens de l'Exode', Bulletin de l'Institut français d'Archéologie orientale 49 (1950), pp. 73 ff.
Helek, W., *Untersuchungen zu Manetho und den ägyptischen Königslisten* (1956), pp. 38 ff.
J. Yoyotte, 'L'Égypte ancienne et les origines de l'antijudaïsme', RHR 163 (1963), pp. 133–43.
van Seters, J., *The Hyksos* (1966), pp. 121 ff.
Fraser, PA I, pp. 505–10.

On *the fragments in Josephus*, cf.:
Müller, J. G., *Des Flavius Josephus Schrift gegen den Apion* (1877), pp. 120 ff., 185 ff., 214 ff.
Krall, *loc. cit.*
v. Gutschmid, A., *Kleine Schriften* IV (1893), pp. 419–62.
Willrich, H., *Juden und Griechen vor der makkabäischen Erhebung* (1895), pp. 53–6.
Reinach, Th., *Textes d'auteurs grecs et romains relatifs au Judaïsme* (1895), pp. 20–34.
Meyer, Ed., *Aegyptische Chronologie* (1904), pp. 71 ff.
Stählin, F., *Der Antisemitismus des Altertums* (1905), pp. 9 ff.
Laqueur, R., *Der jüd. Historiker Flavius Josephus* (1920), pp. 1–6.
Laqueur, R., 'Manethon', RE XIV.1 (1928), cols. 1064–80.
Hospers-Jansen, A. M. A., *Tacitus over de Joden* (1949), p. 119.
Gager, J. G., *Moses in Greco-Roman Paganism* (1972), pp. 113 ff.
Stern, GLAJJ I, pp. 62–92.
Kasher, A., 'The propaganda purposes of Manetho's libellous story about the base origin of the Jews', in B. Oded *et al.*, *Studies in the History of the Jewish People and the Land of Israel* (1974), pp. 69–84 (Heb.).
Troiàni, L., 'Sui frammenti di Manetone nel primo libro del Contra Apionem di Flavio Giuseppe', Studi Classici e Orientali 24 (1975), pp. 97–126.
Troiani, L., *Commento storico al 'Contro Apione' di Giuseppe* (1977).

2. Mnaseas.

According to Josephus, *C. Ap.* ii 9 (112–15), Apion, the enemy of the Jews who is to be further discussed below (no. 6), took the following fiction from an older author. During a war of the Jews against the Idumeans (emending the reading 'Iudaei contra Iudaeos' to 'Iudaei contra Idumaeos') a certain Zabidos from the town of Dora, where Apollo was worshipped, came to the Jews and promised to deliver the god to them, saying that he would come to the Jewish Temple if they would all stay away. Zabidos then made a wooden structure with three rows of lamps, and entered inside it so that it looked as if stars were travelling over the earth. The Jews in amazement kept well away,

598   §33A. Jewish Literature Composed in Greek

whereat Zabidos went into the Temple unhindered and was able to take away the golden asses head and return with it to Dora. Dora is certainly not, as Josephus thinks, the far distant Phoenician Dora, but the Idumean Adora. It is now known from a Greek inscription found in Egypt (OGIS, no. 737) that the Idumeans worshipped Apollo in Hellenistic times (cf. above, vol. II, p. 6). The name of the author from whom Apion took this story is corrupted in the Latin text of Josephus (the only one in which the beginning of the passage has been preserved). The best tradition is Mnafeam, which Niese correctly emended to Mnaseas. Josephus mentions him also elsewhere as a writer on Jewish matters (C. Ap. i 23 (216)); he names him, too, among authors who refer to the flood (Ant. i 3, 6 (94)). Assuming that the same man can be identified in all three mentions with the Mnaseas to whom the Suda refers, s.v. 'Ερατοσθένης, he would seem to have come from Lycian Patara (P. Oxy. 1611, F2, col. 1, lines 127 ff.) and , as a student of Eratosthenes, will have lived at the end of the third century B.C. or the very beginning of the second. He wrote amongst other things a geography, in which he dealt with the curiosities and objects of interest of individual regions and places. The story which Apion quotes was probably part of this work.

Editions

Müller, C., FHG III, pp. 149–58.
Stern, GLAJJ I, pp. 99–100 (texts about Jews only, with English translation).

Bibliography

Willrich, H., Juden und Griechen (1895), pp. 52 ff.
Stähelin, O., Der Antisemitismus des Altertums (1905), pp. 14 f.
Halévy, J., 'La visite d'Apollon au temple juif', Revue sémitique 18 (1910), pp. 218 ff.
Radin, M., The Jews among the Greeks and Romans (1915), pp. 168 ff.
Heinemann, I., 'Antisemitismus', RE suppl. v (1931), cols. 28 ff.
Gutman, Y., in Ziyunim-Simhoni Memorial Book (1929), pp. 181 ff.
Hopfner, T., Die Judenfrage bei Griechen und Römern (1943), pp. 58 ff.
Bickermann, E., 'Ritualmord und Eselskult', MGWJ 71 (1927), pp. 171–87; 255–64 = Studies in Jewish and Christian History (1980), pp. 225–55.
Krappe, A. H., ''Απόλλων "Ονος', CPh 42 (1947), p. 232.
Hospers-Jansen, A. M. A., Tacitus over de Joden (1949), pp. 122 ff.
Tcherikover, V. A., Hellenistic Civilization and the Jews (1959), pp. 365 ff.
Neher-Bernheim, R., 'The libel of Jewish ass-worship', Zion 28 (1963), pp. 106 ff. (Heb.).
Stern, GLAJJ I, pp. 97–8.

3. Apollonius Molon (or Molonis).

Among the literary opponents of Judaism, Josephus frequently refers to 'Απολλώνιος ὁ Μόλων (C. Ap. ii 14 (145); ii 36 (255)) or ὁ Μόλων 'Απολλώνιος (ii 36 (258); cf. ii 7 (79): 'Apollonium Molonis') whose full name he also shortens to 'Απολλώνιος (ii 14 (145); ii 37 (262), twice), or only *Μόλων* (ii 2 (16); cf. ii 33 (236) and ii 41 (295): *Μόλωνες*). This author is undoubtedly identical with the Molon from whom Alexander Polyhistor quotes a passage (in Euseb. *Praep. ev.* ix 19). Elsewhere, frequent mention is made of an orator of the same name (Apollonius Molon) as the teacher of Cicero and Caesar and as a writer on rhetoric.[112] He is to be distinguished carefully from his older contemporary Apollonius who also came from Alabanda in Caria and also taught rhetoric at Rhodes, cf. RE II (1896), cols. 140–1, s.v. 'Apollonios' (84). It seems to have been common though not universal for Roman writers to make the distinction by referring to Josephus' author by the name 'Molon' alone, Strabo, xiv 2, 13 (655); 26 (661). Molon came to Rome as representative of the Rhodians during the dictatorship of Sulla (82–81 B.C.), and Cicero heard him there; later Cicero visited him in Rhodes. He was not only a teacher of rhetoric and a rhetorical writer, but, as was common for rhetorical experts in the Roman empire, also a practical politician and pleader.[113] His full name was *Ἀπολλώνιος ὁ τοῦ Μόλωνος* (Plutarch, *Cicero* 4, *Caesar* 3; Jos. *C. Ap.* ii 7 (79): 'Apollonium Molonis'), or also *Ἀπολλώνιος ὁ Μόλων*, in which, in imitation of Latin nomenclature, he placed his father's name next to his own, following a custom of which other examples have been found.[114]

For an orator living in Caria or Rhodes at the beginning of the first century B.C. there was ample reason for writing a polemical work against the Jews. There were already many Jews there during the second century B.C.[115] The writing of Apollonius was a *συσκευὴ κατὰ Ἰουδαίων* according to Eusebius, *Praep. ev.* ix 19. It is likely that the description reflects Eusebius' usage rather than that of his source, Alexander Polyhistor. The word *συσκευή* usually means 'snare', cf. Euseb. *Hist. eccl.* vi 9, 4; x 8, 5 and 7, but is here transferred to the field of literature to mean 'attack' or 'polemics'. Thus the work did not merely deal occasionally with the Jews, like Manetho's *History of Egypt*, but exclusively. According to Josephus, Apollonius, 'unlike Apion, has not

---

112. Quintilian, *Inst.* xii 6, 7. Suetonius, *Caesar* 4. Quintilian, *Inst.* iii 1, 16. Phoebammon in *Rhetores graeci*, ed. Walz, VIII, p. 494 (here: *Ἀπολλώνιος ὁ ἐπικληθεὶς Μόλων*). In Plutarch, *Cicero* 4, *Caesar* 3, the same teacher of Cicero and Caesar is called *Ἀπολλώνιος ὁ τοῦ Μόλωνος*, for Josephus also has Apollonius Molonis in one passage (*C. Ap.* ii 7 (79)).

113. Cicero, *Brutus*, 87, 312, 316; cf. 245, *Ad Atticum* ii 1, 9. Cicero refers throughout to his teacher as 'Molon'. In contrast Quintilian, in describing Cicero's visit to Rhodes, calls him 'Apollonius Molon' (*Inst.* xii 6, 7).

114. H. Diels, *Doxographi Graeci* (²1929), p. 86.

115. Cf. 1 Mac. 15:16–24, and on this, above, p. 4. 1 Mac. 15:16–24 assumes that Jews lived in the Carian towns of Myndos, Halicarnassus, and Cnidus, and on the neighbouring islands of Cos and Rhodes. On Halicarnassus, cf. also above, pp. 25, 117 (Jos. *Ant.* xiv 10, 23 (256); J. Juster, *Les Juifs dans l'Empire romain* I (1914), p. 191).

grouped his accusations together but scattered them here and there all over his work' (*C. Ap.* ii 14 (148)). Presumably, therefore, this writing was not entirely polemical, but only combined its polemical invective with other statements about the Jews. This is confirmed by the fact that the fragment in Alexander Polyhistor (in Euseb. *Praep. ev.* ix 19) gives objectively the genealogy of the Jews from the flood until Moses. From Josephus' indications it emerges that the history of the exodus from Egypt was also discussed (*C. Ap.* ii 2 (8 ff.)) and that the work contained 'unjust and untrue reports about our Lawgiver Moses' (ii 14 (145)). It appears, too, that Apollonius reproached the Jews for 'not worshipping the same gods as other people' (ii 7 (79)), for refusing fellowship with persons having different ideas about God (ii 36 (258)), for therefore being atheists and misanthropes, besides being cowardly at some times and reckless at others. He accused them of being the most incompetent among the barbarians, who accomplished nothing for the general culture (ii 14 (148)).

Josephus for his part repays Apollonius in kind, reproaching him for a gross lack of understanding, arrogance, and immoral conduct (ii 36 (255); 37 (271)).

Editions

Müller, C., FHG III, pp. 208 ff.
Jacoby, FGrH 728, III C, pp. 687–9.
Stern, GLAJJ I, pp. 150–6 (with English translation).

Bibliography

Reinach, Th., *Textes d'auteurs grecs et romains relatifs au Judaïsme* (1895), pp. 60–4.
Brzoska, J., 'Apollonios (85)', RE II.1 (1896), cols. 141–4.
Radin, M., *The Jews among the Greeks and Romans* (1915), pp. 198 ff.
Portalupi, F., *Sulla corrente rodiese* (1957), pp. 16 ff.
Kennedy, G. A., *The Art of Persuasion in Greece* (1963), pp. 326 ff.
Davies, J. C., 'Molon's influence on Cicero', CQ n.s. 18 (1968), pp. 303–14.
Kennedy, G. A., *The Art of Rhetoric in the Roman World* (1972), pp. 104–5, 155, 285.
Stern, GLAJJ I, pp. 148–9.

4. *Lysimachus (cf. Josephus, C. Ap. i 34–35 (304–20))*.

The fragment quoted by Josephus from the writing of a certain Lysimachus relates to the exodus of the Jews from Egypt and recounts fables similar to, but not apparently derived from, those of Manetho. A few other incidental notices from Lysimachus in Josephus also refer to the same fact (*C. Ap.* ii 2 (16), (20); 14 (145)). He was probably earlier than Apion since the latter is stated by Josephus, *C. Ap.* ii 2 (20), to have guessed the same figure of exiles from Egypt as Lysimachus had done; but otherwise the fragments in Josephus do not give any clear indication of date. Despite the idiosyncrasies of Lysimachus' version of the exodus, his ideas are sufficiently close to those of Manetho for the assumption to be reasonable that he was an Egyptian, and there is explicit, though not entirely trustworthy evidence that the fragments were taken from a work which was probably a 'History of Egypt'.[116]

Two works by an author named Lysimachus are frequently cited elsewhere in ancient literature: *Theban Paradoxes* and Νόστοι ('Return Journeys', i.e. of the Greek heroes from Troy). Since the author of the Νόστοι was an Alexandrian, and lived at some time between *c.* 175 B.C. and the early imperial period, he may be identical with this Lysimachus, but certainty is not possible.[117]

Editions

Müller, C., FHG III, pp. 334–42 (Fragments from Josephus, Theban Paradoxes and Νόστοι).
Jacoby, FGrH 382 (Theban Paradoxes and Νόστοι); FGrH 621 (Fragments from Josephus).
Stern, GLAJJ I, pp. 383–8 (Fragments from Josephus, with English translation).

Bibliography

Gudemann, 'Lysimachus (20)', RE XIV.1 (1928), cols. 32–9.
Fraser, PA II, pp. 1092–3.

5. Chaeremon (cf. Josephus, C. Ap. i 32–33 (288–303)).

The fragment from Chaeremon also relates to the exodus of the Jews from Egypt and as far as its contents is concerned is closer to Manetho's account than to that of Lysimachus, though it also is partly independent. Such stories probably circulated generally in Egypt, as the appearance of a similar antisemitic account in an undated prophecy about Egypt preserved in a papyrus of the third century A.D. seems to indicate (CPJ III, no. 520; cf. Stern, GLAJJ I, p. 420). It may even be that an older Egyptian tradition about the expulsion of a defiled people was only transferred to the Jews at a later stage, cf. the comments of H.-R. Schwyzer, *Chaeremon* (1932), pp. 57 ff., about the apparent introduction of Moses and Joseph into Chaeremon's text only as glosses on the Egyptian names of the leaders of the exodus. At any rate, in this case Josephus says explicitly that the fragment was taken from the *Egyptian History* of Chaeremon (*C. Ap.* i 32 (288)).

This Chaeremon is also known elsewhere as a writer on Egyptian

---

116. Cosmas Indicopleustes, *Topograph. christ.*, lib. xii 4, p. 327 (Winstedt) (ed. W. Wolska-Conus, SC 197, 1973); but Cosmas is not reliable here since he includes among authors of Egyptian histories not only Lysimachus but also, implausibly, Apollonius Molon, for whom no connection with Egypt can be traced.

117. In favour of the identity of the two authors, see A. Gudeman, 'Lysimachus (20)', RE XIV (1928), cols. 32–9; Fraser, PA II, pp. 1092–3. Against identity cf. Jacoby, FGrH 382 and 621.

matters, primarily through the writings of Porphyry. In Porphyry's letter to the Egyptian Anebon, from which Eusebius, *Praep. ev.* iii 4 and v 10, includes two extracts (Porphyry, *Epist. ad Anebonem* ii 12–13 and 8–9, ed. Sodano), two passages are cited from Chaeremon relating to Egyptian mythology and theology, explaining Egyptian divinities as referring to physical things such as the sun and moon. In the second passage (Euseb. v 10, 5), Porphyry describes Chaeremon as a sacred scribe (*ἱερογραμματεύς*). In the surviving writings of Porphyry (*De abstinentia* iv 6–8), a detailed description of the life of Egyptian priests is derived from Chaeremon, introduced with the words: 'Chaeremon the Stoic mentions in his description of the Egyptian priests, who, he says, were considered also as philosophers among the Egyptians, that they chose the sanctuaries as the place to philosophize ... They despised every other occupation and human pursuit and devoted their whole life to the contemplation of divine things etc.'[118] At the end of this account, Porphyry defines Chaeremon as a truth-loving, trustworthy, and intelligent Stoic philosopher (iv 8 *fin.*). All these passages may well have been part of an 'Egyptian History' although, given the lack of book title, another work by Chaeremon is possible. Information on the Egyptian attitude to astrology derived from Chaeremon by Psellus (*πόσα γένη*, pp. 443–4, Kurtz and Drexl = Jacoby, FGrH 618, F7) presumably came from the same source.

However, the same Chaeremon also wrote a work dealing with the meaning of hieroglyphics (*διδάγματα τῶν ἱερῶν γραμμάτων*). This became very influential in late antiquity. The Byzantine writer Tzetzes cites something of it in his historical work (*Chil.*, 5, 395 = Jacoby, FGrH 618, F3) and in his commentary on the *Iliad* (*Exeg. Iliad*, p. 146 (Hermann) = FGrH 618, T6). Tzetzes, too, designates Chaeremon a sacred scribe (*ἱερογραμματεύς*) and says that in Chaeremon's opinion the hieroglyphics exhibit allegorically the *φυσικὸς λόγος* of the gods, their physical meaning. This also characterizes Chaeremon as a Stoic. There can thus be no doubt that this *ἱερογραμματεύς* was identical with the Chaeremon called simply *Στωικός* in a few other citations (e.g. in Origen, *Contra Cels.* i 59, where a book on comets is attributed to him; Apollonius Dyscolus, *De coniunctionibus* 6, where grammatical technicalities are quoted in his name, presumably from an unknown grammatical treatise; Porphyry, quoted in Eusebius, *Hist. eccl.* vi 19, 8).

---

118. The description does not refer to all Egyptian priests but, as indicated in iv, 8, only to the elite among them, the *προφῆται, ἱεροστολισταί, ἱερογραμματεῖς* and *ὡρολόγοι*. Cf. discussion in P. W. van der Horst, *Chaeremon: Egyptian Priest and Stoic Philosopher* (1984), pp. 60–1. Jerome, *Adv. Jovinian* ii 13 (ed. E. Bickel, *Diatribe in Senecae philosophi fragmenta* I (1915), pp. 415–16), is an epitome of this passage in Porphyry except when he quotes verbatim Chaeremon's statement, which does not appear in Porphyry, that Egyptian priests regard eggs as liquid meat, cf. van der Horst, *op. cit.*, p. 61.

He was for this reason a figure characteristic of his age, an Egyptian priest and at the same time a Stoic philosopher. Since he was the teacher of Nero, according to the Suda (s.v. Ἀλέξανδρος Αἰγαῖος), and also the teacher and predecessor of Dionysius of Alexandria, who lived from Nero until Trajan (s.v. Διονύσιος Ἀλεξανδρεύς), he must be placed towards the middle of the first century A.D. He may well be identical with the Chaeremon son of Leonidas who appeared before the Emperor Claudius, presumably in the same sort of quarrel with the Jews that Apion had conducted in the time of Caligula (CPJ II, no. 153).[119] According to the Suda, he was Dionysius' predecessor in the office of librarian in Alexandria and perhaps also keeper of the Alexandrian Museum.[120] At any rate, he cannot be identical with the Chaeremon mentioned by Strabo (xvii 1, 29, p. 806) as the contemporary of Aelius Gallus under Augustus. Besides, the latter is described as someone who made himself ridiculous by his ostentation and ignorance, which does not fit the description of the philosopher. This earlier Chaeremon may well have been his grandfather. The name Chaeremon is very frequent in Egyptian papyri.[121]

Editions

Müller, C., FHG III, pp. 495–9 (lacking the material in Tzetzes and Psellus).
Schwyzer, H.-R., *Chairemon* (1932) (with commentary).
Jacoby, FGrH 618, III C, pp. 145–53.
Stern, GLAJJ I, pp. 419–21 (the fragments from Josephus only).
van der Horst, P. W., *Chaeremon: Egyptian Priest and Stoic Philosopher* (1984) (with English translation, and detailed commentary).

Bibliography

Birch, S., 'On the Lost Book of Chaeremon on Hieroglyphics', Transactions of the Royal Society of Literature, 2nd series, vol. 3 (1850), pp. 385–96.
Bernays, J., *Theophrastos Schrift über Frömmigkeit* (1866), pp. 21 ff., 150 ff.
Zeller, E., 'Die Hieroglyphiker Chäremon und Horapollo', Hermes 11 (1876), pp. 430–3.
Müller, J. G., *Das Flavius Josephus Schrift gegen den Apion* (1877), pp. 203–5.
Schwartz, E., 'Chaeremon⁻(7)', RE III.2 (1899), cols. 2025–7.
Weill, R., *La fin du moyen empire égyptien* (1918), pp. 104–11.
Heinemann, I., 'Antisemitismus', RE suppl. V (1931), col. 27.

119. H. I. Bell, *Jews and Christians in Egypt* (1924), p. 23; H. Stuart-Jones, 'Claudius and the Jewish Question at Alexandria', JRS 16 (1926), p. 18; J. Vergote, 'Clément d'Alexandrie et l'écriture égytienne', Le Muséon 52 (1939), p. 220. Cf. literature cited in CPJ II, pp. 36 f.

120. For succession to the directorship of the Mouseion as the import of the Suda passage, see E. Schwartz, RE III (1899), cols. 2025 f.; *contra*, W. Otto, *Priester und Tempel im hellenistischen Ägypten* I (1905; repr. 1971), p. 199. Cf. H.-R. Schwyzer, *Chaeremon* (1932), p. 11.

121. Cf. F. Preisigke, *Namenbuch* (1922), col. 470; D. Foraboschi, *Onomasticon Alterum Papyrologicum* (1967–71), p. 338.

Schwyzer, H.-R., *Chairemon* (1932).
Wendel, C., 'Zum Hieroglyphen-Buche Chairemons', Hermes 75 (1940), pp. 227–9.
de Liagre Böhl, C. M. T., *Opera Minora* (1953), p. 111.
Strathmann, H., 'Chairemon', RAC II (1959), cols. 990–2.
Stern, M., 'An Egyptian-Greek Prophecy and the Tradition about the Expulsion of the
    Jews from Egypt in the History of Chaeremon', Zion 28 (1963), pp. 223–8 (Heb.).
Roth, L, 'Chaeremon', Enc. Jud. V (1971), cols. 317–8.
Gager, J. G., *Moses in Greco-Roman Paganism* (1972), pp. 120 ff.
Fraser, PA II, pp. 1107–8.
van der Horst, P. W., 'Chaeremon, Egyptisch priester en antisemitisch Stoïcijn uit de tijd
    van het Nieuwe Testament', Nederlands Theologisch Tijdschrift 35 (1981), pp. 265–72.
van der Horst, P. W., 'The Way of Life of the Egyptian Priests According to Chaeremon',
    in M. Heerma van Voss et al., eds., *Studies in Egyptian Religion Dedicated to Prof. Jan
    Zandee* (1982), pp. 61–71.
van der Horst, P. W., *Chaeremon : Egyptian Priest and Stoic Philosopher* (1984).

6. Apion (cf. Josephus, C. Ap. ii 1–13 (1–144)).

The grammarian Apion was an older contemporary and countryman of
Chaeremon who distinguished himself among all the opponents of the
Jews by the depth of his hatred, and was therefore treated with
particular bitterness by Josephus. His nickname was Ἀπίων ὁ
Πλειστονίκης or Πλειστονείκης.[122] The Suda claims that Πλειστονίκης
was the name of his father (s.v. Ἀπίων ὁ Πλειστονίκου), which he
accordingly used as surname, but Julius Africanus (in Euseb. *Praep. ev.*
x 10, 16; and in *Syncellus*, ed. Dindorf, I, pp. 120 and 281), and after
him Ps.-Justin, *Cohortatio ad Graecos* 9, give the father's name as
Ποσειδώνιος. This may be a corruption from Πλειστονίκης, but
otherwise it must be assumed that the Suda is incorrect and that
Πλειστονίκης ('victor in many contests'), or some similar word, was a
nickname.[123]

    According to Josephus, *C. Ap.* ii 3 (29), Apion, born in the Egyptian
oasis—in Upper Egypt, west of Thebes—was not the Alexandrian he

---

122. Clement of Alexandria, *Strom.* i 21, 101 (= Eusebius, *Praep. ev.* x 12, 2): Ἀπίων
τοίνυν ὁ γραμματικὸς ὁ Πλειστονίκης ἐπικληθείς. Cf. Clement of Rome, *Homil.* iv 6; Pliny,
Hist. Nat. xxxvii 5, 75 ; Gellius, *Noct. Att.* v 14; vi 8. The adjective πλειστονίκης is attested
on inscriptions, see e.g. L. Moretti, *Iscrizioni agonistiche greche* (1953), p. 285. H. Jacobson,
'Apion's nickname', AJPh 98 (1977), pp. 413–15, suggests that the original nickname
was πλειστονείκης, 'quarrelsome', and was therefore a pejorative pun on the more
common description πλειστονίκης. There is not in fact any evidence that Apion *was*
'victor in many contests'.

123. The inscription on the Memnon statue near Thebes : Ἀπίων Πλειστον (...) ἤκουσα
τρίς (Dittenberger, OGIS, no. 662 = A. and E. Bernand, *Les inscriptions grecques et latines
du Colosse de Memnon* (1960), p. 165) may refer to our Apion. The missing letters
unfortunately make it uncertain whether Πλειστον (...) refers to Apion's father or his
nickname, but completion of the word as πλειστονίκης is certainly possible, cf.
Dittenberger, *ad loc.* Even so, however, the inscription may refer to a different, less
illustrious Apion since the graffiti on the Colossus mostly date after A.D. 65, by which
time Apion was dead, cf. Jacobson, *art. cit.*, p. 413.

claimed to be. Only afterwards did he receive the rights of Alexandrian citizenship and make a name for himself in Alexandria as a grammarian.[124] He also taught for a while in Rome during the time of Tiberius and Claudius (Suda, s.v. Ἀπίων). During the time of Caligula he travelled throughout Greece as an itinerant orator, lecturing on Homer (Seneca, *Epist.*, 88). It was equally under Caligula that he came to Rome as representative of the Alexandrians on the occasion of their bloody conflict with the Jews (Jos. *Ant.* xviii 8 (257-9)). Josephus writes that he died of gangrene which set in after a therapeutic circumcision made necessary by ulcers on the genitals (*C. Ap.* ii 13 (143)).

Apion was a popular writer (Aulus Gellius, *Noctes Atticae* V 14,2: 'libri non incelebres'), but is described as ridiculously vain. He stated without embarrassment that those to whom he directed a writing would become immortal (Pliny, *N.H.*, praef. 25), and congratulated Alexandria on having a citizen like himself (*C. Ap.* ii 12 (135)).

Apion was the author of a variety of works. His studies on Homer (commentaries and a dictionary) appear to have been best known. Here we are only concerned with his *Egyptian history* (Αἰγυπτιακά), which comprised five books according to Tatian, of which Josephus quotes the third, Tatian and his successors the fourth, and Gellius the fifth.[125] This Egyptian history evidently contained all the polemical invective against the Jews to which Josephus replies (*C. Ap.* ii 1-13 (1-144)). Josephus asserts at the outset of his discussion that it was not easy to summarize Apion's argument because he had advanced everything in the greatest disorder. Three points could nonetheless be distinguished: (1) the fantastic stories concerning the exodus of the Jews from Egypt; (2) the malicious assertions in regard to the Alexandrian Jews; and (3) the accusations regarding worship and legal customs. Josephus says of the latter that they appear mixed up with the first two categories (ii 1 (7)). It is clear therefore that there was only one argument (λόγος) of Apion which contained all these charges, and

---

124. There is no reason to doubt Josephus' references to Apion's origin and to take him for a native Alexandrian; *contra* H. Willrich, *Juden und Griechen vor der Makkabäischen Erhebung* (1895), pp. 172-6; *idem*, Klio 3 (1903), p. 413, n. 2. There is no contradiction between him and Athenaeus i 29, p. 16 F = Jacoby, FGrH 616, T 4b, where Apion is called Ἀλεξανδρεύς. This is entirely explicable as a reference to the fact that he lived in Alexandria, cf. I. Lévy, REJ 41 (1900), pp. 188 ff.

125. Reference to the third book is in Josephus, *C. Ap.* ii 2 (10). There are numerous specific references to the fourth book in other authors besides Tatian, *Or. ad Graecos* 38 = Eusebius, *Praep. ev.* x 11, 14 (= Jacoby, FGrH 616, T 11a); cf. Clement of Alexandria, *Strom.* i 101, 3 (Jacoby, FGrH 616, T 11b) = Eusebius, *Praep. ev.* x 12, 2 (Jacoby, F 2b); Julius Africanus in Eusebius, *Praep. ev.* x 10, 16 = Pseudo-Justin, *Cohortatio ad Graecos* 9 (Jacoby, T 11c). Reference to the fifth book is found in Aulus Gellius, *Noctes Atticae* vi (vii) 8 (Jacoby, F 6).

that Josephus divided it into three classes simply for the sake of order. Having then dealt successively with these three categories—(*C. Ap.* ii 2–3 (8–32) relates to the first; ii 4–6 (33–78) to the second; and ii 7–13 (79–144) to the third)—he leaves Apion and begins the positive presentation of the Mosaic Law. At the start, he incidentally touches once more on Apion, saying of him that he had heaped his accusations together (ii 14 (148)), in contrast to Apollonius Molon, whose polemics pervaded his whole work. There can be little doubt, therefore, that Josephus' argument refers to only one of Apion's writings, and indeed only to one section[126] of one of his larger works. This, as Josephus says explicitly (ii 2, (10)), was the Egyptian history. In it Apion appears to have taken the opportunity to give a hostile account of the exodus of the Jews from Egypt, as Tacitus did later in his *Histories* (*Hist.* v 1–12).

Accordingly, mention by Clement of Alexandria and later Christian writers of a special work of Apion, κατὰ 'Ιουδαίων, rests solely on an incorrect conclusion drawn from Josephus. The very fact that he is silent about it suggests that such a work never existed, and it is clear that these Church writers had no direct knowledge of it. In the passage where he alludes to it (*Strom.* i 21, 101), Clement of Alexandria merely copies Tatian (*Oratio ad Graecos* 38), and Tatian in turn merely quotes Apion's Egyptian history. All subsequent writers who purport to know something about a work of Apion entitled 'Against the Jews', again drew only on Clement or on Josephus.

The mention of Apion's alleged work κατὰ 'Ιουδαίων was introduced simply as a reference by Clement, *Strom.* i 21, 101, while for the rest he merely quotes, like Tatian, Apion's Egyptian history as source for the statement that Amosis reigned during the time of Inachos (*ibid.*). Julius Africanus, however, in Euseb. *Praep. ev.* ix 10, 16 and Syncellus, ed. Dindorf, I, pp. 120, 281, ventures to assert on the basis of Clement's passage that this statement was found in both of the alleged writings of Apion. At the same time he draws in Moses as well, who is not mentioned at all in the passage cited from Apion. Finally the author of Ps.-Justin, *Cohortatio ad Graecos* 9, once more merely copies from Julius Africanus.

Eusebius, *Hist. eccl.* iii 9, 4, asserts, in enumerating the works of Josephus, that 'On the antiquity of the Jews' (i.e. *Contra Apionem*) was written 'against the grammarian Apion, who had at that time composed a λόγος against the Jews'; but this was evidently only

---

126. The concentration of comments about the Jews in the fourth book led Jacoby, FGrH, III C, p. 127, to suggest that the book was entitled κατὰ 'Ιουδαίων. The fact that Josephus assigns Apion's comments on the exodus to the third book (*C. Ap.* ii 2 (10)), even though Julius Africanus in Eusebius, *Praep. ev.* x 10, 16, assigns them to the fourth book, suggests either that Josephus was mistaken or that Apion discussed the matter twice.

inferred from Josephus. The same is true of Jerome, *De viris illustr.* 13 (PL, XXIII, 662). Jerome copied, as was his custom, the account of Eusebius, adding to it from Jos. *Ant.* xviii 8, 1 (257–60) the statement that Apion's book was directed against Philo. The statements in the Suda, s.v. Ἰώσηπος, in turn depend on the Greek translation of Jerome (Sophronius).

When, finally, the Ps.-Clementine Homilies assert that Apion wrote πολλὰ βιβλία against the Jews (*Homil.* v 2), this is of course not to be taken seriously.

Editions

Müller, C., FHG III, pp. 506–16.
Jacoby, FGrH, 616, III C, pp. 122–44.
Fragments about the Jews only in:
Reinach, Th., *Textes d'auteurs grecs et romains relatif au Judaïsme* (1895), pp. 123–4.
Stern, GLAJJ I, pp. 389–416 (with translation and commentary).

Bibliography

Müller, J. G., *Des Fl. Josephus' Schrift gegen den Apion* (1877), pp. 14–17.
Sperling, A., *Apion der Grammatiker und sein Verhältnis zum Judentum* (1886).
von Gutschmid, A., *Kleine Schriften* IV (1893), pp. 356–71.
Cohn, L., 'Apion', RE I.2 (1894), cols. 2803–6.
Willrich, H., *Juden und Griechen vor der makkabäischen Erhebung* (1895), pp. 172–6.
Wellmann, M., 'Aegyptisches', Hermes 31 (1896), pp. 221–53.
Lévy, I., 'Apion était-il Alexandrin?', REJ 41 (1900), pp. 188 ff.
Motzo, B., 'Il κατὰ Ἰουδαίων di Apione', Atti dell'Accademia delle Scienze di Torino 48 (1912–13), pp. 459 ff.
Juster, J., *Les Juifs dans l'Empire romain* I (1914), p. 33.
Radin, M., *The Jews under the Greeks and the Romans* (1915), pp. 199 ff.
de Liagre Böhl, F. M. T., *Opera Minora* (1953), pp. 118 f.
Lévy, I., 'Tacite et l'origine du peuple juif', Latomus 5 (1946), pp. 339 f.
Gager, J. G., *Moses in Greco-Roman Paganism* (1972), pp. 122–4.
Sevenster, J. N., *The Roots of Pagan Antisemitism* (1975), esp. pp. 127–8, 133, 138.
Daniel, J. L., 'Anti-semitism in the Hellenistic-Roman period', JBL 98 (1979), pp. 45–65, esp. p. 56.

7. The literary opponents of the Jews named thus far have been discussed more thoroughly because Josephus' polemics were directed mainly against them. An exhaustive enumeration of all the Greek and Roman writers who until the beginning of the second century A.D. expressed unfriendly sentiments in regard to the Jews would result in another impressive list of names, cf. Stern, GLAJJ. Most pagan authors who spoke about the Jews at all after *c.* 300 B.C. did so in a polemical sense. Hostility was almost universal after the first century B.C. It is hard to establish the extent of literary antisemitism among the earlier authors because of the possibility of interpolations into their work by later antisemites of the early Roman period. It is likely that relations between Jews and gentiles varied from place to place, and it may

therefore be misleading to look for general trends throughout Greek and Roman literature, especially since individual comments by particular authors may not reflect a wider polemic at all but simply a specific need for a literary effect (e.g. Cicero, *Pro Flacco* 66–9; Horace, *Sat.* i 9, 67–72).[127] Among pre-Christian Greek authors, Josephus mentions in particular as adversary of the Jews the distinguished historian and philosopher Posidonius (*C. Ap.* ii 7 (79)). In his great historical work (cf. above, vol. I, pp. 20–2) he may have managed to insert a polemical excursus against the Jews, although, since the charge is derived from Josephus, who was not directly acquainted with Posidonius' writings and therefore presumably relied on Apion's attribution of antisemitic beliefs to his illustrious predecessor, it may be that Posidonius was less hostile. If Josephus is correct, Posidonius will have been a powerful influence, since many later authors depended directly or indirectly on his much-read works.[128] Also polemical were the works of Nicarchus (Jacoby, FGrH 731, F1 = Stern, GLAJJ I, pp. 322–3) and Damocritus (Jacoby, FGrH 730, F1 = Stern, GLAJJ I, pp. 530–1), of which we hardly know more than the titles.[129] Mention should in addition be made here of the literary genre of anonymous stories which survive in papyri about the martyrdoms of Alexandrian pagans during the struggle against the Jews at the hands of the Roman authorities, cf. H. A. Musurillo, *The Acts of the Pagan Martyrs* (1954). Of the Roman historians, Trogus Pompeius and Tacitus should be

127. For pagan literary views of Moses, cf. J. G. Gager, *Moses in Greco-Roman Paganism* (1972), who distinguishes between the favourable view of him in early Hellenistic writers outside Egypt, the hostile accounts to be found in Egypt and in Roman authors after the Judaean revolts, and the picture of Moses as a powerful magician which was widespread throughout the Greco-Roman world. A similar variety can be found in other comments on Jews by pagan authors.

128. Cf. Stern, GLAJJ I, pp. 141–7, esp. 141–3, where the remarks of Diodorus Siculus, xxxiv 1, 1–5, about events in Palestine in 134–132 B.C., usually believed to be derived from Posidonius' history, are discussed. Although the passage contains expressions hostile to the Jews, it does not show sympathy with the characters who express them. Diodorus was anyway sufficiently independent of Posidonius to quote from Hecataeus a description favourable to the Jews, cf. below, VII.4. Justin, xxxvi 2–3 (excerpt from Pompeius Trogus), is unlikely to have used Posidonius; Timagenes is a much more probable source for his comments, cf. Stern, GLAJJ I, pp. 223, 333; above, vol. I, pp. 22–3, on Timagenes.

129. Nicarchus is cited in an anonymous Byzantine lexicon as an authority in his book *On the Jews* for the slander that Moses was called 'Alpha' because of the leprous spots on his body, cf. Jacoby, FGrH, III C, part 2, pp. 691 ff. No date is known for Nicarchus. The same information is found in the works of Ptolemy Chennos of Alexandria, fl. c. A.D. 100 (Photius, *Bibl.*, 279 (ed. Bekker, p. 529b)), but it is likely that the latter authors, who were compilers rather than original writers, used Nicarchus, or that all these writers relied on a common tradition dependent on the antisemitic account of the exodus extant in other Egyptian writers (see below, p. 611). Cf. J. G. Gager, *Moses in Greco-Roman Paganism* (1972), pp. 129–32.

specially indicated. Tacitus describes the Jews (*Hist.* v 2 ff.) with the greatest contempt. Moreover, the Roman satirists Horace, Juvenal, and Martial made Jewish customs the target of their jokes.[130]

2. Jewish Apologetics[131]

Jewish apologetics adopted a twofold course of defence against the manifold attacks which Judaism had to endure: a direct and an indirect one. Some of the historical and philosophical literature of Hellenistic Judaism is indirectly apologetic, aiming to show that the Jews had no reason at all to fear a comparison with other nations. Much of this apologetic, though not all, was directed towards strengthening the confidence of a Jewish audience in their own heritage, and it is doubtful whether a gentile audience was ever intended to read it.[132] But this was not considered sufficient to counteract gentile prejudices, and the attempt was sometimes made to refute the accusations systematically, point after point, and in order to try to stop the slanders at their source, to present them in a way that might not prove rebarbative to a gentile audience. Two such systematically apologetic works are known, one by Philo in only a short fragment, the other by Josephus in a complete text. (1) Eusebius, *Praep. ev.* viii 11, gives the description of the Essenes from Philo's ἀπολογία ὑπὲρ Ἰουδαίων. It is impossible to form an idea of the structure of the whole work from this. It is probably identical with Philo's περὶ Ἰουδαίων, mentioned by Eusebius, *Hist. eccl.* ii 18, 6. The content of Philo's Ὑποθετικά, of which Eusebius, *Praep. ev.* viii 6–7, provides a few

---

130. Cf. the collected texts in Th. Reinach, *Textes d'auteurs grecs et romains relatifs au Judaïsme* (1895) and (much superior) Stern, GLAJJ, I-III. On the remarks of Tacitus, see H. Heubner, *P. Cornelius Tacitus, Die Historien. Kommentar*, vol. V, by H. Heubner and W. Fauth (1982); F. F. Bruce, 'Tacitus on Jewish history', JSS 29 (1984), pp. 33–44.

131. The general works on Jewish apologetics in the Hellenistic and Roman period cover a much wider field than that discussed in this section since they discuss all the Hellenistic Jewish literature of which any part may possibly play an apologetic role when directed towards either a gentile or a Jewish audience. See M. Friedländer, *Geschichte der jüdischen Apologetik als Vorgeschichte des Christenthums* (1903); P. Dalbert, *Die Theologie der Hellenistisch-Jüdischen Missionsliteratur unter Ausschluss von Philo und Josephus* (1954); H. Conzelmann, *Heiden-Juden-Christen* (1981), pp. 121–218. Although the extent to which such apologetics was deliberate varies in each case, it is noticeable that the same themes occur in many of these more general works as can be found in the *explicit* apologetics of Josephus, *C. Ap.*

132. V. A. Tcherikover, 'Jewish Apologetic Literature Reconsidered', Eos 48 (1956), pp. 169–93. The widest net for literature aimed at gentiles is cast by Dalbert, *Die Theologie der hell.-jüd. Missionsliteratur* (1954). He includes in his list of 'Missionsliteratur' Demetrius, Philo the Elder, Eupolemus, Artapanus, Ezekiel the Tragedian, Pseudo-Hecataeus, Aristeas, the Wisdom of Solomon, Pseudo-Aristeas, Aristobulus, and the Sibylline Oracles. Since Tcherikover's article, most scholars would argue that few of these works were primarily aimed at a non-Jewish audience.

fragments, is also apologetic. Since Eusebius himself characterizes the work as apologetic (*Praep. ev.* viii 5 *fin.*: ἔνθα τὸν ὑπὲρ Ἰουδαίων ὡς πρὸς κατηγόρους αὐτῶν ποιούμενος λόγον ταῦτά φησιν) it is presumably identical with the ἀπολογία (cf. below, §34). (2) The work of Josephus belonging to this category is known as *Contra Apionem*. This title does not, however, stem from Josephus himself, and gives a wrong impression of the contents in that it is not only concerned with Apion, but attempts to offer a comprehensive and systematic defence of the Jewish people against all the accusations raised against them (cf. further particulars above, vol. I, pp. 54–5).

In outlining now the main points of the accusations and the defence, it is necessary to keep essentially to the material in Josephus, his being the only extant work which both reviews the accusations and affords an insight into the methods of apologetic argumentation. The disposition of the Greco-Roman world towards the Jews has been described already (pp. 150 ff.). Here, the concern is only with the accusations proper and the Jewish answer to them.[133]

1. In the first section of his work (i 1–23 (1–218)), Josephus presents extensive evidence to prove that the Jews are not inferior in regard to antiquity to other civilized nations. He says that the contention that they are of late origin because Greek historians did not mention them them is foolish, even if this assumption were correct. The silence of all the Greek historians would not disprove the early existence of the nation, since the Jews, living inland, could easily have remained unknown to the Greeks. The truth however is that the Jewish people was noted already in very ancient times by the best historians of Egypt, Phoenicia and Chaldea (Manetho, Dios, Menander, Berossus, and others), indeed even by Greek historians themselves.

Josephus' zeal, and the great amount of material that he devotes to this point, indicates how important the matter was to him. To maintain a late origin was the same as to maintain historical insignificance. A nation which only recently stepped onto the stage of history has of course also no importance in history. It received its culture from the more ancient nations. But this was to strike at the root of Jewish honour. The Jewish apologist therefore regarded it as his primary task to strike out at this fundamental affront.[134]

2. While the Greeks generally were satisfied to deny the antiquity of

---

133. For a complete list of specific charges made against the Jews in antiquity, citing both pagan and Christian sources, see J. Juster, *Les Juifs dans l'Empire romain* I (1914), pp. 45–8.

134. On the proof of antiquity, cf. *C. Ap.* ii 15 (151–6). Christian apologists also lay great stress on this. Cf. Tatian 31, 36–41; Theophilus, *Ad Autol.* iii 20 ff.; Clement of Alexandria, *Strom.* i 21, 101–47; Tertullian, *Apolog.* 19; Pseudo-Justin, *Cohortatio ad Graecos* 9; Eusebius, *Praep. ev.* x 9 ff.

the Jews, Egyptian authors also wrote very unkindly about Jewish origins. According to these writers, the Jews were Egyptian lepers who had managed, very dishonourably, to form themselves into a nation, had left Egypt and settled in Palestine.[135] Faced with this story, Josephus feels himself equal to the situation, and with dignified superiority, proves to the Alexandrians both the absurdity and the intrinsic contradictions of their assertions (i 24–35 (219–320); ii 1–3 (1–32)).

3. To the allegation of the Jews' late origin is connected also the other one, namely that they, the Jews, had made no contribution to civilization. Apollonius Molon says of them that they were the most incompetent of the barbarians, and had therefore contributed no useful invention to the general culture (C. Ap. ii 14 (148)). Apion was of the opinion that they had produced no eminent figures, such as inventors of arts or men distinguished for their wisdom (C. Ap. ii 12 (135)). These reproaches were met by Jewish apologists appealing in their turn to the old Jewish legend that the opposite was rather the case, i.e. that the Jews were the originators of all civilization. According to Eupolemus, Moses was the first sage and the inventor of the alphabet (cf. above, p. 518); according to Artapanus, Abraham instructed the Egyptians in astrology, Joseph improved the cultivation of the land, and Moses introduced all culture (pp. 521 f.). The philosopher Aristobulus declares that Moses was the father of Greek wisdom; Pythagoras, Socrates, Plato, and the others derived their philosophy from him (p. 582). Philo repeats the assertion. Josephus in his apology does not use these older Jewish versions of early Jewish history directly, but he does assume the same general tradition in asserting, like them, that Greek philosophy derived from the Jews (C. Ap. ii 16 (168); 36 (257); 39 (281–2)). This is not however the main thrust of his argument, which concentrates not just on the antiquity of the Mosaic Law but on its wisdom and excellence.

4. Specific accusations against the Jews concerned above all their worship, which was everywhere bound up with a refusal to recognize any other cults as legitimate. In the age of Hellenism such an attitude was scandalous. 'Live and let live' was the password in the field of religion. People were ready to tolerate the most diverse ways of worshipping God provided that the adherents of one cult did not interfere with those of another. In particular, it was taken for granted that, side by side with any possible private worship, the citizens of a town would take part in the worship of the town's gods. The Jewish rejection of all alien worship, and refusal to participate in it, was not

---

135. Thus with much variation in detail: Manetho (C. Ap. i 26, 229 ff. and 233 ff.), Lysimachus (i 34, 304 ff.), Chaeremon (i 32, 288 ff.), Apion (ii 2, 15). Similar stories are also found in Justin xxxvi 2, and Tacitus, Hist. v 3. Cf. also above, pp. 151 f.

only abnormal from a Hellenistic point of view, but synonymous with atheism. If they were citizens, why did they not worship the gods of the city? This accusation of ἀθεότης, of contempt for the gods, recurs in nearly all the opponents of Judaism, from Apollonius Molon and possibly Posidonius, to Pliny and Tacitus;[136] and from it, certainly in large part, arose the conflicts between the Jews and cities, particularly in those where they had established rights.[137] Against these accusations, defence was theoretically easy, but in practice difficult. It was not too hard to demonstrate to an educated reader the advantages of a monotheistic and spiritual understanding of the nature of God, the more so that Greek philosophy offered abundant material to help the Jewish apologist on this point. It is in this sense that Josephus proceeds, simply demonstrating the superiority of the Jewish understanding of God (*C. Ap.* ii 22 (192)). In practice, however, it was not possible to influence the masses with such considerations. The reproach remained that the Jews rejected outright what others regarded as the worship of God. On this point, therefore, the main weapon of Jewish apologists was vigorous attack. If the Jews were rebuked for despising the gods, they for their part showed what kind of gods the others worshipped: impotent images of wood, stone, silver or gold made by man, or all kinds of animals, or at best beings who were burdened with various human weaknesses. Compared with the worshippers of such gods the Jews could certainly feel themselves superior (cf. e.g. *Pseudo-Aristeas* par. 134–9; *Wis.* 13–15; *Ep. Jer.*; frequently Philo; *C. Ap.* ii 33–5 (236–54); and particularly *Sib.* iii 29 ff., and the parallels mentioned there in J. Geffcken's edition).[138]

Of less practical meaning than the charge of atheism were some

---

136. Apion in *C. Ap.* ii 6 (65): 'quomodo ergo, inquit, si sunt cives, eosdem deos, quos Alexandrini, non colunt?' Posidonius and Apollonius Molon, *ibid.*, ii 7 (79): 'accusant quidem nos, quare nos eosdem deos cum aliis non colimus.' (On the possible mistake in this attribution to Posidonius, see Stern, GLAJJ I, pp. 141–4.) Apollonius Molon, *ibid.* ii 14 (148): ὡς ἀθέους ... λοιδορεῖ. Pliny, *N.H.* xiii 4, 46: 'gens contumelia numinum insignis.' Tacitus, *Hist.* v 5: 'contemnere deos.' The same reproach was also made to Christians, cf. A. Harnack, *Der Vorwurf des Atheismus in den drei ersten Jahrhunderten* (TU XIII.4, 1905).

137. Josephus, *Ant.* xii 3, 2 (126): the Ionian cities of Asia Minor asked of M. Agrippa that 'if the Jews were to be their fellows, they should worship their [the Ionians'] gods'. See above, pp. 129–32.

138. Philo's *De vita contemplativa* also begins (par. 1) with a diatribe on the foolishness of idol worship. In explanatory remarks on this, F. C. Conybeare (Philo, *About the Contemplative Life*, 1895) and P. Wendland (Jahrbb. für class. Philologie, suppl. vol. 22, 1896, pp. 707 ff.) collected a great deal of material from parallel passages in Philo, and also from the Sibyllines and other writings. Wendland also pointed out (708 ff.) that 'Jewish and Christian apologetic only continues here the criticism which was already engaged in by gentile philosophy, particularly academic scepticism.' On the other hand it is known that the Old Testament prophets also already paved the way.

absurd stories concerning Jewish worship: that they paid divine honours to *an ass's head*, and, foreshadowing the medieval blood libels, that they annually sacrificed a Greek and ate his intestines (cf. above, pp. 150 ff., notes 8, 9, 19). These fables occur quite frequently, but it can be taken as evidence that they were not totally believed by many gentiles that Josephus reckons to have counteracted them sufficiently once he has shown their silliness (*C. Ap.* ii 7–9 (79–120)).[139]

5. Of greater importance, on the other hand, was another point related to the Jews' ἀθεότης, namely their refusal to worship the emperor. From Augustus' time onwards the provinces competed with one another in the practice of this cult (cf. above, vol. II, p. 34). Zeal for it was a yardstick of loyalty to Rome; its complete rejection was equivalent to a refusal to show the respect due to the authorities. This at least was the view of the Greek population, which, according to the customs of the age, freely offered this worship to the emperor. The Jews were however in a favourable position as the emperors of the first centuries, with the temporary exception of Caligula, did not directly demand this worship. Apart from the short episode under Caligula it was never demanded of them since, from Caesar onwards, their cult was legally protected as part of the legal recognition of their communities (cf. above, pp. 115 f.). It was, however, always a welcome point of attack for the Jews' opponents that they proved themselves to be bad citizens by their refusal to worship the emperor.[140]

Against this accusation, Jewish apologists could appeal to the fact that a daily sacrifice for the emperor was offered in the Temple in Jerusalem (*C. Ap.* ii 6 (76–7); *B.J.* ii 10, 4 (197); cf. above, vol. II, pp. 311–12), and that on special occasions even hecatombs were offered up for the Roman emperor (Philo, *Legat.*, 356). This in fact furnished a certain equivalent for the worship of the emperor, which was impossible to the Jews. In addition, Josephus took advantage of every opportunity to point to the favour which the Jews enjoyed both from the Ptolemies and from the Caesars (*C. Ap.* ii 4–5 (33–64); *Ant.* xiv 10, 1–26 (185–267); xvi 6, 1–7 (161–73)) on the grounds that this certainly would not have been possible if they had not been loyal citizens!

6. A certain degree of social isolation went hand in hand with the

---

139. Cf. E. Bickermann, 'Ritualmord und Eselskult', MGWJ 71 (1927), pp. 171–87; 255–64 = *Studies in Jewish and Christian History* II (1980), pp. 223–55; A. Jacoby, 'Der angebliche Eselskult der Juden und Christen', ARW 25 (1927), pp. 265–82; D. Flusser, 'Blood Libels against Jews', *Commentationes Iudaico-Hellenisticae in Memoriam Iohannis Lewy* (1949), pp. 104–24 (Heb.).

140. Apion in Josephus, *C. Ap.* ii 6 (73): 'derogare nobis Apion voluit, quia imperatorum non statuamus imagines.' Tacitus, *Hist* v 5: 'non regibus haec adulatio, non Caesaribus honor.' For a discussion of the emperor cult in relation to the Jews, cf. J. Juster, *Les Juifs dans l'Empire romain etc.* I (1914), pp. 339–54; J. N. Sevenster, *The Roots of Pagan Anti-Semitism* (1975), pp. 149–52.

religious segregation. Mainstream Judaism explicitly rejected the idea which gained more and more ground during the Hellenistic era that all men are brothers and therefore equal before God. It saw in the unbeliever only the sinner fallen subject to the judgement of God, and associated the fatherly love of God only with the seed of Abraham and righteous proselytes. This particularism was not maintained in its full rigour in all Jewish authors of this period, and was often mitigated in the more philosophical texts by the desire to demonstrate the similarity and interdependence of Greek and Jewish ideas about God and the world. It was however supported by the almost universal Jewish view that a gentile as such is unclean; that dealings with him should be avoided as far as possible in the interest of Levitical purity; and also by the scrupulousness with which contact with anything related to idolatry was abhorred (cf. above, vol. II, pp. 81–4). Since, therefore, the Jew who wished to keep the Law regarded the non-Jew as 'alien', it was in practical terms very hard for him to live in any close social relationship with gentiles. This theoretical and practical ἀμιξία, which ran counter to the whole tendency of Hellenistic times, was a constant and particular reproach against the Jews. To the Greeks and Romans, who did not know the real motives, it could only appear as a lack of humanity and real love of man, indeed a criminal hatred of mankind.[141]

The method adopted by the apologists was on the one hand mainly to stress the humane regulations of the Law, particularly with regard to foreigners (*C. Ap.* ii 28–29 (209–14); Philo, *De Virtutibus*, 12 (76)–15 (88)), and on the other to indicate that the ancient systems of civil law went much further than the Mosaic Law in excluding foreigners (*C. Ap.* ii 36–37 (255–75)).

7. The characteristics of the Jews mentioned so far, their 'atheism' and unsociableness, are those which were most relevant to communal

---

141. Hecataeus (the genuine Hecataeus, about 300 B.C.) emphasizes in his generally sympathetic description of the Jews that Moses 'established a form of life contrary to humanity and hospitality' (Diodorus xl 3, 4; also in C. Müller, FHG II, p. 392; Jacoby, FGrH 264, F6; Stern, GLAJJ I, pp. 26–35). The advisors of Antiochus Sidetes pointed to the ἀμιξία of the Jews (*Ant.* xiii 8, 3 (245, 247) and Diodorus xxxiv 1, possibly after Posidonius). Cf. Justin xxxvi 2, 15: 'caverunt, ne cum peregrinis conviverent.' Apollonius Molon in *C. Ap.* ii 14 (148): 'he reviles us as … misanthropes.' *Ibid.* ii 36 (258): 'Apollonius Molon condemned us for … declining to associate with those who have chosen to adopt a different mode of life.' Lysimachus asserted (*C. Ap.* i 34 (309)) that Moses directed the Jews 'to show goodwill to no-one' etc. According to Apion (*C. Ap.* ii 8 (95)), the Jews used to swear at their annual sacrifice of a Greek 'ut inimicitias contra Graecos haberent', or, as it is said in ii 10 (121): 'to show no goodwill to an alien, especially to Greeks.' Tacitus, *Hist.* v 5: 'adversus omnes alios hostile odium: separati epulis, discreti cubilibus … alienarum concubitu abstinent.' Juvenal, *Sat.* xiv 103–4 (cf. above, p. 153). The sharp opposition in which the Christians stood to the world was also explained as μισανθρωπία, cf. Tacitus, *Annal.* xv 44.

life. Because of them, Jews appeared as enemies of public order and the institutions of the time, indeed as opponents of the whole of human society. The most serious attacks were therefore directed at these points. Other peculiarities lent themselves more to derision and contempt than to actual accusation. Among these were circumcision, abstinence from pork, and the observance of the sabbath.[142] Not even the most malicious of their opponents dared to accuse the Jews of sexual immorality, except Tacitus.[143]

Apologetics countered the mockery of these characteristics with an ideal picture of the whole of the Law of Moses. Thus Josephus, in particular, attempts to show in a well argued and positive discussion that the stipulations of the Mosaic Law are in every respect the purest and most ideal (C. Ap. ii 22–30 (188–219); cf. also Ant. iv 8 1–49 (176–331)). He does not discuss the criticized points, but is content to remind his Egyptian opponent, Apion, of the fact that Egyptian priests are also circumcized and refrain from eating pork (C. Ap. ii 13 (141)). He refers in general, to demonstrate the value and the excellence of the Law, to its great antiquity (ii 15 (154 and 156)), and to the blameless character of the Lawgiver Moses (ii 16 (158–61)); and he emphasizes further that this Law really fulfils its purpose through being known and obeyed by all, which remarkable result follows from its not only being taught but also practised (ii 16–19 (157–181)). Finally Josephus stresses that no Jew ever became unfaithful to his Law, which was another proof of its excellence (ii 31–2 (220–35); 38 (278)). To what is missing here, i.e. a more detailed discussion of those points to which the gentiles objected, Josephus had earlier intended to devote a four-volume work which would have dealt with 'the opinions which we Jews hold concerning God and his nature as well as concerning the laws, that is, why according to them we are permitted to do certain things and forbidden others' (Ant. xx 12, 1 (268)). Among other things, he intended to give here the grounds for circumcision (Ant. i 10, 5 (192)), and the reasons why Moses permitted certain animals to be eaten and others not (Ant. iii 11, 2 (259)). This proposed work, to which Josephus often refers (Ant., Preface 4 (25); i 1, 1 (29); iii 5, 6 (94); 6, 6 (143); 8, 10 (223); iv 8, 4 (198); 44 (302)) was apparently never written, but

---

142. Circumcision: Apion in C. Ap. ii 13 (137); Horace, Sat. i 9, 69 ff. Pork: Apion in C. Ap. ibid.; Juvenal, Sat. vi 160; xiv 98. Observance of the Sabbath: Juvenal, Sat. xiv 105–6; Tacitus, Hist. v 4; cf. R. Goldenberg, 'The Jewish Sabbath in the Roman World up to the Time of Constantine the Great', ANRW II.19.1 (1979), pp. 430–42.

143. Hist. v 5: 'proiectissima ad libidinem gens ... inter se nihil illicitum.' The remark was presumably elicited either by the alleged prolific nature of the Jews or as part of a general prejudice about all Eastern barbarians, cf. Stern, GLAJJ II, p. 40.

there are in his preserved writings many intimations of the deeper meaning of the ritual laws.[144]

Philo likewise sets out in the first place to demonstrate the excellence, humanity, and moral strictness of the Law in general (not only in *Hypothetica* in *Praep. ev.* viii 7, 1–9, but also in his large systematic work on the Mosaic legislation, cf. above, p. 542). He is however at the same time concerned to prove that the special customs which appeared strange to the gentiles, like circumcision, the prohibition of unclean animals, and the keeping of the sabbath, were reasonable and purposeful. In this, he was not writing simply to refute pagan attacks but also to confirm Jews in their beliefs by showing their behaviour to be justifiable in Greek as well as in Jewish terms. Ps.-Aristeas and Aristobulus before him had done much the same.[145]

---

144. For a full account of Josephus' outlook on Judaism, see A. Schlatter, *Die Theologie des Judentums nach dem Bericht des Josefos* (1932); cf. also G. Vermes, 'A summary of the Law by Flavius Josephus', NT 24 (1982), pp. 289–303. On the proposed work, see D. Altshuler, 'The treatise "On Customs and Causes" by Flavius Josephus', JQR 69 (1979), pp. 226–32.

145. On circumcision, cf. Philo, *Spec. Leg.* i 2–7. On the prohibition of unclean animals, cf. Pseudo-Aristeas, 128 ff., 142–69; Philo, *De Specialibus Legibus* iv 17 (100)–24 (125). On the observance of the Sabbath, cf. Aristobulus in *Praep. ev.* xiii 12, 9–16; Philo, *Hypothetica* in *Praep. ev.* viii 7, 10–20. Cf. in general also P. Krüger, *Philo und Josephus als Apologeten des Judentums* (1906), 54 ff.; J. Juster, *Les Juifs dans l'Empire romain* I (1914), pp. 243–390.

VII. Jewish Writings under Gentile Pseudonyms[146]

Approaching the close of this survey, a class of literary productions remains to be discussed which is highly characteristic of Hellenistic Judaism, namely Jewish writings which masquerade as gentile. The works in this category differ greatly in literary form, but all have in common the characteristic of appearing under the name of some gentile authority, be it a mythological authority such as the Sibyl, or a distinguished historian such as Hecataeus or Aristeas. This sort of pretence is also to be found within confessedly Jewish works in the frequent attribution to gentiles of statements or writings which strongly favour Jews or the Jewish view of God.[147] The choice of these pseudonymous forms served a double purpose for their Jewish authors. Firstly, gentiles might be expected to read such writings and accept Jewish ideas more readily to the extent that the names were standard authorities among them, and some of these works, in particular the Sibylline Oracles, certainly were intended for a non-Jewish audience. But, secondly, among hellenized Jews also, the ascription of Jewish ideas to prestigious gentile authors might be expected to confirm them in their Judaism and to prevent apostasy.

It is necessary to distinguish within the literature aimed at gentiles between missionary literature intended to attract converts, and apologetic and general propaganda literature about Jewish ethics and theology. Missionary literature would be unlikely to succeed in a gentile guise. The works examined here therefore offered a more general encouragement towards the acceptance of Jewish attitudes, though in practice the purpose of each writer differed from case to case. Parts of the Sibylline oracles written by Jews certainly set out to exert religious persuasion, trying to make adherents to the Jewish understanding of God in the midst of a heathen world by directly pointing out the foolishness of its idolatry and the depravity of its moral conduct, by threatening punishment and destruction in the case of impenitence, and by promising reward and eternal happiness in the case of conversion. In

---

146. On this whole genre, see W. Speyer, *Die literarische Fälschung im Altertum* (1971), pp. 150–68, with emphasis both on the established tradition of pseudepigraphy in Judaism and on the classical background; M. Hengel, 'Anonymität, Pseudepigraphie und "Literarische Fälschung" in der jüdisch-hellenistischen Literatur', in K. von Fritz, ed., *Pseudepigrapha* I (Entretiens Hardt, XVIII) (1972), pp. 229–308, esp. 285–303; N. Walter, *Pseudepigraphische jüdisch-hellenistische Dichtung* (JSHRZ IV.3) (1983), pp. 175–81.

147. Cf. Speyer, *op. cit.*, p. 164, for a list of literary works falsely attributed to non-Jews in non-biblical texts. On the motives behind such false attributions, see G. W. E. Nickelsburg, JLBBM, pp. 24–5.

contrast, other writings of this category aim at a different, apologetic effect, to draw attention not so much to the faith as to the honour and esteem of the Jewish name. Pseudo-Aristeas, for instance, tries to show in his whole account of the translation of the Jewish Law into Greek what a high opinion Ptolemy II Philadelphus had of the Jewish Law and of Jewish wisdom in general, and that he treated the Jewish scholars with great honour. This author had no directly missionary or propagandistic purpose as regards gentiles. His prime intended audience was almost certainly Jewish, but for gentiles too he might expect his account to create a favourable disposition towards Judaism and the Jewish Law. Despite the variation in the aims of these works, however, all of them in some way were intended to promote Jewish influence, though it may be unwise to take this common characteristic as particularly significant since it is, after all, solely because this is the case that they can all be identified as *Jewish* pseudepigrapha. They are all treated here in one category because of their choice of a gentile mask for the purpose, though they are quite different in form and content.

The discussion begins with the Sibylline oracles, not because they are the oldest writings in this group, but because they are the most important in extent and historical effect.

1. The Sibylline Oracles

The Sibyls belong to the category of semi-mythical and semi-historical figures in the evolution of Greek religion.[148] The etymology of the word is obscure.[149] Since the individual Sibyls are distinguished from each other by particular names, e.g. Herophile, Demo, Sabbe, Sambethe, it can be argued that 'Sibyl' eventually became a common noun, but the view that the original concept referred to a single figure has also been advanced because of the use of the term in this way by the early writer Heraclitus (see below, p. 620).[150] By nature the Sibyls were women who prophesied, and whose ecstatic oracles depended not on any kind of artifice

148. The most important material on the Sibyls is collected in C. Alexandre, χρησμοὶ Σιβυλλικοί, *Oracula Sibyllina*, ed. 1, vol. II (1856), pp. 1–101; J. Geffcken, *Die Oracula Sibyllina* (1902); W. Bousset, 'Sibyllen und Sibyllinische Bücher', HHRE XVIII (1906), cols. 265 ff.; A. Rzach, 'Sibyllen', RE IIA (1923), cols. 2073–2103; *idem*, 'Sibyllinische Orakel', *ibid.*, cols. 2103–83.

149. Varro (in Lactantius, *Inst. div.* i 6) derives it from Doric σιός = θεός, and Aeolic βούλλα = βουλή, hence θεοβούλη, which is clearly only a popular etymology. Other ancient suggestions are however even less plausible (see references in V. Nikiprowetzky, *La Troisième Sibylle* (1971), p. 2, n. 5). Modern linguists have done no better, despite etymologies suggested from semitic and Italian languages as well as Greek. It can at least be said that a Greek origin is most likely, cf. Rzach, RE IIA (1923), cols. 2074–5; Nikiprowetzky, *loc. cit.*

150. A. Kurfess in E. Hennecke and W. Schneemelcher, *N.T. Apocrypha*, ed. R. M. L. Wilson (ET 1965), II, p. 704.

but on divine inspiration (madness, μανία).[151] They lived in grottoes but also wandered throughout the world.[152] In Delphi, the Sibyls were connected with the priesthood.[153] Usually, however, they represented a free, non-priestly prophetic guild. They proved their semi-divinity partly by their origin (Herophile of Erythrae was the daughter of a shepherd and a nymph) and partly by their long life (they reached the age of nearly one thousand years).[154] Although in the representations of a later time they thus towered over the human dimension, being depicted as divine on one coin,[155] the appearance of prophetesses named Sibyls should be regarded as a historical fact. Their later influence in history consisted in part in the written oracles attributed to them, and in part in the places where the oracles were still uttered in their name. Pseudo-Justin, *Cohortatio ad Graecos* 37, writing in the early third century A.D., gives a very picturesque description of the Sibylline grotto at Cumae.[156] It was a basilica hewn from natural stone. In the middle were three cisterns in which the Sibyl used to bathe. After bathing, she passed to the back part of the basilica where a chair stood on a raised area. Seated on this chair, she communicated her oracle. The author of *Cohortatio* had been told this by the local guides. The Sibyl herself had died long ago. Only a bronze flask containing her remains was still shown.[157] It is however very probable that these things once happened as the guides said.

The oldest author to mention a Sibyl is Heraclitus (*Fragmente der*

151. E. Rohde, *Psyche* (ET 1925), pp. 292–3, 596; Rzach, RE IIA (1923), col. 2077.

152. Pausanias, *Descr. Graeciae* x 12, 6; also the inscription of Erythrae, verse 10, cited below in n. 170.

153. Pausanias x 12, 1.

154. Phlegon, *Macrob.* 5 (= Jacoby, FGrH, 257, F 37): Σίβυλλα ἡ 'Ερυθραία ἐβίωσεν ἔτη ὀλίγον ἀποδέοντα τῶν χιλίων. In the inscription from Erythrae, cited below, n. 170, the Sibyl says in verse 9 that she has lived nine hundred years. In Petronius' *Cena Trimalchionis* 48 *fin.*, it is written that the Sibyl of Cumae hung in a bottle ('in ampulla pendere'), and when the children asked, 'Sibyl, what do you wish?', she used to reply: 'I wish to die.' Because of her great age she had shrunk to a diminutive size but was unable to die. (Petronius' description goes back to about the middle of the first century A.D.) Cf. other references to the Sibyl's age given by A. - Kurfess, in E. Hennecke and W. Schneemelcher, *N.T. Apocrypha*, ed. R. McL. Wilson (ET 1965), II, p. 704.

155. B. V. Head, *Historia nummorum* ([2]1911), p. 579.

156. Cf. on this, A. Chiapelli, 'L'antro della Sibilla di Cuma descritto nel IV secolo d. Cr.', *Nuove pagine sul cristianesimo antico* (1902), pp. 315 ff. For the excavation of this Sibylline grotto in 1932, cf. A. Maiuri, *The Phlegrean Fields* (1947), pp. 110–19. Identification of the nearby Roman crypt with this grotto, cf. A. Vogliano, 'Ausgrabung der Grotta della Sibilla', Gnomon 2 (1926), p. 366, was incorrect, cf. Maiuri, *op. cit.*, p. 121. For the influence of this cave on Vergil's description of the Sibyl in *Aeneid* vi 42–50, 77–82, cf. H. W. Parke, *Greek Oracles* (1967), pp. 52–3.

157. φακόν τινα ἐκ χαλκοῦ κατεσκευασμένον, ἐν ᾧ τὰ λείψανα αὐτῆς σώζεσθαι ἔλεγον. φακός (oil or water flasks in the LXX) apparently is the 'ampulla' of Petronius. But a voice no longer sounded from it. Cf. also Pausanias x 12, 8: (Κυμαῖοι) λίθου δὲ ὑδρίαν ἐν 'Απόλλωνος ἱερῷ δεικνύουσιν οὐ μεγάλην, τῆς Σιβύλλης ἐνταῦθα κεῖσθαι φάμενοι τὰ ὀστᾶ.

Vorsokratiker, ed. Diels and Kranz, 92; the fragment is taken from Plutarch, *De Pythiae Oraculis* 6 (*Mor.* 397 A); Clement of Alexandria, *Strom.* i 15, 70), followed by Euripides, Aristophanes, and Plato.[158] They speak of *the* Sibyl, either because they knew of only one, or used the word as a generic concept or a proper noun. Heraclides Ponticus is the first to mention several Sibyls.[159] Later counts vary between two and ten.[160] The best-known in antiquity was Varro's catalogue, which mentioned ten Sibyls, not including a Jewish one.[161] Unique and noteworthy is also the discussion in Pausanias, who mentions four: (1) the Libyan Sibyl, (2) the Herophile of Marpessos or Erythrae, i.e. from Asia Minor, who also prophesied in Delphi, (3) the Demo in Cumae and (4) the Sabbe of the Hebrews in Palestine, who was also called the Babylonian or Egyptian, i.e. the Oriental.[162] It seems that Pausanias has noted that the traditions relating to the Sibyls suggest four different categories of prophecy, and that he has simply assigned a geographical location to each.

The Sibyl from Erythrae was the most famous. For this reason the prophetess in the oldest extant Jewish Sibylline oracle is made to assert that, although she comes from Babylonia, she is identical with the Erythraean seer.[163] It is necessary to comment further on the Erythraean and the Babylonian Sibyls and their relation to the Jewish Sibyl.

The Sibyl of Erythrae (on the Ionic coast opposite the island of Chios) was named by Heraclides Ponticus and by most later authors

---

158. Rzach, RE IIA (1923), cols. 2075 ff.

159. Heraclides Ponticus is quoted in Clement of Alexandria, *Strom.* i 21, 108, and Varro in Lactantius, *Inst.* i 6, 12. A combination of both passages results in three of the Sibyls mentioned by Heraclides: the Phrygian, named Artemis, who also prophesied in Delphi; the 'Ερυθραία 'Ηροφίλη καλουμένη; and the 'Hellespontia in agro Troiano nata vico Marmesso circa oppidum Gergithium.' Heraclides lived in the second half of the fourth century B.C. For the fragments of his historical writings, cf. C. Müller, FHG II, pp. 197 ff.; for the other fragments, including those referring to the Sibyls, see F. Wehrli, *Herakleides Pontikos* (1953), especially pp. 40–1, and H. B. Gottschalk, *Heraclides of Pontus* (1980), p. 130.

160. Cf. the catalogue in Alexandre, *Orac. Sibyll.*, first ed., II, pp. 92–101 and 421–33; Rzach, RE IIA (1923), cols. 2075–6; Nikiprowetzky, *op. cit.*, pp. 1–10; A. Kurfess, *Sibyllinische Weissagungen* (1951), pp. 9–16.

161. Varro in Lactantius, *Div. instit.* i 6 = Varro, *Ant. ser. div.* (ed. B. Cardauns, 1976), F 56a: 'primam fuisse de Persis ... secundam Libyssam ... tertiam Delphida ... quartam Cimmeriam in Italia ... quintam Erythraeam ... sextam Samiam ... septimam Cumanam nomine Amaltheam, quae ab aliis Herophile vel Demophile nominetur ... octavam Hellespontiam in agro Troiano natam vico Marmesso circa oppidum Gergithium ... nonam Phrygiam decimam Tiburtem nomine Albuneam.'

162. Pausanias, *Descript. Graeciae* x 12.

163. Sib. iii 808 ff.

Ἡροφίλη.[164] Her father was a shepherd, Theodorus, and her mother a nymph.[165] But whereas the Erythraeans pointed out a cave near the city as her birthplace, the inhabitants of Troy maintained that she came from Marpessos in the region of Troy and received her name, Ἐρυθραία, from the red soil near Marpessos. As proof of this they referred to four verses of the Sibyl, which end with the words: πατρὶς δέ μοί ἐστιν ἐρυθρὴ Μάρπησσος, μητρὸς ἱερή, ποταμός τ' Ἀϊδωνεύς. The Erythraeans did not acknowledge the end of these verses (from Μάρπησσος on) as genuine,[166] but, since the tradition of the Sibyl of Marpessos is ancient and was well established even down to the time of Tibullus, it is likely that they were wrong, and that there were in fact two competing Sibyls, of whom the Sibyl of Marpessos was probably older than her competitor in Erythrae.[167] It is implausible but possible that the Sibyl's name did not derive from either of these places in Greece but originally referred to the Red Sea.[168]

Whatever the origin of this Sibyl, it is clear that Pausanias was right to describe the prophetess as working in Erythrae at some time in antiquity, for his account was remarkably confirmed by the discovery of the Sibyl's cave near Erythrae in 1891.[169] In addition to some smaller inscriptions, a large and well-preserved inscription from the time of the Antonines (second century A.D.) has come to light there. In it, the Sibyl describes herself as the primeval daughter of a water-nymph and

164. Heraclides Ponticus, cf. above, n. 159. Nicolaus of Damascus, Jacoby, FGrH 90, F 67. Bocchus in Solinus, ii 18, ed. Mommsen (1895), p. 36 (where Herophile Erythraea is to be read and not Herophiles, as the manuscripts have it; Bocchus wrote during the time of Claudius). Pausanias, x 12, 1–7. Plutarch, De Pythiae oraculis 14. Isidorus, Hisp. Etymolog. viii 8, Opp., ed. Arevalo, III, p. 368 (based on Bocchus). Suda, Lex., s.v. Ἡροφίλα. Tibullus ii 5, 68. Martianus Capella ii 159 (both name the Trojan Sibyl of Marpessos Herophile; cf. on this the detailed comments of Pausanias, loc. cit.). Varro in Lactantius, Inst. i 6, 10 (cf. above, n. 161). Eusebius, Chron., ed. Schoene, II, pp. 84, 85 (following Jerome and Syncellus): Σιβύλλη Σαμία Χρησμῳδὸς ἡ καὶ Ἡροφίλα (Helm ed., GCS, Eusebius VII, 2nd ed., pp. 91b, 94b).

165. Pausanias x 12, 7.

166. Pausanias x 12.

167. E. Maass, Hermes 18 (1883), pp. 327–39 and C. Robert, Hermes 22 (1887), pp. 454–9, suggested that the removal of the Erythraean Sibyl's birthplace from Erythrae to Marpessos originated with a local patriotic author from Troy, but A. Rzach, RE IIA (1923), cols. 2081–4, and A. Kurfess, Würzb. Jb. 2 (1948), pp. 402 ff., prefer to accept the evidence that such a Sibyl actually existed (Heraclides Ponticus, Περὶ Χρηστηρ., frg. 97; Tibullus ii 5, 67; Pausanias x 12, 3–6).

168. See K. Mras, '"Babylonische" und "erythräische" Sibylle', Wiener Stud. 29 (1907), pp. 48 ff.

169. Cf. on this and on the inscriptions found there, K. Buresch, 'Die Grabschrift der Erythräischen Sibylle', Wochenschr. für klass. Philologie (1891), pp. 1040–7, 1245 ff.; idem, 'Die sibyllinische Quellgrotte in Erythrae', Mitt. deutsch. arch. Inst., Ath. Abt. 17 (1892), pp. 16–36; S. Reinach, 'La sanctuaire de la Sibylle d'Erythrée', REG 4 (1891), pp. 276–86. See P. Corssen, 'Die erythraeische Sibylle', Mitt. deutsch. arch. Inst., Ath. Abt. 38 (1913), pp. 1–22.

says that her native town is Erythrae and no other, and that Theodorus is her mortal father. The Kissotas (probably the mountain stream near Erythrae) witnessed (actually: bore) her birth. Immediately after birth she uttered oracles to people there. Seated on this rock (i.e. where the statue with the inscription now stands) she sang prophecies to mortals about future suffering. Living for nine hundred years, she wandered throughout the world as an untouched virgin. But now she sits here, etc.[170] The emphasis on Erythrae as her place of birth was clearly to parry the claims of the people of the region of Troy. The same cave yielded another later inscription in which a certain Eutychianos says that he and his son Eutychianos decorated the cave with images (γραφαῖς).[171] A statue of the Erythraean Sibyl has been found in Rome. It may well be a replica of the cult statue in Erythrae.[172]

Literary allusions to the Hebrew Sibyl, as far as they really deal with the Jewish one, probably reflect the existence of Jewish Sibylline poetry.[173] Pausanias mentions her last as the most recent, and there is no notice about her that goes back further than the first century B.C.; whereas the oldest Jewish Sibylline oracle was probably composed already in the second century B.C.[174] It seems, however, that in the accounts of these authors the Jewish Sibyl is merged with a non-Jewish or half-Jewish Chaldean or Egyptian Sibyl called Sabbe, cf. Pausanias, x 12, 9, with commentary in Stern, GLAJJ II, pp. 198–200. The assimilation with the Babylonian and Egyptian Sibyls, and above all the description of Sabbe as a daughter of the Babylonian author

170. For further discussion on the text of this inscription, see Rzach, RE IIA (1923), col. 2085; A. Kurfess, *Sibyllinische Weissagungen* (1951), pp. 11–12. The text is now re-edited by H. Engelmann and R. Merkelbach as IK Erythrai II (1973), no. 224, with translation and commentary.

171. Le Bas, *Inscriptions, Asie mineure*, no. 58 = Buresch, Mitt. deutsch. arch. Inst., Ath. Abt. 17 (1892), pp. 33 ff. = IGR IV, no. 1541 = IK Erythrai II, no. 228. Cf. introd. to nos. 224–8, and note that the Sibyl is referred to in a calendar of sacrifices of the first half of the second century B.C., no. 207, l. 73.

172. R. Herbig, '*ΘΕΑ ΣΙΒΥΛΛΑ*', Jahrb. d. Deutsch. Arch. Inst. 59/60, 1944/5 (1949), pp. 141–7.

173. Cf. on the Hebrew-Chaldean Sibyl: C. Alexandre, *Orac. Sibyll.*, first ed., II, pp. 82–7; A. Bouché-Leclercq, *Histoire de la divination dans l'antiquité* II, pp. 192 ff.; Rzach in RE IIA.2 (1923), cols. 2097–102; A. Peretti, *La Sibilla babilonese nella propaganda ellenistica* (1943); V. Nikiprowetzky, *La Troisième Sibylle* (1970), pp. 9–53.

174. Pausanias x 12, 9. The Jewish Sibyl (ἡ Ἰουδαία) is also mentioned in Aelian, *Varia hist.* xii 35, and at the end. The oldest author to know the Jewish Sibyl was almost certainly Alexander Polyhistor in the first century B.C. (in Eusebius, *Arm. Chron.*, ed. Karst, GCS 20 (1911), p. 12 = Jacoby, FGrH 273, F 79), but he manifestly depended on Book iii of the oracle, for his is the Sibyl who prophesied about the tower of Babel and the confusion of languages. It is not necessary to suggest, as has been done, that both Alexander and the Jewish Sibyl derived their material from a common Babylonian source, cf. below, pp. 632 ff. When Clement of Alexandria spoke of the προφῆτις Ἑβραίων (*Protrept.* vi 70–1), he referred to the Jewish oracle.

Berossus and Erymanthe, show that this tradition is not purely Jewish.[175] It is a mixture of different kinds of material, corresponding to the taste of the Hellenistic era.

Later catalogues have the name Sambethe in place of Sabbe.[176] These all go back to Varro, who says of the Persian Sibyl (Lactantius, *Div. Inst.* i 6, 8): 'primam fuisse de Persis, cuius mentionem fecerit Nicanor, qui res gestas Alexandri Macedonis scripsit.' In the Prologue which the unknown editor has prefixed to the extant collection of the Sibylline oracles (*Oracula Sibyllina*, ed. Geffcken, p. 2) the Chaldean Sibyl, Sambethe, is said to be a daughter of Noah, and is combined with the Persian Sibyl of Varro. Since in the oldest extant *Jewish* fragment, also, the Sibyl designates herself a daughter of Noah (iii 827) and mentions that she came from Babylon and that the Greeks wrongly held her for an Erythraean (iii 809 ff.), the assertions of the anonymous author of the Prologue are partially confirmed by the text of the Jewish oracles, even though the Jewish Sibyl is never given a proper name in the oracles themselves.[177]

The source for the name Sambethe cannot be established[178] but comments on the name in Pausanias prove that it derives from an ancient tradition.

The writer of the Prologue most likely took his information from a somewhat older work. His complete list of Sibyls, and all that follows, exists in nearly identical form in a 'Theosophy' written in the time of

---

175. Pseudo-Justin, *Cohortatio ad Graecos* 37 (= Jacoby, FGrH 680, T 7c) also describes the Sibyl as a daughter of Berossus: ταύτην δὲ ἐκ μὲν Βαβυλῶνος ὁρμῆσθαί φασι, Βηρωσσοῦ τοῦ τὴν Χαλδαϊκὴν ἱστορίαν γράψαντος θυγατέρα οὖσαν. Cf. the same comment in the Suda, s.v. Σίβυλλα Δελφίς. This idea may have originated in the fact that Berossus, as astrologer, was also famous on account of his prophecies (Pliny, *Hist. Nat.* vii 37/123: 'Variarum artium scientia innummerabiles enituere ... astrologia Berosus, cui ob divinas praedictiones Athenienses publice in gymnasio statuam inaurate lingua statuere'). It may however simply originate in the possibility that this particular Sibyl was cited by Berossus as an authority for some of his stories, or from some other confusion, cf. W. Bousset, ZNW 3 (1902), p. 25. H. N. Bate, *The Sibylline Oracles* (1918), p. 19, suggests that Berossus invented Sambethe, hence her designation as his daughter.

176. On the name of the Jewish Sibyl, see the material in C. Alexandre's first ed., vol. II, pp. 421–33; Rzach, RE IIA (1923), col. 2098; Stern, GLAJJ II, p. 199.

177. Despite assertions by some modern scholars, there is no reason to postulate a Babylonian Sibyl separate from the Jewish one at any period, cf. Nikiprowetzky, *op. cit.*, pp. 11–16. See *contra* e.g. S. K. Eddy, *The King is Dead: Studies in the Near Eastern Resistance to Hellenism* (1961), p. 127, who attributes *Sib.* iii 381–7 to a Babylonian Sibyl solely because the passage mentions the destruction of Babylon.

178. For a list of speculative suggestions made by earlier scholars, see Beer, RE II.1 (1920), cols. 2120–1; Nikiprowetzky, *op. cit.*, pp. 12–14; below, p. 626. A. Peretti, *La Sibilla babilonese* (1943), p. 79, preferred a derivation from a Babylonian divinity called Sabitu.

Emperor Zeno (A.D. 474–91), to be discussed below (cf. pp. 628 ff.).[179] The contents of the piece are set out much more clearly in the 'Theosophy' than in the Prologue, so that it cannot be doubted that the latter depends on the former and not vice versa. All later lists mentioning Sambethe depend on one of these sources and have therefore no independent value; but it is noteworthy that they add the designation 'Hebrew' to 'Chaldean'.[180]

It appears almost certain that Sambethe was worshipped as a divinity in the same way as the Erythraean Sibyl (see above, note 172). A list of divinities extant on an ostracon of the late third or early fourth century A.D. includes the name 'Sambathis', who is plausibly identified with the Sibyl Sambethe.[181] It has been argued that the same deity was also worshipped in the Σαμβαθεῖον, which is mentioned in an inscription on a tomb in Thyatira from the time of Trajan (IGR IV, no. 1281 = CIJ II, no. 752, see p. 19 above). The beginning of this inscription reads: Φάβιος Ζώσιμος κατασκευάσας σορὸν ἔθετο ἐπὶ τόπου καθαροῦ, ὄντος πρὸ τῆς πόλεως πρὸς τῷ Σαμβαθείῳ ἐν τῷ Χαλδαίου περιβόλῳ. The expression σαμβαθεῖον could of itself well designate a Jewish synagogue, σαββατεῖον (Jos. *Ant.* xvi 6, 2 (164)), because μβ developed from ββ, as will be shown. The fact that the gentile Fabius Zosimus described the place of his tomb by its proximity to a particular building does not necessarily indicate his participation in worship there, and, although it is true that 'Chaldaeus' in imperial Roman times meant the same as 'astrologer' or 'soothsayer', there is no reason to believe that such a person is concerned here.[182] It is however also possible that the σαμβαθεῖον housed a shrine of Sambethe, for there are no explicit Jewish references in the inscription to deny this. In that case the similar expression used to describe both such a temple and a synagogue may be best understood if both Jews and the worshippers of Sambethe claimed a special relationship to the Sabbath for their places of worship (see below, n. 183). Evidence of a cult of Sambathis or Sambethe can also be found in the σύνοδος Σαμβαθική which was celebrated in Naucratis in

---

179. On the small number of textual variants in the passage about Sambethe in the Theosophy and the Prologue, see K. Mras, *Wiener Studien* 28 (1906), p. 44.

180. This is not yet the case in the Theosophy and the Prologue but see e.g. the Suda, s.v. Σίβυλλα : Σίβυλλα Χαλδαία ἡ καὶ πρὸς τινων Ἑβραία ὀνομαζομένη, ἡ καὶ Περσίς, ἡ κυρίῳ ὀνόματι καλουμένη Σαμβήθη. Other texts in Alexandre, *loc. cit.* (n. 176). The impression that the name Sambethe was originally applied to the Babylonian Sibyl, and only later to the others, is also to be found in *Scholia Platonica ad Phaedrum*, 244 B, which was copied by Photius (PG CI, 811 ff.).

181. H. C. Youtie, 'Sambathis', HThR 37 (1944), p. 213 (= *Scriptiunculae* I (1973), p. 471).

182. On Chaldaei, cf. e.g. Tacitus, *Annal.* ii 27; iii 22; xii 22; 52; 68; xiv 9; xvi 14. Suetonius, *Vitell.*, 14; *Domitian*, 14. Further material in A. Baumstark, 'Chaldaioi', RE III (1899), col. 2059. On the significance of the term here, see CPJ III, p. 49.

Egypt (IGR I, no. 1106 = SB, no. 12). Such a σύνοδος seems to imply a Σαμβαθεῖον as the seat of its activities. The same divinity may be mentioned in a Lydian inscription which mentions a vow made to Σαμβαθικός (Keil and von Premerstein, Denkschr. Akad. Wien 54 (1911), pp. 117 ff.).[183] 'Sabbe' in Pausanias, and 'Sambethe' in the other sources, are certainly two different forms of the same name. An original ββ frequently becomes μβ.[184] This change can be proved especially for the Jewish name *Šabbᵉtay* (Ezr. 10:15; Neh. 8:7; 11:16), which is found for instance in the list of the seventy-two Bible translators, twice in the form Σαββαταῖος, otherwise as Σαββάτιος, but also in the different forms with μβ and νβ.[185] Thus although Σαμβήθη was originally Σαββήθη or

183. On the Sambethe cult, see V. A. Tcherikover in CPJ III, pp. 47–8. Tcherikover, *ibid.*, pp. 47–50, shows a salutary scepticism about the claim by W. Schulze, 'Samstag', Zeitsch. für vgl. Sprachforschung 33 (1895), pp. 366–86 (= *Kleine Schriften* (1934), pp. 281 ff.), that Sambethe was an ancient goddess of Asia Minor with whom the Sibyl was only later identified. The hypothesis is unnecessary and lacks evidence. It is likely that some relationship to the cult of Sambethe should be seen in the worship of ὁ θεὸς ὁ Σαββατιστής attested in an inscription from Elaeusa in western Cilicia (Dittenberger, OGIS, no. 573) and in a smaller fragment of a separate inscription from the same place (E. L. Hicks, JHS 12 (1891), p. 236; cf. Heberdey and Wilhelm, 'Reisen in Kilikien', Denkschriften der Wiener Akademie 44 (1896), p. 67. It is probable that the Σαββατισταί were a pagan fellowship of those who celebrated the Sabbath, cf. Gressmann, 'Sabbatistai', RE II.1 (1920), cols. 1560–6, who also gives other possibilities. If so, many of the proper names such as Σαμβατίς, Σαμβατείς, Σαμβαθοῦς (fem.) and Σαμβατίων or Σαμβαθίων (masc.), which may derive from the name of the Sibyl Sambethe (so Schulze, *art. cit.*, pp. 378 ff.), may also stem directly from the Sabbath, even if the bearers of such names are not Jewish. It is not possible to distinguish, as Schulze tried to do, between the names from one source and those from the other (V. A. Tcherikover, Script. Hier. I (1954), p. 81, n. 11). The names cannot therefore be safely used as evidence for the spread of the Sambethe cult, since they may rather bear witness to the influence, direct or indirect, of the Sabbath. On the evidence for pagan reverence for the Sabbath, see Tcherikover in CPJ III, pp. 43–56. The main testimony lies in names derived from the Sabbath, particularly when they are found in connection with the worship of θεὸς Ὕψιστος as at Tanais on the north-eastern corner of the Sea of Azov, cf. Latyschev, IOSPE II, nos. 446–8, 451. See pp. 38, 161–2, 169 above. Note also the inscription about the Σαββατισταί discussed above. It seems likely from this that Sambethe may have sometimes been worshipped simply as the goddess of Sabbath, with no connection with the Sibyl of the same name (CPJ III, p. 51).

184. Cf. the abundant examples in W. Schulze, *art. cit.*, pp. 366–86; CPJ III, p. 44, n. 3.

185. Σαββαταῖος occurs twice in Pseudo-Aristeas, 48–9. In the Syriac text of Epiphanius, *De Mensuris et Ponderibus* 3, this is rendered as Σαμβαταῖος (Lagarde, *Symmicta* II (1880), p. 161). Examples of both Σαββάτιος and Σαμβάτιος, Σανβάτιος etc. can be found in Schulze, *op. cit.*, pp. 378–84; F. Preisigke, *Namenwörterbuch* (1922), pp. 355–6, 359–60; D. Foraboschi, *Onomasticon Alterum Papyrologicum* (1967–71), pp. 276, 278; CPJ III, pp. 43–87. The name *Shabbethai* (*šbty*) is not infrequent also in later Judaism. Eleven persons with this name are recorded in JE XI (1905), cols. 216 ff.; nineteen in Enc. Jud. I, col. 751. Strictly speaking, it denotes someone born on the Sabbath, as *Numenios* designates someone born at the new moon.

Σαββάθη, Σάββη should probably be taken as an abbreviation of it.[186] The etymology of the name Sambethe for the Sibyl remains however obscure. It is possible that this was originally the name of an independent Babylonian Sibyl and was only later taken over by the Jewish prophetess.[187] In that case, the name from which Sambethe was derived should also be Babylonian, but those derivations that have been suggested are not plausible.[188] A Jewish origin is rather more likely. It is possible that the name refers directly to the Jewish Sabbath. She is the Sibyl who proclaimed the Sabbath, or the Sibyl of those who observed the Sabbath. It is however also possible that the name derives from the Sabbath only through the intermediary goddess Sambethe whose cult has been described above, and that the Sibyl Sambethe was named after this pagan goddess and only subsequently identified with the real Hebrew author of the Jewish oracles. In favour of this latter view is the fact that the oracles of Sambethe proved more acceptable in the pagan world than might have been expected if they were generally treated as purely Jewish.

Written records of alleged Sibylline oracles were in circulation here and there, but the remains that have come down through occasional quotations in authors such as Plutarch, Pausanias and others, are brief and scanty and do not provide a sufficient idea of the contents of the original oracles.[189] What survives is however sufficient to show that the oracles often carried a political message which was usually dire, and that they were grouped into collections in a most disorganized fashion rather than being subjected to careful literary editing.[190] In Asia Minor and Greece these passages moved around in private possession only, without public supervision or official use, but their prestige and

---

186. On the relation between the two names, see Tcherikover in CPJ III, pp. 44, 55. No examples of one man being called both Sambathion and Sambas are known, but the principle behind such a *hypokoristikon* is well established in the case of other names. Of the other Sibyls, Demo too (Pausanias x 12, 8) is an abbreviation of Demophile (Varro in Lactantius i 6, 10), cf. Diels, *Sibyllinische Blätter* (1890), p. 53.

187. W. Bousset, 'Sibyllen und Sibyllinische Bücher', HHRE XVIII (1906), col. 272.

188. The suggestions that the name refers to the Queen of Sheba or to the goddess Siduri-Sabitu are no more than guesses, cf. Rzach, RE IIA (1923), cols. 2097–9. A connection with Aramaic sābā', sābᶜtā, 'old man', 'old woman' (Lewy, Philologus 57 (1898), pp. 350 f.) is ruled out by the duplication of the *b*. Cf. also J. M. Rosenstiehl and J. G. Heintz, 'De Sibtu, la reine de Mari, à Sambèthe', RHPR 52 (1972), pp. 13–15.

189. Cf. the collection in C. Alexandre's first ed. of *Sib*. iii 118–129. Add a χρησμὸς Σιβύλλης of which the text may be found in K. Buresch, *Klaros* (1889), p. 78, and a fragment published by G. Crönert, 'Oraculorum Sibyllinorum fragmentum Osloense', Symbolae Osloenses 6 (1928), pp. 57–9. Cf. Rzach, RE IIA (1923), cols. 2103–5.

190. J. J. Collins, *The Sibylline Oracles of Egyptian Judaism* (1974), pp. 2–19. Collins points out that similar oracle collections were to be found not only elsewhere in the Greek and Roman world but also in Egypt and Persia.

influence should not be underestimated on that account.[191]

In Rome, to which they came from Cumae, they acquired an entirely different importance.[192] King Tarquinius Superbus is said to have obtained a collection of Sibylline oracles from Cumae, which were preserved in the temple of the Capitoline Jupiter.[193] After these were destroyed in the burning of the Capitol in 83 B.C., the Senate, on the suggestion of the Consul C. Curio, sent a delegation to Asia Minor in 76 B.C. to bring back from Erythrae and other places another collection of about one thousand (?) verses which was once again deposited in the Capitol.[194] The collection was later occasionally enlarged and sorted out and still existed in the fourth century A.D. Julian had the Sibylline books consulted in A.D. 363.[195] It was not until about A.D. 404–8 that Stilicho burnt them.[196] Besides the official collection, Sibylline verses in private possession were also passed around, but because of the improper use made of them they were often confiscated or destroyed by the authorities. The official collection was kept secret and only consulted on important occasions, mainly to ascertain what expiations were required on the outbreak of public misfortunes. The alleged 'consultation' was however sometimes nothing other than the preparation of a new passage corresponding to the requirements of the immediate situation.[197]

This Sibyllism was by nature especially liable to exploitation in the interest of religious propaganda. The oracles, of apocryphal origin and circulating without control in private possession, could be complemented or increased at pleasure. What Greeks had done in this respect could just as easily be undertaken by the Jews. In addition, the oracles were highly esteemed among religious minds, not least because of the

191. Cf. on the Sibylline oracles among the Greeks, Alexandre, *op. cit.*, II, pp. 102–47; Rzach, RE IIA (1923), cols. 2104–5.

192. Cf. C. Alexandre in his first ed., II, pp. 148–253; A. Bouché-Leclercq, *Histoire de la divination dans l'antiquité* IV (1882), pp. 286–317; H. Diels, *Sibyllinische Blätter* (1890); E. Hoffmann, 'Die tarquinischen Sibyllen-Bücher', RhM 50 (1895), pp. 90–113; Schultess, *Die sibyllinischen Bücher in Rom* (1895); K. Stützle, *Die Sibyllen und Sibyllinen* I (1904), pp. 15–51; Rzach, RE IIA (1923), cols. 2091–5, 2105 ff.; W. Hoffmann, *Wandel und Herkunft der Sibyllinische Bücher in Rom* (Diss. Leipzig, 1933); R. Bloch, 'L'origine des Livres Sibyllins à Rome: Méthode de recherche et critique du récit des annalistes anciens', in *Neue Beiträge zur Geschichte der Alten Welt* II (1965), pp. 281–92; H. Parke, *Greek Oracles* (1967), pp. 51–5.

193. Dionysius of Halicarnassus iv 62.

194. Lactantius i 6, 14 (cf. i 6, 11). Tacitus, *Annal.* vi 12. Dionysius of Halicarnassus iv 62. The number *circa mille* must be accepted with caution; it is attested only in Lactantius, who refers thereby to the third book of the Jewish-Christian collection.

195. Ammianus Marcellinus xxiii 1, 7.

196. Schultess, *Die sibyllinischen Bücher in Rom* (1904), p. 45.

197. So, for example, the two pieces preserved in Phlegon, *Mirab.* 10 (Jacoby, FGrH 257, F 36) were probably written in the years 207 B.C. and 200 B.C., cf. Diels, *Sibyllinische Blätter* (1890); Jacoby, FGrH, Komm. II BD, p. 846.

mystery surrounding them. Thus it was hoped that widespread attention could be gained by the use of this literary form. When therefore Jewish writers began to use it to express their own religious ideas it can be assumed that religious propaganda was the authors' original intention. As far as can be ascertained, an extensive Sibylline oracle of Jewish origin was first issued in the second century B.C. from Alexandria. The outcome was apparently considered desirable by the Jews concerned, for further oracles were composed in the following centuries. Christians also later respected the value of the forged oracles as a prop for their own apologetic. Not only did they willingly use and highly esteem the Jewish Sibylline oracles; they themselves richly increased those that they had, a production continuing into later imperial times. It is precisely to this tradition of the Christian Church that we are indebted for the possession of the older Jewish Sibylline oracles as well.

The form of these Jewish-Christian Sibylline oracles is the same as that of the old gentile ones.[198] The Jewish or Christian authors allowed the ancient Sibyl to speak to the gentile peoples in Greek hexameters and in the language of Homer. The contents serve throughout to carry a religious message. The Sibyl prophesies the fate of the world from the beginning to the author's own time in order to link it to threats and promises for the near future. She reproaches the gentiles with the sin of their idolatry and with their wickedness, and exhorts them to do penance whilst there is time, for fearful chastisements will overtake the unrepentant.[199]

The first edition of the extant Jewish-Christian Sibyllines was prepared by Xystus Betulejus from an Augsburg (now Munich) manuscript (Basel, 1545). The best critical editions are those by A. Rzach, *Oracula Sibyllina* (1891) (still valuable), and J. Geffcken, *Oracula Sibyllina* (1902) (the best). These are not superseded by A. Kurfess, *Sibyllinische Weissagungen. Urtext und Übersetzung* (1951). All three editions are marred by the incorporation of dubious hypothetical readings into the text.

Of particular importance for the history of the transmission of these oracles, apart from quotations in the Church Fathers (cf. below), is a work entitled Θεοσοφία, written toward the end of the fifth century

---

198. Because the extant pagan oracles are so fragmentary, M. J. Wolff, 'Sibyllen und Sibyllinen', Archiv für Kulturgeschichte 24 (1934), pp. 312–25, preferred to see the prototype of the Jewish Sibyls in the *ex eventu* prophecy enshrined, in the second century A.D., in a long poem called the *Alexandra*, which is attributed to the early third century B.C. author, Lycophron. It is however more likely that [Lycophron] modelled his poem on the Sibyllines than vice versa.

199. On the Jewish Sibyllines as apologetic, cf. P. Dalbert, *Die Theologie der hell.-jüd. Missionsliteratur* (1954), pp. 106–23.

A.D. It was a compilation of gentile testimonies in support of Christian teachings. The original has been lost, but a number of excerpts and fragments have been preserved. The most comprehensive excerpt is given in a Tübingen manuscript.[200] After the introductory comments, which are extant in the excerpt (Buresch, p. 95), the author of the original work wrote first ἑπτα βιβλία περὶ τῆς ὀρθῆς πίστεως, followed by four further books. In these he first shows (i.e. in books 1–3) that 'the oracles of the Hellenic gods, the theological teachings of the Hellenic and Egyptian sages, and finally the oracles of the Sibyls' were in agreement with Holy Scripture. The fourth (or eleventh) book contained the prophecies of Hystaspes with at the end a short chronicle from Adam until the Emperor Zeno. It may be concluded from the last note that the original work was written under Emperor Zeno (474–91). It can have been written at the most only a few years later since, as is likewise noted, the author expects the end of all things in the year six thousand of the world, but places the birth of Christ in the year five thousand five hundred. Not all of this work is given in the Tübingen extract. There is no trace of the fourth book (Hystaspes and the chronicle), but the Sibylline oracles are certainly quoted.[201]

An important fragment of the original Theosophy has probably been preserved in Codex Ottobonianus, Gr. 378.[202] The piece begins with the list of the ten Sibyls, known from the Prologue of the Sibyllines, and subsequently gives an extensive collection of passages from the Sibylline oracles taken, to a large extent, but not completely, from Lactantius, from which the list of the ten Sibyls also derives.[203] The text is parallel to the section of the Tübingen excerpt relating to the Sibyls, but it is much fuller, so that the Tübingen text appears to be only a poor excerpt from *Ottobonianus*.

This material now provides us with a clue to the age of this

---

200. K. Buresch, 'Untersuchungen zum Orakelwesen des späteren Altertums', *Klaros* (1889), appendix, pp. 87–126; cf. K. von Fritz, 'Theosophia', RE V (1934), cols. 2250–1; H. Erbse, *Fragmente griechischer Theosophien* (1941), pp. 1–52.

201. A. Brinkmann attempted to prove that the original work was written by a certain Aristokritos, of whom nothing further is known (RhM 51 (1896), pp. 273–80) except that the θεοσοφία which he wrote attempted to show that Judaism, Hellenism, Christianity and Manichaeism were one and the same. This work cannot be identical to the Theosophy of Tübingen, since the extant version makes no mention of Manichaeism. The existence of Aristokritos' *Theosophia* may however suggest that he and the author of our *Theosophia* both had recourse to the same Christian florilegium, cf. S. N. C. Lieu, 'An Early Byzantine Formula for the Renunciation of Manichaeism', JAC 26 (1983), p. 213.

202. K. Mras, 'Eine neuentdeckte Sibyllen-Theosophie', Wiener Studien 28 (1906), pp. 43–83; Erbse, *op. cit.*, pp. 28 ff.

203. Of the thirty-five Sibylline quotations of the Theosophy, eighteen are to be found in exactly the same length in Lactantius, in ten either Lactantius or the Theosophy has more, and seven do not appear at all in Lactantius. In the readings, too, there are many differences (Mras, 69 f.).

collection. The manuscripts of these Sibyllines fall into three classes.

The first class, designated with Ω by Rzach and Geffcken, gives the Books in a completely different arrangement from the others. The whole collection begins with Books designated as ix and, in some manuscripts, x. These do not correspond to the Books with the same number in the second class and in the editions. Thus Books vi, vii, 1 and viii, 218–428 (in the normal numbering) are included in this class but designated as Book ix, and the normal Book iv is designated in the group, when it is included, as Book x. The more complete representatives of this class have in addition retained Books xi–xiv, which have only been preserved owing to them.

The second class (Φ) preserves very varied readings but is characterized by a prefixed prologue, unique to it. The manuscripts of this class contain Books i–viii in the order of the printed editions.

The third class (Ψ) is more unified. It contains the same Books as the second class except that Book viii stands at the beginning, hence in the order viii, i–vii (although some manuscripts omit vi and vii altogether), without the Prologue.

The manuscripts of classes Φ and Ψ, corresponding to our editions, agree in the enumeration of Books iv–vii. Books i and ii of the editions form only one Book in the manuscripts. Concerning the original division of Books i–iii of the editions, the following may be conjectured from the superscriptions and subscriptions which have been preserved.[204] Immediately preceding Book iii 1, the following note is found in class Φ: πάλιν ἐν τῷ τρίτῳ αὐτῆς τόμῳ τάδε φησὶν ἐκ τοῦ δευτέρου λόγου, as also in class Ψ, except that here the following note is found in the margin: ἐκ τοῦ δευτέρου λόγου. Then Ψ has, after iii 92, the note: ἐνταῦθα ζήτει τὰ λείποντα ἀπὸ τοῦ δευτέρου λόγου καὶ τὴν ἀρχὴν τοῦ τρίτου. Φ, too, notes that something is missing. According to this, there is a large lacuna after iii 92 in this tradition, as is also indicated by the contents. The preceding part formed two Books (λόγοι) which were divided into three τόμοι; what follows equals Book iii, but without a beginning. It can therefore be assumed that iii 1–92 either formed the end of Book ii, as these manuscript notes suggest, or that iii 1–96 constituted a separate new introduction to Book iii, inserted at a late state into the manuscripts to be a link with the present Book ii after the original introductory material and the original Book ii had been

---

204. Cf. on this the introduction in J. Geffcken's ed., pp. l–lii, and especially P. Lieger, *Quaestiones Sibyllinae*, I, *De collectionibus oraculorum Sibyllinorum* (*Gymnasialprogr.*, 1904). These arguments based on the manuscript notes need to be backed by the contents of the relevant sections of the text. The manuscripts claim elsewhere that Book iii contained 1034 verses, which no computation of extant lines can achieve, cf. Nikiprowetzky, *op. cit.*, p. 65.

lost.[205] It will be shown below that this has been preserved through Theophilus.

The placing of Book viii in class Ψ and the thorough rearrangement in class Ω are probably secondary (so Geffcken and Lieger).

In class Φ, in which the original arrangement of the collection is probably best preserved, the editor says in a Prologue that he has assembled the scattered Sibylline oracles. Thus the writer of the Prologue was presumably also the compiler of the extant collection, whether of only the eight Books preserved in Φ or of more. Until that time, single oracles ($\lambda \acute{o} \gamma o \iota$) had been in separate circulation, which agrees with Lactantius' comments (cf. below. It should be noted that this makes it perfectly possible that the other classes of manuscript may preserve better readings in particular cases). However, the largest part of the Prologue, not only the list of the ten Sibyls but all that follows it, appears almost literally in the fragment of the 'Theosophy' published by Mras, and it is highly likely that the 'Theosophy' takes precedence; many of its statements are very well argued (especially lines 75 ff.), whereas this is not true of the Prologue. The author of the Prologue therefore depended on the 'Theosophy', from which it follows that the collection in class Φ was first prepared in the sixth century A.D.

The collection as it is now is chaotic, and even the most astute analysis will probably never succeed in sorting it out and arranging it. It is unfortunately not the case that each Book formed an original whole; individual Books also in part comprised an arbitrary number of individual passages. The curse of pseudonymous authorship seems to have governed these oracles in a quite especial way. Each reader or writer permitted himself to complete what existed at his own discretion and to arrange the scattered leaves thus or otherwise. Obviously, much was at first in circulation as isolated pieces and the

---

205. On the place and function of iii 1–96 see J. J. Collins, *The Sibylline Oracles of Egyptian Judaism* (1974), pp. 24–5. The contents of this section lend credence to the manuscript indications that it should be separated from the rest of the book. Verses 46–96 are probably later than the main corpus of Sib. iii, belonging either to the time of Cleopatra or to a still later date (Collins, *op. cit.*, pp. 64–71). Since J. Geffcken, *Komposition und Entstehungszeit der Oracula Sibyllina* (1902), pp. 47–53, argued convincingly that the present Book ii was originally part of Book i, it is possible that iii 1–96 may comprise part of the lost *second* book of the collection, cf. A. Kurfess, in E. Hennecke and W. Schneemelcher, *N.T. Apocrypha*, ed. R. McL. Wilson (ET 1965), II, p. 707. This hypothesis has the advantage that iii 63–96 would make a good conclusion for a Book, although the function of the last four lines (93–6) is obscure under any hypothesis. V. Nikiprowetzky, *La Troisième Sibylle* (1970), pp. 60–6, 217–22, tries to show that iii 1–96 *could* have belonged originally to Book iii *in addition to* the alternative introduction preserved in Theophilus (see below). The repetitiveness that would ensue is not out of keeping with the nature of these oracles, but Nikiprowetzky's hypothesis fails to account satisfactorily for the manuscript indications discussed here. See below, pp. 639–41.

collection in which they subsequently found a place is fortuitous. Many passages are therefore duplicated in various places.[206]

This being the character of the whole, it is not possible to distinguish between Jewish and Christian material everywhere with certainty. The oldest portions are at any rate Jewish, perhaps with some elaborations of gentile oracles. The bulk of the later books is certainly Christian. But it is only occasionally that the one or the other element appears in a large coherent unit, and the style of the Sibylline hexameters is too homogeneous to permit differentiation on stylistic grounds. As a rule, they are made up of smaller passages which have been strung together quite loosely, often without any connection. It is therefore possible to assess with certainty only whether a few comparatively small pieces are Jewish or Christian. The content of much is so neutral that it can just as well have originated from one side as the other. Each statement of the Sibyl must be subjected to separate scrutiny. The following pieces may be distinguished with some degree of probability as Jewish.

1. In the opinion of all the critics, the oldest and certainly Jewish portions are at all events contained in Book iii. It is generally agreed that the Book as a whole was redacted by Jews, but the extent of Christian interpolations and remaining fragments of pagan oracles is still debated. Views have also differed widely concerning the date of composition and the extent of the Jewish sections. According to Bleek in 1819, Book iii 97–808 is the work of an Alexandrian Jew from the time of the Maccabees (170–160 B.C.), with insertions of older gentile poems (verses 97–161 and 433–88) and later Christian interpolations (verses 350–80). Alexandre in 1841–56 ascribed only passages iii 97–294, 489–818 to an Alexandrian Jew of about 168 B.C., and the intervening section iii 295–488 by contrast to a Christian author. Geffcken, pp. 97–154, held that the first oracle of the building of the tower was gentile. Accepting this earlier work from an oracle of the Babylonian Sibyl, a Jew in around the middle of the second century B.C. composed the older passages which run through the whole Book. A second group is likewise found throughout the Book containing numerous gentile oracles of the Erythraean Sibyl which were revised and completed by a Jew shortly after the Mithridatic war (88–84 B.C.). Despite the confusion and disorder, Geffcken ventured clearly to separate one passage from another. Bousset's view was similar, but he assigned a greater role to a redactor of the mid-first century B.C. who incorporated earlier oracles, as well as adding verses 211–336 and

---

206. A greater degree of literary unity has been asserted for Sibyllines i and ii by J. Geffcken, *Komposition und Entstehungszeit* (1902), pp. 47–53, since he believes they were originally part of a single Book (see preceding note). Nikiprowetzky argues that Book iii is a deliberate unity (see below, p. 633). The general judgement about the incoherence of the collection still however stands.

520–829. According to him, the third Sibyl is 'a work from the time of Alexandra, in which older Jewish Sibylline fragments from the time of Ptolemy VII, a passage of the old Babylonian Sibyl, portions of the Erythraean Sibyl and other Hellenistic Sibylline oracles had been inserted' (cf. HHRE, 3rd ed., XVIII, col. 272). Lieger in 1906 separated two layers, the older one (including iii 97–165, 213–94, 573–615, 652–724, 741–808, 819–29) written 'in or immediately after the year 170', and the more recent one (including all the remaining material) in about 140 B.C. Schürer in 1909 accepted the main elements of Geffcken's analysis but was sceptical about the extent to which gentile oracles had been included. He believed the whole work to have been produced by a Jew in the mid-second century B.C., with only verses 464–70 to be considered a later insertion. Since then, P. Schnabel, *Berossus und die babylonisch-hellenistische Literatur* (1923), pp. 69–93, argued that verses 97–349 cannot be a fragment of an independent prior Babylonian Sibyl since 97–155 are hostile to the Babylonians, and that this section should therefore be assigned to the Jewish authors of the rest of the oracle. A drastically different attitude is put forward by V. Nikiprowetzky, *La Troisième Sibylle* (1970), who dates the entire book to the mid-first century B.C., arguing that it is a unified composition from the time of Cleopatra VII and the second triumvirate (*op. cit.*, p. 216). Only verse 736 (on Camarina) and verses 63–74 (which describe Samaria as 'Sebaste' and therefore date after 25 B.C.) are later additions. J. J. Collins, *The Sibylline Oracles of Egyptian Judaism* (1974), throws doubt on the origins of verses 381–7 in the work of a Persian Sibyl, as asserted by Geffcken. For the rest, he asserts that the original corpus of the Book consisted in verses 97–349 and 489–end, written in the mid-second century B.C., with verses 350–488 added at some time in the first century B.C. (*ibid.*, pp. 27–8).

In order to clarify the issue, the contents will first be surveyed,[207] omitting iii, 1–96 which according to the manuscript tradition belongs to Book ii (cf. above, p. 630). The remainder can be assigned for convenience into three groups (97–294, 295–488, and 489–829) which show a certain coherence because of the fresh starts made at verses 295 and 489. The beginning of the first group is missing. It opens abruptly with a recollection of the building of the tower of Babel and the confusion of languages as the cause of the dispersion of mankind (97–109). When the whole earth was populated, rule over it was divided between three: Chronos, Titan, and Iapetus. At first, they ruled peaceably alongside one another; but Chronos and Titan fell into a conflict which, settled for only a short time by an assembly of the

---

207. Cf. also the survey of contents by Lanchester in Charles, APOT II, pp. 371–2; J. J. Collins, *The Sibylline Oracles of Egyptian Judaism* (1974), pp. 24–8. Cf. also Rzach, RE IIA (1923), cols. 2122–30.

βασιλεῖς, eventually resulted in a battle between the sons of Chronos and the Titans and the destruction of both races. After their annihilation there came into being one after another the kingdoms of the Egyptians, the Persians, the Medians, the Ethiopians, the Assyrians, the Babylonians, the Macedonians, once again the Egyptians, and finally the Romans (verses 110–61). The Sibyl then begins to prophesy, first the golden age of the Solomonic kingdom, followed by the Hellenistic-Macedonian kingdom, and finally the many-headed (176) kingdom of the Romans. After the seventh king of Egypt of the Hellenic race, the people of God will rule again and lead all mortals towards life (162–95). The judgement of God will fall upon all the kingdoms of the world, from the Titans and sons of Chronos onwards. Even the pious from Solomon's kingdom will be afflicted with misfortune. The author makes use of this occasion to present a sketch of the Jewish nation, its worship, and its main fortunes, from the exodus from Egypt until Cyrus (196–294).

The second group is almost entirely taken up with predictions of judgements and calamities, against Babylon (295–313), against Egypt (314–18), against Gog and Magog (319–22), against Libya (323–33). A brief statement of the signs auguring the calamity (334–40) is followed by proclamations of woe on individual cities and lands, and concludes with the promise of a general condition of Messianic prosperity and peace in Asia and Europe (341–80). Added to this are oracles concerning Alexander the Great, adapted to refer to Antiochus Epiphanes and his successors (381–400), and concerning Phrygia, Troy (interspersed with polemic against Homer), Lycia, Cyprus, Italy, and other lands, towns and islands (401–88).

The third group begins with oracles on Phoenicia, Crete, Thracia, Gog and Magog, and the Hellenes (489–572). It then points to the people of Israel, who keep the Law of God and do not take to idolatry and unnatural vices like the other nations (573–600). This is followed by a reiterated prophecy of judgement on the sinful world, ending in promises (601–23) and an exhortation to conversion, together with a description of the ruin which will fall on the ungodly world, especially on Hellas (624–51). The conclusion consists in the promise of the Messianic King, the prophecy of judgement, and a detailed description of the Messianic salvation, interspersed with exhortations to Hellas to abandon its arrogance, and references to the omens of the final judgement (652–808). In the Epilogue the Sibyl says that she comes from Babylon, is wrongly regarded by the Greeks as a native of Erythrae (809–18), is the daughter of Noah and was in the ark with him at the time of the flood (819–29).[208]

---

208. There are no grounds for separating the Epilogue (809–29) from the rest of the

This survey of the contents demonstrates that, despite the arguments
of Nikiprowetzky, it is unlikely that we have here a unified composition.
In the second group, in particular, there is frequently no continuity
between the passages. It is therefore in any case a collection of separate
oracles. Nevertheless, it is at least possible that the bulk derives from
one author, for just as there is little uniformity in the whole, so there is
little certainty in the traces of different hands that have been found in
it. The circumstance which speaks particularly for the essential
homogeneity of the whole is that in all three groups there is reference to
the time of the seventh Ptolemy (191–3, 316–18, 608–10). But this
assumption also needs to take into account the possibility that the
author inserted older, gentile oracles into his own work, and that on the
other hand later writers expanded the original length with larger or
smaller interpolations. The gentile oracles included can scarcely have
been so numerous or extensive, for in that case clearer signs of a
non-Jewish outlook would certainly be expected.[209] The mythological
passage at the beginning, which in a euhemeristic manner makes the
gentile gods into guiltless human kings of antiquity, may also very well
have been written by a Jew. Indeed, this kind of mixture of Greek and
Jewish myths accords precisely with the character of Hellenistic Jewish
writings. Only one line (776) may be a Christian interpolation, in
which case it should be excised, but it is more likely that υἱὸν θεοῖο there
should be read as νηὸν θεοῖο (cf. above, vol. II, p. 501).[210]

The following termini can be provided for the date of composition of
specific oracles within iii, 96–829. Verse 176 presupposes that Rome is
still a republic (πολύκρανος). Verses 191–3, 316–18, and 608–10 assume
a date before the end of the rule of a 'seventh king of Egypt of the
Hellenic race', since, according to these passages, that reign was to
mark the eschatological end of the world. It is hard to believe that such
an assertion could be made after the last king who could be described in
this way had died. The description fits a number of Ptolemies, the
enumeration depending on whether Alexander the Great should be
counted as a king of Egypt, and on the weight to be assigned to

work. The polemic here against the Erythraean Sibyl and the claim to a Babylonian
origin are entirely in keeping with the claims of the Jewish Sibyl elsewhere in the book, cf.
Nikiprowetzky, *op. cit.*, pp. 37–41.

209. Only one passage can be attributed to a pagan oracle with certainty. That is verse
736, which urges that Camarina should not be aroused. This oracle was originally
Delphic and had become proverbial by the late first century B.C., cf. Vergil, *Aeneid* iii
800–1. Cf. H. W. Parke and D. E. W. Wormell, *The Delphic Oracle* I (1956), p. 391;
Nikiprowetzky, *op. cit.*, pp. 207, 353.

210. This emendation, conjectured by Alexandre, is much closer to the context than
the hypothesis that it is a Christian interpolation, cf. Geffcken, *Komposition und
Entstehungszeit* (1902), p. 13; Collins in Charlesworth, OTP I, p. 379; cf. the complete
excision of the line by A. Kurfess, *Sibyllinische Weissagungen* (1951), p. 108.

overlapping reigns. The most likely identification is with Ptolemy VI Philometor (180–145 B.C.), but, since Ptolemy VIII Physcon and Ptolemy VII Philopator are also possible, only a more general date in the mid-second century B.C. can be affirmed for these particular oracles.[211] The term *νέος* (608) is as likely to refer to the king in question as a *new* king, or to be part of his title, as in the case of Philopator, as to refer to his youth, and is therefore of no help in dating.[212]

Verses 350–80, which consist of a sharp polemic against Rome and refer to a great Roman disaster in Asia, may be associated with the massacres of Romans in Asia under Mithridates (88 B.C.)[213] or to the campaign of Cleopatra against Rome.[214] Verses 388–400, which give a complex account of the fate of the warrior who is to conquer Asia and of his descendants, may refer in some detail to Antiochus Epiphanes, in

211. Numerous attempts have been made to establish more accurately the Egyptian king in question and therefore the date of the prophecies. The criteria adopted are the following, which are listed with the objections made to them by their critics. (1) The king in question is likely to have been friendly towards the Jews, therefore Ptolemy VI Philometor is probable (Fraser, PA II, p. 992). Against this, the reference to the king seems to be an indicator of the *date* of the messianic age, not the agent of it, cf. A. Momigliano, 'La portata storica dei vaticini sul settimo re nel terzo libro degli Oracoli Sibillini', *Forma Futuri (Studi in Onore di Cardinale Michele Pellegrino)* (1975), pp. 1077–84. (2) The king may be identified with the 'king from the sun' of verse 652, who will relieve the entire earth from evil war. Such an identification is possible given the role of the sun in Ptolemaic royal titulature and *would* require the Ptolemy in question to have been at least a partial contributor to the messianic age, making his friendship towards the Jews likely. Ptolemy Philometor would again seem probable (Collins, BAAJ, pp. 68–70). Against this, the identification of the kings in the two passages is not inevitable, cf. Momigliano, *art. cit.*, p. 1081. The king from the sun could be a Jewish messiah (though the phrase would be unique in this form, cf. Collins, BAAJ, p. 68), or it could belong to an entirely separate prophecy. (3) The prophecy in verses 175–92 is extremely hostile to Rome and ends by dating the end of Roman power to the rule of the seventh king. This would be very odd for an Egyptian or Judaean Jew between 170 and 160 since both Egypt and Judaea had friendly relations with Rome in this period (Momigliano, *art. cit.*, p. 1082). Either the passage dates the king to a later period (cf. Nikiprowetzky, *op. cit.*, pp. 208–16, who refers the oracle to Cleopatra (!) VII) or it is a late addition (A. Peretti, *La Sibilla Babilonese* (1943), p. 190; cf. Nikiprowetzky, *op. cit.*, pp. 210–12, for arguments in favour of the unity of the text). (4) The reference to the seventh king in lines 608–9 is followed (611–15) by mention of a great king who will come to Egypt from Asia and depart in triumph. If the king is to be identified with Antiochus Epiphanes, the date of the prophecy must be precisely between 170 and 168 B.C., when Antiochus' second invasion of Egypt was threatened by the Romans (Momigliano, *art. cit.*, p. 1081). Against this, the prophecy may be genuine rather than *ex eventu*, and it is odd that no mention of the Maccabaean revolt should be made if the prophecy referred directly to Antiochus (Collins, BAAJ, pp. 65–6). If, as is eminently likely, Jewish oracles of the second century B.C. have been reshaped for a new literary context in the first century B.C. or A.D., precise dating of the original oracles by such means may be impossible.

212. See J. J. Collins, *The Sibylline Oracles of Egyptian Judaism* (1974), p. 30.

213. W. Bousset, 'Sibyllen und Sibyllinische Bücher', HHRE XVIII (1906), col. 271.

214. Peretti, *op. cit.*, pp. 330 ff., 441 ff.; Collins, *Sibylline Oracles*, pp. 57–64.

which case the 'parasite horn' (400) must refer to Zabinas, and at least the section 396–400 of the oracle must be placed after 129 B.C., when Zabinas was proclaimed king, but before 122 B.C., when he perished.[215] Verses 464–9 refer to a disastrous civil war in Italy, which would be unlikely before the Social War of 90–88 B.C. Verses 484 and 487 seem to refer to the destruction of Corinth and Carthage in 146 B.C.[216] Verses 611–15, which describe how a mighty king from Asia will cast down the kingdom of Egypt and bring about mass conversion to God, may refer to Antiochus Epiphanes, in which case they must have been written in the time between his successful campaign against Egypt in 170 B.C. and his failure in 168 B.C. These verses may, however, be a much more general prophecy about the continual threat of Asian kings to Egypt, in which case no precise historical reference is to be sought.[217]

For determining the precise date of composition of the whole Book, none of those passages is decisive. The fact that the references to the seventh king appear in three different sections of the work make attractive the hypothesis of an initial redaction at that date (i.e. probably mid-second century B.C.); in that case, numerous later insertions must be postulated. The dates ascribed to these passages do, however, provide a *terminus post quem* of the mid-first century B.C. for the insertion of those extra passages or the composition of the whole Book. The *terminus ante quem* is the destruction of the Temple in A.D. 70. Composition after that date would be unlikely, given the emphasis put on the Temple cult within the Book. This uncertainty about the date of compilation is clearly not a problem for the interpretation of specific passages if, as argued above, the work is not a literary unity.

External testimony proves an early date only for verses 97–155. The Sibyl's prophecy of the building of the tower of Babel and of the subsequent war between the sons of Chronos and the Titans was already quoted explicitly under the name of the Sibyl (Σίβυλλα δέ φησιν etc.) by Alexander Polyhistor, hence in the first century B.C., in his Χαλδαϊκά, cf. Eusebius, *Chron.*, ed. Schoene, I, p. 23 = Syncellus, ed. Dindorf, I, p. 81 = Cyrill., *Adv. Julian.*, ed. Spanh., p. 9.[218] Quotations

---

215. Identification with Antiochus Epiphanes was originally proposed by Hilgenfeld, *Jüd. Apok.*, pp. 68 ff. The more precise identification of the parasite horn with Zabinas is found in H. H. Rowley, 'The Interpretation and Date of Sibylline Oracles III 388–400', *ZAW* 44 (1926), pp. 324–7.

216. It is not justified to emend verse 484 so that Chalcedon (Χαλκηδών) be read instead of Carthage (Χαρχηδών) as does A. Kurfess, *Sibyllinische Weissagungen* (1951), *ad loc.*, following a conjecture by Meineke.

217. Collins, *Sibylline Oracles*, pp. 29–30.

218. It will be shown below, pp. 646 ff., that Alexander Polyhistor had before him not a Babylonian but our Jewish Sibyl. The quotation was taken by Josephus from Alexander Polyhistor without mentioning his name (*Ant.* i 4, 3 (115–18) = Eusebius, *Praep. ev.* ix 15 and *Onomast.*, ed. Klostermann (1904), 40). Cf. Freudenthal, *Alexander Polyhistor*, p. 25,

from diverse parts of Book iii are found among the oldest patristic writings.[219]

The place of origin of Book iii is normally given as Egypt because of the numerous references to that land, not all of which can easily be explained in terms of its prominence in the Bible (cf. 159–61 on Egypt as a world empire). Specific oracles may however reasonably be assigned a different provenance (e.g. verses 400–88, which may be ascribed to the Erythraean Sibyl in Asia Minor).[220] There are many similarities between the Third Sibyllines and Jewish apocryphal works such as Enoch and Jubilees, which suggests that a Judaean origin for part of the work is possible.[221] Within Egypt, Leontopolis provides a milieu as plausible as Alexandria.[222] As with the dating of the book, it is best to assign a provenance separately to each section of the text.

2. Both the extensive fragments (eighty-four verses in all) given by Theophilus, *Ad Autol.* ii 36 (ed. Grant, pp. 86–9, 90–3) also belong either to the original Book iii or to the lost original Book ii.[223] Verses from the same fragments are also cited by other Church Fathers.[224] These passages are missing from the extant manuscripts because of the break between the present Books ii and iii (cf. above, p. 630). In the early editions they were placed at the head of the whole collection because Theophilus states that they stood at the beginning of the Sibyl's prophecy (ἐν ἀρχῇ τῆς προφητείας αὐτῆς). Because the present Book i and Book ii were almost certainly composed after Theophilus wrote (at the end of the first century A.D.), and it was therefore only much later that

---

note, and the discussion below.

219. Athenagoras, *Leg.* 30. Theophilus, *Ad Autol.* ii 31. Tertullian, *Ad nationes* ii 12. Clement of Alexandria, *Protrept.* vi 70; vii 74. Pseudo-Justin, *Cohortatio ad Graecos* 16.

220. J. Geffcken, *Komposition und Entstehungszeit* (1902), p. 13, followed by Collins, *Sibylline Oracles*, pp. 27–8. The attribution is plausible both because the content of these verses is the same as that attributed to the Erythraean Sibyl by Varro (in Lactantius, *Div. Inst.* i 6) and by Pausanias x 2, 2, and because of the prominence of Asia Minor place names.

221. A. Jaubert, *La Notion de l'Alliance dans le Judaïsme* (1963), p. 331; Nikiprowetzky, *op. cit.*, pp. 70, 128, 132, 137; F. Millar, review of Nikiprowetzky, JThSt n.s. 23 (1972), pp. 223–4.

222. Collins, *Sibylline Oracles*, pp. 47–53.

223. A further fragment of two lines (Theophilus, *Ad Autolycum* ii 3, 2, ed. Grant, p. 24 = Sib. Or., ed. Geffcken, fragm. 2) is assigned to the Prologue by Lanchester in Charles, APOT II, p. 377, where a translation of all three fragments into English is given. (See also Collins in Charlesworth, OTP I, pp. 470–1.) A further three very small fragments from Lactantius and one fragment from Constantine are too brief to be assigned a clear place in the Sibylline corpus, cf. A. Kurfess, 'Wie sind die Fragmenta der Oracula Sibyllina einzuordnen?', Aevum 26 (1952), pp. 228–35.

224. Gnostic fragments in Hippolytus, *Philosophum.* v 16. Clement of Alexandria, *Protrept.* ii 27; *Protrept.* vi 71 = *Strom.* v 14, 108; *Protrept.* viii 77 = *Strom.* v 14, 115; *Strom.* iii 3, 14. Pseudo-Justin, *Cohortatio ad Graecos* 16. Lactantius i 6, 15–16; 7, 13; 8, 3; ii 11, 18 (?); 12, 19; iv 6, 5. *Idem, De ira dei* 22, 7.

they were set at the beginning of the present collection, Book iii is certainly the oldest part and those passages may have constituted the original introduction to it. This surmise is confirmed by the fact that among his numerous quotations, Lactantius only describes such passages as appear in Theophilus' fragments and Book iii, as prophecies of the Erythraean Sibyl, indeed cites them as belonging to one book.[225]

The contents of these verses may be designated as the programme proper of all Jewish Sibyllism: they contain an energetic proclamation of the one true God and an equally energetic polemic against idolatry. The trend of Jewish Sibyllism is to be seen nowhere better than in this proem.[226]

3. The passage given by the editions at the beginning of Book iii (iii 1–92) belongs according to the evidence of the manuscripts to the original Book ii (cf. above, p. 630). The original Book ii appears to have been a composition separate from the extant Book ii, which was originally attached to Book i, cf. Geffcken, *Komposition*, pp. 47–53. If so, the original Book ii probably survives only here, although Kurfess argued that the Theophilus fragments discussed above should also be

225. Cf. Charles, APOT II, pp. 371, 377–8. Lactantius distinguishes the different Books as different Sibyls. When after quoting from one Book he quotes from another, he says: 'alia Sibylla dicit.' Among the approximately fifty quotations which he gives, extending from Book iii to Book viii of the collection, only those from the Prologue preserved in Theophilus and from Book iii are designated as prophecies of the Erythraean Sibyl. From the Prologue: Lactantius i 6, 13–16; i 3; ii 12, 19; iv 6, 5. From Book iii: Lactantius ii 16, 1 (approximately equivalent to *Sib.* iii 228–9, ed. Geffcken); iv 6, 5 (approximately *Sib.* iii 775); iv 15, 29 (= *Sib.* iii 815–18); vii.19, 9 (first half of *Sib.* iii 618); vii 20, 1–2 (= *Sib.* iii 741–3); vii 24, 12 (= *Sib.* iii 788–91, 794). The most instructive, however, is the passage in Lactantius iv 6, 5: 'Sibylla Erythraea in carminis sui principio, quod a summo Deo exorsa est, filium Dei ducem et imperatorem omnium his versibus praedicat: παντοτρόφον κτίστην, ὅστις γλυκὺ πνεῦμα ἅπασιν κάτθετο, χηγητῆρα θεῶν πάντων ἐποίησεν (Geffcken, fragm. 1, verses 5–6). 'Et rursus in fine: ἄλλον ἔδωκε θεὸς πιστοῖς ἀνδρέσσι γεραίρειν' (= approximately *Sib.* iii 775). 'Et alia Sibylla praecipit hunc oportere cognosci: αὐτόν σου γίνωσκε θεὸν, θεοῦ υἱὸν ἐόντα' (= *Sib.* viii 329). Thus it is said quite plainly here that the proem belongs to Book iii.

226. Geffcken (*Komposition und Enstehungszeit*, pp. 69–75) considered this passage to be 'spurious', i.e. one that was never part of a Sibylline manuscript but was fabricated *ad hoc* by a Christian author to serve as a prologue to the oracles. However, nothing in these fragments is necessarily Christian. On the contrary, their content is very similar to iii 1–45 (Collins, BAAJ, p. 153), which Geffcken, *op. cit.*, pp. 15 ff., thought should be retained at the start of Book iii in place of the fragments. It was precisely because of this similarity that Nikiprowetzky, *op. cit.*, pp. 60–6, wished to retain *both* the fragments *and* verses 1–96 in Book iii, and that Kurfess, in Hennecke and Schneemelcher, *N.T. Apocrypha*, ed. R. McL. Wilson (ET 1965), II, p. 707, proposed that the fragments and iii 1–92 together should be treated as the missing original Jewish Book ii of the collection. Whether or not the fragments are an integral part of Book iii, there is no reason to doubt their Jewish origin from before the end of the first century A.D., when Theophilus quoted them. It remains most likely that, if the argument given above, p. 630, that iii 1–96 did *not* belong to the original Book iii, is accepted, these fragments should be assigned to Book iii as the missing introduction to that Book.

assigned to the original Book ii.[227] At any rate, the contents also confirm that verses iii 1–92 are not part of Book iii .[228] It is difficult to pronounce on their origin. At least four passages, which may not be connected, can be distinguished (iii 1–45; 46–62; 63–74; 75–92). Nothing can be said about the date of origin of iii 1–45 except that it shows similarities to the Theophilus fragments, but also to the Jewish Pseudo-Orphic fragments (see below, p. 661) and to Philo.[229] iii 46–62 reads: 'when Rome rules also over Egypt, the great kingdom of the immortal king shall appear among men; a holy king shall come who shall possess the sceptre over the whole earth eternally. Then shall there be pitiless anger of Latin men; three shall destroy Rome with a wretched fate' (iii 46–52). Most critics have interpreted this to mean that the author expected the coming of the Messiah during the second triumvirate (42–32 B.C.), and this remains probable even though the deliberate obscurity of the language leaves open many other possibilities.[230]

The passage that follows (iii 63–74) is certainly not connected with what precedes it. It begins by saying that Beliar will come 'from the Sebastenes' ($\dot{\epsilon}\kappa$ $\Sigma\epsilon\beta\alpha\sigma\tau\eta\nu\hat{\omega}\nu$) and will cause an uproar in nature with marvellous power, will raise the dead and perform many signs. He will delude the Hebrews, both the chosen and those without the law who have not yet heard the word of God.

'Beliar' is clearly Antichrist. $\Sigma\epsilon\beta\alpha\sigma\tau\eta\nu\hat{\omega}\nu$ most probably refers to the inhabitants of Samaria, which was renamed 'Sebaste' in 25 B.C., although a unique use of the word to mean 'from the Sebastoi', i.e. from the line of Augustus, cannot be ruled out. If the reference to Samaria is correct, the prophecy is evidence of Jewish expectation of the emergence of an Antichrist figure from that place, after 25 B.C. but before the rise of a Christian tradition about Simon Magus as a superhuman figure. There is no reason to believe that the passage is of Christian origin.[231] If the reference is to the line of Augustus, Beliar is

227. A. Kurfess in Hennecke and Schneemelcher, *N.T. Apocrypha*, ed. R. McL. Wilson (ET 1965), II, p. 707. See above, n. 226.

228. See, *contra*, Nikiprowetzky, *op. cit.*, pp. 60–6.

229. J. J. Collins, *Sibylline Oracles*, p. 64.

230. Reference to the triumvirs is accepted by Geffcken, Jeanmaire, Kurfess, Volz and Collins. The chief other possibilities are: (1) this is a later Christian interpolation referring to the birth of Christ under Augustus (Bousset, 'Sibyllen', HHRE XVIII, p. 273)—not very likely; (2) the three Romans are a different triad from those of 42–32 B.C., either the Gracchi (?!) or Marius, Sulla and Cinna (Lanchester), or Pompey, Caesar and Crassus (Volz); and (3) the reference to three Roman rulers as bringers of ruin on Rome is simply a traditional motif in Jewish apocalyptic which reappears in many later texts and therefore has no particular historical referent (Nikiprowetzky).

231. In favour of a Christian origin and a direct reference to Simon Magus are Jülicher, ThLZ (1896), p. 379, and Geffcken, *Komposition und Entstehungszeit*, p. 15. Against this, see Nikiprowetzky, *op. cit.*, pp. 140–1, 223–5; cf. pp. 224–5 for the not very

most likely to be identified with Nero as in *Ascension of Isaiah* iii 1.[232] In that case the passage must be dated after A.D. 70.

The final section, iii 75–92, is as it stands closely connected with the preceding prophecy, but may well be considerably earlier in origin, in which case the present connection was brought about simply by the fact that it, too, describes the signs of the end-time. According to this section, a woman who is a widow will rule the whole world. She will sink gold, silver, brass and iron into the sea, but God will destroy earth, sea and heaven by fire. The identity of the widow is much debated. The most plausible hypothesis—and it is no more than that, for the supposed parallels put forward by Tarn and Jeanmaire are very weak—is that the widow is to be identified with Cleopatra, in which case the prophecy belongs to the same period as the second section, iii 46–52, i.e. the period of the second triumvirate.[233] But it may also be that the widow was a mythological figure of the end of time who cannot be further described.[234]

4. With respect to Book iv[235] a far-reaching consensus has developed among scholars concerning its Jewish authorship and a date of about A.D. 80 (e.g. Blass, Geffcken, Bousset, Lanchester). This is probably the correct view, for there is nothing specifically Christian in the Book. The Sibyl's tone is more militant than in the previous Book.

---

considerable early Jewish evidence outside the Sibyllines for such an expectation.

232. R. H. Charles, transl., *The Ascension of Isaiah (1900)*, p. lxviii. See also W. Bousset, *The Anti-Christ Legend*, transl. A. H. Keane (1896); Collins, *Sibylline Oracles*, pp. 86–7.

233. No other connections between the two sections can be discovered. In favour of the Cleopatra identification, see W. W. Tarn, 'Alexander Helios and the Golden Age', JRS 22 (1932), p. 142; H. Jeanmaire, *La Sibylle et la Retour de l'Age d'Or* (1939), p. 210, with the criticisms of Nikiprowetzky, *op. cit.*, p. 146. There is no strong objection to identification with Cleopatra, and the hypothesis is strengthened by her association with Isis, who underwent an annual ritual bereavement (Collins, *Sibylline Oracles*, pp. 69–70). Other less plausible theories are: (1) the widow is to be identified with Rome (C. Alexandre, *Excursus ad Sibyllina* (1856), p. 517; Lanchester in Charles, APOT II, p. 371). Against this, it would be odd to describe the triumphant city as bereaved even when at the height of her power, and it seems forced to take the description as either anticipatory or descriptive of Roman sufferings in the Civil Wars. (2) The widow is a representative of the collective Messiah or the new Jerusalem (Nikiprowetzky, *op. cit.*, pp. 86, 149). Against this, it again seems strange to describe the city thus at a moment of glory, though it may perhaps refer to the belief that Israel will rule although afflicted. (3) The widow is to be identified with Zenobia. This is hardly possible unless the passage is taken to be Christian, as by Bousset, HHRE XVIII (1906), p. 275.

234. This was Schürer's conclusion in 1909, which was followed by A. Rzach, RE IIA (1923), col. 2131.

235. For the content and English translation, see Lanchester in Charles, APOT II, pp. 372 f., 393–7; J. J. Collins in Charlesworth, OTP I, pp. 381–9. Cf. also Rzach in RE IIA (1923), cols. 2131–4; J. J. Collins, 'The Place of the Fourth Sibyl in the Development of the Jewish Sibyllina', JJS 25 (1974), pp. 365–80; V. Nikiprowetzky, 'Reflexions sur Quelques Problèmes du Quatrième et du Cinquième Livre des Oracles Sibyllins', HUCA 43 (1972), pp. 29–58.

Calling herself at the start the prophetess of the true God, she proclaims on his instruction all kinds of calamities through war, earthquake, and other natural phenomena to the cities, lands and peoples of Asia and Europe. Unless they repent, God will destroy the whole world by fire, and will then raise men from the dead and sit in judgement, banishing the ungodly to Tartarus and granting new life on earth to the pious.

Nothing in these words is specifically reminiscent of the Christian sphere of thought, whereas it would hardly have been possible for a Christian author to avoid mentioning the name of Christ in a work on eschatology. Nor is there sufficient basis for assuming that the author was an Essene[236] for the polemic against animal sacrifice in verse 29 is probably only directed against gentile sacrifice,[237] and the baptism to which the gentiles are summoned in verse 165 is either Jewish proselyte baptism (cf. above, p. 174) or, more probably, a baptism of repentance like that provided by John the Baptist.[238] Many critics, particularly Geffcken, have supposed that, as in Book iii, the author has accommodated gentile oracles on a large scale. It is not probable that this occurred to such an extent on the same grounds as there. The fact itself, that gentile oracles have been used here, is of course beyond doubt.[239] Two verses of the Book (97–8) are twice mentioned already by Strabo (i 3, 7 and xii 2, 4) as oracles.

236. An Essene origin was posited by Ewald and Hilgenfeld and is accepted by Lanchester. A. Peretti, 'Ecchi di dottrine esseniche negli Oracoli Sibillini giudaici', La Parola del Passato 17 (1962), pp. 247–95, attempted to confirm the hypothesis by pointing to similarities between the Qumran documents and the Sibyllines, particularly *Sib.* iv. The similarities are however not sufficient to demonstrate any direct connection, cf. B. Noack, 'Are the Essenes Referred to in the Sibylline Oracles?', Studia Theologica 17 (1963), pp. 90–102; V. Nikiprowetzky, *art. cit.*, pp. 35–58.

237. Cf. Nikiprowetzky, *art. cit.*, pp. 34–5; *idem*, *La Troisième Sibylle* (1970), pp. 233–5, based on the parallel attacks on heathen cults to be found in *Sib.* iii 30–2; 564–5; 605–6. It has been argued strongly by J. J. Collins, 'The Place of the Fourth Sibyl in the Development of the Jewish Sibyllina', JJS 25 (1974), pp. 366–9, that *Sib.* iv 24–30 shows a radically different attitude to the *Jewish* Temple than that found in the other Sibylline Books. He argues that the rest of the Book, particularly verse 116, does not seem concerned about the sack of the Temple in A.D. 70 and that it is therefore significant that the author failed to distinguish the Jewish Temple from others when launching his general attack on bloody sacrifices. If Collins is correct, *Sib.* iv is unique among Hellenistic Jewish writings in this respect. It is however only possible to demonstrate the author's lack of concern with the Jerusalem Temple and it remains most probable that verse 29 is an attack upon pagan temples and sacrifices only.

238. Cf. J. Thomas, *Le mouvement baptiste en Palestine et Syrie* (1935), pp. 46–52; A. Jaubert, *La notion de l'alliance* (1963), p. 331; Peretti, *art. cit.* (n. 236), pp. 256–95; Nikiprowetzky, *art. cit.*, pp. 46–7.

239. The use in verses 49–102 and 173–92 of an early Hellenistic oracle about the ten generations since the flood and the four empires of the world is suggested by Geffcken, *Komposition und Entstehungszeit*, pp. 18–19. Cf. D. Flusser, 'The Four Empires in the Fourth Sibyl and in the Book of Daniel', Israel Oriental Studies 2 (1972), pp. 148–75; Collins, *art. cit.* (n. 235), pp. 370–6.

Decisive for the determination of the date of composition is the fact that the destruction of Jerusalem (115–27) and the eruption of Vesuvius of A.D. 79 (130–6) are presupposed.[240] The author also believed with many of his contemporaries in Nero's flight across the Euphrates and his impending return (117–24, 137–9). Accordingly, the oracle must have been composed about A.D. 80 or not much later. Nothing is known of its place of origin.[241]

Patristic citation of this book begins already with Justin.[242]

5. Book v has evoked the same sort of divergent opinions among scholars in assigning a date to the Jewish sections as did Book iii.[243] Friedlieb ascribed the whole of Book v to a Jew from the beginning of Hadrian's reign; similarly Badt, to a Jew of about A.D. 130. Geffcken, *Komposition und Entstehungszeit*, pp. 22 ff., regarded Book v 52–531, at least, to be the work of a Jew about A.D. 80 or a few years earlier. Zahn thought that he could distinguish the work of two Jewish authors, one of whom wrote in about A.D. 71, and the other in about A.D. 120, whereas the whole was edited by a Christian in about 150. Bousset also distinguished two layers of tradition. Schürer in 1909 judged that the book is not a unified whole but a loose conglomerate of different kinds of pieces which therefore cannot be assigned an origin or date in any detail. This opinion was followed by S. Szekely, *Bibliotheca Apocrypha*

240. On the eruption of Vesuvius, cf. S. Herrlich, 'Die antike Überlieferung über den Vesuv-Ausbruch im Jahre 79', Klio 4 (1904), pp. 209–26; E. T. Merrill, 'Notes on the eruption of Vesuvius in 79 A.D.', AJA 22 (1918), pp. 304 ff.; AJA 24 (1920), pp. 262–8; G. B. Alfano and J. Friedlaender, *Die Geschichte des Vesuves* (1929), pp. 11 ff.; H. Sigurdsson, S. Cashdollar and S. R. J. Sparks, 'The eruption of Vesuvius in A.D. 79', AJA 86 (1982), pp. 39–51. The main source is Pliny, *Epist.* vi 16 and 20. The eruption began on the 24th of August. The year is determined by Dio Cass. lxvi 21, 1: 'in the first year of the reign of Titus'. Eusebius, *Chron.*, ed. Schoene, II, pp. 158 ff. (2095), cf. Helm, ed., GCS, Eusebius VII, 2nd ed., p. 189. Plutarch also mentions that the eruption of Vesuvius, like many similar misfortunes, had been foretold by the Sibyl (*De sera numinis vindicta*, p. 566E, *De Pythiae oraculis*, p. 398E). However, a connection between these gentile oracles and the Jewish Sibyl under discussion cannot be proved.

241. The book is more militant than *Sib.* iii and v, cf. P. Dalbert, *Die Theologie der hell.-jüd. Missionsliteratur* (1954), p. 109. This may suggest a different place of origin but might just be due to a different compiler or date. In favour of an origin in the Jordan valley or in Syria is the emphasis on baptism, cf. Thomas, *op. cit.*, p. 223. No good arguments can be put forward for any other place of origin, despite suggestions of Asia Minor (J. B. Frey, DB suppl. I (1928), col. 427).

242. Justin, *Apol.* i 20 (refers to *Sib.* iv 172–7). Clement of Alexandria, *Protrept.* iv 50 and 62. *Paedag.* ii 10, 99; iii 3, 15. *Constit. Apostol.* v 7. Pseudo-Justin, *Cohort.* 16. Lactantius vii 23, 4. *Idem, De ira dei* 23 (three passages).

243. Cf. the summary of the contents and the English translation by Lanchester, in Charles, APOT II, pp. 373, 397–406; Collins, in Charlesworth, OTP I, pp. 393–405. See also Geffcken, *Komposition und Entstehungszeit*, pp. 22–30; Rzach, RE IIA (1923), cols. 2134–40; A. Kurfess, 'Zum 5. Buch der Oracula Sibyllina', RhM 29 (1956), pp. 225–41; V. Nikiprowetzky, *art. cit.*, pp. 30–3; Collins, *Sibylline Oracles*, pp. 73–95; *idem*, BAAJ, pp. 122–8.

(1913), p. 145. Rzach, RE IIA 2 (1923), cols. 2134–40, assigned various sections to older prophecies but opined that most of the book was produced under Domitian, while v 1–50 was produced under M. Antoninus and verse 51 does not belong to the collection at all. Variants of these views have been adopted by all more recent scholars.

The dating of the work depends most on whether the book as it stands should be considered a unity. It is likely that the answer here, unlike the case of Book iii, should be affirmative (Geffcken, Lanchester, Collins). Book v may be divided into the following six sections: 1–51, 52–110, 111–178, 179–285, 286–434, 435–530. Of these, the middle four (52–434) consist of four oracles against the nations, all of which concern the return of Nero as an eschatological figure, his confrontation with a saviour figure, and a terrible destruction (Collins). The opening section has less obviously in common with these oracles (1–51), treating Nero, for instance, as a purely historical person. It may therefore have been added at a different time. The book is certainly of Jewish origin because the sections in which Jewish interests and views come more or less clearly to the foreground are found throughout the book (cf. especially verses 260–85, 328–32, 344–60, 397–413, 414–33). Explicit praise of Jews and Judaism is in fact markedly more obvious in this book than in Books iii and iv, where the gentile guise of the author is rarely shed. Only one Christian interpolation, the remarkable passage (256–9) in which 'an excellent man coming from heaven who spread out his hands on the fruit-bearing tree', i.e. Jesus, was identified with Joshua (Jesus the son of Nave) is probably Christian.[244]

The following criteria can be provided for dating the work. The main prophecies must have been written after A.D. 70, both because the destruction of the Temple in Jerusalem is lamented (150, 397–413) and because of the portrayal of Nero's imminent return. No *terminus ante quem* can be given, although a date before the end of the first century A.D. is likely. The introductory section (1–51) was composed either after the reign of M. Aurelius or, if verse 51 is a later addition,

---

244. 5:256–9. Cf. P. Volz, *Eschatologie der jüdischen Gemeinde* (1934), p. 57; B. Noack, 'Der hervorragende Mann und der beste der Hebräer (Bemerkungen zu Or. Sib. v, 256–259)', ASTI 3 (1964), pp. 122–46. See, *contra*, Nikiprowetzky, *art. cit.*, pp. 58–65, with the identification of the man in question as an entirely Jewish Messiah who amalgamated the attributes of Moses with those of Joshua. According to this hypothesis, this passage also will be Jewish. In verse 258 the future στήσει, conjectured by Geffcken, *Komposition und Entstehungszeit*, p. 29, in place of the manuscript στῆσεν, should perhaps be read (so Nikiprowetzky, *art. cit.*, p. 65, n. 116, against A. Kurfess, *Sibyllinische Weissagungen* (1951), *ad loc.*, and J. J. Collins in Charlesworth, OTP I, p. 399). Also taken by some scholars as Christian passages are verses 62–72 (Bousset, basing the hypothesis on θεοχρίστους in verse 68, which is however quite possible for a Jewish author), and verses 228–46 (Geffcken). In contrast, Str.-B. I, pp. 12–13, take *only* verse 257 as Christian.

during the reign of Hadrian but before A.D. 130.[245] An Egyptian origin is usually proposed for the Book on the grounds of the prominence of Egypt and its towns (60–114, 179–99, 458–89, 484–511) and the claim (53) that the Sibyl is a friend of Isis. Two of the main oracles however lack any Egyptian reference (111–178 and 286–434). It is likely enough that the Book incorporates oracles from an origin different from that of the redactor, and that either an Egyptian redactor used oracles culled from elsewhere or Egyptian oracles were used by a non-Egyptian compiler.[246] Quotations from this book are first found in Clement of Alexandria.[247]

6. Of the remaining Books, vi, vii and viii have been generally and correctly taken as Christian.[248] Books i and ii, which originally formed a single Book, are considered by many to contain Jewish sections re-worked by a Christian. Against this, the complete lack of attestation of the 'Jewish' sections in the Church Fathers of the first three centuries speaks rather for a late origin, in which case it is more likely that they are Christian.[249]

245. Verse 51 refers to M. Aurelius, while verses 46–50 allude in optimistic and friendly terms to Hadrian, which would be unlikely after the Bar Kochba revolt.

246. In the final section (435–530), which refers unambiguously to Egypt, some interpreters have seen a reference to the building and destruction of the Onias Temple (492–511). The idealized picture, based on Isaiah 19:19, is however that of a temple of the most high god built by priests of Serapis in the past and destroyed by the Ethiopians rather than the Romans (Geffcken). The passage may nonetheless also have found a point of departure in the history of the Leontopolis temple (Collins, *Sibylline Oracles*, pp. 93–4, 163). Important for the textual history of this section is the fourth-century papyrus fragment published in G. Vitelli, *Papiri Greco-Egizii* (P.FCor.) III (1915), no. 389.

247. Clement of Alexandria, *Protrept.* iv 50; *Paedag.* ii 10, 99.

248. So A. Kurfess in Hennecke and Schneemelcher, *N.T. Apocrypha*, ed. R. McL. Wilson (ET 1965), II, p. 707. Book viii (217–50) contains the famous acrostic also given in Constantine's *Oratio ad sanctorum coetum* 18 : 'Ἰησοῦς Χριστὸς θεοῦ υἱὸς σωτὴρ σταυρός. Cf. Rzach, RE IIA.2 (1923), cols. 2140–6. It is likely that viii 1–216 preserves a Jewish oracle dated to the reign of M. Aurelius in the mid-second century A.D. (Collins, BAAJ, p. 128).

249. The oldest witness is Constantine's *Oratio ad sanctorum coetum* 18 : ἡ τοίνυν Ἐρυθραία Σίβυλλα φάσκουσα ἑαυτὴν ἕκτῃ γενεᾷ, μετὰ τὸν κατακλυσμὸν, γενέσθαι. Cf. *Sib.* i 283 ff. If *Sib.* xi is a first-century A.D. work (see below, n. 251) this argument from silence about *Sib.* i and ii becomes less compelling. The most persistent advocate of Jewish sections within *Sib.* i and ii has been A. Kurfess, 'Oracula Sibyllina I/II', ZNW 40 (1941), pp. 151–65; *idem*, in Hennecke and Schneemelcher, *N.T. Apocrypha* II, p. 707. In Book i, Kurfess holds verses 1–323 as a Jewish composition from the early first century A.D., apart from a Christian interpolation in verses 137–46. Geffcken, *Komposition und Entstehungszeit*, p. 50, suggested a Phrygian origin for this Jewish section because of verses 196–8 and 261 f. In Book ii, all of verses 6–33, 34–44, 56–176, 184–237, 252–63 and 265–310 *may* be Jewish, but it is scarcely possible to separate the Christian and Jewish elements. Cf. Kurfess, ZNW 38 (1939), pp. 171–81, on *Sib.* ii 34–153, and especially the lengthy insert from Pseudo-Phocylides in verses 56–148. On Books i and ii in general, see A. Rzach, RE IIA (1923), cols. 2146–52; J. J. Collins in Charlesworth, OTP I, pp. 330–4. Translation in Hennecke and Schneemelcher, *op. cit.*, II, pp. 709–19 (*Sib.* i 323–400; ii 1–347 only) and J. J. Collins in Charlesworth, OTP I, pp. 335–53.

Books xi-xiv differ from the others in that their contents are not religious but political. The lists of emperors were apparently constantly updated over the centuries. Book xi offers a mixed series of historical reminiscences particularly from the history of Egypt to the time of Cleopatra. Book xii goes as far as the period of Severus Alexander; Book xiii deals with only a short time-span, approximately A.D. 241–65. Book xiv is fairly worthless. The author 'knows nothing but names of peoples, countries and cities, and mixes these up as he wishes' (Geffcken). It is impossible to disprove the hypothesis put forward by Kurfess that all Books xi-xiv are basically Jewish, but in that case the loyalty of the author to Rome is strikingly more prominent than his Judaism.[250] This attitude to Rome makes the probability of an early, i.e. first century A.D., date for Book xi rather remote and it is better to ascribe it to the third century A.D. along with Book xii, to which it is closely linked.[251] A further treatment of the later evolution of Sibyllism is not part of this work.

The most ancient author to have quoted a Jewish Sibylline Book (and indeed the story of the building of the tower of Babel, *Sib.* iii, 97 ff.) appears to have been Alexander Polyhistor in about 80–40 B.C. Cf. the passage from his Χαλδαϊκά in Eusebius, *Chron.*, ed. Schoene, I, col. 23 = *Syncellus*, ed. Dindorf, I, p. 81 = Cyril, *Adv. Julian.*, ed. Spanh., 9. The almost identical quotation in Josephus, *Ant.* i 4, 3 (115–18), (= Euseb., *Praep. ev.* ix 15, and *Onomast.*, ed. Klostermann, GCS Eusebius III, p. 40), has been copied from Alexander Polyhistor without the mention of his name. Cf. above, p. 637 and note 174.

It is possible that Alexander did not obtain this quotation from the Jewish Sibyl but from Babylonian-Greek Sibylline poetry, cf. Geffcken (NGGW (1900), pp. 88–102), Bousset (ZNW 3 (1902), pp. 26–9) and A. Peretti, *La Sibilla Babilonese* (1942), pp. 289–92 and passim. If so, the Babylonian Sibyl will have been mediated to Alexander through Berossus, cf. Jacoby, FGrH 273, F81, with Komm., p. 289. However there are good arguments to suggest that the source used by Alexander was a Jewish and not a Babylonian Sibyl. In the first place, nothing is

250. Cf. Rzach in RE IIA (1923), cols. 2152–65; A. Kurfess, 'Oracula Sibyllina XI (IX)-XIV (XII) nicht christlich, sondern jüdisch', ZRGG 7 (1955), pp. 270–2; *idem, Sibyllinische Weissagungen* (1951), pp. 333–41; H. Dechent, *Über das erste, zweite und elfte Buch der sibyllinische Weissagungen* (1873), pp. 49–88. Cf. introduction and English translation by Collins in Charlesworth, OTP I, pp. 430–68. On Book xii, see especially Geffcken, 'Römische Kaiser im Volksmunde', NGGW (1901), pp. 183–95; *idem, Komposition und Entstehungszeit*, pp. 56–8; Bousset, 'Sibyllen', HHRE XVIII (1906), p. 278.

251. A first-century A.D. date was favoured by Dechent, *op. cit.*, pp. 49–88, followed by Bousset, Kurfess and Collins. A second- or third-century A.D. date is supported by the reference in verse 161 to the fall of the Parthians in Mesopotamia, which is more likely to be a prophecy *ex eventu* after the campaigns of Septimius Severus, or at least Trajan, than a genuine prophecy about the future. Cf. Rzach, RE IIA (1923), col. 2154.

otherwise known of a Babylonian legend of the building of the tower (A. Jeremias, *Das A.T. im Lichte des alten Orients* (²1906), p. 178). It is unlikely that such a legend was part of Berossus, for Alexander Polyhistor does not ascribe it to him in the extensive passages in which he reproduces Berossus (given in Euseb., *Chron.*, ed. Schoene, I, cols. 7 ff.). Although such an argument from silence is naturally hazardous, it is more likely that Alexander inserted the legend of the building of the tower according to the Sibyl into the material of Berossus. The pagan writer of the second or early third century A.D., Abydenus, is not an independent witness for a Babylonian tradition of the building of the tower, for in the passage in question (Euseb., *Chron.*, ed. Schoene, I, cols. 33–4 = Euseb., *Praep. ev.* ix 14, 2), as elsewhere, he fully depends on Alexander Polyhistor. Secondly, in his Sibylline quotation Alexander Polyhistor gives all the characteristic features of *Sib.* iii 97 ff. (Euseb.: ὁμοφώνων ὄντων... ὅπως εἰς τὸν οὐρανὸν ἀναβῶσι..., the collapse of the tower caused by winds (this is a Jewish tradition, cf. the Book of Jubilees 10:26), ... the naming of the city of Babylon). The dependence of Alexander Polyhistor on the Jewish Sibyl is suggested by the fact that in both (Alexander Polyhistor in Eusebius, following the Armenian), the story of the battle between the Titans and the sons of Chronos follows the tradition of the building of the tower, although it is also possible to claim this relationship for the Chaldean Sibyl. But if this was the case, one Sibyl would become a simple double of the other, and it would have to be assumed that the Jewish Sibyllist copied from a gentile source, namely the Babylonian Sibyl. This would mean that the Jewish author has reproduced from a gentile source the story of the building of the tower well known to him from Jewish tradition, which is unlikely. Thirdly, the fact that in Alexander Polyhistor's quotation (following what is probably the better text of Josephus, which is confirmed by Abydenus as cited by Eusebius), 'the gods' sent the winds (οἱ δὲ θεοὶ ἀνέμους ἐπιπέμψαντες ἀνετρέψαν τὸν πύργον), points to a gentile source. But since Alexander Polyhistor freely reproduced only the contents of the Sibylline prophecy, he might reasonably have changed the immortal God of the Sibyl to gods, just as Eusebius did the opposite in giving Alexander's text and changing the gods to the one God. If Eusebius, who wished to give the text of Alexander, permitted himself such freedom, the same practice of Alexander Polyhistor, who intended to reproduce only the contents, is not at all surprising. See K. Mras, '"Babylonische" und "erythräische" Sibylle', *Wiener Studien* 29 (1907), pp. 25–49; P. Schnabel, *Berossus und die babylonisch-hellenistische Literatur* (1923), pp. 69–93; V. Nikiprowetzky, *La Troisième Sibylle* (1970), pp. 17–36.

The question whether Vergil was influenced by the Jewish Sibyl in his fourth Eclogue is at least worthy of consideration. According to verses

11–12, the poem was written during the consulate of C. Asinius Pollio, hence in 40 B.C., apparently after peace had been concluded between Antonius and Octavian at Brundisium. The poet sees the beginning of a time of peace following the confusion of the civil wars, even of a golden age. 'The last era of the Cumaean poem has already come' (verse 4). 'O pure Lucina, look kindly on the boy as he is born, he with whom the iron race ends and the golden race begins for the whole world' (verses 8–10). 'Already under your consulate, O Pollio, will this glorious time begin' (verses 11–12). 'Under your leadership all lingering traces of our offences will disappear' (verses 13–14). 'He [i.e. the boy] will receive the life of the gods' (verse 15: 'ille deum vitam accipiet') 'and will rule the calmed world with ancestral virtues' (verse 17). There follows a description of the golden era, in which nature, in particular, bestows its gifts in a marvellous way. Christian theology identified 'the boy' with Christ from early times and consequently esteemed Vergil highly as a theologian. (The first certain appearance of this identification is by Constantine, *Oratio ad coetum sanctorum* 19–20, and then by St. Augustine, *Epist. ad Rom. inc. expos.* 3, cf. *Epist.* 137, 12, who attributes the prophecy not to Vergil himself but to his Sibylline source. Cf. also Euseb., *Vit. Const.* v 19; Lactant., *Inst. div.* vii 24; Augustine, *Civ. Dei* x 27.) The reality is clearly different but nonetheless very difficult to pin down. Most scholars agree that Vergil did have in mind a real child, but his identity remains much disputed. The boy may have been a child of Pollio, granted by Vergil a leading position in the new age in honour of his father, cf. Servius in *Servii in Vergilii carmina Commentarii*, rec. *Thilo et Hagen* III.1 (1887), p. 46. If so, he may be identified with Asinius Gallus, consul in 8 B.C., or with a son of Pollio called Saloninus, for whose existence the only evidence is the reference by Servius. Other plausible suggestions have been an expected child of the marriage of Antonius and Octavia, or of Octavian and Scribonia; in favour of such eulogy of an offspring that might not, and in fact did not, appear are traces of the style of the *epithalamium* in the poem. Numerous less plausible references have also been put forward: to a child of Antonius and Cleopatra (hardly suitable for a Roman audience), to the offspring of Octavia by her first husband Marcellus (although the younger Marcellus had probably already been born and the evidence that she was pregnant with another child by her first husband at the time of her marriage to Antonius is not strong), or to Caesar Octavianus himself, cf. *Aeneid* vi 792–5 (even though portrayal of Octavian as a baby would be odd and this identification smacks of hindsight engendered by his later career as Augustus). Other scholars prefer to posit a less specific reference. Vergil may refer to an unknown boy to be favoured by fate, or to a personification of the golden age, or even to his newly-born literary hopes as he pondered writing the

Aeneid. (Cf. R. Coleman, ed., *Vergil Eclogues* (1977), pp. 150–2, and numerous works cited in the bibliography given below.) However, even if a meaning from contemporary history could be firmly established, the question would not be settled whether or not Vergil's description of the golden era rested exclusively on gentile sources. He himself says that this age had been promised by a Sibylline song (for the latter is without doubt the 'Cumaeum carmen'). It is reasonable therefore to think of the Jewish Sibyl. On the other hand, it must be admitted that all Vergil's description can be explained on the basis of pagan traditions, and that in the case of direct dependence on the extant Jewish Sibyl, lines more in accord with *Sib.* iii 787–94 (= Isa. 11) would have been expected. Of particular importance is the fact that it is not the inauguration of the golden age that is ascribed to the expected child, but only a leading position in it. If therefore verse 4, which refers unequivocally to the Cumaean Sibyl, was genuinely based on a Sibylline oracle, it was not one of those still extant, and therefore not necessarily Jewish rather than pagan. There is nothing in the poem that could not possibly have come from the Roman Sibylline traditions. However, a general influence from Jewish prophetic literature should not be ruled out. It was quite possible for Vergil to have read the LXX of Isaiah, though the similarities which can be noted are too vague for it to be shown that he did so. For a dependence on Isaiah, cf. J. B. Mayor, W. Warde Fowler and R. S. Conway, *Virgil's Messianic Eclogue* (1907); T. F. Royds, *Virgil and Isaiah* (1918). It is at any rate probable that the allusiveness of his references to the golden age show Vergil to have been relying on his audience's knowledge of a current prophecy, in which case it was probably contained within the Sibylline corpus, since stylistic similarities between Vergil's prophecy and those of the Sibyl seem to be deliberate. There is no reason to doubt that *Sib.* iii in an early form (i.e. at least without iii 63–74, which was composed after Vergil wrote) was already to be found in that corpus by 40 B.C. along with other Jewish material.

Cf. on Vergil's *Eclogues* in general: Coleman, R., *Vergil Eclogues* (1977); Williams, R. D., *Virgil, The Eclogues and Georgics* (1979); and further works cited in the bibliographies of R. D. Williams, *Virgil* (1967) and *Proceedings of the Virgil Society* (1976–7).

On the fourth eclogue, see:
Jeanmaire, H., 'Le Politique Religieuse d'Antoine et de Cléopâtre', *Revue Archéologique* 5th ser. 19 (1924), pp. 241–61.
Norden, E., *Die Geburt des Kindes* (1924) (with bibliography).
Austin, R. G., 'Virgil and the Sibyl', CQ 21 (1927), pp. 100–05.
Wagenvoort, H., *Virgils vierte Ekloge und das Sidus Iulium* (Mededeelingen der Kon. Akademie) (1929; ET 1956).
Carcopino, J., *Virgile et la Mystère de la IVe Églogue* (1930) (emphasizing the Pythagorean background; cf. pp. 69–72 on the Sibyllines).
Rose, H. J., *The Eclogues of Vergil* (1942).
Kurfess, A., 'Vergil und die Sibyllinen', ZRGG 3 (1951), pp. 253–7.

Kurfess, A., 'Vergils vierte Ekloge und die Oracula Sibyllina', HJ 73 (1954), pp. 120–7.
Kurfess, A., 'Vergils 4. Ekloge und Christliche Sibyllen', Gymnasium 62 (1955), pp. 110–12.
DuQuesnay, I. M. le M., 'Vergil's Fourth Eclogue', Papers of the Liverpool Latin Seminar (1976), pp. 25–99.
Nisbet, R.G.M., 'Virgil's Fourth Eclogue: Easterners and Westerners', Bull. Inst. Class. Stud., London 25 (1978), pp. 59–78.

For further bibliography on the fourth eclogue, see Norden, *op. cit.*, and, for works between 1940 and 1973, *The Classical World Bibliography of Vergil* (1978), pp. 7–8, 38–40, 85–6.

On the use of the Sibyllines by the Church Fathers, cf. the testimonia collected in Alexandre's first ed., vol. II (1856), pp. 254–311; O. Stählin in W. v. Christ and W. Schmid, *Gesch. der Griech. Lit.* II.1 (1920; repr. 1959), pp. 616–17; P. Dalbert, *Die Theologie der hell.-jüd. Missionsliteratur* (1954), pp. 110–23; and especially B. Thompson, 'Patristic Use of the Sibylline Oracles', *The Review of Religion* 6 (1952), pp. 115–36, with lists of patristic references on pp. 130–6.

It is doubtful whether Clement of Rome quoted the Sibyllines, despite Ps.-Justin, *Quaest. et respons. ad orthodoxos*, quaest. 74 (*Corp. apolog.*, ed. Otto, ed. 3, vol. V, p. 108). Cf. J. B. Lightfoot, *The Apostolic Fathers, Part I : S. Clement of Rome* I (1890), pp. 178–80.

Hermas, *Vis.* ii 4, mentions only the Sibyl, not the Sibylline Books, and is exceptional among the patristic writers in not taking the Sibyl as an inspired pagan witness for Christian doctrine but rather identifying with the Church the old woman who is described as appearing to be the Sibyl.

On the other hand, quotations from the Sibyllines themselves are given in the apocryphal Pauline remarks quoted in Clement of Alexandria, *Strom.* vi 5, 42–3 (on the writing which Clement quotes here, cf. below, p. 654, for the remarks on Hystaspes).

Gnostic use of the Sibyllines is recorded in Hippolyt., *Philosophum.* iv 6.

Cf. further: Justin, *Apol.* i 20; Athenagoras, *Leg.* 30; Theophilus, *Ad Autol.* ii 3; 31; 36; Tertullian, *Ad nationes* ii 12, 36; Pseudo-Melito, *Apol.* 4 (in Otto, *Corp. apolog.* IX, pp. 425, 463 ff.); Pseudo-Justin, *Cohortat. ad Graec.* 16; 37–8; *Const. apost.* v 7. Constantine, *Oratio ad sanct. coet.* 18–19, quoted among other things the acrostic of Jesus Christ, *Sib.* viii 217–50.

Quotations are most frequent in Clement of Alexandria and Lactantius.

Clement of Alexandria quotes: (1) The proem: *Protr.* vi 71 = *Strom.* v 14, 108; *Protr.* viii 37 = *Strom.* v 14, 116; *Strom.* iii 3, 14. (2) Book iii: *Protr.* vi 70; vii 74. (3) Book iv: *Protr.* iv 50 and 62; *Paedag.* ii 10, 99; iii 3, 15. (4) Book v: *Protr.* iv 50; *Paedag.* ii 10, 99. Cf. also *Strom.* i 21, 108; 132.

It will be seen from these statistics that, apart from the proem,

Clement knew only the three Books which are considered here on internal grounds to be Jewish. Other patristic quotations until Clement also refer only to these books. They therefore clearly form the oldest Jewish corpus of Sibylline oracles.

Lactantius quotes about fifty passages from the Sibyllines, mostly from Book viii, next from Book iii, only occasionally from Books i, ii, iv, v, vi, and vii, and not at all from the others. Cf. the material in Struve, *Fragmenta librorum Sibyllinorum quae apud Lactantium reperiuntur* (1817); Alexandre's first ed.; Thompson, *art. cit.*, pp. 134–6. It therefore seems that he knew Books iii and viii of the present collection. He must nevertheless also have had some of the material lacking in our manuscripts for apart from the passages from the proem, which in extended quotation is indeed also known only from Theophilus, Lactantius has other quotations which are not attested in our texts, e.g. Lact., vii 19, 2; vii 24, 2. Also, the verses quoted in Lactantius ii 11, 18, which most probably belonged to the proem, are not found in Theophilus.

Lactantius comments in general on the books known to him (*Inst.* i 6, 13) (after an enumeration of the *ten* Sibyls): 'Harum omnium Sibyllarum carmina et feruntur et habentur praeterquam Cymaeae, cuius libri a Romanis occultantur nec eos ab ullo nisi a quindecimviris inspici fas habent. Et sunt singularum singuli libri, quos, quia Sibyllae nomine inscribuntur, unius esse credunt; suntque confusi, nec discerni ac suum cuique adsignari potest, nisi Erythraeae quae et nomen suum verum carmini inseruit, et Erythraeam se nominatuiri praelocuta est, cum esset orta Babylone.'

Celsus also testifies to the esteem in which the Sibyllines were held among Christians (Origen, *C. Cels.* v 61; vii 53; 56). He already accuses the Christians of having forged the oracles, and these charges do not become silent later. Cf. on this the allusions in Constantine's *Oratio ad sanct. coet.* 19, 1; Lact. *Inst.* iv 15, 26; Augustine, *De civ. dei* xviii 46.

On the Sibylline prophecies in the Middle Ages, cf. the following:

C. Alexandre's first ed., II, pp. 287–311.

Lücken, *Die sibyllinischen Weissagungen, ihr Ursprung und ihr Zusammenhang mit den after-prophetischen Darstellungen christlicher Zeit* (Katholische Studien, v) (1875).

Sackur, E., *Sibyllinische Texte und Forschungen. Pseudomethodius, Adso und die tiburtinische Sibylle* (1898; repr. 1963).

Kampers, F., 'Die Sibylla von Tibur und Vergil', HJ 29 (1908), pp. 1–29, 241–63.

Rzach, A., 'Sibyllinische Orakel (späterer Zeit)', RE IIA (1923), cols. 2169–83.

Prümm, K., 'Das Prophetenamt der Sibyllen in kirchlicher Literatur', Scholastik 4 (1929), pp. 54–77, 221–46, 498–533.

Kurfess, A., *Sibyllinische Weissagungen* (1951), pp. 344–8.

Demougeot, E. S., 'Jérôme, les oracles sibyllins et Stilichon', REA 54 (1952), pp. 83–92.

Bischoff, B., 'Die lateinischen Übersetzungen und Bearbeitungen aus den Oracula Sibyllina' in *Mélanges Joseph de Ghellinck* (1951), pp. 121–47.

Alexander, P. J., *The Oracle of Baalbek. The Tiburtine Sibyl in Greek Dress* (1967).

McGinn, B., 'Joachim and the Sibyl', Citeaux 24 (1973), pp. 97–138.
On the representations of the Sibyls in Christian art (particularly of the late Middle Ages), cf. Rzach, RE IIA (1923), cols. 2181 ff.
On the manuscripts, cf.: Alexandre's first ed., I, pp. xliii ff.; Rzach's ed., pp. vii-xvi; Geffcken's ed., pp. xxi-liii; Rzach, RE IIA (1923), cols. 2119–22; V. Nikiprowetzky, *La Troisième Sibylle* (1970), pp. 281–3.

Editions

Alexandre, C., *Oracula Sibyllina, curante C. Alexandre*, 2 vols. (1841–56); second ed.: *Editio altera ex priore ampliore contracta, integra tamen et passim aucta, multisque locis retractata* (1869) (the excursuses of the first edition, which give all the material on the history of Sibyllism more completely than anywhere else, were omitted in the second edition).

Friedlieb, J. H., *Die sibyllinischen Weissagungen vollständig gesammelt, nach neuer Handschriften-Vergleichung, mit kritischem Commentare und metrischer deutscher Übersetzung* (1852).

Rzach, A., *Oracula Sibyllina recensuit* (1891).

Geffcken, J., *Die Oracula Sibyllina* (GCS 8) (1902).

Lieger, P., *Die jüdische Sibylle, griechisch und deutsch, mit erklär. Anmerk.* (*Jahresber. d. Obergymn. zu den Schotten in Wien*, 1908); *Christus im Munde der Sibylle, griechisch und deutsch, mit erklär. Anmerk.* (*Progr. Schottengymn.*, Wien, 1911). Both of these deal with Book iii.

Kurfess, A., *Sibyllinische Weissagungen. Urtext und Übersetzung* (1951) (with only a simplified critical apparatus).

Translations

English:
Terry, M. S., *The Sibylline Oracles* (1899).
Lanchester, H., in Charles, APOT II, pp. 368–406 (Books iii-v and Theophilus fragments, with commentary).
Bate, H. N., *The Sibylline Oracles, books III-V* (1918).
Kurfess, A., in E. Hennecke and W. Schneemelcher, *N.T. Apocrypha* (ET by R. McL. Wilson, 1965), II, pp. 709–45 (Christian Sibyllines only).
Collins, J. J., in Charlesworth, OTP I, pp. 327–472 (with commentary).

German:
The editions of Friedlieb, Lieger and Kurfess are accompanied by translations.
Blass in Kautzsch, APAT II (1900), pp. 177–217 (Books iii-v only) (with commentary).
Riessler, P., *Altjüdisch. Schrift.* (1928), pp. 1014–45 (with commentary).
Merkel in JSHRZ (forthcoming).

French:
Bouché-Leclercq, A., in RHR 7 (1883), pp. 236–48; 8 (1883), pp. 619–34; 9 (1884), pp. 220–33 (Books 1–3).

Hebrew:
Reider, J., in A. Kahana, הספרים החיצונים (²1956).

Bibliography

Dechent, H., *Ueber das erste, zweite und elfte Buch der sibyllinischen Weissagungen* (1873).
Bouché-Leclercq, A., *Histoire de la divination dans l'antiquité* II (1880), pp. 199–214.
Gutschmid, A. v., *Kleine Schriften* II, pp. 322–31.
Susemihl, F., *Gesch. der griech. Litteratur in der Alexandrinerzeit* II (1892), pp. 636–42.
Diels, H., *Sibyllinische Blätter* (1890).
Fehr, E., *Studia in oracula Sibyllina* (1893).
Bousset, W., *Der Antichrist* (1895), pp. 59–63 and elsewhere.

Bousset, W., 'Die Beziehungen der ältesten jüdischen Sibylle zur chaldäischen Sibylle etc.', ZNW (1902), pp. 23–49.

Geffcken, J., Komposition und Entstehungzeit der Oracula Sibyllina (TU vii, 1) (1902).

Oldenburger, E., De oraculorum Sibyllinorum elocutione (1903).

Friedländer, M., Gesch. der jüdischen Apologetik (1903), pp. 31–4.

Harris, J. R., 'Sibylline Oracles', HDB (1904), pp. 66–8.

Lieger, P., Quaestiones Sibyllinae I : De collectionibus oraculorum Sibyllinorum (1904) ; II : Sibylla Hebraea sive de libri III aetate et origine (Gymnasialprogramme, 1906).

Lehmann-Haupt, C. F., 'Geffckens Oracula Sibyllina', Klio 6 (1906), pp. 323–9.

Bousset, W., 'Sibyllen und sibyllinische Bücher' in HHRE XVIII (1906), pp. 265–80.

Székely, S., Bibliotheca apocrypha I (1913), pp. 121–68.

Stählin, O., in W. v. Schmid and O. Stählin, Gesch. der griech. Lit. II.1 (1920), pp. 600–17.

Pincherle, A., Gli Oracoli Sibillini Giudaici (1922).

Schnabel, P., Berossus und die babylonisch-hellenistische Literatur (1923), pp. 69–93.

Rzach, A., RE IIA. 2 (1923), cols. 2073–183.

Rowley, H. H., 'The Interpretation and Date of Sibylline Oracles III 388–400', ZAW 44 (1926), 324–7.

Kugler, F. X., Sibyllinischer Sternkampf und Phaethon (1927).

Frey, J. B., DB supp. I (1928), cols. 423–8.

Bidez, J., and F. Cumont, Les mages hellénisés (1931) I, pp. 215–23 ; II, pp. 359–77.

Wolff, M. J., 'Sibyllen und Sibyllinen', Archiv f. Kulturgesch. 24 (1934), pp. 312–25.

Jeanmaire, H., La Sibylle et le retour de l'âge d'or (1939).

Peretti, A., La Sibilla Babilonese nella propaganda ellenistica (1943).

Lods, Ad., Histoire de la littérature hébraïque et juive (1950), pp. 896–8, 973–5.

Kurfess, A., 'Wie sind die Fragmente der Oracula Sibyllina einzuordnen? Ein Beitrag zu ihrer Überlieferung', Aevum 26 (1952), pp. 228–35.

Kurfess, A., 'Sibyllarum carmina chromatico tenore modulata', Acvum, pp. 385–94.

Kurfess, A., 'Zu den Oracula Sibyllina', in Colligere Fragmenta (1952), pp. 75–83.

Kurfess, A., 'Ad Oracula Sibyllina (ed. J. Geffcken 1902)', Symbolae Osl. 24 (1952), pp. 54–77.

Kurfess, A., 'Alte lateinische Sibyllinenverse', ThQ 133 (1953), pp. 80–96.

Kurfess, A., 'Juvenal und die Sibylle', Judaica 10 (1954), pp. 60–3.

Dalbert, P., Die Theologie der hell.-jüd. Missionsliteratur (1954), pp. 106–23.

Kurfess, A., 'Oracula Sibyllina XI(IX)–XIV(XII) nicht christlich, sondern jüdisch', ZRGG 7 (1955), pp. 270–2.

Kurfess, A., 'Horaz und die Sibyllinen', ZRGG 8 (1956), pp. 253–6.

Kurfess, A., 'Zum 5. Buch der Oracula Sibyllina', RhM 29 (1956), pp. 225–41.

Kurfess, A., 'Juvenal und die Sibylle', HJ 76 (1957), pp. 79–83.

Kocsis, E., 'Ost-West Gegensatz in dem jüdischen Sibyllinen', NT 5 (1962), pp. 105–10.

Peretti, A., 'Echi di dottrine esseniche degli Oracoli Sibillini giudaici', La Parola del Passato 85 (1962), pp. 247–95.

Grant, F. C., 'Sibyllinen', RGG, 3rd ed., VI (1962), 14–15.

Sackur, E., Sibyllinische Texte und Forschungen (1963).

Noack, B., 'Der hervoragende Mann und der beste der Hebräer (Bemerkungen zu Or. Sib. V, 256–259)', ASTI 3 (1964), pp. 122–46.

Nikiprowetzky, V., La Troisième Sibylle (1970).

Denis, IPGAT, pp. 111–22.

Speyer, W., Die literarische Fälschung im heidnischen und christlichen Altertum (1971), pp. 165–6.

Flusser, D., 'The Four Empires in the Fourth Sibyl and in the Book of Daniel', Israel Oriental Studies 2 (1972), pp. 148–75.

Salanitro, G., 'Osservazioni critiche al testo degli "Oracoli Sibillini"', Boletin del Instituto de Estudios Helénicos 6 (1972), pp. 75–8.

Collins, J. J., *The Sibylline Oracles of Egyptian Judaism* (1974).
Hengel, M., *Judaism and Hellenism* (ET 1974), vol. II, p. 125.
Momigliano, A., 'La portata storica dei vaticini sul settimo re nel terzo libro degli Oracoli Sibillini', in *Forma Futuri: Studi in Onore di Cardinale Michele Pellegrini* (1975), pp. 1077–84.
Flusser, D., 'An Early Jewish-Christian Document in the Tiburtine Sibyle', in *Paganisme, Judaïsme, Christianisme* (M. Simon Festschrift) (1978), pp. 153–83.
Nolland, J., 'Sib. Or. III 265–94: An Early Maccabean Messianic Oracle', JThSt 30 (1979), pp. 158–67.
Stern, M., GLAJJ II, pp. 198–200.
Nickelsburg, G. W. E., JLBBM, pp. 162–5.
Collins, J. J., 'The Sibylline Oracles', in JWSTP, pp. 357–81.

2. *[Hystaspes]*

Ammianus Marcellinus relates (xxiii 6, 32–3) that during his stay among the Indian Brahmins, Hystaspes, the father of King Darius, learned from them 'the laws of the movement of the world and pure religious customs *(purosque sacrorum ritus)*' and then communicated some of this to the native Magi, who handed it down to posterity. The Church Fathers also knew a Greek work under the name of this Hystaspes, who was thus regarded by antiquity as an authority in religious matters; they give the following indications regarding the work. According to *Justin*, it prophesied the future destruction of the world by fire. In the *Apocryphum Pauli* quoted by *Clement of Alexandria*, it is asserted that Hystaspes referred clearly to the Son of God and to the conflict between the Messiah and his people with many kings and to his perseverance and glorious parousia. According to *Lactantius*, the fall of the Roman Empire was prophesied in it, and also that in the affliction of the last days the pious and faithful would implore Zeus for help and that Zeus would hear them and destroy the ungodly. Lactantius finds fault here only with the fact that what God will do is ascribed to Zeus, and he regrets at the same time that as a result of deception by the demons, nothing is said of the mission of the Son of God. The anonymous author of the fifth century A.D. Theosophia says that the revelations of Hystaspes dealt with the incarnation of the Saviour.

From these indications it becomes evident that the contents of this writing were apocalyptico-eschatological. Since Lactantius says expressly that it contains no mention of the sending of the Son of God to judge the world, it should be clear that the work is not Christian, despite the remarks of the *Apocryphum Pauli* and the fifth century author of the Theosophy. Either they had a copy of the text revised by a Christian, or, and this is also possible, they read something into Hystaspes by means of Christian interpretation which according to Lactantius was not there. If Christian authorship of the original text is thus ruled out, it is possible that the work is a Jewish forgery. If so, the date, before Justin Martyr in the second century A.D., would make this a product of the same Jewish circles which produced the pseudepigraphic Sibyls. For them, unlike Christians, the choice of Zeus as the name of God was not entirely unnatural. However, Jewish authorship is also most unlikely. The work should be ascribed to Hellenized adherents of Iranian religions whose opposition to the Roman Empire in this period is also well documented. Similarities to Daniel would then be explained by reliance on a common Iranian tradition. Whether Persian or Jewish, the dating limits of composition are, on the one hand, the appearance of the Roman Empire as a great power and, on the other, Justin's knowledge of this book, i.e. between 100 B.C. and A.D. 150.

Justin, *Apol.* i 20: καὶ Σίβυλλα δὲ καὶ Ὑστάσπης γενήσεσθαι τῶν φθαρτῶν ἀνάλωσιν διὰ πυρὸς ἔφασαν. Cf. also 44.

An apocryphal statement of St. Paul quoted in Clement of Alexandria, *Strom.* vi 5, 42–3: Λάβετε καὶ τὰς Ἑλληνικὰς βίβλους, ἐπίγνωτε Σίβυλλαν, ὡς δηλοῖ ἕνα θεὸν καὶ τὰ μέλλοντα ἔσεσθαι, καὶ τὸν Ὑστάσπην λαβόντες ἀνάγνωτε, καὶ εὑρήσετε πολλῷ τηλαυγέστερον καὶ σαφέστερον γεγραμμένον τὸν υἱὸν τοῦ θεοῦ, καὶ καθὼς παράταξιν ποιήσουσι τῷ Χριστῷ πολλοὶ βασιλεῖς μισοῦντες αὐτὸν καὶ τοὺς φοροῦντας τὸ ὄνομα αὐτοῦ καὶ τοὺς πιστοὺς αὐτοῦ καὶ τὴν ὑπομονὴν καὶ τὴν παρουσίαν αὐτοῦ. Since Clement immediately prior to this (*Strom.* vi 5, 39–41) quotes the Gospel of Peter, it has been assumed that this passage was also taken from it (A. Hilgenfeld, ZWTh 35 (1893), pp. 525–31). But he introduces this passage with the words: δηλώσει πρὸς τῷ Πέτρου κηρύγματι ὁ ἀπόστολος λέγων Παῦλος. To the witness of the Gospel of Peter he thus adds words from Paul, although they cannot be assigned to any of the other extant collections of apocryphal Pauline sayings and are accordingly not included in E. Hennecke and W. Schneemelcher, *N.T. Apocrypha*, transl. R. McL. Wilson (1965). Cf. the comments of Harnack, *Gesch. der altchr. Litt.* I, pp. 26, 129; II.1, pp. 491–3, 589.

Lactantius, *Inst.* vii 15, 19, ed. Brandt: 'Hystaspes quoque, qui fuit Medorum rex antiquissimus ..., admirabile somnium sub interpretatione vaticinantis pueri ad memoriam posteris tradidit, sublatu iri ex orbe imperium nomenque Romanum multo ante praefatus est quam illa Troiana gens conderetur.' *Ibid.*, vii 18, 2–3: 'Hystaspes enim, quem superius nominavi, descripta iniquitate saeculi huius extremi, pios ac fideles a nocentibus segregatos ait cum fletu et gemitu extenturos esse ad coelum manus et imploraturos fidem Jovis; Jovem respecturum ad terram et auditurum voces hominum atque impios extincturum. Quae omnia vera sunt, praeter unum, quod Jovem dixit illa facturum, quae Deus faciet. Sed et illud non sine daemonum fraude subtractum, missu iri a patre tunc filium Dei, qui deletis omnibus malis pios liberet.'

In the Theosophy written toward the end of the fifth century, in which are assembled pagan witnesses for the Christian religion, the fourth book was apparently devoted to the prophecies of Hystaspes (cf. on this, above, pp. 628 f.; H. Erbse, *Fragmente griechischer Theosophien* (1941)), but unfortunately the excerpts preserved do not include this book.

Bibliography

Windisch, H., *Die Orakel des Hystaspes* (Verhandelingen der Koninklijke Akademie van Wetenschappen, Amsterdam) (1929).
Cumont, F., 'La fin du monde selon les Mages occidentaux', RHR 103 (1931), pp. 29–96, esp. 64 ff.
Bidez, J., and F. Cumont, *Les Mages hellénisés* (1938) I, pp. 203–28; II, pp. 359 ff.
Perette, A., *La Sibilla Babilonese nella Propaganda Ellenistica* (1943), p. 375.
Altheim, F., *Weltgeschichte Asiens im griechischen Zeitalter* II (1948), pp. 174 f., 179–84.
van Unnik, W. C., 'Hystaspes', RGG, 3rd ed., III (1959), pp. 507 ff.
Eddy, S. K., *The King is Dead* (1961), pp. 16, 59.
Widengren, G., *Die Religionen Irans* (1965), pp. 199–207.
Denis, IPGAT, pp. 268–9.
Momigliano, A., *Alien Wisdom* (1975), p. 146.
Ogilvie, R.M. *The Library of Lactantius* (1978), pp. 54–5.

3. Forged Verses of Greek Poets

Jewish and Christian apologists repeatedly appealed to the most eminent of the Greek poets to prove that the more judicious Greeks held the correct views concerning the nature of God, his unity, spirituality, and supramundane character. Many of these quotations, particularly in Clement of Alexandria, actually come from the genuine writings of those poets and have been skilfully selected and interpreted by the apologists.[252] But interspersed with the authentic quotations are not a few that are clearly forgeries in the interest of Jewish or Christian apologetics. They were not very successful among pagans in passing off the ideas of the forger as those of the original poets, since they are almost never quoted by pagan writers, who evidently recognized them as spurious,[253] so it is likely that here at least Jewish apologetics was originally intended primarily for a Jewish audience. These forged verses are mainly to be found in (1) Aristobulus quoted in Eusebius, *Praep. ev.* xiii 12. (2) Clement of Alexandria, *Strom.* v 14, also given in Eusebius, *Praep. ev.* xiii 13; cf. also *Protrept.* vii 74. (3) Pseudo-Justin, *Cohortatio ad Graecos* 15 and 18. (4) Pseudo-Justin, *De monarchia* 2–4. The poets to whom these verses are ascribed are the great tragic poets Aeschylus, Sophocles, and Euripides; the writers of comedy, Philemon, Menander, and Diphilus; Orpheus, to whom a long passage is ascribed; and

---

252. So e.g. the famous beginning of the *Phaenomena* of Aratus (third century B.C.): 'Ἐκ Διὸς ἀρχώμεσθα, τὸν οὐδέποτ' ἄνδρες ἐῶσιν ἄρρητον etc., from which the saying quoted in Ac. 17:28 also derives: τοῦ γὰρ καὶ γένος ἐσμέν. Already the Jewish philosopher Aristobulus quotes these verses (Eusebius, *Praep. ev.* xiii 12, 6); further Theophilus, *Ad Autol.* ii 8; Clement of Alexandria, *Strom.* v 14, 101 = Eusebius, *Praep. ev.* xiii 13, 26.
253. Cf. Walter in JSHRZ IV.3 (1983), pp. 251–2.

Hesiod, Homer, and Linus (or Callimachus), to whom are attributed some verses on the Sabbath.

For an assessment of the origin of these passages, the following is of importance. Nearly all the pieces under consideration appear both in Clement of Alexandria, *Strom.* v 14, 113–33 (= Eusebius, *Praep. ev.* xiii 13, 40–62) and in Pseudo-Justin, *De monarchia* 2–4. Aristobulus as quoted by Eusebius, and the *Cohortatio ad Graecos*, have only isolated pieces, all of which can also be found in the other writings although their versions of some passages, particularly that ascribed to Orpheus, are significantly different from them. But in both Clement and *De monarchia* the suspect passages are placed together, in *De monarchia* really almost without any other ingredients. It is therefore clear either that one made use of the other, or that both go back to a common source. Closer consideration shows, however, that the first alternative is not acceptable. For although the quoted fragments are nearly all identical, they are given more fully and more exactly sometimes by one and sometimes by the other.[254] Without any doubt, therefore, they both drew either from one common source in which all the presumably suspect pieces were found together or, more likely, from a series of separate collections of such pieces.

What one of these sources was is said plainly by Clement: namely, Pseudo-Hecataeus' book on Abraham and the Egyptians (see below, p. 674), which Clement, *Strom.* v 14, 113 = Eusebius, *Praep. ev.* xiii 13, 40, gives as the origin of a quotation from Sophocles. There is no reason to suppose that *all* the quotations from the tragic and comic poets should be ascribed to this author, but it can at the very least be asserted that this ascription makes it likely that such *florilegia* of pagan testimonia were collected by Jews in the last three centuries B.C. and that there is therefore no *prima facie* reason to suspect the poetic forgeries of being Christian. It is possible but unnecessary to assume that all those quotations not ascribed to Aristobulus (see below) were in fact found in the work of Pseudo-Hecataeus, but it cannot be proved that there were

254. Instructive for example is *De monarchia* 3, compared to Clement, *Strom.* v 14, 121–2 (= Eusebius, *Praep. ev.* xiii 13, 47–8). *De monarchia* first gives a passage from Sophocles here (ἔσται γάρ, ἔσται etc.). Clement has the same passage but in two halves, the second of which is introduced with the formula: καὶ μετ' ὀλίγα αὖθις ἐπιφέρει. Here Clement is undoubtedly more original; the author of *De monarchia* has brought together the two passages which are not directly related. The reverse is true in the following, in Clement the preceding, passage, οἴει σὺ τοὺς θανόντας, all of which Clement ascribes to Diphilus. The author of *De monarchia* assigns the first longer half to Philemon, and the second shorter half to Euripides, the latter correctly, because it includes a few genuine verses from Euripides which are supplemented by spurious ones (cf. Le Boulluec, *Comm. to Clem.*, Strom., *V* (SC 279), pp. 345–6). Thus *De monarchia* has preserved the original; Clement has erroneously ascribed to one author the two passages, which do not belong together.

not *many* such works from which Clement and later authors drew freely. Probably a quite separate collection or collections from that of the drama writers is represented by the large fragments of Orpheus and by the verses of Hesiod, Homer and Linus about the Sabbath, which, according to Eusebius, xiii 12, were quoted by Aristobulus in the second century B.C. The Orphean piece, in rather different recensions, is found both in Clement of Alexandria, *Strom.* v 14, 123 ff. (= Eusebius, xiii 13, 50 ff.) and in *De monarchia* 2, in the midst of the forged verses of the tragic and comic poets. The testimonies of Hesiod and Homer concerning the Sabbath are at least nearby in Clement (*Strom.* v 14, 107 = Eusebius, xiii 13, 34), and in Aristobulus are quoted together with the Orphean piece.

It is however quite unnecessary to assume that this indicates authorship of *all* the pieces by a single author. Aristobulus may well have found the Orphic verses and those on the Sabbath in quite separate collections which he placed together for his own polemical purposes. There is no evidence that Pseudo-Hecataeus was even acquainted with the verses cited by Aristobulus. It is most likely that the citation of all these verses in close proximity is due to the identical use made by the later Jewish and Christian authors of a number of collections of such testimonia.

For the dating of these forgeries only very vague indications can be found in the general similarity of their ideas to those in *Sib.* iii 1–45, Pseudo-Phocylides, and Ezekiel the Tragedian. More accurate dating depends on the evidence for the first attested use of the verses.

For the quotation or quotations that are to be ascribed to Pseudo-Hecataeus, the only fixed date is a time before the composition of the work *On Abraham and the Egyptians* in which the Pseudo-Sophocles verse is quoted. This is not however very helpful since that work can only be *firmly* dated to before Josephus, though if, as is possible, it is referred to by Pseudo-Aristeas, 31, it may be assigned to an earlier date, before *c.* 170 B.C. (see below, section 4). Any period between the third century B.C. and the early first century A.D. is therefore possible for the forgeries. If the unprovable hypothesis is correct that *all* the extant forged verses not explicitly assigned to Aristobulus were originally quoted by Pseudo-Hecataeus (see above), it is likely that the author collected passages from Greek poets, as witnesses for true belief in God, and that, while many of these passages were certainly genuine, they were apparently still not strong enough for the author, so that he either strengthened and completed them by verses of his own composition, or took verses from a Jewish compendium which had already been made for the same polemical purpose. That he would have liked to have proved the acquaintance of the Greek ποιηταί with Moses, or wished to prove this, *may* be shown by the quotation from Hecataeus in

Pseudo-Aristeas, 31, in which Hecataeus is alleged to have asserted that the Greek poets only failed to discuss the Jewish Law because it was too holy for such discussion. It is not however certain whether Pseudo-Aristeas referred to this, pseudonymous, work on Abraham or to the genuine writings of Hecataeus (see below, p. 674). It is however entirely in keeping with other *gnomologia* of this kind that, if Pseudo-Hecataeus found that the Greek poets did not mention Moses explicitly, he should try all the more diligently to show that the contents of their writings agreed with the Mosaic Law. However, it cannot, as already noted, be proved that the works of Pseudo-Hecataeus contained any more forged verses than the single quotation of Sophocles explicitly assigned to him by Clement. The rest of the verses may therefore come from an unknown Jewish source of any period before Clement.

A date for the forged Orphic verses and the verses about the Sabbath is even more difficult to determine since the Orphic verses at least have certainly undergone a number of recensions for different polemical purposes (see below, p. 664). There is however no reason to deny the existence of *some* compilation of such verses before Aristobulus quoted from them, i.e. probably before the mid-second century B.C. Since it is rather unlikely that Aristobulus would have tried to forge the very verses that he used as prime evidence for his assertions about Judaism, it is very likely that he too used an already extant Jewish florilegium of pagan testimonia to Judaism, which may therefore have been composed as early as the third century B.C.[255] A few further verses possibly forged by Jews can be identified scattered in the writings of Pseudo-Justin, Clement, and Eusebius (see below, p. 670). These however cannot be associated with the other known collections and are therefore

---

255. On gnomologia in general, see K. Horna and K. von Fritz, 'Gnome, Gnomendichtung, Gnomologien', RE suppl. VI (1935), cols. 74–9; W. Spoerri, Der Kleine Pauly II (1967), cols. 823–9; Walter, JSHRZ IV.3 (1983), pp. 248–9. In regard to the hypothesis concerning the high antiquity of these forgeries, a related phenomenon should be noted. After showing toward the end of the fifth book of the *Stromata* that the Greeks drew much from the writings of the Old Testament, Clement of Alexandria proceeds at the beginning of the sixth book to argue that they often also 'stole' from each other, meaning thereby to strengthen his main thesis. It is very probable, judging from his whole method of working, that he depended here too on previous studies. The age of his (direct or indirect) source was however indicated by Kaibel on the basis of papyrus discoveries (Hermes 28 (1893), pp. 62–4). In the same way, that is, that *Epicharmus* and *Euripides* are met with in Clement, *Strom.* vi 2, 8, so there is a quite analogous juxtaposition of verses from Epicharmus and Euripides not only already in Philo (*Quaest. in Genes.* iv 203) but even in a papyrus fragment from the third century B.C. (*The Flinders Petrie Papyri*, ed. Mahaffy = *Royal Irish Academy, Cunningham Memoirs*, VIII (1891), table iii, 1). It is possible that this papyrus fragment came from the same florilegium of Greek poets used by Clement. Cf. N. Zeegers-van der Vorst, *Les Citations des Poètes grecs chez les apologistes chrétiens du II* siècle* (Recueil de travaux d'histoire et de philologie, IV, 47) (1972), pp. 27–9.

impossible to date. It is probably significant that only Christian authors, who were naturally prone to believe their witness to Judaeo-Christian values, are known to have accepted these verses as genuine, and that they are not included in the florilegium of any pagan writer.

Edition

Denis, FPG, pp. 161–74.

Translations

German:
Riessler, P., *Altjüd. Schrift.* (1928), pp. 192, 246, 731–2, 1046.
Walter, N., *Pseudepigraphische jüdisch-hellenistische Dichtung* (JSHRZ iv.3) (1983), pp. 235–43, 261–76 (with extensive commentary).

English:
Attridge, H. W., in Charlesworth, OTP II (forthcoming).

Bibliography

Valckenaer, L. C., *Diatribe de Aristobulo Judaeo* (1806), pp. 1–16, 73–125.
Freudenthal, J., *Alexander Polyhistor* (1875), pp. 166–9.
Susemihl, F., *Gesch. der griech. Litteratur in der Alexandrinerzeit* II (1892), pp. 632–5.
Elter, A., *De gnomologiorum graecorum historia atque origine*, parts v-vi (Bonn, *Universitäts-Programme*, 1894), cols. 149–206.
Bousset, W., and H. Gressmann, *Die Religion des Judentums* (^{3}1926), pp. 25, 73. v.
Christ, W. v., O. Stählin and W. Schmidt, *Gesch. der griech. Lit. etc.*^{6} II.1 (1920), pp. 603 ff.
Riessler, P., EJ III, 321 ff.
Pohlenz, M., 'Klemens v. Alexandria u. sein hellenisches Christentum', NAWG (1943), p. 3.
Dalbert, P., *Die Theologie der jüd.-hell. Missionsliteratur* (1954), pp. 102–6.
Cerfaux, L., 'Le hieros logos juif' in *Recueil L. Cerfaux* I (1954), pp. 71–81.
Walter, N., *Der Thoraausleger Aristobulus* (1964), pp. 150–201.
Denis, IPGAT, pp. 223–38.
Zeegers-Vander Vorst, N., 'Les Citations Poètiques chez Théophile d'Antioche', *Studia Patristica* 10 (1970), pp. 168–74.
Speyer, W., *Die literarische Fälschung im heidnischen und christlichen Altertum* (1971), pp. 161–3.
Hengel, M., 'Anonymität, Pseudepigraphie und "Literarische Fälschung" in der jüdisch-hellenistische Literatur', in K. von Fritz, ed., *Pseudepigrapha* I (Entretiens Hardt, XVIII) (1972), pp. 229–329, esp. 294–6.
Zeegers-Vander Vorst, N., *Les Citations des Poètes grecs chez les apologistes chrétiens du IIe siècle* (Recueil de travaux d'histoire et de philologie IV, 47) (1972).

In *De monarchia*, individual passages of the tragic poets and the Pseudo-Orphic verses are arranged according to their essential points of view (the nature of God, future retribution, the necessity of ethical conduct). Since it is probable that, apart from the insertion of the Pseudo-Orphic verses and the two fragments which quote (spuriously) Pythagoras and (genuinely) Plato, the order preserved by Pseudo-Justin is that of the original Jewish collection or collections of such testimonia from the dramatic writers, we have used it as a basis for the following survey.[256]

1. Twelve verses of *Aeschylus* (Denis, FPG, pp. 161–2) on the exalted nature of God above all creatures, *De monarchia* 2 (Otto, *Corpus apologetarum*[3] III, p. 130); Clement of Alexandria, *Strom.* v 14, 131 = Eusebius, *Praep. ev.* xiii 13, 60 (Nauck, *Tragicorum Graec. fragm.*[2] F 464; H.-J. Mette, *Die Fragmente der Tragödien des Aischylos* (1959), p. 223, no. 627).

2. Nine verses of *Sophocles* (Denis, FPG, 162–3) on the unity of God who made heaven and earth, and on the foolishness of idolatry, *De monarchia* 2 (Otto, *Corpus apolog.*[3] III, p. 132); Clement of Alexandria, *Strom.* v 14, 113 = Eusebius, *Praep. ev.* xiii 13, 40; Clement, *Protrept.* vii 74; Pseudo-Justin, *Cohort. ad Graec.* 18. These verses were popular with later patristic writers, cf. Cyril of Alexandria, *Adv. Julian.*, ed. Spanheim, 32a; Theodoret, *Graecarum affectionum curatio* vii 46 (ed. Canivet, I, pp. 308–9), Malalas, *Chron.* II, pp. 40 ff. (PG XCVII, 112); Cedrenus, Bonn ed., I, p. 82. The first two verses appear also in Athenagoras, *Leg.* 5 (Nauck, *Trag. Graec. fragm.*[2], F 1025). Since this excerpt is so widely quoted by itself and is the section of Pseudo-Sophocles attributed to Hecataeus by Clement, *Strom.* v 14, 113, it is possible that it formed part of a separate collection only later incorporated within the main collection of poetic testimonia, especially since the further fragment assigned by *De monarchia* to Sophocles (no. 5 below) is atypically anonymous in the parallel citation by Clement. Cf. Walter, JSHRZ IV.3 (1983), pp. 247–8.

3. Two verses (Denis, FPG, p. 163), ascribed to the comic poet *Philemon* in *De monarchia* 2, but to *Euripides* in Clement of Alexandria, *Protrept.* vi 68, discuss God as one who sees all but is himself unseen. On their spuriousness, cf. Nauck, *Trag. Graec. fragm.*[2], F 1129; Kock, *Comm. att. fragm.*, F 247; Edmonds, *Fragm. Att. Comedy*, F 247; Otto, *Corpus apologetarum*[3] III, p. 132, n. 21. The ascription to Euripides, as by Clement, may be more original according to Walter, *Der Thoraausleger Aristobulus* (1964), p. 187, n. 1, who suggests that the author of *De monarchia* substituted the name 'Philemon' because a forgery of an author as well known as Euripides was too easily detected, cf. also Walter, JSHRZ IV.3 (1983), p. 249, n. 26; p. 251.

4. A long passage attributed to *Orpheus* (Denis, FPG, pp. 163–7) is extant in three essentially differing recensions. (a) The shortest is that in *De monarchia* 2 (Otto, *Corpus apologetarum*[3] III, pp. 132 ff.) and *Cohortatio*

---

256. See Walter, JSHRZ IV.3 (1983), p. 245. For the Orphic fragments as a separate collection, see below, p. 665; for the Pythagorean verse as separate, note the fact that Clement does not refer to it, unlike the other citations. It is noteworthy that *De monarchia* is the only one of the collections of this material in which the forged verses are not mingled with genuine quotations of the poets.

ad Graecos 15. The text is identical in both except for the omission of the two introductory verses in *De monarchia*. The text of the *Cohortatio* is also given, with an abbreviation in the middle, by Cyril of Alexandria, *Adv. Julian.*, I, ed. Spanheim, p. 26. The passage (twenty-one verses in the *Cohortatio ad Graecos*) deals, in the form of a testament, as so often in Jewish pseudepigraphy, with the idea that there is but one God who created everything and still rules, and who is enthroned in transcendent glory in heaven, invisible and yet everywhere present. This theme is closely paralleled in *Sib.* iii 1–45, but, if further proof is needed for the Jewish origin of these verses, it is clearly found in the notion taken from Isa. 66:1 that the heavens are God's throne and the earth his footstool (cf. Mt. 5:34–5; Ac. 7:49):

Οὗτος γὰρ χάλκεον ἐς' οὐρανὸν ἐστήρικται
Χρυσέῳ εἰνὶ θρόνῳ, γαίης δ' ἔπι ποσσὶ βέβηκε.²⁵⁷

It is noteworthy that the author emphasizes that evil is also sent by God:

Οὗτος δ' ἐξ ἀγαθοῖο κακὸν θνητοῖσι δίδωσι
Καὶ πόλεμον κρυόεντα καὶ ἄλγεα δακρυόεντα.

The whole instruction is, according to *Cohortatio ad Graecos* 15, addressed to Musaeus the son of Orpheus. According to *De monarchia* 2, it is contained in the 'Testament of Orpheus', in which the latter, repenting of his former teaching of the existence of 360 gods, proclaimed the one true God. Cf. also *Cohortatio ad Graecos* 15 and 36, and especially Theophilus, *Ad Autol.* iii 2 (365 gods!).

(b) A longer recension of the same Orphean piece is assigned to Aristobulus in Eusebius, *Praep. ev.* xiii 12, 4–5. The beginning is essentially the same as in the above-mentioned recension, but toward the end it has considerably more, in particular a reference to a Chaldean astrologer, probably Abraham,²⁵⁸ who alone saw God and attained true knowledge of him, and the attribution to Moses of a role of prime importance (Denis, FPG, p. 16, lines 25, 41–2). The passage according to which God also inflicts evil is corrected here into the opposite:

Αὐτὸς δ' ἐξ ἀγαθῶν θνητοῖς κακὸν οὐκ ἐπιτέλλει

257. These same verses read, according to Clement of Alexandria, *Strom.* v 14, 124 = Eusebius, *Praep. ev.* xiii 13, 51 (and almost the same, according to Aristobulus in Eusebius xiii 12, 5):
Αὐτὸς δ' αὖ μέγαν αὖτις ἐπ' οὐρανὸν ἐστήρικται
Χρυσέῳ εἰνὶ θρόνῳ, γαίη δ' ὑπὸ ποσσὶ βέβηκεν.
Clement observes the agreement with Isa. 66:1.

258. In the margin of the Tübingen Theosophy, where the same material is included (Buresch, p. 114 = Erbse, p. 181, lines 18–19), the scholiast identifies the Chaldaean as Moses, which Philo, *De Vita Mosis* i 5, show to be a possible identification. However, Clement, *Strom.* v 14, 123, referring to the same passage, explicitly identifies him with Abraham or his son Isaac.

'Ανθρώποις· αὐτῷ δὲ χάρις καὶ μῖσος ὀπηδεῖ,
Καὶ πόλεμος καὶ λοιμὸς ἰδ' ἄλγεα δακρυόεντα.

Aristobulus names as source the poems of Orpheus κατὰ τὸν ἱερὸν λόγον (Eusebius, *Praep. ev.* xiii 12, 4).

Predominantly in agreement with the Aristobulus-Eusebius text is that given in the excerpt from the Theosophia of Tübingen, the work of an author of the fifth century A.D. published by Buresch (Buresch, *Klaros* (1889), the Orphean fragment on pp. 112–15, and, better, H. Erbse, *Fragmente griechischen Theosophien* (1941), pp. 167–201, with the Orphean fragment on pp. 180–2; cf. above, pp. 628 f.). However, this text also includes at particular points lines found in the Pseudo-Justin work but not in Eusebius. It preserves a patently Christian reworking of two lines of the Eusebius text (Buresch, p. 113, 9–114; Erbse, p. 181, 118–19).

(c) A third recension is represented by the quotations in Clement of Alexandria, *Protrept.* vii 74, *Strom.* v 12, 78, and especially *Strom.* v 14, 123–37 = Eusebius, *Praep. ev.* xiii 13, 50–4. Theodoret, *Graecarum affectionum curatio* ii 30–1 (ed. Canivet, I, pp. 146–7), in turn probably drew from Clement.[259] Clement gives the text only piecemeal, broken up into separate quotations. But if all of these are taken together, it becomes quite clear, especially from *Strom.* v 123–4, that he had *some* of the verses preserved in Eusebius under the name of Aristobulus, but not all. Although he agrees with Aristobulus in including the passage on the Chaldean, he lacks any of Aristobulus' material about the role of Moses. It is very unlikely that he deliberately passed over such testimony to Moses if it was known to him. For the rest, Clement, *Strom.* v 12, 78, contains two lines not to be found in Aristobulus, one of which does not appear in any other recension except for the Theosophia, while the other is attested in Pseudo-Justin. There are also agreements in many details with Pseudo-Justin's writings. In particular, Clement has the passage about the infliction of evil by God (*Strom.* v 14, 126 = Eusebius, *Praep. ev.* xiii 13, 53). On Orpheus' writing, from which the passage is taken, Clement says, in agreement with the others, that Orpheus, 'after his preaching of orgies and the theology of idols, introduced a palinode of truth and, though late, sang the teachings which were genuinely sacred (τὸν ἱερὸν ὄντως...λόγον)' (*Protrept.* vii 74).

About the relation of the versions to each other there is still no

---

259. Theodoret cites only thirteen lines, of which eleven are to be found in Aristobulus as quoted by Eusebius. However, two lines quoted by Theodoret are found in Clement but not in Aristobulus. Therefore, although the first three verses quoted by Theodoret agree in part more with Aristobulus than Clement, the fact that the lines in Theodoret are divided into two sections which coincide with those in Clement, *Strom.* v 12, 78 and v 14, 124, makes it most likely that Theodoret took his quotations directly from there.

certainty. It seems clear that the history of transmission was complex.[260] If the versions were developed in a direct line from each other, then the *prima facie* dates of the alleged citation would require Aristobulus (as quoted in Eusebius) to be prior, followed by Clement in the late second century A.D. and by Pseudo-Justin in the early third century A.D. In that case, however, Clement and Pseudo-Justin must have suppressed many lines of Aristobulus, gradually simplifying the quotation to only half its original size. This is not likely. Pseudo-Justin usually includes whatever is in his source uncritically; there is no reason for Clement to have preserved the verses which mention Abraham but not those which refer to Moses; and, above all, both authors preserve some material which is not found in Aristobulus. A simple reduction of the text through these versions is therefore impossible. Such changes could only be explained by the work of numerous intermediaries between Aristobulus and Clement and the hypothesis that they had already drastically changed Aristobulus' text before Clement altered it still further; then Eusebius will have found the genuine Aristobulus text by chance. There is no evidence for this complex series of recensions and the somewhat disjointed nature of Aristobulus' text as Eusebius preserves it tells strongly against the suggestion that it was the original version.

It is possible that all three Christian authors simply selected different material from a large pool of Pseudo-Orphic verses collected by earlier Jewish apologists. However, the extant fragments are much the best explained if it is assumed that the Pseudo-Justin text is the oldest and that the other versions are the result of a series of recensions which added extra material to it. In favour of Pseudo-Justin's as the oldest recension is the lack of obvious later additions to the text. This is the only version which is internally coherent and homogeneous. Furthermore, it is impossible to see how the extra material in Clement could be fitted into Pseudo-Justin's version without awkwardness. The next recension was that used by Clement alongside the original (i.e. Pseudo-Justin's) text. This second recension included the material about the Chaldean and also lines about the presence of the divinity in the forces of nature (Denis, FPG, p. 165, lines 17–20). It is possible but not necessary to see in these later lines a Stoic recension of the text quite separate from the Abrahamic one (so N. Walter, JSHRZ IV.3 (1983), pp. 223 f., 238). The combination of the Abrahamic recension with that

---

260. The number of recensions through which the work went before reaching its present stage has been much debated. A. Elter, *Gnomologia* VI (1894), pp. 178–87, succeeds in distinguishing sixteen stages in the evolution of the work from Pseudo-Justin to Eusebius. Denis, FPG, p. 164, by contrast distinguishes only two recensions. N. Walter, *Der Thoraausleger Aristobulus* (1964), pp. 202–61, distinguishes four main stages. His account is mostly but not entirely followed here.

of Pseudo-Justin may have been the work of Clement himself or, more likely since Clement was only concerned to cite the work in short fragments, it was achieved, rather clumsily, by a compiler before him. Based on the recension used by Clement was that found in Eusebius under the name of Aristobulus, but with the addition by a Jewish author of four verses about Moses as purveyor of the λόγος (FPG, pp. 165–6, lines 21, 25, 41–2) rather uncomfortably tacked onto it. This recension was not known by Pseudo-Justin since it is inconceivable that he would have ignored the verses on Abraham and Moses which would have been congenial to him, particularly when he included other material of dubious orthodoxy about God's relationship with evil in the world. It is also unlikely that Clement knew the recension, but his silence is less significant since anyway he only quoted small sections of the work. Finally, the Tübingen Theosophy preserves a clearly Christian recension.

The dates of these recensions are not firmly established by this analysis of their relationships. There are no clear indications of the date of the original text preserved in Pseudo-Justin. It may quite well go back to before Aristobulus in the second century B.C. since there is no reason to deny his use of *some* collection of Orphic verses,[261] nor to assume that the poem quoted in his name by Eusebius was necessarily the version which he originally cited. It is even possible that he was the first to associate the Orphic verses with the forged verses of Homer and Hesiod, as Eusebius quotes him as having done.

The Abrahamic recension used first by Clement can only be dated between the composition of the original version and the time of Clement (late second century A.D.). The ideas put forward somewhat resemble those in Ezekiel the Tragedian (Collins, BAAJ, p. 206), but this is of little help in dating. There is no reason to suppose that this version was the work of Pseudo-Hecataeus just because Pseudo-Hecataeus wrote about Abraham and quoted one of the forged verses of Sophocles—there is no certainty that the Pseudo-Orphic fragments were associated with the forged verses of the tragic and comic poets until their use by Clement, although it is quite likely that Clement took his own quotations from a previous Hellenistic or early Roman *gnomologion*.

Finally, the Mosaic recension found in 'Aristobulus' in Eusebius has

261. This is only hypothesis. According to Eusebius, *Praep. ev.* xiii 2, 3–4, Aristobulus intended to show how Orpheus and other Greeks spoke about God as creator. This can only be taken in a very vague sense as the subject of the extant Jewish sections in any of the recensions. Aristobulus may have quoted a genuine Orphic verse, or a Jewish forgery which is now lost, rather than the recension preserved in Pseudo-Justin. At any rate, even if Aristobulus *quoted* some forged verses, it is most unlikely that he had the nerve to *compose* them himself before quoting them as evidence for his thesis. See above, p. 584.

been dated by many to the third century A.D. on the grounds that Pseudo-Justin was unaware of its existence. Lobeck proposed that Aristobulus himself be considered an author of the third century A.D. but this cannot be true since Clement cites him at *Strom.* i 150, 1; vi 32, 3. Elter suggested a Christian forger of the same period, to be known as Pseudo-Aristobulus. In fact, however, the recension is clearly that of a Jew, and it is implausible that a Jewish forgery of the third century A.D. would have been accepted by Christian writers at so late a date. The problem can be surmounted if it is recognized that the fact that Clement used a *later* recension of the text than that used by Pseudo-Justin, who probably wrote after him, shows that the different recensions circulated concurrently and that Pseudo-Justin's ignorance of the Mosaic recension therefore does *not* date that recension to after his time. The Mosaic recension may therefore be dated to any time after the Abrahamic recension and before Eusebius; again, a Hellenistic date is not ruled out by its content.

In any case, this Orphean fragment is one of the boldest forgeries which has ever been attempted. It is an alleged testament of Orpheus to his son Musaeus in which, having arrived at the end of his life, he explicitly revokes all his other poems dedicated to polytheistic teachings and proclaims the one true God. According to the Suda (s.v. 'Ορφεύς) there were ἱεροὺς λόγους ἐν ῥαψωδίαις κδ' of Orpheus which will have been intended, as was normal with such works, to explain the origin of Orphic cultic practices. This testament must have been, as Clement says, his true ἱερὸς λόγος.[262]

For the text of this Jewish section, see O. Kern, *Orphicorum fragmenta* (1922), F 245–7 (the texts in Pseudo-Justin, Clement and Aristobulus quoted by Eusebius); Denis, FPG, pp. 163–7 (a composite text of forty-six lines derived from all the fragments). For translation and commentary, see P. Riessler, *Altjüd. Schrift.* (1928), pp. 182 f., 729 f. (not all the recensions); Y. Gutman, *The Beginnings of Jewish-Hellenistic Literature* I (1958), pp. 148–70 (Heb.); E. R. Goodenough, *Jewish*

---

262. The role of Orpheus among Greek-speaking Jews has been shown to be of considerable importance by the finds of illustrations of his figure at Dura-Europus (third century A.D.) and Gaza (early sixth century A.D.), which show that Orpheus was identified with David (E. R. Goodenough, *Jewish Symbols in the Greco-Roman Period*, IX-XI (1964); H. Stern, 'The Orpheus in the Synagogue of Dura-Europus', Journal of the Warburg Institute 21 (1958), pp. 1–6; M. Philonenko, 'David-Orphée sur une mosaïque de Gaza', RHPR 47 (1967), pp. 355–7). Note also the Orphic connotations in the version of Psalm 151 discovered at Qumran, cf. J. A. Sanders, *The Dead Sea Psalms Scroll* (1967), pp. 98–102, 116, and above, p. 189. See Walter, JSHRZ iv.3 (1983), pp. 230–2, with literature cited there; M. Hengel, in K. von Fritz, ed., *Pseudepigrapha I* (1972), p. 293, n. 1. M. L. West, *The Orphic Poems* (1983), p. 35, suggests that Orpheus Frag. 299 (Kern), an Orphic oath in which appears a divine father who created heaven and the whole world by his word, is probably Jewish, though he admits that it may be Hermetic, as asserted by Malalas, *Chronogr.* ed. Dindorff, II, p. 27.

Symbols in the Greco-Roman World IX (1964), pp. 96–7 (Pseudo-Justin and Aristobulus only); and especially N. Walter, *Pseudepigraphische jüdisch-hellenistische Dichtung* (JSHRZ IV.3) (1983), pp. 217–43; M. Lafargue, in Charlesworth, OTP II (forthcoming).

Bibliography

Valckenaer, L. C., *De Aristobulo*, pp. 11–16, 73–85.
Lobeck, C. A., *Aglaophamus* (1829; repr. 1961) I, pp. 438–65.
Elter, A., *De gnomologiorum graecorum historia atque origine* (1893), pp. v–vi, cols. 152–87.
Kern, O., *Orphicorum Fragmenta* (1922), pp. 255–66.
Goodenough, E. R., *By Light, Light!* (1935), pp. 279–82, 296.
Walter, N., *Der Thoraausleger Aristobulus* (1964), pp. 103–15, 202–61.
Georgi, D., *Die Gegner des Paulus in 2 Korintherbrief* (1964), pp. 69, 73–6, 135, 144, 156 f., 181.
Denis, IPGAT, pp. 230–8.
Friedman, J. B., *Orpheus in the Middle Ages* (1971), pp. 13–37.
Speyer, W., *Die literarische Fälschung im heidnischen und christlichen Altertum* (1971), pp. 161 ff., 249.
Hengel, M., 'Anonymität, Pseudepigraphie und "Literarische Fälschung" in der jüdisch-hellenistischen Literatur', in K. von Fritz, ed., *Pseudepigrapha* I (Entretiens Hardt, XVIII) (1972), pp. 293–4.
Collins, BAAJ, pp. 204–7.

On Orpheus and the Orphean literature, cf. in general:
Lobeck, C. A., *Aglaophamus sive de theologiae mysticae Graecorum causis*, 2 vols. (1829).
Abel, E., *Orphica* (1885).
Susemihl, F., *Gesch. der griech. Litt. in der Alexandrinerzeit* I (1891), pp. 375 ff.
Rohde, E., *Psyche* II ([2]1898), pp. 103–36.
Kern, O., *Orphicorum Fragmenta* (1922).
Ziegler, K., 'Orphische Dichtung', RE XVIII.2 (1942), cols. 1321–417.
Guthrie, W. K. C., *Orpheus and Greek Religion* ([2]1952).
Nilsson, M. P., *Geschichte der griechischen Religion* I ([3]1967), pp. 681 ff.; II ([2]1961), pp. 426 ff.
Diels, H., and Kranz, W., *Die Fragmente der Vorsokratiker* I ([8]1956), pp. 1–20, 483.
Prümm, K., 'Mystères: L'orphisme', DB suppl. VI (1957), cols. 55–88.
Burkert, W., *Orphism and Bacchic Mysteries: New Evidence and Old Problems of Interpretation* (1977).
West, M. L., *The Orphic Poems* (1983).

5. The next probably Jewish passage (Denis, FPG, pp. 167–8), quoted in *De monarchia* 3 (Otto, *Corpus apologetarum* III, p. 136), is eleven verses from Sophocles on the future destruction of the world by fire and the twofold fate of the righteous and the unrighteous. (It is possible that the quotation from Pythagoras which intervenes in the *De monarchia* text is also a Jewish forgery but, if so, it came from a separate collection, see above, p. 660; below, p. 670.) In Clement of Alexandria, *Strom.* v 14, 121–2 = Eusebius, *Praep. ev.* xiii 13, 48, these same verses are quoted without mentioning Sophocles, only as the words of the τραγῳδία. It is possible that this indicates that this Sophocles fragment, like the preceding one (no. 2 above), belonged originally to a different

compendium from the main collection of dramatic poets (see above, p. 661). It has even been suggested that the distinctive theology found here of a world conflagration may have originated with a Stoic rather than a Jewish writer, cf. A. C. Pearson, *The Fragments of Sophocles* III (1917), pp. 176–9. Such Stoic ideas would however be quite natural also in a Jewish environment, as is shown by *Sib.* iii 83–92. It is even possible that the forger was influenced by *Sib.* iii 83–92, cf. Walter, JSHRZ IV.3 (1983), pp. 253–4, though this possibility is not strong enough for it to provide a firm date for the composition of these verses. In Clement they have also been divided into two, whereas Pseudo-Justin has united the two halves. The two verses relating to the different destinies of the righteous and the unrighteous are not given by Clement in this context, but in his preceding fragment from Diphilus, where they fit better (*Strom.* v 14, 121 = Eusebius, *Praep. ev.* xiii 13, 47) (Nauck, *Tragicorum Graec. fragm.*², F 1027).

6. Next (Denis, FPG, pp. 168–9) there are ten verses from the comic poet Philemon concerning the certain punishment even of hidden sins by the all-knowing and just God, and ten verses, only six of them spurious, from Euripides on the same theme, *De monarchia* 3 (Otto, *Corpus apologetarum* III, pp. 136–40). In Clement of Alexandria, *Strom.* v 14, 121 = Eusebius, *Praep. ev.* xiii 13, 47, both passages are attributed to the comic poet Diphilus. The text of Clement is given in excerpt also by Theodoret, *Graec. affect. curatio* vi 23 (ed. Canivet, vol. I, pp. 261–2). Denis, IPGAT, p. 229, is inclined to accept the attribution of the verses to Diphilus except for the four verses in Clement, *Strom.* v 14, 121, 2, which are cited by Stobaeus i 3, 15 as an extract from a genuine tragedy of Euripides.

It is certainly difficult to divide the text meaningfully into sections, but Walter, JSHRZ IV.3 (1983), p. 246, argues that the attribution of the fragments to Philemon by *De monarchia* should be accepted, since the separation of the Euripides verses can be explained by the incorporation into the text of a learned scholium by a commentator who observed the presence of the four genuine verses. (Philemon: Kock, *Com. att. fragm.*, F 246 = Edmonds, *Fragm. Att. Comedy*, F 246; Euripides: Nauck, *Tragic. Graec. fragm.*², F 835 (genuine), F 1131 (spurious).)

7. Twenty-four verses (Denis, FPG, pp. 169–70) are ascribed to Philemon by Pseudo-Justin on the theme that moral conduct is more necessary and valuable than sacrifice, *De monarchia* 4 (Otto, *Corpus apologetarum* III, pp. 140 ff.). In Clement of Alexandria, *Strom.* v 14, 119–20 = Eusebius, *Praep. ev.* xiii 13, 45–6, the same verses are ascribed to Menander. It is likely that Clement's ascription reflects the wishes of the original forger since Pseudo-Justin may have had a motive in not referring these verses on the cult to Menander, since his next chapter,

De monarchia 5, is devoted by him instead to Menander's comments on the nature of God, cf. Walter, JSHRZ IV.3 (1983), pp. 246–7. (Kock, *Com. att. fragm.*, F 1130; Koerte, *Menander, quae supersunt*, F 683.)

8. Among the remaining passages from the dramatic poets quoted in *De monarchia* and by Clement are a few more suspect verses (Denis, FPG, p. 171), which in *De monarchia* 5 (Otto, *Corpus apologetarum* III, pp. 150 ff.) are introduced with the formula Μένανδρος ἐν Διφίλῳ. Clement, *Strom.* v 14, 133 = Eusebius, *Praep. ev.* xiii 13, 62, attributes them to Diphilus. Clement is certainly correct, since no play of Menander by this name is known. Walter, JSHRZ IV.3 (1983), pp. 245, 249–50, argues that Pseudo-Justin has tried in *De monarchia* 5 to combine the original collection with a florilegium of quotations from Menander and Euripides by inserting there all material relevant to his subject, i.e. a summons to the worship of the one true God. If so, this would explain the false attribution of these verses to Menander and it is likely that they belong instead with the main compilation of Jewish forgeries preserved in *De monarchia* 2–4.[263] The collection of Menander and Euripides quotations apparently used by Pseudo-Justin seems to have been unknown to Clement. The majority of the citations are genuine. The collection may have been made by a Jew or a Christian and could date to any time before Pseudo-Justin in the third century A.D. (Diphilus: Kock, *Com. att. fragm.*, F 138; Edmonds, *Fragm. Att. Comedy*, F 138). The verses from Sophocles (Denis, FPG, p. 173) in Clement, *Strom.* v 14, 111 = Eusebius, *Praep. ev.* xiii 13, 38, in which Zeus is pictured in a rather unflattering light, are probably also spurious and may come from the main collection of Jewish forgeries of dramatic poets (Nauck, *Tragic. Graec. fragm.*², Fr. Jub. 1026). One further Jewish verse may also be contained under the name of Sophocles in Clement, *Strom.* v 128, 2 (= Eusebius, *Praep. ev.* xiii 13, 55 = Nauck, *Tragic. Graec. fragm.*², F 1028), and another two forged verses of Menander may be found in Pseudo-Justin, *De monarchia* 5 (Koerte, *Menander quae supersunt*, F 64, F 749). Their Jewish origin remains however uncertain, cf. Walter, JSHRZ IV.3 (1983), p. 254.

9. Finally, in this context also belong the verses (Denis, FPG, pp. 171–2) on the number seven and the Sabbath to which Aristobulus (*Praep. ev.* xiii 12, 13–16) and Clement of Alexandria (*Strom.* v 14, 107 = Eusebius, *Praep. ev.* xiii 13, 34), but not Pseudo-Justin, appeal. There are (a) two verses from Hesiod, (b) three verses from Homer, (c) five verses from Linus, for whom Clement has Callimachus. The attribution to Linus is more plausible, since Callimachus, of the third century B.C.,

---

263. N. Walter, *Der Thoraausleger Aristobulus* (1964), p. 184, suggests that the probable Jewish forgery of Euripides in Clement, *Strom.* v 75, 1 (= Denis, FPG, p. 171; Nauck, *Trag. Graec. Frag.*, F 1130), should also be ascribed to this collection even though it is omitted in *De monarchia*. Cf. Walter in JSHRZ IV.3 (1983), pp. 246–7, 250.

was too recent and unserious an author to be worth forging. Linus, a legendary poet in whose name verses were probably being composed from before the end of the third century B.C. when he was already listed as a sage (cf. Diogenes Laertius i 42) is however also rather more obscure a figure than a Jewish forger might have been expected to choose. The attribution to Linus has suggested to Walter that these verses represent a Pythagorean collection of number speculation that had been worked over by a Jew before Aristobulus. Some of the verses may therefore not be Jewish forgeries, either because they are genuine or because they were fabricated by a Pythagorean.[264] On Linus, cf. M. L. West, *The Orphic Poems* (1983), pp. 56–67. At any rate, the verses are a mixture of genuine and invented material. The differences between the texts given by Aristobulus and by Clement are rather unimportant. There are no grounds for connecting the textual tradition of these forgeries with that of the rest of the forged poetry in this section. These verses have different preoccupations in their concern for the uniquely Jewish institution of the Sabbath, and it is likely that they were invented and quoted as a separate collection.[265] Cf. Valckenaer, *De*

264. Walter, *Der Thoraausleger Aristobulus* (1964), pp. 150–71, 177–8. Walter, JSHRZ IV.3 (1983), pp. 255–6, suggests that the function of the Jewish reviser was minimal. M. L. West, *op. cit.*, p. 59, denies the Jewish origin even of the one verse considered Jewish by Walter, preferring to postulate a Stoic author. It should however be noted that there is no certain evidence of Pythagorean interest in the number seven until comparatively late, cf. H. Thesleff, in K. von Fritz, ed., *Pseudepigrapha* I (1972), p. 323. There are no grounds for associating the texts used by the Pythagorean Prorus περὶ τῆς Ἑβδομάδος (= H. Thesleff, ed., *The Pythagorean Texts of the Hellenistic Period* (Acta Acad. Aboensis, ser. A., vol. 30) (1968), pp. 154–5), which was probably a genuine Pythagorean work of the fourth century B.C., with these Jewish forgeries, *contra* W. Speyer, *Die literarische Fälschung* (1971), p. 162. For the date of Prorus, see H. Thesleff, *An Introduction to the Pythagorean Writings of the Hellenistic Period* (Acta Acad. Abeonsis, vol. 24) (1961), pp. 112, 114. The four hexameters cited under the name of Pythagoras in *De monarchia* 2 (= Denis, FPG, p. 167), and a Pseudo-Pythagorean prose fragment cited by Pseudo-Justin, *Contra Gentiles* 19b, and by Clement of Alexandria, *Protrept.* 72, 4b (cf. German translation by Walter, JSHRZ IV.3 (1983), p. 274), are probably the product of the same Jewish interest in Pythagorean writings. It is not possible to be certain whether these are forgeries by Pythagoreans, Christians, or Jews, cf. Walter, JSHRZ IV.3 (1983), pp. 257–8. Note should also be taken of the possibility that Pseudo-Ekphantos, περὶ βασιλείας (= Thesleff, *Pythagorean Texts*, pp. 78–84; L. Delatte, ed., *Les traités de la royauté d'Ecphante, Diotogène et Sthénidas* (1942)), was a Jewish forgery. This work has many points of contact with Philo, which, with other considerations, led Delatte to date it to the early imperial period. Against this, see Thesleff, *Introduction to Pythagorean Writings*, pp. 65–71, with a Hellenistic date. In favour of Jewish authorship because of the Philonic and biblical parallels is W. Burkert, in K. von Fritz, ed., *Pseudepigrapha* I (1972), pp. 48–53, although he suggests, pp. 53–5, that the date of the work may be as late as the early third century A.D.

265. The number of Jewish forgeries of such pagan verses may be much greater than indicated here since forgeries are not always easy to detect and most scholarship on the texts has concentrated on determining whether or not a verse is genuine rather than on the identity of the forger. Walter, JSHRZ IV.3 (1983), p. 258, suggests the following as probable Jewish forgeries: (1) four lines of Pindar in Clement, *Strom.* iv 167, 3 (= Pindar

Aristobulo, pp. 8–10, 89–125; Walter, JSHRZ IV.3 (1983), pp. 271–3, 277–9.

4. Pseudo-Hecataeus

Hecataeus of Abdera,[266] not to be confused with the much more ancient geographer Hecataeus of Miletus of about 500 B.C., was according to Josephus a contemporary of Alexander the Great and of Ptolemy I son of Lagus (*C. Ap.* i 22 (183)). This statement is also confirmed by other witnesses, cf. Jacoby, FGrH, 264. According to Diogenes Laertius ix 69, Hecataeus heard the philosopher Pyrrho, a contemporary of Alexander the Great. According to Diodoros Siculus i 46, he travelled to Thebes during the time of Ptolemy I Soter. He was a philosopher and historian and apparently lived mainly at the court of Ptolemy I Soter. The following are mentioned as his writings: a book about the Hyperboreans (Jacoby, FGrH, 264, FF 7–14), a history of Egypt (Jacoby, FGrH, 264, FF 1–6), and, in the Suda, s.v. 'Ἑκαταῖος, also a work περὶ τῆς ποιήσεως 'Ομήρου καὶ 'Ησιόδου, of which no other trace has been found. Hecataeus referred in some detail to the Jews in the course of his Egyptian history. Much of his description survives in Diodorus Siculus, xl 3 (= Jacoby, FGrH, 264, F 6 = Stern, GLAJJ I, pp. 26–35). Despite the generally friendly attitude of these comments towards the Jews, there is no reason to doubt their genuineness, nor that Diodorus' ascription of them to Hecataeus of Miletus according to the manuscripts should be amended to Hecataeus of Abdera.[267]

Under the name of this Hecataeus of Abdera two further books are quoted, one entitled 'On the Jews', and the other 'On Abraham'. It can

---

F 130, translated by Walter, *op. cit.*, p. 275); (2) two lines of Hesiod in Clement, *Strom.* v 112, 3b and Clement, *Protrept.* 73, 3 (= R. Merkelbach and M. L. West, F 362, translated by Walter, *ibid.*); (3) two lines of an oracle of Apollo cited by Porphyry in Eusebius, *Praep. ev.* ix 10, 4b, translated by Walter, *op. cit.*, p. 276.

266. According to Strabo 644, Hecataeus came from Teos, the mother-city of Abdera. Strabo is probably confused, cf. Fraser, PA II, pp. 718–19.

267. The passage is preserved in Photius, *Biblioth. cod.*, 244. Cf. Jacoby, FGrH, 264, F 6; Stern GLAJJ I, pp. 26–35, esp. 34–5. Only F. Dornseiff, ZAW 56 (1938), p. 76, n. 1, has maintained that the text genuinely belongs to Hecataeus of Miletus, but his arguments are not convincing, cf. Jacoby, FGrH III A, Komm., pp. 46–52. Much of Diodorus Siculus Book i is probably dependent on Hecataeus for the description of Egypt, cf. O. Murray, 'Hecataeus of Abdera and Pharaonic Kingship', JEA 56 (1970), pp. 144–5. Doubts about the extent of this dependence were raised by W. Spoerri, *Späthellenistische Berichte über Welt, Kultur und Götter* (1961), but Hecataeus must still be considered as the most likely source for this book, cf. A. Burton, *Diodorus Siculus Book I: A Commentary* (1972), pp. 1–34, esp. 2–10. It can therefore be assumed that the description of the Jews in Diodorus Siculus i 28 and i 55 also derived from Hecataeus, cf. Stern, GLAJJ I, pp. 167–70. The attitude of Hecataeus towards Jews in Diodorus Siculus lx may be due to his use of a Jewish patriotic source, cf. D. Mendels, ZAW 95 (1983), pp. 96–110.

be proved that the second of these was a pseudonymous work written by a Jew (see below); it has also been argued that the former work, 'On the Jews', was the work of a Jewish forger, but that is more dubious.

The book 'On the Jews' is cited under this name by Josephus (*C. Ap.* i 22 (183), and, implicitly, i 23 (214)) and by Origen (*C. Celsum* i 15). Josephus gives in *C. Ap.* i 22 (183–204) large extracts from this book dealing with the relations between the Jews and Ptolemy I Soter, their faithfulness to the Law, the organization of the priesthood, and the arrangement of their temple. Finally he gives a passage in which Hecataeus relates an anecdote of something he had himself once experienced during an expedition at the Red Sea. A Jewish cavalryman and archer by the name of Mosollamus (Meshullam) who belonged to the expeditionary corps killed a bird whose flight was anxiously observed by a soothsayer, and ridiculed those who were angry about this for their care for the bird which did not even know its own fate beforehand. Eusebius, *Praep. ev.* ix 4, also gives pieces based on these excerpts from Josephus. Josephus further mentions (*C. Ap.* ii 4 (43)) probably from the same book (though this is not explicitly stated), that Alexander the Great had given to the Jews the district of Samaria as a district free of tax in reward for their loyalty.[268] There is no *prima facie* reason to doubt that these fragments came from a genuine book by Hecataeus about the Jews. The long excerpts about Jews cited by Diodorus from his Egyptian history show that he had an interest in the subject, and the somewhat more panegyrical tone of the verse devoted to the Jews may be explained by the use of Jewish sources here and Egyptian sources there. The earliest suggestion that this book was a Jewish forgery was made by Herennius Philo[269] in the early second century A.D. According to Origen, *C. Celsum* i 15 (= Jacoby, FGrH, 790, F 9), Hecataeus took sides with the Jewish people to such an extent in his book 'On the Jews' that Herennius Philo first doubted that the book had been written by the historian Hecataeus, but subsequently said that if it had been written by him, Hecataeus had been carried

---

268. Some scholars have also seen *C. Ap.* ii 4 (42), which deals with the settlement of Jews in Alexandria under Alexander, as part of the quotation from Hecataeus (Denis, IPGAT, p. 264), but it is probably better to regard ii 4 (43) as a single excerpt of Hecataeus inserted within an Alexandrian Jewish work which continues at ii 4 (44–7) (Jacoby, FGrH III A, Komm., p. 74). Cf. also Wacholder, ESJL, pp. 262–73, who sees the passage *C. Ap.* ii 4 (43–7) with *Ant.* xii 1, 1 (3–8) as the product of a separate author later than the (pseudonymous) author of *C. Ap.* i 22–23 (183–205, 213–14) and Pseudo-Aristeas, *Ep.* 83–120, who in turn could be a Jew writing in the late fourth century B.C. See below, n. 272.

269. On Herennius Philo of Byblos, cf. Jacoby, FGrH, 790; Stern, GLAJJ II, pp. 138–45, with literature cited there. See above, vol. I, pp. 41–2, and note now H. W. Attridge and R. A. Oden, *Philo of Byblos: The Phoenician History* (1981); A. I. Baumgarten, *The Phoenician History of Philo of Byblos, a Commentary* (1981).

away by Jewish powers of persuasion and had accepted Jewish teachings. The doubts of Herennius Philo, however, show only how rare such philo-semitic pagan writings were by his time. Such views were far more common in the late fourth century B.C. (cf. Stern, GLAJJ I, p. 24). Arguments against this book as a genuine work of Hecataeus therefore rest entirely on details alleged to be either anachronistic or out of place when uttered by a non-Jew. Anachronisms have been seen in the emphasis on Jewish readiness for martyrdom in defence of the Law (*C. Ap.* i 22 (191)), in the reference to a high priest by the name of Ezekias (*C. Ap.* i 22 (187)), and in the attribution to the priests rather than the levites of the tithes (188).[270] Against these passages as anachronisms is the possibility, given the scarcity of evidence, that Jews may on occasion have indeed faced death under Persian rule, even if not to the extent suffered under Antiochus Epiphanes; the recent discovery of a late Persian or early Hellenistic coin at Beth-Zur bearing the name Hezekiah in Hebrew, which suggests that this name was found in the high-priestly family; and our ignorance of the precise date when tithes began to be paid to the priests rather than the levites.[271] Of statements which seem implausible in the mouth of a non-Jew, the two prime passages are *C. Ap.* i 22 (193), in which Jews are said to have been praised by Hecataeus for destroying pagan temples set up in their country by invaders, and *C. Ap.* ii 4 (43), in which it is stated that the Jews were given the whole of Samaria by Alexander the Great free of tribute. Although it is not totally impossible that both these passages came from the genuine Hecataeus, it may be best to assume that the original genuine text has been slightly altered by a later Jewish reviser.[272]

270. The case for these as anachronisms ?is put most strongly by B. Schaller, ZNW 54 (1963), pp. 15–31. It is suggested that martyrdom is only relevant after the Maccabees, that no high priest called Ezekias is attested in the literary sources (cf. originally H. Willrich, *Juden und Griechen* (1895), p. 31), and that the tithe was not given to the priests until the second century B.C.

271. For the coin, see O. R. Sellers, *The Citadel of Beth-Zur* (1933), p. 73, n. 9, and 74, fig. 9; note also that ἀρχιερεύς may well refer to a member of the high priestly family rather than the high priest (see vol. II, pp. 233–6). On the tithes, see vol. II, pp. 257–70. See also Stern, GLAJJ I, pp. 40–2.

272. So Stern, GLAJJ I, p. 24. The extent to which such a reviser has changed the original is much disputed. Neither of these two last-quoted passages is given by Josephus verbatim, so it is possible that he has himself misunderstood or exaggerated his source (cf. Collins, BAAJ, pp. 139–41), which was therefore the uncontaminated work of Hecataeus. In favour of the book as authentic are H. Lewy, 'Hekataios von Abdera *Peri Ioudaion*', ZNW 31 (1932),pp. 117–32, and J. G. Gager, 'Pseudo-Hecataeus Again', ZNW 60 (1969), pp. 130–9. In favour of almost the entire work as spurious is B. Schaller, 'Hekataios von Abdera über die Juden', ZNW 54 (1963), pp. 15–31. He is followed by N. Walter, *Der Thoraausleger Aristobulus* (1964), pp. 189–94, who accordingly denotes the author of this quite extensive fragment as Pseudo-Hecataeus I, to be distinguished from the Pseudo-Hecataeus II to whom the book on Abraham is assigned (see N. Walter,

Whether the book 'On the Jews' was a Jewish forgery or not, it can be taken as certain that the book on Abraham and the Egyptians, referred to by Josephus, *Ant.* i 7, 2 (159), and Clement of Alexandria, *Strom.* v 14, 113 = Eusebius, *Praep. ev.* xxii 13, 40, was written by a Jew. There is no reason to suppose that the two books were identical or that the book on Abraham was only a small section of the other one, or that its existence was invented to explain the quotation of Sophocles attributed to it. Of the contents of this book it can only be said that it discussed the patriarch in some detail, but that it also included the militantly monotheistic version of Pseudo-Sophocles discussed in the previous section (above, p. 661), and therefore presumably tried to prove that the more noble Greeks agreed with the views of Judaism. It is possible that Josephus was dependent on this work in parts or all of *Ant.* i 7, 1–8, 2 (154–68), as well as simply mentioning its existence at *Ant.* i 7, 2 (159) (Walter), but this is uncertain. It can be assumed that a Jew was more likely to adopt the guise of Hecataeus precisely because of the existence of genuine comments by Hecataeus on the Jews.

For the date of this book on Abraham, it can only be certain that it was written before the reference to it by Josephus. However, it may also be relevant for the date that Pseudo-Aristeas, 31, quotes Hecataeus as authority for the opinion that secular Greek authors did not mention the Jewish Law only because the teachings contained in it were too holy. The passage is also found in Eusebius, *Praep. ev.* viii 3, 3, and, in a freer rendering, in Josephus, *Ant.* xii 2, 4 (38). The quotation from Hecataeus may be taken to extend to the *whole* statement that the Greek poets and the mass of historians did not mention the holy books of the Jews *for the specific reason* that the teachings contained in them were holy, for this is how Josephus understood the words.[273] If the quotation was taken from one of the extant writings of Hecataeus or Pseudo-Hecataeus, it is unlikely to have been the Egyptian history or the work 'On the Jews', since not only is such an attitude not explicitly

---

Fragmente jüdisch-hellenistische Historiker, JSHRZ I.2 (1976), pp. 144–60). Wacholder, ESJL, pp. 262–73, asserts that the two passages in *Contra Apionem* should not be treated together because they reflect different authorial perspectives, thematic interests and attitudes to the Ptolemaic kings. He accordingly posits two pseudonymous authors, of whom the first, author of *C. Ap.* i 22–23 (183–205, 213–14), reflected in Pseudo-Aristeas 31, should be dated to *c.* 300 B.C. This early author would then, according to Wacholder, be a well-informed priestly Palestinian Jew who joined the army of Ptolemy Soter, hence his eye-witness account of Mosollamus. (See below, n. 276, for arguments against this.) Wacholder is certainly right at least when he affirms that neither of these two authors is identical with the writer of the book on Abraham.

273. See e.g. Willrich, *Judaica* (1900), p. 98, *contra* J. Geffcken, *Zwei griechische Apologeten* (1907), p. xii, n. 6, who tries to argue that the only element quoted from Hecataeus is praise for the holy θεωρία of the holy books, and that it was Pseudo-Aristeas, not Hecataeus himself, who used this fact to explain the lack of references in other pagan writers.

attested there, but both writings do in fact contain sections about the Law, although it is possible that Hecataeus made his observation about the reticence of other non-Jewish authors precisely in order to establish his own veracity in his contrasting openness about Jewish customs. The rather tendentious statement would be more characteristic of Pseudo-Hecataeus on Abraham, and, if Aristeas does indeed refer to that work, it must have been written before Aristeas, i.e. before the first century B.C. at the latest and probably before *c.* 170 B.C. However, it can be seen that this relationship is very hypothetical, and it is possible that the reference in Pseudo-Aristeas, 31, was either a free fiction of the author or a reference to yet another, otherwise unattested, work attributed to Hecataeus.[274] The only *terminus post quem* is the date of the invention of the Pseudo-Sophocles verse quoted here by Pseudo-Hecataeus (see above, section 3). The failure of Alexander Polyhistor to mention this book does not show that the work was written after his time since too little survives from Polyhistor's writings for such an argument from silence.[275] The title of the book given by Clement, i.e. 'On Abraham and the Egyptians', suggests that the author may have been an Egyptian Jew, unless it was suggested by Hecataeus' genuine Egyptian history. If Josephus, *Ant.* i 7, 1–8, 2 (154–68), was indeed dependent on this work, the attention given to the Ptolemies there would also make an Egyptian origin likely, though not necessary.

The Jewish reviser, if there was one, of the probably genuine work 'On the Jews' may have written at any time between Hecataeus and Josephus. There is no reason to identify him with the author of the book about Abraham.[276]

---

274. Cf. Walter, JSHRZ I.2 (1976), p. 146. Pseudo-Aristeas is nonetheless used to date Pseudo-Hecataeus by Jacoby, FGrH III A, Komm., pp. 62, 65–6; Fraser, PA II, pp. 968–9. The possible reliance of Pseudo-Aristeas 12–13 on Hecataeus, *On the Jews*, as cited in *C. Ap.* i 22 (186) (cf. Holladay, FHJA I, pp. 289, 297, n. 61), is irrelevant to the dating of Pseudo-Hecataeus if the writing *On the Jews* is seen as the work of the genuine Hecataeus.

275. On possible relations of the author of 'On Abraham' to the forged verses of the Greek poets, see Walter, *Der Thoraausleger Aristobulus* (1964), pp. 173–7, 187–9, 195–201. Walter, pp. 200–1, suggests a date in the first century B.C. at the earliest because of similarities in the image of the world conflagration in the quoted text of Pseudo-Sophocles to that in *Sib.* iii 83–92, but such a date is only possible if the reference in Pseudo-Aristeas is considered irrelevant (so Walter) or Pseudo-Aristeas is assigned an implausible late date. For use as a dating criterion of the silence of Alexander Polyhistor and Philo about Pseudo-Hecataeus see Jacoby, RE VII.2 (1912), col. 2767.

276. For those who judge the work of this reviser to have been very considerable, or the whole work to have been a Jewish forgery, further considerations can be brought for establishing the date. It is unlikely that such a forgery on a large scale originated before the second century B.C., and emphasis on the destruction of pagan temples and Jewish readiness for martyrdom would be more likely subjects for a *Jewish* writer after the Maccabees. Similarly, the assertion that Samaria was given free of tribute to the Jews may reflect the concession by Demetrius II to the Hasmonaeans in *c.* 145 B.C. (1 Mac.

Editions

The fragments of both the genuine Hecataeus of Abdera and the forged Hecataeus can be found in Müller, FHG II, pp. 384–96; Jacoby, FGrH, 264, III A, pp. 11–64.

For the texts referring to the Jews:
Denis, FPG, pp. 199–202 ('On the Jews', with Josephus' testimonia for 'On Abraham'); pp. 162–3 ('On Abraham' from Clement).
Stern, GLAJJ I, pp. 22–4, 35–44 (Egyptian history and 'On the Jews').
Holladay, FHJA I, pp. 277–335 ('On the Jews' and 'On Abraham').

Translations and Commentaries

English:
Stern, *loc. cit.*
Holladay, *loc. cit.*
Doran, R., in Charlesworth, OTP II (forthcoming).

German:
Walter, N., *Fragmente jüdisch-hellenistische Historiker* (JSHRZ I.2) (1976), pp. 154–60 ('On the Jews' and 'On Abraham').

On the genuine Hecataeus, cf. Schwartz, *Hecataeus von Teos* (1885), pp. 223–62; Jacoby, 'Hekataios (4)', RE VII (1912), cols. 2750–69; Fraser, PA I, pp. 496–504.

Bibliography

Freudenthal, J., *Alexander Polyhistor* (1875), pp. 165 f., 178.
Willrich, H., *Juden und Griechen vor der makkabäischen Erhebung* (1895), pp. 20–33.
Willrich, H., *Judaica* (1900), pp. 86–130.
Lévi, I, 'Moïse en Ethiopie', REJ 53 (1907), pp. 201–11.
Geffcken, J., *Zwei griechische Apologeten* (1907), pp. xiii–xvi.
Jacoby, F., 'Hekataios (4)', RE VII (1912), cols. 2750–69.
Christ, W. v., O. Stählin and W. Schmidt, *Gesch. der griech. Litt.*[6] II.1 (1920), pp. 618 ff.
Lewy, H., 'Hekataios von Abdera περὶ 'Ιουδαίων', ZNW 31 (1932), pp. 117–32.
Stein, M., 'Pseudo-Hecataeus, His Time and the Purpose of his Book on the Jews', Zion 6 (1934), pp. 1–11 (Heb.).
Dornseiff, F., *Echtheitsfragen antik-griechischer Literatur* (1939), pp. 52–65.
Jacoby, F., FGrH, Kommentar zu FGrH 264, FF 21–4, III A (1943), pp. 61–74.
Dalbert, P., *Die Theologie der jüdisch-hellenistischen Missionsliteratur* (1954), pp. 65–7.
Walton, F. R., 'The Messenger of God in Hecataeus of Abdera', HThR 48 (1955), pp. 255–7.
Gutman, Y., *The Beginnings of Jewish-Hellenistic Literature* I (1958), pp. 39–73 (Heb.).
Schaller, B., 'Hekataios von Abdera über die Juden', ZNW 54 (1963), pp. 15–31.

11:34). See Schaller, *art. cit.*, p. 31, and Walter, *Der Thoraausleger Aristobulus* (1964), p. 194, for a date in the second century B.C. for 'Pseudo-Hecataeus I'. Jacoby, FGrH, 264, III A, Komm., p. 62, following Willrich, *Juden und Griechen* (1895), p. 32, sees in the High Priest Ezekias in *C. Ap.* i 22 (187–8) a veiled reference to Onias IV who fled to Egypt just before the Maccabaean revolt, and the author of the work as a Palestinian Jewish priest who went to Egypt with him in *c.* 170–168 B.C., but the correctness of seeing Ezekias as a pseudonym for another high priest has been rendered much less likely by the find of the name Hezekiah on a coin at Beth-Zur, see above, p. 673. Wacholder, ESJL, p. 273, attributes part of the work usually considered to come from *On the Jews* to a Jewish priest in Jerusalem *c.* 300 B.C. (see above, n. 272), but the evidence he adduces may be more simply explained by the use of a Jewish source by the genuine Hecataeus in his work *On the Jews* as well as the Egyptian history, cf. Stern, GLAJJ I, p. 21.

Walter, N., *Der Thoraausleger Aristobulus* (1964), pp. 86–8, 172–201, esp. 187 ff.
Spoerri, W., 'Hekataios (4)', *Der Kleine Pauly* II (1967), 980–2.
Gager, J. G., Jnr., 'Pseudo-Hecataeus again', ZNW 60 (1969), pp. 130–9.
Denis, IPGAT, pp. 262–7.
Speyer, W., *Die literarische Fälschung im heidnischen und christlichen Altertum* (1971), pp. 160–1.
Hengel, M., 'Anonymität, Pseudepigraphie und "Literarische Fälschung" in der jüdisch-hellenistischen Literatur', in K. von Fritz, *Pseudepigrapha* I (1972), pp. 295, 301–3, 324–5.
Gager, J. G., *Moses in Greco-Roman Paganism* (1972), pp. 26–37.
Stern, M., and O. Murray, 'Hecataeus of Abdera and Theophrastus on Jews and Egyptians', JEA 59 (1973), pp. 159–69.
Stern, GLAJJ I, pp. 20–5.
Mortley, R., 'L'historiographie profane et les pères', in *Paganisme, Judaïsme, Christianisme* (Festschrift M. Simon) (1978), pp. 315–27.
Conzelmann, H., *Heiden, Juden, Christen* (1981), pp. 164–70.
Collins, BAAJ, pp. 42–3.
Gauger, J.-D., 'Zitate in der jüdischen Apologetik und die Authentizität der Hekataios-Passagen bei Flavius Josephus und im Ps. Aristeas-Brief', JSJ 13 (1982), pp. 6–46.
Mendels, D., 'Hecataeus of Abdera and a Jewish "patrios politeia" of the Persian Period (Diodorus Siculus XL, 3)', ZAW 95 (1983), pp. 96–110.

5. Pseudo-Aristeas

The famous letter (or, more accurately, διήγησις, i.e. narrative[277]) of Aristeas to Philocrates on the translation of the Jewish Law into Greek also belongs among the group of writings under discussion here. The legend forms only the work's outer framework. The whole is in fact a panegyric on Jewish Law, Jewish wisdom, and the Jewish name in general, from the mouth of a gentile. The two men Aristeas and Philocrates are not known from history. Aristeas describes himself in the narrative (40, 43) as an official of King Ptolemy II Philadelphus (285–246 B.C.) who was highly esteemed by the king. Philocrates is his brother (7, 120), an inquisitive and serious-minded man who wishes to acquire all the education and culture of the time. Both are obviously to be taken as non-Jews (Aristeas says of the Jews in par. 16: 'For they worship the same God, overseer and creator of the universe, as all other men, as we ourselves, though we call him by different names such as Zeus and Dis.'

Aristeas, as a participant and an eye-witness, tells his brother Philocrates how the translation of the Jewish Law into Greek came about. The librarian Demetrius of Phalerum drew the attention of King Ptolemy II Philadelphus (cf. 12–13) to the fact that the Law of the Jews was still missing from his great library and that its translation into

---

277. Cf. M. Hadas, *Aristeas to Philocrates* (1951), pp. 56–9, who notes that the work does not have the form of a letter and was never described as such in antiquity; cf. also Jellicoe, SMS, p. 30: an 'epistle'.

Greek was desirable so that it could be included in his royal collection. The king complied with this suggestion, Aristeas taking the opportunity of this royal favour towards the Jews to put in a successful plea for the emancipation of Jewish slaves kept in Egypt after the Syrian campaigns of Ptolemy I Soter (12–27). The king sent Andreas, the captain of his bodyguard, and Aristeas (40, 43) as envoys to Eleazar, the Jewish high priest, to Jerusalem with rich presents and with the request that Eleazar should send him experienced men capable of undertaking this difficult task. Eleazar immediately prepared to do as the king wished. He despatched seventy-two Jewish scholars, six from each of the twelve tribes. In this connection Aristeas now also gives a detailed description of the lavish presents which Ptolemy sent to Eleazar, and also of the city of Jerusalem, the Jewish Temple, Jewish worship, and even of the Jewish land, as he had seen them on the occasion of that embassy. The whole description tends to glorify the Jewish people with its excellent institutions and its sumptuous prosperity. With the same intention, Aristeas then imparts the content of a conversation which he had with the high priest Eleazar concerning the Jewish Law. On the strength of this conversation Aristeas is so fully convinced of the superiority of the Jewish Law that he considers it necessary to expound 'its holiness and its natural (reasonable) meaning' to his brother Philocrates also (171 : τὴν σεμνότητα καὶ φυσικὴν διάνοιαν τοῦ νόμου). In particular, the foolishness of idolatry, especially that of the Egyptians (138), and the reasonableness of the Jewish laws of purity are dealt with exhaustively, with the use of allegorical exegesis.

When the Jewish scholars arrived in Alexandria, they were received by the king with special honours and were invited to the royal table day after day for seven days. During these seven banquets the king directed to the Jewish scholars in turn seventy-two questions on the most important topics of politics, ethics, philosophy and worldly wisdom which were so excellently answered that the king was full of amazement at the wisdom of these Jewish men and expressed his gratitude for the lesson given him in the art of kingship (293). Aristeas, who took the text of these conversations from the official records (297–300), was himself very astonished by the wisdom of these men, who replied extempore to the most difficult questions which would otherwise have required long consideration.

After these festivities, a splendid residence was appointed for the seventy-two translators on the island of Pharos far from the noise of the city, where they eagerly set to work. Every day, a section of the translation was finished in such a way that a harmonious common text was arrived at by comparing what each had written independently (302; cf. also 39). By this means, the whole was completed in seventy-two days. When it was finished, the translation was first read to the assembled Jews, who declared it so excellent, sacred and accurate that no alteration should ever be made to it (310). It was then also read to the king, who 'admired the intelligence of the Lawgiver very much indeed' (312), and commanded that the books should be carefully preserved in his library. Finally, the seventy-two interpreters were set free to return to Judaea, taking with them rich presents for themselves and the high priest Eleazar.

This outline of the contents shows that the purpose of the narrative is a dual one. First and foremost, the story teaches how highly even gentile authorities such as King Ptolemy and his envoy Aristeas respected and praised the Jewish Law and Judaism in general. The work seen from this angle was obviously intended primarily for gentile readers, though Jews might also enjoy basking in the esteem of eminent gentiles. The gentiles were to be shown the interest evinced in the Jewish Law by Ptolemy, the promoter of learning, and the admiration with which his high-ranking official, Aristeas, spoke of it, and of Jewish matters in general, to his brother Philocrates. Secondly, despite the remarkable brevity of the passage which after such long digressions finally describes the actual work of translation of the Law (302–7), it is clear, from the emphatic declaration, that the accuracy of the translation was also recognized by the Jews, and that a further aim of the book was to commend the Greek rendering of the Law as a genuine equivalent of the Torah to those Jews whose knowledge of Hebrew was deficient and to all gentile readers.[278]

There is still no consensus among critics about the *date* of this book. It is not possible to tell to what extent the narrative has been invented by the author. Some degree of historicity for the basic framework is possible since an Alexandrian Greek version of the Pentateuch was certainly produced in the third century B.C. (see above, p. 476). Some passages in the present book, however, are only loosely connected with the main story, and it is likely that they originated quite separately. In particular, the account of the Jewish Law given to Aristeas by the High Priest Eleazar (130–71), in which allegorical interpretations are used in a way quite different from the rest of the work, may have been

---

278. When reproducing the story of the translation, Philo (*Vita Mosis* ii 25–40) insinuates that the LXX is divinely inspired and thus identical to the original Hebrew text. P. Kahle, CG, pp. 212 f., claims that the main aim of Aristeas was Jewish propaganda to ensure the substitution of the standard LXX for all earlier, more imperfect Greek translations of the Law, but it is more likely that the imperfect texts of the Law which, according to the words of Demetrius quoted by Aristeas (29–32), needed to be supplanted by the genuine version of the LXX were *Hebrew* texts available in Alexandria, cf. D. W. Gooding, 'Aristeas and Septuagint Origins: A Review of Recent Studies', VT 13 (1963), pp. 158–80, and above, p. 475.

borrowed from elsewhere,[279] and it is likely that the philosophical
questions asked and answered at the king's banquet (187–292) derived
either from an earlier non-Jewish ethical treatise or, more probably,
from the common clichés of contemporary pagan philosophy.[280]
However, the style of the whole work as it survives now is uniform and
there are no grounds for positing that these sections are later
interpolations. For the date of the present work, a strongly argued
theory assumes that it originated at the beginning of the second century
B.C. The legend that Demetrius of Phalerum suggested the whole
undertaking to Ptolemy Philadelphus is unhistorical, not only in details
but also in its main points, for Demetrius of Phalerum almost certainly
did not live at the court of Alexandria during the time of Ptolemy
Philadelphus (cf. above, p. 475). Therefore, when the Jewish
philosopher Aristobulus in c. 180–145 B.C. also designates Demetrius of
Phalerum as the originator of the undertaking (Eusebius, *Praep. ev.* xiii
12, 2) it is possible that he already had the book before him.[281] An early
second century date may also be supported by internal considerations.

279. This section is entirely omitted by Josephus in his paraphrase and has therefore
been claimed as an interpolation by a writer at the time of, and in the style of, Philo (J.
G. Février, *La Date de Composition et les sources de la lettre d'Aristée à Philocrate* (1925), pp. 24
ff., 63 ff.). Josephus, however, also omitted much else and this cannot be a decisive
argument, cf. Fraser, PA II, p. 980.

280. G. Zuntz, 'Aristeas Studies I: "The Seven Banquets"', JSS 4 (1959), pp. 121–36,
claims that Pseudo-Aristeas used a single source in which a doctrine of kingship was
systematically formulated, cf. also W. W. Tarn, *The Greeks in Bactria and India* (1938), pp.
414–36 (suggesting a hypothetical 'Questions of Ptolemy Philadelphus' written by a Jew
in the reign of Ptolemy Euergetes); Hadas, *op. cit.*, pp. 40–3. *Contra*, in favour of the
section as the work of Pseudo-Aristeas himself using common ideas, cf. O. Murray,
'Aristeas and Ptolemaic Kingship', JThSt 18 (1967), pp. 337–71; V. A. Tcherikover,
'The Ideology of the Letter of Aristeas', HThR 51 (1958), pp. 59–85; Fraser, PA II, p.
982. Cf. also J. J. Lewis, 'The Table-Talk Section in the Letter of Aristeas', NTSt 13
(1966), pp. 53–6.

281. The dependence of Aristobulus on Pseudo-Aristeas is strongly argued by, among
others, Fraser, PA I, pp. 694, 700, both on the grounds that all later antiquity saw
Pseudo-Aristeas and no other source as the origin of the story about Demetrius and
Ptolemy Philadelphus, and also because of an apparent coincidence between the plan of
the two works. An inverse relationship, Pseudo-Aristeas using Aristobulus, is possible, cf.
G. Zuntz, 'Aristeas Studies II', JJS 4 (1959), p. 125, but unlikely, given the elaboration in
Pseudo-Aristeas of fantastic testimonia to Judaism from other gentile literary figures
roughly contemporary with Demetrius (e.g. Menedemus, Theopompus of Chios,
Theodectes) compared to the casual allusion to the story in Aristobulus. However, the
third possibility that both writers used a common oral tradition which each elaborated
differently is perhaps the most likely of all, cf. N. Meisner, *Aristeasbrief*, JSHRZ II.1
(1973), p. 39. In that case, despite the argument of Walter, *Der Thoraausleger Aristobulus*
(1964), pp. 100, 146–7, that the priority of Aristobulus is demonstrated by the
appearance of the same material in concentrated form in Aristobulus but scattered in
Pseudo-Aristeas, and by the differences between the authors in their allegorical exegesis, it
is better to admit that the fragmentary survival of Aristobulus' writings prevents any
proper argument derived from his date being used to fix the time of Pseudo-Aristeas.

The background of the account appears to be a time in which the Jewish people, under the leadership of its high priest and with only slight dependence on Egypt, enjoyed a peaceful and happy existence, hence the time before the conquest of Palestine by the Seleucids. Nowhere is there any intimation of the complications and difficulties which began soon after the Seleucid conquest. Politically, the Jewish people and their high priest seem almost independent. It is an age of peace and prosperity. The weight to be given to this general picture depends however on the extent to which the picture was ever intended to reflect contemporary reality. Many of the geographical details are impossible, and inspired by biblical accounts rather than by anything in the author's own day.[282] Nonetheless it is reasonable to assume that those details for which no biblical or Egyptian sources, and no apologetic reason for invention can be found, are more likely to derive from contemporary conditions than the author's imagination. It is therefore noteworthy that the fortress of Jerusalem was in the possession of the Jews (100–4). The fortress described here was directly connected with the Temple, which it was its purpose to protect, and lay higher than the latter (*ibid.*, especially 101). These details cannot apply to the fortress erected by Antiochus Epiphanes, the seat of a Syrian garrison until the High Priest Simon conquered it, and subsequently levelled by a later Hasmonean (1 Mac. 1:33; 13:49–52; Jos. *Ant.* xii 5, 4 (252); xiii 6, 7 (215–17); *B.J.* v 4, 1 (136–41); cf. above, vol. I, pp. 154–5, 192). This fortress of the Syrians lay on the site of the former city of David, south of the Temple, probably on the southern spur of the Eastern hill at Jerusalem, cf. above, vol. I, p. 154, n. 39. By contrast, the fortress mentioned by Aristeas was evidently situated in the same place where the later Antonia stood, immediately to the north of the Temple. One has here to look for the Temple fortress already mentioned by Neh. 2:8; 7:2. This same fortress is also meant when it is said that the Egyptian general Skopas placed a garrison in the fortress of Jerusalem which was subsequently expelled by Antiochus the Great (Jos. *Ant.* xii 3, 3 (133 and 138)). It is also mentioned in 2 Mac. 4:12, 27; 5:5, which deals with the time *before* the erection of the Syrian fortress. It continued to exist under the Hasmoneans, was renewed by them, and was later reconstructed under the name Antonia by Herod.[283] Since in Ptolemaic

---

282. M. Hadas, *op. cit.*, p. 64; V. A. Tcherikover, *art. cit.*, pp. 77–9. The choice of particular biblical passages, e.g. at 116, from Joshua 3:15, was sometimes dictated by the attempts of the author to point up parallels between Judaea and Egypt (Tcherikover, pp. 108–11).

283. Renewal by Hyrcanus I (*Ant.* xviii 4, 3 (91)) or more generally by the Hasmonaeans (*Ant.* xv 11, 4 (403)). Existence during the time of Aristobulus I (*Ant.* xiii 11, 2 (307); *B.J.* i 3, 3–5 (75–80)) and of Alexandria (*Ant.* xiii 16, 5 (426); *B.J.* i 5, 4 (117–19)).

682 §33A. *Jewish Literature Composed in Greek*

times troops were clearly only temporarily placed in the fortress for military purposes (which can be seen quite plainly from *Ant.* xii 3, 3 (133)), Aristeas' allusions to the fortress are compatible with a date around 200 B.C. Even the position occupied by the high priest is in agreement with this. He stands at the head of the community but is not a worldly ruler in the style of the Hasmoneans. Neither is there any clear trace in the book of the circumstances of Herodian and Roman times. It is noteworthy that in the lengthy conversations at table (187–300), in which reference is made to God's guidance of human destiny, there is nowhere any expression of belief in immortality as is the case in many later Jewish writings.[284] But given the variety of Jewish attitudes to the afterlife in this period, it is unwise to rely too much on this as evidence for dating the book.

These arguments cannot, however, be accounted entirely decisive, and other dates have been plausibly suggested.[285] The latest is that proposed by Momigliano on the basis of the similarity between the phrasing of the official letter in Pseudo-Aristeas 37 and that in 1 Mac. 10:37. Momigliano argues that Pseudo-Aristeas relied directly on the document in 1 Maccabees and therefore wrote after the publication of that book in *c.* 110 B.C.[286] The similarity is, however, not close enough to show a direct connection, and it is anyway most likely that the document quoted in 1 Maccabees (a genuine letter of 151 B.C.) was available in Egypt before the incorporation of that work. Rather stronger grounds have been proposed by Bickermann for a date

---

284. M. Friedländer, *Die religiösen Bewegungen innerhalb des Judentums im Zeitalter Jesu* (1905), pp. 241 f.

285. To be rejected as entirely implausible are all suggestions of a date after 100 B.C., cf. e.g. H. Grätz, 'Die Abfassungszeit des Pseudo-Aristeas', MGWJ (1876), pp. 289–308, 337–49 (in the time of Tiberius because of the references to informers in verse 167); L. Herrmann, Latomus 25 (1966), pp. 58–77 (in the time of Titus). The only argument to be taken seriously for such a late date is that based on verse 115, where the Jewish area is said to have, in Ascalon, Joppa, Gaza, and Ptolemais, harbours well situated to supply its needs. If the geographical excursus is based on reality (see above, p. 681), and *if* this passage refers to Jewish *political* control of these ports, the passage must date after 96 B.C., when Gaza was captured by Alexander Jannaeus (P. Wendland, *Aristeae ad Philocratem Epistula* (1900), p. xxv) or, even later, to the Roman period, after Gaza had been rebuilt under Pompey (Willrich, *Judaica* (1900), p. 124). However, verse 115 probably does not refer to political control but only geographical proximity and the passage of trade (which would not be affected by the ports being in gentile hands), in which case it is irrelevant for the dating of the book.

286. A. Momigliano, 'Per la data e la caratteristica della lettera di Aristea', Aegyptus 12 (1932), pp. 161–73 = *Quarto Contributo* (1969), pp. 213–24. If the work *was* written so late, it was probably still composed before 104 B.C., when the Hasmonaean high priest assumed the title of βασιλεύς, cf. B. Motzo, Att. Acad. Torino 50 (1915), pp. 210–25 = *Ricerche sulla letteratura e la storia giudaico-ellenistica* (1924, repr. 1977), pp. 513–28.

between 145 and 127 B.C.[287] These limits are primarily fixed by the attested use in dated official Ptolemaic documents on papyrus of the titles and epistolary greeting formulae which are found in Pseudo-Aristeas. The criterion would be decisive if it could be shown that these formulae *never* appeared before 145 B.C., but in fact, although they seem to have been regularized around that date into the form in which they are found in Pseudo-Aristeas, sufficient earlier examples can be found which go back to the third century B.C. to leave open the possibility of an earlier date.[288] There are no positive historical reasons for dating the work to the later second century, though neither are there any such reasons to deny such a date.[289] If Pseudo-Aristeas did write as late as this, his work cannot have been read by Aristobulus, if Aristobulus is correctly dated to the time of Philometor, but we have already seen (above, p. 580) that Aristobulus' dependence on the letter is not certain, though it is likely. No such objection can be raised against the next, slightly earlier, period proposed for the composition of the work, namely the reign of Philometor (180–145 B.C.).[290] In favour of such a date is the generally peaceful picture of Jerusalem already noted which, however unreal, is most implausible after the Seleucid occupation of their fortress in the early 160s B.C., and the high rank of the author at the Ptolemaic court as revealed by his detailed and accurate knowledge of court procedure and royal administration.[291] Such royal favour towards a Jew was most likely in the second period of Philometor's rule (after 164 B.C.),[292] but would also be possible before

287. E. J. Bickermann, 'Zur Datierung des Pseudo-Aristeas', ZNW 29 (1930), pp. 280–98 = *Studies in Jewish and Christian History* I (1976), pp. 108–36. Taking Bickermann's evidence to permit a date shortly after 127 B.C., N. Meisner, *Aristeasbrief*, JSHRZ II.1 (1973), p. 43, proposes that the letter was written by Alexandrian Jews to distance themselves from the Jews of Leontopolis and their Bible translation during the struggle between Ptolemy VIII Physcon and Cleopatra II during 127–118 B.C. There is however no evidence of a separate Greek version of the Bible having been produced at Leontopolis (see below, n. 289).

288. A further review of the papyrological evidence in Fraser, PA II, pp. 970–1.

289. Hadas, *op. cit.*, p. 54, relies mostly on the linguistic arguments of Bickermann in preferring 130 B.C. Collins, BAAJ, pp. 83–4, notes that the account of the liberation of Jewish slaves, the attack on informers and open disapproval of Jews acting as soldiers would all make sense in the context of the unhappy relations of the military followers of Onias with Ptolemy VIII Physcon in the period, but this is pure speculation, as is the suggestion by S. Jellicoe, 'The Occasion and Purpose of the Letter of Aristeas: A Re-Examination', NTSt 12 (1965/6), pp. 144–50, that the letter was composed to endorse a Greek translation which came from Jerusalem against the claim of a (hypothetical) translation from Leontopolis. See above, n. 287.

290. Fraser, PA II, pp. 970–2.

291. *Ibid.*, I, pp. 698–700.

292. Hence this period is preferred by Fraser, *op. cit.*, II, p. 971. It should be noted that this does not preclude a rather later date either, since a Jew in favour under Philometor might have written the letter at a later time, cf. Collins, BAAJ, p. 82.

170 B.C.[293] The author can therefore only be dated with certainty to some time in the second century B.C.; a position of such authority would be most unlikely for a pious Jew in the third century B.C. All scholars at any rate agree that the author must have been an Egyptian, and probably an Alexandrian, Jew, because of this detailed knowledge of Ptolemaic court life.[294]

The legend of this book was readily taken over and widely repeated by Jews and Christians. The first person to betray an acquaintance with the story, though not necessarily the book, was Aristobulus (Eusebius, *Praep. ev.* xii 12, 2). The next was Philo (*Vita Mosis* ii 26–40), who also mentions a yearly commemoration festival at Pharos (41–44) and again may write independently of Pseudo-Aristeas but against the background of the tradition, cf. R. Tramontano, *La lettera di Aristeo* (1931), pp. 170*–184*. Josephus by contrast reproduces almost literally a large section of the book in *Ant.* xii 2, 1 (12 ff.). Cf. also *Ant.* i *Proem* 3 (10–11), *C. Ap.* ii 4 (45–7). In rabbinic literature there are also some, admittedly confused, echoes of this legend (*yMeg.*, i 71d; *bMeg.*, 9a; *Massekhet Sopherim*, i 7–10); cf. Hadas, pp. 79–84.

Passages from the Church Fathers and from Byzantine authors have been collected in Wendland's edition (1900), pp. 121–66. A few testimonia from oriental sources not given by Wendland may be found in French or Latin translation or paraphrase in A. Pelletier, *Lettre d'Aristée à Philocrate* (1962), pp. 95–6. English translations of the more important passages are given in H. St. J. Thackeray, *The Letter of Aristeas* (1917), pp. 89–116. Cf. R. Hanhart, VT 12 (1962), pp. 146–9. The legend is reproduced here with various modifications, in particular the following two: (1) that the translators worked independently of each other and yet arrived at verbal agreement in their translations (this is Philo's version; Aristeas has the exact opposite, namely that agreement was reached by way of comparison); (2) that not only the Law but the entire Holy Scriptures were translated by the LXXII (in Aristeas there is question only of the Law).[295] Cf. on the various forms

293. This is the view of H. M. Orlinsky, 'Review of Hadas, *Aristeas to Philocrates* (1951)', Crozer Quarterly 29 (1952), pp. 201–5.
294. On his use of technical language see Bickermann, ZNW 29 (1930), pp. 280–98 (n. 287 above). Cf. in general, Fraser, PA I, pp. 698–700, 703.
295. Jerome already called attention to both differences. (1) *Praef. in vers. Genes.* (PL XXVIII, 181–2): 'nescio quis primus auctor septuaginta cellulas Alexandriae mendacio suo exstruxerit, quibus divisi eadem scriptitarent, quum Aristeas eiusdem Ptolemaei ὑπερασπιστής, et multo post tempore Josephus, nihil tale retulerint, sed in una basilica congregatos, contulisse scribant, non prophetasse.' (2) *Comment. in Ezech.* 5:12 ff. (CCL, LXXV, p. 60): 'quamquam et Aristaeus et Iosephus et omnis schola Iudaeorum quinque tantum libros Moysi a Septuaginta translatos asserant.' Similarly *Comment. in Mich.* 2:9 ff. (CCL, LXXVI, pp. 446–7); *Praefat. in librum quaest. hebr.* (CCL, LXXII, p. 2). Jerome's aim was to call into question the supposed divine origin of the Septuagint text in order to

of the legend: R. Tramontano, *La lettera di Aristeo* (1931), pp. 193 ff.;
Hadas, *op. cit.*, pp. 73–9; Jellicoe, SMS, pp. 41–7. The fullest list of
references may be found in C. Oikonomos, Περὶ τῶν ὁ Ἑρμηνευτῶν τῆς
παλαιᾶς θείας Γραφῆς, 4 vols. (1844–9). The most important of these are
the following: Justin, *Apol.* i 31. *Dial. c. Tryph.* 68. Pseudo-Justin,
Cohortatio ad Graecos 13. Irenaeus, *Adv. haer.* iii 21, 2 (Greek in Eusebius,
Hist. eccl. v 8, 11–15). Clement of Alexandria, *Strom.* i 22, 148 ff.
Tertullian, *Apologet.* 18 (the first Christian writer to mention Aristeas by
name). Anatolius in Eusebius, *Hist. eccl.* vii 32, 16. Eusebius gives long
passages from the book of Aristeas in an unadorned epitome in his
Praeparatio evangelica viii 2–5 and 9; cf. also viii 1, 8; ix 38. *Chronic.*, ed.
Schoene, II, cols. 118 ff. (*ad ann. Abrah.*, 1736). Cyril, *Hieros. cateches.* iv
34. Hilarius, *Prolog. ad librum psalmorum* 8; *Idem, Tractat. in psalmum* ii
and cxviii. Epiphanius, *De mensuris et ponderibus* 3; 6; 9–11 (a fantastic
elaboration typical of the author, cf. Hadas, *op. cit.*, pp. 76–8; M.
Stone, HThR 73 (1980), pp. 331–6 on the Armenian version). Jerome,
Praefat. in version. Genes. (PL XXVIII, 181–2). *Idem, Praefat. in librum
quaestion. hebraic.* (CCL LXXII, 2). Augustine, *De civitate dei* xviii 42–3.
Chrysostom, *Orat. I adversus Iudaeos. Idem, Homil. in Matt.* v 2.

On the manuscripts of the book of Aristeas, see Wendland's ed.
(1900), pp. vii-xxiii; Thackeray's ed. in H. B. Swete and R. R. Ottley,
IOTG, pp. 533–50; A. Pelletier, *Lettre d'Aristée à Philocrate* (1962), pp.
8–22.

Editions

Wendland, P., *Aristeae ad Philocratem epistula* (1900) (still not entirely superseded).
Thackeray, H. St. J., in Swete, IOTG, pp. 533–606.
Pelletier, A., *Lettre d'Aristée à Philocrate* (1962).

Translations and Commentaries

English:
Thackeray, H. St. J., in JQR 15 (1903), pp. 337–91, revised as *The Letter of Aristeas*
   (1917).
Andrews, H. T., in Charles, APOT II, pp. 94–122.
Meecham, H. G., *The Oldest Version of the Bible* (1932), pp. 12–86.
Hadas, M., *Aristeas to Philocrates* (1951).

German:
Wendland, P., in Kautzsch, APAT II (1900; repr. 1921), pp. 1–31.
Riessler, P., *Altjüd. Schrift.* (1928), pp. 193–233; 1277–9.
Meisner, N., *Aristeasbrief* (JSHRZ II.1) (1973), pp. 35–87.

French:
Pelletier, *op. cit.*

Italian:
Tramontano, R., *La Lettera di Aristea a Filocrate* (1931).

justify his own revision based on the Hebrew. Cf. W. Schwartz, *Principles and Problems of
Biblical Translation* (1955), pp. 26–34.

Hebrew:
Kahana, A., הספרים החיצונים (²1956).

Bibliography

Hody, H., *Contra historiam Aristeae de LXX interpretibus dissertatio* (1685).
Freudenthal, J., *Alexander Polyhistor* (1875), pp. 110–12, 124 ff., 141–3, 149 f., 162–5, 203 ff.
Grätz, H., 'Die Abfassungszeit des Pseudo-Aristeas', MGWJ (1876), pp. 289 ff., 337 ff.
Kuiper, K., 'De Aristeae ad Philocratem fratrem epistola', Mnemosyne 20 (1892), pp. 230–72.
Willrich, H., *Juden und Griechen* (1895), pp. 33–6.
Willrich, H., *Judaica* (1900), pp. 118–27.
Motzo, B., 'Aristea', *Atti Acad. Torino* 50 (1915), pp. 202–26, 547–70.
Willrich, H., *Urkundenfälschung in der hellenistisch-jüdischen Literatur* (1924), pp. 86–91.
Février, J.-G., *La date, la composition et les sources de la Lettre d'Aristée à Philocrate* (1925).
Tracy, S., 'III Maccabees and Pseudo-Aristeas', YCS 1 (1928), pp. 241–52.
Guttmann, J., EJ III (1929), 316–20.
Bickermann, E. J., 'Zur Datierung des Pseudo-Aristeas', ZNW 29 (1930), pp. 280–98 (reprinted in *Studies in Jewish and Christian History* I (1976), pp. 123–36).
Stählin, G., 'Josephus und der Aristeasbrief', ThStKr 102 (1930), pp. 324–31.
Michel, O., 'Wie spricht der Aristeasbrief über Gott?', ThStKr 102 (1930), pp. 302–6.
Stein, M., 'The Author of the Letter of Aristeas as a Jewish Apologist', Zion 1 (1926), pp. 129–47 (Heb.).
Martin, J., *Symposion. Die Geschichte einer literarischen Form* (1931), pp. 266–70.
Momigliano, A., 'Per la data e la caratteristica della lettera di Aristea', Aegyptus 12 (1932), 161–72 (= *Quarto contributo* (1969), pp. 213–24).
Meecham, H. G., *The Letter of Aristeas, A Linguistic Study with Special Reference to the Greek Bible* (1935).
Dornseiff, F., *Echtheitsfragen antik-griechischer Literatur* (1939), pp. 69 ff.
Wilcken, U., 'Urkunden-Referat (II PER Inv. 24552 gr.)', Arch. f. Pap. 12 (1937), pp. 221–3.
Joüon, P., 'Ὄχλος au sens de "peuple, population" dans le grec du Nouveau Testament et dans la Lettre d'Aristée', RSR 27 (1937), pp. 618 ff.
Joüon, P., 'Imparfaits de "continuation" dans la Lettre d'Aristée et dans les Évangiles', RSR 28 (1938), pp. 93–6.
Westermann, W. L., 'Enslaved Persons who are Free. Rainer Papyrus (PER) Inv. 24, 552', AJPh 59 (1938), pp. 1–30.
Wilhelm, A., 'Zu dem Judenerlasse des Ptolemaios Philadelphos', Arch. f. Pap. 14 (1941), pp. 30–5.
Bickerman, E. J., 'The colophon of the Greek Book of Esther', JBL 63 (1944), p. 343.
Hadas, M., 'Aristeas and III Maccabees', HThR 42 (1949), pp. 175–84.
Tarn, W. W., *The Greeks in Bactria and India* (²1951), pp. 414–36.
Schubart, W., 'Spicilegium criticum', Aegyptus 31 (1951), pp. 148–57.
Orlinsky, H. M., 'Review of Hadas, *Aristeas to Philocrates* (1951)', Crozer Quarterly 29 (1952), pp. 201–5).
Dalbert, P., *Die Theologie der hell.-jüd. Missionsliteratur* (1954), pp. 92–102.
Stricker, B. H., *De Brief van Aristeas* (Verhandelingen der Koninklijke Akademie van Wetenschappen te Amsterdam, 62, 4, 1956).
Altheim, F., and R. Stiehl, 'Alexander the Great and the Avesta', East and West 8 (1957), pp. 123–35, pl. 125–7.
Tcherikover, V. A., *Corpus Papyrorum Judaicarum* I (1957), pp. 1–47.
Tcherikover, V. A., 'The Ideology of the Letter of Aristeas', HTR 51 (1958), pp. 59–85.
Zuntz, G., 'Zum Aristeas-Text', Philologus 102 (1958), pp. 240–6.
Kahle, P. E., *The Cairo Geniza* (²1959), pp. 209–14.

Tcherikover, V. A., *Hellenistic Civilization and the Jews* (1961), pp. 351, 527.

Zuntz, G., 'Aristeas Studies I: "The Seven Banquets"', JSS 4 (1959), pp. 21–36.

Zuntz, G., 'Aristeas Studies II: "Aristeas on the Translation of the Torah"', JSS 4 (1959), pp. 109–26.

Jellicoe, S., 'St. Luke and the "Seventy(-Two)"', NTSt 6 (1959/60), pp. 319–21.

Jellicoe, S., 'St. Luke and the Letter of Aristeas', JBL 80 (1961), pp. 149–55.

Jellicoe, S., 'Aristeas, Philo and the Septuagint *Vorlage*', JThSt 12 (1961), pp. 261–71.

Bickermann, E. J., 'Notes sur la chancellerie des Lagides', Revue Internationale des Droits de l'Antiquité 9 (1962), pp. 251–67.

Hanhart, R., 'Fragen um die Entstehung der LXX', VT 12 (1962), pp. 139–63.

Pelletier, A., *Flavius Josèphe adaptateur de la 'Lettre d'Aristée': une réaction atticisante contre la Koiné* (1962) (SC 89) (1962).

Zuntz, G., 'Aristeas', IDB I (1962), pp. 219–21.

Gooding, D. W., 'Aristeas and Septuagint Origins: A Review of Recent Studies', VT 13 (1963), pp. 357–79.

Jaubert, A., *La Notion de l'Alliance dans le Judaïsme* (1963), pp. 322–9.

Klijn, A. F. J., 'The Letter of Aristeas and the Greek Translations of the Pentateuch in Egypt', NTSt 11 (1965), pp. 154–8.

Jellicoe, S., 'The Occasion and Purpose of the Letter of Aristeas: a Re-examination', NTSt 12 (1965/6), pp. 144–50.

Herrmann, L, 'La Lettre d'Aristée à Philocrate et l'empereur Titus', Latomus 25 (1966), pp. 58–77.

Lewis, J. J., 'The Table-Talk Section in the Letter of Aristeas', NTSt 13 (1966/7), pp. 53–6.

Murray, O., 'Aristeas and Ptolemaic Kingship', JThSt 18 (1967), pp. 337–71.

Préaux, C., 'De la Grèce Classique à l'Égypte Hellénistique. Traduire ou ne pas traduire', Chron. d'Égypte 42 (1967), pp. 369–83.

Van't Dack, E., 'La date de la Lettre d'Aristée', *Studia Hellenistica* XVI (1968), pp. 263–78.

Jellicoe, SMS, pp. 29–58.

Rost, L., 'Vermutungen über der Anlage zur griechischen Übersetzung der Torah', Abhandlungen zur Theologie des Alten und Neuen Testaments 59 (1970), pp. 39–44.

Rappaport, U., *Studies in the History of the Jewish People* (1970), pp. 37 ff. (Heb.).

Speyer, W., *Die literarische Fälschung* (1971), p. 163.

Howard, G. E., 'The *Letter of Aristeas* and Diaspora Judaism', JThSt 22 (1971), pp. 337–48.

Meisner, N., *Untersuchungen zum Aristeasbrief* (1972).

Murray, O., 'Aristeas and his Sources', *Studia Patristica* XII.1 (1975), pp. 123–8.

Orlinsky, H. M., 'The Septuagint as Holy Writ and the Philosophy of the Translators', HUCA 46 (1975), pp. 89–114.

Shutt, R. J. H., 'Notes on the Letter of Aristeas', Bulletin of the International Organization for Septuagint and Cognate Studies 10 (1977), pp. 22–30.

Schwartz, D. R., 'The priests in *Ep. Arist.* 310', JBL 94 (1978), pp. 567–71.

Sabugal, S., 'La exégesis bíblica de Aristóbulo y del seudo-Aristeas', Revista Agustiniana de Espiritualidad 20 (1979), pp. 195–202.

Mendels, D., '"On Kingship" in the "Temple Scroll" and the ideological *Vorlage* of the seven banquets in the "Letter of Aristeas to Philocrates"', Aegyptus 60 (1980), pp. 127–36.

6. Pseudo-Phocylides

The gnomic poet Phocylides of Miletus lived in the sixth century B.C. according to the Suda (ed. Adler IV, p. 754), and Eusebius, *Chron. ad Olymp.* 60, ed. Schoene, II, col. 98. Little has been preserved of his genuine poems,[296] but references in Plato (*Republic*, 407a7), Isocrates (*Ad Nicoclem*, 42 ff.) and Aristotle (*Politics* iv 11, 1295b34) show him to have been considered an authority in ethical matters from the fourth century B.C. A poem which gives moral instructions of the most diverse kinds in 230 hexameters was circulated under his name in the Hellenistic period. It is very likely, though not yet certain (see below), that the author of this work was a Hellenistic Jew. As the work was often used as a schoolbook in the Byzantine period, it has been preserved in numerous manuscripts, and since the sixteenth century has often been printed.

The contents of these verses are almost exclusively ethical. Only occasionally are there references to the one true God and future retribution. The moral teachings which the author enjoined extend to the most varied areas of practical life in the manner of Jesus ben Sira. But in detail they are affiliated most closely with the Old Testament, particularly with the Pentateuch, whose precepts relating to civil life (property, marriage, public welfare, etc.) resound throughout. One even finds here such special rules as those laying down that only the young birds may be taken from a nest, while the mother must be permitted to fly away (84–5; Dt. 22:6–7) and that the meat of fallen animals or animals killed by beasts of prey should not be eaten (Dt. 14:21; Exod. 22:30 = Phoc. 139, 147–8).

It is nonetheless still not entirely clear whether the author was Jewish. The hypothesis of a pagan author assumes either that the work is genuinely of the sixth century B.C. (most recently, Dornseiff) or that a pagan writer of the Hellenistic period came under considerable Jewish influence through the LXX whether as a god-fearer or in some less formal relation. The first suggestion is rendered untenable by the existence of numerous late words and word-forms, despite the old Ionic dialect in which the poem is couched. The latter idea is possible but cannot be proved. It is certainly no more plausible than the hypothesis of a Jewish author and it is unlikely that a pagan author wishing to influence other pagans towards Jewish ethics would be so reticent in ascribing his work to a pagan rather than to a Jewish author. A Christian author is rather unlikely since neither Clement nor Eusebius quotes the work. The earliest references are in Stobaeus and classical scholia, though the silence of the patristic writers may be due to the fact that they were only interested in quoting pagan authors who testified to Christianity more explicitly than does Pseudo-Phocylides. More significantly, the moral teaching in the work coincides only with the Old Testament and ignores the Gospels, which would be unlikely for a

---

296. Collected in E. Diehl, ed. R. Beutler, *Anthologica Lyrica Graeca*, 3rd ed., fasc. 1 (1949), pp. 57–60, and in B. Gentili and C. Prato, *Poetarum Elegiacorum testimonia et fragmenta* I (1979), pp. xii, xxxviii, 130–40.

Christian author discussing morals. Passages referring to 'gods' in the plural (98, 104) do not show, as was once thought, either Christian or pagan origin : line 98 is to be emended,[297] and line 104, which says that the dead will become 'gods' at the consummation, is just as possible, if uncomfortable, in a Jewish context (especially since the revelation of the eschatological ideas prevalent at Qumran) as it would be in a Christian or pagan text.[298]

The hypothesis of a Jewish origin is further suggested by Pseudo-Phocylides' independent use of material also used, probably later than him, by the early Christian literature including the Didache, e.g. the motif of the Two Ways.[299] It is also confirmed by his selection for emphasis of the same elements of the Jewish Law as were selected by Philo in the *Hypothetica* and by Josephus, *C. Ap.* ii 22–30 (188–219).[300]

The work is most likely therefore to be the product of a Hellenistic Jew. It is all the more striking that no serious attempt is made to stress specifically Jewish ideas. The two basic religious ideas of Judaism, the unity of God and future retribution, are only referred to in passing, and the author's concentration is on ethical maxims to which any

---

297. Verses 97–8 exhort :

μὴ δὲ μάτην ἐπὶ πῦρ καθίσας μινύθῃς φίλον ἦτορ.
μέτρα δὲ τεῦχε θεοῖσι· το γὰρ μέτρον ἐστὶν ἄριστον.

In line 98, θεοῖσι is impossible to translate in any way consonant with the context (*contra* Ludwich and Ranston). Various emendations have been proposed (cf. van der Horst, *ad. loc.*). Bernays's conjecture is the most appealing : γόοισι (lamentations) in place of θεοῖσι. The lines can then be translated : 'Sit not in vain beside the fire, weakening your heart. Be moderate in your grief, for moderation is best' (van der Horst). Alternatively, Young in the Teubner edition has ἔθ' ἑοῖσι, meaning : 'Set limits to (the grief of) your family'.

298. Verses 103–4 :

καὶ τάχα δ' ἐκ γαίης ἐλπίζομεν ἐς φάος ἐλθεῖν
λείψαν' ἀποιχομένων· ὀπίσω δὲ θεοὶ τελέθονται

'For in fact we hope that the remains of the departed will soon come to light again out of the earth.' Bernays wanted to emend θεοὶ to νέοι, but unnecessarily. The concept is perfectly possible among Jews, cf. M. Hengel, *Der Sohn Gottes* (1975), pp. 67–89, and the note *ad loc.* in van der Horst's edition.

299. This has been aptly shown by Funk, *Doctrina duodecim apostolorum* (1887), pp. xviii-xxii. The relationship between Phocylides and the *Didache* may be explained by the fact that both go back to a common Jewish source, namely the presumably Jewish 'Two Ways', of which many traces are found in early Christian literature. Cf. on the 'Two Ways' in general, above, pp. 172 f., and on its use by Phocylides, Alfr. Seeberg, *Die beiden Wege und das Aposteldekret* (1906), pp. 24 ff. ; *idem, Die Didache des Judentums und der Urchristenheit* (1908), pp. 11–15, 23–34. See also G. Klein, *Der älteste christliche Katechismus und die jüdische Propaganda-Literatur* (1909), pp. 143–53. For the relation of Pseudo-Phocylides to the New Testament in general, see P. W. van der Horst, 'Pseudo-Phocylides and the New Testament', ZNW 69 (1978), pp. 187–202.

300. Cf. Wendland, Jahrbb. für class. Philologie, suppl. vol. 22 (1896), pp. 709–12. See also the connections in all these texts with Jewish wisdom literature emphasized by M. Küchler, *Frühjüdische Weisheitstraditionen* (1979), pp. 236–302; cf. pp. 211–15 (parallels with Josephus), pp. 223–6 (parallels with Philo).

well-intentioned contemporary, no matter his religious affiliation, might be expected to assent. The work would therefore clearly fail as missionary literature to gentiles for Judaism and, if intended by a Jew for a pagan audience, can only have hoped to influence them, not towards Judaism, but towards a general morality as understood by Jews, i.e. the seven Noachide laws, of which Pseudo-Phocylides mentions five, excluding (tactfully?) blasphemy and idolatry. If so, the work presumably survives only because the ascription to Phocylides was believed genuine. Alternatively and more likely, the poem was written by a Jew for Jews. It is not necessary for this that the superscription attributing it to Phocylides be a late addition, which is linguistically implausible, since among Hellenized Jews the attribution to an ancient Greek author of notions that they already accepted as valid through the Old Testament will have reinforced their attachment to Judaism and their belief in the possibility of reconciling their religion with the surrounding Greek culture that they had already adopted.

For the date of composition there are no other limits than those given for Hellenistic-Jewish literature in general. It is a reasonable argument that a text of this sort is likely to have expanded over the centuries and that, besides any possible later Christian interpolations (cf. the athetized verses in the Teubner text), the manuscripts also include material that may go back to the genuine Phocylides in the sixth century B.C. (Farina). But it is reasonable to enquire more precisely about the date of the Hellenistic Jewish contribution to such a corpus of gnomic sayings. The later appearance in other texts of some word-forms found in Pseudo-Phocylides suggests a date after 100 B.C., as would his knowledge of the LXX and Stoicism, and agreements between his ideas and those in Philo and Cynic-Stoic diatribe (van der Horst).

For the place of composition, the polemic against the dissection of human corpses (verse 102) would be very appropriate in Alexandria in the Hellenistic period since the anatomical investigations there were celebrated, cf. F. Kudlien, 'Anatomie', RE supp. XI (1968), cols. 38–48, but it cannot be ruled out that dissection of corpses occurred elsewhere, nor that such dissection continued in Alexandria and other places in the Roman period. The reticence of later non-Alexandrian doctors about such interference with corpses may reflect not the cessation of the practice but the same disgust among lay persons which is mirrored by Pseudo-Phocylides, cf. J. Scarborough, *Roman Medicine* (1969), pp. 168–70. If so, the forgery need not be Alexandrian, and could conceivably have been written quite late in the Roman period, though clearly before the first citations in the fifth century A.D.

A passage from this poem (verses 5–79) has been interpolated in the text of the Sibylline Oracles (ii 56–148) in the Ψ group of manuscripts. The insertion is older than the Suda, s.v. *Φωκυλίδης*, who thought that

Phocylides' verses had been 'stolen' from the Sibylline Oracles. This however is clearly wrong since only one manuscript of the Sibylline Oracles contains the interpolation. It has nonetheless been suggested that the Sibylline insertion preserves an older and better text than the extant Pseudo-Phocylides manuscripts (Sitzler, Kurfess), and certainly the omission of verses 70–5, as in Sibylline manuscript group Ψ, removes one of the main reasons for suggesting that the ideas of the poem may be polytheistic. On the whole, however, it is probable that the Pseudo-Phocylides verses in Oracula Sibyllina were themselves interpolated there by a Christian editor with modifications of the Pseudo-Phocylides text to fit the Sibylline context. This would explain the omission of verses 70–5. The main manuscript tradition should therefore probably be preferred, but the question is not vital to the understanding of Pseudo-Phocylides and should be left open at present.

Editions

Diehl, E., ed. R. Beutler, *Anthologia Lyrica Graeca*, 3rd ed., fasc.2 (1950), pp. 91–108.
Young, D., ed., *Theognis, Pseudo-Pythagoras, Pseudo-Phocylides, Chares, Anonymi Aulodia, Fragmentum Telecambicum* (^{2}1971) (best).
Denis, FPG, pp. 149–56 (prints Young's text).
van der Horst, P. W., *The Sentences of Pseudo-Phocylides* (1978) (prints Young's text).

Translations and Commentaries

English:
Easton, B. S., 'Pseudo-Phocylides', AnglThR 14 (1932), pp. 222–8.
van der Horst, *loc. cit.*
van der Horst in Charlesworth, OTP II (forthcoming).

German:
Riessler, P., *Altjüd. Schrift.* (1928; repr. 1966), pp. 862–70, 1318–21.
Ebener, D., *Griechische Lyrik in einem Band* (1976), pp. 440–8, 592 f.
Walter, N., *Pseudepigraphische jüdisch-hellenistische Dichtung* (JSHRZ IV.3) (1983), pp. 182–216.

Italian:
Farina, A., *Silloge Pseudofocilidea* (1962).

Bibliography

Bernays, J., *Ueber das phokylideische Gedicht, ein Beitrag zur hellenistischen Litteratur* (1856; reprinted in Bernays, *Gesammelte Abhandlungen*, ed. Usener, I (1885), pp. 192–261).
Bernhardy, G., *Grundriss der griechischen Litteratur* II.1 (^{3}1867), pp. 517–23.
Goram, O., 'De Pseudo-Phocylide', Philologus 14 (1859), pp. 91–112.
Bergk, Th., 'Kritische Beiträge zu dem sog. Phokylides', Philologus 41 (1882), pp. 577–601.
Sitzler, J., 'Zu den griechischen Elegikern', Jahrbb. für class. Philol. 129 (1884), pp. 48–53.
Bergk, Th., *Griech. Literaturgesch.* II (1883), pp. 298–302.
Dieterich, A., *Nekyia. Beiträge zur Erklärung der neuentdeckten Petrusapokalypse* (1893; reprinted 1969), pp. 173–84.

Wendland, P., 'Die Therapeuten und die philonische Schrift vom beschaulichen Leben', Jahrbb. für class. Philol. Supplementband 22 (1896), pp. 693–772.

Lincke, K. F. A., *Samaria und seine Propheten* (1903), pp. 40–102.

Ludwich, A., *Ueber das Spruchbuch des falschen Phokylides* (Königsberger Vorlesungsverzeichniss, 1904).

Ludwich, A., *Quaestionum Pseudophocylidearum pars altera* (Königsberger Univ.-Programm, 1904).

Beltrami, A., 'Ea quae apud Pseudo-Phocylidem Veteris et Novi Testamenti vestigia deprehenduntur', Rivista di filologia 36 (1908), pp. 411–23.

Seeberg, A., *Die beiden Wege und das Aposteldekret* (1906).

Lincke, K. F. A., 'Phokylides und die Essener', Die Grenzboten (Zeitschrift für Politik, Literatur und Kunst) 68 (1909), pp. 128–38 (a pan-Zoroastrian theory).

Klein, G., *Der älteste christliche Katechismus und die jüdische Propaganda-Literatur* (1909), pp. 143–50.

Rossbroich, M., *De pseudo-Phocylideis* (1910) (stressing the classical background—an important study).

Lincke, K. F. A., 'Phokylides, Isokrates und der Dekalog', Philologus 70 (1911), pp. 438–42.

Beltrami, A., 'Spirito giudaico e specialmento essenico della silloge pseudofocilidea', Riv. di Fil. 41 (1913), pp. 513–48.

Stählin, O., in W. v. Christ, O. Stählin and W. Schmidt, *Geschichte der griech. Litt.* II.1 (⁶1920), p. 621.

Ranston, H., *Ecclesiastes and the Early Greek Wisdom Literature* (1925), chap. 3.

Guttmann, M., *Das Judentum und seine Umwelt* (1927), pp. 98 ff.

Spinner, S., *Herkunft, Entstehung und antike Umwelt des hebräischen Volkes* (1933), pp. 380–494 (for the poem as authentic).

Kurfess, A., 'Das Mahngedicht des sog. Phokylides', ZNW 38 (1939), pp. 171–81.

Dornseiff, F., *Echtheitsfragen antik-griechischer Literatur* (1939), pp. 37–51.

Kroll, W., 'Phokylides', RE XX.1 (1941), cols. 505–10.

Lewis, J. J., 'The Teaching of Pseudo-Phocylides', The London Quarterly and Holborn Review (October 1953), pp. 295–8.

Dalbert, P., *Die Theologie der jüd.-hell. Missionsliteratur* (1954), pp. 9–11.

Alon, G., 'The Halakhah in the Teaching of the Twelve Apostles', in *Studies in Jewish History* (²1967), pp. 274–94 (Heb.).

Denis, IPGAT, pp. 215–19.

Hengel, M., 'Anonymität, Pseudepigraphie und "literarische Fälschung"', in K. von Fritz, ed., *Pseudepigrapha* I (Entretiens Hardt, 18) (1972), pp. 296–8.

Crouch, J., *The Origin and Intention of the Colossian Haustafel* (1972).

Christ, F., 'Das Leben nach dem Tode bei Pseudo-Phokylides', ThZ 31 (1975), pp. 140–9.

van der Horst, P. W., 'Pseudo-Phocylides and the New Testament', ZNW 69 (1978), pp. 187–202.

Fischer, U., *Eschatologie und Jenseitserwartung im hellenistischen Diasporajudentum* (1978), pp. 125–43.

Küchler, M., *Frühjüdische Weisheitstraditionen* (1979), pp. 236–302.

Derron, P., 'Inventaire des manuscrits de Pseudo-Phocylide', Revue d'histoire des textes 10 (1980), pp. 237–47.

7. *Pseudo-Menander*

In 1862, J. P. N. Land published a collection of aphorisms from a seventh-century Syriac manuscript in the British Museum entitled, 'The Wise Menander Said'. Little attention was paid to it until W.

Frankenberg (1895) attempted to demonstrate that it was 'a product of Jewish aphoristic wisdom' despite the fact that A. Baumstarck had tried to show the previous year that the basis of the collection lay in genuine quotations from the comedies of the Athenian fourth century B.C. comic writer Menander. The contents are in fact entirely compatible with the Judaism of the Old Testament Proverbs and Ecclesiasticus, and parallels can be noted with Job and the story of Ahikar. In both cases, value is attached to the duties of humanity as divine commandments, which in both cases appear in the same characteristic association with the most obvious, common-sense rules of daily life. In both cases there is indifference towards the cultic element in religion, yet without concealing in any way what is specifically Jewish. In both cases, there is the notion of divine retribution, or of the usefulness lying at the basis of all exhortations and divine warnings. Nothing obviously Christian is contained in these aphorisms, so at issue is only whether they are Jewish or pagan. There is nothing surprising for a Jewish author to mention Homer (Audet, p. 63, section 13), and the polemics against priests who despise their own gods and behave greedily when invited to a meal (Audet, p. 70, section 43) are at least possible for a Jew, given the equally hostile attitude towards the Jerusalem priests at Qumran. Nonetheless it is most likely that the collection is of basically gentile materials of a general ethical nature which have been collected by a monotheistic writer of Jewish sympathies and some knowledge of the Jewish wisdom traditions. It must be admitted that the ethic of this author is entirely down-to-earth and that the specifically religious matters revert so far into the background that the assertion of Stählin that nothing specifically Jewish is to be found in the work cannot be disproved.

It is very improbable that the author is a Jew by the name of Menander. The name of the famous Attic comic poet Menander played a large role in the history of the literature of maxims; see below, p. 695, for other collections; above, p. 669, for the Pseudo-Menander verses collected with those of other dramatic poets. Because numerous verses from Menander are included in the collections of Greek maxims collected from the poets, later copyists and revisers simply attributed such collections to him. His name thus became typical for this kind of literature. Insofar, therefore, as this Menander is certainly meant in the title of this Jewish or Judaizing collection, it is pseudonymous. If the title originated with the author himself, he must have written when Menander's name had already acquired this prestige. However, it is also possible that the title was not provided until later as a label for an originally anonymous work, for not even one certain allusion to the work of the genuine Menander can be identified in the work as it now stands (but cf. Audet, *art. cit.*, p. 78, for one possible exception).

The dating of the work can only be suggested from internal references. A Roman date before Constantine is likely from a probable reference to crucifixion (Audet, section 50) and to the gladiatorial schools, which are portrayed as still in operation (Audet, section 6). A time after Hadrian is suggested by the statement that a master cannot put a slave to death (Audet, section 24). The term *nomos* is taken in Audet, section 65, to refer to an administrative district which, if the work is indeed of the Roman period, suggests Egypt as the place of composition. The author could be a gentile god-fearer (Audet), but he could just as well be a Jew. The original language was certainly Greek.

Bibliography

Land, J. P. N., *Anecdota Syriaca* I (1862), Syriac text pp. 64–73, Latin translation pp. 156–64, notes pp. 198–205.

Baumstark, A., 'Lucubrationes syro-graecae', suppl. to Jahrbb. für class. Philol. 21 (1894), pp. 473–90.

Frankenberg, W., 'Die Schrift des Menander, *Land. anecd. syr.* I, 564 ff., ein Produkt der jüdischen Spruchweisheit', ZAW 15 (1895), pp. 226–77.

Schulthess, F., 'Die Sprüche des Menander aus dem Syrischen übersetzt', ZAW 22 (1912), pp. 199–202.

Stählin, O., in W. v. Schmid and O. Stählin, *Gesch. der griech. Lit.* II.1 ([6]1920), p. 623.

Riessler, P., *Altjüd. Schrift.* (1928), pp. 1047–57, 1328–9.

Audet, J. P., 'La sagesse de Ménandre l'Egyptien', RB 59 (1952), pp. 55–81 (the best version of the text, in French).

Treu, K., 'Aspekte Menanders', Kairos 19 (1977), pp. 22–34.

Küchler, M., *Frühjüdische Weisheitstraditionen* (1979), pp. 207–318.

There are extant other collections of gnomic sayings attributed to Menander but of which there is no reason to suspect a Jewish origin, cf. in general, A. Koerte, *Menandri quae supersunt* II (1959), pp. viii-xiii. The Γνῶμαι μονόστιχοι of Menander exist in several redactions which differ radically from each other, cf. G. Lanowski, 'De monostichis Menandri quae dicuntur, quaestiones selectae', Eos 44.1 (1950), pp. 35–74.

The so-called *Comparatio Menandri et Philistionis*, of the fourth to sixth centuries A.D., has also been preserved in various redactions which differ radically from each other. Cf. the three versions published by G. Studemund, *Menandri et Philistionis Comparatio cum appendicibus edita* (1887), pp. 3–42; on a fourth version, cf. W. Meyer, 'Die athenische Spruchrede des Menander und Philistion', AAM 19.1 (1891), pp. 225–95.

8. Dubious Fragments under Gentile Names for which a Jewish Origin has been claimed

1. [Letters of Heraclitus]

The view that the fourth and seventh of the letters attributed to the pre-Socratic philosopher, Heraclitus of Ephesus (*c.* 500 B.C.), were edited or even written by an author, Jewish or Christian, who believed in the Bible, was based on the polemic found there against the worship of images and the taking of 'live' flesh from animals (Bernays). However, it is now generally accepted that Jewish authorship would present many difficulties and that such views can be better understood as part of the Cynic-Stoic element in the letters. This view of a Cynic origin is strongly supported by the discovery of a longer version of the seventh letter in a papyrus of the second century A.D. or earlier, where it is found included in a collection of Cynic diatribes (V. Martin, Museum Helveticum 16 (1959), pp. 77–117).

Editions

Denis, FPG, pp. 157–60 (without the new papyrus evidence in Museum Helveticum 16 (1959), pp. 77–117).
Cappelletti, A. J., *Epistolas pseudo-Heracliteas* (1960), pp. 26–31, 36–45 (also lacking the new papyrus).
Attridge, H. W., *First-Century Cynicism in the Epistles of Heraclitus* (1976), pp. 58–61, 66–79 (with English translation).

Bibliography

Bernays, J., *Die heraklitischen Briefe, ein Beitrag zur philosophischen und religionsgeschichtlichen Litteratur* (1869).
Heinemann, I, 'Herakleitos (16a)', RE suppl. V (1931), cols. 228–32.
Denis, IPGAT, pp. 220–2.
Strugnell, J., and H. Attridge, 'The Epistles of Heraclitus and the Jewish Pseudepigrapha: A Warning', HThR 64 (1971), pp. 411–13.
Attridge, H. W., *First-Century Cynicism in the Epistles of Heraclitus* (1976), pp. 3–39.
Malherbe, A. J., 'Pseudo Heraclitus, Epistle 4: The divinization of the wise man', Jahrbuch für Antike und Christentum 21 (1978), pp. 42–64.

2. [A Letter of Diogenes]

J. Bernays thought that of the fifty-one alleged letters of Diogenes, he could trace one—the twenty-eighth—to the same source as the seventh letter of Heraclitus. It admittedly contains a sermon on morality which is similar to the latter, but can as easily have originated with a Cynic as with a Jew.

Edition

Hencher, R., *Epistolographi Graeci* (1873), pp. 241–3.

Bibliography

Bernays, J., *Lucian und die Kyniker* (1879), pp. 96–8.

3. [Hermippus]

Hermippus Callimachius, who lived under Ptolemy III and IV, hence in the second half of the third century B.C., wrote a large number of sensational biographies of famous men. Two of the notes preserved from these arouse attention. According to Origen (*Contra Celsum* i 15), it was said in the first book, 'On the Lawgivers', that Pythagoras took his philosophy from the Jews. According to Josephus (*C. Ap.* i 22 (164–5)), a similar statement was contained in the first book, 'On Pythagoras'. Josephus' note is however much more specific and exact than that of Origen. According to Josephus, that is to say, Hermippus reported that Pythagoras taught that a person should 'not pass by a place where an ass had sunk to its knees, should abstain from thirst-producing water,[301] and should avoid all blasphemy'. To which Hermippus then remarked: 'Pythagoras did and taught these things, imitating and adopting the opinions of the Jews and Thracians'. Thus Hermippus did not describe the philosophy of Pythagoras in general as borrowed from the Jews but only those specific teachings. For the words which follow in Josephus—in fact it is actually said that that man, i.e. Pythagoras, introduced many points of Jewish law into his own philosophy—are no longer the words of Hermippus but those of Josephus himself, and reflect the current view among Hellenistic Jews about the relation of their religion to Greek philosophy.

In the formulation reported by Josephus, Hermippus' words contain nothing that he might not really have written, and there is no need to postulate a Jewish forger. Origen's citation is not direct from Hermippus but derives from 'what is said', and hence it is not surprising that he too attributes to Hermippus a belief that Pythagoras brought his own philosophy to the Greeks from Judaism. He cites a different work, 'On Legislators', and is therefore probably independent of Josephus in this case, but it is very likely that he relied on another Jewish source. It is also possible that Hermippus genuinely made this rather vague connection between Pythagoras and Judaism. There is no reason to believe that a separate Jewish forgery entitled 'On Legislators' ever existed.

Bibliography

Müller, C., FHG III, pp. 35–54.
Reinach, T., *Textes d'auteurs grecs et romains relatifs au Judaïsme* (1895), pp. 39 ff.
Stern, GLAJJ I, pp. 93–6, with commentary.
Jacobson, H., 'Hermippus, Pythagoras and the Jews', REJ 135 (1976), pp. 145–9.

4. [Numenius]

The Pythagorean and Neo-Platonist Numenius (second half of the

---

301. δυψίων ὑδάτων should mean 'thirsty water'. A. v. Gutschmid, *Kleine Schriften* IV (1893), p. 559, explained this as 'making thirsty' on the analogy of δυψώδης and δυψητικός. Cf. Thackeray, Loeb ed., pp. 228–9, for other possibilities; S. Lieberman, *Ha-Yerushalmi Kiphshuto* I.1 (1934), p. 49, suggests 'uncovered' water.

second century A.D.), knew the Holy Scriptures of the Jews and indeed Jewish tradition (e.g. on Jannes and Jambres, cf. below, pp. 781 ff.), and made use of them in his own way. The most certain evidence of this comes from Origen, who says in *Contra Celsum* iv 51 that he knows that Numenius 'quotes sayings of Moses and the prophets in many passages of his works and explains them allegorically in a convincing way as, e.g., in the work called "Epops" and in the books "On Numbers" and in those "Concerning Place"'. Cf. also Origen, *Contra Celsum* i 15. There is no reason to mistrust this testimony. It has been suspected that Numenius could not actually have expressed his opinion in the precise words, 'For what is Plato but Moses speaking in Attic', which Clement of Alexandria and others attribute to him (Clement, *Strom.* i 22, 150; Eusebius, *Praep. ev.* ix 6, 9; xi 10, 14; Theodoret, *Graec. Aff. Cur.* ii 114 (ed. Canivet I, p. 169); Suda, s.v. Νουμήνιος). It is therefore proposed that the statement in Eusebius, *Praep. ev.* xi 10, 14, should be taken literally and that the saying in question should be understood as only *attributed* to Numenius, i.e. by oral tradition, and not actually written by him. In fact, not even this is necessary. In the relatively philo-semitic atmosphere of Apamea, sympathy with Judaism was perfectly possible even at so late a date, especially in an author so respectful of oriental religious beliefs in general. There is no reason therefore to believe either that Numenius himself was Jewish or that the work has been tampered with by a Jewish forger.

Editions of Numenius on the Jews

des Places, E., ed., *Numénius, Fragments* (1973) (all the fragments, with notes).
Stern, GLAJJ II, pp. 206–16 (with commentary).

Bibliography

Bigg, C., *The Christian Platonists of Alexandria* (1913), p. 300, n. 1 (Numenius a Jew).
Puech, H.-C., 'Numenius d'Apamea', *Mélanges J. Bidez* (1934), pp. 745–78.
Leemans, A. E., *Numenios v. Apamea* (1937), pp. 159 ff.
Beutler, R., 'Numenios (9)', RE suppl. VII (1940), cols. 663–78.
Dodds, E. R., in *Les Sources de Plotin* (Entretiens Hardt, 5) (1957), p. 6.
Schneider, C., 'Numenius', RGG IV (³1960), col. 1542.
Martano, G., *Numenio d'Apamea* (²1960).
Gager, J. G., *Moses in Greco-Roman Paganism* (1972), pp. 63–9.

5. [Hermes Trismegistus]

The Egyptian god Thoth, identified by the Greeks as Hermes, counted in a large corpus of writings as the inventor of writing and the protector of science. Works on astrology, magic and alchemy are attributed to him. According to Clement of Alexandria, *Strom.* vi 4, 37, there were forty-two books of Hermes, thirty-six of which contained the entire philosophy of the Egyptians, the remaining six being devoted to medicine. Tertullian, *De anima* 2 and 33, knew books of Mercurius Aegyptius, which taught a Platonizing psychology. It is clear already from the latter fact that the 'philosophy' of the later Greek books of Hermes was of a Platonizing nature. This is indeed also the case in regard to the extant Hermetic works, which were first quoted by Lactantius and were written between *c.* 100 B.C. and *c.* A.D. 300, most probably in the second or third centuries A.D. A connection with Judaism is suggested by the clear signs of direct use of the LXX in Tractate I (*Poimandres*), Tractate III (The Sacred Discourse) and Tractate VII. There is also evidence in these and the other tractates of considerable indirect influence from the LXX and of biblical interpretation similar to Philo's. Nonetheless, there is no reason to believe that the author of these works was himself a Jew. The tractates deliberately combine a variety of different religious traditions. Babylonian, Iranian and Greek religious ideas are mixed with those of Judaism. There is also an Egyptian element, though that appears to be confined to the astrological books. This is essentially the pagan literature that it purports to be, based primarily not on Judaism but on Greek philosophy and the Gnostic attitudes popular in the period. This Gnostic element renders it probable that Jewish influence helped indirectly to form some of the ideas in the Hermetica, but it cannot be proved that Jewish hands actually cooperated in the production of this literature. On the other hand, the involvement of a rather unusual Jew as author of Tractate III cannot be disproved (Dodd).

Editions

Scott, W., and Ferguson, S. A., *Hermetica* I-IV (1924–36).
Nock, A. D., and Festugière, A. J., *Corpus Hermeticum* I-IV (1945–54) (the best text).

Translations

English:
Mead, G. R. S., *Thrice Greatest Hermes* (1907).
Scott, W., and Ferguson, A. S., *loc. cit.*

French:
Nock, A. D., and Festugière, A. J., *loc. cit.*

Bibliography

Reitzenstein, R., *Poimandres. Studien zur griechisch-ägyptischen und frühchristlichen Literatur* (1904).
Kroll, W., 'Hermes Trismegistos', RE VIII.1 (1912), cols. 792–823.
Dodd, C. H., *The Bible and the Greeks* (1935), pp. 99–248.
Festugière, A. J., *La révelation d'Hermès Trismégiste* I-IV (1944–54).

6. [Greek Chronographers]

There can be no doubt that most of the fragments of the pagan chronographers Manetho, Apollodorus and Eratosthenes were transmitted in their original form. It is however possible that in some places a Jewish writer has altered these texts in order to make them conform with biblical chronology. Jewish insertions at some time before Josephus into the text of the Egyptian Manetho preserved in *C. Ap.* i 14 (74–92) are suggested by Laqueur, 'Manethon', RE XIV.1 (1928), cols. 1088 ff. (= Jacoby, FGrH, 609, F 8), but the extent of such interpolations is not clear (see above, p. 595, n. 107). It is also possible that the fusion of Berossus' Babylonian chronicle and other documents of oriental history with the Greek chronicle of the Athenian Apollodorus, who wrote *c.* 150 B.C., was the work of a Jew, since the extant fragments of that fused chronicle, preserved by Eusebius, Syncellus and Clement of Alexandria (= Jacoby, FGrH, 244, FF 83–7), show some knowledge of biblical history. If so, this Pseudo-Apollodorus will have written before Alexander Polyhistor, who used his work. It is equally likely that a Pseudo-Berossus or Pseudo-Eratosthenes could have been responsible for the incorporation of this biblical material into the genuine history of Apollodorus. Such a forgery, or forgeries, might also be responsible for the deliberate alterations to the lists of ancient kings preserved in Christian authors, but it is difficult to disentangle Christian alterations in these lists from Jewish ones, cf. E. J. Bickermann, 'Origines Gentium', CPh 47 (1952), p. 80, n. 70. In any case however, though an interest of this sort in reconciling pagan and Jewish chronologies is quite plausible among Jewish writers of this period, there is no certain evidence that a Jew was responsible for the changes and additions, and it is quite possible to assume pagan authorship of these fragments.

Bibliography

Jacoby, FGrH, 244, II B komm., p. 752.
Wacholder, B. Z., 'Biblical Chronology in the Hellenistic World Chronicles', HThR 61 (1968), pp. 451–81, esp. 464–5.
Speyer, W., *Die literarische Fälschung im Altertum* (1971), p. 165.
Hengel, M., 'Anonymität, Pseudepigraphie und "Literarische Fälschung" in der jüdisch-hellenistischen Literatur', *Pseudepigrapha I* (Entretiens Hardt, 18) (1972), pp. 236–7.
Wacholder, ESJL, p. 113, n. 72.

9. Pseudo-Tages

A note given by the fifth- or sixth-century A.D. scholiast Lactantius Placidus in explanation of Statius, *Thebaid* iv 515, seems to rely on the testimony of a Jewish work, which praised Moses and Isaiah along with Orpheus as authorities for the need to keep secret the name of God. This Jewish work apparently circulated under the venerable name of Tages, the legendary founder of Etruscan divination, and it is also probably the work which is summarized by the Suda, s.v. *Tυρρηνία*, where a cosmogony similar to that in Genesis is attributed to an expert Etruscan.

Edition

Bidez, J., and F. Cumont, *Les Mages Hellénisés*, 2 vols. (1938), pp. 225–38, with discussion of both fragments.

Among the Greek men of letters in Rome there were a number of freedmen who, born in the east, came to the west as slaves, and after obtaining their freedom through their scholarly activity, won for themselves a certain esteem. One of these, Caecilius of Calacte, may be mentioned here since he was probably of Jewish parentage and apparently did not completely disavow his origin even later.

Athenaeus names him twice to the same effect (vi, p. 272 ff.; xi, p. 466a) Καικίλιος ὁ ῥήτωρ ὁ ἀπὸ Καλῆς ἀκτῆς. The town Caleacte, or Calacte, lay on the north coast of Sicily. Caecilius was therefore also called Σικελιώτης. The two writings mentioned by Athenaeus are of a historical nature, vi, pp. 272 f.: περὶ τῶν δουλικῶν πολέμων (concerning the slave wars in Sicily) and xi, p. 466a: περὶ ἱστορίας. It is however likely that Athenaeus is confused in attributing these histories to the orator, and that they should be ascribed instead to a quite separate man of the same name who flourished much earlier in the first century B.C. (see below, p. 703, on the references by Cicero to this earlier Caecilius). The later Caecilius is best known as a writer on themes of rhetoric, and, in particular, on questions of authenticity in the Attic orators and on figures of speech. With his friend Dionysius of Halicarnassus he belonged to the first representatives of 'Atticism' and was frequently quoted as a specialist by later writers, e.g. in περὶ ὕψους, wrongly attributed to Longinus, in Quintilian's *Institutio*, and in *De decem oratoribus*, which goes under the name of Plutarch.[302] [Longinus'] περὶ ὕψους was occasioned by Caecilius' work dealing with the same theme, as becomes clear from the prologue. It was judged unfavourably by [Longinus] because it did not fulfil its own purpose. Caecilius attempted to show by means of countless examples, as for the ignorant, what the sublime is, but failed to reveal how it could be achieved.

Further information relating to the person of Caecilius is given by the Suda, s.v. Καικίλιος: 'A Sicilian of Calacte (Calacte is a city of Sicily). A rhetor who practised in Rome under Augustus [and until the time of Hadrian] and from slave stock, as some say, and previously called Archagathus, but by religion Jewish.' A list of the books written by Caecilius follows, in which the Suda, like Athenagoras, may also confuse the orator with the earlier Caecilius, attributing to him a work

302. [Longinus],*Περὶ ὕψους*, ed. Russell, 1, 1; 4, 2; 8, 1;4; 31, 1; 32, 1; 8. Quintilian, *Inst.* iii 1, 16; iii 6, 48; v 10, 7; viii 3, 35; ix 1, 12; ix 3, 38; 46; 89; 91; 97. Cf. for the passages from Pseudo-Plutarch, *De decem oratoribus*, Müller, FHG III, p. 332.

περὶ τῶν καθ' ἱστορίαν ἢ παρ' ἱστορίαν εἰρημένων τοῖς ῥήτορσι. The transmitted text of the Suda is very corrupt, cf. apparatus to text in Jacoby, FGrH, 183, T 1, and it is therefore reasonable to athetize the words 'until the time of Hadrian' (Jacoby, *ad. loc.*). The statement that Caecilius lived in Rome under Augustus is correct since it is confirmed not only by other passages in the Suda (cf. s.v. Ἑρμαγόρας and Τιμαγένης) but also by the testimony of Dionysius of Halicarnassus, who calls him his 'friend' (Dionysius of Halicarnassus, *Ad Cn. Pompeium epistola* 3, 20). But there is no reason to mistrust the Suda's statement that he was descended from slaves, was really called Archagathos, and was a Jew by religion. If his father was taken to Rome by Pompey as a Jewish slave and was sold to Sicily, and if the son received his Greek upbringing there and was freed by a Roman named Caecilius, all the personal details are accounted for quite easily. It is of course also possible that Caecilius was not a Jew by birth, but a proselyte. But the words ἀπὸ δούλων, on the one hand, and on the other the fact that Caecilius' Judaism retreated to the background in his literary works, speak rather for the present interpretation. A proselyte would in prolific writing have exhibited more zeal for his newly-gained convictions.

Two further reasons may support the Suda's statement that Caecilius was a Jew. (1) In περὶ ὕψους, in which otherwise only examples from Greek literature are produced, appears the following reference to Moses (ix 9): 'A similar effect was achieved by the Lawgiver of the Jews—no mean genius, for he both understood and gave expression to the power of the divinity as it deserved—when he wrote at the very beginning of his laws, I quote his words: "God said—what? 'Let there be light.' And there was. 'Let there be earth.' And there was."' Since [Longinus] περὶ ὕψους did not originate with the neo-Platonist Longinus but is considerably older (written either in the time of Augustus or soon after), the reference to Moses is quite surprising. Older scholars therefore took it for a Jewish or Christian interpolation. But a Christian would not have made the mistake of quoting γενέσθω γῆ καὶ ἐγένετο, which is not in the text of Genesis at all.[303] The same argument applies against suggestions that [Longinus] might himself have been a Jew.[304] It is quite possible that a pagan author could have gained this amount of knowledge of the Bible directly from Jews without himself having any

---

303. See the discussion about the authenticity of the passage in D. S. Russell, *'Longinus' On the Sublime* (1964), pp. 92–4.

304. G. P. Goold, 'A Greek professorial circle at Rome', TAPhA 92 (1961), p. 177: 'Longinus is in some sense a Jew.' The language and some of the ideas in [Longinus] are close to Philo. Goold also suggests that the orator Theodorus of Gadara might have been Jewish, but there is no evidence for this. Cf. Russell, *op. cit.*, pp. xxix–xxx.

inclinations towards Judaism.[305] It is also possible that the author took a large part of his material from the work of his predecessor Caecilius, which dealt with the same theme, and that therefore the biblical example came, somewhat misread, from this predecessor's work.[306] If this were the case, the quotation in [Longinus] would confirm the Jewish origin or upbringing of Caecilius.

(2) Cicero's *Divinatio in Caecilium* and Pseudo-Asconius' commentary to it allude to a Q. Caecilius Niger who claimed the right to accuse Verres in order to free him from the serious charge which Cicero, as advocate for the Sicilians, had raised against him. He was a Sicilian by birth and had served under Verres as quaestor. Plutarch relates the following anecdote with regard to Cicero's legal suit against Verres (Plutarch, *Cicero* 7): 'The Romans call a castrated pig "Verres" (βέρρην). When a freedman suspected of Judaizing, by the name of Caecilius, wished to take over from the Sicilians the prosecution of Verres (τοῦ βέρρου), Cicero said, "What interest has a Jew in a castrated pig?"' Verres' administration of Sicily fell in 73–71 B.C. His quaestor Caecilius could not therefore be identical with the orator of the same name if the latter flourished under Augustus. Clearly Plutarch, like Athenaeus and the Suda, has confused the two Caecilii, and is speaking here of the earlier Caecilius to whom the historical works already mentioned should probably be attributed (see above, p. 701). The quaestor of whom Cicero spoke could hardly be a Jew like the later Caecilius, for it is inconceivable (1) that a freedman would have attained to the office of quaestor of Sicily, and (2) that Cicero would not have ridiculed Caecilius' Judaism in his dispute against him if this had been a fact. The fact that both men were Sicilian or at least connected with Sicily will have helped to bring about the confusion, and the bon mot 'Quid Iudaeo cum Verre?' will not have originated with Cicero but have been put in his mouth by a later person on the basis of the confusion. In that case we find here, too, confirmation of the orator's Judaism, since it must have been well enough known for a later wit to be tempted to invent the joke.[307]

305. Stern, GLAJJ I, p. 363, who points to the likelihood that [Longinus] knew more about Moses than what is contained in this quotation. It cannot be assumed that pagan authors never quoted the Septuagint directly, cf. Stern, GLAJJ I, p. 131, on a probable allusion to the Septuagint of Genesis by Ocellus Lucanus, a Pythagorean writer of the second or first century B.C..

306. Th. Reinach, REJ 26 (1893), pp. 42 f. See the bibliography on the passage in Stern, GLAJJ I, p. 363.

307. The Jewishness of the quaestor mentioned by Cicero was still maintained by L. Friedländer, *Darstellungen aus der Sittegeschichte Roms* III (1923), p. 212, but it is wholly implausible at so early a date in Roman history.

Editions

Müller, FHG III, pp. 330-3 (the fragments probably to be assigned to the older Caecilius).

Jacoby, FGrH, 183, II B, pp. 911-12 (only the fragments probably to be assigned to the older Caecilius).

Ofenloch, E., *Caecilii Calactini fragmenta* (1907; repr. 1967) (including much dubious material with all the genuine fragments).

Bibliography

Rothstein, M., 'Caecilius von Kalakte und die Schrift vom Erhabenen', Hermes 23 (1888), pp. 1-20.

Weise, R., *Quaestiones Caecilianae* (1888).

Reinach, Th., 'Quid Judaeo cum Verre?', REJ 26 (1893), pp. 36-46.

Brzoska, 'Caecilius (2)', RE III.1 (1897), cols. 1174-88.

Rhys Roberts, W., 'Caecilius of Calacte: A Contribution to the History of Greek Literary Criticism', AJPh 18 (1897), pp. 302-12.

Kennedy, G., *The Art of Rhetoric in the Roman World* (1972), pp. 364-9.

[Longinus] περὶ ὕψους.

Editions

Rhys Roberts, W., *Longinus on the Sublime* (1899).

Prickard, A. O., *Libellus de Sublimitate* ... (²1947).

Russell, D. A., *'Longinus' On the Sublime* (1964) with commentary and references to earlier editions on p. li. (Text also printed separately as *Libellus de Sublimitate* ... (1968).)

Translations

Prickard, A. O., *Longinus, On the Sublime* (1906).

Russell, D. A., *On Sublimity* (1965). References to earlier translations are given on p. lii of his edition (1964).

Bibliography

Kennedy, G., *The Art of Rhetoric in the Roman World* (1972), pp. 369-77, with bibliography at p. 369, n. 91.